Family Law

PRINCIPLES, POLICY
AND PRACTICE

To
Louis, Natasha and Daniel
with love

Family Law

PRINCIPLES, POLICY AND PRACTICE

Mary Hayes BA (Law), JP
Professor of Law, University of Sheffield
of Lincoln's Inn, Barrister

Catherine Williams LLB
Senior Lecturer in Law,
University of Sheffield

 LexisNexis®

Members of the LexisNexis Group worldwide

United Kingdom	LexisNexis UK, a Division of Reed Elsevier (UK) Ltd, Halsbury House, 35 Chancery Lane, LONDON, WC2A 1EL, and 4 Hill Street, EDINBURGH EH2 3JZ
Argentina	LexisNexis Argentina, BUENOS AIRES
Australia	LexisNexis Butterworths, CHATSWOOD, New South Wales
Austria	LexisNexis Verlag ARD Orac GmbH & Co KG, VIENNA
Canada	LexisNexis Butterworths, MARKHAM, Ontario
Chile	LexisNexis Chile Ltda, SANTIAGO DE CHILE
Czech Republic	Nakladatelství Orac sro, PRAGUE
France	Editions du Juris-Classeur SA, PARIS
Germany	LexisNexis Deutschland GmbH, FRANKFURT, MUNSTER
Hong Kong	LexisNexis Butterworths, HONG KONG
Hungary	HVG-Orac, BUDAPEST
India	LexisNexis Butterworths, NEW DELHI
Ireland	LexisNexis, DUBLIN
Italy	Giuffrè Editore, MILAN
Malaysia	Malayan Law Journal Sdn Bhd, KUALA LUMPUR
New Zealand	LexisNexis Butterworths, WELLINGTON
Poland	Wydawnictwo Prawnicze LexisNexis, WARSAW
Singapore	LexisNexis Butterworths, SINGAPORE
South Africa	LexisNexis Butterworths, DURBAN
Switzerland	Stämpfli Verlag AG, BERNE
USA	LexisNexis, DAYTON, Ohio

© Reed Elsevier (UK) Ltd 1999
 Reprinted 2004
Published by LexisNexis UK

A CIP Catalogue record for this book is available from the British Library.

ISBN 0 406 90597 5

Printed and bound in Great Britain by Antony Rowe Ltd, Chippenham, Wiltshire

Visit LexisNexis UK at www.lexisnexis.co.uk

Preface

Producing the second edition of this book has proved in many respects more challenging and exciting than producing the first. The impact of Family Law on society, and society on Family Law, has attracted a growing volume of public and political debate and is increasingly seen as a pivotal area of legal scholarship. Our aim has been to keep abreast with this momentum, and to highlight and explore significant developments as they are reflected in the fast-changing content of Family Law.

The social trends will be familiar to our readers. More marriages are ending in divorce. More couples are living together outside marriage. More children are being born into single parent families. More couples of the same sex are living openly together. Some who live in this country have traditions and norms which differ from those which have shaped our Family Law. Sadly, many family members are victims of cruel and destructive behaviour. Physical, sexual and emotional abuse continues to haunt the lives of a significant number of children, and there seems to be no decline in the number of victims of domestic violence. Family Law must therefore transform itself to respond to all of these trends and must serve the interests of all affected by it.

Family Law must also have an international dimension: international conventions have an increasing impact on the shape and content of legal rules. With the growth in the unlawful removal of children from one jurisdiction to another it is important that lawyers have knowledge and understanding of the law of international child abduction. We have therefore included a fresh chapter devoted entirely to this topic.

We were naturally delighted when reviewers, students and practitioners alike all praised the original text for its readability and accessibility. We have tried to maintain the same reader-friendly style throughout this greatly enlarged new edition. We have taken account of the flood of case law, especially from the Court of Appeal and the House of Lords, and have considerably extended the citation of recent legal literature. We have, however, retained the deliberately selective policy of the first edition. This book aims to cover in depth those areas of Family Law which arise frequently in practice, or which best illustrate the intellectual challenge faced by legislators, judges and academics in determining how the law should best respond to family difficulties.

Our comments are aimed at encouraging readers to look at the law with a critical eye, and we suggest at various points that either fresh legislation is needed, or that the judiciary are failing to give sufficient weight to those principles which, in our view, should properly inform decision making in relation to the particular point in issue. Readers might also care to reflect on why courts tend to treat some cases as raising matters of general public importance, but operate very tight controls over appeals in others. It surely gives rise to more than a sense of unease that the House of Lords was prepared to adjudicate on a child's surname in *Dawson v Wearmouth*, but that in *Re M and R (Child Abuse: Evidence)* counsel was strongly criticised for taking serious child protection issues to the Court of Appeal, and was refused leave to appeal to the House of Lords.

A major question we had to face in preparing this edition was how best to treat the divorce provisions in the Family Law Act 1996. The results of the various pilot projects are still being analysed, and rumour has it that implementation is likely to be delayed until some of the difficulties exposed by these projects have been resolved. We have therefore decided to retain brief coverage of the law of divorce under the Matrimonial Causes Act 1973 as this may remain in force for some considerable time to come. We do, of course, describe in detail the new practices and procedures brought about by the 1996 Act, and explain the philosophies underlying the changes in divorce law. However, we question how far the new law is likely to achieve its very mixed purposes.

Most readers will be able to relate to the contents of at least some of the chapters of this book because most families have some involvement with Family Law. This may be through a joyful experience, such as when a child joins the family through the process of adoption, or through a sad experience, such as when a marriage is terminated by divorce.

This book aims to be of particular use to students. Law students can become overwhelmed by the volume of material that they are expected to read and absorb. We have tried to produce a book that guides students carefully through the legislation and case law, explains the principles and policies informing the law, and helps the reader fully to understand the topics under discussion. It is also designed to raise the level of critical awareness of students and to whet their appetite for further study.

We think that those practitioners who are new to the practice of Family Law, and those who are familiar with its day-to-day application, will also find this volume helpful. It gives a detailed and up-to-date account of the substantive law, adopts a problem-solving approach, and incorporates recent evidential and practical developments.

Our families have proved stoical and supportive while this second edition has been in preparation and we are grateful for their kindness and endless patience. We also owe a debt of gratitude to those colleagues who have generously commented on chapters when in draft form.

The law is stated as at April 1999

Mary Hayes and Catherine Williams.

Contents

Chapter 2 Section 8 orders, and orders under the High Court's inherent jurisdiction 57

Chapter 3   Children needing services, care or protection   *133*

Chapter 7   Ending a marriage – the law of nullity, divorce and separation   *479*

Chapter 9 Money and property for unmarried partners and all children *683*

Table of statutes

Page references in **bold** type indicate where a section of an Act is set out in part or in full.

Table of cases

PAGE

B

PAGE

PAGE

PAGE

PAGE

Chapter 1

Responsibility for bringing up children

Chapter 1

Responsibility for bringing up children

The responsibility to decide about a child's upbringing

When there is disagreement over a child's upbringing, various persons may have an interest in, or views about, what should happen to the child. These persons may include the child, the parents, a step-parent, grand-parents and other relatives, a local authority, a foster parent, an 'expert' such as a paediatrician, psychologist or psychiatrist, and other concerned individuals. Normally, such disagreement is best resolved through dis-cussions and compromise. Indeed, agencies and systems exist to encourage conciliatory methods of resolving children cases.[1] However, it is inevitable that circumstances will occur in which an amicable resolution of conflict cannot be achieved. Identifying who has the responsibility to make decisions about a child's upbringing may then be of crucial importance. It will be seen in the pages which follow that much of child law centres around this issue.

Parental responsibility

'Parental responsibility' is a key principle and a key concept in child law.[2] It permeates the Children Act 1989. This Act provides the statutory framework around which most of child law is based, and is the bedrock in which burgeoning ideas and principles relating to the upbringing of children are firmly rooted.[3] Parental responsibility is defined in section 3(1) to mean:

> 'All the rights, duties, powers, responsibility and authority which by law a parent of a child has in relation to the child and his property.'

1 See ch 4.
2 See J Eekelaar *Parental responsibility: state of nature or nature of the state?* [1991] JSWFL 37.
3 Any statutory references in this chapter are to the Children Act 1989 unless otherwise stated.

This definition reveals that parental responsibility is a compilation of attributes of parenthood. It is a concept which can be encapsulated in the notion that it is those with parental responsibility who have the power and responsibility to determine how a child is brought up. Babies and young children cannot make decisions about their own upbringing because they lack the capacity to do so. In the case of older children, they may have the intellectual capacity to make decisions, but they are nonetheless likely to be dependent on adults to provide them with their basic needs. Also, while older children may have the ability to understand and make choices, they may lack the maturity and foresight to make decisions which are wise and in their own interests.[4] The law therefore throws a ring of care around children by imposing parental responsibility for their upbringing on specified persons until the children reach adulthood.[5] However, recognising that those with parental responsibility have the right to control most aspects of a child's upbringing does not imply that the means used will always be acceptable. 'The principle of law ... is that parental rights are derived from parental duty and exist only so long as they are needed for the protection of the person and property of the child.'[6] Thus parental responsibility can be challenged, and even overridden, when parents and others with parental responsibility act in violation of this principle.[7]

There is no definitive list of the 'rights, duties, powers, responsibility and authority' which belong to those with parental responsibility; essentially they comprise those attributes of parenthood which are needed to enable parents to perform their duty properly to bring up their children until the children are capable of looking after themselves. However, these powers are not unlimited and they cannot be exercised in a way which infringes the rights of others.[8] Because there are no written rules about the nature and scope of parental responsibility this creates some degree of uncertainty.[9]

---

4 See below in relation to '*Gillick* competent' children.

5 Not only do persons with parental responsibility have all the responsibilities of parenthood, they also are not allowed to surrender or transfer any part of that responsibility to another: s 2(9). Only a court can deprive a person of parental responsibility.

6 *Gillick v West Norfolk and Wisbech Area Health Authority* [1985] 3 All ER 402 per Lord Scarman at p 420.

7 See ch 3 in relation to child abuse. See also the extremely important ruling in *A v UK (Human Rights: Punishment of Child)* [1998] 2 FLR 959, where the European Court of Human Rights unanimously held that the beating of a child with a garden cane with considerable force on more than one occasion amounted to 'inhuman or degrading treatment or punishment' in breach of Art 3 of the European Convention for the Protection of Human Rights and Fundamental Freedoms.

8 See *Re M (Care: Leave to Interview Child)* [1995] 1 FLR 825 for an analysis of how this limit also limits the powers of local authorities where they share parental responsibility with parents.

9 See N V Lowe *The meaning and allocation of parental responsibility – A common lawyer's perspective* (1997) 11 IJLPF 192. Lowe argues that a meaningful definition of parental responsibility can and should be given.

This tension between flexibility and certainty is endemic in child law. On the one hand it will be seen that Parliament and the courts have resisted formulating rules which would create certainty about the responsibilities of parents, in order to enable the law to respond flexibly to changing social circumstances, and to be sensitive to alterations in customs and values relating to the upbringing of children. On the other hand it is desirable that others who have dealings with a child know what is, or is not, permissible without parental agreement, and it will be seen that the courts have been responsive to this pressure too.[10]

Parents and parental responsibility

A mother always has parental responsibility. The position of fathers is more complicated. Section 2(1) of the Children Act 1989 provides:

> 'Where a child's father and mother were married to each other at the time of his birth, they shall each have parental responsibility for the child.'

Clearly this means that a father who was married to the child's mother at the time when the child was born has automatic parental responsibility. However, on its face, this provision is slightly misleading because the meaning of 'being married to each other at the time of the child's birth' is extended by section 1 of the Family Law Reform Act 1987 to include relationships in which the parties clearly were not married to each other at the time of the child's birth. Thus parents who are parties to a void marriage fall within section 2(1) provided that at the time of the child's conception, or the time of the marriage if later, either or both of them reasonably believed that the marriage was valid.[11] This means, for example, that both parents enjoy parental responsibility if one of the parents was aged under 16 at the date of the marriage, if either or both of them did not realise this. It means that a man who is already married to someone else, and who knowingly enters into a bigamous marriage, has parental responsibility for any child of the new marriage if his 'wife' reasonably believed that their marriage was valid at one of the relevant times.

Furthermore, it is relatively common for parents who were not married to each other at the time of the child's birth subsequently to marry. Such parents are treated as if they were married to each other at the time of the child's birth.[12] The father's status alters from being a parent without parental responsibility to being a parent with parental responsibility

---

10 For example, the law relating to the medical treatment of children, see below. For a general analysis, see *Report on Family Law*, Scot Law Com No 135, paras 2.1–2.13.
11 Legitimacy Act 1976, s 1. Void marriages are explained in ch 7.
12 Legitimacy Act 1976, s 2.

through the act of marrying. Parents of adopted children are included within the definition of parents married to each other at the time of the child's birth.[13] This reinforces the principle that, where the adopters are a married couple, an adopted child shall be treated in law as if he had been born as a child of the marriage.[14] Finally, parents of any person who is otherwise treated in law as legitimate also fall within section 2(1).[15] This provision draws in those cases, usually where there is a foreign element, where a child is treated by law as a child of parents who are married at the time of his birth even though this is not factually the case.

Unmarried fathers and parental responsibility

All other parents are treated as parents who were not married to each other at the time of the child's birth. In relation to unmarried parents, section 2(2) provides:

> 'Where a child's mother and father were not married to each other at the time of his birth—
> (a) the mother shall have parental responsibility for the child;
> (b) the father shall not have parental responsibility for the child, unless he acquires it in accordance with the provisions of this Act.'

However, although unmarried mothers enjoy all the rights, duties, powers, responsibility and authority of parenthood to the exclusion of the father, the fact that the father does not have parental responsibility for a child does not affect any obligations he may have, in particular the statutory duty to maintain the child. Nor does it affect any rights he may have in the event of the child's death in relation to the child's property.[16]

It has been seen that a child's father automatically has parental responsibility if he was married to the mother at the time of the child's birth. Why is an unmarried father treated differently? In 1979 the Law Commission suggested in a working paper on the reform of the law relating to illegitimacy that unmarried fathers should have the same rights in relation to their children as married fathers.[17] However, the process of consultation which followed publication of the working paper revealed that there was widespread opposition to this proposal, and by the time the Law Commission published its final report it had moved away from its original suggestion.[18] The Law Commission pointed out

---

13 Family Law Reform Act 1987, s 1(3)(c).
14 Adoption Act 1976, s 39.
15 Family Law Reform Act 1987, s 1(3)(d).
16 Children Act 1989, s 3(4).
17 Law Com WP No 74.
18 *Illegitimacy*, Law Com No 118.

that in most other countries an unmarried father did not automatically have the full range of rights, powers and authority enjoyed by a married father, and it gave reasons why a similar approach should be taken in England.

These reasons took account of the response that the Law Commission had received from organisations representing single parents which stated that each year they received numerous enquiries from unmarried mothers seeking reassurance about their rights over their children, and whether these could be challenged, particularly by the father. The Law Commission reported that some respondents had indicated that there was reason to fear that mothers would be tempted to conceal the identity of the child's father in order to ensure that he did not have any rights in relation to the child's upbringing. Other respondents had pointed out that the welfare of children could be imperilled by conferring rights on all fathers.[19] After balancing the advantages and disadvantages of alternative proposals, the Law Commission recommended that unmarried fathers should not have rights automatically, but that they should be entitled to apply to a court for such rights. This recommendation led to the enactment of section 4 of the Family Law Reform Act 1987 which enabled an unmarried father to apply to a court for a parental rights and duties order. Such an order gave him the same status as a married father.

This provision has been repeated in very similar terms in section 4 of the Children Act 1989.[20] A further innovation is that an unmarried father may obtain parental responsibility by agreement with the child's mother, provided certain provisions in the Act are complied with. Section 4 provides:

'(1) Where a child's father and mother were not married to each other at the time of his birth—
(a) the court may, on the application of the father, order that he shall have parental responsibility for the child; or
(b) the father and mother may by agreement ('a parental responsibility agreement') provide for the father to have parental responsibility for the child.'

Should unmarried fathers be afforded equal treatment?

There is a strong body of opinion which would afford equal treatment to unmarried fathers which is matched by an equally strong body of opinion which is resistant to any alteration in the present law.[1] It has been suggested that English law may be out of line with Articles 8 and 14 of

---

19 M Hayes *Law Commission Working Paper No 74: Illegitimacy* (1980) 43 MLR 299.
20 Parental responsibility orders are discussed in detail below.
1 See A Bainham *Children: The Modern Law* (Family Law, 1998, 2nd edn) pp 168-174 for a helpful account of the literature on this debate.

the European Convention on Human Rights and Fundamental Freedoms.[2]
Article 8(1) provides that:

> 'Everyone has the right to respect for his private and family life,
> his home and his correspondence.'

Article 14 provides that:

> 'The enjoyment of the rights and freedoms set forth in this
> Convention shall be secured without discrimination on any ground
> such as sex, race, colour, language, religion, political or other
> opinion, national or social origin, association with a national
> minority, property, birth or other status.'

This latter article has no independent existence, rather it complements
the other articles. There has been no direct consideration of the question
whether the Convention demands that an unmarried father should be as
equally entitled to exercise his parental role as a parent with parental
responsibility. It is clear from the ruling of the European Court of Human
Rights in *Marckx v Belgium*[3] that the Convention draws no distinction
between the married and the unmarried family life when interpreting
'respect for ... family life'. However, the Law Commission took the view
that the *Marckx* case only required English law to prevent discrimination
against the *child* of unmarried parents, rather than against the father, in
order to bring it into line with its treaty obligations.

More recently, Article 18 of the United Nations Convention on the Rights
of the Child provides under the heading *'parental support'* that:

> 'States Parties shall use their best efforts to ensure recognition of
> the principle that both parties have common responsibilities for
> the upbringing and development of the child. Parents, or as the
> case may be, legal guardians, have the primary responsibility for
> the upbringing and development of the child. The best interest of
> the child will be their basic concern.'

This is one factor which influenced the Scottish Law Commission to
recommend that 'in the absence of any court order regulating the position,
both parents of the child should have parental responsibilities and rights
whether or not they are or have been married to each other'.[4] However, no
provision to this effect was included in the Children (Scotland) Act 1995.

---

2   A Bainham *'When is a parent not a parent?' Reflections on the unmarried father and his
     child in English law* (1989) 3 IJLF 208; for a contrary view, see R Deech *The unmarried
     father and human rights* (1992) 4 JCL 3.
3   Series A No 31 (1979) 2 EHRR 330, ECtHR; and see S Maidment *The Marckx Case*
     (1979) 9 Fam Law 228.
4   Scot Law Com No 135 recommendation 5. For their more general reasoning, see paras
     2.36–2.49.

Clearly there is a divide between the English and Scottish Law Commissions, and in the populace generally, between those who support and those who oppose the automatic conferment of parental responsibility on all fathers. Each group advances the notion that the welfare of children is best served by adopting their point of view. Those in favour of removing all discrimination assert that it is wrong to deprive a child of a parent who has the normal parental responsibilities and rights in relation to the child, merely because that parent, perhaps through no fault of his own, was not married to the mother. Furthermore, they assert that, by discriminating against unmarried fathers, the law may be fostering irresponsible parental attitudes which it ought to be doing everything possible to discourage.[5]

Those who take the contrary view point to how conferring parental responsibility on all fathers may damage the rights and interests of children. When parents are married the identity of the father of a child conceived, or born, in wedlock is either known to be, or is presumed by law to be, the husband of the mother.[6] There can be no such presumption in the case of unmarried fathers, and in some cases, for example when a child has been conceived as a result of a casual relationship, or when one of several men could be the father of the child, it may be difficult to identify who the father is. Often this will not matter. But sometimes it will. Once rights have been given to a father they must be accorded respect by law. An inevitable consequence of conferring parental responsibility on all fathers is to add to the persons who have the right to be consulted in relation to the child's upbringing.[7] This is liable to cause delays in decision-making about the child whilst steps are taken to trace, and in some cases to identify, the father.[8] Yet there is a general principle that any delay in determining a question in relation to a child's upbringing is likely to prejudice the welfare of a child, as section 1(2) of the Children Act 1989 recognises and stresses.

Other reasons advanced for opposing the automatic conferment of parental responsibility on all fathers include the offence this could cause to unmarried mothers struggling to bring up their children without support from the children's fathers, and the fears of some mothers that they might be at risk of interference and harassment. The Scottish Law Commission was fairly dismissive of the former objection, pointing out that it is not the feelings of one parent which should determine the content of the law but rather the interests of children and responsible parents. It said that the answer to the latter problem is for the law to remove or regulate parental rights. But it could be maintained that this response ignores the

---

5   Ibid, paras 2.45 and 2.43.
6   See below.
7   For example, in adoption proceedings if unmarried fathers had the same rights as married fathers it would be essential to obtain the father's agreement to his child's adoption, or to find grounds for dispensing with that agreement: see further ch 4.
8   Cf *Re P (Adoption) (Natural Father's Rights)* [1994] 1 FLR 771.

issue of the delay which will occur while legal proceedings are taken, and fails to give weight to the potential for disruption of the child's upbringing. It is also open to the more profound objection that it makes too many assumptions about the efficacy of legal proceedings in dealing with family conflict, and the ability of the principle that the child's welfare must be the court's paramount consideration when an issue arises with respect to his upbringing adequately to embrace strife of this nature.[9] The Lord Chancellor's Department is reviewing whether some or all unmarried fathers should have parental responsibility for their children. It seems likely that a compromise position will be presented to Parliament.[10]

Parental responsibility agreements

English law effects what the Scottish Law Commission described as a 'second best solution',[11] namely section 4(1)(b) of the Children Act 1989. This enables the unmarried father to acquire parental responsibility by making an agreement with the mother. This is a formal agreement which must be made on a set form, be signed and witnessed, and be registered in the Principal Registry of the Family Division in London.[12] Because the Children Act Advisory Committee, which was established to monitor the working of the Act, detected that there had been some attempts to forge a mother's signature to an agreement, it proposed that agreements should be witnessed by a lay justice or an officer of the court,[13] which proposal was implemented.[14] Both parties are advised to seek legal advice before signing the agreement. Any person giving legal advice to the mother would need to explain to her that once a parental responsibility agreement has been made it cannot be revoked by either party.[15] Only a court may bring a parental responsibility agreement to an end, and it may only do this if an application is made either by any person who has parental responsibility for the child, or by the child himself who has

---

9   See M Hayes *Law Commission Working Paper No 74: Illegitimacy* (1980) 43 MLR 299. On the application of the welfare principle to disputes between parents over the upbringing of their children, see ch 4.

10 The suggestion which appears to command the most support is that parental responsibility should automatically be conferred on all fathers who accompany the child's mother to register the birth.

11 Scot Law Com No 135, para 2.51.

12 Parental Responsibility Agreement Regulations 1991 (SI 1991/1478). These forms are not readily available or widely publicised. See further, M Hayes and C Williams *Parental responsibility agreements – successfully combining research with teaching* (1999) 33 Law Teacher 1.

13 Children Act Advisory Committee annual report 1992-93, p 13.

14 See now form C(PRA), inserted by SI 1994/3157, which comes with explanatory notes.

15 This can be contrasted with the appointment of a guardian for a child by deed or will or other formal document, which can be revoked at any time before the guardianship takes effect. On guardianship generally, see below.

been given leave of the court to apply.[16] A court cannot either make or end a parental responsibility agreement using its own motion powers.

An important aspect of this legal solution to the formalisation of human relationships is that many parents, particularly those living together in a stable union, are unaware of the relative lack of status of the unmarried father in the eyes of the law. Even fewer unmarried parents know about parental responsibility agreements,[17] or about the importance of making such an agreement.[18] It is therefore hardly surprising that the number of agreements entered into has been low.[19] This lack of knowledge is particularly unfortunate when it is borne in mind that the agreement procedure is open to all, whatever their means, because no fee is imposed when the agreement is registered at the Principal Registry of the Family Division.[20]

Parental responsibility orders

When an agreement with the mother cannot be effected for whatever reason, an unmarried father is entitled to apply for a parental responsibility order.[1] There is no specific guidance in section 4 on how a court should determine whether to confer parental responsibility, and the court is not required to apply the checklist in section 1(3) which identifies those matters to which a court must have regard when deciding what course of action will best promote a child's welfare.[2] However, who should have parental responsibility is undoubtedly a question with respect to the upbringing of a child, and the child's welfare is therefore the court's paramount consideration in determining the issue.[3] But parental responsibility is also a matter of status, and the issue for the court to resolve is whether the father should be treated in the same way by law as a married father. Those who have parental responsibility have an advantage when decisions must be made about a child's future because they are

---

16 S 4(3).
17 See S McRae *Cohabiting mothers: changing marriage and motherhood?* (1993) Policy Studies Institute, at p 71.
18 By contrast, many unmarried parents understand the importance of appointing a guardian for their children when making a will, but unmarried fathers often do not appreciate that such an appointment has no effect unless they have parental responsibility, see below.
19 Statistics show that in 1996 only 3,590 parental responsibility agreements were registered with the Principal Registry of the Family Division: see *The Children Act Advisory Committee Final Report* (1997) Lord Chancellor's Department, 1997.
20 Court fees, by contrast, are payable when an application is made to a court for a parental responsibility order.
1 S 4(1)(a).
2 See ch 4, where the provisions in the checklist are explained.
3 S 1(1), *Re G (A Minor) (Parental Responsibility Order)* [1994] 1 FLR 504; *Re C and V (Contact and Parental Responsibility* [1998] 1 FLR 392.

entitled to be consulted. By contrast, the status of being a parent without parental responsibility does not always afford a father the same protection of his interest to be involved in decisions about his child's upbringing. This can be of crucial importance where a local authority is treating a child as a child in need of accommodation,[4] or if there are adoption proceedings about the child.[5]

Guidance from case law on when it is appropriate for a court to make a parental responsibility order stems both from cases decided under section 4 of the Family Law Reform Act 1987, and from cases decided under section 4 of the Children Act 1989 which replaced it. In *Re CB (A Minor) (Parental Responsibility Order)*[6] Waite J said that, in his view, Parliament intended to carry forward the case law decided under the 1987 Act, and thus it will be seen that the earlier case law has been influential on how cases brought under section 4 of the Children Act 1989 have been approached. Importantly, the courts have taken the view that an application for a parental responsibility order is a discrete application which must be determined separately from other matters which may have arisen in the proceedings.[7]

Under the law which preceded the Children Act 1989 an unmarried father did not have the right to apply for contact with his child who was in local authority care, and there was no other way open to him to challenge the decision of the local authority to deny him contact. Clearly this placed him at an enormous disadvantage by contrast with mothers and married fathers who were entitled to challenge a refusal to allow contact. In *D v Hereford and Worcester County Council*[8] an unmarried father wished to apply for contact with his child in care. He therefore applied for a joint parental rights and duties order under section 4 of the Family Law Reform Act 1987 in order to obtain the *locus standi* to make a further application challenging the decision to refuse him contact. Ward J ruled that the essence of the question to be determined by the court when making a parental responsibility order was: 'can [the natural father] show that he is a father to the child, not in a biological sense, but in the sense that he has established or is likely to establish such a real family tie with the child that he should now be afforded the corresponding legal tie'.[9] He said that another way of framing the question is to ask: 'Has he behaved or will he behave with parental responsibility towards the child?'[10] He added

---

4 S 20; and see ch 3.
5 See ch 4.
6 [1993] 1 FLR 920.
7 As applications for parental responsibility are often made alongside applications for contact it is important to appreciate that the applications are entirely separate and involve distinct questions. See particularly *Re C and V (Contact and Parental Responsiblity)* [1998] 1 FLR 392.
8 [1991] 1 FLR 205.
9 Ibid, at p 212.
10 Ibid.

that the burden of proof was on the father, and there may be obvious reasons for rejecting his application, such as when the mother is implacably hostile to the intervention of the father into her life, perhaps after the most casual of relationships. He said that if the father had nothing to offer the child it would be right to refuse his application.

An unmarried father without parental responsibility was, and still is, at a disadvantage in adoption proceedings in comparison with a married father. Neither his agreement to an order which would free his child for adoption, nor his consent to an adoption order, is required.[11] In *Re H (Illegitimate Children: Father: Parental Rights) (No 2)*[12] an unmarried father was seeking a parental rights and duties order under the Family Law Reform Act 1987 in the course of proceedings to free his children for adoption. Such an order would give him the *locus standi* to oppose the freeing order. It would also give him residual rights under the Adoption Act 1976 to receive progress reports on the children, and to apply for the freeing order to be revoked if the children were not placed for adoption within twelve months.[13] Balcombe LJ said that in determining whether to make an order the court should take account of the degree of commitment the father had shown towards the child, the degree of attachment that existed between father and child, and the reasons why the father was applying for the order.[14] The court found that there had been contact between the father and his children and that there was evidence of some attachment between them. It therefore determined that a parental rights and duties order should be made. However, it went on to rule that grounds for dispensing with the father's agreement to the freeing order had been established.

Re H (Illegitimate Children: Father: Parental Rights) (No 2) illustrates the principle that a court may think it right to confer parental responsibility on a father even if during the course of the same legal proceedings that responsibility is then removed. Whether a father should be given all the responsibilities of a married father is determined by one set of principles; whether he should then be deprived of these responsibilities is a completely separate question which is determined by a different set of principles. These latter principles relate to the nature of the proceedings which have been brought. In relation to the application for parental responsibility, the concern of the court is whether the

---

11 A parent for the purposes of the Adoption Act 1976, ss 18 and 16 means a parent with parental responsibility: see Adoption Act 1976, s 72. An unmarried father is, however, afforded lesser measures of protection: see ch 4.
12 [1991] 1 FLR 214.
13 Adoption Act 1976, ss 19 and 20.
14 In *Re G (A Minor) (Parental Responsibility Order)* [1994] 1 FLR 504 Balcombe LJ, when told that this list 'had become used almost as if it were a statutory definition', said that it was certainly not so intended, and that the factors were not intended to be exclusive (at p 507). However, it is clear that this test, whilst not definitive, has nonetheless been relied upon in subsequent cases.

unmarried father should be afforded the same status, and therefore the same rights, as a married father. In relation to dispensing with agreement to adoption, the concern of the court is to determine whether a parent who enjoys the privileges of parental responsibility is unreasonably withholding his agreement to an adoption order being made.[15]

The principle that an application for parental responsibility is a discrete application was illustrated in a different way in *Re C (Minors) (Parental Rights)*,[16] which was also decided under the Family Law Reform Act 1987. Here the issue to be resolved was whether a court should make a parental rights and duties order even though some, or all, of the rights given to the father would be incapable of being enforced. Unmarried parents of two children had parted and there was medical evidence to the effect that the mother's mental stability would be at risk if the father was allowed contact with the children. The court therefore determined that contact should be denied for the time being. However, in relation to the parental rights and duties order Waite J said that the question to ask was: 'was the association between the parties sufficiently enduring, and has the father by his conduct during and since the application shown sufficient commitment to the children, to justify giving the father a legal status equivalent to that which he would have enjoyed if the parties had been married'.[17] Waite J said that the order 'will have real and tangible value, not only as something [the father] can cherish for the sake of his own peace of mind, but also as a status carrying with it rights in waiting, which it may be possible to call into play when circumstances change with the passage of time'.[18] The court concluded that it could never be right to refuse a parental rights and duties order on the automatic ground that it would be vitiated by an inability to enforce it.

A similar approach has been adopted in cases decided under section 4 of the Children Act 1989. In *Re CB (A Minor) (Parental Responsibility Order)*[19] the court ruled that magistrates hearing an application brought in care proceedings should have given independent assessment to whether the father should have a parental responsibility order. In determining this matter the court should have regard to the father's commitment and attachment to the child and to his motives. In *Re H (A Minor) (Parental Responsibility)*,[20] in which a father was seeking parental responsibility and contact orders, the Court of Appeal found that the trial judge could not be faulted in the reasoning which led him to deny contact by the father with his child, but held that he had been plainly wrong to apply the same kind of reasoning to whether the father should be given a parental responsibility order. In *Re H (A Minor)*, measuring the order against the child's best interests, the judge had found that it would have no benefits and some disadvantages. He took the view that a parental responsibility order might raise false hopes in the father, and

15 See ch 4.
16 [1992] 1 FLR 1.
17 Ibid, at p 8.
18 Ibid, at p 4.
19 [1993] 1 FLR 920.
20 [1993] 1 FLR 484.

would tend to disrupt relationships in the mother's household with her new husband to the child's disadvantage in the same way as allowing contact would. The Court of Appeal held that this approach had been wrong. The evidence showed that the father had shown commitment and attachment to the child, and that in the light of the authorities a parental responsibility order should therefore have been made.[1]

In *Re C and V (Contact and parental responsibility)*[2] the Court of Appeal again had occasion to remind the lower courts of the discrete nature of a parental responsibility order which is designed to do no more than confer on the natural father the same legal status of fatherhood which a father has when married to the mother. Ward LJ explained why normally it is in the best interests of the child that a parental responsibility order is made. 'A child needs for its self-esteem to grow up, wherever it can, having a favourable positive image of an absent parent; and it is important that, wherever possible, the law should confer on a concerned father that stamp of approval because he has shown himself willing and anxious to pick up the responsibility of fatherhood and not to deny or avoid it.'[3]

The willingness of courts to separate the responsibility of a father to foster his personal relationship with his child from his duty to take on the more onerous obligations of parenthood was demonstrated in *Re H (Parental Responsibility: Maintenance)*.[4] The trial judge had adjourned a father's application for parental responsibility to enable the father to demonstrate his commitment to the children by assisting in their financial upkeep. The Court of Appeal held that the father's deliberate failure to pay maintenance did not disqualify him from having a parental responsibility order. 'The court ought not to use the weapon of withholding a parental responsibility order for the purpose of exacting from the father what may be regarded as his financial dues ... Though he is failing the children by not putting his money where he says his heart is, it must ... be in the children's best interest that their natural father should at least

---

1 Subsequently, in *Re G (A Minor) (Parental Responsibility Order)* [1994] 1 FLR 504 the Court of Appeal accepted for the purposes of the case that the welfare principle applies to parental responsibility orders; see, too, the observations of Butler-Sloss LJ in *Re T (A Minor) (Parental Responsibility: Contact)* [1993] 2 FLR 450.

2 [1998] 1 FLR 392, in which the child frequently needed to attend hospital for treatment and the father's main reason for seeking the order was so that he could make his own inquiries about his child's medical condition and be sent reports.

3 At p 397, per Ward LJ. Contact was refused because the child had a medical condition which meant that he needed constant and informed medical attention which the mother, but not the father, was able to provide. See also *Re G (A Minor) (Parental Responsibility Order)* [1994] 1 FLR 504 at p 508 where Balcombe LJ emphasised that it is normally for the welfare of a child that an attached and committed father is given parental responsibility; and *Re M (McKenzie Friend)* [1999] 1 FLR 75 where the link between parental responsibility and the child's welfare was again emphasised. Cf *Re J (Parental Responsibility)* [1999] 1 FLR 784 where a father's appeal from the refusal by justices to make a parental responsibility order was dismissed despite the justices having shown some lack of understanding of the true purpose of the order. The father had demonstrated minimal attachment and commitment and his 12-year-old daughter did not wish to see him.

4 [1996] 1 FLR 867.

be accorded that voice in their future which is implicit in a parental responsibility order.'[5] It is questionable whether it is wise for courts to allow an unmarried father to enjoy the rights associated with parental responsibility in circumstances where he has shown himself determined not to pay towards his child's support. For courts to adopt an approach which divests the notion of parental responsibility of any significant moral content gives an undesirable message to fathers about what having responsibility for a child entails. Such a message, which is permissive of irresponsible behaviour, is of little assistance in promoting the idea that children are entitled to receive a good standard of care from their parents.

A mother who is alienated from the father is likely to fear that a parental responsibility order will lead to the father interfering in the day-to-day upbringing of her child. However, in *Re P (A Minor) (Parental Responsibility Order)*,[6] Wilson J held that this was to misunderstand the effect of the order. He emphasised that a parental responsibility order does not permit the father to interfere in the day-to-day management of the child's life; it is the mother who has the right to determine such matters. Nor does it give him the power to override the mother's decisions. Furthermore, he pointed out that if a father were to misuse the rights given to him under section 4, they could be controlled by orders made under section 8 of the Children Act 1989.[7] As a last resort, the parental responsibility order itself could be discharged.[8] In relation to the case before him, Wilson J held that the fact that there was acrimony between the parties was not a reason for denying the father parental responsibility. He found that the father had shown great love and concern for the child, and it was therefore in her interests that both parents should have parental responsibility for her.[9]

It can be seen from the above analysis that courts are normally not prepared to deny parental responsibility to a father who is able to demonstrate some degree of commitment and attachment to his child. Once such commitment and attachment has been established, the courts have been reluctant to pass moral judgments on a father's behaviour when exercising their discretion, as was illustrated by *Re S (A Minor) (Parental*

---

5 Per Leggatt LJ at p 872.
6 [1994] 1 FLR 578. See also *Re C and V (Contact and Parental Responsibility)* [1998] 1 FLR 392, where the Court of Appeal held that it is perfectly proper for the court to inquire into the reasons which impelled the application, but unless these reasons were demonstrably improper and wrong, the court should not seek to regulate how parental responsibility was exercised on an application for a parental responsibility order.
7 These allow a court to control with whom the child will live and with whom he may have contact, to prohibit the manner in which a parent is otherwise entitled to exercise his parental responsibility, and to deal with any specific issue which has arisen. Such orders may contain directions and impose conditions. For a full account, see ch 2.
8 A parental responsibility agreement or order may be brought to an end by order of a court, but only on application by a person with parental responsibility for the child, or, with the leave of the court, the child himself (s 4(3)); and see *Re P (Terminating Parental Responsibility)* [1995] 1 FLR 1048.
9 See too *Re E (A Minor) (Parental Responsibility)* [1994] 2 FCR 709.

Responsibility).[10] In that case an order was made despite the fact that the father had been convicted of possessing obscene literature and was failing to pay child maintenance. However, this non-judgmental approach has been tempered in very serious cases. In *Re P (Parental Responsibility)*[11] the father had committed a serious robbery while on home leave from prison, for which he was sentenced to fifteen years' imprisonment. The children were taken to see him in prison and contact was settled by agreement. However, the judge declined to make a parental responsibility order. Refusing the father's appeal, the Court of Appeal emphasised that a prisoner does not lose his personal rights when sentenced to imprisonment. However, it held that if a father behaves in a manner which is likely to result in a long sentence he should be taken to realise that this has a damaging effect on his children. It is an act of irresponsibility on his part. It devalues his commitment and a long sentence means, inevitably, that the level of attachment is minimal. Similarly, in *Re H (Parental Responsibility)*[12] an order was refused where the father had deliberately injured the child in a sadistic manner.[13] Further, in *Re P (Terminating Parental Responsibility)*[14] Singer J granted an application to terminate a parental responsibility agreement in circumstances where the father had very seriously injured the child. However, Singer J also made it clear that such a step 'should not be allowed to become a weapon in the hands of the dissatisfied mother of the non-marital child: it should be used by the court as an appropriate step in the regulation of the child's life where the circumstances really do warrant it and not otherwise'.[15]

Although abuse of parental responsibility can be controlled by section 8 orders, as was emphasised in *Re S (Parental Responsibility)*[16] and *Re C and V (Contact and Parental Responsibility),*[17] where a father's reasons for seeking parental responsibility are demonstrably improper and wrong an order will be denied at the outset. This was the position in *W v Ealing London Borough Council.*[18] The children were in the care of the local authority, and leave had been given to the authority to terminate contact between the children and their parents prior to placing the children with long-term foster parents with a view to their adoption. The children had

10 [1995] 2 FLR 648, which contains a useful summary of how the case law has developed. For comment see F Kaganis *Responsible or feckless fathers? – Re S (Parental Responsibility)* (1996) 8 CFLQ 165. See also J Eekelaar *Parental responsibility – a new legal status* (1996) 112 LQR 233.
11 [1997] 2 FLR 722.
12 [1998] 1 FLR 855. See also *Re P (Parental Responsibility)* [1998] 2 FLR 96 where the father was deeply confused about sexual boundaries and about the difference between abusive and appropriate sexual behaviour.
13 The child had bruising to various parts of the body including the inner ear, penis and scrotum. Disturbingly, the judge nonetheless made a supervised contact order.
14 [1995] 1 FLR 1048.
15 At p 1052.
16 [1995] 2 FLR 648.
17 [1998] 1 FLR 392.
18 [1993] 2 FLR 788.

been prepared for separation from their parents, and two possible adoptive families had been found, neither of whom wanted contact between the children and their mother and father to continue. The father applied for contact and for a parental responsibility order.[19] Refusing his application, the court found that an order for contact would inevitably be disruptive of plans for the children's future, and that the father's only reason for applying for a parental responsibility order was the hope that he might thereby thwart the making of an adoption order. Similar reasoning was applied in *Re P (Parental Responsibility)*[20] where an attached and committed father made unfounded allegations about the mother's care to the social services department. The court found that he intended to use his parental responsibility inappropriately to try to interfere with, and possibly undermine, the mother's care for her child, and refused to make an order even though his likely abuse could have been controlled by a prohibited steps order.[1]

Who, in law, *are* a child's parents?

Almost all children know with certainty who their mother is, and the great majority of children know who their father is; however, in some cases the identity of a child's parents may be in doubt. This situation may arise for a variety of reasons. Sometimes a woman deceives a man into thinking that he is the father of her child, and sometimes the woman herself may not know which of two (or more) men is the child's father. The position is further complicated because modern methods of assisted conception mean that a woman may conceive a child other than through having sexual intercourse with a man. She may become pregnant by means of artificial insemination. The semen used to fertilise her egg may have been donated by a man who is not her husband or, in the case of unmarried couples, not the man with whom she is living. Instead, the donor of the semen is likely to be anonymous. Eggs, as well as semen, can be donated, and this can result in a woman giving birth to a child which has grown from another woman's egg.

The Human Fertilisation and Embryology Act 1990 brings clarity to this area of scientific development and its implications for family life. The Act provides a system of tight controls over which fertility procedures are acceptable. The Human Fertilisation and Embryology Authority, which was set up by the Act, operates a compulsory licensing system for those who wish to provide treatment services, to store sperm and eggs (gametes)

---

19   Because the children were in care, the contact application was made under s 34 of the Children Act 1989: see ch 3.
20   [1998] 2 FLR 96.
1   Under s 8, see ch 2. In this case the court was clearly influenced by the fact that the father was fifty years older than the mother and that photos of his pre-pubescent grandchildren in obscene or suggestive poses had been found in his possession.

or to create or use embryos for the purposes of research, and provides guidance for licensees by means of a code of practice. Where a child has been conceived by artificial methods, it is to that Act that attention must be given when looking for answers to the question 'who in law are the child's parents?'.[2]

Who is the child's mother?

The only situation in which the question 'who is a child's mother?' arises is when a woman has sperm and eggs implanted in her, or an embryo which uses eggs obtained from another woman. This means that the child contains none of the woman's genetic material. Is the woman who gives birth the mother of the child, or is the woman who donated her egg the mother?[3] The law answers this question without equivocation. Section 27(1) of the Human Fertilisation and Embryology Act 1990 provides:

> 'The woman who is carrying or who has carried a child as a result of the placing in her of an embryo or of sperm and eggs, and no other woman, is to be treated as the mother of the child.'

Section 29(1) further provides that a woman treated as the child's mother under section 27 is to be treated in law as the mother of the child for all purposes. Thus here there is certainty. The woman who gives birth to a child is the child's mother whether or not the child is genetically related to her.[4]

Occasionally a woman may be willing to act as a surrogate mother for a married woman who is unable to carry a child to term herself, with the intention of handing the child over to her and her husband after birth. In a situation of this kind there is no doubt that the woman who gives birth is the child's mother. But, in some instances, section 30(1) of the Human

---

2   For a detailed account of the law shortly after the passing of the Human Fertilisation and Embryology Act, see G Douglas *Law, Fertility and Reproduction* (Sweet and Maxwell, 1991). With the burgeoning interest in medical law there are now a number of medical law texts which consider assisted conception in considerable detail. See also R Deech *Family law and genetics* (1998) 61 MLR 697 for a very wide ranging discussion concerning genetic knowledge.

3   For a fascinating account of some research into egg donation, which reveals that 'egg donors actively envisage future children born of their donation, and have expectations and concerns about both these children and the women who will give birth to them', see F Price and R Cook *The donor, the recipient and the child – human egg donation in UK licensed centres* (1995) 7 CFLQ 145.

4   The Warnock Committee *Report of the Committee of Inquiry into Human Fertilisation and Embryology* (1984) Cmnd 9314, took the view that the law should always regard the carrying mother as the child's real mother. However, there is one exception to this rule: s 29(4) provides that the rule does not apply to 'the succession to any dignity or title of honour'.

Fertilisation and Embryology Act 1990 provides that a court may make an order in favour of the commissioning couple 'providing for a child to be treated in law as the child of the parties to a marriage'.[5] Before such an order can be made a court must be satisfied that the child has been carried by a woman other than the wife as the result of placing in her of an embryo, or sperm and eggs, or her artificial insemination, and that the gametes of the husband or the wife, or both, were used to bring about the creation of the embryo. In addition it must be satisfied that various conditions specified in subsections (2) to (7) of section 30 have been complied with. These conditions include that the application for the order has been made within six months of the child's birth; that both the woman who carried the child and the father[6] of the child agree unconditionally to the making of the order; and that no money or other benefit has been given or received by the commissioning couple for the purposes of the surrogacy arrangements and the making of the order.[7]

Once an order is made under section 30 the child becomes the child of the commissioning parents, and the woman who gave birth to him is no longer recognised by law as his mother. However, it should be noted that proceedings under section 30 are family proceedings for the purposes of the Children Act 1989,[8] so a court could make an order under section 8 of that Act[9] in addition to the section 30 order, or instead of a section 30 order. This is an important safeguard, which would allow a court to base any order it made on the principle that the child's welfare is the court's paramount consideration. However, it seems most unlikely that an order under section 8 would be made unless either an issue arose over contact with the child, or one or other of the child's legal parents changed his or her mind about agreeing to the section 30 order during the course of the proceedings.

Who is the child's father?

Identifying a child's father can be complicated,[10] although it is less complicated than hitherto. Modern forensic methods can determine with certainty whether a man is a child's father where genetic samples are available for

---

5   Thus avoiding the situation which occurred in *Re W (Minors) (Surrogacy)* [1991] 1 FLR 385, which arose before s 30 came into force.

6   For these purposes the 'father' includes the man who is recognised by law as being the child's father under s 28 (see below) where he is not the commissioning father: s 30(5), and see *Re Q (Parental Order)* [1996] 1 FLR 369.

7   For an analysis of some of the technical difficulties which can arise in relation to consents to a parental order, and for a moving description of the anguish experienced by a surrogate mother when parting with her child, see *Re Q (Parental Order)* [1996] 1 FLR 369.

8   S 30(8).

9   See ch 2.

10   As Shakespeare (who understood more than most about the vagaries of family life) realised when he commented through the mouthpiece of Young Gobbo in *The Merchant of Venice* 'it is a wise father that knows his own child'.

analysis. The question 'who is the child's father?' may arise in various contexts, the most commonplace being when a married woman gives birth to a child and there is doubt about whether her husband is the child's father; when an unmarried woman gives birth to a child and the man whom she alleges is the father denies paternity; and when a child is conceived either as the result of the artificial insemination of the mother, or by some other method of fertilisation not involving sexual intercourse.

The presumption of legitimacy

When a married woman gives birth to a child, the law dictates that the child should be presumed to be the offspring of her husband unless or until it is proven to be otherwise. This presumption of legitimacy applies to children conceived during a marriage, to children conceived before marriage but born during the marriage, and to children born within the normal gestation period after a marriage has ended by death or divorce. The presumption, which is a presumption of law, may be rebutted by evidence which shows that it is more probable than not that the husband is not the father.[11] Before issues relating to paternity could be resolved through blood tests and, more recently, DNA profiling, a body of case law had developed around this presumption and how it could be rebutted. This case law is now mainly of historic interest. However, if the husband has died, or cannot be traced, and if doubt is thrown on his paternity, it may be necessary to have recourse to this body of law because forensic testing will not be available.[12] There is no corresponding presumption relating to the paternity of a child who is born of parents who are unmarried.

Forensic testing

Nowadays, when doubt is cast on a husband's paternity, or when a man denies that he is the father of a child, a court has a discretion to direct blood testing under the Family Law Reform Act 1969, section 20. The court may exercise this power either of its own motion or on an application by any party to the proceedings. However, jurisdiction to make a direction for blood tests only arises where there are civil proceedings before the court in which the paternity of a child is in issue.[13] A court cannot make a direction for blood tests on a free-standing application. It seems likely that cases in which paternity is in issue will continue regularly to be brought before the courts because of the implications of the Child Support Acts 1991 and 1995. These Acts impose an obligation on all absent parents

---

11 Family Law Reform Act 1969, s 26.
12 For an account of the case law see Bromley and Lowe *Bromley's Family Law* (Butterworths, 7th edn) pp 240-244.
13 *Re E (A Minor) (Parental Responsibility)* [1994] 2 FCR 709.

to support their children financially, and provide for tracing and enforcement methods which have the potential to draw far more unmarried
fathers into the net of child support than hitherto.[14] They also give fathers
a stronger motive than hitherto to deny paternity because the amount
they are likely to be ordered to pay may be substantial, in which case the
matter can be referred to a court for determination.[15]

Forensic evidence is far preferable to evidence relating to whether the
man and woman had sexual intercourse around the time when the child
is believed to have been conceived, and to evidence relating to whether a
wife had sexual intercourse with another man or men as well as her
husband during the relevant period. Unless forensic evidence is available,
the evidence is likely to consist of statements made by the mother, and by
the man she alleges to be the father, and of statements made by other
witnesses. These statements will mainly relate to whether the alleged
father had the opportunity and the inclination to have sexual intercourse
with the mother. As people normally have sexual intercourse in private,
such witness statements are usually of limited assistance. The disadvantage of placing reliance on this type of evidence is manifest. Apart
from the fact that such evidence is often somewhat distasteful, embarrassing to all concerned, and may sometimes cause distress to the
parties because of the type of detail about the parties' sexual activities
which is required in a contested case, it is also not the best evidence
available. Forensic evidence is the best evidence and, of the choices
available, DNA testing is preferable to blood-matching testing because it
can establish paternity with certainty. By contrast, a blood-matching test
can establish that a man is not the child's father, but can only give a
statistical likelihood of whether he is the father.

The discretion to order blood tests

Guidance on the discretion to direct blood testing was given by the House
of Lords in *S v S; W v Official Solicitor*.[16] The point of law to be resolved

---

14 See ch 9.
15 There is, however, a risk that a man may sometimes be dissuaded from asking for
DNA testing, even though he has reasonable cause for believing that he is not the
father, because the court could order him to pay the costs, which are substantial
(currently about £500). *T v Child Support Agency* [1997] 2 FLR 875 provides a
salutary warning against not contesting paternity where the man correctly believes
that he is not the father. Pursuant to s 27 of the Child Support Act 1991, a family
proceedings court made a declaration of paternity against T. Subsequent DNA tests
proved that T was not the child's father. There is no right of appeal from a declaration
made under s 27. However, the court was prepared to exercise its discretion to
grant a declaration under RSC Ord 15, r 16, as no other form of redress was open to
T. But it should be noted that this is a discretionary power, and one which the court
may not always be prepared to exercise where the man has failed to avail himself of
his normal statutory rights.
16 [1970] 3 All ER 107.

was whether a test could be ordered despite the fact that the child might not benefit from the outcome of the test. The House of Lords made it clear that the paramountcy of the child's welfare is *not* the governing principle. Rather, the principle to be applied was expressed by Lord Hodson:[17]

> 'The court in ordering a blood test in the case of an infant has, of course, a discretion and may make or refuse an order for a test in the exercise of its discretion, but the interests of other persons than the infant are involved in ordinary litigation. The infant needs protection but that is no justification for making his rights superior to those of others.'[18]

Their Lordships ruled that where there is, or may be, a conflict between the interests of the child and the general requirements of justice, justice requires that available evidence should not be suppressed. It held that a court's duty to protect children will not ordinarily provide a ground for refusing to order forensic testing merely because it might, in revealing the truth, prove that the child is not the husband's child, and thus not born in lawful wedlock.[19] In relation to the child's interests, Lord Reid said: 'On the one hand, it is said that with rare exceptions it is always in the child's interests to have a decision that it is legitimate. On the other hand, it is said that the value to the child of a finding of legitimacy is now much less than it used to be, and that it is generally better for the child that the truth should out than that the child should go through life with a lurking doubt as to the validity of a decision when evidence, which would very likely have disclosed the truth, has been suppressed.'[20]

Despite the recognition by the House of Lords in *S v S; W v Official Solicitor* that to allow the truth to emerge normally serves both the interests of justice and the welfare of the child, the child's interests may occasionally demand that forensic testing does not take place. In *Re F (A Minor) (Blood Tests: Parental Rights)*[1] the mother was having a sexual relationship with both her husband and another man during the period when the child was conceived. The child had been brought up by her mother and the mother's husband since her birth, and had had no contact with the other man. This man, believing that he was the child's father, applied for a parental responsibility order, an order allowing him to have contact with the child, and for blood tests to determine her paternity. Clearly, unless the man was the child's father, the applications for parental

---

17 Ibid, at p 124.
18 See too Lord Reid: 'I would, therefore, hold that the court ought to permit a blood test of a young child to be taken unless satisfied that it would be against the child's interests,' ibid, at p 113.
19 Although the law does not distinguish between children born inside and outside marriage, in some circles there is still a stigma attached to illegitimacy.
20 [1970] 3 All ER 107, at p 111.
1 [1993] 3 All ER 596. For a critique, see J Fortin *Re F: 'The gooseberry bush approach'* (1994) 57 MLR 296.

responsibility and contact would be without basis. The trial judge dismissed the man's application for blood tests to be carried out, and the man's appeal was dismissed. The Court of Appeal held that the judge had properly exercised his discretion to refuse the application for blood tests. It held that the probable outcome of his application for a parental responsibility and contact order was that both orders would be refused because they could not possibly benefit the child. It said that the decisive factor was the child's welfare, and that the stability of the family unit on which the child's security depended might be disturbed if blood testing was ordered.[2] It further held that a court will not order a blood test to be carried out on a child against the will of a parent who has had sole parental responsibility for the child since the child's birth.[3]

A similar approach was taken in *O v L (Blood Tests)*.[4] The issue of the paternity of the youngest child of the family arose in divorce proceedings. Until the parties separated the child was brought up on the basis that the husband was her father, and it was only when the child was three that the wife alleged that the man with whom she was currently living was the father of the child. The trial judge found that the mother's application for blood tests was premature. He found that the child had a good relationship with the husband and that it was in her interests to maintain this relationship. Contact between the child and the husband was strongly opposed by the mother, and the judge took the view that there would be a much greater risk of contact being damaged or frustrated if it were proved that the husband were not the father. He therefore refused to direct blood tests. Confirming the judge's approach, the Court of Appeal held that to order blood tests which might show that the husband was not the child's father was a matter of considerable importance which should not be undertaken lightly. Here, information derived from the tests might be used to undermine contact, and it was not necessary for the precise nature of the relationship between the child and the husband to be defined by blood tests in order for contact to be fostered. Interestingly, however, Wall J stated that as the mother and the man she alleged was the father of the child had now married, were they to apply to the court for a declaration that the child was their legitimated daughter an order for blood tests would be almost inevitable. It therefore followed that 'the time is likely to come sooner rather than later when it will undoubtedly be in [the child's] interests for the question of her paternity to be resolved so that all her relationships within the family can be properly defined'.[5]

2 See also, *K v M (Paternity: Contact)* [1996] 1 FLR 312.
3 However, this aspect of the ruling has been thrown into doubt by the judgment of Hale J in *Re R (Blood Test: Constraint)* [1998] 1 FLR 745, where she held that a court can override the refusing parent and require the child to be tested. See below, and ch 2, where exercise of the inherent jurisdiction is considered.
4 [1995] 2 FLR 930.
5 At p 937.

The fact that a parent is adamant in refusing to be tested, or to allow her child to be tested, may in itself influence the court in its decision whether to order tests. In *Re CB (A Minor) (Blood Tests)*,[6] when refusing the applicant's request that orders for blood tests be made in respect of the mother, a married woman, and her youngest child, Wall J held that if blood tests were to establish that the applicant was the child's father, but if as a consequence the adults became involved in a bitter dispute over the child's upbringing, this would be contrary to the child's interests. However, in the light of the Court of Appeal's subsequent ruling in *Re H (Paternity: Blood Test)*,[7] it seems likely that courts will refuse to direct a blood test only in those cases where the facts are exceptional. In *Re H (Paternity: Blood Test)* the court reiterated that the child's welfare was not the dominant issue, and that while the outcome of any proceedings for parental responsibility and contact were obviously factors which would impinge on the child's welfare, they were not determinative of the blood testing question. Moreover, the court stated that the child has a right to know who his parents are 'unless his welfare clearly justifies the cover up', and drew an analogy between the need for a child to know the truth about his origins with the call for greater openness in adoption.[8]

Refusing forensic testing

Section 20 of the Family Law Reform Act 1969 empowers a court to give a direction for the use of blood tests to ascertain paternity, it does not give the court power to make an order requiring that tests be taken. Section 21(1) makes it clear that a court cannot force an adult to undergo forensic testing, his or her consent is necessary.[9] In relation to children, a child of 16 can give consent to the taking of a bodily sample.[10] Where the child is under 16 a sample can be taken if the person who has care and control of him consents.[11] Thus a direction can be given even where it is clear that it may never carried into effect. What inferences may a court properly draw from the refusal of a person to be tested or to agree to the child being tested in the face of the court's direction? Section 23(1) of the Family Law Reform Act 1969 provides that:

---

6   [1994] 2 FCR 925.
7   [1996] 2 FLR 65. This case contains a full and helpful analysis of the case law and the issues of principle to be resolved. For comment see B Gilbert *Paternity, truth and the interests of the child – some problems of Re H (Paternity: Blood Test)* (1996) 8 CFLQ 361.
8   Ward LJ pointed to the risks to the child where he does not discover the truth early in childhood, and referred to Art 7 of the UN Convention on the Rights of the Child to support his view that a blood test should be ordered.
9   See *Re H (Paternity: Blood Test)* [1996] 2 FLR 65 for discussion of this issue.
10 S 21(2).
11 S 21(3); it may also be the case that a '*Gillick* competent' child can consent to giving a bodily sample: see below.

'Where a court gives a direction under section 20 of this Act and any person fails to take any step required of him for the purpose of giving effect to the direction, the court may draw such inferences, if any, from that fact as appear proper in the circumstances.'

Section 23(2) provides that:

'Where in any proceedings in which the parentage of any person falls to be determined by the court hearing the proceedings there is a presumption of law that that person is legitimate, then if—
(a) a direction is given under section 20 of this Act in those proceedings, and
(b) any party who is claiming relief in the proceedings and who for the purposes of obtaining that relief is entitled to rely on the presumption fails to take any step required of him for the purpose of giving effect to the direction,
the court may adjourn the hearing for such period as it thinks fit to enable that party to take that step, and if at the end of that period he has failed without reasonable cause to take it the court may, without prejudice to subsection (1) of this section, dismiss his claim for relief notwithstanding the absence of evidence to rebut the presumption.'

Section 23(3) provides that:

'... where any person named in a direction under section 20 of this Act fails to consent to the taking of a bodily sample from himself or from any person named in the section over whom he has care and control he shall be deemed for the purposes of this section to have failed to take a step required of him for the purpose of giving effect to the direction.'

In *Re A (A Minor) (Paternity)*[12] the Court of Appeal held that the court's powers to draw inferences under section 23(1) are wholly at large and unconfined, including about the fact in issue, namely the child's paternity. It concluded that where an alleged father chooses to exercise his right not to be tested, the inference that he is the father of the child would be virtually inescapable. It pointed out that, in the light of recent scientific advance, a man cannot be forced against his will to accept paternity of a child whom he does not believe is his. But, as Waite LJ said, 'any man who is unsure of his own paternity and harbours the least doubt as to whether the child he is alleged to have fathered may be that of another man now has it within his power to set all doubt at rest by submitting to

---

12 [1994] 2 FLR 463.

a test'.[13] Equally, it seems that a court could properly draw the inference that a particular man is the child's father in a case where the mother denies this, but refuses to be tested, or to allow her child to be tested.

Subsequently, courts have adopted a robust approach where one of the parties has refused to be tested, or to allow the child to be tested, and have taken full advantage of their entitlement to draw such inferences as appear proper. As Ward LJ has said: 'common sense seems to me to dictate that if the truth can be established with certainty, a refusal to produce the certainty justifies some inference that the refusal is made to hide the truth'.[14] In *Re G (Parentage: Blood Sample)*[15] the Court of Appeal was firmly of the opinion that 'the forensic process is advanced by presenting the truth to the court. He who obstructs the truth will have the inference drawn against him. The inexorable advance of science cannot be ignored.'[16] In *Re R (Blood Test: Constraint)*[17] an even stronger stance was taken. It has been seen that forcing a person to submit to a blood test would normally be an assault, and that an adult cannot be forced to provide a blood sample against his or her will. It had hitherto been the view of the courts that blood cannot be taken from a child without the consent of the parent with care and control.[18] However, this has been thrown into doubt by Hale J's ruling that just as a parent can lawfully require that a young child submit to a blood test, so too can the court.[19] She could find nothing in principle against the court authorising the use of physical constraint against the child to achieve this purpose. Her suggested mechanism was to make a direction under the Family Law Reform Act 1969 to order the delivery of the child into the care and control of the Official Solicitor and to make it plain that he was permitted to consent on the child's behalf.

Where paternity proceedings arise in relation to a child who is born to a married woman, and where consent to blood testing is refused by one of the adults concerned, the legal position is made more complicated by the presumption of legitimacy. It can be seen that the drafting of section 23(2) separates the presumption of legitimacy from claiming relief in reliance on the presumption. In a case in which a party who is relying on the

---

13 Ibid, at pp 472-473.

14 *Re H (Paternity: Blood Test)* [1996] 2 FLR 65 at p 77.

15 [1997] 1 FLR 360.

16 Ibid, per Ward LJ at p 366.

17 [1998] 1 FLR 745.

18 See *S v S; W v Official Solicitor* [1970] 3 All ER 107, per Lord Reid at p 112: 'No case has yet occurred in which a court has ordered a blood test to be carried out against the will of the parent who has the care and control of the child, and I am not at all certain that it would be proper to do that or that it will be possible to do that after Part III of the Act of 1969 comes into operation.' See also, *K v M (Paternity: Contact)* [1996] 1 FLR 312; *Re H (Paternity: Blood Tests)* [1996] 2 FLR 65.

19 Hale J drew an analogy with cases where blood products have been administered to children against the express wishes of the parents, as in *Re R (A Minor) (Blood Transfusion)* [1993] 2 FLR 757. For further discussion of *Re R (Blood Test: Constraint)*, see the consideration of the use of the inherent jurisdiction of the High Court in ch 2.

presumption refuses to be tested, or to allow the child to be tested, the court may dismiss the claim for relief even though there may be an absence of evidence to rebut the presumption. An example might be where a married woman alleges that a man other than her husband is the father of her child for child support purposes. Where the man denies paternity, but refuses to be tested, it seems that it would be possible for a court to order that the man should be liable to make child support payments, even though there is an absence of evidence to rebut the presumption of legitimacy.[20] However, where a husband relies on the presumption of legitimacy and refuses to be tested, the inference will be drawn that he is not the father of the child.[1]

Courts have increasingly taken the view that the truth about a child's paternity should emerge, and that attempts by a parent (including an alleged parent) to obstruct this process should be met by the drawing of adverse inferences. Commentators have generally welcomed this development in the law, taking the view that it is the 'right' of the child to know his or her paternity.[2] Whilst 'secrets and lies' are not normally beneficial to inter-personal relationships, it is none the less arguable that courts have become over-confident that a 'truth must out' approach benefits all children.[3] Whether this confidence is borne out by experience, and whether it should be applied in almost a blanket fashion to the multiplicity of parent/child relationships which exist within English multi-cultural society is questionable.[4] There has been no direct research on whether directing blood tests against a parent's wishes is of benefit to children, and it may be that too many assumptions are being made about the impact on children of knowing that their father is not their father extrapolated from research conducted in other contexts. In particular, analogies have been drawn with adoption in cases where a child's paternity has been put in issue. There is a body of reputable research which favours an open, honest approach to adoption and for adopted children to be brought up in

20 This could only occur in a case where the husband is unavailable for testing but where there is evidence that he could be the father, for otherwise whether or not the husband is the child's father could be established with certainty by taking samples from him and the child.

1 *Re G (Parentage: Blood Sample)* [1997] 1 FLR 360.

2 For a particularly perceptive and sensitive discussion of the significance of the blood tie, see J Fortin *Children's Rights and the Developing Law* (Butterworths, 1998) ch 14.

3 See, for example, Ward LJ's approach to the anxieties of the 'father' in *Re G (Parentage: Blood Sample)* [1997] 1 FLR 360. The father took the view that for his little girl to discover 'that the only thing she has got left in her life that has not changed is not real any more, I think that would do more damage to her that can be said', was dismissed with the statement that it was not for the father to assess what is best for the child but for the court. 'I am in entire agreement with the opinion of the court welfare officer that it is essential for the ultimate well-being of this child both that she knows the truth about who her father is, and that she knows it sooner rather than later.'

4 See, for example, the mother's evidence in *Re H (Paternity: Blood Test)* [1996] 2 FLR 65 at p 69. 'I shall lie to [the child]. I shall do that to protect [the child]. In my mind my husband is the father.'

the knowledge that their parents are not their birth parents. However, the factual position in adoption is very different from one where a wife's ex-lover is claiming paternity of a child who is being treated by her husband as his own, and where both husband and wife are experiencing the alleged father's unwelcome intrusion into their family life as destabilising.[5] If forcing blood tests on an unwilling married couple has a destructive effect on their personal relationship, or on the husband's relationship with the child, this may be more harmful to the child than giving him knowledge of the true facts.[6] While some men may have no difficulty in treating another man's child as their own even where there is doubt about the child's paternity, other men may find it emotionally impossible to continue to respond to the child as their own where the fact of their non-paternity is established by incontrovertible evidence.

It is suggested, therefore, that care should be taken before too much certainty is vested in the notion that a child will *always* (as distinct from normally) benefit from knowing that the man whom he believes is his father is not his father,[7] particularly in those cases where contact between the child and the alleged father is likely to be denied.[8] In the context of artificial insemination of a wife by a donor with her husband's agreement, which is equally analagous to adoption, the law treats the husband as the father of the child and takes the view that disclosure to the child of his true paternity is a matter for the couple themselves.[9] This approach acknowledges the complexity of adult personal relationships and gives choice to the parents as to whether, when and how this disclosure is made. Family dynamics vary from one household to another, particularly over an issue as sensitive as contested paternity. Directions for blood tests may force disclosure at a time which may not fit in with the child's peace and sense of security, or may deliver a body blow to a recovering marriage which is still fragile with regard to the previous relationship which led to the child's birth. It therefore seems desirable that courts should feel free to respond flexibly to a request that blood tests be directed and in a manner which is perceptive of the family life of the particular child concerned.

5   See, for example, *Re F (A Minor) (Blood Tests: Parental Rights)* [1993] 1 FLR 598; *Re H (Paternity: Blood Test)* [1996] 2 FLR 65.
6   As was recognised in *O v L* [1995] 2 FLR 930, although the Court of Appeal also acknowledged that at some stage the child's true paternity needed to be determined.
7   Such a child could, for example, feel an outsider, especially where his siblings suddenly become his half siblings.
8   As in *Re F (A Minor) (Blood Tests: Parental Rights)* [1993] 3 All ER 596.
9   Human Fertilisation and Embryology Act 1990, s 28(2) and see below. For a discussion of whether this is the 'right' approach see S Maclean and M Maclean *Keeping secrets in assisted reproduction – the tension between donor anonymity and the need of the child for information* (1996) 8 CFLQ 243; S Wilson *Identity, genealogy and the social family: The case of donor insemination* (1997) 11 IJLPF 270; and E Blyth *Donor assisted conception and donor offspring rights to genetic origins information* (1998) 6 Int JCR 237.

Assisted conception and paternity

It has been seen that methods of assisting an infertile couple to conceive a child may include impregnating the woman with sperm from a man who is not the woman's husband, or partner. However, despite the lack of genetic relationship between the husband, or partner, and the child, these men can be accorded the status of father of the child as a matter of law provided that they fall within the provisions of the Human Fertilisation and Embryology Act 1990.

Assisted conception and husbands

Section 28(2) of the Human Fertilisation and Embryology Act 1990 provides that if at the time of the placing in her of the embryo or the sperm and eggs or of her insemination, the woman was a party to a marriage, and the creation of the embryo carried by her was not brought about with the sperm of the other party to the marriage, her husband shall be treated as the child's father,[10] unless he has not consented to the artificial form of treatment she received to bring about conception. Consent must be given in writing, and the husband must be given a suitable opportunity to receive counselling and any relevant information.[11] Where he has not consented, the common law presumption of legitimacy will nonetheless apply unless rebutted by evidence to the contrary.[12]

The issue of consent was crucial in the case of *R v Human Fertilisation and Embryology Authority, ex p Blood*.[13] After the applicant, Diane Blood, and her husband had been married for about three years they decided that they would like to have a child. However, the husband contracted meningitis and died a few days later. While he was unconscious in hospital doctors, at the request of Mrs Blood, removed a sample of his sperm and stored it at a licensed clinic. Subsequently, Mrs Blood wished to be artificially inseminated with her late husband's sperm in order to have his child.[14] However, the Human Fertilisation and Embryology Authority refused to release the sperm to her on the grounds that the husband had not consented to its removal and use, and therefore to authorise the wife's insemination with his sperm would be contrary to the provisions of the Human Fertilisation and Embryology Act 1990. It was accepted by the Authority that it had discretion to authorise the export of the sperm so that Mrs Blood could be treated abroad. However, the Authority took the

---

10 Consequently the husband's position in relation to contact with his child is identical to that where the child is biologically his own child; see *Re CH (Contact: Parentage)* [1996] 1 FLR 569.
11 Sch 3, para 3.
12 Human Fertilisation and Embryology Act 1990, s 28(5)(a).
13 [1997] 2 FLR 742.
14 The husband's family gave the wife's request their full support.

view that they should not give her permission to take the sperm to Belgium where she might be able to be treated.

Mrs Blood sought to challenge the Authority's decision by way of judicial review. Sir Stephen Brown, President, felt unable to accede to her application but granted leave to appeal. The Court of Appeal held that storage of sperm could only take place lawfully pursuant to a licence where the donor had given written consent, been given the opportunity to receive counselling, and had been provided with proper information. Therefore, the sperm should never have been preserved and stored and the decision of the Authority to refuse to release the sperm was correct. However, the Authority had a wide discretion to authorise the export of sperm, and by refusing the request to export the sperm to Belgium, the Authority had failed to consider the effect of Articles 59 and 60 of the EC Treaty. These provisions gave the wife a right directly enforceable by her (and therefore part of English law) to receive medical treatment in another Member State. The Authority's prohibition of the export of the late husband's sperm was an interference with the freedom to provide and receive cross-border services in other Member States.[15] Such a decision could be justified, and would not be an infringement of Article 59, provided that it had been reached in accordance with well-established principles applying to administrative decisions.[16] However, the Authority had not taken account of Article 59 when coming to its decision. Moreover, once judgment was given on the instant case there should be no further cases where sperm was preserved without written consent, as such a practice was illegal. Therefore, any decision in favour of the applicant would not create an undesirable precedent. These findings persuaded the Court of Appeal to remit the matter to the Authority for reconsideration.[17]

This simple, tragic situation attracted widespread controversy and publicity, and deep sympathy was expressed by many for Diane Blood's

15 Married couples are not affected by whether the treatment takes place outside the United Kingdom. Section 28(8) confirms the husband's paternity regardless of the location of the treatment: see *U v W (A-G Intervening)* [1997] 2 FLR 282, at p 292.

16 For full analysis of the position under the EC Treaty, and the principles applying to administrative decisions, see [1997] 2 FLR 742, pp 766-773.

17 The *Blood* case attracted considerable comment and one academic, Professor Sheila McLean, was specifically invited to review some of the workings of the Human Fertilisation and Embryology Act 1990 in the light of the decision: see S McLean *Consent and the Law – Consultation Document and Questionnaire* (DOH, 1997). See too R Deech *Infertility and ethics* (1997) 9 CFLQ 337 (this article is of particular interest as the author was (and still is) Chairman of the HFEA throughout the time the case proceeded through the courts); S J Treece and D Savas *More questions than answers? R v Human Fertilisation and Embryology Authority ex parte Blood* (1997) 3 Med Law Int 75; D Morgan and R G Lee *In the name of the father? Ex parte Blood: Dealing with novelty and anomaly* (1997) 60 MLR 840; M E Rodgers *Gametes: storage, consent and treatment* [1997] 3 Web JCLI. Also see T Hervey, *Buy baby: The European Union and regulation of human reproduction* (1998) 18 OJLS 207, in which the author considers the extent to which EC law affects the regulation of human reproduction in Member States.

position.[18] The Authority gave fresh consideration to Mrs Blood's application in the light of the guidance issued by the Court of Appeal, and agreed to allow her to take her late husband's sperm to Belgium, where she was able to obtain the fertility treatment she had so fervently pursued. This is one of those rare cases where the end of the story is known, because of the publicity it engendered. Shortly before Christmas in 1998 Diane Blood gave birth to a son, whom she named Liam Stephen.[19] It would be desirable to add the phrase 'after his father' which, of course, is the reality of what occurred. However, as a matter of law, Liam Stephen is fatherless. Section 28(6)(b) of the Human Fertilisation and Embryology Act 1990 provides that where:

'... the sperm of a man, or any embryo the creation of which was brought about with his sperm, was used after his death, he is not to be treated as the father of the child'.

The desirability of the inclusion of section 28(6) in the legislation has undoubtedly been raised by the birth of Diane Blood's child. The subsection appears to be more concerned with difficulties relating to the administration of the estates of deceased persons, and related problems of inheritance and succession than with the welfare of children born posthumously. It is suggested that any legislation which deliberately renders a child fatherless where his genetic parentage is known is in urgent need of review.[20]

Assisted conception and unmarried couples

In the case of a child born to an unmarried couple as a result of artificial methods of conception, section 28(3) provides that a man who is not the child's genetic father (because his sperm did not create the embryo) is nonetheless treated by law as father of the child, provided that the methods used to assist conception were carried out 'in the course of treatment services provided for [a woman] and a man together by a person to whom a licence applies'.[1] There is clearly a mental element in 'treatment together', and if the man at all material times were to believe that the treatment which was being provided was treatment in which his sperm alone was to be used, and if the woman were to agree to the use of donor sperm without the man's knowledge or consent, such services would not

---

18 See also the compassionate remarks by Sir Stephen Brown P [1997] 2 FLR 742, at p 757; the affidavit of Lord Winston, Professor of Fertility Studies, at p 754; and the statement of Baroness Warnock, who chaired the Committee of Inquiry into Human Fertilisation and Embryology (1994), at pp 749-750.
19 Mr Blood's name was Stephen.
20 S 28(6)(a) provides that where a deceased man's sperm is used the child is fatherless despite the fact that his consent was properly given under Sch 3, para 5.
1 That is, a licence issued by the Human Fertilisation and Embryology Authority.

amount to 'treatment services provided for them together'.[2] However, the test in section 28(3) 'is not whether the man consented either to be deemed in law to be the father of the prospective child or to become legally responsible for him: it is whether the relevant treatment services were provided for the woman and him together'.[3] Thus the man's status is dependent on whether the unmarried couple have together been able to secure the placing in the woman of an embryo, or sperm and eggs, or artificial insemination with the assistance of a licensed clinic. Where, applying these rules, the man is the child's father, this has the consequence that he takes on all the obligations of paternity, including, of course, the obligation to maintain the child.[4]

The requirement that the treatment is provided by a person to whom a licence applies is the other crucial requirement in section 28(3). In *U v W (A-G Intervening)*[5] Miss U and Mr W (who was married to another woman) travelled to Rome where they received fertility treatment together,[6] which resulted in the birth of twins. Tests confirmed that Mr W was excluded from genetic paternity. In the meantime the relationship between Miss U and Mr W came to an end, and Miss U sought a declaration that Mr W was father of the twins so that she could obtain a maintenance assessment under the Child Support Act 1991.[7] The issue for the court was whether Mr W fell within section 28(3) in view of the fact that the treatment had been provided abroad. Dismissing Miss U's application, Wilson J held that although the treatment services had been provided by the parties together, it had not been at a licensed clinic. In relation to the question of whether this requirement was restrictive on the freedom to provide services for all nationals of Member States within the European Union under Article 59 of the Treaty of Rome, the court ruled that it was, but that the restriction could be justified for policy reasons. Member States had been given considerable discretion under Community law to determine which restriction was proportionate to their own legitimate objectives, and the licensing system with its code of practice was a restriction which was not out of proportion to the reasons which justified that restriction. There was no direct restriction on couples seeking fertility treatment; the only effect of section 28(3) was to withhold from couples who received successful treatment the legal consequence that the man was the father of the child. Therefore there was no infringement of Article 59. Consequently the twins were fatherless, and Mr W was not liable to maintain them. It is important that unmarried couples who obtain fertility treat-

---

2 See *U v W (A-G Intervening)* [1992] 2 FLR 282, at p 294.
3 Ibid, per Wilson J, at p 295.
4 *Re B (Parentage)* [1996] 2 FLR 15. However, like any other unmarried father, he does not have automatic parental responsibility unless he acquires it as provided by s 4 of the Children Act 1989.
5 [1997] 2 FLR 282.
6 Artificial insemination by an anonymous donor.
7 See ch 9.

ment abroad are made aware of the implications of this ruling, so that they can make provision for any children born by legal means which do not turn on the man's paternity.[8]

Where a child is conceived in accordance with the provisions of the Human Fertilisation and Embryology Act 1990, the donor of the sperm is not treated as the child's father for any purposes.[9] By contrast, where a woman conceives through donor insemination using self-help methods, then it is the donor, not her partner, who is the child's father.[10] This outcome is inevitable, for there is no regulated framework within which the conception occurs. However, where such self-help methods have been used, and where the woman's partner holds himself out as the child's father with the agreement of the mother, he will of course be recognised and treated by others as the father because no one will have cause to think otherwise. Where couples disguise the truth about the child's paternity in cases of this kind, the true position is unlikely to emerge provided that the family relationships remain stable. However, serious questions may arise about whether forensic testing should be ordered in a case where the relationship between the man and the woman subsequently breaks down, and where the 'father' denies paternity. Is it in the best interests of a child for tests to take place where the child has had a relationship of many years with the man, and where he believes that the man is his father? Should a man who has agreed to the donor insemination of his partner be entitled to avoid having any further responsibility for the upbringing of the child?[11] And if the mother refuses to undergo forensic testing, or to allow the child to be tested, because she does not want her partner to be able to avoid the financial obligations of parenthood which he initially agreed to undertake, what inferences, if any, would it be proper for the court to draw under section 23(1) of the Family Law Reform Act 1969?

Transsexuals and parenthood

English law defines a person's sex by reference to biological criteria at birth and does not recognise that it can be changed by reassignment

---

8   For example, the mother could appoint the man as guardian to the children, so that he would acquire parental responsibility for them in the event of her death. The mother and the man might also be able to secure parental responsibility for the man by applying for a joint residence order, see chs 2 and 4. Should the man and the mother subsequently marry, they could apply jointly to adopt the children, see ch 4. It would clearly be in the interests of the mother to arrange for a contract to be drawn up between herself and the man to secure the children's future maintenance. The woman should also seek to ensure that the man makes provision for the children in his will.

9   S 28(4), s 28(6)(a) and Sch 3, para 5.

10   Self-help may involve the woman having sexual intercourse with a man on the understanding that any child conceived will not be treated as his child; or by the man producing his sperm and the woman inserting it into her body by a syringe.

11   This question is particularly likely to arise where an unmarried mother is claiming child support from the 'father'. Unless the man is indeed the child's father, he has no duty to support the child: see further ch 9.

surgery.[12] As a result of this principle, a female to male transsexual is not permitted to marry a woman and cannot be regarded as father of a child. The refusal of English law to recognise the relationship between a transsexual male and the child born to his female partner as a result of artificial insemination by donor was challenged in the European Court of Human Rights in the case of *X, Y and Z v United Kingdom*.[13] The applicants (X, a female to male transsexual, his female partner Y, and Z the child born to Y) submitted that the refusal by the Registrar General to register X as the father of Y's child amounted to a violation of Article 8 of the European Convention on Human Rights. Article 8 provides:

'(1) Everyone has the right to respect for his private and family life, his home and his correspondence.
(2) There shall be no interference by a public authority with the exercise of this right except such as is in accordance with the law and is necessary in a democratic society in the interests of national security, public safety or the economic well-being of the country, for the prevention of disorder or crime, for the protection of health or morals, or for the protection of the rights and freedoms of others.'

The Court was unanimous in finding that Article 8 applied to the applicant's position. The notion of 'family life' was not confined solely to families based on marriage; it may encompass other family relationships. Relevant factors included whether the couple live together, the length of their relationship and whether they had demonstrated their commitment to each other by having children together or by any other means. Here the couple applied jointly for, and were granted, treatment for artificial insemination to allow Y to have a child. X was involved throughout that process and had acted as Z's father in every respect since the birth. However, the Court also held that it must have regard to the fair balance which must be struck between the competing interests of the individual and of the community as a whole, and in both cases the State enjoys a certain margin of appreciation. The Court observed that there was no common European standard with regard to granting parental rights to transsexuals. In addition, it had not been established before the Court that there existed any generally shared approach amongst the Contracting States with regard to the manner in which the social relationship between a child conceived by artificial insemination by donor should be reflected by law. Consequently, the United Kingdom must be afforded a wide margin of appreciation, and in the circumstances was justly cautious of changing the law. The Court therefore ruled by 14 votes to 6 that given that transsexuality raised complex scientific, legal, moral and social issues in respect of which there was no generally shared

12 *Corbett v Corbett (Otherwise Ashley)* [1971] P 83, and see further the law of nullity of marriage, ch 7.
13 [1997] 2 FLR 892.

approach among the Contracting States, there had been no violation of Article 8.

When considering this ruling it is important to bear in mind the points made in the concurring opinion of Judge Pettiti.[14] In his view too much emphasis had been placed on the personal demands of X and Y which were specific to their individual situations. As this was the first case in which the Court had had to deal with both transsexualism and a child's right to know his biological origins, more thought should have been given to the conflict of interests between parents and children. If there was a family, as there appeared to have been in the case before the Court, could the object being sought by X be imposed on Z? The case touched on the conflict between the demand of a transsexual to be registered as a child's father and the demand which could in due course be made by Z to find out who her biological father was.[15] As Judge Pettiti commented:

> 'The growing number of precarious and unstable family situations is creating new difficulties for children of first and second families, whether legitimate, natural, successive or superimposed, and will in the future call for thoughtful consideration of the identity of the family and the meaning of family life which Article 8 is intended to protect, taking into account the fact that priority must be given to the interests of the child and its future.'[16]

Parental responsibility and third parties

The concept of parental responsibility underpins decision-making about children. It is the fact that a decision-maker enjoys this responsibility, which gives him or her the power and the authority to make choices about a child's upbringing. Consequently, it may be essential for persons other than parents to have parental responsibility so that they are empowered to act on the child's behalf. Unless a decision is made by a person with parental responsibility it is not normally a decision which can safely be acted upon. Parental responsibility can be acquired by persons who are not parents of the child in the following circumstances: when a person is appointed as guardian of the child; when a court makes a residence order to a third person; when a local authority obtains a care order, including an interim care order; or when an emergency protection order is made. In each of these circumstances there are reasons why the fact that the child's

14 At p 905.
15 The judge suggested that should a similar case arise in the future, it would be desirable for the Commission and the Court to suggest to the parties that a lawyer be instructed specifically to represent the interests of the child alone.
16 For further critical discussion, see the arguments presented by the applicants, the responses to them in the majority ruling, and the dissenting opinions. See also C Lind *Perceptions of sex in the legal determination of fatherhood – X, Y and Z v UK* (1997) 9 CFLQ 401.

mother, and sometimes his father, have parental responsibility provides insufficient safeguards for the child.[17] In the case of guardianship, a parent with parental responsibility will be dead.[18] In the case of a residence order to a third party, a court will have made an order that the third party is the person with whom the child is to live because the child's welfare requires this.[19] In the case of a care order, or an emergency protection order, it will have been established that the child is suffering, or is likely to suffer, significant harm attributable to a lack of reasonable parental care, or because the child is beyond parental control, and that it is for the welfare of the child that parental responsibility is given to the local authority.[20] With the exception of guardianship, parental responsibility can only be conferred on a person other than a parent by means of a court order.

Sharing parental responsibility

A person who already has parental responsibility for a child does not cease to have that responsibility solely because some other person subsequently acquires it.[1] The Children Act 1989 makes it explicit that more than one person may have parental responsibility for the same child at the same time.[2] This is a vital principle which underpins much of the thinking in the Children Act 1989.[3] It means that parental responsibility is not only shared between parents, but also that it may sometimes be shared between parents and a third party. But if each person with parental responsibility has 'all the rights, duties, powers, responsibilities and authority which by law a parent of a child has in relation to the child and his property',[4] how can such persons exercise parental responsibility independently of the other where their parental responsibility is shared? This question is answered in various provisions in the Act, and in the accompanying regulations and guidance.

Section 2(7) provides that:

> 'Where more than one person has parental responsibility for a child, each of them may act alone and without the other (or others) in meeting that responsibility; but nothing in this Part shall be

---

17 It has been explained above how an unmarried father can acquire parental responsibility either by making a formal agreement with the mother, or by a court order.
18 Guardianship is considered below.
19 See ch 2.
20 Care orders and emergency protection orders are considered in detail in ch 3.
1   S 2(6).
2   S 2(5).
3   In particular, it underpins the notion that local authorities who are looking after a child in their care, and for whom they therefore have parental responsibility, should work in partnership with parents: see ch 3.
4   The meaning of parental responsibility given in s 3(1).

taken to affect the operation of any enactment which requires the consent of more than one person in a matter affecting the child.'

Section 2(7) clearly allows unilateral decisions to be made about a child's upbringing by a person with parental responsibility. This is essential for practical reasons. If every time a decision was made about a child which required authorisation from someone with the requisite authority, it would often be impossible to proceed if agreement was first required from all persons with parental responsibility. There may also be psychological benefits in the notion that each person with parental responsibility may act alone in meeting that responsibility. When parents are estranged, they often disagree over matters relating to the upbringing of their children. There are advantages in the notion that one parent is not entitled to dictate to the other parent how he or she looks after the child when that child is in the other's care.[5] If a residence order is made to a third party, which means that the child will have his home with that third party, he or she is likely to need to have the authority to make decisions about the child without prior consultation with the parents.

On the other hand there are disadvantages in allowing unilateral decision-making by persons with parental responsibility. Some decisions about the upbringing of a child are so important that it may be thought right that all persons with parental responsibility should have the opportunity to express an opinion before action on the decision is taken. Thus in *Re G (Parental Responsibility: Education)*[6] Glidewell LJ had no doubt that the mother ought to have been consulted by the father before he made the important decision to remove the child from his day school and to send him to a boarding school.[7] However, section 2(7) affords protection to the parent who acts unilaterally in a case of this kind, and no sanction can be imposed on a parent who fails to consult the other. Indeed, the court may feel that it is inappropriate to intervene once a decision about the child's upbringing has been made by one parent.[8] Furthermore, where the issue is discussed, but where agreement cannot be reached, a person with parental responsibility who objects to the exercise by the other of his or her parental responsibility has the burden of pursuing the matter before a court. An exception to this general principle applies where the law dictates that the consent of all persons with parental responsibility is required. The law requires the consent of both parents

---

5   For example, after divorce the child will normally live with one parent and have contact with the other. When the non-residential parent looks after the child on a contact visit he or she is entitled to care for the child in whatever manner he or she chooses.

6   [1994] 2 FLR 964.

7   A different example might be where the child requires medical treatment, and where there are different views about whether such treatment is in the child's best interests.

8   Thus in *Re G (Parental Responsibility: Education)* [1994] 2 FLR 964, the court refused to make an ex parte prohibited steps order to prevent the child attending the boarding school, despite finding that the mother should first have been consulted.

with parental responsibility to change of the child's surname,[9] to the child's adoption,[10] or to his permanent removal from England.[11] In other cases the law normally requires the consent of both parents to the child's marriage while he is a minor,[12] to his temporary removal from England,[13] or to his reception into local authority accommodation.[14] But it will be seen that these matters are affected by whether one parent has the benefit of a residence order.[15]

The other way in which the sharing of parental responsibility is made workable is through the 'incompatibility' principle which is embodied in section 2(8). This provides that:

'The fact that a person has parental responsibility for a child shall not entitle him to act in any way which would be incompatible with any order made with respect to the child under this Act.'

Thus when a court has made a decision about a child which has been embodied in a court order, that decision takes priority over the parental responsibility of the parents and others. For example, the parents might not wish the child to have contact with his grandparents. Normally parents have the power to decide whether such contact should take place. But where that decision is challenged in a court, and the court rules that contact should be permitted, the court's order must be obeyed. Similarly, a local authority which is looking after a child in care is normally entitled to decide whether a child has contact with his grandparents. However, if the grandparents successfully challenge this decision in a court, the local authority must allow such contact to take place in accordance with the court's ruling. Any other outcome would be incompatible with the court's order. Or one parent might be empowered by a court order to make all decisions about a child's medical treatment in a case where the other parent holds strong views against traditional forms of medical intervention.[16] Thus the incompatibility principle diminishes the decision-making powers of those with parental responsibility, and in some cases determines how decision-making will be shared.

Where a child is in care under a care order, which means that the local authority have parental responsibility for him, the general principles in

---

9 See ch 4. And see J Eekelaar *Do parents have a duty to consult?* (1998) 114 LQR 337.
10 Adoption Act 1976, s 16 and see ch 4.
11 Child Abduction Act 1984, s 1; Children Act 1989, s 13 and see ch 4.
12 Marriage Act 1949, s 3(1A).
13 Children Act 1989, s 13.
14 Children Act 1989, s 20(7)(8).
15 See ch 2.
16 See *Re S (Minors)* (1995) 8 February, Lexis, where the Court of Appeal prohibited a Jehovah's Witness mother from requiring her four daughters to carry a card stating that they could not have a blood transfusion in the event of an accident. The father, who was not a Jehovah's Witness, did not object to blood transfusions.

section 2 apply. The local authority must share their parental responsibility with the parents. However, the provisions in section 2 are qualified by section 33(3)(b). This provides that the local authority have the power to determine the extent to which the parents may meet their parental responsibility for a child where a care order has been made. However, provisions in Part III of the Act, and regulations and guidance issued under the Act, require local authorities to work in partnership with parents, and to involve them in decision-making about their child's upbringing.[17] Periodic reviews must be held about the child, and the views of the parents must be sought.[18] Procedures must be established which enable a parent to make representations, including any complaint, to the local authority about their child's upbringing, and at least one person who is not a member or officer of the local authority must be a member of such a reviewing body.[19] Thus mechanisms have been put in place which are designed to ensure that responsibility between parents and the local authority is shared, despite the fact that it is the local authority which has the primary responsibility to make decisions about the child.[20]

Delegating parental responsibility

It is often necessary for persons who have dealings with the day-to-day care of a child to be empowered to make decisions on the child's behalf despite the fact that they do not have parental responsibility. Relatives, school teachers, child-minders and nannies are obvious examples of such persons. Section 2(9) specifically stipulates that a person who has parental responsibility for a child may not surrender or transfer any part of that responsibility to another, but the subsection does allow a person with parental responsibility to arrange for some or all of it to be met by one or more persons acting on his behalf. For example, it is common practice for schools to receive written authority from parents delegating their power to give consent to medical treatment for children to the teachers. When the main body of care for a child is provided in an institution, such as when a child is accommodated in a boarding school, or in a local authority children's home, a wide variety of decisions about the child's upbringing will be formally delegated to the persons running these institutions.

In the usual course of daily living, parents do not normally make formal provision for the day-to-day arrangements they make with others about the care of their children. However, this can sometimes cause problems. The Act places considerable emphasis on the concept of parental res-

---

17 See ch 3.
18 S 26(2).
19 S 26(3)(4) and see ch 3.
20 However, just as parents do not have unlimited powers over the upbringing of their children, neither do local authorities: *Re M Care (Leave to Interview Child)* [1995] 1 FLR 825.

ponsibility as providing the basis for decision-making, and this is gradually permeating into public awareness.[1] In the context of medical treatment there is evidence that some hospital personnel refuse to provide medical treatment for a child until they receive parental authority to do so (unless the situation is one of an emergency).[2] It would be most unfortunate if medical decisions about a child were to be delayed whilst parents are contacted if such delay would cause a child avoidable pain and suffering. It is suggested that such an approach to the formal provision of consent from a parent stems from a misunderstanding of the formality which is required by law for the delegation of parental responsibility. For the law to be workable, it would appear essential for the delegation of parental responsibility to be capable of being implied. It is suggested that if a relative, nanny, child-minder or other person is caring for a child, and has been told informally to seek medical assistance if the child needs it, that this should be sufficient to amount to delegated authorisation from the parent to consent to whatever type of medical treatment is suggested until the parent can be contacted.

The position of persons without parental responsibility

Many people have the day-to-day care of children without having parental responsibility for them. Yet it has been seen that only those with parental responsibility have all the responsibilities of parenthood, and the position of others who have the care of children therefore requires some clarification. Can they make important decisions about the child? If such a person were to smack the child, would this be an assault on the child?[3] If not, where does the power to smack or otherwise punish the child come from?[4] Section 3(5) contains only a partial answer to these and other questions. It provides:

'A person who–
(a) does not have parental responsibility for a particular child; but

---

1   For example, in *B v B (A Minor) (Residence Order)* [1992] 2 FLR 327 a local education authority was refusing to accept the consent of a grandmother to her grandchild going on school trips, and was demanding the written consent of the mother: see ch 2.

2   The evidence is anecdotal, rather than derived from a properly conducted research study. However, it seems highly unlikely that a doctor would ask a father whether he is married to the child's mother and, if not, whether he has a parental responsibility order, before obtaining his consent to treat the child! In this way, strict law and day-to-day practice completely part company for obvious and practical reasons.

3   Cf the position of child-minders under Part X of the Act, and see *Sutton London Borough Council v Davis* [1994] 1 FLR 737.

4   This aspect of the nature and scope of parental responsibility, and to whom it can be delegated, has taken on greater significance since the ruling of the European Court of Human Rights that a step-father who beat a child with a garden cane on a number of occasions had violated the child's right under Art 3 of the European Convention for the Protection of Human Rights and Fundamental Freedoms, see *A v United Kingdom (Human Rights: Punishment of Child)* [1998] 2 FLR 959.

(b) has care of the child,
may (subject to the provisions of this Act) do what is reasonable
in all the circumstances of the case for the purpose of safeguarding
or promoting the child's welfare.'

This is a broadly based provision the scope of which has yet to be ascertained. It is suggested that reliance could be placed by medical personnel on section 3(5) where persons with parental responsibility cannot be contacted, but where others who have care of the child consent to medical treatment. It is suggested that section 3(5) could be wide enough to encompass giving consent to most orthodox forms of medical treatment. Furthermore, it might be a sustainable argument that the doctor himself 'has care of the child' and can do what is reasonable to safeguard or promote the child's health, which is an aspect of his welfare, until the parents can be found. Such an approach gives respect to the notion that parental responsibility is conferred in order to enable a parent to fulfil his parental duties. When a parent is not available to do this, then there is merit in allowing other persons, who are motivated by the purpose of safeguarding the child's welfare, to step in. The alternative approach, namely that persons cannot normally act until a parent agrees, may give too much weight to the notion that parents have *rights* in respect of their children rather than *responsibilities*, and give insufficient weight to the right of the child to be treated as an autonomous individual, who is entitled to receive the aid and assistance of others who are acting in the course of their professional duties.

Whether section 3(5) permits a person with care of the child to take steps for the purposes of safeguarding or promoting the child's welfare contrary to the express wishes of a person with parental responsibility is more controversial. The context in which this question is most likely to arise is where the person with care forms the view that it would be against the interests of the child to return him to the care of a parent. For example, if parents returned home drunk, and a baby sitter formed the opinion that it would be unsafe to leave the child in the house with them, could she lawfully remove the child from the premises and take the child to her own home? It would seem desirable that the law should authorise such a properly motivated action, and section 3(5) would almost certainly cover this situation. More difficult is the position when a child is being accommodated by a local authority under section 20, and a parent wishes immediately to remove his child from that accommodation. A local authority does not have parental responsibility for an accommodated child, and section 20(8) specifically states that any person who has parental responsibility may at any time remove the child from accommodation provided by the local authority under that section.[5] Whether section 3(5) would allow a foster parent, or a person in charge of a children's home,

5   See further ch 3.

to refuse to hand the child over in express disregard of section 20(8) has yet to be determined. It would seem desirable that section 3(5) should provide such persons with protection for a short period, provided that during that period steps were being taken to obtain a court order authorising the retention of the child.

Guardians and parental responsibility

Many parents are anxious to make provision for a person to have parental responsibility for their children in the event of their death. They can achieve this by appointing a person to be the child's guardian. The law relating to the appointment of guardians is contained in section 5 of the Act. In the case of married parents, each parent is entitled to appoint an individual to be the child's guardian in the event of his or her death. In the case of unmarried parents, the father may not appoint a guardian unless he has parental responsibility. Guardians can be appointed in a relatively informal manner. The appointment can be made by deed or will, but it is also sufficient if it is 'made in writing, is dated and is signed by the person making the appointment'.[6]

When does the appointment of a guardian take effect?

Although the purpose of appointing a guardian is to arrange for someone to act in the deceased's place, section 5 provides that the actual appointment does not take effect unless both parents with parental responsibility have died.[7] When parents are living together in harmony this rule creates no difficulties, although it may be that the surviving parent would sometimes have welcomed sharing parental responsibility with the guardian appointed by his deceased spouse. The benefits and burdens of bringing up children are often easier to manage when the task is shared. It is suggested that the Law Commission, when it recommended that the law be changed from the common law position under which the testamentary guardianship took effect from death, may have been unduly influenced by the notion that the deceased spouse was seeking to rule the other from the grave.[8]

In the event of estrangement or divorce, neither party may be content with the notion that the surviving spouse will have sole responsibility for their child's upbringing, and they may wish to appoint a guardian to have parental responsibility in conjunction with the survivor. This is particularly likely where a parent anticipates his or her premature death, and where he or she wants a relative to have care of his or her children; or

6   S 5(5).
7   S 5(7), (8); a person can disclaim his appointment 'within a reasonable time of his knowing that the appointment has taken effect': s 6(5).
8   Law Com No 172, para 2.27.

where a parent has remarried, and wants the new spouse to be the children's guardian. However, it has been seen that normally guardianship does not take effect where there is a surviving parent with parental responsibility.[9] The only way in which the appointment of a guardian can take immediate effect is when the deceased parent had a residence order. Section 5(7)(b) provides that where:

> '... immediately before the death of any person making such an appointment, a residence order in his favour was in force with respect to the child, the appointment shall take effect on the death of that person.'

When such an appointment takes place, parental responsibility is shared by the guardian with the surviving spouse. Where they cannot agree over the child's upbringing, for example whether the child should have his home with the parent or with the guardian, the matter in dispute will have to be resolved by an application for an order under section 8.[10]

Where a child has no parent with parental responsibility for him, or where a parent with a residence order has died, an application may be made by any individual to a court, and the court may appoint that individual to be the child's guardian.[11] A court may also exercise this power in any family proceedings where it considers that a guardianship order should be made, even though no application has been made for the order.[12] Such an appointment may have an advantage over a residence order in a case where a child has been orphaned, because a guardian obtains greater powers. He can himself appoint a guardian for the child,[13] and his agreement to the child's adoption is required.[14]

Only an 'individual', as distinct from a 'person', may be appointed a child's guardian. This means that a local authority may not apply for guardianship in respect of an orphaned child. Furthermore, it was held by Thorpe J in *Birmingham City Council v D and M*[15] that the mere fact of being an orphan does not mean that a child is suffering, or is likely to suffer, significant harm for the purposes of section 31 of the Act, and therefore a care order cannot be made in respect of such a child conferring parental responsibility on the local authority. It is suggested that there is a gap here in the law which creates difficulties for local authorities seeking to make the most appropriate provision for orphaned children.[16]

---

9   S 5(7), (8).
10 The guardian is entitled to apply for a section 8 order, and need not first obtain the leave of the court. The implications of having entitlement, as distinct from requiring the court's leave, are explained in ch 2.
11 S 5(1).
12 S 5(2).
13 S 5(4). See ch 2 in relation to local authority foster parents and guardianship.
14 Adoption Act 1976, ss 16 and 18.
15 [1994] 2 FLR 502.
16 For a fuller discussion of the position of orphans and local authorities, see ch 3.

Competent children, parental responsibility and decision-making

So far in this chapter the assumption has been made that it is parents, and others with parental responsibility, who are the persons who are entitled to make decisions about a child's upbringing. But of course children themselves hold strong opinions about their own upbringing, and these opinions may not coincide with the opinions of the persons who have parental responsibility for them. It seems likely that the large majority of parents will normally discuss important matters about their children's upbringing with their children. The extent to which, in any particular household, decisions are made in an authoritarian manner by parents, in a more relaxed and consultative manner by parents and children together, or by the children themselves, will depend on how the parents see their role as parents. It will also depend on whether the children are old enough to understand and to express a point of view, and how forceful they are in asserting their own wishes and feelings. Where others have parental responsibility for a child under a residence order, or through guardianship, it seems likely that the dynamics of decision-making about the child's upbringing will operate in a similar manner. In most families some degree of conflict occurs between parents and children over the exercise of parental responsibility and authority, and each family handles this conflict in its own way. It is only where areas of disagreement between children and those who have parental responsibility for them cannot be resolved within the family, by whatever means, that the law may have a part to play.[17]

Where a child is being looked after by a local authority, conflict is just as likely to occur between the child's carers and the child himself as it does in families. Whether the child is being looked after by foster parents, or is living in residential accommodation, day-to-day decisions about the child's upbringing must be made by the persons who are looking after him. Furthermore, it should be borne in mind that children being looked after by local authorities have often suffered at the hands of those who have hitherto had charge of them, and this may make such children less amenable to the assertion of adult authority than those children who come from more stable home backgrounds. The responsibility of a local authority when making decisions about children is somewhat different from the responsibility of parents, because the manner in which this responsibility is exercised is governed in part by the Children Act 1989, and its associated regulations. A local authority has a duty to consult with children. They must, so far as is reasonably practicable, ascertain the child's wishes and feelings before making any decision with respect to a child whom they are looking after, or are proposing to look after.[18] They are obliged by law

---

17 It will be seen in ch 2 that a child may be given leave by a court to bring proceedings under s 8 of the Children Act 1989 for an order which interferes with the exercise of his or her parents' parental responsibility.

18 S 22(4).

periodically to review the position of a child whom they are looking after and, when holding such a review, must take steps to ascertain the child's views.[19]

In the case of a young child it is inevitable that adults will make decisions on the child's behalf because the child does not have the requisite competence to decide himself. However, as children grow older they become increasingly capable of making their own choices about their own upbringing. When adults are in serious conflict with the child over a matter relating to a child's upbringing, difficult issues arise about who has the right to determine what should happen to the child.

The '*Gillick*' case

The starting point of any discussion about decision-making by children is the House of Lords' decision in *Gillick v West Norfolk and Wisbech Area Health Authority*.[20] The case itself was concerned with whether a doctor could lawfully give contraceptive advice and treatment to a girl aged under 16 without the knowledge and consent of her parents.[1] Mrs Gillick sought a declaration stating that such action would be unlawful. Various arguments were advanced on her behalf. These included the assertion that it would be unlawful to provide such advice and treatment, because a child below the age of 16 lacks the capacity to give valid consent to medical treatment; and the assertion that to give advice and treatment without parental consent would be inconsistent with Mrs Gillick's rights as a mother. The House of Lords ruled by a majority that, in relation to when a child acquires capacity to make decisions, 'a minor's capacity to make his or her own decision depends on the minor having sufficient understanding and intelligence to make the decision and is not to be determined by reference to any judicially fixed age limit.'[2] In relation to the notion that parents have rights in relation to the upbringing of their children which cannot be displaced by others, the House of Lords acknowledged that parental rights clearly do exist, and that they do not wholly disappear until the age of majority. However, it then affirmed the centrality of the principle that 'the common law has never treated such rights as sovereign or beyond review or control. Nor has our law ever treated a child as other than a person with capacities and rights recognised by law. The principle

---

19 S 26(2).
20 [1985] 3 All ER 402. It is impossible here to do justice to the complexity of the ruling in *Gillick* which has been the subject of extensive analysis. See, for example, J Eekelaar *The eclipse of parental rights* (1986) 102 LQR 4; J Eekelaar *The emergence of children's rights* (1986) 6 OJLS 161; A Bainham *The balance of power in family decisions* (1986) 45 CLJ 262.
1   The reason why the age of 16, rather than 18, was the age in issue is because the Family Law Reform Act 1969, s 8 specifically provides that the consent to medical treatment of a minor aged 16 is a valid consent.
2   [1985] 3 All ER 402, per Lord Scarman, at p 423.

of law ... is that parental rights are derived from parental duty and exist only so long as they are needed for the protection of the person and property of the child.'[3] Accordingly, the House of Lords refused to grant the plaintiff the declaration which she sought.

Gillick v West Norfolk and Wisbech Area Health Authority was undoubtedly an enormously important decision even when restricted to its material facts. As a consequence, a child is entitled to have a confidential relationship with her doctor and to obtain contraceptive advice and treatment without parental consent.[4] Guidance on when it would be justifiable for a doctor to proceed in this manner was given by Lord Fraser; this guidance includes the prerequisites that the girl 'is very likely to begin or to continue having sexual intercourse with or without contraceptive treatment', 'that unless she receives contraceptive advice or treatment her physical or mental health or both are likely to suffer' and that 'her best interests require him to give her contraceptive advice, treatment or both without parental consent'.[5] Clearly this guidance encompasses additional factors to those which a doctor would have in mind when deciding whether to prescribe contraception for an adult. A doctor who sought to ascertain from an adult patient whether she was 'very likely to begin or to continue having sexual intercourse' before he would agree to prescribe for her might risk receiving a fairly hostile response! It might therefore be argued that all the House of Lords did in *Gillick* was to substitute professional decision-making by a doctor for parental decision-making, and that it did not give a child a positive right to make her own choices irrespective of the view taken by adults of their desirability. However, whilst such an argument has some merit in respect of the confines of the actual decision in *Gillick* itself, it ignores the wide impact which the ruling has had on the development of child law in recent years.

Essentially what *Gillick* achieved was to create a climate of expectation that a child will be consulted, and his or her wishes and feelings will be taken into account, when any important decision is made in respect of his or her upbringing.[6] What *Gillick* did *not* achieve was to create a rule that the wishes and feelings of a child will always prevail over the wishes and

3   Ibid, per Lord Scarman, at p 420.
4   However, for a view that, in the realm of sex education, the legacy of the *Gillick* case has been ignored in relation to children's rights to sexual knowledge and advice, see J Pilcher *Contrary to Gillick: British children and sexual rights since 1985* (1997) 5 Int JCR 299.
5   At p 413. This guidance has been incorporated in DOH guidelines. More general guidance on the level of capacity required in the child was given by Lord Scarman at pp 423-424. This was put at a very high level of comprehension, and appreciation, of the issues involved.
6   This situation can, of course, arise in very varying circumstances. For a different consideration of the *Gillick* principle see E Mumford, *Bone marrow donation – the law in context* (1998) 10 CFLQ 135. The author considers the difficult issue of where a child wishes, or parents wish the child, to become a donor for a sibling.

feelings of the persons with parental responsibility, even though the child has sufficient competence to understand the full implications of the decision to be made. The opportunity to suggest the incorporation of such a rule in legislation was afforded during the massive review of child law which took place before the Children Act 1989 was enacted, but no suggestion for such a rule was made. Rather, the definition of parental responsibility was made in terms that it means 'all the rights, duties, powers, responsibility and authority which by law a parent has in relation to the child and his property'.[7] The use of the phrase 'which by law a parent has in relation to the child' allows for development and change in the law, and gives scope for further judicial interpretation of what the phrase encompasses.

Competent children and medical decisions

The question of who has the responsibility to decide when there is disagreement between a competent child and the persons with parental responsibility for him has arisen mainly in the context of medical decisions.[8] It should be recalled that *Gillick v West Norfolk and Wisbech Area Health Authority*[9] was concerned with whether a competent child could *consent* to medical treatment, and whether such consent could be countermanded by a person with parental responsibility. Subsequently two serious cases involving very sick children came before the courts in which the children concerned were *refusing* medical treatment, and where there was doubt about whether there was authority to treat the children without their consent.[10] In *Re R (A Minor) (Wardship: Medical Treatment)*[11] the girl concerned was aged 15 and in *Re W (A Minor) (Wardship: Medical Treatment)*[12] she was 16.

In *Re R (A Minor) (Wardship: Medical Treatment)* the child had a history of serious mental illness such that, in the past, she had been ill enough to be admitted to hospital under sections 2 and 3 of the Mental Health Act 1983. Subsequently she was placed in an adolescent psychiatric unit. Concern grew about her mental state such that the senior consultant in the unit stated that he believed R to be in a psychotic state, and he wanted the permission of the local authority, who had parental responsibility for R under a care order, to administer anti-psychotic medication to her. This consent was given, but R refused to take the drugs. A social worker, who

---

7   S 3(1).
8   See M Brazier and M Bridge *Coercion or caring: analysing adolescent autonomy* (1996) 16 Legal Studies 84; C Smith *Children's rights: judicial ambivalence and social resistance* (1997) 11 IJLPF 103.
9   [1985] 3 All ER 402.
10   See too *Re E (A Minor) (Wardship: Medical Treatment)* [1993] 1 FLR 386; *Re S (A Minor) (Consent to Medical Treatment)* [1994] 2 FLR 1065.
11   [1991] 4 All ER 177.
12   [1992] 4 All ER 627.

had experience with cases involving persons who are mentally ill, then had a three-hour telephone conversation with R after which he decided that R sounded lucid and rational and he did not regard her as 'sectionable'.[13] The local authority therefore took the view that they could not give permission for R to have drugs administered against her will. As a consequence of this refusal of permission, the adolescent unit took the view that they could not continue to care for R unless they were given a free hand in relation to the administration of medication. The psychiatrist was of the opinion that, without medication, R was likely to lapse into a fully psychotic state under which she would be a serious suicidal risk, and potentially very violent and unpredictable in her behaviour. He was also of the opinion that R was currently mature enough to understand the nature and the implications of the treatment proposed, and of sufficient understanding to make a decision in her own right. The local authority therefore made the child a ward of court, and asked the court to determine whether R could be treated without her consent in the light of the House of Lords' ruling in *Gillick v West Norfolk and Wisbech Area Health Authority*.

In *Re R (A Minor)* there were three issues to be resolved: did R have the capacity to refuse consent to medical treatment; if she did, could she nonetheless be treated if a person with parental responsibility gave consent; and did the court have the power to override the decision of a child irrespective of whether the child was competent to give consent?

In relation to capacity, the Court of Appeal ruled that R did not have the capacity to make decisions about her own medical treatment. It was by no means satisfied that R understood the implications of the treatment being withheld, as distinct from understanding what was proposed to be done by way of treatment. The evidence had established that R's mental state fluctuated, so that even if, on a good day, she was capable of reaching the standard of competence required to meet the *Gillick* criteria, on other days she was not only *Gillick* incompetent, she was actually sectionable. Lord Donaldson MR ruled that 'no child in that situation can be regarded as "*Gillick* competent"... "*Gillick* competence" is a developmental concept and will not be lost or acquired on a day-to-day or week-to-week basis. In the case of mental disability, that disability must also be taken into account, particularly where it is fluctuating in effect.'[14]

13 That is, liable to be made the subject of an application under ss 2 and 3 of the Mental Health Act 1983.
14 [1991] 4 All ER 177, at pp 187-188. The concept of 'competence' was subsequently developed in *Re C (Refusal of Medical Treatment)* [1994] 1 FLR 31 where Thorpe J ruled that the decision-making process should be approached in three stages: (i) comprehending and retaining treatment information; (ii) believing it; and (iii) weighing it in the balance to arrive at a choice. This test was applied in *A Metropolitan Borough Council v DB* [1997] 1 FLR 767 where the court ruled that a 17-year-old pregnant girl who was addicted to drugs, living in squalid conditions and had a phobia against needles failed to satisfy each stage of the test. Compulsory medical treatment of the girl was therefore authorised.

In relation to whether a person with parental responsibility had the power to override the refusal to consent to medical treatment by a competent child, only Lord Donaldson expressed a view. He was clearly of the opinion that in a case where a *'Gillick* competent' child refuses treatment, but someone with parental responsibility consents, that treatment can lawfully be given to the child. He acknowledged that the child's refusal of consent will be a very important factor in the doctor's decision whether or not to treat, but held that it does not stop treatment going ahead if consent is obtained from another person with parental responsibility. In relation to the court's position, all of the judges had no hesitation in finding that a court has the power to override the refusal of consent by a competent child.[15]

In *Re W (A Minor) (Wardship: Medical Treatment)*[16] the girl was suffering from anorexia nervosa. By the time the case came to court her weight had dropped to such a low level that, should she continue to lose weight for more than a few days, her capacity to have children in later life would be put seriously at risk, and a little later her life itself might be in danger. The court granted the local authority leave to make an application for the exercise by the court of the inherent jurisdiction of the High Court.[17] The local authority applied for leave to move the girl from the clinic in which she was currently being treated to a specialist unit for the treatment of eating disorders, and for leave to treat the girl without her consent. The girl wished to remain where she was. This case differed from the case of *Re R (A Minor)* in two significant respects: the girl concerned was aged 16; and the trial judge, Thorpe J, had found that she was of sufficient understanding to make an informed choice, a finding that was accepted by the Court of Appeal.[18] By contrast with *Re R (A*

---

15 The ruling in *Re R (A Minor) (Wardship: Medical Treatment)* was subject to considerable criticism. See, for example, C Dyer (ed) *Doctors, Patients and the Law* (Blackwell, 1992) pp 60-61 and 156-157; R Thornton *Multiple keyholders – wardship and consent to medical treatment* (1992) 51 CLJ 34. For an example of where a court has authorised medical treatment, see *Re L (Medical Treatment: Gillick Competency)* [1998] 2 FLR 810. A 14-year-old girl urgently needed a blood transfusion to save her life. She was a Jehovah's Witness, and would not consent. Sir Stephen Brown P ordered that the medical treatment take place without her consent. He found that she was not *Gillick* competent because she had led a sheltered life largely influenced by the Jehovah's Witness congregation. This limited her understanding and she had not been able constructively to formulate an opinion in the manner which would occur with adult experience. Moreover, it was appropriate to authorise treatment even if the girl were *Gillick* competent, because this was an extreme case and she was facing a particularly horrible death. See also, *Re E (A Minor) (Wardship: Medical Treatment)* [1993] 1 FLR 386, where the refusal of consent of a 15-year-old boy to blood transfusions was overriden.

16 [1992] 4 All ER 627.

17 For the use of the High Court's inherent jurisdiction, see ch 2.

18 Although Lord Donaldson MR expressed doubt whether Thorpe J had taken sufficient account of the fact that it is a feature of anorexia nervosa that it is capable of destroying the ability to make an informed choice.

Minor), the determination in *Re W (A Minor)* was made against the background that section 8 of the Family Law Reform Act 1969 enables a person who has attained the age of 16 to give a valid consent to medical treatment.

The two main questions for the court to resolve were: could persons with parental responsibility for a competent minor aged 16 authorise medical treatment in the face of the minor's refusal; and did the court's power to override the wishes of a competent minor who *refuses* treatment extend to a minor aged over 16? The court also considered whether a court could override a competent minor's *consent* to medical treatment. Lord Donaldson MR and Balcombe LJ were of the view that the consent of a person with parental responsibility, and a fortiori a consent by the court, suffices to authorise the medical treatment of a minor of whatever age, and that no minor by refusing consent to medical treatment has the power to override such consent. Nolan LJ appeared to have some reservations about this point.[19] The court was united in its view that a court has the power to override a minor's consent to medical treatment. In relation to whether a court can override the consent of a competent child, Lord Donaldson asserted that this was accepted by all parties in *Gillick v West Norfolk and Wisbech Area Health Authority*.

When the rulings in *Re R (A Minor) (Wardship: Medical Treatment)* and *Re W (A Minor) (Wardship: Medical Treatment)* are separated from their factual context they raise all sorts of alarming possibilities of invasive forms of medical treatment being forced on unwilling teenagers who have the competence to make their own choices. The possibility that sedative medication will be forced on resisting adolescents with behavioural difficulties, who are being looked after in residential homes and treatment units run by local authorities or health trusts is particularly disturbing. An example arose in *Re K, W and H (Minors) (Medical Treatment)*[20] in which Thorpe J said that applications for orders authorising medical treatment, made by a hospital in respect of three highly disturbed 15-year-old girls who might not wish to consent in the future to the emergency use of medication, had been misconceived and unnecessary. He ruled that the girls were not '*Gillick* competent' to make decisions about their own medical treatment but that, even if they were, it was clear that the law allowed treatment to be given provided that someone with parental responsibility had given consent. An alarming feature of this case was that the judge took the view that the law was 'perfectly clear in this field', and that 'where more than one person has the power to consent, only a refusal by all having that power will create a veto'. He rejected the hospital's appraisal of the situation as being highly complex and confusing.

19 See below.
20 [1993] 1 FLR 854, which occurred after *Re R (A Minor)* but before *Re W (A Minor)*.

The weight to be given to the competent child's wishes in medical cases

It is suggested that Thorpe J's certain approach in *Re K, W and H (Minors),*[1] coupled in that case with a finding that the girls did not have sufficient competence to instruct their own lawyers, despite the beliefs of their lawyers to the contrary,[2] bodes ill for competent and incompetent children who are in conflict with persons with parental responsibility in relation to medical decisions.[3] It illustrates the dangers of translating reasoned judgments, in which various reservations are expressed, into a simplified rule of law. It is important, therefore, that some of the thinking of the judges in *Re W (A Minor) (Wardship: Medical Treatment)* about the weight to be given to the competent child's wishes in medical cases is not lost.

The Court of Appeal clearly expected great weight to be given by medical practitioners to the wishes of the competent child. However, the court's pronouncements in this regard were made in the context of what Lord Donaldson MR described as the 'hair-raising' possibility, which had been canvassed before him, of abortions being carried out by doctors with the consent of parents on unwilling 16- and 17-year-olds. Lord Donaldson MR had no doubt that the wishes of a competent child were of the greatest clinical importance, and was content to place reliance on medical ethics to act as a restraining influence in cases of this kind. Balcombe LJ was also of the opinion that a doctor would not terminate the pregnancy of a mentally competent 16-year-old merely upon the consent of the child's parents. He added that it would seem inevitable that the matter would have to come before the court in such highly unlikely circumstances. Nolan LJ offered the child the strongest safeguard when he said:

'We are not directly concerned with cases in which the jurisdiction of the court has not been invoked, and in which accordingly the decision on treatment may depend upon the consent of the child or of the parent. I for my part would think it axiomatic, however, in order to avoid the risk of grave breaches of the law that in any case where time permitted, where major surgical or other pro-

---

1 Even though at the time of his judgment the only ruling on parental consent and *Gillick* competence had been in *Re R (A Minor) (Wardship: Medical Treatment)*, on which only Lord Donaldson MR had expressed a concluded view. For further comment, see P Bates, *Children in psychiatric units: Re K, W and H –'out of sight, out of mind'?* (1994) 6 JCL 131.

2 See further ch 2.

3 See too *South Glamorgan County Council v W and B* [1993] 1 FLR 574 which is discussed in ch 2. C Bridge, in *Adolescents and mental disorder: who consents to treatment?* (1997) 3 Med Law Int 51, suggests that differentiation should be made between three different categories of adolescent disturbance: the competent young person who refuses treatment that an adult may refuse; the rebellious teenager, whose refusal is triggered by simple teenage angst; and the mentally ill teenager, whose refusal is triggered by illness. She submits that adolescent autonomy needs to be more fully understood and the Mental Health Act 1983 more readily used in treating young people.

cedures (such as an abortion) were proposed, and whereby the parents or those in loco parentis were prepared to give consent but the child (having sufficient understanding to make an informed decision) was not, the jurisdiction of the court should always be invoked.'[4]

Furthermore, Balcombe LJ was clearly unhappy with the approach which had been taken by Thorpe J when trying *Re W (A Minor)* at first instance. Thorpe J had treated the case 'as one for the unfettered exercise of his discretion, in which W's views were merely a relatively unimportant factor'. Balcombe LJ, by contrast, stressed that 'the judge should approach the exercise of the discretion with a predeliction to give effect to the child's wishes on the basis that prima facie that will be in his or her best interests'.[5] He added that W's wishes should have been respected 'unless there were very strong reasons for rejecting them'. Nolan LJ was certain that a court had not only the power, but also the inescapable responsibility, of deciding what should be done in W's case, guided by the welfare principle in section 1(1) of the Children Act 1989, and the checklist of matters in section 1(3) to which a court is required to have regard.[6] However, he commented:

'I am very far from asserting any general rule that the court should prefer its own view of what is in the best interests of the child to those of the child itself. In considering the welfare of the child, the court must not only recognise but if necessary defend the right of the child, having sufficient understanding to make an informed decision, to make his or her own choice.'[7]

This thinking gives great weight to the wishes and feelings of the competent child, and affords the child's interest in the decision-making process some considerable protection when a case comes before a court. However, what it also exposes is that a child may not obtain the benefit of such protection where a person with parental responsibility authorises medical treatment. Whilst persons with parental responsibility may generally be presumed to make decisions in a child's best interests, this is not inevitably the case. Such a person's perception of a child's best interests may be misguided. It may give insufficient weight to the wishes and feelings of the child. Or it may be over-influenced by the consenting person's own wishes and feelings.

In *Re C (Detention: Medical Treatment)*[8] a cautious and conscientious approach was taken by Wall J to ordering the detention of a minor (aged

4   [1992] 4 All ER 627, at pp 648-649.
5   Ibid, at p 644.
6   See further ch 4.
7   [1992] 4 All ER 627, at p 648.
8   [1997] 2 FLR 180.

16) against her will for the purpose of giving her medical treatment for anorexia nervosa. He held that in the exercise of the inherent jurisdiction of the court he had power to direct that the girl reside at a clinic, and to authorise the use of reasonable force (if necessary) to detain her in the clinic.[9] He also found that while he must have regard to the child's wishes and feelings, he could override these if they were not in her best interests, but that where the child had capacity to give or refuse consent, then the weight which the court should give to her wishes and feelings would increase. However, Wall J acknowledged that an order for the detention of a minor aged 16 against her will was a Draconian remedy, and although the powers of the court when exercising the inherent jurisdiction were theoretically limitless, there were recognised boundaries beyond which the jurisdiction should not be exercised. In the instant case, because the girl's civil liberties were involved, he held that the order should be time-limited and have built into it stringent safeguards to protect the girl's interests.[10] Leave was given to the doctors concerned 'to furnish such treatment and nursing care as in their opinion may be necessary and as may be appropriate to ensure that the said minor suffers the least distress and retains the greatest dignity'.[11]

This and other rulings, despite their concern for the welfare of the children concerned, are nonetheless open to criticism. By exercising the inherent jurisdiction of the High Court in those cases where the child is suffering from a mental illness or serious mental disturbance, judges are by-passing the protective measures which are built into the Mental Health Act 1983, and they may as a result be exposing children to medical and behavioural regimes and treatment processes to which far more stringent safeguards apply where adults are involved.[12] Even more disturbing is the ability of parents to give permission for their children to be confined, institutionalised and treated in clinics where none of the checks and balances provided by statutorily authorised regimes for intervention apply, and where courts are not involved.[13]

What might a '*Gillick* competent' child do when medical or psychiatric treatment is authorised by persons with parental responsibility, but

---

9   See also, *Norfolk and Norwich Healthcare (NHS) Trust v W* [1996] 2 FLR 613, where Johnson J held that he had power under the common law to authorise a Caesarian section (in that case on an adult).

10 Interestingly, Wall J took the view that the girl's 'best safeguard is legal representation and access to the court though her lawyers' and that any order should give her liberty to apply at short notice. In this way, Wall J gave open endorsement to the view that children, like adults, should be entitled to turn to the courts when their liberties are at stake. Courts have not generally been so ready to accept that children should have easy access to the courts; see ch 2.

11 [1997] 2 FLR 180, at p 200.

12 For further discussion of these and other aspects of the medical treatment of children, see C Bridge 'Parental Powers and the Medical Treatment of Children' in *Family Law Towards the Millenium; Essays for PM Bromley*, ed C Bridge (Butterworths, 1997); J Fortin *Children's Rights and the Developing Law* (Butterworths, 1998), ch 5.

13 As in *Re K, H and W* [1993] 1 FLR 854.

without the child's consent? It is suggested that he or she would be best advised to seek leave to apply either for a specific issue order, or for a prohibited steps order, under section 8 of the Children Act 1989, or that he or she should seek leave to make an application for the exercise by the High Court of its inherent jurisdiction. Similarly, where the child concerned is younger and unable to initiate proceedings, a relative or other interested third party anxious about the child's predicament could seek leave to invoke the jurisdiction of the courts. Court involvement would act as a safeguard to detect whether those exercising parental responsibility for the child were abusing their powers and whether any decisions made were giving paramountcy to the interests of the child. The availability and use of section 8 orders in a wide range of matters concerning the care and upbringing of children, and the inherent jurisdiction of the High Court, are each discussed in the next chapter.

Chapter 2

Section 8 orders, and orders under the High Court's inherent jurisdiction

Chapter 2

Section 8 orders, and orders under the HighCourt's inherent jurisdiction

Court orders about children

Where opposing points of view about a child's upbringing are being expressed by persons who have equal parental responsibility for a child, and when neither will give way, then legal proceedings to resolve the matter in dispute may become inescapable. Persons without parental responsibility may also feel compelled to go to court when they disagree with those who have the right to decide about some matter concerning the child's upbringing. Local authorities have specific statutory duties to take steps to protect children, and in some cases these may warrant the institution of legal proceedings. The Children Act 1989 contains a range of orders which can be made about children. Between them, they cover almost all aspects of a child's upbringing, and the areas of disagreement which are likely to arise.[1] In this chapter the making of private law orders under section 8 of the Act is discussed. This is followed by an analysis of when the inherent jurisdiction of the High Court can be invoked.

No order unless better for the child

It will be seen that courts have wide powers to make orders and that, in some cases, there are few restraints on how these powers should be exercised. But there is a risk, therefore, that a court might be tempted to be too interventionist, and to make orders about matters which should normally be decided by those with parental responsibility. For example, it has not been unknown for a court to think that it properly falls within its powers to order at what time a child should be put to bed![2] A restraining feature on the use and misuse of orders is embodied in section 1(5) which provides that:

---

1   Adoption law is the main exception; this is covered by the Adoption Act 1976: see ch 4. Parental responsibility and guardianship orders have been considered in ch 1; public law orders under Parts IV and V are considered in ch 3.
2   *B v B (Custody: Conditions)* (1979) 1 FLR 385.

'Where a court is considering whether or not to make one or more orders under this Act with respect to a child, it shall not make the order or any of the orders unless it considers that doing so would be better for the child than making no order at all.'

These words encapsulate an important principle, namely that a court should not make an order which will influence the upbringing of a child unless it is satisfied that the order will improve matters for the child. Another way of expressing this might be to say that court orders are designed to achieve a purpose and should not be granted automatically and without thought as to their consequences.[3]

Before the enactment of the Children Act 1989 court orders were used in almost all divorce cases involving children.[4] The relationship between parents and children was formalised and characterised in legal language without much thought as to whether this was either desirable in the interests of children, or wanted by their parents. In court the following dialogue would be typical – 'The children are living with you, Mrs Smith?' 'Yes.' 'They see their father regularly?' 'Yes.' 'You have no objection to Mr Smith having reasonable access to them?' 'No.' 'The court orders custody, care and control to Mrs Smith and reasonable access to Mr Smith.' This approach had the major disadvantage of putting labels on the forthcoming relationship between parents and children. While, legally speaking, each parent would still be entitled to be involved in major decisions about the child's upbringing,[5] this was not generally realised and the language of 'custody' and 'access' made the situation appear to be otherwise. The very fact that a court order was made appeared to reduce the parental responsibility of the non-custodial parent to one of having a right of access only, and to diminish his or her future role in the child's life. Consequently the non-custodial parent may have been both physically and emotionally distanced from his child, sometimes with damaging consequences for the child if this led to a loss of contact. Furthermore, some parents experienced the role of courts as being unnecessarily, and sometimes offensively, intrusive in cases in which they could agree over arrangements for their children; such parents were sometimes forced to accede to court orders which they did not necessarily want.

The Children Act 1989 turns its face away from this approach. It recognises that a court order may be neither necessary nor helpful where there is agreement between the parties about the upbringing of a child. In many cases parents are able to make arrangements about their children without assistance from either conciliators or lawyers. Indeed, intervention from an outsider may sometimes cause annoyance and distress to the

---

3 For discussion of how other commentators have approached s 1(5), see A Bainham *Changing families and changing concepts* [1998] 10 CFLQ 1.
4 See further J Priest and J Whybrow *Custody Law in Practice in the Divorce and Domestic Courts* supplement to Law Com WP No 96.
5 *Dipper v Dipper* [1980] 2 All ER 722.

divorcing parents. Conciliators or lawyers may be useful in those cases where the parents cannot agree; and where acceptable arrangements prove difficult to negotiate it may be advisable for the lawyers to incorporate the arrangements in a written agreement, so that they are on record, and no one has any doubt about their exact nature. But again no court order may be necessary. Indeed, an order could in some circumstances be counter-productive, because it might create, or exacerbate, hostility between the adults.

The concern of the law is to identify those cases where the proposed order will be better for the child than making no order. Just as there are likely to be many cases where an order is unhelpful or unnecessary, so too it is probable that there will be many cases when an order will prove beneficial. For example, a parent may be determined to fight a case, or just be utterly unreasonable in the arrangements he or she proposes. Even where the parties can be persuaded to agree, it may be sensible for their understanding of the agreed arrangements to be embodied in a court order, for the avoidance of doubt, and so that it puts an imprint of authority on the agreement.[6] Sometimes a court order might be needed to satisfy a bureaucratic requirement for 'evidence' that a certain state of affairs exists. An example might be a case where a court order would assist a parent to obtain local authority housing, or to be granted other types of public, or charitable, assistance which will benefit the child. Here the order will be better for the child not because it resolves an argument, but because it increases the child's chances of being properly housed, or otherwise well looked after.[7]

The principle in section 1(5) applies to all orders made under the Children Act 1989, be they orders made between private individuals or orders made in public law proceedings when a local authority is involved. This means that in all cases the applicant has the burden of proving why making the order sought will improve matters for the child. The 'no order' approach means that persons seeking an order must normally explain to the court why an order is needed, and what they will do with the order if it is granted. In the case of applications for orders made by a local authority this may have the desirable effect of promoting considered forward planning for children, and introducing a measure of accountability in an area of decision-making which normally is not subject to judicial scrutiny. It will be seen below that courts may not make certain orders once a child has been placed in the care of a local authority. Hence there may be all the more reason for a court to be satisfied, at the outset, that an order which vests major decision-making powers in a local authority will be better for the child than making no order at all.

---

6   Cf *Re A (A Minor)(Parental Responsibility)* [1996] 1 FCR 562.
7   In *B v B (A Minor) (Residence Order)* [1992] 2 FLR 327 it was held to be appropriate to make a residence order in favour of a grandmother so that, amongst other matters, she had authority to consent to her grandchild going on school trips. See too *Re S (Contact: Grandparents)* [1996] 1 FLR 158.

Section 8 orders

The four orders which can be made under section 8 are designed to deal with practical issues concerning a child's upbringing in a flexible fashion. The Act explains what each order means in the following manner:

'A residence order' means an order settling the arrangements to be made as to the person with whom a child is to live.

'A contact order' means an order requiring the person with whom a child lives, or is to live, to allow the child to visit or stay with the person named in the order, or for that person and the child otherwise to have contact with each other.

'A prohibited steps order' means an order that no step which could be taken by a parent in meeting his parental responsibility for a child, and which is of a kind specified in the order, shall be taken by any person without the consent of the court.

'A specific issue order' means an order giving directions for the purpose of determining a specific question which has arisen, or which may arise, in connection with any aspect of parental responsibility for a child.

On its face, a specific issue order could be made in most of the situations which are covered by the meanings given to the other three section 8 orders. Identifying the person with whom the child is to live, or the persons with whom he is to have contact, are each specific questions which may arise in connection with the exercise of parental responsibility. However, section 9(5) provides that:

'No court shall exercise its powers to make a specific issue or prohibited steps order—
(a) with a view to achieving a result which could be achieved by making a residence or contact order.'

It is clear, therefore, that the orders are not interchangeable.[8] Consequently it is important to know exactly what each order covers, and the legal consequences of each order.

---

8   The reason for this is explained below; essentially it is to prevent local authorities from by-passing the care framework when intervening in a child's family life. See too *Re B (Minors) (Residence Order)* [1992] 3 All ER 867.

A residence order

A residence order is easily explained. As the Act states, a residence order means:

'... an order settling the arrangements to be made as to the person with whom a child is to live.'

An increasing number of children born both in and outside marriage are experiencing the breakdown of their parents' relationship. Discord over where the children are to have their main home may be one of the more distressing and difficult issues to be resolved through court proceedings. Other persons such as relatives or foster parents may also be caught up in this type of strife. In some cases it may be appropriate for more than one person to have a residence order, for example where two relatives such as grandparents are looking after their grandchild.

Normally when more than one person has a residence order the persons concerned will live together in the same household, but this is not essential. Section 11(4) provides that:

'Where a residence order is made in favour of two or more persons who do not themselves all live together, the order may specify the periods during which the child is to live in the different households concerned.'

This provision may have particular significance for parents who each wish to provide a home for the child. It is easy to understand why it may occasionally be important to a child, and to the parent who spends less time with the child than the other parent, that their time spent together is dignified by the word 'residence' rather than 'contact'. Residence is a concept which brings with it connotations of shared care, similarity of status and the equal exercise of parental responsibility. The emotional impact of a court order on the parties to the proceedings is one of the many considerations a court may have in mind when assessing whether the order proposed will advance a child's best interests. The Court of Appeal has confirmed that there is no reason in principle why a parent who has his child to stay for regular periods of time, on an agreed or defined basis, should not have the arrangement incorporated in a residence order rather than a contact order. However the court also said that an order in which residence was shared between the parents would be unusual, and there would have to be positive benefit to the child in making such an order.[9]

---

9   *A v A (Minors) (Shared Residence Order)* [1994] 1 FLR 669. See *Re H (A Minor) (Shared Residence)* [1994] 1 FLR 717 where Cazalet J expressed his views in much the same terms, but where Purchas LJ thought a shared residence order should only be made in 'exceptional circumstances'. See, also *Re R (Residence Order)* [1995] 2 FLR 612 where the judge was partly influenced by financial considerations. For further discussion, see ch 4.

A residence order has specific legal consequences in addition to settling the person(s) with whom the child is to live. These are broadly (i) that it confers parental responsibility on persons who would not otherwise have it; (ii) it diminishes the existing parental responsibility of the non-residential parent; and (iii) it discharges a care order.

A residence order confers parental responsibility

It has been explained already that an unmarried father is a parent without parental responsibility, but that he can acquire parental responsibility for his child either by making a formal agreement to this effect with the mother, or by obtaining a parental responsibility order.[10] Where a court makes a residence order in favour of an unmarried father it must also make an order giving him parental responsibility under section 4.[11] This has the advantage for the father that not only does he have parental responsibility for his child while the residence order is in force, he also retains his parental responsibility where the residence order is subsequently brought to an end. The law in this way recognises that once a court has decided that an unmarried father is suitable to act as a residential parent, it is only logical that he should henceforth be treated in the same way as a father who was married to the child's mother. It also means that he is in the position to appoint a guardian for his child in the event of his death.[12]

When a person who is not the child's parent or guardian obtains a residence order, section 12(2) provides that he or she shall have parental responsibility for the child, but only while the residence order remains in force. The reason why a residence order confers parental responsibility on such a person is because the person who provides the child with a home will normally make most, or all, of the day-to-day decisions about the child's upbringing, and he or she is therefore likely to need parental responsibility. The value of this provision is illustrated by *B v B (A Minor) (Residence Order)*.[13] A grandmother had applied for a residence order in the family proceedings court. The magistrates, applying the 'no order unless better for the child' principle in section 1(5),[14] had refused to make the order on the grounds that it was not necessary since the child was already living with the grandmother, and the matter was not in dispute. On appeal it was held that the court had been wrong to refuse to make a residence order. The grandmother had found that her lack of parental responsibility was giving rise to practical difficulties, in particular the local education authority were unwilling to accept her consent to the child

10 S 4, and see ch 1.
11 S 12(1).
12 See ch 1.
13 [1992] 2 FLR 327. And see *Re AB (Adoption: Joint Residence)* [1996] 1 FLR 27.
14 See above.

going on school trips, and were demanding the written consent of the mother. It was also pointed out that she might need the power to consent to the child receiving both routine and emergency medical treatment. The grandmother needed parental responsibility for the child while she had charge of the child's upbringing, and this could only be conferred by means of a residence order.

The status of having had parental responsibility for a child is relevant if the child subsequently goes into local authority care. Although section 12(2) provides that a non-parent has parental responsibility only while the residence order remains in force, and although the making of a care order discharges any order made under section 8,[15] the preceding parental responsibility of a non-parent continues to be recognised. Section 34 provides that a local authority shall allow the child reasonable contact with 'a person in whose favour a residence order was in force immediately before the care order was made'. It also entitles such a person to apply for a contact order when there is a dispute with the local authority about what arrangements are reasonable.[16] More generally, when a child is being looked after by a local authority they must involve any person with parental responsibility in decision-making about the child.[17]

A residence order diminishes the parental responsibility of the non-residential parent

Part of the rhetoric surrounding the period preceding the implementation of the Children Act 1989 was that residence orders would 'lower the stakes', and avoid the impression that the 'loser takes all' when parents part.[18] It is certainly the case that each parent still retains parental responsibility whether or not a residence order is made in his or her favour. However, a residence order, like any other order, is covered by the incompatibility principle in section 2(8). This provides that:

'The fact that a person has parental responsibility for a child shall not entitle him to act in any way which would be incompatible with any order made with respect to the child under this Act.'

The incompatibility principle inevitably affects the exercise of parental responsibility by the non-residential parent because the person with whom the child lives will make the day-to-day decisions about the child's upbringing. Nonetheless it is clear that the non-residential parent has the right to act independently in meeting his or her parental responsibility[19]

---

15 S 91(2).
16 S 34(3)(a).
17 S 22(4)(c), and see further ch 3.
18 See R White, P Carr and NV Lowe *A Guide to the Children Act 1989* (Butterworths, 1990) para 3.3.
19 S 2(7).

and, when there is disagreement between parents on any major aspect of the child's upbringing, neither has the absolute right to decide. However, it is suggested that it is somewhat misleading to state that a residence order does not award a 'bundle of proprietorial rights in the child' to the residential parent.[20] A residence order undoubtedly does give additional rights to the residential parent, and does diminish the parental responsibility of the non-residential natural parent in various ways.

It is normally the case that a person who takes, or sends, a child out of the United Kingdom without the consent of a parent with parental responsibility commits an offence.[1] However, such a person does not commit an offence where he has a residence order, and where he takes or sends the child from the United Kingdom for less than one month.[2] The aim of the one-month provision is to allow holidays abroad to be taken without prior consent or the court's approval. But a law which permits the removal of some children from the United Kingdom by a residential parent, or other person with a residence order, runs the risk that occasionally a child will not be returned. Because no consent is needed, the non-residential parent does not need to be notified about the residential parent's intentions, and he or she may therefore be in no position to take action to prevent the removal by applying for a prohibited steps order.

A residence order affects the appointment of a guardian. Each parent with parental responsibility is entitled to appoint a person to act as guardian of the child in the event of his or her death. However, such an appointment does not take effect when there is a surviving parent with parental responsibility *unless* the deceased parent had a residence order.[3] It is only in the latter situation that the guardian shares parental responsibility with the surviving parent. This could expose the non-residential parent to forms of interference in the child's upbringing which he would not experience where no residence order had been made, and to that extent it may diminish his or her parental responsibility. A parent may also take the view that his responsibility has been diminished when he discovers that the normal rule that the consent of each parent with parental responsibility to the marriage of their child aged under 18 is abrogated when a residence order is in force. It is only the consent of the person who has a residence order which is needed.[4] A residence order also affects who may confer entitlement to apply for a residence or contact order on a third party.[5]

The parental responsibility of the non-residential parent can be seriously affected in a case where a person with a residence order wishes to make use of accommodation provided for children in need by a local authority. The law makes it clear that a local authority may not provide

20 B Hoggett *Parents and Children* (Sweet and Maxwell, 4th edn) p 67.
1   Child Abduction Act 1984, s 1.
2   Child Abduction Act 1984, s 1(4); Children Act 1989, s 13(2).
3   Children Act 1989, s 5(7), (8).
4   Marriage Act 1949, s 3.
5   This is explained below.

accommodation for a child if any person with parental responsibility is willing and able to provide, or to arrange for accommodation to be provided, for the child.[6] Furthermore, any person with parental responsibility may remove the child at any time from local authority accommodation.[7] The thinking behind these provisions is that the state should not be able to keep a child away from a parent with parental responsibility who is offering to care for the child unless there are grounds for a care order. However, this rule does not apply when a residence order is in force.[8] Thus, for example, if parents divorce and no residence order is made, the parent who does not have the day-to-day care of the child can prevent the child going into local authority accommodation, and can remove the child who is being accommodated at any time. But where there is a residence order and the residential parent wants the child to be accommodated, the local authority have a discretion as to whether to accommodate the child against the wishes of the non-residential parent. The extent to which these accommodation provisions diminish parental responsibility is therefore dependent on the approach adopted by the local authority. When the authority is insistent on accommodating the child, the remedy for the aggrieved parent is to apply for a residence order.[9]

A residence order discharges a care order

When a child is the subject of a care order only a very limited class of persons are entitled to apply for the order to be discharged.[10] Fathers without parental responsibility, relatives and other interested persons fall outside this class. However, section 91(1) provides that a residence order discharges a care order. It will be seen below that a fairly wide group of persons are entitled to apply for a residence order, and that any other person may seek the court's leave to apply for a residence order.[11] Thus it may be possible for a relative, or other interested person, to take steps to bring a care order to an end by obtaining a residence order.[12] This is a vitally important provision where a relative wishes to look after a child, but where a local authority refuse to place the child in the care of that relative.[13]

6   Children Act 1989, s 20(7).
7   S 20(8).
8   S 20(9).
9   See ch 3 for a fuller examination of the accommodation provisions in s 20.
10 S 39(1). These are any person who has parental responsibility for the child, the child, or the designated local authority.
11 An exception to this rule is made in relation to local authority foster parents to whom special provisions apply: see below.
12 For the converse of this situation see the unusual case of *Re K (Care Order or Residence Order)* [1995] 1 FLR 675, where the local authority invited the court to make supervision orders and residence orders in favour of the grandparents, with whom the children were living. The grandparents opposed this and invited the court to make care orders.
13 This opens up a jurisdiction to relatives aggrieved by a local authority's decision about a child in care, which was denied to them under the law preceding the Children Act 1989; see *W v Hertfordshire County Council* [1985] 2 All ER 301.

Directions and conditions in a residence order

The decision that the child should live with one parent rather than the other inevitably gives the residential parent the greater say in the day to day care of the child.[14] This raises the question whether the courts should have additional powers to control the exercise of the residential parent's parental responsibility. Section 11(7) permits a court to supplement any section 8 order by giving directions about how it is to be carried into effect and by imposing conditions on specified persons. Often proposals made for the upbringing of children after divorce or parental separation are not ideal and it may be tempting for courts to attempt to remedy this by making orders under section 11(7). However, although section 11(7) appears to confer wide discretionary powers, the court's jurisdiction is not unfettered.

In *Re E (Residence: Imposition of Conditions)*[15] the Court of Appeal made it plain that a general imposition of conditions in residence orders was clearly not contemplated by Parliament, and that the temptation to include them should therefore be resisted. It ruled that although the court's powers under section 11(7) were wide enough to restrict residence to a particular place, such a restriction was normally an unwarranted imposition on the right of the parent to choose where to live. Where there were cross-applications for a residence order, the correct approach was to look at where the children would live as one of the relevant factors in choosing what order to make. In a finely balanced case, the proposals put forward by each parent would assume considerable importance. However, Butler-Sloss LJ said that in exceptional cases, such as where a court has concerns about the ability of the parent with a residence order to care for the children in a satisfactory manner, 'the court might consider it necessary to keep some control over the parent by way of conditions which include a condition of residence'.[16]

Section 11(7) does not permit the court to make an order which has the effect of interfering with a clear right of occupation of property,[17] nor does it permit a court to make a residence order to a parent containing either a condition that the children are not brought into contact with her partner, or a condition ordering her not to allow her partner to reside at her address.[18] A parent is entitled to choose with whom she wishes to live and a court cannot prevent this. The question for the court where a parent does choose to live with someone whom the court regards as presenting a risk to the children, or who is otherwise unsuitable to have contact with them, is whether a residence order should be made in that parent's favour

---

14 For example, in most cases the child will go to school in the area where the residential parent lives.
15 [1997] 2 FLR 638.
16 Ibid, at p 642.
17 *Re D (Prohibited Steps Order)* [1996] 2 FLR 273.
18 *Re D (Residence: Imposition of Conditions)* [1996] 2 FLR 281.

or whether it would be better for the children to live elsewhere, normally with the other parent.[19]

It is suggested that this cautious approach to conditions in section 8 orders is sensible. It strikes a proper balance between recognising that courts have extensive powers to make orders for the benefit of children and acknowledging that parents have a right to conduct their lives in the manner they choose. At the same time it warns parents that should they decide to move away from an area where the children are settled and where they have close links with the wider family and friends, or should they choose to set up home with an unsuitable partner, this may lead to them losing the day to day care of their children.

If the courts were to approve the practice of making residence orders containing the condition that a parent should not allow her children to come into contact with a third person, this would put unrealistic faith in the efficacy of such a protective measure to safeguard the children from harm. Only the residential parent would be under a duty to ensure that the condition was obeyed and no-one would have a duty to inform the court where the condition was broken. Therefore, such a condition could be broken with impunity, possibly placing the child at risk, yet the inclusion of the condition might generate a false sense of security that the child was being properly protected.

A contact order

A contact order means:

> '... an order requiring the person with whom a child lives, or is to live, to allow the child to visit or stay with the person named in the order, or for that person and the child otherwise to have contact with each other.'

Contact can be maintained with a child in a variety of ways. Normally it involves the person with the order visiting the child, taking the child out for the day, or having the child to stay overnight or for much longer periods. In some situations, however, it may not be possible, or it may not be appropriate, for direct physical contact to take place. In these circumstances a court may order indirect contact by means of letters, cards, presents for birthdays and Christmas, and telephone calls.[20] Occasionally

---

19 Where a court is concerned that the children will be at risk of suffering significant harm which ever alternative is chosen it may give a direction to the local authority under s 37(1) to undertake an investigation with a view to initiating care proceedings, see ch 3.

20 See, for example, *Re J (A Minor) (Contact)* [1994] 1 FLR 729, and *Re L (Contact: Transsexual Applicant)* [1995] 2 FLR 438, where in each case the court allowed the fathers to send letters and presents but not to have direct contact. Itemisation of telephone bills should make orders of this type easier to make because the recipient of calls from a child could agree to pay for their cost.

it may be thought that contact should be informally supervised by a relative. Many court welfare services and charitable organisations provide contact centres which are aimed at facilitating contact. These centres provide a particularly useful service where contact poses some risk to the child and must therefore be carefully observed, or where there is so much distrust and animosity between the parents that contact will only be possible if it takes place in a neutral setting.[1]

Directions and conditions in a contact order

The courts' powers under section 11(7) to give directions and impose conditions when making a section 8 order are probably most often used when contact orders are made. However, while a section 8 order may 'be made to have effect for a specified period, or contain provisions which are to have effect for a specified period',[2] and while the court may 'make such incidental, supplemental or consequential provision as the court thinks fit',[3] this does not entitle the court to give directions and impose conditions which fall outside the scope of the main order. In *D v N (Contact Order: Conditions)*[4] a judge attached conditions to a defined contact order which were intended to be injunctive in character and to which he attached a penal notice.[5] The 'conditions' included, inter alia, orders relating to obtaining a passport for the child, entering or telephoning the mother's place of work, entering premises owned by relatives of the mother and molesting these relatives, removing the child from the mother's care and control, and telephoning the mother. Sir Stephen Brown P held that these orders were outside the powers of the court when adding conditions to a contact order. He stated that very great care should be exercised before what were in effect injunctive orders were brought under the umbrella of section 11(7) powers.[6]

The onus to facilitate contact is placed on the person with whom the child is living. It requires that person to allow the child to have contact with the person in whose favour the contact order has been made. In *Re M (A Minor) (Contact: Conditions)*[7] magistrates directed a mother to write a letter every three months to the child's father, who was in prison, telling

1 See further E Halliday *The role and function of child contact centres* (1997) 19 JSWFL 53.
2 S 11(7)(c).
3 S 11(7)(d).
4 [1997] 2 FLR 797.
5 Such a notice informs the respondent of the consequences of disobedience. This includes the risk of committal to prison in the event of breach.
6 However, in circumstances of this kind the applicant parent is not entirely without a remedy. Sir Stephen Brown P voiced the opinion that such orders could properly be made by the High Court in the exercise of its inherent jurisdiction, see [1997] 2 FLR 797 at pp 802 and 803. The inherent jurisdiction of the High Court is examined below.
7 [1994] 1 FLR 272.

him about the progress of his child. They also ordered the mother to read letters from the father to the child. Wall J held that the magistrates had acted beyond their powers. He said that the effect of their order would have been to require the parents to have contact with each other, and that the court had no power to make such an order.[8] Moreover, he was 'profoundly unhappy' about orders which required a parent to be pro-active in facilitating contact, and said that although the court may have had jurisdiction to give such a direction, nonetheless it should not have done so unless satisfied that the other parent consented, and was willing to undertake the task. He ruled that the direction was wrong in principle, and unwise on the facts, and therefore that it could not stand. However, Wall J's judgment can no longer be relied upon in the light of Sir Thomas Bingham MR's trenchant remarks in *Re O (Contact: Imposition of Conditions)*.[9] Commenting robustly on the mutual obligations of parents to facilitate contact by doing such things as reading letters and sending photographs and reports, he said:

> 'If the caring parent puts difficulties in the way of indirect contact by withholding presents or letters or failing to read letters to a child who cannot read, then such parents must understand that the court can compel compliance with its orders; it has sanctions available and no residence order is to be regarded as irrevocable. It is entirely reasonable that the parent with the care of the child should be obliged to report on the progress of the child to the absent parent.'

Sir Thomas Bingham MR added that he disagreed with Wall J's approach because it was 'tantamount to saying that a mother's withholding of consent and expression of unwillingness to do something is enough to defeat the court's power to order that it should be done.'

The two cases of *Re M (A Minor) (Contact: Conditions)* and *Re O (Contact: Imposition of Conditions)* highlight the inevitable fact that, when a young child is involved, it will often be impossible for a contact order to take effect without the co-operation of the caring parent. But when parents are badly estranged such co-operation may not be forthcoming. During the course of his judgment Wall J commented that the magistrates had rejected any suggestion that the child should be taken to see his father in prison.[10] But what would the position have been if the court had taken the view that such an arrangement would have been in the interests of the child? These cases leave open the question of whether, and in what circumstances, a parent or other person can be ordered to take active

---

8 Similarly, a court cannot order that parents do not have contact with one another; see *Croydon London Borough Council v A* [1992] 2 FLR 341.
9 [1995] 2 FLR 124, at p 130.
10 Nor can this be achieved by making a family assistance order and requiring a member of the court welfare service to take the child to the prison; see *S v P (Contact Application: Family Assistance Order)* [1997] 2 FLR 277.

steps to facilitate direct contact. The wording in section 8, which explains what a contact order means, simply requires the person with whom the child lives 'to allow the child to visit or stay with the person named in the order, or for that person and the child otherwise to have contact with each other'. In *Re M (A Minor) (Contact: Conditions)* the court was clear that there was power under section 11(7) to direct the residential parent to keep the other parent informed of the child's whereabouts as a necessary condition of contact taking place. In *Re O (Contact: Imposition of Conditions)* the Court of Appeal was certain that a mother must comply with an order to send photographs at regular intervals.[11] But these orders were a long way away from requiring the residential parent to take the child to visit the non-residential parent. Perhaps the solution lies in making this kind of co-operation a condition of making the residence order to that parent, thus squarely placing the burden of facilitating direct contact on the residential parent. However, the problem of enforcing the order if the residential parent refused to co-operate would remain. Threatening to remove the child is usually an empty threat since to do so would normally be against the child's best interests.

Ordering no contact

When a court wishes to order that no contact should take place it is not always clear whether it should make no order, a no contact order or a prohibited steps order. This is a real issue because section 9(5)(a) provides that a prohibited steps order cannot be made with a view to achieving a result which could be achieved by making a residence or contact order. In *Re H (A Minor)*[12] the question of which order should be made was not raised, but Scott Baker J took the view that the appropriate order to prevent contact between parent and child was a prohibited steps order. In the particular case with which he was dealing he stated that the order should be drafted in the nature of an injunction, with a penal notice attached, stating that the natural parents should not assume physical possession of, or contact with, their child in any way without the court's further order. However, in the later case of *Nottinghamshire County Council v P*[13] it was held that the sensible and appropriate construction

---

11 Similarly, the court's powers are broad enough to require the person with whom the child is living to send a copy of the child's school report to the non-residential parent, and to notify him or her of any special activities in which the child is taking part, such as a sporting event, play or concert. In *Re O (Contact: Imposition of Conditions)* the Court of Appeal appeared totally to ignore the mother's reasons for not wishing the child to have any type of contact: the parties were unmarried, had separated before the child was born, the father had given undertakings not to pester or molest the mother which he had broken and the child, aged two, had been upset by visits to the contact centre.

12 [1993] Fam Law 205; see too *Croydon London Borough Council v A* [1992] 2 FLR 341 where contact was prevented by a prohibited steps order.

13 [1993] 2 FLR 134.

of the term 'contact order' included a situation where a court was required to consider whether any contact at all should be allowed. It was further held that an order for no contact fell within the general concept of contact and that, applying section 9(5)(a), a prohibited steps order could not be made where it would be a disguised form of contact order. In *Re J (A Minor) (Contact)*[14] the judge ruled that there should be no order on the father's application for contact, and the Court of Appeal made no comment on the choice of no order as a means to deny contact.

The position is complicated by the existence of the special rule in section 9(2) which prevents a local authority from applying for a contact order and prevents such an order being made in their favour. The reason for this rule is to prevent a local authority from using a private law order to supervise a child (for contact could be used in a supervisory way). When a local authority believe that a child is in need of supervision they must apply for a supervision order under Part IV. On the other hand, a local authority may apply for a prohibited steps order provided that they first obtain the court's leave. In *Nottinghamshire County Council v P*[15] the Court of Appeal took the view that the local authority were attempting to by-pass the rule in section 9(2) by applying for a prohibited steps order to prevent a father from having contact with his daughters. The court ruled that to make a prohibited steps order which prohibited contact was in essence to make a no contact order.

The same issue of law arose in *Re H (Prohibited Steps Order)*.[16] The trial judge in an application brought in care proceedings had left the children in the care of their mother and had made a supervision order. He made a prohibited steps order against the mother to prevent the children from having contact with the abuser of one child, attached a condition of no contact to the supervision order, but declined to make a prohibited steps order against the abuser on the ground that he had no jurisdiction as the abuser was not a party to the proceedings. On appeal, the Court of Appeal held that the judge was in error in making a prohibited steps order against the mother because this directly contravened section 9(5), since a prohibited steps order against the mother would achieve the same result as a contact order requiring the mother not to allow contact with the abuser, and could be enforced in the same way. The judge had no power to attach a condition of no contact to the supervision order.[17] However, a prohibited steps order which required the abuser not to seek contact with the children did not contravene section 9(5). Butler-Sloss LJ explained the Court's reasoning:

> 'If a "no contact order" had been made in this case to the mother the order would be directed at the mother as the subject of the

14 [1994] 1 FLR 729; the Court of Appeal held that such a ruling gave the father an automatic right of appeal: RSC Ord 59, r 1B(1)(f)(ii), (iii).
15 [1993] 2 FLR 134.
16 [1995] 1 FLR 638.
17 See Sch 3.

order and the obligation would be placed on her to prevent any contact by the children with [the abuser]. There could not be a "no contact order" which would direct [the abuser] not to have nor to seek contact with the four children since he does not live with the children. A contact order directed at the mother would not in this case achieve the required result.'

In the light of this reasoning, the Court of Appeal made a prohibited steps order against the abuser.[18]

Which approach is preferable? Contact orders are drafted in a positive manner in section 8 and, on the face of it, to order that a child should not have contact with his parent appears to be a clumsy way of expressing this positive drafting in negative terms. Prima facie, therefore, applying the no order principle under section 1(5) and making no order for contact seems to be the better solution.[19] However, where there have been contested proceedings about contact it is very important that the parties understand exactly what the court has ruled. Although courts must give reasons when making no order, just as they must when making an order,[20] for the sake of clarity it is important that the applicant should receive from the court a written form on which it is made absolutely plain that contact is not allowed. A prohibited steps order appears particularly appropriate where it is thought desirable to add a penal notice, as in *Re H (A Minor)*.[1] However, in *Re H (Prohibited Steps Order)*[2] Butler-Sloss LJ was confident that a no contact order could be enforced in the same way as a prohibited steps order.

It is suggested that the importance of determining which of a no contact order, a prohibited steps order, or simply declining to make an order, applying the 'no order' approach in section 1(5), should most appropriately be used to deny contact is probably limited to those situations in which a local authority are involved. In that regard the issue has been resolved by the rulings in *Nottinghamshire County Council v P*[3] and *Re H (Prohibited Steps Order)*[4] and a prohibited steps order should be used.

---

18 The court confirmed that it had this power despite the fact that the abuser was not a party to the proceedings. See [1995] 1 FLR 638 at p 642 for discussion of the procedural difficulties which might arise in such ex parte proceedings, and the court's suggested solution to them. See too M Roberts *Ousting abusers – Children Act 1989 or inherent jurisdiction? Re H (Prohibited Steps Orders)* (1995) 7 CFLQ 243.

19 See *Re J (A Minor) (Contact)*, above; and *Re W (A Minor) (Contact)* [1994] 1 FLR 843 where such an approach by magistrates was accepted without comment by the Court of Appeal. (The case was remitted for other reasons.)

20 Family Proceedings Rules 1991, r 4.21(4). It seems doubtful whether a penal notice could be issued when a court declines to make an order, although it might be possible to attach this to the statement of reasons.

1 [1993] Fam Law 205.

2 [1995] 1 FLR 638.

3 [1993] 2 FLR 134.

4 [1995] 1 FLR 638.

A prohibited steps order

A prohibited steps order means:

> '... an order that no step which could be taken by a parent in meeting his parental responsibility for a child, and which is of the kind specified in the order, shall be taken by any person without the consent of the court.'

It can be seen that this is an order which can impose limits on the exercise of parental responsibility by a parent, but that it can also be used to control the behaviour of 'any person' towards a child, which therefore includes a person who does not have parental responsibility. The purpose of a prohibited steps order is to enable a court to play a continuing parental role in relation to the child by empowering it to identify those matters of parental responsibility which must be referred back to the court.[5]

The scope of a prohibited steps order

It is important to realise that a prohibited steps order cannot be used to forbid any action which the applicant or court wish to prevent, for the order is confined to controlling those steps which could be taken by a parent in meeting his parental responsibility for a child.[6] In *Croydon London Borough Council v A* [7] it was held that while the trial court had been correct to make an order prohibiting a father from having any contact with his children, and prohibiting the mother from allowing him to have contact with the children, it had been plainly wrong to make an order that the parents could not have contact with each other, as contact between parents has nothing to do with the exercise of parental res-ponsibility. It is for this reason, too, that a prohibited steps order cannot be used as a means to oust a parent from the home.[8] Nor may such an order be made where its purpose is to prevent a father from staying overnight at the matrimonial home at the conclusion of contact with his children.[9] Such use of a prohibited steps order would amount to the importation by the back door of an occupation order, which is governed by Part IV of the Family Law Act 1996.[10]

---

5 See the Law Commission Review of Child Law, Guardianship and Custody, Law Com No 172, para 4.20.
6 For example, it could not be used to prohibit publicity about a child; an injunction under the court's inherent jurisdiction would be the proper remedy.
7 [1992] 2 FLR 341.
8 *Nottinghamshire County Council v P* [1993] 2 FLR 134.
9 *Re D (Prohibited Steps Order)* [1996] 2 FLR 273.
10 See ch 6.

It appears that a prohibited steps order can be used to require a parent to prevent a person who has no legal entitlement to go on the premises from entering her home. In *W v Hertfordshire County Council*[11] justices made an order prohibiting a mother from allowing her partner, who had allegedly caused her child's injury, into her house. This was referred to without comment when the case was appealed on other grounds. It is suggested that an order of this type could be valuable because it places a burden of responsibility on the parent, but that such an order should also be made against the partner so that it is clearly he who is in breach of the court's order, as well as the mother.[12]

Removal of children from the United Kingdom without the consent of all those with parental responsibility is a criminal offence,[13] but parents and others may either not be aware of this, or they may be prepared to break the criminal law. In addition, section 13 of the Children Act 1989 provides that a person with a residence order can take or send the child out of the United Kingdom for a period of less than one month without either the consent of all those with parental responsibility or the court's leave.[14] In some situations any removal from the jurisdiction could expose the child to the risk of being taken permanently abroad and a prohibited steps order may therefore be necessary to obviate this risk. Certainly it is advisable that such an order is sought by a person with parental responsibility where there is a perceived risk of the child being taken overseas without consent, for once a child has been taken from the country it may be extremely difficult to secure his return.[15] A person without parental responsibility, such as an unmarried father or other close relative, may be particularly well-advised to apply for a prohibited steps order preventing removal from the jurisdiction, for such persons have no right to prevent a child being taken abroad. Where they enjoy a close relationship with the child, a court could well be persuaded to prohibit the child's removal unless those with parental responsibility first gained the permission of the court.[16]

The relationship between prohibited steps orders and public law orders

The full scope of prohibited steps orders has yet to be explored by the courts, in particular their relationship with the public law orders under Parts IV and V. Local authorities are encouraged to work in partnership with parents, and to take the least intrusive steps into the family life of a child which are consistent with protecting him from harm, and private

11 [1993] 1 FLR 118.
12 See *Re H (Prohibited Steps Order)* [1995] 1 FLR 638, and see the discussion above about the inter-relationship between prohibited steps orders and no contact orders.
13 Child Abduction Act 1984, s 1.
14 See also, the Child Abduction Act 1984, s 1(4).
15 International child abduction, and the efforts made to control it by international conventions, is examined in ch 5.
16 See *Re WB (Residence Orders)* [1995] 2 FLR 1023.

law orders are far less threatening to parents than public law orders.[17] It is not clear whether prohibited steps orders may ever be used as a substitute for the initiation of care proceedings. This approach was certainly disapproved in *Nottinghamshire County Council v P*,[18] but it is uncertain how far that ruling extends. There may be occasions when a more limited form of intervention than an application brought in care proceedings might be sufficient to protect a child. For example, if the feared risk of significant harm to a child was from too severe forms of punishment, but otherwise the child was properly looked after, and if a local authority were to obtain the leave of the court to apply for an order that a parent did not use any form of corporal punishment on a child, it remains to be seen whether a court would be willing to make such an order.[19]

Controversy over whether a prohibited steps order may be used to restrain a local authority in the manner in which they are exercising their statutory powers and duties in relation to a child arose in *D v D (County Court Jurisdiction: Injunctions)*.[20] The Court of Appeal ruled that the trial judge did not have jurisdiction to issue a direction which had the effect of inhibiting a local authority from carrying out their investigative function in response to a suspicion of child abuse in proceedings brought by parents for residence orders.[1] This investigation had been set in motion when the father made an allegation of child abuse against the mother.[2] However, the court also ruled that if a parent was exercising her parental responsibility in a way which was detrimental to the welfare of the child, she could be restrained by an order under section 8 from doing so. Importantly, there is obiter dicta in *D v D (County Court Jurisdiction: Injunctions)* to the effect that a court may make a prohibited steps order against a person with parental responsibility where she is permitting her child to be exposed to unnecessary interviews and examinations. The court added that once such a prohibited steps order has been made, neither the local authority nor the police [3] could take any step which was invasive of the life of the child without first applying to the court.

The ruling in *D v D (County Court Jurisdiction: Injunctions)* may have significant implications for a local authority where they have reasonable cause to suspect that a child is suffering, or is likely to suffer, significant harm and where they are carrying out an investigation.[4] Where such an

---

17 See the several volumes of *The Children Act 1989 Guidance and Regulations* issued by the Department of Health (HMSO, 1991).
18 [1993] 2 FLR 134.
19 It is suggested that a prohibited steps order made in these circumstances would not fall foul of s 9(5).
20 [1993] 2 FLR 802.
1   Whether a High Court judge has such power was doubted, but left open: ibid, at p 811.
2   The trial judge clearly suspected the father's motives, and described the intervention by the police and social services department as 'ham-fisted'.
3   Except in the exercise of their emergency powers under s 46: and see ch 3.
4   Under s 47: see ch 3.

investigation requires the co-operation of a parent with parental responsibility, and where the parent has been prohibited by the court from
permitting the child to be medically examined or otherwise investigated
without the leave of the court, the local authority will either be forced to
abandon the investigation, or it will require permission from the court to
proceed with the investigation.[5]

A specific issue order

A specific issue order means:

> '... an order giving directions for the purpose of determining a
> specific question which has arisen, or which may arise, in con-
> nection with any aspect of parental responsibility for a child.'

A specific issue order may be of particular value to a parent in a situation
where the child has his home elsewhere. Clearly, the parent in charge of
the day-to-day care of the child will make most decisions about the child's
upbringing, but the other parent still retains an interest in these decisions
and, where they are in dispute, the issue can be placed before a court and
the court asked to decide. Examples of when a specific issue order might
be useful are where parents disagree over where their child is to be
educated,[6] over the religion in which he is to receive instruction, or over
which name he is to be called.[7] It was stated in *Re C (A Minor) (Leave to
Seek Section 8 Orders)*[8] that specific issue orders should be reserved for
the resolution of matters of importance. The court therefore refused to
give leave to a child to apply for an order determining whether she could
go on holiday to Bulgaria with the family with whom she was living,
against the wishes of her parents.

A specific issue order may also be of value to a third party who wishes
to challenge a decision of a person with parental responsibility. In *Re F
(Specific Issue: Child Interview)*[9] a father was accused of assaulting the
mother of two children and had been committed for trial. His solicitor
wished to interview the children because they may have witnessed the
alleged assault. The mother, who had sole parental responsibility for the
children, refused to consent to the interview taking place. Dismissing the
mother's appeal against the granting of a specific issue order permitting
the solicitor to interview the children, the Court of Appeal held that the

---

5   See ch 3 for further discussion of the implications of *D v D (County Court Jurisdiction:
    Injunctions)* [1993] 2 FLR 802.
6   See, for example, *Re G (Parental Responsibility: Education)* [1994] 2 FLR 964.
7   See ch 4 for detailed discussion of how courts have approached change of a child's
    surname.
8   [1994] 1 FLR 26. See below.
9   [1995] 1 FLR 819.

interview would be an ordeal the boys would want to be spared if possible, but that that consideration had to be weighed against the advantages of securing a fair trial.[10]

Each of the section 8 orders is concerned with an aspect of parental responsibility, and although the orders are wide enough to cover most matters relating to a child's upbringing, some issues clearly fall outside the scope of the order. Thus in *Re J (Specific Issue Order: Leave to Apply)*[11] a child claimed to be a 'child in need' for the purposes of section 17 of the Act.[12] He sought leave to apply for a specific issue order which would deem him to be such a child, his purpose being to compel a local authority to make appropriate provision for his upbringing. Wall J ruled that, as a matter of statutory construction, it was clear that it was the intention of Parliament that the exercise of a local authority's powers and duties under Part III of the Act should not be subject to judicial scrutiny or control except by means of judicial review.[13] Accordingly, a specific issue order was inapposite to determine the question whether or not the applicant was a child in need. Moreover, the decision whether a child was a child in need was not a specific question which arose 'in connection with any aspect of parental responsibility'. Such a question must relate to the application of the exercise of parental responsibility to particular facts.

Specific issue orders and medical treatment

Decisions relating to medical treatment can pose particular difficulties when persons with parental responsibility disagree. In this situation it should be recalled that each person with parental responsibility may act alone in meeting that responsibility, which means that a medical practitioner is authorised to provide treatment with the consent of one parent alone.[14] However, unless asked to do so in an emergency, it is most unlikely that a medical practitioner would be willing to give medical treatment in a situation where the persons with parental responsibility are in conflict, because the ethics of so doing may not be clear. Consequently, the person who wishes the treatment to take place might feel impelled to ask a court to rule that the treatment is in the best interests of the child, and that the consent of one parent alone is all that is required in the circumstances.

---

10 In relation to balancing the welfare of children against other profoundly important principles: see ch 4.
11 [1995] 1 FLR 669.
12 See ch 3.
13 It was accepted by the court that the local authority's decision that the applicant was not a child in need was susceptible to judicial review. It is suggested, however, that any such challenge would first have to made under the complaints procedure established by s 26: see further ch 3.
14 S 2(7); *Re R (A Minor) (Wardship: Medical Treatment)* [1991] 4 All ER 177; *Re W (A Minor) (Medical Treatment: Court's Jurisdiction)* [1993] Fam 64.

Parents may also seek a form of medical treatment for their child which raises profound moral and ethical dilemmas. In *Re HG (Specific Issue Order: Sterilisation)*[15] a girl aged nearly 18 had severe epilepsy and a form of chromosomal deficiency which meant that she was an infant in terms of abilities. She lived in a school which meant she was likely at some time to be at risk of sexual relationships leading to pregnancy. The contraceptive pill was not suitable because of her epilepsy. It was accepted by all that it would be disastrous for the girl if she were to become pregnant because she would not be capable of understanding what was happening to her. Her parents wished to raise the question of whether their daughter could be sterilised by making an application as the child's next friend for a specific issue order. Their application raised two matters of principle: first, whether sterilisation was a matter which fell within the scope of a specific issue order because, the argument ran, parental responsibility did not extend to authorising a sterilisation operation to take place; and secondly, whether a specific issue order could be made when there was no issue between the persons having parental responsibility. The court ruled that the fact that a High Court judge must rule on sterilisation did not take from the parents their responsibility to form their own conclusion and to take the necessary steps to implement that conclusion. Indeed, the court suggested that it may be one of the responsibilities of parenthood to bring the issue of sterilisation before a judge. On the second matter the court ruled that a specific question had arisen which had given rise to the issue to be resolved and the parents could, and indeed should, bring the issue before the court. It was not necessary for there to be protagonists on either side of the debate.

Re HG (Specific Issue Order: Sterilisation) is illustrative of how an application for a specific issue order can be made by a child who does not have the capacity herself to initiate proceedings. Section 10(7) entitles any person who falls within a category of persons prescribed by rules of court to apply for a section 8 order, and rules of court provide that a person under a disability may begin and prosecute proceedings by her next friend, in this case the parents.[16] The parents could, of course, have made their own application for a specific issue order; however, they were not entitled to legal aid to make an application themselves, and legal proceedings in the High Court are very expensive. On the other hand they could obtain legal aid to bring proceedings on behalf of their child. The court found this approach to be acceptable.

As with a prohibited steps order, the court's order must relate to an aspect of parental responsibility, and a specific issue order cannot be used to achieve a result which could be obtained by making a residence or contact order.[17] The courts have been on their guard to prevent these orders

15 [1993] 1 FLR 587.
16 Family Proceedings Rules 1991 (SI 1991/1247), r 9.2 (as amended).
17 S 9(5).

from being used for ulterior purposes because in theory any issue about a child can be characterised as a specific issue. Thus in *Pearson v Franklin*[18] the court refused to accept the argument that a specific issue order could be used to oust a father from the home because such an order would be in the best interests of the child. Ouster orders were governed by different statutes, and the Court of Appeal ruled that they could not be made under the guise of a specific issue order.[19]

Specific issue orders and local authorities

Cases in which all persons with parental responsibility are refusing to agree to a child receiving medical treatment may be of the utmost gravity. Any decision of the court to order medical treatment may run counter to the most profound and sincerely held beliefs of the parents. In *Re O (A Minor) (Medical Treatment)*[20] and *Re R (A minor) (Blood Transfusion)*[1] it was held that such cases should be determined, wherever possible, by a High Court judge, and that strenuous efforts should be made to ensure an inter partes hearing. Usually it will be the local authority who will initiate legal proceedings on behalf of the child because they are under a statutory duty to intervene when a child is at risk of significant harm. This raises questions about which proceedings are the most appropriate when a local authority is the applicant; should they apply under the public law provisions in Part IV of the Act; under the inherent jurisdiction of the High Court; or for a specific issue order?

In *Re O (A Minor) (Medical Treatment)* parents who were Jehovah's Witnesses were refusing to authorise blood transfusions for their gravely ill child. A family proceedings court made an emergency protection order[2] in ex parte proceedings followed by an interim care order, and the case was then transferred for hearing to the High Court. Johnson J was asked to express a view about the most appropriate legal framework in which such decisions should be made. He agreed with counsel, who had been unanimous in rejecting all proceedings governed by the Children Act 1989, and ruled that the inherent jurisdiction of the High Court was the only one appropriate.[3] However, when *Re R (A Minor) (Blood Transfusion)*, a case with similar facts, came before Booth J, she distinguished *Re O (A Minor) (Medical Treatment)* on the grounds that it was a case in which the local authority had already obtained parental responsibility for the

18 [1994] 1 FLR 246.
19 See now Part IV of the Family Law Act 1996, discussed in ch 6.
20 [1993] 2 FLR 149.
1   [1993] 2 FLR 757.
2   It was pointed out in the appeal that it was difficult to bring the case within any of the three situations envisaged by s 44(1): see ch 3.
3   See [1993] 2 FLR 149 at p 154 for Johnson J's reasoning on why the inherent jurisdiction was preferable.

child, and held that the case before her could be determined on an application for a specific issue order. She ruled that it is unnecessary, and inappropriate, for the court to exercise its inherent jurisdiction where there is no need for the court to intervene otherwise to safeguard the child.

Emergency protection orders, interim care orders and care orders all confer parental responsibility on the local authority, which means that the local authority become entitled to give consent to a blood transfusion. However, in *Re R (A Minor) (Blood Transfusion)* and *Re O (A Minor) (Medical Treatment)*, the courts have taken the view that such a decision should be made by a High Court judge where it is to be made against the strongly held beliefs of the child's parents. The difficulty which arises once the child is in the care of a local authority is that a court is prevented by section 9(1) from making any section 8 order other than a residence order.[4] Consequently, a High Court judge cannot make a specific issue order about a child in care. Therefore, once a child is in care, which was the position in *Re O (A Minor) (Medical Treatment)*, the only possible way of transferring decision-making powers from the local authority to a High Court judge was for the local authority to make an application for leave to apply under section 100 for the exercise of the court's inherent jurisdiction.

The choice of which proceedings are appropriate *at the outset* depends on the nature of the local authority's concerns about the child. Where the local authority's only anxiety about the child's well-being relates to medical treatment, it seems that they are best advised to apply for leave to apply for a specific issue order, and for the leave court to direct that the matter should come before a High Court judge as a matter of urgency. This approach follows Booth J's reasoning in *Re R (A Minor) (Blood Transfusion)*. Where the local authority have other concerns about significant harm to the child it is suggested that they should commence care proceedings and take steps to ensure that the case is immediately transferred to the High Court. The High Court can then make rulings about any medical treatment and also determine what order if any should be made in the care proceedings. It should, however, be appreciated that unless the local authority commence care proceedings, the High Court is powerless to place the child in the authority's care as this is specifically prohibited by section 100(2).[5]

A family assistance order

A family assistance order complements orders made under section 8. It may be made with respect to any child where, in family proceedings, the

4   This provision is to prevent a court from exercising decision-making powers which properly belong to a local authority.
5   The inherent jurisdiction of the High Court, and the limits placed on the court's powers by s 100 are explained at the conclusion of this chapter.

court has power to make an order under Part II of the Act, irrespective of whether or not it makes such an order. The purpose of the order is to provide assistance for the family, for a relatively brief period.[6]

Features of a family assistance order

Section 16(1) provides that a court may make an order requiring:

'(a) a probation officer to be made available; or
(b) a local authority to make an officer of the authority available,
to advise, assist and (where appropriate) befriend any person named in the order.'

The persons who may be named in the order are any parent or guardian; any person with whom the child is living, or in whose favour a contact order is in force; and the child himself. The court may not make an order unless satisfied that the circumstances of the case are exceptional.[7] The meaning of this provision has yet to be clarified; however, it recognises that welfare resources are scarce, and that were probation officers and social workers frequently to be called upon to provide assistance under these orders, it would put an intolerable strain on these resources.[8] It has been made clear that a family assistance order cannot be made for the ulterior purpose of requiring a local authority to undertake to escort a child to visit a parent in prison, or otherwise facilitate contact arrangements.[9]

An order cannot be made without the prior consent of every person named in the order, with the exception of the child. Thus it can be seen that the purpose of the order is to provide *voluntary* assistance, for a maximum period of six months. It seems most likely to be made where parties have separated or divorced, and where they need help with coping with the changes in their personal relationships. Where both a family assistance order and an order under section 8 are in force in respect of the same child, the supervising officer may refer to the court the question of whether the section 8 order should be varied or discharged. For example, where a defined contact order has been made, and where this order is not working and is causing distress to the child, the supervising officer could

---

6   For an account of a small research study, see L Trinder and N Stone *Family assistance orders – professional aspiration and party frustration* (1998) 10 CFLQ 291.

7   In *Re L (Contact: Transsexual Applicant)* [1995] 2 FLR 438, the applicant for contact was a father who had made the transition from the male to the female gender. The mother had found it extremely difficult to adapt to this change, and Thorpe J, making a family assistance order said 'if ever there was a family that needed assistance it is this'. The order would also help them to resolve serious housing and financial problems.

8   In *Re C (A Minor) (Family Assistance Order)* [1996] 3 FCR 514 a local authority successfully complained that it did not have the resources to implement the order, which was therefore discharged.

9   *S v P (Contact Application: Family Assistance Order)* [1997] 2 FLR 277.

refer the matter back to court. Similarly, he could refer back an order where one of the parties was refusing to obey it. It would then be a matter for the court to determine whether the order should be varied or discharged.[10]

Applying for a section 8 order

A section 8 order can be made when someone makes a free-standing application for an order under section 10(2), on an application made in family proceedings under section 10(1)(a), and when the court makes an order of its own motion under section 10(1)(b). It is often the case that an issue about a child arises in the context of other proceedings, yet it is wasteful of time and resources if different proceedings are commenced to resolve inter-related family matters; also a proliferation of court hearings can cause extra anxiety and stress for the parties concerned. The Children Act 1989 recognises this, designates certain proceedings as 'family proceedings', and empowers a court to make a section 8 order 'in any family proceedings in which a question arises with respect to the welfare of any child'.[11] 'Family proceedings' means any proceedings 'under the inherent jurisdiction of the High Court in relation to children'[12] or under any of the enactments listed under section 8(4). These enactments are:

- Parts I, II and IV of the Children Act 1989;
- the Matrimonial Causes Act 1973;
- the Adoption Act 1976;
- the Domestic Proceedings and Magistrates' Courts Act 1978;
- Part III of the Matrimonial and Family Proceedings Act 1984;
- the Family Law Act 1996

The availability of section 8 orders in family proceedings allows a court to choose how best to respond to an application for a different order. It is not limited to making, or refusing to make, the order which has been requested. For example, a court might decide that there is sufficient evidence to enable it to make a care order under section 31, but that the child's interests would better be served by making a residence order in favour of a concerned relative. Similarly it might be satisfied that although an adoption order could be made under the Adoption Act 1976, a residence order to the applicants to adopt, coupled with a contact order to the natural mother, would better promote the welfare of the child.

A court in free-standing or family proceedings has power to make a section 8 order of its 'own motion'. This means that where the court takes

---

10 Guidance on how court welfare officers should approach family assistance orders is provided in *National Standards for Probation Service Family Court Welfare Work* (HMSO, 1994).
11 S 10(1)(a).
12 S 8(3).

the view that a section 8 order would be in the child's best interests then it can make such an order even though no application for an order has been made.[13] It has been held in the context of contact orders with children in care, when a court may also make an order of its own motion, that normally a court should give a party to the proceedings the opportunity to oppose an order before it exercises its own motion powers, but that where an adjournment would be contrary to the child's welfare, the court can make the order despite the fact that no advance warning has been given.[14]

Applying for a section 8 order – entitlement and leave

When there is disagreement over a child's upbringing the person, or persons, with parental responsibility are entitled to decide what should happen. Where those with parental responsibility are resolute about their decision then, unless their decision can be reviewed and, where appropriate, overturned by a court, those without parental responsibility have no choice but to abide by the will of those with the power to decide. It has been seen that section 8 orders are designed to provide solutions to areas of disagreement which cover all practical aspects of a child's upbringing. On its face it may seem an attractive proposition that the law should be so structured that the door to the court is open to everyone who has an interest in the child. However, there are various objections to such an approach.

There is the pragmatic objection that it could lead to a flood of applications, some of which might be wholly without merit, which would use up valuable court time and divert attention and resources from those genuine cases in need of resolution. A more powerful objection is that an open door policy would be against the best interests of children. Section 8 orders are powerful orders, with the potential to have a major impact on the life of a child, and on those with parental responsibility for him. Consequently, even the suggestion that an application for an order will be made could cause distress to a child and undue anxiety to his parents or others with parental responsibility. Opening the door of the court to all might also be disruptive, and prevent arrangements for a child's upbringing from being implemented until the litigation had been completed. But, as section 1(2) of the Act recognises, any delay in determining a question about a child's upbringing is likely to prejudice the welfare of the child.

On the other hand to deny access to the courts to anyone other than a limited and named class of persons also has disadvantages. This approach could prevent excluded persons with a genuine interest in a child's

---

13 S 10(1)(b).
14 *Re SW (A Minor) (Care Proceedings)* [1993] 2 FLR 609; see further ch 3.

upbringing from pursuing the matter, and challenging the decisions of parents and others with parental responsibility in the courts. This approach could operate to the disadvantage of the child and could put his or her welfare at risk. The law therefore seeks to strike a delicate balance between making courts readily accessible to all with a genuine interest in the child, and exposing the child, and others, to unnecessary and possibly damaging litigation. This balance is achieved by designating certain persons as entitled to apply for section 8 orders, and by allowing all other persons to apply only if the court is first prepared to give them leave. In addition, there are special rules which apply to children, local authorities and local authority foster parents.

Persons entitled to apply for any section 8 order

Section 10(4) provides:

'The following persons are entitled to apply to the court for any section 8 order with respect to a child—
(a) any parent or guardian of the child;
(b) any person in whose favour a residence order is in force with respect to the child.'

The entitlement of all parents to apply for any section 8 order recognises their prime position. It is also a provision which comes to the assistance of the unmarried father. He is entitled to apply whether or not he has parental responsibility.[15] However, once parents cease to be their child's parents because their child has been adopted, or has been freed for adoption, they cease to fall within section 10(4) and are therefore not entitled to apply for an order.[16] The other entitled persons, namely a guardian or a person with a residence order, already have parental responsibility for the child which is why they too are especially favoured. In the case of a guardian, difficulties are most likely to arise when his or her appointment takes place despite the fact that there is a surviving parent, a position which arises when the deceased parent had a residence order.[17] In this situation, parental responsibility is shared between the guardian and the surviving parent, and where they cannot agree about any aspect relating to the child's upbringing a court ruling may be the only way of resolving the matter.

It has already been explained that parental responsibility is acquired incrementally, and that acquisition of parental responsibility by a third

---

15 *M v C and Calderdale Metropolitan Borough Council* [1993] 1 FLR 505.
16 Ibid; *Re C (A Minor) (Adopted Child: Contact)* [1993] 2 FLR 431.
17 See ch 1.

party does not diminish the parental responsibility of parents.[18] Rather, parental responsibility is shared, and its exercise inhibited only by the incompatibility principle enshrined in section 2(8). Plainly, there will be occasions when the person with a residence order finds himself in disagreement with parents. When this occurs it may then be essential for either party to have access to a court to resolve the matter by means of a section 8 order. Hence a person with a residence order is also entitled to apply for any section 8 order.

Persons entitled to apply for a residence or contact order

Section 10(5) identifies a privileged group of persons who are entitled to apply for a residence or contact order. It provides:

> 'The following persons are entitled to apply for a residence or contact order with respect to a child—
> (a) any party to a marriage (whether or not subsisting) in relation to whom a child is a child of the family;
> (b) any person with whom the child has lived for a period of at least three years;
> (c) any person who—
>   (i) in any case where a residence order is in force with respect to the child, has the consent of each of the persons in whose favour the order is made;
>   (ii) in any case where the child is in the care of a local authority, has the consent of that authority; or
>   (iii) in any other case, has the consent of each of those (if any) who have parental responsibility for the child.'

Why are these persons accorded special treatment? What is their uniting characteristic? According to the Law Commission they were selected because to require such persons to seek the court's leave to apply would amount to a meaningless formality because it would almost invariably be granted.[19] However, the applicant who falls within section 10(5) is only entitled to apply for those orders which are concerned with where the child lives and whom he sees. This is presumably because such matters are determined by the quality of the applicant's personal relationship with the child, and the perceived value of that relationship to the child. However, in this regard it is curious that such persons are not also entitled to apply for a specific issue or prohibited steps order, for it would seem that the same reasoning applies to these orders too.

18 See ch 1.
19 Law Com No 172, para 4.45.

Any party to a marriage in relation to whom a child is a child of the family

A step-parent who is, or has been, married to a parent is entitled to apply for a residence or contact order provided that he or she has treated the child as a child of their family.[20] Sometimes a husband may falsely believe that he is the father of his wife's child and not discover the true facts until after the marriage has broken down. In a case of this kind the child will nonetheless be a child of the family because he will have been treated as such, albeit on a mistaken basis.[1]

In the past, if a custodial parent remarried and she and her second husband applied to adopt her child a court would sometimes make a joint custody order as an alternative to adoption. Indeed, legislation specifically required an adoption court to consider that option.[2] Under the present law the only way in which a step-parent can obtain parental responsibility for a step-child (other than through adoption, or appointment as the child's guardian), is by applying for a residence order. Section 10(5)(a) entitles a step-parent to make such an application without first obtaining the court's leave. This has the beneficial result that the step-parent acquires parental responsibility jointly with the natural parent(s).

Re H (Shared Residence: Parental Responsibility)[3] has resolved any doubt over whether a residence order can be made where its true purpose is not to settle the arrangements to be made as to the person with whom the child was to live, but is to confer parental responsibility on the step-parent. The Court of Appeal held that it would sometimes be appropriate to make a shared residence order to a step-parent simply in order to give him parental responsibility.[4] In a case of this kind it would, however, be important that the natural parent made a joint application with the step-parent for a residence order. Otherwise, if the step-parent's application was successful, he or she would have more rights in relation to the child than the natural parent.[5]

Any person with whom the child has lived for a period of at least three years

Any person with whom the child has lived for a period of at least three years is entitled to apply for a residence or contact order.[6] Section 10(10)

---

20 A child of the family is defined in s 105(1).
1   *W (RJ) v W (SJ)* [1971] 3 All ER 303. Cf *Re H (A Minor) (Contact)* [1994] 2 FLR 776, where a husband who knew he was not the father of the child was given a contact order with the child.
2   Adoption Act 1976, s 14(3).
3   [1995] 2 FLR 883.
4   It could be argued that such an arrangement would be desirable in many families because the step-parent may need parental responsibility in order properly to care for the child.
5   See above on the impact of a residence order on parental responsibility where this is shared.
6   S 10(5)(b).

provides that the period of three years need not be continuous but must not have begun more than five years before, or ended more than three months before, the making of the application. This three-year provision recognises that it is in the interests of children that persons who have provided a child with a home over a considerable period of time are able to apply for an order, either to secure that position, or to ensure that contact with the child is maintained. Furthermore, no one is able to pre-empt an application simply by removing the child, as there is the three-month period of grace within which proceedings can be commenced. Three years is an arbitrary period which may bear no relationship either to a child's sense of time, or to the strength of his personal attachments. These will vary considerably according to the child's particular circumstances, and will be influenced by the child's age, personality and stage of development. However, the chosen period seeks to strike a balance between recognising the importance of a child's attachments to persons other than parents, and not exposing parents to the threat of legal proceedings, and the fear of losing their children to substitute carers, without the pre-liminary safeguard of an application for leave.[7]

Any person who has the necessary consents

The third category of persons entitled to apply for a residence or contact order are those who have obtained the necessary consents. By providing that it is only the consent of each of the persons in whose favour the residence order was made which must be given in order to confer entitle-ment on an applicant, section 10(5)(c)(i) is another example of how a residence order gives increased authority to a parent or third person who has the benefit of such an order.[8] Others who share parental responsibility for the child have no power to give or withhold consent. This can be illustrated by the following example: after divorce a mother obtains a residence order; later she falls ill and is unable to look after her child. A friend of the mother offers to care for the child, but the child's father disagrees because he wishes to care for the child himself. Provided that the friend has the mother's consent, she is entitled to apply to a court for a residence order. By contrast, if the facts were the same, but no residence order had been made, the consent of *both* parents would be required under section 10(5)(c)(iii) to confer entitlement to apply; without these consents the friend would first need to obtain the leave of the court to make an application.

In a case where the child is in the care of a local authority it is the consent of the authority which confers entitlement to apply. Section 9(1)

---

7   The conferment of the right to apply for an order which will secure the child's position after the lapse of three years is not new; it was first introduced by the Children Act 1975.
8   See above.

prohibits a court from making any section 8 order other than a residence order with respect to a child in care, so in fact an application for a residence order is the only one which can be made in relation to a child in care. The reason for this exception is because a residence order goes to the source of the local authority's power and not to the manner in which it is exercised; the effect of a residence order is to discharge the care order.[9] Contact with a child in care is governed by section 34 (which has its own provisions about entitlement and leave to apply).[10] In a case where the child is merely being accommodated by a local authority and a person is seeking to apply for a section 8 order it is the consent of those with parental responsibility under sub-paragraphs (i) and (iii) which is needed to confer entitlement to apply for an order and not that of the local authority.[11]

In any other case, that is to say when there is no residence order in force and the child is not in local authority care, a person is entitled to apply who has the consent of each of those (if any) who have parental responsibility for the child. Where there is no one with parental responsibility there is no one with the capacity to give consent, which means that anyone is entitled to apply for a residence or contact order. When parents are unmarried, normally the mother alone has parental responsibility, so it is her consent which is needed. If she has died, no one has parental responsibility for the child despite the fact that the unmarried father survives. The effect of this, in practice, can be illustrated by the following example: an unmarried mother dies and her parents wish to apply for a residence order in respect of their granddaughter. If the child's father has parental responsibility they will need his consent to entitle them to apply for the order. Without that consent they must obtain the leave of the court to make their application. But if the father does not have parental responsibility, then the grandparents are entitled to apply for a residence or contact order.

Leave to apply for a section 8 order

It has been seen already that the class of persons who are entitled to apply for section 8 orders is limited. However, this does not necessarily mean that the door of the court is closed to non-entitled persons. Any person, apart from local authorities and local authority foster parents to whom special rules apply,[12] may seek the leave of the court to apply for any section 8 order either in family proceedings or on a free-standing application.[13] An alternative route to a hearing for a non-entitled person

9   S 91(1).
10   See ch 3.
11   In relation to how this might affect the entitlement to apply of a local authority foster parent, see below.
12   See below.
13   S 10(1)(a)(ii); s 10(2)(b).

is to apply to be joined as a party to existing family proceedings. As a party, a non-entitled person has the opportunity to adduce evidence and to make submissions with a view to persuading a court to exercise its own motion powers to make a section 8 order in his or her favour. Rules of court[14] which permit an application to be made to be joined as a party provide no guidelines as to the test to be applied in determining the application. However in *G v Kirklees Metropolitan Borough Council*[15] Booth J stated that the criteria which apply to an application for leave are equally applicable to an application to be joined as a party.

The criteria for an application for leave

Section 10(9) provides:

'Where the person applying for leave to make an application for a section 8 order is not the child concerned, the court shall, in deciding whether or not to grant leave, have particular regard to—

(a) the nature of the proposed application for the section 8 order;

(b) the applicant's connection with the child;

(c) any risk there might be of that proposed application disrupting the child's life to such an extent that he would be harmed by it; and

(d) where the child is being looked after by a local authority—

(i) the authority's plans for the child's future; and

(ii) the wishes and feelings of the child's parents.'

In *Re A (Minors) (Residence Order)*[16] the trial judge held that a court must give paramount consideration to the welfare of the child on an application for leave. The Court of Appeal held that in this regard the judge had been plainly wrong. It ruled that the court must be guided by the specific criteria contained in section 10(9) when deciding whether to grant leave and held that the paramountcy principle did not apply. It held that in granting, or refusing, leave a court is not determining a question with respect to the upbringing of the child concerned, and therefore section 1(1) was not applicable.[17] The court reinforced its argument by pointing out that some of the criteria in section 10(9) would be otiose if the whole matter were subject to the overriding provisions of section 1(1).

---

14 Family Proceedings Court (Children Act 1989) Rules 1991, r 7; Family Proceedings Rules 1991, r 4.7.

15 [1993] 1 FLR 805; see too *North Yorkshire County Council v G* [1993] 2 FLR 732.

16 [1992] 3 All ER 872.

17 The court cited *F v S (Adoption: Ward)* [1973] 1 All ER 722 in support of this ruling.

Whether leave is granted to a non-entitled person is usually of crucial importance to that person. Often an applicant for leave has already been excluded from the child's life by the persons who have parental responsibility, or plans for the child's future involve his or her exclusion from having any say in the child's upbringing. Unless the applicant for leave can get through the door of the court to obtain a hearing there is no other way in which the merits of decisions of this nature can be challenged and subjected to judicial scrutiny.

The nature of the proposed application, and the applicant's connection with the child

While the nature of the proposed application, and the applicant's connection with the child, are distinct criteria they are usually closely interrelated. They indicate that any person who can demonstrate a genuine relationship with, and a legitimate concern about, some matter relating to the child's upbringing will normally be granted leave. For example, in *G v F*[18] the applicant who had lived in a lesbian relationship with the child's mother had behaved towards the child[19] as a joint parent. After the couple separated the applicant continued to play a substantial part in the little boy's upbringing until he was three, when staying contact with the applicant ceased. Because the applicant was not a parent she required the court's leave to make applications for a shared residence order and contact. When granting the leave requested, Bracewell J emphasised that there was no presumption of any kind that if the applications for leave were granted that thereafter the substantive orders sought would be made. The question of the merits of the applications would arise at a later stage. However, the applicant's close connection with the child made this a clear case where leave should be granted.[20]

The fact that the applicant has close family ties with a child is not determinative however, and it may not outweigh different considerations in the other paragraphs. Thus in *Re A (A Minor) (Residence Order: Leave to Apply)*[1] a request was made by an aunt for leave to apply for a residence order in the course of care proceedings which were already under way. The trial court took the view that sufficient persons were already involved in the case, and that to join another would not be in the interests of the child because it would lead to delays and be disruptive. This approach was confirmed on appeal.

When a child has been adopted then, as a matter of law, his natural parents are no longer his parents.[2] Consequently if a natural parent wishes

---

18 [1998] 2 FLR 799.
19 Who had been conceived by artificial insemination.
20 See too *Re A (Section 8 Order: Grandparent Application)* [1995] 2 FLR 153.
1 [1993] 1 FLR 425.
2 Adoption Act 1976, s 39(2).

to apply for a section 8 order he or she must first obtain the court's leave.[3] It is easy to understand why it could be manifestly undesirable if an application for, say, contact could be made by a natural parent of an adopted child without the prior screening of leave. This could cause emotional turmoil and feelings of insecurity both for the child and for the adoptive parents. Difficulty then arises as to who should be notified about the leave application, because these feelings could be generated merely by the knowledge that a leave application was being made.

In *Re C (A Minor) (Adopted Child: Contact)*[4] the court was of the opinion that the vast majority of leave applications by natural parents would fail. It was concerned to shield the adoptive parents from unnecessary anxiety, and it took the view that an application for leave could safely be refused without the adoptive parents' involvement. It therefore ruled that the Official Solicitor should be brought in as respondent in a case of this kind, his function being to represent the child's interests. In addition the local authority, which had been a party to the adoption proceedings, should be invited to take part where they had a relevant contribution to make. Only if, having heard from the applicant, and from the Official Solicitor and/or the local authority, the court was satisfied that the natural parent had made out a prima facie case for leave should notice be given to the adoptive parents. In this way the court would ensure that no application for leave was granted without the adoptive parents having first been given an opportunity to oppose it. In *Re C (A Minor) (Adopted Child: Contact)* itself, the court refused the natural parent leave to apply for either a specific issue order, which would result in her learning the identity of the adoptive parents, or a contact order. It held that adoption orders are intended to be permanent and final, and that a fundamental question such as contact should not be subsequently reopened unless there is some fundamental change in circumstances.[5]

The use of leave as a sifting process to prevent undesirable applications coming before a court applies not only when an individual is the applicant, but also when an application for leave is made by a local authority. Local authorities are limited by section 9 in respect of the applications they may make,[6] however they may apply for leave to apply for specific issue

---

3   *Re C (A Minor) (Adopted Child: Contact)* [1993] 2 FLR 431; *M v C and Calderdale Metropolitan Borough Council* [1993] 1 FLR 505.

4   Above.

5   See *Re T (Minors) (Contact after adoption)* [1995] 2 FLR 792 where such a change did occur. Adoptive parents informally agreed at the time of the adoption hearing to supply the applicant, a half-sibling, with a yearly report on the children. She therefore withdrew her application for leave to apply for contact. The adopters later failed to provide a report, but gave no explanation for that failure. The Court of Appeal held that in such a situation, where the contact envisaged is of such a nature as to be most unlikely to be disruptive of the children's lives, it is not appropriate for the court to accept that position without more. See also *Re S (Contact: Application by Sibling)* [1998] 2 FLR 897 where a child of nine (acting by her best friend and adoptive mother) was refused leave to apply for a contact order to her adopted half-brother.

6   See below.

and prohibited steps orders. There is a risk in allowing local authorities to do this, namely that an authority might apply for leave to apply for one of these orders in inappropriate circumstances, and refrain from exercising their statutory powers and duties to apply for appropriate orders under Part IV of the Act. This risk materialised in *Nottinghamshire County Council v P*.[7] In that case the Court of Appeal ruled that the local authority's application for a prohibited steps order with the aim of excluding an allegedly abusive parent from the home, rather than a care order, had been inappropriate and misconceived. The court took the view that it was likely that the local authority's leave application would have been refused if the matter had been referred to the county court. It therefore gave a direction that, in future such proceedings should be transferred to the county court and should be dealt with inter partes.

Does the applicant have an arguable case?

Where an application for leave is frivolous or vexatious or otherwise an abuse of the process of the court it will, of course, fail. However, most applications have some merit, and different expressions were originally used to describe the extent to which the court must be satisfied that the application is likely to succeed before granting leave. Clearly, if the prospects of success are remote the application is unsustainable, but this does not mean that the applicant must show that it is more probable than not that the application will succeed before leave is granted. It now appears clear that the test to be applied is 'does the applicant have an arguable case'?

The nature of the proposed application and the applicant's connection with the child are usually relevant to whether the applicant has an arguable case. In *G v Kirklees Metropolitan Borough Council*[8] an aunt had acted for a short period as an approved foster parent for her nephew, but then had ceased to have contact with him. Subsequently the local authority had instituted care proceedings, and the aunt was seeking to be joined as a party to these proceedings with a view to obtaining a residence order. The court's findings that the child's mother was strongly opposed to any family placement, coupled with opposition from the local authority to the aunt having further involvement with her nephew, were fatal to her application. However, the weight to be attached to the ruling in *G v Kirklees Metropolitan Borough Council* has been put in doubt because Booth J stated that the applicant had to establish 'a case that was reasonably likely to succeed' before the court would grant her leave.

Subsequently, in *Re M (Care: Contact: Grandmother's Application for Leave)*,[9] the Court of Appeal held that Booth J had imposed too high a

---

7   [1993] 2 FLR 134.
8   [1993] 1 FLR 805. See too *F v S (Adoption: Ward)* [1973] 1 All ER 722; *Re G (Adoption: Freeing Order)* [1996] 2 FLR 398.
9   [1995] 2 FLR 86, commented on further in ch 3.

test. Ward LJ was anxious to ensure that the standard to be satisfied is not too stringent. He said that the applicant must satisfy the court that there is a serious issue to be tried and must present a good arguable case. He emphasised the importance of not fettering the court's discretion and explained that a 'good arguable case' means a case that is better than merely arguable yet not necessarily one which has a better than even chance of success.[10] The door of the court appears to have been opened even wider by Butler-Sloss LJ's statement (obiter) in *Re G (Child Case: Parental Involvement)*[11] that the test for an application for leave was whether there was 'an arguable case' and not whether there was a reasonable likelihood that the substantive application would succeed.[12]

Any risk of harm or disruption

It has been explained already that one reason why the door of the court is not open to all is because this could have the potential to cause disturbance to the child's life. When determining whether to grant leave, the court is required to have particular regard to 'any risk there might be of the proposed application disrupting the child's life to such an extent that he would be harmed by it'. 'Harm' for these purposes means harm as defined by section 31(9).[13] It will sometimes be the case that a court cannot properly determine whether disruption and harm will be caused unless it considers the child's wishes and feelings, and some or all of the other factors specified in the checklist in section 1(3). The question then arises as to what extent a court, at the leave stage, may hear evidence which relates to the merits of the substantive application.

In *Re A (A Minor) (Residence Order: Leave to Apply)*[14] it was recognised that a court may inevitably be drawn into considering matters of substance when considering the disruption issue in the leave criteria. In *Re A (A Minor) (Residence Order: Leave to Apply)* the aunt of a child aged seven was requesting leave to apply for a residence order. On an appeal against a refusal by magistrates to grant the aunt's request, Hollings J held that it had been correct for a court to consider the child's wishes and feelings when

---

10 In *Re G (Child Case: Parental Involvement)* [1996] 1 FLR 857, the Court of Appeal extended this approach to applications for leave under s 91(14). Such applications arise where a litigant has behaved unreasonably, or is likely to do so in the future and where a court has specifically prohibited that person from making any further applications to the court without the leave of the court; see below.

11 Above, at p 866.

12 See also, *G v F (Contact and Shared Residence)* [1998] 2 FLR 799, where Bracewell J acknowledged that an application for shared residence of a child by the former lesbian partner of the respondent was 'more problematical' but held that there was a serious issue to be tried and that the applicant for leave had a good arguable case.

13 *Re A (Minors) (Residence Order)* [1992] 3 All ER 872. S 31(9) provides: '"harm" means ill-treatment or the impairment of health or development'.

14 [1993] 1 FLR 425.

determining whether the proposed application would be disruptive and harmful to him. He also held that a court is entitled to consider matters which relate to the substantive application when considering whether the application might prove to be disruptive, and that the amount of cross-examination allowed is essentially a matter for the court. Similarly, in *North Yorkshire County Council v G*[15] the court ruled that the tests the court should apply are the criteria in section 10(9) coupled with those in section 1(3). In *Re A (Minors) (Residence Order)*[16] a former foster mother of several children in local authority care was applying for leave to apply for a residence order. The Court of Appeal admitted information from the Official Solicitor relating to the wishes and feelings of the children. It took account of the inevitable delay a successful leave application would cause in making long-term arrangements for the children; and it took account of the disruption and harm which would occur if all the children had to be examined by a psychiatrist and were caught up in proceedings which were bound to be bitter. In the light of these findings the court refused leave.

In *Re S (Contact: Application by Sibling)*,[17] an application was made on behalf of a nine year old adopted child for leave to apply for a contact order to her seven year old adopted half-brother.[18] The half-brother's adoptive mother strongly opposed the application. The child applicant was represented by the Official Solicitor and her application was supported by evidence from two child psychologists. Thus once again information relevant to the substantive order was placed before the court at the leave stage. The court, refusing leave, held that where there was a risk that the proposed application would disrupt the child concerned's life to such an extent that he would be harmed by it, such a risk was 'an important and weighty factor against granting leave'.[19]

The local authority's plans for the child

In a case where a child is being looked after by a local authority a court is required to have particular regard to the authority's plans for the child's future. In *Re A (Minors) (Residence Order)*[20] counsel for the local authority, relying on pre-Children Act 1989 authority,[1] submitted that, save in the most exceptional circumstances, a court should not allow an application for leave to apply for a residence order where a child is in the care of a local authority when this would interfere with the authority's care of the

---

15 [1993] 2 FLR 732.
16 [1992] 3 All ER 872.
17 [1998] 2 FLR 897.
18 The court had to have regard to the matters listed in s 10(9) when considering the girl's leave application because the half-brother was the 'child concerned'.
19 [1998] 2 FLR 897, at p 916, per Charles J. See also, *Re M (Care: Contact: Grandmother's Application)* [1995] 2 FLR 86, at pp 95-96 where Ward LJ states that the risk of harm or disruption is a factor of crucial significance.
20 [1992] 3 All ER 872.
1 *A v Liverpool City Council* [1981] 2 All ER 385.

child. The Court of Appeal rejected this submission, pointing out that while that principle is maintained in relation to most matters concerning a child in care, an application for a residence order is expressly excepted because section 9(1) specifically permits an application for a residence order. However, the court added that this does not mean that the court should give no weight to the authority's plans. On the contrary, section 10(9)(d)(i) requires a court to have particular regard to the authority's plans. The court went on to explain how a court should approach a case where a local authority have plans for the child's future which are inconsistent with the application for leave. It reasoned as follows: a local authority have a duty under section 22(3) to safeguard and promote the welfare of any child in their care:

> 'Accordingly, the court should approach the application for leave on the basis that the authority's plans for the child's future are designed to safeguard and promote the child's welfare and that any departure from those plans might well "disrupt the child's life to such an extent that he would be harmed by it".'[2]

This ruling highlights the dilemma faced by courts when a challenge is made to the way in which a local authority is choosing to exercise its statutory powers, namely when is it proper for a court to substitute its own judgment for the judgment of the authority about what decision will best promote the welfare of the child? An analysis of the ruling in *Re A (Minors) (Residence Order)* reveals that it is clear that the decision whether or not to grant leave is one for a court to make, and the fact that a child is in care does not detract from the court's decision-making function. However, the Court of Appeal ruled that a court must take as its starting point the notion that the local authority are under a statutory duty to promote the child's welfare, and a fortiori the authority's plans are therefore designed to advance the welfare of the child. Thus the court created what appears to amount to a presumption in favour of not disrupting the authority's plans for the child, and put the burden of rebutting that presumption squarely on the applicant. It seems that this will be an extremely difficult burden to discharge, since it should be borne in mind that there are often conflicting views about how the child's interests will best be served, and a court may be no better equipped to identify where the welfare of the child lies than the local authority.

It is not clear how much evidence a court ought to be prepared to accept on a leave application, which is, of course, a preliminary application only. It is, nonetheless, an application of enormous importance to the parties, and it seems likely that where an applicant is in conflict with a local authority he or she will need to take advantage of the rulings in *Re A (A Minor) (Residence Order: Leave to Apply)*[3] and *North Yorkshire County*

Council v G[4] that information relating to the welfare checklist, as well as that relating to section 10(9), can be put before the court. It also seems likely that the applicant will need to seek the indulgence of the court to allow the cross-examination of witnesses.[5]

It is suggested that where there is evidence which might open a local authority to challenge in judicial review, that this could provide a sound base on which to question the judgment of the local authority. In *R v Hereford and Worcester County Council, ex p D*[6] it was held in judicial review proceedings to have been wrong to remove a child without warning from her aunt who was acting as her foster parent. The removal occurred during the course of care proceedings. Initially, the understanding with the aunt had been that the child would be placed on a long-term basis with her, but there was a change of care plan, and the child was taken from her without consultation. In that case the court ruled that any decision about the child's future should be made on the fullest information, and that the local authority had been wrong not to listen to the aunt and to give her views due weight. The Children Act 1989 was not in force when *R v Hereford and Worcester County Council, ex p D* was decided, so the only remedy for the aunt was in judicial review. Now she would be able to apply for leave to apply for a residence order.

The phrase 'being looked after' by a local authority embraces both a child being provided with accommodation by the authority and one in their care under a care order.[7] In relation to an accommodated child the authority do not have parental responsibility, and it could be somewhat anomalous to give significant weight to the local authority's plans for a child's future in circumstances when they do not have the power to implement these plans. It might therefore be maintained that less weight ought to be given to the authority's plans for an accommodated child than when the child is in care.

The wishes and feelings of the child's parents

Curiously, section 10(9) requires the wishes and feelings of the child's parents to be taken into account only when the child is being looked after by the local authority. Yet parents will normally have the greatest interest in whether or not an application is allowed to proceed.[8] In *Re A (Minors) (Residence Order)*[9] a foster mother had applied for a residence order in respect of four children who were in the care of a local authority. No

---

4   [1993] 2 FLR 732.
5   *Re A (A Minor) (Residence Order: Leave to Apply)* [1992] 3 All ER 872. Expert witnesses were called at the leave stage in *Re S (Contact: Application by Sibling)* [1998] 2 FLR 897, and the leave hearing appears to have been lengthy.
6   [1992] 1 FLR 448.
7   S 22(1).
8   As, indeed, will any other person who has parental responsibility for the child.
9   [1992] 3 All ER 872.

notification of her application had been given to the children's mother. The Court of Appeal stated that the children's mother should have been notified of the leave application although there was no notification requirement under the rules, and that by failing to give the mother notice the judge had deprived himself of information which was necessary for the proper exercise of his discretion. It seems that while this somewhat anomalous provision[10] ensures that the views of parents are taken into account when the child is being looked after by a local authority, it is unlikely that it can be used in a negative manner to exclude the wishes and feelings of the parents in other cases.

Ex parte or inter partes applications for leave

A request for leave to apply for a section 8 order can be made ex parte before a single magistrate or judge, or at an inter partes hearing. It seems probable that a request for leave which is made ex parte is more likely to succeed than an application made at an inter partes hearing, bearing in mind that the applicant will not draw to the attention of the court any risk that the application might prove disruptive and harmful to the child. The ex parte nature of the leave process has caused anxiety to judges hearing contentious and difficult cases. In *Re S (Adopted Child: Contact)*[11] Thorpe J stated that where a natural mother of an adopted child is seeking leave to apply for a contact order, the request should always be heard in the Family Division and not be granted on an ex parte application. In *Nottinghamshire County Council v P*[12] the Court of Appeal stated that it was wholly inappropriate for a local authority to apply ex parte before a single justice for leave to issue an application for a prohibited steps order. The court added that, in future, any such application should be transferred to the county court and that it should not be dealt with ex parte. In *Re SC (A Minor) (Leave to Seek Residence Order)*[13] the court held that where the applicant for leave is a child, it was desirable that everyone with parental responsibility should be given notice of the application even though an application for leave can be made ex parte. In *Re M (Prohibited Steps Order: Application for Leave)*[14] Johnson J emphasised the importance of the leave decision. He stated that while there may well be cases of urgency, or other circumstances, which make it right to grant leave on an ex parte application, in the ordinary case the interests of justice require that notice of the application should be given to other parties who are likely to be affected if leave is granted. He added that such persons should be given the opportunity to adduce evidence and to make submissions.

---

10 Particularly bearing in mind that in the case of an accommodated child, it is the parents who have parental responsibility, not the local authority.
11 [1993] 2 FCR 234.
12 [1993] 2 FLR 134.
13 [1994] 1 FLR 96.
14 [1993] 1 FLR 275.

A court at the leave stage, whether the hearing is ex parte or inter partes, may find itself confronted with a difficult choice between either granting, or refusing, an application for leave after allowing only brief evidence, or holding a 'trial within a trial' in which issues relating to the substantive application are put before the court at this preliminary stage. A court may have difficulty in determining whether a person ought to be granted leave on minimal information provided by the applicant. However, obtaining adequate information upon which to base a ruling is liable to be time-consuming, which in itself could be disruptive and harmful to the child. Exercising judicial restraint, and refusing leave because the alternative is to embark on a detailed enquiry, may sometimes be just as proper a way of advancing a child's best interests as allowing the leave application to be conducted at an inter partes hearing.

The child concerned and leave

No one has a greater interest in decisions about a child's future than the child him- or herself.[15] The Children Act 1989 recognises that in some instances children should be given the opportunity to communicate their own views by initiating proceedings on their own behalf. Children do not fall within the categories of persons who are entitled to apply for a section 8 order, but a child is entitled to make a leave application, subject to the proviso in section 10(8) that:

> '... where the person applying for leave to make a section 8 application is the child concerned, the court may only grant leave if it is satisfied that he has sufficient understanding to make the proposed application for the section 8 order.'

The 'child concerned' means the child with respect to whom the court may make a section 8 order.[16] The constraint in section 10(8) is the only statutory restriction imposed where the 'child concerned' is also the applicant; the criteria for leave in section 10(9) do not apply.[17] This may be of advantage to the child in a case where, as in *Re SC (A Minor) (Leave to Seek Residence Order)*[18] she wishes to live with a person who, because of section 10(9), would be unlikely to succeed on her own leave application. In that case it was made clear that while a residence order could not be made in favour of the child herself, the child could nonetheless seek leave to apply for a residence order in favour of someone else. However, where the child seeking leave is not 'the child concerned', the applicant child must satisfy the criteria in section 10(9) in the same way as any other

---

15 See generally J Roche *Children's rights: in the name of the child* (1995) 17 JSWFL 281.
16 *Re S (Contact: Application by Sibling)* [1998] 2 FLR 897.
17 *Re C (Residence: Child's Application for Leave)* [1995] 1 FLR 927, but see below in relation to the welfare of the child and applications for leave by children.
18 [1994] 1 FLR 96.

applicant for leave.[19] Moreover, in *Re S (Contact Application by Sibling)*[20] it was held that the court was not required to have exclusive regard to the criteria in section 10(9) where the case concerned an applicant child. The child's understanding remained a relevant consideration, as did her chances of success, and the fact that she and her brother had been adopted by different adoptive parents.

In relation to a child's understanding, in *Re S (A Minor) (Independent Representation)*[1] the Court of Appeal stated that a balance must be struck between two considerations. First is the principle that the child's views, wishes and feelings should command serious attention, and are not to be discounted simply because he is a child. Second is the fact that a child is liable to be vulnerable and impressionable which is why the law is particularly solicitous in protecting his interests. A child may lack the maturity and experience to weigh the longer term against the short term, or the insight to know how he may react to certain outcomes, or how others will react in certain situations. Different children have differing levels of understanding at the same age, and understanding must be assessed relative to the issues in the proceedings. The court concluded that where any sound judgment on the issues calls for insight and imagination which only maturity and experience can bring, both a court and a solicitor should be slow to conclude that the child's understanding is sufficient to enable him to take an independent part in the proceedings.[2]

Thus the degree of understanding required under section 10(8) appears to be relatively high. Yet if a court is too ready to assume that a child lacks the capacity to institute proceedings on his own behalf this could amount to a denial of the child's right to be treated as an autonomous individual.[3] It is suggested that, in many cases, the only understanding he ought to be required to demonstrate is an understanding that he wants a court to intervene in his life, and for the court to substitute its own view of his best interests for the view of the person(s) who have parental responsibility for him.

Leave and the welfare of the child where the child is the applicant

The limit on children applying for a section 8 order, on its face, is concerned simply with whether the child has sufficient understanding to make an

---

19 *Re S (Contact: Application by Sibling)* [1998] 2 FLR 897.
20 Ibid.
1   [1993] 2 FLR 437.
2   See too *Re H (A Minor)* [1992] Fam Law 368, where, in the context of care proceedings, the court held that if there was any real question as to whether the child's emotional disturbance was so intense that he could not give instructions, it should be the subject of expert opinion.
3   As established in *Gillick v West Norfolk and Wisbech Area Health Authority* [1986] AC 112 (see ch 1). Consider, too, how far denying a child access to the courts may be in breach of Art 6 of the European Convention for the Protection of Human Rights and Fundamental Freedoms.

application, where the applicant child is also the 'child concerned'.[4] However, in *Re SC (A Minor) (Leave to Seek Residence Order)*[5] Booth J pointed out that a court has a discretion whether to grant leave even if it has been established under section 10(8) that the child has sufficient understanding to make the application. But she added that as the initial application for leave did not raise any question about the child's upbringing, the child's welfare was not the court's paramount consideration when exercising its discretion in deciding whether or not to grant leave.[6] In that regard, she said, no distinction could be drawn between an application by a child for leave, and an application made by any other person. On the other hand she held that it was right for the court to have regard to the likelihood of success of the proposed application, and to be satisfied that the child was not embarking on proceedings which were doomed to failure.

By contrast, in *Re C (A Minor) (Leave to Seek Section 8 Orders)*[7] Johnson J extended the application of the welfare principle to the whole question of leave on an application made by a child. A 15-year-old girl was seeking leave to apply for a residence order to live at the home of a friend and her family, and for a specific issue order to go on holiday with them to Bulgaria. Johnson J ruled that as the considerations laid down in section 10(9) did not apply where the applicant was the child concerned, he must be guided in respect of both leave applications by the paramountcy of the child's welfare.[8] In relation to the residence order he took the view that there was no identifiable advantage in making a residence order at the present time. He therefore adjourned the child's application for leave. In relation to the application for leave to apply for a specific issue order, he recognised that the question whether the child should be allowed to go on holiday to Bulgaria had important significance both for her and for her parents. However, he took the view that this was not the kind of issue which Parliament had envisaged as being litigated in a court when it allowed children to make applications for leave. He therefore refused the child's leave application.[9]

In *Re C (Residence: Child's Application for Leave)*,[10] in a third examination by the High Court of the relevance of the child's welfare to an

---

4 Discussed above, and see *Re S (Contact: Application by Sibling)* [1998] 2 FLR 897. Where s 10(9) applies, when considering the likelihood of success, the court approaches this question on the basis that at the substantive hearing the child concerned's interests will be the court's paramount consideration.

5 [1994] 1 FLR 96.

6 Following *Re A (Minors) (Residence Order)* [1992] 3 All ER 872.

7 [1994] 1 FLR 26.

8 *Re A (Minors) (Residence Order)* [1992] 3 All ER 872, in which the Court of Appeal ruled that the welfare principle does not apply to leave applications made under s 10(1), (2), does not appear to have been brought to the court's attention.

9 See A Bainham *'See you in court, Mum': children as litigants* (1996) 6 JCL 127 for a discussion of these cases.

10 [1995] 1 FLR 927.

application by a child for leave, a 14-year-old girl was seeking the leave of the court to apply for an order which, if granted, would enable her to live with her mother. Granting the application, Stuart White J declined to follow Johnson J's approach. He held that while the best interests of the child were 'very much at the centre of the court's thinking' they were not paramount. However, he agreed with Johnson J that a leave application by a child should be approached 'cautiously', and he also agreed that the jurisdiction should be exercised only in matters of importance.[11]

It is suggested that treating a child differently from an adult in the area of rights, particularly when these have apparently been given to the child by Parliament, requires stronger justification than that advanced in *Re C (A Minor) (Leave to Seek Section 8 Orders)*,[12] and that the approach taken by Booth J in *Re SC (A Minor) (Leave to Seek Residence Order)*[13] and Stuart White J in *Re C (Residence: Child's Application for Leave)*[14] is preferable. It seems correct that, normally, it should only be at the trial of the substantive issue that a court should be influenced by whether a child's wishes coincide with his or her best interests, and not at the stage of leave. Any other approach brings with it the danger that the children will be denied the right to litigate about their upbringing, which is a right enjoyed by adults.

It is, however, acknowledged that there are strong arguments in favour of adopting a more cautious approach to permitting children to litigate. There is undoubtedly a risk that a child could be manipulated by a parent, and be drawn into proceedings which are essentially between the adults. The Court of Appeal was clearly determined to prevent the personal involvement of children becoming a common practice when it roundly condemned the swearing of an affidavit by a 12-year-old girl in support of her father's application for residence.[15] Moreover, where a child is made a party to proceedings which involve her parents, or is given leave to make her own application in proceedings which will involve her parents, she is likely to be present when evidence is given by her parents, and to hear them being cross-examined, 'hearing perhaps of many matters which, at the tender age of the child, it would be better for her not to hear'.[16] The child, too, could face cross-examination by a parent about the contents of her own statement.

Where the child is the applicant for leave this may also create a difficult practical problem namely, where is the child to live in the period between

---

11 Though, as he said at p 932, in relation to the matter before him, 'few things can be more important to a child, even a child in her teenage years, than with which parent she should make her home'.

12 [1994] 1 FLR 26.

13 [1994] 1 FLR 96.

14 [1995] 1 FLR 927.

15 *Re M (Family Proceedings: Affidavits)* [1995] 2 FLR 100. See the critique of this ruling in J Fortin *Children's Rights and the Developing Law* (Butterworths, 1998) at pp 171-172.

16 *Re C (Residence: Child's Application for Leave)* [1995] 1 FLR 927 at p 931.

the application for leave and the hearing? Apart from the normal notice requirements (which can in certain circumstances be abridged), a case of this nature is likely to be difficult and may take several days to prepare. Also, such cases must be heard by a High Court judge which may add to the delay. In the meanwhile the child may be living with a parent or other person, such as a step-parent, in circumstances of considerable animosity. An interim order, temporarily to settle the arrangements as to the person with whom the child is to live, would seem essential. An interim order may be made at any stage during the course of the proceedings in question,[17] but it is doubtful whether one can be made at the leave to apply stage. Furthermore, the difficulty presented in taking this step is that it interferes in a parent's parental responsibility on the basis of incomplete information, and makes an order which could be influential against the parent when the case comes for trial. Therefore, where the child should live pending the hearing for leave raises some awkward questions of principle as well as the practical question of what should be done.

Who should represent the child?

Shortly after the Children Act 1989 came into force a number of cases occurred in which the child was the applicant for leave either to be joined as a party to existing family proceedings, or to make a free-standing application. Some senior judges expressed the view that such applications raised issues which were more appropriate for determination in the High Court and subsequently a *Practice Direction* was issued requiring such cases to be transferred there.[18] This Direction has significant procedural implications. Under the High Court and County Court Rules, a child must seek leave to institute or participate in existing proceedings through a next friend or guardian ad litem,[19] who is normally the Official Solicitor.[20] A child, for the purposes of the Rules, is treated as a person under a disability. However, the Rules also provide that when the child has sufficient understanding, or is represented by a lawyer, he may be a party to the proceedings without this assistance;[1] indeed, he cannot be represented by both.

It is important to keep distinct the question of whether leave to take part in the proceedings should be granted to a child from who, if anyone, should represent the child. There are significant differences between not

---

17 S 11(3).
18 *Practice Direction (Family Proceedings Orders: Applications by Children)* [1993] 1 All ER 820.
19 Family Proceedings Rules 1991, r 9.2.
20 R 9.2(3)(7); this replicates the long-standing practice of the wardship jurisdiction which allows the ward's best interests to be examined independently of the competing claims or arguments of the main parties.
1 R 9.2A.

allowing a child to take part in existing family proceedings; not allowing him to do so unless represented; not allowing him to conduct the remaining stages of existing proceedings without a guardian ad litem; and not allowing him to commence proceedings at all. Where a child is applying for leave to make a free-standing application for a section 8 order, the matter relating to his upbringing which he wishes to have investigated will never come under the scrutiny of a court if leave is refused.[2] In Children Act 1989 proceedings initiated by adults, issues about the child are already before the court and, where these are contested, the court is bound to have regard to the child's wishes and feelings before formulating its judgment.[3] Usually it will have a report from a court welfare officer which gives an account of the child's views.[4] Where the court takes the view that the child's interests demand assessment from another professional with particular expertise it may order a report from that person.[5] In cases brought in the High Court, the Official Solicitor can be asked to represent the child. This means that the voice of the child will be heard in some way. However, it may not always be expressed in the manner which the child would prefer. The difficulty for a child where her voice is mediated through a court welfare officer is that the officer's duty to the court is twofold: it is to give an account of the child's wishes and feelings and to interpret them.[6] This may be highly objectionable to an articulate teenager.[7]

Where a child applies for leave to participate in proceedings without a next friend or guardian ad litem, it is the judge, not the solicitor, who is required to assess the individual child's understanding in the context of the proceedings in which he has applied to take part.[8] However, in *Re CT (A Minor) (Wardship: Representation)*[9] Waite LJ said that he would hope, and expect, that instances where a challenge is directed to a solicitor's

---

2   As in *Re C (A Minor) (Leave to Seek Section 8 Orders)* [1994] 1 FLR 26.
3   S 1(3)(a), and s 1(4).
4   A court is entitled to request reports under s 7(1) and it is the duty of the local authority or a probation officer to comply with this request (s 7(5)).
5   S 7(1), and see *Re W (Welfare Reports)* [1995] 2 FLR 142.
6   In *Re M (Family Proceedings: Affidavits)* [1995] 2 FLR 100, the Court of Appeal stated that it was not the practice in family proceedings for children to give evidence, and it strongly deprecated an attempt to introduce into the proceedings an affidavit sworn by a 12-year-old child. The girl said that she wished to live with her father. However, the court welfare officer expressed the view that it would be better for the girl to remain with her mother in the former matrimonial home. The view of the court welfare officer was accepted by the court.
7   In *Re C (Residence: Child's Application for Leave)* [1995] 1 FLR 927 Stuart White J acknowledged that a 14-year-old girl had very decided views on her own wishes about with which parent she wanted to live, and why she did so wish, and that she was not content to have these put forward by the court welfare officer, albeit in the utmost good faith.
8   See *Re S (A Minor) (Independent Representation)* [1993] 2 FLR 437; *Re CT (A Minor) (Wardship: Representation)* [1993] 2 FLR 278.
9   Above. For comment see J Murphy *Re CT: litigious mature minors and wardship in the 1990s* (1993) 5 JCL 186.

view of his minor client's ability to instruct him would be rare, and that cases where the court felt bound to question such ability of its own motion would be rarer still.[10] In *Re S (A Minor) (Independent Representation)*[11] the Court of Appeal held that a court would be unlikely to grant leave to a child to take part in proceedings without a next friend or guardian ad litem unless the child had already instructed a solicitor. When, as in *Re S (A Minor)(Independent Representation),* a next friend or guardian ad litem had been appointed, and the child wished to continue the proceedings without that person's participation, this too required the court's leave, and whether leave was granted was also dependent on the child's capacity to understand. Consequently, at the leave stage a court has two issues to resolve: does the child have sufficient understanding to make the proposed application?; and what form of representation, if any, should the child have?

There may be a vital difference for the child in being represented by a guardian ad litem or next friend, and having a solicitor to conduct his case. The role of a guardian ad litem is to listen to the child, understand his point of view and explain it to the court, but the guardian's overriding duty is to safeguard and represent the child's best interests. Where the guardian ad litem forms the opinion that the child's welfare will not be served by taking steps which accord with the child's wishes and feelings, the guardian has a duty to protect the child against himself.[12] However, the role of the solicitor is to take the child's instructions and to pursue the case simply on the basis of those instructions.[13]

A disturbing example of a court refusing to allow children to be separately legally represented in existing legal proceedings, and instead requiring them to be represented by a guardian ad litem, arose in *Re K, W and H (Minors) (Medical Treatment).*[14] Three 15-year-old girls were being looked after in a specialist unit for disturbed adolescents. A question arose over whether they were consenting to emergency medication and whether they might not wish to consent to such treatment in the future. The hospital therefore applied for orders under section 8 to confirm that they could treat the girls in reliance on the consent of a person with parental responsibility. Thorpe J ruled that he was confident that none of the girls was '*Gillick* competent'[15] for the purposes of giving consent to medical treatment. But he also said that, even if they were, the application

---

10 But cf *Re K, W and H (Minors) (Medical Treatment)* [1993] 1 FLR 854.

11 [1993] 2 FLR 437.

12 See *Re CT (A Minor) (Wardship: Representation)* [1993] 2 FLR 278.

13 See also, *Re P (Representation)* [1996] 1 FLR 486, which concerned a child's right to separate representation in care proceedings where he disagreed with the guardian ad litem's proposals. For the role of the guardian ad litem in care proceedings, see ch 3. See generally C Sawyer *The competence of children to participate in family proceedings* (1995) 7 CFLQ 180. The author conducted research into how solicitors undertake an assessment of competence of children.

14 [1993] 1 FLR 854. For comment see P Bates *Children in secure psychiatric units: Re K, W and H – 'out of sight, out of mind'?* (1994) 6 JCL 131.

was misconceived because the doctors had the necessary consents from the persons with parental responsibility. When the case had first come before the court each of the girls had applied to be independently represented by her own lawyers. Although the lawyers were of the opinion that all the girls had sufficient understanding to instruct their own legal representatives, Thorpe J preferred the view of the childrens' previous guardians ad litem, who had expressed the opinion that the children did not have sufficient understanding to participate in the proceedings without a next friend or guardian ad litem. The girls' applications for independent representation were therefore refused, and they were represented by the Official Solicitor for the remainder of the proceedings.

It is suggested that by preventing the girls from being independently represented in a case where the question of compulsory medication of an unwilling and possibly '*Gillick* competent' child was in issue, and where the consent being relied upon was that of the parent rather than the court, the court was depriving the children of the separate representation of their voice in exactly the type of case where this safeguard is needed.

Restricting applications for orders under section 91(14)

It has been seen that the structure of section 10 permits parents and other persons to apply to a court for a section 8 order as a matter of right. This entitlement accords with Article 6 of the European Convention for the Protection of Human Rights, which states that 'In the determination of his civil rights and obligations ... everyone is entitled to a fair and public hearing within a reasonable time by an independent and impartial tribunal established by law'; and Article 8 which states that 'Everyone has the right to respect for his private and family life ...'. However, a bar may be placed on future applications under the Act being made unless the leave of the court is first obtained. Section 91(14) provides:

'On disposing of any application for an order under this Act, the court may (whether or not it makes any other order in response to the application) order that no application for an order under this Act of any specified kind may be made with respect to the child concerned by any person named in the order without leave of the court.'

This bar was eloquently described by Waite LJ in *B v B (Residence Order: Restricting Applications)*:[16]

'Tucked away ... as one of the 17 subsections of a section whose general purpose is largely administrative, the power under s 91(14)

---

15 For the meaning of this phrase, see ch 1.
16 [1997] 1 FLR 139, at p 146.

... represents a substantial interference with the fundamental principle of public policy enshrined in our unwritten constitution that all citizens enjoy a right of unrestricted access to the Queen's courts.'

When may section 91(14) orders be made?

It is clear that courts should exercise considerable caution before making an order under section 91(14). It is a power which should be exercised sparingly and with extreme care, it should not be made as a run-of-the-mill type of order,[17] and should not be used merely because there is bitterness between the parties which is inevitably detrimental to the child.[18] The applicant must have 'crossed the line from making applications which it is his right to make, to making applications which are in one sense oppressive, or might be said to be vexatious'.[19] The purpose of the bar is to prevent issues relating to a child's upbringing being the subject of constant disruptive, unnecessary and often highly contentious, litigation.[20] An order made under section 91(14) should do nothing to prevent a meritorious application.[1] Although it may be used sparingly this should only be where the applicant has acted unreasonably or would be likely to do so in the future.[2] What the order should do is serve to remind the applicant not to make applications which have no realistic chance of success and which could have harmful effects on the child.[3]

Re R (Residence: Contact: Restricting Applications)[4] graphically illustrates the frequency with which some parents may seek to bring proceedings under

---

17 *F v Kent County Council* [1993] 1 FLR 432, at p 438 per Sir Stephen Brown P.

18 See *Re H (Child Orders: Restricting Applications)* [1991] FCR 896, at p 899; *B v B (Residence Order: Restricting Applications)* [1997] 1 FLR 139.

19 *B v B (Residence Order: Restricting Applications)* [1997] 1 FLR 139, at p 145 per Butler-Sloss LJ.

20 See, for example, *Re N (Section 91(14) Order)* [1996] 1 FLR 356.

1 Although it is clearly desirable that applications for leave pursuant to an order under s 91(14) should be resolved at an inter partes hearing, see *Re N (Section 91(14) Order)* [1996] 1 FLR 356, at pp 359-360.

2 *Re G (Child Case: Parental Involvement)* [1996] 1 FLR 857. This case illustrates the possibility of future decision-making being based on false findings of facts as a direct result of a parent being denied access to the courts. In earlier proceedings the father had alleged that the mother took drugs and was guilty of undue chastisement of the children. The judge's view of these allegations was that they were a farrago of lies and he formed a very unfavourable opinion of the father. In later proceedings it transpired that the mother was guilty of both types of behaviour.

3 In *Re R (Residence Order: Contact: Restricting Applications)* [1998] 1 FLR 749, at p 758 the proposition was accepted by the Court of Appeal that a restraint under s 91(14) is more likely to be apt where there is no de facto relationship between a father and a child. However, Wilson J went on to observe that 'if proper application of the principles to be collected from the jurisprudence leads to a certain conclusion, factual differences will not invalidate it'.

4 [1998] 1 FLR 749.

section 8 of the Children Act 1989. Between 1993 and 1996 a father had made no less than eighteen applications for orders, fifteen to review contact arrangements with his child and three for residence. When hearing the father's latest application, the judge refused to make a residence order, and made an order under section 91(14) restricting his right to bring further applications before the court. Dismissing the father's appeal against this restriction, the Court of Appeal held that when exercising its discretion to make an order under section 91(14), the best interests of the child must be weighed against the applicant's fundamental freedom of access to the courts without going through an initial screening process. The court found that this particular father was committed to his child and had steadily built up a relationship with him. It acknowledged that a section 91(14) order was a substantial interference with the applicant's fundamental right to raise issues affecting his child's welfare before a court, but it ruled that such a right had to be exercised consistently with the welfare of the child. In this regard, a court had to take account of the emotional effect on the residential parent of frequent applications to change a child's residence. As Wilson J said, 'nothing can raise the temperature of a family dispute more than an ill-considered, unfounded application for a residence order ... Even worse can be the effect of a residence application when the applicant expresses himself or herself in intemperate and bilious terms'.[5]

Duration of a section 91(14) order

It is sometimes the practice of courts when ordering that no further application should be made without the court's leave to make the order last for a specific period of time. While not objecting to this practice in principle, the Court of Appeal has pointed out that it has the potential to create difficulties.[6] For example, apart from the difficulty in forecasting what would be the appropriate length of time before the applicant's rights revived, an order of fixed duration almost invites a fresh application at the expiry of the specified term. The Court of Appeal recommended that, generally speaking, a section 91(14) order should simply state that leave must be sought before a further application can be issued, as such an approach gives the courts the greatest flexibility.

There appears to be only one reported case where a term preventing the applicant seeking the leave of the court for a specific period was included in a court order. In *Re T (A Minor) (Parental Responsibility: Contact)*[7] an order was made by a High Court judge that there should be no application by a father of a child for three years. The order did not state that there should be no such application within three years without

---

5   Ibid, at p 759.
6   *Re R (Residence: Contact: Restricting Applications)* [1998] 1 FLR 749.
7   [1993] 2 FLR 450.

the leave of the court. The Court of Appeal discussed this ruling in *Re R (Residence: Contact: Restricting Applications)*[8] and concluded that the order could not have been made under section 91(14), as the section envisages that an application for leave to apply may be made at any time in the future. Rather, said the Court of Appeal, this case was an example of the High Court exercising its inherent jurisdiction on exceedingly unusual facts.

When a court is determining whether to grant an application for leave to apply for the section 91(14) restriction to be lifted, or for leave to proceed notwithstanding the bar, what factors should influence the court's discretion? In *Re A (Application for Leave)*[9] the Court of Appeal held that an application under section 91(14) is a distinct application which should not be subjected either to the criteria in section 10(9) or to the elaboration of those criteria which have been introduced by subsequent decisions of the courts. Thorpe LJ said that he favoured 'the simplest of tests. Does this application demonstrate that there is any need for renewed judicial investigation? If yes, then leave should be granted'.[10] He further expressed the opinion that, in appropriate cases, the application for leave to proceed could be determined at a directions appointment. In this way, all the court commits itself to is to survey the material presented in the form of statements supporting the application for leave, and probably a report from a court welfare officer.

Local authority foster parents and section 8 orders

Where a local authority foster parent has had the care of a child for a considerable period of time she may wish to apply for a residence order so that the child will continue to have his home with her. There are special, and somewhat complicated provisions which apply to local authority foster parents. The first question to be resolved is: 'is the foster parent entitled to apply for a residence order?' The answer to this question is discovered in section 10(5). If she falls within the scope of the provisions in that subsection, then she is entitled to apply for a residence order.[11] Thus where the child has lived with the foster parent for a period of at least three years, not ending more than three months before the date of the application, she is entitled to apply for an order under section 10(5)(b).[12] Where she has looked after the child for less than three years, and where the child is being looked after by the local authority under a care order, she

---

8 [1998] 1 FLR 749, at p 760.
9 [1998] 1 FLR 1.
10 Ibid, at p 4.
11 She is also entitled to apply for a contact order unless the child is in the care of the local authority. In practice this will almost certainly be the situation. Contact applications in relation to children in care are governed by s 34. A foster parent would need the leave of the court to apply for a contact order under that section.
12 As qualified by s 10(10).

would need the consent of the local authority under section 10(5)(c)(ii) in order to be entitled to make an application for a residence order.[13] But where the child is an accommodated child, then before the foster parent can be entitled to apply, she would either have to obtain the consent of each person with a residence order under section 10(5)(c)(i); or in any other case, the consent of each of those (if any) who have parental responsibility for the child under section 10(5)(c)(iii).

Where an accommodated child has lived with the foster parents for some considerable period (but less than the three years which would entitle them to apply), and where the relationship between the foster parents and the natural parent(s) is good, the provisions relating to the consent of persons with parental responsibility could be important. Local authorities sometimes operate fostering policies which do not necessarily command the full support of the parents of the children whom they are looking after: treating children of mixed race parentage as being black being one such policy which does not necessarily enjoy widespread acceptance. On the one hand a local authority might wish to alter the child's placement in pursuance of such a fostering policy.[14] On the other hand, the natural parent(s) might prefer the child to stay with the foster parents to whom he has become attached. In a case of this kind the parents might be willing to consent to the foster parents making an application for a residence order despite objections from the local authority.[15]

While this is likely to be a rare occurrence, it reinforces an important principle: local authorities only have power to determine the course of the lives of other people's children either because this power has been conferred on them by Parliament, or by a court, or because those with parental responsibility agree. In the case of accommodated children, foster parents are in a somewhat curious position. Their relationship with a local authority is controlled by regulations and they must abide by the authority's instructions.[16] However, where foster parents are in disagreement with a local authority over residence and contact, the ultimate decision-making power about conferring entitlement on the foster parents

---

13 S 10(5)(c)(ii) requires the consent of the local authority only where the child is in the care of the local authority; this provision should be contrasted with the consent provision in s 9(3)(a), which also applies where the child is accommodated, and which is discussed below.

14 It is not fanciful to state that local authorities have sometimes vigorously pursued such policies despite there having been apparently compelling reasons to allow the child to remain where he was: see, for example, *Re A (A Minor) (Cultural Background)* [1987] 2 FLR 429; *Re N (A Minor) (Adoption)* [1990] 1 FLR 58; *Re P (A Minor) (Adoption)* [1990] 1 FLR 96; *Re JK (Adoption: Transracial Placement)* [1991] 2 FLR 340. These cases are discussed in ch 4.

15 In such a situation there would need to be a strong degree of trust between the parents and foster parents. The latter would acquire parental responsibility if a residence order was made, and the parents would be likely to experience difficulty in persuading a court to substitute an order restoring the child's residence to them at a later date, unless the foster parents were in agreement.

16 Foster Placement (Children) Regulations 1991 (SI 1991/910).

to apply for a residence, or contact order, rests with the person(s) who have parental responsibility, which in the case of accommodated children is not the local authority.

Foster parents and leave to apply for a section 8 order

A foster parent who is not entitled to apply for an order must, like any other non-entitled applicant, apply to the court for leave to apply for the order. However, special rules apply to foster parents. Section 9(3) provides that:

'A person who is, or was at any time within the last six months, a local authority foster parent of a child may not apply for leave to apply for a section 8 order with respect to the child unless—
(a) he has the consent of the authority;
(b) he is a relative of the child; or
(c) the child has lived with him for at least three years preceding the application.'

Why are local authority foster parents who require the court's leave singled out for special treatment? One of the many aims of the Children Act 1989 is to instil confidence in parents in state provision of social services for children in need and in care. Parents are encouraged to work in partnership with local authorities for the benefit of their children. Foster parents may often have more material possessions than a natural parent, and the opportunities afforded in the foster home to develop and enhance a child's physical, emotional and educational progress may be superior to those that a natural parent is able to provide. These are all matters which are relevant to the application of the welfare principle which governs the determination of applications for section 8 orders.[17] If a foster parent could apply like any other person for leave to apply for a residence order a natural parent might be fearful of making temporary arrangements for his or her child with a local authority. This could rebound to the general disadvantage of children in need and in care, because parents might be tempted to make private arrangements for their children which are less appropriate to their child's needs, or they might become hostile to a foster placement simply because it appeared to be particularly well-suited to their child's circumstances.

Unless a foster parent is a relative, or has looked after the child for at least three years, he or she must obtain the consent of the local authority to apply to the court for leave to apply for a section 8 order. Unless that consent is forthcoming, the foster parent is precluded from seeking a section 8 order. The requirement of local authority consent is included to reassure parents that it is safe to allow their children to go into foster

17 See ch 4.

care. It operates, too, as a reminder to foster parents that normally their role is to work alongside parents, so far as is reasonable and possible, in all aspects of the child's upbringing. If foster parents could seek a court's leave to apply for an order that the child should live with them, without further restraint, some might be tempted to exclude the natural parents, rather than to work co-operatively with them. The consent provision is also there to reassure local authorities that they can develop their fostering services without losing control over the children.[18]

In *Re P (A Minor) (Leave to Apply: Foster Parents)*[19] the question arose whether the local authority had the entitlement to give consent under section 9(3)(a) where the child was an accommodated child, and where the local authority therefore did not have parental responsibility for the child. It was argued that if a local authority were able to give leave under section 9(3), this would, in effect, allow the authority to circumvent the clear prohibition in section 9(2) that no application may be made by a local authority for a residence order or a contact order.[20] Hale J dismissed this argument. She said that it was absolutely plain from the wording that the consent of the local authority accommodating the child was the consent which was needed. While this ruling was unremarkable on the point of law which it settled, the argument raised by counsel that this was a back-door way of allowing a local authority to apply for a residence order was uncomfortably close to the mark. Of course, it was not the local authority who were applying for the residence order, it was the foster parents. Furthermore, it would be the court which would decide whether leave should be given for the foster parents to make the substantive application; and it would be for the court to decide whether to make a residence order in their favour. However, it does expose an uncomfortable tension between the various policies which underpin different provisions in the Act. The ruling makes it clear that a local authority, where they take the view that the welfare of the child requires that he should remain in the care of his foster parents, but where they also take the view that they do not have sufficient grounds to satisfy the test for making a care order,[1] can encourage the foster parents to make their own application for a residence order, and give them the leave to do so.[2] Were this to happen with any frequency, it could undermine confidence in the accommodation

---

18 Where a child has been orphaned, or when a parent with a residence order has died, many of these arguments do not apply; in these circumstances there is nothing in s 5 of the Children Act 1989 to prevent a foster parent from applying for a guardianship order; see below.

19 [1994] 2 FCR 1093.

20 See below.

1 S 31(2), and see ch 3.

2 Which indeed was close to what happened in *Re P (A Minor) (Leave to Apply: Foster Parents)*. The local authority were also acting as an adoption agency in respect of the child. The parents, who were Orthodox Jews, objected to the foster parents as adoptive parents because they were Roman Catholics. The court granted the foster parents leave to apply for a residence order.

provisions in the Act which section 9(2) and (3), amongst other provisions in the Act, are designed to promote.[3]

A relative[4] who acts as local authority foster parent may apply to a court for leave to apply for a section 8 order without first obtaining the local authority's consent. This provision could come to the assistance of a relative in circumstances similar to those that occurred in *R v Hereford and Worcester County Council, ex p D*.[5] In that case a local authority had initially decided to place a child (about whom care proceedings had been commenced and who was in their care under an interim care order) with her aunt as foster parent. However, the child's guardian ad litem formed the opinion that the aunt would not be able to protect the child from her mother. This led the local authority to change their mind about the suitability of the placement, and to the removal of the child from her aunt's care. Prior to the Children Act 1989 the only possible redress open to the aunt was in judicial review. Nowadays a relative in a similar position would be able to apply to a court for leave to apply for a residence order.[6] However, a relative might still find that access to a full court hearing would be prevented by the refusal of leave under the criteria in section 10(9).[7]

Section 9(3)(c) allows a local authority foster parent with whom the child has lived for at least three years to apply to a court for leave to apply for a section 8 order without first obtaining the consent of the local authority. What is the difference between that provision and the provision in section 10(5)(b) which entitles anyone to apply for a residence or contact order after the child has lived with the applicant for at least three years? The answer is found in a close examination of sections 10(10) and 9(4). Under both provisions the three-year period must have begun not more than five years before the making of the application, but *entitlement* to apply for an order arises only when the three-year period has ended not more than three months before the application. Thus if the child has been removed from the foster parents, and more than three months elapses before they make their application, they must overcome the hurdle of leave before they can get through the door of the court.

It should be noticed that the requirements in section 9(3) apply only to a person who is, or was at any time within the last six months, a local authority foster parent of the child in question. Once six months have elapsed since the foster parent last looked after the child, the foster parent is free to apply to the court for leave to apply for a section 8 order without

---

3 Particularly s 20(8): see ch 3. See also, *Re R-J (Minors) (Fostering: Person Disqualified)* [1999] 1 FLR 618, where local authority foster parents who had become disqualified to act as foster parents because of new regulations were given the leave of the local authority to seek the leave of the court to apply for a residence order. The court's leave was also given. See further ch 3.

4 For the definition of 'a relative', see s 105.

5 [1992] 1 FLR 448.

6 She could also make use of the complaints procedure under s 26: see ch 3.

7 See above.

first obtaining the consent of the local authority. Thus, for example, a local authority foster parent who had looked after a child for two years, and who is not a relative of the child, could not apply for leave to apply for a section 8 order. But if the child were to be taken from her, and six months were to elapse, she could then apply directly to a court for leave to apply for a residence order. Of course her difficulty in overcoming the hurdle of the criteria in section 10(9) would almost certainly be accentuated by the lapse of time. However, a foster parent who was determined to apply for leave once the six months had elapsed might persuade the local authority to consent to her making a leave application at once. This would resolve the matter at an early stage and allow the child's future to be planned without the threat of future litigation.[8]

Foster parents and adoption as an alternative to a residence order application

Where a child has been in the care of a foster parent for more than twelve months the foster parent becomes eligible under section 13(2) of the Adoption Act 1976 to apply for an adoption order. It may sometimes be appropriate, therefore, to advise a foster parent to make an application for an adoption order where the local authority are threatening to remove the child. The Court of Appeal held in *Re C (A Minor) (Adoption)*[9] that the grant of leave to remove a child once an application for an adoption order had been made was governed by the welfare test in section 6 of the Adoption Act 1976, and that any decision about whether adoption by the foster parents was in the child's interests should not be brought to a premature conclusion by the local authority's application to remove the child. It was in the best interests of the child that the foster mother's application to adopt should be determined after a proper investigation and full court hearing. Thus the decision-making power about the child's future was a matter for the court, and not solely for the local authority, once the adoption application had been made.[10]

It was argued before the trial judge that it was anomalous that section 13(2) of the Adoption Act 1976 enabled the foster mother to apply to adopt the child after he had been in her care for twelve months when this was contrasted with the requirement in section 9(3) of the Children Act 1989 that she must have looked after the child for three years under the section before being able to apply for a residence order without the permission of the local authority. Dismissing this argument, Butler-Sloss LJ said:

---

8 In *Re A (Minors) (Residence Order)* [1992] 3 All ER 872 the local authority gave their consent to the foster mother applying for the court's leave to apply for a residence order, but opposed her application to the court for leave.
9 [1994] 2 FLR 513.
10 Adoption, and the special rules relating to removal of a child from an applicant to adopt, are considered in ch 4.

'There is no basis for importing the Children Act by analogy into the Adoption Act when Parliament has chosen not to make a specific amendment. However anomalous with the Children Act 1989 it may be, the Adoption Act continues to give a person in the position of the foster mother the right to apply for an adoption order after a shorter period of residence of the child with the carer than is required for an application for a residence order under the provisions of the Children Act 1989, and the courts have to apply the law as it is.'[11]

Local authority foster parents and guardianship

Guardianship is another route by which foster parents might be able to circumvent the restraints in section 9(3) on their obtaining a court hearing. There is no control or filtering mechanism over who is entitled to make an application for guardianship. Section 5(1) provides that any individual may apply to a court for appointment as guardian if the child has no parent with parental responsibility for him. An application for guardianship may also be made where a residence order has been made in favour of a parent or guardian of the child, and that person has died while the residence order was in force.[12] Thus, in these circumstances, there is nothing to prevent an application for guardianship being made by foster parents, or anyone else in respect of a child, who is being looked after by a local authority.[13] The application must come before the court despite any objections from the local authority, or from other members of the child's family.[14]

Where a guardianship order is made it confers parental responsibility on the applicant. However, a guardianship order has no other effect on any existing orders. In particular, it has no effect on an existing care order, so that even if the foster parents were appointed guardians of the child the child would still remain in local authority care. Guardianship proceedings are family proceedings, consequently the court, if so minded, could make any section 8 order of its own motion during their course, including a residence order which would have the effect of discharging the care order.[15] The advantage to the foster parents of a court hearing in guardianship would be that a new decision-maker, the court, would be

11 [1994] 2 FLR 513, at p 515.
12 On guardianship generally, see ch 1.
13 S 22(1) provides that a child is being 'looked after' by a local authority whether the child is merely being accommodated by the local authority under s 20 or is the subject of a care order under s 31. See further ch 3.
14 The situations when this may arise, although narrow, are not exceptionally narrow. Residence orders are clearly sometimes made after divorce. Also, where the child's mother has died, and where she was unmarried, it is unlikely that the child's father would have parental responsibility.
15 S 91(1).

entitled to consider the merits of their case. Decision-making would be vested in the court and not in the local authority. If the court were to contemplate using its own motion powers to make a residence order in addition to a guardianship order, and where the effect of the order would be to discharge a care order, a guardian ad litem would have to be appointed to protect the child's interests.[16] This would mean that the local authority's plans for the child would be subjected to an independent professional assessment, and occasionally the alternative plans offered by the foster parent might be thought by the guardian ad litem to be more in the interests of the child than those offered by the local authority. While it is unlikely that a court would make a guardianship order to a foster parent in a case where the local authority were opposed to the application, an application for guardianship might be worth pursuing in a case where the foster parent has been looking after an orphaned foster child for some considerable length of time,[17] and where the local authority are planning to remove the child from her care.

Local authorities and section 8 orders

Local authorities do not fall within the categories of persons who are entitled to apply for section 8 orders but they, like anyone else, may apply to a court for leave to apply for an order. However, section 10(3) provides that section 10 is subject to the restrictions imposed by section 9, and section 9(1) and (2) impose specific restrictions on local authorities.

A court may only make a residence order with respect to a child in care

Section 9(1) provides that:

> 'No court shall make any section 8 order, other than a residence order, with respect to a child who is in the care of a local authority.'

Why may a residence order be made with respect to a child in care but none of the other section 8 orders? A residence order not only settles the arrangements as to the person with whom the child is to live, it also discharges the care order and brings to an end a local authority's parental responsibility for the child.[18] Thus a residence order goes to the source of the local authority's powers, and not to the manner in which they are being exercised. By contrast, the other three orders are each directed to the manner in which those with parental responsibility are able to exercise

---

16 S 41(6).
17 But for less than three years, otherwise the foster parents would be entitled to apply for a residence order under s 10(5)(b).
18 S 91(1).

that responsibility, and where a child is in care it is the local authority which has parental responsibility.[19]

The reason for the prohibition on a court making a specific issue order, or a prohibited steps order, is because when a child is in the care of a local authority, not only do the authority have parental responsibility for the child, but also they have the power to determine the extent to which a parent or guardian may meet his parental responsibility for the child.[20] Thus the position of local authorities is different from that of others who share responsibility for a child's upbringing. It is they who can determine all matters relating to the child's upbringing.[1] Section 9(1) reflects this. It also reflects the constitutional rule that normally the day-to-day decision-making of local authorities should not be subject to review and interference by courts. If courts were permitted to make specific issue and prohibited steps orders in respect of a child in care this would give power to courts to dictate to local authorities how they should carry out the duties imposed on them by statute. Such power would conflict with orthodox principle.[2]

Section 9(1), by preventing specific issue and prohibited steps orders being made, therefore enshrines an important constitutional principle, namely that where Parliament has imposed duties on a local authority, and given them corresponding powers to put them into effect, courts may only interfere in the exercise of those powers and duties where Parliament has authorised this. Otherwise the only challenge which can be directed to the exercise by the local authority of their statutory functions is where the authority's behaviour has been such as to render them liable to an action in judicial review.[3]

Although a contact order cannot be made under section 8 in relation to a child in care the Act does allow for judicial interference in a local authority's decisions about contact, but it does so under section 34. Contact arrangements are a vital aspect of the relationship between a child and his parents and members of his wider family. Unless contact is allowed on a reasonably frequent basis it will normally be impossible to secure the rehabilitation of the child with his parents, and the eventual discharge of the care order. Thus although orders about contact go to the manner in which a local authority exercise their powers over a child in care, contact is an issue of such importance in relation to the right of the child and his parents to enjoy one another's company that Parliament has authorised that questions about contact with a child in care may be determined by the courts.[4]

---

19 Which the authority shares with the parents.
20 S 33(3).
1   Apart from issues relating to contact; and see s 33(3) which puts other limits on the local authority's powers.
2   *A v Liverpool City Council* [1981] 2 All ER 385; *W v Hertfordshire County Council* [1985] 2 All ER 301.
3   Parliament could, of course, have controlled supervision by courts of the day to day care of children through the mechanism of leave, which would have permitted some s 8 applications to proceed, but not others. However, it decided otherwise.
4   See ch 3.

A local authority may not apply for a residence or contact order

Section 9(2) provides that:

'No application may be made by a local authority for a residence order or contact order and no court shall make such an order in favour of a local authority.'

Why are these restrictions imposed? Why is a local authority prohibited from seeking leave to apply for either a residence or contact order, yet permitted to apply for leave to apply for a specific issue or prohibited steps order? The first point to realise is that section 9(2) is directed at those cases where a local authority do not have a care order. The reason why a local authority may not apply for, or be granted, a residence order is to prevent a local authority from obtaining parental responsibility for a child otherwise than through making an application in care proceedings. Without this prohibition a local authority might be tempted to by-pass making an application in care proceedings under Part IV of the Act, and instead to seek a residence order. A local authority may not apply for a contact order for similar reasons. Such an order could enable the authority to have enforceable contact with a child other than through obtaining a supervision order in an application brought in care proceedings.

Significantly too, it was held in *F v Cambridgeshire County Council*,[5] that it is wrong for a local authority to be made a party to contact proceedings, and it is not open to a local authority to invite a court to refuse to make a contact order applied for in private law proceedings between a mother and father. As Stuart-White J explained, the only means by which the local authority can seek to interfere in relation to residence and contact is by bringing public law proceedings under Parts IV or V of the Children Act 1989. This principle applies even though at an earlier stage in the private law proceedings the court has directed the authority to conduct an investigation into whether, inter alia, the authority should apply for a care or supervision order.[6]

Good intentions, a genuine motive, and a different view about where a child should live, and whether he should be supervised by a social worker, are not regarded as sufficient reasons for permitting a local authority to obtain control over a child's upbringing. If a local authority wish to obtain such control, they must prove that there are sufficient grounds to justify this type of intervention. The law relating to care proceedings contains many checks and balances designed to limit state intervention in family life. Courts are empowered to order the removal of children from their homes, and to give parental responsibility to local authorities, only in those cases that can be justified on carefully formulated criteria including, among other things, proof of actual or anticipated significant harm to the

---

5 [1995] 1 FLR 516, following *Nottingham County Council v P* [1993] 2 FLR 134.
6 S 37: see ch.3.

child.[7] By contrast, residence and contact orders are governed solely by the application of the principle that the child's welfare is paramount.

There may, however, be some potential for the restriction in section 9(2) to be circumvented through indirect means. Many children who are being accommodated on a voluntary basis by a local authority are placed with foster parents.[8] It may be, in a particular case, that the local authority and foster parents form the view that there are insufficient grounds to institute proceedings for a care order, but that nonetheless the child's interests will best be served by remaining in foster care. Where the child, too, is strongly expressing a wish to remain where he is, this view will be compounded. In these circumstances there is nothing to prevent a local authority from consenting to the foster parents applying for leave to apply for a residence order, and supporting the foster parents in their leave application.[9] Alternatively they could encourage a child of sufficient age and understanding to see a lawyer and initiate his own application for leave to apply for a residence order.

There is a tension here between the interests of the individual child to have his upbringing looked into by a court on the basis of the paramountcy of his welfare, and the more general public law principle that the state should not intervene in the private family life of those with parental responsibility without sufficient cause. If, in a case like the one given above, the foster parents were to obtain a residence order, and if the local authority were to continue to make contributions towards the foster parents' costs of accommodating the child,[10] and perhaps to continue to supervise the child on a voluntary basis too, this public/private divide could become blurred, arguably to an unacceptable degree.

A local authority may apply for a specific issue order, or a prohibited steps order

A local authority may seek a court's leave to apply for a specific issue or prohibited steps order (except when they already have a care order, and section 9(1) therefore applies).[11] Why are these orders treated differently from residence and contact orders? This question is best answered by recalling the various philosophies which underpin the Children Act 1989. These include the belief that it is normally in the best interests of a child to be brought up by his own parents; that parents and state should work in partnership to further a child's welfare; and that any state intervention which results in the conferment of parental responsibility on a local

---

7   S 31(2): and see ch 3.
8   Under the accommodation provisions in s 20: see ch 3.
9   S 9(3)(a); and see above.
10   Sch 1, para 15(1).
11   They may, however, be given leave to invoke the inherent jurisdiction of the High Court, see below.

authority should be limited to those occasions when the child is suffering, or is likely to suffer, significant harm. Having the freedom to apply for leave to apply for specific issue or prohibited steps orders affords local authorities the opportunity to seek a court's assistance to make a ruling on one aspect of the exercise of parental responsibility, without otherwise interfering in the day-to-day control exercised by parents, and others, over a child's upbringing. As Johnson J accepted in *Re O (A Minor) (Medical Treatment)*,[12] where the issue to be resolved was whether the child should have a blood transfusion, it is wholly inappropriate for a court to make even an interim care order where the child's parents are 'caring, committed and capable and where only one issue arises for decision, albeit one of the gravest significance'.[13] In *Re R (A Minor) (Blood Transfusion)*[14] the issue to be resolved was also whether a child should have a blood transfusion. Booth J ruled that a local authority should make an application for a specific issue order before a High Court judge where there was no need for any other order to safeguard the child.

Where a local authority are seriously concerned about an aspect of a child's upbringing they must strike a proper balance between applying for one or both of the two private law orders under section 8, and using the public law provisions under Part IV or PartV. The choice is not always easy bearing in mind the non-interventionist philosophy of the Act. In *Nottinghamshire County Council v P*[15] the Court of Appeal held that a local authority which believed a child to be at risk of suffering significant harm should proceed by way of an application for a care or supervision order and not use the private law provisions. The court also warned against the local authority attempting to use a prohibited steps order for the purpose of controlling a father's contact with his daughters, stating that this was disallowed under section 9(2) and (5).[16] This ruling means that where a local authority take the view that it is safe to leave a child with one parent, but that the other parent presents a serious risk to the child, that they must seek to persuade the caring parent to apply for orders which will be effective to protect the child. This is likely to include orders under section 8 and under legislation which permits a court to oust a parent from the home.[17] Where the caring parent refuses, or is too frightened, to take such action, the local authority then has no alternative but to apply for an order in care proceedings.[18] Where a local

12 [1993] 2 FLR 149.
13 However, in *Re O (A Minor) (Medical Treatment)* Johnson J also ruled that the inherent jurisdiction was the most appropriate legal framework in which to consider the issue.
14 [1993] 2 FLR 757.
15 [1993] 2 FLR 134.
16 See above.
17 Under Part IV of the Family Law Act 1996: see ch 6.
18 This dilemma for local authorities may be alleviated if, and when, s 60 of the Family Law Act 1996 is implemented. This states that rules of court may provide for a 'representative' to apply for an occupation order or a non-molestation order, on behalf of another: see further ch 6.

authority will not take such steps, it appears that a court is powerless to direct them to do so.[19]

The inherent jurisdiction of the High Court

The inherent jurisdiction of the High Court in children cases dates back to feudal times. Its origins lie in the duty of the king, as *parens patriae*, to take care of those who are not able to take care of themselves. The situations in which the court can act under its inherent jurisdiction to protect a child have never been defined. The most usual way of invoking the High Court's inherent jurisdiction is by making a child a ward of court. A child becomes a ward as soon as an application is made, that is to say the jurisdiction takes effect even before any order is made. In wardship the High Court takes control over the child's upbringing, but then delegates powers to make decisions about the child to the persons who are responsible for looking after him. However, once a child has been warded no important step in the child's life can be taken without the court's leave. The difference between asking the High Court to exercise its inherent jurisdiction and warding a child is that the court, when exercising its inherent jurisdiction, simply adjudicates on a particular aspect of the child's welfare; it does not place the child under the long-term control of the court.[20]

The inherent jurisdiction and a court's powers under the Children Act 1989

The purpose of the Children Act 1989 is to provide a comprehensive framework within which decision-making about children may best proceed, and it has been seen that it makes available a variety of orders designed to encompass all aspects of a child's upbringing. In particular, a court can take long-term control over the child by making a prohibited steps order, and it can choose to use this power either on application or in the exercise of own motion powers.[1] This parallels the continuing control exercised by the High Court where the child is a ward. In cases of difficulty the lower courts are empowered, and sometimes required, to transfer proceedings upwards to the High Court, and even the most delicate and difficult decisions, such as whether a child should be sterilised,[2] or whether a child

---

19 See the concluding remarks of Sir Stephen Brown P in *Nottinghamshire County Council v P* [1993] 2 FLR 134.

20 For an historical analysis, see N V Lowe and R White *Wards of Court* (Butterworths, 1986).

1   Children Act 1989, s 10(1)(b). A prohibited steps order directs that 'no step which could be taken by a parent in meeting his parental responsibility for a child, and which is of a kind specified in the order, shall be taken by any person without the consent of the court': s 8(1), and see above.

2   *Re HG (Specific Issue Order: Sterilisation)* [1993] 1 FLR 587.

should receive life-saving treatment,[3] have been heard by High Court judges in proceedings brought under the 1989 Act.[4]

Why, therefore, should an applicant wish to invoke the inherent jurisdiction, or ward the child, rather than institute proceedings under the Act? First, it is clear that there is nothing in the Children Act 1989 to prevent any individual, but *not* a local authority,[5] who has a genuine interest in the upbringing of a child from warding the child, or from otherwise asking the High Court to exercise its inherent jurisdiction to deal with a specific issue which has arisen. It is also clear that because proceedings brought under the inherent jurisdiction fall within the definition of family proceedings, the High Court is entitled to make any section 8 order when exercising its inherent jurisdiction.[6] Nonetheless there appears to be an acceptance that sensitive areas of parental responsibility, and their scrutiny in legal proceedings, should best be handled under the inherent jurisdiction of the High Court. Thus it has normally been thought appropriate to invoke the inherent jurisdiction in those tragic cases where the issue for the court has been whether a child's medical treatment, or placement on a life support system, should continue or be withdrawn.[7] Similarly, the inherent jurisdiction is normally invoked where a request is being made for the court to authorise medical treatment against opposition from the child's parents, and sometimes the child, which is based on strongly held religious beliefs.[8] These situations give rise to

---

3   *Re R (A minor) (Blood Transfusion)* [1993] 2 FLR 757.
4   International child abduction is one area where retention of the wardship jurisdiction is invaluable because of its speed, and because High Court judges are familiar with the complex legal framework, see ch 5. For an example of the inherent jurisdiction being used to handle a specific issue, see *Re A-K (Foreign Passport: Jurisdiction)* [1997] 2 FLR 569 where, in a case with a background of child abduction, an order was made requiring the surrender of an Iranian father's passport to his solicitors.
5   See below.
6   S 8(3).
7   Controversial rulings relating to the withdrawal of treatment from babies include: *Re B (A Minor) (Wardship: Medical Treatment)* (1981) 3 FLR 117; *Re C (A Minor) (Wardship: Medical Treatment)* [1989] 2 All ER 782; *Re J (A Minor) (Wardship: Medical Treatment)* [1990] 3 All ER 930; *Re T (Wardship: Medical Treatment)* [1997] 1 FLR 502. For comment see S Michalowski *Is it in the best interests of a child to have a life-saving liver transplantation? Re T (Wardship: Medical Treatment)* (1997) 9 CFLQ 179. The kind of acute dilemma cases of this kind involve was poignantly illustrated by *Re C (Medical Treatment)* [1998] 1 FLR 384 where, against the wishes of the child's parents, the court gave leave for the withdrawal of artificial ventilation of a child of 16 months and her non-resuscitation in the event of respiratory arrest. See J Fortin *Re C (Medical Treatment) A baby's right to die* (1998) 10 CFLQ 411. See also, *Re C (A baby)* [1996] 2 FLR 43 where similar facts occurred. For further discussion, see A Bainham *Children – The Modern Law* Family Law, 2nd ed (1998) ch 8; J Fortin *Children's Rights and the Developing Law* Butterworths (1998) chs 5 and 11.
8   See, for example, *Re L (Medical Treatment: Gillick Competency)* [1998] 2 FLR 810, where a 14-year-old girl's refusal of medical treatment on religious grounds was overridden by the High Court exercising inherent powers. See also, *Re C (Detention: Medical Treatment)* [1997] 2 FLR 180, where Wall J held that the Court exercising its inherent powers could direct that a 16-year-old girl should remain a patient at a clinic and be treated by the use

extraordinarily difficult moral, ethical and legal dilemmas and High Court judges and lawyers have therefore often found it appropriate that they should be resolved under an ancient jurisdiction which has traditionally commanded public confidence and respect.

Situations not covered by the Children Act 1989

The High Court has been jealous to preserve its role to come to the assistance of children where the law is otherwise powerless or inadequate. By refusing to define the scope of the jurisdiction, the High Court has reserved to itself the power to respond to circumstances as they arise. Examples have arisen in the context of press freedom where the wardship jurisdiction has been invoked to prevent the publication of information in the press which could be harmful to the child.[9] In cases of this nature the court has needed to balance the interest in freedom of information against the welfare of the child.[10] Another arose where a contract for surrogate parenthood was involved, and where there appeared to be a need to throw a ring of care around the child, but where care proceedings were inappropriate.[11] A third example arose in *D v N (Contact Order: Conditions).*[12] There is no power under the Children Act 1989 to attach conditions to a contact order which are designed to protect a parent and others from molestation by another parent, and this led the Court of Appeal to state that where such a non-molestation order was needed the inherent jurisdiction should be invoked.[13]

of reasonable force if necessary. The competence of children to make their own decisions, and their consent to, or refusal of, medical treatment are considered in ch 1. More detailed discussion of the principles which have been applied in medical treatment cases involving adolescents and young children is beyond the scope of this book.

9　*Re M and N (Minors) (Wardship: Freedom of Publication)* [1990] 1 All ER 205; *Re X (A Minor) (Wardship: Jurisdiction)* [1975] 1 All ER 697.

10　In *Re Z (A Minor) (Freedom of Publication)* [1995] 4 All ER 961, a distinction was drawn between those situations where the freedom to publish was the prevailing interest, and where the material to be published was only indirectly referable to the child. It was stated that in such a case the court, in practice would normally decline to exercise its powers. However, where the material to be published was an act of parental responsibility directed to the child, or to an aspect of her upbringing, so that the paramount concern of the court was the child's welfare, the court would exercise its powers to refuse to permit the exercise of parental responsibility in a manner which might harm the child. See also *Re W (Wardship: Publicity)* [1995] 2 FLR 466; and see J Moriarty *Children, privacy and the press* (1997) 9 CFLQ 217.

11　*Re C (A Minor) (Wardship: Surrogacy)* [1985] FLR 846.

12　[1997] 2 FLR 797.

13　It is suggested that this response was an example of the High Court being prepared to come to the assistance of an applicant even though many, if not all, of the orders requested by the applicant were, and are, available under the general law. The judge had purported to attach conditions to a defined contact order under s 11(7), which, inter alia, included orders forbidding the father to enter specified property; assaulting or otherwise molesting the mother; initiating investigations by the police or the DSS into the mother's conduct; obtaining a passport for the child; and from entering and damaging the premises of the mother's relatives. Much of this behaviour could now be controlled under Part IV of the Family Law Act 1986, see ch 6.

In *Re X (A Minor) (Adoption Details: Disclosure)*[14] a situation arose where, if any jurisdiction to intervene existed at all, it could only be under the inherent powers of the High Court. Under the Adoption Act 1976, the Registrar General has a mandatory duty to keep a register of adopted children and must allow any person to search the index and to have a certified copy of any entry.[15] The fear in this case was that the birth mother, who was an aggressive and violent woman, of whom the child was terrified, would discover the child's whereabouts if she had access to this inform-ation. The Court of Appeal ruled that the High Court could order that the Registrar General should not reveal details of the adoption recorded on the register to any person without the leave of the court.[16]

In *S v S; W v Official Solicitor*[17] the House of Lords was certain that an adult cannot be forced to provide a blood sample against his or her will, the reason being that 'English law goes to great lengths to protect a person of full age and capacity from interference with his personal liberty'.[18] However, as Lord Reid pointed out, a parent can lawfully require a child to submit to a blood test, 'and if the parent can require that, why not the court?'[19] Nonetheless, Lord Reid acknowledged that no case had occurred in which the High Court, exercising its inherent jurisdiction, had ordered a blood test against the will of the parent with care and control. Moreover, section 21(3) of the Family Law Reform Act 1969 specifically provides that 'a bodily sample may be taken from a person under the age of sixteen … if the person who has care and control of him consents'. However, despite this apparently clear and unequivocal requirement for consent from a parent, or other person with care and control of the child, Hale J, in a robust judgment, found a way of ordering blood tests without parental consent in *Re R (Blood Test: Constraint)*.[20] Having decided that it was in the best interests of a child for her paternity to be determined, she said that there were two possible approaches. One was to make a direction for blood tests under the Family Law Reform Act 1969 but to deal with the question of the child under the inherent jurisdiction. The other was to make a direction under the Act, but to order the delivery of the child into the care and control of the Official Solicitor and to make it plain that the Official Solicitor was permitted to consent on the child's behalf.[1]

---

14   [1994] 2 FLR 450.
15   Adoption Act 1976, s 50.
16   See also *Re W (Adoption Details: Disclosure)* [1998] 2 FLR 625.
17   [1970] 3 All ER 107.
18   Ibid, per Lord Reid, at p 111. He continued: 'We have too often seen freedom disappear in other countries not only by coups d'etat but by gradual erosion; and often it is the first step that counts. So it would be unwise to make even minor concessions'. The use of blood tests to determine paternity is discussed in ch 1.
19   Ibid. Lord Reid said that in the case of a child there was no overriding requirement of public policy as there was with an adult.
20   [1998] 1 FLR 745. Hale J acknowledged that she had only had a very brief time to consider the point, which had not hitherto been directly addressed.
1   It is not clear from the body of the judgment which course her Ladyship took. However, the headnote indicates that she chose the latter.

It is suggested that whichever solution commended itself to the court, the outcome of the child being tested against the wishes of the person with care and control could only be achieved by Hale J exercising the High Court's inherent powers. Provisions of the Children Act 1989 would not have provided a solution because a specific issue order could surely not have been in the face of the express provision in section 21(3) of the Family Law Reform Act 1969. A lower court has no power to make an order which departs from an express provision in a statute, and in relation to Children Act orders the three levels of court exercise a concurrent jurisdiction.[2] Nor was there any statutory basis for the court's direction that the child be delivered into the care and control of the Official Solicitor.

Because there is no statutory restriction placed on individuals making an application to the High Court for the exercise of the inherent jurisdiction, the question arises whether an individual may seek the assistance of the High Court when other remedies under the Children Act 1989 are denied, or have been used and exhausted. While there appears to be no direct authority on this point, it can be predicted with confidence that a court would not allow the inherent jurisdiction to be used to circumvent restrictions which are included within the statutory framework. For example, if grandparents were to be refused leave to apply for a residence order in relation to their grandchild under section 10(9), it is suggested that it is inconceivable that they would be able to obtain a hearing on the merits under the inherent jurisdiction for an order to be made that the child should live with them. For a court to rule otherwise would be to turn the inherent jurisdiction into an alternative code for resolving disputes about children, with its own body of case law separate and distinct from cases decided under the Act. This would seriously undermine the Act and its associated procedures and be constitutionally unsound because the court would be overriding the will of Parliament.[3]

The inherent jurisdiction and local authorities

Historically, local authorities could invite the High Court to exercise its inherent jurisdiction in wardship to make up for apparent deficiencies in the statutory child protection framework. Wardship was used to safeguard children when other procedures and remedies were unavailable, or had failed. In return, the local authority relinquished some of their control over a child to the court, and before they took any important step in the child's life which related to his upbringing they were required to refer the matter back to the court. Section 100 of the Children Act 1989 makes it plain that

2   Any exercise of the inherent jurisdiction with respect to children is only exercisable by the High Court, see *Devon County Council v B* [1997] 1 FLR 591.
3   See *W v Hertfordshire County Council* [1985] 2 All ER 301. It would also be a method of circumventing the normal appeals procedure, and the limits imposed by the House of Lords in *G v G* [1985] 2 All ER 225 on allowing appeals against the exercise of judicial discretion: see further ch 4.

it is no longer open to local authorities to ask the High Court to exercise the inherent jurisdiction as an alternative to taking proceedings under the Act. Section 100(2) provides that no court shall exercise the inherent jurisdiction to put a child in care, under local authority super-vision, or into local authority accommodation. Nor may the jurisdiction be used for the purpose of conferring on any local authority the power to determine any question which has arisen, or which may arise, in con-nection with any aspect of parental responsibility for the child.[4] The High Court may only grant a local authority leave to apply for the exercise of the court's inherent jurisdiction if it is satisfied both that the desired result cannot be achieved by any other order for which the local authority are entitled to apply, and that there is reasonable cause to believe that if the court's inherent jurisdiction is not exercised the child is likely to suffer significant harm.[5]

The reason for this restriction on the High Court's powers is that if a local authority could invoke the inherent jurisdiction, or make a child a ward of court, whenever it wished to do so, this could enable the authority to obtain parental responsibility for a child other than by satisfying the threshold test for care proceedings.[6] The threshold test lays down a minimum standard which, if established, allows a court to authorise the removal of children from their homes and for their placement in the care of a local authority. It is a universal standard applicable in all cases to all local authorities and the structure of the Children Act 1989 makes it absolutely clear that the test cannot be circumvented.

In *Devon County Council v S*,[7] Thorpe J drew a distinction between a local authority seeking to have protective powers conferred upon them through resort to the inherent jurisdiction, which is prohibited by section 100(2)(d), and a local authority inviting the court to exercise its inherent powers to make an order which does not give any powers to the local authority. He held that, because of the Court of Appeal's judgment in *Nottinghamshire County Council v P*,[8] there was no jurisdictional found-ation for making a prohibited steps order on an application from a local authority, where the purpose of the order was to prevent a child sex abuser from having contact with children living at home with their mother.

---

4   S 100(2).
5   S 100(4). For the application of this principle to the detention of children in order to secure medical treatment in secure accommodation, which is normally covered by s 25, see *A Metropolitan Borough Council v DB* [1997] 1 FLR 767; *Re C (Detention: Medical Treatment)* [1997] 2 FLR 180. For comment on these cases see A Downie *A Metropolitan Borough Council v DB* and *Re C (Detention: Medical Treatment): Extra-statutory confinement – detention and treatment under the inherent jurisdiction* (1998) 10 CFLQ 101.
6   S 31(2); see ch 3.
7   [1994] 1 FLR 355.
8   [1993] 2 FLR 134. The Court of Appeal ruled that a local authority could not apply for a prohibited steps order to stop contact between an abusive father and his daughters because this was, in effect, to apply for a contact order. A prohibited steps order would therefore evade the restrictions imposed by s 9(2) and (5) of the Children Act 1989, which are designed to ensure that the threshold test is not circumvented, see above.

However, the local authority could invite the court to exercise its own powers under the inherent jurisdiction in order to protect the child.[9] The exercise of this power to invite the court to intervene in those cases where the local authority is otherwise powerless may be the only way, or the most appropriate way, to promote the welfare of the child.[10]

Restrictions on the power of a court to make orders in favour of a local authority either under the Children Act 1989, or under the inherent jurisdiction, may sometimes present a local authority with a predicament. Section 9(1) provides that a court may not make a section 8 order other than a residence order in respect of a child in care.[11] Yet a specific question may arise in connection with an aspect of the authority's parental responsibility where they take the view that a court should be the decision-maker rather than themselves. Examples might be where a child in care is seeking an abortion against her parents' wishes;[12] where sterilisation is believed to be in a child's best interests;[13] where a '*Gillick* competent' child is refusing consent to medical treatment;[14] or where a child and his parents are refusing to consent to medical treatment on religious or other grounds.[15] The strict legal position is that because the local authority have parental responsibility they have the right to give the requisite consents to the medical treatment which is in issue. But these questions raise sensitive and controversial moral dilemmas, and it may be thought that a court, rather than the local authority, ought to be the final decision-maker. Indeed, in the case of sterilisation there is a practice direction to the effect that the matter must be resolved by a High Court judge.[16] Because a local authority with care of a child cannot apply for a specific issue order in relation to that child, it is in this type of case that they may properly turn to the High Court for assistance. Section 100(4) enables a court to grant a local authority the leave of the court to apply for the exercise of the inherent jurisdiction where the result is not one which can be achieved by any kind of order, and where it can be shown that the child is likely to suffer significant harm if the jurisdiction is not exercised.

9   The scope of the distinction drawn in *Devon County Council v S* is unclear. In any event, it appears to have been overtaken by ss 44A and 38A of the Children Act 1989 (added by the Family Law Act 1996) which enable courts to add exclusion requirements to emergency protection orders and interim care orders, see chs 3 and 6.

10 See, for example, *Re RJ (Wardship)* [1999] 1 FLR 618 where regulations prevented a local authority continuing a placement for three children with foster parents in whose care they were happy and settled. The court made orders in wardship proceedings vesting care and control of the children with the foster parents. See further ch 3.

11 S 9(1) formally clarifies the division of powers and responsibilities between local authorities and courts: see above.

12 *Re B (Wardship: Abortion)* [1991] 2 FLR 426.

13 The sterilisation of a minor in virtually all cases requires the prior sanction of a High Court judge: *Practice Note* [1990] 2 FLR 530; *Re B (A minor) (Wardship: Sterilisation)* [1987] 2 FLR 314.

14 *Re R (A Minor) (Wardship: Medical Treatment)* [1991] 4 All ER 177; *Re W (A Minor) (Medical Treatment)* [1992] 4 All ER 627: see ch 1.

15 *Re B (A Minor) (Wardship: Medical Treatment)* [1981] 1 WLR 1421; *Re E (A Minor) (Wardship: Medical Treatment)* [1993] 1 FLR 386.

16 *Practice Note, Sterilisation* [1993] 2 FLR 222.

More controversial is the situation when the inherent jurisdiction is invoked because an effort to protect a child is apparently being thwarted by statute. It has been seen that since the enactment of section 100 of the Children Act 1989 it is clear that the inherent jurisdiction cannot be used to replace, or supplement, a local authority's statutory powers of intervention. It is against this background that the ruling in *South Glamorgan County Council v W and B*[17] presents difficulties. During the course of care proceedings a judge made an interim care order, and gave directions under section 38(6) for the child, a girl of 15, to undergo a psychiatric examination and assessment and, if necessary, to be treated at an adolescent unit and to remain there during the assessment. Section 38(6) provides that 'if the child is of sufficient understanding to make an informed decision, he may refuse to submit to the examination or other assessment'. The girl refused to comply with the court's direction and the court found that she was competent to make an informed decision.[18] The court therefore gave leave to the local authority to bring proceedings to invoke the exercise of the court's inherent jurisdiction to authorise that the child be assessed and treated without her consent. Leave was granted because the court was satisfied that the result which the local authority wished to achieve could not be achieved through the making of any order made otherwise than in the exercise of the court's inherent jurisdiction, and for which the local authority were entitled to apply. It therefore fulfilled the requirements of section 100(5). It was put to the court that the court's power under the inherent jurisdiction to override in a proper case the wishes of a child, and to give consent for medical treatment, had been abrogated by section 100 of the Children Act 1989. This view was rejected by the court on the ground that the court had always been able to override the wishes of a competent child, and that it would require very clear words in a statute to take that right away.

There were compelling reasons why the child in *South Glamorgan County Council v W and B* should receive psychiatric assessment and treatment, and it is easy to appreciate why the court was determined to override her refusal. However, the difficulty with the ruling is that Parliament had specifically legislated, in section 38(6), that a child with sufficient competence could refuse to comply with a direction *from a court* that she undergo such an assessment. Thus Parliament appeared deliberately to have circumscribed the powers *of a court* in the face of a refusal from the child. The ruling in *South Glamorgan County Council v W and B* allowed the inherent jurisdiction to be used to give powers to the court which were denied it by statute. The court's justification for this was that when in a particular case other remedies within the Children Act 1989 had been used, and exhausted, and found not to bring about the result desired by the court then, in these exceptional circum-

17 [1993] 1 FLR 574.
18 The court expressed this in the negative, that is that it was not prepared to find that she was not competent.

stances, the court could have resort to the inherent jurisdiction. In this regard the ruling in *South Glamorgan County Council v W and B* parallels the pre-Children Act 1989 rulings that the powers of the High Court should be made available to a local authority when this is deemed necessary in the interests of a child.[19] However, it seems that the inherent jurisdiction may not be used as an alternative to the statutory framework in cases involving a local authority unless the authority request this, even though the result desired by the court cannot otherwise be achieved. Certainly the Court of Appeal appears to have held this view in *Nottinghamshire County Council v P*,[20] because it held that it was powerless to compel a local authority to take care proceedings, and where it further held that it could not make a care order of its own motion.

What is the position where a parent or a third party wishes to invoke the inherent jurisdiction in order to challenge a decision made by a local authority in the exercise of their parental responsibility? By placing a prohibition on specific issue orders being made in respect of children in care, section 9(1) makes it plain that Parliament did not intend that parents, or others, should be able to bring proceedings under the Act to challenge any of the many day to day decisions made by local authorities with respect to the children for whom they are responsible.[21] Where, by contrast, the issue to be resolved does not involve an exercise of parental responsibility by the local authority the High Court may be able to intervene. In *Re M (Care: Leave to Interview Child)*[1] a solicitor acting for a father in criminal proceedings wished to interview the father's two sons for the purpose of preparing his defence. The boys were the subject of interim care orders, and while the local authority did not object to them being interviewed, there was disagreement about the conditions under which the interview should be carried out. The issue for the court was whether it could intervene under its inherent jurisdiction, or whether the decision was one for the local authority alone. Hale J held that local authorities have the same powers as parents when exercising their parental responsibility. These powers are not unlimited, and they may not be exercised in ways which infringe the rights of others. Here justice required that the father, who faced very serious charges, should be permitted properly to prepare his defence. The court had powers under its inherent jurisdiction to determine how the solicitor should interview the children and it would exercise these powers whether or not the local authority agreed.

On the other hand, it is equally clear that an individual who seeks to question the manner in which a local authority are exercising their

---

19 *A v Liverpool City Council* [1981] 2 All ER 385; *W v Hertfordshire County Council* [1985] 2 All ER 301.
20 [1993] 2 FLR 134.
21 A parent or other interested party is not entirely without redress, as each local authority must establish a complaints procedure: Children Act 1989, s 26: see ch 3.
1   [1995] 1 FLR 825.

statutory powers and duties over a child in care cannot circumvent the prohibition in section 9(1) by having resort to the inherent jurisdiction. It was recognised by the House of Lords in *A v Liverpool City Council*[2] that it is a fundamental principle of law that the High Court will not exercise its inherent jurisdiction where this would interfere with the discretionary powers which Parliament has clearly given to local authorities.[3]

A common feature of children cases is that there are choices to be made between viable alternatives, and often there is no obviously right decision. Rather one course of action will seem preferable to one decision-maker, and a different decision will seem preferable to another. Who has the right to have the final word about a child's upbringing, and the rules and values which such decision-makers apply to the decision-making process, is therefore an issue of very great importance in child law. This chapter has been concerned with whether an aggrieved person can get through the door of the court in private law proceedings. Where the applicant is successful, it is the court which is the final arbiter of the matter in dispute. How local authorities, which have special responsibilities towards children in need and children suffering, or likely to suffer, significant harm, have responded to the child care and protection framework, and how courts have approached child care and protection cases, are both considered in the next chapter.

2   [1981] 2 All ER 385.
3   See also *W v Hertfordshire County Council* [1985] 2 All ER 301 where this 'profoundly important principle' was re-affirmed.

Chapter 3

Children needing services, care or protection

Chapter 3

Children needing services, care or protection

Children needing services, care or protection

Many persons caring for children are unable properly to fulfil their parental responsibilities without the assistance of services. The Children Act 1989 recognises that families sometimes require help in bringing up children, and it imposes specific duties and powers on local authorities to facilitate this process and expects them to work in partnership with parents.[1] The Act also recognises that children who need care or protection may sometimes be the same children who need the provision of services. It will be seen that the guiding principle lying behind the duty to provide services is to promote the upbringing of children by their families,[2] that these services should be used to prevent children from suffering ill-treatment or neglect,[3] and that some services should be designed to reduce the need to bring care proceedings.[4] Thus the inter-relationship between providing services for children in need, and protecting children from suffering significant harm, is firmly established. The importance of this inter-relationship should not be under-estimated; it influences not only the manner in which local authorities exercise their statutory powers and duties, but also the way in which courts approach care proceedings.[5]

---

1   See particularly DOH *The Challenge of Partnership in Child Protection: Practice Guide* (HMSO, 1995); F Kaganis, M King and C Piper (eds) *Legislating for Harmony – Partnerships under the Children Act 1989* (Jessica Kingsley, 1996).
2   Children Act 1989, s 17(1); further statutory references in this chapter are to the Children Act 1989 unless otherwise stated.
3   Sch 2, para 4.
4   Children Act 1989, Sch 2, para 7.
5   It has been estimated that approximately 350,000 children each year will be in an environment of low warmth and high criticism, an environment which is particularly damaging to children. These children are in need to the extent that their health and development will be significantly impaired if their families do not receive some help. See M Smith, P Bee, A Heverin and G Nobes *Parental Control Within the Family: the nature and extent of parental violence to children* (Thomas Coram Research Unit, 1995).

Part III of the Children Act 1989 is concerned with the duty of every local authority to provide support for children and their families. Much of Part III, which is developed under Part 1 of Schedule 2, is devoted to the duty of every local authority to provide services for children in need and their powers to provide services for other children. The Act itself provides only part of the legal and administrative framework within which services for children and their families are provided. A large body of regulations and guidance has been issued which gives detailed instructions on how this Part (and other Parts) of the Act should be implemented.[6]

Fundamental to the thinking in Part III of the Children Act 1989 is the principle that it is normally in the best interests of children to be brought up by their own families. Section 17, the opening provision, states that:

'(1) It shall be the general duty of every local authority... –
(a) to safeguard and promote the welfare of children within their area who are in need; and
(b) so far as is consistent with that duty, to promote the upbringing of such children by their families,
by providing a range and level of services appropriate to those children's needs.'

Who are 'children in need'?

Section 17(10) provides that a child shall be taken to be in need if:

'(a) he is unlikely to achieve or maintain, or to have the opportunity of achieving or maintaining, a reasonable standard of health or development without the provision for him of services by a local authority under this Part;
(b) his health or development is likely to be significantly impaired, or further impaired, without the provision for him of such services; or
(c) he is disabled,
and "family", in relation to such a child, includes any person who has parental responsibility for the child and any other person with whom he has been living.'

Section 17(11) explains what is meant by 'disabled', 'development' and 'health'. It provides:

---

6 For the status of regulations and guidance, see *The Care of Children, Principles and Practice of Regulations and Guidance* (HMSO). Some details concerning the provision of services under Part III, the regulation of child-minding, private foster care, community homes and voluntary homes are beyond the scope of this book. For greater detail, see the Department of Health volumes on *The Children Act 1989 Guidance and Regulations* (HMSO, 1991). See too, MDA Freeman, *Children, Their Families and the Law* (Macmillan, 1992); A Bainham *Children – The Modern Law* (Family Law, 1998).

'For the purposes of this Part, a child is disabled if he is blind, deaf or dumb or suffers from mental disorder of any kind or is substantially and permanently handicapped by illness, injury or congenital deformity or such other disability as may be prescribed; and in this Part –
"development" means physical, intellectual, emotional, social or behavioural development; and
"health" means physical or mental health.'

Thus it can be seen that the definition of a child in need focuses both on a child who is disabled, and on a child who is at risk of impaired health or development unless preventive steps are taken. These steps may include not only the provision of services for the child himself, but also their provision for any member of his family, if they are provided with a view to safeguarding or promoting the child's welfare.[7]

Provision of services – duties and discretion

Part III and Schedule 2 of the Children Act 1989 use the language of 'shall' and 'may' when specifying the nature of the services to be provided by a local authority. The difference in the words is important – 'shall' means that a local authority *must* provide the service; 'may' gives them a discretion. Where a local authority fail to provide a service for a child in need which they 'shall' provide, then they are in breach of their statutory duty. However, discretion is also built into many of the 'shall' provisions; often the provision made must either be 'reasonable' or 'as is appropriate'. Because local authority social services departments are under a duty not only to provide services for children in need in their area, but also for other needy members of the community, and because they are operating with limited budgets, standards of reasonableness and appropriateness may sometimes be low.[8] Limited budgets may also affect the ability of local authorities to make full use of their powers under section 17(6) to give assistance in kind or in exceptional circumstances in cash.

A local authority 'shall' provide day care for pre-school and other children in need; they 'may' provide such care for other children.[9] They 'shall' provide accommodation for specified children in need, including a child who has reached the age of 16 whose welfare is otherwise likely to be seriously prejudiced; they 'may' provide accommodation for other

7   S 17(3).
8   Hence the frequent complaint that the principles in Part III are excellent, but that the resources to implement them have not been provided. See too *R v Royal Borough of Kingston upon Thames, ex p T* [1994] 1 FLR 798, where the local authority were unable to accommodate two Vietnamese sisters together, partly because of resource constraints.
9   S 18; this is qualified by 'as is appropriate'.

children.[10] They 'shall' provide family centres in relation to children within their area[11] where the child, his parents, any person with parental responsibility and any other person who is looking after him may attend for occupational, social, cultural or recreational activities; advice, guidance and counselling; and where such a person may be provided with accommodation while he is receiving such advice, guidance or counselling.[12] In relation to children in need who are living with their families, a local authority 'shall make such provision as they consider appropriate' for the following services: advice, guidance and counselling; occupational, social, cultural or recreational activities; home help (which may include laundry facilities); facilities for, or assistance with, travelling to and from home for the purpose of taking advantage of any other service provided under the Children Act 1989 or of any similar service; and assistance to enable the child concerned and his family to have a holiday.[13] They 'shall' also take reasonable steps designed to prevent any children within their area suffering ill-treatment or neglect, and to reduce the need to bring care or other legal proceedings with respect to such children.[14] Where it appears that a child is suffering, or is likely to suffer, ill-treatment at the hands of another person who is living on the same premises the local authority 'may' assist that person to obtain alternative accommodation, and such assistance may include the provision of cash.[15]

There are many children in need, and a local authority may not have the resources to provide a service which has been requested; or they may have other reasons for failing or refusing to provide a service. Each local authority is required to establish a procedure for considering any representations, including any complaint, made to them by certain specified persons. Where such a person is dissatisfied with the provision offered by the local authority he or she should make use of this procedure. A complainant will not be given leave to pursue an action in judicial review unless this remedy has first been exhausted.[16]

---

10 S 20(1), (3), (4), (5).
11 Not merely children in need.
12 Sch 2, para 9; qualified by 'as they consider appropriate'.
13 Children Act 1989, Sch 2, para 8.
14 Children Act 1989, Sch 2, paras 4 and 7. The National Commission of Inquiry into the Prevention of Child Abuse, *Childhood Matters,* Chairman: Lord Williams of Mostyn (HMSO, 1996), recognised that public agencies who wish to make a shift towards prevention find it difficult to do so. It recommended that greater emphasis should be given to supporting children and families before abuse occurs. The Inquiry commissioned studies on a wide range of issues, including the law; the cost of child abuse; what can be learned from child survivors; children and young people's views; a review of recent research; the impact of race and culture; social worker attitudes; employment policies; parliamentary attitudes; and the media.
15 Children Act 1989, Sch 2, para 5.
16 *R v Royal Borough of Kingston upon Thames, ex p T* [1994] 1 FLR 798. See further below on the complaints procedure.

Co-operation between different authorities

The effective provision of services for children and their families may require inter-departmental collaboration within a local authority at all levels. The Children Act 1989 promotes a structure which not only requires different local authorities to assist one another, but also requires different bodies within the same local authority to co-operate with one another, to assist the local social services department to fulfil their general duty to provide services for children in need. Section 27 provides that a local authority may request help in the exercise of any of their functions under Part III from any local authority, local education authority, local housing authority, health authority or National Health Service trust, or any other authorised person. An authority whose help is so requested 'shall' comply with the request 'if it is compatible with their own statutory or other duties and obligations and does not unduly prejudice the discharge of any of their functions'.[17]

The policy of the Children Act 1989 is to encourage corporate arrangements and clear procedures with respect to inter-departmental collaboration. Guidance issued under the Act clearly contemplates that a social services department within a local authority can request help from another department within the same local authority.[18] At one stage this policy appeared to have been severely undermined by *R v Tower Hamlets London Borough Council, ex p Byas*,[19] which concerned a request made by a social services department for assistance from the housing department of the same local authority in providing housing for some children in need and their parents. The Court of Appeal ruled that section 27 applies only to requests for help from other local authorities, and that a local authority cannot request help from itself under that section. However, this restricted construction of section 27 appears to have been wrong. In *R v Northavon District Council, ex p Smith*,[1] where a similar request had been made under section 27 by a county council to a district housing authority, Lord Templeman said, 'the present appeal concerns two authorities...Where one and the same authority is both housing authority and social services authority, the same problems of the interaction of the two statutory codes would arise as between the housing department and the social services department of that authority.'[2] Their Lordships do not appear to have had their attention drawn to the ruling in *R v Tower Hamlets London Borough Council, ex p Byas* and, strictly, Lord Templeman's statement is obiter

---

17 S 27(2).
18 *The Children Act 1989 Guidance and Regulations* Vol 2, para 1.13.
19 [1993] 2 FLR 605; see too *R v Oldham Metropolitan Borough Council, ex p Garlick* [1993] AC 509. For comment on these and other cases on the link between the Children Act 1989 and the Housing Act 1985 see Gilbert *Housing for children* (1993) 5 JCL 166.
1 [1994] 3 All ER 313.
2 Ibid, at p 318.

only. However, it is suggested that his statement must be right, and that the Court of Appeal's construction of section 27 was wrong.[3]

Clearly there are difficult issues for both social services departments and housing authorities where children and their parents are threatened with homelessness. In *R v Northavon District Council, ex p Smith*, the housing authority decided that the applicant and his wife were homeless, and in priority need because they had five children, but that they had become homeless intentionally within section 60(1) of the Housing Act 1985. The housing authority therefore declined to provide accommodation in response to a request made under section 27 by the social services department. The House of Lords ruled that section 27 did not enable a local authority to require a housing authority to exercise its powers to provide housing. Instead it imposed a duty of co-operation between social services and housing authorities, both of which had together to do the best they could to carry out their respective responsibilities for children and housing.[4]

Provision of accommodation for children

It has been seen that the primary purpose of the provision of services under Part III of the Children Act 1989 is to keep children and their families together. However, sometimes this may not be possible and a child may need instead to live away from home. Local authorities have a duty to provide accommodation for certain children. Section 20(1) provides:

> 'Every local authority shall provide accommodation for any child in need within their area who appears to them to require accommodation as a result of –
> (a) there being no person who has parental responsibility for him;
> (b) his being lost or having been abandoned; or
> (c) the person who has been caring for him being prevented (whether or not permanently, and for whatever reason) from providing him with suitable accommodation or care.'

Subsection (4) provides:

> 'A local authority may provide accommodation for any child within their area (even though a person who has parental responsibility

---

3   The language of s 47(9)-(12) is similar, though not identical, to that used in s 27. S 47 is concerned with inter-agency co-operation where there is a suspicion of child abuse. The crucial wording in s 27(3) which refers to any local authority and any local housing authority is identical with that in s 47(11). It is inconceivable that the duty to co-operate under s 47 is imposed only when two separate local authorities are involved; such a construction would entirely defeat the requirement that agencies in the same authority work together in matters relating to child protection. It is suggested that not only should the same reasoning apply to children in need of services, but also that, for consistency, ss 27 and 47 should be construed in the same manner.

4   The issue of homelessness is further discussed in ch 5.

for him is able to provide him with accommodation) if they consider that to do so would safeguard and promote his welfare.'[5]

It can be seen that a range of children is covered by those for whom there is a duty to provide accommodation, but that they all must fall within the definition of a 'child in need'. The discretion to accommodate a child arises when the local authority consider that to do so would safeguard and promote his welfare. The influence of the notion that the child himself should be involved in important decisions which are made about his upbringing can be seen in section 20(6), which requires a local authority to take reasonable steps to ascertain the child's wishes and feelings on the matter, and to give them due consideration having regard to his age and understanding. Clearly, while the child may have strong negative wishes and feelings about whether he should be accommodated at all, the practicalities of his situation may appear to leave room for no alternative. It is in this regard that attempts to involve members of the child's extended family who have not previously been looking after him may be of great importance in preserving the child's family links, and in keeping him out of foster care or a residential home. Where this cannot be arranged, it is important that the child's views on the type of accommodation to be provided for him are also taken into account.

The voluntary nature of accommodation

The philosophy of Part III of the Children Act 1989 is to encourage local authorities to work in partnership with parents and persons with parental responsibility, and to promote mutual confidence and trust. The thinking is that parents and others should be able to turn to local authorities for positive help and support in bringing up their children, and that they should not have cause to fear that they may lose their children into state care if they take advantage of the services provided. Such fear may be very real in a case where a person with parental responsibility is encouraged to agree to his child being accommodated under section 20, because he or she thereby loses a measure of control over the child's upbringing. Reassurance is provided by subsections (7) and (8), which together make it clear that accommodation under section 20 may only be provided, or continue to be provided, if the persons with parental responsibility for the child are willing to agree.

Section 20(7) provides that:

'A local authority may not provide accommodation under this section for any child if any person who –
(a) has parental responsibility for him; and

5 Accommodation for certain children aged over 16 and up to the age of 21 may also be provided under sub-ss (3) and (5).

(b) is willing and able to –
    (i) provide accommodation for him; or
    (ii) arrange for accommodation to be provided for him,
objects.'

It can be seen that section 20(7) does not require a local authority to obtain the consent of persons with parental responsibility before a child is received into accommodation. Such a provision would prove unworkable for the practical reason that it may not always be possible to contact such persons. However, where there is a positive objection from a person with parental responsibility, the local authority may not accommodate the child where the objecting person can make his own arrangements for the child.

It is not clear how suitable the accommodation arrangements offered by the objecting person with parental responsibility must be. Where the local authority take the view that they are entirely unsuitable, the question then arises whether the authority are entitled to accommodate the child in the face of such an offer. It is suggested that the local authority are not so entitled. The accommodation provisions in section 20 are built around the principle that the arrangement is voluntary. Should the local authority go ahead and accommodate the child in the face of an objection from a person with parental responsibility, there is nothing to prevent the objecting person from removing the child immediately. In this regard, section 20(8) gives a person with parental responsibility an unqualified right to remove the child. It provides that:

'Any person who has parental responsibility for a child may at any time remove the child from accommodation provided by or on behalf of the local authority under this section.'

It is therefore suggested that the same voluntary principle applies to section 20(7), and that the local authority are not entitled to accommodate a child where he or she disapproves of the accommodation arrangements proposed. Where the local authority are unhappy with this outcome, and where they have reasonable cause to believe that the child is likely to suffer significant harm if he is not accommodated by them, or if he is removed from accommodation which they are providing, they should take steps to obtain the authority to keep the child by applying for an emergency protection order, or for an order in care proceedings.[6]

Exceptions to the voluntary principle

The uncompromising language in which subsections (7) and (8) are couched makes it clear that the accommodation arrangements made under section 20 are entirely voluntary. However, there are three qualifications to this

---

6 See below.

principle: the subsections only apply to persons with parental responsibility; they do not apply where a residence order, or an order under the High Court's inherent jurisdiction, has been made; and they do not apply when the child concerned is 16 or over.

The unmarried father

The first of these exceptions places an unmarried father in a vulnerable position because he is usually a parent without parental responsibility.[7] An unmarried father has no enforceable right to object to his child being accommodated, and he is not entitled to remove his child from accommodation at any time. However, the general duty of a local authority is to promote the upbringing of children by their families,[8] and they are not required to receive the child into accommodation when a family member is offering to look after the child. In a case where the child is already being accommodated they can bring the accommodation arrangement to an end, or where they continue to accommodate the child,[9] they 'shall' make arrangements to enable an accommodated child to live with a parent unless that would not be reasonably practicable or consistent with his welfare. Thus an unmarried father should only find himself in conflict with the local authority when placement with him appears to the authority to be against the interests of the child. Where this is the case, the father's remedy would be to apply for a residence order.[10] In determining the merits of his application, the court would give paramount consideration to the welfare of the child, but normally it would give considerable weight to the fact that a parent was offering to provide a home for a child in a case where the alternative offered was foster care, or accommodation in a residential home.[11]

Where there is a residence order, or an order made by the High Court

A parent with parental responsibility is placed in a similar position to an unmarried father where there is a residence, or other, order settling the arrangements as to the person with whom the child is to live. Section 20(9) provides that:

'Subsections (7) and (8) do not apply while any person –
(a) in whose favour a residence order is in force with respect to the child; or

---

7   See ch 1.
8   S 17(1), above.
9   Under s 23(6).
10 He is entitled to apply by virtue of s 10(4)(a): see ch 2.
11 On the application of the welfare principle generally, see ch 4.

(b) who has care of the child by virtue of an order made in the exercise of the High Court's inherent jurisdiction with respect to children,

agrees to the child being looked after in accommodation provided by or on behalf of the local authority.'

Where more than one person has the benefit of a residence order, all such persons must agree.[12]

The thinking lying behind subsection (9) is that it is the voice of the person who has had the benefit of the residence order which should prevail in dealings with the local authority. Where there has been an estrangement between parents, between parents and others, or where some other reason has led to a residence order being made, a court must have decided that it is better for the child to make a residence order than not to make an order.[13] The thinking is that it is normally in the interests of the child that the person with the residence order should be able to make arrangements about where the child will live, including placing him with a local authority, in spite of the objections of a parent or other person with parental responsibility.

Subsection (9) has been the subject of criticism on the ground that it undermines the notion of continuing parental responsibility. It has been said that the purpose of a residence order is simply to regulate where the child is to live but otherwise to leave intact the full parental responsibility of both parents.[14] It is suggested that this criticism of subsection (9) is flawed because it fails to draw an analogy between a person with a residence order using local authority accommodation and that person choosing to make his own private arrangements to place the child with a relative or other person. In the latter situation, the person with a residence order is able to delegate parental responsibility, and make such an arrangement in the confident knowledge that a parent with parental responsibility is not entitled to remove the child. Such a removal would violate the incompatibility principle in section 2(8).[15] Similarly, section 20(9) enables a person with a residence order to feel free to place the child in local authority accommodation without fear that another person with parental responsibility will be entitled to remove him. Treating local authority accommodation as different from making private arrangements is arguably to perpetuate the pejorative association between turning to the state for the provision of services for children rather than making one's own arrangements.

In fact the reality is that persons with a residence order are in a relatively weak position when approaching a local authority to accommo-

---

12 S 20(10).
13 S 1(5): see ch 2; or the High Court has intervened in the exercise of its inherent jurisdiction.
14 A Bainham *Children – The New Law* (Family Law, 1990) para 4.26; A Bainham *Children – The Modern Law* (Family Law, 1998) p 339.
15 See ch 1.

date a child in comparison with the situation where they make their own private arrangements. Where there is a residence order, but where a parent with parental responsibility is offering to look after the child, the local authority's position is identical to the one described where an unmarried father is offering to care for the child. The local authority are only obliged to accommodate the child where they take the view that this would be in the child's best interests. Where the local authority do so agree, a parent who is aggrieved by the decision should apply under section 10 for the discharge of the existing residence order and for a residence order to be made in his or her favour.

Where the child is 16

The third exception to the voluntary principle is where a child who has reached the age of 16 agrees to being accommodated. Section 20(11) provides that in these circumstances subsections (7) and (8) do not apply. Subsection (11) is an important example of how the law has moved towards allowing a child to determine his own upbringing in the face of objections from a parent or other person with parental responsibility. It respects the right of the competent child to be treated as an autonomous individual as established in *Gillick v West Norfolk and Wisbech Area Health Authority*,[16] and gives the decision-making power about the child's future upbringing to the child. It assumes that a child of 16 is old enough, and has reached a sufficient level of understanding, to make an informed choice about where he wishes to live.[17] In many cases this will be correct. The thinking is that a child of 16 is approaching full adulthood so that he should be entitled to leave home and to seek assistance from a local authority in obtaining properly regulated accommodation.[18] Where the child is already being accommodated, he should be entitled to remain with the persons with whom he has been living in the face of parental objection. Subsection (11) also assists the local authority, because they need not consider instituting care proceedings to assist the mature child in a case where the persons with parental responsibility refuse to agree to the child being accommodated.

The disadvantage of subsection (11) is that it may sometimes place parents and others with parental responsibility in an intolerable position in a case where they do not wish the child to be accommodated. The fact

---

16 [1985] 3 All ER 402.
17 For further discussion of a child's competence to make decisions about his or her own upbringing, see ch 1.
18 The local authority must accommodate a child aged 16 who is in need and whose welfare 'is likely to be seriously prejudiced if they do not provide him with accommodation' (s 20(3)). It may accommodate any child aged between 16 and 21 where to do so would 'safeguard or promote his welfare' (s 20(5)), and see *Re T (Accommodation by Local Authority)* [1995] 1 FLR 159 where a local authority's decision to refuse formally to accommodate a 17 year old child was quashed in proceedings for judicial review.

that a child chooses to put himself into, or to remain in, local authority accommodation may be a matter of very great concern to them. Children being looked after by a local authority come from a variety of backgrounds, some of which are very disturbed. An accommodated child who comes from a 'good home' may live on premises where he or she associates with children who have been involved in prostitution, drug abuse and various types of crime. The child's desire to remain in accommodation may be because these alternative forms of life style seem attractive at an age which is notoriously associated with rebellion against parental norms. While those charged with the duty of looking after older accommodated children make every effort to ensure that such children are not involved in unhealthy, dangerous and criminal forms of activity, there may be little they can do to prevent a determined child from becoming so involved. Local authorities do not have the power to restrict the liberty of delinquent children who they are looking after unless given specific authority to do so by a court.[19]

While it has been observed that, since the ruling in *Gillick*, 'children will now have, in wider measure than ever before, that most dangerous but most precious of rights: the right to make their own mistakes',[20] it is suggested that, during a child's minority, such rights should not include those which may lead to the permanent impairment of the child's health, to imprisonment, or even death. In an extreme case of this kind, a child's desire to be accommodated is associated with reasons which an objective observer would characterise as being against the child's best interests. It would seem that the obvious solution would be for the persons with parental responsibility to apply for a residence order, as this would have the effect of overriding the child's decision to be accommodated. However, such persons are normally powerless to obtain a residence order once a child is 16. Section 9(7) provides that a court shall not make any section 8 order with respect to a child who has reached the age of 16 unless it is satisfied that the circumstances of the case are exceptional. It is suggested that a person with parental responsibility should either seek to persuade a court to treat the case as exceptional under section 10(7),[1] or should seek the leave of the High Court to invoke the exercise of the inherent jurisdiction.[2] Once decision-making power had been taken from the child and placed in the court, the court's decision would be determined by the view it took of the child's best interests, in relation to which the child's wishes and feelings would be but one element.[3]

---

19 S 25 enables a court to make a secure accommodation order on specified grounds for a maximum period of three months.
20 J Eekelaar *The emergence of children's rights* (1986) 6 OJLS 161 at p 182.
1   It would probably be wise to ask a lower court to transfer the case to the High Court.
2   See ch 2.
3   See generally ch 4 on the application of the welfare principle.

Accommodated children who need care or protection

Providing accommodation for a child forms part of a local authority's strategy to provide services for a child in need, to prevent him suffering ill-treatment or neglect, and to reduce the need to bring care or other proceedings about his upbringing.[4] In this regard, accommodation may be used by a local authority as an alternative to bringing care proceedings in a case where there are concerns and fears about the manner in which a child is being looked after. While the voluntary nature of accommodation arrangements made under section 20 is in keeping with the partnership philosophy of the Act, in some cases subsections (7) and (8) may be difficult to reconcile with a local authority's child protection duties.

It has been seen that a local authority cannot prevent a child's removal from accommodation where they are unable to persuade a person with parental responsibility to agree to this. Where such a person is obdurate, the local authority must either release the child to that person's care or they must institute proceedings to obtain the authority to retain the child. Where the local authority have reasonable cause to believe that the child is suffering significant harm, or that he is likely to suffer significant harm if he is removed from his present accommodation, they may make an application in care proceedings for an interim care order.[5] Where the local authority have reasonable cause to believe that the child is likely to suffer significant harm if he does not remain in the place in which he is then being accommodated, and the situation is one of emergency, the authority may apply for an emergency protection order.[6] Either order will authorise the local authority to retain care of the child for a limited period[7] while an assessment is made of whether an application for a care order should be further pursued.

In an emergency, where a person is demanding instantly to remove the child, there will be a short period between the demand to remove the child and the obtaining of an emergency protection order from a court.[8] The question then arises whether the local authority may refuse to release the child into the care of the person exercising his right of removal bearing in mind that section 20(8) states that the child may be removed 'at any time'. There is no authority on this point. It is suggested that the local authority might be protected for a brief period by section 22(3). This places a general duty on a local authority which is looking after a child to safeguard and promote the child's welfare. Alternatively it is suggested

4   Including criminal proceedings: Sch 2, para 7.
5   S 38(1): see below.
6   S 44(1)(a)(ii): see below.
7   Under an interim care order the maximum period is eight weeks (s 38(4)(a)); under an emergency protection order it is eight days (s 45(1)).
8   In this context a court includes a single magistrate or judge to whom an application may be made outside court hours.

that they could rely on section 3(5). This permits a person who does not have parental responsibility for the child, but who has his care, to do what is reasonable in all the circumstances for the purpose of safeguarding or promoting the child's welfare.[9] There are overwhelming policy reasons why either section 22(3), or section 3(5), or both, should apply. If the position were otherwise, and the local authority were compelled to hand the child over immediately, the child might suffer the feared significant harm which had formed the basis of the application for the emergency protection order. This reasoning is assisted by the Court of Appeal's ruling in *F v Wirral Metropolitan Borough Council*[10] that there is no separate tort of interference with parental rights. If a local authority were to be sued for retaining a child in breach of section 20(8), the plaintiff would have the burden of establishing that a tort had been committed against the *child*, and not against the person with parental responsibility.

A separate possibility might be to involve the police. A constable has emergency powers to prevent the removal of a child from the place in which he is being accommodated where he has reasonable cause to believe that the child would otherwise be likely to suffer significant harm.[11] The advantage of invoking police powers over applying for an emergency protection order is that the police will attend at the situation and no court is involved, whereas an application for an emergency protection order must either be made at a court, or at the home of a magistrate or judge.

The accommodation plan

Some of the difficulties outlined above might better be overcome by careful forward planning between the local authority and the persons with parental responsibility. Regulations provide that a scheme of arrangements should be agreed between the local authority and a person with parental responsibility for the child whenever a child is accommodated.[12] This scheme, which must be drawn up in writing,[13] should include details about 'the expected duration of arrangements and the steps which should apply to bring the arrangements to an end, including arrangements for rehabilitation of the child with the person with whom he was living before the voluntary arrangements were made or some other suitable person ...'.[14] This type of planning enables the local authority and persons with parental responsibility to agree in advance about any problems which might arise through the strict enforcement of rights under section 20(8). For example, a parent might be prepared to

9   See ch 1.
10   [1991] 2 All ER 648; for a useful comment see A Bainham *Interfering with parental responsibility – a new challenge for the law of torts?* (1990) 3 JCL 3.
11   S 46(1).
12   Arrangements for Placement of Children (General) Regulations 1991, reg 3 and Sch 4.
13   Reg 3(5).
14   Sch 4, para 9.

agree that the best interests of a child are not normally served by a precipitate and unplanned removal from accommodation, and that at least a brief period of notice is normally better for the child. Furthermore, the guidance on agreements issued by the Department of Health suggests that it should include a statement of the steps each party should take if the other party were to decide to change the agreement. In this context the guidance suggests that the persons with parental responsibility should be warned that the local authority would consider applying for an emergency protection order if one of them were to decide to take action which was harmful to the child.[15]

The advantage of this type of formal planning between a local authority and persons with parental responsibility is that it reinforces the philosophy that local authorities, parents and others should work together in partnership, and that each should trust the other. In this regard, warning parents and others in a written agreement that precipitate removal might lead to an application for an emergency protection order is honestly to reflect the reality. It tells them in no uncertain terms that a 'voluntary' arrangement might be transformed into a compulsory arrangement if their co-operation is withdrawn. Injecting this note of realism into accommodation arrangements may better promote the child's sense of security with his current carers, and the child can be reassured that his wishes and feelings will be taken into account before there is any sudden change of plan.

The disadvantage of agreements of this kind is that terms which require persons with parental responsibility to give a period of notice before removing a child from accommodation[16] undermine the principle that the arrangement is voluntary. Parliament was insistent that no notice period should be included in section 20(8) in the face of very great pressure to include at least a brief period.[17] Local authorities are in a much stronger position than parents when suggesting what terms should be included, and they are likely to tell parents what the arrangements will be, however much this is couched in the language of mutual agreement. There is a risk that written accommodation agreements will take on a spurious authority in the eyes of those who are party to them, so that local authorities may feel that they can 'contract out' of the law's provisions, and parents and others may feel 'bound' by the terms, and not be aware of their rights under section 20(8).

Representations and complaints

Local authorities are required to establish procedures for considering representations, including complaints, about how they are discharging

---

15 *The Children Act 1989 Guidance and Regulation* Vol 3, para 2.66.
16 As suggested in para 2.66 of the *Guidance*, above.
17 *House of Commons Debate, Standing Committee B*, 18 May 1989, cols 137-154; *House of Lords, Official Report*, 20 December 1988, col 1335.

their functions under Part III of the Children Act 1989.[18] The introduction of this procedure was a new legislative initiative. Its effectiveness is continuously monitored by the Social Services Inspectorate, which has established a benchmark for good practice which indicates the steps which must be taken in order to meet 16 standards.[19] Those entitled to use the procedures are any child being looked after by the local authority, a child in need, the child's parent, any other person who has parental responsibility for the child, any local authority foster parent, and 'such other person as the authority considers has a sufficient interest in the child's welfare to warrant his representations being considered by them'.[20] Representations and complaints relating to matters which fall outside Part III strictly ought not to be dealt with under the procedure established by section 26. However, guidance stipulates that it is good practice for local authorities to extend the procedure to complaints about child protection issues, and more specifically 'about inter-agency case conferences and their recommendations'.[1] This view is reiterated in 'Working Together',[2] where it is recommended that area child protection committees should establish procedures to handle representations and complaints, in particular about child protection conferences. The procedures established under section 26 must be publicised.[3] Regulations set out the way in which they should operate and each authority must use the regulations as the basis for the creation of their own procedure.[4]

The procedure has three possible stages. The first is the informal stage, where an attempt is made to solve the problem through discussion, reconsideration and explanation.[5] Where this fails, and a formal rep-

---

18 S 26(3). These include complaints about day care, services to support children within the family home, accommodation of a child, after care and decisions relating to the placement of a child or the handling of a child's case: *Children Act 1989 Guidance and Regulations, Vol 3, Family Placements*, para 10.8.

19 *The Inspection of the complaints procedures in local authority social services departments*, (SSI, HMSO, 1993); *The second overview report of the complaints procedures in local authority social services departments*, (SSI, HMSO, 1994); *SSI inspection of complaints procedures in local authority social services departments – third overview report*, (SSI, HMSO, 1996).

20 S 26(3).

1   *Children Act 1989 Guidance and Regulations, Vol 3, Family Placements*, para 10.10.

2   *Working Together under the Children Act 1989: A guide to arrangements for inter-agency co-operation for the protection of children from abuse* (DoH, HMSO, 1991), para 6.21. Some local authorities have embraced a wide interpretation of when the procedure should be available and who should be permitted to use it, see C Williams and H Jordan *The Children Act Complaints Procedure: A study of six local authority areas* (University of Sheffield, 1996). See also B Schwehr *A complaint about complaining under the Children Act 1989* (1992) 11 Litigation 331, who argues that 'the jurisdictional line is hard to draw'.

3   S 26(8). For research showing the variable nature of this publicity, see C Williams and H Jordan *Factors relating to publicity surrounding the complaints procedure under the Children Act 1989* (1996) 8 CFLQ 337.

4   Representations Procedure (Children) Regulations 1991, SI 1991/894.

5   Ibid, para 10.13-10.14.

resentation is made, an investigation must take place. At this stage the local authority must appoint an independent person to take part in considering the complainant's representations, and a response should be formulated within 28 days.[6] Where this fails to placate the complainant the matter moves on to the third stage where a panel, which must include at least one person who is independent of the local authority, is established to consider the complaint.[7] The complainant is entitled to attend the meeting of the panel and he may be accompanied by another person of his choice who may speak on his behalf.[8] Alternatively he may make written submissions. The local authority may also make oral or written submissions, as may the independent person, if different from the independent person appointed to the panel.[9] This last is a very strange arrangement and does not appear to comply with the normal rules of natural justice. How can a panel member be truly independent where he or she has already been involved in the complaint at an earlier stage and has already formed an opinion on the complaint?

After considering the complaint, the panel must decide on their recommendations, record them with their reasons and notify the complainant, the local authority, the independent person and any other person who the local authority considers has sufficient interest in the case.[10] The local authority, together with the independent person on the panel, must consider what action, if any, should be taken in relation to the child and the independent person must take part in any decisions about any such action.

This procedure goes some way towards mitigating the limited role of the courts in supervising how local authorities carry out their statutory duties to children in need, children being accommodated and children in care. The courts have no involvement with children in need and accommodated children, and later in this chapter it will be seen that once a care order is made, the court's role comes to an end and it has no jurisdiction to intervene in how the local authority is looking after a child. It is therefore crucial that a person with a grievance about a child's treatment by the local authority should have somewhere to turn, and that there should be at least some independent element in the conduct of an inquiry into that grievance. It should also be stressed that one purpose behind the establishment of this procedure was to give children being looked after by local authorities an avenue for making complaints about the care they are receiving. Tragically, some children, particularly those in residential care, are victims of abuse from the very people with whom they have been placed to protect them

6   Regs 5 and 6. In practice, local authorities find it extremely difficult to observe this time limit and the procedure normally takes far longer.
7   Reg 8(3).
8   Reg 8(6). Therefore the complainant is entitled to bring a lawyer with him.
9   Reg 8(5).
10   Reg 9.

from harm. Although the procedures set up by section 26 are not designed to investigate allegations of child abuse, it is one method open to children to bring what is happening to them to the attention of others in the local authority.

Prior to the introduction of the representations and complaints procedure, the only possible avenue open to an aggrieved party was to seek judicial review. This avenue is now closed unless and until all other avenues of complaint have been exhausted. For this reason judicial review was refused where a local authority failed to provide suitable accommodation for a severely disturbed child,[11] closed a day care nursery attended by children in need,[12] and placed a Vietnamese child away from her sister, who was also being looked after by them, and put her in a home with no suitable provision for her needs.[13] Where the complaints procedure is fully pursued and where the panel makes recommendations then normally the local authority must abide by those recommendations unless they have substantial reasons for not doing so, and their failure to do so may be actionable in judicial review.[14]

Investigating whether a child is suffering, or is likely to suffer, significant harm

It has been seen that children in need are those children who are disabled, or those children whose health or development will be put at risk without the provision of services.[15] An even more serious situation arises where there is reasonable cause to believe or suspect that a child is suffering, or is likely to suffer, significant harm. When such a suspicion is brought to the attention of a local authority[16] they are under a duty to investigate.[17] Section 47(1) of the Children Act 1989 provides:

'Where a local authority –
(a) are informed that a child who lives, or is found, in their area –

---

11 *R v Birmingham City Council, ex p A* [1997] 2 FLR 841. Moreover, judicial review may be inappropriate, and the complaints procedure an entirely appropriate response to the grievance. See further, C Williams *R v Birmingham City Council, ex p A: An unsuitable case for judicial review?* (1998) 10 CFLQ 89.

12 *R v London Borough of Barnet, ex p B* [1994] 1 FLR 592.

13 *R v Kingston-upon-Thames Royal Borough, ex p T* [1994] 1 FLR 798.

14 *R v Avon County Council, ex p M* [1994] 2 FLR 1006.

15 S 17(10).

16 See H Cleaver and P Freeman *Parental Perspectives in Cases of Suspected Child Abuse* (HMSO, 1995). They identify five types of family whose characteristics might be borne in mind when abuse is suspected: multi-problem families; specific problem families; acutely distressed families; infiltrating perpetrators; and outside perpetrators.

17 It is estimated that about 160,000 s 47 enquiries take place in England each year, including 25,000 where the suspicions are unsubstantiated. See J Gibbons, B Gallagher, C Bell and D Gordon *Development After Physical Abuse in Early Childhood: A follow-up study of children on protection registers* (HMSO, 1995).

(i) is the subject of an emergency protection order; or
(ii) is in police protection; or
(b) have reasonable cause to suspect that a child who lives, or is found, in their area is suffering, or is likely to suffer, significant harm,
the authority shall make, or cause to be made, such inquiries as they consider necessary to enable them to decide whether they should take any action to safeguard and promote the child's welfare.'[18]

The value of different agencies working together in the early detection and prevention of child abuse is emphasised in the guidance issued under the Act.[19] Each local authority, under the auspices of their area child protection committee,[1] must draw up child protection procedures to which all collaborating agencies and persons are expected to adhere. Section 47(9) and (11) emphasise the importance of inter-agency co-operation by placing a duty on specified persons to assist the local authority in conducting their inquiry.[2] The focus of the inquiry must be directed in particular towards establishing whether the local authority should initiate any court proceedings or exercise any of their other powers under the Act.[3]

The conduct of an investigation under section 47 requires not only the co-operation of other agencies, but also the co-operation of persons with parental responsibility for the child. Section 47 does not give a local authority any coercive powers. There is nothing in section 47 which empowers a local authority to enter premises, despite the fact that one of their duties when conducting their investigation is to take such steps as are reasonably practicable to obtain access to the child.[4] Rather, the local authority are reliant on the person who has care of the child allowing them to see the child. However, co-operation from such a person may be forthcoming when it is explained to him that if a person conducting an inquiry under section 47 is refused access, or denied information as to the

---

18 The local authority have an identical duty where they themselves have obtained an emergency protection order with respect to a child: s 47(2).
19 *Working Together under the Children Act 1989* (DOH, 1991); the absolute necessity for inter-agency co-operation has been demonstrated many times in the reports of official inquiries into the deaths of children where child protection procedures have failed.
1   Which are multi-disciplinary bodies.
2   Unless it would be unreasonable in all the circumstances of the case (s 47(10)). The persons specified are any local authority, any local education authority, any local housing authority, any health authority, and any other person authorised by the Secretary of State. Surprisingly, and arguably wrongly, the police are omitted from this list. See further E Birchall and C Hallett *Working Together in Child Protection* (HMSO, 1995); C Hallett *Inter-Agency Co-ordination in Child Protection* (HMSO, 1995).
3   S 47(3). H Cleaver and P Freeman *Parental Perspectives in Cases of Suspected Child Abuse* (HMSO, 1995) highlight the fine balance which has to be drawn between the benefits of intervention and its potential for doing harm.
4   S 47(4).

child's whereabouts, 'the authority *shall*[5] apply for an emergency protection order, a child assessment order, a care order or a supervision order with respect to the child unless they are satisfied that his welfare can be satisfactorily safeguarded without them doing so'.[6] It is suggested that only rarely should a local authority be so satisfied without actually seeing and talking to the child. Tragically, many children who have died at the hands of those looking after them are those children to whom social workers and others have not insisted on having proper access.[7]

Once a suspicion has been raised that a child is suffering, or is likely to suffer, significant harm, the local authority have a duty to consider whether some kind of continuing surveillance of the child is necessary. If, at the conclusion of their inquiries, the local authority decide not to apply for a court order in respect of the child, they must decide whether it is appropriate to review the case at a later date and, if so, set a date for the review.[8] There may be no need for legal intervention even where significant harm is discovered. Where parents and other persons caring for the child are willing to work with social workers and other professionals in addressing the concerns which have arisen, it may be decided that the child can be adequately protected if he remains at home while work with the family is attempted.[9]

Can a court prohibit a section 47 investigation?

In *D v D (County Court Jurisdiction: Injunctions)*[10] a county court judge attempted to prevent a local authority and the police from pursuing their inquiries under section 47 by issuing an injunction against both. There were proceedings before the judge for a residence order, and he was clearly

5   Emphasis added.
6   S 47(6).
7   See particularly *A Child in Mind: The report on the death of Kimberley Carlile*, Greenwich London Borough Council (1987). See too *A Child in Trust: Report on the death of Jasmine Beckford*, London Borough of Brent (1988); *Whose Child: Report on the death of Tyra Henry*, London Borough of Greenwich (1987); *Child Abuse: A study of inquiry reports 1973-1981* (HMSO, 1982).
8   S 47(7).
9   A Government commissioned programme of research into child protection, stemming from public anxiety about the safety of children and agency responses, was initiated following the Cleveland Inquiry *Report of the Inquiry into Child Abuse in Cleveland 1987*, Cm 412 (1988). A summary of the findings of 20 studies from that research programme was published in 1995: *Child Protection: Messages from Research* (HMSO, 1995); for a critique see C Wattam *The social construction of child abuse for practical policy purposes – a review of Child Protection: Messages from Research* (1996) 8 CFLQ 189. Allied with the research, an extensive review of the literature available up to 1992 on the effectiveness of agency interventions was undertaken. This was designed to inform the planning of future studies, and also had an influence on the way the DOH programme was originally conceived. See D Gough *Child Abuse Interventions: A review of the research literature* (HMSO, 1993).
10 [1993] 2 FLR 802.

incensed at the manner in which the local authority were carrying out their investigation at a time when the court was seised of matters relating to the welfare of the children.[11] On appeal the judge was held to have exceeded his jurisdiction in issuing the injunctions. However, the Court of Appeal stated, obiter, that the judge could have made a prohibited steps order to prevent a person with parental responsibility from allowing the child to be interviewed, or examined in a way which the court thought would be detrimental to his welfare. Thus although a court has no power to prohibit an investigation by a local authority, it can frustrate it by prohibiting a parent from consenting to the child being investigated. It has been seen that the co-operation of persons caring for the child is normally needed for a section 47 inquiry to be effective. Were a court to exercise powers to prohibit such co-operation, the inquiry would almost certainly have to be abandoned. Unless the court is entirely confident that it is in possession of all relevant information about the child and his family, it is suggested that it is a very risky step indeed for a court to seek to inhibit a local authority from carrying out their investigative duties. The main purpose of a section 47 inquiry is to discover whether there are grounds for initiating care or other proceedings. Without the necessary evidence, any application for an order will inevitably fail. While in *D v D (County Court Jurisdiction: Injunctions)* itself the judge may have had good cause to be critical of the local authority,[12] it is suggested that the power to issue a prohibited steps order in this context should be exercised with the greatest of caution.[13]

Local authority responses to significant harm

Determining which is the most effective response to a discovery that a child is suffering, or is likely to suffer, significant harm is not easy for local authorities. The main system which is used to protect children is to hold a multi-agency case conference. At that case conference, persons with knowledge of the child and his family pool information about the child, make recommendations for future action, and decide whether the child should be put on a child protection register.[14] This register lists all the

---

11 On the difficulties that are posed generally for the courts where a child is thought to be at risk, but proceedings other than Part IV proceedings are before the court, see N Wall *The courts and child protection – the challenge of hybrid cases* (1997) 9 CFLQ 345.
12 The Court of Appeal was divided on this.
13 *D v D (County Court Jurisdiction: Injunctions)* is also discussed in ch 2.
14 See E Farmer and M Owen *Child Protection Practice: Private risks and public remedies – Decision making, intervention and outcome in child protection work* (HMSO, 1995) where those factors which are particularly important in deciding whether to register a child are discussed. J Gibbons, S Conroy and C Bell *Operating the Child Protection System: A study of child protection practices in English local authorities* (HMSO, 1995) found it was universally the case that the families of those children who were registered received significantly more in the way of services than those where the decision was taken not to register.

children in the locality for whom there is an inter-agency protection plan.[15] The plan itemises the steps which have been agreed about what should be done to protect the child and it is for the agency representatives to decide how responsibility for implementing the various parts of the plan is to be allocated. A date for reviewing how the plan is working will be set. The child of sufficient age and understanding is encouraged to attend at the conference, though normally not to be there throughout, so that his voice about his own future is properly heard. Parents and persons with parental responsibility should also be invited to attend unless there are exceptional reasons for their exclusion.[16]

The choice for a local authority where they have reasonable cause to believe that a child is suffering, or is likely to suffer, significant harm, is either to leave the child where he is and to put resources into protecting the child at home, or to take care proceedings. In making this choice there are various issues to be balanced.[17] Some have argued that:

> 'Every child must have the basic right of remaining in his own family unless there are compelling reasons which justify his removal. This presumption in favour of parental autonomy should only be rebutted by proof of some specific harm to the child or of the disruption or absence of parental ties. Even when this is proved, however, there should be a presumption against removal of the child from his home; such intervention should be a last resort. Removal should require a thorough investigation of alternative ways of dealing with the situation (for example by voluntary services and support) and evidence that such measures are inadequate.'[18]

---

15 In 1996, 28,000 children were registered on the child protection register: see (1997) 9 Children's Services News 5. In *R v Hampshire County Council, ex p H* (1998) 142 Sol Jo LB 188, the Court of Appeal held that there must be sufficient evidence of actual or likely significant harm to a child, and of its cause, before registration.

16 A detailed account of the working of case conferences is given in *Working Together* (HMSO, 1991). For some of the difficulties surrounding case conferences see D Savas *Parental participation in case conferences* (1996) 8 CFLQ 57; J Thoburn, A Lewis and D Shemmings *Paternalism or Partnership? Family Involvement in the Child Protection Process* (HMSO, 1995).

17 See E Sharland, D Jones, J Aldgate, H Seal and M Croucher *Professional Intervention in Child Sexual Abuse* (HMSO, 1995). Sharland et al undertook a study of families where sexual abuse was suspected. Their concern was to investigate whether the process of investigating sexual abuse might be capable of doing harm over and above that caused by the abuse itself. The team came increasingly to doubt whether protection procedures were always adequate to deal with sexual abuse referrals, because the cross currents of general need and specific risk were often very complex and sometimes impossible to distinguish one from the other. They concluded that there was a need both to improve services generally, and to redress the balance between child protection on the one hand and child welfare on the other.

18 A Morris, H Giller, E Zwed and H Geach *Justice for Children* (Macmillan, 1980) p 128.

The Children Act 1989, in part, reflects this thinking. It has been seen that a local authority are under a duty to provide services for children who would otherwise be at risk of sustaining impaired health or development, and that such services must be directed to preventing the need to take care proceedings.[19]

However, the sting in the tail in the reasoning in the above quotation is in the last sentence. There is evidence that children who have suffered significant harm through sexual abuse and other forms of ill-treatment will often continue to be abused even though the adults in the family receive treatment. Information gathered prior to the implementation of the Children Act 1989 revealed that neglecting families can drift for years beyond the boundaries of acceptable parenting without a systematic assessment being made of the situation, or legal proceedings being instituted.[20] For the law to require that evidence should be produced in *all* cases to demonstrate that services and other measures are inadequate could mean that some children who are suffering significant harm will continue to suffer for some considerable period before there is legal intervention. Yet placing a child in care may not be the best solution for the child. Research has demonstrated that 'far from remedying existing deficiencies ... periods in public care have further impaired the life chances of some children and young people because of poor educational achievement, uncorrected health problems and maladjustment'.[1]

The dilemma for child protection law and procedures is how to 'ensure that a child shall not be separated from his or her parents against their will, except when competent authorities subject to judicial review determine, in accordance with applicable law and procedures, that such separation is necessary for the best interests of the child'.[2] The law must strike a proper balance between giving due weight to the right of everyone to respect for his private and family life,[3] and giving due weight to the rights and freedoms of the child. The dilemma is made more complex because the rights and freedoms of the child are inextricably bound up with the rights and freedoms of the parents. The notion that every child

---

19 S 17; Sch 2, para 7; and see above. For an account of different European approaches to child protection see B Luckock, R Vogler and H Keating *Child protection in France and England – authority, legalism and social work practice* (1996) 8 CFLQ 297; and *The Belgian Flemish child protection system – confidentiality, voluntarism and coercion* (1997) 9 CFLQ 101.

20 *Protecting Children* (HMSO, 1988) p 7.

1 *Patterns and Outcomes in Child Placement, Messages from Current Research and their Implications* (HMSO, 1991) p 7. J Gibbons, B Gallagher, C Bell and D Gordon *Development After Physical Abuse in Early Childhood: A follow-up study of children on protection registers* (HMSO, 1995) found that while for a majority of children placed in substitute care there were measurable gains in their physical growth and vocabulary, there was no evidence of general advantage in their mental well-being or behaviour.

2 See Art 9 of the United Nations Convention on the Rights of the Child.

3 A right embodied in Art 8 of the European Convention on Human Rights and Fundamental Freedoms.

has the right to be brought up by his own family is a notion which normally accords with the child's wishes and feelings, and is generally believed to promote his best interests. Yet, when taken to an extreme, such a notion may identify a child's interests too closely with his parents, and create a climate of unwillingness to remove a child from his home even when this is necessary to protect the child.[4] It may lead to responses to significant harm failing to give adequate respect to the child's right to be treated as an autonomous individual.

The power of a court to direct a section 37 investigation

One of the times when the welfare of a child may come under scrutiny is when an application is made to a court in family proceedings. The question of the welfare of a child may arise in any family proceedings, but the most common occasion is when persons are divorcing. Parties to a divorce are required to provide a fairly extensive statement of arrangements about the future upbringing of any children of their family who are under the age of 16. This statement will be scrutinised by the court, and in every case the court must consider whether it should exercise any of its powers under the Act with respect to any of the children.[5] Sometimes these arrangements give rise to concern, or even alarm, and the court may take the view that the position of a child should be further investigated. One response is to request a welfare officer's report under section 7. Such a request may be made in any case where the court feels in need of assistance in determining the welfare of a child, and is the appropriate response where the matter can be handled in purely private law proceedings.

Where there is serious concern about the upbringing of a child, such that the court takes the view that it may be appropriate to make a care or supervision order with respect to him, section 37 provides that the court may direct a local authority to undertake an investigation of the child's circumstances. In responding to this direction, and when undertaking their investigation, the local authority must consider whether they should apply for a care or supervision order, provide services or assistance for the child or his family, or take any other action with respect to the child.[6]

---

4   E Farmer and M Owen, in *Child Protection Practice: Private risks and public remedies – Decision making, intervention and outcome in child protection work* (HMSO, 1995), found there was a close link between the adequacy of the initial child protection plans and the child's safety. Whereas in 80% of cases the child was protected where the original plan was sound, in 50% of cases the child was subsequently re-abused or neglected when the original plan was deficient. They also found that in some circumstances children who stayed at home were exposed to serious continuing risks where social workers had developed high thresholds of tolerance of parenting standards of families well known to them.

5   Matrimonial Causes Act 1973, s 41(1); in exceptional circumstances the court may direct that the decree nisi is not made absolute (s 41(2)).

6   Children Act 1989, s 37(2).

Because it is the court which is instigating the inquiry, it may wish to specify particular matters which it would like the local authority to look into. In *Re H (A Minor) (Section 37 Direction)*,[7] which concerned a residence order application by a lesbian couple who were looking after an eight-month-old child under what amounted to a quasi-surrogacy and backdoor adoption arrangement, Scott Baker J particularly wanted the local authority to consider the emotional and other difficulties the child was likely to face as she grew up. He asked the local authority to inform him of whether the applicants were likely to be able to handle such difficulties; what counselling or psychiatric help might be available; and if such difficulties could not be overcome with help, how these should be weighed against the possibility of removing the child from her present carers. Scott Baker J stated that a child's circumstances should be widely construed, and should include any situation which may have bearing on the child being likely to suffer significant harm in the future.[8]

Where a local authority undertake an investigation under a direction given under section 37 and decide not to apply for a care or supervision order, they must give the court their reasons. They must also inform the court of any service or assistance which they have provided, or intend to provide, for the child and his family, and of any other action which they have taken, or propose to take, in relation to the child.[9] However, it was held in *Nottinghamshire County Council v P*[10] that a court has no power to direct the local authority to initiate care proceedings where it is not satisfied with the authority's reasons for failing to do so. *Nottinghamshire County Council v P* is an example of a case where who had the final decision-making power was crucial to its outcome. On the one hand the trial judge and the Court of Appeal were in no doubt that a care order was necessary to prevent the children from suffering further significant harm; on the other hand the local authority were obdurate in their refusal to pursue an application for a care order. The decision-making power lay with the local authority and, as Sir Stephen Brown P said, 'if a local authority doggedly resists taking the steps which are appropriate to the case of children at risk of suffering significant harm it appears that the court is powerless'.[11] By way of contrast, the local authority's duties under section 37 do not include the duty or power to advocate any point of view in relation to the private law dispute between the original parties.[12] Any other approach might enable local authorities to circumvent the principle

---

7   [1993] 2 FLR 541.

8   See *Re CE (Section 37 Direction)* [1995] 1 FLR 26 for guidance both on the appointment of a guardian ad litem when a s 37 direction has been given, and on the appointment and funding of a guardian ad litem in private law proceedings.

9   S 37(3); they must provide this information within eight weeks unless the court directs otherwise (s 37(4)).

10 [1993] 2 FLR 134.

11 Ibid, at p 148.

12 For this reason, local authorities are prohibited from seeking leave to apply for a residence or contact order (s 9(2)).

that it is only where significant harm has been established that an authority can seek to interfere in where the child is to live and with whom the child is to have contact. Consequently, local authorities are not permitted to be made parties to the private law proceedings in which a section 37 direction is made, nor may the authority attempt directly to influence the outcome of these proceedings by adducing evidence.[13] The authority's role is confined to providing reports for the court.[14]

Where, during the course of their section 37 inquiries, the local authority uncover matters which lead them to believe that a child is being abused they can, of course, take steps to protect the child by making an application in care proceedings. Difficulty occurs where the alleged abuser denies harming the child but the non-abusing parent accepts the local authority's opinion and promises to prevent the alleged abuser having contact.[15] In such a case the local authority may choose not to institute care proceedings because the non-abusing parent's control over contact renders the child safe. However, such an outcome places the alleged abuser in an invidious position. He is being refused contact in the absence of a proper forensic determination of whether the behaviour of which he is accused did in fact occur. This is what happened in *Re S (Contact: Evidence)*.[16] The father sought to challenge an allegation of sexual abuse made in a section 37 report requested in contact proceedings. He applied for a *subpoena duces tecum* to obtain copies of the evidence held by the police with a view to it being examined by an expert. The judge refused his application because of the costs which would be incurred and made an order for supervised contact. Allowing the father's appeal, the Court of Appeal held that the effect of the judge's ruling was to deprive the child of unsupervised contact with her father simply on the basis of what the local authority had said. A court should not accept a local authority's allegation in a section 37 report that a parent has harmed his child without giving the parent a proper opportunity to challenge what is said against him.

Child assessment orders

It has been seen that an assessment of whether a child is suffering, or is likely to suffer, significant harm can normally only be made if the child is seen and examined and, where appropriate, interviewed. Persons with parental responsibility, and other persons caring for the child, also need to be interviewed, and their part in the cause for concern about the child needs to be explained to them. However, such persons are sometimes uncooperative in allowing access to the child; or they may prevent a proper

---

13 *F v Cambridgeshire County Council* [1995] 1 FLR 516; see too, ch 2.
14 The content of such reports may, however, influence the court in relation to the matter in dispute.
15 Or promises to ensure that contact is supervised.
16 [1998] 1 FLR 798.

assessment from taking place by refusing to allow the child to be medically, or otherwise, examined. Where access is denied, or the person making enquiries is denied information as to the child's whereabouts, the local authority must apply for a court order unless they are satisfied that the child's welfare can otherwise be satisfactorily safeguarded.[17] It is suggested that this latter response should be most unusual, because it is a dangerously optimistic reaction to a suspicion of abuse which has not been properly investigated. Normally the most appropriate response where access is denied is to apply for an emergency protection order.[18] Where access is allowed, but where an assessment of the child is being frustrated, the most appropriate response might be to apply for a child assessment order.[19] The effect of this order is to place any person who is in a position to produce the child under a duty to produce him to the persons named in the order, and to comply with the court's directions.[20]

Section 43(1) provides that a child assessment order may be made if, but only if, the court is satisfied that:

'(a) the applicant has reasonable cause to suspect that the child is suffering, or is likely to suffer, significant harm;
(b) an assessment of the child's health or development, or the way in which he has been treated, is required to enable the applicant to determine whether or not the child is suffering, or is likely to suffer, significant harm; and
(c) it is unlikely that such an assessment will be made, or be satisfactory, in the absence of an order under this section.'

It can be seen that the standard of proof which must be satisfied is one of reasonable suspicion only. Because this standard of proof is relatively low, the type of intervention allowed is strictly limited. The order gives the local authority a time-limited period of a maximum of seven days in which to discover whether there is any real foundation to their suspicion.[1] It is the court which takes control over the type of assessment which should take place. The court may give such directions as it thinks fit, and the order authorises any person carrying out an assessment to do so in accordance with the terms of the order.[2] Those carrying out the assessment are limited as to where the assessment is carried out: a child may only be kept away from home where this is in accordance with directions specified in the order; where it is necessary for the purposes of the assessment; and where it is for such period, or periods, as may be specified in the

---

17 S 47(6).
18 S 44(1)(b): see below.
19 For a general evaluation of the child assessment order see R Lavery, *The child assessment order – a reassessment* (1996) 8 CFLQ 41.
20 S 43(6); this person may not, of course, be a person with parental responsibility.
1   S 43(5).
2   S 43(6), (7).

order.[3] Where a child is to be kept away from home, the court must give directions about contact arrangements.[4] The voice of the child may also be determinative in a case of this kind. A child who has sufficient understanding to make an informed decision may refuse to submit to a medical, psychiatric or other assessment.[5]

It can be seen from this structure that it is up to the court to determine how far a child assessment order can be used as a 'fishing expedition' to discover whether the suspicion that the child is suffering, or is likely to suffer, significant harm is soundly based. It is not clear to what extent it would be appropriate for the court to be very specific in the type of assessment it authorises, and to what extent it can leave this to the discretion of the local authority. Very little use has been made of the child assessment order[6] and there is no reported case law.[7] It seems that the court is expected to be cautious about authorising removal of the child from the home. A fine balance must be struck between taking the steps which are needed to discover whether or not the local authority's decisions can be verified, and causing unnecessary distress and anxiety to a child and his parents in a case where there is nothing untoward happening. The caution surrounding the structure of child assessment orders can be partly explained by the crisis which occurred in Cleveland in the period immediately preceding the passing of the Children Act 1989. A large number of children were suspected of being sexually abused, and many children were subjected to forms of interviewing which in some cases could more properly be described as interrogations.[8] Hence the control given to courts to be very specific about the manner in which the investigation is carried out.[9]

If, on hearing an application for a child assessment order, the court is satisfied that there are grounds for making an emergency protection order, it may make such an order, and it must not make a child assessment order where it feels that it ought to make an emergency protection order.[10] This provision is designed to obviate the risk of children being left in a

---

3   S 43(9).

4   S 43(10).

5   S 43(7); and see above ch 2, on the power of the High Court to overrule decisions made by a competent child.

6   See *Children Act Reports* (1992/93) Cm, 2584, Table 3.1. Less than 100 applications for such an order were made in 1993, and about a quarter of these were subsequently withdrawn.

7   There is information which suggests that social workers are unhappy about the alienating effect of such an order, and consider that there is no need for an order where parents can be persuaded to co-operate: see J Dickens, *Assessment and the control of social work: analysis of reasons for the non-use of the child assessment order* [1993] JSWFL 88 .

8   *Report of the Inquiry into Child Abuse in Cleveland 1987*, Cm 412 (1988).

9   For an account of the effect of the Cleveland Inquiry on the work of those involved with child sexual abuse see A Bentovim, *Cleveland 10 years on – A mental health perspective* [1998] Fam Law 153-157, 202-207 and 267-269.

10 S 43(4).

position of immediate danger because the wrong proceedings have been commenced. For the same reason, a court may treat an application for a child assessment order as an application for an emergency protection order.[11]

Protecting children in an emergency

Normally, when it is believed that a child is suffering, or is likely to suffer, significant harm, a social worker, or other person, should explain to the child what steps are going to be taken to protect him. Before a child is removed from his home and familiar surroundings he should be given the opportunity to discuss this, and to come to terms with proposed changes in his upbringing before these changes are implemented. Ideally he needs to know in advance when he will be taken from his parents, and he should meet the persons who will be looking after him before any transfer to their care is made. However, sometimes there will be very great concern about the child's situation, and its urgency may therefore justify immediate steps being taken to protect him. It is in these circumstances that an application can, and indeed should, be made under section 44 for an emergency protection order.

The effect of an emergency protection order is that it operates as a direction to any person who is in the position to do so to comply with a request to produce the child. In addition, it authorises either the child's removal to accommodation provided by the applicant, or the prevention of his removal from any hospital or other place in which he is currently being accommodated.[12] Clearly an order which authorises the sudden removal of a child from his home, often without any prior warning, is a powerful order which could have a traumatic effect on the child and his parents. Other relatives of the child are also likely to be shocked, angry or distressed when an emergency protection order is obtained. Therefore there is tight legal control over when an emergency protection order may be granted, the purpose of this control being to limit the availability of the order to those circumstances which merit such urgent intervention. There is further tight control over the duration of such an order and over the powers which may be exercised in relation to the child while an order is in force.

The grounds for an emergency protection order

Section 44(1) provides that where an application is made for an emergency protection order the court may make the order if, but only if, it is satisfied that:

11 S 43(3).
12 S 44(4).

'(a) there is reasonable cause to believe that the child is likely to suffer significant harm if –
   (i) he is not removed to accommodation provided by or on behalf of the applicant; or
   (ii) he does not remain in the place in which he is then being accommodated;
(b) in the case of an application made by a local authority –
   (i) enquiries are being made with respect to the child under section 47(1)(b); and
   (ii) those enquiries are being frustrated by access to the child being unreasonably refused to a person authorised to seek access and that the applicant has reasonable cause to believe that access to the child is required as a matter of urgency.'[13]

Paragraph (a) requires the applicant to raise the anxiety level of the court to the point where the court has reasonable cause to believe that the child is likely to suffer significant harm unless an emergency protection order is made. In doing this the applicant can put any information he wishes before the court, and the court can take it into account regardless of any enactment or rule of law which would otherwise prevent it from doing so, provided that, in the opinion of the court, it is relevant to the application.[14] The applicant must further persuade the court that there is a causative link between the harm being likely to occur and the child being removed from, or remaining in, his present accommodation. Thus, for example, if the child is reasonably believed to have suffered a serious non-accidental injury, but if the person who is suspected of having injured the child has been remanded in custody pending trial, and the person presently caring for him is not implicated in the abuse in any way, it is suggested that it is most unlikely there are grounds for making an emergency protection order. On the other hand, where the alleged abuser has moved out of the home, but where there is uncertainty about where he is living, or whether he will stay away from the child, there may be grounds for an order being made. Where the alleged abuser is still in the home, or intends to discharge the child from hospital, there are likely to be very clear grounds for making the order.[15]

Paragraph (b) is aimed at those cases where a local authority have reasonable cause to suspect that a child in their area is suffering, or is

13 Para (c) makes similar, but not identical, provisions in the case of an application made by an authorised person, presently only the NSPCC.
14 S 45(7).
15 Munchausen syndrome by proxy, ie where a parent fabricates illness on behalf of a child, often occurs in hospital. For a general discussion of the many problems associated with the syndrome see J Horwath and B Lawson (eds) *Trust Betrayed* (National Children's Bureau, 1995); see also C Williams and V T Bevan *The secret observation of children in hospital* (1988) Lancet 780; T Thomas *Child protection, privacy and covert video surveillance* (1995) 17 JSWFL 311.

likely to suffer, significant harm, and where they are therefore under a duty under section 47(1)(b) to make enquiries about the child in order to decide what action they should take to safeguard or promote his welfare.[16] In conducting such an enquiry, the local authority must normally obtain access to the child.[17] This provision reflects the findings made in various inquiries which have been conducted into cases where child protection procedures have failed to protect children from being killed as a result of ill-treatment and neglect. These inquiries have emphasised that it is usually imperative that access is obtained to a child where there is a suspicion that he is suffering, or is likely to suffer, significant harm.[18] Unless the child is seen, and in the case of a young child physically examined for signs of injuries, ill-treatment or neglect, and in the case of an older child spoken to in private as well, it may be very easy for a parent to conceal significant harm to the child from a concerned professional. It should be noted that when an application is made under section 44(1)(b) a court is empowered to make an emergency protection order on the basis that the applicant has reasonable cause to *suspect* that the child is suffering, or is likely to suffer, significant harm[19] and has reasonable cause to believe that access to the child is urgently required. This is a lesser standard than the requirement that the court should have reasonable cause to *believe* that such harm is likely to occur, which must be proved in relation to applications made under section 44(1)(a). Clearly, where access is being refused, it may be impossible for the applicant to obtain the evidence to substantiate a belief, and therefore a reasonable suspicion provides an adequate basis for an order being made.

Including an exclusion requirement in an emergency protection order

Sometimes a preferable response to removal of the child is for action to be taken against the person who is alleged to be endangering him. Provisions introduced in October 1997 allow for this. Section 44A(1)[20] provides that the court may include an exclusion requirement in an emergency protection order provided that the conditions in section 44A(2) are satisfied. In essence these conditions require the court to be satisfied that there is reasonable cause to believe that the child will not be likely to suffer significant harm, or that enquiries about him and access to him will cease to be frustrated, if a person is excluded from the house where the child lives.[1] The court must also ensure that another person living in the same

---

16 On s 47 generally, see above.
17 S 47(4).
18 See particularly *A Child in Mind: The report on the death of Kimberley Carlile*, Greenwich London Borough Council (1987).
19 As this is the wording of s 47(1)(b) under which the enquiry was initiated.
20 Inserted, together with s 44B, by the Family Law Act 1996, s 52, Sch 6 para 3.
1 Including, where appropriate, a defined area around the house (s 44A(3)).

house consents to the exclusion order and is able and willing to care properly for the child. The reason why an exclusion order is in addition to, rather than an alternative to, an emergency protection order is to give the local authority the power immediately to remove the child where the co-operation of the person caring for the child is withdrawn, or the order is otherwise broken.

The attraction of using an exclusion requirement is much stronger where the applicant can be confident that it will be backed up by strong enforcement powers. This is recognised in the legislation. A power of arrest may be added to an exclusion requirement. This permits a police officer to arrest without warrant any person who he has reasonable cause to believe to be in breach of the requirement.[2] Consequently, any breach of the order should lead to the arrest of the person excluded and this should avoid the necessity to remove the child, except in those cases where the person caring for the child has colluded in the breach.

A court may accept an undertaking from the relevant person in any case where it has power to include an exclusion requirement in the emergency protection order, but a power of arrest may not be added to an undertaking.[3] As this power appears essential to ensure full protection of the child it is to be hoped that the power to accept undertakings will only rarely be exercised.[4]

Powers of entry and police powers

Sometimes an applicant for an emergency protection order may be unsure of the child's whereabouts, or be denied entry on to premises where he suspects the child to be. Sometimes he may have reasonable cause to believe that there is another child on the premises with respect to whom an emergency protection order ought to be made. In cases of this kind the applicant should apply for orders under section 48(3) and (4) which authorise him to enter premises and search for the children concerned. However, such orders do not authorise the applicant to break into premises by force; where force is needed the police must be involved and a warrant obtained under section 48(9).[5] The police have their own separate powers to remove children to suitable accommodation and to keep them there, or to prevent the child's removal from hospital or any other place.[6] A police

2   S 44A(5).
3   S 44B.
4   Undertakings are permitted despite a firm recommendation to the contrary by the Law Commission, see *Domestic Violence and Occupation of the Family Home* Law Com No 207, para 6.15.
5   See too the Police and Criminal Evidence Act 1984, s 17(1)(e), which authorises the police to enter premises without a warrant where there is an immediate risk to life or limb.
6   Dame Margaret Booth *Delay in Public Law Children Act Cases – Second Report* (1996) found that in some areas police protection powers, rather than emergency protection orders, were used when the crisis arose out of hours: at para 8.15.

constable may exercise these powers where he has reasonable cause to believe that the child would otherwise be likely to suffer significant harm.[7] Section 46 provides a code of guidance on how the police should exercise their powers, and how they should inform the parents and liaise with the local authority once they have taken the child into police protection. In difficult cases, particularly where it is anticipated that those looking after the child will respond to being served with an emergency protection order with violence, police involvement is likely to be an added feature of the implementation of an emergency protection order.

Court control over emergency protection orders

In urgent child protection cases the law seeks to strike a proper balance between protecting children from suffering significant harm by authorising their immediate removal to, or retention in, a place of safety, and allowing those who are caring for a child to have the opportunity to give an explanation for the child's condition before the child is taken from them. Clearly, because emergency protection orders are, as their title makes manifest, for emergency situations only, it is often essential that the application is made ex parte. Indeed, in some cases if the person caring for the child were to be alerted in advance to the fact that an application for an order was being made, this could expose the child to an even greater risk of suffering significant harm. Most applications for emergency protection orders are made to magistrates, and the justices' clerk has an important role in determining whether the application should be heard at an inter partes or ex parte hearing. Rule 4(4) of the Family Proceedings Court (Children Act 1989) Rules 1991 provides that an application may be made ex parte with the leave of the justices' clerk. The clerk therefore acts as a filter to which proceedings are allowed to proceed without the normal safeguard of allowing all interested parties the opportunity to be heard. An ex parte application made during court hours will normally be heard by a bench of magistrates, or a single magistrate, at the court; one made in the evening, during the night, or at a weekend will normally be heard by a magistrate at his or her home. The magistrate must supply reasons why he or she has made, or refused to make, the order.[8] Where the single magistrate, or bench of magistrates, refuse to make an order on an ex parte application they may direct that the application be made inter partes.[9]

The child, a parent, anyone with parental responsibility for the child, or any person with whom the child was living immediately before the making of the order may apply for the emergency protection order to be discharged, but not until at least 72 hours have elapsed since the order

---

7   S 46(1).
8   Family Proceedings Court (Children Act 1989) Rules 1991, r 21(5).
9   R 4(5).

was made.[10] However, this provision does not apply in a case where such a person was given at least one day's clear notice of the hearing at which the order was made, and was present at that hearing.[11] Allowing the order to be challenged after 72 hours gives some measure of safeguard to the interests of those persons affected by an ex parte application; whereas those persons who had the opportunity to attend the hearing, and did attend it, are not further entitled to challenge the order. An emergency protection order lasts for a maximum period of eight days.[12] It can be extended for up to another seven days, but only where the court has reasonable cause to believe that the child is likely to suffer significant harm if the order is not extended, and it may only be extended once.[13]

When making an emergency protection order the court may direct that the applicant, on exercising any powers conferred by the order, be accompanied by a general practitioner, nurse, or health visitor, if he so chooses.[14] This latter provision may assist in preventing removal of a child from the home in a case where fears about his health and safety prove to be unfounded. Section 44(5)(a) provides that the applicant shall only exercise the power to remove, or to prevent the removal of, the child in order to safeguard the welfare of the child. In a case where a doctor is willing to accompany the applicant (who will normally be a social worker) to the child's home, a medical examination of the child in the home might sometimes reveal that there is nothing to give rise to concern that the child is suffering, or is likely to suffer, significant harm. In such a case the child should be left where he is. In a case where the child has been removed or retained under an emergency protection order, and where it appears to the applicant that it is safe to return the child, or to allow him to be removed, the child must be returned or his removal must be allowed.[15]

Parental responsibility and emergency protection orders

An emergency protection order gives the applicant parental responsibility for the child.[16] However, section 44(5)(b) provides that:

> '... the applicant shall take, and shall only take, such action in meeting his parental responsibility for the child as is reasonably required to safeguard or promote the welfare of the child (having regard in particular to the duration of the order).'

---

10 S 45(8), (9).
11 S 45(11); also, an application to discharge cannot be made where the order has been extended under s 45(5): see below.
12 S 45(1), (2), (3).
13 S 45(5), (6).
14 S 45(12).
15 S 44(10).
16 S 44(4)(c).

Thus the applicant should not make a major decision having long-term effects on the child unless it must be made as a matter of urgency. The applicant's parental responsibility is also circumscribed by section 44(13) which requires the applicant to allow the child to have reasonable contact with his parents and other specified persons. This provision reflects the assumption which permeates the Act that maintaining contact between a child and his parents, and others who have parental responsibility for him, is normally in the best interests of the child and must therefore be permitted unless a court authorises otherwise. Such contact may not, of course, be in the interests of the child, and it is important that the applicant draws this to the attention of the court where he believes this to be the case. The court has the power to exercise control over contact arrangements by directing what contact, if any, is or is not to be allowed between the child and any named person.[17]

An applicant for an emergency protection order may sometimes want the child to be medically or psychiatrically examined or otherwise assessed while the emergency protection order is in force. Without such an examination or assessment it may not be possible to establish whether the child is indeed suffering, or likely to suffer, significant harm, and to what that harm is attributable. One of the attributes of parental responsibility is the power to give permission for a child to be examined, or otherwise assessed, and therefore an applicant who has been granted an emergency protection order undoubtedly has this power. However, in 1988 the Cleveland inquiry[18] had concluded that a local authority, and the doctors concerned, had been examining and otherwise assessing children subject to place of safety orders[19] without having proper regard either for the interests and welfare of the children, or for the responsibilities of their parents. This inquiry was highly influential on parts of the Children Act 1989, and one outcome was that courts may now choose whether or not to exercise control over the medical or psychiatric examination or other assessment of children who are the subject of emergency protection orders. Section 44(6)(b) provides that where the court makes an emergency protection order it may give such directions, if any, as it considers appropriate with respect to the medical or psychiatric examination or other assessment of the child. Section 44(8) further provides that such a direction may be to the effect that there should be no such examination or assessment of the child, or no such examination or assessment unless the court directs otherwise.[20] In the face of such a direction, the parental

17 S 44(6)(a).
18 *Report of the Inquiry into Child Abuse in Cleveland 1987,* Cm 412 (1988), which concerned an investigation into the management of cases in Cleveland in which an exceptionally large number of children were suspected of having been sexually abused.
19 Which preceded emergency protection orders.
20 S 44(6)(b) and s 44(8). The child may, if he is of sufficient understanding to make an informed decision, refuse to submit to the examination or other assessment (s 44(7)); see further ch 1.

responsibility of the applicant to permit such an examination or assessment must yield to the superior decision-making powers of the court.

Another of the attributes of parental responsibility is the power to give permission for a child to have medical or psychiatric treatment. The extent to which this power may be exercised by an applicant for an emergency protection order is not entirely clear, because of the limiting impact of section 44(5)(b). It is suggested that this section would appear to mean that the applicant should not normally arrange for the child to have any major medical or psychiatric treatment without the agreement of a parent or other person with parental responsibility, unless the child is in urgent need of such treatment. In such a case, where the parent refuses to agree to the child receiving treatment, and where to authorise the treatment would conflict with the strongly held religious or other beliefs of the parents, it has been held that the matter should be determined, wherever possible, by a High Court judge.[1]

Challenging the making of, or refusal to make, an emergency protection order

Section 45(10) provides that no appeal may be made against the making of, or refusal to make, an emergency protection order, or against any direction given by the court in connection with such an order. In *Essex County Council v F*,[2] Douglas Brown J held that section 45(10) allows no scope for the use of the appellate process, and he ruled that if magistrates act unreasonably in refusing to make an order the only possible remedy is in proceedings brought in judicial review. But of course judicial review proceedings are totally impracticable in an emergency situation; they are not designed to provide speedy relief. Douglas Brown J arrived at his ruling in *Essex County Council v F* with considerable regret because the facts 'cried out for the intervention of the court'; however, he took the view that the words of the statute gave him no alternative.

It is suggested that the combined effect of section 45(10) and the ruling in *Essex County Council v F* is particularly alarming when it is recalled that applications for an emergency protection order are often heard by a single magistrate in his or her own home. It cannot be acceptable that nothing further can be done to protect a child in a case where, as in the *Essex* case, the court's decision is plainly wrong. In that case, the mother promised the local authority that she would not remove the child from her foster parents until the hearing of the application in care proceedings, which would come before the court a few days later. However, other mothers might not be so compliant, and the fact that the child was secure

---

1 See *Re O (A Minor) (Medical Treatment)* [1993] 2 FLR 149 and *Re R (A Minor) (Blood Transfusion)* [1993] 2 FLR 757.
2 [1993] 1 FLR 847.

in the *Essex* case may have lulled the judge into a false sense of security. It is the precedent force of *Essex County Council v F* in relation to other cases which makes the decision so disturbing. A child could be put in grave danger by the wrongful refusal of a court to make an emergency protection order. He might even be badly injured or killed. It cannot be acceptable that the courts are apparently powerless to protect a child in circumstances of this kind.[3]

It is therefore necessary to search for possible solutions and to consider what might be done if a case such as this arose again. One possibility might be for the local authority to make a fresh application for an emergency protection order to a judge, probably a High Court judge. However, there are obstacles to this. It seems implicit in the judgment in *Essex County Council v F* that this is not possible, for otherwise the court hearing the appeal in the *Essex* case could itself have made an ex parte emergency protection order. Also, the Children (Allocation of Proceedings Order) 1991[4] requires such applications to be made in a magistrates' court with only limited exceptions. However, it is nonetheless suggested that, where a child's safety is gravely at risk, a judge might find that he has the power to make the order requested. There is no actual precedent which prevents the judge from making such an order, and he would be likely to be very aware of his own personal responsibility for any possible tragic outcome of his refusal to do so.

Another possibility might be to make an application under the inherent jurisdiction of the High Court. It seems, on its face, that recourse to the inherent jurisdiction would be barred where the applicant is the local authority. Section 100(2) prohibits the exercise of the inherent jurisdiction so as to require a child to be placed in the care of, or to be accommodated by or on behalf of, a local authority, or to give the local authority power to determine any aspect of parental responsibility for the child. However, section 100(4) might possibly come to the assistance of the child. This allows the High Court to grant leave to a local authority to apply for the exercise of the court's inherent jurisdiction where the court is satisfied that the result which the authority wish to achieve could not be achieved through the making of any order other than in the exercise of the court's inherent jurisdiction. It is therefore suggested that the local authority might rely on section 100(4) and ask the court to make an order placing the child in the care of an individual (but not of course an order which placed the child in the care of the local authority, or in local authority accommodation, as this is prohibited). It is suggested that the court might, for example, order that the child be kept in hospital, or live with a relative

---

3 The position is identical where a court refuses to extend an emergency protection order. See *Re P (Emergency Protection Order)* [1996] 1 FLR 482, where justices refused to extend the emergency protection order in the face of firm medical evidence pointing to a risk of life-threatening abuse.

4 SI 1991/1677.

or friend of the family, or possibly even with the local authority foster parents with whom he has been living, but only in their personal capacity and not as agents of the local authority. These suggestions are all devices which might be attempted in order to overcome section 45(10), and the ruling in *Essex County Council v F.* It is regrettable to be put in the position where it seems necessary to suggest the use of such devices to circumvent specific provisions in a statute. However, taking action of this kind may be essential where the safety of a child is at stake.

Local authority standards for intervention

When a local authority, other agencies or a court are deciding whether a child is suffering, or is likely to suffer, significant harm what is it that they are looking for?[5] The Act provides a very clear meaning of the phrase. Section 31(9) provides:

> '"Harm" means ill-treatment or the impairment of health or development;
> "development" means physical, intellectual, emotional, social or behavioural development;
> "health" means physical or mental health; and
> "ill-treatment" includes sexual abuse and forms of ill-treatment which are not physical.'

It can be seen that the definition of harm is very wide and covers all types of conceivable harm to the child.[6] It is qualified by the adjective 'significant' which means that not any falling off in standards of parenting causing harm to the child will fall within the definition. A resilient child, who is able to withstand forms of ill-treatment or other types of unacceptable parenting, may fall outside the scope of the meaning of 'significant harm' where the harm he is presently suffering is not serious. However, where the standards of parenting of those who are looking after him show no sign of being capable of change, so that the child will sustain the effects of poor parenting continued over a considerable period of time, it is suggested that such a child might be one whom a local authority should take steps to protect on the basis that he is 'likely' to

5   Many of the most important topics relating to child abuse and child protection, seen from a medical, legal and social work perspective, are looked at in Allan Levy QC (ed) *Re-Focus on Child Abuse* (Hawksmere, 1994). See also T Stephenson *Child protection – the paediatrician's contribution* (1995) 7 CFLQ 95.
6   For example, it is increasingly being recognised that harm can arise to a child from being a member of a household where domestic violence occurs. See *Domestic Violence and Social Care* (SSI/DOH, 1995); P Parkinson and C Humphries *Children who witness domestic violence: the implications for child protection* (1998) 10 CFLQ 147.

suffer significant harm, because the harm he is presently suffering is likely to become 'considerable, noteworthy or important'.[7]

Further assistance on the meaning of significant harm is provided by section 31(10). This subsection creates a yardstick against which to make an assessment of whether a child's health or development is being significantly impaired. It states that the child's health or development 'shall be compared to that which could reasonably be expected of a similar child'. According to guidance issued under the Act, the meaning of 'similar' in this context needs to take account of environmental, social and cultural characteristics of the child.[8] It seems that a similar child is a child with similar attributes, that is a child of the same age, sex and ethnic origin. Where a child has learning difficulties he should be compared with a child with similar learning difficulties. Where the child was born prematurely the child's achievement of developmental milestones should be compared with those achieved by other premature babies. Where the child has a spurt in growth in weight and height if put into hospital or foster care, and comparison is made with a similar child, the question to be asked is would a similar child demonstrate such a growth spurt under these conditions. Where such a child would not, the question then arises whether the first child has been malnourished, or otherwise treated in an abusive manner which has led to him failing to grow and put on weight, or whether there is some organic cause for his condition.

More contentious is the question of how far a disadvantaged child should be compared to a similar disadvantaged child, and how far he should be compared to a child who has benefited from greater material, social and intellectual advantages. An example might be of children living in deprived circumstances in an inner city area. It might be expected that some such children will be poorly clothed, have few toys or books, be fed on a diet which is not very healthy and not receive much intellectual stimulus from those who are caring for them. It is suggested that it could probably be maintained that a child who is looked after in this way is being treated in no worse a manner than many other children living in deprived circumstances, and that the standard of care he is receiving amounts to good enough parenting in the light of his background. However, it is suggested that deprivation and relative poverty do not provide a reasonable excuse for a child being dressed in filthy clothing, for complete lack of attention to his personal hygiene, for not seeking medical attention when he is ill, for no interest being taken in his intellectual and emotional development,

---

7   See *Humberside County Council v B* [1993] 1 FLR 257 in which this dictionary definition of 'significant' was approved.

8   *The Children Act 1989 Guidance and Regulations* Vol 1 Court Orders, para 3.20. M Smith and M Grocke *Normal Family Sexuality and Sexual Knowledge in Children* (Royal College of Psychiatrists/Gorkill Press, 1995) studied parental behaviour and attitudes on sexual matters, and children's concepts and sexual thinking, in order to provide a baseline from which to view the deviant attitudes or behaviour in sexually abusing families.

or for the child running out of control and becoming involved in serious criminal activity. Decision-makers must, of course, take account of poverty, but where one or more of these conditions applies to a child, then it seems proper to conclude that the level of care has fallen below the minimum standard which is acceptable.[9]

Children are too young and immature to protect themselves, and it is adults who must determine whether the manner in which they are living is such that they are suffering significant harm. The setting of standards by local authorities of when it is appropriate to intervene is undoubtedly the most difficult issue to be resolved, and the question of what amounts to significant harm inevitably turns on value judgments. If standards are set too high, too many children and their families may be drawn into the net of child care and protection processes; if standards are set too low, children may be forced to endure a life style which is intolerable by any objective criteria.[10]

Where a child is not presently suffering significant harm, it may be even more difficult for the local authority to determine when it is appropriate to intervene on the basis that a child is 'likely' to suffer significant harm. The main benefit of the inclusion of likely harm as a basis for taking child protection action is that it allows for intervention before any actual harm is suffered. Clearly local authorities and guardians ad litem of the child will approach legal intervention on this basis with great caution. Local authorities may sometimes be uncertain about what type of evidence will be sufficient to satisfy a court that a child is likely to suffer significant harm, and therefore whether it is appropriate to pursue a case in care proceedings. It is suggested that assistance on this can usefully be derived not only from cases which have occurred since the Children Act 1989,[11] but also from the law which preceded the Act. Under the Children and Young Persons Act 1969 it was possible for a court to make a care order on the basis of risk, but it defined the evidence which had to be adduced to substantiate that risk. Either a child had to be a member of the same household as another child for whom the grounds for care proceedings had been proved;[12] or a care order could be made where a person who had been convicted of an offence under Schedule 1 of the Children and Young Persons Act 1933 had joined, or might be going to join, the household where the child was living.[13] These provisions allowed

---

9 The message from several research teams, summed up in *Child Protection: Messages from Research* (HMSO, 1995), was that abuse was better understood if the focus of concern was on behaviour which children ordinarily encountered, but which in certain circumstances could be defined as maltreatment.

10 See generally N Wall (ed) *Rooted Sorrows* (Family Law, 1997), which gathers together the papers and discussions held at a conference for judges and mental health pro-fessionals in September 1995. In particular see R Kennedy *Assessment of Parenting*, p 74.

11 See below on how courts have approached the meaning of likely harm.

12 This wording is a paraphrase of the Children and Young Persons Act 1969, s 1(2)(b).

13 Children and Young Persons Act 1969, s 1(2)(bb); the offences were offences against the person of a child, including offences involving the taking of indecent photographs: Protection of Children Act 1978, s 1(5).

babies to be removed at birth, siblings within a family to be protected, and orders to be made when a child abuser moved from one household to another. In the case of a Schedule 1 offender, they allowed for swift intervention even before the convicted person joined the household, for example when he was due for release from prison. It is suggested that this is exactly the type of evidence which can properly substantiate a claim under the Children Act 1989 that a child is 'likely' to suffer significant harm.

However, the Children Act 1989 does not impose any evidential restrictions on the establishment of likely significant harm, so there can be intervention outside this narrow range of circumstances. Professionals who engage in child protection work are aware that parents and other carers may have little appreciation of the vulnerability of babies and small children to suffering significant harm. In the case of babies a shaking which is relatively mild by adult standards may lead to disastrous consequences such as brain damage, impairment of sight, or even death. A parent with learning difficulties may not be able to be trusted always to test that water in which a child is bathed is of the correct temperature, yet for a child to be scalded may be fatal, or it may have permanent serious consequences for the child's appearance, health and development. When setting standards, and evaluating the risk of harm occurring to a child, the question to be resolved is: 'when should the parents and others be allowed the opportunity to demonstrate whether it is safe for the child to remain in their care, and when is it proper to intervene to prevent predicted harm from occurring?' In some cases this question arises even when no such harm has occurred already.

Interim care and supervision orders

Where the local authority conclude that the only way to provide the child with the protection he needs is for them either to share parental responsibility for him with his parents, or to have the power formally to supervise his upbringing, they must bring an application in care proceedings. Section 31(2) of the Children Act 1989 provides:

> 'A court may only make a care order or supervision order if it is satisfied –
> (a) that the child concerned is suffering, or is likely to suffer, significant harm; and
> (b) that the harm, or likelihood of harm, is attributable to –
>   (i) the care given to the child, or likely to be given to him if the order were not made, not being what it would be reasonable to expect a parent to give to him; or
>   (ii) the child's being beyond parental control.'

When an application is first made in care proceedings it would be most unusual for either the local authority, or the other parties to the proceedings, to be in a position fully to present their case. Of greater significance is the fact that the court will not have sufficient information on which to base a final order until an independent investigation of the child's circumstances has been conducted by a guardian ad litem appointed for the child. In the meanwhile arrangements must be made about where the child will live and with whom he may have contact. Sometimes the local authority will be satisfied that the child can be protected from harm if he remains living at home pending the final hearing of their application. They may, for example, be able to persuade the person whom they allege is causing significant harm to the child to move away from the premises.[14] Sometimes a relative or friend of the child will offer to look after him and this may give the child the protection he needs. In a case of this kind it may be appropriate to make a residence order to the person offering to care for the child, in which case section 38(3) provides that the court must make an interim supervision order unless satisfied that the child's welfare will be satisfactorily safeguarded without such an order being made. Sometimes the local authority will offer to accommodate the child under section 20, and his parents, and any others with parental responsibility, may be willing to comply with this arrangement. It is where voluntary arrangements of this nature cannot be agreed, or where the local authority take the view that they will not give the child sufficient protection, or where the local authority take the view that they need to have parental responsibility for the child during the period preceding the final hearing, that they are likely to make an application for an interim order.

Section 38(1) provides that where in any proceedings for a care order or a supervision order the proceedings are adjourned, or where the court gives a direction under section 37(1) that the local authority should investigate the child's circumstances,[15] the court may make an interim care order or an interim supervision order. Section 38(4) makes provision for various time limits to be imposed when an interim order is made; in essence these provide that the maximum period for the initial interim order is eight weeks and that subsequent orders may be made to last for a maximum of four weeks.[16] The temporary nature of an interim order allows the court to maintain a degree of control over the steps taken by the local authority in the interim period. Issues can be raised about how the local authority are exercising their parental responsibility under the order each time an application is made for the renewal of the order. Where the court is dissatisfied with action taken by the local authority it can refuse to make a further interim order.[17]

14 They may assist that person to obtain alternative accommodation under Sch 2, para 5. They may also assist a parent to bring proceedings under Part IV of the Family Law Act 1996 for an occupation order excluding a spouse, partner or other 'associated person' from the home; see ch 6.
15 See above.
16 The position is slightly more complicated than as described; however there is nothing in s 38 which prevents a number of consecutive interim orders from being made. The Family Proceedings Courts (Children Act 1989) Rules 1991 (SI 1991/1395), r 28 allows for the continuation of interim orders by consent, and without the attendance of the parties.
17 See *Re G (Minors) (Interim Care Order)* [1993] 2 FLR 839.

Interim care and supervision orders – the standard of proof

There is a gradation in the standard of proof which must be satisfied before a court may make an order under Parts IV or V of the Children Act 1989. It has been seen that the standard which must be satisfied before a court may make a child assessment order is one of a reasonable suspicion only.[18] The standard of proof which must be discharged in relation to an application for an interim order in care proceedings is higher. Section 38(2) provides that a court shall not make an interim care order or an interim supervision order unless it is satisfied that there are reasonable grounds for believing that the child is suffering, or is likely to suffer, significant harm. In *Re B (A Minor) (Care Order: Criteria)*,[19] Douglas Brown J held that this test means that the court does not have to be satisfied in fact that the grounds exist but simply that there are reasonable grounds for believing that they do. He also held that evidence which might not be sufficient to satisfy the court at a final hearing may be acceptable to discharge the lower standard for an interim care order. An application for an interim order is not a trial run for the final hearing, and the courts have ruled that evidence, and the cross-examination of witnesses, should be restricted to the issues which are essential at the interim stage.[20]

Interim care orders are neutral orders

Parents and other family members will probably view an application for an interim care order with apprehension, and the making of such an order as a judgment in advance on the merits of the local authority's case. Where an interim care order is made they may take the view that the court's mind is already made up. In *Re G (Minors)(Interim Care Order)*, Waite LJ was keen to dispel this view. He said 'the making of an interim care order is an essentially impartial step, favouring neither one side nor the other, and affording no one, least of all the local authority in whose favour it is made, an opportunity for tactical or adventitious advantage'.[1] He said that in a case in which all the parties accept that the threshold requirements in section 31 are satisfied, the making of an interim care order is a neutral method of preserving the status quo.

Despite this reassurance about the function of an interim care order parents, or other persons such as a relatives, may wish the child to have his home with them in the period leading up to the final hearing while the local authority's assessment of the child and his family takes place. This situation raises the question of law whether the threshold test for

---

18 S 43(1)(a); see above. See below for the standard of proof in care proceedings.
19 [1993] 1 FLR 815.
20 *Hampshire County Council v S* [1993] 1 FLR 559; *Re W (A Minor) (Interim Care Order)* [1994] 2 FLR 892.
1 *Re G (Minors) (Interim Care Order)* [1993] 2 FLR 839, at p 845.

care can be established where a person who has not harmed the child is offering to look after him. This question was resolved by the House of Lords in *Re M (A Minor) (Care Order: Threshold Conditions).*[2] Their Lordships made it clear that the test for care relates to when the local authority first took steps to protect the child. Consequently, an interim care order can be made despite the fact that a parent, relative or other person who has not caused the child to suffer, and is not likely to cause the child to suffer, significant harm is offering to look after the child pending the final hearing.[3]

Interim care orders and assessment

In the period between first making an application in care proceedings and the final hearing a local authority will normally wish to carry out a careful assessment of the child, his parents, his siblings and others, such as relatives, who are important persons in his life. The purpose of this assessment is to give the local authority a clearer idea about the nature of the harm which the child is suffering, or is likely to suffer, and to whom it can be attributed. The local authority also need to give close attention to whether a care or supervision order is the most appropriate response to the child's circumstances, and to decide on the arrangements they wish to make for the future care of the child should they obtain a care order. In many cases the local authority are likely to take the view that they can only carry out a proper assessment of the child if they have all the rights and powers which are conferred under an order which gives them parental responsibility. Where this is the position the local authority are likely to apply for an interim care order.

Sometimes it is the court which requests information which can only be obtained by a thorough assessment of the child and other family members. Difficult questions of law have arisen over how much control a court can properly exercise over the assessment child and his family once it has handed over interim responsibility for the child to the local authority. The basic principles are clear: where a court makes a care order, be it an interim order or a final order, it loses its powers over the child's upbringing and gives control to the local authority.[4] A care order is a 'care order' whether the order made is interim or final[5] and a court cannot normally attach conditions or give directions about where the child shall live once

2   [1994] 3 All ER 298, discussed below.

3   *Re B (A Minor) (Care Order: Criteria)* [1993] 1 FLR 815 is therefore no longer applicable. However, it contains commentary on how a relative's attitude to the assessment process may influence a court's choice of order pending the final hearing.

4   This principle stems from the pre-Children Act 1989 ruling of the House of Lords in *A v Liverpool City Council* [1982] AC 363; and see M Hayes *The proper role of courts in child care cases* (1996) 8 CFLQ 201. For a different view see J Dewar *The courts and local authority autonomy* (1995) 7 CFLQ 15.

5   S 31(11).

a care order has been made.[6] However, an exception to this principle arises where statute confers specific powers on the court to intervene, and it will be seen that section 38(6) and (7) of the Children Act 1989 empowers the courts to exercise a large measure of control over the assessment process, despite the fact that an interim care order is in force.

Section 38(6) provides:

'Where the court makes an interim care order, or interim supervision order, it may give such directions (if any) as it considers appropriate with regard to the medical or psychiatric examination or other assessment of the child.'

Section 38(7) provides:

'A direction under subsection (6) may be to the effect that there is to be –
(a) no such examination or assessment; or
(b) no such examination or assessment unless the court directs otherwise.'

These directions may be given when the interim order is made, or at any time when it is in force, and an application may be made at any time for a direction to be varied.[7] Subsection (6) reflects the need of the court to obtain information and guidance from doctors, social workers and others about the child and his circumstances in order to assist it to determine whether the threshold test has been crossed, and to decide what order, if any, to make. In *Re O (Minors) (Medical Examination)*[8] Rattee J had no doubt that a direction given under section 38(6) or (7) is mandatory. This means that a local authority must comply even though they object to the direction and despite the fact that all other decisions relating to the placement and general welfare of children who are the subject of interim care orders are vested in the authority.

The scope of the court's powers under section 38(6) and their inter-relationship with the powers of the local authority at the interim stages of a child protection case were considered by the House of Lords in *Re C (Interim Care Order: Residential Assessment).*[9] The case highlights the tensions which can arise where a local authority disagrees with the views

---

6   *Re T (A Minor) (Care Order: Conditions)* [1994] 2 FLR 423; *Re L (Interim Care Order: Power of Court)* [1996] 2 FLR 742.

7   S 38(8).

8   [1993] 1 FLR 860. The local authority were unsuccessful in their appeal against a direction from justices that the children concerned should be tested to discover whether they were HIV positive. In *Re HIV Tests* [1994] 2 FLR 116 a direction was given that the question whether there should be HIV tests of children should always come before a High Court judge.

9   [1997] 1 FLR 1. For further discussion, see C Smith *Judicial power and local authority discretion– the contested frontier* (1997) 9 CFLQ 243.

of the judge. C had suffered very serious and unexplained injuries while being looked after by his parents. An interim care order was made and C was placed with foster parents. C's parents, who were immature, lacked family support and had a difficult relationship with each other, nonetheless had extensive contact with C and showed progress in caring for him. Social workers involved in the case, with the support of a clinical psychologist and the guardian ad litem, were firmly of the view that a proper evaluation of the parents' ability to care for C should be carried out before a final order was made, and that such an evaluation could only be carried out by means of an in-depth assessment at a residential unit. The local authority submitted that the court's powers under section 38(6) did not extend to directing that the proposed residential assessment take place. Initially the local authority's refusal to agree to, or pay for, this type of assessment appeared to be for financial reasons, but subsequently it became clear that the authority took the view that any consideration of rehabilitation of C would expose him to an unacceptable level of risk. Moreover, the authority's care plan was a permanent alternative placement with a view to C's adoption. Hogg J ordered that the residential assessment take place, rejecting the local authority's submission that the court had no jurisdiction to make such an order. The Court of Appeal reluctantly allowed the authority's appeal and gave leave to appeal to the House of Lords.

The point of construction for the House of Lords was whether the Court of Appeal had been correct to take a narrow view of the words 'other assessment of the child' in section 38(6) and to rule that they had to be construed as ejusdem generis with the words 'medical or psychiatric examination'. Their Lordships held that this narrow construction was wrong, that the words were wide enough to embrace a joint assessment of the child and his parents together. Accordingly, they ruled that Hogg J did have jurisdiction to order a residential assessment.[10] Lord Browne Wilkinson, who delivered the sole speech, pointed out that the interaction between a child and his parents and others looking after him is an essential element in making any assessment of the child.[11] He stated that section 38(6) should be construed purposively so as to give effect to the underlying intentions of Parliament, namely to enable the court to obtain the information necessary for its own decision.[12] However, subsequently the

---

10 Their Lordships accepted that orders under s 38(6) have significant cost implications but held that this was not a reason for refusing to make an order, rather it was a matter the court should take into account when exercising its discretion. In *Re W (Assessment of Child)* [1998] 2 FLR 130, the Court of Appeal commented that local authority resources, both human and financial, and legal aid funds should all be borne in mind. Consequently, such applications should not be encouraged. See too, *Berkshire County Council v C* [1993] 1 FLR 569; *Re M (Residential Assessment Directions)* [1998] 2 FLR 371.

11 The court has no power to order the parents to take part in any assessment against their wishes.

12 The court is to have such powers to override the views of the local authority as are necessary to enable the court to discharge properly its function of deciding whether or not to accede to the local authority's application to take the child away from its parents by obtaining a care order' [1997] 1 FLR 1 at p 7.

Court of Appeal in *Re B (Psychiatric Therapy for Parents)*[13] made the important disctinction between assessment, which involved the child, and treatment or therapy for the parents. While the former came within section 38(6), the latter did not. Therefore, a treatment programme, proposed by the guardian ad litem, that would simply address the parents' disabilities was outside the scope of the subsection.

It is now plain that section 38(6) gives the courts jurisdiction to override powers over a child which a local authority would otherwise have under an interim care order. Specifically, the court can also direct that the assessment under section 38 be undertaken by a named individual.[14] However, the full extent of the courts' powers remain unclear. A key unresolved question is whether a court has power to couple an interim care order with a direction that a child should be assessed while living at home with his parents. There is Court of Appeal authority, which preceded *Re C (Interim Care Order: Residential Assessment)* which states that the principle that a court may not order that a child should reside at home when making a final care order equally applies where an interim care order is made.[15] The House of Lords did not directly comment on whether this authority remains valid.[16] However, their Lordships did make it clear that a direction which specified the venue at which a residential assess-ment was to take place did not wrongly interfere with the local authority's power under section 23 of the Children Act 1989 to determine a child's place of residence under a care order, including an interim care order. In their Lordships' opinion, section 23 is concerned with a child's placement, not his assessment.

Approaching the question from a purposive point of view, prima facie there is no difference between a court directing a residential assessment in a special unit and directing that the child be assessed at home. A home assessment may be just as necessary to provide a court with the inform-ation it needs at the final hearing to enable it to decide whether the threshold test is established, and what order, if any, will best promote the child's welfare. The difficulty with adopting such a broad interpretation of section 38(6) is that it fails to acknowledge that home assessments, unlike residential assessments, involve taking far greater risks. A local authority's opposition to a home assessment is normally made on the

13 [1999] 1 FLR 701. See too *Re M (Residential Assessment Directions)* [1998] 2 FLR 371.
14 *Re W (Assessment of Child)* [1998] 2 FLR 130. However, the court's jurisdiction is limited by the fact that it cannot direct an individual to carry out the assessment who is either unable or unwilling to do so.
15 *Re B (Minors) (Care: Contact: Local Authority's Plans)* [1993] 1 FLR 543, following *A v Liverpool City Council* [1982] AC 363; *Re W (A Minor) (Wardship Jurisdiction)* [1985] AC 791; *Re L (Interim Care Order: Power of Court)* [1996] 2 FLR 742. In *Re T (A Minor) (Care Order: Conditions)* [1994] 2 FLR 423 the trial judge gave a direction that the child be assessed at home. On appeal the Court of Appeal left unclear whether he had jurisdiction to do so.
16 Lord Browne-Wilkinson simply commented that *Re L (Interim Care Order: Power of the Court)* (above) raised no question on the powers of the court to order residential assessments under s 38(6).

grounds that they fear that the child will not be safe in the care of his parents. Can it, therefore, be correct in principle for a court to be able to require a local authority, on which it is conferring parental responsibility, to act against their better judgment and to take risks with which they disagree? In these circumstances should it not be the court which takes its own steps to secure the safety of the child during the assessment period, for example by making an interim residence order (which could contain conditions and directions) coupled with an interim supervision order?[17]

The child's right to refuse to be assessed

Subsection (7) was included in the Act partly in response to matters raised in the Cleveland inquiry.[18] The report revealed that children who were suspected of having been sexually abused were subjected to repeated medical examinations and prolonged interviews which caused them a considerable degree of distress. Now the type and duration of such assessments can be strictly controlled by a court. Additional safeguards for the child appear in the final words of section 38(6), which provide that where a child is of sufficient understanding to make an informed decision he may refuse to submit to a medical or psychiatric examination or other assessment. However, the scope of this safeguard for the child has been limited by the ruling in *South Glamorgan County Council v W and B.*[19] During the course of care proceedings a court gave directions under section 38(6) for the child, a girl of 15, to undergo a psychiatric examination and assessment and, if necessary, to be treated at an adolescent unit and to remain there during the assessment. The girl refused to comply with the court's direction, and the court found that she was competent to make an informed decision. Leave was therefore given to the local authority to institute proceedings to invoke the exercise of the High Court's inherent jurisdiction to authorise that the child be assessed and treated without her consent. The constitutional implications of the ruling in *South Glamorgan County Council v W and B* do not appear to have been considered by the court. Section 38(6) clearly contemplates that a competent child can refuse to comply with a direction made by a court in relation to examinations and assessments. Whether the High Court, in the exercise of its inherent jurisdiction, should be able to override the right of a child to refuse to consent to an assessment directed by a court under statutory powers, raises profound issues relating to the inter-relationship between the courts and Parliament.[20]

17 In *Re T (A Minor) (Care Order: Conditions)* [1994] 2 FLR 423, at p 435, it was acknowledged by Nourse LJ that a placement at home could be achieved in this fashion, though he went on to say: 'In our judgment the local authority were wise to accept the court's jurisdiction to give directions to them in the context of an interim care order.'
18 *Report of the Inquiry into Child Abuse in Cleveland 1987* Cm 412, HMSO, 1988.
19 [1993] 1 FLR 574.
20 *South Glamorgan County Council v W and B* is more fully discussed in ch 2.

Interim care orders and excluding the alleged abuser from the home

Since October 1997 courts have had the power to add an exclusion requirement[21] to an interim care order provided that the conditions in section 38A(2) are satisfied. These conditions are:

'(a) that there is reasonable cause to believe that, if a person ("the relevant person") is excluded from a dwelling house in which the child lives, the child will cease to suffer, or cease to be likely to suffer, significant harm, and

(b) that another person living in the house (whether a parent of the child or some other person)-
   (i) is able and willing to give the child the care which it would be reasonable to expect a parent to give to him, and
   (ii) consents to the inclusion of the exclusion requirement.'

This reform of the law is designed to spare a child who is suffering, or is likely to suffer, significant harm the additional trauma of being removed from the family home. Where the child can be protected by an order which ousts the alleged abuser, or prohibits the abuser from living in the family home, this response may better promote the child's welfare.[1] The alleged abuser may also be excluded from a defined area around the child's home. This useful additional safeguard means that the child can be protected when outside, for example, when he goes to school, as well as within the home itself. Furthermore, the court may attach a power of arrest to an exclusion requirement[2] and a police constable may arrest without warrant any person whom he has reasonable cause to believe to be in breach of the requirement.[3] No guidance is given in the Children Act 1989 on how the court should exercise its discretion to attach a power of arrest. It is suggested that this is a very important power within the armoury of child protection measures, that it better enables the police to work in co-operation with the social services department and that courts should not normally hesitate to exercise it.

An exclusion requirement can only be made as an addition to, and not as an alternative to, an interim care order.[4] Why is this? One reason is

---

21 S 38A(3). Ss 38A and 38B were inserted by the Family Law Act 1996, s 52, Sch 6, para 1. For further discussion, see Domestic Violence and Occupation of the Family Home, Law Com No 207, paras 6.15-6.22.

1 Another advantage of this provision is that in many instances the non-abusing parent may, herself, be the victim of violence. She may be too frightened to take her own steps to have the abuser ousted from the home, but welcome the local authority taking action. See further E Farmer and M Owen *Child protection practice: private risks and public remedies – decision making, intervention and outcome in child protection work* (HMSO, 1995) ch 13.

2 S 38A(6).

3 S 38A(8).

4 It can also be made as an addition to an emergency protection order, s 44A, see above.

that new information might come to light once the court proceedings have ended, for example, it might transpire that the ousted adult was not the sole abuser and that another adult in the household was also suspected of harming the child. Similarly, the person in the home who was able and willing to give the child care, and who consented to the inclusion of the exclusion requirement, might secretly start to allow the excluded person to have contact with the child. Unless the local authority have parental responsibility they cannot remove the child without first obtaining a court order and any delay while this was obtained could place the child at risk.

It will be seen below that a local authority may not deny a parent reasonable contact with his child unless they have the prior authority of a court.[5] It is therefore suggested that courts, when including an exclusion requirement in an interim care order, should ensure that the local authority have been given adequate powers to regulate contact arrangements. Difficulties could arise unless issues concerning contact between an excluded person and the child are anticipated, particularly where the excluded person is a parent.

Section 38(B) allows for exclusion from the home to be regulated by undertakings rather than a court order. The child is still afforded the protection of an interim care order and an undertaking is enforceable as if it were an order of the court. However, undertakings have the disadvantage that a power of arrest cannot be attached. It is therefore to be hoped that little use will be made of undertakings in this context. The aim of the provisions is to spare the child the distress of being taken from the home and the best way of achieving this is by threatening the alleged abuser with arrest. As the Law Commission has explained, 'The parent looking after the child at home will have little incentive to report a breach of the undertaking if the only real sanction is the instant removal of the child.'[6]

Although it will normally be the local authority which requests the insertion of an exclusion order into an interim care order there appears to be nothing to prevent the child's guardian ad litem or parent from asking the court to make such a direction using its own motion powers. These new powers therefore have the potential to give rise to difficulties where a local authority is opposed to the insertion of an exclusion requirement. In the light of the House of Lords' ruling in *Re C (Interim Care Order: Residential Assessment)*[7] it seems plain that the court has the power to make such an order whether or not the local authority agrees.[8] However, similar difficulties over the proper division and exercise of powers and responsibilities seem likely to arise where a court insists on making such an order in the face of local authority opposition.

---

5   S 34(1). In an emergency, this rule does not apply (s 34(6)).
6   *Domestic Violence and Occupation of the Family Home*, Law Com No 207, para 6.15.
7   [1997] 1 FLR 1, discussed above.
8   Despite the special regulations which govern the placement at home of a child who is the subject of a care order, Placement of Children with Parents etc Regulations 1991, SI 1991/893.

Which order should be made – an interim order or a final order?

Decision-making about the future upbringing of a child passes from the court to the local authority once a final care order is made. It has therefore been stressed that a court should not divest itself of decision-making powers and make a final care order until it is in possession of all relevant information. Where a further assessment of the situation is needed in order to determine whether it will be safe to allow the child to live with members of his family,[9] or where, as in *Hounslow London Borough Council v A,*[10] an application for a residence order is made at a late stage in the proceedings, and the local authority and the guardian ad litem have not had the opportunity to assess the merits of the applicant's case, no final decision should be made. The child may be protected in the meanwhile by an interim order. This order may be an interim care order, an interim supervision order, or an interim residence order, and in the case of the latter two orders it can be strengthened by the imposition of conditions which afford additional safeguards for the child. The disadvantage of an interim order is that it delays proper arrangements being made for the child's future. Normally delay is prejudicial to the welfare of the child.[11] But where it is a planned and purposeful delay, designed to ensure that the correct decision is reached, then it is justifiable.[12] At the date of the final hearing it is essential that a court has full information on which to determine what order, if any, it should make.

In *C v Solihull Metropolitan Borough Council,*[13] Ward J emphasised that just as it may be wrong for a court to make a final order giving parental responsibility to a local authority on the basis of insufficient information, so too lack of information makes it equally wrong for a court to make a final order which leaves sole parental responsibility with the parents. Initially magistrates had allowed a child, who had been seriously injured in unexplained circumstances, to be returned to her parents. The only safeguard in place was a supervision order, with no further safeguards attached. On appeal, the court held that a further assessment was necessary to discover why the child had suffered such a serious non-accidental injury.[14] It ordered that the child should be returned home under an interim residence order conditional upon the parents undertaking a programme of assessment, allowing access to their home at all reasonable times, and co-operating with all reasonable requests made by the local authority.

9 *C v Solihull Metropolitan Borough Council* [1993] 1 FLR 290.
10 [1993] 1 FLR 702.
11 S 1(2).
12 Such a situation may arise, for example, where the parent is suffering from a serious illness, such as post-natal depression, but where the prognosis is that she will make a good recovery.
13 [1993] 1 FLR 290.
14 The child had a spiral fracture of the right femur, which the local authority alleged was attributable to the application of considerable force by one or other of her parents.

It is clear that the court can no longer monitor the administration of a child's upbringing by a local authority once a care order is made.[15] The only way in which the court can again be involved is if an application is made to discharge the care order,[16] or if there is disagreement over contact arrangements.[17] The child's guardian ad litem has no further part to play, and a court may not direct that the guardian continues his involvement in the case.[18] What is the position where a court is satisfied that a care order is the appropriate order, but where it disagrees, or is unhappy, with aspects of the care plan which the local authority have in mind? Here the issue to be resolved is whether the court should nonetheless make a care order, or whether it should make an interim order, or orders, until satisfied that the care order is working. This was the question which arose in *Re J (Minors) (Care: Care Plan)*[19] and, as the court recognised and emphasised, it went to the heart of the division of responsibility between courts and local authorities in determining the upbringing of a child.

The reasoning of Wall J in *Re J (Minors) (Care: Care Plan)* developed as follows. Before making an application for a final order the local authority should have prepared a care plan for the child which should be explained to the guardian ad litem, and which must be presented to the court.[20] A court is not in the position to assess whether a care order will be in the child's best interests unless it is able carefully to examine the care plan, and Wall J said that local authorities should be left in no doubt that in each case the care plan will be subject to rigorous scrutiny. However, he added that the court must not engage in an over-zealous investigation into matters which properly fall within the administrative discretion of the local authority. When determining what order, if any, to make, the court must apply the welfare principle, it must consider the effect any further delay would have, it must apply the checklist, and it must be satisfied that to make an order would be better for the child than not to make an order. Where it is not satisfied that the care plan is in the best interests of the child it may refuse to make a care order.[1] It had been suggested to Wall J in *Re J (Minors)* that he should make a series of interim care orders until he could be satisfied that the local authority's care plan was working well in practice. He rejected this suggestion. He said that a court should be wary of using interim orders to exercise a supervisory function over a local authority. He emphasised that a court has no such supervisory function. It cannot review a care order to see if it

---

15   And see *Re B (Minors) (Care: Contact: Local Authority's Plans)* [1993] 1 FLR 543.
16   S 39, or if an application for a residence order is made under s 10, which if granted would discharge the care order (s 91(1)).
17   S 34.
18   *Kent County Council v C* [1993] 1 FLR 308.
19   [1994] 1 FLR 253.
20   In accordance with *The Children Act 1989 Guidance and Regulations*, Vol 3, para 2.62; and see *Manchester City Council v F* [1993] 1 FLR 419n.
1   In other words it must apply s 1(1), (2), (3), (4), (5). These provisions are further discussed in chs 2 and 4.

is working, and it cannot direct the local authority to make a different plan where the original care plan is not working. These are matters which Parliament has entrusted to local authorities. Rather the court's function is to entrust the execution of the care plan to the local authority and then to step back.[2]

Subsequently, in *Re L (Sexual Abuse: Standard of Proof),*[3] the Court of Appeal approved Wall J's analysis and conclusions and emphasised that an interim care order is to be used for its intended purpose and should not be extended in order to provide continuing control over the actions of the local authority. Butler-Sloss LJ acknowledged that the point at which the court withdraws control is linked to its powers to direct an assessment under section 38(6) and she accepted that where a court refuses to accept the care plan it may make a further interim care order and direct a further assessment. However, she stated that an interim care order is inappropriate where it is clear that a care order is essential and where the child cannot return home within a short period of time. A court should not make a series of interim care orders while the local authority embarks on further investigations into the prospect of rehabilitating a child with his parents. This assessment and this decision is for the local authority.[4]

An interim order may be an appropriate way of handling the phased return of a child in a case where the local authority and guardian ad litem have recommended that a care order be made on a final application in care proceedings, but where the court has concluded that a care order is not in the child's best interests, and that the child should be rehabilitated with a parent. This was the situation in *Buckinghamshire County Council v M.*[5] The Court of Appeal held that the trial judge had been plainly wrong to make no order because, without an order, there would be no continuing proceedings to which a review of the child's position could be attached. It would also end the professional work of the guardian ad litem in relation to the child. An interim order, by contrast, would allow a structured scheme of phased rehabilitation to take place over a specified period.[6] It would be necessary to renew the interim care order every 28 days, but the renewal

---

2 Despite his clear recognition of the division of functions between the local authority and the court, it is interesting that Wall J nonetheless felt sufficiently anxious about the case to urge the local authority to appoint a member of its senior management as co-ordinator in overall charge of it. See further, P Kidd and P Storey *The role of the guardian ad litem – reality or myth?* [1996] Fam Law 621.

3 [1996] 1 FLR 116.

4 It is the duty of the judge to ensure that all necessary evidence is before the court before he finally disposes of the case, otherwise he is unable properly to carry out his judicial function, see *Re CH (Care or Interim Care Order)* [1998] 1 FLR 402. The point at which the court withdraws from further control of the child and passes responsibility to the local authority is a matter for the court's discretion. However, it was re-emphasised in *Re R (Care Proceedings: Adjournment)* [1998] 2 FLR 390 that this decision should be reached where there is no realistic alternative to making a full care order.

5 [1994] 2 FLR 506.

6 Three months was the suggested period.

hearing would enable the court to determine whether the rehabilitation process was working, or whether it was floundering, in which case the court would be able to reconsider its decision.[7]

Concurrent criminal and civil proceedings

The question of whether an interim or final order is appropriate arises where there are concurrent civil and criminal proceedings concerning the child. There is a body of authority which makes it plain that a final hearing in care proceedings should not be adjourned merely because criminal proceedings are pending.[8] It has been stressed that applications made in care proceedings should be dealt with swiftly and that delay is prejudicial to the welfare of the child.[9] Nonetheless, in *Re S (Care Order: Criminal Proceedings)*[10] the Court of Appeal (overruling the trial judge) held that the criminal proceedings should come before the care proceedings where the parents of a small boy faced a charge of murder in respect of his sister. By contrast, in *Re TB (Care Proceedings: Criminal Trial)*[11] the Court of Appeal stated that the detriment to the family of the care proceedings taking place first was not in itself a reason for delaying the final hearing. Rather it needed to be shown that there will be some detriment to the children unless the care proceedings were delayed until after the trial. The Court of Appeal emphasised that each case must be decided on its own facts and own merits.[12]

The role of the guardian ad litem

Where an application is made in care proceedings it will often be the case that the interests of the child and the interests of the persons who are

---

7   The difficulty with *Buckinghamshire County Council v M* is that the Court of Appeal appeared to be directing the local authority to place the child at home against the wishes of the authority. This appears wrong in principle, see the discussion above, and against the approach taken by the Court of Appeal in *Re L (Sexual Abuse: Standard of Proof)* above. It is suggested that a more principled way of achieving the court's aims would be to set up a structured scheme using interim private law orders coupled with conditions and a supervision order; for an example, see *C v Solihull Metropolitan Borough Council* [1993] 1 FLR 290.

8   *R v Exeter Juvenile Court, ex p DLH and RKH; R v Waltham Forest Juvenile Court, ex p B* [1988] 2 FLR 214; *Re TB (Care Proceedings: Criminal Trial)* [1995] 2 FLR 801.

9   The prejudicial effect of delay is emphasised in s 1(2).

10   [1995] 1 FLR 151.

11   [1995] 2 FLR 801.

12   It was stated in *Re TB (Care Proceedings: Criminal Trial)* that while the judgment in *Re S (Care Order: Criminal Proceedings)* was correct, the court had been mistaken to say that in a case as serious as murder it would be preferable for the criminal trial to come first unless there were exceptional circumstances requiring the child's long-term future to be arranged without delay.

looking after him do not coincide. Significant harm to the child, attributable to a lack of reasonable parental care, is being alleged against those persons, and a conflict of interest between the child and his carers should therefore almost always be assumed. It may not be in the best interests of the child that a care order is made, even where the application for the order is unopposed. It might, for example, be better for the child if a residence order were made to a relative. However, unless there is someone who has the duty to be the voice of the child, and who has a duty to safeguard the child's interests before the court, there is a risk that the child's perspective will be inadequately represented. Because care proceedings usually involve babies and children who lack the capacity properly to instruct a lawyer, the normal safeguards afforded by separate legal representation do not assist the child to any great extent. A lawyer has only limited opportunities to make a close and independent investigation into the circumstances surrounding a child client's case, and he is likely therefore to feel obliged to support the local authority's perception of the case unless he receives instructions from someone who has the authority to make enquiries and to represent the child's position.[13] A guardian ad litem for the child is such a person.[14] He or she is trained and experienced in social work, and has the knowledge and skills necessary to investigate the child and his family, to ask questions of other persons, and to assess the merits of the local authority's case. He or she must be independent of the local authority, or any other body concerned in the case (such as the NSPCC), and must not have been involved professionally as a social worker with the child at any time during the last five years.[15]

It is not only in relation to applications for a care order that it is important that the child's position is fully and independently examined. The dangers inherent in an unopposed application to discharge a care order being allowed to proceed without any separate investigation being conducted on behalf of the child was graphically illustrated by the tragic circumstances surrounding the death of Maria Colwell.[16] At that time no one had the duty to give an account of Maria's wishes and feelings to the court, and no one had the duty to make an assessment, independent of the one made by the local authority, of whether Maria's mother and step-

---

13 The solicitor should nonetheless always remember that it is the child who is his client, and note the recommendation made in *A Child in Trust: The report of the panel of inquiry into the circumstances surrounding the death of Jasmine Beckford*, London Borough of Brent (1985) (Chairman Louis Blom-Cooper QC), that a solicitor acting in care proceedings should see, and if possible talk to or play with the child. It is suggested, however, that this should only be done after consultation with the guardian ad litem; the child may already be frightened and confused by being spoken to by a number of strange adults.

14 See generally *The Children Act Guidance and Regulations Vol 7 – Guardians ad Litem* (1991) HMSO; DOH *A Guide for Guardians ad Litem in Public Law Proceedings under the Children Act 1989* (1995).

15 The Family Proceedings Courts (Children Act 1989) Rules 1991, r 10(7).

16 *Report of the Committee of Inquiry into the Care and Supervision provided in relation to Maria Colwell* (1974, HMSO) (Chairman: T G Field-Fisher QC).

father might ill-treat her, or otherwise cause her harm, were she to be returned to their care. Guardians ad litem for children were first introduced as a result of Maria Colwell's death, initially in respect of unopposed applications to discharge a care order. Gradually the appointment of guardians ad litem to safeguard and represent the interests of children has been extended to other proceedings. Section 41 of the Children Act 1989 provides that a court must appoint a guardian ad litem for the child unless satisfied that it is not necessary to do so in order to safeguard his interests in the following proceedings: on an application to make or discharge a care order, including when the court is considering making a residence order with respect to a child who is the subject of a care order; on an application to make, vary or discharge a supervision order; when a direction has been made in family proceedings and the court has made, or is thinking of making, an interim care order; when an application is made with respect to contact with a child in care; in respect of any proceedings brought under Part V; and on an appeal in relation to any of the above proceedings.[17]

The duty of the guardian ad litem is to safeguard the interests of the child in a manner prescribed by rules of court.[18] The manner in which the guardian ad litem discharges his or her duty to apply the principle that delay will normally be prejudicial to the child's welfare, and applies the checklist in section 1(3) to the circumstances of the child's case, will of course turn on the individual discretion of the person concerned.[19] However, the rules direct that he must carry out such investigations as may be necessary for him to carry out his duties, and in particular he must contact or seek to interview such persons as he thinks appropriate, or as the court directs. He has a right to inspect and take copies of any local authority records and, where he thinks that they may assist in the determination of the case, he may bring them to the attention of the court. He may also obtain such professional assistance, such as a report from an expert, which he thinks appropriate, or which the court directs him to obtain.[20] In addition the guardian ad litem must appoint a solicitor to represent the child,[1] attend all directions, appointments and hearings unless excused from so doing,[2] and advise the court on various specified matters.[3] Where the local authority's care plan is adoption, the guardian ad litem has the right to see the case record in relation to the prospective adopters even

---

17 S 41(6).
18 S 41(2)(b); the Family Proceedings Courts (Children Act 1989) Rules 1991, r.11; and the Family Proceedings Rules 1991, r 4.11. For the avoidance of confusion, all references in this section are to the former rules.
19 R 11(1).
20 R 11(9).
1   Unless such a solicitor has already been appointed: r 11(2).
2   R 11(4).
3   R 11(4)(a)-(f); these include the level of the child's understanding, his wishes in relation to court attendance, the appropriate forum for the proceedings and their timing, and the options available in respect of the child.

though this is normally confidential. As the Court of Appeal held in *Re T (A Minor) (Guardian ad Litem: Case Record)*,[4] unless the guardian ad litem can see this record, and include relevant information derived from it in his report to the court, he cannot properly fulfil his duties.

Occasionally the child may wish to give instructions to his solicitor which conflict with those of the guardian ad litem. This is most likely to arise where the guardian ad litem forms the view that it would be in the interests of the child if a care order were made and the child does not want to go into care. In such a case, provided that the solicitor is satisfied that the child is able, having regard to his understanding, to give instructions on his own behalf, the rules provide that the solicitor must conduct the case in accordance with the instructions received from the child.[5] The guardian ad litem will nonetheless continue to investigate the case on behalf of the child, and must perform all his duties set out in the rules other than his duty to appoint a solicitor for the child.[6] The guardian ad litem may also, with the court's leave, obtain his own legal representation.[7] These provisions are an example of how the law seeks to balance giving due weight to the child's right to be respected as an individual, and to have access to the type of legal safeguards which are given to adults, and the concern of the law to ensure that the welfare of children is afforded proper protection in proceedings designed to secure their safety and well-being.

It is undoubtedly improper for a court to refuse to appoint a guardian ad litem at the request of one party to the proceedings when the other party is acting on the assumption that such an appointment will be made. It is also improper for a court to refuse to make such an appointment in the exercise of its discretion in a case where the proceedings are strongly contested, and where the case for the child's interests being separately represented are clear. These principles are illustrated by *R v Pontlottlyn Juvenile Court, ex p R*[8] which concerned two teenage boys who were in local authority care. Their mother was applying for contact with her sons but the local authority were strongly opposed to her obtaining such contact. The local authority, without informing the mother, successfully opposed the appointment of a guardian ad litem on the grounds that such an appointment would unsettle the children. In proceedings brought by the mother in judicial review, an order of *certiorari* was granted on the grounds that the justices had been thoroughly unreasonable and perverse when they refused to appoint a guardian ad litem. The court held that the case for someone to speak for the boys, and to investigate their views and

---

4   [1994] 1 FLR 632.
5   R 12(1)(a), and see *Re H (A Minor) (Care Proceedings: Child's Wishes)* [1993] 1 FLR 440; *Re P (Representation)* [1996] 1 FLR 486.
6   See *Re M (Minors) (Care Proceedings: Child's Wishes)* [1994] 1 FLR 749 where Wall J laid down guidelines to be followed where the views of the guardian ad litem conflict with those of the child.
7   R 11(3).
8   [1991] 2 FLR 86.

interests with an open mind, was overwhelming. Furthermore, the court's decision had been made at a hearing at which the mother had been encouraged not to attend, in circumstances in which she had been led to believe that there was no point in issue over the appointment of a guardian ad litem. Clearly this was wrong, and the Divisional Court held that the procedure adopted by the justices had been so unfair and contrary to natural justice that their decision should therefore be quashed.

When the guardian ad litem has completed his investigation he must provide a report for the court for the final hearing. The parents and other parties must have the opportunity to read the report in advance of the hearing. This is particularly important where the guardian ad litem is supporting the local authority's application for a care order, for the persons affected are entitled to know details of the case which is being made against them, so that they can prepare their own case properly.[9]

The final hearing in care proceedings – how courts have interpreted the threshold test

It has been seen that at early stages in an investigation the court is empowered to make an order where there is a reasonable suspicion, or a reasonable belief, that the child is suffering, or is likely to suffer, significant harm.[10] At the final hearing the court must be satisfied, on the balance of probabilities, that the threshold test for care has been made out before it can make either a care or a supervision order. It must therefore be confident that the facts of the case as presented fulfil the criteria specified in section 31(2). This provides that:

> 'A court may only make a care order or a supervision order if it is satisfied –
> (a) that the child is suffering, or is likely to suffer, significant harm; and
> (b) that the harm, or likelihood of harm, is attributable to –
>   (i) the care given to the child, or likely to be given to him if the order were not made, not being what it would be reasonable to expect a parent to give to him; or
>   (ii) the child's being beyond parental control.'

The language of child care legislation must seek to avoid the pitfalls which are the hallmarks of all legislation: too precise drafting of the grounds for making an order may inadvertently create loopholes through which some children may fall leaving them incapable of being protected; too loose

---

9 *R v West Malling Juvenile Court, ex p K* [1986] 2 FLR 405.

10 The reasonable suspicion of the applicant is sufficient to justify a child assessment order; the court must have a reasonable belief that the grounds exist before an emergency protection order, or an interim care order, can be granted: see above.

drafting may permit intervention where there are insufficient reasons for it. The aim of the language of section 31(2) was to strike the correct balance between these extremes. Courts, when they construe the meaning of the words in the Children Act 1989, must similarly take care to avoid the pitfalls associated with the construction of child protection statutes, namely too literal or narrow an interpretation may leave some children unprotected, but too wide a construction may extend the law beyond the scope of the mischief which the law is designed to address. There is often a tension between a literal and a purposive way of construing statutory provisions, and in *Newham London Borough v AG*[11] Sir Stephen Brown P issued a warning against courts taking a too legalistic approach to the analysis of the language of section 31(2). He said 'of course, the words of the statute must be considered, but I do not believe that Parliament meant them to be unduly restrictive when the evidence clearly indicates that a certain course should be taken in order to protect the child'.[12]

The threshold test can be broken down into parts. It will be satisfied where it is shown that the child 'is suffering' significant harm or it will be satisfied where it is shown that he is 'likely to suffer' such harm. The harm suffered must be 'significant harm'. In either case it must be shown that the significant harm is 'attributable either to a lack of reasonable parental care, or to the child's being beyond parental control'. 'Harm' means ill-treatment or the impairment of health or development; 'development' means physical, intellectual, emotional, social or behavioural development; 'health' means physical or mental health; and 'ill-treatment' includes sexual abuse and forms of ill-treatment which are not physical.[13]

Split hearings

Where factual issues are disputed, for example, whether the child's injuries occurred accidentally or non-accidentally and, if the latter, who was the perpetrator of harm to the child, it is not possible for any firm recommendations to be made as to what should happen to the child until these issues have been resolved. In the annual report of the Children Act Advisory Committee 1994-95[14] the committee suggested that judges and practitioners should be alert to identify those cases where an early hearing should be held to decide contested factual issues.[15] Where this is the position, the court should give directions, on request, or in the exercise of own motion powers, about the filing of medical evidence and statements by the parties, and direct an early hearing as to the factual issues in dispute. Experts in the same field of expertise should be fully briefed

11 [1993] 1 FLR 281.
12 Ibid, at p 289.
13 S 31(9).
14 LCD (1995) at p 19.
15 For a general discussion of the advantages and disadvantages of split hearings see I Hamilton *The case for split hearings* [1997] Fam Law 22.

upon joint instructions setting out the issues in the case, and be requested to meet and discuss the issues in advance of the hearing in order to identify areas of agreement and dispute. These should be incorporated into a schedule for the court.[16] This procedure is designed to prevent delay in determining a child's future and the ill-focused use of scarce expert resources.[17]

Because the whole purpose of a split hearing is to enable a court swiftly to determine whether the threshold criteria are satisfied, evidence which is relevant to the assessment of parents or other family members should not be permitted at this stage of the proceedings, unless for some reason it is of direct relevance to the issues being tried. However, a split hearing should not inhibit a local authority from adducing relevant factual evidence relating to the history of the case and the background of the parents. Such evidence is usually necessary for a proper understanding of the case.[18]

The meaning of 'significant' harm

The meaning of 'significant' is not defined in the Act. In *Humberside County Council v B*[19] Booth J accepted that significant should be construed in accordance with its dictionary meaning of being either 'considerable, or noteworthy or important'. Where the question of whether harm suffered by a child is significant turns on the child's health or development, section 31(10) provides that his health and development should be compared with that which could reasonably be expected of a similar child.[20]

In *Re O (A Minor) (Care Order: Education: Procedure)*[1] the meaning of significant harm, in the context of a child's intellectual, emotional, social and behavioural development was considered, and parallels were drawn with a similar child. *Re O* concerned a 15-year-old girl who had been truanting from school for three years. Considerable efforts had been made by the local education authority to secure the girl's attendance at school, but to no avail. The main thrust of the local authority's application for a care order, which was supported by the guardian ad litem, was that if the girl's absenteeism was not arrested it would have a profound effect on her ability to cope in adult life. Although there was anxiety about her intellectual and educational development,[2] the real

---

16   Guidance on the use of experts in contested cases is given in several cases, see particularly, *Re C (Expert Evidence: Disclosure: Practice)* [1995] 1 FLR 204; *Re CB and JB (Care Proceedings: Guidelines)* [1998] 2 FLR 211.
17   *Re S (Care Proceedings: Split Hearing)* [1996] 2 FLR 773.
18   *Re CB and JB (Care Proceedings: Guidelines)* [1998] 2 FLR 211. This case contains extensive guidance on the conduct of care proceedings.
19   [1993] 1 FLR 257.
20   For criticism of the similar child concept, see M D A Freeman *Care After 1991* in D Freestone (ed) *Children and the Law* (Hull University Press, 1990).
1   [1992] 2 FLR 7.
2   The evidence was that the girl had in fact acquired educational skills so that, in comparative terms, she was of about average ability.

concern related to her emotional and social development. It was said that her refusal to go to school 'will have a major impact on her self-esteem, her self-confidence and her perception of herself ... it will also seriously impair her ability to relate to peers and adults in a more formal way. This will inhibit [the girl's] development because school is, of course, not only about intellectual learning, it also provides young people with necessary social and relationship skills.'[3]

On appeal from magistrates who made a care order, Ewbank J ruled that it had been entirely open to the magistrates to come to the view that the girl's intellectual and social development was suffering, and was likely to suffer, significant harm. He said 'if a child does not go to school and is missing her education, it is not difficult to draw the conclusion that, if she had gone to school and had not truanted, she would have improved her intellectual and social development'. With regard to the comparison to be made with a similar child he said 'in the context of this type of case, "similar child" means a child of equivalent intellectual and social development, who has gone to school, and not merely an average child who may or may not be at school'.[4] Ewbank J therefore confirmed the care order, and the care plan that the girl should go to a children's home and should be taken to school from there until a pattern of attendance had been achieved, when consideration would be given to sending her home.[5]

Orphans and abandoned children

The question whether the threshold criteria can be established where children from two different families were orphans, where no family members were available to be appointed as their guardians, and where they were being accommodated by the local authority, arose in *Birmingham City Council v D and M*.[6] The local authority argued that the absence of parental responsibility in any person imperilled the children because they would not be fully empowered to deal with crises and emergencies, and that therefore the children were at risk of suffering significant harm. The application was resisted by the children's guardians ad litem, who said that the needs of orphans were addressed by the accommodation provisions in the Act.[7] Thorpe J rejected the local authority's application. He said that 'section 31 is plainly designed to protect families from invasive care

3   [1992] 2 FLR 7 at pp 11-12.
4   Ibid, at p 12.
5   For comment on, and criticism of, *Re O (A Minor) (Care Order: Education: Procedure)*, see J Fortin *Significant harm revisited* (1993) 5 JCL 151, in which, amongst other things, she argues that the facts did not justify removing a child from her parents, that it was wrong to use removal into state care to deal with a child's lack of self-esteem and self-confidence, and that an application for an education supervision order would have been the appropriate response. See too R White (1992) 142 NLJ 396.
6   [1994] 2 FLR 502.
7   Ss 20, 22 and 23.

orders unless there is a manifest need evidenced by a perceptible risk of significant harm ... in these cases the local authority does not seek to invade, but to protect and compensate children who have been bereft of parental support. I have every sympathy with the local authority's motives and their aims, but I must construe section 31 sensibly and realistically. If there is some shortcoming in the statutory framework it is not for me to remedy the deficiency by a strained construction of section 31, particularly in the light of the opposition of the guardians ad litem.'[8] This case is illustrative of the principle that even where the proposals made by a local authority are entirely well-meaning, and arguably in the child's best interests, they cannot be authorised by a court unless the grounds for an order are first established. Here Thorpe J took the view that the language of the relevant provision prevented the court from intervening, even had it wished to do so.

In *Re SH (Care Order: Orphan)*[9] the court was faced with a similar situation: the child was being accommodated by the local authority, he was an orphan and no member of his extended family was prepared to care for him. However, the facts differed in one vital respect, there was evidence that the child was already suffering significant harm when the local authority first took steps to rescue him, and therefore the threshold criteria were met independently of the fact that he was an orphan.[10] However, the fact that no one had parental responsibility for the child was influential on Hollis J. When giving his reasons for concluding that a care order was in the child's best interests, he said that although the local authority had extensive powers under Part III of the Children Act 1989 they did not have the powers they might need when caring for the boy. Moreover, the guardianship provisions in section 5 were not apt to cover the situation because they were designed to confer guardianship upon an individual, not on an artificial individual such as the director of social services.

In the case of an orphaned child, whether the threshold test can be established appears, therefore, to turn on the court's view of the child's total situation. Being an orphan is not enough to overcome the threshold test, but where the fact of being an orphan is linked to other facts together they may provide sufficient evidence to establish that the child is suffering, or is likely to suffer, significant harm.[11]

Cazalet J applied similar reasoning to an abandoned child in *Re M (Care Order: Parental Responsibility)*.[12] He held that the threshold test was established in the case of a baby who had been abandoned when only a few days old. He reasoned that the fact of abandonment, with all the

---

8   [1994] 2 FLR 502, at pp 504-505.
9   [1995] 1 FLR 746.
10   Following *Re M (A Minor) (Care Order: Threshold Conditions)* [1994] 2 AC 424, discussed below.
11   The Children Act Advisory Committee has recommended that the position of children for whom no-one has parental responsibility is in urgent need of review, CAAC Report 1994/95, p 32.
12   [1996] 2 FLR 84.

risks it entailed, meant the child was suffering significant harm immediately before it was found. Furthermore, and importantly, he held it
was likely that the child would suffer significant harm in view of the fact
that he would grow up having no knowledge of his background. Such lack
of knowledge would probably cause him to have distressing fantasies about
his origins and he would be deprived of a sense of belonging. In *Re M
(Care Order: Parental Responsibility)* the child had been abandoned in
circumstances which placed him at risk and hence there were grounds for
legal intervention under the first limb of section 31(2)(a). However, some
parents leave their children in a safe place when abandoning them.
Therefore, the reasoning which led Cazalet J to the conclusion that the
fact of abandonment, in itself, makes it likely that a child will suffer
significant harm could be crucial in those cases where an abandoned child
is not already suffering significant harm when the local authority take
steps to protect him.

A similar situation arose in *H v Trafford Borough Council,*[13] where the
mother, who engaged in prostitution and was addicted to drugs, asked
neighbours to baby-sit for her baby and then disappeared for six weeks.
Although the mother reappeared briefly, she disappeared again and the
following year she indicated that she did not now wish to resume care of
her child. The local authority decided to commence care proceedings even
though the child was being properly looked after by the neighbours. Wall
J held that magistrates were entitled to find that the child would be likely
to suffer significant harm at the time when the local authority first
intervened, and that there should not be a narrow construction of section
31 which would prevent intervention to protect such a child. He added 'a
care order in the ultimate event may not be the right order but to deprive
the court of the jurisdiction to make such an order on the facts of this case
would appear to me to be a very limited misinterpretation of the statute'.[14]

The harm is attributable to a lack of reasonable parental care

The second limb of section 31(2) focuses on the source of the harm. It
requires proof that:

> '... the harm, or likelihood of harm, is attributable to –
> (i) the care given to the child, or likely to be given to him if the
> order were not made, not being what it would be reasonable
> to expect a parent to give to him.'

It can be seen that the test to be applied is an objective test. It is not
whether the child's actual parents or carers have fallen below standards

---

13 [1997] 3 FCR 113.
14 Ibid, at p 119. The child was living with the neighbours in what was, in effect, a private
    fostering arrangement and the mother could at any time have reclaimed the child.

of acceptable parenting, but whether they have fallen below the standard of care which it would be reasonable to expect 'a parent' to give to the child. In a case where parents, or others, do not have the capacity to care for the child without the child suffering, or being likely to suffer, significant harm, the test is satisfied even though any harm to the child is entirely unintentional. This is not to say that the motive of the person who has harmed the child is irrelevant; clearly harm which is caused intentionally or recklessly will be viewed with far greater concern than harm which occurred accidentally. Rather, it is to say that the caring person's motive is only partly relevant to proof of the second limb of the threshold test. Although this may seem harsh, it is suggested that any test which would always require some kind of intentional, reckless or negligent behaviour on the part of the person who had caused the child significant harm could put the child at serious risk. It would mean that a child could not be protected from persons with serious physical incapacities, serious or unpredictable mental illness, or severe learning difficulties.

The harm is attributable to the child's being beyond parental control

Occasionally a child may be suffering, or be likely to suffer, significant harm not because of a failure of reasonable parental care, but because he is beyond parental control.[15] An example might be where a child has become addicted to drugs, or is sexually promiscuous, or has developed anorexia nervosa, and where the parents are powerless to influence the child's behaviour. An example arose in *M v Birmingham City Council*[16] where the child, aged 13, was very seriously disturbed and behaving in an uncontrollable fashion, such that she was posing a serious risk to herself and those around her. It is suggested, however, that those initiating care proceedings, and courts when determining an application brought in care proceedings, should be wary of improper reliance being placed on the beyond control provision. Where parents, or others, have truly tried their best to make reasonable arrangements for the child's upbringing it is right that they should not be stigmatised as causing the child to suffer, or to be likely to suffer, significant harm because the care they have given the child, or are likely to give the child, is not what it would be reasonable to expect a parent to give to him. However, it is equally stigmatising for the child to be found to be beyond parental control in a case where the fault lies with those who have brought him up. Such a finding is likely to influence the arrangements which are made about how the child will be looked after if a care order is made, or the types of activities in which the child will be required to take part if a supervision order is made.

Justice to a child requires that he should only be labelled as beyond control where there is cogent evidence to support this allegation. Where a

---

15   S 31(2)(b)(ii).
16   [1994] 2 FLR 141.

child is badly behaved, or otherwise apparently out of control, it may be comparatively easy to prove that the child is bringing harm upon himself. It may be far harder to prove wrongdoing or other failure by a parent which has led to the child coming to harm, or to be likely to come to harm. It seems likely that there is a risk that the attribution of harm to the child, rather than the parent, might sometimes be selected as the basis for bringing proceedings, or making an order, because it is easier to prove. However, just as it is wrong to label a parent as having caused his child to come to harm unless there is evidence to substantiate this, so too it is wrong to label a child as being beyond parental control if the true cause of his coming to harm is because his parents, or others, have failed to give him reasonable parental care.

At what stage must the grounds for the threshold test be established?

Before a final application is made in care proceedings there is always some considerable lapse of time between the commencement of the case and the final hearing while enquiries are made on behalf of the child by the child's guardian ad litem. In the meanwhile the child will normally have lived for several weeks, and often months, with local authority approved foster parents, or on an agreed basis with relatives. Indeed, local authorities are positively charged with the duty to place a child whom they are looking after with a member of his family, unless this would not be reasonably practicable or consistent with his welfare.[17] Consequently, by the time of the final hearing, when full evidence is given to substantiate the allegation that the child is suffering, or is likely to suffer, significant harm, steps will already have been taken to protect him. Indeed the child may be positively thriving in his new environment and clearly not so suffering in a literal sense. Difficult questions about the proper interpretation of section 31(2) have therefore arisen in cases where a relative, or other person, is offering to care for the child, and where there is no evidence to suggest that the child would positively come to harm if cared for by that person. Such cases not only give rise to awkward questions about the proper meaning of the language of section 31(2), they also raise fundamental issues of social policy, and go to the root of child protection practices and procedures. Essentially they pose the question 'when is it right for the state to be allowed to impose its own view on what would be best for the child when this view is at variance with the sincerely held wishes of members of the child's family?'[18]

Where the court is satisfied that the relatives would be unable to protect the child from suffering further significant harm, even though the relatives themselves are caring persons, the threshold test is clearly established.[19]

17 S 23(6).
18 This is a dilemma to which social workers and other professionals are constantly exposed when discussing a child's future at a child protection case conference.
19 *Newham London Borough v AG* [1993] 1 FLR 281.

A more difficult situation arose in *Northamptonshire County Council v S*.[20] The court had found that the significant harm which the child was suffering was attributable to the care provided by the mother. However, the children's grandmother was offering to look after the children and the question arose whether the court should consider the care offered by the grandmother when determining whether both limbs of the threshold condition had been proved. Ewbank J said that the answer to this was clearly 'no'. He ruled that the threshold test related only to the parent or other carer whose lack of care has caused the harm referred to in section 32(1)(a). He said that the care which other carers might give to the child only became relevant after the threshold test had been met.

Whether Ewbank J was correct, the point in time in which the first limb of section 31(2) must be established, and the proper response of the courts when a relative is offering to look after the child, all came under close scrutiny in the leading case of *Re M (A Minor) (Care Order: Threshold Conditions)*.[1] The complex issues raised in *Re M* can better be understood after the facts have been outlined in some detail. It concerned a two-year-old child. His parents were married and he had three half siblings. In October 1991, when M was four months old, his father murdered his mother in a very brutal manner in the presence of all the children. It was the police who immediately obtained a place of safety order in respect of all the children.[2] After a week the three half-siblings went to live with Mrs W who was the mother's maternal cousin, and in August 1992 she obtained a residence order which gave her parental responsibility for them.[3] However Mrs W, who was a lady in her mid fifties, felt unable to care for M because he was so young and because of the special needs of the older children. M was therefore accommodated by the local authority and placed with a short-term foster mother. In May 1992 the local authority applied for a care order in respect of M. Members of the father's family and Mrs W separately applied for residence orders, but before the final hearing the paternal relatives had discontinued their application. The final hearing was not until February 1993. Mrs W, who had managed to care for the older children, now felt able to care for M. The local authority were also of the opinion that Mrs W could care for M. They therefore supported her application and were no longer pursuing their application for a care order. However, M's guardian ad litem recommended that a care order be made with a view to M being adopted outside the family.[4]

---

20 [1993] 1 FLR 554.
1 [1994] 3 All ER 298.
2 Under the Children and Young Persons Act 1969, s 28. That Act has since been repealed and place of safety orders have been replaced by emergency protection orders under the Children Act 1989, s 44: see above. The police have their own separate powers under s 46.
3 Children Act 1989, ss 8 and 12(2), and see ch 2.
4 The father, who had by now been sentenced to life imprisonment for murder, supported the guardian ad litem's recommendation.

The question therefore arose whether the grounds for making a care order had been made out and, if they had, whether such an order should be made in the light of the suggestion that the child should be adopted.[5]

Bracewell J found that the threshold conditions for making a care order had been established and found that the child's interests would best be served by a care order being made with a view to his adoption. Mrs W appealed, supported by the local authority.[6] The Court of Appeal disapproved Bracewell J's interpretation of the wording of the statute; it also disagreed with her judgment for reasons of social policy. Balcombe LJ, who gave the judgment of the court, said that the facts of *Re M* were analogous with a case where a child's parents have both been killed in a motor accident, but where relatives offer to care for the child, and said for it to be open to a court to say that the second threshold condition was satisfied on facts of this kind would amount to a form of 'social engineering'.[7]

Issues of law and policy raised by *Re M (a Minor) (Care Order: Threshold Conditions)*

The House of Lords reversed the decision of the Court of Appeal and restored the care order which had been made by Bracewell J.[8] The House condemned the Court of Appeal's apparent pre-occupation with whether the present tense drafting of the statute was satisfied at the date of the final hearing. Rather, Lord Mackay LC ruled that:

'Where, at the time the application is to be disposed of, there are in place arrangements for the protection of the child by the local authority on an interim basis which protection has been contin-

---

5   A difficult feature in analysing this case is that the local authority were not seeking a care order, and although the court could make a care order on the recommendation of the guardian ad litem, she could not impose her view on the local authority on what should happen to the child if the care order was made.

6   One of the many curious features of this case is that once a care order is made it is up to the local authority, and not the court, to decide about the child's future upbringing. Therefore, the local authority could have chosen to disregard the judge's opinion that the child should be placed for adoption and have placed the child in the care of Mrs W, thus obviating the necessity for an appeal. However, for reasons which are not explained, the local authority appear to have conceded their decision-making powers to the court, and to have treated Bracewell J's view that adoption would best promote the welfare of the child as a ruling which was binding upon them.

7   [1994] 1 All ER 424, at p 432.

8   Somewhat curiously, the appeal to the House of Lords was pursued not by the child's guardian ad litem but by the father. It is suggested that it was wrong for anyone other than the child to have been allowed to pursue the appeal. It is suggested that the fact that the father took the same view of the child's interests as the guardian ad litem should have been treated as irrelevant. It was a classic situation where the court should have assumed that there might at some stage be a conflict of interest between parent and child.

uously in place for some time, the relevant date with respect to which the court must be satisfied is the date at which the local authority initiated the procedure for protection under the Act from which these arrangements followed. If after a local authority had initiated protective arrangements the need for these had terminated, because the child's welfare had been satisfactorily provided for otherwise, in any subsequent proceedings it would not be possible to found jurisdiction on the situation at the time of the initiation of these arrangements. It is permissible only to look back from the date of disposal to the date of initiation of protection as a result of which local authority arrangements had been continuously in place thereafter to the date of disposal.'[9]

This is not an easy passage to understand, but when it is read in the context of the remainder of Lord Mackay's speech it seems clear that he is stating that where there has been a continuum of protective measures between the first initiation of proceedings and the final hearing, the fact that the child is being currently well cared for does not preclude the making of a care order. He endorsed the view that the point of time at which the court has to consider whether a continuing situation exists is at the moment in time immediately before the process of protection is first put into motion.

By the time the appeal reached the House of Lords the child had been living for several months with Mrs W and, because he was thriving in her care, all parties were agreed that there was no question of the child being taken from her at the present time and placed for adoption. The issue for the House of Lords, once it had resolved the jurisdiction question, was whether it should confirm the residence order to Mrs W, or restore the care order made by Bracewell J. Somewhat astonishingly, their Lordships restored the care order. Lord Mackay gave as his reason for so doing that there was a possibility in the longer term of difficulties, and the care order would enable the local authority to monitor the progress of the child. Also, a care order would give them the power to determine the extent to which the father should be allowed to meet his parental responsibility for the child.[10] Lord Templeman said that a care order would have the advantage for Mrs W that it would enable her to turn to the local authority for advice and help if necessary. He also expressed the view that it would have the advantage for the child that the local authority would be able to monitor his progress, and intervene with speed if anything went wrong.

It is regrettable that there was virtually no discussion in the House of Lords of the important and controversial social policy issues raised by the case. No attempt was made to deal with Balcombe LJ's telling analogy with a case where a child's parents have been killed in a motor accident. No comparison was made between the results which would be produced by the

9   Ibid, at p 305.
10 Under s 33(3)(b).

competing interpretations of section 31(2).[11] At no stage did their Lordships address the question of fundamental difficulty posed by Bracewell J's ruling, namely when is it a proper application of the welfare principle to make an order which will result in a child being adopted when a relative is offering to care for him'? However, it was accepted by most commentators that the House of Lords' ruling on the issue of the proper construction of the threshold test was in accordance with the purpose of the legislation, and that it struck the correct balance between giving respect to the rights of families to make provision for children who are suffering, or at risk of suffering, significant harm, and allowing local authority and court involvement with such children.[12]

It is suggested, however, that the ruling was unsatisfactory with respect to their Lordships' approach to the choice of orders available. Their Lordships were at pains to emphasise that the fact that the threshold test for care can be established, even though satisfactory arrangements are currently in place for the child, does not preclude the court from taking these arrangements into account when deciding whether or not to make a care order. They emphasised that the conditions which must be established under section 31(2) merely confer jurisdiction on a court to make a care order; and pointed out that after applying the welfare principle, and considering the factors in the checklist in section 1(3), the court may choose to make an order under section 8 instead.[13] It is nonetheless suggested that the justification given by Lords Mackay and Templeman for making a care order was an untenable application of the welfare principle. The statement that a care order would enable Mrs W to turn to the local authority for help and advice was undoubtedly correct. But such help and advice would almost certainly have been forthcoming in any event, and even if it were not, surely its desirability cannot justify permitting the state to take over parental responsibility? In relation to the court's continuing concerns about the child, these could adequately have been alleviated by making a residence order to Mrs W, possibly with conditions attached, and coupling it with a supervision order. The supervisor would have been charged with the duty to advise, assist and befriend the child,[14] which would inevitably have involved giving help and advice to the child's carer. Moreover it was Mrs W, not the local authority, who would have responsibility for making the day-to-day decisions about the child's upbringing, but the House of Lords was expecting her to carry out this

---

11 For example, where significant harm is caused by one parent at a time when the other parent is absent from the home, and where the local authority take steps to protect the child during that parent's absence, on his return the absent parent would not be able to claim that the court has no jurisdiction to make a care order. The local authority would be able to overcome the threshold test and the absent parent would be in the same position as Mrs W.

12 M Hayes (1995) 58 MLR 878; A Bainham, *The temporal dimension of care* (1994) 53 CLJ 458; J Whybrow, *Care, supervision and interim orders* (1994) 6 JCL 177. For a contrary view, see J Masson, *Social engineering in the House of Lords: Re M* (1994) 6 JCL 170.

13 Or indeed no order at all, applying the principle in s 1(5).

14 S 35(1).

function without the benefit of a residence order, and without the parental responsibility which such an order confers. The statement that a care order would enable the local authority to determine the extent to which the father should meet his parental responsibility for the child does not bear close examination. He was serving a life sentence for murder, and had been recommended for deportation on his release. Thus he would have no part to play in the child's life in the foreseeable future, if at all. Also, the child's siblings similarly needed protection from the father exercising parental responsibility at some time in the future, but it would have been inconceivable that anyone could have successfully pleaded that this would justify making a care order in respect of them too. Any problems could clearly have been dealt with by orders under section 8.[15]

Likely significant harm

The inclusion of 'likely' significant harm within the threshold test allows for an order to be made where no significant harm to the child has yet occurred. In *Re H (A Minor) (Section 37 Direction)*,[16] Scott Baker J ventured the opinion that when considering whether facts exist to make a care or supervision order, and when looking at the likelihood of significant harm, the court is not limited to looking at the present and the immediate future. He said 'if a court concludes that a parent, or a carer, is likely to be unable to meet the emotional needs of a child in the future – even if years hence – my view is that the condition in section 31(2) would probably be met'.[17]

In an extreme case the inclusion of likely significant harm enables a baby to be removed from her mother at birth, as in *F v Leeds City Council*[18] where the court found that the mother's dangerously egocentric behaviour posed an unacceptable risk to her child. Clearly, any removal of a baby from her mother without giving the mother the opportunity to demonstrate that she has the capacity to care for the child is a Draconian decision, and one which should only be reached where there is compelling evidence that the child is likely to suffer significant harm.

In *Re H (Minors) (Sexual Abuse: Standard of Proof)*[19] the meaning of the word 'likely' was considered by the House of Lords. Their Lordships

---

15 The orders available on an application made in care proceedings are discussed in greater detail below. For further commentary, see M Hayes *Care by the family or care by the state?* (1995) 58 MLR 878.

16 [1993] 2 FLR 541.

17 He did not need to resolve the question because no application had been made for a care or supervision order. The case concerned an application by a lesbian couple for a residence order in respect of a baby girl. Scott Baker J ordered the local authority to undertake an investigation under s 37(1).

18 [1994] 2 FLR 60; see also *Re A (A Minor) (Care Proceedings)* [1993] 1 FCR 824 where three children had already been removed from their mother. When a fourth child was born, the local authority immediately obtained an emergency protection order and commenced care proceedings on the basis of likely significant harm.

19 [1996] 1 All ER 1.

were unanimous that 'likely' in the context of the threshold test did not mean more likely than not. They ruled that for the purposes of section 31(2)(a) 'likely' is being used 'in the sense of a real possibility, a possibility that cannot sensibly be ignored having regard to the nature and gravity of the feared harm in the particular case.'[20] As Lord Nicholls, who gave the speech for the majority explained, if the word 'likely' were given the meaning more likely than not it would have the effect of preventing courts from making care and supervision orders in cases where the court was satisfied that there was a real possibility of significant harm to the child in the future.[1]

The occasions when likely significant harm can be relied upon was further considered in *Re CB and JB (Care Proceedings: Guidelines)*.[2] A child had been injured when in the care of both parents and the issue for the court was whether her sibling could be protected even though it was not possible to establish which parent had caused the first child to suffer significant harm. Wall J ruled that where the actual culprit cannot be identified the court may nonetheless properly conclude that an injured child has suffered significant harm attributable to the care, or lack of care, which she has received while living with both parents. Applying the same reasoning to the sibling who had not been harmed, he held that a finding that the first child's injuries must have been caused by either the mother or the father gave rise to a real possibility, a possibility which could not sensibly be ignored, that the unharmed sibling would also suffer significant harm were he to be left in the care of both or either of his parents.[3]

Standard of proof where child abuse is alleged

The standard of proof in children cases is the civil standard of the balance of probabilities. However, cases in which a parent or another family member is alleged to have harmed, or to be likely to harm, a child are exceptionally difficult because 'they bring into contrast two stark principles which everyone would acknowledge as fundamental to our society. One is the basic requirement of justice that nobody should have to face a finding by any court of serious parental misconduct without the opportunity of having the allegations against him clearly specified

---

20 [1996] 1 All ER 1 per Lord Nicholls at p 15, approving *Newham London Borough v AG* [1993] 1 FLR 281.

1 See below for more extensive discussion of *Re H (Minors) (Sexual Abuse: Standard of Proof)*.

2 [1998] 2 FLR 211.

3 As Wall J said, 'the argument to the contrary ... strikes at the whole philosophy of child protection embodied in the Children Act 1989 and seeks to import into care proceedings the unsatisfactory rule of criminal law that if a jury cannot decide which of two people is responsible for the death of a child, or serious injury of a child, each is entitled to an acquittal', at p 220.

and cogently proved.[4] The other is the public interest in the detection and prevention of parental child abuse as conduct which is liable, if persisted in, to do serious damage to the emotional development of the victim and to his or her capacity to form stable and satisfying relationships in adult life.'[5]

In civil cases the courts have taken the view that the degree of probability required to discharge the burden of proof in any particular context may vary and must be 'commensurate with the occasion' or 'proportionate' with the subject matter.[6] Applying this approach to children cases, the Court of Appeal ruled in *Re W (Minors) (Sexual Abuse: Standard of Proof)*[37] that the more serious the allegation which is made against a parent by a child the more convincing must be the evidence to establish the truth of what is alleged. A similar approach to the standard of proof was adopted in *Re M (A Minor) (No 2) (Appeal)*[8] in which the trial judge justified his finding that the child's mother and her cohabitee had not seriously injured and otherwise ill-treated the child on the ground that 'given the seriousness of the nature of the allegation and the personalities and relationships involved, it is a proportionately higher standard of probability than otherwise for less serious allegations'. The Court of Appeal confirmed the judge's approach.[9] However, as one critic has said when fiercely criticising *Re M (A Minor) (No 2)*:

> 'The consequence of finding that the parents nearly killed their child when they did not will be that the child will be removed from them. The consequence of finding that they did not do it when they did is likely to be the refusal to make a care order, and the child being returned to the people who nearly killed her. In this context, [this theory] about the standard of proof is worse than just not sensible: it is actually perverse. In practice it means that the worse the danger the child is in, the less likely the courts are to remove her from it.'[10]

---

4   In this regard, the rules relating to the admissibility of hearsay evidence in children cases may appear to conflict with the ordinary principles of natural justice. Courts have the discretion to refuse to issue witness summonses requiring the attendance at court of children who have made allegations of, inter alia, sexual abuse against the person caring for them but to allow such allegations to be adduced in evidence. This discretion has been exercised, see *R v B County Council, ex p P* [1991] 1 FLR 470; *Re P (Witness Summons)* [1997] 2 FLR 447, and see further ch 4.

5   *Re W (A Minor) (Child Abuse: Evidence)* [1987] 1 FLR 297 at 298.

6   Adopting the approach of Denning LJ (as he then was) in *Bater v Bater* [1951] P 35.

7   [1994] 1 FLR 419; see too *Re H (A Minor); K v K (Minors) (Child Abuse: Evidence)* [1989] 2 FLR 313.

8   [1994] 1 FLR 59.

9   Although it expressed the test slightly differently. See too, *Re P (A Minor) (Care: Evidence)* [1994] 2 FLR 751.

10   J R Spencer *Evidence in child abuse cases – too high a price for too high a standard? Re M (A Minor) (Appeal) No 2* (1994) 6 JCL 160.

An opportunity arose in *Re H (Minors) (Sexual Abuse: Standard of Proof)*[11] for the House of Lords to reconsider the standard of proof in child protection cases. Care proceedings were instituted in respect of three younger daughters in a family on the ground that they were likely to suffer significant harm.[12] The local authority's case was based solely on the alleged sexual abuse of their eldest sister, D. The trial judge held that he could not be sure to the requisite standard of proof, namely the more serious or improbable the allegation the more convincing was the evidence required to prove it, that D's allegations of rape and sexual abuse were true. He therefore found that the threshold criteria had not been made out in respect of the younger children. However, he added 'This is far from saying that I am satisfied that [D's] complaints are untrue... If it were relevant, I would be prepared to hold that there is a real possibility that her statement and her evidence are true.'

The House of Lords was split 3:2 on crucial issues of law.[13] All their Lordships agreed that the ordinary civil standard applies to proof of the threshold test. However, they were divided on whether it should be a simple balance of probabilities test without any further gloss. Lord Nicholls, who gave the only speech expressing the majority opinion, took the view that a generous degree of flexibility is built into the preponderance of probability standard, and he reasoned that a court when assessing probabilities should have in mind that 'the more serious the allegation the less likely it is that the event occurred and, hence, the stronger should be the evidence before the court concludes that the allegation is established on the balance of probability'.[14] He emphasised that this does not mean that the standard of proof is higher than the balance of probabilities; rather he asserted that 'it means only that the inherent probability or improbability of an event is itself a matter to be taken into account when weighing the probabilities and deciding whether, on balance, the event occurred'.[15]

Lord Lloyd, in his dissenting speech, expressed the opinion that proof of the threshold test can be established on the balance of probabilities, and no more, even where there is a serious allegation (in this case of sexual abuse). It is suggested that Lord Lloyd's opinion was correct and

---

11 [1996] 1 All ER 1. For further comment, see M Hayes *Reconciling protection for children with justice for parents* (1997) 17 LS 1; I Hemingway and C Williams *Re M and R: Re H and R* [1997] Fam Law 740; C Keenan *Finding that a child is at risk from sexual abuse: Re H (Minors) (Sexual Abuse: Standard of Proof)* (1997) 60 MLR 857; H Keating *Shifting standards in the House of Lords – Re H (Minors) (Sexual Abuse: Standard of Proof)* (1996) 8 CFLQ 157.

12 The eldest daughter was being accommodated by the local authority with the agreement of her parents.

13 Lord Nicholls gave the speech for the majority with which Lords Goff and Mustill agreed, Lords Lloyd and Browne-Wilkinson dissenting. Kennedy LJ dissented in the Court of Appeal.

14 Ibid at p 16.

15 At p 17.

that an approach to the standard of proof in children cases which endorses the view that 'the more serious the allegation, the more cogent is the evidence required to overcome the unlikelihood of what is alleged'[16] is misconceived. Unless the threshold criteria are met the local authority can do nothing to protect the child however grave the anticipated injury to the child, or however serious the apprehended consequences, and as Lord Lloyd commented:

> 'This seems to me to be a strong argument in favour of making the threshold test lower rather than higher. It would be a bizarre result if the more serious the anticipated injury, whether physical or sexual, the more difficult it became for the local authority to satisfy the initial burden of proof, and thereby ultimately, if the welfare test is satisfied, secure protection for the child.'[17]

Once a child has made an allegation of serious abuse the argument that such abuse does not often occur has no bearing on whether it occurred in the particular case before the court. Of course, when looking at the sample of the whole population of step-fathers and step-daughters up and down the country what Lord Nicholls said about probability must be correct. It is extremely unlikely that a substantial proportion of step-fathers are raping and having oral sex with their step-daughters. But that is not the sample under consideration. Step-daughters do not normally make such an allegation against their step-fathers. Once the allegation has been made the court is dealing with an entirely different sample of children, namely those who are willing to make a complaint that they have been sexually abused. Thus the question of probability relates to this sample, and not to the population as a whole. It is suggested that Lord Nicholl's reasoning fell into the trap of equating the seriousness of an allegation with its likelihood and that this led him to concentrate on the likelihood of a parent being wrongly accused rather than on the likelihood of a child making a false allegation.[18]

Their Lordships were also divided over whether evidence which had failed to satisfy the court that the eldest daughter was currently suffering significant harm could nonetheless be relied upon to establish that her

---

16 These words, taken from the judgment of Ungoed-Thomas J in *Re Dellow's Will Trusts, Lloyds Bank Ltd v Institute of Cancer Research* [1964] 1 All ER 771 at p 773, were approved by Lord Nicholls. All three leading counsel in *Re H* had agreed that this was the appropriate test.

17 [1996] 1 All ER 1 at p 8.

18 Another solution might be for the courts to apply a simple balance of probabilities test to whether the applicant has proved that a child has been abused, but to require the applicant to adduce more cogent evidence to prove that a particular person is the abuser. One standard is about child protection, the other is about casting grave imputations on a parent or other person. This suggestion is based on the approach taken by Sheldon J in the pre-Children Act case of *Re G (A Minor) (No 2)* [1988] 1 FLR 314. However, it is logically difficult to apply where there is only one possible abuser of the child.

younger sisters were likely to suffer significant harm. Their Lordships' difficulties arose because the case had been fought solely on the basis that the eldest girl, D, had been sexually abused.[19] It has been seen above that all their Lordships were agreed that the test for likely significant harm is whether there is a real possibility of significant harm occurring. However, the majority view was that once the trial judge had rejected D's evidence that she had actually suffered significant harm there was no evidence upon which he could make a finding that the younger girls were likely to suffer significant harm. The judge's suspicions or lingering doubts could not form a proper basis for concluding that likely significant harm had been established.[20]

The dissenting Law Lords took a different view. Lord Lloyd expressed the opinion that evidence which is insufficient to establish the truth of an allegation to a required standard of proof, nevertheless remains evidence in the case. It need not be disregarded. The trial judge's conclusion that there was a real possibility that the evidence of D was true was a finding based on her evidence coupled with a number of other 'micro' facts which supported her account. It was not a mere suspicion that Mr R was an abuser, it was a finding of risk based on facts. Therefore, it was open to the judge to find that the younger daughters were likely to suffer significant harm.[21] Lord Browne-Wilkinson, in an unusually forceful dissenting speech, supported Lord Lloyd and said: 'My Lords, I am anxious that the decision of the House in this case may establish the law in an unworkable form to the detriment of many children at risk.'[1]

The implications of *Re H (Minors) (Sexual Abuse: Standard of Proof)* for proof of harm at the disposal stage of an application made in care proceedings were considered by the Court of Appeal in *Re M and R (Child Abuse: Evidence).*[2] The threshold test had been passed because the children had been emotionally abused. However, the trial judge declined to make a final care order because although there was a real possibility that sexual abuse

---

19 *Re P (A Minor) (Care: Evidence)* [1994] 2 FLR 751 is another instance of a case where likelihood of harm turned on an allegation relating to a sibling. The child's younger brother had died from subdural bleeding. The medical evidence was conflicting as to whether the child's condition had occurred naturally or non-accidentally. Douglas Brown J held that, as the local authority had failed to prove that the child's injuries had been deliberately caused, he had no jurisdiction to make a protective order in relation to the older brother.

20 See also, *Re P (Sexual Abuse: Standard of Proof)* [1996] 2 FLR 333. For an example of where a local authority failed to prove that the children had been sexually abused but where there was substantial other evidence of significant harm to the children, see *Re G and R (Child Sexual Abuse: Standard of Proof)* [1995] 2 FLR 867.

21 For further analysis of difficulties of proof in child protection cases, and for an account of the dissenting Law Lords' explanation of how a court could find that incidents did not occur and then go on properly to find that a child is likely to suffer significant harm by reason of those incidents, see M Hayes *Reconciling Protection of Children With Justice for Parents* [1997] 17 LS 1.

1 [1996] 1 All ER 1 at p 4.

2 [1996] 2 FLR 195.

had occurred, the judge ruled that the evidence of sexual abuse was not sufficient to prove the allegations to the requisite standard.[3] The local authority appealed, supported by the guardian ad litem. The question of law was whether the judge's conclusion that there was a real possibility that sexual abuse had occurred could be taken into consideration when the court was considering what order (if any) to make. Paragraph (e)[4] of the welfare checklist directs the court to have regard to 'any harm which [the child] has suffered or is at risk of suffering' and it was asserted on behalf of the child that there was sufficient evidence of sexual abuse for the purposes of that paragraph'. The Court of Appeal held that where there is a dispute at the welfare stage of the proceedings over whether the child has suffered, or is at risk of suffering, significant harm the court must apply the same reasoning as in *Re H (Minors) (Sexual Abuse: Standard of Proof)*. It must reach a conclusion based on facts, not on suspicion or doubts. 'If the court concludes that the evidence is insufficient to prove sexual abuse in the past, and if the fact of sexual abuse in the past is the only basis for asserting risk of sexual abuse in the future, then it follows that there is nothing (except suspicion or mere doubts) to show a risk of future sexual abuse.'[5]

Orders on an application made in care proceedings

The grounds for instituting care proceedings are commonly referred to as the 'threshold test' for care because, once established, they allow the court to make a care order. But proof of the grounds is permissive only. It by no means follows from proof of the grounds for care that a care order will always be in the child's best interests, and the court has a choice between a variety of orders. It may of course make a care order, in which case parental responsibility for the child is given to the local authority. Or it may decide that a supervision order will afford the child sufficient protection against suffering further significant harm, and that to allow him to remain in his present home will best promote his interests. In some cases the court may determine that no useful purpose will be served by the local authority continuing to have involvement with the child, and that it is better for the child if no order at all is made. Sometimes a residence order may be thought to be the most appropriate response, particularly where a relative is offering to look after the child.[6] A residence order can be made subject to conditions, or it could be coupled with a supervision order where this seems necessary for the purpose of protecting

---

3 Despite the unanimous opinion evidence of three consultant psychiatrists that two children of the family had probably been abused.

4 S 1(3)(e).

5 Per Butler-Sloss LJ, at p 203. For a critique, see I Hemingway and C Williams *Re M and R: Re H and R* [1997] Fam Law 740; contra see D Bedingfield *The Child in Need* (Family Law, 1998), at p 343.

6 Cf *Re D (Care: Natural Parent Presumption)* [1999] 1 FLR 134.

the child.[7] A family assistance order may be a helpful adjunct to a residence order, particularly where there may be difficulties about contact arrangements with the child.[8] Such an order, which requires either a probation officer or an officer of the local authority to advise, assist and befriend any person named in the order, may only be made with the consent of any adult named in the order, and only in exceptional circumstances. It lasts for six months unless a shorter period is specified.[9] A specific issue order might afford the child sufficient protection against further harm, for example where the issue precipitating the care proceedings relates to the child receiving medical treatment, and where the court authorises such treatment to take place without the consent of the parents.[10] Or a prohibited steps order might suffice, where a specified person is prohibited from having any contact with the child. However, it has been made clear that a prohibited steps order cannot be used to order a parent to leave home,[11] or to prevent parents from having contact with each other.[12] Should the court wish to order that an unmarried father should have parental responsibility for his child, without wishing to grant him a residence order, it can do so only on the father's application. It does not have own motion powers in this regard. Similarly, where a child has no parent with parental responsibility, it may only order that a person is appointed guardian of the child if an application is made by an individual.[13]

Whatever the court chooses, its decision must be governed by the principle that the child's welfare is its paramount consideration. It is bound to apply the checklist in section 1(3), and it must be satisfied that to make an order or orders will be better for the child than making no order at all.[14] Even when parties to the proceedings agree about which order is most suitable, the decision is nonetheless one for the court to make. The parties might, for example, all agree that the threshold for care is established but that the child can be adequately protected by a supervision order. The court, on the other hand, might be unhappy with this arrangement, and take the view that a care order is the only order which will properly safeguard the child from suffering further significant harm. In these circumstances it should make a care order. However, there must in general be cogent and strong reasons to force a more Draconian order upon the local authority than that for which they have asked, and it is wrong to make a care order simply to encourage or oblige a local authority to fulfil their statutory duties towards children in need.[15] Similarly, the

---

7 See *Re DH (A Minor) (Child Abuse)* [1994] 1 FLR 679; *Re FS (Child Abuse: Evidence)* [1996] 2 FLR 158.
8 See *Leeds City Council v C* [1993] 1 FLR 269.
9 S 16(1)(3)(5). See further, ch 2.
10 Cf *Re E (A Minor) (Wardship: Medical Treatment)* [1993] 1 FLR 386.
11 *Nottinghamshire County Council v P* [1993] 2 FLR 134.
12 *Croydon London Borough Council v A* [1992] 2 FLR 341.
13 On guardianship orders generally, see ch 1.
14 S 1(5).
15 *Oxfordshire City Council v L (Care or Supervsion Order)* [1998] 1 FLR 70.

court can, of course, refuse to make a care order even though the local authority's application is supported by the guardian ad litem. However, where a court departs from a recommendation made by the guardian ad litem it must give particularly full and clear reasons for reaching a different decision.[16]

The implications of making a care order

Where a court makes a care order it may also make an order in relation to contact with the child under section 34, but in all other respects the court must step back and allow the local authority to decide how to implement their care plan. The court cannot attach any conditions to a care order, or ask the guardian ad litem to report back on how the order is working, for this would amount to an attempt to regulate the manner in which a local authority exercise their powers under the order.[17] Once the order is made, parental responsibility lies with the local authority and all decision-making powers about the child are henceforth vested in the local authority and taken from the court.[18] The court will only become involved in further litigation about the child where an application is made which would have the effect of discharging the care order,[19] or where an application is made for a contact order under section 34.

The court therefore needs to have a clear idea of the nature of the local authority's plans for the child before it transfers decision-making powers to the authority.[20] In *Manchester City Council v F*[1] Eastham J stated that the local authority should submit a care plan which should accord, so far as possible, with guidance on the format and content of such a plan which has been issued by the Department of Health.[2] In *Re J (Minors) (Care: Care Plan)*[3] Wall J said that, wherever possible, evidence to support the care plan should be provided, though he acknowledged that the extent and nature of the evidence will vary from case to case, and that the local authority may have been inhibited from formulating long-term plans until

---

16 *S v Oxfordshire County Council* [1993] 1 FLR 452; *Leicestershire County Council v G* [1994] 2 FLR 329.

17 *Kent County Council v C* [1993] 1 FLR 308; *Re B (A Minor) (Care Order: Review)* [1993] 1 FLR 421; *Re T (A Minor) (Care Order: Conditions)* [1994] 2 FLR 423.

18 Once a care order is made it lasts until the child reaches 18 unless it is brought to an end earlier by order of a court (s 91(12)).

19 As when a direct application is made to discharge the care order under s 39; where an application is made for a residence order, which, if made, would have the effect of discharging the care order (s 91(1)); or in adoption proceedings, when a freeing order or an adoption order is made: Adoption Act 1976, ss 12 and 18; see ch 4.

20 This sometimes gives rise to the question whether the court is in a position to make a final order or whether it should make an interim order: see above.

1 [1993] 1 FLR 419n.

2 *Guidance and Regulations*, Vol 3, para 2.62; this paragraph is reproduced in its entirety in *Re J (Minors) (Care: Care Plan)* [1994] 1 FLR 253 at p 259.

3 Above.

sure of obtaining a care order.[4] Where the court disagrees with the care plan it can refuse to make a care order, though of course this gives rise to the dilemma that unfettered parental responsibility will therefore remain with those who already have it, and this too may be an unsatisfactory outcome.[5]

This was made clear in stark form in *Re S and D (Children: Powers of Court)*[6] where the judge was in the unenviable position of disagreeing with the local authority's plan to place the children at home because he was convinced that it would place the children at grave risk of suffering further significant harm.[7] He therefore purported to protect the children through coupling a supervision order with private law orders designed to prevent the children's removal from their foster parents, but in this regard he acted outside his powers.[8] Balcombe LJ, when asked to provide guidance to other courts faced with a similar dilemma, gave the unequivocal response:

> '[The judge] has only two alternatives: He may make a care order knowing that the local authroity will then act in a way which he considers to be undesirable; or he may make no care order, which will often, as here, leave an unsuitable parent with parental responsibility for the children.'[9]

Parents and guardians do not lose their parental responsibility when a care order is made because parental responsibility is not lost solely because some other person subsequently acquires it.[10] However, section 33(3)(b) provides that the local authority have the power to determine the extent to which a parent or guardian of the child may meet his or her parental responsibility for the child.[11] Thus it can be seen that local authority and parents are not equal holders of parental responsibility; decision-making

---

4 For example, they are unlikely to arrange a potential adoption placement until certain that they will obtain a care order, but they could give the court some idea of how easy such an arrangement would be to make.

5 Parental responsibility could be given to a third party under s 8, and control over the exercise of parental responsibility by parents could be imposed by other s 8 orders, but there are no administrative mechanisms for ensuring that the court's orders are obeyed.

6 [1995] 2 FLR 456.

7 There was overwhelming evidence that the mother could not provide an adequate standard of parenting, and a suggestion that she was suffering from Munchausen's syndrome by proxy.

8 The Court of Appeal held that the orders were in breach of ss 9(5) and 100(2)(b); see further ch 2.

9 [1995] 2 FLR 456 at p 463. Balcombe LJ regretted that this was the position. For a similar example of local authority obduracy, see *Nottinghamshire County Council v P* [1993] 3 All ER 815.

10 S 2(6).

11 There are some limits imposed on the exercise of parental responsibility by a local authority in s 33(6)-(9) which relate to maintaining the child's religious upbringing, giving consent to adoption, appointing a guardian, changing the child's surname and removing him from the United Kingdom.

has been firmly vested by statute in the local authority. However, the local authority do not have an unfettered discretion on whether they continue to involve parents in the upbringing of their children. Part III creates a framework in which local authorities are expected to work in partnership with parents where this is consistent with the welfare of the child. Section 22(3) imposes a general duty on a local authority in relation to a child whom they are looking after to safeguard and promote the child's welfare, and section 22(4) imposes on the authority the more specific duty to consult with the child and his parents, so far as is reasonably practicable, before making any decision about the child. When choosing the child's placement, the local authority 'shall' make arrangements to enable him to live with a parent, a person with parental responsibility, the holder of a residence order immediately before the care order was made, or a relative, friend or other person connected with the child. They must also seek to secure that the child is accommodated near his home and that siblings are accommodated together. Understandably, these requirements are subject to the proviso that they should be followed only when to do so would be reasonably practicable and consistent with the child's welfare.[12]

It has been seen that a child is able to live at home with his parents despite the fact that he is in the care of the local authority. Indeed, a significant proportion of children in care live at home with their parents for all or part of the time, where the local authority's purpose is to rehabilitate the child with his family. Clearly, where it was the parents who caused, or failed to protect, the child from suffering, or being likely to suffer, significant harm, safeguards are needed to ensure the safety of the child when this arrangement is made. There are special regulations about such placements which impose stringent requirements on the local authority to be sure that the placement of the child is the most suitable way of performing their duty to safeguard and promote the child's welfare,[13] to make proper inquiries, to ensure all interested persons are notified of the placement and to supervise the placement at regular intervals.[14] The child should, if possible, be seen alone when visited,[15] and the local authority are under a duty to remove the child immediately if the child's welfare or safety is at risk.[16] Because the local authority have parental responsibility, it is they who are accountable for ensuring that the child receives an upbringing which secures his safety and promotes his welfare.

---

12 S 23(4)-(7); see too Sch 2, Part II and *Guidance and Regulations*, Vol 4.
13 S 22(3).
14 Placement of Children with Parents etc Regulations 1991 (SI 1991/893).
15 Reg 9; the importance of seeing and talking to the child alone has been stressed in a number of inquiries where children have been killed or come to harm when being cared for by parents or foster parents: see particularly *A Child in Mind: The Report on the Death of Kimberley Carlile*, Greenwich London Borough Council (1987); *A Child in Trust: Report on the death of Jasmine Beckford*, London Borough of Brent (1988).
16 Reg 11.

The Children (Protection from Offenders) (Miscellaneous Amendments) Regulations 1997[17] affect the qualification and approval of prospective adopters and foster parents of children being looked after by local authorities. Persons who have been convicted of a specific offence or have been cautioned for a specific offence, or where any other member of the household over 18 has been so convicted or cautioned, are disqualified from caring for a child.[18] This appears to be an enduring bar and the Regulations do not allow for the exercise of discretion. This was illustrated in *Lincolnshire County Council v RJ, X intervening.*[19] A local authority foster parent, with whom three children had been placed during the pendency of care proceedings, had been cautioned five years earlier in respect of an assault on a previous foster child.[20] On an application to determine whether he could continue acting as a foster parent, the court ruled that he was barred from so acting. The local authority, anxious that the children should stay with the same foster parents where they were happy and thriving, thereupon, with the support of the guardian ad litem, proposed that the foster parents should apply for residence orders. Sir Stephen Brown P ruled that this was a solution designed to circumvent the effect of a regulation which was both specific and mandatory, and for the court to grant the applications would be an abuse of the court's role and contrary to public policy. However, the Court of Appeal overruled the President's decision and held that there was no reason why, in an exceptional case, a private law application for a residence order should not be granted to a person disqualified by the regulations from adopting or fostering a child.[21] The regulations were not directed to the powers of the court under the Children Act 1989, they were directed to the exercise by local authorities of their powers under that Act.[22]

While this solution resolved the difficulties which arose in the particular case, the impact of the Regulations are likely to be far-reaching. They will lead to the termination of existing placements and will prevent the selection of some persons who put themselves forward to act as foster parents. The restrictions imposed by the Regulations are generally desirable, since persons who have a conviction or caution for a sexual offence, or one involving violence, are clearly unsuitable to have the care of children. However, there will be occasions where to move a happily settled child is likely to cause the child more harm than any risk posed by leaving him where he is. It is

---

17 SI 1997/2308.
18 The specified offences are set out in Sch 2.
19 [1998] 2 FLR 82 and 110.
20 The foster father had nonetheless been subsequently permitted to adopt the child.
21 *Re R-J (Minors) (Fostering: Person Disqualified)* [1999] 1 FLR 605. The foster parents could only bring the proceedings where they had the consent of the local authority and the leave of the court; Children Act 1989, s 9(3) and see further ch 2 for the position of local authority foster parents and private law orders.
22 At the full hearing, the court dismissed the local authority's application for a care order, and the foster parents' application for a residence order, and made orders in wardship vesting care and control in the foster parents; *Re J (Wardship)* [1999] 1 FLR 618.

suggested that it is unfortunate that there is no provision within the Regulations which enables the local authority to seek court authority to make, or continue with, an otherwise forbidden placement.[1]

Supervision orders

When the only practical choice for the court is between making a care order or a supervision order, the question to be resolved is whether a supervision order will afford the child sufficient protection. A supervision order gives a local authority far less power in relation to the child than a care order, and correspondingly imposes a far less onerous duty on the authority. The duty of the supervisor is to advise, assist and befriend the child and to take such steps as are reasonably necessary to give effect to the order.[2] A supervision order does not require the supervisor to keep the child safe; such a requirement would be unreasonable because the supervisor does not have the powers and resources to do this, and it is misguided to think of a supervision order as 'a sort of watered-down version of care'.[3] A supervisor cannot enforce compliance with the order, but where the order is not wholly complied with, or where it appears no longer to be necessary, the supervisor must consider whether an application should be made to vary or discharge the order.[4] Clearly, if the supervisor becomes anxious that supervision is not enough to protect the child from suffering significant harm, he should set in motion the process which will lead to a fresh application in care proceedings being made, this time for a care order. In an emergency, steps should be taken to obtain an emergency protection order.

Provisions within Schedule 3 enable a highly-structured supervision order to be made which may afford the child adequate protection without the need to give parental responsibility to the local authority. A supervision order can be supplemented and strengthened by giving the supervisor additional powers. He may require the supervised child to comply with directions about where the child is to live, places he should go to, persons he should meet and activities in which he should take part. These directions can be given to the child without the child's consent; indeed it

---

1 In *Re A (Protection from Offenders)* [1999] 1 FLR 697, Hogg J held that the court had power to waive reg 3(4A) which prohibits the approval of a foster parent who has committed a specified offence. However, in *Re RJ (Fostering: Person Disqualified)* [1999] 1 FLR 605 the Court of Appeal appeared to regard the regulations as binding, and its solution was to permit an application for a section 8 order to be made. In *R v Secretary of State for Health and Kent County Council, ex p B* [1999] 1 FLR 656, the court held that the regulations were not ultra vires the Children Act 1989 or the Adoption Act 1976. However, because of hasty drafting and lack of any discretion in the local authority the effect of the regulations had led to undesirable results, of which the court gave eleven examples. The court was advised that the regulations were being reviewed.
2 S 35(1)(a).
3 *Re S(J) (A Minor) (Care or Supervision Order)* [1993] 2 FLR 919 at p 950, per Judge Coningsby QC; see too *Leicestershire County Council v G* [1994] 2 FLR 329.
4 S 35(1)(c).

will only be in the case of an older child that his willingness to comply with such directions will be a relevant consideration.[15] The order may also require the child to submit to medical or psychiatric examination and treatment.[6] In the large majority of cases the child will be too young to control his own upbringing in any way and to express a view on the directions and requirements imposed. Directions are likely to include such matters as that the child should go to a day nursery, attend a clinic and go to a family centre on specified days. Co-operation from the persons looking after the child is therefore normally essential if the supervision order is to work. Consequently, there is power to impose obligations on a 'responsible person'[7] to ensure that the supervised child complies with the directions imposed and any examination or treatment ordered. The order may also include a requirement that the responsible person complies with any directions given by the supervisor that he attends at certain places for the purpose of taking part in specified activities. However, these obligations can only be imposed if the responsible person consents. But even where he does, the supervisor has no powers to make him comply. The supervisor's only 'sanction' in the case of non co-operation is to consider seeking variation or discharge of the order.[8] It is therefore entirely inappropriate for a supervision order to be made where it is the court's intention that the local authority should be able to control the situation.[9]

In *Re H (Supervision Order)*,[10] the children concerned were living with their mother and having contact with their father. He had served a sentence of imprisonment for sexual assaults on his step-child. He was anxious to receive treatment for his behaviour and therefore readily agreed to attend at a specialist clinic. It was agreed by all parties, and by the court, that a supervision order was appropriate. But the mother, father and guardian ad litem sought an order under Schedule 3 that the local authority should direct the father to attend a particular course of treatment at the clinic. The local authority contended that the court had no power to make such a direction. Bracewell J upheld the local authority's contention. She drew a contrast between the power of the court to direct that the child submit to a medical or psychiatric examination or treatment, and its powers to make orders in respect of a responsible person. She held that requirements as to treatment of the child are wholly the responsibility of the court, and must be specified in the order itself. However, she held that the imposition of obligations on a responsible person fell into a wholly different category, namely that such directions are solely a matter for the

---

5   This may be particularly relevant where the significant harm is attributable to the child's being beyond parental control.
6   The usual proviso about the competent child agreeing to such examination or treatment applies: Sch 3, paras 4(4) and 5(5).
7   A responsible person means any person who has parental responsibility for the child and any other person with whom the child is living: Sch 3, para 1.
8   S 35.
9   *Re R and G (Minors) (Interim Care or Supervision Orders)* [1994] 1 FLR 793.
10 [1994] 2 FLR 979.

supervisor, and that it is not open to the court to order the local authority to give any such directions. Clearly, if a court were entitled to impose such an obligation on a local authority, this would amount to a form of court control over local authority expenditure. Services provided by clinics of this kind are an expensive resource, and therefore it is for the local authority, rather than the court, to decide whether use should be made of such services as part of the authority's child protection strategy.

Care order or supervision order?

Where the choice for the court, after applying the check-list in section 1(3), is whether a care order or a supervision order is the most appropriate response, normally the question to be resolved is whether a supervision order will afford the child adequate protection against coming to harm. In *Re D (A Minor) (Care or Supervision Order)*[11] Ewbank J held that where a local authority take the view that a care order would undermine working co-operatively with parents, that this is not a proper reason for making a supervision order rather than a care order where a supervision order would not afford the child sufficient protection. On the other hand, in *Re M (A Minor) (No 2) (Appeal)*[12] Ward J justified declining to make a supervision order on the ground that confidence between the parents and the local authority had been 'irredeemably destroyed'. He reached this conclusion despite having found that the mother, by failing to obtain medical attention for the child, had caused the child to suffer, and to be likely to suffer, significant harm, and that the child was dangerously ill by the time she was taken to hospital.[13] It is suggested that the approach in *Re D (A Minor) (Care or Supervision Order)* is preferable. Unless the local authority are authorised to make regular checks on a child's progress, there are real dangers that the child may slip through the net of child protection procedures. There is clear authority for the proposition that it is appropriate for a court to make a care order even though the parties, the guardian ad litem and the court itself all agree that the child should not be removed from his parents; and even where the local authority only wish and propose that there should be a supervision order.[14]

11 [1993] 2 FLR 423.
12 [1994] 1 FLR 59.
13 *Re M (A Minor) (No 2) (Appeal)* is a highly disturbing case in which the Court of Appeal confirmed the finding of the trial judge that a child aged five had not been seriously non-accidentally injured, beaten and sexually abused. The child became hysterical on being told that she was to be returned to her parents, and the professionals and the child's grandparents were convinced that the child had been the victim of serious and repeated abuse. For critical commentary, see J R Spencer *Evidence in child abuse cases – too high a price for too high a standard? Re M (A Minor) (Appeal) No 2* (1994) 6 FLR 160, and the editorial by M Hayes in the same issue.
14 *Re B (Care or Supervision Order)* [1996] 2 FLR 693. For a full analysis of the distinction between the two types of order, see particularly *Re S(J) (A Minor) (Care or Supervision Order)* [1993] 2 FLR 919.

It is equally clear from the authorities that a care order rather than a supervision order should be made only if the stronger order is necessary for the proper protection of the child.[15] As Hale J pointed out in *Re O (Care or Supervision Order)*,[16] where the children are to remain at home it would be normal to assume that a supervision order is the appropriate order. Hale J stressed that the choice of order is linked to the powers and duties of local authorities under Part III of the Children Act 1989 to provide services to prevent children in their area suffering ill-treatment or neglect and to reduce the need to take proceedings for care or supervision orders, and she emphasised that Parliament intended that these services should be offered. She further stated that the court should begin with a preference for the less interventionist rather than the more interventionist approach[17] and that this should be considered to be in the better interests of the child unless there are cogent reasons to the contrary.

The power to remove a child under a care order is a major factor likely to influence the court one way or the other when choosing the most appropriate response. A care order is particularly apposite where it is anticipated that a dangerous situation may rapidly arise where the child's immediate removal is necessary.[18] While the local authority may, of course, apply for an emergency protection order, it may be in the interests of the child that the authority should not have first to take this step before intervening. A care order may also act as an incentive to parents to comply with the care plan because they know that non-compliance may lead to their child being taken from them. Such strong pressure cannot be exerted where a supervision order is in place. A factor which may be influential in persuading a court to make a supervision order rather than a care order is that final control over the child is not ceded to the local authority. The court retains an opportunity to reassess the situation either where the local authority apply for the order to be extended, or where they seek a care order in substitution for a supervision order.[19]

Discharge of care orders

Care orders may be discharged on the application of any person who has parental responsibility for the child, the child himself[20] or the local authority.[1]

---

15 *Re W (A Minor) (Interim Care Order)* [1994] 2 FLR 892; *Oxfordshire County Council v L (Care or Supervision Order)* [1998] 1 FLR 70.

16 [1996] 2 FLR 755.

17 Hale J related this approach to the 'no order unless better for the child' principle in s 1(5) (see ch 2), though for criticism of the 'seductive' notion that s 1(5) predicates a non-interventionist approach, see A Bainham *Changing families and changing concepts – reforming the language of family law* (1998) 10 CFLQ 1 at pp 2-4.

18 *Re S(J) (A Minor) (Care or Supervision Order)* [1993] 2 FLR 919.

19 *Re O (Care or Supervision Order)* [1996] 2 FLR 755.

20 The child does not first require the leave of the court to make an application, (unlike the position in private proceedings under s 10): *Re A (Care: Discharge Application by Child)* [1995] 1 FLR 599.

1   S 39(1).

There is no obligation on the applicant to satisfy the court that the threshold requirements no longer apply. The court has a dis-cretionary jurisdiction from the outset and the welfare principle and welfare check-list applies.[2] The requirement in section 1(3)(e) that the court shall have regard to any harm which the child has suffered or is at risk of suffering normally takes on a particular significance in discharge cases. The relevant time at which the risk must be considered is the risk current at the date of the discharge hearing.[3] Where, after hearing from the applicant, the court feels that the application stands no realistic prospect of success it is entitled to exercise its discretion and stop the case without hearing all the evidence.[4]

In *Re S (Discharge of Care Order)*,[5] the Court of Appeal acknowledged that there are instances where justice to both children and adults requires the court which is hearing the discharge application to question not merely the relevance but also the soundness of the findings of fact made in the original proceedings. Although this amounts to a relaxation of the ordinary rules of issue estoppel, the court explained that such willingness 'does not originate from laxity or benevolence but from recognition that where children are concerned there is liable to be an infinite variety of circum-stances whose proper consideration in the best interests of the child is not to be trammelled by the arbitrary imposition of procedural rules'.[6]

Contact with a child in care

Generally speaking a child is likely to find it easier to cope with living away from his parents and wider family if he believes that these persons are concerned about his upbringing, and wish to see him on a regular basis. Furthermore, unless the child maintains regular contact with his parents and wider family it is unlikely that he will be rehabilitated home again. The encouragement of contact between a child in care with his parents and other persons is therefore of the greatest importance. The public law part of the Children Act 1989 is built around the notion that contact between a child in care and his family is in his interests. Paragraph 15(1) of Schedule 2 positively promotes the maintenance of contact by providing that:

> 'Where a child is being looked after by a local authority, the authority shall, unless it is not reasonably practicable or consistent with his welfare, endeavour to promote contact between the child and –

2   Discharge applications can cause particular problems where it is clear that the local authority's care plan is not working, yet it cannot be said that the parents have improved sufficiently for it to be safe to return the child to their care, see G Posner, *Applications to discharge care orders* [1998] Fam Law 623.
3   *Re S (Discharge of Care Order)* [1995] 2 FLR 639.
4   *Re S and P (Discharge of Care Order)* [1995] 2 FLR 782.
5   [1995] 2 FLR 639.

(a) his parents;
(b) any person who is not a parent of his but who has parental responsibility for him; and
(c) any relative, friend or other person connected with him.'

Other provisions in the Act reinforce this general principle: local authorities are required to make efforts to secure that a child is accommodated near his home;[7] parents and persons with parental responsibility should be told where the child is living;[8] and it is recognised that parents, relatives and friends of a child in care may be too poor to afford the travelling costs involved in visiting the child, and the local authority have a discretion to make payments towards defraying these and other expenses.[9] More generally, the guidance to local authorities issued under the Act encourages them to work in partnership with parents, to share parental responsibility with them and to seek to ensure that contact between the child and his family is maintained in a positive manner.[10] The guidance emphasises that the first weeks during which a child is looked after by a local authority are likely to be particularly crucial to the success of contact because it is at this time that patterns of behaviour are set.[11]

Because contact is of such significance to both the child and his family, there is a framework of provisions in Parts IV and V of the Children Act 1989 within which those who are caring for the child must operate. The law takes as its starting point the rule that a child must be allowed to have reasonable contact with his parents and other important persons in his life even though he has been removed from their care.[12] However, while the maintenance of contact between a child and his family is normally regarded as beneficial to the child, in some cases it is in the interests of the child that contact between him and his family should be heavily restricted, or even denied. It is in cases of this kind, where the child needs protection from contact with his family, or where there is disagreement between interested persons such as the local authority, the child, his parents and others over contact with a child in care, that the courts become involved.

Contact and emergency protection orders

The first occasion where a question about contact arrangements is likely to arise is when a court makes an emergency protection order under section 44.[13] Section 44(13) provides that a successful applicant for an emergency

---

6   Ibid, at p 646. See ch 4 for a fuller discussion of issue estoppel.
7   S 32(7).
8   Unless, in the case of a child in care, this would prejudice the child's welfare: Sch 2, para 15(2), (3), (4).
9   Sch 2, para 16.
10 *Guidance and Regulations*, Vol 3, para 6.10.
11 Ibid, para 16.
12 S 34(1); see below.
13 Emergency protection orders are discussed above.

protection order must allow the child to have reasonable contact with certain specified persons.[14] The applicant, who can be anyone, but who is almost always the local authority, does not have the power to refuse contact unless the court authorises this by an order made under section 44(6)(a). This provision states that the court may give such directions (if any) as it considers appropriate with respect to the contact which is, or is not, to be allowed between the child and any named person. Emergency protection orders are made either ex parte or at an inter partes hearing. In the case of the former, the court (which will normally be a single magistrate) is likely to make no order about contact and to leave the question of what amounts to reasonable contact to be decided at the discretion of the local authority. However, where the local authority wish to deny contact altogether they must obtain a direction from the court permitting them to do so at the time the order is made. Where an emergency protection order is made at an inter partes hearing, parents and others may wish to raise questions about how much contact they should be permitted to have with their child, and whether it must always be supervised. In such a case, where parents disagree with what the local authority are proposing, the court may give more specific directions about contact.[15]

Contact and interim care orders

The next occasion when an issue may arise about contact with a child is when an application has been made in care proceedings, where no final order has yet been made, and where the child is being looked after under an interim care order. In such a case the local authority must allow reasonable contact between a child and his parents and other specified persons.[16] What amounts to 'reasonable contact' is not the same as contact at the discretion of the local authority. In *Re P (Minors) (Contact with Children in Care)*,[17] Ewbank J stated that 'reasonable' implies contact which has been agreed between the local authority and the parents, or, if there is no such agreement, contact which is objectively reasonable. Clearly, this will vary according to the child's particular circumstances, but must be in accordance with the local authority's general duty to promote contact and must take account of the wishes and feelings of the child and his parents.[18] Where the local authority and the parents, or

---

14 These are: parents, persons with parental responsibility, persons with whom the child was living, persons with a contact order, and persons acting on behalf of the above persons.

15 Emergency protection orders are, in any event, of only limited duration. They last initially for a maximum period of eight days (s 45(1)), but can be extended for a further period of up to seven days (s 45(5)).

16 S 34(1).

17 [1993] 2 FLR 156.

18 S 22(4).

other specified persons, cannot agree over contact arrangements an application can be made under section 34 for the court to determine the matter. Guidance was given in *A v M and Walsall Metropolitan Borough Council*[19] on how courts should approach such an application. Ewbank J ruled that contact should not normally be terminated at an interim stage in care proceedings; rather, he said, contact should be maintained save in circumstances of exceptional and severe risk. Thus where the child can be kept safe, for example by the contact being supervised, then contact should be permitted, for any other conclusion anticipates the decisions to be made at the final hearing of the application for the care order, and to do this is premature at an interim stage.

Regulating contact with a child in care

Once a care order has been made the general principle that courts are not permitted to intervene in a local authority's day-to-day plans for the upbringing of a child in care is tempered by the rival principle that any major intervention in a person's family life should only be authorised after a judicial hearing at which the rights and interests of all the persons concerned are properly represented.[20] The starting position in relation to contact with a child in care is stated in section 34(1). This prevents a local authority from exercising an unrestrained discretion over contact arrangements by providing that:

> 'Where a child is in the care of a local authority, the authority shall (subject to the provisions of this section) allow the child reasonable contact with –
> (a) his parents;
> (b) any guardian of his;
> (c) where there was a residence order in force with respect to the child immediately before the care order was made, the person in whose favour the order was made; and
> (d) where, immediately before the care order was made, a person had care of the child by virtue of an order made in the exercise of the High Court's inherent jurisdiction with respect to children, that person.'

In the event of disagreement the local authority may apply to the court to make such order as it considers appropriate with respect to the contact which is allowed between the child and any named person.[1] Any person mentioned in section 34(1)(a)-(d) is similarly entitled to apply for a contact

19 [1993] 2 FLR 244.
20 See too the European Convention on Human Rights, Arts 6 and 8.
1   S 34(2).

order.[2] Any other person who is aggrieved about the amount of contact which he is allowed with a child in care is not entitled to this preferential treatment. However, such a person may apply for a contact order provided that the court first gives leave.[3] In some cases it could be disruptive and damaging to the child if a non-entitled person were to apply for a contact order. It is therefore somewhat surprising that the Children Act 1989 does not contain specific criteria for determining whether an application for leave under section 34 should be granted. Detailed guidance on how this vacuum should be filled was given in *Re M (Care: Contact: Grandmother's Application for Leave)*.[4] Ward LJ stated that while it is clear that section 10(9) which deals with leave to apply for section 8 orders[5] does not govern contact with a child in care, it is equally clear that it could be anomalous were the court not to take account of the factors specified in section 10(9) when exercising its discretion to grant leave.[6]

Orders under section 34 are, of course, only appropriate where the views of the local authority about contact with the child are in conflict with the wishes of the child, with the wishes of his parents, or with the wishes of any other person who is wanting to have contact with the child. Where, unusually, parents of a child in care are refusing to have anything to do with him they cannot be compelled to have contact with him. However, there is a remedy where parents are preventing a child in care from having contact with siblings. The child may seek the leave of the court to apply for a contact order under section 8.[7] However, such a remedy may be of

2   S 34(3)(a). An order that contact should be at the discretion of the local authority made in relation to a person who falls within s 34(1) means that the local authority must allow and arrange reasonable contact between the child and that person, and it is not inapt for the court to indicate the frequency which it has in mind, see *L v London Borough of Bromley* [1998] 1 FLR 709. However, where a court in earlier proceedings has made an order authorising that there should be no contact between a child and his parent, if an application is later made under s 34 a court is entitled to act robustly and to dismiss the application without hearing oral evidence: *Cheshire County Council v M* [1993] 1 FLR 463.

3   S 34(3)(b). As such persons are not entitled to contact within s 34(1), an order that their contact should be at the discretion of the local authority means only that the authority should endeavour to promote it unless it is not practicable or consistent with the welfare of the child (Sch 2, para 15(1)(c)); see *L v London Borough of Bromley* [1998] 1 FLR 709.

4   [1995] 2 FLR 86. The guidance identifies the main factors which are material to an application to leave. Amongst other approaches, Ward LJ adopted the words used by Butler-Sloss LJ in *Re B (Minors) (Care: Contact: Local Authority's Plans)* [1993] 1 FLR 543 at p 551D. However, it should be noted that Butler-Sloss LJ also stated, obiter, at p 550F that there is no statutory requirement to have particular regard to the local authority's plans for the child's future on a leave application.

5   See ch 2.

6   For example, a court might be faced with an application by a grandparent for leave to apply for a residence order in relation to a child in care, or alternatively a contact order. For the first application, she would need leave of the court under s 10(9); for the second under s 34(3).

7   Such an application does not fall foul of s 9(1) (see ch 2) because any s 8 contact order would be made in respect of the siblings, not 'with respect to a child who is in the care of a local authority', and see *Re F (Contact: Child in Care)* [1995] 1 FLR 510.

little value to the applicant child. In the section 8 proceedings the welfare of the applicant child must yield to the welfare of the child who is the subject matter of the application. It is that child's welfare which is the court's paramount consideration.[8]

Authorising the local authority to deny contact

At the time when an application is made for a final care order, the local authority's attitude towards contact between the child and his parents will normally form part of their care plan for the child. Section 34(11) provides that before making a care order the court must consider the contact arrangements which the local authority have made, or propose to make, and must invite the parties to the proceedings to comment on those arrangements. The court is empowered at this stage to make any order it thinks appropriate in relation to contact, either on the application of one of the parties, or in the exercise its own motion powers.[9] Generally speaking, a court is unlikely to make a contact order at the time when it makes a care order because contact is normally a matter to be arranged by agreement between the local authority, the child, the parents and other interested persons. However, there may be occasions when an order about contact is appropriate right at the outset of a care order. In *Re SW (A Minor) (Care Proceedings)*,[10] Booth J held that justices were correct to exercise their own motion powers to order no contact between a child and his mother in circumstances where there was no realistic chance that the child would return to live with her, where the local authority's plan was to find a permanent substitute family for the child, and where the guardian ad litem supported this plan.

Where the question whether contact should be denied arises at the outset of the operation of a care order a balance must be struck between allowing time for the parents to explore with the local authority whether the rehabilitation of the child with his family will be attainable under the changed circumstances of a care order, and recognising that any delay in determining a question about the child's upbringing is likely to prejudice the welfare of the child.[11] Where the long-term plan for the child is to place him for adoption, the more swiftly any questions about contact are resolved, the sooner steps can be taken to place a child with potential adoptive parents.[12] Where it is believed that the child needs the security

8   *Re F (Contact: Child in Care)* above. The Law Commission recommended that the welfare of 'any child likely to be affected' should be the court's only concern, Review of Child Law, Guardianship and Custody, Report No 172 (HMSO 1998) and clause 1(2) of the attached draft Bill. This provision was not adopted by Parliament, consequently a child in care's welfare cannot be given equal weighting.

9   S 34(2), (3), (4), (5), (10).

10 [1993] 2 FLR 609.

11 S 1(2).

12 Research informs us that the chances of an adoption being successful start to diminish the older the child becomes, see J Fratter, J Rowe, D Sapsford and J Thoburn *Permanent Family Placement* (BAAF, 1991).

of a settled placement, the difficulty is to know how much opportunity, if any, should be given for alternative arrangements which continue to involve the parents to be attempted before an order authorising the reduction or termination of contact is made.[13]

The presumption that contact with parents is in the best interests of the child is displaced where the child is likely to be injured by the parent. In such a case, the local authority may decide to abandon any attempt to rehabilitate the child with his or her family, and adoption may be their long-term plan for the child. In *Birmingham City Council v H*[14] the mother of the child was herself a child in the care of the local authority. She had very serious behavioural problems, and her behaviour towards her baby caused great anxiety about his safety. Connell J concluded that it was very unlikely that the mother would make significant progress in her ability to care for the child, and that it was important that he should be adopted as soon as possible and given a stable long-term home. He therefore authorised the local authority to refuse contact. The case raised the point of law as to whose welfare was paramount where both parent and child were children. The House of Lords ruled that it was the welfare of the baby which must be the court's paramount consideration. Applying the paramountcy test to the facts, their Lordships concluded that Connell J had given due weight to the fact that an order prohibiting contact between a mother and a young child should rarely be made, and that it was impossible to say that he had erred in the exercise of his discretion when authorising the refusal of contact.

Terminating contact is a Draconian decision and one which courts will not make lightly. It is recognised that contact is for the benefit of children in care because by retaining a link with their biological parents, children sustain a continuing knowledge of their parents as real people rather than as figments of their memory or imagination. However, the courts also recognise that contact must not be allowed to destabilise or endanger the local authority's plans for a child. As Thorpe J said in *Re N (Minors) (Care Orders: Termination of Parental Contact)*[15] 'it is always tempting to keep doors open against possible developments in an uncertain future, but the future must be surveyed in terms of probabilities and not low possibilities'. The three children concerned had suffered very severe significant harm at the hands of their parents, and as a consequence had special needs and would be difficult to place with long-term foster or adoptive parents. Thorpe J found that the search for a permanent new family would be made more difficult if the children continued to have a relationship with their parents in the interim. He therefore concluded that the need for an order authorising the refusal of contact had been plainly established.

13 See *L v London Borough of Bromley* [1998] 1 FLR 709 allowing an appeal from justices who had failed to take account of the unlikelihood of finding adopters who could tolerate a high level of contact.
14 [1994] 1 FLR 224.
15 [1994] 2 FCR 1101 at p 1107.

Questions about contact may arise at any time while a child is in the care of a local authority. Because any decision by the authority to refuse contact between a child and the persons specified in section 34(1) is a judgment of such major importance to both the child and those persons, section 34(6) provides that it cannot be implemented without the authority of a court order, except in a case of urgency, and then only for up to seven days.[16] Where the authority wish to bring contact to an end they must apply to the court under section 34(4). Where the court agrees to the local authority's application it makes an order which authorises the local authority to refuse to allow contact between the child and any person named in the order. This puts the local authority, not the court, in control over when contact is actually brought to an end. It allows the authority to determine whether, for example, contact should be gradually phased out, whether there should be a final 'good bye' visit, or whether contact should terminate forthwith.

An order authorising a local authority to terminate contact is not a final order. As with any order made under section 34, an application may be made for the order to be varied.[17] The burden is on the applicant to show that there has been some material change in circumstances and that the application is not a disguised form of appeal. The courts do not welcome applications which seek to reopen decided questions and it is up to the court to decide the extent to which it will consider the application to rescind the local authority's power to refuse contact. The greater the apparent change in circumstances, the more intensively will the court be prepared to consider whether the section 34(4) order should remain in place. The child's welfare is the court's paramount consideration, but when considering the child's welfare courts have in mind that children are often troubled by the fact that court proceedings are taking place.[18] Where adoption is the care plan and where the local authority remain committed to that plan, it is unlikely that the court would order renewal of contact between parent and child. A second termination of contact would be likely to cause the child unnecessary distress.[19]

Contact, the local authority's plans and the court's jurisdiction

Any decision by a court to order contact against the wishes of a local authority is likely seriously to interfere with the authority's plans for the child's future upbringing. It was acknowledged by the Court of Appeal in *Re B (Minors) (Care: Contact: Local Authority's Plans)*[20] that such a decision therefore raises profound questions about the inter-relationship between

16 S 34(6).
17 S 34(9). The only express statutory restriction on making any kind of s 34 order is that provided by s 91(17).
18 *Re T (Termination of Contact)* [1997] 1 FLR 517.
19 *Greenwich London Borough Council v H* [1996] 2 FLR 736.
20 [1993] 1 FLR 543.

the plans of the local authority, the jurisdiction of the court and the proper exercise of the court's discretion. The interchange between the judicial control of children who are the subject of applications to the court, and the responsibility of local authorities for children in their care, is a difficult and sensitive area of law. The fundamental principle that courts have no reviewing power over how local authorities exercise their discretionary powers when carrying out their statutory functions remains intact.[1] However, in *Re B (Minors) (Care: Contact: Local Authority's Plans)*, and subsequently in *Re E (A Minor) (Care Order: Contact)*,[2] the Court of Appeal unhesitatingly rejected the argument that the court cannot go behind the long-term plans of the local authority unless they were acting capriciously, or were otherwise open to scrutiny by way of judicial review. In *Re B (Minors)*, Butler-Sloss LJ said that it is clear that the discretion to refuse to allow contact, or otherwise to determine what contact is reasonable, is firmly vested in the courts and not in the local authority.[3] She said that the proposals of the local authority, based on their appreciation of the best interests of the child, must command the greatest respect and consideration from the court, but that the duty to decide is in the court. 'Consequently', she said 'the court may have the task of requiring the local authority to justify their long-term plans to the extent only that those plans exclude contact between parent and child.' It is for the court to determine whether such a plan is in the best interests of the child.[4] However, it is also plain that orders about contact should not be made where their purpose is to enable the court to review the implementation by the local authority of its care plan. At this point the judge would be 'straying into the forbidden territory of supervising the administration of the local authority's arrangements for rehabilitation.'[5]

Re L (Sexual Abuse: Standard of Proof)[6] provides an illustration of the application of these principles. The local authority's care plan was to remove the children from their parents and to place them for adoption. The trial judge held that a final care order rather than an interim care order was the appropriate order even though he took the view that there was a possibility of rehabilitation of the children with their mother. The Court of Appeal approved his decision. It held that it was for the judge to determine whether the point had been reached where responsibility for the child's future should be passed to the local authority. However, the

---

1 *A v Liverpool City Council* [1981] 2 All ER 385.
2 [1994] 1 FLR 146.
3 Butler-Sloss LJ said that her own earlier judgment in *Re S (A Minor) (Access Application)* [1991] 1 FLR 161 should be read 'with considerable caution'. *West Glamorgan County Council v P (No 2)* [1993] 1 FLR 407 in which Rattee J had applied an even more stringent test was disapproved in both *Re B (Minors) (Care: Contact: Local Authority's Plans)* and *Re E (A Minor) (Care Order: Contact)* above.
4 Hence the dismissal of the local authority's appeal against the making of a contact order in *Berkshire County Council v B* [1997] 1 FLR 171. See too the emphasis on the scrutinising role of the court in *Re E (A Minor) (Care Order: Contact)* above.
5 *Re S (A Minor) (Care: Contact Order)* [1994] 2 FLR 222, per Simon Brown LJ at p 226.
6 [1996] 1 FLR 116 .

parents' appeal against the judge's order authorising the local authority to terminate contact between them and their children was allowed.[7] The judge's motive in making an order under section 34(4) was to save the local authority the necessity of making a further application to the court should the authority wish to bring contact to an end. The Court of Appeal held that the judge had been wrong. The effect of the order was to hand over to the local authority the residual responsibility for contact arrangements which still vested in the court, and in the circumstances of the case it was premature. The local authority had no immediate intention to bring contact to an end and the judge had indicated that rehabilitation with the mother was a possibility.[8]

When the converse position applies, so that it is the court which wishes to prevent contact between a child and his parent, or another person, in a case where a local authority are content to allow such contact to continue, the position is more complex. It is clear that a court has power to order that no contact should take place.[9] However, regulations allow the terms of any order made under the section to be departed from by agreement between the local authority and the person in relation to whom the order has been made.[10] Thus, theoretically at least, a court could make a 'no contact' order on one day and the local authority could, with the agreement of the person concerned, depart from such an order the following day. Clearly it is wrong that a court is put in the position that an order which it has made on the merits is overridden by a decision made subsequently by agreement between the person concerned and the local authority, and therefore in *Kent County Council v C*,[11] Ewbank J said that a court ought not in the ordinary way make an order for no contact between parent and child.

It can be seen that there are subtle distinctions in the provisions in section 34 relating to the interplay between a court's powers to make orders about contact and a local authority's powers to make decisions about a child's upbringing free from supervision by the courts. These can be summarised as follows. Only a court has the power to authorise a local authority to terminate contact with the persons specified in section 34(1). A court may exercise this power either on an application made by the local authority or in the exercise of its own motion powers. Where the court believes that it is in the best interests of a child that contact should be refused or terminated it may authorise the local authority to do so, but it cannot compel the authority to do so. Therefore a court would be unwise to make a no contact order using its own motion powers without first ascertaining whether the local authority would welcome it. Similarly, where the court makes an order under section 34(2) regulating contact

---

7   The local authority had not sought a s 34(4) order; it was made at the request of the guardian ad litem.

8   See too *Re D and H (Children in Care)* [1997] 1 FLR 841; *Re T (Termination of Contact: Discharge of Order)* [1997] 1 FLR 517.

9   S 34(2), and see *Kent County Council v C* [1993] 1 FLR 308.

10 S 34(8) and the Contact with Children Regulations 1991 (SI 1991/891), reg 3.

11 [1993] 1 FLR 308.

arrangements between the child and a specified person, these can only be altered by the local authority where the person affected by the contact order agrees. However, an order of the court can be overridden where such an agreement is made. When a court is determining the merits of a contact application it must apply the principle that the child's welfare is its paramount consideration.[12]

Child safety orders

The child safety order is intended to enable local authorities and courts to intervene where a young child behaves anti-socially or disruptively. Preventing offending by children and young persons is part of the wider youth crime reduction strategy contained in the Crime and Disorder Act 1998,[13] and the new order is founded on the belief that early intervention is more effective than waiting until the child is old enough to be dealt with under the youth justice system.[14] Application for an order is made by a local authority to the Family Proceedings Court. The order can only be made in respect of children under 10, and the court must first be satisfied that one or more of the conditions in section 11(3) of the Crime and Disorder Act 1998 are met. These are:

'(a) that the child has committed an act which, if he had been aged 10 or over, would have constituted an offence;
(b) that a child safety order is necessary so as to prevent the child committing an act which, if the child were above the age of criminal responsibility, that is 10 years old, would constitute an offence;
(c) that the child has contravened a ban imposed under a local child curfew scheme as established under section 15 of this Act; or
(d) that the child has acted in a manner that caused or was likely to cause harassment, alarm or distress to a person or persons not of the same household as himself.'

The standard of proof is the civil standard despite the fact that the conditions are crime-related.

The order is not available nationwide. It is being piloted in selected areas to allow the Government time to assess its effectiveness and its financial implications. The aim is to implement the order nationally during 2000-2001,

---

12 Ch 4 discusses the inter-relationship between contact with children in care and adoption. See also, *Contact Orders Study: A study of local authority decision making around contact applications under section 34* (SSI/DOH, 1994).

13 See further, C Piper *The Crime and Disorder Act 1998: child and community 'safety'* (1999) 62 MLR 397.

14 For the background to the youth offending part of the Act, see *No More Excuses – A new approach to tackling youth crime in England and Wales* (1997, Cm 3809).

subject to the outcome of the pilot schemes. Guidance issued to local authorities advises on the type of information a local authority might put before the court in support of their application. It suggests that under paragraph (a) evidence is given of the 'offence' and the child's deliberate involvement in it, together with a commentary on the likely causes of this 'offending' behaviour, such as negative peer group pressure and poor parental supervision. Under (b) it suggests that the type of information which indicates that a child is at risk of becoming involved in 'offending' behaviour might include evidence of truancy, poor educational attainment or exclusion from school. Under (c) there would need to be evidence of when and how the local curfew was breached and why a child safety order might usefully be imposed as a result of the breach. Under (d) it suggests that the local authority, in addition to giving evidence relating to the child's behaviour and its detrimental effect on the people concerned, should also provide information on the apparent causes of the child's behaviour.[15]

The local authority and the child's parents are parties to the proceedings. The child is not. Child safety order proceedings are not specified proceedings for the purposes of section 41 of the Children Act 1989. This means that a guardian ad litem will not be appointed to safeguard the child's interests and investigate how any order would promote his welfare, and a lawyer will not be appointed to represent him. No one will have the duty to give the child's account of what occurred, his explanation for why it occurred, and his wishes and feelings about what should happen to him should the court decide that an order is needed. The proceedings are family proceedings,[16] consequently the court could respond to a child safety order application by making an order under section 8 of the Children Act 1989,[17] either on application or using its own motion powers. The grounds for seeking a child safety order cover situations where the strengths of the wider family could, in theory, be brought into good use to assist the child, and to guard against his involvement in offending. An appropriate court response might, therefore, be to make a residence order to a relative so that parental responsibility is shared between the relative and the child's parents. However, it seems unlikely that this power will be used unless it is specifically drawn to the court's attention. Instead it seems probable that the court will focus on whether the proposed content of the child safety order is appropriate when considering the proper disposal for the child.

Section 12(1) of the Crime and Disorder Act 1998 states that before making a child safety order, the court must obtain information about the child's family circumstances and the likely effect of the order on those circumstances. It must explain to the parents the effect of the order, the requirements proposed to be included in it, and the consequences which

---

15 The type of behaviour envisaged is the same as that which would support an anti-social behaviour order available for children aged 10 and over. It is intended to cover persistent vandalism and the intimidation of elderly people.
16 Children Act 1989, s 8(4).
17 Residence, contact, specific issue and prohibited steps orders.

may follow if the child fails to comply with any of the requirements.[18] The court should also explain to the parents that the court has power to review the order on the application of the parents or of the supervising officer responsible for the child. Where appropriate, the order should also be explained to the child.

Requirements in a child safety order and the role of the responsible officer

The requirements imposed under a child safety order are entirely a matter for the court, however the guidance states that they should relate to, and be proportionate to, the reasons why the application for an order was made, and must take account of local facilities and schemes. The court is expected to ensure that the requirements are desirable in the interests of securing that the child receives appropriate care, protection and support and is subject to proper control, or that they are desirable in the interests of preventing the repetition of the kind of behaviour which led to the child safety order being made. Suggested requirements include: attendance at school or extra curricular activities such as sporting activities or homework clubs; avoiding contact with disruptive and possibly older children; not visiting areas such as shopping centres unsupervised; being inside the home in the evenings; attending courses or sessions designed to address specific problems such as behaviour management or the provision of educational support. The guidance gives the following example:

> 'An 8 year old girl was found shoplifting with a group of older girls in the local shopping centre and was referred by the police to the social services department. The local authority applied to the court for a child safety order. The order required the girl to stay away from the shopping centre, not mix with the older girls and (with the agreement of the organisers) to attend a local youth programme to make constructive use of her leisure time.'

Whether this proposed response is 'proportionate', gives the child 'appropriate care, protection and support' or 'proper control' is debatable. On its face it seems a Draconian response which focuses on the child in a punitive manner and places no burden of responsibility on the parents to give the child the kind of firm care and attention which protects her from the temptation to go shoplifting. However, it is most unlikely that a child safety order will be made in isolation. Instead the child's parents will be required to support her in complying with the order by means of a parenting order and they risk a fine of up to £1,000 or any other sentence available for non-imprisonable offences should they fail to comply.[19]

---

18 Any requirements imposed under s 11(1) should avoid any conflict with the parents' religious beliefs and any interference with the child's attendance at school, s 12(3).
19 Parenting orders are described below.

The responsible officer's role is to supervise the child and to ensure that he complies with any requirements in the order which the court decides are appropriate. The responsible officer may be a social worker or a member of a youth offending team. He or she must prepare a plan on how the order is to be implemented and monitored and explain this to the child and her parents. The responsible officer is expected to work with the child's parents and, unless there is good reason to the contrary, the parents should be encouraged to take proper responsibility for their child and to support the child during the period of the order. The normal maximum duration is three months. However, section 11(4) provides that where the local authority believe that there are exceptional circumstances relating to the child, his or her family circumstances, or the behaviour, such that they cannot be successfully addressed within the timescale of a typical length order, they may apply for a longer order. This can be for up to a year's duration.

The local authority or the parents may apply for the order to be varied or discharged.[20] Where the reason for the application is because the requirements are not achieving their objectives, other requirements can be inserted in the order. Conversely, where the behaviour which led to the order being made has been 'nipped in the bud' this may be a reason for the order to be discharged ahead of time.

Breach of a child safety order

An application for breach of the order is initiated by the responsible officer who is expected to express a view about how the court might respond to the breach. The court may either make another child safety order or it may discharge the order and make a care order under section 31(1)(a) of the Children Act 1989. It is disturbing to discover that there is no requirement that the threshold test conditions for making a care order must first be overcome.[21] At the time of the Act's enactment the then Lord Chancellor said:

'[The threshold] conditions are the minimum circumstances which the Government considers should always be found to exist before it can ever be justified for a court even to begin to contemplate whether the state should be enabled to intervene compulsorily in family life ... once the court becomes involved in intervention from outside the family, and especially where state intervention is proposed, I do not believe that a broad discretion without defined minimum criteria, whatever its guiding principle, can be justified.'[1]

---

20 Crime and Disorder Act 1998, s 12(4).
21 Children Act 1989, s 31(2).
1   Lord MacKay LC, delivering the Joseph Jackson Memorial Lecture, (1989) 139 NLJ 505.

The minimum criteria which must be overcome in child safety order cases are those contained in section 11(3) of the Crime and Disorder Act 1998, so it is possible to argue that Lord Mackay's concerns have been addressed. However, child safety orders were designed to achieve a different purpose, namely to prevent children under the age of 10 being drawn into criminal and anti-social behaviour and, prima facie, the grounds for intervention are not related to the threshold test. However, significant harm includes impairment of a child's emotional, social or behavioural development[2] and the harm must be attributable either to a lack of reasonable parental care or to the child's being beyond parental control. There appears, therefore, to be no sound reason why a local authority should not be required to overcome the threshold test before a care order can be made where a child safety order has been breached. It is certainly arguable that the language of section 11(3) of the Crime and Disorder Act 1998 fits with some of the situations which the Children Act 1989 envisaged. It will be most unfortunate if the principled safeguards in Parts IV and V of the Children Act 1989 are undermined by the later legislation.

It may be that there is not too much cause for concern because the existing arrangements for applications brought in care proceedings come into effect where the court decides that a care order appears appropriate. The guidance states that, at this stage, the court should consider whether to appoint a guardian ad litem, and the local authority should draw up a care plan. However, the opportunity is there to bypass the appointment of a guardian ad litem and there may well be financial and resource pressures to do so because the child already has a supervising officer. Furthermore, the court merely has to be satisfied that there has been a breach of the order and that a care order is in the interests of the child having regard to the welfare principle and check-list. It is not clear whether the court will be entitled to investigate whether the order was properly made in the first instance and whether it was proportionate to the behaviour complained about. Care orders are not necessarily experienced as benevolent orders by children; they involve loss of liberty and separation from the family. There is a real risk that the Crime and Disorder Act 1998 will see a reintroduction of the use of care orders in a punitive sense.[3]

Parenting orders

Section 8(1)(a) of the Crime and Disorder Act 1998 provides that a parenting order may be imposed where a child safety order has been made.[4] Research

2 Children Act 1989, s 31(9).
3 This was possible under the Children and Young Persons Act 1969.
4 A parenting order may also be made where the court makes an anti-social behaviour order or sex offender order in respect of a child or young person; where a child or young person has been convicted of an offence; and where a person has been convicted of an offence involving non-attendance at school. These circumstances are beyond the scope of this book.

has shown that inadequate parental supervision is strongly associated with youth offending.[5] The same research has also shown that the quality of the relationship between parent and child is crucial.[6] The purpose of the order is to require parents to attend courses which will assist them to prevent their children offending.[7] As with the child safety order, a parenting order is supervised by a responsible officer who is a social worker, a probation officer or a member of a youth offending team,[8] and it would normally be appropriate for the same officer to supervise both the child and the parents. The order is made by the family proceedings court exercising own motion powers. Before making an order the court must first be satisfied that the order would be desirable in the interests of preventing a repetition of the kind of behaviour which led to the child safety order being made.[9] It may be made against one or both parents or against the child's 'guardian'. For the purposes of the order, 'guardian' has the meaning ascribed to it in section 107 of the Children and Young Persons Act 1933; consequently the order may be made against any person who, in the opinion of the court, has for the time being the care of the child or young person. Clearly there is no point in making an order against a parent who is not in the position to support the child because he or she has very little contact with the child.

Requirements in a parenting order

Before making an order the court must obtain information about the parent's family circumstances and the likely effect of the order on those circumstances.[10] Any requirements should, as far as is practicable, avoid any conflict with the parent's religious beliefs and interference with the times when the parent normally works or attends an educational establishment.[11]

---

5   J Graham and B Bowling, *Young People and Crime* Home Office Research Study 145, (1995). This study showed that 42% of juveniles who had low or medium levels of parental supervision had committed offences, whereas only 20% of juveniles had offended where they experienced high levels of parental supervision.

6   For research which reveals that children of parents whose behaviour towards them is harsh or erratic are twice as likely to offend as other children, see D P Farrington *Family backgrounds of aggressive youths* in L Hersov et al *Aggressive and anti-social behaviour in childhood and adolescence* (Pergamon Press, 1978).

7   Research in the United States as early as in 1973 showed that by training parents in negotiation skills, in sticking to clear rules and rewarding good behaviour, offending rates among children were halved, see J F Alexander and B V Parsons, *Short term behavioural intervention with delinquent families: Impact on family process and recidivism* (1973) 81(3) Journal of Abnormal Psychology. See also, *Families and Crime,* NACRO (1997).

8   Established by the local authority under s 39 of the Crime and Disorder Act 1998.

9   S 8(6).

10 S 9(2). Normally the social services department will provide the information where a child safety order has been made.

11 S 9. However, some parents might find it helpful to be involved in some follow up work after the order has been formally completed, and it is suggested that provision should be made for parent support groups or similar activities to be attended on a purely voluntary basis.

The order can impose two types of requirement on the parent. The first is that the parent attends counselling or guidance sessions as directed by the responsible officer. These can last for up to three months but should not involve attendance more than once a week.[12] The second is any other requirement which encourages the parent to exercise a measure of control over the child and to address the behaviour which convinced the court that a child safety order coupled with a parenting order was needed. For example, the parent might be ordered to ensure that his or her child attends school or any extra curricular activities; that the child avoids contact with disruptive and possibly older children; that the child avoids visiting certain areas, such as shopping centres, unless supervised; that the child attends at any courses or sessions; or that the child is at home and properly supervised during the evening.[13]

Parenting orders can be varied or discharged in the same way as child safety orders.[14] Breach of the order is a criminal offence and there is an obligation on the responsible officer to report any failure to comply with any of the requirements in the order to the police. Any prosecution is heard in the magistrates' court, and where the parent is found guilty the normal sentencing powers open to a court for a non-imprisonable offence are available to the court.[15]

Part of the thinking informing child safety and parenting orders is protection of children. Responsible adults normally take the view that young children should not be out late at night, should not be involved in offending behaviour and should be properly looked after by their parents. However, it will sometimes be the case that a child who avoids being at home in the evenings is keeping out of the way of domestic violence. Moreover, the child who associates with offenders may be modelling his behaviour on that of his parents. Requiring such children to spend more time in the company of their parents may not, therefore, always be in the child's best interests. Indeed, it may put some children at greater risk of suffering significant harm. Whether counselling for parents will address these concerns remains to be seen. Much will depend on how the super-vising officer sees his or her role. If it contains a child protection and child welfare element then, maybe, there is no need to fear for the children. If the role focuses solely on tackling crime and disorder and general anti-social behaviour by children, then the suffering of some children may be increased. It remains to be seen whether what may turn out to be mainly punitive orders will best handle the control of children under the age of 10 and prevent them 'offending', truanting or otherwise behaving dis-ruptively. It might be better to increase the resourcing and funding of services for children in need and their families under Part III of the Children Act 1989.

---

12 Guidance suggests that they should be no less than six or seven two-hourly sessions.
13 These examples are suggested in the guidance to the Act.
14 There is a right of appeal against both child safety and parenting orders to the Divisional Court of the Queen's Bench Division.
15 The sentence could be an absolute or conditional discharge, a fine of up to £1,000, a probation order, a curfew order (available in certain areas only), or a community sentence.

Chapter 4

Approaches to welfare in children cases

Enforcement of contact in the face of parental obduracy
Where contact is likely to destabilise the child's present family unit
Concealing a child's true paternity
Contact where a parent has caused harm to the child
Authorising the child's removal from the jurisdiction
The child's wishes and feelings
The weight given to the child's wishes and feelings
Change of a child's surname
Change of surname and parental responsibility
Change of surname and the child's welfare
Adoption and welfare
'Open adoption'
The welfare test in adoption
Placement for adoption and selection adopters
Removal of a child from prospective adopters
Agreement to adoption
Freeing for adoption
Revocation of a freeing order
Applying for an adoption order
The unmarried father and agreeing to adoption
Dispensing with agreement to adoption
The parent is withholding his or her agreement unreasonably
Baby adoptions and dispensing with agreement
Is adoption by a step-parent in the child's interests?
Step-parent adoption and dispensing with agreement
Adoption with contact
Adoption as a child's care plan
Children in care and dispensing with agreement

Chapter 4

Approaches to welfare in children cases

Civil child law proceedings and welfare

Where a child is directly or indirectly involved in legal proceedings the law, and procedures associated with the law, are likely to impinge on the child's welfare. During the second half of this century increasing respect and regard has been given to the rights and interests of children who are caught up in the civil process and this is reflected both in the development of various aspects of the substantive law and in the processes which are designed to resolve family and other disputes.[1] Giving consideration and weight to the welfare of the child sometimes gives rise to tension in those cases where the child's welfare appears to conflict with principles which also command high regard. Sometimes the child's welfare must be treated as the paramount consideration, but at other times there is no statutory or common law principle which states what importance should be given to welfare considerations. In this chapter the weight given to the welfare of the child is considered in a variety of contexts.[2] It commences with the vexed question of whether certain types of conflicts involving children should ever come before the courts, or whether they are better handled outside the court system through private ordering.

Agreed arrangements are normally in the child's best interests

Before a court can make an order in family proceedings it must be satisfied that it would be better for the child than making no order at all.[3] This

---

1   This is also being reflected in criminal proceedings where a child is a witness. Some attempts have been made to reduce the trauma this causes by allowing a child to give evidence in court shielded by screens, or by allowing the child's evidence to be recorded on video tape from a separate room.
2   For an interesting account of how the law in Australia, which was altered by the Family Law Reform Act 1995 and requires the court to take into account the child's 'best interests', can be compared and contrasted with the approach to welfare contained in the Children Act 1989 see R Bailey-Harris and J Dewar *Variations on a theme – child law reform in Australia* (1997) 9 CFLQ 149.
3   Children Act 1989, s 1(5).

principle reflects an increasing realisation that courts are not always the most appropriate forum within which decisions about the upbringing of children should be made. This is particularly true in those cases where the persons in dispute are the parents and where there is no issue about whether the state should intervene to protect the child. In cases of this kind the law seeks to promote a climate in which parents and others are encouraged to take steps to find their own solution to the matter in dispute. The thinking behind this approach is that if parents are able to agree about the child's upbringing they are more likely to abide by their agreement, and therefore an agreed outcome will better promote the child's welfare than a solution imposed by a court. But when parents are quarrelling, and where they are grappling with the myriad of feelings which usually accompany relationship breakdown, they often may not be capable of reaching agreement about the upbringing of their children without the assistance of a third party.

Sometimes the third party will be a lawyer, and intervention by lawyers on behalf of their clients often leads to an agreed outcome. When parents instruct separate lawyers they become involved in a process of negotiation: they tell their lawyers about what they want to achieve, and whether and how they are prepared to reach a compromise. This process, in which the parties are kept at arm's length, and in which the lawyers act as inter-mediaries, may achieve a satisfactory outcome for all, including the child.[4] But there is a risk that lawyers will use their skills in such a way that the quality of the parents' relationship is further undermined, and so that the chances of them maintaining a reasonable association with one another in the future is further diminished. Certainly, if negotiation fails and the case comes before a court, even the most sensitive and careful of lawyers, who is mindful that an aggressive and point-scoring approach is usually unhelpful, must nonetheless present his client's case in a manner which is favourable to the client's position.[5] This usually involves not only promoting the client's strengths, but also emphasising the opposing party's weaknesses and seeking to discredit him or her as a parent. As Sir Thomas Bingham has said, it is 'notorious that, when marriages break down and problems arise affecting the children, resolution of these problems through the ordinary processes of adversarial litigation often leads to exaggerated accusations and counter-accusations with, in consequence, an exacerbation of feelings and a heightening of tension'.[6] Thus the legal process may sometimes aggravate existing hostilities, store up trouble for the future and give rise to further litigation. When this occurs, the aim of the legal process to conclude the dispute in the interests of the child is defeated.

4   However, no-one has the task of ascertaining the wishes and feelings of the child and the lawyers will rely on their clients accurately to reflect the child's wishes. See C Piper *Ascertaining the wishes and feelings of the child* [1997] Fam Law 796.
5   The Solicitors' Family Law Association operates a code of practice which encourages lawyers to approach family cases in a constructive and non-aggressive manner.
6   *Re D (Minors) (Conciliation: Disclosure of Information)* [1993] 2 All ER 693, at p 695.

Where the parties cannot reach a solution with the assistance of their lawyers, and where the matter is then placed before a court, the court will normally impose a solution on the parties by making an order. But children cases are different from most other types of civil litigation in which court orders provide a remedy for wrongs which have occurred in the past. By contrast, the majority of court orders in children cases are not concerned with the past, but state what arrangements must be made for the child in the future. But of course whilst courts can anticipate what is likely to happen in relation to the child and his parents they cannot know what will happen. Yet it is inevitable that the personal circumstances of the parents and their children will alter.[7] Sometimes these changes in circumstances will mean that a solution imposed by court order, which was acceptable to all at the time it was made, suddenly becomes un-acceptable to one of the parties, or to the child.[8] When this occurs, a major disadvantage of a court-imposed order is likely to become apparent, namely the order is probably inflexible and incapable of making provision for the altered circumstances. Consequently, where the parents cannot agree on alternative arrangements, the party who wants the arrangements to be changed must apply to the court for the original order to be varied, and thus the parents and the child become embroiled in further litigation about the child's upbringing. Such a process can rarely be in the child's best interests, and in many cases it may be positively harmful to the child.

Conciliation and mediation

A recognition that the legal process is often not the most appropriate system for resolving conflict about the upbringing of children has, in recent years, led to a growing movement to encourage parents to make use of conciliation and mediation services.[9] Conciliation and mediation do not form part of the legal process but as a matter of practice they are becoming an important tool in the procedure of many courts.[10] Proponents of these services explain that often it is only after a parent in a failed relationship has been able to voice his or her anger, anxiety, distress and fears within a safe and non-judgemental environment that he or she becomes capable of making sensible decisions about the upbringing of the children. Proponents also explain that parties to a broken relationship are often

---

7　The mere fact that the children grow older may make a court order inappropriate or unenforceable.

8　This problem usually arises in cases concerning contact arrangements.

9　For an account of the development of conciliation as a recognised process, see University of Newcastle Conciliation Project Unit *Report to the Lord Chancellor on the Costs and Effectiveness of Conciliation in England and Wales* (1989). See too, G Davis *Partisans and Mediators* (1988, Oxford University Press); J M Eekelaar and R Dingwall (eds) *The development of conciliation in England*, in *Divorce Mediation and the Legal Process* (1988, Clarendon Press).

10　See *Practice Direction: Conciliation – Children* [1992] 1 FLR 228.

unable to communicate with one another about their children because of the level of misunderstanding and mistrust which has grown up between them, and that an invaluable aspect of the service provided by conciliation and mediation is that it facilitates parents to communicate with one another.[11] Conciliation and mediation provide a structured setting in which parents, and sometimes the children and other relatives,[12] meet with an independent third party and explore whether they can reach an agreement. Sometimes it is only where spouses and partners have been able to work through their feelings about the ending of their relationship that they are capable of negotiating reasonable contact arrangements for the children.

Marriage or relationship breakdown often precipitates one or both of the parties into a state of emotional turmoil, which varies in its intensity, and the parties may not have the energy to concentrate on the emotional needs of their children. When suffering the pain and anger associated with relationship breakdown, some parents behave in ways which they would not normally contemplate. They may regress into child-like behaviour which includes an aggressive determination to pursue their own personal needs. Disputes over contact can give rise to some of the most bitter and difficult conflicts over the upbringing of children, and the warring of the adults is often at the expense of their children. Consequently the process of conciliation may be particularly suited to resolving contact issues. The process is designed to empower those using the service to arrive at their own solution, and in this way the responsibility for making decisions about the upbringing of children stays where it belongs, with the parents and children themselves.

Conciliation also provides a process in which people can resolve their differences without feeling under pressure of time, and without feeling that unless they agree the court may impose an unacceptable arrangement on them.[13] For this reason some take the view that the provision of conciliation and mediation services under a court-directed system, with persons being pressured into making use of these services, could be self-defeating, because an agreement reached under these conditions might not be one to which the parties had freely given their consent. It also could be unfair to one of the parties. On the other hand it is said that there is evidence that many parents who reach a mediated agreement, and who then check the arrangements with their own solicitor in order to obtain reassurance that it is fair and appropriate, abide by the decision they have reached. This is clearly for the benefit of all parties.

11 Although conciliation services must carefully be distinguished from services which are designed to assist spouses and unmarried couples to explore whether they can be reconciled, reconciliation is sometimes the outcome of conciliation because, through using the process, the couple start to speak to one another about matters which go to the heart of their relationship.
12 For example, grandparents seeking contact with their grandchildren.
13 For example, where people arrive at an agreement 'at the door of the court' under some pressure from their counsel, solicitor and sometimes from the judge himself.

The notion that parents are free to arrive at their own decision within a process assisted by a third-party conciliator has, however, been doubted. This notion pre-supposes that the conciliator is neutral, and does not seek to impose his or her views on the parties. But, as has been pointed out, all such arrangements are arrived at 'within the shadow of the law'[14] and it has been asserted that 'the conciliator is clearly not neutral but the purveyor of certain ideologies and practices';[15] and that 'the common thread of an idea can be almost lost through the speed with which it is modified to suit the purposes of practitioners in different fields'.[16]

Which courts hear children cases?

Family proceedings arise in the High Court, county court and magistrates' court and are widely defined.[17] In family proceedings the court hearing the substantive application may also make orders under section 8 of the Children Act 1989 in relation to the children. The courts also exercise a concurrent jurisdiction in relation to freestanding applications brought under the Act, and questions then arise concerning which court is the most appropriate forum for hearing particular cases. The Children (Allocation of Proceedings) Order 1991 provides that care and other public law proceedings should normally commence in the magistrates' court.[18] However, that court has power to transfer any such proceedings upwards, and should do so where this would obviate delay, or where the proceedings are exceptionally grave, important or complex and for other specified reasons.[19] It has been held that magistrates should transfer a case to the county court where there is conflicting evidence, or where the case involves a very difficult assessment of risk to the child.[20] That court can in turn decide whether the case is more suited to be heard by a High Court judge. Private law proceedings, by contrast, can commence in any court. Where they are started in the magistrates' court they can be transferred to the county court, and in *R v South East Hampshire Family Proceedings Court, ex p D*[1] it was held that when a magistrates' court is determining whether to transfer a case its main function is to consider which court is most

---

14 A famous phrase first coined by R Mnookin and L Kornhauser in *Bargaining in the shadow of the law: the case of divorce* (1979) 88 Yale Law Journal 950.
15 A Bottomley *Resolving family disputes: a critical view* in *State, Law and the Family: Critical Perspectives*, ed. M D A Freeman (1984, Stevens).
16 G Davis *Mediation in divorce: a theoretical perspective* [1983] JSWL 131.
17 Children Act 1989, s 8(3), (4).
18 Art 3.
19 Art 7; examples of particular circumstances are included in the article. Directions are sometimes given that certain decisions should always be made by a High Court judge; see for example, *Re HIV Tests* [1994] 2 FLR 116.
20 *C v Solihull Metropolitan Borough Council* [1993] 1 FLR 290; *S v Oxfordshire County Council* [1993] 1 FLR 452.
1 [1994] 2 All ER 445.

appropriate, and what would be in the interests of the child. It is not limited to transferring cases solely where this would prevent delay.

Evidence in children cases and welfare

Before a court can make a decision it must first be supplied with information upon which to base its ruling. In children cases this information may come from a variety of sources. Parents, relatives and other persons with a personal interest in the child may give evidence about past incidents relating to the child and what each of them has to offer the child in the future. Other persons may give evidence in support of one of the parties. An expert witness may be asked to give his or her opinion; this may be about a contested issue of fact, such as whether injuries to a child were caused deliberately or whether they could have occurred accidentally, or it may be about which course of action the witness, in his or her professional judgment, thinks would best promote the child's welfare. In a contested private law case a court is likely to request a court welfare officer to make enquiries into the child's present circumstances, to interview the parties and other relevant persons and to supply the court with a report on his or her findings. The courts are highly dependent upon this investigative service; without it they would often lack the necessary material upon which to make an informed decision. In public law cases where a local authority is a party to the proceedings a guardian ad litem for the child will normally have been appointed and he or she will provide a report for the court, and will often give oral evidence too. During the course of the hearing the court may itself take the view that it needs more information before it arrives at its decision. It may find out what it needs to know simply by putting questions to the witnesses, or it may adjourn the case for further inquiries to be made, or for an expert witness to be approached to assist the court.

Court control over evidence which can be adduced

Parties to proceedings about the upbringing of a child often wish to obtain a report from an expert or experts about the child's health or development. This gives rise to a risk that a child might be exposed to unnecessary and upsetting medical, psychiatric or other assessments for the purpose of legal proceedings, particularly where such an assessment would include an intimate physical examination. This risk, and the realisation that some children were seriously harmed in Cleveland during the period when there were intensive investigations into allegations of child sexual abuse,[2] led to rules being made which prevent such examinations and assessments

---

2   *Report of the Inquiry into Child Abuse in Cleveland 1987*, Cm 412 (1988).

being conducted without the court's leave.[3] Where such an examination or assessment does take place without leave first being obtained, no evidence arising from it may be adduced without the leave of the court.[4] These rules are a major invasion into the normal right of a litigant to prepare his or her case in the manner which the litigant regards as most appropriate, and they apply uniquely to children cases. It is suggested that they can be justified on the basis that it is the child who is the subject matter of the proceedings even though he or she is not a party to them, and therefore there must be procedural safeguards which protect the child's rights and interests. As the court's inquiry is focused on what decision will advance the child's welfare the court is empowered to control the preparation of a party's case where it appears to conflict with the child's welfare.

The parties must submit witness statements and other documentary evidence supporting their case well in advance of the hearing, the actual timing being as directed by the court.[5] In a case where a guardian ad litem has been appointed, once he completes his investigation he must file a written report advising on the interests of the child which must be served on the parties to the proceedings at least seven days in advance of the hearing.[6] These time periods are intended to afford all parties to the proceedings the opportunity to deal with any allegations made in witness statements, in the guardian ad litem's report, in experts' reports and in reports prepared by the local authority, either by arranging to call witnesses in rebuttal or by taking other steps. If these rules are not complied with, and if an adjournment is refused, an aggrieved party might have grounds for proceeding in judicial review on the basis that he has been denied a fair hearing because he has not received sufficient notice of the case.[7]

A distinctive feature of proceedings brought under the Children Act 1989 is their semi-inquisitorial nature. Increasingly this has led to courts taking firm directive control over the way in which proceedings before them are conducted. Such control occurs where the court exercises its powers under the rules to give, vary or revoke directions for the conduct of the proceedings.[8] Directions may be given about a wide range of matters and directions hearings are not merely a formality; their purpose is to enable the court firmly to come to grips with the case.[9] Court control also occurs when the court asks a child's guardian ad litem to obtain an expert's report or otherwise to assist the court.[10] The House of Lords has made it plain that children cases fall into a special category because the welfare

---

3 Family Proceedings Courts (Children Act 1989) Rules 1991, r 18(1); Family Proceedings Rules 1991, r 4.18. The rules are virtually identical and reference will therefore be made to the former rules only, unless otherwise stated.
4 R 18(3).
5 R 17.
6 R 11(7).
7 *R v West Malling Juvenile Court, ex p K* [1986] 2 FLR 405.
8 R 14.
9 *B v B (Child Abuse: Contact)* [1994] 2 FLR 713.
10 R 11(9), (10).

of the child is paramount.[11] Consequently, the court may, for example, call a witness of its own motion,[12] or it may give leave for a person not a party to intervene in the proceedings.[13] It may be essential for a court to exercise such powers so that it is acquainted with as much relevant information as possible before it arrives at an adjudication.[14]

Expert evidence

The evidence of an expert differs from that of an ordinary witness of fact because he may give opinion evidence. The role of the expert is not to promote a particular cause or point of view; such an approach is to advance an argument and not an opinion. Rather, the court looks for objectivity and impartiality in an expert witness and for his expression of opinion to be properly researched so that the court can place reliance on it.[15] In some cases this may mean that an expert may find that he has to give an opinion adverse to his client.[16] Fundamentally, it is the duty of an expert not to mislead the court. As Cazalet J said in *Re R (A Minor) (Experts' Evidence)*[17] 'an absence of objectivity may result in a child being wrongly placed and thereby unnecessarily put at risk'. In *Re M (Minors) (Care Proceedings) (Child's Wishes)*[18] Wall J emphasised the non-adversarial nature of children's proceedings, and stressed the vital importance of expert evidence in assisting the judge to arrive at the correct decision.[19] The court must be satisfied that the expert has the appropriate qualifications and

11 *Re L (Police Investigation: Privilege)* [1996] 1 FLR 731.
12 'In my experience, where fairness requires that an advocate should be able to cross-examine rather than suffer the handicap of examination-in-chief, the court will itself occasionally call the witness so that cross-examination can take place' *Re P (Witness Summons)* [1997] 2 FLR 447 at p 453, per Wilson J.
13 *Re S (Care: Residence: Intervener)* [1997] 1 FLR 497.
14 In *Re S (Care: Residence: Intervener)* above, the Court of Appeal affirmed that there will be cases where a court should exercise its powers in order to ensure that the interests of a person who is alleged to have harmed a child, but who is not a party to the proceedings, are adequately protected within the judicial process.
15 See G Brasse *The expert rules – Ok?* [1996] Fam Law 547, for a consideration of proposals relating to expert evidence as they apply to children cases, detailed in the Woolf Report *Access to Justice* (LCD).
16 See the detailed guidance given to experts by Cazalet J in *Re R (A Minor) (Experts' Evidence)* [1991] 1 FLR 291n; and by Wall J in *Re M (Minors) (Care Proceedings: Child's Wishes)* [1994] 1 FLR 749. See generally, J R Spencer and R Flin *The Evidence of Children* (Blackstone Press, 2nd edn, 1993); C Keenan and C Williams *Expert witnesses in child sexual abuse cases* (1993) 1 Med Law Int 57; D Ormerod *Expert witnesses in children's cases* (1992) 4 JCL 122; and the opposing views of M N Howard and J R Spencer [1991] Crim LR 98 and 106.
17 [1991] 1 FLR 291n.
18 [1994] 1 FLR 749.
19 Wall J has also given extensive guidance on the preparation of cases for trial when expert witnesses are involved, *Re M (Minors) (Care Proceedings) (Child's Wishes)* above; *Re DH (A Minor) (Child Abuse)* [1994] 1 FLR 679; *Re M and TD (Minors) (Time Estimates)* [1994] 2 FLR 336; *Re G (Minors) (Expert Witnesses)* [1994] 2 FLR 291.

experience to be accepted as an expert in the field of expertise relevant to his testimony.[20] Where the expert does not satisfy these requirements his opinion evidence is liable to be discounted. Sometimes so-called 'experts' give evidence based on no properly conducted research[1] and on no clinical information, and courts and lawyers need to be very wary of this. Thus in *Rochdale Borough Council v A*[2] Douglas Brown J was dismissive of the testimony of the expert witness called by the local authority in relation to allegations of child sexual abuse, including satanic abuse, because, he said 'she is not a child psychologist, she is a clinical psychologist, dealing mainly with adults. She has had no experience of ritual or satanic abuse, and bases her views almost entirely on her understanding of writings on the subject.'

A witness may sometimes be asked to give an opinion about a child's mental state and whether the child has a propensity to fantasise, or otherwise invent information which is presented to the court as an accurate statement of fact. It is clear that it lies within the scope of a witness's professional competence to express an opinion about whether what a child has said to the witness is credible. Where the case turns on whether or not a child is telling the truth, the proper limits on what an expert may say to the court about the child's credibility has been the subject of a number of decisions, and at one stage the approach of the courts was extremely narrow.[3] The legal position was clarified in *Re M and R (Child Abuse: Evidence)*[4] where it emerged that earlier judgments of the Court

---

20 See C A Kaplan et al *The use of expert witnesses – trials and tribulations* [1997] Fam Law 735 for an account of some research conducted into how legal professionals select experts and use their expertise, and how health professionals work in the legal arena. Also, see K Weir *Evaluating child sexual abuse* [1996] Fam Law 673 for a description of the framework which one consultant psychiatrist has developed in order to assist the court in demonstrating how he forms an expert opinion as to whether or not a child has been sexually abused.

1 For an extreme example of this see *Re AB (Child Abuse: Expert Witnesses)* [1995] 1 FLR 181 in which Wall J was severely critical of an expert witness who propounded a theory about brittle bone disease. The witness had omitted to take into account a vital piece of information inconsistent with his theory, had given no indication that his theory of causation was a matter of controversy and ignored credible material which contradicted his views. In commenting on his evidence Wall J said: 'I regard that omission as a grave breach of Dr Paterson's duty to the court as an expert witness in putting before it an opinion upon which he invites the court to rely'. (At p 195).

2 [1991] 2 FLR 192, at p 216; contrast his approach to the testimony of this witness with his acceptance of the evidence of another witness whom he described as very experienced in the field; see too *Re E (A Minor) (Child Abuse: Evidence)* [1991] 1 FLR 420 in which a police surgeon admitted in evidence that he had neither the knowledge nor experience to reach a definite conclusion that a child had been anally penetrated.

3 Obiter dicta in *Re S and B (Minors) (Child Abuse: Evidence)* [1990] 2 FLR 489 was particularly influential, and as a consequence the approach of the civil courts was in danger of becoming more restrictive to the reception of expert evidence than under the rules relating to criminal trials, see Butler-Sloss LJ in *Re M and R (Child Abuse: Evidence)* [1996] 2 FLR 195, at p 208.

4 [1996] 2 FLR 195. Commenting on *Re FS (Child Abuse: Evidence)* [1996] 2 FLR 158 and *Re N (Child Abuse: Evidence)* [1996] 2 FLR 214, Butler-Sloss LJ said, at p 210, 'we do not believe those courts would have expressed themselves in the terms they did had they been aware of [the provisions of the Civil Evidence] Act'.

of Appeal had been made per incuriam because the court had never been referred to the Civil Evidence Act 1972. It is, of course, not for the experts to decide the case, the final decision is always a matter for the judge but nevertheless section 3 of the Civil Evidence Act 1972[5] makes it clear that expert opinion evidence is admissible on the ultimate issue in a case. Thus, 'in cases involving children, expert medical and psychiatric evidence from paediatricians and allied disciplines is often quite indispensable to the court' and the court is entitled to receive 'all the help it can get' in arriving at its decision.[6]

Legal professional privilege

When a person who is a party to legal proceedings asks an expert witness to prepare a report for actual or contemplated legal proceedings usually that person will want to rely on the report at the hearing. However, sometimes the expert's report, far from assisting the person who has commissioned it, may in fact be adverse to his case. The general rule relating to civil litigation is that the report is covered by legal professional privilege and therefore only the party concerned can waive the privilege and choose whether to disclose the information to other parties to the proceedings. The reason for this privilege is to encourage experts to give their opinions fully and frankly to the persons who engage them, and to enable them to comment on the case, with all its strengths and weaknesses, without fear that the other side will be able to take advantage of this openness.

In relation to children cases the arguments in favour of privilege are overriden by other, stronger, policy considerations. The thinking which justifies treating children cases differently is that courts should not decide such cases in ignorance of material facts. It was made clear in *R v Hampshire County Council, ex p K*[7] that local authorities do not have the benefit of legal professional privilege in respect of experts' reports in care proceedings. They are obliged to disclose to all parties all relevant documents and experts' reports which are in their possession. In *Oxfordshire County Council v M*[8] this principle was extended to the other parties

---

5 S 3(1) provides – '… where a person is called as a witness in any civil proceedings, his opinion on any relevant matter on which he is qualified to give expert evidence shall be admissible in evidence'.

6 *Re M and R (Child Abuse: Evidence)* [1996] 2 FLR 195, per Butler-Sloss LJ, at pp 205-206. See too N Wall, 'Issues arising from the involvement of and expert evidence given by psychiatrists and psychologists in proceedings involving children' in N Wall (ed) *Rooted Sorrows* (Family Law, 1997), at pp 37-41.

7 [1990] 2 All ER 129.

8 [1994] 2 All ER 269, following the ruling of Thorpe J in *Re R (A Minor) (Disclosure of Privileged Material)* [1993] 4 All ER 702. For a commentary on the Oxfordshire case see J McEwan *Privilege and the Children Act 1989 – confusion compounded?* (1995) 7 CFLQ 236.

to care proceedings. The Court of Appeal ruled that children cases fall into a special category in which the welfare of the child is the court's paramount concern. It said that if a party was able to conceal, or withhold from the court, important matters relevant to the future of the child, there would be a risk that the welfare of the child would not be promoted as the Children Act 1989 requires. The court therefore concluded that the court has power to override legal professional privilege in relation to experts' reports in care proceedings when it gives leave to the parties to obtain them.

The Court of Appeal did not expressly cover the question whether counsel has a duty to make voluntary disclosure of an expert's report on which he is not intending to rely. It is a matter of fundamental principle that there should be confidence between a client and his advocate, and it would normally be regarded as an extremely serious breach of professional practice if a lawyer were to disclose material which was against his client's interests, and contrary to instructions. Nonetheless, in *Essex County Council v R*[9] Thorpe J said: 'For my part I would wish to see case law go further and to make it plain that the legal representatives in possession of such material relevant to determination but contrary to the interests of their client, not only are unable to resist disclosure by reliance on legal professional privilege, but have a positive duty to disclose to the other parties and to the court.' In *Re DH (A Minor) (Child Abuse)*,[10] Wall J stated (obiter): 'In my judgement ... the answer is that the client needs to be told authoritatively at an early stage in the relationship that whilst the advocate has a duty to present the client's case to the best of his or her ability, the advocate has a higher duty to the court and to the child whose interests are paramount to disclose relevant material to the court even if that disclosure is not in the interests of his client.' He concluded that practitioners should therefore be under a duty to disclose all material, unless and until the Court of Appeal ruled otherwise.[11]

Clearly the extent and scope of legal professional privilege was a matter of fundamental importance which needed to be resolved at the highest level. An opportunity arose in *Re L (A Minor) (Police Investigation: Privilege)*.[12] Interim care orders were granted in respect of a child, L, after she was found to have ingested methadone. L's mother, who was an addict, claimed that the child had accidentally taken the drug on one occasion. The mother's solicitor advised her that a report from a consultant chemical pathologist should be obtained. The parents applied for leave to disclose the court papers to this expert[13] and leave was granted by the district

---

9   [1993] 2 FLR 826, at p 828.
10 [1994] 1 FLR 679, at p 704.
11 Wall J dealt with some of the practical difficulties this approach can cause, ibid, at p 704; he also said that the letter of instruction to an expert is not privileged, and should therefore be disclosed.
12 [1996] 2 All ER 78.
13 As required by the Family Proceedings Rules, r 4.23.

judge, on condition that the expert's report would be filed with the court. The report was not favourable to the mother. It cast doubt on her account of events and on her claim that the ingestation had been accidental. However, the report was filed without any attempt being made by the mother's solicitor to vary the terms of the district judge's order. Meanwhile the police, who were not parties to the proceedings, came to hear of the report at a case conference. They sought an order authorising disclosure of the report to them for the purpose of making enquiries into whether a crime had been committed.

The issue for the House of Lords was whether disclosure of the report would infringe the mother's legal professional privilege. Their Lordships, by a 3:2 majority, ruled that it would not. A distinction was drawn between communication between a solicitor and his client, to which absolute legal professional privilege applies, and the privilege attaching to reports by third parties prepared on the instructions of a client for the purposes of litigation, which the House of Lords described as litigation privilege. Litigation privilege is an essential component of adversarial proceedings.[14] However, the essence of children proceedings is that they are primarily non-adversarial; rather, they are investigative. The role of the court is to to make a decision which is in the best interests of the child in question. This investigative, child-focused approach is illustrated by the power of the court to make orders exercising own motion powers,[15] and by its powers in care proceedings to require the guardian ad litem to obtain experts' reports and other assistance. The court's leave is required before an expert can examine a child for the purpose of preparing a report for the court and leave must be given before reports already filed with the court can be disclosed to the expert. The majority of their Lordships therefore concluded that litigation privilege has no place in children proceedings.[16]

It still remains uncertain whether there is a positive duty on a party to proceedings concerning children to make voluntary disclosure of all matters likely to be material to the welfare of the child, and whether this duty extends to legal representatives in possession of such material, even though such disclosure is contrary to the interests of their client. The imposition of such a duty would be a dramatic inroad into the area of legal professional privilege. Lord Jauncey, speaking for the majority in Re *L (A Minor) (Police Investigation: Privilege)*, said that while it might

---

14 In adversarial proceedings the judge must decide the case in favour of one party or the other upon such evidence as they choose to adduce, however much he may wish for further evidence on any point to be placed before the court.

15 Children Act 1989, ss 10(1)(b), 31(5), 34(5).

16 For further commentary on the decision in Re *L (A Minor) (Police Investigation: Privilege)* see C Tapper, *Evidential privilege in cases involving children* (1997) 9 CFLQ 1; B Walsh *Beyond legal professional privilege* [1996] Fam Law 412; D Burrows *Disclosure in children cases* [1996] Fam Law 566; G Brasse *The duty of disclosure in children cases* [1996] Fam Law 358.

well be that such a development would be welcome in cases where the welfare of children is involved, he did not find it necessary to come to a conclusion on the point.[17]

Public interest immunity and confidential information

Information obtained by local authorities and others in the course of their duties towards children is confidential and covered by the umbrella of public interest immunity.[18] Public interest immunity arises where confidentiality cannot be waived because this would be against the public interest. Consequently, the rule that there should be full disclosure of reports and statements for the purpose of legal proceedings is qualified where public interest immunity will justify withholding specific information. Local authorities must be able to carry out their statutory child care functions without fear that they will be forced to divulge highly sensitive information. Where the public interest in ensuring that all relevant information is disclosed comes into conflict with the public interest that children are protected from suffering significant harm, the former may have to yield to the latter. Thus in *D v National Society for the Prevention of Cruelty to Children*[19] the House of Lords ruled that if a local authority were to be forced to name the person who has passed information about a child to the NSPCC, this might deter others from coming forward to give information on a confidential basis. It can be seen here that the broader principle that the law should safeguard the welfare of all children prevailed against the claim of an individual litigant to obtain access to material information relating to proposed litigation.[1]

There is, however, no absolute rule against the disclosure of information protected by public interest immunity to parties to legal proceedings. It is for the court to decide whether disclosure is in the pubic interest. Guidance

17 [1996] 2 All ER 78, at p 87. Contrast *R v Derby Magistrates' Court, ex p B* [1995] 4 All ER 526 where a man charged with murder wanted to have access to proofs of evidence given by his stepson so that he could better defend himself. The House of Lords held that once legal professional privilege attaches to any communication the privilege is absolute and cannot be overridden by the court for any reason. See also Lord Nicholls' powerful dissent in *Re L (A Minor) (Police Investigation: Privilege)*.

18 *Re D (Infants)* [1970] 1 WLR 599. It is clear that confidential information can be disclosed to fellow members of a child protection team engaged in the investigation of a possible case of child abuse, for any other approach would prevent the inter-agency co-operation which is essential for good professional practice. See *Re G (A Minor) (Social Worker: Disclosure)* [1996] 2 All ER 65; *Re W (Disclosure to Police)* [1998] 2 FLR 135. Access to confidential information by the different agencies with duties towards children is the subject of comprehensive guidance in Working Together (HMSO, 1991).

19 [1977] 1 All ER 589.

1 See too *Re D (Minors) (Wardship: Disclosure)* [1994] 1 FLR 346, in which it was said that social work case notes, medical records and other documents in the possession of the local authority, and health authority, probably attracted public interest immunity.

was given in *Re M (A Minor) (Disclosure of Material)*[2] on how courts should approach an application for the production of records and other documentary material about a child. *Re M (A Minor) (Disclosure of Material)*[3] was about the future care of S, a child of five. S had been made a ward because her half sister, A, had made an allegation of sexual abuse by her father, who was also S's father. The father strenuously denied the allegations.[4] He applied in the wardship proceedings for the production by the local authority of, inter alia, all social services case records, reports, notes and memoranda relating to A.[5] Waite J refused to order discovery. The Court of Appeal held that the judge had been wrong to impose a blanket refusal on disclosure, for while an application for general discovery was inappropriate, an application for disclosure of specific documents might be appropriate. Social work and analagous records are in a special category of public interest immunity justified by the underlying principle of the welfare of the child, but this principle may require disclosure to other parties and to the court. Accordingly, it may be necessary for local authorities to volunteer disclosure of certain records, such as contemporaneous notes in a neglect case or the actual notes of interviews in a sexual abuse case. The local authority does not need the leave of the court to make such disclosure because of the nature of the immunity they enjoy. 'The wider interests of the child may require consideration of the position of the parents as well as the narrower concerns of the case put forward by the local authority for the protection of the child.'[6] In a disputed case the judge has a duty to weigh up the competing public interests when determining whether to order disclosure.[7]

The power of the court to give leave for protected information to be disclosed means that it is never safe for parties and witnesses to assume that wardship or Children Act proceedings are totally confidential. In *Re Manda*[8] a child had been made a ward of court when he was twelve, because it was suspected that he had been sexually abused, and had been committed to the care of a local authority. Evidence had been given in the wardship proceedings by a consultant paediatrician who had examined the child. Subsequently the boy was returned to his parents and the wardship was discharged. The parents, who had always vehemently denied abusing their son, wished to institute proceedings on his behalf in negligence or trespass to the person.[9] The parents'

---

2   [1990] 2 FLR 36.
3   Which preceded the Children Act 1989 and was brought in wardship proceedings.
4   He was prosecuted and acquitted on charges of incest and rape.
5   He also applied for the disclosure of all medical and psychiatric notes and records relating to A which were the subject of separate proceedings.
6   [1990] 2 FLR 36, at p 43.
7   It may be necessary for the judge to inspect the documents in order to decide whether production should be ordered.
8   [1993] 1 All ER 733.
9   The child himself reached majority during the course of the litigation and would therefore be able to pursue his own claim.

solicitors had in their possession papers relating to the wardship proceedings, and the parents sought leave to disclose these documents to solicitors acting on their child's behalf in the proposed civil action. Thus a conflict existed between the interests of the particular child who wished to pursue litigation, and the general public interest in preserving confidentiality in relation to wardship proceedings.[10] In this case the interests of the child litigant prevailed. The Court of Appeal ruled that the public interest in seeing that he had available to him all relevant information outweighed the public interest in preserving witness confidentiality. Balcombe LJ also gave a warning to professionals giving evidence in children cases that they should not assume that this evidence would always be treated as confidential.

Similarly, in *Re K (Minors) (Disclosure)*[11] a father sought leave to disclose at his trial for rape evidence adduced in proceedings brought under the Children Act 1989. The court, granting him leave, held that while it had to have regard for the interests of the children concerned, it had to balance the importance of confidentiality and frankness in children proceedings against the public interest in ensuring that persons receive a fair trial and that the interests of justice are properly served. It was in the interests of justice that the defendant in a criminal trial should have available all relevant and necessary material for the conduct of his defence.[12]

The courts are extremely wary of extending the notion of confidentiality in children cases to situations where a court welfare officer, or a guardian ad litem, wishes to place information before the court, but asks that the contents of that information should not be disclosed to the parties to the proceedings. It is a fundamental principle of natural justice that persons should be informed of the nature of any allegations made against them. A court should not make a decision in reliance on information which is adverse to one of the parties unless that party has been given the opportunity to challenge it, or to address the court about it. However, occasionally a situation arises when an application is made that information before the judge should not be disclosed to the parties because it is alleged that it will be harmful to the child. Here the principle that there should be full disclosure must be balanced against the interests of the child.

The leading case on confidentiality within proceedings is the House of Lords' ruling in *Official Solicitor to the Supreme Court v K*,[13] which was heard in wardship, where it was held that parties to the proceedings

---

10 It was a matter of importance that although the litigation was unlikely to succeed, it was not bound to fail.
11 [1994] 1 FLR 377; following *Re D (Minors) (Wardship: Disclosure)* [1994] 1 FLR 346.
12 See too, *Re F (A Minor) (Disclosure: Immigration)* [1994] 2 FLR 958 in which leave was given for the disclosure to the special adjudicator in immigration proceedings, of documents used, and a transcript of the evidence given, in proceedings which had been brought under the Children Act 1989.
13 [1965] AC 201.

have no right to see confidential reports. As the welfare of the child is the court's paramount consideration, disclosure of such reports must remain a matter for the court's discretion.[14] The principles in that case have since been extended to proceedings brought under the Children Act 1989.[15] In *Re B (A Minor) (Disclosure of Evidence)*[16] the Court of Appeal confirmed that a court has power in a child case to act on evidence adduced by one party, or given by a welfare officer, which is not disclosed to the other party. However, it stated that this power should only be exercised in most exceptional circumstances, and only where the court is satisfied that the disclosure of the evidence would be so detrimental to the welfare of the child as to outweigh the normal requirements for a fair trial. In *Re G (Minors) (Welfare Report: Disclosure)*[17] the Court of Appeal reinforced this approach in a case where a welfare officer, who had given a promise of confidentiality to certain informants, wished to place what the informants had said before the court, but for that information not to be disclosed to the parties. The Court of Appeal stated that the court welfare officer was not entitled to protect her sources of information; it is only the judge who can decide whether information should be treated as confidential. It further emphasised that the evidence of the welfare officer was compellable, and that once she had put documentary evidence before the court she was not in the position to be able to withdraw that evidence. The evidence was compellable unless the witness could properly claim privilege, and that was for the court to decide.

In *Re M (Minors) (Disclosure of Evidence)*[18] the question arose whether an addendum to a report from a court welfare officer about the wishes and feelings of the children could properly be treated as confidential to the court. The children had expressed fears and reservations to the welfare officer about their mother's reaction if she saw the contents of the report, and had asked that it be revealed to the judge alone. The judge acceded to this request holding that a 'real significant risk of harm' to the children would be occasioned were the addendum to be disclosed. The Court of Appeal held that whilst a court does have the power to order that evidence should not be disclosed to a party, it must be sure that such disclosure would be so detrimental to the child as to outweigh the normal requirement for a fair trial that all evidence is fully disclosed, so that all parties can consider it and, if necessary, seek to rebut it.[19] Following the House of Lords

---

14 However, their Lordships emphasised that the occasions when the judge will decide against disclosure on the ground that the welfare of the child outweighs the principle that a case should not be decided on information that a party has not seen, and cannot challenge, will be rare.

15 *Re C (A Minor) (Irregularity of Practice)* [1991] 2 FLR 438; *Re B (A Minor) (Disclosure of Evidence)* [1993] 1 FLR 191; *Re M (Minors) (Disclosure of Evidence)* [1994] 1 FLR 760.

16 [1993] 1 FLR 191.

17 [1993] 2 FLR 293.

18 [1994] 1 FLR 760.

ruling in *Official Solicitor to the Supreme Court v K*,[20] the Court of Appeal held that the welfare of the children was paramount, but that to withhold evidence is an exceptional procedure. A judge should not conclude that the paramount interests of the child outweigh the right of a properly interested party, particularly a parent, to disclosure of information submitted to the judge save where he is satisfied that 'real harm to the child must otherwise ensue'. It pointed out that this is a far more stringent test than the test of whether there was a 'real significant risk of harm'. Thus it is clear that the courts, when applying the welfare principle, will nonetheless exercise their discretion to withhold information from parties to the proceedings only where the circumstances are most exceptional, because any other approach undermines the basic principle of natural justice that parties to proceedings must know the case which they have to meet.[1]

Adoption proceedings present particular difficulties because the Adoption Rules recognise their essentially strictly confidential nature. However, as in other children proceedings, it is for the court to determine whether disclosure of all, or part, of a report should be directed.[2] There is a strong presumption in favour of disclosing to a party any material relating to that party since: 'the opportunity to know about and respond to adverse materials is at the heart of a fair hearing'.[3] Where it is suggested that disclosure may harm the child 'a powerful combination of likelihood and seriousness of harm will be required before the requirements for a fair trial can be overridden'.[4]

From the above analysis, it can be seen that it can never be proper for the child's guardian ad litem to promise a child that information will be withheld from the court. This principle applies regardless of the nature of the proceedings. The guardian ad litem can properly tell the child that he will inform the judge that the child does not wish a particular party to be told details of the child's conversations with the guardian ad litem. However, it is essential that any party to whom information is not to be revealed should be given the opportunity to make representations to the court.[5]

---

19 See *Official Solicitor to the Supreme Court v K* [1965] AC 201; *Re C (A Minor) (Irregularity of Practice)* [1991] 2 FLR 438; *Re B (A Minor) (Disclosure of Evidence)* [1993] 1 FLR 191; *Re G (Minors) (Welfare Report: Disclosure)* [1993] 2 FLR 293.
20 [1965] AC 201.
1 Secrecy may also prevent material information being fully canvassed and so possibly prevent a decision being arrived at which would truly be in the interests of the child
2 *Re D (Adoption Reports: Confidentiality)* [1995] 2 FLR 687.
3 Ibid, at p 694, per Lord Mustill.
4 Ibid. For further discussion, see E Hess *Re D and disclosure – the result* [1996] Fam Law 39. See also *Re C (Disclosure)* [1996] 1 FLR 797 where a guardian ad litem in care proceedings was given leave to withhold information given by the child from the child's mother.
5 In *Official Solicitor at the Supreme Court v K* [1965] AC 201, approval was given to the practice whereby the judge declares his willingness to disclose the contents of reports to the parties' legal advisers provided that they are not disclosed to the parties themselves. In an extreme case this may be a reasonable compromise, though the lawyer will have difficulty in knowing how to handle such confidential information.

Parties and witnesses should be warned that evidence given in wardship proceedings and Children Act 1989 proceedings must be treated as confidential by the parties, and any breach of this rule is a contempt of court. However, it is also clear that the strict control exercised by courts over documents which are held by the court, and which relate to the proceedings, does not extend to information recorded in case notes or in a report which does not reach the court. There is no bar on the exchange of information between those professionally engaged in the investigation of an allegation of child abuse. Any such bar would seriously undermine child protection procedures which depend for their efficiency on professionals working together, and on close inter-agency co-operation.[6] However, once information is put into writing and filed with the court it falls within rule 4.23 and must not be disclosed to another agency unless the leave of the court is first obtained.[7] Guidance was given in *Re EC (Disclosure of Material)*[8] on the factors to be taken into account in the balancing operation. In particular, it is clear that the public interest in the prosecution of serious crime, especially where the offence is against a child, means that there is a strong public interest in making available to the police material which is relevant to a criminal trial.[9]

Statements made in conciliation proceedings

The courts have taken the view that statements made in the course of conciliation proceedings should be treated as confidential and privileged and may not be adduced without the consent of both parties. Here the public interest in encouraging parties to a dispute about their children to come to their own arrangements outweighs any right of one party to rely on concessions and admissions made during the course of conciliation in any subsequent litigation. In *Re D (Minors) (Conciliation: Disclosure of Information)*[10] the Court of Appeal held that statements made by one or other of the parties in the course of meetings held, or communications made, for the purpose of conciliation may not be used in evidence in any proceedings brought under the Children Act 1989. Because otherwise 'it is plain that the parties will not make admissions or conciliatory gestures,

---

6   Consequently, in *Re G (A Minor) (Social Worker: Disclosure)* [1996] 2 All ER 65 the
     Court of Appeal held that there was no legal restraint on a social worker revealing
     information disclosed by a child's parents about their child's injuries to the police.
     Butler-Sloss LJ provided convincing reasons for the adoption of this approach, at p 72;
     and see N V Lowe *Guardians ad Litem and disclosure* [1996] Fam Law 618. See also,
     Re W (Disclosure to Police) [1998] 2 FLR 135.
7   *Re G (A Minor)(Social Worker: Disclosure)* left in doubt whether r 4.23 extended to
     documents created for the purpose of the proceedings. *Re W (Disclosure to the Police)*
     [1998] 2 FLR 135 clarified this: documents not held by the court do not come within the
     ambit of the rule.
8   [1996] 2 FLR 725.
9   See also *Re W (Disclosure to Police)* [1998] 2 FLR 135.
10   [1993] 2 All ER 693.

or dilute their claims, or venture out of their entrenched positions unless they can be confident that their concessions and admissions cannot be used as weapons against them if conciliation fails and full-blooded litigation follows'.[11] The only exception to this rule is where the maker of the statement has said something which indicates that he has caused, or is likely to cause, serious harm to the child. Where this is the case, it is for the judge to determine whether the evidence can be admitted.

Hearsay

The normal rule in civil proceedings is that evidence given by one witness of a statement made by another person, which is tendered to prove the truth of the statement, is inadmissible. However, this rule has been relaxed in children cases. Section 96(3) of the Children Act 1989 empowers the Lord Chancellor to make provision for the admissibility of evidence which would otherwise be inadmissible under any rule of law relating to hearsay, and Article 2 of the Children (Admissibility of Hearsay Evidence) Order 1993[12] provides that in:

'(a) civil proceedings before the High Court or a county court; and
(b) (i) family proceedings, and
    (ii) civil proceedings under the Child Support Act 1991 in a magistrates' court,
evidence given in connection with the upbringing, maintenance or welfare of a child shall be admissible notwithstanding any rule of law relating to hearsay.'

Thus Parliament has taken the view that cases 'in connection with the upbringing, maintenance or welfare of a child' should be treated differently from other civil cases because it is in the interests of children that all possible relevant information should be placed before the courts. The scope of this provision came under scrutiny in *Re C (Minors) (Hearsay Evidence: Contempt Proceedings)*.[13] Here it was alleged in contempt proceedings that a father had breached a non-molestation injunction. The mother wished to introduce in evidence statements made by the children of the family about the alleged breach which were contained in a court welfare officer's report, and which were therefore hearsay. Whilst the Court of Appeal held that hearsay evidence could be introduced in contempt proceedings, it ruled that the courts would only allow this where a substantial connection between the proposed evidence and the welfare of the child had been established, and that this will be a matter of fact in each case. In this case the connection was held to be insufficiently substantial.

11 Ibid, per Lord Bingham MR, at p 695.
12 SI 1993/621.
13 [1993] 4 All ER 690.

It is suggested that this ruling was unduly narrow even within the context of contempt proceedings, which traditionally have been surrounded by stringent safeguards because the penalty for contempt may be imprisonment. In *Re C (Minors)* the children's statements would have pointed to breaches of an injunction by the father not to enter the former matrimonial home in which the children were living with their mother. It seems unhelpful to draw a distinction between cases in which the injunction is designed to protect the child himself, and one in which it is designed to protect the parent with whom the child is living, which distinction was drawn by the Court of Appeal. Furthermore, the Order does not state that a 'substantial' connection must be established between the hearsay evidence and the welfare of the child; it is drafted in far more neutral terms. It is suggested that this judicial gloss on the wording of Article 2 may lead to hearsay evidence being inappropriately excluded in cases concerning children, and that it was a strange finding of fact in *Re C (Minors)* that the children would not be affected by any breaches of the injunction.[14]

The dilemma for the court in those cases where the Order does apply is not whether a hearsay statement can be admitted, because article 2 states that it *shall* be admissible, but how much weight the court should give to this type of evidence. A first-hand account from a witness of what he saw, heard or otherwise experienced can be given significant probative weight because it can be tested for its veracity. By contrast, a hearsay statement has two major disadvantages which tend to diminish its probative value: it cannot be tested in cross-examination, and the person reporting what the maker of the statement has said may do so inaccurately, or even deliberately falsely.[15] It is suggested that very little, or no, probative weight should be given to a prejudicial hearsay statement when the statement was made by an adult who could be called as a witness. For example, if a social worker were to give evidence that a teacher told her that she, the teacher, saw the child's mother beat the child such a statement is prejudicial because it appears to establish that the child has been beaten. But where the mother is denying beating the child, such a statement clearly needs to be tested in cross-examination, and the only way in which this can be done is if the teacher herself is called to give evidence. Unless this happens, it is suggested that no probative weight can properly be given to a statement of this kind.

It is nevertheless almost inevitable in children cases that hearsay information will be presented by witnesses as true accounts of what has occurred. For example, a consultant paediatrician may give a clinical

14 In the light of this ruling it would also seem wise for a parent who is the subject of domestic violence to seek a non-molestation order which embraces the children as well as herself where appropriate, see further ch 6.
15 See, for example, *Re E (A Minor) (Child Abuse: Evidence)* [1987] 1 FLR 269, where the court found that oral evidence of an interview bore little resemblance to the video recording of the same interview, and that the expert witness's conclusions bore no relationship with the actual questions asked.

description of a child's physical condition when first admitted to hospital, and of changes observed in the child's growth and development whilst under his care. Parts of this information will come from the paediatrician's own observations, and his own examination of the child, but other parts are likely to have been taken from notes compiled by other medical personnel such as nurses and more junior doctors. Similarly a social worker who is called as a witness by a local authority may have taken over the child's case from a previous worker. He may be called upon to give an historical account to the court of incidents involving the child and his family which have given rise to professional concern, and of action taken by the local authority in response to these incidents. His source of information will be the file kept on the child, and conversations with other persons. In either case, the paediatrician, or the social worker, is relying on reports and findings made by others, he does not have first-hand knowledge of the facts he is recounting. Normally no problem arises with the hearsay element in the witness's statement where the facts recounted are non-controversial. It is when facts are disputed, or when an account is given of actions and statements made by the child which is challenged by a party to the proceedings, that difficulties arise about how much weight and probity should be given to hearsay evidence.

Sometimes the court may be faced with whether a child should be called to give evidence in contested proceedings. The court has a discretion whether or not to order the attendance of a witness, and may decline to issue the summons if to do so would be oppressive.[16] Since the question whether to issue a summons against a child is not a question which relates to his or her upbringing, the paramountcy of the child's welfare principle does not apply either to the child witness or to the child who is the subject of the proceedings. Nonetheless the courts are likely to be heavily influenced against issuing such a summons by the child-orientated purpose behind the introduction of the Children (Admissibility of Hearsay Evidence Order) 1993[17] which was to spare children the stress of appearing in court to give evidence concerning, inter alia, sexual abuse. Where a court refuses to issue a summons it must approach any hearsay account of what the child has said with great caution and in full awareness that it has been precluded from testing in cross-examination.[18] In those cases where fairness requires that an advocate should be able to cross-examine a witness rather than merely carry out an examination-in-chief, the court will itself occasionally call the witness so that cross-examination can take place.[19]

16 See *R v B County Council ex p P* [1991] 1 FLR 470 where the court declined to authorise the issue of a witness summons against a girl aged 17 who had made allegations of sexual abuse against her stepfather.
17 SI 1993/621, art 2.
18 See *Re P (Witness Summons)* [1997] 2 FLR 447, where the court refused to order the attendance of a twelve-year-old girl who made allegations of sexual abuse against the stepfather of another twelve-year-old child who was the subject of an application made in care proceedings.
19 Ibid, at p 453.

Statements made by a child

A child can be treated as a competent witness in civil proceedings even though he or she does not, in the opinion of the court, understand the nature of the oath.[20] Section 96(2) provides that:

> 'The child's evidence may be heard by the court if, in its opinion—
> (a) he understands that it is his duty to speak the truth; and
> (b) he has sufficient understanding to justify his evidence being heard.'

However, it is extremely rare for a child to give evidence in a civil child case because it is the generally held view that it is an ordeal for a child to appear in court as a witness.[1] Consequently, someone else will tell the court what the child has said about his experiences. But the court's task in assessing a child's credibility is not made easier by the fact that any statements from the child presented to the court will therefore almost invariably be in the form of hearsay. There is guidance in *Re W (Minors) (Wardship: Evidence)*[2] in relation to the weight to be given to remarks made by children, and reported to the courts by adults. A note of caution was sounded by Neill LJ when he said 'this evidence and the use to which it is put has to be handled with the greatest care and in such a way that unless the interests of the child make it necessary, the rules of natural justice and the rights of parents are properly observed'. He said that a court 'will be very slow indeed to make a finding of fact adverse to a parent if the only material before it has been untested by cross-examination'.[3] McCowan LJ expressed similar caution when he said 'it would be wrong for a judge to find sexual abuse proved against a particular person solely on the basis of hearsay evidence'. However he continued 'what he can do, however, is to have regard to hearsay evidence to assist him to form a view as to the degree of risk involved for the future in permitting children to return to their parents'.[4] Thus it can be seen that only rarely will the unsupported statements of a child be sufficiently cogent and reliable to satisfy a court that the person the child identifies as a perpetrator of abuse against him is in fact such a perpetrator.[5]

---

20 S 96(1).
1   This ordeal for the child cannot be avoided in criminal proceedings where the hearsay rule still applies (though see s 23 of the Criminal Justice Act 1988). There is some amelioration of the process through the use of live TV-link evidence and video recorded evidence: Criminal Justice Act 1988, ss 32 and 32A. The use of screens to shield the child in court is governed by the common law: see *R v X, Y and Z* (1989) 91 Cr App Rep 36. See generally JR Spencer and R Flinn *The Evidence of Children* (Blackstone Press, 1993); *The Pigot Report* (HO, 1989). On the competence of children generally to participate in proceedings see ch 2.
2   [1990] 1 FLR 203, decided in wardship. Hearsay evidence was admissible in wardship prior to it becoming admissible in all children cases.
3   Ibid, at p 228.
4   Ibid, at p 222.
5   See too *Re M (A Minor) (No 2) (Appeal)* [1994] 1 FLR 59.

Video taped interviews

Making a video recording of interviews with the child is one way of overcoming some of the disadvantages and difficulties which arise where otherwise the only evidence adduced of what the child has said is hearsay evidence. Clinicians experienced at working in the field of child abuse have pointed out that the value of video taped recordings may be diminished by poor technology.[6] They have also expressed anxiety about judges interpreting interviews, a task which traditionally has been the exclusive territory of experts.[7] Nonetheless, in *Re M (Child Abuse: Evidence)*[8] Latey J explained why courts much prefer this evidence. Not only can the court see and hear the child's responses to questions, and detect changes in the child's vocal inflection, it can also observe the child's non-verbal responses such as body movements and gestures.[9] This reasoning was reinforced in the Cleveland Report, which includes amongst the points to be observed in conducting interviews with children the requirement that there must be careful recording of what the child says, whether or not there is a video recording.[10] Furthermore, the advantage of a video taped recording is that the court can see and hear for itself whether the child discloses information about abuse spontaneously, or whether he is pressurised by the interviewer into responding in a particular way.[11] As Butler-Sloss LJ said in *H v H and C; K v K (Child Abuse: Evidence)*:[12] 'The conduct of the interviews would inevitably have a marked effect on the weight to be attached to the evidence adduced. Frequent repetitive interviews with young, suggestible children, reminding them of what they had previously said, would be likely to have decreasing evidential value. The spontaneous statements of a child at an early stage have far greater impact ... The pressure or absence of pressure upon the child can be seen by the observer, including the judge.'

Issue estoppel in children cases

Sometimes findings of fact made in one set of proceedings concerning children are relevant, even crucial, to subsequent proceedings concerning the same, or different, children. The question then arises whether the later court is bound by the findings of fact made in the earlier case or

---

6   E Vizard *Interviewing young sexually abused children* (1987) 17 Fam Law 28.
7   E Vizard, A Bentovim and M Tranter *Interviewing sexually abused children* (1987) 11 Adoption and Fostering 20.
8   [1987] 1 FLR 293n.
9   Some of the many difficulties associated with the video-taped, as opposed to live, testimony of children in criminal proceedings are examined by A Wade, A Lawson and J Aldridge in *Stories in court – video-taped interviews and the production of children's testimony* (1998) 10 CFLQ 179.
10   Report of the Inquiry into Child Abuse in Cleveland 1987, Cm 412, para 12.34.
11   See *Re E (A Minor) (Child Abuse: Evidence)* [1991] 1 FLR 420.
12   [1989] 3 All ER 740, at p 752.

whether these findings can be reopened in the later case. The Court of Appeal has emphasised that courts have an inquisitorial, as distinct from an adversarial, function in children cases and that their role is to investigate the circumstances of the child and to arrive at a conclusion which will best serve the child's interests. Therefore the court has ruled that a strict application of the doctrine of issue estoppel,[13] has no place in family proceedings.[14] However, the Court of Appeal has also recognised that were courts to have unfettered powers to reopen past disputes this 'would be a recipe for chaos and open the floodgates'.[15]

Where a party to one set of proceedings wishes to rely on, or to dispute, findings made in previous proceedings in order to prove or defend a case, the issue for the court is whether this should be permitted and, if so, how the later proceedings should be handled. The courts have given comprehensive guidance on the principles to be applied and the factors to be taken into account in such cases.[16] These factors include whether the previous findings are so significant that they are bound to affect the outcome of the current proceedings; whether there is any reason to think that a rehearing of the issues will result in any different findings from those made in the earlier trial; whether the previous findings were made after a full hearing in which the person concerned took part; and whether the evidence was tested in the usual way. The court will also want to know whether there is any new evidence or information casting doubt upon the accuracy of the original findings. These factors must be balanced when the court is considering how far it should apply the broad principle that it is in the public interest that litigation is brought to an end, and how far it should be influenced by the fact that any delay in a child case is likely to be prejudicial to the welfare of the child. Thus the principle that decisions should be certain may have to yield to the countervailing notion that the welfare of the child is unlikely to be served where a court relies on determinations of fact which turn out to have been erroneous. Essentially, the court should exercise its discretion so as to achieve justice rather than injustice.[17]

---

13 Ie the principle that no-one is allowed to litigate afresh issues which have already been determined.

14 *Re S (Discharge of Care Order)* [1995] 2 FLR 639; *B v Derbyshire County Council* [1992] 1 FLR 538; *Re S, S and A (Care Proceedings) (Issue Estoppel)* [1995] 2 FLR 244; *K v P (Children Act Proceedings)* [1995] 1 FLR 248.

15 *Re S (Discharge of Care Order)* above, at p 645.

16 See especially, Hale J in *Re B (Children Act Proceedings) (Issue Estoppel)* [1997] 1 FLR 285. Care proceedings had been instituted in respect of two boys whose parents had separated. The boys had been living with their mother. The father wished to look after his sons. However, it came to light that in earlier care proceedings a judge had found that he had sexually abused two different children. The issue for the court was whether the father was bound by the findings of fact made in those proceedings.

17 *K v P (Children Act Proceedings)* [1995] 1 FLR 248, at p 257.

Identifying the welfare of the child

The principle that the child's welfare must be the court's paramount consideration in children cases is not new. Equity adopted this approach towards the end of the last century, and the paramountcy of the child's welfare was given formal statutory recognition in section 1 of the Guardianship of Infants Act 1925. Thus courts have long been grappling with the difficult task of determining what decision will best promote the child's interests. However, whilst the principle is long-established, responses to it have altered radically as succeeding generations have applied different norms and values to the choices to be made. Growth in knowledge about human development, and how certain experiences have affected that development, means that comments made by judges applying the welfare principle in the early part of this century may be viewed with amazement by later generations.

An illustration arose in *Re W (Infants)*[18] which concerned two children who had been looked after for many years by a couple who were seeking to adopt them. Their application was opposed by the children's father, and the issue for the court was whether the children would be positively harmed if taken from the care of the potential adopters and returned to their father's care. *Re W (Infants)* came before Cross J in 1965. Similar facts had come before Eve J in 1925 in *Re Thain*,[19] in which the child's mother had died and the child had been brought up for many years by her uncle and aunt, Mr and Mrs Jones. Her father was seeking to recover her care. Restoring the child to her father, Eve J said 'it is said that the little girl will be greatly distressed and upset at parting from Mr and Mrs Jones. I can quite understand it may be so, but, at her tender age, one knows from experience how mercifully transient are the effects of partings and other sorrows and how soon the novelty of fresh surroundings and new associations effaces the recollection of former days and kind friends.' Cross J, commenting on these words in *Re W (Infants)*, in which he ordered that the children should remain with the potential adopters, said:

> 'When I was called to the Bar some 35 years ago, it was not, as I remember, usual to have medical evidence as to the effect which the order of the court would be likely to have on the infant ...But child psychiatrists who give evidence in these cases nowadays, though they do not always agree in detail, all emphasise the risks involved in transferring young children from the care of one person to another ...while as to the views of Eve J, Dr S,[20] when they were put to him, plainly regarded them much as Thomas Huxley

18 [1965] 3 All ER 231.
19 [1926] All ER Rep 384, which was emphatically approved by the Court of Appeal.
20 The child psychologist who had interviewed the children.

would have regarded the suggestion that the world came into being in the manner set out in the first chapter of Genesis.'[1]

This example is not merely an issue of historical or even contemporary interest. Rather it illustrates how difficult it can be to advise on the likely outcome of a contested child case where that outcome turns on differing perceptions of a child's welfare.

Precedent and the welfare principle

When a court determines what decision will best promote the welfare of the child it is expressing a preference which is likely to be founded on a variety of norms. It may be that a case with similar facts has already come before the courts, and that the Court of Appeal has given a ruling on how such facts should be approached. The question then arises whether such a ruling can ever set a precedent which must be followed. Strictly the answer to this question is 'no'. Every child case is unique and therefore one case cannot be a precedent for another. As Stamp LJ has said 'although one may of course be assisted by the wisdom of remarks made in earlier cases, the circumstances in infant cases and the personalities of the parties concerned being infinitely variable, the conclusions of the court as to the course which should be followed in one case are of little assistance in guiding one to the course which ought to be followed in another case'.[2] However, there may be situations in which an approach to a similar problem has become so firmly established that it appears to take on precedent force. Thus in *Belton v Belton*[3] the Court of Appeal ruled that the trial judge had erred when he formed the view that it was not in the child's welfare to grant her mother leave to remove her from the jurisdiction because the child would thereby lose contact with her father and paternal relatives. Purchas LJ stated that the judge had failed to appreciate 'the force of the authorities' in which leave had been granted, and added that 'these authorities are quite clear in the course the court must take'. But affording such weight to earlier case law decided on the welfare principle is unusual, and the Court of Appeal is generally loth to give precedent force to a particular view about the factors which will serve a child's best interests. An example arose in *Re A (A Minor) (Custody)*[4] in which the trial judge, apparently following what he thought to be precedent, namely a statement made by Butler-Sloss LJ in *Re S (A Minor) (Custody)*,[5] had taken as his starting point that it is natural for a mother to have the care of a six-year-old daughter. Butler-Sloss LJ disapproved this approach stating that:

1   [1965] 3 All ER 231, at pp 248-249.
2   *Re K (Minors) (Wardship: Care and Control)* [1977] 1 All ER 647, at p 649.
3   [1987] 2 FLR 343.
4   [1991] 2 FLR 394.
5   [1991] 2 FLR 388, at p 390.

'There is no starting point that the mother should be preferred to the father and only displaced by a preponderance of evidence to the contrary ... The welfare of the child is paramount, and each parent has to be looked at by the judge in order to make as best he can the assessment of each, and to choose one of them to be the custodial parent. In so far as the judge appears to have started with the proposition that little girls naturally go to their mothers, the judge was in error and applied the wrong test.'[6]

In family law cases, perhaps more than in any other branch of the law, there are several examples of the Court of Appeal apparently not following its previous decisions. One illustration may be seen in cases relating to the change of a child's surname.[7] Another is where a mother is refusing to allow her child contact with his natural father. At one stage, where the mother was living with her new husband and where the child believed that the husband was his father, the courts were unwilling to upset an apparently stable family unit by coercing the mother into allowing the truth to emerge and this approach was confirmed by the Court of Appeal.[8] Almost immediately afterwards, on very similar facts, the Court of Appeal ordered that steps should be taken to make a child aware of her actual parentage.[9] Hence it is important to keep up to date not only with the latest developments in the legal framework but also with changing fashions in how welfare decisions are approached.

The role of the appeal court

The precedent value of a children case cannot properly be ascertained unless the role of an appeal court in children cases is also understood. Because the determination of welfare is a decision which turns on the exercise of judicial discretion, an appellate court is not entitled to interfere with the ruling of the trial court unless the grounds for appeal fall within the scope of the principles laid down by the House of Lords in *G v G*.[10] The fact that the trial court has reached a decision with which the appellate court might reasonably disagree is not enough. In order to intervene, the appellate court must be satisfied that the trial court has taken account of

---

6 [1991] 2 FLR 394, at p 400.
7 See below. This is not a recent development: it was commented upon by Professor Peter Bromley in his introduction to the 6th edition of *Bromley's Family Law* (Butterworths, 1981).
8 *Re SM (A Minor) (Natural Father: Access)* [1991] 2 FLR 333.
9 *Re R (A Minor) (Contact)* [1993] 2 FLR 762.
10 [1985] 2 All ER 225; an appeal court is reluctant to interfere with a trial court decision because it is the judge who has seen and heard the witnesses and it is he who has formed an opinion of their truthfulness, strengths and weaknesses. It is recognised that impressions of the personalities of the contenders for a child can be a highly material influence on the exercise of discretion in a child case.

matters it ought not to have taken into account, has failed to take account of matters it ought to have taken into account, or that the decision was so plainly wrong that the only legitimate conclusion is that the court has erred in the exercise of its discretion.[11]

Re J (A Minor) (Contact)[12] provides an example of how this principle operates. The trial judge had ordered that there should be no order on the father's application for contact with his son because of the mother's implacable hostility to the father, and her vehement opposition to contact taking place. The father appealed. The Court of Appeal confirmed that the principles which should be applied to cases of this kind are well established, namely that 'contact with the parent with whom the child is not resident is the right of the child, and very cogent reasons are required for terminating such contact'. Balcombe LJ went on to state that 'it was undoubtedly open to the judge to have made an order for contact, and there are ... strong policy reasons for saying that a recalcitrant parent should not be allowed to frustrate what the court considers the child's welfare requires. Had the judge made such an order, I do not see how the mother could successfully have appealed from it'.[13] However, the trial judge in the exercise of his discretion had concluded that the making of a contact order would cause the child harm, and the Court of Appeal, applying the ruling in *G v G*, was unable to say that he was plainly wrong within the *G v G* principle. The father's appeal was therefore dismissed.

This example demonstrates how the determination of the precedent force of a Court of Appeal ruling can be extremely complex. It would clearly be wrong to treat *Re J (A Minor)* as a precedent for saying that where one parent is implacably hostile to the other parent having contact, and where that contact may cause harm to the child, that contact will therefore be denied. On the contrary, Balcombe LJ stated that had the trial judge made a contact order the Court of Appeal would have felt equally unable to intervene. Furthermore, he was at pains to point out that courts should be very reluctant to allow parental hostility to deter courts from making contact orders. But nevertheless in *Re J (A Minor)* the mother won, and the father was denied contact, and to that extent it is a precedent for saying that a judge will not be plainly wrong if he refuses contact on the grounds that it will cause the child harm. It is suggested that the value of *Re J (A Minor)* is as much to reaffirm the precedent force of *G v G* as it is on giving guidance on how courts should approach contact cases. The case illustrates the vital importance of the first instance ruling in children cases, and how an appellate court may reluctantly dismiss an appeal even where it takes the view that one parent has suffered an injustice at the hands of the other parent.

It can be seen from this analysis that it is not easy to state with confidence how much weight should be given to previous case law when

---

11 See too, *Re F (A Minor) (Wardship: Appeal)* [1976] Fam 238.
12 [1994] 1 FLR 729.
13 Ibid, at p 735.

advising on cases which turn on the welfare principle. The task is made harder because previous cases are often relied on by the higher courts to support and justify their rulings, despite the fact that precedent does not determine the course to be followed. It is undoubtedly true to say that it is essential to be familiar with the up-to-date approach of courts to the welfare principle in a similar context, because of course advising on the law is a predictive exercise, and the best guide to the future is what the courts have done already. Where the courts, and particularly the Court of Appeal, have adopted a consistent approach to similar facts a lawyer can feel fairly confident, though not certain, that the same approach will be adopted in relation to the child case on which he is giving advice.

Research studies

The study of child development is a growing science and this, coupled with studies on the impact of marriage and relationship breakdown on children, has led to a better understanding of the types of upbringing which best advance a child's physical, intellectual, emotional and social development.[14] This research underpins many contemporary studies.[15] But of course legal proceedings are usually concerned with circumstances in which the child's upbringing cannot be ideal, and applying the welfare principle often means choosing the least damaging alternative for the child. Here too research studies can assist.[16] However, research studies should always be viewed with caution. As one commentator has said, 'present debates in child welfare lack a sense of history and this may make policy makers and practitioners vulnerable to swings and fashions which are not soundly based'.[17] The findings made in different studies may lead to the formation of genuinely held opposing views about which outcomes are in the best interests of children. Moreover, in some cases there can be real disagreement between researchers about the relative

---

14 It is commonly reported that children from 'broken' homes suffer in a number of ways, including educationally and financially. Much research has been undertaken on the impact upon such children who then go on to live in stepfamilies. G Bar-Hava and J Pryor in *Cinderella's challenge – adjustment to stepfamilies in the 1990s* (1998) 10 CFLQ 257 examined 19 of the key studies on stepchildren, drawing out the outcomes for the children and considering the factors influencing the children's adjustment to stepfamily living.

15 Some of this research is also gathered together in the area of child protection. See, for example, *Studies in Child Protection*, DoH (HMSO, 1995), *Messages from Research*, DoH (HMSO, 1995).

16 They may, for example, throw light on the likely impact on a child of separating her from the adults who have cared for her for many years; or they may give guidance on the advantages or disadvantages of seeking to preserve contact between a child and the parent with whom he is not living after divorce. Useful research material is referred to in C Piper *'Looking to the Future' for children* (1994) 6 JCL 98.

17 Olive Stevenson, 'Recent research in child welfare: implications for policy and practice' in *Divided Duties* (Jordans, Family Law, 1998), at p 45.

validity and significance of findings made in identical studies.[18] This divergence of opinion can be of considerable practical significance when plans are made for the future care of children. For example, where 'the emphasis on "permanency placement" seems to conflict with the need to develop a sense of identity through connectedness to one's origins and birth family',[19] a difficult choice may have to be made. Should a child's links with the members of his birth family be severed where they have failed to meet his needs? Or should these links be maintained at the cost of finding him a potentially stimulating and stable alternative family placement?

Flawed research is particularly dangerous because it deceives. In some studies the researcher's methodology is beyond reproach, but in others the researcher may arrive at conclusions which are scientifically invalid, and which ignore contradictory research.[20] Even greater caution should be exercised where there is reason to believe that the researchers hold a particular ideological theory about the upbringing of children which they wish to advance. Sometimes this leads them, either consciously or unconsciously, to extrapolate findings from their own and others' research which are not supported by the data that has been collected.[1] The risk created by research which is methodologically unsound is that it may lead to misguided judgments being made about what decisions will serve a child's best interests. On the other hand, where well-conducted research is referred to in evidence by a highly qualified expert, this may have a very persuasive impact on the outcome of a case.[2]

Courts must give reasons for their decisions

The determination of what decision will best promote a child's welfare cannot be a science because the decision revolves around the behaviour

---

18 Contrast the views of M Ryburn *In whose best interests? – post-adoption contact with the birth family* (1998) 10 CFLQ 53 and D Quinton, J Selwyn, A Rushton and C Dance *Contact with birth parents in adoption – a response to Ryburn* (1998) 10 CFLQ 349 on the weight to be given to studies about the value to adoptees of retaining contact with their birth families. On this debate, see also B Lindley *Open adoption – is the door ajar?* (1997) 9 CFLQ 115.

19 Olive Stevenson 'Recent research in child welfare: implications for policy and practice' in *Divided Duties* (Jordans, Family Law, 1998) p 45, at p 47.

20 See the review by J Kelly and R Emery in (1989) 19 Fam Law 489 of Wallerstein and Blakeslee *Second Chances: Men, Women and Children a Decade after Divorce* (Bantam Press, 1989); see too Elliott et al *Divorce and children: a British challenge to the Wallerstein view* (1990) 20 Fam Law 309.

1 This has occurred in the area of trans-racial adoption where some researchers have alleged that the adoption of white children by black parents is harmful to the children, despite the fact that this conclusion is unsupported either by the researchers' own findings or by the findings of other researchers: see E Bartholet *Where do black children belong? The politics of race matching in adoption* (1991) 139 University of Pennsylvania Law Review 1164; P Hayes *The ideological attack on transracial adoption in the USA and Britain* (1995) 9 IJLF 1.

2 See, for example, the research studies on lesbian mothers cited in *B v B (Minors) (Custody, Care and Control)* [1991] 1 FLR 402, at p 406.

and personalities of the child, the parents, and any other persons who are offering to care for the child. Essentially, therefore, the determination of welfare is a matter of personal preference. However, there are mechanisms which are designed to ensure that such a determination is arrived at in a structured way. One such mechanism is the requirement that courts give reasons for their decisions.[3] A court must make findings of fact and articulate the values which are informing its ruling. It must indicate the nature of the evidence which supports its findings and the conclusions which it draws from these findings. Where evidence is presented which is rejected by the court as unproved, irrelevant or unconvincing, it must explain why it arrived at this conclusion.[4] The requirement to give reasons therefore naturally exerts a discipline on decision-making. It is mandatory and any failure to observe the rule vitiates the decision.[5] This principle applies with just the same force to an application for leave to apply for an order.[6]

The welfare principle

The welfare principle is the golden thread which runs through decision-making by courts in children cases. Section 1 of the Children Act 1989 provides that:

'When a court determines any question with respect to
(a) the upbringing of a child; or
(b) the administration of the child's property or the application of any income arising from it,
the child's welfare shall be the court's paramount consideration.'

This simple statement means that a court must give overriding weight to the welfare of the child when determining any question with respect to the child's upbringing.[7] However, the very simplicity of the welfare principle conceals two often highly complex problems. The first is which questions are questions 'with respect to the upbringing of a child'. It has been explained elsewhere that the welfare principle does not apply to

---

3   The Family Proceedings Court (Children Act 1989) Rules 1991, r 21; The Family Proceedings Rules 1991, r 4.21.
4   See, for example, *Leicestershire County Council v G* [1994] 2 FLR 329.
5   *W v Hertfordshire County Council* [1993] 1 FLR 118; *Re W (A Minor) (Contact)* [1994] 1 FLR 843. It is suggested that this is a particularly valuable requirement in the case of magistrates who are lay persons and unaccustomed to having to justify their judgments.
6   *T v W* [1996] 2 FLR 473.
7   For a useful and oft-quoted description of the meaning of 'paramount' see Lord MacDermott's speech in *J v C* [1970] AC 668, at p 710. In *Birmingham City Council v H* [1994] 1 All ER 12, the House of Lords ruled that when both the parent and the parent's child are children, the welfare principle applies only to the parent's child because it is that child who is the subject of the application; see too *F v Leeds City Council* [1994] 2 FLR 60.

applications made under section 10 of the Children Act 1989 for leave to apply for a section 8 order;[8] to orders for financial and property provision made under section 15 and Schedule 1 of the Act;[9] or to applications for occupation orders,[10] and it will be seen below that other disputes involving the upbringing of children are not governed by this principle either. The second problem faced by courts is how is the goal of promoting the child's best interests best achieved, and it is to this question that attention is now turned.

The 'checklist'

A mechanism leading to the controlled exercise of discretion and structured decision-making is the requirement that courts consider a 'checklist' of factors before giving judgment. Section 1(4) provides that where a court is considering whether to make, vary or discharge a section 8 order, and the making, variation or discharge is opposed by any party to the proceedings, or where the court is considering whether to make, vary or discharge an order under Part IV of the Act, the court must have regard to a list of factors before arriving at its decision. Section 1(3) provides that:

> 'In the circumstances mentioned in subsection (4), a court shall have regard in particular to—
> (a) the ascertainable wishes and feelings of the child concerned (considered in the light of his age and understanding);
> (b) his physical, emotional and educational needs;
> (c) the likely effect on him of any change in his circumstances;
> (d) his age, sex, background and any characteristics of his which the court considers relevant;
> (e) any harm which he has suffered or is at risk of suffering;
> (f) how capable each of his parents, and any other person in relation to whom the court considers the question to be relevant, is of meeting his needs;
> (g) the range of powers available to the court under this Act in the proceedings in question.'

This checklist seeks to ensure that judicial preferences are properly informed, and that judicial rulings are based on reasoning which takes account of all relevant considerations. Witnesses in children cases often give evidence in a self-serving and highly persuasive manner. Were such evidence to be received within a completely free and unstructured discretionary framework it could add to the risk, which is inherent in all

8   See ch 2.
9   See ch 9.
10 See ch 6.

discretionary decision-making, that a particular ideology, an idiosyncratic point of view, or a feeling of sympathy for an adult witness, could be given more weight than is merited, and lead to the court making a decision in which the child's welfare has become subordinated to other values. The advantage of the checklist is that it focuses the attention of the court on those factors which are widely accepted to be relevant to the promotion of a child's welfare. It is a mechanism which is designed to achieve balanced decisions after the court has consciously weighed all the factors which it ought to take into account.

Where all, or most, of the factors in the checklist point in one direction the decision on what will best promote the child's welfare may be relatively straightforward, and indeed a court ruling is unlikely to be necessary. However, the complexity of children cases often turns on the fact that the matters listed in the checklist are pulling the courts in different directions. For example, the age and sex of a child may point to an order being made that she should live with her mother rather than an older relative, but there may be evidence to suggest that the mother might cause the child to suffer harm. The court must then determine whether the factor specified in paragraph (d) should be given greater weight than the factor specified in paragraph (e) and in this it must be guided by the factors in the other paragraphs, which again are likely to conflict, and to point to different outcomes. Thus opinion evidence may have been given that the child is likely to be badly affected by a change in her circumstances, which raises the considerations in paragraphs (b) and (c), but that if she were to remain with the mother it is unlikely that the mother could meet some of her needs, which raises paragraph (f).

An analysis of case law assists in the prediction of how a court is likely to approach the resolution of a case where the factors in the checklist point to different outcomes. While each child case is unique, the majority of children cases can nonetheless be divided into loose categories. The analysis below discusses how courts have approached cases within different contexts.

Residence and welfare

When a marriage breaks down, and where parents no longer live together, both may wish to provide the children with a home. In many cases each parent is perfectly capable of caring for the children (paragraph (f)), neither parent is likely to harm the children (paragraph (e)), and when parents part there is inevitably a change of circumstances for the children (paragraph (c)), although if one parent remains in the former matrimonial home, he or she has a clear advantage under that head. But because each parent can usually provide a reasonable standard of care for the child, the decision about which parent will better provide for the child's welfare often turns on considerations relating to the child's physical, emotional and educational needs (paragraph (b)), and the child's age, sex, background and any characteristics of his which the court considers relevant (paragraph (d)). Courts, when choosing between parents, are therefore inevitably drawn into making value judgments about the roles of mothers and fathers, about different lifestyles,[11] and about which factors make the most important contribution to a child's well-being.[12] During this century, society has gained increasing insight into the physical and psychological needs of children and how provision can best be made for these needs. Studies of children whose parents have divorced or separated reveals that children are usually deeply saddened by their parents' parting and wish that they had remained together; that those who suffer most are those whose parents remain in conflict; but that those who suffer least are those who are able to retain a good relationship with each parent.[13] One commentator at least has therefore suggested that where both parents are able to provide the child with a reasonable upbringing, the child's welfare will normally best be served if he lives with the parent who will most encourage the continuing role of both parents as parents after divorce, and who will foster the child's links with his wider family.[14] This approach was reflected by Butler-Sloss LJ, when in *Re A (A Minor) (Custody)*[15] she said that the approach of a parent to contact is highly relevant to the determination of whether the child should live with him or her.

Shared residence

Many parents recognise that their children need to maintain positive links with each of them and some are able to organise their lives so that care of the children is shared between them. Where such an arrangement breaks down, or where parents cannot agree over with whom the children will live, and where their disagreement leads to an application for a residence order being made to a court, the court normally makes a residence order in favour of one of the parties and a contact order in favour of the other.[16] However, the parent who is most likely to obtain contact rather than

---

11 For a striking example of a difference in judicial attitude towards nudity in the home see *Re W (Residence order)* [1998] 1 FCR 75.

12 See, for example, *May v May* [1986] 1 FLR 325 where the welfare officer said that the conflict was not as to the competence of either of the parents, it was a conflict of different values. She concluded that she was confident that the children would be well cared for by either party. Research shows that no one factor can be isolated as being of unequivocal significance in establishing the ultimate welfare of the child, but that the factors interrelate and all need to be weighed in the balance. See J Pryor and F Seymour *Making decisions about children after parental separation* (1996) 8 CFLQ 229.

13 A Mitchell *Children in the Middle: Living through Divorce* (Tavistock, 1985); M P M Richards and M Dyson *Separation, Divorce and the Development of Children: A Review* (DHSS, 1982). Further useful material is gathered together by C Piper in 'Looking to the Future' for children (1994) 6 JCL 98.

14 M P M Richards *Joint custody revisited* (1989) 19 Fam Law 83.

15 [1991] 2 FLR 394, at p 400.

16 Provided that the court is satisfied that to make an order will be better for the children than to make no order at all: s 1(5); see ch 2.

residence may find this unsatisfactory and may wish to share providing the child with a home with the other parent. Prior to the Children Act 1989 the Court of Appeal had ruled in *Riley v Riley*[17] that it was not open to a court to make a joint care and control order. However, this ruling has since been overtaken by section 11(4) which specifically contemplates a residence order being made to both parents despite the fact that they are living apart. It provides:

> 'Where a residence order is made in favour of two or more persons who do not themselves all live together, the order may specify the periods during which the child is to live in the different households concerned.'

Although courts have acknowledged that they now have power to make orders in which a child's residence is shared, they have stated that such orders are unusual, and that there must be some positive benefit to the child before such an order is made.[18] Courts have taken the view that where parents cannot agree, it is not in the child's best interests to make a shared residence order because of the difficulties which such an arrangement can cause. The nature of the concern about the effect of shared residence orders on the welfare of the child was illustrated in *Re J (A Minor) (Residence)*.[19] Here residence was strictly divided between the parents. However, the child was playing one parent off against the other, and was developing such a degree of anxiety and stress as to lead the court welfare officer to recommend that the child should spend the greater part of the week with one parent and a smaller proportion with the other. In *Re H (A Minor) (Shared Residence)*[20] Purchas LJ took the view that the establishment of two competing homes only leads to confusion and stress and is contrary to the paramount interests of the child, and he stated that such an order 'would rarely be made and would depend upon exceptional circumstances'. In the same case Cazalet J said that there may be circumstances in which a shared residence order is appropriate because it may reduce the differences between the parties, but that where there are differences between them, a child should normally make his settled home with one parent.

In *A v A (Minors) (Shared Residence Order)*[1] the conflict was not over the amount of time which the children should spend with their mother and their father; that had already been agreed. For the previous twelve months the children had spent the school week with their mother and divided their weekends and holidays between their parents. However, the parents had great difficulty in communicating with one another, and

---

17 [1986] 2 FLR 429.
18 *A v A (Minors) (Shared Residence Order)* [1994] 1 FLR 669. For further general commentary see I Weyland *Judicial attitudes to contact and shared residence since the Children Act 1989* (1995) 17 JSWFL 445.
19 [1994] 1 FLR 369.
20 [1994] 1 FLR 717.
1 [1994] 1 FLR 669. See H Conway *Shared residence orders* [1995] Fam Law 435.

when the father applied for a shared residence order the mother strongly opposed this. The issue for the court, therefore, was whether the children should continue to see their father under the auspices of a contact order or under the auspices of a shared residence order. The trial judge confirmed the existing arrangements and made a residence order in favour of each parent. Dismissing the mother's appeal, the Court of Appeal found that the judge had not exceeded the generous ambit within which reasonable disagreement is possible, and therefore there was no evidence that he had been plainly wrong.[2] However, Butler-Sloss LJ disagreed with Purchas LJ's approach in *Re H (A Minor) (Shared Residence)* in so far as he had imported a general test of 'exceptional circumstances' into the interpretation of section 11(4), and emphasised that each case must be decided on its own facts.[3] She stated that a shared residence order is an unusual order which should only be made in unusual circumstances, but that a judge should exercise his discretion in accordance with the checklist. Giving guidance on where a shared order would *not* be appropriate, she said:

> 'A shared residence order would, in my view, be unlikely to be made if there were concrete issues still arising between the parties which had not been resolved, such as the amount of contact, whether it should be staying or visiting contact or another issue such as education, which were muddying the waters and which were creating difficulties between the parties which reflected the way in which the children were moving from one parent to another in the contact period.'[4]

It is clear that orders for shared residence are still unusual orders and the conventional wisdom remains that if an order is required at all it is usually a residence order for one parent and a contact order for the other.[5] A shared residence order may, however, be appropriate where one of the parties is not a parent of the child and therefore does not have parental responsibility. This was the position in *Re H (Shared Residence: Parental Responsibility)*.[6] The mother's husband was not the father of the elder son of the family but he had accepted the boy as his own. The Court of Appeal held that in these circumstances it was appropriate to make a shared residence order for the purpose of conferring parental responsibility on the husband.[7]

---

2   *G v G* [1985] 2 All ER 225. On the role of the appeal court, see above.

3   [1994] 1 FLR 669, at p 678.

4   Ibid, at p 677.

5   For a general discussion of the pros and cons of shared residence see C Bridge *Shared residence in England and New Zealand – a comparative analysis* (1996) 8 CFLQ 12; A Baker and P Townsend *Post-divorce parenting – rethinking shared residence* (1996) 8 CFLQ 217.

6   [1995] 2 FLR 883.

7   Other factors influencing the court's decision were that a shared residence order had originally been made by agreement between the parties, and that it was in the interests of the boy for the law to give a stamp of approval to the husband's wish to treat the boy as his own. Cf *Re WB (Residence Orders)* [1995] 2 FLR 1023.

Should the children live with their mother or their father?

Although the law does not favour mothers over fathers in the sense that there is no presumption that a child should live with his mother, past surveys of practice have revealed that mothers retain care of the children far more often than fathers.[8] These surveys were carried out prior to the Children Act 1989, but there does not appear to be any evidence to suggest that patterns have undergone any marked alteration. In the past judges felt able to express a bias towards women using language which would not be acceptable today. Thus in *M v M*,[9] when comparing the claim of the father against the mother to look after their four-year-old daughter, Stamp LJ stated 'I would entertain no doubt whatsoever that this little girl of four and a half years old ought to be brought up by her mother that *nature has ordained* should look after her own little girl'.[10] He added, 'however good a man [the father] may be, he cannot perform the functions which a mother performs by nature in relation to her own little girl'. While Ormrod LJ expressed the opinion that '[the mother] can give up work much more easily than the father can if the child is ill'. It is inconceivable that the Court of Appeal would speak of the role of a mother in this manner today. Indeed, in *Re A (Children: 1959 UN Declaration)*[11] the Court of Appeal found that the trial judge was plainly wrong to rule that because the child was of tender years he should therefore naturally go to his mother.

The present approach of the Court of Appeal was articulated by Butler-Sloss LJ in *Re S (A Minor) (Custody)*[12] where she said 'it is natural for young children to be with their mothers but, where it is in dispute, it is a consideration but not a presumption'. She subsequently elaborated on what she meant by this in *Re A (A Minor) (Custody)*.[13] She explained that where a young child has lived throughout with the mother in an unbroken relationship, such a relationship is very difficult to displace unless the mother is unsuitable to care for the child.[14] However, she distinguished the situation where there has been a continuum of care by the mother from that where mother and child have been separated, and where the mother seeks the return of the child. She said that in these circumstances other considerations applied, and there is no starting point that the mother should be preferred to the father and only displaced by a preponderance of evidence to the contrary. She emphasised that there is no presumption

---

8 See J A Priest and J C Whybrow *Custody Law in Practice in the Divorce and Domestic Courts* Supplement to Law Com WP No 96 (HMSO, 1986).
9 (1978) 1 FLR 77.
10 Emphasis added.
11 [1998] 1 FLR 354.
12 [1991] 2 FLR 388, at p 390.
13 [1991] 2 FLR 394.
14 Thus, in this regard, Butler-Sloss LJ was confirming the approach that mothers have an inherent advantage in relation to young children, but using more moderate language than in *M v M* (1978) 1 FLR 77.

which requires the mother, as mother, to be considered as the primary caretaker in preference to the father.[15]

It is clear that a mother starts with an advantage over a father in a case where a baby or young child is involved. In *Re W (A Minor) (Residence Order)*,[16] the Court of Appeal held that while there is no presumption of law that a child of any given age is better off with one parent there is a rebuttable presumption of fact that a baby's interests are best served by being cared for by his mother. As Balcombe LJ said, 'it hardly requires saying that a baby of under four weeks old would normally be with his or her natural mother'. Furthermore the court emphasised the risks of delaying a decision while full welfare reports were prepared. In *Re W (A Minor)* the baby had been separated from her mother and was in the care of her father. A judge had ordered that the status quo be maintained pending the preparation of reports. Allowing the mother's appeal, the Court of Appeal substituted an interim residence order in favour of the mother.

In *Brixey v Linus*,[17] where parents were disputing the custody of a young child, the sheriff had given custody to the father because he took the view that, 'as a member of the father's family the child would have all the advantages of comfort, education and a strong and stable moral framework which they can offer'.[18] Allowing the mother's appeal, the Court of Session the First Division found that the sheriff had failed to take account of the important factor that during infancy the child's need for her mother is stronger than the need for a father. Dismissing the father's appeal to the House of Lords, their Lordships' view of how gender considerations should influence the determination of a contest between parents of a young child was neatly encapsulated in the expression of opinion by Lord Jauncey that 'to ignore the fact that in normal circumstances, and I stress the word normal, a mother is better able than a father to fulfil the needs of a very young child is to ignore what is generally accepted to be reality'.[19]

---

15 In *Re K (Residence order: securing contact)* [1999] 1 FLR 583 this type of reasoning led the Court of Appeal to uphold a residence order in favour of a father with regular staying contact to the mother in relation to the parties' two-year-old son. The court acknowledged that the order was unusual bearing in mind the child's age; it was influenced by the risk that the mother might take the child to India, and difficulties which the mother had made over contact between the child and his father.

16 [1992] 2 FLR 332.

17 [1996] 2 FLR 499. The concept of custody was still applicable in Scotland. For commentary see E Sutherland *The unequal struggle – fathers and children in Scots law* (1997) 9 CFLQ 191.

18 The parents were unmarried, very young and came from different social backgrounds. The child was happy, healthy and well cared for in the mother's house, but the mother had none of the educational and social advantages of the father.

19 At p 503. See too the unusual facts of *Re P* [1987] 2 FLR 421 where a mother of five-month-old twins had entered into a private surrogacy arrangement but refused to hand the babies over to the commissioning couple. Although the couple could offer the children an advantageous upbringing in terms of intellectual stimulus, material benefits and a two-parent household, these factors did not outweigh the advantage of preserving the children's link with their mother to whom they were bonded.

Choosing between parents may give rise to particular difficulties where there are several children of the family and where either the children have expressed different wishes about which parent they would like to live with, or where the interests of the children appear to demand that they should be separated. Normally courts are reluctant to separate siblings; such an outcome means that not only do the children lose their day to day relationship with the non-residential parent, they also experience the sadness of losing this relationship with a brother or sister to whom they are attached. However, where the best interests of each child point in different directions then an order splitting the siblings between the parents is appropriate. The interests of one child to be with one parent should not be subordinated to those of another.[20]

A parent's sexual orientation

Occasionally questions have arisen about the relevance of a parent's sexual orientation to the welfare of the child.[21] In *C v C (A Minor) (Custody: Appeal)*[1] the court had to choose between parents of a six-year-old girl who both clearly loved the child and could give her good physical care. The father had remarried and was living with his new wife, the mother was living with a lesbian partner. The trial judge gave the care of the child to the mother, holding that her lesbian relationship was not a matter to put into the balancing exercise since its impact on the child would be much the same whether she visited her mother from time to time or lived with her permanently. Allowing the father's appeal and remitting the case for a fresh hearing the Court of Appeal ruled that the judge had been plainly wrong to engage in the balancing operation as if there were no lesbian relationship. Balcombe LJ stated that a judge must not allow his subjective views to affect his decision on what a child's welfare requires when approaching sensitive issues on which different views are held, rather he should apply the moral standards which are generally accepted in society. Taking this approach, he said:

'It is still the norm that children are brought up in a home with a father, mother and siblings (if any) and, other things being equal, such an upbringing is most likely to be conducive to their welfare. If, because the parents are divorced, such an upbringing is no longer possible, then a very material factor in considering where

---

20 *B v B (Residence Order: Restricting Applications)* [1997] 1 FLR 139.
21 Cases of this nature have tended in the past to lead to less than temperate language being used by the judges; see Lord Wilberforce's speech in *Re D (An Infant)* [1977] AC 602, at p 609 where he refers to children, at critical ages, being exposed to homosexual ways of life which may lead to 'severance from normal society, to psychological stresses and unhappiness and possibly even to physical experiences which may scar them for life'. Surely the same could be said for heterosexual encounters too?
1   [1991] 1 FLR 223.

the child's welfare lies is which of the competing parents can offer the nearest approach to the norm. In the present case it is clearly the father.'[2]

Later he added 'if her home was to be with the father that would be a normal home by the standards of our society; that would not be the case if the home were with the mother'. Glidewell LJ expressed the same view in even stronger language. He said 'despite the vast changes over the past 30 years or so in the attitudes of our society generally to the institution of marriage, to sexual morality, and to homosexual relationships ... a lesbian relationship between two adult women is an unusual background in which to bring up a child'. He continued:

'The judge had no evidence, and thus we have none, about the effect on a young child of learning the nature of a lesbian relation- ship and of her friends learning about it. Nevertheless, it seems the judge accepted, and it is certainly my view, that this child should learn or understand at an early age the nature of her mother's relationship .... Moreover, he seems to have disregarded the effect on [the child] of her school friends learning of the relationship. If or when they do, she is bound to be asked questions which may well cause her distress or embarrassment.'[3]

It is suggested that much of the reasoning in *C v C (A Minor) (Custody: Appeal)* relied on assertions about what is 'normal' stemming from a narrow perspective of normality, and was based on speculation about how living with a lesbian parent is likely to affect a child. There was neither empirical nor research evidence to support the judges' assertions, and there was no evidence before them on the impact which a lesbian up-bringing would be likely to have on the child's relationship with her peers, or on the development of her own sexuality.[4] It is suggested that where a parent's sexual orientation is homosexual or lesbian he or she might be well advised to adduce expert evidence that this will not harm the child. Evidence of this nature was very persuasive in *B v B (Minors) (Custody, Care and Control).*[5] Here a highly qualified expert witness was able to assure the court that there is no increased incidence of homosexuality amongst the children of homosexual parents. In relation to stigmatisation and reputation, the witness was further able to reassure the court that children tend to be teased about matters about which they show sensitivity relating to them

2   Ibid, at p 231.
3   Ibid, at pp 228-229.
4   Which was another matter of concern to the court. It is interesting to note that when the case was reheard by a Family Division judge that he ordered that the child should live with her mother: see F Tasker and S Golombok *Children raised by lesbian mothers* (1991) 21 Fam Law 184. See too, K Standley *Children and lesbian mothers: B v B and C v C* (1992) 4 JCL 134.
5   [1991] 1 FLR 402.

personally, and that it was very rare for children to show an interest in the background of other children. There is nonetheless a body of authority to the effect that a parent's sexual orientation is a relevant matter in the assessment of a child's welfare, and that, all other things being equal, a child will benefit more from being brought up in a heterosexual household.[6]

Continuity of care

Paragraph (c) directs courts to consider the likely effect on the child of any change in his circumstances, and where present arrangements are working it is unlikely that a court will be willing to alter the status quo.[7] Continuity of care is generally regarded as desirable for a child because it assists in giving him a sense of security at a time when he is feeling vulnerable and threatened by his parents' separation. Courts are reluctant to interfere with established arrangements because bonds are likely to exist not only between the child and the parent with whom he is living, but also between the child and other members of the household, neighbours, friends and companions at school.[8] This means that the parent who keeps the children in the immediacy of marriage breakdown is the parent who is most likely, all other things being equal, to obtain a residence order. It is in cases of this kind that a father has tended to be successful in obtaining an order that the care of young children should remain with him.[9] *Re B (Residence Order: Status Quo)*[10] is illustrative of this. The trial judge transferred residence from the father to the mother because the child's happiness and related sense of security depended on what the judge termed 'comfortable contact'. The judge took the view that the child could only enjoy such contact if it was under the control of the mother. Allowing the father's appeal, the Court of Appeal held that the judge had misdirected himself, and that maintaining the status quo was of overwhelming importance for securing the child's future.

---

6   *Re P (A Minor) (Custody)* (1983) 4 FLR 401; *S v S (Custody of Children)* (1978) 1 FLR 143. In *Re H (A Minor) (Section 37 Direction)* [1993] 2 FLR 541 a lesbian couple applied for a residence order in respect of a baby girl whom they had been looking after for eight months. There were various serious concerns about the suitability of the applicants, including about the impact on the child of being brought up in a lesbian household, and the court directed that an investigation under s 37(1) of the Children Act 1989 take place: see ch 3. Interestingly, in relation to adoption the courts have adopted an increasingly 'liberal' attitude: see in particular *Re W (Adoption: Homosexual Adopter)* [1997] 2 FLR 406, further below.
7   For a pre-Children Act 1989 example, see *D v M* [1982] 3 All ER 897. Retention of the status quo is also highly relevant to paragraphs (b) and (e). Where a child has formed settled relationships, to move the child may be positively harmful to his or her future mental health and ability to relate normally to people: see, for example, *Re JK (Adoption: Transracial Placement)* [1991] 2 FLR 340 which is discussed below.
8   See the comments by Ormrod LJ in *Dicocco v Milne* (1983) 4 FLR 247.
9   *Re A (A Minor) (Custody)* [1991] 2 FLR 394; see too *Stephenson v Stephenson* [1985] FLR 1140.
10 [1998] 1 FLR 368.

The status quo position is reinforced when a court requests the preparation of reports in order to assist it in arriving at its decision. Owing to the pressures on court welfare officers it is unlikely that a report will be prepared in less than two months, and three months is a more common minimum preparation time.[11] In addition, although children cases take priority in court listing arrangements, the pressure on courts also leads to delay in the hearing of cases. Therefore the parent who has care of the child in the meantime inevitably has a built-in advantage, because by the time the case is heard, the status quo will have assumed even greater importance.

It is suggested that parents seeking legal advice should be made fully aware of this bias towards the status quo. In particular a father or mother, who might otherwise be willing to leave the matrimonial home pending divorce, needs to appreciate the implications of doing so in relation to the children. However, a short period of separation from the children may not be problematic. Where the parties have separated fairly recently the status quo argument does not carry the same weight, and a court is more likely to be willing to order a transfer of residence.[12]

Where parents continue to live close by to one another after they have parted, contact between the child and the non-residential parent is normally easy to arrange, and other links can readily be maintained. By contrast, where one parent plans to move to another part of the country this will inevitably cause disruption to existing arrangements and the desirability of retaining the child's links with both sides of his family takes on a particular magnitude. In *Re E (Residence: Imposition of Conditions)*[13] the Court of Appeal held that it is normally wrong to make an order which prevents the residential parent moving house. Rather, the correct approach is to treat the issue of where the child will live as one of the relevant factors in determining who should obtain the residence order.[14] Where a parent wishes to move children to a part of the country which is less suitable for them, in some cases this might persuade the court to make a residence order in favour of the other parent.

'Snatching' and ex parte applications

Courts are anxious to prevent children from becoming pawns in a battle between their parents, particularly where this develops into a situation where parents are literally pulling the child from one home to the other.

11 The National Standards For Probation Service Family Court Welfare Work (Home Office, 1994) states, at para 4.28 that a report should normally be filed within 10 weeks of the receipt of the relevant papers from the court.
12 *Allington v Allington* [1985] FLR 586.
13 [1997] 2 FLR 638.
14 In *Re E (Residence: Imposition of Conditions)*, it was held that s 11(7) was wide enough to enable a court to make an order with restrictions on where the parent caring for the child could reside. However, normally such an order would be an unwarranted imposition on the right of the residential parent to choose where she would live, and with whom, see *Re D (Minors) (Residence: Imposition of Conditions)* [1996] 2 FLR 281.

Married parents, of course, enjoy equal parental responsibility and, in the absence of a court order, each is entitled to exercise all aspects of that responsibility. But in *Re B (Minors) (Residence Order)*[15] the Court of Appeal made it clear that this does not mean that a parent is free to take the children away from their settled home. Nor does it mean that a parent is entitled to refuse to return a child after a contact visit where the child's home is with the other parent.[16] The courts have expressed grave displeasure at behaviour of this kind, and are likely to counter it by making an interim order restoring the child to the parent who had de facto residence pending a fuller investigation and the preparation of welfare reports.[17]

In *W v D*[18] a father had refused to return his daughter aged four to her mother after a contact visit. The mother applied for an order restoring the child to her care, but the judge adjourned the case pending the preparation of a welfare report, and ordered that the child should stay in her father's care pending the final hearing. Allowing the mother's appeal, the Court of Appeal ruled that against the background of snatch the principles are these: where a child of tender years has spent her life in the care of her mother then, unless it appears on credible evidence that there is something so prejudicial to the life of the child flowing from the care of the mother so that it would be dangerous to restore the pre-existing situation, the court should order that the child is restored to the situation that existed before the snatch.[19] In *Re R (Minors) (Interim Custody Order)*[20] Balcombe J criticised the use of the word 'principle' in this context, pointing out that the only principle to be applied in children cases is the paramountcy of the child's welfare. But in *Townson v Mahon*[1] the Court of Appeal reasserted the approach that a judge making an interim order ought to restore the status quo in the absence of particular reasons to the contrary. As Wood J pointed out, one of the arguments which had been put for the father at the hearing before the judge was that the child had settled with him after he had wrongfully kept her after a contact visit. Thus when the judge had dismissed the mother's application to have the child returned to her forthwith, the effect of that was to consolidate the position created by the father's wrongdoing.

---

15 [1992] 3 All ER 867.
16 *Re H (A Minor) (Interim Custody)* [1991] 2 FLR 411.
17 *Jenkins v Jenkins* (1978) 1 FLR 148.
18 (1979) 1 FLR 393; although this case preceded the implementation of the Children Act 1989 by a decade it is suggested that the approach of the Court of Appeal has not altered.
19 The court asserted these principles on the assumption that the child had been snatched from the mother; it is not clear whether it would have adopted the same approach if the mother had snatched a young child from the father. In view of the approach of the Court of Appeal in *Re S (A Minor) (Custody)* [1991] 2 FLR 388 that, where there has not been a continuum of care by the mother, there is no presumption in favour of the mother as primary caretaker (see above), the principles should now apply equally if the mother is the 'snatcher'.
20 (1980) 2 FLR 316.
1 [1984] FLR 690.

Where allegations are made by the 'snatching' parent against the residential parent the court may adopt a less rigorous approach to snatching. In *Re J (A Minor) (Interim Custody: Appeal)*[2] the snatching father had made allegations against the mother in relation to her care of the child in swiftly heard inter partes proceedings, and the trial judge had concluded that the child should stay with her father during the short period pending a fuller hearing. Dismissing the mother's appeal, Butler-Sloss LJ emphasised that there was no principle that where a child has been retained beyond the agreed time that the court should automatically order that the child be returned pending a final decision. However, and by contrast, in *Re H (A Minor) (Interim Custody)*[3] Butler-Sloss LJ reproved the trial judge for making an order in ex parte proceedings transferring the care of a child from the mother to the father. The father had alleged that the child had been non-accidentally injured by being kicked by her mother's partner, and had supported this allegation with opinion evidence to that effect from a doctor who had examined the child. Butler-Sloss LJ said that she deprecated the use of an ex parte order for changing the child's home from one parent to another unless the circumstances were very exceptional. She drew an analogy with a case where a local authority wished to obtain an emergency order to protect a child from immediate danger, and said that unless the facts justified such an order the court should not transfer the child from one parent to the other until after an urgent inter partes hearing.

It is suggested that the analogy drawn with an application by a local authority for an emergency order[4] was not apt to proceedings involving parents. When an emergency protection order is made the child is taken from home and placed in unfamiliar surroundings and parental responsibility is given to the applicant, who is usually a social worker. This is traumatic for the child and involves state interference in family life which must be carefully controlled for reasons of broad policy.[5] By contrast, when a non-residential parent takes, or retains, care of a child, the child will not be moving to a strange environment where he is cared for by people whom he does not know. Rather, he will be with a parent who enjoys de jure, or at least de facto, parental responsibility for him, and with whom he is familiar. Whilst it may be upsetting for the child, the child may well be unaware of what is taking place because he is merely staying longer with a known and trusted adult. Where, as in *Re H (A Minor)*, a general practitioner gives evidence that there is a prima facie case of child abuse, and the non-abusing parent is wanting to care for the child, it is suggested that the welfare of the child should normally point

---

2   [1989] 2 FLR 304.
3   [1991] 2 FLR 411.
4   In *Re H (A Minor) (Interim Custody)* Butler-Sloss LJ drew an analogy with an application for a place of safety order under the Children and Young Persons Act 1969. This has since been replaced by the emergency protection order under the Children Act 1989, s 44.
5   See ch 3.

to the child being transferred to that parent for a very short period while further enquiries are made, this being the safest alternative for the child. It is suggested that the approach taken in *Re H (A Minor)* may sometimes fail to serve a child's welfare, and that a judge, in the exercise of his discretion, should not feel inhibited from ordering that a child's residence is *temporarily* transferred from one parent to another in ex parte proceedings where there is an allegation of child abuse, while further investigations take place.[6]

Where the choice is between a parent and a third party

The principle that the child's welfare must be the court's paramount consideration can sometimes exist uneasily alongside the principle that it is parents who enjoy parental responsibility, and it is they who have the right to bring up their own children. Where a child is being cared for by a parent, and where he is well looked after and happy, it would be most unusual for a court to order that the child should live with someone else, even his other parent, because courts are quite properly reluctant to disturb an arrangement which is working well. However, where a third party such as a relative, friend or foster parent is bringing up a child within a loving and stable environment, and where that third party is seeking to retain care of the child against the opposition of the child's natural parents, a real tension can arise. In a case of this kind the court is often faced with a choice between leaving the child in the care of persons whom he loves, and with whom he has formed bonds of attachment, and returning him to parents who usually live in more disadvantaged circum-stances, and to whom the child's attachment links may have been weakened. Thus the welfare principle and the principle that parents have a right to bring up their own children may sometimes be pulling in different directions.

The principle to be applied in such a situation is clear: the child's welfare must be the court's paramount consideration. In 1969 the House of Lords ruled in *J v C*[7] that just as the paramountcy principle applies between parent and parent, so too it applies to disputes between parents and strangers. Lord MacDermott's speech provides helpful guidance on the practical application of this principle. The issue in *J v C* was whether a ten-year-old Spanish boy should be returned to the care of his natural parents or whether he should remain with his English foster parents, with whom he had spent most of his childhood. In this regard Lord MacDermott stated that the rights and wishes of the parents must be assessed and weighed as to their bearing on the welfare of the child in conjunction with all other factors relevant to that issue. He added that 'such rights and wishes, recognised as they are by nature and society, can be capable of ministering to the total welfare of the child in a special way, and must therefore preponderate in many cases'. However, he

6   See too *Re B (Minors) (Residence Order)* [1992] 3 All ER 867.
7   [1969] 1 All ER 788.

stated that there is no rule of law that the rights and wishes of unimpeachable parents must prevail, and that experience shows that serious harm can sometimes be occasioned to children by moving them from one home to another. He added that a child's future happiness and sense of security are always important factors, and that the effect of such a change will often be worthy of close and anxious attention.

The weight to be given to the wishes and feelings of parents came under further scrutiny from the House of Lords in 1988 in *Re KD (A Minor) (Ward: Termination of Access)*.[8] Here a local authority had applied to terminate contact between a child and his mother so that they could place the child for adoption. The issue to be resolved was whether the welfare principle applied to the termination of contact between a child and his parent, or whether such an approach was inconsistent with the European Convention on Human Rights and Fundamental Freedoms, to which the United Kingdom is a party. Article 8 of the Convention provides:

'1. Everyone has the right to respect for his private and family life, his home and his correspondence.
2. There shall be no interference by a public authority with the exercise of this right except such as is in accordance with the law and is necessary ... for the protection of health or morals, or for the protection of the rights and freedoms of others.'

The House of Lords ruled that there is no conflict between the Convention and giving paramountcy to the child's welfare. Lord Oliver stated that pronouncements made by the European Court of Human Rights[9] and the principles laid down by the House of Lords in *J v C* could be reconciled, and that:

'Such conflict as exists is, I think, semantic only and lies in differing ways of giving expression to the single common concept that the natural bond and relationship between parent and child gives rise to universally recognised norms which ought not to be gratuitously interfered with and which, if interfered with at all, ought to be so only if the welfare of the child dictates.'

Lord Oliver was at pains to point out that 'parenthood, in most civilised societies, is generally conceived as conferring on parents the exclusive privilege of ordering, within the family, the upbringing of children of tender age, with all that that entails'. But he added 'it is a privilege circumscribed by many limitations imposed both by the general law, and, where the circumstances demand, by the courts or by the authorities on whom the legislature has imposed the duty of supervising the welfare of children and young persons'.[10]

8 [1988] 1 All ER 577.
9 *R v United Kingdom* [1988] 2 FLR 445, E Ct HR.
10 [1988] 1 All ER 577, at p 588.

Like Lord Oliver, Lord Templeman found no difficulty in reconciling the paramountcy principle with Article 8 of the Convention. He said:

'In my opinion there is no inconsistency of principle or application between the English rule and the convention rule. The best person to bring up a child is the natural parent. It matters not whether the parent is wise or foolish, rich or poor, educated or illiterate, provided the child's moral or physical health are not endangered …. In terms of the English rule the court decides whether and to what extent the welfare of the child requires that the child shall be protected from harm caused by the parent, including harm which could be caused by resumption of parental care after separation has broken the parental tie. In terms of the Convention rule the court decides whether and to what extent the child's health or morals require protection from the parent and whether and to what extent the family life of parent and child has been supplanted by some other relationship which has become the essential family life for the child.'[11]

Whilst the guiding principles are undoubtedly clear, the cases where the conflict over the child is between a parent and a third party are undoubtedly the most difficult for the courts to resolve. There is often a strong tension between having regard to the wishes and feelings of the parents and giving paramountcy to the child's welfare. An example arose in *Re K (A Minor) (Custody)*.[12] The child had gone to live with his uncle and aunt, Mr and Mrs E, after the suicide of his mother. When the child's father sought to recover the care of his son the trial judge asked himself the question: 'who would provide the better home for the child, the father or Mr and Mrs E?' and decided that Mr and Mrs E would do so. Reversing the judge's decision, Fox LJ said that this approach had been wrong. The question was not where the child would get the better home. The question was: 'was it demonstrated that the welfare of the child positively demanded the displacement of the parental right.'[13] Waite J stated that the speeches in *Re KD (A Minor)* 'make it plain that the term "parental right" is not there used in any proprietary sense, but rather as describing *the right of every child*, as part of its general welfare, to have the ties of nature maintained wherever possible with the parents who gave it life'.[14]

11 Ibid, at p 578.
12 [1990] 2 FLR 64.
13 Fox LJ acknowledged that the word 'right' was not accurate in so far as it might connote something in the nature of a proprietary right, which, he emphasised, it is not.
14 Ibid, at p 70, emphasis added. For an application of this reasoning, see *Re D (Care: Natural Parent Presumption)* [1999] 1 FLR 134. The father was found suitable to care for the child provided that a care order was made; the grandparents who were looking after the child's two half-siblings were seeking a residence order. The Court of Appeal held that the trial judge had been wrong to conduct a balancing exercise between the two households; he should have first considered the father as a potential carer and only rejected him in favour of the grandparents where there were good grounds for doing so. The child's relationship with his siblings could be maintained through contact.

In *Re K (A Minor) (Wardship: Adoption)*,[15] the Court of Appeal warned against a court making an order which could offer the child an advantageous style of upbringing with substitute parents where this would prevent the natural parents caring for their child themselves. The case concerned a child of seven months whose mother was being treated for heroin addiction and who, with her husband, was seeking to recover the child from a couple to whom the mother had handed her over when she was six weeks old. Reversing the trial judge's decision to leave the child in a 'warm and loving family who are currently caring for her admirably and wish to continue to do so' and where 'if she moves there will be inevitable upheaval and upset for the child', Butler-Sloss LJ said 'the mother must be shown to be entirely unsuitable before another family can be considered, otherwise we are in grave danger of slipping into social engineering'.[16]

It is suggested that if the courts maintain their recent antipathy to social engineering it is unlikely that a court would again make a ruling like the one in *Re H (A Minor: Custody)*[17] in which a 'warm and loving' Indian mother was unable to regain the care of her son from her brother-in-law and sister-in-law. In *Re H* the child aged seven and a half had been placed with these relatives by his father, and they had looked after him for the last two and a half years. During this time the mother had had regular contact with her son, apart from a period of nine months at the outset, when the father very improperly cut off contact. The case is illustrative of how the considerations in the checklist which relate to the child's sense of security, and its link with the status quo, may point in one direction, and the claim of a parent to bring up her own child may point in another. The child was living in a secure and stable environment, and had settled well at school, and the court was unwilling to upset this arrangement even though nothing could be said against the mother as a mother. However, the ruling in *Re H* was disturbing because of the manner in which the claims of the mother to care for her own child, and the interests of the child to be brought up by his own mother, were so readily displaced.

Cases of this kind are profoundly difficult. It is clear that the court's starting point that there is 'a strong supposition that, other things being equal, it is in the interests of the child that it shall remain with its natural parents'[18] is not readily displaced. This was forcibly illustrated in *Re M (Child's Upbringing)*[19] which raised cross-cultural issues similar to those which arose in *J v C*.[20] Great weight was given by the trial judge and the

---

15 [1991] 1 FLR 57.
16 Ibid, at p 62. However, care must be taken over the weight to be given to this authority. The couple caring for the child were not themselves entirely suitable as carers because of their age, and they had attempted to circumvent the safeguards surrounding the placement of children for adoption.
17 [1990] 1 FLR 51.
18 *Re H (A Minor) (Custody: Interim Care and Control)* [1991] 2 FLR 109 at 113, per Lord Donaldson.
19 [1996] 2 FLR 441. This case received considerable publicity in the press.
20 [1969] 1 All ER 788.

Court of Appeal to the notion that a ten year old South African boy's development 'must be, in the last resort and profoundly, Zulu development and not Afrikaans or English development'.[1] The boy had been living in England with a South African woman and her family[2] for about four years during which time he had only intermittent contact with his natural family. Expert evidence was given that abrupt separation from his 'psychological' family would cause him severe trauma. Nonetheless the court ordered that he be returned to South Africa. Neill LJ justified this conclusion by asserting that the boy had a right to be reunited with his Zulu parents. Similarly, Ward LJ asserted that the child's roots were in South Africa and that he therefore ought to return to his family there.[3]

By labelling the notion that a child should be brought up by his parent as the 'right of the child', and by stating that the court must beware of 'social engineering', the courts have been able to give considerable weight to the parents' claims to bring up their own children without appearing to come into conflict with the paramountcy of the child's welfare. However, there are dangers in taking a rights approach to the welfare principle. A child's right to family life is separate and independent of that of his parents, and the child may, or may not, agree with the characterisation of his right to family life as the 'right to be brought up by the parents who gave birth to him'. The child's views are likely to be coloured by the strength of his attachment to his 'natural' parents and the strength of his attachment to those who have been caring for him as substitute parents.[4] Where he has little attachment to his natural parents, and where he is much loved by his substitute parents and they have been making very considerable provision for his physical, emotional and educational needs, the child may have reservations, or even strong negative views, about the perceived advantages of his returning to live with his natural parent against his remaining with his substitute 'psychological' parents.[5] He certainly may not regard it as his 'right' to be brought up by his parents, who, to him, may be the strangers

1   [1996] 2 FLR 441 at p 453 per Thorpe J.
2   There was evidence to suggest that the woman had deceived the boy's parents as to her intentions when bringing him to England.
3   For further discussion, see Jane Fortin, *Children's Rights and the Developing Law* (Butterworths, 1998), pp 351-359. Subsequently, the boy returned back to England, to his foster mother.
4   As Wall J said in *Re B (Adoption: Child's Welfare)* [1995] 1 FLR 895, at p 902, 'a child has in principle a right to be brought up by his or her parents in the way of life and in the religion practised by the parents. That principle, however, is not absolute. It is an expression of what would ordinarily be in the child's interests and falls to be displaced where the welfare of the child requires it to be displaced.' For a consideration of both *Re M (Child's Upbringing)* (above) and *Re B (Adoption: Child's Welfare)* see I Weyland *Attachment and the welfare principle* [1996] Fam Law 686.
5   A phrase first used by J Goldstein, A Freud and A Solnit in their highly influential book *Beyond the Best Interests of the Child* (Collier Macmillan, 1973). For a review of this and other important works of these authors, published under the general title *The Best Interests of The Child: The Least Detrimental Alternative* (New York, Free Press, 1996) see, M D A Freeman, *The best interests of the child: is The Best Interests of the Child in the best interests of children?* (1997) 11 IJLPF 360.

rather than his substitute parents whom he regards as his family. Thus the definition of what is meant by 'family' or 'parents' turns on whether the blood tie defines the relationship, or whether the child's experience, wishes and feelings define it.[6] In a case where the dispute is between parents and third parties what a court is often doing is determining whether the parents are capable of providing the child with a good enough standard of parenting; where they can, the court must find strong reasons for preventing the parents from providing that care. Where the child has formed strong attachment bonds, the question for the court is whether returning the child to the parents is likely to cause him psychological harm. Where it is, such a finding is likely to justify leaving the child where he is.[7]

It is suggested that when a decision is characterised as one which upholds the rights of the child this can tend to inhibit discussion about the thinking which is informing the decision. It would be preferable if it were more openly acknowledged that courts are applying ideologies and values when choosing between parents and strangers, because such an acknowledgment would better encourage debate about whether these ideologies and values command widespread acceptance. It might aid clarity if courts found it easier to state that parents do indeed have 'rights' as part of their parental responsibility, and that for a court to interfere in these rights without good cause would be to implement a dangerous social policy amounting to unwarranted state interference in private family life. It seems undoubtedly to be the case that where a court takes as its starting point that it is the right of the child to be brought up by his parents, and that a court should turn its face against social engineering unless there are good reasons, it is applying norms which command international acceptance.[8]

Placement with a parent or placement for adoption

Conflict between the principle that the welfare of the child is paramount, and the principle that it is normally the responsibility of the parent to bring up his or her own child, may arise where one parent wishes the child to be given up for adoption, and the other wishes to look after the child. In *Re M (A Minor) (Custody Appeal)*[9] the Court of Appeal adopted a

6 See further I Weyland *The blood tie: raised to the status of presumption?* (1997) 19 JSWFL 173 for a consideration of recent decisions and a criticism of any blood tie 'presumption'.

7 As in *J v C* [1969] 1 All ER 788; see too *Re N (A Minor) (Adoption)* [1990] 1 FLR 58 and *Re A (A Minor) (Cultural Background)* [1987] 2 FLR 429 (which concerned a dispute between a grandmother and third parties). Both are discussed below. See also *Re O (Adoption:Withholding Agreement)* [1999] 1 FLR 451 for a painfully difficult decision, made harder for the court because it was faced with conflicting expert evidence on the value to the child of preserving the blood tie.

8 It is suggested that this approach is consistent with Arts 5, 9 and 18 of the United Nations Convention on the Rights of the Child. The Convention was adopted, without a vote, on 20 November 1989.

9 [1990] 1 FLR 291.

very different approach to that of Lord Templeman in *Re KD (A Minor) (Ward) (Termination of Access)*,[10] and gave very considerable weight to the perceived advantages to a child of being brought up by strangers rather than by his own family. In *Re M* the mother and father were at school and aged 16 and 17 when the child was born. The mother decided that the child should be adopted so the father, supported by his parents, applied for custody of the child.[11] The trial judge found that the father's application was sincere and that the grandparents could provide the child with a good home, but he nonetheless concluded that it would be in the child's best interests to be placed for adoption. The reasons given for refusing the father custody were speculative and based on a particular view of 'normal' family life and the behaviour of young men. Nothing was said against the father or grandparents which suggested that they were unfit to care for the child; indeed the grandparents were described as 'excellent'. In relation to the father's claim to bring up his own child, the trial judge had said 'I do not give particular weight to the blood tie, although I take it into account, but I do not think it should be the decisive factor'.[12]

It is suggested that this was a case which gives cause for considerable unease. The approach taken in *Re M (A Minor) (Custody Appeal)* to the paramountcy of the child's welfare was far removed from Lord Templeman's strictures in *Re KD (A Minor)* that a natural parent is the best person to bring up his or her own child, and that the natural bond between parent and child should only be interfered with where the child's moral or physical health is endangered. By contrast, the trial judge in *Re M* appeared intent on optimising the child's position by means of adoption by a two-parent family. Perhaps the greatest cause for unease is that the father's appeal was dismissed not simply for the usual reasons, namely that the matter was one for the trial judge in the exercise of his discretion, and that the appellant had failed to establish that he had been plainly wrong. Rather, in *Re M* the Court of Appeal fully endorsed the trial judge's approach and said that, had the decision been for the Court of Appeal to make, it would have arrived at the same conclusion.

Subsequently the Court of Appeal has reverted once more to the approach taken in *Re KD (A Minor)*, and in *Re K (A minor) (Custody)* and *Re K (A Minor) (Wardship: Adoption)*. In *Re O (A Minor) (Custody: Adoption)*[13] Butler-Sloss LJ used the phrase 'social engineering' to describe the authorisation of adoption in a case where a parent was offering to care for the child. In *Re O* a married woman had conceived in the course

---

10 [1988] 1 All ER 577.

11 The modern equivalent would be to make an application for a residence order.

12 Virtually no weight at all appears to have been given to the notion of extended family rights and the claim of the grandparents to be involved in the upbringing of their grandchild; contrast with the approach in *Re L (A Minor) (Care Proceedings: Wardship) (No 2)* [1991] 1 FLR 29 in which grandparents were offering to care for their grandchild. Judge Willis, sitting as a deputy High Court judge, stated 'adoption should only be the last resort when no-one in the wider family is available and suitable to look after a child.'

13 [1992] 1 FLR 77.

of an adulterous relationship. She became reconciled with her husband and, after much heart-searching, she placed her child with an adoption agency with a view to his adoption. The child's father was seeking to look after the child, but the mother, who was very hostile to the father, strenuously opposed his application. The trial judge made an order in favour of the father giving him the care of the child, and the Court of Appeal dismissed the mother's appeal. Butler-Sloss LJ said that the test to be applied was whether the father was a fit and suitable person to care for his son, and that if he was adoption did not arise. She stated that no distinction should be drawn between the married and the unmarried father because, so far as the child was concerned, he was the other parent, and added 'the judge quite correctly posed to himself the test that if the mother and father were married and the mother could not care for the child, would one say that the child should not go to the father? Quite simply, the answer would be that one could not say that.'

However, it is suggested that just as *Re M (A Minor) (Custody: Adoption)*[14] gives cause for unease so too *Re O (A Minor) (Custody: Adoption)*, in which the contrary decision was reached, also gives cause for unease. This time the anxiety arises because of the manner in which the mother's strongly held views were discounted by the court. In *Re M* there was no suggestion that the natural parents were hostile to one another, or that the father had behaved badly towards the mother. By contrast, whilst the court did not accept all the mother's allegations against the father in *Re O*, it found as a fact that the mother felt very strongly that the father had behaved dishonourably towards her, and that she was vehemently opposed to the father bringing up her child. It is suggested that *Re O* has serious impli-cations for any unmarried mother who is considering placing her child with an adoption agency. It seems essential that she should be warned that her wish that the child should be brought up by an adoptive couple who can offer the child a two-parent family may be frustrated by an application for a residence order from the father. Where she is passionately opposed to the father having care of her child, she also needs to know that, in the light of *Re O,* her opposition is unlikely to prevent an order being made in the father's favour.

Re O (A Minor) (Custody: Adoption) poses the broader question whether courts would be wise to treat all unmarried fathers in an identical fashion to married fathers where the mother wishes the child to be adopted, or whether they would be better to adopt the approach taken in *Re M (A Minor) (Custody: Adoption)*. It is suggested that there *is* a distinction between married and unmarried parenthood. When a man and a woman marry, they agree implicitly to share parental responsibility for any child of their union. When an unmarried woman becomes pregnant by a man there is no such implicit agreement; how the mother sees the father's role in the child's life is likely to turn on the length and quality of her relationship with the father. Where that relationship has been relatively fleeting, and where she feels betrayed or otherwise ill-used by the father, she is unlikely to want

---

14 Discussed above.

him to have sole responsibility for the upbringing of their child. If courts too readily make residence orders in favour of unmarried fathers in cases where the mother wishes the child to be adopted by third parties, the knowledge that such an order could be made is likely to deter some unmarried mothers from placing their children for adoption. It seems likely that some mothers will not be prepared to risk the fathers obtaining a residence order. If this results in more babies being brought up by single mothers who would otherwise prefer that their children are adopted, it can be questioned whether this promotes the general welfare of children.

A child's ethnic origin

When making plans about a child's welfare, virtually all local authority social services departments take the view that it is self-evident that the child's interests are best served if he has his home with persons of the same ethnic origin.[15] The Children Act 1989 itself makes reference to religious, racial and cultural matters,[16] and guidance on the implementation of the Act provides that 'it may be taken as a guiding principle of good practice that, other things being equal and in the great majority of cases, placement with a family of similar ethnic origin and religion is most likely to meet a child's needs as fully as possible and to safeguard his or her welfare most effectively'.[17] The guidance adds the proviso that this principle should be applied with proper consideration for the circumstances of the individual case, and that there may be circumstances where placement with a family of a different ethnic origin may be the best choice for a particular child. It gives as examples where a child has formed strong links with prospective foster parents, or where he is related to them; where siblings who have different ethnic origins need to be placed together; where the child needs to remain close to his family, school and friends; or where he has special needs. However, the guidance takes it as axiomatic that placement in a family which reflects as nearly as possible the child's ethnic origins is likely to be the best choice in most cases. Indeed, it goes so far as to advise that, when exploring a child's wishes and feelings on the matter, 'responsible authorities should be ready to help the child with any confusion or misunderstandings about people of different ethnic groups which may have arisen through previous family or placement experience.

15 Including when the local authority are acting as adoption agency. The number and the nature of placements of children from different ethnic backgrounds who are privately fostered is very difficult to estimate, as it is frequently the case that private foster-parents fail to notify the local authority when they have such a child in their care. See further *Private fostering: Development of policy and practice in three English local authorities* (Save the Children, 1997).

16 S 22(4) and (5)(c) provide that before making any decision with respect to a child whom they are looking after, or proposing to look after, a local authority must take into consideration the child's religious persuasion, racial origin, and cultural and religious background.

17 *Children Act 1989 Guidance and Regulations*, vol 3, Family Placements, para 2.40.

Children of mixed ethnic origin should be helped to understand and take pride in both or all elements of their cultural heritage and to feel comfortable about their origins.'[18] In relation to the selection of persons to care for children, the guidance states that carers must be able to provide children with such help.

This view on child rearing, which is presented in the guidance in terms of having a universal and objective value,[19] has been highly influential not only on the manner in which local authorities select foster parents and adoptive parents, but also in the manner in which they, and the courts, have approached litigation about a child who is already living with a family of a different ethnic origin. Several highly contentious cases have come before the courts in which the child's ethnicity has been treated by one of the parties as an issue of great importance.

In *Re A (A Minor) (Cultural Background)*[20] a Nigerian child was sent to live with her grandmother in England. For various reasons relating to her work and her health the grandmother was unable to care for the child so she placed her with foster parents who were white. For the next five and a half years the child lived with the foster parents and their daughter, with whom she formed a very close relationship, and she came to look upon them as her family. The grandmother visited the child from time to time, and after one such visit, when the child was nine, she sought to recover the care of the child. The child was adamant that she wished to stay with her foster parents and so the matter came before the court in wardship. The case for the grandmother was that for a Nigerian child to be brought up by a white English family stored up trouble for the child in the future. A senior social worker, with extensive experience of the fostering and placement of children from Africa, gave evidence as an expert witness. She expressed the view that 'any child of West African background, regardless of the length of time that a child has been in an alternative family, must be placed back with a West African family'. Indeed, she went so far as to say that although she had not examined the details of the care which would be provided for the child if she were to return to live with her grandmother 'she felt so strongly that a Nigerian child should be returned to her own family that she would be quite sure that the arrangements would be satisfactory'. The case for the foster parents was that the child was happy and contented living with them and that they loved her as if she was their own daughter.

18 Ibid, para 2.42.
19 Despite the fact that several studies have consistently found that trans-racial adoption has a long-term aggregate success rate similar to the success rate of adoption in general. There is a brief analysis of the relevant studies by J Thoburn in *Review of Adoption Law – A Consultation Document* (DOH, 1992). There appear to be no research studies to say whether a black child placed with a black family is better able to withstand discrimination and racial prejudice than a black child placed in a white family. This may be the case, but until research establishes this, it is merely a matter of opinion. Yet it is presented as authoritative: see, for example, J Triseliotis (1989) 13 Adoption and Fostering 21. For a critique, see P Hayes *The ideological attack on transracial adoption in the USA and Britain* (1995) 9 IJLF 1.
20 [1987] 2 FLR 429.

A social worker who knew the child well gave evidence that she thought it would be catastrophic if the child was removed from the care of her foster parents. In arriving at his judgment, Swinton Thomas J stated that he had to balance the need of the child to have stability, love and security against the loss to her of her Nigerian culture and background and her own family. He found that to remove the child from the family with whom she had lived for so long would have a devastating effect on her, and that the best prospect for the child was for her to enjoy a happy and secure childhood leading to a well-adjusted adulthood. He therefore concluded that the child should remain in the care of the foster parents and that her grandmother should continue to have contact with her.

Analysing *Re A (A Minor)*, it can be seen that the court was presented with totally divergent views on what factors would serve the child's best interests. It is suggested that the opinion of the expert witness that great weight should be given to the child's ethnicity when identifying the child's long-term needs, and that, save in extreme circumstances, this should outweigh other considerations, is illustrative of the powerful hold which a particular ideological approach to the upbringing of children has over some persons who work for local authorities in the child-care field. The court, by contrast, took a more balanced approach, and whilst it gave weight to the child's origins, it weighed this factor against the likely harmful effect on the child of bringing about a change in her circumstances, and it gave respect to the child's wishes and feelings.

Similar opinion evidence about the importance to a Nigerian child of living with persons of the same ethnic origin, and that black children should not be brought up by white parents, was placed before Bush J in *Re N (A Minor) (Adoption)*[1] in a case where a father was seeking in wardship proceedings to recover the care of his black daughter aged four and a half who had been living with the same white foster parents since she was a baby. An application by the foster parents to adopt the child was also before the court. In a powerful judgment, Bush J resoundingly rejected the emphasis on colour rather than cultural upbringing in the assessment of the welfare of a child, stating that such an approach was 'highly dangerous'. After commenting that he had been 'bombarded with a host of theories and opinions by experts who derive their being from the political approach to race relations in America in the 1960s and 1970s' which had persuaded most local authorities not to place black children with white foster parents, Bush J said that other expert evidence presented to the court had pointed out that there is little real evidence, other than anecdotal, that black-white fosterings are harmful. He pointed out that some local authorities 'even go in for what one advocate described as colour co-ordination, that is if the child is three parts white and one part black, then you try to get the same combination in foster parents'. He added 'I have only to cite this doctrine to show the ridiculous nature of a dedication to dogma'. He concluded that to separate the child from her foster parents would be cruel to the child and likely to cause her serious psychological

1   [1990] 1 FLR 58.

damage both at present and in the future. He therefore ordered that she should remain living with them. However, he gave weight to Nigerian cultural patterns when considering whether the child should be adopted. He found that in the father's culture adoption was regarded as a form of slavery and that the father would feel shame and distress if such an order were made. Furthermore, he found that the father had an important part to play in the child's life in the future, when she was likely to seek out her cultural roots. Balancing these factors against the security which an adoption order would give to the child, Bush J concluded that it would not be in the child's interests to make an adoption order.

The single-mindedness with which some local authorities pursue same race policies for the children whom they are looking after was further illustrated in *Re JK (Adoption: Transracial Placement)*.[2] A local authority had placed a Sikh child with short-term white English foster parents soon after her birth while they looked for adopters of the same ethnic origin. Three years later the child was still living with the foster parents because they had been unable to find a suitable matching placement. Meanwhile the child had become deeply attached to her foster parents, who asked to be considered as prospective adoptive parents. They were rejected as such a proposal was contrary to the local authority's same race policy. When the local authority decided to move the child to a bridging family until suitable adopters could be found, the foster parents issued wardship proceedings and sought care of the child. The issue for the court was whether three years' settled attachment, or racial and cultural considerations, should determine where the child should live until adulthood.[3] Evidence was given by a child psychiatrist that in the depths of her being the child understood the foster parents as having been her parents all her life. He expressed the firm view that to move the child at this stage from the only home she had ever known would be likely to cause her irreparable psychological damage and that she would probably never trust anyone again. He said 'the separation from a much loved home at the age of three will always leave a profound pining for the rest of the child's life'. In the light of this evidence the court committed the child to the care of the foster parents with a view to her adoption by them.[4]

Re A (A Minor), *Re N (A Minor)* and *Re JK (Adoption: Transracial Placement)*, although they preceded the implementation of the Children Act 1989, are illustrative of the value which the checklist may have in

2   [1991] 2 FLR 340.
3   The local authority were investigating three families as possible adoptive families; all were Asian, two were Hindus, the third was Roman Catholic. Yet the child's religious heritage was Sikh. It is hard to see how such an arrangement would have paid regard to the child's religious and cultural heritage. There is evidence in the cases that the same race policies operated by some local authorities are related to colour, and are otherwise crude: see Bush J in *Re N (A Minor) (Adoption)* [1990] 1 FLR 58, at p 63.
4   Cf *Re P (A Minor) (Adoption)* [1990] 1 FLR 96 where the trial judge sanctioned the removal of a black child aged 16 months from white foster parents where he was thriving. The Court of Appeal held that he had been entitled to conclude that the advantages of bringing up a child of mixed race in a black family outweighed the importance of maintaining the status quo for the child.

preventing one consideration in the matters itemised in the checklist being given undue weight. Paragraph (d) requires a court to consider the child's background and any characteristics of his which the court considers relevant, and it seems clear that considerations relating to a child's ethnic origin fall within its scope. Where considerations relating to a child's background and characteristics dominate planning for a child, there is a danger that other equally important factors will be ignored or undervalued. This is what happened in *Re M (Child's Upbringing)*[5] where a ten year old boy was labelled as a Zulu child and stereotyped on the basis of his colour and cultural origins. The normal considerations relating to a child's deeply felt attachments and respect for a child's strongly held feelings were displaced by the notions that the child's development 'must be in the last resort and profoundly, Zulu development and not Afrikaans or English development'[6] and that 'he has a right to be reunited with his Zulu parents and with his extended family in South Africa'.[7] The Court of Appeal ordered the child's immediate return to South Africa despite receiving expert evidence from a child psychiatrist that this would be deeply traumatic for the child.[8] However, by requiring a court to consider all factors which are relevant to the welfare of the child, the checklist should normally act as a safeguard against an unbalanced concentration on one factor only occurring.

Contact and welfare

Litigation over contact normally centres around whether any contact at all should take place and, if so, when, where and how often this should be. Disputes arise not only about the frequency and venue of contact,[9] but also over whether the child should stay overnight with the non-residential parent (a form of contact which is often referred to as 'staying' contact), and over whether contact visits should be supervised by a third party. The disadvantage of an order in which contact arrangements are closely defined is that it is rigid, and unable to respond flexibly to changing circumstances. Therefore contact provisions which are responsive to the child's developmental needs, and to the needs of the parties, are normally preferable.[10] Where direct contact

5   [1996] 2 FLR 441, also discussed above.
6   Per the trial judge, Thorpe J, quoted at p 453.
7   Per Neill LJ, at p 454.
8   The outcome of the court's ruling proved disastrous, and the child was eventually returned to his foster mother in England with whom he had formed strong attachments since he was a baby.
9   This tension has led to a very significant increase in the establishment of child contact centres. For a discussion of the role of these centres see E Halliday *The role and function of child contact centres* (1997) 19 JSWFL 53.
10 Prior to the Children Act 1989 it was normal for courts to make orders for reasonable contact in favour of the non-residential parent, and the courts left it to the parties to negotiate what was reasonable. However, s 1(5) requires the court to be satisfied that making an order will be better for the child than making no order at all, and as a result the automatic making of reasonable contact orders has mainly fallen out of use.

is impossible or undesirable the relationship with the child may be sustained through indirect contact. This usually involves the sending of letters and cards to the child and sometimes telephone calls. Obligations may be imposed on the residential parent, for example he or she may be required to send photographs of the child and copies of school reports to the non-residential parent, and to inform that parent before making any major decision concerning the child's upbringing.

Courts have also increasingly recognised that a child's psychological links with an adult whom he or she looks on as a parent but who is not a parent may be equally, if not more, important to the child.[11] The leave of the court must normally be given before a third party can apply for a contact order.[12] However, the granting of leave does not imply that the third party, like a parent, can normally expect to be given contact.[13] In the case of third parties, be they grandparents, other relatives, or friends of the child, the burden lies on the person who wishes to have contact to establish reasons why a contact order should be made. Only if that person establishes a case for contact will it be necessary for the parent(s) to show why there should be no contact. When determining the matter the court, as with every other case, must apply the test of the paramountcy of the child's welfare and apply the checklist.[14]

Contact is the right of the child

For more than two decades the courts have emphasised that contact with a parent is the right of the child. In *M v M (Child: Access)*[15] the Court of Appeal affirmed the principle that no court should deprive a child of contact with either parent unless it is wholly satisfied that it is in the interests of the child that contact should cease.[16] It held that a court should be extremely slow to arrive at such a conclusion. Courts have taken the view that the companionship of a parent is of such immense value to a child that there is a basic right in him to such companionship.[17] In *Re R (A*

---

11 See, for example, *Re C and V* [1998] 1 FLR 392.

12 A third party may be entitled to apply under s 10(5). The criteria for granting leave are in s 10(9). The entitlement and leave provisions are discussed in ch 2.

13 Therefore, the argument that a third party applicant should have contact unless there are cogent reasons for denying contact is plainly wrong; *Re A (Section 8 Order: Grandparent Application)* [1995] 2 FLR 153; *Re W (Contact: Application by Grandparent)* [1997] 1 FLR 793.

14 S 1(3).

15 [1973] 2 All ER 81.

16 The importance of the ruling was its emphasis on depriving *the child* of contact with the parent, rather than the parent of contact with the child.

17 A considerable amount of research has been conducted around parental separation. Thus although it may be reasonable to start with a presumption in favour of contact, studies have shown that it is futile to seek simple answers to whether ongoing contact is beneficial or detrimental for children and that it is important to take each case on its own merits. For a discussion, see K Hewitt *Divorce and parental disagreement* [1996]

Minor) (Contact)[18] Butler-Sloss LJ stated that this principle has been repeatedly stated by the appellate courts, that it is endorsed in the Children Act 1989, and that it is underlined in the United Nations Convention on the Rights of the Child. The principle applies whether the court is deciding whether contact should cease or whether it should be reintroduced. In the latter situation it was held in *Re H (Minors) (Access)*[19] that the court should *not* ask the question whether any positive advantages were to be gained by the resumption of contact. Rather, the test to be applied is whether there are any cogent reasons why a child should be denied the opportunity to have contact with a parent.[20] It is often the case that a mother opposes contact because her relationship with the father involved domestic violence. However domestic violence is not of itself a bar to contact, even where the mother has genuine and rational reasons for wishing to terminate the children's relationship with their father. It is a matter for discretion and where, as in *Re H (Contact: Domestic Violence)*,[1] the judge takes the view that any short-term harm to the children if supervised contact is reintroduced is outweighed by the benefits of re-establishing the father's relationship with them, the Court of Appeal is most unlikely to rule that his judgment was plainly wrong.

Where the residential parent is implacably opposed to contact

The principle that contact is the right of the child has been highly influential on the manner in which courts have approached cases where the residential parent is implacably opposed to contact taking place with the other parent. Thus in *Re E (A Minor: Access)*[2] the mother and her new husband had made their hostile feelings towards the child's father known to the child, thereby causing the child unnecessary suffering and conflict, which had manifested itself in disturbed behaviour at school and at home. The Court of Appeal nonetheless held that contact should continue. It took the view that the fact that the attitude of the mother and step-father had led to distress on the child's part could not of itself render inimical an order which was made in the child's best interests.

A similar approach to contact in the face of the mother's implacable hostility was taken in *Re W (A Minor) (Contact)*.[3] Here contact between

Fam Law 368, who refers to further helpful literature. The author, a clinical psychologist, considers some of the issues faced by psychologists when dealing with warring parents.

18 [1993] 2 FLR 762.

19 [1992] 1 FLR 148.

20 An example might be where a child needs constant medical care which the parent seeking contact is unable to give, see *Re C and V* [1998] 1 FLR 392.

1 [1998] 2 FLR 42. An influential factor was that unless there was a contact order there was a real risk that the children would be brought up in the belief that their step-father was their father.

2 [1987] 1 FLR 368.

3 [1994] 2 FLR 441.

the father and the child of the marriage had been a constant source of difficulty, and after the mother remarried she made a conscious and deliberate decision to prevent the child from having contact with his father. The boy, who was aged four, was being brought up to believe that his step-father was his father. The mother and step-father had stated that they would rather go to prison than obey a contact order. The trial judge, relying on the no order presumption in section 1(5), refused to make a contact order on the ground that it would cause harm and destabilising un-happiness for the child. In this the Court of Appeal found the judge to have been plainly wrong. It emphasised that contact with his parent was the fundamental right of the child, that the mother had no right what-soever to deny the child contact with his father, and that the judge was therefore under a positive duty to make an order despite the obduracy of the mother. The court added that it was an abdication of judicial res-ponsibility to decline to make an order simply on the basis that the mother would not obey it. A court could not simply allow a parent to defy an order of the court.[4]

The Court of Appeal's determination that contact should only be refused in exceptional cases was emphasised and reinforced by Sir Thomas Bingham MR in *Re O (Contact: Imposition of Conditions)*.[5] Responding to the suggestion that direct contact would put a child at serious risk of major emotional harm, he said:

> 'The courts should not at all readily accept that the child's welfare will be injured by direct contact. Judging that question the courts should take a medium-term and long-term view of the child's development and not accord excessive weight to what appear likely to be short-term or transient problems. Neither parent should be encouraged or permitted to think that the more intransigent, the more unreasonable, the more obdurate and the more unco-operative they are, the more likely they are to get their own way.'

In *Re M (Contact: Supervision)*,[6] applying and developing Sir Thomas Bingham's approach, Ward LJ held that the trial judge had been wrong to

---

4   See too *Re S (Minors: Access)* [1990] 2 FLR 166. For a discussion of *Re W (A Minor) (Contact)*, and other 'implacable hostility' cases, see J Wallbank *Castigating mothers* (1998) 20 JSWFL 357. The author argues that once the idea of the mothers' hostility has been latched on to it takes precedence over, and sometimes negates, the mothers' reasons for wanting to frustrate contact, even where there is strong evidence to suggest paternal contact may not be in the children's best interests.

5   [1995] 2 FLR 124, at p 129. For a comment on *Re O (Contact: Imposition of Conditions)*, see S Jolly *Implacable hostility, contact, and the limits of the law* (1995) 7 CFLQ 228.

6   [1998] 1 FLR 727. See also, *Re P (Contact: Supervision)* [1996] 2 FLR 314, where the relationship between the parents had been characterised by bouts of excessive drug taking and drinking by both parents and serious unremitting physical violence by the father towards the mother. Since leaving the father, the mother's mental and physical health had considerably improved and she was providing stable care for the children. The father's behaviour too had improved and he had stopped drinking and abusing drugs. Contact was ordered despite the mother's opposition, which went well. The

deny a father immediate supervised contact with his child because she could not envisage when the time would come when it would be safe for the father to have unsupervised contact. This finding led her to conclude that therefore it would not be in the child's interests to build up a relationship with her father. Ward LJ said that the flaw in the judge's reasoning was that 'she addressed as a *present* concern the issue of unsupervised contact, but she had no evidence to justify a conclusion that it was impossible to envisage a time coming when the step from supervised to unsupervised contact could take place without harm to the child'.[7] Furthermore, the judge had failed to address the medium and long-term benefits to the child of having effective and meaningful contact with her father.

However, despite the determination of the courts to prevent a parent's obduracy from being an obstacle to contact they are faced with an extremely difficult dilemma where the hostility between the parents makes contact a very stressful experience for the child. A child is able to benefit from visiting the other parent where a parent conceals his or her negative feelings about contact arrangements. But where the occasion of visits is accompanied by tension, anger and tears on the part of the residential parent, a child will normally wish to avoid precipitating these emotions.[8] In *Re J (A Minor) (Contact)*[9] the ten-year-old child's experience of contact arrangements was associated with acrimony, recrimination and family upset. The boy told the court welfare officer that he did not wish to see his father again, and she concluded that it would not be in the child's best interests to be forced into a situation which was fraught with anxiety and insecurity for him. The trial judge said that the mother's hostility to contact was about as great as he had ever come across, and that she would continue to communicate this implacable hostility to her son. He therefore concluded that 'for me to make a contact order would cause such disturbance and distress within this boy's home and such disturbance and distress for the boy himself that it is not possible for me to say that it is in the best interests of the boy ... that such an order be made. I come to the conclusion with the utmost reluctance.' He added 'if I am satisfied, as I am, that this child would be caused deep disturbance by my making the order then I must not make it'. The Court of Appeal refused to upset the judge's decision. It said that there were no grounds for finding that the judge had been plainly

mother applied for contact to be terminated. The issue for the court was whether the detriment to the children in not seeing their father outweighed the risk of the detriment to them of the risk that their mother's health would deteriorate because of her stress and anxiety. The Court of Appeal held that the weight given to the risk to the mother's health was not warranted by the evidence and that the mother's intransigent opposition to contact could not justify its termination.

7   At p 732, emphasis added.
8   For one possible solution to this problem, see H Conway *Implacable hostility – seeking a breakthrough* [1997] Fam Law 109. The author argues that the creation of a children's officer, who would provide a child with information concerning both his legal rights and his emotional needs, could create a breakthrough in implacable hostility cases.
9   [1994] 1 FLR 729.

wrong in how he had balanced the harm caused by making an order against the harm which would be caused to the child by being deprived of contact with his father. However, Balcombe LJ made the general observation that courts should be very reluctant to allow the implacable hostility of one parent to deter them from making a contact order where they believe the child's welfare requires it.

There is a risk that judicial antipathy towards those parents who oppose contact for no good reason could be misunderstood by practitioners negotiating about contact arrangements within the shadow of the law. In particular, the label 'implacable hostility' has tended to become an umbrella term extending to those cases where there are authentic reasons for a parent's opposition to contact. In *Re D (Contact: Reasons for Refusal)*[10] the Court of Appeal was anxious to ensure that the phrase 'implacable hostility' is not wrongly used. It emphasised that where the court is satisfied that the opposing parent has genuine and rationally held fears for the child's or for her own safety, and where the court is satisfied that there is a serious risk of harm to the child or that parent, the court may properly conclude that it is not currently in the child's best interests for contact to take place.[11] However, there are few reported cases where contact has been denied even where there has been serious domestic violence.[12]

In *Re H (Contact: Domestic Violence)*[13] the father had behaved in an appalling manner and the mother had real and genuine fears concerning the reintroduction of contact. Although the Court of Appeal refused the mother's appeal against an order for supervised contact, it was not happy with the manner in which the trial judge had exercised control over the structure of the reintroduction process. The judge had imposed requirements on the mother but had not required the father to demonstrate that he could behave appropriately with the children. Remitting the case, the Court of Appeal invited the trial judge to consider imposing directions requiring the father to recognise the corrosive effect of his constant denigration of the mother, to recognise the real basis of her justified fears, to show that he was not a threat to the children or their mother and not to undermine her relationship with them. It further stated that this was a case where the trial court should keep control over the contact arrangements and that a review hearing should be ordered.

---

10 [1997] 2 FLR 48.
11 In *Re D (Contact: Reasons for Refusal)* the court found that the mother had real fears of violence not only for herself but also for her son.
12 *Re D (A Minor) (Contact: Mother's Hostility)* [1993] 2 FLR 1 is an example of where there were cogent reasons why the child should not have contact with his father in the light of the mother's hostility. The mother had left the father before the child was born because of his violence, dabbling with drugs and excessive drinking. He had behaved in an intimidating manner to the mother and her parents and his past conduct had left an indelible impression on them. The fact that the father had not seen the child since his birth was another matter which the court took into account. See also *Re A (Contact: Domestic Violence)* [1998] 2 FLR 171.
13 [1998] 2 FLR 42.

This is an interesting development. By placing an expectation on the father, as well as the mother, to make contact work, and by inviting the judge to adopt a pro-active, overseeing approach, the Court of Appeal acknowledged the significance of the father's destructive behaviour. Directions of this kind would require the father to admit that he had largely caused the mother's hostility, and the burden would lie on the father at the review hearing to demonstrate that he was genuinely committed to the children's welfare.[14]

Enforcement of contact in the face of parental obduracy

Parental obduracy may continue despite the fact that numerous applications for contact have been made and numerous contact orders have been granted. Cases of this kind are extremely difficult for practitioners to handle and for courts to manage. Normally, where there is real intransigence, it is important that every effort is made by the court welfare service to suggest methods of facilitating contact which acknowledge and address any fears which the obdurate parent may have concerning her own or her child's safety.[15] Where, despite such efforts (which almost invariably take place over months and even years rather than weeks) the residential parent continues to refuse to allow contact other steps may be taken to bring about her compliance. One such step is for the court to threaten to transfer residence from one parent to the other. The restraint, of course, on such a course of action is that it is likely to harm the child, at least in the immediacy. However, this must be balanced against the long-term interests of the child to enjoy a relationship with both parents.[16] In so far as research findings tell us that many children suffer powerful feelings of rejection in the absence of regular and frequent contact visits, and in so far as contact with an absent parent makes a significant contribution to the emotional well-being of the child, such a Draconian decision may occasionally be appropriate.[17]

14 At such a hearing, counsel could place reliance on *Re A (Contact: Domestic Violence)* [1998] 2 FLR 171 where a decision of magistrates that the father had not changed sufficiently to make it in the interests of the children to reintroduce contact was confirmed by Connell J.

15 For example, by involving relatives or other sympathetic third parties, or by using a contact centre to which the child can be taken and from which he can be collected without the parents being forced to meet, and where the contact visit can be supervised. For further commentary see C Willbourne and L-A Cull *The emerging problem of parental alienation* [1997] Fam Law 807; S Maidment *Parental alienation syndrome – a judicial response?* [1998] Fam Law 264.

16 See the pre-Children Act 1989 cases of *V-P v V-P* (1980) 1 FLR 336; *Williams v Williams* [1985] FLR 509.

17 See the pre-Children Act 1989 case of *Cutts v Cutts* (1977) 7 Fam Law 209. Research studies have consistently shown that children of separating parents wish to remain in contact with both parents. See in particular J Pryor and F Seymour *Making decisions about children after parental separation* (1996) 8 CFLQ 229 which usefully refers to, and assesses, much of the research.

Sometimes an application to commit the obdurate parent to prison for contempt may be made. Such an application presents the court with an extremely difficult dilemma: on the one hand a parent cannot be permitted to continue to flout the court's orders with impunity; on the other hand, concepts of damage to the dignity of the court should not enter into consideration in this kind of case where the welfare of the child is at stake. Furthermore, it is plain that an order committing the parent to prison is likely to cause harm to the child and as Ormrod LJ said in the pre-Children Act case of *Churchard v Churchard*:[18]

'To accede to the father's application for the committal order would not conceivably be in the best interests of the children ... their mother would be taken away from them for a time and their father would be branded in their eyes as the man who had put them in prison. That is a brand from which no parent in my experience can ever hope to recover. It is the most deadly blow a parent can inflict on his children.'

However, when this quotation was put to the Court of Appeal in the post Children Act 1989 case of *A v N (Committal: Refusal of Contact)*,[19] whilst the court accepted that the child's welfare was a material consideration on an application to commit, it rejected the submission that the child's welfare was the paramount consideration. In *A v N* the mother had 'flagrantly set herself upon a course of collision with the court's order' and had been given 'endless opportunities to comply' and the judge had 'bent over backwards to accommodate her'. Eventually the judge's patience ran out and he put into effect a suspended order committing the mother to prison for 42 days. Dismissing the mother's appeal, Ward LJ said:

'It is perhaps appropriate that the message goes out in loud and clear terms that there does come a limit to the tolerance of the court to see its orders flouted by mothers even if they have to care for their young children. If [the mother] goes to prison it is her fault, not the fault of the judge ... The Children Act 1989 makes it [the judge's] duty ... to determine what is in the child's best interests. He, not this mother, has to decide whether contact will promote this child's welfare ... He did not commit this mother to preserve his own dignity. He was concerned to preserve the due administration of justice which depends on orders of the court being obeyed.'[20]

In *A v N* the Court of Appeal made it plain that courts should not shirk from imposing the sanction of imprisonment where all other reasonable

18 [1984] FLR 635, at p 638.
19 [1997] 1 FLR 533.
20 At pp 541-542. See too, *Re O (Contact: Imposition of Conditions)* [1995] 2 FLR 124.

steps to obtain compliance with the court's order have failed.[21] However, the courts have accepted that this sanction should be used sparingly in children cases and in *Re F (Contact: Enforcement)*[1] the Court of Appeal adopted a cautious approach. Although Hale J expressed the opinion that 'it would be unwise to rule out any form of enforcement for all time in any case whether or not it involved a disabled child',[2] she held that the judge had been correct not to add a penal notice to a contact order. Furthermore, in relation to the welfare of the child, she commented 'if a court is to put enforcement above the risk of harm to the child, it must be very clear indeed about the correctness of the orders it is seeking to enforce,' and acknowledged that there are usually two perceptions of a contested contact case when she remarked 'a child will not thank any parent who makes the life of the people carrying out the major burden of looking after him even more difficult than it already is'.[3]

It is to be hoped that Hale J's more understanding approach to the wishes and feelings of the parent with day to day care of the child will lead judges to be more discriminating in the ways in which they respond to a parent who opposes contact.[4] The danger presented to children and their mothers by a well-publicised robust judicial response is that it will filter down to other professionals involved in disputed contact cases. Indeed, a study by Smart and Neale[5] has found that 'the crusade against the "implacably hostile" mother is evident at every level of the legal process, including the private arena where it has infiltrated the thinking of mediators and solicitors'. Commenting critically on the increasing coercion being placed on mothers who have suffered domestic violence to agree to contact arrangements,[6] they assert that a mother's own fears and personal welfare are deemed irrelevant:

---

21 For an example, see *F v F (Contact: Committal)* [1998] 2 FLR 237. See too the letter of concern from a solicitor representing an allegedly 'implacably hostile' mother at [1997] Fam Law 62.
1   [1998] 1 FLR 691. The child was disabled and the father was having weekly supervised contact at the grandmother's house until he abandoned his visits because he could not stand the grandmother's hostility towards him.
2   At p 698.
3   Ibid. As Hale J pointed out, the child was not being denied a relationship with his father, it was the father who found the contact arrangements intolerable. She said that the welfare officer had wrongly characterised the case as one involving implacable hostility because although the mother and grandmother were undoubtedly hostile to the father, contact was continuing weekly until the father gave it up.
4   In *Re M (Contact Order: Committal)* [1999] 1 FLR 810, a judge exercising own motion powers had himself initiated the committal hearing, for which he drafted the particulars of the breach. The Court of Appeal held that although the judge had jurisdiction to proceed of his own motion, he should not thereafter have sat in judgment. Allowing the mother's appeal, the Court of Appeal stated that committal was always exceptional, and in relation to breach of a contact order, a remedy of the very last resort. Moreover, the mother's failure to produce the children in the right psychological state of mind was not, in any event, a sufficiently clear breach to justify committal.
5   C Smart and B Neale *Arguments against virtue – must contact be enforced?* [1997] Fam Law 332.

'Such mothers are likely to be offered little legal support or protection. Their allegations against their partners may not be taken seriously and may be regarded as an excuse to avoid contact. In this way abusive behaviour is rendered invisible and is treated as harmless.'[7]

As Smart and Neale point out, all mothers who oppose contact for whatever reason are likely to be labelled 'implacably hostile' and the use of this term implies that the only bar to a child's true welfare is his mother's irrational and spiteful hostility.[8] Furthermore, where a mother refuses to allow contact because she 'wrongly' believes that she is thereby acting in the best interests of her child, even her own solicitor will seek to force her to comply, and may not tell her that it is unlikely that a court would enforce its order by committing her to prison.

Judicial certainty that contact will virtually always promote the child's welfare lies uneasily with research into the effect of domestic violence on children.[9] Studies both in the UK and abroad reveal that the impact of domestic violence on family life is wide-ranging and that children whose mothers have violent partners are significantly at risk of being physically, sexually and emotionally abused.[10] Furthermore, research into the likelihood of violence continuing after parents separate reveals that violent men often continue to attack their ex-partners and sometimes the children.[11] This link has been recognised in New Zealand and reflected in legislation which creates a presumption against unsupervised contact where there has been violence to a partner or child.[12] It is suggested that

6   See, for example, *Re P (Contact: Supervision)* [1996] 2 FLR 314 where the father had been persistently violent towards the mother and had been imprisoned for attempting to strangle her. He had also allegedly threatened to kill the children. He was an extreme racist with anti-Semitic attitudes and behaviour, which included dressing his sons in Nazi regalia. Nonetheless the Court of Appeal described the mother's opposition to the continuance of contact as 'implacable hostility'.

7   [1997] Fam Law 332, at p 334.

8   See also C Piper, *Divorce reform and the image of the child* (1996) 23 Journal of Law and Society 364, at p 372, where she comments 'it is the "implacably hostile" mother who continues to be the bogey "man" of family law'.

9   The significant research is usefully summarised in M Hester and C Pearson, *Domestic violence and children – the practice of family court welfare officers* (1997) 9 CFLQ 281. See also L Anderson *Contact between children and violent fathers* (Rights of Women, 1997).

10   See L Bowker, M Arbitell and J McFerron, 'On the relationship between wife-beating and child abuse' in M Bograd and K Yllo (eds) *Feminist perspectives on child abuse* (Sage, 1988); K Browne, 'Violence in the family and its links to child abuse' in C Hobbs and J Wynne *Child Abuse* (Bailliere Tindall, 1993).

11   M Hester and C Radford, *Domestic Violence and Child Contact in England and Denmark* (Bristol University Policy Press, 1996); F Kaganis and C Piper *Domestic violence and divorce mediation* (1994) 16 JSWFL 265.

12   Guardianship Act 1968, s 16B; and see M Kaye *Domestic violence and contact* (1996) 8 CFLQ 285 where the author contrasts the English position with that in New Zealand and Australia. It is suggested that many English members of Parliament might be startled and disturbed to learn that it is they who have allegedly recommended imprisonment as the proper approach to the enforcement of a contact order even though

serious judicial consideration should be given to whether it would be for the benefit of children if a similar approach were to be adopted in England.[13]

Where contact is likely to destabilise the child's present family unit

Where a child has never known his father, and where his mother has formed a secure family unit with another partner, the normal notion that maintaining contact with both natural parents is in a child's best interests may not apply. The court has been anxious not to destabilise the family unit of mother, step-father and child where the child concerned is very young, has no comprehension of relationships and where the step-father is acting as a father to him or her. In *Re H (A Minor) (Parental Res-ponsibility)*[14] the step-father of a two-year-old boy wrote to the natural father saying that his marriage to the mother would be put at risk if the father continued to have contact with the child. The court therefore refused contact on the ground that the child's welfare would not be served if he lost his present home and security because his mother's marriage broke down. In *Re W (A Minor) (Access)*[15] an intermittent relationship between the parents had ended before the child was born, and the father had enjoyed only a brief period of contact shortly after the child's birth. Meanwhile the mother was living with another man whom she planned to marry. The child, who was two, had grown up in the belief that his mother's partner was his father. Magistrates made a contact order to the father, but their decision was reversed by Heilbron J. She found that the magistrates should have considered whether contact would have a destabilising effect on the family unit and on the marriage of the mother and step-father. She said they should have considered the confusion and disturbance which the child would probably feel. She found that the child was presently developing well both physically and emotionally, said that his life should be kept free from conflict as far as possible, and ruled that no contact should therefore be allowed between the child and his father.

The fear that contact would destabilise the mother's marriage was also highly influential on Sir Stephen Brown P in *Re SM (A Minor) (Natural*

---

the mother, in the past, has been a victim of the father's domestic violence. However, Ward LJ, responding in *A v N (Committal: Refusal of Contact)* [1997] 1 FLR 533, at p 541, to a mother who opposed contact because she was fearful of the father's violent behaviour, confirmed that the judge had been correct to commit her to prison for six weeks because, in his view, the mother's fears were unfounded, and backed up his decision with the assertion that 'If [the mother] goes to prison it is her fault, not the fault of the judge who did no more than his duty to the child which is imposed on him by Parliament'.

13   For a sensitive account of some of the difficulties faced by the court in such cases, see His Honour Judge Victor Hall *Domestic violence and contact* [1997] Fam Law 813.

14   [1993] 1 FLR 484. However, the court did make a parental responsibility order.

15   [1989] 1 FLR 163.

Father: Access).[16] The facts were similar to those in *Re W (A Minor) (Access)*, but were more favourable to the father because he had enjoyed contact once a month until the child was 22 months old. The mother stopped contact when she resumed her relationship with her former husband, whom she intended to remarry. The court welfare officer stated in her report that 'experience shows that if [contact] is established while the child is still young, it can become an accepted and pleasurable part of life and a good relationship formed with the absent parent. Disruption is more likely to occur if the child learns the truth at a later date.' She recom-mended that contact take place and the magistrates made a contact order. Allowing the mother's appeal, Sir Stephen Brown P said that the welfare officer and the magistrates had applied the theoretical general principle that contact was beneficial to a child without considering the particular facts of the case. He found that the only bonds the child had were with her mother and step-father, and held that the magistrates had failed to take account of the risk of destabilising this family unit, and causing the child confusion, if the natural father were reintroduced into the child's life.

Despite the approach in these cases it will be seen below that the courts have become increasingly determined that a child is told the truth about his or her paternity. However, although there has been a strong shift of emphasis towards the truth emerging, it remains the position that contact will be denied where the court has substantial grounds for fearing that the child's family life will be disrupted if contact were to take place. Indeed, in *Re B (Contact: Stepfather's Opposition)*[17] the Court of Appeal held that the judge had been justified at a directions hearing in summarily dismissing an application by an ex-husband father for contact, even though the father had neither been present in court nor been given any warning that his application might be dismissed. The stepfather was implacably opposed to contact and was threatening to reject the mother as well as the child. The court took the view that the serious harm that the break up of the family would cause the child outweighed the real injustice to the father and therefore ruled that the interests of the child must prevail.[18]

Concealing a child's true paternity

Where the mother has had a relatively fleeting relationship with the father of her child, and where she has subsequently married or formed a stable unmarried relationship with another man, she may choose to conceal the

---

16 [1991] 2 FLR 333.
17 [1997] 2 FLR 579.
18 It may be that the precedent value of this case is limited to cases raising difficult cultural considerations. The family were Sikhs, and within sectors of that community it is accepted that there should be no contact between a child and his or her non-residential parent. The court found that the step-father's hostility to contact, and his real threat to abandon the child and the marriage were it to take place, was not an attempt to threaten or blackmail the court. Rather, it was a genuine manifestation of his uncompromising belief that a child should only have one family.

child's true paternity from the child so that the child believes that his step-father is his father. This was the position in both *Re SM (A Minor) (Natural Father: Access)*[19] and in *Re W (A Minor) (Access)*.[20] It is suggested that a disturbing feature of these cases is the way in which the courts appeared to connive at the continuance of this fantasy. They appeared to be supporting the view that it would be confusing for young children to be brought up knowing the truth, and that they should be left in ignorance of their true paternity until some later date. During the course of her judgment in *Re W (A Minor) (Access)*, Heilbron J said:

> 'The court should consider [the child's] welfare not only now and in the short term but in the long term, as, for instance, how will he begin to understand these matters at such an early age, and how will he explain to himself and to his friends that he has a living-in as well as a visiting father with whom he has, and can only have, a very tenuous relationship.'[1]

This appears to imply that the child would wish to conceal his parentage from his friends, almost as if this was a matter for embarrassment. But surely this was a very unhealthy attitude to foster? It is very hard for a child to cope with a feeling that he is different from others, and even harder if it is implied that his situation is in some sense shameful. It is suggested that it is far better for a child if he is brought up to realise that many children are conceived in similar circumstances to his own, and if he is encouraged to feel confident about his origins. The literature on adopted children suggests that those who grow up in the knowledge that they are adopted right from the start are the children who make the most comfortable transition into adulthood. It is those children who learn about their birth parents at a later stage who become emotionally disturbed. Heilbron J surmised that the mother might need to seek psychiatric or psychological help when it became appropriate for the child to know who his true father was at some time in the future. Yet it is inevitable as a child grows up that he will learn that his step-father is not his father, and it is suggested that when courts collude at the concealment of a child's origins, and take no steps to discourage a step-father from passing himself off as the child's natural father, as distinct from his psychological father, they may themselves be creating the child's need for future professional assistance.[2]

In recent years, however, the courts have become increasingly unwilling to allow the concealment from a child of his or her true paternity. In *Re W (A Minor)(Contact)*,[3] Sir Stephen Brown P commented 'it is disturbing to

19   [1991] 2 FLR 333.
20   [1989] 1 FLR 163.
1   Ibid, at p 172.
2   The problems such concealment can cause is illustrated in *Re R (A Minor) (Contact)* [1993] 2 FLR 762, which is discussed below.
3   [1994] 2 FLR 441, which concerned a four-year-old child whose parents had divorced shortly after his birth, whose mother had remarried, and where the court made a contact order despite the mother's implacable hostility: see above.

read in the report which has been made available to us, that [the child] has apparently regarded Mr C, the second husband of the mother, as his father and refers to him as "daddy"'.[4] He added that a child and adolescent consultant psychiatrist had pointed out that difficulty now arose as to how to explain to the child that his step-father was not his father and that his sister was his half sister. In *A v L (Contact)*[5] Holman J was confident that it was in the best interests of a child to know the truth from an early age so that he could gradually assimilate that he had two fathers. He therefore held that justices were plainly wrong to deny a father indirect contact with his three-year-old son for the reason that the child believed that his mother's partner was his father. He gave this ruling despite finding that the justices 'had clearly approached their decision with great conscientiousness and care', despite the fact that the parents had separated before the child's birth because the father had inflicted frequent serious violence on the mother, and despite the fact that the father was currently serving a long sentence of imprisonment for other offences of violence.[6]

Re R (A Minor) (Contact)[7] illustrates the difficulties which can arise if a child is not told who her real father is from a very young age. It concerned an application by a divorced father for contact with his five-year-old daughter who was living with her mother and step-father. The mother had refused to allow the father to have contact with his daughter on the basis that this would destabilise the new family unit, and because the child had been brought up to believe that her step-father was her father. The mother could not bring herself to tell her daughter the truth about her paternity. The court welfare officer had expressed the view that to reintroduce the child to her father was potentially seriously disruptive of the child's settled environment and welfare, and that it might go so far as to wreck the family unit. The judge had concluded that the child could not see her father for the time being without considerable risks and therefore he had denied contact at the present time. The Court of Appeal approved that part of the judge's ruling denying the father contact in the present circumstances. However, Butler-Sloss LJ emphasised that it was the right of the child to have contact with her father, and therefore that she ought to be informed about her true parentage soon. She was anxious, too, that the child might accidentally discover that her step-father was not her father, and was not prepared to leave the decision about when the child should be told the truth to the mother. Instead she joined the child as a party to the proceedings

4   This was a rather different approach to the one which Sir Stephen Brown P had taken in *Re SM (A Minor) (Natural Father: Access)* [1991] 2 FLR 333 in which the little girl was being brought up to believe that her step-father was her father. He had voiced no criticism in that case of the mother's decision to conceal from her child the truth about her paternity for the time being.
5   [1998] 1 FLR 361.
6   Similarly, in *Re H (Contact: Domestic Violence)* [1998] 2 FLR 42, the fact that the child would be unlikely to discover who his true father was unless the court made a contact order appears to have been influential on Wall J's refusal to allow an appeal from an order for contact where there had been extremely serious domestic violence.
7   [1993] 2 FLR 762.

and invited the Official Solicitor to become her guardian ad litem. She invited the Official Solicitor to instruct a child psychiatrist to assess the family and to assist the mother to inform the child of her true paternity. If that proved impossible she requested that the psychiatrist tell the child if he or she thought this was appropriate. She also asked the Official Solicitor and the psychiatrist to advise the court on the best way to implement a period of renewed contact between the father and his daughter, or to give any reasons why such contact should not take place.

It is suggested that the lengths to which the Court of Appeal was prepared to go in order to ensure that the child discovered her father's true identity were quite remarkable, bearing in mind that the function of the court is to act as an appellate jurisdiction. These lengths were illustrative of the seriousness with which the court viewed the right of the child to know her own father, and of a growing antipathy by some judges towards the concealment from a child of his or her true origins.

Contact where a parent has caused harm to the child

Paragraph (e) of the checklist directs a court to consider any harm which the child has suffered, or is at risk of suffering, before making an order. Where the parent seeking contact has behaved in a violent and threatening manner towards the residential parent this may provide sound reasons for denying contact. The risk of physical harm to the child or to the residential parent must be balanced against the advantage to the child of knowing his own parent. It is for the judge to balance these risks and advantages and to see where their preponderance lies.[8] The burden of proving that a parent has harmed his or her child is on the person who makes the allegation. The House of Lords has ruled that the standard to be overcome when the court is deciding whether past harm has been proved is the civil balance of probabilities test. However, this standard is commensurate with the seriousness of the allegation.[9] In relation to the direction under paragraph (e) that the court should consider the risk of future harm, it is clear since the ruling of the Court of Appeal in *Re M and R (Child Abuse: Evidence)*[10] that where the evidence relied on to establish such a risk relates to alleged past abuse of the child, such past abuse must be proved to the civil standard applying the commensurate seriousness test. However, where, by contrast, the risk of future harm relates solely to fears that such harm will occur, a

---

8   See *Re D (Contact: Reasons for Refusal)* [1997] 2 FLR 48 where the mother had a real and genuine fear of the father.

9   *Re H ((Minors) (Sexual Abuse: Standard of Proof)* [1996] 1 All ER 1. Thus in *Re P (Sexual Abuse: Standard of Proof)* [1996] 2 FLR 333 an attempt by the judge to exercise his discretion under s 1(3)(e) of the checklist on the basis of finding that there was a substantial risk that past abuse had occurred was a fundamental error which vitiated his decision.

10 [1996] 2 FLR 195. For criticism of this decision see I Hemingway and C Williams *Re M and R: Re H and R* [1997] Fam Law 740; but see contra, D Bedingfield *The Child in Need* (Family Law, 1988), at p 343.

lower standard applies. In *Re H (Minors) (Sexual Abuse: Standard of Proof)*[11] the House of Lords held that 'likely' significant harm for the purposes of establishing the threshold test in care proceedings does not require the applicant to establish that it is 'more likely than not' that such harm will occur.[12] So, by analogy, a risk of suffering harm cannot mean that the applicant must prove that the occurrence of the risk is more likely than not. It is suggested, therefore, that an identical test to proof of likely significant harm applies. Accordingly, risk means 'a real possibility, a possibility that cannot sensibly be ignored having regard to the nature and gravity of the feared harm in the particular case'.[13]

Where the risk to the child is from a parent who has sexually abused the child, the court must balance the importance to the child of maintaining a relationship with the parent against the risk to the child if contact takes place. The harm caused to a child as a result of sexual abuse has often resulted in a parent being denied any form of contact with the child. In *Re R (A Minor) (Child Abuse: Access)*[14] the Court of Appeal was firmly of the view that any benefit to the child of maintaining the blood tie had no weight against the risk to her of being further sexually abused. In *S v S (Child Abuse: Access)*[15] the trial judge made a finding that a father had sexually abused the eldest of his three daughters. He therefore refused the father contact with that daughter, but allowed him supervised contact with the younger children. Allowing the mother's appeal, Fox LJ ruled that the father should be denied contact with all three girls. He found that an order which distinguished between the children would be destructive of family cohesion and likely to cause tensions in the household.

It was proposed on behalf of the fathers in *Re R (A Minor) (Child Abuse: Access)* and *S v S (Child Abuse: Access)* that strictly supervised contact would resolve any risk of further sexual abuse of the children. However, as the Court of Appeal pointed out, limited contact under supervised conditions has the disadvantage that it takes place infrequently and in artificial surroundings. Furthermore, at some stage a child is likely to enquire why contact is taking place under these conditions, and if given the true answer could suffer psychological damage. However, courts are so strongly of the view that contact with a parent is normally of benefit to a child that, despite the reservations expressed in *Re R (A Minor)* and *S v S*, they have nonetheless made supervised contact orders. In *Re H (Minors) (Access: Appeals)*[16] the Court of Appeal confirmed the decision of a trial

11 [1996] 1 All ER 1.
12 S 31(2), fully discussed in ch 3.
13 [1996] 1 All ER 1, at p 15, per Lord Nicholls. In *Re W (Residence Order)* [1999] 1 FLR 869, the Court of Appeal held that the fact that a mother and her partner had been uninhibited in their approach to nudity did not raise child protection issues. Nudity and communal bathing are not abuse, but in some cases it may be wise for the local authority to investigate because the behaviour may hide abusive conduct. For further discussion of proof of child abuse, see ch 3.
14 [1988] 1 FLR 206.
15 [1988] 1 FLR 213.
16 [1989] 2 FLR 174.

judge to allow two successive periods of contact between a father and his daughters before making a final decision as to what was in the best interests of the children, and in *L v L (Child Abuse: Access)*[17] the Court of Appeal upheld a contact order to a father who had abused his daughter, despite the opposition to it from both the mother and the supervising local authority. The court found that there was a close bond between the child and her father, that she enjoyed contact visits, that she was socially well adjusted and that she showed no disturbance after the abuse. It therefore concluded that contact was in her best interests.

In *Re H (Minors) (Access: Appeals)* and *L v L (Child Abuse: Access)* the courts acknowledged the strongly held feelings of the mothers against contact taking place but they were not persuaded by these feelings to deny contact between the children and their abusing fathers. Indeed, the mother in *L v L* was severely criticised for breaking the court's order and refusing the father contact pending the appeal. It is suggested that the courts failed to appreciate the level of fear, disgust and repulsion that mothers are likely to feel at the thought of their children having contact with fathers who have sexually abused them. Sexual abuse is such a serious betrayal of a child's trust that the notion that a child will benefit from having further contact with the abuser is likely to be totally alien to the majority of residential parents.[18] It may be that some courts are failing to recognise the magnitude of the distress suffered by the non-abusing parent when sexual abuse is discovered, and the impact any contact order will have on her and therefore on her ability to relate properly to the child. An anxious and distressed residential parent, who is fearful for her child's safety, is unlikely to be able to give an abused child the balanced and calm care which such a child needs. It is suggested that courts should exercise great caution before making orders which conflict with the fundamental values of the parent who is called upon to allow contact, particularly where, as in *L v L*, the local authority are also of the view that contact should not be allowed.[19]

Authorising the child's removal from the jurisdiction

If a child is taken out of the jurisdiction by a parent or some other person it is almost inevitable that the child will be unable to enjoy regular contact with the other parent. Moreover, where the child is young it is likely that

---

17 [1989] 2 FLR 16.

18 Indeed, research demonstrates that the victims of child sexual abuse often suffer serious and long-term psychological damage: see A Bentovim, et al *Child Sexual Abuse Within the Family* (Wright, 1992). Furthermore, research also indicates that even where contact is supervised that this may not protect the child from further abuse by the parent, and that the abuser may use the contact session to try and persuade the child to retract her story: see E Jones and P Parkinson *Child sexual abuse, access and the wishes of children* (1995) 9 IJLF 54.

19 See generally on child sexual abuse cases, I Weyland *The response of civil courts to allegations of child sexual abuse* (1989) 19 Fam Law 240.

contact will be brought to an end entirely, or at least until he or she is old enough to travel long distances alone. The most serious risk to a parent is that the child will be taken out of the country without either his or her knowledge or agreement. The Child Abduction Act 1984 provides a measure of safeguard against this occurring. It is a criminal offence under the Act for a person to take or send a child out of the United Kingdom without 'the appropriate consent'.[20] This safeguard means that before such removal is legal, either all persons with parental responsibility for the child must have consented to the child's removal, or the leave of the court must first have been obtained. Section 13(1)(b) of the Children Act 1989 reinforces this safeguard by providing that:

> 'Where a residence order is in force with respect to a child, no person may—
> (b) remove [the child] from the United Kingdom;
> without either the written consent of every person who has parental responsibility for the child or the leave of the court.'

However, families commonly travel abroad for holidays, and the stringent nature of this provision could prove very disruptive and inconvenient for the parent with whom the child is living. Section 13(2) therefore contains some amelioration by providing that a person with a residence order may take the child out of the jurisdiction for a period of up to one month without first obtaining such consents or the court's leave. Also, when making the residence order, the court may grant the leave required by section 13(1)(b), either generally or for specified purposes.[1] Where a parent is anxious that his child will be permanently removed if allowed to travel abroad he or she is also entitled to apply under section 10 for a prohibited steps order[2] under which the court could either prohibit the child's removal absolutely, or it could control when and to where the child was taken by the imposition of conditions in the order.[3]

The decision to remove a child from the jurisdiction is undoubtedly a matter which concerns the child's upbringing; the welfare principle therefore applies, and the likely effect on the child of this change in his circumstances falls squarely within paragraph (c) of the checklist. *Poel v Poel*[4] is the leading case on how courts should approach an application for leave by one parent which is opposed by the other parent. Although decided 20 years before the implementation of the Children Act 1989 it is nonetheless highly influential on current practice.[5] In *Poel v Poel* the Court

---

20   Defined in s 1(3).
1   S 13(3).
2   Under s 8.
3   S 11(7).
4   [1970] 1 WLR 1469.
5   See *Re H (Application to Remove from Jurisdiction)* [1998] 1 FLR 848, at p 853, where Thorpe LJ said 'the approach that the court must adopt in these cases has not evolved or developed in any way since the decision of this court in *Poel v Poel*'.

of Appeal ruled that a child of two, who had been enjoying regular contact with his father, should be allowed to emigrate to New Zealand with his mother and step-father. Sachs LJ reasoned as follows:

'Once custody is working well, the court should not lightly interfere with such reasonable way of life as is selected by that parent to whom custody has been rightly given ... The way in which the parent who properly has custody of the child may choose in a reasonable manner to order his or her way of life is one of those things which the parent who has not been given custody may well have to bear.'

He explained the connection between this approach and the welfare principle by saying that any such interference 'may produce considerable strains which would not only be unfair to the parent whose way of life is interfered with but also to any new marriage of that parent. In that way it might well in due course reflect on the welfare of the child'.

Subsequently, a body of case law has grown up in this area in which the courts have followed and developed the *Poel v Poel* line of reasoning.[6] Indeed, in *Belton v Belton*,[7] when reversing the decision of the trial judge to refuse leave for the time being to a mother and step-father to emigrate to New Zealand with the three-year-old daughter of the mother's previous marriage, Purchas LJ said that the judge, by refusing leave:

'... had misapplied the authorities and the law which dictate that the hard and difficult decision which must be made once it is established that the custodial parent genuinely desires to emigrate and, in circumstances in which there is nothing adverse to be found in the conditions to be expected, those authorities are quite clear in the course that the court has to take, whatever the hardship and distress that may result.'[8]

The thinking which has informed the approach since *Poel v Poel* is that the welfare of children is best served by bringing them up in a happy and secure family atmosphere. Where, after divorce, a parent remarries, the children then become members of a new family and it is on the happiness and security of that family that their security will depend. But a parent and step-parent would be likely to feel frustrated and resentful were the courts to refuse them leave to emigrate and this sense of resentment could spill over on to the children. Moreover, it might sometimes put the stability of the second marriage at risk, which clearly would be harmful to the

---

6   *Nash v Nash* [1973] 2 All ER 704; *Chamberlain v De La Mare* (1982) 4 FLR 434; *Lonslow v Hennig* [1986] 2 FLR 378; *Re F (A Ward) (Leave to Remove Ward Out of the Jurisdiction)* [1988] 2 FLR 116.

7   [1987] 2 FLR 343.

8   Ibid, at pp 349-350.

children.[9] Therefore, if the decision to leave is in itself reasonable, the court must take account of how the unhappiness, distress or even bitterness which the parent and step-parent are likely to feel if refused permission will rebound upon the child.[10]

A striking feature of the cases in which leave has been granted is that the mother was the applicant and she had either remarried or was planning to do so.[11] This feature appeared to be particularly crucial in *Re H (Application to Remove from the Jurisdiction)*[12] where the father had played an unusually large role in caring for his daughter and where the Court of Appeal acknowledged that he had a very strong case.[13] The father nonetheless failed in his application to prevent the child being taken to America by the mother and her new husband, considerable weight being given to the damage which would be done to the mother's relationship with her husband if leave to remove the child were to be refused. The court emphasised that applications for permanent removal required profound investigation and judgment, but stated that there had to be some compelling reason to justify a court preventing the residential parent from taking a reasonable decision to live outside the jurisdiction.[14]

By contrast, leave has been refused in three cases in which the mother was living as a single parent.[15] In *Tyler v Tyler*[16] the mother applied for leave to take her two sons to Australia where she had been brought up and where her parents and extended family lived. Her ex-husband had enjoyed frequent contact with the boys who were aged six and eight and there was a close bond between them and their father. The trial judge found that the mother's desire to emigrate was genuine and not motivated by spite, or a desire to take the children away from their father without herself having any reasonable wish to emigrate. However, he nonetheless was persuaded that the mother should be refused leave to take the children to Australia because of the warm and loving relationship between the father and his sons, and because they would leave behind their roots in

9   See Griffiths LJ in *Chamberlain v De La Mare* (1982) 4 FLR 434, at p 445.
10 See Kerr LJ in *Re F (A Ward) (Leave to Remove Ward Out of the Jurisdiction)* [1988] 2 FLR 116.
11 *Re F (A Ward) (Leave to Remove Ward Out of the Jurisdiction)* was an exception; the mother had not remarried in that case. The mother had also not remarried in *Re K (Application to Remove from Jurisdiction)* [1998] 2 FLR 1006, but a significant part of her motivation for wishing to return to Nigeria was her desire to try and develop her relationship with her boyfriend.
12 [1998] 1 FLR 848.
13 The father looked after his daughter when the mother returned to full-time work when the child was six months old, and although the child lived with the mother when the parents parted about two years later, the father continued to share responsibility for her care.
14 The Court of Appeal rejected the submission that reasoning in *Poel v Poel* [1970] 1 WLR 1469, which continues to dominate decision-making in leave to remove applications, gives too little weight to the welfare of the child.
15 *Tyler v Tyler* [1989] 2 FLR 158; *K v K (A Minor) (Removal from Jurisdiction)* [1992] 2 FLR 98; *M v A (Wardship: Removal from Jurisdiction)* [1993] 2 FLR 715.
16 [1989] 2 FLR 158.

the family farm where the father lived and where they had been brought up. The judge therefore took the view that the mother's desire to remove the boys from the jurisdiction at this age was not reasonable. The judge also considered whether the undoubted bitterness and frustration of the mother would have an adverse effect on the boys. He found that she would cope with the decision and would not allow her feelings about it to destroy her relationship with the boys, or that between the boys and their father. The Court of Appeal held that there were no grounds for upsetting the judge's ruling.

In *K v K (A Minor) (Removal from Jurisdiction)*[17] the mother who was born in the USA applied to take the child of the marriage, who was nearly four, to the USA so that she could pursue postgraduate education. Thorpe J held that the principles to be applied were established in *Poel v Poel*, namely the approach of the court was to sanction the realistic proposals of the residential parent unless these proposals were inconsistent with the child's welfare. He found that the mother would feel despair or disenchantment if not allowed to return to the USA with her daughter, but that she had an underlying resilience which would enable her to cope. He refused the mother leave on two grounds. First and foremost, he found that the continuation of the relationship between the child and her father was of very great importance and that to reduce contact to annual visits would be a retrograde step. Secondly, he refused leave on the ground that the mother's proposals were ill thought out, and because she had paid insufficient attention to the practicalities of pursuing postgraduate studies in the USA.

In *M v A (Wardship: Removal from Jurisdiction)*[18] a mother who wished to return to Canada with her sons aged twelve and nine was similarly refused leave. She had lived with the boys' father for many years, and after the parties separated they had shared the care of the children, although their principal home remained with the mother. The boys themselves loved both homes and wished to remain in England. Bracewell J said that although the test remained the same as in *Poel v Poel*, the Children Act 1989 had increased the emphasis to be placed on the wishes of the children where they were of sufficient age and understanding to be able to express their own views. She found that the mother's plans were ill thought out and little researched, and that they were not reasonable because they did not accommodate the needs and wishes of the children.[19]

It is suggested that courts have been too ready to indulge the selfish feelings of mothers and second husbands in those cases where they have granted them leave to take the children of a previous marriage or long term relationship out of the jurisdiction. By granting leave, the courts

---

17 [1992] 2 FLR 98.
18 [1993] 2 FLR 715.
19 See too *M v M (Minors) (Jurisdiction)* [1993] Fam Law 396, where an Israeli mother was refused leave to take her children permanently to Israel because they did not want to be uprooted from their father, schools and this country.

have deprived the children of contact with their natural fathers, yet time and again courts have emphasised that contact is the *right* of the child as well as being in the child's best interests. A large number of marriages end by divorce whilst the children are young, and many children live in reconstituted families. It is suggested that one of the many responsibilities of parenthood is to put the interests of the children first, and that this often requires parents and step-parents to negate their own wishes and feelings. A woman who marries again cannot simply substitute her second husband as father for her children and expect the children to have no need or desire to know their natural father. A man who marries a woman who already has children knows that she has responsibilities to those children, and that they have a father with whom they have a relationship which ought to be maintained. If the second husband is a foreign national that in itself should not entitle him to take another man's children out of the jurisdiction simply because he has married their mother. It is suggested that a parent and step-parent are not entitled to feel bitter, frustrated and resentful if they cannot live in the country of their choice during the minority of the children. These are natural responses, but they are also self-indulgent emotions and ones which should not be countenanced by courts unless the circumstances are exceptional.[20] Restrictions on mobility should simply be regarded as one of the burdens of bringing up children, and a recognition that the parental responsibility of the natural parents is shared throughout the children's minority. Childhood passes rapidly, and when the children are old enough to express an informed opinion they can be asked whether the benefits of visiting a loved parent outweigh the opportunities offered by moving to a new country.[1]

The child's wishes and feelings

The first paragraph in the checklist, which states that a court must have regard to the ascertainable wishes and feelings of the child concerned (considered in the light of his age and understanding), recognises that children are entitled to be treated as persons in their own right and not merely as the subject matter of legal proceedings in which only the adults have a voice. It recognises that children have an appreciation of their own situation, that they have views about what should happen to them,

---

20 It is suggested that if the marriage were to break down because leave was refused such a marriage would in any event be likely to collapse if some other stress was placed upon it.

1 It is salutary to note that the children wished to maintain their relationship with their father in those cases where they were old enough to express a view. It is suggested that the approach of the trial judge in *Belton v Belton* [1987] 2 FLR 343, in which he adjourned the application until the child was five so that real bonds between her father and extended family could be established before the child left was wise, and that it truly gave paramount consideration to the child's interests.

and that such views should be accorded respect when the child's welfare is determined. A child is not a party to private law proceedings, unless a court orders otherwise, and therefore he is not entitled to independent legal or other representation. How then are the child's views to be made known to the court? Normally a court welfare officer is asked to undertake the task of ascertaining the child's wishes and feelings.[2] He or she is usually a probation officer, and the court may ask the officer 'to report to the court on such matters relating to the welfare of the child as are required to be dealt with in the report'.[3] Whilst a report from one person about the wishes and feelings of a different person suffers from the disadvantages inherent in all hearsay information, namely that it may be incomplete, inaccurate and cannot be tested in evidence, the alternative is for children to appear before courts and give evidence themselves, or to see the judge, or magistrates, in private. However, it is generally regarded as highly undesirable to expect children to give evidence, or for them to be inter-viewed in private, because of the stress, and sometimes distress, such an experience is likely to cause them. This practice is discouraged in the case of judges[4] and is positively frowned upon in the case of magistrates.[5] Using a court welfare officer to transmit the child's wishes and feelings to the court provides an alternative system which appears to operate in an acceptable and reliable manner. Any questions about the child's strength of feeling, or reasons for it, can be put to the court welfare officer.

Where proceedings are brought under Parts IV and V of the Children Act 1989 the child's voice is afforded greater protection because the child is a party to the proceedings. However, most children are not capable of safeguarding their own interests before a court, and therefore a guardian ad litem for the child will normally be appointed whose duty it is to safeguard the child's interests in the manner specified in the court rules.[6] This includes the duty to advise the court about the child's wishes and feelings, and to appoint a solicitor for the child.[7] The solicitor must represent the child in accordance with instructions received from the guardian ad litem unless the child wishes to give instructions which conflict with those of the guardian ad litem. In such a case the rules provide that where the solicitor considers that the child is able, having regard to his understanding, to give instructions on his own behalf, the solicitor

---

2   For even the most experienced of child welfare officers, ascertaining a child's wishes and feelings can be a very delicate task and practices vary widely as to when, where and how often children should be seen. See A James and W Hay *Court welfare in action* (Harvester Wheatsheaf, 1993).

3   S 7. Alternatively, the court may ask a local authority to arrange for an officer of the authority, or some other appropriate person, to report to the court.

4   *B v B (Minors) (Interviews and Listing Arrangements)* [1994] 2 FLR 489.

5   *Re M (A Minor) (Justices' Discretion)* [1993] 2 FLR 706; *Re W (A Minor) (Contact)* [1994] 1 FLR 843 in which Wall J said 'in my judgment, there have to be unusual circumstances before any tribunal interviews any child'.

6   S 41; and see ch 3.

7   The Family Proceedings Court (Children and Young Persons) Rules 1991, r 11.

must conduct the case in accordance with the instructions he receives from the child, and not the guardian ad litem.[8] In *Re H (A Minor) (Care Proceedings: Child's Wishes)*,[9] Thorpe J stated that the court should apply the rules in a manner which ensures that 'not only is the professional voice of the guardian heard through an advocate's presentation, but that also the wishes and feelings of the child, however limited the horizon, should be similarly presented'.[10]

The weight given to the child's wishes and feelings

Section 1(3)(a) is drafted cautiously. It refers to the *ascertainable* wishes and feelings of the child concerned because, of course, a very young child is unable to articulate these. Nonetheless, even in the case of a baby it may be possible to ascertain the child's feelings in an indirect manner. For example, an expert witness might be called to give factual evidence about the child's behaviour, appearance and body language when in the presence of an adult, and opinion evidence about what, in the expert's view, this means in terms of the child's feelings.[11] An older child may have no difficulty in expressing a point of view, but may not fully appreciate the significance of what he or she is saying. Paragraph (a) puts the child's wishes and feelings into the context of his age and understanding, and greater weight is likely to be given to the child's point of view where he has the maturity properly to understand what the outcome would be if his wishes and feelings were allowed to influence the court's decision in a particular direction.[12]

But even children who are very close to adulthood may be found not to have sufficient comprehension fully to understand what it will mean if their wishes and feelings are allowed to prevail. In *Re E (A Minor) (Wardship: Medical Treatment)*,[13] the 'child' was a youth aged 15 years and 9 months who was suffering from leukaemia and very likely to die unless he received a transfusion of blood or blood products. He and his

---

8 R 12(1)(a). For further discussion see ch 2.
9 [1993] 1 FLR 440. For a consideration of the decision in *Re H (A Minor) (Care Proceedings: Child's Wishes)* see the wide ranging discussion by M D A Freeman in *The next Children's Act?* [1998] Fam Law 341. Freeman considers the underlying ideology of the Children Act and then goes on critically to look at a number of aspects relating to the competence of children.
10 Ibid, at p 450. He ruled on the facts that the level of understanding that enables a child to make an informed decision whether to refuse to submit to a psychiatric examination is, in all practical senses, a much higher level of understanding than is required to enable him to give instructions to a solicitor on his own behalf.
11 Thus a paediatrician might describe a child's face as being in a state of 'frozen awareness' when in the presence of a particular adult and interpret this to mean that the child is in fear of that adult.
12 For a detailed discussion see J Fortin *Children's Rights and the Developing Law* (Butterworths, 1998), at pp 207-222.
13 [1993] 1 FLR 386.

parents were devout Jehovah's Witnesses and it was contrary to the tenets of their faith to permit transfusions of blood. Ward J found that whilst the youth was of sufficient intelligence to be able to make decisions about his own well-being, and that he knew that he might die as a result of his decisions, he was nonetheless not fully able to grasp the implications of the views he was expressing. Even when a child has the intelligence and understanding to make his own decision about the matter in question this does not mean that the child's wishes and feelings will be allowed to dominate the court's ruling; the child's wishes and feelings and the child's welfare may pull in opposite directions, and where this happens the child's welfare must be the court's paramount consideration, and welfare is for the court, not the child, to determine.[14] However, the Court of Appeal has emphasised that the court should always listen to the child and has stated that a mature child's views will be given very considerable weight.[15]

Courts have expressed considerable caution about the weight to be given to a young child's wishes and feelings because they have doubts about the reliability of what the child is saying. Whilst they have probably moved away from the thinking that persuaded the Court of Appeal to state in 1981 that 'cases that come to this court show only too well that children of tender years are apt to express their wishes upon no truly reasonable grounds'[16] they are nonetheless likely to be anxious as to whether a child has been put under pressure by a parent to express a particular point of view, particularly the parent with whom the child is currently living.[17] Sometimes a child may choose to live with the parent whom the child thinks needs him most, or because his siblings are living with the other parent and the child therefore feels sad and anxious about the parent who will be living on his or her own. In *Guery v Guery,*[18] the Court of Appeal said that it would be dangerous to give decisive weight to the wishes of a boy of twelve, because at that age a child can be extremely suggestible, reluctant to upset a parent and very protective towards him or her. The courts have therefore been careful about giving significant weight to the views of children.[19]

However in *M v M (Transfer of Custody: Appeal)*[20] a strong-minded child, who was determined in her views about the parent with whom she

---

14 See *Re R (A Minor) (Wardship: Medical Treatment)* [1991] 4 All ER 177; *Re W (A Minor) (Medical Treatment)* [1992] 4 All ER 627, which are discussed in ch 1. See too *Re S (Minors) (Access: Religious Upbringing)* [1992] 2 FLR 313.

15 *Re P (A Minor) (Education)* [1992] 1 FLR 316, in which the wishes of a boy of 14 about where he should be educated had a crucial influence on the court's determination.

16 *Cossey v Cossey* (1980) 11 Fam Law 56.

17 See *Doncheff v Doncheff* (1978) 8 Fam Law 208; *M v M* (1977) 7 Fam Law 17. It is submitted that the thinking in these, and the other pre-Children Act 1989 cases cited below, carry equal force today because the anxieties about the veracity of what the child is saying remain the same. See further B Cantwell and S Scott *Children's wishes, children's burdens* (1995) 17 JSWFL 337.

18 (1982) 12 Fam Law 184.

19 See *Re B (Change of Surname)* [1996] 1 FLR 791 for an extreme example relating to change of the surname of teenage children, discussed below.

20 [1987] 2 FLR 146.

wished to live, effectively forced the court to make an order which was against its own perception of the child's best interests. *M v M* provides an example of a sense of realism by courts in their approach to older children. Where a child disagrees with the court's ruling he or she is likely to disobey it, or to cause so much trouble, or to become so unhappy, that the order becomes unworkable. Furthermore, the courts are increasingly aware of the requirement to pay heed to the wishes and feelings of the children. As Butler-Sloss LJ said in *Re P (Minors) (Wardship: Care and Control)*[1] 'in all family cases it is the duty of the court to listen to the children, ascertain their wishes and feelings and then make decisions about their future having regard to but not constricted by those wishes'. Similarly, in *Re A (A Minor) (Cultural Background)*[2] Swinton Thomas J stated that although it is important that decisions about a child's future should not be dictated by the child herself, the views of a nine-year-old child expressed to an experienced court welfare officer were nonetheless of considerable importance, and where the child was adamant about where she wished to live any court would be bound to hesitate very long before it made an alternative placement. In *Re F (Minors) (Denial of Contact)*,[3] the Court of Appeal held that the trial judge had rightly given the views of boys aged twelve and nine very considerable and not disproportionate weight when deter-mining not to make a contact order in favour of their father, who was a transsexual. The boys were steadfast in their present wish not to see their father and the judge was not prepared to force them to do so.[4]

Despite the growing recognition of the importance of heeding the wishes and feelings of the child, young children who cannot control their own destiny are still vulnerable to having their strongly held wishes and feelings discounted or ignored by courts. In *Re M (A Minor) (No 2) (Appeal)*[5] the trial judge had declined to make a care order in respect of a child aged six because he did not believe that the mother and her partner had beaten and sexually abused the child.[6] The local authority appealed and asked leave to call further evidence relating to the child's hysterical reaction on being told that she was going to go back to live with her mother. The Court of Appeal refused to allow this evidence to be called on the ground that it only tended to confirm that the child had ambivalent feelings about returning home and that 'the only way to the true feelings of this troubled child is through the experienced eyes of the trial judge who saw and heard

1 [1992] 2 FCR 681.
2 [1987] 2 FLR 429.
3 [1993] 2 FLR 677.
4 See too *M v A (Wardship: Removal from Jurisdiction)* [1993] 2 FLR 715 and *M v M (Minors) (Jurisdiction)* [1993] Fam Law 396, discussed above. The wishes and feelings of the children were strongly influential on the outcome of both of these cases.
5 [1994] 1 FLR 59.
6 He had nonetheless found the threshold test for care proved because the mother did not seek medical attention for her daughter until a very late stage, and by the time the child was admitted to hospital with a very severe haematoma and other bruising she was dangerously dehydrated.

over a long period the numerous witnesses'. However, as a critic of this approach to the wishes and feelings of the child has pointed out:

> 'It seems impossible to justify the Court of Appeal's refusal to hear evidence of the child's extreme reaction to the judge's order. To say, as they did, that assessing the child's true feelings is a matter for the trial judge who has heard the evidence is quite illogical. This was an important piece of evidence which the judge never heard and could not possibly have heard, because the incident had not yet happened.'[7]

Whilst it is generally accepted that it is right that children should be consulted when decisions are being made which will intimately affect their future, court welfare officers, guardians ad litem and other professionals working with children, and the courts themselves, are anxious about the burden of responsibility which an insensitive handling of section 1(3)(a) could sometimes place on children.[8] *M v M (Defined Contact Application)*[9] is an example of sensitive judicial handling of the child's wishes and feelings. It concerned a girl, aged eight, who was strongly opposed to contact with her mother. The mother was seeking defined contact and alleging that the child's antipathy had been instilled by the father. Judge Hallon (sitting as a High Court judge) held that a defined contact order would not provide a solution to the situation, as such an order would not prevent the father from disrupting contact. Furthermore, it would have the disadvantage of putting the child in the position of being able to flout the court's order. Such an outcome would give the child inappropriate power and inappropriate responsibility, as would a form of order to which she agreed, or making no order at all. The judge took the view that the child needed the guidance and support of both parents, not coercion. She therefore made what she described as an 'unusual order'. The wishes and feelings of the parents would be set out in a preamble to the contact order. In this way the child would know her parents were setting the framework and that they expected her to co-operate with their joint wish that she have regular contact with, and develop a better relationship with, her mother.

Research tells us that many children blame themselves for the breakdown of their parents' marriage, and for the fact that their parents are in dispute about their upbringing, and that they suffer badly from unwarranted feelings of guilt and shame. Most children love each of their parents and do not like to have their loyalties divided. Therefore there is a risk that a provision which expects a court welfare officer to ask a child to voice his or her wishes and feelings about, for example, residence and

---

7   See J R Spencer *Evidence in child abuse cases – too high a price for too high a standard?* (1994) 6 JCL 160.
8   See *B v B (Minors) (Interviews and Listing Arrangements)* [1994] 2 FLR 489.
9   [1998] 2 FLR 244.

contact arrangements could increase the child's sense of personal responsibility for what has happened, cause the child pain and add to his or her feelings of guilt. Indeed, it has been argued that one of the rights of a child in this context is the right not to make a decision.[10] There is also a danger that children will be asked to express their wishes and feelings in circumstances where the chances that the court will be able to give weight to their expressed preferences are remote because they are unrealistic in the light of other evidence. For example, if a child is asked whether he or she wants to leave local authority care and return home in a case where the parent is so ill, or so disturbed, that this is an impossibility, such a question may simply add to the child's sense of loss and rejection. Moreover, children have strong emotional ties to their parents even where they have been abused by them, so that 'listening to children is a much more complicated process than simply obtaining a view from the child about where they want to live or with whom. If we do not take what is at the same time a more comprehensive and more subtle approach, it could be that taking on board the child's express wish, such as to be at home, gives us false reassurance. It may make us much less concerned rather than much more inclined to intervene and protect ... A child who says "I am fine, thank you", may nevertheless need help'.[11] A delicate balance must therefore be struck between taking proper account of the child's wishes and feelings and burdening the child with choices which should be made on his or her behalf by adults.

Change of a child's surname

It has long been customary for a woman to take her husband's surname on marriage. In recent years this custom has been observed to a lesser extent; but in those cases where a married woman retains her maiden or professional surname it is still normally customary for the child to be registered in his or her father's surname. With the increase in the number of parents living together outside marriage, many children of unmarried parents are also registered in their father's surname. One anxiety of an

---

10 *M v M* (1977) 7 Fam Law 17, per Sir George Baker P, referring to law reform proposals in Canada. See also H Schaffer *Making Decisions about Children: Psychological Questions and Answers* (Blackwell Publishers, 1990); T Campbell, 'The Rights of the Minor', in P Alston, S Parker and J Seymour (eds) *Children, Rights and the Law* (Clarendon Press, 1992), at pp 21-22.

11 G Schofield, *Making sense of the ascertainable wishes and feeings of insecurely attached children* (1998) 10 CFLQ 363, at p 364. In an illuminating article, the author explains why a careful assessment of children's development and relationships should always be made alongside any consultation with the children themselves. She explains the many ways in which a child's cognitive capacity can be damaged, and how this affects the child's capacity to make sense of available options, and analyses the reasons for the 'particular need to understand the internal world, the thoughts, wishes and beliefs, of children whose early experiences of neglect or abuse have left them distressed and confused'.

ex-husband or ex-partner on the breakdown of a relationship is that his ex-wife or ex-partner will change his child's surname. He is particularly likely to find this objectionable where he discovers that the child's surname has been changed to that of a new husband or partner, thus severing all official acknowledgment of the father's parental link with the child.

Change of surname and parental responsibility

Until recently, there was some confusion as to whether the consent of only one person with parental responsibility was needed before a child's surname could lawfully be changed.[12] The issue was resolved in *Re PC (Change of Surname)*[13] where Holman J expressed the opinion that any suggestion that a parent with parental responsibility could unilaterally change his child's surname was 'little short of bizarre'. As Holman J pointed out, all that section 13(1) of the Children Act 1989 does is to make it clear that a residence order no more carries a right or power to change the surname of a child than had a custody order before it.[14]

Where a child is born to unmarried parents under the provisions of the Births and Deaths Registration Act 1953 the mother alone has the duty and the right to register the child's surname with the surname of her choice. The unmarried father can take no part in this without the mother's consent and co-operation. Once the mother has exercised her right there is nothing in the 1953 Act to permit that registration to be changed. A child's birth certificate may only be altered within twelve months of original registration.[15] However, formal steps may be taken by the mother to record a new surname through the execution and enrolment of a deed poll and only the consent of all those with parental responsibility is required to authorise this process.[16] Prima facie, therefore, an unmarried

---

12 Texts produced for practitioners were uncertain about the effect of ss 2(7) and 13(1) of the Children Act 1989 on the previous law, which had clearly provided that previously married parents must agree over any change of name, see *Re PC (Change of Surname)* [1997] 2 FLR 730, at pp 732 and 735, and Matrimonial Causes Rules 1973, r 92(8).

13 [1997] 2 FLR 730.

14 See *Family Law: Review of Child Law: Guardianship and Custody*, Law Com No 172, para 4.14, where the Law Commission made it plain that change of surname was clearly not a matter on which the parent with whom the child lived should be able to take unilateral action. The Enrolment of Deed (Change of Name) Regulations 1994, reg 8(5) also reflect this approach. Although consent to change of name need not be given in writing unless a residence order is in force so that s 13(1) applies, the practical effect of a Practice Direction (11 April 1994) is to require written consent before the enrolment of a deed poll. In *Re PC (Change of Surname)* Holman J gave guidance to schools, doctors and other holders of official or formal records on how they should respond to a request to change the child's surname on their records or to start using a new surname for the child. He advised them to find out whether any other person has parental responsibility for the child, and where this is the position, only to record or use the new surname where either that person consents or the change has been authorised by a court.

15 Births and Deaths Registration Act 1953, s 13.

16 *Practice Direction: Child: Change of Surname* [1995] 1 FLR 458, para 2.

mother may lawfully change her child's surname; a married mother may not. However, the extent to which an unmarried mother has this right as part of her parental responsibility has been thrown into doubt by the decision of the House of Lords in *Dawson v Wearmouth*.[17] Their Lordships approved the ruling of the Court of Appeal that the registration or change of a child's surname is a profound and not a merely formal issue, whatever the age of the child. 'Any dispute on such an issue must be referred to the court for determination whether or not there is a residence order in force *and whoever has or has not parental responsibility*. No disputed registration or change should be made unilaterally'[18] .Consequently 'there is a heavy responsibility on those who seek to effect the change, first, as a matter of prudence if not direct law to take the issue of dispute for the resolution of the judge'.[19]

It is therefore clearly wrong to advise a mother that she is entitled to change her child's surname provided that she alone has parental responsibility. Her legal position is much weaker than this. It is correct that she may lawfully change her child's surname without the father's consent, but may only do so where the issue is not disputed by the father. Furthermore, it appears that a disputed case includes the situation where the mother anticipates that the father would oppose the change of surname were he to be told that this was her intention.[20] The father is entitled to challenge any actual or anticipated change of name by applying for either a specific issue order or a prohibited steps order, and it now seems as if the mother should apply for a specific issue order in a disputed case rather than relying on the father to initiate proceedings. It cannot be emphasised too strongly, therefore, that an unmarried mother should give the most careful consideration to her choice of surname when registering her child at birth.

Change of surname and the child's welfare

The courts have held that the surname by which a child is known is a matter of profound importance to the child. Consequently any exercise of parental responsibility to cause the child to be known by a new surname must be in the best interests of the child. Where the matter is disputed it should be brought before a court and the court will exercise its discretion applying the welfare principle as guided by the considerations in the

---

17 [1999] 2 All ER 353.
18 At p 635, emphasis added. See also, *Re T (Change of Surname)* [1998] 2 FLR 620.
19 *Re C (Change of Surname)* [1998] 2 FLR 656, at p 667 per Ward LJ.
20 This was strongly emphasised in *Re C (Change of Surname)* above, where the mother and her solicitors were criticised for their lack of frankness with the father. The Court of Appeal reinforced the point that even though a child's surname may lawfully be changed where only the mother has parental responsibility, she nonetheless was not entitled to make a change where the matter is in dispute. 'I would endorse the view of the court that disputed issues ought to be referred to the court. Whether that is simply a matter of wisdom, common decency, courtesy or whatever and not a binding obligation, I leave on one side' per Ward LJ, at p 663.

checklist.[1] The judges have stated on a number of occasions that permission should be sought in advance of any change of name. However, despite such strictures, in practice the majority of the reported cases have been concerned with the situation where the child's name has already been changed and where the child is using the new name informally within the family, and more formally at school.[2] The difficulty facing the courts where an application is made at this stage is that once change of name has occurred there may be powerful emotional, psychological, social and practical reasons why a child's name should remain as it is, and this is true whether the original change was made lawfully or unlawfully.

What factors have the court taken into account? Delay by the father in the initiation of proceedings for the child's name to be changed back is an influential factor. Delay occurred in *Re C (Change of Name),*[3] and the Court of Appeal held that the proper approach was to ask whether it was in the interests of the child that her name be changed at the time when the change took place. However, where the change had already taken place, the question for the court was whether it should interfere judging the matter at the time the matter came before the court. The wishes and feelings of the children (the first consideration in the checklist) are also undoubtedly important. In *Re PC (Change of Surname)*[4] Holman J said of children aged twelve and a half and ten that 'it would be wrong of me even to contemplate trying to effect any reversal of the position which has now been reached without knowing their wishes and feelings and degree of understanding'. However, in *Re B (Change of Surname)*[5] the Court of Appeal confirmed the trial judge's refusal to permit the names of three teenage children to be changed to that of their step-father despite the fact that they strongly wished this, despite their hostility towards their father, despite the fact that they had not had contact with him for five years and despite the fact that 'orders nowadays which run flatly counter to the wishes of normal children aged 16, 14 and 12 are virtually unknown to family law'.[6] Wilson J drew a distinction between an appli-

---

1   In *Dawson v Wearmouth* [1997] 2 FLR 629, where the Court of Appeal reversed the trial judge's order that the child should be known by his father's name, the court held that no difference should be drawn between an application made for a specific issue order under s 8, to which the checklist applies, and an application under s 13, to which the checklist does not technically apply. In each situation the child's welfare is the court's paramount consideration and thus any distinction is more theoretical than real. This part of the ruling was not taken on appeal to the House of Lords.

2   It seems likely that cases of this kind will diminish when the significance of Holman J's judgment in *Re PC (Change of Surname)* [1997] 2 FLR 730 permeates into schools. He advised those responsible for altering records to find out which people have parental responsibility for the child and only to record or use the new surname where all those with parental responsibility consent or where the change has been authorised by a court.

3   [1998] 2 FLR 656.

4   [1997] 2 FLR 730, at p 740.

5   [1996] 1 FLR 791.

6   Per Wilson J, at p 794. The strength of the children's hostility can be measured by their practice of destroying birthday and Christmas cards without opening them and their habit of referring to their father as 'him at Blyth'.

cation by the children's mother to lift an existing prohibition on change of name and imposing an order on the children in the teeth of their opposition.[7] He pointed out that the order did not oblige the children to do anything which they were refusing to do and that they could not be prevented from informally using their step-father's name. However, he asserted that only the father's name should be recorded on formal documents and that the order prevented the *mother* from causing the children to be known by a new surname. Dismissing the 'traditional' argument that it is embarrassing for children to be known by a surname other than that of the adults in their household, he concluded:

> 'In my judgment the grant of leave to the mother to effect a formal change in the surname of the children would not only have been unwarranted on pragmatic grounds but, more importantly, would have sent out a wholly inappropriate message to the children, namely that the court agreed with them that their father was of the past, not of the present. Save following adoption, a father, while he lives, is always of the present. Far from being clearly wrong, the judge was, I believe, right.'[8]

Despite this reasoning, which emanated from the basic principle that it is of fundamental importance for every child to have an enduring relationship with both parents, it is nonetheless hard to accept that the court's decision was a sensible exercise of judicial discretion. It seems strange in the light of the House of Lords' ruling in *Gillick v West Norfolk and Wisbech Area Health Authority*[9] that the court should take the view that it had an unfettered right to impose its own view of welfare on competent adolescent children in order to prevent them from choosing the name by which they wished to be known formally as well as informally.[10] Adolescent children are usually very certain that they know their own minds, know what is good for them and know what will cause them harm. It may be that the children's decision in *Re B (Change of Surname)* was mistaken, and that they would come to regret it. But their choice would not lead them positively to suffer harm and therefore surely the principles in *Gillick* ought to apply?[11] It is further suggested that such an approach is probably

7　The prohibition had automatically been imposed at the time of the divorce.
8　At p 796. A similar approach was taken in *W v A (Child Surname)* [1981] 1 All ER 100; *Re F (Children: Surname)* [1994] 1 FCR 110.
9　In which the House of Lords not only accorded considerable respect to adolescent competence, but their Lordships also recognised and declared that children have the right to make many decisions *as a matter of law*. See the discussion of *Gillick* competence in ch 1.
10　The reasoning that the prohibition was an existing order directed to the mother was technically correct, but failed to give weight to the fact that the impact of the prohibition was on the children and to the fact that the Act makes specific provision for such an order to be lifted.
11　Unlike, for example, experimenting with illegal drugs which clearly falls outside the scope of competent adolescent decision-making.

not conducive to promoting the child's welfare, because where a court prevents a determined adolescent child from formally changing his or her name the child's resentment is likely to be counter-productive to fostering good interpersonal relationships with the father. Where, by contrast, a court respects a teenager's wishes and feelings it seems more likely that at some stage in the future he or she might attempt to form some kind of relationship with the discarded parent.[12] It is also suggested that a sad feature of the ruling in *Re B (Change of Surname)* is that it appears to reflect judicial antipathy towards the use of a step-father's surname,[13] and to have placed no value on the children taking enjoyment in the step-parent relationship or on their positive approach to living in a reconstituted family.

Dawson v Wearmouth[14] underlines the importance of the choice of surname which appears on a child's birth certificate. The mother was a married woman and she registered her child under her married surname notwithstanding that the child was born as a result of her relationship with another man. The father objected to his son being registered in this surname and was successful in obtaining a specific issue order directing that the child should be known by the father's surname. The trial judge based his decision on the reasoning that the child was in the day to day care of his mother, his interests would best be served by being reminded of his father's place in his life, and this could be achieved through bearing his father's surname. Allowing the mother's appeal, the Court of Appeal accepted that the factors which had swayed the judge were routine considerations which would apply in virtually every case involving unmarried parents. Instead, said the Court of Appeal, 'registration is a profound matter, and consequently in our judgment a major factor to be taken into account in the exercise of the court's discretion'.[15] This consideration, coupled with the consideration that the child's chosen name was also the name by which the mother was known at the time his name was registered, and continued to be the name by which the child's two half siblings were known, persuaded the court to reject the father's application.[16] Dismissing the father's appeal, the House of Lords ruled that the paramount consideration was the welfare

12 Which, of course, is what really matters. Wilson J's understandable anxiety that to agree to the change of name would be interpreted by the child as an endorsement of the child's negative opinion of the father could have been handled through the careful giving of reasons for the court's decision.

13 'The principle that the stamp of parenthood upon the children represented by their having the same surname as the parent should not lightly be erased by the name's replacement with that of a non-parent', per Wilson J commenting on *Re B (Change of Surname)* in *Re C (Change of Surname)* [1998] 1 FLR 549, at p 552.

14 [1999] 2 All ER 353, .

15 [1997] 2 FLR 629, at pp 635-636.

16 In *Re C (Change of Surname)* [1998] 2 FLR 656 the mother changed the name of her child originally registered in an unmarried father's name. The father's appeal from a judge's refusal to order that the name be changed back was rejected because the initial change had been made lawfully, albeit deceitfully, and by the time the case came to court it was feared that any order to change it back would have a deleterious effect on contact arrangements.

of the child, that the criteria in section 1(3) of the Children Act applied, and that a court should not make an order to change a child's name unless there was evidence that this would lead to an improvement from the point of view of the welfare of the child. As Lord Hobhouse said: 'the name appearing upon a child's birth certificate is not without importance. It has practical implications and, other things being equal, it is in the long term interest of the child that the name by which he is known should also be the name which appears on his birth certificate.'[17] The Court of Appeal was, however, criticised by the House of Lords for appearing to elevate registration into an overriding factor because such an approach would be liable to distort a proper evaluation of the criteria on section 1. Their Lordships held that registration was relevant but that it was not 'all-important'. It is clear from the combined effect of the speeches of Lords Mackay, Jauncey and Hobhouse,[18] that registration does not render irrelevant the considerations which weigh in favour of a child having the same surname as his natural father, and does not alter the need for making an overall assessment of where the child's interests lie.

The ruling of the Court of Appeal in *Re C (Change of Surname)*[19] is both interesting (and arguably controversial) when viewed alongside the assertion that initial registration is a relevant and sometimes important factor.[20] The facts were unusual because the application was brought by a mother against her former unmarried partner. The children, aged eight and seven, had originally been known by their mother's maiden name. When the parents parted the father obtained a residence order and he subsequently caused the children to be known by his surname (not realising that he was prohibited from making this change). Proceedings were issued and the father was granted leave to cause the children to be known by his surname. The mother sought leave to appeal. She did not seek to prevent the daily use by the children of their father's name, but she did want them to retain her name for official purposes. Refusing the mother's application, the Court of Appeal distinguished *Re B (Change of Surname)*[21] on the grounds that the mother had since married, had taken her husband's surname and no longer used her maiden name. Therefore, although the stamp of parenthood reflected by a surname should not lightly be erased, retention of the mother's maiden name would not significantly assist in preserving the link between her and her children. Wilson J stated that nothing in *Re B (Change of Surname)* should be taken as indicating that it was desirable that children should have a different official name from the name in general use. On the contrary, in principle this was undesirable. In *Re B (Change of Surname)* the children were of an age

17 [1999] 2 All ER 353, at p 365.
18 Lords Slynn and Clyde agreed with the reasons given by Lord Mackay. Lord Jauncey expressed doubt as to whether the Court of Appeal had given proper weight to the fact that the child bore the name of a man with whom he had no connection.
19 [1998] 1 FLR 549.
20 *Dawson v Wearmouth* [1999] 2 All ER 353.
21 [1996] 1 FLR 791.

where they could not be prevented from using their preferred surname even though the parent with whom they lived was prevented from using it. In *Re C (Change of Surname)* the children were eight and seven and the court agreed with the father's submission that for children of that age to be free to choose what name they wished to be known by, but for the parent with whom they were living to be under a restraint, 'is particularly artificial and not conducive to easy operation'.[20]

It is suggested that this decision sits uneasily alongside earlier rulings which have focused on the importance of initial registration and which have emphasised that neither parent is allowed unilaterally to change their child's surname.[1] The use by children of their mother's maiden name would undoubtedly confirm their links with her whether or not the mother herself has chosen to adopt a new surname. It would also reflect that at the time of initial registration an unmarried mother alone has parental responsibility and is entitled to choose her children's surname. Surely, therefore, the importance of initial registration should be treated as even more profound where the parents have never been married, where the registered name belongs to the children's mother, and where the father has subsequently married another woman who has changed her name to his?[2] It is suggested that the courts are ambivalent about the value they place on the formal recognition of reconstituted families and that this is reflected in an inconsistency in their rulings on change of name.

It would appear to be unprecedented for a court to permit a parent without parental responsibility to cause a child to be known by his surname. However, the thrust of the authorities on parental responsibility orders set a low threshold for the father to overcome in order to obtain such an order.[3] Consequently, where, as in *Re P (Parental Responsibility)*,[4] a court declines to make a parental responsibility order it is unlikely to order that a child should revert to being known by his father's name, even if this is the name in

---

22 [1998] 1 FLR 549, at p 552, per Wilson J. It is interesting to note that Wilson J could detect no flaw in the judge's exercise of discretion, which he described as copy-book even though it appeared to depart so radically from his own judgment in *Re B (Change of Surname)*.

1 Cf *Re T (Change of Surname)* [1998] 2 FLR 620, where the mother's argument that all her children should have the same surname, that they had been known by their new surname for more than a year, and that it would be convenient for the purpose of medical and school records, failed to persuade the court not to order that the name be changed back.

2 It would therefore be easy falsely to pass off the second wife as the mother of her step-children. It may be that one factor affecting the decision in *Re C (Change of Surname)* [1998] 1 FLR 549 was that, in a compromise gesture, the father had offered to use the mother's maiden name as each child's middle name.

3 See the analysis in ch 1.

4 [1997] 2 FLR 722. The father had been sentenced to a long term of imprisonment and was refused a parental responsibility order because his behaviour amounted to 'an act of irresponsibility on his part towards his children'. The court concluded that even though the children were being taken to the prison to see their father it was to their advantage to be known by the name of their mother, as she was the only person who had their effective care.

which the child was originally registered. In a case of this kind, other factors appertaining to the child's welfare will probably take on a greater significance including the length of time for which the children have been known by their new name, and whether official records have already been altered.

It should, however, be noted that the ruling in *Re P (Parental Responsibility)*, like the rulings discussed above, concerned the position where a unilateral change of surname had already been made. It seems likely that cases of this kind will diminish and that applications for leave to change the child's name in advance of any formal change will increase when the significance of Holman J's judgment in *Re PC (Change of Surname)*[5] permeates into schools. He advised those res-ponsible for altering records to find out who has parental responsibility for the child and only to record or use the new surname where all those with parental responsibility consent, or where the change has been authorised by a court. It also seems likely, now that the House of Lords has made it clear that the criterion in section 1(3) applies to the change of a child's surname, that the argument that use of the non-residential parent's name raises the child's awareness that he has two parents, and acts as a constant reminder to him, will be more persuasive where an advance application is made remains to be seen.[6]

Adoption and welfare

Adoption applications can raise complex questions relating to the welfare of children. When an adoption order is made it ends the status relationship between the child and his or her natural parents. The child is treated by law as the child of the adopters, and as if he or she had been born to them in lawful wedlock even where the child is adopted by a single person.[7] It is a final order, and once properly made cannot be annulled, revoked or otherwise set aside.[8] This conceptual framework applies to all adoptions irrespective of the factual circumstances of the child, the natural parents and the adopters.

---

5   [1997] 2 FLR 730.

6   See *Dawson v Wearmouth* [1999] 2 All ER 353. It should, however, be noted that in *Re C (Change of Surname)* [1998] 1 FLR 549 the Court of Appeal commented that the father's arguments for change would still have been powerful even if the children had not already adopted the use of his name.

7   Adoption Act 1976, s 39. S 39(4) specifically states that the section prevents an adopted child from being illegitimate. S 12(3) provides that the making of an adoption order operates to extinguish any previously held parental responsibility, any order under the Children Act 1989, and any maintenance obligation made by agreement or court order. All statutory references hereafter in this section are to the Adoption Act 1976, unless otherwise stated.

8   *Re B (Adoption: Setting Aside)* [1995] 1 FLR 1. The only cases where adoption orders have been set aside is where there has been some procedural irregularity, although cf *Re M (Minors) (Adoption)* [1991] 1 FLR 458; or where there has been a fundamental breach of natural justice, as in *Re K (Adoption and Wardship)* [1997] 2 FLR 221, which involved the inter-country adoption of a Bosnian child. Even then, the child's psychological attachments to the applicants to adopt may require that she should remain in their care for the foreseeable future, as in *Re K (Adoption and Wardship)*.

Adoption is traditionally associated with the early transfer of parental responsibility for a baby from the child's unmarried mother to married adoptive parents. Adoption continues to make provision for such children, but the number of babies available for adoption has undergone a rapid decline. On the other hand, adoption is one of the options open to a local authority when planning the upbringing of a child in care, and there has been an increase in the adoption of older children, and children with special needs. Furthermore, the growth in the number of children born outside marriage, and the increase in the number of divorces which are followed by remarriage, has led to a steady demand from step-parents to be able to adopt the children of a previous relationship.[9] Many children for whom adoption is considered as the most appropriate way of giving them a secure childhood have existing links with their natural parents, and sometimes it may be thought important to preserve these links. In the context of adoption difficult questions can then arise in relation to whether the complete severance of the relationship between the child and his or her natural family necessarily promotes the child's welfare. The significant advantage of adoption is that it can give a child much needed stability and permanency; its disadvantage is that it is inconsistent with the child remaining a member of his or her birth family.

'Open adoption'

In the past adoption tended to be shrouded with secrecy and the notion that it could be in the interests of the child to maintain links with his or her birth parents was alien to what was essentially a secretive arrangement. Currently the view is taken that more openness is needed in the adoption process. In recent years, adoption law has been the subject of a major review, and this review recognised that amongst the many factors which have influenced changes in the approach of professionals to adoption is the increasing value which they place on a child maintaining some kind of links with his or her birth family. As the *Review of Adoption Law* explained:

> 'For many years now, there has been an increasing recognition that a child's knowledge of his or her background is crucial to a formation of positive self-identity, and that adoptive families should be encouraged to be open about the child's adoptive status and the special nature of the adoptive relationship. There has also been a move towards enabling some children to maintain contact with their birth families.'[10]

9 See NV Lowe, *The changing face of adoption- the gift/donation model versus the contract/services model* (1997) 9 CFLQ 371, and the figures quoted, at p 372.
10 *Review of Adoption Law* (1992) DOH, para 4.1. For a comparative survey, see C Bridge *Changing the nature of adoption: law reform in England and New Zealand* (1993) 13 LS 81; see too C Bridge *Adoption and contact: the value of openness* (1994) 6 JCL 147.

This thinking undoubtedly influences the selection of adopters by adoption agencies. It is also a factor which has become of increasing importance to courts when they are assessing whether an adoption order should be made at all, and if so, whether it should be made on the basis that the child will continue to have contact with his birth family.

The welfare test in adoption

Section 6 of the Adoption Act 1976 states that:

> 'In reaching any decision relating to the adoption of a child a court or adoption agency shall have regard to all the circumstances, first consideration being given to the need to safeguard and promote the welfare of the child throughout his childhood; and shall so far as practicable ascertain the wishes and feelings of the child regarding the decision and give due consideration to them, having regard to his age and understanding.'

Adoption proceedings are family proceedings,[11] consequently the court may make an order under section 8 of the Children Act 1989 if the court considers that the order should be made even though no such application has been made.[12] Therefore, when determining whether adoption will safeguard and promote the welfare of a child throughout his childhood the court should consider not only the nature and effect of an adoption, order on the child's welfare, but also whether an alternative order, almost always a residence order, would better promote the child's best interests.

> 'It is essential that adoption is regarded not as a means of determining with whom a child is to live, but as a way of making a child legally part of a new family and severing any legal relationship with the birth family.'[13]

This is a vital distinction; there may be cases where there is no doubt that the child should continue to live with the applicants to adopt, but where a residence order, not an adoption order, is the most appropriate way of safeguarding the child's future.[14] Moreover, adoption should not be used merely as a means of securing a right of abode for a child in this country and avoiding normal immigration procedures. This is to confuse the purpose of adoption with the benefits of residence. However, where adoption will safeguard and promote the welfare of the child, and give him the secure

---

11 Children Act 1989, s 8(4).
12 S 10(1).
13 *Review of Adoption Law* (1992) DOH, para 3.6.
14 For a particularly compelling and complex example, see *Re M (Adoption or Residence Order)* [1998] 1 FLR 570.

family upbringing he needs, then adoption is appropriate. Section 6 applies and must be considered quite independently of any benefits which will accrue to the child through acquiring British nationality.[15]

Section 6 of the Adoption Act 1976 should be contrasted with the principle enshrined in section 1 of the Children Act 1989 which provides that when a court determines any question with respect to the upbringing of a child the welfare of the child shall be the court's *paramount* consideration. In the case of adoption the child's welfare is the court's *first* consideration; this means that whilst it is of first importance it does not always and necessarily override all other considerations and determine the course to be followed. The reason why the child's welfare is not paramount is because the welfare test in adoption is bound up with the question whether the objection of a parent to his or her child being adopted can ever be reasonable. Clearly if a court is satisfied that adoption would otherwise be in the best interests of the child, and if the child's welfare were to be paramount, the fact that a parent is objecting to the adoption would not be a reason for refusing to make the order.[16] However, the essence of an adoption order is that it gives parental responsibility for the child to the adopters and extinguishes the parental responsibility of the natural parents. That is why considerations other than the child's welfare, including considerations relating to the wishes and feelings of the child's parents are taken into account before an adoption order is made.[17]

The difference between a child's interests being the court's paramount consideration and a child's interests being the court's first consideration was critical in *Re T and E (Proceedings: Conflicting Interests)*.[18] Two half sisters, T and E, had the same mother and different fathers.[19] The father of E, with whom the mother was living, had sexually abused T. Consequently, care orders had been made in respect of both children. Two conflicting plans concerning the future of the children were placed before the court. T's father had applied for the discharge of the care order so that T could live with him and his second wife and children. The local authority had made applications to free both children for adoption, their plan being to place the children together. They took the view that E's welfare in particular required that she remain with her sister, because T represented

15 *Re H (Adoption: Non-Patrial)* [1982] 3 All ER 84; *Re K (A Minor) (Adoption Order: Nationality)* [1994] 2 FLR 557; *Re H (Adoption: Non-Patrial)* [1996] 2 FLR 187; *Re B (Adoption Order: Nationality)* [1998] 1 FLR 965. These rulings should be contrasted with *Re J (Adoption: Non-Patrial* [1998] 1 FLR 225 and *Re I (Adoption: Nationality)* [1998] 2 FLR 997 where the distinction was drawn between applications solely designed to achieve a legal status, and applications designed to create the psychological relationship between parent and child with all its far reaching consequences.

16 See the *Report of the Departmental Committee on the Adoption of Children (The Houghton Committee)* Cmnd 5107, HMSO, (1972).

17 See the discussion by Wall J in *Re B (Adoption Child's Welfare)* [1995] 1 FLR 895.

18 [1995] 1 FLR 581.

19 The facts were unusual because the fathers were brothers, and the mother had married each in turn. She remained living with E's father and therefore there was no question of returning the children to her care.

the only stability in E's otherwise disrupted upbringing. The application to free E for adoption was unopposed. T's father did not feel able to offer himself as an adopter for E, but there was evidence that it would be in the interests of T to live with her father. The issue for the court, therefore, was how to resolve the conflict of interest between the two children. The application by T's father to revoke the care order was governed by the paramountcy principle; the application for a freeing order fell to be determined under section 6 of the Adoption Act 1976. The court was therefore driven to the conclusion that T's interests had to prevail over those of E.[20]

Placement for adoption and selection of adopters

Every local authority is under a duty to establish and maintain an adoption service within their area. Local authorities themselves act as adoption agencies and provide the requisite services, or they secure that they are provided by approved adoption societies.[1] Adoption agencies have exclusive responsibility for selecting adopters and placing children for adoption. Section 11(1) provides that no person other than an adoption agency shall make arrangements for the adoption of a child. Private adoption place-ments are illegal except where the prospective adopter is a relative of the child, or where the placement is made in pursuance of a High Court order. No court has power retrospectively to authorise a placement in breach of section 11.[2] However, this does not prevent the High Court making an adoption order in an appropriate case.[3] Section 11 is clearly intended to protect children, and 'having regard to the provisions of section 6, it cannot seriously be suggested that Parliament considered that an illegal place-ment, however innocent, should be an absolute bar to the adoption of a child'.[4] Where there has been a breach of section 11, the court must take the breach into account, give first consideration to the welfare of the child pursuant to section 6, and

---

20 Consequently, the court granted the father's application, refused the application for the freeing order in respect of T, but granted it in respect of E. For further comment, see V Cromack and M Parry, *Welfare of the child – conflicting interests and conflicting principles* (1996) 8 CFLQ 72. As the authors point out, by giving a higher priority to T's interests the court also gave higher priority to her father's interests. They are also critical of the court for placing greater value on the parent/child relationship than on the sibling relationship.

1 S 1.

2 *Re G (Adoption: Illegal Placement)* [1995] 1 FLR 403. Balcombe LJ stated that in so far as any previous cases had suggested that any court has power retrospectively to authorise a placement in breach of s 11, they had been wrongly decided.

3 Only the High Court has this power, and the power to authorise in advance a placement which would otherwise be prohibited by s 11, *Re S (Arrangements for Adoption)* [1985] FLR 579; *Re G (Adoption: Illegal Placement)* [1995] 1 FLR 403.

4 *Re G (Adoption: Illegal Placement)* [1995] 1 FLR 403, at p 406.

consider whether public policy requires that the order should be refused because of the applicant's criminal conduct.[5]

Section 13(1) lays down the requirement that in the case of family placements, or where the child has been placed by an adoption agency or order of the High Court, an adoption order shall not be made unless the child is at least 19 weeks old and at all times during the preceding 13 weeks had his home with the applicants or one of them. Section 13(2) allows a court to make an adoption order where the child has not been placed with the applicants by an adoption agency, but where the child has had his home with the applicants at all times during the preceding twelve months. This provision covers cases where a child has, for example, been for a long time with foster parents and where they subsequently wish to adopt the child.[6]

In the case of agency placements there are few legal restrictions relating to a person's eligibility to adopt a child. Sections 14 and 15 of the Adoption Act 1976 impose lower age limits,[7] requirements relating to domicile, and in the case of adoption by two persons states that the parties must be married.[8] It was emphasised in *Re W (Adoption: Homosexual Adopter)*[9] that there is nothing in the Act to suggest that adoption by a single applicant should not take place, or that the general law seeks to impose any specific restrictions relating to the personal characteristics of the adopter. The simplicity of the provisions in sections 14 and 15 enables the law to adapt to changing social attitudes. It was acknowledged in *Re W (Adoption: Homosexual Adopter)* that it was unlikely that the framers of the legislation contemplated that a single homosexual applicant might apply for, and obtain, an adoption order, but the reason for this lay not in the legislation but in the likely attitude of adoption agencies two decades ago when selecting persons as potential adopters.[10] Singer J therefore concluded: 'the Adoption Act 1976 permits an adoption application to be made by a single applicant, whether he or she at the time lives alone, or

---

5 *Re Adoption Application (Non-Patrial: Breach of Procedures)* [1993] 1 FLR 947. See also, *Re MW (Adoption: Surrogacy)* [1995] 2 FLR 759 where the applicants to adopt were a husband and wife who had made a surrogacy arrangement. As the wife was not a relative within the meaning of s 11, the placement was illegal. However, there were glowing reports as to how the care of the applicants had promoted the child's welfare and an adoption order was made in their favour despite the illegal placement, and despite the fact that they had made payments which were illegal under s 57.

6 But this provision does not contemplate an adoption order being made where there has been an illegal placement (as was wrongfully suggested in *Re ZHH (Adoption Application)* [1993] 1 FLR 83), see Balcombe LJ in *Re G (Adoption: Illegal Placement)* [1995] 1 FLR 403, at p 405. However, *Re ZHH (Adoption Application)* is correct in so far as it stated that the fact that an illegal placement is a criminal offence did not preclude the High Court from making an adoption order.

7 21, except where one of joint adopters is a parent and has reached the age of 18.

8 But see *Re AB (Adoption: Joint Residence)* [1996] 1 FLR 27.

9 [1997] 2 FLR 406.

10 See Review of Adoption Law (DOH 1992), paras 26.9–26.14 for more current views on who make suitable applicants to adopt.

cohabits in a heterosexual, homosexual or even an asexual relationship with another person who it is proposed should fulfil a quasi-parental role towards the child. Any other conclusion would be both illogical, arbitrary and inappropriately discriminatory in a context where the court's duty is to give first consideration to the need to safeguard and promote the welfare of the child throughout his childhood.'[11] However, the restriction that joint adopters must be married remains, and may sometimes have a limiting effect.[12]

Adoption agencies, nevertheless, have tended to operate very specific criteria when determining eligibility to adopt which are neither laid down in the primary legislation nor in the associated Regulations.[13] Many have rejected would-be adopters for reasons such as that they are too old, they already have natural children, because they follow the wrong religion, or have no religion, or are the wrong race or colour to adopt the child in question, or because they smoke or are obese, or are undergoing fertility treatment. Agencies have applied these and other criteria to the selection process because they have taken the view that such factors relate to the welfare of the children who are available for adoption. However, in recent years, Government has taken an active interest in adoption policy and practice and has given advice on the recruitment of prospective adopters. In the White Paper on adoption it was recognised that some local authorities had adopted too rigid a stance on 'same race placements' and that race was only one factor to be considered alongside all the other factors which are relevant to the child's welfare.[14] In a letter written to all directors of social services in 1996, it was drawn to their attention that children from ethnic, cultural and religious minorities were sometimes being allowed to drift in the care system. Such an outcome was against Government policy and the directors were advised that long-term plans for such children should not exclude placements with families not sharing the children's heritage.[15] In 1998, in a circular, it was re-emphasised that it was unacceptable for a child to be denied loving adoptive parents solely on the ground that the child and adopters did not share the same racial or cultural background.[16] Moreover, all directors of social services were advised both in 1996 and in 1998 that age should not be the main or sole

11 [1997] 2 FLR 406, at p 413. In *Re W (Adoption: Homosexual Adopter)* the applicant was living with a lesbian partner. See also, *Re E (Adoption: Freeing Order)* [1995] 1 FLR 382 where the potential adopter was a lesbian single woman.

12 The difficulties this may present can be overcome, see *Re AB (Adoption: Joint Residence)* [1996] 1 FLR 27 where an adoption order was made in favour of the foster father, and a joint residence order was made to him and his female cohabitee.

13 The Adoption Agencies Regulations 1983, regs 10(1)(c) and 11(1) simply require that the agency is satisfied about the suitability of the prospective adopter and that she would be a suitable adoptive parent for a particular child.

14 *Adoption: The Future,* White Paper Cm 2288, HMSO, (1993), at para 4.32.

15 The letter was sent from the Chief Inspector of the Social Services Inspectorate, Sir Herbert Laming. The letter also advised that a high level of education, time consuming jobs or a high income should not preclude persons from selection.

16 *Adoption – Achieving the right balance* LAC(98)20.

determinant in assessing suitability to adopt, and that the important considerations were whether prospective adopters had the health[17] and vigour to meet the many and varied demands of children in their growing years, and that they would be there for the children when they reached adulthood.

Where persons are rejected as prospective adopters there is no formal appeal system available to them. The complaints procedure established under section 26(3) of the Children Act 1989 does not apply to prospective adopters. However, it may be that a local authority would be willing to allow this procedure to be used even though there is no obligation on the authority to make it available.[18] Otherwise the only way of challenging the agency's decision would be in judicial review. This is a jurisdiction which enables the High Court to review the behaviour of a public authority where it has acted illegally, with procedural impropriety or irrationally. It is a jurisdiction which is exercised with great caution. Courts are generally extremely reluctant to intervene in the way in which public authorities carry out their duties and powers. Furthermore, the court does not have an appellate function; it is confined to determining whether there has been an abuse of power.

Illegality might be established if it could be shown that the adoption agency have fettered their discretion by adopting a rigid policy which allows for no exceptions. The agency is entitled to follow a general policy, but they must consider each case on its merits.[19] However, it is likely to be extremely difficult to satisfy the court that a rigid policy has been adopted. Thus in *R v Lancashire County Council, ex p M*[20] foster parents sought to challenge the decision of the local authority to reject them as suitable adopters for a foster child who had lived with them from shortly after his birth until he was two years old. The foster parents alleged that the primary reason for moving the child from their care was to implement a rigid policy, namely that children ought to be placed with families of the same cultural or ethnic background as the child. It was further alleged that the authority had taken account of matters which it ought not to have taken into account, and had refused or neglected to take account of matters which it ought to have done, and therefore that they had come to a decision at which no reasonable authority could have arrived. Refusing to grant the adopters leave to bring an action in judicial review, the Court of Appeal stated that they had failed to establish that the authority's decision was so unreasonable that no authority could ever have come to it. It emphasised that judicial review proceedings are not concerned with what the court would have done had it been applying the welfare principle.

---

17 The 1998 circular advises that a local authority may have to restrict adoption of some children to non-smokers, particularly where the child is a baby or very young, or where the child has a chest or heart complaint or a history of asthma.

18 See C Williams and H Jordan *The Children Act Complaints Procedure: A Study of Six Local Authority Areas* (Sheffield University, 1996), at p 45.

19 Cf *R v Lewisham London Borough Council, ex p P* [1991] 2 FLR 185.

20 [1992] 1 FLR 109.

In the context of judicial review the role of the court was simply to determine whether the authority had acted in such a way as to be almost perverse. Thus decision-making about the choice of adopters is vested firmly in adoption agencies, and it is most unlikely that a successful challenge could be mounted against a refusal to select a person or couple as suitable where the child is not living with them.

Removal of a child from prospective adopters

Parents who arrange for their child to be placed for adoption by an adoption agency may subsequently change their minds and seek the return of the child. Until an adoption order is made the natural mother, and sometimes the natural father, have parental responsibility for the child and, prima facie, this entitles them to recover the care of the child from prospective adopters or the adoption agency.[1] The Act therefore contains various provisions which are designed to protect the child from the disruptive and possibly harmful effects of precipitate removal by a parent. It also contains provisions which give the prospective adopters a measure of security against the child being taken from them by the local authority or adoption agency against their will.

Section 27(1) provides that:

> 'While an application for an adoption order is pending in a case where a parent or guardian of the child has agreed to the making of an adoption order – the parent or guardian is not entitled, against the will of the person with whom the child has his home, to remove the child from the home of that person except with the leave of the court.'

This protection only arises where agreement to adoption has been given. In *Re T (A Minor) (Adoption: Parental Consent)*[2] the Court of Appeal held that such agreement could be given orally or in writing, and that in either case the agreement falls within the scope of section 27(1). It is the institution of legal proceedings which triggers the protection from removal; thus where applicants to adopt are fearful that the parent will change her mind, they can make an application for an adoption order at an early stage. It is suggested that whether they are well-advised to do so depends on all the circumstances of the case, but particularly on whether the court is likely to regard the application as premature, such as where the child has been with the applicants for only a relatively short time. Where foster parents or relatives have looked after a child for some considerable length of time, and where the parent has needed some persuasion to agree to the making

---

1 Whether an unmarried father has parental responsibility depends on whether he has a parental responsibility agreement or order: see ch 1.
2 [1986] 1 All ER 817.

of an adoption order, it would normally seem wise to make a swift application for an order so that the protection afforded by section 27(1) immediately comes into play. It should however be realised that although the protection afforded by this section arises only when agreement has been given, in those cases where parental agreement is not forthcoming the child is often in local authority care. The child is therefore protected against removal from the prospective adopters because of the effect of the care order.

Where a parent has not agreed to the child being adopted, the child is vulnerable to being taken by a parent at any time from the home of the persons who have been caring for him, and who would like to adopt him. Once a child has been taken from the home of the applicants to adopt it is inevitable that they will fail to satisfy section 13 which requires that the child should have lived with them for a specified period during the weeks or months preceding the making of the adoption order.[3] Section 28(1) affords some protection to the child in circumstances of this kind. It provides that while an application for an adoption order is pending, and where the child has had his home with the applicants for the five years preceding the application, no person is entitled to remove the child from the applicants' home against the will of the applicants except with the leave of the court.[4] However, five years is a considerable length of time before the protection arises, and it is the initiation of adoption proceedings which operates as the trigger to prevent removal. Unless and until an adoption application has been made, there is nothing in the Adoption Act 1976 to prevent the child from being taken by the parents from the prospective adopters' care.

However, it should be remembered that the child is afforded protection against precipitate removal from a settled home under section 10 of the Children Act 1989. Any person with whom the child has lived for a period of at least three years is entitled to apply for a residence order.[5] Furthermore, where persons have looked after the child for a lesser period they can seek the leave of the court to apply for a residence order.[6] However, this will only assist persons who are seeking an adoption order if they are able to obtain a residence order, or an order restraining the child's removal under section 29(2), before the child is taken from their home.[7] Once the child has gone, even if he is restored to the potential adopters' care by a court, it seems that they will no longer be able to fulfil the requirements of section 13, and therefore no adoption order can be made, at least for the time being.

---

3 S 13(1) states that the child must have had his home with the applicant for the preceding 13 weeks where the application is made by a parent, step-parent or relative, or where the child was placed by an adoption agency, or in pursuance of a High Court order. S 13 (2) states that in any other case the child must have had his home with the applicant during the preceding twelve months.

4 Or under authority conferred by any enactment or on the arrest of the child. This proviso also applies to s 28(2) below.

5 Children Act 1989, s 10(5)(b) and (10).

6 Unless they are local authority foster parents to whom special rules apply: see ch 2.

7 Where a child has been removed in breach of ss 27 and 28, a court may order the person who has removed the child to return the child: s 29.

It may not only be parents who wish to remove a child from persons who wish to adopt him. For example, where the child is in the care of a local authority the authority may have plans for the child which do not include continuing care by the foster parents who are currently looking after the child. Section 28(2) imposes additional restrictions on the removal of the child where a person has provided a home for a child for at least five years. It provides:

> 'Where a person ("the prospective adopter") gives notice to the local authority within whose area he has his home that he intends to apply for an adoption order in respect of a child who for the preceding 5 years has had his home with the prospective adopter, no person is entitled, against the will of the prospective adopter, to remove the child from the prospective adopter's home, except with the leave of the court or under authority conferred by any enactment, ... before:
> (a) the prospective adopter applies for the adoption order, or
> (b) the period of three months from the receipt of the notice by the local authority expires,
> whichever occurs first.'

This prohibition safeguards the child against removal by anyone, including the local authority, without the leave of the court once notice of intention to adopt has been given. However, the applicants must apply for an adoption order before three months expire or they lose this protection.[8]

In *Re H (A Minor) (Adoption)*[9] it was held that the court ought not to exercise its discretion under the adoption legislation to refuse a local authority leave to remove the child where the applicant's purpose was to frustrate the local authority's plans. However, it is suggested that the court mistakenly applied the principle in *A v Liverpool City Council*[10] in this case and that it therefore should not be followed. Section 28(2) contemplates a situation where the decision-making function on the merits of removal is clearly vested in the court, and since the implementation of the Children Act 1989 the courts have been careful to preserve their powers where it is they, and not the local authority, who have the right to determine the case on the merits.[11]

Further provisions preventing the child's removal from his present home by either an adoption agency or a local authority without the leave of the court are contained in sections 30 and 31. The placing adoption agency is charged with the duty of ensuring that the child's placement is in the interests of the child. Sometimes the agency may form the view that the

---

8   A fresh notice of intention to adopt cannot be issued until 28 days have elapsed after the expiry of the original notice: s 28(6).
9   [1985] FLR 519.
10   [1981] 2 All ER 385.
11   *Re C (A Minor) (Adoption)* [1994] 2 FLR 513, see below; see too on this general principle, *Re B (Minors) (Termination of Contact: Paramount Consideration)* [1993] 1 FLR 543.

child should not be allowed to remain in his present placement. Where this is the position, section 30(1) provides:

> 'Subject to subsection (2), at any time after a child has been placed with any person in pursuance of arrangements made by an adoption agency for the adoption of the child by that person, and before an adoption order has been made on the application of that person in respect of the child—
> b)   the agency may cause notice to be given to that person of their intention not to allow the child to remain in his home.'

Subsection (2) provides:

> 'No notice under paragraph (b) of subsection (1) shall be given in respect of a child in relation to whom an application has been made for an adoption order except with the leave of the court to which the application has been made.'

Again it should be noted that it is the application for an adoption order which brings section 30(2) into play. Where no such application has been made, the agency may issue a notice under section 30(1)(b) requiring the return of the child within seven days without the leave of the court. Where this occurs, it seems that the prospective adopters have no means of challenging the merits of the agency's decision. In *Re W (A Minor) (Adoption Agency: Wardship)*[12] prospective adopters who received such a notice thereupon made the child a ward of court. Discharging the wardship without considering the merits of the prospective adopters' application for care and control of the child, the court ruled that the principle in *A v Liverpool City Council*[13] applied, namely that the court had no power to intervene in wardship proceedings to review the merits of an adoption agency's decision to give notice of removal made in pursuance of its statutory powers under section 30(1)(b). This ruling was subsequently approved by the Court of Appeal in *Re C and F (Adoption: Removal Notice)*.[14] It is only where an application has been made for an adoption order that the court becomes involved, and section 30(2) comes to the assistance of the applicants. In this event, the adoption agency must obtain the court's leave before it can require the applicants to return the child within seven days.[15] Thus applicants to adopt who fear that the agency may require them to return the child to the agency's care are best advised to make an adoption application at the first available opportunity.

---

12   [1990] 2 FLR 470.
13   [1981] 2 All ER 385.
14   [1997] 1 FLR 190.
15   S 30(3). Refusal to comply is a criminal offence, s 30(7).

The fact that an adoption agency is afforded powers and responsibilities by statute to make discretionary decisions, the merits of which may not be subjected to scrutiny by the courts, does not mean that the agency has total freedom to act as it wishes. An adoption agency carries out a public function pursuant to its statutory powers. Consequently, should the agency abuse its powers, it may lay itself open to an application for judicial review. In *R v Devon County Council, ex p O (Adoption)*[16] the applicants to adopt had looked after a child placed with them for adoption for two years and five months when they received formal notice to return the child to the adoption agency within seven days.[17] In proceedings brought in judicial review, it was established that there was no suggestion that the child was in danger and therefore no urgent need to remove him. The agency failed to consult with the applicants before arriving at its decision to issue the notice.[18] Moreover, the agency failed to consult the child, aged nine, as to his wishes and feelings on being adopted by the applicants.[19] Both of these omissions rendered the agency's decision-making process flawed and therefore the decision to remove the child was quashed.[20]

Section 31 makes provision for those cases where a child has not been placed for adoption by an adoption agency. It provides that section 30 shall apply as if the child had been placed in pursuance of such arrangements:

'Where a person gives notice in pursuance of section 22(1) to the local authority within whose area he has his home of his intention to apply for an adoption order in respect of a child—
(a) who is (when the notice is given) being looked after by a local authority.'

The effect of this provision is to prevent a local authority who are looking after the child from giving notice of their intention not to allow the child to remain in the applicant's home without the leave of the court. This is a significant provision, because where a local authority are looking after a child under a care order it is normally the local authority who are entitled to make all decisions about the child, including the decision to remove the child from his present foster parents and to place him elsewhere. Local authority foster parents are not entitled to challenge the decision in the

16 [1997] 2 FLR 388.
17 Adoption Act 1976, s 30(1).
18 They were not invited to the strategy meeting where the decision to remove the child was made. Of this behaviour, Scott Baker J said: 'individuals who take on the care of damaged and difficult children from local authorities are entitled not only to be treated fairly but to be seen to be treated fairly' [1997] 2 FLR 388, at p 394.
19 In Scott Baker J's view, at p 396, the child's views were 'crucially important'.
20 Judicial review does not, of course, enable a court to substitute its own view of the merits; the court's concern is only with the lawfulness of the decision. The applicants remained vulnerable to the agency simply confirming its original decision. However, the agency would have to reconsider the matter giving due regard of the matters to which Scott Baker J had referred in his judgment.

courts unless the child has been living with them for at least three years.[1] However, foster parents who wish to be considered as a child's adopters may be assisted by the combination of provisions in section 13(2), section 22(1) and section 31. Section 13(2) provides that an adoption order can be made where the child has had his home with the applicants at all times during the preceding twelve months; section 22(1) states that the applicants to adopt must notify the local authority of their intention to apply for an adoption order at least three months before the date of the order; and section 31(2) prevents the child being removed from the home of applicants who have notified the local authority under section 22(1) without the leave of the court.

This combination of provisions has a critical impact on what is often the key question in children cases, namely whether it is the local authority, or the court, which has the final word about who can look after the child. This was illustrated in *Re C (A Minor) (Adoption)*.[2] A foster mother had been rejected by the local authority as either a long-term carer or adopter of a child who had been living with her since he was a few days old, and who was now aged two years and four months. The local authority were in the process of moving the child away from her home to other adoptive parents when the foster mother served notice of intention to apply to adopt under section 22(1) and issued the adoption application. The effect of the foster mother's action was to halt the removal of the child to his new home. The local authority therefore applied for leave to serve notice on the foster mother of intention to remove the child from her home under sections 30(2) and 31.

There were two issues for the court to resolve when considering the leave application: first, whether the welfare test in section 6, which required the court to give first consideration to the welfare of the child, applied to applications for leave to remove a child under Part III of the Act; and secondly, if it did, whether the court had a free discretion when considering the welfare of the child, or whether it must limit its function to interfering with the local authority's plans only if the authority were acting perversely. The trial judge found that the court should not take steps which were tantamount to a review of the adoption agency and local authority's powers and decisions, and granted the local authority leave to serve the notice of removal. Allowing the foster mother's appeal, the Court of Appeal ruled that an application by a local authority for leave under section 30(2) was 'a decision relating to the adoption of a child' and therefore that section 6 applied.[3] In relation to how much weight should be given to the local authority's plans for the child, Butler-Sloss LJ said that they had to be given the weight they deserved and that the court was

---

1 See ch 2.
2 [1994] 2 FLR 513.
3 It distinguished *F v S (Adoption: Ward)* [1973] 1 All ER 722 and *Re A (Residence Order: Leave to Apply)* [1992] 2 FLR 154 (see ch 2) on the grounds that they were applications to initiate proceedings, whereas the application by the foster parent had already triggered the procedure to be followed under the adoption legislation.

entitled to assume that the local authority had the welfare of the child to the forefront of their thinking when making plans for the child. However, she said:

'A court determining a section 30(2) application must give most careful consideration to the plan of the local authority but it has the task to decide whether that plan should go ahead or whether the child should remain with its existing carer even if the consequence of its decision may be to frustrate the local authority's arrangements. It is never the task of the court to rubber stamp the local authority. Either it has no duty to interfere or it has the duty to decide.'[4]

The court stated that where the application by the foster parent was a genuine one, with reasonable prospects of success, it was in the best interests of the child that it should be determined by a full hearing and not brought to a premature conclusion without a proper investigation.

Agreement to adoption

Normally an adoption order cannot be made unless each parent agrees to the child being adopted. For adoption purposes, 'parent' means any parent who has parental responsibility for the child under the Children Act 1989, thus the agreement of an unmarried father is not necessary.[5] There are two methods of obtaining parental agreement to adoption: under section 18, through a procedure known as 'freeing' the child for adoption; and under section 16, where the parent agrees to a specific adoption order being made, whether or not she knows the identity of the applicants.

Freeing for adoption

Under the freeing procedure an application is made by an adoption agency for an order declaring the child free for adoption. The parents must consent to the application being made and, under section 18(1)(a), the court must be satisfied that each parent:

'... freely, and with full understanding of what is involved, agrees generally and unconditionally to the making of an adoption order'.

On the making of a freeing order, parental responsibility for the child is given to the adoption agency until the child is adopted. The parents lose

---

4   [1994] 2 FLR 513, at pp 522-523. Butler-Sloss LJ added that a guardian ad litem can be appointed in a case of this kind under the Adoption Rules 1984, r 47(8).
5   Adoption Act 1976, s 72; the position of the unmarried father is explained below.

their parental responsibility, and therefore have no subsequent entitlement to withhold their agreement to the child's adoption.[6]

The freeing procedure has advantages for the child, the parents and the potential adopters. Because all issues about agreement are resolved at an early stage, it means that the child can be placed with applicants to adopt without any risk that the birth parent will change her mind and seek the return of the child. This has undoubted advantages for the child, who will be able to form attachments to his adoptive family without any danger of these being broken through his removal from the adopters and return to his birth mother. It also may take some of the strain of the adoption process away from the parent who has decided that her child should be adopted. Freeing allows a parent to make a relatively speedy decision, and it may make her experience of giving up her child for adoption less distressing than under the alternative process which takes considerably longer. The mother of a new-born baby is given special protection against making such a momentous decision at a time when she may not be in a proper mental and physical state to arrive at an informed choice; at least six weeks must elapse after the child's birth before her consent can be effective.[7] But once this period has elapsed, a mother can relinquish her parental responsibility for the child to the adoption agency, and thus from any further involvement in the arrangements for the child. The advantage for the potential adopters is that the child is not normally placed with them until all matters relating to agreements to adoption have been resolved. Consequently from the outset they are free of the fear that the mother may wish to have the child restored to her care, and able to feel secure in their relationship with the child as soon as the child is placed. In cases where there are issues over whether there are grounds for dispensing with a parent's agreement to the child's adoption, these can be dealt with in the context of freeing proceedings, which means that the adoption agency bears the costs of legal proceedings rather than the applicants to adopt.

It has become relatively common for a freeing application to be made after prospective adopters have been identified and their adoption of the child has been approved in principle by the adoption agency. A freeing application may also be used to determine whether adoption by strangers, or present foster carers, will be for the welfare of the child or whether the child should continue to maintain his links with his natural family in the hope that rehabilitation may eventually occur. The fact that an adoption agency has decided that adoption is in the child's interests and has applied to the court for a freeing order does not mean that the court is bound to make the order; it must first consider under section 6 whether adoption would safeguard and promote the interests of the child throughout his childhood. The court should only make a freeing order where it is satisfied that the child's welfare will be served by adoption. Thus in *Re U (Appli-*

6 Dispensing with parental agreement to a freeing application is explained below.
7 S 18(4). This does not prevent the child being placed for adoption before he or she is six weeks old.

cation to Free for Adoption)[8] the adoption agency wished the child to be freed for adoption by strangers. The paternal grandparents wished themselves to adopt the child. The court, applying section 6, decided that the paternal grandparents would make suitable adopters and it therefore rejected the adoption agency's application for a freeing order. However, because adoption proceedings are family proceedings for the purposes of the Children Act 1989,[9] the court could choose to make a section 8 order under that Act rather than a freeing order, and here the court made a residence order in favour of the paternal grandparents with the purpose of eventually enabling them to apply for an adoption order.

Revocation of a freeing order

Parental agreement to a freeing order can be dispensed with just as it can to the making of an adoption order itself.[10] However, no agreement may be dispensed with unless the child is already placed for adoption, or the court is satisfied that it is likely that the child will be placed for adoption.[11] Moreover, where no adoption order has been made within a year of the freeing order, and the child does not have his home with a person with whom he has been placed for adoption, the former parent may apply for the freeing order to be revoked on the ground that he wishes to resume parental responsibility.[12] Where the child concerned was in the care of the local authority prior to a freeing order being made the care order is discharged by the freeing order and does not automatically revive when the freeing order is discharged.

The combination of these provisions has the potential to cause problems, as was acknowledged by the House of Lords in *Re G (Adoption: Freeing Order)*.[13] In some cases the parent may be entirely suitable to resume full and unfettered parental responsibility for her child, but in others she may not. The solution in the latter situation is for an order revoking the freeing order to be made conditional upon such consequential orders being made under the Children Act 1989 as are appropriate, or under the inherent jurisdiction of the High Court.[14] Where the parent has made a declaration under section 18(6) that she prefers not to be involved in future questions concerning the adoption of the child this too can cause difficulties should the child not be adopted. Section 9(1) makes it plain that such a parent is no longer a 'former parent' for the purposes of the Act and therefore she cannot apply for the freeing order to be revoked. As a result,

---

8 [1993] 2 FLR 992.
9 See ch 2.
10 S 16, discussed below.
11 S 18(3).
12 S 20(1).
13 [1997] 2 FLR 202.
14 In *Re G (Adoption: Freeing Order)* the local authority agreed to apply for a care order, which the mother indicated she would not oppose.

a child may find himself in adoptive limbo with no one in the position o apply for revocation of the freeing order, and the local authority unable to apply for a care order as care orders and freeing orders are mutually exclusive. This was the situation in *Re C (Adoption: Freeing Order)*,[15] and Wall J resolved it by exercising the inherent jurisdiction of the High Court to revoke the freeing order.

Applying for an adoption order

The alternative procedure for giving agreement to adoption is where a parent agrees to a specific adoption order being made. Section 16(1) provides that:

'An adoption order shall not be made unless—
(a) the child is free for adoption by virtue of an order made—
(i) in England and Wales, under section 18;
....; or
(b) in the case of each parent or guardian of the child the court is satisfied that—
(i) he freely, and with full understanding of what is involved, agrees unconditionally to the making of an adoption order (whether or not he knows the identity of the applicants).'

Under this procedure the court must be satisfied at the time that it makes the adoption order that each parent agrees to the order being made. Inevitably there is some time lapse between the child being placed for adoption and the adoption hearing. In all adoptions the child must be at least 19 weeks old and at all times during the preceding 13 weeks have had his home with the applicants, or one of them.[16] In practice the time gap between the child's placement and the adoption hearing is likely to be much longer, because health and other reports must be prepared, and the relationship between the child and the applicants to adopt scrutinised, in order to ensure that adoption will be for the welfare of the child.

The advantage of this procedure over the freeing procedure is that the child can be placed as soon as the parent has given her preliminary agreement, and this means that the attachment links between the child and the prospective adopters can be established from an early stage which is clearly in the interests of the child. It allows the birth mother a longer period of reflection before she finalises her agreement to her child's adoption, and thus

---

15 [1999] 1 FLR 348. C had been freed for adoption when aged 7, and was now 15. All were agreed that it would be appropriate for the freeing order to be revoked, and for the mother and the local authority to share parental responsibility for C under a care order. Wall J held that an order made in the exercise of the inherent jurisdiction would not transgress s 100 of the Children Act 1989; see ch 2.

16 S 13(1).

provides safeguards against her making a decision which she later regrets. Also, the parent gives her agreement in the knowledge that suitable adopters have been chosen, and she can have the reassurance of knowing that the professionals dealing with the child are satisfied that the adoption placement will serve the child's best interests. However, the requirement that parental consent should be forthcoming at the time that the adoption order is made can be stressful for all parties: the birth parent may be asked on several occasions whether she agrees to her child being adopted and this may compound her pain;[17] a child who is old enough to understand the process will not be certain whether the adoption will take place; and the potential adopters may find that parental agreement is withdrawn at the last minute.[18]

The unmarried father and agreeing to adoption

It is only where an unmarried father has parental responsibility that his agreement to his child's adoption is required, or must be dispensed with, before an adoption order can be made.[19] However, the interests of a father who has forged links with his child are afforded protection in freeing proceedings by section 18(7). This states that before a court makes a freeing order the court shall satisfy itself in relation to any person claiming to be the father that he has no intention of applying for either a parental responsibility order or a residence order, or that if he did make any such application it would be likely to be refused.[20] Also, if the father is liable by virtue of any order or agreement to contribute to the child's maintenance he must be made a respondent to freeing and adoption proceedings, he is entitled to attend the hearing, and he is entitled to be heard on whether an adoption order should be made.[21] Furthermore, the court has a general discretion to add any person as a party to freeing and adoption proceedings, and may exercise this in favour of the unmarried father.[1] In any event, the court is likely to obtain information about the father in the report supplied by either the adoption agency or local authority covering matters specified in paragraph 2 of Schedule 2 of the Adoption Rules 1984. Schedule 2 states that, so far as is practicable,

17 It is the duty of the reporting officer, who must be appointed in all cases where parental agreement is forthcoming, to ensure that consents have been freely given: Adoption Rules 1984, r 17. Notice of the hearing must be served on the parent, but she is not required to attend: r 21(1). Once the application has been made and the parent has agreed to the child being adopted, the child cannot be taken from the potential adopters pending the adoption hearing: Adoption Act 1976, s 27; see above.

18 Cf *Re G (A Minor) (Adoption: Parental Agreement)* [1990] 2 FLR 429.

19 See the definition of parent in s 72, and see *Re C (Adoption: Parties)* [1995] 2 FLR 483. A court may make a parental responsibility order even where it is inevitable that the father's agreement to adoption will be dispensed with: see *Re H (Illegitimate Children: Father: Parental Rights) (No 2)* [1991] 1 FLR 214.

20 A father will normally fulfil the requirement that he would be likely to obtain a parental responsibility order where he has been attached and committed to the child. Cases on parental responsibility orders are analysed in ch 1.

21 Adoption Rules 1984, rr 4(1)(f),10(1),15(2)(h) and 23(1).

1 R 15(3).

this report shall include information about each natural parent's wishes and feelings in relation to the adoption, 'including where appropriate the child's father who was not married to the child's mother at the time of his birth'.[2]

However, unless the father is entitled to be a respondent to the proceedings, these safeguards of the unmarried father's position may not always assist him. In *Re B (A Minor) (Adoption)*[3] a county court judge refused to allow an unmarried father to be joined as a party to adoption proceedings. The Court of Appeal held that there was no presumption that the father should be made a party where he had no right to be a party, and that it was a matter for the court's discretion whether it allowed him to be joined. Similarly, in *Re C (Adoption: Parties)*,[4] where the father's application for parental responsibility and contact had already been refused, the Court of Appeal ruled that it was not mandatory for a father without parental responsibility to be joined as a party to the application.

In *Re L (A Minor) (Adoption: Procedure)*[5] the mother of a child was very anxious that the unmarried father did not discover that the child existed. She had placed the child with a local authority in their capacity as an adoption agency. The child had been placed with potential adopters and they had applied for an adoption order. During the course of the adoption proceedings the judge directed that the father be discreetly interviewed to ascertain his wishes and feelings. The local authority appealed against this direction, because they feared that the mother might withdraw her agreement to the adoption if the father was told of the child's existence. Allowing the appeal, the Court of Appeal held that the words 'where appropriate' in Schedule 2 were highly significant. It held that they were intended to confer a discretion upon the adoption agency preparing the report whether to include particulars of the unmarried father. Furthermore, it held that this discretion was that of the adoption agency alone, and that the court had no power to interfere unless it had been improperly exercised. As the local authority were convinced that adoption was in the child's best interests, and as they were concerned that it should not fall through because of an approach to the father which the mother did not want, it was impossible to say that they had improperly exercised their discretion. Thus whether the father learns of the adoption application is a matter for the adoption agency and not for the court.

It is suggested that the decision in *Re L (A Minor) (Adoption: Procedure)* is worrying. Unless the court is told why no details about the father have been provided it is lacking a piece of information which may be relevant to its assessment of whether the child's welfare will be served by adoption. Whilst it is clear from the rules that the decision whether to pursue enquiries about the father is one for the agency, the court's duty under

2 In *Re Adoption Application (No 2) 41/61* [1964] Ch 48 it was held that no one has a duty positively to seek out the father, and see *Re C (Adoption: Parties)* [1995] 2 FLR 483.
3 [1991] Fam Law 136.
4 [1995] 2 FLR 483.
5 [1991] 1 FLR 171.

section 6 of the Act is to be satisfied that adoption is for the welfare of the child, and it is suggested that it should not arrive at this finding on the basis of incomplete knowledge. The scope of the Court of Appeal's ruling is not clear, but if it is taken to mean that a court should make no enquiries as to why information about the father has been omitted from the Schedule 2 report that is surely to leave too much power in the hands of the agency. While in the particular case the mother's reasons for denying the father knowledge of his paternity may have been valid, in other cases she may have improper motives of which the court should be aware. It is suggested that fresh consideration should be given to whether it should be the adoption agency, or the court, which finally determines whether a father who can be identified and traced should nonetheless be excluded from being involved in the adoption proceedings.

Dispensing with agreement to adoption

Section 16(1) of the Adoption Act 1976 enables a court to dispense with a parent's agreement to the making of the adoption order where it is satisfied that one of the grounds in section 16(2) has been established. Similarly, the court may dispense with the parent's agreement to adoption in a freeing application brought under section 18.

The grounds for dispensing with agreement are:

'... that the parent or guardian—
(a) cannot be found or is incapable of giving agreement;
(b) is withholding his agreement unreasonably;
(c) has persistently failed without reasonable cause to discharge his parental responsibility for the child;
(d) has abandoned or neglected the child;
(e) has persistently ill-treated the child;
(f) has seriously ill-treated the child.'

Paragraphs (c) to (f) are each concerned with fault on the part of the parent, and in practice are rarely relied upon. Paragraph (a) is concerned with those cases where a parent cannot be traced or where he or she lacks the mental capacity to give agreement. The provision which is almost always relied on in practice is paragraph (b) and the discussion below concentrates on that provision.[6]

The parent is withholding his or her agreement unreasonably

Unlike paragraphs (c) to (f), paragraph (b), which allows a court to dispense with parental agreement on the ground that it is being unreasonably

6   For an account of the case law on the other provisions see the *Inter-Departmental Review of Adoption Law, Discussion Paper No 2, Agreement and Freeing* (DOH, 1991).

withheld, contains no built-in standards of behaviour which have been breached. The meaning of the phrase has been the subject of much judicial exposition. The classic statement is contained in Lord Hailsham's speech in *Re W (An Infant)*[7] and it needs to be quoted extensively in order to capture the essence of the test which the courts must apply. Lord Hailsham approved as authoritative the passage from the judgment of Lord Denning MR in *Re L (An Infant)*[8] in which he said:

> 'In considering the matter I quite agree that: (1) the question whether she is unreasonably withholding her consent is to be judged at the date of the hearing; and (2) the welfare of the child is not the sole consideration; and (3) the one question is whether she is unreasonably withholding her consent. But I must say that in considering whether she is reasonable or unreasonable we must take into account the welfare of the child. A reasonable mother surely gives great weight to what is better for the child. Her anguish of mind is quite understandable; but it may still be unreasonable for her to withhold consent. We must look to see whether it is reasonable or unreasonable according to what a reasonable woman in her place would do in all the circumstances of the case.'

Lord Hailsham said:

> 'From this it is clear that the test is reasonableness and not anything else. It is not culpability. It is not indifference. It is not failure to discharge parental duties. It is reasonableness and reasonableness in the context of the totality of the circumstances. But although welfare per se is not the test, the fact that a reasonable parent does pay regard to the welfare of his child must enter into the question of reasonableness as a relevant factor. It is relevant in all cases if and to the extent that a reasonable parent would take it into account. It is decisive in those cases where a reasonable parent must so regard it.'[9]

Later in his speech Lord Hailsham said:

> '...it does not follow from the fact that the test is reasonableness that any court is entitled simply to substitute its own view for that of the parents. In my opinion, it should be extremely careful to guard against this error. Two reasonable parents can perfectly reasonably come to opposite conclusions on the same set of facts without forfeiting their right to be regarded as reasonable. The

7   [1971] 2 All ER 49.
8   (1962) 106 Sol Jo 611: see *Re W (An Infant)* [1971] 2 All ER 49, at p 55.
9   Ibid, at p 55.

question in any given case is whether a parental veto comes within the band of possible reasonable decisions and not whether it is right or mistaken. Not every reasonable exercise of judgment is right, and not every mistaken exercise of judgment is unreasonable. There is a band of decisions within which no court should seek to replace the individual's judgment with his own.'[10]

The House of Lords' ruling in (*Re W*) (*An Infant*) thus made it plain beyond doubt that a court cannot dispense with a parent's agreement to her child's adoption simply because it does not agree with the parent's view of the situation. When considering the question of the reasonableness of the parental veto it should be remembered that the Adoption Act 1976 imposes two conditions which must be complied with before an adoption order can be made. The first is under section 6, which requires that the court be satisfied before making an adoption order that adoption will safeguard and promote the welfare of the child throughout his childhood. It is only after the court has made a positive finding in favour of adoption that the court moves to the second consideration, namely whether the parental veto to adoption falls within or outside the band of possible reasonable decisions.[11] These considerations are distinct and separate, and it is solely where the veto falls outside this band that the court may dispense with the parent's agreement, despite the fact that the court has already determined that adoption would be in the interests of the child.

It is clear that reasonableness is an objective, not a subjective test.[12] It involves consideration of how a parent in the actual circumstances of the parent opposing the adoption, but hypothetically endowed with a mind and temperament capable of making reasonable decisions, would approach the question.[13] In considering parental reasonableness, it is wholly relevant for the judge to consider the basis upon which he had found adoption to be in the child's best interests.[14] An influential factor in determining whether the parent is unreasonable in withholding his or her agreement to adoption is what the consequences for the child will be if an adoption order is refused. The nature of the placement and the importance of security for the child must be considered.[15] In baby adoption cases the normal outcome will be that the child will return to the care of his or her mother; in step-parent adoptions the child will normally remain with the parent and step-parent regardless of whether an adoption order is made; in cases involving children in care who are enjoying contact with their birth families reasonableness is likely to revolve around contact arrange-

---

10 Ibid, at p 56.
11 *Re D (A Minor) (Adoption: Freeing Order)* [1991] 1 FLR 48.
12 'Would a reasonable parent have refused consent?', per Lord Reid in *O'Connor v A and B* [1971] 2 All ER 1230, at p 1232.
13 *Re D (An Infant)* [1977] AC 602.
14 *Re E (Adoption: Freeing Order)* [1995] 1 FLR 382. The court had found that neither rehabilitation nor contact with the mother were in the child's best interests.
15 *Re AB (Adoption: Joint Residence)* [1996] 1 FLR 27.

ments, and whether a form of 'open adoption' is thought desirable. It is therefore suggested that care should be taken before statements made in one context are extrapolated and applied in a different context.

Baby adoptions and dispensing with agreement

It has been seen that delay is built into the adoption process and that adoption orders under section 16 are not normally made until several months, and often as much as a year, after the placement of the child with the prospective adopters. Where a mother of a baby agrees to her child's adoption the law indicates that she can withdraw her agreement at any time until the adoption order is made. However, once the mother sets the adoption process in motion her action has an impact not only on herself, but also on the child and the applicants to adopt. The difficulty facing the courts is that the child, in the time between his placement and the adoption hearing, will almost certainly have formed close bonds of attachment with the prospective adopters. Expert opinion evidence is likely to be given that to remove the child from the only home he has ever known and to place him with his mother, who is a stranger to him, is likely to cause him serious psychological damage, particularly where there are unstable features about the mother's household, as was the situation in *Re W (An Infant)*[16] itself. The adopters, too, will have had their hopes and expectations raised, and as Lord Reid said in *O'Connor v A and B*[17] 'the adopting family cannot be ignored either. If it was the mother's action which brought them in in the first place, they ought not to be displaced without good reason.' Thus although the mother has in no sense been culpable in her behaviour towards her child it may nonetheless be unreasonable for her to change her mind and to seek to recover the care of her child. The dilemma in a case of this kind is how to balance the welfare of the child against the prima facie reasonableness of the mother's decision to bring up her own child herself.

In circumstances where the child's welfare positively demands that he be adopted the House of Lords ruled in *Re W (An Infant)* that a reasonable mother may be expected to put aside her own anguish of mind and to agree to the child's adoption. In *Re H (Infants) (Adoption: Parental Consent)*[18] Ormrod LJ pointed out that 'it ought to be recognised by all concerned with adoption cases that once formal consent has been given, or perhaps once the child has been placed with adopters, time begins to

---

16 [1971] 2 All ER 49.
17 [1971] 2 All ER 1230, at p 1232.
18 [1977] 2 All ER 339n, at p 340. In *Re O (Adoption: Withholding Agreement)* [1999] 1 FLR 451 the consent of an 'impeccable' father was dispensed with because of the distress and trauma which would be caused to the child if he was taken at the age of eighteen months from the only family he had ever known. The father had only become awae of his child's existence when he learned of the adoption proceedings on the court's instructions.

run against the mother and, as time goes on, it gets progressively more and more difficult for her to show that the withdrawal of her consent is reasonable'. The fact that the mother has vacillated in her intentions is not conclusive that she is being unreasonable, but it is a further factor which weighs against her.[19]

However, the majority of contested baby cases were decided some time ago, when the pendulum then had swung markedly in favour of giving considerable weight to the child's welfare. For example, in *Re P (An Infant)*[20] the Court of Appeal considered the quality of the mother's lifestyle, compared it unfavourably with the opportunities offered to the child by the adopters and concluded that the mother was withholding her agreement unreasonably. Since then the Court of Appeal has stated that there must be a limit to this shift towards the prioritising of the child's welfare, and the indications are that it is swinging back towards giving greater consideration to the parent's position. Thus in *Re E (A Minor) (Adoption)*[1] the mother of two children accepted that adoption was in the best interests of her younger child who had been taken into care, but nonetheless opposed it. Allowing the mother's appeal against the decision of the trial judge to dispense with her agreement, the Court of Appeal said that he had failed to consider properly what weight the hypothetical reasonable parent would give to the interests of her other child, who had a loving relationship with his half brother. Furthermore, the fact that two witnesses, a teacher and a social worker, held the view that the mother was capable of looking after the child was something she was entitled to take into account when reaching her decision, as was the fact that although the local authority had prospective adopters in mind, the placement had not, as yet, been tested. The court therefore concluded that the mother's refusal to consent to the adoption was within the band of possible reasonable decisions. 'She may have been wrong, she may have been mistaken, but she was not unreasonable.'[2]

It is not clear how far this approach would be applied in a case where the mother initially agrees to her child being adopted and subsequently changes her mind. As has been stated a crucial factor in this type of case is that the child, in the meanwhile, has formed strong attachment bonds with the prospective adopters, and the issue for the court is likely to focus on whether severing these bonds will cause him psychological damage. Thus in *Re MW (Adoption: Surrogacy)*[3] the mother had acted as a surrogate for the applicants to adopt, but after handing her baby over to their care she changed her mind and wished to recover the care of the child. By the time the application came before the court the child was nearly two and a half years old and had spent all of his life in the care of the adopters. The

19 *Re P (Adoption: Parental Agreement)* [1985] FLR 635; *Re G* [1990] 2 FLR 429.
20 [1977] 1 All ER 182.
1 [1989] 1 FLR 126.
2 Ibid, per Balcombe LJ, at p 133.
3 [1995] 2 FLR 759.

court held that to disturb the present arrangements would so clearly be contrary to the welfare and interests of the child that the mother was being unreasonable in withholding her consent to his adoption. By contrast, in *Re E (A Minor) (Adoption)*[4] the child was in foster care, and had not forged links with an alternative family. However, there is evidence to suggest that the courts are now more sympathetic towards parents who wish to retain links with their children, and less prepared to give considerable weight to the child's welfare.[5]

Is adoption by a step-parent in the child's interests?

Many children live in families with a birth parent and a step-parent. This situation arises where the mother or father has had children by a previous unmarried relationship, or where an earlier marriage has ended by divorce, or where the mother or father of the children has died. Sometimes couples who already have children by different partners marry and thus each spouse is both a birth parent and a step-parent. Where the birth parent and step-parent wish for their family relationship to be cemented through the process of adoption they must apply jointly for an adoption order. If the step-parent were the sole applicant an adoption order to him would sever the child's legal relationship with both his birth parents, and not merely the parent he was replacing.[6] The question whether adoption by step-parents is normally in the best interests of children is controversial. In step-parent cases there is no issue about whether the child will continue to have his home with his parent and step-parent; and in an opposed case the court does not face the difficulty that the child will be removed from the applicants if an adoption order is not made. The welfare question revolves around the key question whether altering the child's status relationship with his natural parent and his step-parent will be of more benefit to him than retaining the status quo.

The advantages of adoption are mainly in the intangible consequences of the order on the emotional links between the parties. A step-parent who adopts is committing himself to a relationship with the child which has as much to do with putting into legal form the expression of his love for the child, and of the child's love for him, as it has with altering the parties' status. Adoption is also an expression of commitment to the marriage, and it may be seen by the spouses as a method of publicly affirming the permanence of their relationship and of the viability of their family as a unit. A consequence of adoption may therefore be an improvement in the relationships between members of the family because they feel more secure as a result of the step-parent's de facto

---

4   [1989] 1 FLR 126.
5   See too *Re H; Re W* (1983) 4 FLR 614.
6   The *Review of Adoption Law*, para 19.3, recommends that a new order should be available only to step-parents which does not make the birth parent an adoptive parent.

commitments having been legally recognised. A more practical benefit flows from the legal consequence that the child's name can be changed to that of the step-parent. Research reveals that the lack of a common surname is important to the majority of those seeking step-parent adoption orders.[7]

Anxieties that step-parent adoption orders may not promote the welfare of the child relate to concerns about the impact on the child of the severance by law of his ties with his birth parent and one half of his natural family.[8] Thus where a child is adopted by his step-father not only does he lose a birth father and acquire an adoptive father, he also loses his legal relationship with his paternal grandparents and other paternal relatives.[9] Prior to the Children Act 1989, the court was required to dismiss an application to adopt by a parent and step-parent where it considered that the matter could better be dealt with by orders for custody and access.[10] It is clear that this leaning against step-parent adoptions continues. As Thorpe LJ has explained:

'Cautionary dicta[11] are still apt since applications in step-parent adoptions may be driven or complicated by motives or emotions derived from conflict within the triangle of adult relationships. They may also be buoyed up by quite unrealistic hopes and assumptions as to the quality of the marriage replacing that into which the children were born.'[12]

In the Adoption Law Review, the opinion is expressed that:

'Where the prime motivation behind an adoption application is the wish to cement the family unit and put away the past, this may be confusing and lead to identity problems for the child, especially if (as is statistically not unlikely) the new marriage breaks down. It is also possible that the step-parent's family has little or no involvement or interest in the adopted child, so that the child loses one family without really gaining another.'[13]

---

7   J Masson, D Norbury and S G Chatterton *Mine, Yours or Ours? A Study of Step-Parent Adoption* (1983, HMSO). After divorce a parent is not entitled to change a child's surname without the agreement of the other parent or the leave of the court, and the courts have been very reluctant to grant such leave; see above.

8   See s 14(3) of the Adoption Act 1976, which the Children Act 1989 repealed.

9   Whether in practice these are lost will depend on whether the adoptive parents are willing to maintain these links for the child, at least until the child is old enough to make his own decisions.

10 Under the Matrimonial Causes Act 1973. Residence and contact orders are the nearest equivalent to those orders.

11 See, for example, *Re D (An Infant) (Parent's Consent)* [1977] AC 602, at p 627, per Lord Wilberforce; *Re B (A Minor) (Adoption Jurisdiction)* [1975] 2 All ER 449.

12 *Re PJ (Adoption: Practice on Appeal)* [1998] 2 FLR 252, at p 260.

13 Para 19.2.

Other anxieties relate to the reasons why the parent and step-parent are applying to adopt. So, for example, the child's guardian ad litem and the court are likely to wish to discover whether they are making the application in order to conceal a previous failed marriage, or the fact that a child was born when the mother was unmarried, or to cut the birth father out of the child's life, rather than because they take the view that the child will benefit from the change in status.[14] The impact of the Child Support Act 1991 has created a different ground for concern about motives, namely whether the natural father's agreement to his child's adoption is influenced by the financial consideration that his support obligation will come to an end, and not because he no longer is interested in the child.

The court is specifically directed in section 6 to consider the wishes and feelings of the child and to give due consideration to them before making an adoption order. The question whether the child has sufficient age and understanding to appreciate what he is being asked takes on a special significance in the context of step-parent adoptions because of the far-reaching effects of an adoption order. Thus in *Re S (Infants) (Adoption by Parent)*[15] the views of three children aged between six and eleven were largely discounted because they were thought to be too young to understand the full effects of adoption.

Dispensing with agreement to a step-parent adoption

Where after divorce and remarriage a parent and step-parent apply to adopt, and where the application is opposed by the other parent, it is very unlikely that the court will find that adoption will promote the child's welfare.[16] The order extinguishes for ever the father's parental responsibility for the child and cuts him out of the child's life and it is therefore almost invariably against the child's interests. As Cumming-Bruce LJ said in *Re B (A Minor) (Adoption: Jurisdiction)*:[17]

'Where there has been a divorce and the parent ... has married again, and seeks with her new husband by adoption to extinguish the relationship between the children and their father, against the will of the father who honestly wishes to preserve his relationship, and who is not said to be culpable, it is likely to be difficult to discover any benefit to the child from the adoption commensurate with the probable long-term disadvantages.'

---

14 *Re S (Infants) (Adoption by Parent)* [1977] 3 All ER 671.
15 Above.
16 See *Re PJ (Adoption: Practice on Appeal)* [1998] 2 FLR 252 where the Court of Appeal found that a father's consent was not unreasonably withheld despite the strongly expressed wishes of the children aged 17 and 11 to be adopted. However, the court decided not to set aside the adoption orders as to do so would probably be more harmful to the children.
17 [1975] 2 All ER 449, at p 461.

He continued 'it is quite wrong to use the adoption law to extinguish the relationship between the protesting father and the child, unless there is some really serious factor which justifies the use of the statutory guillotine'.

It is only where the court decides that adoption by a parent and step-parent is in the child's interests that the question arises whether the parent is being unreasonable in withholding his agreement. In *Re S*[18] the husband had deserted his wife before the child was born so that the child had never known his father, the mother was living in a stable relationship with the step-father and they applied to adopt the child. The husband refused his consent. The Court of Appeal said that the question to ask was 'would a reasonable father who had not seen the child at all, apart from a short visit when the child was three weeks old, withhold his consent to adoption, the adoption being plainly to the advantage of the child?' Ormrod LJ took the view that just as Lord Denning in *Re L (An Infant)*[19] had said that a reasonable mother gave great weight to what was best for her child, so too a reasonable father would surely give great weight to the nature of the relationship existing between him and the child, and what it was likely to be in the future. He held that if that test was applied to the facts of the case there was only one answer, the father was unreasonably withholding his agreement.

Adoption with contact

Section 12(6) of the Adoption Act 1976 enables a court to attach such terms and conditions to an adoption order as the court thinks fit. Also, because adoption proceedings are family proceedings, an order for contact can also be made under the Children Act 1989, section 8. Prior to the House of Lords' ruling in *Re C (A Minor) (Adoption: Conditions)*[20] the courts took the view that they only had power to make an adoption order with a condition that contact be allowed in exceptional circumstances.[1] Since that ruling it has been clear that it is possible to make an adoption order with a condition of contact where such a condition is in the child's best interests.[2] However, Lord Ackner, who made the main speech, emphasised that in normal circumstances there should be a complete break between the child and his natural family. He added:

18 (1978) 9 Fam Law 88.
19 (1962) 106 Sol Jo 611.
20 [1988] 1 All ER 705.
1   See, for example, *Re M (A Minor) (Adoption Order: Access)* [1986] 1 FLR 51, at p 61.
2   An order was made that a 13-year-old girl should be adopted subject to the condition that she should continue to have reasonable contact with her brother. The condition was attached with the full support of the applicants to adopt. The case was further complicated by the fact that the mother was refusing to agree to the adoption because it would weaken the relationship between the children. The lower courts took the view that she was therefore being reasonable in withholding her agreement. The mother's refusal to agree to the adoption was no longer reasonable once contact could be preserved, and the House of Lords dispensed with it.

'The court will not, except in the most exceptional case, impose terms or conditions as to access to members of the child's natural family to which the adopting parents do not agree. To do so would be to create a potentially frictional situation which would be hardly likely to safeguard or promote the welfare of the child. Where no agreement is forthcoming the court will, with rare exceptions, have to choose between making an adoption order without terms or conditions as to access, or to refuse to make such an order.'[3]

Although the House of Lords' ruling was made only a decade ago, adoption practice has moved forward since then. It is increasingly being recognised that the many older children who are eventually placed for adoption have positive as well as negative memories of their birth families, and that it is important to such children that some kind of link with the birth family is preserved. It is therefore no longer unusual for an adoption order to be made where it is intended that residual contact between the child and one or members of the natural family should be maintained.[4]

It is important to appreciate, however, that the House of Lords differentiated between cases where contact was agreed and where it was not, and it would be most unlikely for a contact order to be thrust upon adopters against their express wishes. Moreover, once an adoption order without contact has been made, the issue of contact cannot normally be revisited. In *Re C (A Minor) (Adopted Child: Contact)*,[5] Thorpe J refused a birth mother leave to apply for contact with her adopted child.[6] He emphasised that adoption orders are intended to be permanent and final. He said that 'a fundamental question such as contact, even if confined to the indirect, should not subsequently be reopened unless there is some fundamental change in circumstances'.[7] A similar approach was taken in *Re E (Adopted Child: Contact: Leave)*.[8] At a hearing to dispense with the consent of parents to their child's adoption reassurances were given to the birth parents that they would receive photographs of the child, and that if they experienced any problems about this they could take the matter back before the judge. The adoption application itself was not made until two months later, at which stage the adoption order was made with no conditions attached.[9]

---

3 [1988] 1 All ER 705, at p 712. This reasoning was applied in *Re MW (Adoption: Surrogacy)* [1995] 2 FLR 759. The surrogate mother originally had the prospect of having contact with her child by agreement, but by her behaviour seeking publicity for her own and her child's position she caused anguish to the applicants and brought the child himself into the limelight. The court refused to make a contact order, largely because of the mother's behaviour.

4 According to a study by the Social Services Inspectorate, *Moving Goalposts* (SSI, 1995) in approximately 70% of the adoptions in the areas studied there was some form of direct or indirect contact with the birth family.

5 [1993] 2 FLR 431.

6 The mother sought leave under s 10(9) of the Children Act 1989; see ch 2 for discussion of the leave provisions.

7 At p 436.

8 [1995] 1 FLR 57.

Nothing was said about photographs and none were sent. The birth parents subsequently applied for leave to apply for a contact order, not with a view to having direct contact with the child, but in order to ensure that the photographs were sent. The adopters opposed the application because they feared that their identity might be discovered by the birth parents. Thorpe J found that the unfairness to the parents was real and not merely apparent. However, he held that this unfairness did not mean that the parents should be granted leave. The adopters had always been opposed to indirect contact, and there were no exceptional circumstances to justify making an order for indirect contact against their wishes.[10]

The unfairness to the natural parents which occurred in *Re E (Adopted Child: Contact: Leave)*[11] also has a potential to arise in those cases where some kind of contact arrangement is found to be in the child's best interests. The court must decide whether the child's link should be preserved by means of an order for contact, or whether the court should rely on the adopters to honour any promise they make about preserving links between the child and his birth family.

In *Re T (Adoption: Contact)*[12] adopters had always agreed that the birth mother should have contact once a year, but they opposed this agreement being incorporated in a court order because they wished to be in control and for there to be flexibility in when contact took place.[13] The trial judge made a contact order, taking the view that this had the advantage that the matter could come back to court in the event of a dispute. The Court of Appeal rejected the judge's approach and ruled that no contact order should be made. It recognised that the mother had consented to the adoption on the understanding that she would see her child at least once a year, and that she therefore wished to know with some degree of certainty that this contact would take place. However, it took the view that the security the mother sought had to be found in the trust she had in the adopters.[14] It also took the view that in the event of any dispute, it should not be the adopters who would have to go back to court to ask to have an order varied. The burden should be on the mother to apply to the court to have her contact restored where the adopter's reasons for denying contact were inadequate, wrong or unjust.

The approach in *Re T (Adoption: Contact)* appears highly desirable where there is trust and co-operation between all parties. However, what

9   Somewhat curiously, the adoption took place in a 'split hearing', rather than through the orthodox freeing procedure, and Thorpe J commented on the pitfalls to which this procedure could give rise.
10 Thorpe J stated that the remedy the parents had, if any, was to appeal the adoption order on the grounds that it was unfair, flawed and deficient, or to apply for the order to be amended.
11 [1995] 1 FLR 57.
12 [1995] 2 FLR 251.
13 The adopters were supported in this view by the social worker and guardian ad litem.
14 The court also relied heavily on the principle in the Children Act 1989, s 1(5) that a court should not make an order unless satisfied that it would be better for the child than making no order at all.

should the court's response be where the adopters promise to allow contact but then go back on that promise? This situation arose a few months later in another case also known as *Re T (Adoption: Contact)*.[15] An elder sibling, D, of children placed for adoption withdrew her application for a contact order with the children on the express understanding that the adopters would send her an annual report about the children's welfare. However, the adopters resiled on their agreement, and D therefore applied for leave to make a contact application for the annual reports to be provided.[16] Allowing D's application for leave, the Court of Appeal held that the behaviour of the adopters was not acceptable. If adopters, having agreed to some form of indirect contact, were simply able to change their minds and resile from the agreement without good cause, this could lead to more contested adoptions and other undesirable consequences.[17]

In *Re O (Transracial Adoption: Contact)*[18] an adoption order was preferred to a residence order in contested adoption proceedings, and the consent of the parents was dispensed with. However, the court took the view that there would be two benefits for the child, a girl aged ten, in having contact with her mother. The child had no memory of her mother, and had developed fantasies about her founded on the conviction that the mother had abused and abandoned her. These fantasies, if left uncorrected, would cause her emotional disturbance in adolescence and beyond. Moreover, the child's parents were Nigerian, and the child was living in a locality where it would be very difficult to buttress her Nigerian heritage and identity. If the child had contact with her mother she would in this way be exposed to her Nigerian heritage. The issue for the court was whether contact arrangements should be left to the discretion of the adopters, or whether an order containing a specific provision for contact should be made. Thorpe J took the view that this was an occasion when a contact order should be made. He said that the order did not imply any lack of trust in the adopters, but if made it would stand for the remainder of the child's minority, and 'if it is not so expressed, it becomes procedurally and as a matter of prospects very difficult for the biological parent to obtain by a subsequent application'.[19]

One solution to the difficulty over whether contact arrangements should be incorporated in a court order is for a written agreement to be drawn up

---

15 [1995] 2 FLR 792. There is no connection between the two cases. For a most useful commentary comparing the two, see M Richards, *It feels like someone keeps moving the goal posts – regulating post-adoption contact* (1996) 8 CFLQ 175.

16 Children Act 1989, s 10(9).

17 Balcombe LJ was at pains to explain to the adopters that courts understand the stresses and strains which adoptive parents face, and said that 'a simple explanation of their reasons in non-legal terms would usually be all that is necessary'.

18 [1995] 2 FLR 597.

19 At p 610. The court not only made a specific order for contact, it also directed that it would be for the local authority to decide when the first contact visit should take place, 'as will be the determination of date and venue of further meetings. It is necessary in current circumstances for contact to be supervised by them'. *Sed quaere* whether the court acted in excess of its powers in view of the prohibition in s 9(2) of the Children Act 1989 of contact orders being made in favour of a local authority; see further, ch 2.

between the adopters and the birth parent or other family member.[20] This has the advantage of introducing clarity and formalising the expectations of both sides. But, as one commentator has pointed out, legal advisers have difficulty in advising their clients on the enforceability of such agreements. Moreover, 'there are dangers in using contact as a weapon in negotiations with birth relatives or in assuming that indirect contact in particular is to be implied for the sake of others, whether or not it is of benefit to the child. Adoption itself necessitates the legal and emotional separation of children from their birth parents, and unless this is acknowledged and internalised, contact may be harmful to all involved.'[1]

Adoption as a child's care plan

Where a child is being looked after by a local authority adoption may be the authority's care plan from the outset, or it may become their plan at a later stage. Adoption is normally selected as the best outcome for the child where the view is taken that the child needs long-term security.[2] While a residence order may in some measure achieve these purposes, only adoption can finalise arrangements for the child's future, prevent further court proceedings and end undesired social work involvement. Adoption may therefore be the most appropriate plan where the child has formed deep psychological attachments to her foster parents and wishes to be a member of their family.[3] Indeed, where the child's need to remain in the security of her foster home is clearly established, a reasonable parent would recognise this and accept that it is a decisive consideration and that it cannot be met by anything less than adoption.[4] Therefore, the parent's consent to adoption, if not forthcoming, may be dispensed with.

The question whether it is for the welfare of a child in care to be adopted is often inextricably linked with the question whether it is in

---

20 *Moving Goalposts* (Social Services Inspectorate, 1995) para 3.3.
1 M Richards, *It feels like someone keeps moving the goal posts – regulating post-adoption contact* (1996) 8 CFLQ 175, at p 179.
2 Directors of social services have been advised that the perception that every effort should be made, and all possibilities exhausted, to try to secure the return of the child to his family, no matter how long this may take, is ill-advised and lacks proper balance. Once it becomes clear that a child can no longer live with his or her birth family, decisions about placing children with permanent families should be made as a matter of priority; see Local Authority Circular, *Adoption – Achieving the Right Balance* LAC(98)20.
3 *Re O (Transracial Adoption: Contact)* [1995] 2 FLR 597. In *Re AB (Adoption: Joint Residence)* [1996] 1 FLR 27, adoption by the child's foster parents, who were unmarried, was considered so important for the child that the court was willing to make an adoption order to the foster father and a joint residence order to him and his partner. The couple had lived together for more than twenty years and brought up two children of their own, and the court was satisfied that theirs was a 'happy, responsible and secure family home in the best sense of those words.'
4 *Re O (Transracial Adoption: Contact)* [1995] 2 FLR 597, at p 609.

his interests to continue to have contact with his parents.[5] Where continued contact is desirable, a long-term foster placement may provide the child with the security he needs without severing the links with his natural family.[6] The determination of whether fostering or adoption will better serve the child's welfare is further complicated by the fact that there are differing views on whether 'open adoption', which allows for some kind of continuing contact between the child and his natural parents, is a desirable outcome. It may not be realistic to think that prospective adopters will be found who will encourage such contact. Some adopters may be prepared to countenance a form of open adoption, but many find continuing parental contact inconsistent with the concept of adoption itself, and they are not willing to offer themselves as adopters unless the arrangement is exclusive. Thus the continuation of parental contact may undermine the adoption process itself because suitable applicants are not forthcoming.[7]

In some cases the question whether a child in care should have contact with his parents is determined at the time when the care order is made. The local authority may take the view that rehabilitation with the parents will not be possible, and that adoption will therefore be the best arrangement for the child, in which case they should state this in their care plan. Where this is the local authority's position they may seek an order authorising them to terminate contact with the parents at the same time as they apply for the care order.[8] Where the children have suffered serious harm, as in *Re N (Minors) (Care Orders: Termination of Parental Conduct)*[9] the court may decide that the case is one which requires 'robust management', and that the interests of the children dictate that there should be an immediate termination of contact. However, in most cases a local authority will initially attempt to rehabilitate a child with his parents. But where attempts at rehabilitation fail, the authority may then conclude that contact should be terminated, their purpose being to end the child's family links so that a closed adoption can be considered as the long-term plan for the child.

In *Re B (Minors) (Care: Contact: Local Authority's Plans)*[10] Butler-Sloss LJ said that:

---

5 Under s 34 of the Children Act 1989 a local authority are under a duty to allow a child reasonable contact with his parents unless a court authorises otherwise; see ch 3.
6 See J Gibbons et al, *Development after Physical Abuse in Early Childhood – a follow up study of children on protection registers* (HMSO, 1995) and the review article which discusses this research by C Edwards, *Are children better off following protective intervention?* (1995) 7 CFLQ 136. Amongst other matters, the research looks at whether children removed from their parents and placed in new families show better life outcomes than those who remain at home.
7 See Butler-Sloss LJ in *Re A (A Minor) (Adoption: Contact)* [1993] 2 FLR 645, at pp 649-650.
8 Children Act 1989, s 34(4).
9 [1994] 2 FCR 1101.
10 [1993] 1 FLR 543, at p 551. See also *L v London Borough of Bromley* [1998] 1 FLR 709 in relation to the child known as A.

> 'The presumption of contact, which has to be for the benefit of the child, has always to be balanced against the long-term welfare of the child and particularly where he will live in the future. Contact must not be allowed to destabilise or endanger the arrangements for the child and in many cases the plans for the child will be decisive of the contact application.'

However, in a significant ruling on the division of responsibility for decision-making between the courts and local authorities, she stated that the denial of contact is a decision for the court and not the local authority, and that a court is not bound to make an order which is consistent with the local authority's plan that the child should be adopted. Where the court takes the view that the benefits of contact outweigh the disadvantages of disrupting the local authority's plan that the child should be adopted it must refuse the authority's application to terminate contact.

This was the position in *Re E (A Minor) (Care Order: Contact)*.[11] The local authority, in an agreed application for a care order, applied at the same time for an order authorising them to refuse the children contact with their parents. Their plan was that contact should gradually be reduced and finally terminated when the children were placed with prospective adoptive parents. However, the guardian ad litem took the view that the children would benefit from continuing face-to-face contact with their parents, and that the parents would not undermine the children's placement whether it was in an adoption setting or a long-term fostering setting. The trial judge held that the court should not make an order which was incompatible with the local authority's care plan unless the children's welfare demanded otherwise. The Court of Appeal, following *Re B (Minors) (Care: Contact: Local Authority's Plans)* ruled that this approach was incorrect, and that the decision to terminate contact was one for the court to make after considering the merits of the application. It held that section 34 of the Children Act 1989 created a strong presumption in favour of continuing parental contact, and that the onus was on the local authority to show why it should be discontinued. It held that it was premature for the court to authorise the termination of contact until the local authority had made some positive efforts to find prospective adopters who would accept some form of parental contact with the children. It added that it was not enough for the local authority to dismiss the likelihood of obtaining suitable adopters who were prepared to entertain an open adoption on the basis that there were none on the register at the time. In relation to the value to the children of continuing parental contact when adoption was planned, Simon Brown LJ said:

> 'Even when the section 31 criteria are satisfied, contact may well be of singular importance to the long-term welfare of the child:

11 [1994] 1 FLR 146.

first, in giving the child the security of knowing that his parents love him and are interested in his welfare; secondly, by avoiding any damaging sense of loss to the child seeing himself abandoned by his parents; thirdly, by enabling the child to commit himself to the substitute family with the seal of approval of the natural parents; and fourthly, by giving the child the necessary sense of personal and family identity. Contact, if maintained, is capable of reinforcing and increasing the chances of success of a permanent placement, whether on a long-term fostering basis or by adoption.'[12]

Where the parents will not agree to the child being adopted and wish to maintain contact, difficulty sometimes arises as to how the matter should proceed. Should the authority take steps to free the child for adoption and seek an order dispensing with the parents' agreement, or should they first apply for an order authorising the termination of contact? In *Re E (Minors) (Adoption: Parental Agreement)*[13] the Court of Appeal held that until the question of contact had been decided it was premature to issue a freeing application. This approach was reaffirmed in *Re C (Minors) (Adoption)*[14] in which Balcombe LJ stated 'with all the emphasis at our command' that where children are in care, but are enjoying beneficial contact with a parent, it is premature to make an application for a freeing order until the issue of contact is first determined. He further stated that it is wholly inappropriate to assert that a parent who seeks to continue such contact at the date of the freeing application is unreasonably withholding her agreement to an order freeing the child for adoption. Subsequently Butler-Sloss LJ in *Re A (A Minor) (Adoption: Contact)*[15] held that these cases have been overtaken now that it is possible under the Children Act 1989 to attach a contact order to a freeing order. However, the sentiments expressed in the cases on the association between contact and the appropriateness of adoption continue to be applicable. Procedurally it is now deemed to be appropriate for a freeing application to be heard concurrently with an application to terminate contact.[16]

---

12 Ibid, at pp 154-155. It is unclear how far these assertions by Simon Brown LJ are supported by empirical studies. See the differing views of M Ryburn *In whose best interests? – post-adoption contact with the birth family* (1998) 10 CFLQ 53 and D Quinton, J Selwyn, A Rushton and C Dance, *Contact with birth parents in adoption – a response to Ryburn* (1998) 10 CFLQ 349. For a review of research findings relating to adoption, see the analysis by J Thoburn in *The Review of Adoption Law* (DOH, 1992) appendix C.

13 [1990] 2 FLR 397.

14 [1992] 1 FLR 115.

15 [1993] 2 FLR 645.

16 In *G v G (Adoption: Concurrent Applications)* [1993] 2 FLR 306 Cazalet J, following *Re G (A Minor) (Adoption and Access Applications)* [1980] FLR 109, held that where there were competing contact and adoption applications both applications should be heard concurrently so that all available options were open to the court when it was making its decision as to what the child's welfare required. The case concerned an application by a mother and step-father to adopt, and where the unmarried father sought contact.

Children in care and dispensing with agreement

It can be seen from the above analysis that the question whether it is in the interests of a child in care to continue to have contact with his parents is highly relevant when a court is determining whether it is reasonable for a parent to refuse to agree to the child's adoption. In *Re H; Re W (Adoption: Parental Agreement)*[17] Purchas LJ said that the chances of a successful reintroduction to, or continuance of contact with, the natural parent is a critical factor in assessing the reaction of the hypothetical reasonable parent.[18] In *Re E (Minors) (Adoption: Parental Agreement)*[19] a mother of children in care had done everything within her limited power to preserve contact with her children. However, the local authority terminated contact and the magistrates' court adjourned the mother's contact application pending the outcome of the local authority's application to free the children for adoption.[20] The Court of Appeal held that the mother was not unreasonable if she withheld her agreement to her children being freed for adoption until issues relating to contact had been resolved, and until she had had a proper opportunity to demonstrate that continuing contact with her children would benefit them. It was further held that since the prospective adopters had stated that they would not abandon the children if they could not adopt them that this was also a factor which a reasonable parent could take into account. A similar approach to contact was taken by the Court of Appeal in *Re C (Minors) (Adoption)*.[1] It held that where a child in care was enjoying beneficial contact with a parent it was wholly inappropriate to assert that a parent who was showing a keen interest in continuing having such contact at the date of the freeing application was unreasonably withholding his agreement. In *Re E (A Minor) (Adoption)*[2] a mother of a child in care refused to agree to her child's adoption because his elder brother was devoted to him and had regular contact with him. The Court of Appeal held that was not being unreasonable. As Balcombe LJ said 'she may have been wrong, she may have been mistaken, but she was not unreasonable'.

In *Re A (A Minor) (Adoption: Contact)*[3] the Court of Appeal took a fresh look at the reasonableness of a parent's refusal to agree to a freeing application made in respect of her child in care in the light of changes in

---

17 (1983) 4 FLR 614.
18 See also, *Re E (Adoption: Freeing Order)* [1995] 1 FLR 382 where there was very strong evidence supportive of adoption, and where, were the mother to have contact, it was clear that she would destabilise the child's placement. The mother's refusal of consent was therefore found to be unreasonable.
19 [1990] 2 FLR 397.
20 The mother's application was made under s 12C of the Child Care Act 1980, which preceded the Children Act 1989. It is not clear whether a local authority can continue to refuse contact under s 34(6) of the Children Act 1989 once an application is pending in the court.
1 [1992] 1 FLR 115.
2 [1989] 1 FLR 126.
3 [1993] 2 FLR 645.

the law brought about by the Children Act 1989. Applications had been made by the local authority for a freeing order and for leave to terminate contact between the child and his mother.[4] Both applications were heard together. At the hearing the guardian ad litem advised the judge that the child should be freed for adoption, but that continuing contact between the child and his mother and other family members was in the child's best interests. The judge found that there was no prospect of the child being rehabilitated with his natural family, that long-term fostering was a less suitable option for the child than adoption, and that adoption would still be in the child's best interests even if the adopters chosen for him could not tolerate any contact with the mother. He found that a reasonable mother would recognise that adoption was the right decision for her son and he therefore made an order freeing the child for adoption, and dispensed with the mother's agreement on the grounds that it was being unreasonably withheld. However, in addition he exercised powers under section 8 of the Children Act 1989 to order that the child should have monthly contact with his mother until the adoption took place.

The mother appealed against the freeing order arguing that continuing substantial contact and freeing were inconsistent and therefore that her refusal to agree to the freeing application was reasonable. The Court of Appeal held that since the implementation of the Children Act 1989 a court has the opportunity not only to free a child for adoption, but also to preserve contact between the child and his natural family pending adoption by making a contact order under section 8. It therefore held that all issues relating to contact did not have to be resolved before a freeing order was made, and that the judge had been correct to dispense with the mother's agreement. Butler-Sloss LJ made it clear that the contact order would not survive the making of an adoption order, but stated that, in theory at least, a section 8 contact order could be imposed on the adopters when the adoption order was made.[5] She added that in the adoption proceedings, although the mother would no longer have parental responsibility she would have the right to be heard on whether she should have continuing contact after the adoption order was made.

It is suggested that the decision in *Re A (A Minor) (Adoption: Contact)* to use Children Act 1989 powers to make a contact order in freeing proceedings, when the local authority did not already have potential adopters who were prepared to enter into an open adoption, did little to promote the welfare of the child. Indeed the contact order appears to have been positively counter-productive in furthering the adoption plans for the child. The general principle enshrined in section 1(2) of the Children Act 1989 is that any delay in determining a question about a child's

4   The father too was involved, but the issues taken on appeal concerned the mother only.
5   She said that this would be an alternative to making an adoption order with conditions under s 16 of the Adoption Act 1976. However, she foresaw dangers in different judges being involved in future applications concerning the adoption and the continuance of contact, and said that steps should be taken to guard against different courts arriving at different decisions.

upbringing is likely to prejudice the welfare of the child. In the case of a young child who needs to form permanent attachments as soon as possible, such delay may be extremely damaging.[6] Yet eight months after the freeing order a suitable adoptive family had not been found for the child, and evidence was given that this was because of the effect of the contact order on the willingness of prospective adopters to put themselves forward. Sections 18(5) and 12(3)(a) of the Adoption Act 1976 state that parental responsibility is given to the adoption agency on a freeing order being made, and that the order operates to extinguish the parental responsibility which any person has for the child immediately before the order was made. It is suggested that for a court to free a child for adoption and at the same time to make a contact order under section 8 should normally be regarded as being inconsistent with these provisions unless it knows that there are adopters who are willing to accept the child on these terms.

A similar problem arose in *Re P (Adoption: Freeing Order)*[7] where the trial judge combined a freeing order, in which he dispensed with the mother's agreement, with a contact order. However, the case differed from *Re A (A Minor) (Adoption: Contact)* because the judge not only found that it was in the interests of the children for contact with their mother to continue but, crucially, he also found that the mother would not be unreasonable in withholding her agreement to the adoption if it meant that she would lose contact with her children. Allowing the mother's appeal against the freeing order, Butler-Sloss LJ held that a court cannot guarantee that adoption with contact will be possible at the time that it makes a freeing order. She therefore held that the judge had been wrong to dispense with the mother's agreement where he had concluded that he did not have grounds to do so unless contact would continue. She said that the judge had:

> '... fallen between two stools in not saying either "adoption in any event although contact is highly desirable", or leave it to the adoption application where the mother can fight her corner as to whether or not at that stage the adopters should be accepting contact or there should not be an adoption order.'[8]

Thus it is clear from *Re P (Adoption: Freeing Order)* that a court should not free a child for adoption against the wishes of the parent where it takes the view that adoption should only be authorised on the condition that contact with the parent continues to take place. Moreover, as Butler-Sloss LJ pointed out, the effect of the freeing order had been to tie the local authority's hands as to the persons they could select as adopters for the children. Although optimism had been expressed at the original hearing that suitable adopters would be forthcoming, seven months after the judge's order such adopters had not been found. The ruling also

6   In *Re A (A Minor) (Adoption: Contact)* the child concerned was three.
7   [1994] 2 FLR 1000.
8   Ibid, at p 1004.

illustrates the difficulties faced by local authorities when planning for children in care. The Court of Appeal recognised that the children were difficult to place for adoption because there was a history of serious mental illness in the family. It also recognised that adopters might be found for the children who could accept the risk of the children developing mental illness, but who would not be able to tolerate continuing contact with the mother. But, in a case of this kind, unless a court makes an unconditional freeing order, the decision whether contact is more important than adoption is delayed until the application to adopt is made. This in itself may make it difficult to obtain prospective adopters for children who are continuing to have contact with their natural parents. Adopters may not be prepared to put themselves forward unless they are satisfied that questions relating to consent, and to contact, have been resolved. Yet, at the same time, it may be in the interests of the children to have contact with their natural mother until an alternative family is found, and perhaps after it has been found. However, a parent may not be unreasonable in withholding her agreement to adoption unless and until such an alternative family is found. Thus the problem can become circular, and identifying at which point the circle should be broken may be an extremely difficult decision to make.

This chapter has revealed that stating that the welfare of the child should be treated as the court's paramount consideration (or its first consideration in adoption cases) is easy, but that determining how to give effect to those principles is infinitely more complex. The resolution of children cases in a manner which secures that children are given the opportunity to develop into secure, confident, well-balanced and happy adults is a formidable task. It can sometimes demand a degree of wisdom and foresight with which the best-intentioned of decision-makers, and those who advise them, are not necessarily endowed. Indeed, and sadly, the realistic dilemma which often faces parents, social workers, judges and other decision-makers is not whether the proposed outcome of the case will give paramountcy to the child's welfare, but which of the available options represents the least detrimental choice for the child.

Chapter 5

International child abduction

Chapter 5

International child abduction

The law's response to international child abduction

When a marriage between persons of different nationalities breaks down the adult who is living in the 'foreign' country may wish to return to his or her country and to take the children as well. It has been seen already that it is an offence for a child to be taken from the United Kingdom for more than a month without either the consent of all persons with parental responsibility or the leave of the court.[1] However, this provision may not deter a determined parent from leaving the United Kingdom with the children. Equally, a British citizen who is living in a foreign country may return to this country with his or her children in breach of that country's domestic laws. Or a parent may agree to a child spending time in a foreign country with the intention that the child's stay should be temporary only. But when the time comes for the child to return to his country of habitual residence, the persons looking after the child in the foreign country may retain him there. The United Kingdom is a signatory to two international Conventions which are designed to achieve a common response to cases of this nature where a child is wrongfully removed or retained. The Child Abduction and Custody Act 1985 gives force of law to both the Convention on the Civil Aspects of International Child Abduction, hereinafter referred to as the 'Hague Convention', and the European Convention on Recognition and Enforcement of Decisions concerning Custody of Children and on the Restoration of Custody of Children, hereinafter referred to as the 'European Convention'. The purpose of the Hague Convention is to secure the prompt return of children wrongfully removed or retained in any Contracting State; and to ensure that any dispute over custody rights takes place in the State where the child had his habitual residence prior to his removal. The purpose of the European Convention is to secure the recognition or enforcement of judgments concerning custody of children and it only applies where there has been a court order. Where both

---

1   Child Abduction Act 1984, s 1.

Conventions apply, an application under the Hague Convention takes precedence over one made under the European Convention.[2]

The Hague Convention

The philosophy informing the Hague Convention is contained in Article 1 which provides that its objects are:
'(a) to secure the prompt return of children wrongfully removed to or retained in any Contracting State, and
(b) to ensure that rights of custody and access under the law of one Contracting State are effectively recognised in other Contracting States.'

With this purpose in mind, each contracting state has established a central authority which is charged with the duty to take measures to secure the prompt return of children and to achieve the other objects of the Convention.[3] Thus if, for example, a child has been wrongfully removed from England, a request for assistance can be made to the central authority for England and Wales. The authority will approach the central authority of the country to which the child has been taken and that authority should take steps to secure the child's immediate return to England. Alternatively, an approach may be made directly to the central authority of the country to which the child has been taken. Similarly, if a child is retained in England in breach of the Convention, the central authority for England and Wales will take steps to secure the return of the child to the country in which the child was habitually resident before the wrongful retention.[4]

Article 3 provides that:

'The removal or retention of a child is to be considered wrongful where—
(a) it is in breach of rights of custody attributed to a person, an institution or any other body, either jointly or alone, under the law of the State in which the child was habitually resident immediately before the removal or retention; and
(b) at the time of removal or retention those rights were actually exercised, either jointly or alone, or would have been so exercised but for the removal or retention.

The rights of custody mentioned in sub-paragraph (a) above may arise in particular by operation of law or by reason of a judicial or

2   Child Abduction and Custody Act 1985, s 16(4)(c), and see *Re R (Abduction: Hague / European Convention)* [1997] 1 FLR 663.
3   Art 7. A list of signatories to the Convention can be found in the Child Abduction and Custody (Parties to Conventions Order) 1986 (SI 1986/1159). This has been amended as new States have become signatories; see, for example, SI 1998/256.
4   For an account of changes in the pattern of abductions, and how foreign jurisdictions, as well as the English courts, have applied the Convention, see D McClean, *International child abduction – some recent trends* (1997) 4 CFLQ 387.

administrative decision, or by reason of an agreement having legal effect under the law of that State.'

Article 5(a) provides that:

'... rights of custody' shall include rights relating to the care of the person of the child and, in particular, the right to determine the child's place of residence.'

'Rights of custody'

An English court must look to the law of the country in which the child was habitually resident immediately before the removal or retention to determine whether the case before it is in breach of 'rights of custody'. The key concepts which determine the scope of the Convention are not dependent for their meaning on any single legal system. Thus the expression 'rights of custody' does not coincide with any particular concept of custody in domestic law, but draws its meaning from the definition, structure and purposes of the Convention.[5] It is for the requested state to determine whether such rights amount to 'rights of custody',[6] and whether they were being 'exercised'.[7] Where the abduction violates an existing court order there is no difficulty in establishing breach of rights of custody. However, a child may be taken abroad before any order has been made, or it may not be customary to make court orders about children at the time of marriage or relationship breakdown,[8] or the parents may be unmarried and the father may not have any rights unless, or until, they are granted by court order. In each of these circumstances there may be difficulty in establishing a breach of Article 3. Unless there is such a breach, the court does not have jurisdiction under the Convention to order the child's return to the requesting state.[9]

The leading case on 'rights of custody' is the House of Lords' ruling in *Re J (A Minor) (Abduction: Custody Rights)*.[10] The mother and father were

---

5   *Conclusion of the second meeting of the Special Commission to discuss the operation of the Convention, 1993.* See also, Vienna Convention of the Law of Treaties, Art 31(1), 'a treaty shall be interpreted in good faith in accordance with the ordinary meaning to be given to the terms of the treaty in their context and in the light of its object and purpose'.

6   It may be assisted in this where a decision or other determination is made pursuant to Art 15 in the country of the child's habitual residence that the child's removal or retention was wrongful. However, such a decision is not determinative, but is provisional only: *Re P (Abduction: Declaration)* [1995] 1 FLR 831.

7   The purpose of this provision is to prevent applications succeeding where the person with such rights does not make use of them.

8   As is the position in England in the light of the Children Act 1989, s 1(5).

9   It may, however, be able to order the return of the child relying on common law principles: see below.

10 [1990] 2 AC 562.

not married and lived together with their child in Australia. The mother brought the child to England. After she left, the father obtained an order in the Family Court of Western Australia giving him sole custody and guardianship of the child. Although the father had been sharing de facto custody of the child, when the mother took the child from Australia she alone had the legal rights of custody under Western Australian law.[11] The House of Lords held that the father had no legal rights of custody at the time that the child was removed and therefore that the mother had not unlawfully removed the child for the purposes of the Convention. Moreover, the child's retention outside the jurisdiction had not been wrongful either, because the mother had come to England with the settled intention of remaining here, and therefore the child had ceased to be habitually resident in Australia before the order conferring custodial rights on the father had been made.[12]

This strict ruling on when 'rights of custody' can be claimed was ameliorated to some extent by the Court of Appeal's decision in *Re B (A Minor) (Abduction)*.[13] The crucial point for determination was whether the father had 'rights of custody' at the date of the child's removal from Australia. Under Australian law he had no parental rights at the time of the child's removal, and no order by a court had yet been made in his favour. However, he had looked after the child over a period of time. On its face, therefore, the father's legal position appeared identical to that of the father in *Re J (A Minor) (Abduction: Custody Rights)*. None the less the Court of Appeal ruled, by a majority, that *Re B (A Minor) (Abduction)* was distinguishable.[14] It stated that the issue to be determined was whether the concept of 'rights of custody' was confined to rights propounded by law or conferred by court order, or whether the concept was capable of describing the inchoate rights of a person who had been acting as a parent without the benefit of either official status or a court order. The Court of Appeal held that the authorities established that the Convention must be construed broadly as an international agreement according to its general tenor and purpose, without attributing to any of its terms a specialist meaning which the word, or words, in question may have acquired under the domestic law of England.[15] It ruled that where, before the child's abduction, the aggrieved parent was exercising parental functions in the requesting state, it must in every case be a question for the court of the requested state to determine whether these amounted to 'rights of custody'

11 Family Law Act of Western Australia 1975-1979, s 35.
12 See below for a discussion of habitual residence.
13 [1994] 2 FLR 249.
14 Waite and Staughton LJJ; Peter Gibson LJ dissenting. In his view the House of Lords had insisted on legal rights of custody being violated, and the father only had de facto rights of custody at the time of the child's removal. D McClean, *International child abduction – some recent trends* (1997) 4 CFLQ 387 at p 390 comments 'it is difficult not to agree with that analysis'.
15 See *Re C (A Minor) (Abduction)* [1989] 1 FLR 403; *Re J (A Minor) (Abduction: Custody Rights)* [1990] 2 AC 562.

within the terms of the Convention.[16] The majority concluded that the expression 'rights of custody' should be construed in the sense which would best accord with the purpose of the Convention and that 'in most cases this will involve giving the term the widest sense possible.'[17] They therefore held that inchoate rights could properly be called 'rights of custody' in the Convention sense in those cases where a court in the requesting state would be likely to uphold them in the interests of the child concerned, at least to the point of not allowing them to be disturbed without due opportunity to consider issues relating to the child's welfare.[18]

Re B (A Minor) (Abduction)[19] and the subsequent decision of *Re O (Child Abduction: Custody Rights)*[20] are difficult to reconcile with the House of Lords' ruling in *Re J (A Minor) (Abduction: Custody Rights)*[1] that de facto joint custody was not enough to give rise to 'rights of custody'.[2] It was undoubtedly significant that in *Re B (A Minor) (Abduction)* an agreement relating to custody was about to be perfected, and in *Re O (Child Abduction: Custody Rights)* custody proceedings were pending. However, even without these features, these rulings expanded the English concept of 'rights of custody' to include more than strictly legal rights. A purposive approach to the Convention was adopted, the courts taking the view that children who were already suffering distress and disruption should be spared from suffering the further distress and disruption which would be caused by their arbitrary removal from their settled environment and the persons who had been looking after them for a considerable period of time.[3]

The outcome of these decisions is to be welcomed. Families care for children in various ways and the primary carer of a child may not enjoy the strict legal right to do so. Unmarried fathers are particularly vulnerable to falling outside a narrow and legalistic definition of 'rights of custody'. It must surely be right that where, as in *Re B (A Minor)*

---

16 Waite LJ gave as examples, at one end of the scale a transient cohabitee of the sole custodial parent whose status and functions would be unlikely to qualify for recognition as 'rights of custody' within the terms of the Convention, and at the other a relative or friend who had assumed the role of a substitute parent in place of the legal custodian, where the opposite would be true.

17 Per Waite LJ, [1994] 2 FLR 249, at p 261.

18 And see the crucial wording in the last paragraph of Art 3, which Waite and Staughton LJJ did not explicitly discuss, but the generous interpretation of which was implicit in their judgments. In relation to whether the father had 'consented' to the child's removal, the court found that it was not a true consent because it had been obtained by a cruel deceit. This case was followed by Cazalet J in *Re O (Child Abduction: Custody Rights)* [1997] 2 FLR 702.

19 [1994] 2 FLR 249.

20 [1997] 2 FLR 702. This case concerned maternal grandparents who had exercised full parental responsibilities for the child for a considerable period of time.

1 [1990] 2 AC 562.

2 See too, *Re W; Re B (Child Abduction: Unmarried Father)* [1998] 2 FLR 146, at p 155, where Hale J stated that she had difficulty in reconciling the decision in *Re B (A Minor) (Abduction)* with *Re J (A Minor) (Abduction: Custody Rights)*, 'even though I recognise that the merits in *Re B* were all on the father's side'.

3 See particularly, Waite LJ in *Re B (A Minor) (Abduction)* [1994] 2 FLR 249, at p 260.

(Abduction), a father had looked after his child for some considerable period, or where, as in *Re O (Child Abduction: Custody Rights)*, a grandmother was caring for the child on a daily basis, the mother playing no part except for short periods of contact, that such examples of de facto exercise of parental responsibility should be treated as 'rights of custody' for Convention purposes.[4] Any other view means that the very many children who live in homes which do not conform with conventional norms would automatically fall outside the Convention's protective scope.[5]

The position of English unmarried fathers

Under English law, an unmarried father does not have automatic parental responsibility for his child.[6] Accordingly, an unmarried father's consent is not necessary to authorise any removal of his child from England unless or until he obtains parental responsibility.[7] Because applications involving unmarried fathers whose children have been taken from England by their mothers raise particular difficulties, an attempt to clarify their position was made in a *Practice Note* issued in 1998.[8] This was followed by *Re W; Re B (Child Abduction: Unmarried Father)*.[9] In these two cases two unmarried fathers sought declarations under Article 15 of the Convention that the removal of their children was wrongful within the meaning of Article 3. The cases were heard together by Hale J. Under English domestic law it was clear that at the time when each child was removed from the jurisdiction there was nothing preventing their mothers from taking this action,[10] and it is clear that it is not the intention of the Convention that every child who is removed from his country of habitual residence without the consent of both

---

4 The child in *Re B (A Minor) (Abduction)* was, of course, from Australia and therefore the court was concerned with how the law of Western Australia should be interpreted under the Convention, not English law. However, the rights given by the domestic law in both countries appear to be virtually identical.

5 For a helpful discussion of the policy of the law, the role of courts and the impact of the European Convention of Human Rights on domestic law as it applies to unmarried fathers, and the effect of these considerations on how the Convention should be applied, see *Re W; Re B (Child Abduction: Unmarried Fathers)* [1998] 2 FLR 146, at pp 163-168, per Hale J.

6 An unmarried father acquires parental responsibility either by making a formal agreement to this effect with the mother, or by obtaining an order conferring parental responsibility under provisions of the Children Act 1989: see ch 1. Clearly, where an unmarried father has acquired parental responsibility by agreement or court order, whether interim or final, he has 'rights of custody'.

7 Children Act 1989, s 13(1); Child Abduction Act 1994, s 1(1)(3).

8 *Practice Note: Hague Convention: Application by Fathers without Parental Responsibility* [1998] 1 FLR 491.

9 [1998] 2 FLR 146.

10 Neither father had parental responsibility at the time of their children's removal, nor was any court order in force prohibiting their removal.

parents, or the court's leave, is to be summarily returned.[11] It was none the less argued on behalf of both fathers that the removal of the children was in breach of their 'rights of custody'.

In Hale J's judgment, neither father had 'rights of custody' which had been breached. She emphasised that there is a substantial difference between having rights of custody and rights of access. The latter give no remedy of speedy return of the child to his country of habitual residence.[12] Rights of access are protected under Article 21, which is limited to providing remedies to organise and secure their effective exercise in the country in which the children are living. Of course, it is often the case that applications under Article 3 are made by married or divorced parents who, in practice, are exercising rights of access only, the abducting parent being the primary carer. But under English law married and divorced parents have parental responsibility and therefore have the right to veto their child's removal to another country. Thus, for Convention purposes they enjoy 'rights of custody'. Unmarried fathers do not have this right of veto, and unless and until a court orders otherwise, what rights they have are rights of access only.[13] The two concepts are distinct.

All may not be lost, however, for an unmarried father (or other applicant) who, as a matter of law, does not have rights of custody.[14] Where litigation concerning the child's upbringing is pending and the child is removed without the court's leave, this may amount to a breach of the rights of custody of the court for Convention purposes.[15] The mere issue of proceedings is not sufficient to establish interference with the court's rights of custody.[16] Nor does the existence of a court order automatically clothe the court with rights of custody.[17] However, Hale J ruled in *Re W; Re B (Child Abduction: Unmarried Father)* that where the court was actively seised of relevant proceedings concerning the child, removal of the child from the jurisdiction without the court's leave was in breach of the court's rights of custody because the court had the right to determine the child's place of residence.[18] The mother in *Re W* had given no hint that she was

---

11 *Explanatory Report on the Convention*, by Professor Perez-Vera.
12 Under Art 12, see below.
13 *Re B (Abduction) (Rights of Custody)* [1997] 2 FLR 594.
14 Including where he is the primary carer and therefore has inchoate rights, as in *Re B (A Minor) (Abduction)* [1994] 2 FLR 249.
15 Art 3 is not only concerned with the rights of individuals, it also covers the rights of custody of 'an institution or any other body' which arise by 'operation of law or by reason of a judicial or administrative decision'.
16 Cf *C v C (Minors) (Child Abduction)* [1992] 1 FLR 163.
17 *Re F (Child Abduction: Risk if Returned)* [1995] 2 FLR 31, at p 36. (In that case, however, the abducting mother was in breach of the father's rights of custody.)
18 Art 5(a). Relevant proceedings include proceedings for residence, parental responsibility or to prohibit removal of the child, as these are 'rights of custody' under the Convention, and 'it may be that they should extend to any proceedings for an order relating to the child' [1998] 2 FLR 146, at p 162. See also *B v B (Abduction)* [1993] 1 FLR 238, where removal of a child by a mother from Canada to England was held to be in breach of an Ontario court's rights of custody. There were pending custody proceedings in which the

actively considering leaving the country and had gone out of her way to frustrate the process of the court. A declaration was therefore made that the child's removal had been wrongful.[19] By contrast, the father in the *Re B* case had never applied for a parental responsibility order, and orders prohibiting the removal of the child from the jurisdiction had been discharged. The proceedings between the parents had been concluded and a final determination of the mother's custody rights had been made. Therefore, there was nothing to prevent her taking the child abroad or changing her habitual residence should she choose to do so.

The *Practice Note*[20] details those situations where the Child Abduction Unit (which undertakes the duties of the Central Authority for England and Wales) takes the view that removal by a mother with sole parental responsibility is in breach of a court's rights of custody. The Child Abduction Unit does not support the view that once the court becomes actively seised of any family proceedings the court has rights of custody for Convention purposes merely because it has own motion powers to make residence orders. The Unit operates on the basis that an application for a residence order involves the court's rights of custody because it invokes the court's powers to determine the child's place of residence. It takes the same view about an application for an order restraining removal of a child from the jurisdiction.[1] However, the *Practice Note* states that 'an application for a parental responsibility order ... does not require the court to determine the child's place of residence, and thus would not involve an exercise by the courts of rights of custody within the meaning of the Convention'.[2] It is suggested that this is a very narrow view of how the concept of parental responsibility ties in with 'rights of custody' for Convention purposes. A parental responsibility order confers on a father all the rights of a married father, including the right to veto his child's removal from the jurisdiction. The notion that there is a significant distinction between an application for a residence or prohibited steps order and an application for a parental responsibility order fails to acknowledge that a parental responsibility order may have a marked impact on the right of the child's mother to reach unilateral decisions about her child's upbringing, including the child's place of residence.

Another possibility which may be open to an applicant who lacks rights of custody at the time of the initial removal is to claim that the child's retention in the country to which he has been taken has become unlawful. Wrongful removal and wrongful retention are distinct and mutually

---

Ontario court had already made orders giving interim custody to the mother and access to the father. Summary return was ordered despite the fact that the mother had interim custody when she removed the child, because the final determination of where the child should live was a matter for the Ontario court.

19 Art 15.
20 [1998] 1 FLR 491.
1   This would normally be a prohibited steps order; and see *Re C (A Minor) (Abduction)* [1989] 1 FLR 403.
2   [1998] 1 FLR 491, at p 493.

exclusive concepts.[3] What is initially a lawful removal may become a wrongful retention, for example, where a parent agrees to his child going abroad for a visit for a specific period and where the person caring for the child refuses to return him home when that time expires. Where an applicant acquires 'rights of custody' by court order after the child's lawful removal and demands the child's summary return, the retention may instantly become wrongful. This is what occurred in *Re S (Custody: Habitual Residence).*[4] A child of unmarried parents was taken to Ireland by his grandmother immediately after the death of his mother. An originating summons to make the child a ward of court was issued on behalf of the father. Wall J gave interim care and control to the father and ordered that the child be returned to the jurisdiction. The House of Lords ruled that as a result of Wall J's order the father acquired rights of custody within the meaning of Articles 3 and 5 of the Convention, and the child's retention in Ireland thenceforth became wrongful.

How did the situation in *Re S (Custody: Habitual Residence)* differ from that in *Re J (A Minor) (Abduction: Custody Rights)*[5] where, after the child had lawfully been removed from Australia by his mother and brought to England, the father was awarded sole custody rights by an Australian court, but where the House of Lords held that there was no wrongful retention? The critical difference between the cases was that in *Re S (Custody: Habitual Residence)* the child remained habitually resident in England at the time of Wall J's order and thus the retention in Ireland was wrongful, whereas in *Re J (A Minor) (Abduction: Custody Rights)* the child had ceased to be habitually resident in Australia at the time of the Australian court's order giving custody to his father, and as a result the child's retention in England was lawful.[6]

'Habitual residence'

It can be seen from the contrast between the above House of Lords' decisions that 'habitual residence' is a key concept for the purposes of the Convention.[7] The place of a child's habitual residence is a question of fact

---

3   *Re H (Minors) (Abduction: Custody Rights)* [1991] 2 AC 476. But both can occur on the facts in relation to the same child at different times, *Re S (Custody: Habitual Residence)* [1998] 1 FLR 122.

4   [1998] 1 FLR 122.

5   [1990] 2 AC 562.

6   See also *Re B-M (Wardship Jurisdiction)* [1993] 1 FLR 979 where even if the removal was not unlawful the retention was wrongful when the mother failed to return the child in accordance with orders of the English court, the child having been habitually resident in England at the time the wardship proceedings began.

7   Art 3 revolves around the law of the state in which the child was habitually resident immediately before the removal or retention. Art 4 states: 'The Convention shall apply to any child who was habitually resident in a contracting State immediately before any breach of custody or access rights.' The Convention ceases to apply once the child reaches 16.

and, as with the other expressions in the Convention, is to be understood according to the ordinary and natural meaning of the words.[8] In *Re J (A Minor) (Abduction: Custody Rights)*[9] the child's retention in England would only be wrongful where it was in breach of the rights of custody 'under the law of the state in which the child was habitually resident immediately before ... the retention'. The issue for the House of Lords, therefore, was whether the child's habitual residence had ceased to be in Australia during the three weeks that had elapsed between his mother lawfully bringing him to England and his father obtaining an order for custody and guardianship in the Australian court.[10] It was clear from the evidence that when the mother removed the child she had a settled intention of residing in England on a long-term basis. Their Lordships stated that there was a significant difference between a person ceasing to be habitually resident in a country and acquiring habitual residence in a new country. A person can lose habitual residence 'in a single day' when he or she leaves with the settled intention not to return. However, habitual residence cannot be acquired in a day. 'An appreciable period of time and a settled intention will be necessary to enable him or her to become [habitually resident].'[11] As the mother had ceased to be habitually resident in Australia as soon as she left with the child there was never any wrongful retention of him in England within the meaning of Article 3.

In *Re S (Custody: Habitual Residence)*[12] the House of Lords held that where the person removing the child did not have parental responsibility for him, such removal could not extinguish the child's existing habitual residence and create a new habitual residence for him in the country to which he was taken.[13] Nor did ex parte orders made by a foreign court, giving custody to the person who had taken the child, have the effect of depriving the child of his habitual residence in England.

When married parents are living together the habitual residence of their young children is the same of that of the parents themselves. Neither parent may change a child's habitual residence unilaterally.[14] However, where parents agree to change a child's habitual residence, it does not require the continued agreement of both parents to make that situation

8   *Re J (A Minor) (Abduction: Custody Rights)* [1990] 2 AC 562.
9   [1990] 2 AC 962.
10 It was *not* whether the child had become habitually resident in England before the Australian court order was made.
11 Ibid, per Lord Brandon, at p 578. During that period of time a person will not be habitually resident in either country. See also *Re M (Minors) (Residence Order: Jurisdiction)* [1993] 1 FLR 495; *Re A (Abduction: Habitual Residence)* [1996] 1 FLR 1.
12 [1998] 1 FLR 122.
13 It was also held that the power conferred by s 3(5) of the Children Act 1989 on a person without parental responsibility to do what is reasonable in all the circumstances for the purpose of safeguarding and promoting the child's welfare did not include the power to change the child's habitual residence merely by taking him out of the country.
14 *Re A (Wardship Jurisdiction)* [1995] 1 FLR 1. It was open to parents to change their child's habitual residence without changing their own, but an agreement to send the child to a boarding school abroad was not sufficient.

continue.[15] The parents' habitual residence is 'their abode in a particular place or country which they have adopted voluntarily and for settled purposes as part of the regular order of their life for the time being whether of short or long duration'.[16] In *Re J (A Minor) (Abduction: Custody Rights)*[17] the House of Lords refrained from indicating what an 'appreciable period of time' would be for the purposes of acquiring a new place of habitual residence. Subsequently, Waite J has said 'logic would suggest that provided the purpose was settled, the period of habituation need not be long';[18] the Court of Appeal has approved a finding that a family had acquired a fresh habitual residence only one month after arrival in a new country;[19] and Stuart White J has said, obiter, that the three weeks a child had spent in Greece was not sufficient time in the circumstances of the case for his residence to have borne the characteristic of being habitual.[20]

It is suggested, therefore, that the obiter dictum by Lord Slynn in *Re S (Custody: Habitual Residence)*[1] that where a parent with parental rights 'leaves one country to go to the other with the established intention of settling there permanently her habitual residence and that of the child may change very quickly' should be treated with caution. Acquisition of habitual residence should not, of course, be confused with acquisition of a domicile of choice. Habitual residence does not require a combination of residence and the intention that it should be permanent or indefinite. However, in so far as Lord Slynn's statement implies that a young child in the sole lawful custody of a parent acquires habitual residence in the new country almost instantaneously, it does appear to ignore the ordinary and natural meaning of the word 'habitual'.

Article 12 – Peremptory return

Where a court is satisfied that the case before it is a Convention case then, under the provisions of Article 12, it *must* order the return of the child forthwith provided that the application was brought within twelve months of the child's unlawful removal or retention. The essence of the

---

15 *Re M (Abduction: Habitual Residence)* [1996] 1 FLR 887. 'The idea that a child's residence can be changed without his ever leaving the country where he is resident is to abandon the factual basis of habitual residence and to clothe it with some metaphysical or abstract basis more appropriate to a legal concept such as domicile', at p 895, per Sir John Balcombe, disapproving dicta to the contrary by Hale J in *Re A (Wardship Jurisdiction)* above.

16 *Re B (Minors) (Abduction) (No 2)* [1993] 1 FLR 993.

17 [1990] 2 AC 562.

18 *Re B (Minors) (Abduction) (No 2)* [1993] 1 FLR 993, at p 995.

19 *Re F (A Minor) (Child Abduction)* [1992] 1 FLR 548. See also, *Re A (Abduction: Habitual Residence)* [1996] 1 FLR 1, where the children and their mother had acquired habitual residence in Iceland because the father had been posted to a naval base there.

20 *Re A (Abduction: Habitual Residence)* [1998] 1 FLR 497, at p 505.

1 [1998] 1 FLR 122, at p 127.

jurisdiction is peremptory, as distinct from the child eventually being returned following a more detailed investigation of his future by negotiated agreement or court order.[2] The English court must cede the jurisdiction to hear the merits of the case to the country of the child's habitual residence in the interests of international co-operation and comity, in order to deter other parents from abducting their children, and in order to minimise the effect an abduction has on a child. The Convention is built on the assumption that the courts of all of its signatories are equally capable of handling the case, and that they will apply proper procedures and principles to its resolution. Arguments that peremptory return may be against the best interests of the particular child concerned are therefore to no avail.[3]

The date when a child was wrongfully removed is a question of fact, and it may be crucial for the purpose of calculating whether twelve months had elapsed before proceedings under the Convention were initiated. In *Re S (Child Abduction: Delay)*[4] a child was wrongfully removed from Germany, but three months later returned to Germany for three days before again being removed. Wall J ruled that wrongful removal is not a continuing state of affairs, and that as the child had remained habitually resident in Germany throughout, her second removal was a second wrongful removal on which the wronged parent could rely and from which time started to run.[5]

Once twelve months have elapsed, the question of which court should determine the child's future upbringing does not disappear. Article 12 further provides that the court must order the return of the child even where proceedings are commenced more than a year after the child's removal or detention 'unless it is demonstrated that the child is now settled in its new environment'. Thus at this stage an element of discretion creeps in, but it is a limited discretion. The burden is on the abducting parent to establish such a settlement. In *Re N (Minors) (Abduction)*[6] the court was asked to determine the meaning of 'now'. Did it mean the 'date of the hearing' or the 'date of commencement of proceedings'? Bracewell J ruled that it meant the latter, otherwise any delay in hearing the case might affect the outcome. She held that 'settlement' involved a physical element

2   A detailed description of the impressively speedy time-tabling of cases and related procedures adopted by the Child Abduction Unit, the High Court and the Court of Appeal is given in *Re S (Child Abduction: Delay)* [1998] 1 FLR 651, at p 660.
3   *Re N (Minors) (Abduction)* [1991] 1 FLR 413; *Re L (Child Abduction) (Psychological Harm)* [1993] 2 FLR 401. However, see Art 13 below and a discussion of when summary return may be refused.
4   [1998] 1 FLR 651.
5   Attractive arguments were presented for the alternative approach: the child had lived in England for over a year and was settled. It was also pointed out that if the abducting parent took a train journey in which she passed through Germany this would amount to a fresh wrongful removal. Of this, Wall J said: 'The argument that mere physical presence, however transient, can form the basis of a wrongful removal under Art 3 must await a case in which those facts arise.'
6   [1991] 1 FLR 413.

of being established in the community and environment, and an emotional constituent denoting security and stability. In relation to the degree of settlement which must be demonstrated, she ruled that it meant that the present position imports stability when looking at the future. She further held that the word 'new' encompassed place, home, school, people, friends, activities and opportunities, but not the relationship with the abducting parent which had always existed in a close, loving attachment.

Article 13 – Grounds for refusing peremptory return

The absolute nature of Article 12 is tempered by Article 13 which provides three grounds for releasing the court or administrative authority of the requested state from its duty to order the summary return of the child. They are given a discretion where the person, institution or other body which opposes the child's return establishes that there has been consent or aquiescence to the removal or retention, or where there is a grave risk that returning the child will expose him to physical or psychological harm or otherwise place him in an intolerable position, or where a child of sufficient age and maturity objects.

Consent or acquiescence

Article 13(a) states that summary return of the child is not mandatory where:

> '... the person, institution or other body having care of the person of the child was not actually exercising the custody rights at the time of removal or retention, or had consented to or subsequently acquiesced in the removal or retention.'

Where the child's removal is consensual it clearly is not wrongful, nor is retention wrongful where the initially wronged parent acquiesces in the arrangement. Prior consent or subsequent acquiescence on the part of the parent from whose custody the child has been removed can be active, signified by express words or conduct, or it can be passive and inferred from inactivity or silence.[7] It must be positive and unequivocal, and although it has been stated that consent must be evidenced in writing, the preferred view seems to be that this is not necessary; nor is it necessary that there should be an express statement of consent.[8] Once consent has been given it cannot be withdrawn. Similarly, acquiescence is not a

---

7   See *Re O (Abduction: Consent and Acquiescence)* [1997] 1 FLR 924 for an example of positive consent being given.
8   Contrast *Re W (Abduction: Procedure)* [1995] 1 FLR 878 with *Re C (Abduction: Consent)* [1996] 1 FLR 414 and *P v P (Abduction: Acquiescence)* [1998] 1 FLR 630.

continuing state of affairs, and once it has occurred a subsequent change of mind cannot alter the position.[9]

In *Re H (Abduction: Acquiescence),*[10] the House of Lords held that consent and acquiescence were matters of fact and this depended upon the wronged person's subjective state of mind.[11] Any construction of Article 13 which reflected purely English law rules on the meaning of acquiescence was to be deplored. 'The Convention must have the same meaning and effect under the laws of all Contracting States,'[12] and a subjective approach was reflected in decisions in other jurisdictions.[13] The burden of proof was on the abducting parent to establish the wronged parent's subjective intention. 'The trial judge, in reaching his decision on that question of fact, will no doubt be inclined to attach more weight to the contemporaneous words and actions of the wronged parent than to his bare assertion in evidence of his intention. But that is a question of weight to be attached to evidence and is not a question of law.'[14]

Giving guidance on how courts should engage in this fact finding exercise, Lord Browne-Wilkinson stated that it would be a matter for ordinary judicial common sense to attach more weight to the express words or conduct of the wronged parent than to possibly self-serving evidence of undisclosed intentions. Judges should be slow to infer an intention to acquiesce from attempts by the wronged parent to effect a reconciliation or to reach an agreed voluntary return of the abducted child.[15] Acquiescence is not normally to be found in passing remarks or letters written by a parent who has recently suffered the trauma of the removal of his children.[16] Nor is it to be found in a request for access, in negotiations for the voluntary return of the child, or in the parent pursuing the dictates of his religious beliefs.

There is one exception to this approach. On rare occasions there may be cases where the wronged parent did not, in fact, acquiesce, but where, by his unequivocal words or actions, he so conducted himself as to lead the abducting parent to believe that the wronged parent was not going to insist on the child's summary return. Normally behaviour of this kind would be likely to lead the judge to find that the actual intention of the

---

9 *Re K (Abduction: Consent)* [1997] 2 FLR 212; *Re D (Abduction: Acquiescence)* [1998] 2 FLR 335.

10 [1997] 1 FLR 872. Lord Browne-Wilkinson gave the sole speech with which the other Law Lords agreed. Prior to this ruling, the Court of Appeal had drawn a distinction between the intention needed for active and passive acquiescence and had introduced elements of objectivity into the law.

11 Approving Neill LJ's approach in *Re S (Minors) (Abduction: Acquiescence)* [1994] 1 FLR 819; and Millett LJ's approach in *Re R (Child Abduction: Acquiescence)* [1995] 1 FLR 716.

12 [1997] 1 FLR 872, at p 881.

13 Ibid, see the examples given at p 882.

14 Ibid, at p 884.

15 The Convention places weight on the desirability of negotiating a voluntary return of the child, Art 7(c) and Art 10.

16 See *Re S (Child Abduction: Acquiescence)* [1998] 2 FLR 893; *Re I (Abduction: Acquiescence)* [1999] 1 FLR 778.

allegedly wronged person was to acquiesce in the wrongful removal or retention. 'The wronged parent, knowing of his rights, ... cannot be heard to go back on what he has done and seek to persuade the judge that, all along, he has secretly intended to claim the summary return of the children.'[17] However, there may be occasions where, despite the wronged parent's outward behaviour to the contrary, the judge is satisfied that he did not in fact acquiesce. In the face of this inconsistent behaviour, Lord Browne-Wilkinson stated that justice requires that the wronged parent be held to have acquiesced.[18] However, he added that 'these will be strictly exceptional cases'.[19]

Where a parent delays in bringing proceedings this may amount to acquiescence. In *Re S (Abduction: Acquiescence)*[20] the Court of Appeal was of the view that 'delay as such is not relevant if within the twelve month period, although ... the reasons for the delay may be an indication of the subjective state of mind of the applicant.' For example, in *W v W (Child Abduction: Acquiescence)*[1] a father took no steps for ten months to secure his son's return after learning of the mother's decision not to return him to Australia, and this was held to amount to acquiescence in his unlawful retention. However, where an aggrieved parent's inactivity arises because he has been given erroneous legal advice this may negate any inference of acquiescence.[2] But a parent does not have to know his precise legal rights and have specific knowledge of the Convention in order to acquiesce.[3] In *Re A (Minors) (Abduction: Acquiescence)*[4] Stuart-Smith LJ stated that:

'A party cannot be said to acquiesce unless he is aware, at least in general terms, of his rights against the other parent. It is not necessary that he should know the full or precise nature of his legal rights under the Convention: but he must be aware of the factual situation giving rise to those rights, the court will no doubt readily infer that he was aware of his legal rights, either if he could reasonably be expected to have known of them or taken active steps to obtain legal advice.'[5]

---

17 [1997] 1 FLR 872, at p 883.
18 See *Re AZ (A Minor) (Abduction: Acquiescence)* [1993] 1 FLR 682, where the father had made a clear decision to leave the child where he was for the time being. See also, *Re D (Abduction: Acquiescence)* [1998] 2 FLR 335 where the father, who lived in Australia, consented to residence orders being made by a court in Wales.
19 Attempts to bring the facts within this situation have normally failed, see *P v P (Abduction: Acquiescence)* [1998] 2 FLR 835; *Re S (Child Abduction Acquiescence)* [1998] 2 FLR 893.
20 [1998] 2 FLR 115, at p 123, per Butler-Sloss LJ.
1 [1993] 2 FLR 211.
2 *Re S (Minors) (Abduction: Acquiescence)* [1994] 1 FLR 819.
3 *Re AZ (A Minor) (Abduction: Acquiescence)* [1993] 1 FLR 682; *Re S (Abduction: Acquiescence)* [1998] 2 FLR 115.
4 [1992] 2 FLR 14.
5 Ibid, at p 26; see also Waite J in *W v W (Child Abduction: Acquiescence)* [1993] 2 FLR 211, at p 217.

Where a parent received legal advice about the Convention, but was told (realistically) that it was not worth pursuing an application for summary return because the child would most probably ultimately be sent back from the requesting state to the requested state, he was held to have acquiesced in his child's retention when he failed, at this stage, to seek the child's summary return and sought contact only.[6]

In *Re B (Minors) (Abduction) (No 2)*[7] an English father and German mother came to England from Germany for a holiday, and during this period the father issued proceedings for the dissolution of the marriage and for a residence order. He also obtained an ex parte order restraining the removal of the children from England. The mother made a cross-application in family proceedings and consented to an order prohibiting the removal of the children pending the hearing in family proceedings. On the same day she made an application under the Hague Convention for the immediate return of the children to Germany. Dismissing the claim of the father that it was not he who had retained the children in England, but the order of the court, Waite J said:

> 'The Convention is not, in my view, an instrument to be construed semantically but purposively. Full and sensible effect can only be given to it if the term "retention" is construed as wide enough to comprehend not only acts of physical restraint on the part of the retaining parent but also juridical orders obtained on his initiative which have the effect of frustrating a child's return to the jurisdiction of its habitual residence.'[8]

Waite J was similarly dismissive of the father's claim that, by consenting to the order prohibiting the removal of the children until the family proceedings hearing, the mother had acquiesced in their wrongful detention. He held that the mother's consent to the direction given for trial of the case in England could be relied on only for the purpose of demonstrating that she had so far, and without prejudice to any issue of forum conveniens[9] which might arise in the future, agreed that the courts in England would be the forum in which issues about the children would be tried, and that her agreement to this could not possibly be interpreted as consent on her part to the children remaining in the meantime in England. As Waite J explained:

> 'Parents should ... be encouraged ... to proceed as rapidly as possible with family welfare proceedings designed to settle the children's future at the earliest achievable date. It would be very injurious to that encouragement if a parent's participation in

6   *Re S (Abduction: Acquiescence)* [1998] 2 FLR 115.
7   [1993] 1 FLR 993.
8   Ibid, at p 1000.
9   That is the place of jurisdiction appropriate for the purposes of determining the merits of the case.

family proceedings involved the risk of depriving him or her of a right to the children's return in the meantime, which would otherwise be theirs under the terms of the Convention.'[10]

The risk that a parent who had attempted to compromise might thereby lose his right to seek redress under the Convention was acknowledged in *P v P (Abduction: Acquiescence).*[11] The mother had brought the child to England from Cyprus without the father's consent. The father attempted to negotiate arrangements about the child's upbringing and these included a proposal that the mother have custody of the child in England with the father having regular access. The parties failed to achieve a settlement, and the father thereupon issued proceedings under the Convention. It was argued on behalf of the mother that the father had been willing to contemplate that the child would remain where he had been taken and therefore that he had acquiesced. Hale J stated that this was a difficult case which was finely balanced. In her view, it appeared to fall between the examples given by Lord Browne-Wilkinson in *Re H (Abduction Acquiescence)*[12] of where a wronged parent's outward behaviour was inconsistent with his actual intentions. Hale J arrived at her conclusion that there had been no clear and unequivocal behaviour on the part of the father amounting to acquiescence by adopting a purposive approach. She stated that where parents seek to achieve a negotiated settlement which involves the child remaining in England, this should not necessarily lead the court to conclude that the wronged parent was in a subjective state of mind that was wholly content for the child to remain in England.

Grave risk to the child

Article 13(b) allows the court discretion not to return the child where:

'... there is a grave risk that his or her return would expose the child to physical or psychological harm or otherwise place the child in an intolerable situation.'

Thus there are two issues for the court: first, whether a ground for the exercise of discretion has been established and, secondly, whether the child should be sent back in the exercise of that discretion.

---

10 Ibid, at p 999. The reference to the issue of forum conveniens is puzzling. The whole thinking informing the Convention is that it is the country of the child's habitual residence which should determine the merits of the case. And see the even more puzzling, and indeed almost certainly wrong, decision in *H v H (Child Abduction: Stay of Domestic Proceedings)* [1994] 1 FLR 530 in which Thorpe J, despite making a finding of wrongful retention, nonetheless ordered that the merits of the case should be investigated in England.
11 [1998] 2 FLR 835, confirming Hale J's judgment at [1998] 1 FLR 630.
12 [1997] 1 FLR 872.

It is in the context of Article 13(b) that issues relevant to the welfare of the child can legitimately be advanced. However, it must be understood at the outset that the child's welfare is *not* the court's paramount consideration. A *grave* risk of physical or psychological harm must be established, or the child must be placed in an *intolerable* situation. Lord Donaldson MR acknowledged in *Re C (A Minor) (Abduction)*[13] that a child caught up in a case which involves operating the machinery of the Convention is bound to suffer some psychological harm if he or she is returned. But he said that it is the concern of the state to which the child is returned to take steps to minimise or eliminate this harm, and in the absence of compelling evidence to the contrary the courts should assume that this will be done.

Courts have been extremely wary of accepting the claim that a child will suffer psychological harm if his or her return is ordered because by doing so they could rapidly undermine the whole purpose of the Convention. As Bracewell J said in *Re N (Minors) (Abduction)*,[14] 'it is plain that it is not a trivial risk and it is not a trivial psychological harm which is envisaged and which has to be justified and, furthermore, I am satisfied that the intolerable situation envisaged has to be something extreme and compelling'. In *P v P (Minors) (Child Abduction)*[15] the mother claimed that if the court ordered the return of the children to the USA she would at once become a deeply unhappy person, and that an unhappy mother means unhappy children. Of this claim Waite J said:

> 'Arguments of this kind are commonly raised within this jurisdiction. They are really, however, beside the point. That is not because the jurisdiction is inhumane. On the contrary there is a humane purpose underlying it in ensuring that children are not subjected to disruption through arbitrary movement by one parent or the other. The reason why evidence of that kind is beside the point at this stage is the underlying assumption of the Convention ... that the courts of all its signatories are equally concerned to ensure, and equally capable of ensuring, that both parties receive a fair hearing, and that all issues of child welfare receive a skilled, thorough and humane evaluation.'[16]

In *Re C (A Minor) (Abduction)*[17] the mother said that she would refuse to accompany the child if he was returned to Australia and she asserted that the child would therefore suffer severe psychological harm. The Court of Appeal rejected this contention stating that the parent could not crea

---

13 [1989] 1 FLR 403.
14 [1991] 1 FLR 413, at p 419; see also *Re C (A Minor) (Abduction)* [1989] 1 FLR 403.
15 [1992] 1 FLR 155; see also *B v B (Abduction)* [1993] 1 FLR 238 in which the severity of the harm, and high degree of intolerability, was emphasised.
16 [1992] 1 FLR 155, at p 161; see also *Re L (Child Abduction) (Psychological Harm)* [1993] 2 FLR 401; *Re O (Child Abduction: Undertakings)* [1994] 2 FLR 349.
17 [1989] 1 FLR 403.

a psychological situation and then seek to rely on it.[18] However, although the conduct of the abducting parent is crucial and often determinative, and although to allow a parent to profit from her own wrong-doing is an anathema to the courts, there have been rare occasions where the court, despite its strong disapproval of the parent's conduct, has looked beyond it to the manifest needs of the children and not ordered summary return.[19]

An objecting parent may be fearful about the manner in which she and the children will be treated by the other parent and the foreign legal system if the court orders the return of the children to the requesting state. In *Re A (Minors) (Abduction: Acquiescence)*[20] the mother declared that if she and the children were to return to Australia they would have no home and no financial support from the father. She contrasted this situation very unfavourably with the support she was receiving from her family in England. The Court of Appeal found that the mother would be eligible to claim Australian state benefits and therefore it held that this assertion came nowhere near to establishing what the Convention meant by an 'intolerable' situation. In *Re S (Child Abduction: Acquiescence)*[1] the mother raised fears in relation to herself. The father acknowledged that in the past he had treated the mother with violence though 'only in circumstances when he was unwell'. Sir Stephen Brown P dismissed the suggestion that this indicated that the child would be at risk if returned to California. In *Re O (Child Abduction: Undertakings)*[2] the mother expressed the fear that the Greek courts would never allow her to bring the children to England if they were returned to Greece. Singer J ruled that reliance could be placed on this consideration under Article 13(b), but only if it were established in relation to a given country that there was some fixed embargo on allowing the removal of children to another country, or precluding the removal of children by a parent who had once wrongly removed them.

A method often used by courts to handle these and other fears is to obtain undertakings from the applicant, which are binding promises made to the court, breach of which is punishable by fine or imprisonment. The efficacy of this method of protecting the returning parent and children is not clear because undertakings are, of course, only enforceable in the jurisdiction in which they are given. However, courts have generally been satisfied that they afford sufficient safeguards for the respondent,[3] arguably to the point of complacency. Can there really be any value in an

---

18 See also *Re L (Child Abduction) (Psychological Harm)* [1993] 2 FLR 401.
19 See, for example, *Re M (Abduction: Psychological Harm)* [1997] 2 FLR 690.
20 [1992] 2 FLR 14.
1 [1998] 2 FLR 893.
2 [1994] 2 FLR 349.
3 *Re C (A Minor) (Abduction)* [1989] 1 FLR 403; *Re G (A Minor) (Abduction)* [1989] 2 FLR 475; *G v G (Minors) (Abduction)* [1991] 2 FLR 506; *P v P (Minors) (Child Abduction)* [1992] 1 FLR 155; *Re O (Child Abduction: Undertakings)* [1994] 2 FLR 349; *Police Comr of South Australia v Temple (No 2)* [1993] FLC 92; *Re K (Abduction) (Child's Objections)* [1995] 1 FLR 977.

undertaking given by a person living outside the jurisdiction who has admitted to treating a parent with violence 'not to harass or pester the mother',[4] or 'to vacate the former matrimonial home in Cyprus and not to threaten, assault, harass or pester the mother in England or in Cyprus'?[5]

For all of the reasons given above there have been relatively few cases in England where an application under Article 13(b) has succeeded. Courts are generally sceptical of attempts by abducting parents to invoke the provisions of Article 13 to try to stave off the almost inevitable requirement to return the child. *Re M (Abduction: Psychological Harm)*[6] is one example of where such an attempt did succeed. There was no doubt that the mother was in breach of Article 3; she had wrongfully retained the children aged nine and a half and seven for a second time. Evidence was given that the children had a particularly close attachment to their mother and did not settle with their father, who had an interim custody order made in the Greek courts. Their reaction to being returned to Athens after periods of contact with their mother in England had been particularly strong.[7] Reports from an English and a Greek psychologist and an English psychiatrist all expressed deep concern about the children's current psychological well-being and the effect on them of an order returning them to Greece, and the Court of Appeal accepted that there was cogent evidence to support a finding under Article 13(b).

Where the child objects

Article 13 provides that:

> 'The judicial or administrative authority may also refuse to order the return of the child if it finds that the child objects to being returned and has attained an age and degree of maturity at which it is appropriate to take account of its views.'

This provision allows children a voice in the proceedings. It does not lay down any age below which a child is to be treated as too immature to voice an opinion, and therefore it is for the judge to determine whether the child objects, and to decide whether the child has attained the age and degree of maturity at which it is appropriate to take account of his or her views.[8]

---

4   As in *Re S (Child Abduction: Acquiescence)* [1998] 2 FLR 893.
5   *P v P (Abduction: Acquiescence)* [1998] 2 FLR 835.
6   [1997] 2 FLR 690.
7   The father took the children 'kicking and fighting' into the departure lounge at Heathrow airport.
8   See *Re G (A Minor) (Abduction)* [1989] 2 FLR 475; *S v S (Child Abduction) (Child's Views)* [1992] 2 FLR 492. In *B v K* [1993] 1 FCR 382, Johnson J exercised his discretion not to return two 'sensible and intelligent' children aged nine and seven to Germany, holding that they were of an age and maturity where it would be appropriate to take account of their views.

The courts are hesitant about accepting the views of young children because of their relative lack of maturity,[9] but in *S v S (Child Abduction) (Child's Views)*[10] the Court of Appeal accepted that a nine year old girl's objections to returning to France had substance, and were not confined to a desire to remain in England with her mother.[11] The child's objection is an entirely separate matter from paragraph (b) of Article 13, the words are to be read literally without any additional gloss, and that there is no need to establish that the child would be at risk of physical or psychological harm before the discretion comes into play.[12] However, where the child's objections are closely related to the considerations which are relevant to paragraph (b), it is more likely that the court will exercise its discretion not to return the child.[13]

Article 12(1) of the UN Convention on the Rights of the Child 1989 has undoubtedly been influential upon how courts have approached objections by a child under Article 13.[14] It provides that:

> 'States Parties shall assure to the child who is capable of forming his or her own views the right to express those views freely in all matters affecting the child, the views of the child being given due weight in accordance with the age and maturity of the child.'

Article 12(2) further provides that the child should be given an opportunity to be heard, either directly or through a representative. It is a matter for the judge whether to authorise an investigation into the child's views and to determine how such an investigation should be carried out; but the courts have held that it is contrary to the purpose of the Hague Convention if such an investigation is allowed to delay the prompt return of the child to any significant extent.[15] If, on the other hand, the child has already made his objection apparent, as in *Re M (A Minor) (Child Abduction)*,[16]

---

9   *Re K (Abduction: Child's Objections)* [1995] 1 FLR 977.

10 [1992] 2 FLR 492.

11 Similarly, in *Re M (Abduction: Psychological Harm)* [1997] 2 FLR 690, the views of a nine and a half year old boy 'had, at least, to be listened to'. The court found that the boy's objections were well-founded in view of his psychological state. As it had never been suggested that the brothers be parted, the younger boy's position had to be considered alongside his older brother.

12 *S v S (Child Abduction) (Child's Views)* [1992] 2 FLR 492. The Court of Appeal stated that the extra gloss put on the word 'object' in *Re R (A Minor) (Abduction)* [1992] 1 FLR 105 at pp 107-108 had been unwarranted. See also, *Re R (Abduction: Hague/European Convention)* [1997] 1 FLR 663, where the court concluded that the objections of a ten and a half year old girl should be taken into account.

13 *Ontario Court v M and M (Abduction: Children's Objections)* [1997] 1 FLR 475.

14 See particularly, *S v S (Child Abduction) (Child's Views)* [1992] 2 FLR 492; *Re B (Abduction: Children's Objections)* [1998] 1 FLR 667, where Stuart White J, after referring to the Article 12, concluded that boys of twelve and seven were sufficiently mature for the court to consider their views, and exercised his discretion not to order their return to Ireland.

15 *P v P (Minors) (Child Abduction)* [1992] 1 FLR 155; *Re G (A Minor) (Abduction)* [1989] 2 FLR 475.

16 [1994] 1 FLR 390.

then the matter should be investigated before such a return is ordered.[17] It may be appropriate for an objecting child to have separate representation, for the matter to be investigated by a court welfare officer, and a guardian ad litem for the child to be appointed.[18]

Exercise of discretion under Article 13

Once the mandatory requirement in Article 12 has been relaxed by a finding under Article 13 the court has a discretion whether to order the child's return or whether to permit the merits of the case to be heard in England. The question then arises whether, at this stage, the court can take account of the interests of the child, and if so, how much weight can be given to his or her interests. The final paragraph provides that:

> 'In considering the circumstances referred to in this Article, the judicial and administrative authorities shall take into account the information relating to the social background of the child provided by the Central Authority or other competent authority and the child's habitual residence.'

Clearly if a court finds that to order the child's return would expose the child to a grave risk of physical or psychological harm or otherwise place the child in an intolerable position it is extremely unlikely that it would ever order that the child should nonetheless be restored to his or her country of habitual residence. Thus in *Re M (Abduction: Psychological Harm)*[19] the Court of Appeal confirmed the trial judge's exercise of discretion not to order summary return of the children despite its strong disapproval of the mother's behaviour and despite its anxiety to uphold the notion that foreign courts can be trusted to handle cases properly and, in the interests of comity with Greece, to emphasise that it had no reservations about how the Greek courts might deal with the case.[20] However, where the child has expressed a wish to remain in this country the court must decide how much weight to give to the child's views bearing in mind the purpose of the Convention. In *S v S (Child Abduction)*[1] the

---

17 In *Re M (A Minor) (Child Abduction)* [1994] 1 FLR 390, the Court of Appeal ruled that the wording of Art 13 does not inhibit the objection of a child to returning to a parent rather than to a country.

18 See *Re P (Abduction: Minor's Views)* [1998] 2 FLR 825. There was evidence that the child, a boy aged 13, was very disturbed with possible suicidal tendencies. It was also possible that he had been manipulated by his mother to make statements designed to deceive the court. The Court of Appeal was not prepared to order the child's summary return without further investigation as the decision, if wrong, 'could be disastrous'.

19 [1997] 2 FLR 690.

20 An important feature was that no practical proposals had been made as to how the mother might go with the children and remain with them in Greece pending a hearing in the Greek courts.

1 [1992] 2 FLR 492.

court was alert to the danger that Article 13 could be interpreted in a manner which would undermine the notion that it is normally in the best interests of children that they should be promptly returned to the country from which they have been wrongfully removed. Thus Balcombe LJ stated that:

> 'If the court should come to the conclusion that the child's views have been influenced by some other person, eg the abducting parent, or that the objection to return is because of a wish to remain with the abducting parent, then it is probable that little or no weight will be given to those views. Any other approach would be to drive a coach and horses through the primary scheme of the Hague Convention.'[2]

In *Re R (Minors) (Child Abduction)*[3] the Court of Appeal emphasised that in exercising the discretion, the policy of the Convention, and its faithful implementation by the courts, should always be a weighty factor to be brought into the scales. On the other hand the weight to be attached to the views of the child would clearly vary with his age or maturity: the older the child the greater the weight, the younger the child the less weight.[4] It is, however, clear that where the court finds the child has valid reasons for his or her objections to being returned then it may refuse to make an order, as in *S v S (Child Abduction)* itself, where the child aged nine had given strong and independent reasons why she did not want to return to France.[5] Where it seems likely that the requesting State would give leave to the 'abducting' parent to remove the child from its jurisdiction and bring the child back to this country this would be another important consideration against ordering summary return.[6]

The background litigation leading to Hale J's judgment in *Re HB (Abduction: Children's Objections) (No 2)*[7] makes salutary reading. It is suggested that this case went badly wrong at the initial hearing.[8] Hale J, at that stage, gave great weight to the policy consideration that parents

---

2   Ibid, at p 501.
3   [1995] 1 FLR 717.
4   The court took account of the wishes of boys aged seven and a half and six to stay in England with their mother, but exercising its discretion, ordered that they be returned to Illinois.
5   See too *Re A (Minors) (Abduction: Acquiescence)* [1992] 2 FLR 14; *Re M (Minor)* (25 July 1990, unreported) in which the court refused to order the return of three children aged 11, 9 and 8 to America. In *Re M (A Minor) (Abduction)* [1994] 2 FLR 126 the dispute was between a 13-year-old boy and his mother who was seeking his return to Ireland under the Convention. The boy was made a party to the proceedings and in the light of his allegations of ill-treatment and the validity of his objections the court refused to order his return to Ireland.
6   *Re B (Abduction: Children's Objections)* [1998] 1 FLR 667.
7   [1998] 1 FLR 564; following the Court of Appeal decision in *Re HB (Abduction: Children's Objections)* [1998] 1 FLR 422 to remit the case back to Hale J.
8   *Re HB (Abduction: Children's Objections)* [1997] 1 FLR 392.

should feel able to send their children abroad for holiday visits secure in the knowledge that they would be returned when the visit ends. As a result she ordered the return of children aged thirteen and eleven to Denmark against their very strong objections.[9] The older boy flew back to Denmark (although it was he who had the strongest reasons for objecting) but then reverted to his previous delinquent behaviour and ended up living with foster parents. The younger girl voted with her feet and refused to get on the plane. There appears to be no doubt that both children were harmed by the attempt to return them under the Convention.[10] At the very least the order for summary return led to the children's separation, and there was other information placed before the courts at the subsequent hearings indicating how each child had suffered. The chain of events illustrated the danger that court orders may be flouted by children where their strongly expressed objections to return are discounted in the interests of promoting the policy of the Convention. The outcome of this case supports the view that considerable attention should be payed to the views of mature, objecting children. A Convention designed to protect children's rights should also respect their wishes, as the framers of the Convention recognised.[11]

Where a parent has consented or acquiesced in the child's otherwise wrongful removal, but where he or she is requesting that the child should nonetheless be returned, and for the merits of the case to be heard in the country from which the child was taken, it is less clear what approach the court should take to the exercise of its discretion. In *Re A (Minors) (No 2) (Abduction: Acquiescence)*[12] the question arose whether the court can take account of the welfare of the child when exercising its discretion. The Court of Appeal ruled that the final paragraph of Article 13 makes it clear that it is appropriate for the court to consider the welfare interests of the child at this stage. However, the court added that the court need not treat the welfare of the child as paramount. In *W v W (Child Abduction: Acquiescence)*[13] Waite J itemised various matters which appeared to him to be relevant to the exercise of his discretion, including the emotional effect on the child in ordering his peremptory return, and the extent to which the purpose and philosophy of the Convention would be at risk of frustration if a return order were to be refused. Another factor which has influenced the courts is whether the children are likely to be removed

---

9   The evidence concerning the children's views and their reasons for them was very powerful. The court concluded that they were sincerely held and not the result of pressure from the abducting parent. The children had gone so far as to consult a solicitor with a view to participating in the proceedings.

10   Though much of the responsibility for this lay with the parents, not the courts. Certainly the girl's views about her mother altered considerably, and the case became increasingly polarised. See also, Thorpe LJ at [1998] 1 FLR 422, at p 427.

11   It will be interesting to observe whether greater weight is given to children's objections in the light of the Human Rights Act 1998.

12   [1993] 1 FLR 396.

13   [1993] 2 FLR 211.

back to their country of habitual residence only for that court to order that they should be allowed to leave again.[14]

The European Convention

The aim of the European Convention on Recognition and Enforcement of Decisions concerning Custody of Children and on the Restoration of Custody of Children is to ensure the mutual recognition and enforcement of decisions relating to the custody of children between Contracting States.[15] It may be invoked where a child has been improperly removed across an international frontier in breach of a decision relating to his or her custody which has been given in a Contracting State and which is enforceable in such a State.[16] Application for the recognition or enforcement of a decision is made to the central authority in the relevant Contracting State which is then under a duty to take all appropriate steps, if necessary by instituting proceedings before its competent authorities, in order:

'(a) to discover the whereabouts of the child;
(b) to avoid, in particular by any necessary provisional measures, prejudice to the interests of the child or of the applicant;
(c) to secure the recognition or enforcement of the decision;
(d) to secure the delivery of the child to the applicant where enforcement is granted;
(e) to inform the requesting authority of the measures taken and their results.'[17]

A person with custody rights conferred by another Contracting State may apply under section 16 of the Child Abduction and Custody Act 1985 for the decision to be registered in an appropriate court in the United Kingdom.[18] Once registered, section 18 provides that the court in which it is registered shall have the same powers for the purpose of enforcing the decision as if it had been made by that court. It is a mandatory requirement that a subsisting decision relating to custody which is enforceable in its country of origin should be registered, recognised and enforced in England.
    Article 12 provides that:

---

14 See Staughton LJ in *Re A (Minors) (No 2) (Abduction: Acquiescence)* [1993] 1 FLR 396; *W v W (Child Abduction: Acquiescence)* above.
15 Art 7. Thus s 15(2) of the Child Abduction and Custody Act 1985 (which ratifies the Convention) provides that a custody decision made in a Contracting State shall be recognised in each part of the United Kingdon as if it had been made by a United Kingdom court. This section also applies to orders made under Art 12, see below.
16 Art 1(d). For a list of Contracting States, see Child Abduction and Custody (Parties to Conventions) Order 1986 (SI 1986/1159). This is amended as new States become signatories; see, for example, the amendments made by SI 1997/1747.
17 Art 5.
18 Indeed, the decision is not enforceable unless it has been registered; Child Abduction and Custody Act 1995, s 15(2)(b).

'Where, at the time of the removal of a child across an international frontier there is no enforceable decision given in a Contracting State relating to his custody, the provisions of the Convention shall apply to any *subsequent*[19] decision relating to the custody of that child and declaring the removal to be unlawful, given in a contracting State at the request of any interested person.'

The advantage of this provision is that it enables an order (commonly known as a 'chasing order') to be made after the child has left the jurisdiction which is just as enforceable as if it had been made before the removal took place.

Unmarried fathers and unlawful removal

Article 12 may be of particular importance to unmarried fathers. It has been seen that under domestic English law an unmarried father does not enjoy automatic parental responsibility, his consent to his child's removal from the jurisdiction is therefore not required and any such removal against his wishes is legal. However, once the court is involved the father's position alters, as was illustrated by *Re S (Abduction: European Convention)*.[20] The father had issued proceedings for parental responsibility under section 4 of the Children Act 1989 before the mother removed the child to Denmark. When the father discovered that the child had gone he obtained an ex parte order giving him interim residence and requiring the mother to return the child to him in England. The father then applied for a declaration under section 23(2) of the Child Abduction and Custody Act 1985 that the mother's removal was unlawful under Article 12.[1] The declaration was made despite the fact that the father did not have the right to determine the child's residence at the time the child was removed.[2]

In *Re S (Custody: Habitual Residence)*[3] relatives removed a child to Ireland within a few days of her mother's death without the father's knowledge or consent. The trial judge immediately granted the father interim care and control but rejected the father's contention that there

---

19 Emphasis added.
20 [1996] 1 FLR 660.
1   'Where in any custody proceedings a court in the United Kingdom makes a decision relating to a child who has been removed from the United Kingdom, the court may also, on an application made by any person for the purposes of Art 12 of the Convention, declare the removal to be unlawful if it is satisfied that the applicant has an interest in the matter and that the child has been taken or sent or kept out of the United Kingdom without the consent of the person … having the right to determine the child's place of residence under the law of the part of the United Kingdom in which the child was habitually resident.'
2   Contrast with the Hague Convention, above, where the Art 3 criteria must always be present at the time of removal or retention.
3   [1998] 1 FLR 122.

had been a breach of Article 12 of the European Convention.[4] Meanwhile an aunt had obtained an order in a Dublin court for care and control of the child. The issue for the House of Lords to resolve was whether there had been an unlawful removal of the child from the jurisdiction contrary to Article 12. It was contended on behalf of the relatives that under section 23 of the Child Abduction and Custody Act 1985, the only person who could make an application or whose consent was relevant was the child's mother, and that Article 12 could not create rights for the person seeking the declaration which were not in being prior to the removal. The House of Lords rejected this contention. It held that, as a matter of law, where there was a failure to return a child at the end of the period during which the child had been lawfully outside the jurisdiction, at this stage the removal became retrospectively unlawful under Article 1(d). Therefore, once the judge had given interim care and control to the father, the father had the right to determine the child's place of residence and the retention of the child in Ireland became unlawful. Accordingly, the court had power to declare that for the purposes of the Convention the child's removal had become an improper removal.

Refusal of recognition and enforcement

Recognition and enforcement may be refused on various limited grounds specified in Articles 9 and 10.[5] In the case of a decision given in the absence of the defendant or his legal representative, it may be refused where the decision-making body failed to observe proper procedural requirements in relation to the service of notice on the defendant: Article 9(1)(a).[6] It may be refused in the case of a decision made in the absence of the defendant or his legal representative if the competence of the authority giving the decision was not founded on the habitual residence of the defendant, or of one or both of the child's parents, or of the child: Article

---

4 Proceedings were also issued under the Hague Convention, the outcome of which is discussed above.

5 The United Kingdom entered a reservation under Art 17 with the result that it will not give effect to Art 8 and therefore has a discretion under Arts 9 and 10. Art 8 requires steps to be taken forthwith to restore the custody of the child where an improper removal has occurred within six months. The United Kingdom took the view that this provision was incompatible with the Hague Convention and could lead to the return of the child when it might not be in the child's interests to be returned.

6 In *Re S (Abduction: European Convention)* [1996] 1 FLR 660, Art 9(1)(a) did not assist the mother because the court was satisfied that the mother had been served with notice of the Children Act 1989 proceedings before she removed the child. Moreover, although the mother had not, of course, been served with notice of the ex parte proceedings and although the interim orders had been made in her absence, this did not debar the father's application because service could not be effected because the mother had concealed her whereabouts, and because both father and child were habitually resident in England at the time of the child's removal: Art 9(1)(b).

9(1)(b). Article 9(1)(c) permits the exercise of discretion where the decision to recognise and enforce is incompatible with a decision relating to custody which became enforceable in the State addressed before the removal of the child, unless the child's habitual residence was in the territory of the requesting State for one year before his removal.

Article 9(3) provides that 'in no circumstances may the foreign decision be reviewed as to its substance'. In *Re A (Foreign Access Order: Enforcement)*[7] the French courts made an order giving parental authority to both parents, the children to reside with their mother in England and the father to have staying access in France. Subsequently the English courts made an order at the mother's instance that the children should not be removed from the jurisdiction. The father applied under section 15 of the Child Abduction and Custody Act 1985 for the order of the French court to be enforced. Allowing the father's application, the Court of Appeal held that the radical change by the English court to the French court order, by giving the father staying access in England not France (which he could not afford to take up), amounted to review of the substance of the French court's decision, which was specifically prohibited by Article 9(3).

The child's welfare

Article 10(1)(b) allows considerations relating to the welfare of the child to influence the requested State's decision. It provides that registration or enforcement may be refused:

'... if it is found that by reason of a change in the circumstances including the passage of time but not including a mere change in the residence of the child after an improper removal, the effects of the original decision are manifestly no longer in accordance with the welfare of the child.'[8]

Article 15(1) provides that before reaching a decision under Article 10(1)(b), the court or administrative authority:

'... shall ascertain the child's views unless this is impracticable having regard in particular to his age and understanding.'

It is clear that not only must it be established that the order is no longer in accordance with the child's welfare, but that it must 'manifestly' no longer be so. Moreover, although Article 15 makes it mandatory for the court to discover the child's views before making a decision under Article 10(1)(b), this requirement only arises where the court is satisfied that

---

7   [1996] 1 FLR 561.
8   See too Art 10(1)(d) and how it was applied in *Re M (Child Abduction) (European Convention)* [1994] 1 FLR 551.

there has been a change of circumstances including the passage of time. A change in the child's residence may not be taken into account if it is the sole change that has taken place, but where there are other factors, a change of residence may be coupled with those other factors.[9]

The meaning of 'the effects of the original decision are manifestly no longer in accordance with the welfare of the child' was considered by Latey J in *Re K (A Minor) (Abduction)*.[10] The child concerned was aged seven, she had a Belgian mother and an English father who were unmarried. The father was violent towards the mother and the parties separated, the mother taking the child. Shortly afterwards the father abducted the child to England. The mother obtained a custody order in a Belgian court and 16 months later she applied to have the order registered and enforced in the High Court under the Child Abduction and Custody Act 1985. The mother was not responsible for the delay in taking these proceedings. The father defended the action under Article 10(1)(b). Evidence was given that the child had settled happily in England, was progressing well at school, that she was being very well cared for by her father and enjoyed the company of her paternal grandparents. Evidence was also given that the mother was a very good and loving mother who could offer the child a happy home surrounded by members of the wider family. The issue for the court was whether the effects of the decision of the Belgian court to award custody to the mother were manifestly no longer in accordance with the child's welfare. Latey J said that this test was not the same as whether it was in the child's best interests for the order to be enforced. Moreover, it was a question which required a speedy resolution without the type of full investigation which was necessary where the welfare of the child was paramount.[11] The length of time the child had spent in England was an important consideration; however, the evidence suggested that the child would adjust well if she returned to Belgium. Latey J therefore made an order recognising, registering and enforcing the order of the Belgian court.

In *Re L (Child Abduction: European Convention)*[12] the parents were Irish, married and lived in Ireland with their three children. The mother, who had brought two of the children from Ireland to England in breach of an Irish court order giving custody to the father, asked the court to exercise its discretion under Article 10(1)(b), relying on the fact that the children had lived with her since she left the matrimonial home over a year previously. She also sought an adjournment to enable the court to exercise its powers under Article 15 to ascertain the views of the children. Booth J rejected both of the mother's applications and ordered the registration and enforcement of the order of the Irish court. She emphasised that proceedings under the Child Abduction and Custody Act 1985 should be

9   *Re R (Hague and European Conventions)* [1997] 1 FLR 663.
10 [1990] 1 FLR 387.
11 Latey J did however state that, had the welfare of the child been the paramount consideration, the court would have concluded that she should return to Belgium.
12 [1992] 2 FLR 178.

taken swiftly, that decisions should be made by courts expeditiously, and that the court should only exercise its discretion not to comply with the spirit and terms of the Convention in a very clear case. She added that a very high burden of proof rests on the party who seeks to satisfy the court that Article 10(1)(b) applies.

Thus it can be seen that the attitude of the courts is firmly to reinforce the purpose of the Convention by making summary orders without engaging in prolonged enquiries into the position of the children. The first question for the court is whether the order of the foreign court should be recognised and enforced. In *Re H (A Minor) (Foreign Custody Order)*[13] the Court of Appeal held that recognition and enforcement should be interpreted disjunctively, and that enforcement does not automatically follow recognition where the provisions of Article 10(1)(b) apply.[14] Where the child's views are known, and where the child objects to the enforcement of the order, this does not decide the matter. The child's views are not determinative. It must be shown that it is manifestly no longer in accordance with the welfare of the child for the order to be enforced.[15]

Non-Convention cases

Where a child is taken from England and Wales to a country which is not a signatory to the Hague or European Convention, or where a child from a non-Convention country is brought to this country without lawful authority, the legal position is more difficult to describe and predict. In relation to children who are wrongfully removed, the law's response is to seek to prevent this happening by criminalising the behaviour. Under section 1 of the Child Abduction Act 1984, it is an offence to take a child under the age of 16 out of the United Kingdom without the appropriate consents.[16] Because an offence is committed where a child

---

13 [1994] 1 FLR 512.
14 Thus although an order providing for a 13-year-old girl to have staying access with her father in Belgium was registered under s 16 of the Child Abduction and Custody Act 1985, the court applied Art 10(1)(b) and refused to enforce it as this would have been manifestly no longer in accordance with the welfare of the child.
15 Contrast *Re A (Foreign Access Order: Enforcement)* [1996] 1 FLR 561, where the views of young children which had 'hardened' against having access with their father in France were held to be insufficient to amount to the change of circumstances to bring Art 10(1)(b) into play with *Re R (Hague and European Conventions)* [1997] 1 FLR 663, where the real change of circumstances coupled with the strong views of a 13-year-old girl led to the court's refusal to enforce an order made by a Swiss court.
16 Child Abduction Act 1984, s 1. In the case of married and divorced parents both must consent, but where the mother is unmarried she may remove the child without the father's consent unless he has parental responsibility for the child under the Children Act 1989, s 4. The consent of persons other than the child's parents is required where there is a residence order to a third party, where the child has a guardian or where any person has custody of the child. Where the courts have been involved the leave of the court may also be required. No ward of court may ever be removed without the court's consent. See ch 4 for a discussion of applications for leave to take a child out of the jurisdiction.

is wrongfully taken abroad, the police are willing to take preventive action. They will inform the port authorities where there is a real threat that a child is about to be removed unlawfully from the country.[17] It is not necessary first to obtain a court order before the police will assist. However, a court order may be influential in persuading decision-makers in the country to which the child has been taken to order his return to England.[18] Moreover, the Child Abduction Act 1984 applies to children aged under 16 only. Therefore, in relation to a child between 16 and 18 a court order is essential. Courts will hear cases of this kind very speedily. An ex parte application can be made for a prohibited steps order,[19] or the child can be made a ward of the High Court. The court may require the surrender of any United Kingdom passport which has been issued to, or contains particulars of, the child.[20] The passport office should be notified that passport facilities should not be provided in respect of a child without either the requisite consents or the court's leave. Assistance in tracing the abductor can be obtained from government departments.[1]

Children wrongfully abducted to England

Where a child is abducted to England from a non-Convention country the question arises whether an English court should determine issues relating to the child's upbringing or whether it should order the child's immediate return to the country of the child's habitual residence. The difference between a Convention case and a non-Convention case is that in a Convention case the child's welfare is *not* the court's paramount consideration while in a non-Convention case it *is*. It may, of course, best promote the child's welfare to order the child's immediate return to the non-Convention country without investigating the merits, but welfare is the only proper reason for making such an order.[2] At one stage, the Court

---

17 When the police are asked to institute a port-alert, they must first be satisfied that the danger of removal is 'real and imminent'. 'Imminent' means within 24 to 48 hours, and 'real' means that the port-alert is not being sought by the applicant merely by way of insurance; see *Practice Direction* [1986] 1 All ER 983, where full details of the appropriate steps to take are detailed.
18 Sadly, however, once a child has been taken to a non-Convention country he may never be recovered; or many years may pass while proceedings to secure his return drag on, and meanwhile the child becomes settled in his new way of life, new culture and makes new family attachments, so that his return becomes increasingly unlikely.
19 Children Act 1989, s 8.
20 Family Law Act 1986, s 37.
1 *Practice Direction* [1989] 1 All ER 765.
2 *McKee v McKee* [1951] AC 352. 'To this paramount consideration (of welfare) all others yield. The order of a foreign court of competent jurisdiction is no exception.' Per Lord Simonds, at p 365; and *J v C* [1970] AC 668 'the existence of [an order of a foreign court] will not oust the jurisdiction or preclude the application of [the paramountcy of the welfare principle]'. Per Lord MacDermott, at p 714. See also, *Re L (Minors) (Wardship: Jurisdiction)* [1974] 1 WLR 250.

of Appeal appeared to decide that the application of the paramountcy principle led to the conclusion that the general principles of the Hague Convention should be applied in non-Convention cases too.[3] However, in *D v D (Child Abduction)*,[4] the Court of Appeal sounded a note of caution. The trial judge had applied the principles and Articles in the Convention to the facts of the case and had not considered the welfare of the children separately from this. Of this approach Butler-Sloss LJ said:

> 'The courts have always set their face against condoning the abduction of children from their rightful homes and have for many years provided a summary procedure to determine whether to return them. Nonetheless it is important to remember that the Articles of the Convention are not to be applied literally in the wardship jurisdiction and the court retains discretion to consider the wider aspects of the welfare of the wards.'[5]

Balcombe LJ expressed a similar caveat when he said:

> 'His judgment is open to criticism in that [the judge] appears to have sought to apply the detailed provisions of the Convention to a non-Convention case ... However, I should stress that, in a non-Convention case, the welfare of the children remains the paramount consideration, and the principles of the Convention are applicable only to the extent that they indicate what is normally in the interests of the children.'[6]

The reason why it is undesirable for courts to apply Convention principles to non-Convention cases[7] is because the Convention is built around administrative structures which are designed to achieve mutual

---

3 *Re F (A Minor) (Abduction: Jurisdiction)* [1991] 1 FLR 1; *G v G (Minors) (Abduction)* [1991] 2 FLR 506, adopting the view that it is in the interests of all children that parents and others should not abduct them from one jurisdiction to another.
4 [1994] 1 FLR 137.
5 Ibid, at p 140.
6 Ibid, at p 144. The Court of Appeal nonetheless ruled that the trial judge had been right to apply the general principles of the Convention to the case before him. However, the mother's situation had changed by the time of the appeal, and the Court of Appeal held that the welfare of the children now required that their future should be decided by an English court.
7 As in *S v S (Child Abduction: Non-Convention Country)* [1994] 2 FLR 681, where the court ordered the return of a child to South Africa even though the mother's removal was not in breach of the father's custody rights, and therefore Art 12 would not have applied had the case been a Convention case. Similarly, in *Re M (Abduction: Non-Convention Country)* [1995] 1 FLR 89 the Italian father was not married to the mother, yet there was no inquiry into whether, if Convention principles were going to be applied, the mother's removal of the children to England was in breach of his 'rights of custody' for the purposes of Art 3. Both States are now Contracting States; South Africa in 1997, and Italy in 1995.

co-operation between states parties, including in particular rights of access,[8] and these will not be in place where children are returned to a non-Convention country. Also, a child may be returned to a country where the principles governing the resolution of children cases are significantly different from the welfare principle as operated by the English courts. Of this fear Lord Donaldson MR said in *Re F (A Minor) (Abduction: Jurisdiction)*:[9]

> 'Which court should decide depends ... on whether the other court will apply principles which are acceptable to the English courts as being appropriate, subject always to any contra-indication such as those mentioned in Article 13 of the Convention, or a risk of persecution or discrimination, but prima facie the court to decide is that of the state where the child is habitually resident immediately before its removal.'

There is a common assumption linking the several cases concerned with the summary return of children that the foreign court will apply law and practice in a broadly comparable manner to the English courts. In *Re S (Minors) (Abduction)*,[10] Balcombe LJ stated that the general principles of the Hague Convention should apply in an 'appropriate' non-Convention case. Quoting Lord Donaldson, he said: 'Which court should decide depends ... on whether the other court will apply principles which are acceptable to the English courts as being appropriate'.[11]

In the light of that general principle the ruling in *Re S (Minors) (Abduction)* was disturbing because of the approach taken by the Court of Appeal to what other systems were 'appropriate'. The case concerned whether children of Muslim parents should be returned to Pakistan. Their mother, although born in Pakistan, had been brought up in England, but had gone to live in Pakistan after marrying, and had had three children there. Later she brought the two younger children to England without the father's knowledge or consent and he sought their return to Pakistan. Expert evidence was given that although the Pakistani courts would apply a similar welfare principle to the determination of the upbringing of the children, the attitude of the Pakistani courts towards the welfare of the children would differ considerably from an English court. The Pakistani court would try to give effect to the children's welfare from a Muslim point of view and this point of view would exclude a Muslim mother from entitlement to bring up her children in certain specified circumstances. Of this approach to welfare, Nolan LJ said:

---

8   Arts 7 and 21.
9   [1991] 1 FLR 1 at p 5. Cf *C v C (Abduction: Jurisdiction)* [1993] Fam Law 185 in which Cazalet J refused to return a child to Brazil because of the delay which would occur before the merits of the case would be tried in the Brazilian courts.
10 [1994] 1 FLR 297, at p 303.
11 *Re F (A Minor) (Abduction: Jurisdiction)* [1991] 1 FLR 1, at p 5.

'... that seems to me to be neither surprising nor, in the circumstances of these children, objectionable. They are the children of
Muslim parents who are part of a Muslim family ... In my
judgment, [the trial judge] was fully entitled to take the view that,
for Muslim children of Muslim parents whose home hitherto has
been in Pakistan, the principles of Pakistani law are appropriate
by English standards.'[12]

Thus the Court of Appeal was prepared to order children aged three and
seven, who were living with their mother and grandmother in England, to be
returned to a country where, according to the expert evidence, the law would
allow the children to be deprived of the care of their mother if she concluded
a subsequent marriage, or formed a liaison with another man other than a
close relative to the children, or if she was deemed to be unsuitable, for
instance if she had a way of life which the court would consider un-Islamic.

It is suggested that the general justification relied on for the summary
return approach, namely that these were children who were being
alienated from their background, home, school, friends and relations[13]
was not borne out by the facts.[14] A child of three has no sense of country
and nationality. A little girl of seven would be far more likely to wish to
remain in the same country as her mother and maternal family rather
than experience the further upheaval of returning to her original home
country. If the child were to learn that there was a possibility that she
would be deprived of her mother's care if she returned to Pakistan it is
surely inconceivable that she would wish to return there. The underlying
assumption of the Convention is that 'the courts of all its signatories are
equally concerned to ensure, and equally capable of ensuring, that both
parties receive a fair hearing, and that all issues of child welfare receive
a skilled, thorough and humane evaluation'.[15] However, although the Court
of Appeal claimed that it was acting in the best interests of the children,
in *Re S (Minors) (Abduction)* it was allowing them to return to a system
which would take account of matters which an English court would regard
as incompatible with the welfare principle. What in reality it was doing
when it applied the Hague Convention philosophy in this non-Convention
case was preserving comity between nations, giving respect to a different
judicial system, giving respect to the tenets of a non-Christian religion,
and deterring parents wishing to return to England after a failed marriage
from bringing their children to this country. Furthermore, it was ordering
the return of children with none of the safeguards built into the system
as it operates between Contracting States. In particular Article 19 makes
it clear that a decision under the Convention concerning the return of the
child must not be taken to be a determination of any custody issue. A non-

12 Ibid, at pp 304-305.
13 See Buckley LJ in *Re L (Minors) (Wardship: Jurisdiction)* [1974] 1 WLR 250 at p 264.
14 Indeed, it is suggested that this justification for the approach of the Hague Convention
    does not survive close examination in the case of young children.
15 *P v P (Minors) (Child Abduction)* [1992] 1 FLR 155 per Waite J, at p 161.

Convention state on the other hand might well be influenced by the English court's order when adjudicating on the merits.[16]

Re S (Minors) (Abduction) was not a unique example of the sub-ordination of the child's welfare to other principles. In *Re M (Abduction: Non-Convention Country)*,[17] Waite LJ stated that the principle of comity applies to this area of law. He repeated this view in *Re M (Abduction: Peremptory Return Order)*.[18] It was put to him that the court should have regard to the way in which issues relating to the child's welfare would be likely to be resolved in the country of the competing jurisdiction, so that the court could be satisfied that the principles that would be operated by the judicial system of the non-Convention country[19] would be principles acceptable to an English court. Rejecting that argument, he said:

> 'Underlying the whole purpose of the peremptory return order is a principle of international comity under which judges in England will assume that facilities for a fair hearing will be provided by the court of the other jurisdiction, and that due account will be taken by overseas judges of what has been said, ordered and undertaken to be done within the English jurisdiction. ... Very exceptional circumstances would be needed to show that in a particular case the English court would be justified in parting from that general principle.'

In *Re JA (Child Abduction: Non-Convention Country)*[20] the child was habitually resident in the United Arab Emirates prior to coming to England with both parents. Reviewing the law which would be applied in the United Arab Emirates, the Court of Appeal found that there was no indication that the child's welfare would be the test. Moreover, the mother's health as well as her happiness would be put at risk if she was to return there with the child. The court held that the authorities clearly established that it was 'an abdication of the responsibility and an abnegation of the duty of this court to the ward under its protection to surrender the determination of its ward's future to a foreign court whose regime may be inimical to the child's welfare.'[1] It therefore found that the ordinary expectation that a court of the child's habitual residence would decide a child's future was not of sufficient benefit to the child to outweigh the risks associated with ordering his return.[2]

The discrepancies in the rulings in the above cases reveal that there is an undoubted tension in the Court of Appeal over what should be the court's

---

16 It is suggested that, at the very least, expert evidence should be obtained on this point.
17 [1995] 1 FLR 89.
18 [1996] 1 FLR 478.
19 In that case, the United Arab Emirates.
20 [1998] 1 FLR 231.
1   At p 243, per Ward LJ.
2   That decision did not, of course, decide the issue of the child's future residence. It meant only that an English court would determine the case on the merits. However, English law would apply, and the child's welfare would be the court's paramount consideration.

proper response in non-Convention cases.[3] It is therefore not easy to predict with exactness how a court might approach a non-Convention case. Certainly, the manner in which Waite LJ elevated international comity to be the guiding principle in *Re M (Abduction: Peremptory Return Order)*[4] was at odds with what had been said in the Privy Council and House of Lords about the paramountcy of the welfare principle being the deciding factor.[5] Indeed, in *Re JA (Child Abduction: Non-Convention Country)*[6] Ward LJ went so far as to say that, if driven to it, he would reluctantly say that the Court of Appeal's decision in *Re M (Abduction: Peremptory Return Order)*[7] was made per incuriam. However, and somewhat surprisingly, Ward LJ stated in *Re P (Abduction: Non-Convention Country)*[8] that the trial judge correctly directed himself when he approached a non-Convention case concerning a five-year-old child on the basis that he should deal with the matter peremptorily and summarily. However, Ward LJ was in no doubt that the paramountcy principle applied to the question of whether peremptory return would best serve the child's interests, and he claimed that this approach was supported by 'the overwhelming burden of authorities'.[9]

This resurgence of the paramountcy principle cannot disguise the fact that much of the case law supports the view that the welfare of the child normally requires that decisions about children are best taken in the jurisdiction in which they have resided.[10] Nor can the fact that other courts have been persuaded by appeals to notions of comity be ignored. The association between peremptory return and the welfare principle has not usually been closely related to the individual circumstances of the particular child, but has been treated as a matter of general good policy. 'The fact that there is jurisdiction to grant peremptory return in child abduction cases where the Convention does not apply, is itself based upon nothing else but an appreciation of the general demands of the best interests of all children.'[11] Courts appear to take no account of the child's age when adopting this

---

3   See D McClean and K Beevers, *International child abduction – back to common law principles* (1995) 7 CFLQ 128; D McClean, *International child abduction – some recent trends* (1997) 9 CFLQ 387.
4   [1996] 1 FLR 478.
5   In *McKee v McKee* [1951] AC 352 and *J v C* [1970] AC 668 respectively.
6   [1998] 1 FLR 231.
7   [1996] 1 FLR 478.
8   [1997] 1 FLR 780.
9   At p 787.
10 Stemming from the judgment of Buckley LJ in *Re L (Minors: Wardship Jurisdiction)* [1974] 1 All ER 913. See also *T v T (Child Abduction: Non-Convention Country)* [1998] 2 FLR 1110, where the court ordered that children wrongfully removed and retained by the father in England should be returned to their mother in the United Arab Emirates. The court said that the dilemma it faced was whether the welfare of the children demanded immediate return or whether their welfare required further investigation. The court was not persuaded that further inquiry was necessary because the welfare principle also required that children were not separated from a caring parent.
11 *Re M (Abduction: Non-Convention Country)* [1995] 1 FLR 89 at p 98, per Waite LJ; *Re F (A Minor) (Abduction: Jurisdiction)* [1991] 1 FLR 1; *Re S (Minors) (Abduction)* [1994] 1 FLR 297.

policy view.[12] Moreover, there has been a tendency to presume that the courts to which the child will be returned will adopt procedures and apply principles which are compatible with the paramountcy principle, even where the court has received evidence to the contrary.[13] However, in *Re P (Non-Convention Country)*[14] the Court of Appeal rejected an approach to the child's welfare which applied Article 13 of the Convention to a non-Convention case, and firmly stated that:

> '... to elevate Article 13 into the test which governs return (or rather no return) is to fly in the face of the established authority because ... one does not proceed on the basis that it is necessary to establish that the child would be in some obvious moral or physical danger if returned. That is not the criterion: welfare, wide-ranging concept that it is, is the only criterion.'[15]

This more positive attitude to the welfare principle and more focused approach to its application to individual children is to be welcomed. Those courts which are overly concerned with ensuring that international child abduction is discouraged should beware of making hard decisions about some children in order to discourage the parents of other children from taking them across jurisdictional borders. Notions of general deterrence should have no part to play in decision-making about children. In their eagerness to promote comity in non-Convention cases where none of the safeguards built into the Convention can be relied upon to be applied, some courts may have come perilously close to making orders which are incompatible with the individual human rights of both children and parents.[16]

---

12 Were such an approach to be taken to paramountcy in domestic children proceedings, it is suggested that it might well be held to be an improper application of the welfare principle. In family proceedings there is an expectation that a perceptive approach to the unique position of each child will be taken in accordance with the guidance in s 1(3) of the Children Act 1989; see ch 4.

13 *Re S (Minors) (Abduction)* [1994] 1 FLR 297; *Re M (Abduction: Peremptory Return Order)* [1996] 1 FLR 478; *Re M (Abduction: Non-Convention Country)* [1995] 1 FLR 89.

14 [1997] 1 FLR 780. See also *Re JA (Child Abduction: Non-Convention Country)* [1998] 1 FLR 231.

15 *Re P (Non-Convention Country)* [1997] 1 FLR 780 at p 789, per Ward LJ. In the same case he described as 'excellent' an article by D McClean and K Beevers, *International child abduction – back to common law principles* (1995) 7 CFLQ 128, in which the authors advocate that the welfare principle should have full rein in non-Convention cases.

16 Where courts refuse to give leave for evidence to be adduced about a child's wishes and feelings before ordering summary return this appears to fly in the face of Art 12(2) of the UN Convention on the Rights of the Child 1989: 'the child shall in particular be provided the opportunity to be heard in any judicial and administrative proceedings affecting the child, either directly or through a representative or an appropriate body in a manner consistent with the procedural rules of national law.'

Chapter 6

Personal protection and regulating the occupation of the family home

Arrest
Provision for third parties to act on behalf of victims of domestic
          violence
Persons not protected under the Family Law Act 1996
Protection from Harassment Act 1997
Homelessness
    Priority need
    Intentional homelessness

Chapter 6

Personal protection and regulating the occupation of the family home

The law's response to domestic violence

One of the most dangerous symptoms of conflict in personal relationships is when it escalates into domestic violence. A large literature has developed over the past twenty years upon the problems of domestic violence, its nature, causes and extent and the effectiveness of various responses to it.[1] Domestic violence occurs between people of all social classes, amongst all racial and religious groupings and in all age groups.[2] Crime and other statistics provide only a rough estimate of the nature and extent of the suffering which is endured by families behind closed doors,[3] but there can be no doubt that parents and children living in households in which assaults take place are damaged by this behaviour, both physically and emotionally. Victims of domestic assaults often do not complain of violence, either through fear of being further assaulted, or because they are too embarrassed and ashamed to reveal their plight to professionals who might be able to assist them. Wife beating is not regarded with the same revulsion as child beating; indeed, until recently it was not identified as a social problem which required addressing by agencies concerned with the welfare of families. It was during the late 1960s that the pernicious nature of

---

1   *Domestic Violence and Occupation of the Family Home,* Law Com No 207, para 2.1. The Report contains extensive references. An introduction to much of the research can be found in L J F Smith *Domestic Violence: an overview of the literature* (Home Office Research Study No 107, 1989). See also S Edwards *Sex and gender in the legal process* (Blackstone Press, 1996, Cch 5).

2   Law Com No 207, para 3.1. See further M Russel *Taking Stock: Refuge provisions in London in the late 1980s,* Southwark Council (1989); United Nations Centre for Social Development and Humanitarian Affairs *Violence against Women in the Family* (1989).

3   It is estimated that one in ten women who have lived with a male partner have, at some time, experienced domestic violence and that over one-third of these incidents happen after separation. See C Mirrlees-Black *Estimating the extent of domestic violence: findings from the 1992 British Crime Survey* (Home Office Research and Statistics Dept, Research Bulletin No 37, Whiting and Birch, 1995).

domestic violence started to exercise the minds of law reformers,[4] but not until the 1970s that the political will was found to create a legislative framework designed to meet the needs of battered women.[5] Of course women are not the only victims of domestic assaults; men, children and the elderly are vulnerable to domestic violence too. However, there is an abundance of evidence to show that it is women and children who are the main victims. Children who themselves suffer violence at the hands of a parent are in the main protected by the state through child protection procedures.[6] The remedies provided by the civil law are therefore generally used to obtain protection for an adult victim. But where that victim is looking after children, any orders or injunctions which she obtains will normally assist the children too. For children to witness violence is undoubtedly a damaging experience, and it will be seen that the welfare of such children will influence the courts in the exercise of their discretion.

The role of the criminal law

Domestic assaults are criminal offences and a man who has attacked his wife can be prosecuted for his actions. He may be charged with one or more of various offences against the person,[7] including the offence of rape.[8] The Protection from Harassment Act 1997 introduced strong measures to assist those who are victims of a course of conduct which amounts to harassment and made such conduct a crime. However, victims of domestic violence and harassment may be reluctant to become involved in the prosecution process for a number of reasons.[9] These include the realisation by the victim that the matter is no longer under her control once she has reported an attack to the police. It will be up to the police to decide whether and how they wish to investigate her complaint, and it will be the decision

4   Who were stimulated into taking action by such pioneering women as Erin Pizzey who opened the first women's refuge in Chiswick, and who subsequently published a dramatic account of the horrors of domestic violence and the failure of the law to provide safeguards for its victims in *Scream Quietly or the Neighbours Will Hear*, Harmondsworth (Penguin Books, 1974).

5   House of Commons Select Committee on Violence in Marriage *Report, Minutes of Evidence and Appendices* (HMSO, 1974-75). In the reported case law on domestic violence the woman is virtually always the complainant, and the use of the personal pronouns 'he' and 'she' in this chapter reflects this fact.

6   See ch 3.

7   See the major textbooks on criminal law for details of these offences.

8   It was not until 1991 that the House of Lords ruled that a man could be convicted of the offence of rape when the victim was his wife: see *R v R (Rape: Marital Exemption)* [1991] 4 All ER 481. The House took a far more radical approach than the Law Commission which, somewhat timidly and conservatively, had recommended that such a change in the common law would require legislation; see Law Commission Working Paper No 116 *Rape Within Marriage* (1989).

9   See D Lockton and R Ward *Domestic Violence* (Cavendish Publishing, 1997) pp 20-25 for a useful summary of much of the literature.

of the Crown Prosecution Service whether or not to go ahead and press charges. This loss of control acts as a disincentive to women to report incidents of violence, as they may well fear the consequences of their action if the police and Crown Prosecution Service fail, as they see it, to respond in an appropriate fashion. In the past the police have been unwilling to intervene in cases of domestic violence, and to prosecute offenders. This perception of the police as unwilling to come to the assistance of victims of domestic assaults is still evident today, even though domestic violence is taken much more seriously by the police than in the past, and even though police practices in many areas have changed radically in favour of the victim.[10]

Other factors which may deter a woman from becoming involved in the criminal process include the fear of further, and perhaps more vicious, assaults on her person in retaliation for her action; anxiety about the financial hardship which the family would suffer if the man were to lose his job; and a more general reluctance to be instrumental in the man gaining a criminal record, and perhaps being sent to prison. Although a woman may wish to take steps to stop a man from assaulting her, such steps may not include taking the risk that the man (who is often the father of her children) will be sent to prison. Furthermore, the criminal law is concerned with identifying and punishing criminals, whereas what the victim of domestic violence needs is protection against further assaults once the punishment process has come to an end.

Criminal injuries compensation

The question of whether a woman might be entitled to receive criminal injuries compensation is an important factor which should be taken into account when advising a woman whether to press for the prosecution of her assailant. Any victim of an assault is potentially able to make a claim under the criminal injuries compensation scheme. However, where the victim lives in the same household as the perpetrator, as a member of the same family, she can only claim compensation if she satisfies certain conditions.[11] Amongst these conditions there is one stating that the perpetrator of the violence must either have been successfully prosecuted for the offence, or the Criminal Injuries Compensation Board must be satisfied there are good reasons why such a prosecution has not taken place. Clearly the amount of compensation the woman would be likely to

---

10 See generally A Sanders *Personal violence and public order: The prosecution of 'domestic' violence in England and Wales* (1988) 16 Int J Soc L 359; D Lockton and R Ward *Domestic Violence* (Cavendish Publishing, 1997). Lockton and Ward record that after their study of the police in Leicester was concluded the Leicestershire police force changed its policy and training.

11 See the 26th Report of the Criminal Injuries Compensation Board, Cm 1365, 1990, App C.

receive if her application to the Board were successful, and what amounts to good reasons for the Board's purposes, should influence any advice given.

Non-molestation orders

The solution offered by the civil law to the brutality of domestic violence and to other forms of personal molestation is to confer powers on the courts to make non-molestation orders.[12] Non-molestation orders are aimed at providing a speedy remedy for the victim which can be enforced through contempt proceedings, or through police involvement. Magistrates, who exercise a local jurisdiction which is easily accessible, have the same powers as circuit judges and designated district judges sitting in county courts.[13] In practice the majority of applications for protection against violence and other forms of molestation are made to the county courts. This is partly for historical reasons relating to the limits which used to be placed on the powers of magistrates under the law which preceded the Family Law Act 1996;[14] and partly because of the influence of legal aid considerations.

Meaning of molestation

'Molestation' is not defined in the Family Law Act 1996.[15] It covers the obvious case where the victim is subject to an assault or battery which could give rise to criminal proceedings. But, despite the reference to 'violence' in the heading to Part IV of the Family Law Act 1996, it is clear that the court is not limited to granting orders in those cases where violence or threats of violence occur. 'Violence is a form of molestation, but molestation may take place without the threat or use of violence and still be serious and inimical to mental and physical health.'[16] Any conduct which is a sufficient harassment of the victim as to call for intervention of the court can be the subject of an injunction.[17] Harassment can take a variety of forms. In *Horner v Horner*[18] the molestation by the husband took the form of handing the wife upsetting notes, and intercepting her on her

---

12 Family Law Act 1996, s 42.
13 The High Court also has jurisdiction.
14 Domestic Proceedings and Magistrates' Courts Act 1978, ss16-18 (now repealed). This bias towards the use of the county court would alter if the Lord Chancellor exercises his power to specify the circumstances in which proceedings must be commenced in, or transferred to, a particular level or class of court, Family Law Act 1996, s 57.
15 Following the recommendation of the Law Commission, Law Com No 207, para 3.1. Contrast the position in New Zealand where in the Domestic Violence Act 1996, s 3 the meaning of 'domestic violence' is closely defined.
16 *Davis v Johnson* [1978] 1 All ER 1132, per Viscount Dilhorne at p 1144.
17 See generally Judge Nigel Fricker QC *Molestation and harassment after Patel v Patel* (1988) 18 Fam Law 395.
18 [1982] 2 All ER 495.

way to the station. In *Spencer v Camacho,*[19] after a series of other activities for which the woman had obtained non-molestation orders, riffling through her handbag was held to be sufficient conduct to amount to molestation. Other activities that have given rise to injunctions have included writing abusive letters and shouting obscenities,[20] and following the applicant around and making a 'perfect nuisance' of oneself.[1] In *C v C (Non-Molestation Order: Jurisdiction)*[2] the applicant was unsuccessful. The former wife of the applicant spoke to two national newspapers complaining about her husband's conduct during the marriage, which allegations the newpapers published. Sir Stephen Brown was clear that such action came 'nowhere near' molestation as envisaged by section 42. What the applicant suffered was not molestation, but feared damage to his reputation for which he could mount appropriate proceedings. Where a non-molestation order is made the actual wording of the order will clearly be tailored to the needs of the particular case. However, a usual form of wording is that the respondent is restrained from 'assaulting, molesting, annoying or otherwise interfering with the applicant or any child living with the applicant'.

At least one commentator believes that the 'anachronistic' term 'non-molestation order' should have been replaced with modern and clear terminology which accurately portrays the harm at which non-molestation orders are aimed.[3] The police had similar concerns because they had information to suggest that either the people seeking protection, or those to whom they turned for assistance, did not fully understand what the term means. They took the view that some kind of definition, designed to be inclusive, not exclusive, could usefully have been provided containing such words as 'pester', 'threaten' or 'harass'.[4] It is suggested that the anxieties of the police give real cause for concern. There is a real risk that the phrase may be narrowly interpreted by the police when they are initially called to intervene in a domestic situation, or when called upon to enforce a non-molestation order, because of lack of any clear indication of how wide the term's meaning is meant to be.

Non-molestation orders between 'associated persons'

Although a non-molestation order can be made in respect of any 'relevant child', where adults are concerned the benefits of the Act are restricted to

---

19 (1984) 4 FLR 662.
20 *George v George* [1986] 2 FLR 347.
1   *Vaughan v Vaughan* [1973] 1 WLR 1159.
2   [1998] 1 FLR 554, which appeared to be the first reported case under the Family Law Act 1996.
3   See the written evidence of M L Parry to the Special Public Bill Committee on the Family Homes and Domestic Violence Bill (1994-95) HL Paper 55, p 66. He suggested that words like 'no harm', 'non-abuse' or 'protection' orders would be more appropriate.
4   Ibid, oral evidence, p 41.

a limited class of applicants. Section 42(2) provides that a court may make a non-molestation order:

'(a) if an application for the order has been made (whether in other family proceedings or without any other family proceedings having been instituted) by a person who is associated with the respondent; or

(b) if in any family proceedings to which the respondent is a party the court considers that the order should be made for the benefit of any other party to the proceedings or any relevant child even though no such application has been made.'

Paragraph (a) makes it clear that before an applicant can take proceedings she must establish that she is 'associated with' the respondent. Paragraph (b) extends the court's own motion powers to those cases where family proceedings are already underway. However, own motion powers may only be exercised where the people concerned are both parties to the proceedings, or where there is a relevant child. It is suggested that these limits on the court's jurisdiction may have undesirable consequences. For example, where a witness is threatened with violence or otherwise molested by a party to family proceedings, unless the witness is associated with that party, she is not entitled to apply for a non-molestation order, and the court cannot make a non-molestation order of its own motion.[5]

The meaning of 'associated persons' is explained in section 62. This section should be read in conjunction with section 63 which provides guidance on the interpretation of the words and phrases used in Part IV of the Act.

Section 62 provides that for the purposes of Part IV:

'(3) A person is associated with another person if-

(a) they are or have been married to each other;

(b) they are cohabitants or former cohabitants;

(c) they live or have lived in the same household, otherwise than merely by reason of one of them being the other's employee, tenant, lodger or boarder;

(d) they are relatives;[6]

(e) they have agreed to marry one another (whether or not that agreement has been terminated);

---

5 Such behaviour may, of course, amount to contempt of court as well as being criminal.

6 S 63 provides that 'relative' in relation to a person means the parents, step-parents, children, step-children, grandparents, grandchildren, siblings, uncles and aunts and nephews and nieces (whether of the full blood or half blood or by affinity) of that person or of that person's spouse or former spouse. Somewhat startlingly, in relation to a person who is living or has lived with another person as husband and wife, relative includes any person who would fall within the above list if the parties were married to each other.

    (f) in relation to any child, they are both persons falling within subsection (4); or

    (g) they are parties to the same family proceedings (other than proceedings under this Part).[7]

(4) A person falls within this subsection in relation to a child if-

(a) he is a parent of the child; or

(b) he has or has had parental responsibility for the child.[8]

(5) If a child has been adopted or has been freed for adoption by virtue of any of the enactments mentioned in s 16(1) of the Adoption Act 1976, two persons are also associated with each other for the purposes of this Part if-

(a) one is a natural parent of the child or a parent of such a natural parent; and

(b) the other is the child or any person-

    (i) who has become a parent of the child by virtue of an adoption order or has applied for an adoption order, or

    (ii) with whom the child has at any time been placed for adoption.'

The Law Commission recommended, and Parliament accepted, that the availability of non-molestation orders should be limited to persons with some kind of domestic connection.[9] Whether this was wise is debatable. The 'associated persons' provisions are extremely complicated[10] and they are bound to leave gaps.[11] As the Commission itself recognised, restricting the law's remedies can give rise to strange results. It gave the example of four friends sharing a flat. Where they are all joint tenants a remedy may be available to any one of them. Yet where one of them took the tenancy and then sublet to his friends, the remedy would not be available to him. It seems unfortunate to legislate knowing in advance the difficult problems that are liable to arise, particularly if those difficulties can be avoided. Limiting the scope of the Act's provisions to associated persons also prevents the courts from dealing in an even-handed manner with potential litigants where molestation is making someone's life a misery. Where the behaviour is such that the law should provide a remedy, why limit that

---

7   The Law Commission recommended that the list of associated persons should include 'persons who have or have had a sexual relationship with each other (whether or not including sexual intercourse)'. This was rejected by Parliament, perhaps fortunately as there is a risk that it could have become known as the 'Clinton' clause.

8   Sub-s (6) provides that 'a body corporate and another person are not, by virtue of sub-s (3)(f) or (g), to be regarded for the purposes of this Part as associated with each other.' Thus a local authority with parental responsibility for a child is not an associated person for the purposes of the Act.

9   Not all close relatives are covered. For example, cousins do not fall within the list.

10   Note also the evidence provisions relating to an agreement to marry in s 44.

11   Eg, in relation to adopted children, s 62(5)(a) may allow for the inclusion of the natural grandparent of an adopted child, but only where the natural parent has died, and it does not include natural siblings. However, experience tells us that domestic violence does not fit naturally into such closely defined categories.

remedy to a certain class of applicant?[12] It is suggested that a simple, accessible remedy available to all who are subject to molestation, not just to those in a 'familial' relationship, should have been provided. Parliament subsequently took this view when it enacted the Protection from Harassment Act 1997.[13]

Paradoxically, there may be advantages for those who are entitled to apply under the Family Law Act 1996 to apply instead under the 1997 Act. Harassment and putting a person in fear of violence on at least two occasions are criminal offences under the 1997 Act. Thus, damages may be awarded; injunctions may be granted; restraining orders may be made; warrants of arrest may be issued; and, as breach of an injunction is a criminal offence, the courts have sentencing powers, which are of up to five years' imprisonment.[14]

The child as applicant for a non-molestation order

The plight of child victims of domestic violence was of particular concern to Parliament. Children will normally fall within the definition of an associated person and children on the threshold of adulthood are just as entitled as adults to apply for non-molestation orders. The position of a child under 16 is governed by section 43 which states that the child (i) must first obtain the leave of the court; and (ii) that the court may grant leave only if it is satisfied that the child has sufficient understanding to make the proposed application. No guidance is given to the court on what criteria it should apply to such a leave application. However, it is probable that parallels will be drawn with applications for leave to apply for section 8 orders made by children under the Children Act 1989, where the same restriction applies. It also seems likely that the direction that such children must apply to the High Court will be extended to children applying for leave under the Family Law Act.[15] Furthermore, it appears likely that the court will take steps to encourage an adult to make an application on the child's behalf relying on the broad provisions relating to 'relevant children'.[16] Persuading a parent or other adult associated with the

---

12 For example, if a university student becomes the object of the obsessive attentions of an unbalanced lecturer (or vice versa) why should not he or she be able to obtain a non-molestation injunction under this Act? For further criticism, see M Hayes and C Williams *Domestic violence and occupation of the family home: proposals for reform* [1992] Fam Law 497 at 498; M Hayes *Non-molestation protection – only associated persons need apply* [1996] Fam Law 134.

13 See below.

14 The details of this Act are beyond the scope of this book. For a fuller account, see T Lawson-Cruttenden and N Addison *Blackstones Guide to the Protection from Harassment Act 1997*. The position of persons who fall outside the scope of the 1996 Act is discussed, briefly, below.

15 For the implications of this, see the discussion in ch 2.

16 See above.

respondent to apply for a non-molestation order, particularly where the application is coupled with an application for an occupation order,[17] might sometimes avoid the necessity to institute care proceedings on behalf of a child who is suffering, or who is likely to suffer, significant harm, as a result of domestic violence.[18] It also avoids the child becoming embroiled in taking legal proceedings against his or her own parent. The parent/child relationship is complex and delicate and the courts are properly hesitant about permitting the initiation of proceedings which could lead to the permanent estrangement of a child from his parent, as this will not normally be in the long-term best interests of the child.

Criteria for granting non-molestation orders

The Law Commission suggested, and Parliament accepted, that the criteria for the grant of a non-molestation order should focus on the effect of the respondent's behaviour on the applicant and on the applicant's need for protection.[19] Consequently, section 42(5) of the 1996 Act provides that:

> 'In deciding whether to exercise its powers under this section and, if so, in what manner, the court shall have regard to all the circumstances including the need to secure the health, safety and well-being-
> (a) of the applicant or in a case [where the court proposes to make an order of its own motion], the person for whose benefit the order would be made; and
> (b) of any relevant child.'

A very wide definition of molestation, and a victim-focused approach to the criteria to be applied to the exercise of judicial discretion is to be welcomed. Any conduct which has the express purpose of harassing another family member should be subject to regulation by the law if sufficiently serious. These criteria ensure that the court is concerned to protect the applicant's health and safety, and it must also consider her well-being, which widens the scope of relevant considerations. However, there are two undesirable precedents which could survive the alterations brought about by the 1996 Act. In *Johnson v Walton*[20] the court was of the opinion that molestation involving harassment includes an intent to cause distress or harm. It is suggested that any restriction which requires that the conduct must be intentional would be unfortunate. It is certainly the case that where the respondent is physically violent towards the applicant an order can be granted regardless of intention, as demonstrated in *Wooton*

17 See below.
18 See ch 3 for when care proceedings can be taken to protect children from harm.
19 *Domestic Violence and Occupation of the Family Home* LC No 207, para 3.6.
20 [1990] 1 FLR 350.

v Wooton,[1] where the respondent only became violent during epileptic episodes. The Court of Appeal held that the court had jurisdiction to grant an injunction because it was the actual violence, and the consequences suffered by the applicant, which were the important factors to be considered by the court. There seems to be every reason in principle why the same reasoning should apply to non-violent behaviour. A husband who, perhaps due to mental illness, is behaving in such a way that the court would normally intervene, may be causing just as much distress as a husband who is acting out of spite. While concern and compassion should always be extended to the mentally ill, if a victim is finding a mentally ill person's behaviour intolerable she should be just as much entitled to the protection of the law as a victim of intended action. Of course, in cases where the respondent is so ill that he is incapable of understanding the nature and consequences of a non-molestation order it ought not to be granted. The order would not have a deterrent effect because the respondent would not be capable of complying with it, and any breach could not be subject to effective enforcement proceedings since the respondent would have a clear defence to an application for committal for contempt, as in *Wookey v Wookey*.[2]

Normally a woman who is seeking a non-molestation order on the grounds of violence, or other serious misbehaviour, will also be seeking an order which gives her exclusive occupation of the matrimonial home for a temporary period. However, this will not necessarily be the case. Sadly, it is a fact that people get locked into destructive relationships and find it enormously difficult to break free from them. Some people, mainly but not exclusively women, wish to stay with their partners even though they are the victims of persistent violence. They may, therefore, still wish to remain living in the same household but be seeking an order to restrain any further violence being committed upon them. This situation arose in *F v F (Protection From Violence: Continuing Cohabitation).*[3] Judge Nigel Fricker QC[4] held that an injunction cannot be granted to an applicant who is living, and intends to continue living, in full cohabitation with the respondent. The judge thought that Parliament cannot have intended that injunctions should be used to direct conduct between cohabiting couples under the threat that disobedience would amount to contempt of court. However, there is nothing in the wording either of the previous legislation or in the Family Law Act 1996 to limit the court's jurisdiction to grant non-molestation orders in this way, and it is suggested that the decision was wrong. Many women continue to live with their violent partners. They should be afforded the protection of an order in appropriate cases.[5]

---

1   [1984] FLR 871.
2   [1991] 3 All ER 365.
3   [1989] 2 FLR 451. This is a rare example of a county court judgment being reported, rather than an appeal from such a judgment.
4   Who is an acknowledged expert on domestic violence injunctions and who has written extensively in this field.
5   For a critique of *F v F* see R Stevens *Protection or not?* [1989] Fam Law 464.

Non-molestation of a child

A non-molestation order may be made in respect of any 'relevant child'.[6] Section 62(2) provides that a 'relevant child' means:

'(a) any child who is living with or might reasonably be expected to live with either party to the proceedings;
(b) any child in relation to whom an order under the Adoption Act 1976 or the Children Act 1989 is in question in the proceedings; and
(c) any other child whose interests the court considers relevant.'

There is no requirement that the child must be a child of the family or otherwise associated with the applicant; indeed the child need not have a defined relationship with either the applicant or the respondent.[7] By including within its protective scope all children who live, or who might reasonably be expected to live, with either party to the proceedings, the Act recognises that a child who has not been treated as part of the family is liable to be a child at risk. Jealousy and anger directed at a child who has no blood relationship with the man living in the household has led to tragedy in a number of well-known cases.[8] A non-molestation order is also available where the applicant has moved out of the home, perhaps because of the respondent's violence, and where the children remain living with the respondent. Consequently, where a woman has fled the home and is living in a refuge she can apply for an order where she fears for the safety of her children despite the fact that the children are no longer with her.

The door of the court is widened even further by the inclusion of a child in relation to whom an order under either the Adoption Act 1976 or the Children Act 1989 is in question in the proceedings. Indeed, Parliament was so concerned to ensure that all relevant children fell within the scope of the protection afforded by non-molestation injunctions that it included the catch-all provision in paragraph (c). This gives courts a discretion to make orders to protect 'any other child whose interests the court considers relevant'. The gate-keeping role is vested in the court. It is for the court to decide whether the application is misconceived.

Occupation orders and entitled applicants

The breakdown of a personal relationship often occurs over a long period of time and it may be punctuated by incidents of violence and molestation. Victims of domestic assaults do not necessarily want their relationship

---

6   S 42(1)(b).
7   Thus, for example, children such as foster-children are afforded protection.
8   See for example the reports into the deaths of Jasmine Beckford *A Child in Trust* (London Borough of Brent, 1985), and Kimberley Carlile *A Child in Mind* (London Borough of Greenwich, 1987), both of whom were killed by their step-fathers.

with their spouse or partner to come to an end; rather they may want it to continue but for the violence and threatening behaviour to cease. Or they may decide that the position has become so unbearable that the only solution is to end the relationship. In the case of a married victim she may decide to institute divorce proceedings. In the case of an unmarried victim she may start to take steps to sort out the parties' personal affairs. In either situation, a spouse or partner who is being assaulted, harassed, threatened or otherwise abused and molested may reach the stage where she can no longer tolerate living under the same roof with the man. Indeed, many victims of domestic violence are forced to flee the home because of the risks to which they are exposed. The question of whether an order can be obtained to oust one of the parties from the home and, where one party has been driven from the home, an order obtained which will entitle her to return and live on the premises unmolested, then arises as a matter of real urgency. This is particularly true where the parties have few assets and a relatively low income; in a case of this kind the parties often cannot agree about who should stay in the home and who should leave, because the person who leaves may have nowhere suitable to go.

Where there are children, a spouse or partner may insist on remaining in the home because he takes the view (probably correctly) that to leave would prejudice any chance he has of obtaining a residence order in respect of the children.[9] Where violence is alleged against one of the parties (usually against the man) he may refuse to leave the home because he may take the view that to do so would amount to an admission of his guilt. It has been seen that non-molestation orders can be granted which focus solely on the person of the victim, but these may have little value if the perpetrator of an assault (or other form of molestation) is living in the same household as the victim. The law therefore makes provision for the temporary ousting of one of the parties from the home.[10]

Spouses and others with an estate or interest in the family home

Section 33 covers those people who have an estate or interest in the family home. It needs to be understood at the outset that the scope of section 33 extends beyond spouses, to include any situation where the applicant 'is entitled to occupy a dwelling house by virtue of a beneficial estate or interest or contract or by virtue of any enactment giving him the right to remain in occupation'[11] provided that the respondent is an 'associated

9   On residence orders and the status quo, see ch 4.
10 The situation may arise that the parents are in dispute about with which parent the child will live as well as about the occupation of the home. In *Re T (A Minor), T v T (Ouster Order)* [1987] 1 FLR 181 it was held that normally the court should first decide who is to be the parent with whom the children are to have their home, and then go on to decide whether or not to oust the other parent.
11 S 33(1)(a)(i).

person'.[12] Thus section 33 may embrace an application between a variety of associated persons, for example, siblings, unmarried partners, and same sex couples. This has nothing to do with the nature of the applicant's personal status. Whether section 33 applies depends on whether the applicant has a proprietary right to live in the property or 'matrimonial home rights' and has shared the home with another person with whom she is associated.

Section 33 provides:

'(1) If -
(a) a person ("the person entitled")-
  (i) is entitled to occupy a dwelling house by virtue of a beneficial estate or interest or contract or by virtue of any enactment giving him the right to remain in occupation, or
  (ii) has matrimonial home rights in relation to the dwelling-house, and
(b) the dwelling-house
  (i) is or at any time has been the home of the person entitled and of another person with whom he is associated, or
  (ii) was at any time intended by the person entitled and any such other person to be their home,
the person entitled may apply to the court for an order containing any of the provisions specified in subsections (3),(4) and (5).'

A spouse is almost always able to apply for an occupation order because he or she almost always has a personal right to occupy the matrimonial home (known as 'matrimonial home rights').[13] The nature of this personal right is described in section 30(2) of the 1996 Act. A spouse who is not entitled to occupy the home by virtue of a beneficial estate or interest or contract or by virtue of any enactment has the following 'matrimonial home rights':

'(a) if in occupation, a right not to be evicted or excluded from the dwelling house or any part thereof by the other spouse except with the leave of the court given by an order under section 33;

---

12 The meaning of 'associated person' is defined in s 62(3); it is discussed above in relation to non-molestation orders. Persons who have agreed to marry (whether or not that agreement has been terminated) are associated, but where the agreement has been terminated, no application may be made under s 33 by reference to that agreement after the end of the period of three years beginning with the day on which it is terminated (s 33(2)).

13 Where the spouses are bare licensees or squatters they are both non-entitled. Spouses have matrimonial home rights simply because they are married. For the purpose of obtaining occupation orders it does not matter whether these rights have been registered. It is only where a third party is claiming rights in the family home that notification of matrimonial home rights by registration becomes a crucial issue: see ch 8.

(b) if not in occupation, a right with the leave of the court so given
to enter into and occupy the dwelling-house.'

This is a crucial provision because it not only gives a non-owning spouse
the right to live in the matrimonial home, it also gives that spouse rights
against third party purchasers. Any purchaser from the entitled spouse
will take the property subject to the other spouse's matrimonial home
rights (provided these have been registered in accordance with the Act's
provisions).[14]

What order(s) can be made?

Sometimes it may not be clear whether an applicant who is not a spouse
has a sufficient property interest to be entitled to apply for an order.
Consequently provision is made for this first to be clarified by an order
declaring that the applicant is so entitled under section 33(a)(i), or has
matrimonial home rights.[15] It does not matter whether the dwelling house
is currently the applicant's home provided that at any time it has been, or
was intended to be, her home and the home of the person with whom she
is associated.[16]

In the case of any entitled applicant the court may make a variety of
orders. Section 33(3) provides that the court may:

'(a) enforce the applicant's entitlement to remain in occupation
as against the other person ("the respondent");
(b) require the respondent to permit the applicant to enter and
remain in the dwelling-house or part of the dwelling-house;
(c) regulate the occupation of the dwelling-house by either or both
parties;
(d) if the respondent is entitled as mentioned in subsection
(1)(a)(i), prohibit, suspend or restrict the exercise by him of
his right to occupy the dwelling-house;
(e) if the respondent has matrimonial home rights in relation to
the dwelling-house and the applicant is the other spouse,
restrict or terminate those rights;
(f) require the respondent to leave the dwelling-house or part of
the dwelling-house; or
(g) exclude the respondent from a defined area in which the
dwelling-house is included.'

Together these provisions give the court wide powers to control occupation
of the dwelling-house where either the applicant alone, or both the

14 Ss 31, 32 and see ch 8.
15 S 33(4).
16 S 33(1)(b).

applicant and the respondent are entitled to live there. In some instances it may be that a respondent husband might offer to share the accommodation with his wife with each being allowed only to use certain rooms. Where there has been no violence on the respondent's part, and the house is sufficiently large, this is a proposal to which the court might give a sympathetic hearing, particularly in view of the general approach that ouster orders are Draconian orders.[17] It is suggested that it may also make sense on the part of the wife to accept such an offer, as the difficulties in gaining an ouster order are such that parties are frequently left living together. To have an order restricting occupation may be better than no order at all.[18] Where there has been violence sufficient to justify ouster then it is suggested that the court ought not normally to take up this option in view of the risk to the wife, although exceptionally it may do so. In *E v E (Ouster Order)*,[19] despite accepting the evidence of the wife that her husband had attempted to rape her, the Court of Appeal confirmed the trial judge's decision simply to exclude the husband from one of the two bedrooms in the house. In her evidence-in-chief the wife had said: 'separate rooms would help, yes. I don't necessarily want him to go. I want my safety and peace. I don't want any more aggravation.' The Court of Appeal considered that normally it should be expected that an ouster order would follow where the judge finds allegations of rape or attempted rape proved. However, the evidence of the wife, coupled with other factors,[20] indicated that it was not possible for them to say that the judge had been plainly wrong in the exercise of his discretion. However, despite *E v E (Ouster Order),* it is suggested that the smaller the accommodation the less possibility there should be of such an order being made.

Where there are children involved the court is required to think very carefully about how an order might affect them.[1] This can be illustrated by *Anderson v Anderson*[2] where an order to share the property had been made at first instance despite the fact that the parties lived in a two-bedroomed flat, the wife was pregnant, they already had a two-year-old child, and there was a history of violence. This was overruled on appeal, where it was held that the trial judge had been wrong to put the onus on the wife to establish that it would probably be disastrous for the couple to stay under the same roof and he should have assessed the risks to the family.

---

17 See below.
18 See, for example, *G v J (Ouster Order)* [1993] 1 FLR 1008, where the man successfully appealed against an ouster order despite allegations of violence. He originally offered to live separately from the woman under the same roof.
19 [1995] 1 FLR 224.
20 A living pattern whereby the parties were not in the house together very often, no children, and the wife's uncertain immigration status, which meant she might be reluctant to bring divorce proceedings. This latter consideration meant that the wife was in a particularly vulnerable position; it is therefore worrying that the court was so ready to accept at face value her evidence that separate bedrooms would give her adequate protection.
1 S 33(7).
2 [1984] FLR 566.

Paragraph (g) is a particularly useful additional power because it enables the court to throw a ring around the property and order the respondent not to come within its vicinity.[3] In *Tuck v Nicholls*[4] the order stated that the respondent should not enter 'that area of King's Lynn in which lies the matrimonial home'. Such an injunction confers considerable additional protection on a battered wife or other entitled applicant. She can take action to have the respondent brought before the court for breach of the court's order before he comes near enough to attack her. Thus, if he is hanging around in the road outside the house, or threatening her when she goes to the shops, or harassing her when she goes to collect the children from school, and an injunction is in force prohibiting him from being in that area, she can have him brought back before the court for contempt.[5]

In the case of spouses two additional orders are available, and each may have a radical effect on a 'non-entitled' spouse's position. Section 33(3)(e) allows the court to restrict or terminate a spouse's matrimonial home rights. Such an order not only ends the non-entitled spouse's right to live in the dwelling house, it also frees the spouse who is the sole beneficial owner of the property to dispose of the property as he wishes. By contrast, section 33(5) is a protective provision which enables a court to order that a spouse's matrimonial home rights are not brought to an end by the death of the other spouse, or the termination (otherwise than by death) of the marriage.[6] However, such an extension of matrimonial home rights may only be ordered during the subsistence of the marriage, so where death or divorce are anticipated care should be taken to make the application in time.

Section 40 specifies additional orders which may be included where an occupation order is made under section 33.[7] Either party can be obliged to take responsibility for the repair and maintenance of the dwelling-house, or the discharge of rent, mortgage payments or other outgoings.[8] The party

---

3 For example, where the home is in a block of flats, the respondent could not only be ordered to keep away from the home, but also from the block in which the home is situated.

4 [1989] 1 FLR 283. The order was discharged on appeal, but not for excess of powers in this regard.

5 Clearly, care must be taken that the power is not used oppressively; also attention may need to be given to how contact with the children will be arranged so that any order is not breached when they are collected and returned from contact visits.

6 Which is when they normally terminate, s 30(8).

7 S 40 also applies to orders made under ss 35 and 36. The criteria to be applied relate to the needs and financial resources and obligations of the parties (s 40(2)).

8 S 40(1). This provision is particularly important where spouses are joint owners of the property. Until any order to the contrary is made, both will continue to be liable for the mortgage payments. Thus where a woman is driven from the home and forced to take refuge elsewhere, and having to pay rent, she will also continue to be liable for the mortgage payments. Furthermore, because correspondence is normally only sent to the first named person on a joint mortgage, which will usually be the man as the order of names is almost always Mr and Mrs, the woman will not receive automatic notification of any change in payments due to alteration in interest rates.

in occupation can be required to pay an occupation rent. Either party can be given possession or use of the furniture or other contents, or be required to take reasonable care of these items and to keep them secure, along with the house itself. One of the main concerns of a spouse in a financially weak position is to keep a roof over her head and not to fall behind with payments owed to third parties, as default may entitle them to take possession proceedings. These orders could be particularly useful to such a spouse to tide her over pending any financial provision and property adjustment order made in divorce proceedings, or more generally in cases where spouses have parted and where negotiations about their financial affairs are proving protracted. Section 40 orders are likely to be less useful to unmarried partners and other persons entitled to apply for orders under sections 35 and 36, as any provision ceases to have effect when the occupation order to which it relates comes to an end.[9]

Factors influencing the court's discretion

Prior to the Family Law Act 1996, a court was guided by section 1(3) of the Matrimonial Homes Act 1983 when determining how to exercise its powers to make orders about the occupation of the matrimonial home. This Act applied only to spouses, but the criteria were extended to include orders relating to unmarried partners.[10] Section 1(3) directed the court:

'... to make such order as it thinks just and reasonable having regard to the conduct of the spouses in relation to each other and otherwise, to their respective needs and financial resources, to the needs of any children and to all the circumstances of the case.'

A ruling by the House of Lords in *Richards v Richards*[11] made it plain that the welfare principle did not apply to applications for ouster orders where children were involved. After that decision the Court of Appeal inserted its own gloss on the language of section 1(3) by insisting that an order ousting a spouse from the home was a Draconian order which required strong justification, and declaring that it should be made only where the judge was satisfied that no lesser measure would suffice to

---

9   S 40(3). Orders under s 33 may be made for a specified period, until the occurrence of a specified event or until further order (s 33(10)). In the first instance orders relating to former spouses under s 35 cannot last for longer than six months, although they may be extended on one or more occasions for a further six months (s 35(10)). However, orders between unmarried partners made under under s 36 may be extended by six months on one occasion only (s 36(10)).

10 Made under the Domestic Violence and Matrimonial Proceedings Act 1976.

11 [1983] 2 All ER 807, where their Lordships rejected the submission that the needs of the children were paramount and held that each of the factors in s 1(3) should be given equal weight.

protect the wife and children.[12] In *Burke v Burke*[13] an ouster order was described by Lloyd LJ as 'a drastic order and an order which should only be made in cases of real necessity. It must not be allowed to become a routine stepping-stone on the road to divorce on the ground that the marriage has already broken down and that the atmosphere in the matrimonial home is one of tension.' The Family Law Act 1996 has not altered this approach. In *Chalmers v Johns*[14] the Court of Appeal held that the string of authorities which emphasise the Draconian nature of an ouster order had not been overtaken by the new provisions in the 1996 Act, and that an order which overrides proprietary rights was only justified in exceptional circumstances.

It was also held that it was wrong to use ouster to achieve an ulterior purpose. In *Summers v Summers*[15] the trial judge found that the repeated loud quarrels between the parents were frightening and adversely affecting the children. In deciding to oust the husband the judge included in his considerations the fact that 'at this time it might be beneficial for there to be a break for a while. It may be a forlorn hope but might ease a reconciliation'.[16] On appeal he was criticised for taking into account the prospect of reconciliation, but failing to take into account the Draconian nature of an ouster order.[17]

The ruling in *Summers v Summers*[18] that 'allowing the dust to settle', in the admittedly forlorn hope of effecting a reconciliation, fell outside the scope of the criteria appears narrow and excessively legalistic. The court was (and still is) specifically required to have regard to all the circumstances and, where a judge, after evaluating the witnesses and the evidence, thinks that ouster may achieve an improvement in the parties' relationship in the particular case then it is most unfortunate if he is prevented from testing out this theory. Indeed, if in *Summers v Summers* a short-term ouster order had succeeded in achieving the judge's purpose this would have been of positive benefit both to the parties and to their children.[19] It is suggested that courts should be encouraged to take the prospect of achieving a reconciliation into account in appropriate cases rather than be castigated for adopting this approach.

Section 33(6) of the Family Law Act 1996 introduces new criteria to guide the courts on whether and when one of the parties should be ordered

---

12 *Reid v Reid* (1984) Times, 30 July, which was the first reported Court of Appeal decision after *Richards v Richards*. See also, *Wiseman v Simpson* [1988] 1 All ER 245; *Shipp v Shipp* [1988] 1 FLR 345; *Blackstock v Blackstock* [1991] 2 FLR 308.
13 [1987] 2 FLR 71 at p 73.
14 [1999] 1 FLR 392.
15 [1986] 1 FLR 343.
16 Ibid, at p 347.
17 The case was sent back for retrial by another judge; the outcome of the proceedings is not known.
18 [1986] 1 FLR 343.
19 Contrast the obiter dicta of Glidewell LJ in *Scott v Scott* [1992] 1 FLR 529 at p 537, in which he recognised that an order requiring one of the parties to leave the home can sometimes give rise to a positive outcome in respect of their relationship.

from the home. In deciding whether to exercise its powers to make an order and (if so) in what manner, the court must have regard to all the circumstances including:

'(a) the housing needs and housing resources of each of the parties and of any relevant child;
(b) the financial resources of each of the parties;
(c) the likely effect of any order, or of any decision by the court not to exercise its powers under subsection (3), on the health, safety or well-being of the parties and of any relevant child; and
(d) the conduct of the parties in relation to each other and otherwise.'

Viewed in isolation, these criteria do not appear substantially to alter the previous criteria. However, they do not stand alone. They must be applied alongside section 33(7), which provides:

'If it appears to the court that the applicant or any relevant child is likely to suffer significant harm attributable to conduct of the respondent if an order under this section containing one or more of the provisions mentioned in subsection (3) is not made, the court shall make the order unless it appears to it that -
(a) the respondent or any relevant child is likely to suffer significant harm if the order is made; and
(b) the harm likely to be suffered by the respondent or child in that event is as great as, or greater than, the harm attributable to conduct of the respondent which is likely to be suffered by the applicant or child if the order is not made.'

This structure means that the four matters itemised in subsection (6), ie, housing needs and resources, financial resources, the effect of any order on the health, safety or well-being of the parties and any children, and conduct are subject to the balance of harm test in subsection (7). This test places a court under a *duty* to make an order where it appears that the applicant or a child is likely to suffer significant harm if an order is not made *unless* the respondent or a child are likely to suffer equal or greater significant harm if an order is made. Where the latter is the case, the court retains a discretion. The analysis which follows examines how any tension between relatively minor acts of misconduct by the respondent and the needs of the applicant and her children have been handled in the past, and considers what changes in this balance are likely to occur as a result of the new legislation.

Richards v Richards[20] was the leading case prior to the Family Law Act 1996. The trial judge found that Mrs Richards had no reasonable grounds for refusing to return to live with her husband in the matrimonial home.[21]

20 [1983] 2 All ER 807.
21 Indeed, a reading of the facts reveals that any 'misconduct' by one of the spouses had been on the part of the wife, not the husband.

He nonetheless made an order excluding Mr Richards from the home, commenting: 'I think it is thoroughly unjust to turn out this father, but justice no longer seems to play any part in this part of the law.' His reason for making the order was because the wife would not live under the same roof as the husband, and she could only find temporary accommo-dation for herself and the children in a caravan, which was unsuitable for the children. Allowing Mr Richards's appeal, the House of Lords ruled that the specified criteria for the exercise of discretion should be given equal weight, and that the welfare of the children was not the court's paramount consideration in ouster cases.[1]

Some of this thinking appears to survive the new legislation. The factors in subsection (6) are given equal weight and it is clear that the welfare of any children, while highly relevant, is not the court's paramount con-sideration. Significant harm to the applicant or child must be shown before the balance of harm test comes into play, and the test applies only where it is established that the harm is attributable to the respondent's conduct. This emphasis on the causative nature of the respondent's conduct did not form part of the Law Commission's recommendations,[2] and its inclusion means that the balancing exercise is not morally neutral. It means that the test does not apply where the significant harm is brought about by the applicant's decision to move out without good cause, which is what appeared to be the position in *Richards v Richards*. It is difficult to predict how the appellate courts would respond if facts similar to those in *Richards v Richards* were to arise and be taken on appeal. It is nonetheless suggested that the fresh weighting given to the interests of the applicant and the children in the new legislation will not force the judges to arrive at a decision to oust a parent from the home where they believe this to be unjust.

Housing and financial needs and resources

The needs and financial resources of the parties are of major importance, particularly the need of both parties to be adequately housed. However, it is abundantly clear that ouster orders are not to be regarded simply as housing matters. In *G v J (Ouster Order)*[3] Purchas LJ commented:

'The decision which the judge made would appear to most people to be fair and sensible if the task of the court was to decide who, in fairness, between the man who is going to work and the woman

---

1 Lord Scarman gave a short, but powerful, dissenting speech at pp 819-821. Three of the Law Lords were of the view that even if the paramountcy of the children's welfare applied, it would not be in their interests to evict their father from the home. It should also be appreciated that by the time the issue of law reached the House of Lords, the parties had resolved their domestic living arrangements by sharing care of the children in the family home. The wife occupied it from Monday to Friday, and the husband from Friday to Monday.
2 *Domestic Violence and Occupation of the Family Home* Law Com No 207, para 4.34.
3 [1993] 1 FLR 1008 at pp 1015-1016.

who has the care of the child, should have the flat to live in. As a matter of housing policy the judge's answer may well be right. But the court has no power to decide such a case simply as a matter of housing policy.'

The question to be resolved is whether the order can be sustained under all of the criteria of the Family Law Act 1996. Thus although the court may consider the ability of the respondent to rehouse himself, even where this is thought to be feasible this is by no means a guarantee that the court will make an order ousting him from the home, despite the fact that the court may accept that it is impossible for the two parties to carry on living together under the same roof. In *Shipp v Shipp*[4] the wife had made a successful application for ouster in proceedings based on affidavit evidence only. Allowing the husband's appeal, the Court of Appeal took account of the possible practical impact of a temporary ouster order on the husband, and stated that ouster for a period of two months 'might make it practically impossible for the husband to reverse the arrangements which he would be bound to make in the intervening period and go back to live in the matrimonial home, if it was held at the adjourned hearing that he should be allowed to do so'.[5] In the result, the husband was left living alone in the three-bedroomed house, while the wife and child were living in very cramped conditions at the house of her sister. A wife in a case such as *Shipp* could now pray in aid both the provisions in subsection (6)(c)[6] and the balance of harm test. However, as explained above, for the balance of harm test she would have to establish that she or the children were suffering *significant* harm and that the harm was attributable to the respondent's conduct.

On the other hand, if the respondent actually has suitable accommodation available to move into the court may more readily grant the order, as in *Scott v Scott,*[7] where the husband, who was a property developer, owned another house as well as the matrimonial home. Similarly in *Baggott v Baggott*[8] the Court of Appeal confirmed the decision to oust the husband, commenting that it was obvious that he was in a position to find himself a home, or somewhere to live, because he had put in the forefront of his case an offer to raise £20,000 in order to provide a fund to enable either himself, or the wife, to live elsewhere. It is also worth remembering that in some instances it may be possible for the parties to continue to share the accommodation, with orders made restricting either or both parties' use to certain rooms.

There are grounds for suggesting that in the past the Court of Appeal has generally been far more concerned about the impact of an ouster order

4   [1988] 1 FLR 345.
5   Per Nourse LJ at p 347. Why it would be 'practically impossible' to 'reverse' any arrangements was not explained, nor was it explained why the respondent husband could not simply seek a short tenancy of two months' duration.
6   See below.
7   [1992] 1 FLR 529.
8   [1986] 1 FLR 377.

on the husband than it has been about the impact of a refusal to make an order on the wife and children. In *Summers v Summers*[9] if the husband were to be ousted from his home he would be reduced to sleeping on the settee at the home of his grandmother. Clearly this would have a major impact on him, and the court commented sympathetically on these 'difficult' living conditions. By contrast, in *Shipp v Shipp*[10] the court had very little empathy for the wife's position. It merely stated that it was up to her to decide whether she wished to return to the matrimonial home with her child, under the protection of an undertaking given by the husband that he would not molest her, or whether she and the child would continue living with her sister in very cramped conditions. However, more recently it appears that the mood of the Court of Appeal had altered. In *Brown v Brown*[11] evidence was given that the wife and child had been driven out of the house and were sleeping in sleeping-bags on the floor. The trial judge found this to be a highly important factor in the exercise of his discretion to oust the husband, where there had been no violence, and the Court of Appeal rejected the husband's appeal. The approach in *Brown v Brown* seems to anticipate the provisions in subsection (3)(c).

Where the parties live in accommodation provided by a local authority the court may be influenced by the authority's housing policies in determining whether or not to make an ouster order.[12] Where the court is satisfied that suitable alternative accommodation will be provided for the respondent the decision to evict him from the home then becomes less Draconian. However, if ousting a husband will render him homeless this is an extremely serious matter.[13] In *Wooton v Wooton*[14] the court found that if the man were to be ousted he would become homeless and the local authority would be under no obligation to rehouse him,[15] whereas if the woman and her children were to leave they would be treated by the local authority as in priority need for rehousing. Consequently, as the court felt that there was no urgent need to protect the applicant, they refused to oust the man, who was the sole tenant. By contrast, in *Thurley v Smith*[16] the man was ousted for a period of three months, even though he would be rendered homeless as a consequence. His position as a single man was contrasted with that of the woman and her eight-year-old son. The man was a violent alcoholic, whom the court felt could be justly condemned to

9   [1986] 1 FLR 343.
10 [1988] 1 FLR 345.
11 [1994] 1 FLR 233.
12 Cf *Jones v Jones* [1997] 1 FLR 27 which states that there is an expectation that the court will consider a local authority's housing policy when considering the transfer of a tenancy on divorce.
13 See further below, homelessness.
14 [1984] FLR 871.
15 Although they were probably incorrect in this view, as the man appeared to fall within the definition of priority need, now found in the Housing Act 1996, s 189(1)(c), as he was suffering from epilepsy which was difficult to control.
16 [1984] FLR 875.

a substantial extent for his conduct. The woman was living in wholly unsuitable accommodation, and although the court thought that she had a prospect of eventually being granted more satisfactory local authority accommodation, they also recognised that it was likely that it would not approach the standard afforded by the matrimonial home because of severe pressures on the authority's housing resources.

The effect of the court's decision on the health, safety or well-being of the parties or a child

The requirement in subsection (6)(c) that the court should take into account the effect of its decision either to grant, or to refuse to grant, an order is a new requirement. As discussed above, in some of the cases which revolved around the issue of housing while the courts were prepared to consider the effect of their decisions on the respondent, they were less ready to consider the effect of failing to make an order. This unsympathetic approach also manifested itself in other cases. Thus in the 1979 case of *Hopper v Hopper*[17] a wife appealed against an order which ousted her husband from the home, but which was not to take effect for one month. The wife stressed that her daughter was presently suffering severely; she was living in very cramped conditions, and having to sleep on a camp bed. The child's situation was made very much worse by the fact that she was suffering from a broken arm. The wife claimed that twenty four hours would have been sufficient time for her husband to find alternative accommodation. In relation to this, Stamp LJ commented: 'I cannot think that the harm that may be done to this girl by having to sleep on a camp bed with a broken arm after being in hospital can possibly outweigh the undesirability of driving her step-father out of the home at very short notice.'[18] Generally, however, it was unusual for the Court of Appeal to express quite such a very unsympathetic attitude towards children, and a few years later, in *Lee v Lee*,[19] the Court took a more generous stance. In that case the wife had left the home and was unable to find accommodation for herself and her children all to live together as a family. It was held that the needs of the children to be together, and to be with their mother, were sufficient to establish the necessity for an order.

However, although the courts expressed sympathy towards applicants the Draconian nature of an ouster order was emphasised on many occasions. In *Tuck v Nicholls*,[20] despite evidence that the child may have been at risk living with the 'wife'[21] at the home of her parents, the emphasis was on the effect on the man of being ousted. The trial judge had made an ouster order

17 [1979] 1 All ER 181.
18 Ibid, at p 183.
19 [1984] FLR 243.
20 [1989] 1 FLR 283.
21 The couple were unmarried.

on the basis of affidavit evidence alone on the grounds that it was unsafe to leave the parties together; because of allegations that the woman's father might be a child sex abuser; and because the reason why the couple had been granted a council tenancy was because they had a young baby. Allowing the man's appeal, the Court of Appeal ruled that although 'nobody would wish to leave a baby in circumstances where that child might be at risk', this evidence had been produced in an affidavit at the last moment, and nothing had been done to alert the man in advance to the allegations made against the wife's father. For this and other reasons the court therefore discharged the ouster injunction and remitted the case for a fresh hearing.

It is suggested the Court of Appeal adopted a rigid and un-compromising position in *Tuck v Nicholls* and that it gave far too little weight to the health, safety and well-being of the mother and her child. Of course it would be Draconian to oust the man, but the woman had left the home and she needed a proper roof over her head for herself and her baby. It is understandable that courts are reluctant to base orders on affidavit evidence only, and even more reluctant to do so where the contents of the affidavit have not been served in advance on the other party. But ouster orders are often sought in an emergency, and where the applicant has left the home, either she or the respondent will suffer the Draconian consequences of being out of the home pending a hearing at which oral evidence can be tested in cross-examination. One party will always suffer temporary inconvenience in cases of this kind, yet it is suggested that the Court of Appeal was refusing to recognise that the woman out of the house had an equal claim to live in it pending a full hearing as did the man. The 1996 Act has not altered the Court of Appeal's approach to making an ouster order at an interim stage of proceedings. In *Chalmers v Johns*[22] it held that unless the balance of harm test applied under section 33(7),[1] an ouster order applying the criteria in section 33(6) should only be made in exceptional circumstances.

Tuck v Nicholls appears to be just the kind of case where the new criteria in section 33(6), particularly paragraph (c), might well tip the balance in favour of the applicant. A woman's claim to be restored and for the respondent to be ousted must be very strong where she has children whom she says are at risk of harm in their present accommodation. If the applicant's allegations prove to be groundless, the respondent will eventually be permitted to return to the property. Although the provisions in subsection (6) have equal weighting, where they pull in different directions so that there is a choice between an adult or a child suffering in the interim period, the wording in paragraph (c) makes it plain that the health and well-being of the children are important factors. These factors must be taken into account in all cases, whether or not the balance of harm test also applies.[2]

22 [1999] 1 FLR 392.
1   See below.
2   In *Tuck v Nicholls*, the balance of harm test would not have applied because the cause of the anticipated significant harm to the child was the behaviour of the applicant's father, not the respondent's conduct.

While *Tuck v Nicholls* may be a case that would be decided differently under the Family Law Act 1996, it nonetheless seems likely that while courts regard occupation orders as an extremely serious invasion of the rights of the ousted spouse, considerations relating to the well-being of the applicant and any children whom she is looking after will not, on their own, persuade the court to oust the respondent; more will be required.[3] In *G v J (Ouster Order)*[4] the Court of Appeal declined to give decisive weight to the interests of the child where the merits of the case were evenly divided between the adult parties. The trial judge had adopted the approach that if the needs of the child combined with the needs of the mother together added up to a greater need than that of the father, then an order for ouster could be justified. He found as a fact that neither party was significantly more to blame than the other for the break-up in the relationship. In the end what, for the judge, 'tipped the balance' in favour of ousting the man was 'the primacy of J's [the child's] interest. Not primacy in the sense of overriding other considerations, but the combination of needs of [the mother] and J in my view indicates that the balance is in favour of them residing in the house.' However, the Court of Appeal ruled that this 'tipping of the balance' approach was not the correct test and fell short of what is required to justify the making of a Draconian order.[5] It seems likely that section 33(6), despite the matters to which the court must have regard under subsection (c), will similarly not be satisfied by a mere tipping of the balance.

Cases in which it is said that the parties' present living circumstances are having a detrimental effect on the child tend to be based on assertions and counter-assertions made by the parties, and these have had little evidential force. In *Wiseman v Simpson*[6] the mother claimed that the continual arguing between the parents was retarding the development of the child, then aged 18 months. She brought no evidence from a doctor, or other expert, to support her allegation. Although the Court of Appeal accepted that expert evidence was not necessarily essential before a finding on such a matter could be reached, it considered the wife's assertions to be a most uncertain basis for making a finding that the child's development was being retarded by the circumstances in the home. It is suggested that it would therefore seem wise for an applicant using subsection (6)(c) to bring medical, or other, evidence to substantiate any allegation that the child's health is being affected or that he is otherwise suffering harm.[7]

---

3   Cf *Chalmers v Johns* [1999] 1 FLR 392.
4   [1993] 1 FLR 1008.
5   See also *E v E (Ouster Order)* [1993] 1 FLR 1008.
6   [1988] 1 All ER 245.
7   Similarly, if the wife has been driven out of the home and is now living in highly unsuitable accommodation, and the poor living conditions are such as either to cause, or aggravate, illness or disability in the child, she would be well advised to bring the appropriate evidence to substantiate her case.

Conduct

As has been noted, a new 'principle' took root after the House of Lords' decision in *Richards v Richards*,[8] namely that ouster orders were 'Draconian' orders which should only be made in exceptional circumstances. However, in *Richards v Richards* itself the court stated that all four criteria in section 1(3) of the Matrimonial Homes Act 1983 should be considered, none of them being pre-eminent. Lord Hailsham LC, giving the leading judgment of the majority stated:

'The facts in matrimonial proceedings are so varied in their nature that courts should be extremely careful before reading into judgments which are uttered in the context of a particular case universal principles which may have the virtue of simplicity but which if so treated are at variance with the fuller and more appropriate criteria prescribed by Parliament, and in particular with the requirement that the total result should be just and reasonable.'[9]

This was a clear exhortation to be cautious in extracting general principles from the cases. Yet *Burke v Burke*[10] laid claim to the idea that an order should only be made in a case of 'real necessity' although there was nothing in section 1(3) which forced such an interpretation.[11] The section simply stated that the order must be one that was 'just and reasonable', which was by no means the same thing. Of course there was force in the argument that an order requiring one of the parties to leave the home should not be made lightly, and it was probably the case that the pendulum had swung too far in some of the cases which preceded *Richards v Richards*.[12] However, in subsequent cases, the courts tended to focus almost entirely on whether the respondent's conduct was sufficiently grave to justify his exclusion, and in this regard it is suggested that the pendulum had swung back too far in the other direction.

The inclusion in the Family Law Act 1996 of 'the conduct of the parties in relation to each other and otherwise'[13] as a relevant consideration means

8 [1983] 2 All ER 807.
9 Ibid, at p 817.
10 [1987] 2 FLR 71.
11 This approach was repeated time and again; see particularly *Tuck v Nicholls* [1989] 1 FLR 283; *Shipp v Shipp* [1988] 1 FLR 345; *Blackstock v Blackstock* [1991] 2 FLR 308; and *G v J (Ouster Order)* [1993] 1 FLR 1008.
12 One line of cases had adopted an essentially pragmatic approach, whereby applications were treated as issues of housing. If it was found that a woman needed a home for herself and the children she would be allowed to stay in the house and the husband would be ousted. Little attention was paid to the merits of the application: see, for example, *Spindlow v Spindlow* [1979] 1 All ER 169; *Samson v Samson* [1982] 1 WLR 252. The other approach was very different. Before an order would be granted the court would require evidence that it was impossible for the spouses to remain together under the same roof: see, for example, *Elsworth v Elsworth* (1978) 1 FLR 245; *Myers v Myers* [1982] 1 WLR 247.
13 S 33(6)(d).

that there will continue to be a tension in the law between those cases where, after balancing all the factors, decisive weight is given to whether the respondent's conduct has been sufficiently serious to justify making an order ousting him from the home, and those cases where the financial and housing needs of the applicant and her children appear to demand an order requiring the respondent to leave.[14] The analysis which follows examines how this tension was handled under the previous legislation and considers whether the same approach should be adopted under the Family Law Act 1996.

Although, in 1988, the Court of Appeal ruled in *Wiseman v Simpson*[15] that it was not necessary to prove violence or other adverse behaviour to the applicant or a child living with the applicant in order to be granted an ouster injunction, it is disturbing to note that the Law Commission pointed out in 1989[16] that there appeared to be no reported cases in the Court of Appeal since *Richards v Richards* of ouster in circumstances other than violence, although before that time there had been several. In *Wiseman v Simpson* itself the Court allowed an appeal against the making of an ouster order, and sent the case back for a retrial, Ralph Gibson LJ stating that 'it can only be "just and reasonable" to make an ouster order if the case of the party claiming the order is not only stronger on those matters than the other party's case but is such as to justify making an order that a man or woman be ousted from his or her home'.[17] Subsequently, there were cases in which ouster orders were made without proof of violence,[18] but the courts continued to emphasise the drastic nature of the order.

The Court of Appeal's tendency to focus on misconduct, coupled with a determination that trial courts should discover which of the parties was responsible for the misconduct, was highlighted in *Blackstock v Blackstock*.[19] The trial judge accepted that there had been an 'horrendous' incident of violence, and that both parties had had severe injuries inflicted upon them.[20] The wife had left home with the three children and since

---

14 In *Chalmers v Johns* [1999] 1 FLR 392, Thorpe LJ commented that the gravity of making an ouster order had been recognised prior to the passing of the Family Law Act 1996 and that 'the order remains Draconian'. However, see also *O'Connell v O'Connell* (1998) LEXIS 28 August, for an example of a case where despite the husband being unemployed, there only being one incident of violence and the husband having nowhere to go, the needs of the wife and children to live free of fear was held to justify making an ouster order.

15 [1988] 1 All ER 245.

16 *Domestic Violence and Occupation of the Family Home,* Law Com Working Paper No 113 at p 22.

17 [1988] 1 All ER 245 at p 251.

18 See *Brown v Brown* [1994] 1 FLR 233.

19 [1991] 2 FLR 308. See too *Shipp v Shipp* [1988] 1 FLR 345, where it was hotly contested as to who was responsible for the one serious incident of violence. The Court of Appeal criticised the trial judge for granting a short-term ouster order in proceedings on the basis of affidavit evidence without having explored in depth who was to blame for the incident.

20 The wife sustained a fracture of the shaft of the ulna of the right forearm. The husband suffered scalding and a broken cheekbone with pinning through the nose.

then they had been living in highly unsatisfactory accommodation. The wife applied for an ouster order so that she and the children could return. The judge refused her application on the ground that he was unable to say which party was to blame for the incident and, in view of that lack of finding, he could not justify the making of an ouster order. He accepted that the children were living in unsatisfactory accommodation, but found that they were in no danger from the husband and did not need any protection from him if they were living under the same roof. The husband offered to give an undertaking not to molest the wife, and the judge found that such an undertaking would be sufficient to protect her.[1] On appeal it was argued on behalf of the wife that the high level of violence justified her staying away, irrespective of where the fault might lie. The Court of Appeal refused to accept this argument. It ruled that the court could not ignore the source of the violence, that the burden had been on the wife to prove culpability on the part of the husband, and that she had failed to discharge this burden. The court therefore concluded that an order should not be granted, since it was not clear who was responsible for the initiation of the violence, and because there was a real possibility that the wife herself might have been its instigator.

It is suggested that the Court of Appeal's approach in *Blackstock v Blackstock* was dangerously misguided.[2] It is normally the case that violence in the home is not witnessed by outsiders and therefore, where both parties have injuries, it is easy for each to accuse the other of being the main assailant. Even if it had been established that it was the wife who had instigated the violence it was clearly extremely risky for the parties to continue to live together under the same roof. The notion that the giving of an undertaking not to be violent provides adequate protection where serious violence has already occurred flies in the face of all the evidence about the recidivist nature of domestic assaults. It is suggested that it should be the role of the civil law to afford protection in cases of domestic violence by contrast with the role of the criminal law, which is to apportion blame and to punish. Therefore, in a case of this kind, one of the parties ought to be be evicted from the home regardless of who was responsible for initiating the assaults. An ouster order is in the interests of the personal safety of each of the parties. In relation to the children, the fact that they are not physically at risk does not mean that the violence has no impact upon them. It cannot be in the interests of children to live in a household where the parents have attacked one another in the manner in which they did in *Blackstock v Blackstock*. Such children would clearly be vulnerable to serious psychological damage were they to witness such violence.[3]

---

1 A factor influencing the judge in reaching this decision was that he was not satisfied that this was a marriage in which there had been a long history of violence.
2 As it was to a lesser extent in *Shipp v Shipp* [1988] 1 FLR 345.
3 On the impact of domestic violence on children, see in particular M Hester and L Radford *Domestic violence and child contact arrangements in England and Denmark* (The Policy Press, 1996); M Hester, C Pearson and L Radford *Domestic violence: A national survey*

The Court of Appeal's decision in *Scott v Scott* [4] was in marked contrast to that in *Blackstock v Blackstock* and the majority of other reported decisions. Here there was no evidence that the husband had treated his wife with violence, or had behaved with any other misconduct towards her. Rather, the wife's complaint was that her husband could not accept that their marriage had irretrievably broken down, and that he was constantly pressing her to resume their relationship, despite the fact that she had obtained a decree nisi of divorce. This difference between the parties as to the state of their marriage had been in existence for some considerable time, and in earlier proceedings the husband had given undertakings not to interfere with his wife, which had been followed by an injunction to this effect. Eventually the trial judge took the view that the only way of enforcing the court's injunction was to make an order excluding the husband from the house which they jointly owned. The Court of Appeal clearly found the judge's approach difficult to reconcile with existing principles. As Glidewell LJ said, having considered the criteria in section 1(3) (apart from conduct) and having reminded himself that ouster orders are Draconian orders:

'The final question is, is this conduct sufficiently serious to justify the making of an ouster order? This has greatly troubled me, because I take the view that it is wrong that ouster injunctions should be used too widely or too commonly, and I think there is a risk that they are. I recognise the force of the previous decisions of this court to the effect that they are only to be used in cases of real necessity. In the end I am persuaded that, knowing as he did all about the history ..., the judge was justified in concluding that he had to keep these parties apart if that injunction was not going to be broken in the future, and this was the way in which he could do it. Therefore I cannot say that the judge was wrong to reach the conclusion to which he came.'[5]

Scott v Scott was an important decision because of its essentially pragmatic approach. It recognised the reality that marriages are often brought to an end by the unilateral decision of one of the parties. One spouse wants to be free of the relationship, and to move on, the other clings to what has been between the parties, and is unable to accept that the marriage has irretrievably come to an end.[6] Where this is the case, the question then

---

of court welfare and voluntary sector mediation (The Policy Press, 1997); G Hague, L Kelly, E Malos and A Mullender *Children, domestic violence and refuges: A study of needs and responses* (Women's Aid Federation, 1996). Also see NCH Action for Children *The Hidden Victims – Children and Domestic Violence* (NCH, 1994).

4   [1992] 1 FLR 529.

5   Ibid, at pp 536-537.

6   Glidewell LJ himself adverted to this at the end of his judgment when he attempted to offer the husband sympathetic and constructive advice. The courts will be faced with similar moral dilemmas when the new divorce law measures are implemented. The courts will be empowered to make orders regulating the occupation of the home during the period of consideration and reflection: see ch 7.

arises whether the court is entitled to treat reconciliation overtures made by the spouse who cannot accept that the marriage is finished as a form of molestation. In *Scott v Scott* the trial judge was prepared to treat such overtures in this way and to accept undertakings and to make orders against further such reconciliation attempts. When the husband persisted, the judge was prepared to enforce the court's order by evicting the husband from the home, and the Court of Appeal was not willing to find that he had been plainly wrong. The ruling was in marked contrast with the Court of Appeal's desire in *Blackstock v Blackstock* to discover who was to blame for the violence which, in that case, had erupted between the parties. In *Scott v Scott* the court was not concerned to allocate blame; indeed, in relation to blame Glidewell LJ said 'of course, the rights and wrongs are not all on one side and [not on] the other. It is the conduct of both parties that has led to the breakdown of the marriage.'[7] It is suggested that it was a radical decision to allow a court to be used to assist a wife to avoid having to listen to her husband's repeated requests for a reconciliation. It was even more radical to enforce the court's order by evicting the husband from his home before the decree nisi had been made absolute. If, instead, contempt proceedings had been instituted, it may have been difficult to prove that the husband's behaviour amounted to contempt, bearing in mind the court's concession that the husband's behaviour arguably 'did not go so far as molestation'.[8]

Scott v Scott was an unusual decision and did not follow the general pattern of cases whereby misconduct had to be established. There is a very real danger in normally requiring proof of some type of serious misconduct, usually violence, on the part of the respondent before he can be ousted as happened under the previous legislation. It is arguable that such an approach creates the risk that a wife who is determined to leave her husband, but who has nowhere to go, may feel forced to take steps to goad him into assaulting her. This could have serious consequences for both parties. The wife could be badly injured, and the husband could acquire a criminal record. Furthermore, requiring the applicant to prove that the respondent is at least equally, if not more, to blame for the violence, as the Court of Appeal did in *Blackstock v Blackstock*,[9] is to give greater priority to the conduct element in the criteria than to the other considerations. From the point of view of any children it matters not who is the instigator of violence between the parents. Their concern is to have a safe and comfortable roof over their heads. They need to be living in a household where they are not subjected to scenes of violence. Violence not only has the potential to be extremely damaging to the mental well-being of any children, but also exposes them to the risk of becoming personally involved, particularly where they feel the need to try and step in to protect one of their parents, as in *Jordan v Jordan*.[10]

7   [1992] 1 FLR 529 at p 536.
8   Ibid.
9   [1991] 2 FLR 308.
10 [1993] 1 FLR 169. See also P Parkinson and C Humphries *Children who witness domestic violence – the implications for child protection* (1998) 10 CFLQ 147.

An approach which concentrates on proof of misconduct penalises those spouses and partners whose relationships have broken down but who do not attack or otherwise molest one another. It is suggested that it is absurd for a court to arrive at the conclusion that it is impossible for the parties to remain together under the same roof, but to refuse to assist them to part, as it did in *Wiseman v Simpson*.[11] Parties often cannot engage in self-help and negotiate an agreed arrangement in cases of this kind. Where each has an interest in remaining in the property they are likely to need an independent arbitrator to determine who should go and who should be allowed to remain, at least for the time-being.[12]

The balance of harm test

It has been seen that, in the past, some courts have tended to give little weight to the fact that a woman has felt compelled to leave the home and to live in highly unsuitable accommodation, often with the children. This approach ignored the Draconian consequences for the applicant of refusing to make an order. It is not just section 33(6)(c) which has amended the approach to this issue. In addition, the balance of harm test should also alter this balance because it makes it incumbent on the court, where significant harm is alleged, to consider the practical consequences for both parties and any children of making, or refusing to make, an order. Section 33(7) ensures that, in these circumstances, the living conditions of the applicant merit just as much attention as those of the respondent. It provides:

> 'If it appears to the court that the applicant or any relevant child is likely to suffer significant harm attributable to conduct of the respondent if an order under this section containing one or more of the provisions mentioned in subsection (3) is not made, the court shall make the order unless it appears to it that -
> (a) the respondent or any relevant child is likely to suffer significant harm if the order is made; and
> (b) the harm likely to be suffered by the respondent or child in that event is as great as, or greater than, the harm attributable to conduct of the respondent which is likely to be suffered by the applicant or child if the order is not made.'

This balance of harm test states that the court *shall* make an order where it appears that the applicant or any relevant child is likely to suffer significant harm attributable to conduct of the respondent if an order is not made. The court must, therefore, make an order in favour of the applicant. However, where the harm likely to be suffered by the respondent or child if

11 [1988] 1 All ER 245.
12 See further M Hayes *The Law Commission and the family home* (1990) 53 MLR 222.

an order were to be made is as great as, or greater than, the harm which is likely to be suffered by the applicant or child if the order is not made, then the court has a choice about what order(s), if any, to make and does not have to make an order in favour of the applicant. Where the balance of harm test does come into play the courts will face some difficult decisions in comparing the needs of different children. In *B v B (Occupation Order)*[13] the wife had been forced out of council property due to the husband's serious violence and was living in bed and breakfast accommodation. She took their baby with her but left the husband's six-year-old son by a previous relationship with the husband. Allowing the husband's appeal against an occupation order made in favour of the wife, the Court of Appeal found that all that the baby needed was to be securely with her mother. Although the baby's present accommodation was unsuitable it was likely to be temporary, and the local authority were bound to treat the wife as homeless and in priority need.[14] However, the local authority's duty to the husband, at its highest, was to secure temporary accommodation for him, and the husband did not have the resources to rent accommodation in the private sector. The court found that if the husband was ordered out of the house this would cause his son to suffer significant harm. It would result in the boy changing school for the fifth time in eighteen months, and this would be very damaging and disruptive to his mental and emotional well-being. The boy's security depended not just on being with his father, but on his other day to day support systems of which his home and school were plainly the most important. Thus, when the respective likelihoods of harm to the two children were weighed, the balance came down on the son suffering the greater harm if an occupation order was made.[15]

The balance of harm test only applies where 'likely significant harm attributable to conduct of the respondent' is established. The test is taken from the threshold criteria which apply to child protection proceedings under Parts IV and V of the Children Act 1989.[16] Harm in relation to both adults and children is defined as ill-treatment or the impairment of health; but in relation to a child it also includes impairment of the child's development.[17] For the purposes of the Children Act 1989, 'significant' has been taken to mean 'considerable, noteworthy or important'.[18] 'Likely' harm need not be established on the balance of probabilities; establishing a real possibility that significant harm will occur is sufficient.[19] The Law Commission did not

---

13 (1999) 1 FLR 715 (the first case on Part IV of the Family Law Act 1996 to reach the Court of Appeal).
14 Housing Act 1996, s 188(1), and see below on homelessness.
15 The Court of Appeal was emphatic that the husband's behaviour had been disgraceful, and it stressed that fathers who treat their partners with domestice violence and cause them to leave home cannot expect to remain in shared accommodation. A critical factor in *B v B (Occupation Order)* was that the son was not the child of both parties, and there was no question of him being cared for by anyone other than the father.
16 See ch 3.
17 Family Law Act 1996, s 63(1).
18 *Humberside County Council v B* [1993] 1 FLR 257 at 263, per Booth J.
19 *Re H (Minors) (Sexual Abuse: Standard of Proof)* [1996] 1 All ER 1.

find it easy to strike an acceptable balance between what it termed a 'balance of hardship' test and a test which made the welfare of the children paramount,[20] but it was persuaded that paramountcy was not the appropriate principle to apply to occupation order cases.[21] It was, however, convinced that violence and other forms of abuse required an immediate and urgent response and it took the view that a test which gave the court a duty to make an order where significant harm was anticipated was the right approach. However, section 33(7) leaves open what type of protective action the court should take. The orders under section 33(3) range from simply enforcing the applicant's right to live in the house to excluding the respondent, and normally, of course, it is only the latter order which affords the applicant and child adequate protection. It is disturbing, therefore, that there is nothing in the reforming legislation to prevent a court responding as it did in the pre-Act decision of *C v K (Inherent Powers: Exclusion Order)*.[22] Despite finding that there was a risk of significant harm to the child, Wall J nonetheless took the view that the powers of the court to exclude a person with a proprietary interest must be exercised with extreme caution. This caution led him to make injunctive orders short of excluding the respondent from the property, and to adjourn the application for an exclusion order for a period of three months. It is to be hoped that courts will adopt a more robust approach to the occupation claims of respondent property owners than hitherto, and that they will apply the balance of hardship test in a manner which has real practical advantages for victims of domestic violence.[1]

The Law Commission was careful not to link the test to the respondent's conduct for, as it explained, 'by placing an emphasis on the need for a remedy rather than on the conduct which gave rise to that need, the criteria will not actually put a premium on allegations of violence and thus may avoid the problems which would be generated by a scheme which focuses upon it'.[2] However, Parliament thought otherwise and introduced conduct as an element to be considered both under the general criteria in section 33(6) and where the balance of harm test is in issue. As a result, it is only where the respondent's conduct is causative of the likely harm that he is bound to have an order made against him. In all other circumstances the judge retains a discretion.[3]

---

20 See the discussion in *Domestic Violence and Occupation of the Family Home*, Law Com No 207, paras 4.20-4.34.

21 'It might lead to more specious applications by fathers for custody, and encourage more mothers to use "I've got the kids so kick him out" arguments,' ibid at para 4.31.

22 [1996] 2 FLR 506.

1 It could be maintained that it is implicit that a finding of hardship to the applicant under s 33(7) must lead to an order which, at a minimum, regulates the respondent's occupation of the home, because this is what the court must do in a case of an applicant former spouse with no existing right to occupy; see s 35(5), (8).

2 Ibid at para 4.34. See also M Hayes *The Law Commission and the family home* (1990) 53 MLR 222.

3 And see the decision of *Tuck v Nicholls* [1989] 1 FLR 283 (above) which is illustrative of a situation where the balance of harm test would not come to the applicant's aid, despite the child being at risk of suffering significant harm.

The test's concentration on conduct and causation in addition to proof of significant harm gives ample scope for argument on behalf of the respondent. The requirement that the harm should be 'significant' rules out more minor types of harm. As a consequence, are the courts likely to take the view that a child with a broken arm is unlikely to suffer significant harm if she continues to sleep on a camp bed, or has to live in a caravan, or is a witness to violence between her parents?[4] Indeed, it is only in the third example that the harm to the child could be attributed to the respondent's conduct and therefore the balance of harm provision will not assist the child in the other two. Moreover, the respondent has scope to claim that the violence witnessed by the child was caused by the applicant, and where the court is persuaded of this the significant harm to the child does not take precedence over the respondent's interests.[5] How will courts respond to a mother who seeks an order to oust the father where she suspects that he is sexually abusing their child and he denies it? Ousting the father from the home could prevent the instigation of care proceedings. However, proving sexual abuse is notoriously difficult, and where sufficient evidence is not forthcoming there is no factual basis for reliance on the balance of harm test.[6]

Duration of orders made in favour of entitled applicants

The Law Commission recommended that a distinction should be made between entitled and non-entitled applicants on the question of the duration of an order.[7] They took the view that where an applicant is entitled to occupy the home an order of unlimited duration may be appropriate. This view is reflected in section 33(10) which provides: 'An order under this section may, in so far as it has continuing effect, be made for a specified period, until the occurrence of a specified event or until further order'. The reasoning behind this provision, as it applies to spouses, was explained by Hale J when giving evidence to the Special Public Bill Committee which considered the original version of the Bill:[8]

'Think of the circumstances in which the Matrimonial Homes Act was first passed, it was to preserve and enforce the so-called deserted wife's equity. In other words, the wife who was left in the matrimonial home by a husband who had abandoned her and who might otherwise dispose of the home leaving her homeless could be protected in her right to live there. In some of those cases there are no divorce proceedings and there is no intention to divorce. So of course her rights of occupation should be protected and [she]

---

4   *Hopper v Hopper* [1979] 1 All ER 181; *Richards v Richards* [1983] 2 All ER 807; *Jordan v Jordan* [1993] 1 FLR 169.
5   Cf *Blackstock v Blackstock* [1991] 2 FLR 308.
6   See ch 3, and *Re H (Minors) (Sexual Abuse: Standard of Proof)* [1996] 1 All ER 1.
7   Law Com No 207, paras 4.35-4.37.
8   Family Homes and Domestic Violence Bill (1995, HL 55) question 51.

may need an order to protect [her] for the foreseeable future unless and until there is a divorce and possibly even thereafter.'[9]

Entitled 'cohabitants'

It has already been explained that any person who is entitled to occupy a dwelling-house by virtue of a beneficial estate or interest or contract or by virtue of any enactment is entitled to apply for an occupation order, provided that the house is, was, or was intended to be, the home of the person entitled and of another person with whom he is associated.[10] Apart from spouses, the persons most likely to fall within this provision are unmarried 'cohabitants' who share the ownership of their home. Cohabitants are defined to mean 'a man and a woman who, although not married to each other, are living together as husband and wife'; thus only hetorosexual relationships are recognised.[11] Unlike spouses, unmarried partners do not enjoy matrimonial home rights regardless of how long they have lived together. Therefore the question whether the applicant is 'a person entitled' will arise in those cases where the property is conveyed into the name of one partner only, and he or she refuses to accept that the other partner has a beneficial interest in the property. Section 33(4) makes provision for this by empowering the court to make a declaratory order that the applicant is entitled within the provisions of section 33(1)(a)(i).[12] An entitled unmarried partner may apply for an order containing any of the provisions in subsection (3) and the court's discretion is governed by the criteria in subsections (6) and (7).[13]

It was where cohabitants were co-owners of the property that the deficiencies of the previous law were particularly apparent. Under general property law principles one co-owner does not have a right of occupation in preference to the other.[14] Consequently, although temporary relief could be granted[15] it was not long-term, even if the result was that the victim of violence was driven from property of which she was a co-owner. In *Davis v Johnson*[16] the parties were joint tenants of their council house, and the man treated the woman with extreme brutality, yet Lord Salmon commented:

---

9   Hale J also expressed the hope that the substantive law would not be glossed by a practice direction on the duration of orders.

10 S 33(1)(a)(i).

11 S 62(1)(a).

12 See further ch 9. Where this is a complicated issue, a cohabitant may meanwhile seek an order under s 36, and the fact that there are proceedings pending between the parties to determine the legal or beneficial ownership of the home is directly relevant to the exercise of the court's discretion to make an order securing the roof over her head until the matter is determined (s 36(6)(i)).

13 See above.

14 *Ainsbury v Millington* [1986] 1 All ER 73.

15 Under the Domestic Violence and Matrimonial Proceedings Act 1976.

16 [1978] 1 All ER 1132.

'There is no doubt that under the Act[17] a violent man may be excluded for a limited period from the "matrimonial home". I cannot however agree that his exclusion can properly be made to continue for as long as there is a danger that if he returns he will assault his former mistress. This might well be forever. I do not think that the purpose of the Act is to punish the violent.'[18]

It was therefore commonplace under the Domestic Violence and Matrimonial Proceedings Act 1976 for an injunction affording a joint owner protection to be made to last for a maximum period of three months. This outcome could be highly unsatisfactory because the violent partner was able to manipulate the situation to his own benefit. On his return to the home where he was sufficiently unpleasant, but where his behaviour fell short of violence or molestation, he could effectively drive his property owning partner from the home. Furthermore, even though the parties were joint tenants, delay in bringing the proceedings greatly reduced, if not entirely extinguished, the applicant's chance of successfully ousting her abusive partner from the home. The Court of Appeal took the view that the 1976 Act provided a short-term remedy only. It was designed to give the woman a home while the parties resolved their long-term problem of accommodation.

All of this has been altered by section 33 of the Family Law Act 1996. In the case of entitled cohabitants (and other entitled applicants) an occupation order has a purpose beyond the short-term protection of the applicant. Where two people are each entitled to live under the same roof, it may be necessary to regulate that right until a long-term solution can be found.[19] It is therefore suggested that any attempt by the courts routinely to limit the duration of orders between joint occupants should be strongly resisted.[20] The applicant's long-term solution is to apply under section 14 of the Trusts of Land and Appointment of Trustees Act 1996 for an order that the property be sold[1] or, where the entitlement to occupy arises by virtue of a relevant tenancy, to apply for the tenancy to be transferred into her sole name.[2] Where she does make such an application,

---

17 That is the Domestic Violence and Matrimonial Proceedings Act 1976.
18 At p 1152.
19 Where the cohabitants are tenants of the property, one of the dangers a cohabitant may face is that before she has made her application to regulate the tenancy her partner may give notice to quit, thereby terminating the tenancy altogether. The House of Lords confirmed, in *Harrow London Borough Council v Johnstone* [1997] 1 FLR 887, that where notice is given by a single joint tenant this operates to terminate the tenancy. This is despite the fact the other tenant does not consent and wishes to remain in the property.
20 This was clearly the Law Commission's intention, see Law Com No 207, para 4.36.
1 Replacing the Law of Property Act 1925, s 30. By virtue of s 15, the Act introduces criteria for determining an application for an order under s 14. These include the court having regard to the intentions of the parties, the purposes for which the property is held and the welfare of any minor.
2 S 53 and Sch 7 of the Family Law Act 1996: see further ch 9. For a consideration of the difficulties arising out of a transfer of tenancy, see S Bridge *Transferring tenancies of the family home* [1998] Fam Law 26.

it is suggested that the court should normally be willing to grant her an order ousting the respondent pending its outcome.[3]

Unfortunately sale will by no means always supply a satisfactory solution. It is not unusual for an applicant to find herself in the same situation as the woman found herself in *G v J (Ouster Order)*.[4] Here the court recognised that the parties could no longer live together, and thought sale the obvious answer. However, there was a negative equity in the house. The court therefore advised that the 'parties will have to reach some other suitable solution'.[5] What other solution they had in mind they did not indicate, but the situation would seem to be a desperate one. The parties will obviously not wish to sell and be left with a large debt and no housing. It might be possible for one of them to agree to buy the other one out. However, this would not appear to be feasible in all but the most unusual of cases, as it would mean one person either having, or raising, a large sum of capital. Clearly that person would not be able to raise the money on mortgage, so his only other option would be to raise the money from some other source, where he is liable to be charged a very high rate of interest. Another possibility would be to negotiate with the mortgage lender and try and arrange a transfer of the mortgage to two separate properties. Quite apart from the difficulty of persuading the mortgage lender that this is a practical proposition, the parties would inevitably end up very considerably out of pocket if they could secure such an arrangement. They would still be the owners of property with a negative equity, and may well subsequently find that they are not in fact able to afford to finance such an arrangement. There therefore appears to be no obvious solution to the problem where there is a negative equity.

Where the party seeking an order is solely entitled he or she can, of course, take proceedings for possession and for the eviction of the other under the general law, for once the respondent's licence to live there is withdrawn he or she is a trespasser on the property. Where the issue is solely concerned with the parties' property rights, the applicant is not required to establish good cause to evict the respondent. The court is likely to allow the respondent a breathing space in which he can find alternative accommodation, but where he refuses to go, the applicant is entitled to an order which ousts him permanently. In this regard the cohabitant applicant has an advantage over a married applicant because the respondent has no legally recognisable right to live in the property. However, there are advantages in a solely entitled cohabitant seeking an occupation order under the Act rather than taking possession proceedings, particularly where there is violence, because more speedy relief is obtainable backed up by strong enforcement provisions.

---

3   By analogy with the court's willingness to grant an ouster order to a married woman pending the outcome of divorce proceedings and cf *Gibson v Austin* [1992] 2 FLR 437.
4   [1993] 1 FLR 1008.
5   Ibid, at p 1019.

Non-entitled cohabitants

A more difficult situation arises where a cohabitant who has no proprietary right to remain in the house has either evicted, or wishes to evict, the owning cohabitant. Here she is in a far more vulnerable position. Since 1976 the law has recognised that the civil law should come to the aid of unmarried partners who are victims of domestic violence whether or not they have a proprietary right in the home. However, cohabitants seeking orders under the Domestic Violence and Matrimonial Proceedings Act 1976 were excluded from the court's protective jurisdiction unless they could show that they were 'living together as husband and wife'.

An important improvement brought about by the Family Law Act 1996 is the inclusion of 'former cohabitants' among the persons entitled to apply for an occupation order. For example, a cohabitant who moves out, ceases to have any form of communal living with her ex-partner, and subsequently moves back into the house but does not resume living with him as husband and wife, would now be entitled to apply for an order under section 36[6] should her ex-partner evict her.[7] The difficulties caused by the present tense drafting of living together as husband and wife were dramatically illustrated in *McLean v Nugent*.[8] The parties had a relationship which resulted in the birth of a child. Subsequently the woman moved into accommodation away from the man because she did not want to continue her association with him. However the man found her and forced his way in. He then treated her with violence and, on her account, raped her.[9] After three months the woman left. The Court of Appeal held that the parties were cohabitants because 'there can be no doubt in fact, as I think, that willy nilly she was living with him as husband and wife in the same household'.[10] Clearly this decision was aimed at granting the woman a remedy in very needy circumstances, and on that basis it is to be applauded.[11] It is nonetheless distasteful and offensive to state that a woman who is being forced against her will to live with a man who is also raping her is living in the same household with him as 'husband and wife'. Therefore the inclusion of former cohabitants is particularly to be welcomed because it means that in the large majority of cases there will

6 Or s 33 where she has a proprietary right to live there.
7 The situation which arose in *McLean v Burke* (1982) 3 FLR 70, and under the old law the former cohabitant was therefore denied a remedy.
8 (1980) 1 FLR 26.
9 Ormrod LJ, ibid at p 28, says: 'He treated her with some violence. He forced her to have intercourse, she says against her will, from time to time.'
10 Ibid, at p 31.
11 In *McLean v Nugent* the woman was in fact seeking a non-molestation injunction, rather than an order for ouster. It is perhaps best to rationalise the decision by stating that one of the crucial factors in deciding whether the parties are, or were, cohabitants is to ask whether at least one of the parties possessed the intention to live together with the other at some point in their relationship. Provided that this test is satisfied at the relevant date, it seems that this should be sufficient to bestow jurisdiction upon the court.

no longer be any need to strain the proper interpretation of the present tense drafting of 'living together as husband and wife'.[12]

The Select Committee on Violence in Marriage,[13] which produced its report in 1975, revealed that there were grounds for serious disquiet about the lack of protective safeguards for women abused by their violent spouses or partners. Sadly, the home continues to be a dangerous place to live in, and cohabitants and former cohabitants have an undoubted need for protection from eviction, and to be able to evict their abusive partners. However, the thrust of the House of Lords' ruling in *Davis v Johnson*[14] was that the purpose of domestic violence relief is to provide a swift but temporary response to an urgent situation and to give the applicant a secure roof over her head while she looks for alternative accommodation.[15] Consequently, the courts were normally unwilling to interfere with the undoubted right of the respondent to live in his own home except on the most temporary of bases. The Family Law Act 1996 continues to reflect this view. The Law Commission was of the opinion that placing severe restrictions on the rights of a property owning cohabitant can more readily be justified where both parties have occupation rights in the property than where the applicant has no such rights.[16]

Section 36 governs the situation where one cohabitant or former cohabitant is entitled to occupy the dwelling-house in which they live, used to live, or intended to live, as their home, and the other cohabitant or former cohabitant is not so entitled. The provisions in the section have a progressively stronger impact on the owner cohabitant's property rights. First the section makes provision for an order that the applicant be permitted to remain in the home; then provision is made for an order that the applicant be permitted to enter the home; and lastly the section provides for an order restricting the right of the entitled cohabitant to occupy the home.

The discretion to allow a non-entitled cohabitant to remain in or enter the home

Section 36(3) provides that where the non-entitled cohabitant is in occupation, she may apply for an order:

---

12 This was largely resolved by the Court of Appeal's decision in *O'Neill v Williams* [1984] FLR 1 that the parties must have been living together at the date of the violence complained of. The applicant in *McLean v Nugent* might have been able to establish that she was living with the respondent as husband and wife before the birth of their child.
13 HC 553 (1974-75).
14 [1978] 1 All ER 1132.
15 Perhaps looking to the local authority for council housing; and see *Freeman v Collins* [1984] FLR 649 where the court limited the order to a period of one month.
16 Law Com No 207, para 4.7.

'(a) giving the applicant the right not to be evicted or excluded from the dwelling-house or any part of it by the respondent for the period specified in the order; and

(b) prohibiting the respondent from evicting or excluding the applicant during that period.'

Subsection (4) covers the converse situation, and provides that where the cohabitant is not in occupation, an order must contain provisions:

'(a) giving the applicant the right not to be evicted or excluded from the dwelling-house or any part of it by the respondent for the period specified in the order; and

(b) requiring the respondent to permit the exercise of that right.'

When the court is determining whether to make an order under either of these subsections and (if so) in what manner, subsection (6) directs it to have regard to all the circumstances including:

'(a) the housing needs and housing resources of each of the parties and of any relevant child;

(b) the financial resources of each of the parties;

(c) the likely effect of any order, or of any decision by the court not to exercise its powers under subsection (3) or (4), on the health, safety or well-being of the parties and of any relevant child;

(d) the conduct of the parties in relation to each other and otherwise;

(e) the nature of the parties' relationship;

(f) the length of time during which they have lived together as husband and wife;

(g) whether there are or have been any children who are children of both parties or for whom both parties have or have had parental responsibility;

(h) the length of time that has elapsed since the parties ceased to live together; and

(i) the existence of any pending proceedings between the parties-

(i) for an order under paragraph 1(2)(d) or (e) of Schedule 1 to the Children Act 1989 (orders for financial relief against parents);

(ii) relating to the legal or beneficial ownership of the dwelling-house.'

Orders made under subsections (3) and (4), which give the applicant a right to live in the property but do not otherwise interfere with the owning cohabitant's rights, are the least intrusive on his otherwise sole right of occupation. Where the court decides to make an order under either subsection it is explicitly stated that the court *must* make orders giving the applicant occupation rights and prohibiting the respondent from interfering with those rights. The criteria governing the exercise of the court's discretion in paragraphs (a) to (d) are identical to those which apply to spouses and other entitled applicants. The additional criteria in paragraphs (e) to (i) focus on the nature and duration of the personal relationship between the cohabitants, whether they have children, and whether proceedings designed to resolve the financial and property owning issues stemming from their joint occupation and joint parenthood are pending. These criteria enable the court to take account of matters which reflect the parties' legitimate expectations according to the circumstances of their case.[17] In cases where the cohabitation has lasted for a short period of time the claim of the non-entitled cohabitant to oust the respondent from his home is relatively weak. However, the court is also directed to take account of both the respondent's conduct and the applicant's needs and these considerations may give the applicant a strong case for immediate relief.[18]

Particular attention should be given to paragraph (e). This requires the court to consider the nature of the parties' relationship and, when doing so, the court is specifically directed by section 41 'to have regard to the fact that they have not given each other the commitment involved in marriage'. As one commentator has said of this 'useless ...or pernicious'[19] provision:

> 'It is an ideological statement with its roots in the Daily Mail-inspired opposition to the 1995 Bill. Whether it will assist courts or even whether they will seek assistance in it is dubious. But there are clear dangers that myth will be dressed up as fact and cohabitants be labelled as uncommitted because, for example, she has not taken his surname or they have retained separate bank accounts.'[20]

The reason why the authors of this book also find the provision in section 41 objectionable is because the language in which it is phrased denigrates unmarried unions,[1] and because it adds an unnecessary gloss to the flexible response to the parties' individual circumstances, including their commitment to one another, for which, in our view, paragraphs (d), (f) and (g) already make more than adequate provision.

The discretion to regulate the entitled cohabitant's occupation of the home

Section 36(5) allows the court to interfere directly with the entitled cohabitant's right to occupy the home and will therefore be experienced by him as a far more Draconian order. An order under this subsection may:

---

17 Law Com No 207, para 4.12.
18 For example, where there has been serious violence and the applicant is pregnant by the respondent.
19 Earl Russell (*Hansard*), HL Vol 570, col 115).
20 M D A Freeman, Family Law Act 1996, Current Law Statutes. He partly bases this fear on the facts and the court's interpretation of them in *Helby v Rafferty* [1978] 3 All ER 1016.
1   That cohabitation involves less commitment than marriage is stated as an uncontested matter of *fact*.

'(a) regulate the occupation of the dwelling-house by either or both of the parties;

(b) prohibit, suspend or restrict the exercise by the respondent of his right to occupy the dwelling-house;

(c) require the respondent to leave the dwelling-house or part of the dwelling-house;

(d) exclude the respondent from a defined area in which the dwelling-house is included.'

The criteria guiding the court in the exercise of this discretion differ from those applying to subsection (3) and (4) orders. Subsection (7) provides that in deciding whether to include a subsection (5) provision and (if so) in what manner, the court should have regard to all the circumstances including:

'(a) the matters mentioned in subsection (6)(a) to (d); and

(b) the questions mentioned in subsection (8).'

This structure excludes the matters mentioned in paragraphs (e) to (h) of subsection (6). This is important, because those paragraphs contain considerations which may be unhelpful to the applicant's case. It is plain that once paragraphs (e) to (h) have been overcome, and an order has been made allowing the applicant to enter and remain in the dwelling-house, they should not be revisited when consideration is given to making a more Draconian order containing a subsection (5) provision.

Subsection (8) contains a parallel balance of harm test to that enacted in section 33(7).[2] The questions are:

'(a) whether the applicant or any relevant child is likely to suffer significant harm attributable to conduct of the respondent if the subsection (5) provision is not included in the order; and

(b) whether the harm likely to be suffered by the respondent or child if the provision is included is as great as or greater than the harm attributable to conduct of the respondent which is likely to be suffered by the applicant or child if the provision is not included.'

There is, however, a crucial distinction between the application of the balance of harm test where the applicant is entitled to apply for an order under section 33 (which, as we have seen, always includes married couples) and where the applicant is a non-entitled cohabitant. In the former situation the court *shall* make an order where the likely harm to the applicant or child exceeds the likely harm to the respondent or child.[3] In the case of cohabitants, the questions in subsection (8) must merely be taken into

2   See above.
3   S 33(7).

account by the court when exercising its discretion; they do not determine what, if any, order should be made. Is this distinction acceptable? While there are legitimate reasons for distinguishing between property owning and non-property owning applicants, such a distinction is unacceptable when applied to relevant children living with the cohabitant. Subsection (8) reads like a legacy from the past, where 'illegitimate' children were afforded fewer rights than children born into a marriage. Surely the balance of harm test should benefit the children of cohabitants just as much as it benefits the children of married applicants and those other applicants who have occupation rights in the home concerned?

Duration and nature of orders where the applicant is non-entitled

Orders made on the application of a cohabitant with no existing right to occupy are limited in duration. In the first instance they can last for up to six months, but may be extended on one occasion for a further maximum period of six months.[4] This means that a cohabitant will be protected in her occupation of the home in which she lived with her partner as 'husband and wife' at the most for a year irrespective of the length of their cohabitation, their relative need for accommodation, or the nature of the conduct which led to the breakdown of their relationship. The court has no residual discretion so, for example, where the couple have lived together for most of their adult life and have brought up children who are now no longer dependent, the non-entitled partner must leave at the end of the specified period.[5] The six-month period, with the possibility of its extension, is intended to give the applicant time in which to sort out her financial affairs, to claim a beneficial entitlement to the property where the evidence to support this is disputed, or otherwise to make new housing arrangements.

One former spouse with no existing right to occupy

When spouses divorce the non-entitled spouse's matrimonial home rights come to an end.[6] This leaves the non-entitled spouse in a vulnerable position where the entitled spouse asserts his sole right to occupy the former matrimonial home. She, and any children living with her, may have nowhere to go and may need to remain in the matrimonial home until any pending financial provision and property adjustment arrange-ments within the divorce proceedings are resolved;[7] immediate steps to

---

4   S 36(10).
5   Where the children continue to be dependent, she may be able to obtain an order maintaining a roof over the children's (and therefore her own) head until their dependency ends: see Sch 1 of the Children Act 1989 and ch 9.
6   Unless they have been extended under s 33(5).
7   See ch 8.

protect either her or the children from domestic violence may also be essential. Section 35 gives a former spouse similar, but not identical, protection to that which is afforded to a non-entitled cohabitant.[8] The criteria governing the exercise of the court's discretion are (where relevant) the same, and a similar distinction is drawn between the factors to be taken into account where the court is giving the non-entitled former spouse a right to live in the dwelling-house, and where it is regulating the entitled former spouse's right of occupation.[9] However, the balance of harm test is more protective of a former spouse and child than it is of a cohabitant and child. The same test applies as that which applies where the applicant is an entitled applicant, namely that the court *must* make an order regulating the entitled spouse's occupation rights where failure to do so would be likely to lead to the applicant or child suffering greater significant harm than the respondent.[10]

Orders where neither party is entitled to occupy the dwelling-house

In a case where neither party is entitled to occupy the dwelling-house, the court is not interfering with property rights, it is merely adjusting occupation rights as between the parties themselves. Section 37 governs the situation where the parties are spouses or former spouses, and section 38 where they are cohabitants or former cohabitants. Either party may apply for an order against the other containing the usual regulatory provisions. In the case of spouses and former spouses the court's discretion is governed by subsections (6) and (7) of section 33.[11] The order must initially be limited to six months, but may be extended on one or more occasions for a further specified period of not more than six months.[12] In the case of cohabitants and former cohabitants Parliament's determination to distinguish a cohabitation relationship from marriage, and consequently to discriminate against the applicant and any relevant child, continues, even though in this instance there are no property rights involved.[13] The same factors must be taken into account, but the balance of harm test is not mandatory and must merely be considered as a question affecting the exercise of discretion. The six-month maximum duration of any order applies, but the order may be renewed on one occasion only.[14]

8   S 35(3), (4), (5).
9   S 35(6), (7).
10 S 35(8). The courts took a similar, sympathetic approach to the needs of the children prior to the Act, by holding that where there are still children living in the home they could exercise their inherent jurisdiction. They were able to oust the ex-husband from the home solely on the basis of protection of the interests of the children. See *Quinn v Quinn* (1983) 4 FLR 394; *Wilde v Wilde* [1988] 2 FLR 83.
11 That is the criteria affecting orders where the applicant is an entitled applicant.
12 S 37(5).
13 See above.
14 S 38(6).

Occupation orders in private and public law proceedings involving children

An occupation order can be made on a free standing application brought under section 33 or sections 35 to 38 of the Family Law Act 1996. Where an application is made under the wrong section the court may make an order under the correct section.[15] Proceedings for non-molestation and occupation orders are family proceedings,[16] and consequently an order under the Children Act 1989, section 8 may be made in addition to, or instead of, the order(s) being requested.[17] Non-molestation and occupation orders may also be made in other family proceedings.[18] Non-molestation orders may be made both on application and in the exercise of the court's own motion powers;[19] occupation orders may be made only on application.[20] Treating orders under the Family Law Act 1996 as family proceedings continues the process of rationalising, simplifying and unifying family law generally, and enables different matters involving parents and children to be resolved by the same court at the same time. For example, it enables a court in one and the same private law proceedings to make orders settling the arrangements as to the person with whom a child is to live (a residence order),[1] protecting parent and child from actual or threatened violence, or other unwelcome behaviour (a non-molestation order), and permitting them to stay in the family home and evicting the respondent from it and from the neighbourhood in which the home is situated (an occupation order).

Where parents are in dispute about the person with whom the child is to live the question arises whether this issue should first be resolved before any occupation order is made regulating the occupation of the family home. In *Re T (A minor), T v T (Ouster Order)*[2] it was held that, normally, the court should first decide the residence issue and then go on to decide whether or not to oust the other parent. The applicant must couple her application for residence with an appropriate application for an occupation order. If she does not, the court has no power to make an occupation order in the same proceedings.[3]

---

15 S 39(3).
16 Sch 8, para 60.
17 Children Act 1989, s 10(1). A court may make residence, contact, specific issue and prohibited steps orders.
18 Family Law Act 1996, s 39(2).
19 Family Law Act 1996, s 42(2)(b).
20 Family Law Act 1996, s 39(2).
1   Children Act 1989, s 8.
2   [1987] 1 FLR 181.
3   Although this may be rectifiable on appeal: see *Re M (Minors) (Disclosure of Evidence)* [1994] 1 FLR 760. In *Re M* the Court of Appeal shared the concern of the trial judge as to the extreme effect of the conduct of the mother on the children, and the urgent need to protect them. Thus although the father had not originally applied for an ouster order they confirmed the judge's decision to oust the mother. They were satisfied that the judge had been fully apprised of all the relevant criteria, and since the appropriate application had now been made, they could, without risk of injustice, make their own decision and exercise their own discretion.

Occupation orders and care proceedings

Under the Children Act 1989 courts may make orders ousting alleged abusers from the home when making emergency protection orders or interim care orders.[4] These ouster orders enable a child to be protected without removing her from her home. However, they terminate when the substantive orders come to an end, and there is nothing in the Children Act 1989 which directly empowers a court to make an ouster order either as ancillary to, or as an alternative to, a final care order. It has been seen that the only way in which a non-molestation or occupation order can be made is by application between associated persons in accordance with the provisions of the Family Law Act 1996. Despite this limitation on who may apply for non-molestation and occupation orders, there is real potential for their use to assist children where care proceedings are contemplated, or have already been started. Where a local authority take the view that an occupation order would adequately protect a child from suffering further significant harm, they could encourage the non-abusing parent to apply for orders giving her a right to occupy the family home and evicting the person believed to have abused the child. The non-abusing parent, faced with choosing between applying for an occupation order in order to keep her children, or remaining with her spouse or current partner and losing her children, might well be persuaded to take this action to prevent the initiation of care proceedings. The court would almost certainly come to her assistance were she to apply for an occupation order, because there can be little doubt that a court would resolve the balance of harm test in her favour once the alleged abuser's misconduct towards the children was established.[5] An occupation order would have distinct advantages for the children; it would spare them the trauma of removal from the home, or being prevented from returning to the home, and would give the parent looking after them the support and enforcement powers she needs to protect them from further significant harm.

Non-molestation and occupation orders could also come to the aid of children at the final stage of an application made in care proceedings. As care proceedings and occupation order proceedings are both family proceedings an application for an occupation order can be made and granted within the care proceedings. Where a non-abusing parent obtained an order evicting the abuser from the home this might persuade the court not to make a care order. Where this course of action was opposed by the local authority and the child's guardian ad litem, leading the court to take the view that it would involve too much risk, the court might still take the view that an occupation order in favour of the non-abusing parent would be beneficial to the children as it might lead to their eventual rehabilitation home. Furthermore, where the non-abusing parent agreed

---

4   Children Act 1989, ss 38A and 44A, and see ch 3.
5   Family Law Act 1996, ss 33(7), 35(7), 36(8), 37(4) and 38(5).

to apply for an occupation order, the local authority in their turn might agree to put forward a care plan which would allow the children to be placed at home immediately.

The negative side of this approach is that the duration of an occupation order depends upon the status of the applicant. Where the applicant is married to the respondent, or otherwise has a proprietary right in the property (and is, of course, associated with the respondent) there is no limit placed on the order's duration, and therefore it may be sufficiently protective.[6] However, where the applicant is a non-entitled cohabitant the maximum duration of an occupation order is twelve months.[7] Nevertheless, even the shorter period would give the non-abusing parent time in which to obtain alternative accommodation, and for the children to be protected in the home in the meanwhile.

Ex parte orders

Normally a respondent to an application for an order in civil proceedings must be given adequate notice of the proceedings in accordance with rules of court. However, in an emergency, the normal notice procedure can be dispensed with. Section 45 provides that in any case where the court considers it just and reasonable to do so it may grant a non-molestation order or an occupation order in ex parte proceedings. In determining whether to exercise its powers the court must have regard to all the circumstances including:

'(a) any risk of significant harm to the applicant or a relevant child, attributable to conduct of the respondent if an order is not made immediately;
(b) whether it is likely that the applicant will be deterred or prevented from pursuing the application if an order is not made immediately; and
(c) whether there is reason to believe that the respondent is aware of the proceedings but is deliberately evading service and that the applicant or relevant child will be seriously prejudiced by the delay involved-
　(i) where the court is a magistrates' court, in effecting service of proceedings; or
　(ii) in any other case effecting substitute service.'

These criteria stress that ex parte applications should only be granted where there are compelling reasons for doing so. As the Law Commission pointed out: 'The danger of a misconceived or malicious application being

---

6　S 33(10).
7　S 36(10).

granted or the risk of some other injustice being done to the respondent is inevitably greater where the court has only heard the applicant's side of the story and the respondent has had no opportunity to reply.'[8]

Other inherent drawbacks in ex parte orders mentioned by the Law Commission included that 'the judge has no opportunity to try to resolve the parties' differences by agreed undertakings or otherwise to reduce the tension of the dispute'; and 'there is no opportunity to bring home the seriousness of the situation to the respondent and to underline the importance of complying with the order or undertaking'.[9] Accordingly, ex parte orders will be rare, although courts are likely to be more ready to make ex parte non-molestation orders than occupation orders; the former simply restrain the respondent from doing that which he is prohibited from doing under the general law, while the latter involve a balancing act which is difficult to carry out without the respondent also presenting evidence.

The criteria concentrate on those situations where ex parte orders may be necessary or desirable. Paragraph (a) focuses on cases where the respondent's conduct is creating a risk of significant harm to the applicant or a relevant child unless the order is made immediately. This clearly covers situations where imminent physical violence is threatened. In addition, an ex parte order may be particularly appropriate where the applicant is frightened that the respondent will have a violent reaction to service of the proceedings. In *G v G (Ouster: Ex Parte Application),*[10] Lord Donaldson MR voiced the general hostility of the Court of Appeal to ex parte orders ousting a party from the home, and expressed the opinion that as the wife, against whom the order was sought, was readily available for service, there was no reason why the judge could not simply have granted an ex parte non-molestation order, which could have been served on the wife at the same time as notice of an inter partes hearing for ouster.[11] It is suggested that courts should be cautious in taking the view that a widely couched non-molestation injunction will be sufficient protection for the applicant where a violent reaction to service of the summons is feared. In highly volatile domestic situations fear of being in breach of an injunction is unlikely to deter many respondents from assaulting their spouse, and an ex parte order for ouster may therefore be advisable.

Paragraph (b) is a significant provision as it recognises and acknowledges the real risk that many applicants may be deterred from pursuing an application if an order is not made immediately. It also ties in with paragraph (c) which is aimed at the difficult situation where the

8   Law Com No 207, para 5.6.
9   Ibid, though it is doubtful whether the Commission's confidence in the efficacy of the judicial role is realistic in the majority of cases. See too *Loseby v Newman* [1995] 2 FLR 754.
10 [1990] 1 FLR 395.
11 This was despite the fact that the husband had stated in evidence that recently the wife had been inviting a 'gentleman' to the house, of whom the husband was so frightened that on one occasion he had jumped out of a first floor window.

respondent is deliberately evading service, sometimes as a device to wear down the applicant's resolution by causing delay and making it even more difficult than it already is to pursue proceedings against him.[12]

Where an ex parte order is granted it should be strictly limited in time until a full hearing can be arranged.[13] In *G v G (Ouster: Ex Parte Application)*[14] the Court of Appeal stated that setting a hearing date seven weeks hence was completely unjustifiable; the hearing should be treated as an emergency. The Court of Appeal has a similar antipathy to courts granting ouster injunctions solely on the basis of affidavit evidence alone, laying down stringent conditions for the granting of such an order in *Whitlock v Whitlock*.[15] Additionally, the court's powers to attach a power of arrest are more circumscribed in ex parte proceedings than in a full hearing.[16]

Enforcement of orders

Court orders designed to protect the applicant against violence and other forms of molestation may be worthless unless they are backed up by strong enforcement powers which courts are prepared to use, and the police to operate in practice. Enforcement of orders under Part IV of the Family Law Act 1996 can be handled under the general law of contempt, through the giving of undertakings, and by the attachment of a power of arrest to one or more provisions within the order.

Contempt of court

Breach of an injunction is a contempt of court and can be punished accordingly. The sanctions that may be imposed are a fine or imprisonment.[17] Imprisonment for contempt may well afford some protection for the applicant, but in *Ansah v Ansah*[18] Ormrod LJ stated that committal orders are remedies of last resort, particularly in family cases. He observed that they could damage the complainant spouse almost as much as the offending spouse, for example by alienating the children. *Ansah v Ansah* has proved to be a highly influential case. Since *Ansah v Ansah* there has been a general reluctance on the part of the courts to use imprisonment as a sanction. Nonetheless, counsel for the contemnor in *Jones v Jones*[19]

---

12 The Law Commission was informed by a number of respondents that this evasion gives rise to considerable problems and expense, Law Com 207, para 5.9.
13 *Ansah v Ansah* [1977] 2 All ER 638.
14 [1990] 1 FLR 395.
15 [1989] 1 FLR 208; see also *Shipp v Shipp* [1988] 1 FLR 345.
16 S 47(3), and see below.
17 Contempt of Court Act 1981, s 14(1). The maximum fine is currently £5,000 and the maximum sentence two years.
18 [1977] 2 All ER 638.
19 [1993] 2 FLR 377.

failed in his attempt to persuade the Court of Appeal to lay down the principle that imprisonment should not be imposed on a first breach. Russell LJ made it clear that each case depended on its own individual facts, and no such general principle could be extracted from the observations of Ormrod LJ.[20]

Contempt of court is a civil matter and the Court of Appeal has made it clear that a court should only exercise its powers in a manner that reflects the gravity of the contempt, and not go on to punish any criminal offence that may have been committed.[1] In view of this, expressions of remorse on the part of the contemnor have played a significant part in the attitude of the Court of Appeal to the use of committal to prison as a sanction. Thus in *Jones v Jones*,[2] the Court of Appeal, despite the fact that it recognised that it was faced with a 'blatant and aggravated contempt by a man who had been told over and over again of the possible consequences if he defied the order of the court', nonetheless reduced the contemnor's period of imprisonment from six to three months because of the husband's 'contrition and remorse'. Similarly in *Jordan v Jordan*,[3] where on appeal it was stated that 'this is about as bad a case as it is possible to imagine, short of any permanent injury being caused to the wife',[4] the Court of Appeal nevertheless ordered that the husband's period of imprisonment should be reduced to three months, as this would not only reflect the gravity of the offence but also the husband's expressions of remorse.

Committal proceedings for contempt are hedged round with procedural technicalities.[5] Where there has been a breach of these technicalities the appeal court has a number of options. First, it can uphold the appeal and release the alleged contemnor. In view of the fact that the liberty of the subject is at stake the courts in the past have taken a very strict line and have released the man on a number of occasions. For example, in *B v B (Contempt: Committal)*[6] it was stated by the Court of Appeal that where there was a blatant error it would need to be a wholly exceptional case for the court to cure the error, despite the fact that the court was satisfied that the man ought to be serving the remainder of an appropriate sentence for contempt. However, in recent years there has been a move away from such a technical approach. In *Nicholls v Nicholls*[7] the Court of Appeal said that in future it should not be necessary to revisit any authority prior to that of *M v P (Contempt of Court: Committal Order); Butler v*

---

20 See also *Thorpe v Thorpe* [1998] 2 FLR 127 where it was reiterated that there is no principle that a first breach could not result in a sentence of imprisonment.
1 *Smith v Smith* [1991] 2 FLR 55.
2 [1993] 2 FLR 377.
3 [1993] 1 FLR 169.
4 Per Lord Donaldson MR at p 171.
5 For a detailed account of applications for committal see Fricker et al *Emergency Remedies in the Family Courts* (Jordan Publishing, 1997).
6 [1991] 2 FLR 588.
7 [1997] 1 FLR 649.

Butler[8] and that it should be recognised that the courts have a discretion which they are required to exercise. Lord Woolf MR commented:

'If committal orders are to be set aside on purely technical grounds which have nothing to do with the justice of the case, then this has the effect of undermining the system of justice and the credibility of the court orders ... As long as the order made by the judge was a valid order, the approach of this court will be to uphold the order in the absence of any prejudice or injustice to the contemnor as a consequence of doing so.'[9]

Another option open to the court is to reverse or vary the decision of the court below and make such order as it considers to be just.[10] Thus where the effect on the contemnor has been slight, as in *Mason v Lawton*,[11] the court will be prepared to correct the error. In *Delaney v Delaney*[12] the judge stated that a custodial sentence was inevitable in respect of a deliberate and frightening breach of a non-molestation order with a power of arrest attached.[13] He took the view that the husband would be liable to repeat the serious breach if he remained at liberty. However, the judge was concerned about the position of the children, as one child was living with the husband. The judge therefore committed the husband to prison for contempt, but did not specify any sentence. Instead he directed that the husband should be brought back before the court on a specified date by which time a report from the probation service could be prepared. The Court of Appeal allowed the contemnor's appeal, holding that there was no power to detain after a finding of contempt but before passing sentence. However, it also held that there was no injustice to the contemnor in imposing such order as the court below could have ordered, since he was sentenced to imprisonment on his first appearance and could be in no doubt that he faced a further term of imprisonment when brought back before the court.[14]

A third option is to order a retrial. This power was used for the first time in *Duo v Osborne*[15] where the Court of Appeal was satisfied that the partial sentence already served by the husband would be inadequate if

8 [1993] Fam 167.
9 [1997] 1 FLR 649 at p 660. Cf *Loseby v Newman* [1995] 2 FLR 754, at p 756, where Balcombe LJ commented: 'I regret to say that [the order] is deficient in so many respects that it would be very difficult to cure.'
10 Administration of Justice Act 1960, s 13. See *Linnett v Coles* [1987] QB 555.
11 [1991] 2 FLR 50.
12 [1996] 1 FLR 458.
13 The husband hid in the wife's car and when she opened it he threatened to stab her with some scissors and to kill her with a gun.
14 After taking account of the fact that the contemnor had now served a number of days in prison and that he was said to be genuinely remorseful the court imposed a sentence of 6 months, suspended for 18 months.
15 [1992] 2 FLR 425.

the wife's allegations were made out. This approach was subsequently confirmed in *Nicholls v Nicholls*[16] where the Court of Appeal ruled that where a defect has occasioned an injustice the court will consider ordering a new trial except where circumstances indicate that it would not be just to do so.

The Court of Appeal's ruling in *Duo v Osborne* and approach in *Delaney v Delaney* were welcome decisions. It is highly offensive that a man who has been committed for contempt should be released on a technicality where there is clear evidence that he is a wife batterer, as in *B v B (Contempt: Committal)*. While it is of course essential that proper procedures are followed where the liberty of the subject is at stake, the remedy for failure to observe these procedures should also take account of the effect it will have on the victim. It is suggested that correction of the error where the injustice will be slight, or an order for a retrial, best balances and protects the rights and interests of both parties.

Further difficulties arise where the breach of the civil order gives rise to criminal proceedings. It may be argued on behalf of the contemnor that he will be seriously prejudiced at trial if the contempt proceedings go ahead. In *M v M (Contempt: Committal)*[17] Lord Bingham CJ held that three principles apply to the exercise of judicial discretion in these circumstances: first, there is no absolute rule that civil proceedings (including contempt proceedings) should not proceed when criminal proceedings are pending; secondly, there is a general rule that contempt proceedings should be dealt with swiftly and decisively; and thirdly, the test as to whether or not contempt proceedings should proceed in advance of criminal proceedings is whether there is a real risk of serious prejudice leading to injustice if the contempt proceedings go ahead. In the last situation the court would normally stay the contempt proceedings.

When a respondent is brought before the court for breach of the court's order, or for failing to comply with an undertaking given to the court, the court must decide on the penalty. The Court of Appeal's ruling in *Wilson v Webster*[18] acknowledged the plight of victims, and made it clear that courts should take incidents of domestic violence very seriously indeed. The parties were former cohabitants and Mr Webster had given undertakings to the court not to assault or threaten to assault Ms Wilson. Shortly afterwards Mr Webster attacked Ms Wilson in the street, causing very severe bruising which required hospital treatment. At the subsequent committal proceedings for breach of the undertakings the judge said: 'If you had not admitted [causing these injuries] you would have been sentenced to three months' imprisonment. This is so serious that a custodial sentence cannot be avoided. In the circumstances that you admitted it and are in work, the sentence is one of 14 days' imprisonment.' Ms Wilson appealed, alleging that the sentence was too short, and that it

16 [1997] 1 FLR 649.
17 [1997] 1 FLR 762 at p 764. See also *Keeber v Keeber* [1996] 1 FCR 199.
18 [1998] 1 FLR 1097.

failed to reflect the serious nature of the offence. The Court of Appeal agreed with Ms Wilson. It ruled that there was no jurisdictional bar to the court increasing the sentence, held that the judge's sentence was wholly inadequate and substituted a sentence of three months imprisonment. Commenting on the approach which courts should adopt, Sir Stephen Brown P said: 'It should be understood by those who have to exercise this jurisdiction that quite deliberate violent attacks of this nature should be marked by condign punishment ... It is important that the court should mark the gravity of a deliberate breach of undertaking of this kind ... I hope that county court judges will take seriously the views of this court that matters of this kind are to be dealt with seriously.'[19]

Undertakings

Where, prior to the Family Law Act 1996, an application was made to a court for a non-molestation order, it was frequently the case that pressure was put on the applicant to withdraw her application in return for the respondent giving an undertaking to the court not to molest her. Similarly, when faced with an application for (what is now) an occupation order, the respondent often agreed to leave the home, thus obviating the necessity for the court to make an order. An undertaking is a promise given to the court. Theoretically, the protection afforded by it is as effective as a court order, and breach of an undertaking can give rise to proceedings for contempt.[20] However, it was often to the respondent's advantage to give an undertaking because the court did not make any findings of fact about his alleged behaviour. It was also to his advantage because there was evidence to suggest that undertakings were not viewed as seriously as injunctions by either the courts or the police.[1] Moreover, even where the court did make the requisite findings of fact against the respondent, it could still deal with his case by accepting an undertaking from him not to repeat the behaviour. Where an undertaking was broken, and the issue was brought back to court, in some cases the court simply accepted a further undertaking from the respondent; or it granted an order in the same or similar terms to the undertaking, rather than committing the respondent to prison for breach.

The Family Law Act 1996 allows the practice of accepting undertakings in non-molestation and occupation order cases to continue.[2] However, the

---

19 At p 1100.
20 Family Law Act 1996, s 46(4). Also see *Hussain v Hussain* [1986] 2 FLR 271; *Roberts v Roberts* [1990] 2 FLR 111.
1   See J Barron *Not Worth the Paper: the effectiveness of legal protection for women and children experiencing domestic violence* (Women's Aid Federation, 1990).
2   Unfortunately the Law Commission failed to address the issue of undertakings in their report on domestic violence, Law Com No 207. S 46 did not appear in the Law Commission Draft Bill, or in the original Family Homes and Domestic Violence Bill 1995, but was introduced at Committee stage.

Act recognises that the major disadvantage of undertakings from the view point of the applicant is that no power of arrest can be attached.[3] As a result, the occasions when a court may accept an undertaking are now carefully controlled by section 46(3), which states: 'The court shall not accept an undertaking ... in any case where apart from this section a power of arrest would be attached to the order.'

Arrest

A non-molestation or occupation order is only of value to the applicant if it is obeyed. A person who assaults his spouse or partner in the privacy of the home is unlikely to be deterred from repeating his behaviour by court order, unless the order is backed up by swift and effective enforcement procedures. Similarly, where the court issues occupation orders requiring the respondent to permit the applicant to enter and remain in the matrimonial home, excluding the respondent from the home, or forbidding him from a specified area in which the home is included, such orders only have 'teeth' if steps can readily be taken to enforce them should the respondent choose to ignore them.

Civil courts do not normally have sufficient personnel available to enforce their orders and to bring a respondent before the court for contempt. Normally the man must be served personally with notice of an application to commit him for breach.[4] He may only be arrested by officers of the court, but they of course go home in the evenings and at weekends. Yet these are exactly the times when domestic violence is most likely to occur. Clearly, where a crime has been committed, and where a man is threatening to assault and batter a woman, the police have powers of arrest under the Police and Criminal Evidence Act 1984.[5] However, historically the police have sometimes been reluctant to become involved in domestic violence cases (because of the difficulties they face in mounting a successful prosecution). Furthermore, in some cases, the powers of the police do not encompass the behaviour which has been forbidden by court order. This gap in the enforcement process was recognised by the Select Committee on Violence in Marriage, and it recommended that the police should become involved in the enforcement of domestic violence orders, despite the fact that non-molestation and occupation orders are made in civil proceedings. This recommendation was accepted, and since 1976 courts have had power to attach a power of arrest to court orders restraining the respondent from using violence or excluding him from the home.[6] However, although the introduction of the power of arrest un-

---

3   Family Law Act 1996, s 46(2).
4   CCR Ord 29, r 1(4) and r 1(7).
5   Ss 24 and 25.
6   Magistrates' courts had slightly more limited powers.

doubtedly assisted victims of domestic violence, the Law Commission found that powers of arrest were being attached to a relatively small proportion of orders.[7]

Reluctance to make use of the power of arrest stemmed from the Court of Appeal's decision in *Lewis v Lewis*[8] which was made shortly after the Domestic Violence and Matrimonial Proceedings Act 1976 came into force. The court ruled that attaching a power of arrest to an injunction should not be a routine remedy and that the use of this power was quite plainly intended for the exceptional situation 'where men or women persistently disobey injunctions and make nuisances of themselves to the other party and to others concerned'.[9] This set the pattern for the approach in subsequent cases, and the courts consistently stated that the power of arrest should only be attached in exceptional circumstances.[10]

This gate-keeping attitude failed to recognise the very dangerous nature of domestic violence, and tacit within it was the assumption that victims of assaults within the privacy of the home could be expected to put up with illegal and immoral behaviour unless it was extremely serious. Such an approach was unacceptable and wrong. It failed to afford battered women adequate protection and was far too solicitous of the civil liberties of their assailants. It also failed to recognise that a power of arrest is a 'simple, immediate and inexpensive means of enforcement which under-lines the seriousness of the breach to the offending party'.[11] The Law Commission consulted widely on whether the power of arrest should be more readily attached to non-molestation and occupation orders, and reported that a sizeable and varied group of respondents suggested that powers of arrest should generally be attached where there had been violence or threatened violence.[12] This response was hardly surprising,

---

7   In 1989, the latest year for which figures were available to the Law Commission, injunctions were attached to only 29% of orders made under the 1976 Act: Law Com 207, para 5.11.

8   [1978] 1 All ER 729. Similarly, in *Widdowson v Widdowson* (1982) 4 FLR 121, it was held that magistrates should only attach a power of arrest where it was really necessary, and they should specifically state their reasons for so doing.

9   Ibid, at p 731. This wording suggested that a power of arrest should only be attached to an injunction where there had already been a breach. The choice of the word 'nuisance' was an extraordinarily gentle euphemism for the behaviour being considered.

10 See *Harrison v Lewis; R v S* [1988] 2 FLR 339. In *McLean v Nugent* (1980) 1 FLR 26 it was stated that a power of arrest should not be attached unless the respondent had been forewarned of the application, because he might not otherwise bother to turn up at court if he thought that only an injunction was going to be made, whereas he might well do so if he thought that a power of arrest would be attached.

11 Law Com 207, para 5.13.

12 Including the Magistrates' Association, Women's Aid Federation, Rights of Women, Institute of Legal Executives, Children's Legal Centre, Association of Women Solicitors, Law Society, Family Law Bar Association, National Council for One Parent Families, Association of Chief Police Officers and the Metropolitan Police; see Law Com 207, para 5.12. It is interesting to note such unanimity bearing in mind that not all of these organisations are noted for their sympathetic approach to victims of domestic violence.

as what can be objectionable about giving courts the authority to attach a power of arrest to injunctions which prohibit physical violence or threatened violence? The respondent can only be arrested if he is in breach of the injunction, and as any such breach would be a crime, why should he not therefore be vulnerable to immediate arrest?

The Family Law Act 1996 reflects this thinking. Section 47(2) provides that where, on making an occupation order or a non-molestation order, it appears to the court that the respondent has 'used, or threatened, violence against the applicant or relevant child', it *shall* attach a power of arrest to one or more provisions of the order. A court is only permitted to ignore this requirement where it is satisfied that the applicant or child will be adequately protected without such a power of arrest. Violence is not defined. Under the previous legislation, 'actual bodily harm' to the applicant or to the child had to be established. This phrase was held to encompass both physical violence and psychological violence in *Kendrick v Kendrick*.[13] In that case the Court of Appeal held that actual bodily harm could be established provided that there was clear evidence that the person assaulted has suffered real psychological damage, causing a real change in her condition. However, the test was a stringent one, and in that particular case being very frightened of the husband was held to be insufficient. The 1996 Act has clearly extended the occasions when a power of arrest *shall* be attached by including threatened as well as actual violence. This is an important change because it recognises that the applicant or child should not first have to be physically assaulted before the law extends its protective arm, and acknowledges that living in constant fear of assault can be as harmful, or even more distressing, than actual attacks themselves. Thus the power of arrest should now be attached in situations similar to *Kendrick v Kendrick*. The arrest must be for a breach of the provision of the order to which the power of arrest is attached. Accordingly, the pre-Act decision in *Bowen v Bowen*[14] is still relevant. There it was held that where the respondent subsequently molested the applicant in a way which did not amount to violent molestation the power of arrest could not be exercised.

A more cautious approach to the power of arrest applies where an ex parte order is made. The court may (not shall) attach a power of arrest where it appears that the respondent has used or threatened violence and that there is a risk of significant harm to the applicant or child attributable to conduct of the respondent if a power of arrest is not attached immediately to one or more of the provisions of the order.[15] Where the applicant succeeds in having a power of arrest attached to orders made in either ex parte or inter partes proceedings, it is suggested that a lawyer advising her should always ensure that a copy of the court's order, with

13 [1990] 2 FLR 107.
14 [1990] 2 FLR 93.
15 S 47(3). In this instance, the court may also provide that the power of arrest is to have effect for a shorter period than other provisions in the order (s 47(4)).

its power of arrest, is sent to her local police station, with a letter explaining exactly what powers the court's order confers on a constable. The lawyer should also ensure that the woman has her own copy of the order so that she can show it to a constable should she need to seek the constable's assistance.

A constable may arrest without warrant a person whom he has reasonable cause for suspecting to be in breach of the provisions in the order to which the power of arrest is attached.[16] The respondent must be brought before a judge or justice of the peace within twenty four hours, and where the matter is not disposed of forthwith he may be remanded either in custody or on bail (to which conditions may be attached).[17] In cases where no power of arrest has been attached, if at any time the applicant considers that the respondent has failed to comply with the order she may apply on oath for a warrant of arrest.[18] A difficulty may arise where the respondent claims that he is not in breach and wishes to call witnesses to prove it. It could well be impossible for him to organise his witnesses within 24 hours. In these circumstances it was held by the Court of Appeal in *Roberts v Roberts*[19] that the proceedings should be adjourned 'to a convenient date a short way further on' and in the meanwhile the man should be released. It is suggested that this was unduly lenient towards the alleged contemnor. While it may have given him plenty of time to arrange his witnesses, it gave very little protection to the applicant. A more satisfactory course would have been to direct an adjournment to the earliest date possible, with the court imposing a very tight limit indeed on the amount of time given to either party to gather information or to contact witnesses.

Provision for third parties to act on behalf of victims of domestic violence

Section 60 of the Family Act 1996, which at the time of writing has not been implemented, states that rules of court may provide for prescribed persons to act on behalf of another for an occupation order or a non-molestation order. Any such rules will also prescribe the details of how this provision will be put into practice. This provision stems from the Law Commission's recommendation that where the police have been involved in an incident of molestation or actual or threatened violence, or its aftermath, they should have power to apply for civil remedies on behalf of the victim.[20] The Commission modelled its recommendation on that pertaining in several Australian states where it has been found to be a

---

16 S 47(6).
17 S 47(7), (12). No account is taken of Christmas Day, Good Friday or any Sunday in reckoning this period or time.
18 S 47(8). The same remand provisions apply. For further details, see Law Com 207, para 5.15.
19 [1991] 1 FLR 294.
20 Law Com No 207, paras 5.18-5.23.

useful and valuable provision.[1] The purpose behind involving the police is to remove the burden of taking action from the victim, to reduce the scope for further intimidation by the perpetrator and to lead to far fewer cases being withdrawn: 'The fact that the police are initiating the proceedings also has the beneficial effect of bringing home to the respondent the seriousness of the matter and giving civil proceedings the "weight" they can lack in the eyes of some of the less law abiding members of society.'[2]

The Commission found the question of whether the victim's consent should be necessary before the police can bring civil proceedings a difficult one to resolve.[3] It concluded that the best solution was to require the police to consult the woman concerned and take account of her views, but not to make her consent or approval the decisive factor in determining whether or not civil proceedings are issued. This approach has the advantage that the police can emphasise to the assailant that the decision to initiate civil proceedings is out of the victim's hands. Similarly, the Commission recommended that in cases where the proceedings are brought by the police, the court should have the duty to take the victim's views into account before making any order.

Persons not protected under the Family Law Act 1996

It has been seen that the Law Commission took the view that it was inappropriate to remove all restrictions on applicants and open the jurisdiction to all in genuine need of protection, as has been done in some Australian states.[4] Consequently, neighbours, colleagues in the work place, tenants, members of Parliament, doctors, school teachers and others who are particularly vulnerable to threats of violence, sexual harassment and other forms of molestation are excluded from the 1996 Act's provisions.[5] Unless the behaviour was obviously criminal or tortious, such as where there had been violence, persons falling outside the 1996 Act were not protected under the general criminal or civil law either. A breakthrough occurred when in *Burris v Azadani*[6] the Court of Appeal declared that there was a tort of harassment, and another appeared to occur in *Khoransandjian*

---

1   D Chappell and H Strang *Domestic violence – findings and recommendations of the National Committee on Violence* [1990] Australian J Fam L 211.
2   Law Com No 207, para 5.18. Giving the police these powers may also encourage them to upgrade the importance of domestic violence and become more aware and sensitive in relation to it. They may also be more prepared to arrest for breach if they themselves have initiated the proceeding and obtained the order.
3   Ibid, para 5.22.
4   In New South Wales it has been possible since 1989 for anyone to apply for an 'apprehended violence order' regardless of their connection with the applicant.
5   Mistakenly, it is suggested. For further comment, see M Hayes *Non-molestation protection – only associated persons need apply* [1996] Fam Law 134.
6   [1995] 4 All ER 802; cf *Patel v Patel* [1988] 2 FLR 179.

v Bush,[7] where the Court of Appeal moved away from limiting an action in nuisance to those who had an interest in land, and opened up the possibility of future developments. In the latter case the plaintiff was a young woman whose friendship with the defendant had ceased. Since the end of their relationship the defendant had, amongst other acts, persecuted both her, and also her mother and current boyfriend, with telephone calls. The defendant conceded that the mother could complain about the persistent telephone calls made to the parental home, if she had a freehold or leasehold interest in the property, as such conduct would fall within the tort of private nuisance. However, he claimed that as the plaintiff was a mere licensee in her mother's property, with no proprietary interest, she did not fall within the scope of the law. In a robust judgment Dillon LJ commented, 'to my mind, it is ridiculous if in this present age the law is that the making of deliberately harassing and pestering telephone calls to a person is only actionable in the civil courts if the recipient of the calls happens to have the freehold or a leasehold proprietary interest in the premises in which he or she has received the calls'.[8] He went on to approve the wording of the injunction granted by the judge which prohibited the defendant from 'using violence to, harassing, pestering or communicating with' the plaintiff.

The decision in *Khoransandjian v Bush* was widely welcomed.[9] As one commentator wrote:

> 'For too long harassment of women has been treated as part of the "rough and tumble" of male/female relationships. If a woman complains of sexual or other forms of harassment she is told not to take it seriously; it is a sign of "affection". This case suggests a greater sensitivity to the real harm that is done by such harassment and in so doing provides women not protected by the 1976 Act with a legal remedy. [There] is, as the majority recognised, a pressing social concern that needs redressing; a new tort of unreasonable harassment would go some way to doing that.'[10]

However, any pleasure derived from this development was short-lived because *Khoransandjian v Bush* was overruled by the House of Lords in *Hunter v Canary Wharf Ltd.*[11] Their Lordships held that a person who has no right in the land affected by the nuisance, such as a licensee or occupier, cannot bring an action in nuisance. Moreover, it was wrong to treat actions

---

7   [1993] 3 All ER 669.
8   Ibid, at p 675.
9   See E Cooke *A Development in the tort of private nuisance* (1994) 57 MLR 289; S Cretney [1993] All ER Annual Review 231; A Mullis [1993] All ER Annual Review 473; J Ford *Squaring analogy with principle, or vice versa* (1994) 53 CLJ 14; J Murphy *The emergence of harassment as a recognised tort* (1993) 143 NLJ 926; M Noble *Harassment – a recognised tort?* (1993) 143 NLJ 1685; J Bridgeman and M A Jones *Harassing conduct and outrageous acts* (1994) 14 Legal Studies 180.
10 A Mullis [1993] All ER Annual Review 473, at p 473-474, although it undoubtedly raised questions which would require future clarification.
11 [1997] 2 All ER 426.

in respect of discomfort, interference with personal enjoyment or personal injury suffered by the plaintiff as actions in nuisance.[12]

Protection from Harassment Act 1997

Fortunately, many of the limitations of both the 1996 Act and the common law have been addressed by the Protection from Harassment Act 1997. This creates an arrestable offence[13] of harassment and gives victims of harassment and those who are put in fear of violence both criminal and civil remedies, including the right to claim damages.[14] Section 1 states that a person must not pursue a course of conduct which amounts to harassment of another, and which he knows or ought to know amounts to harassment of the other.[15] Such a person will be taken to know that his behaviour amounts to harassment 'if a reasonable person in possession of the same information would think the course of conduct amounted to harassment of the other'.[16] This provision focuses on the defendant's behaviour as well as its impact on the victim. Harassment plainly covers speech and includes alarming a person and causing that person distress.[17] It is suggested that harassment also encompasses the same types of behaviours as those which amount to molestation for the purposes of the 1996 Act.[18] A person who pursues a course of conduct which amounts to harassment is guilty of an offence; and an actual or apprehended breach of section 1 may also be the subject of a claim in civil proceedings by the person who is, or may be, that person's victim.[19] Various responses are open to the civil court. Damages may be awarded for (among other things) any anxiety or financial loss caused by, or resulting from, the harassment.[20] Injunctions may be granted to restrain the defendant from pursuing the course of conduct, any breach of which may be enforced by the issue of an arrest warrant in ex parte proceedings brought by the victim.[1] Breach of an injunction amounts to an offence as well as contempt of court, but where the defendant is convicted he may not also be punished for contempt, and vice versa.[2] Section 4 of the Act makes it an offence for a person to

---

12 See further I Anderson *Hunter and Others v Canary Wharf Ltd, the tort of nuisance – not for women or children?* (1998) 10 CFLQ 201.
13 S 2(3).
14 S 3(2). Damages may be awarded for (among other things) any anxiety caused by the harassment and any financial loss resulting from the harassment. A full account is beyond the scope of this book. See further, T Lawson-Cruttenden and N Addison *Blackstones' Guide to the Protection from Harassment Act 1997.*
15 S 1(1).
16 S 1(2).
17 S 7.
18 See above.
19 S 3(1).
20 S 3(2).
1 S 3(3), (5).
2 S 3(6), (7) and (8).

engage in a course of conduct on at least two occasions which causes another to fear that violence will be used against him. No warrant is needed where there is a breach because the offence falls within the normal arrest powers given to the police.[3] This Act clearly has widespread civil and criminal law implications, and where the victim wishes to pursue an action in damages it may be advantageous to her to apply under this Act even though she is entitled to apply for orders under the Family Law Act 1996.

Homelessness

Persons who are the victims of domestic violence, or who otherwise have been driven from their homes, may turn to their local housing authority for assistance. Under the Housing Act 1996,[4] a local authority are obliged to provide accommodation for certain categories of person whom the law deems to be 'homeless'. In order to qualify for the provision of emergency accommodation, the applicant must establish that she has no reasonable home to go to, that she is in priority need, and that she is unintentionally homeless.[5]

Under the Housing Act 1996, section 175(2)(a), a person is deemed to be homeless if he has accommodation but he cannot secure entry to it. Further, under section 175(3):

'A person shall not be treated as having accommodation unless it is accommodation which it would be reasonable for him to continue to occupy.'

Whether it is reasonable to continue to occupy accommodation is defined in section 177(1) which states:

'It is not reasonable for a person to continue to occupy accommodation if it is probable that this will lead to domestic violence against him, or against-
(a) a person who normally resides with him as a member of his family, or
(b) any other person who might reasonably be expected to reside with him.

---

3 Police and Criminal Evidence Act 1994, s 24(6). Indeed, this provision does not create new law since such behaviour must at least amount to a common assault and may fall within the provisions of the Public Order Act 1986.

4 Which was preceded by the White Paper, *Our Future Homes: Opportunity, Choice, Responsibility* (HMSO, 1995), and a Consultation Paper, *More Choice in the Social Rented Sector* (DOE, 1995).

5 The homelessness provisions are complex and have given rise to a considerable body of case law, the analysis of which is beyond the scope of this book. The outline below provides merely a brief overview.

For this purpose "domestic violence", in relation to a person, means violence from a person with whom he is associated, or threats of violence from such a person which are likely to be carried out.'

'Associated person' is defined in section 178, the definition being almost identical to that contained in section 62 of the Family Law Act 1996.[6] In sum, the Act makes provision both for a person who has been locked out of the home, and for a person who is too frightened either to stay in the home,[7] or to return there. A woman who takes shelter in a refuge is nonetheless homeless.[8]

Priority need

If a woman is regarded as homeless under the criteria in section 175 she must then show that she is in priority need of accommodation. Section 189(1) provides:

'The following have a priority need for accommodation—
(a) a pregnant woman or a person with whom she resides or might reasonably be expected to reside;
(b) a person with whom dependent children reside or might reasonably be expected to reside;[9]
(c) a person who is vulnerable as a result of old age, mental illness or handicap or physical disability or other special reason, or with whom such a person resides or might reasonably be expected to reside;
(d) a person who is homeless or threatened with homelessness as a result of an emergency such as flood, fire or other disaster.'

Dependent children do not qualify as being in priority need in their own right. Neither will they qualify as being vulnerable either because of their youth or because of some sort of disability.[10] 'Dependent child' is not defined in the Act, but the *Code of Guidance* issued under the previous legislation[11] suggested that it should cover children under 16, and those aged 16-18

---

6 See above. The only significant difference is that where the parties live or have lived in the same household, then employees, tenants, lodgers and boarders are not excluded.
7 See *R v Broxbourne Borough Council, ex p Willmoth* (1989) 22 HLR 118.
8 *R v Ealing London Borough Council, ex p Sidhu* (1982) 80 LGR 534.
9 Cf *B v B (Occupation Order)* [1999] 1 FLR 715.
10 *R v Oldham MBC, ex p Garlick; R v Bexley LBC, ex p Bentum; R v Tower Hamlets LBC, ex p Begum* [1993] AC 509. For a fierce criticism of the judgment of the House of Lords, see I Loveland *The status of children as applicants under the homelessness legislation – judicial subversion of legislative intent?* (1996) 8 CFLQ 89.
11 Housing Act 1985. See *Homelessness – Code of Guidance for Local Authorities* DOE (HMSO, 1992).

who are still in full-time education or training, or who are unable to support themselves and live at home.[12]

'Vulnerable' is also not defined. The *Code of Guidance* gave advice as to how it should be interpreted. It stated that it is good practice for a local authority to 'secure wherever possible that accommodation is made available for men and women without children who have suffered violence at home or are at risk of further violence if they return home.'[13] This left it to the discretion of a local authority whether or not to classify a woman without dependent children as being in priority need. Research in the past has found that local authority policy and practice has been variable, and that whereas some authorities operated a generous interpretation of this provision, other authorities were very restrictive when considering a single woman's application for housing.[14] However, in *R v Kensington and Chelsea LBC, ex p Kihara*[15] the Court of Appeal was quite clear that the phrase 'or other special reason' was intended to cover all battered wives.

It may also be possible for a woman to establish that she is in priority need under the category of vulnerability where she has a child living with her, but that child is now over 18 years, if the child himself is vulnerable. Where the child is severely handicapped he may not be able to make an application for housing on his own behalf, as he may be considered to lack the capacity to do so.[16] However, section 189(1)(c) also encompasses the carer of a vulnerable person. Provided that her homelessness is not intentional, she will qualify for an offer of accommodation which will enable her to continue looking after her vulnerable child.

Intentional homelessness

If the woman is found to be homeless and in priority need a local authority must then assess whether or not she is intentionally homeless. Where her homelessness is unintentional, the authority are under a duty to secure that accommodation becomes available for her occupation.[17] If, however, the local authority decide that she is intentionally homeless[18] their duty is limited to securing her some temporary accommodation, simply in order

---

12 Para 6.3. The Code of Guidance was considered in *R v Royal Borough of Kensington and Chelsea, ex p Amarfio* (1995) 27 HLR 543. The Court of Appeal held that a young person on a youth training scheme ought to be regarded as being in full-time employment and not dependent.

13 Para 6.17.

14 See E Malos and G Hague *Domestic Violence and Housing: Local authority responses to women and children escaping violence in the home* (Women's Aid Federation and School of Applied Social Studies, University of Bristol, 1993), at para 3.16.

15 (1997) 29 HLR 147.

16 *R v Oldham MBC, ex p Garlick; R v Bexley LBC, ex p Bentum; R v Tower Hamlets LBC, ex p Begum* [1993] AC 509.

17 S 193(2).

18 S 191.

to enable her to have a reasonable opportunity of securing her own accommodation, and to furnishing her with advice and assistance.[19] The relevant date for determining whether or not homelessness is intentional is the date a person leaves the accommodation, and the cause of homelessness must be assessed as at that date.[20]

Local authorities are, of course, anxious to preserve scarce resources for those who cannot make provision for themselves. Research has revealed that some authorities will not assist a woman unless she has taken her own steps to secure an exclusive right to occupy her present accommodation. They have put pressure on the woman, and will not classify her as being homeless unless she has taken such steps.[1] If a woman fleeing violence is offered accommodation, but rejects it as being unsuitable, she may then find that the local authority classify her as being intentionally homeless. When offering accommodation, the local authority must comply with the terms of section 193 and make her an offer of 'suitable' accommodation. Where the local authority consider that they have fulfilled their duty under section 193, the woman may find it very difficult to challenge their decision that she is now intentionally homeless.[2]

Where a woman has dependent children and is driven from the home by domestic violence, she does not automatically qualify for assistance if the local authority take the view that her complaint of violence has not been substantiated. In *R v Westminster City Council, ex p Bishop*[3] the applicant had a ten-year-old daughter living with her. She claimed that she had been driven from the home by her partner's violence, but was nonetheless classified by the local authority as being intentionally homeless. However, the mother successfully challenged the council's decision in judicial review on the grounds that they had never properly addressed the position of the daughter. The Court of Appeal commented that the position of the daughter was of 'great significance'. This welcome ruling suggests that it would be most unwise for a local authority to deem a woman to be intentionally homeless where she has dependent children living with her, except where they have strong evidence, and unless they have considered the position of the children with great care.

In *R v Oldham MBC, ex p Garlick*[4] the parents had been declared intentionally homeless by their local authority. The parents therefore used the device of making their children the applicants for accommodation on the basis of homelessness and priority need. The children

---

19 S 190(2).
20 *Din v Wandsworth London Borough Council* [1983] 1 AC 657.
1   *R v Westminster City Council, ex p Bishop* [1993] 2 FLR 780. See further E Malos and G Hague, op cit, ch 5; R Thornton *Homelessness through relationship breakdown: the local authorities' response* [1989] JSWL 67.
2   *R v Lewisham London Borough Council, ex p D* [1993] Fam Law 277; *R v London Borough of Brent, ex p Awua* [1996] AC 55.
3   [1993] 2 FLR 780.
4   *R v Oldham MBC, ex p Garlick; R v Bexley LBC, ex p Bentum; R v Tower Hamlets LBC, ex p Begum* [1993] AC 509.

were then aged four. The local authority refused to accept the children's application, so an action was then brought in judicial review to compel them to do so. The application was dismissed on the basis that the provisions in the (then) Housing Act 1985 were not intended to confer any rights to housing directly upon dependent children. The House of Lords ruled that the intention of the legislation was that the parents of children, or those looking after them, would provide the children with accommodation, and it was to those carers that any offer of accommodation should be made. In dismissing the application, Lord Griffiths commented: 'I wish however to point out that there are other provisions of our social welfare legislation that provide for the accommodation and care of children and of the duty of co-operation between authorities in the discharge of their duties.'[5]

However, the provisions to which Lord Griffiths was referring do not directly overcome the difficulties experienced by families who have been declared intentionally homeless. The provisions to which he was referring are sections 20 and 27 of the Children Act 1989.[6] Section 27 states that a local authority may request another authority to assist them in the exercise of any of their functions under Part III of the Act.[7] In *R v Northavon District Council, ex p Smith*[8] the House of Lords ruled that where a local housing authority has turned down a request for housing on the grounds that the applicants are intentionally homeless, the authority cannot be required to supply such housing in response to a request made by the social services department of the local authority under section 27. The two authorities had different responsibilities, one being responsible for children and the other for housing. They should co-operate for the benefit of the children, but, the House of Lords ruled, it was up to them to decide what form that co-operation would take.

Where a person is already a local authority tenant, the Housing Act 1996, section 145,[9] introduced a new ground for possession proceedings which can be of particular significance. Ground 2A provides that the local authority may now take possession proceedings where:

> 'The dwelling-house was occupied (whether alone or with others) by a married couple or a couple living together as husband and wife and-
> (a) one or both of the partners is a tenant of the dwelling-house,
> (b) one partner has left because of violence or threats of violence by the other towards-

5   Ibid, at p 518
6   Which are discussed in ch 3. S 20 is concerned with a local authority's duty to accommodate children, but not their parents.
7   This Part is mainly concerned with the provision of services for children in need and other children.
8   [1994] 3 All ER 313. For comment see D Cowan and J Fionda *Housing homeless families – an update* (1995) 7 CFLQ 66.
9   Which amended the Housing Act 1985, Sch 2.

(i) that partner, or
(ii) a member of the family of that partner who was residing
with that partner immediately before the partner left, and
(c) the court is satisfied that the partner who has left is unlikely
to return.'

The effect of this provision is that the local authority can now obtain a possession order against the violent partner. The significant point for the battered woman is that, where she so desires, she may well be able to negotiate with the local authority that she be granted a new tenancy of the same premises in her sole name.[10] In view of the fact that the local authority will be obliged to house her in any event, this may well be acceptable to the authority in a large number of cases.

However, while the new provision in section 145 has the potential to be a significant step forward for battered women, another new provision in the Housing Act 1996 has the potential to be a significant step backwards. Section 193, which imposes a duty on the local authority to house the unintentionally homeless, also provides in sub-section(3):

'The authority are subject to the duty under this section for a period of two years ("the minimum period"), subject to the following provisions of this section.

After the end of that period the authority may continue to secure that accommodation is available for occupation by the applicant, but are not obliged to do so (see section 194).'

This provision was designed to reduce the rights of homeless people. However, following the House of Lords decision in *R v London Borough of Brent, ex p Awua*[11] that although accommodation must be 'suitable', there is no requirement that it must be permanent, it may not be the reduction it was first thought to be. Nonetheless, the introduction of a statutory limit of two years on the duty to house is certainly of considerable importance. The rationale behind this provision was that the then Government felt that some homeless people were 'jumping the queue' in obtaining permanent accommodation. They therefore wished to regularise the situation. The serious nature of the provision is further confirmed by section 207(1), which provides that in discharging their housing function under this Part of the Act the authority *shall not* provide accommodation for more than two years. However, it should be noted there is a discretion in the authority to continue to provide housing by virtue of the words in section 193(3) 'the authority *may* continue to secure that accommodation',

---

10 A battered woman may have good reason not to wish to return to the home. For example, where she has fled from severe violence she may not wish her partner to know her new address.
11 [1996] AC 55.

although this is subject to the limitations contained in section 194.[12] Furthermore, section 193(9) also provides that where a person has ceased to be owed a duty under the section, that person may make a fresh application for accommodation, or assistance in obtaining accommodation.

12 The limitations are that the applicant must continue to be in priority need; there must be no other accommodation available for occupation in the district; and the applicant must wish the authority to continue to secure accommodation for her. Also, any continuation may only last for up to two years at a time, when it must be reviewed: s 194(2). Cf *B v B (Occupation Order)* [1999] 1 FLR 715.

Chapter 7

Ending a marriage – the law of nullity, divorce and separation

Chapter 7

Ending a marriage – the law of nullity, divorce and separation

The law of nullity

The concept of nullity

The law of nullity stems from the Canon law administered by the Ecclesiastical Courts prior to the Reformation. At that time, annulment was the only means by which a marriage could be brought to an end; divorce was then unheard of. The law relating to void marriages was, and still is, built around the notion that there is an impediment to the marriage which prevents it from coming into existence. In the eyes of the law there is no marriage. Parties to a void marriage are therefore free to marry whenever they please, and neither needs to apply for a decree to annul their existing 'marriage' before remarrying. Because there is no legally recognised union to annul, it may seem curious that a decree of nullity can nonetheless be obtained in respect of a void marriage. This is justified on the basis that a decree resolves uncertainty. It is a judgment in rem, and therefore binding on future courts. Nullity decrees can be granted not only to the parties to the 'marriage' themselves, but also to third parties who have an interest in whether or not the marriage is a valid marriage.[1] Third parties can challenge the validity of a marriage even where the 'spouses' are dead. Thus it can be seen that there is a need for a legal framework within which the validity, or otherwise, of a particular marriage can be clarified. The remedy could, of course, simply be a declaration as to the status of the parties. The advantage to the 'spouses' of the availability of a nullity decree is that the court has the same powers to make financial provision and property adjustment orders as it has when a marriage is ended by divorce. This is an important safeguard, for a void marriage may last for many years, and children may be born. One, or sometimes both, parties to a void marriage may be completely unaware that their marriage is an invalid marriage, and as such either of the parties may

---

1   This is most likely to arise in a dispute involving succession rights.

have financial claims and needs which can only fairly be resolved within a financial provision and property adjustment framework when the invalidity of their union is exposed.

Void marriages

Section 11 of the Matrimonial Causes Act 1973 provides that:

> 'A marriage celebrated after 31 July 1971 shall be void on the following grounds only, that is to say—
> (a) that it is not a valid marriage under the provisions of the Marriage Acts 1949 to 1986 (that is to say where—
>   (i) the parties are within the prohibited degrees of relationship;
>   (ii) either party is under the age of sixteen; or
>   (iii) the parties have intermarried in disregard of certain requirements as to the formation of marriage);
> (b) that at the time of the marriage either party was already lawfully married;
> (c) that the parties are not respectively male and female;
> (d) in the case of a polygamous marriage entered into outside England and Wales, that either party was at the time of the marriage domiciled in England and Wales.
> For the purposes of paragraph (d) of this subsection a marriage may be polygamous although at its inception neither party has any spouse additional to the other.'[2]

Each of these grounds goes to the very root of the concept of marriage in the eyes of English law and renders the marriage void from the outset.

Marriage within the prohibited degrees of relationship

English law prohibits marriage between certain blood relations; this is known as a relationship of consanguinity.[3] A person may not marry his or her parent, grandparent, child, grandchild, sibling, aunt or uncle, niece or nephew. However, cousins are entitled to marry because the blood tie link is sufficiently distant. The prohibition on marriage between persons related closely by blood is founded on biological, social and moral reasons. The biological reasons are based on genetic factors: inherited disorders

---

2   Whether or not a marriage is polygamous may involve difficult issues of the conflict of laws, which are beyond the scope of this book.
3   Part I, Sch 1, of the Marriage Act 1949 lists the prohibited degrees of relationship of consanguinity.

are more liable to arise within the same genetic pool. For this reason an adopted child may not marry his or her birth relatives who fall within the prohibited degrees of relationship. An adopted child also may not marry his or her adoptive parents for social and moral reasons. However, there is no prohibition on marriage between a child and siblings to whom he or she is related through adoption. Clearly there is no genetic reason why such a marriage should not take place, and because adoption arises in a variety of contexts, it could be unduly restrictive if adoptive siblings were unable to marry.[4] The reasons of morality and social policy which forbid certain marriages relate closely to what is acceptable to public opinion. These reasons are therefore not susceptible to proof that they are 'right' or 'wrong'. People have a strong sense of taboo about sexual relationships taking place between persons who are closely related, even though they fall outside of the scope of the criminal law of incest. Thus on relationships of consanguinity, the Law Commission posed the question: 'would public opinion tolerate or object to marriages between uncle and niece or nephew and aunt? ... There are some matters of conviction on which men hold strong feelings of right and wrong though they cannot place their fingers on any particular reason for this conviction.'[5]

There is also a prohibition on marriage between certain persons who are related through marriage, known as a relationship of affinity.[6] The historical basis of the prohibition is that, by marriage, a relationship becomes equivalent to a relationship by blood. While this thinking is no longer one which holds sway, the rule that certain marriages should be prohibited turns on the notion that such unions are morally wrong, and therefore that they should not be permitted. When the Law Commission produced its Report on Nullity of Marriage in 1970, it concluded that there should be no change in the law relating to the prohibited degrees of affinity as there was no evidence that public opinion had altered since the question had last been canvassed in 1955.[7] The Commission found that the almost unanimous view of those who had commented on its Working Paper[8] was that the law should remain as it was. Somewhat surprisingly, therefore, the law was made less restrictive than hitherto by the Marriage (Prohibited Degrees of Relationship) Act 1986. It is now permissible for a man to marry his step-daughter, that is the daughter of his former wife if, but only if, both parties are over 21, and provided that he has never treated her as a child of the family before she reached the age of 18. He may also marry his son's former wife if, but only if, both parties are over 21 and both his son, and the mother of his son, have died.[9] Should a man wish to marry his mother-in-law, this is permitted

---

4 On adoption generally, see ch 4.
5 *Report on Nullity of Marriage*, Law Com No 33, 1970, at p 24.
6 Parts II and III, Sch 1, of the Marriage Act 1949 list the prohibited degrees of affinity.
7 See the Report of the Royal Commission on Marriage and Divorce, 1956, Cmd 9678.
8 Law Commission Working Paper No 20.
9 Marriage Act 1949, s 1(5)(b).

only if his former wife, and the father of his former wife, are both dead.[10] These prohibitions are clearly based on social policy considerations designed to discourage sexual relationships within the family which cut across taboos of what is generally regarded as acceptable behaviour. But the law of marriage cannot, of course, prevent a man from having sexual intercourse with his step-daughter before she reaches the age of 21, or committing adultery with his daughter-in-law. All that the law can do is to refrain from putting any kind of stamp of approval on the relationship through the orthodoxy of marriage.[11]

Marriage under the age of 16

Under English law, a person only acquires the capacity to marry when he or she reaches the age of 16. The view has been taken that it is 'essential that the minimum age for marriage and the age of consent for sexual intercourse should be the same'.[12] It is a criminal offence to have sexual intercourse with a girl aged under 16. The notion that a man should nonetheless be entitled to have sexual intercourse with a girl under the age of 16, under the cloak of marriage, offended law reformers when the age of marriage was raised from 12 for girls, and 14 for boys, in 1929, and it continues to cause similar offence today. There are social reasons too for discouraging marriage between young persons. There is evidence to suggest that the youthfulness of parties to a marriage may lead to it breaking down, and it is generally thought advisable for persons to delay the commitment which marriage entails until they have acquired greater maturity. Before producing their Report on Nullity, the Law Commission considered whether an under-age marriage should be voidable rather than void, because of the hardship which the rule rendering it void might cause. They concluded that, on balance, the arguments against this proposal were the more compelling.[13]

Failure to observe certain formalities

The formal requirements for entering into a valid marriage are contained in the Marriage Act 1949. Because English law recognises both civil and religious ceremonies of marriage, the law relating to the civil and religious preliminaries, and to the solemnisation of the marriage itself, is involved and somewhat puzzling.[14] However, despite there being an abundance of rules to

---

10 Marriage Act 1949, s 1(5)(a). The equivalent provisions apply to a woman.
11 For further discussion, see S M Cretney and J M Masson *Principles of Family Law* (6th edn, Sweet and Maxwell, 1996), ch 2.
12 *Report of the Committee on the Age of Majority*, Latey Committee (1967) Cmd 3342, para 177.
13 *Report on Nullity of Marriage*, Law Com No 33, paras 16-20.
14 For a detailed account, see S M Cretney and J M Masson, *Principles of Family Law* (6th edn, Sweet and Maxwell, 1997), pp 14-37.

be observed, failure to observe them may have no impact on the validity of the marriage. Thus, for example, the consent of parents is needed where the parties to the marriage are aged under 18.[15] But where the parties succeed in evading this restriction, and marrying without obtaining the requisite consents, their marriage is a valid marriage. Other defects render the marriage void, but only where the parties 'knowingly and wilfully intermarry'.[16] Thus it is impossible innocently to contract a marriage which is void for lack of formality. Whether a decree will be granted where a marriage is void for lack of formality turns on whether the parties, having undergone the ceremony of marriage, regard themselves as married. Where they do, they fall within section 11(a)(iii); where following the ceremony the parties do not regard themselves as married, there is no marriage to annul.[17]

Bigamous marriages

Where a person marries whilst he or she is already validly married to someone else, the marriage will be bigamous, and therefore void. The crucial date for determining whether a marriage is bigamous is the date of the marriage, and thus the supervening death of the first spouse will not validate the second 'marriage'. The marriage is void even though the bigamous party held an honest and reasonable belief that the first marriage had been lawfully terminated at the time of the second 'marriage', or that the first spouse was dead.[18] Where a nullity decree is granted the court has power to make financial provision and property adjustment orders. However, where in *Whiston v Whiston*[19] a party to a 'marriage' deliberately deceived her 'spouse' and married knowing that she was already married the court would not exercise its discretion to make orders in the bigamist's favour. As the Court of Appeal pointed out, had the applicant not committed the crime 'which strikes at the very heart of the institution of marriage' she would have had no claim for financial and property provision, she would have been in the same position as an unmarried cohabitee; and 'for a litigant to have to rely on his or her own criminal behaviour in order to get a claim on its feet is in my judgment offensive to the public conscience and contrary to public policy'.[20]

Bigamy is an imprisonable offence.[1] It is doubtful, however, whether the position of the deceived spouse and that of the first spouse is assisted

---

15 Marriage Act 1949, s 3.
16 Marriage Act 1949, s 25 in respect of marriages according to the rites of the Church of England; s 49 in respect of civil marriages by superintendent registrar's certificate.
17 *Gereis v Yagoub* [1997] 1 FLR 854.
18 This will, however, provide a defence to the crime of bigamy: see *R v Gould* [1968] 1 All ER 849.
19 [1995] 2 FLR 268. See S M Cretney *Right and wrong in the Court of Appeal* (1996) 112 LQR 33.
20 [1995] 2 FLR 268, at p 275, per Russell LJ.
1 Offences against the Person Act 1861, s 57.

by jailing the offender, and it may in fact be harmed. The rationale for involving the criminal law lies in the general public policy that society is entitled to express its disapproval of such behaviour.[2] Where bigamy results in grave social consequences it can be argued that there is still a place for the criminal law to operate. However, beyond that it is suggested that the criminal law no longer has any place. As one commentator has written: 'The only anti-social consequences that are necessarily involved in the mere celebration of a bigamous marriage are (1) the falsification of the State records, and (2) the waste of time of the Minister of Religion or Registrar.'[3]

Decree of presumption of death and dissolution of the marriage

A difficult situation arises where a spouse completely disappears, where the other spouse does not know whether he or she is alive or dead, and where that spouse wishes to marry again. If the second marriage goes ahead, it will be void where the first spouse is still alive. In a case of this kind, a spouse can be assisted by the decree of presumption of death and dissolution of the marriage. Section 19 of the Matrimonial Causes Act 1973 provides that:

'(1) Any married person who alleges that reasonable grounds exist for supposing that the other party to the marriage is dead may present a petition to the court to have it presumed that the other party is dead and to have the marriage dissolved, and the court may, if satisfied that such reasonable grounds exist, grant a decree of presumption of death and dissolution of the marriage.
(2) In any proceedings under this section the fact that for a period of seven years or more the other party to the marriage has been continually absent from the petitioner and the petitioner has no reason to believe that the other party has been living within that time shall be evidence that the other party is dead until the contrary is proved.'

The court can grant the decree before the seven years have elapsed, but any shorter period does not raise the presumption that the absent person has died. Consequently the evidential burden on the petitioner is considerably higher. The decree both presumes death and dissolves the marriage. Thus, if the missing person should reappear after the second

---

2   The traditional rationale was stated by Cockburn LJ in *R v Allen* (1872) LR 1 CCR 367, at pp 374-375: 'It involves an outrage on public decency and morals, and creates a public scandal by the prostitution of a solemn ceremony, which the law allows to be applied only to a legitimate union, to a marriage at best but colourable and fictitious, and which may be made and too often is made, the means of the most cruel and wicked deception.'

3   Glanville Williams *Language and the law* (1945) 61 LQR 71, at pp 77-78.

marriage has taken place, his reappearance has no effect on the validity of the second marriage. In *Chard v Chard*[4] the court held that, before a decree can be granted, the petitioner must establish that there are persons who would be likely to have heard from the missing spouse during the seven-year period; that those persons have not heard from him or her; and that all due enquiries appropriate to the circumstances have been made.

The parties are not male and female

Because under English law marriage can only take place between a man and a woman, the requirement that the parties be respectively male and female seems, at first sight, to be self-evident. However, difficulties arise when the gender of one of the parties is unclear, because he or she is a transsexual. A transsexual is a person who has many of the fundamental characteristics of one sex, gonadal, chromosomal and genital, and who will thus have been registered as a member of that sex as a baby. However, he or she will function psychologically as a member of the opposite sex. Such a person may then undergo operative and hormonal treatment to enable him or her to function totally, to all outward appearances, as a member of his or her psychological sex. If such a person wishes to marry, the question then arises as to whether or not the marriage can be classified as a valid marriage.

The leading case is *Corbett v Corbett*[5] in which it was determined that a person's biological sex is fixed at birth at the latest, on the basis of the gonadal, chromosomal and genital biological criteria, and that whatever artificial means are subsequently taken to alter the situation, this cannot take effect so as to alter the registration of a person's birth.[6] Accordingly, as the respondent was registered as a male at birth, the marriage she entered into with the petitioner 'husband' was void. This decision was subsequently challenged in the European Court of Human Rights in *Rees v United Kingdom*[7] and *Cossey v United Kingdom*.[8] In both cases the complainant argued that the British Government was in breach of Articles 8 and 12 of the Convention for the Protection of Human Rights and Fundamental Freedoms. Article 8 provides:

> 'Everyone has the right to respect for his private and family life, his home and his correspondence.'

4 [1956] P 259.
5 [1971] P 83.
6 Except in cases where there has been 'a clerical error, or where the apparent and genital sex of the child was wrongly identified or in a case of biological intersex': see *Cossey v United Kingdom* [1991] 2 FLR 492 at p 498. This is not what is claimed in the case of a transsexual.
7 [1987] 2 FLR 111.
8 [1991] 2 FLR 492.

Article 12 provides:

> 'Men and women of marriageable age have the right to marry and to found a family, according to the national laws governing the exercise of this right.'

In both instances the complainant was living a life as a member of his or her psychological sex, having undergone both hormonal and operative treatment. Both had changed their names by deed poll, and both had acquired various documents which established their new identity.[9] In essence the only differences between the two complainants were that one of them was now a man, Mr Rees, and one a woman, Miss Cossey. Mr Rees had no partner whom he wished to marry, whereas Miss Cossey had intended to marry a man at the time of her application to the European Commission, and had subsequently purported to undergo a ceremony of marriage with a different man. This latter distinction between the two complainants was held by the European Court of Human Rights to be of no legal relevance, as Articles 8 and 12 are not dependent on the existence, or otherwise, of a willing marriage partner. In dismissing the applications the court held that, as regards Article 8, the refusal to alter the register of births, or to issue a new, altered, birth certificate was not an interference with a person's private life; that what the applicant was arguing was not that the State should abstain from acting, but simply that the State should take steps to modify its existing system. As regards Article 12, it was argued that persons in the position of the applicants would be completely unable to marry. However, it was held that their inability to marry a person of the opposite biological sex to the one to which each applicant had been assigned at birth did not stem from any *legal* impediment. It therefore could not be said that the right to marry was impaired as a consequence of domestic law. Further, the Court ruled that the criteria adopted by English law with regard to marriage was in conformity with the concept of marriage to which the right guaranteed by Article 12 referred, that is the traditional marriage between persons of the opposite biological sex.

In *Sheffield and Horsham v United Kingdom*[10] a further attempt was made to persuade the European Court of Human Rights that the United Kingdom was in breach of Articles 8 and 12 the European Convention on Human Rights and Fundamental Freedoms in refusing to alter the birth certificates of two women. They had been registered as male at birth, and had undergone gender reassignment surgery and treatment and had adopted a new identity. The Court was not persuaded that it should depart

---

9 By acquiring new names by deed poll, these names could thereby be used in documents such as driving licences, car registration books, national insurance cards, medical cards, tax codings and social security papers.

10 [1998] 2 FLR 928.

from its decisions in *Rees* and *Cossey,* and it ruled that in view of the lack of any shared approach among Contracting States towards transsexualism, the United Kingdom was entitled to rely on the margin of appreciation to defend its refusal to alter the birth certificates. The Court therefore held that there was no breach of Article 8, but only by the slim majority of 11 votes to 9. Moreover, the Court acknowledged that there had been an increased social acceptance of transsexualism, and the United Kingdom was reminded of its obligation to keep the issue under review. However, in relation to the alleged violation of the right to marry, the Court ruled that there had been no such violation by 18 votes to two.[11]

The result of these decisions is that a transsexual is unable to marry a person of the same sex as that which is recorded on the transsexual's birth certificate. Such a marriage is void. English law conforms with that of many other countries in refusing to recognise the validity of the marriage of a transsexual. However some countries, states, and provinces have adopted a different attitude, and have afforded transsexuals full legal recognition of change of status, including the ability to marry.[12] It is suggested that it is time for English law to change.[13] Where a person has undergone the radical hormonal and operative treatment that is necessary to bring about a change of sex it is inhumane not to allow such a person to enter into a valid marriage.[14] In any event, the biological test propounded by Ormrod J in *Corbett v Corbett*[15] may not be medically correct. To the non-scientist the terms biological and psychological sex appear to be two entirely different things. Psychology is to do with the functioning of the mind, whereas biology is to do with the make-up of the body. However, it has been argued that psychological sex, psycho-sexuality and behaviour is hormone determined and consequent upon the sex of the brain, and is therefore biological.[16] Research by scientists has been done on the sex differentiation of the brain, and experts in the field have written:

'Infants are not blank slates on whom we scrawl instructions for sexually appropriate behaviour. They are born with male or female minds of their own. A male foetus will have enough male hormones to trigger a development of male sex organs though they may not be able to push the brain into the male pattern. This being so, his brain will stay female so that he could be born with a female brain in a male body.'[17]

11 The partly dissenting opinions make particularly interesting reading.
12 For example, Denmark, South Australia and New Jersey.
13 In *Sheffield and Horsham v United Kingdom* [1998] 2 FLR 928, the ECHR made it clear that the UK was under an obligation to review the law in this area.
14 Indeed, a court has held that the fact that a woman has an artificial vagina does not prevent the natural act of sexual intercourse taking place: see *S Y v S Y* [1963] P 37.
15 [1971] P 83. Interestingly, Ormrod J practised medicine before he became a lawyer.
16 See C M Armstrong and T Walton, *Transsexuals and the law* (1990) 140 NLJ 1384.
17 A Moir and D Jessell *Brain Sex* (Michael Joseph Ltd, 1989).

If this statement is valid (and transsexualism is becoming less of a mystery than it once was, so it may well be) then the arguments in favour of altering the law become all the more compelling.[18]

It has already been explained that a party to a void marriage is entitled to apply for financial relief on the grant of a nullity decree. In *J v S-T (Formerly J) (Transsexual: Ancillary Relief)*[19] a female to male transsexual had gone through a ceremony of marriage with a woman with whom he subsequently lived for about 17 years. The marriage was annulled on the grounds that the parties were not respectively male and female, and the issue for the Court of Appeal was whether the 'husband' should be entitled to financial relief. Ward and Potter LJJ and Sir Brian Neill were unanimous in refusing the applicant the property adjustment order which he sought, but they reached their judgments for different reasons. Ward LJ took the view that the husband was seeking to benefit from his own wrongdoing, and that his application must fail for reasons of public policy. Potter LJ and Sir Brian Neill disagreed with this approach. They dismissed the husband's application on its merits, but not for reasons of public policy which, they held, should only operate as a disqualifying factor in a very restrictive manner. Both judges were anxious that the court should retain its discretionary powers to make orders on the grant of a nullity decree, whether in favour of a guilty or innocent applicant. In their view, the fact that the 'husband' had deceived his 'wife' did not necessarily bar him from obtaining ancillary relief.[20]

Children of void marriages

The status of a child of a void marriage is determined by section 1(1) of the Legitimacy Act 1976, which provides that:

> 'The child of a void marriage, whenever born, shall ... be treated as the legitimate child of his parents if at the time of the insemination resulting in his birth, or where there was no such insemination, the child's conception (or at the time of the celebration of the marriage if later) both or either of the parties reasonably believed that the marriage was valid.'

The child will be treated as a legitimate child notwithstanding that the belief that the marriage was valid was due to a mistake as to the law; furthermore, there is a presumption that one of the parties reasonably

---

18 See *Re P and G (Transsexuals)* [1996] 2 FLR 90 for a brief survey of the literature. The applicants, who had undergone gender reassignment surgery, failed in their application to have their entries in the register of births altered.

19 [1997] 1 FLR 402.

20 They limited the rule in *Whiston v Whiston* [1995] 2 FLR 268 to cases of bigamy, where the marriage itself constituted a criminal act.

believed that the marriage was valid.[1] Where the child of a void marriage wishes to establish his legitimacy he may apply to a court for a declaration of legitimacy.[2] The burden of proof is on the person seeking to establish his or her status. In *Re Spence*[3] the Court of Appeal held that section 1 of the Legitimacy Act 1976 applies only where the parents have entered the void marriage before the birth of the child. Where, after the birth of their child, unmarried parents marry, but their marriage is a void marriage, the child will not be legitimated whatever their belief about the validity of the marriage. It is suggested that it is unfortunate that legitimacy turns upon the reasonableness, or otherwise, of the beliefs of a person's parents. If one of them honestly, but unreasonably, believes that the marriage was valid, it appears harsh that the child should be adversely affected. In similar vein, in *Re Spence*, Nourse LJ thought it was not easy to see why Parliament should have legislated to discriminate against the child whose parent reasonably believes that he or she has contracted a marriage which, if valid, would legitimate a pre-marital child.

Voidable marriages

A voidable marriage is a valid, subsisting marriage unless and until a decree of nullity is obtained. It can only be annulled during the lifetime of both parties, and the parties to the marriage are the only parties who are able to petition. In common with a void marriage, on a decree being granted all the court's powers are available as if the marriage had been terminated by divorce. Section 12 of the Matrimonial Causes Act 1973 provides that a marriage shall be voidable on the following grounds only:

'(a) that the marriage has not been consummated owing to the incapacity of either party to consummate it;

(b) that the marriage has not been consummated owing to the wilful refusal of the respondent to consummate it;

(c) that either party to the marriage did not validly consent to it, whether in consequence of duress, mistake, unsoundness of mind or otherwise;

(d) that at the time of the marriage either party, though capable of giving a valid consent, was suffering (whether continuously or intermittently) from mental disorder within the meaning of the Mental Health Act 1983 of such a kind or to such an extent as to be unfitted for marriage;

(e) that at the time of the marriage the respondent was suffering from venereal disease in a communicable form;

---

1 Legitimacy Act 1976, s 1(3), (4). Sub-s (4) applies in relation to a child born after s 28 of the Family Law Reform Act 1987 came into force.
2 Family Law Act 1986, s 56.
3 [1990] 2 All ER 827.

(f)   that at the time of the marriage the respondent was pregnant
by some person other than the petitioner.'

Thus the grounds for avoiding a marriage have a similar conceptual base
to the void marriage, namely that there is an impediment to the marriage
which prevents it from coming into being. However, in the case of a voidable
marriage, the impediment has a subjective dimension. For example, many
people may enter into a marriage in the full knowledge that one of the
parties is incapable of having sexual intercourse. It would be appalling if
this lack of capacity were to render such a marriage void. Sexual intercourse between spouses is essentially an entirely personal and private
matter between the couple themselves. There is no public interest in
whether or not marriages are consummated, thus there is no question of
such a marriage being rendered void. Yet equally, non-consummation of a
marriage may cause a considerable amount of anguish and distress to
one or both of the parties to the marriage. A sexual relationship is what
marks out marriage from the other forms of intimacy which people bring
to their personal relationships. Where that sexual relationship is lacking
in a marriage, for some couples there will be a real sense that their
relationship does not amount to a marriage. It may also be important to
such persons that their marriage is brought to an end by annulment,
rather than by divorce, for spiritual reasons. Many faiths recognise
annulment as an acceptable way of withdrawing from a marriage which
has never, in the eyes of the particular faith concerned, properly come
into existence.

Incapacity and wilful refusal to consummate

For the purposes of consummation, sexual intercourse must be 'ordinary
and complete, and not partial and imperfect'.[4] The courts have concentrated entirely on whether there has been a physical union between
the parties. Thus a marriage is consummated where there is coitus
interruptus,[5] or where the husband is incapable of ejaculation.[6] The use
of contraceptives does not prevent consummation occurring,[7] and the fact

---

4   *DE v AG* (1845) 1 Rob Eccl 279, per Dr Lushington at p 298. This should be contrasted
with the law of rape, and adultery, in which sexual intercourse occurs where the penis
makes the slightest penetration of the vagina.
5   That is, where the husband withdraws before ejaculation. See *White v White* [1948] 2
All ER 151; *Cackett v Cackett* [1950] 1 All ER 677. (But see contra, *Grimes v Grimes*
[1948] 2 All ER 147.)
6   *R v R (Otherwise F)* [1952] 1 All ER 1194.
7   *Baxter v Baxter* [1947] 2 All ER 886. The decision leads to a difficult question: what is
the position if one party is only willing to consummate the marriage if contraceptives
are used, and the other is only willing if they are not. Has either party wilfully refused
to consummate the marriage?

of intercourse is the sole issue, not whether it is qualitatively satisfactory.[8] In *S v S (Otherwise W) (No 2),*[9] as the wife was willing to undergo an operation to enable her vagina to be artificially extended, making penetration possible, the husband's petition based on her incapacity to consummate was dismissed.[10] This strict, and somewhat technical, approach to consummation is in keeping with its canonical origins. However, there is no need to prove that the spouse who has failed to consummate the marriage is incapable of having sexual intercourse with anyone; it need only be established that he or she is incapable of sexual intercourse with his or her spouse. This accords with medical science in that non-consummation may well have a psychological, rather than a physical, cause.

Where wilful refusal to consummate is being relied upon, 'a settled and definite decision not to consummate without just excuse' must be established.[11] It is this requirement that led to the failure of the wife in *Potter v Potter*[12] to have the marriage annulled on the basis of her husband's wilful refusal to consummate it. After the parties married in October 1969 they attempted to consummate the marriage on many occasions. Unfortunately, the wife had a physical defect which made her unable to have sexual intercourse. In August 1970 she had an operation curing this defect, and the husband again attempted to consummate the marriage. However he failed once more, not due to unwillingness on his part, but principally due to the wife's emotional state. Thereafter he refused to make another attempt. On the wife's petition on the ground of her husband's wilful refusal to consummate, the trial judge found that the failure to consummate was due to the husband's loss of ardour, which was something that had happened naturally, not deliberately. Accordingly the wife failed to establish wilful refusal on his part.

---

8   *S v S (Otherwise W) (No 2)* [1962] 3 All ER 55. If the husband is incapable of sustaining an erection this may not amount to consummation: *W (Otherwise K) v W* [1967] 3 All ER 178n.

9   Above.

10 At common law relief would only be granted where the impotence of the party was incurable. *S v S (Otherwise W) (No 2)* imports the same notion into the word incapacity. How far this notion can be taken is not clear. If the respondent refuses to undergo any treatment the petitioner should be able to plead either incapacity or wilful refusal. But what if it is the petitioner who refuses treatment? Where this will involve the petitioner in risky, or highly speculative, medical intervention there would be no reason to deny the petitioner a remedy. But where the treatment is relatively minor, and has a high success rate, it might be argued that the petitioner cannot then complain.

11 *Horton v Horton* [1947] 2 All ER 871. This test was applied in *Ford v Ford* [1987] Fam Law 232 where the marriage took place after the respondent husband was imprisoned. The husband lacked any reasonable opportunity to consummate the marriage, but by his conduct showed an unswerving determination not to consummate the marriage, or to live with the petitioner as husband and wife. The petitioner successfully pleaded wilful refusal.

12 (1975) 5 Fam Law 161.

Clearly, incapacity to consummate, and wilful refusal to consummate, are very closely linked even though, conceptually, the two grounds are quite different. Incapacity is a pre-existing condition which exists at the date of the marriage, whereas wilful refusal, by its very definition, cannot arise until after the celebration of the marriage. However, where a petitioner wishes to plead that the marriage has not been consummated, he or she may well be unsure which of the two grounds is the relevant one, and may indeed plead them in the alternative.[13] However, in the case of incapacity to consummate, the impotent spouse may present a petition in reliance on his or her own lack of capacity.[14] By contrast, wilful refusal can only be pleaded by the 'innocent' spouse; a petitioner cannot rely on his or her own wilful refusal to consummate the marriage. It has been argued that wilful refusal to consummate should not be available as a ground for nullity because it offends against the principle that the impediment to the marriage should exist at the date of the marriage, and not arise subsequently. However, the fact that the petitioner may not know whether the reason why the marriage has not been consummated is as a result of incapacity, or wilful refusal, is a powerful reason for retaining wilful refusal as a ground for nullity.

It is particularly in the area of arranged marriages that questions have arisen as to whether the reason why a marriage has not been consummated is due to incapacity or wilful refusal on someone's part. In relation to marriages other than those celebrated in accordance with the rites of the Church of England, it is often the practice that the civil ceremony of marriage is followed by an appropriate religious ceremony. For persons of many faiths it is only after the religious ceremony has taken place that the marriage is deemed to exist, and that consummation should take place. It will normally, therefore, amount to wilful refusal if one party either refuses to go through with the religious ceremony,[15] or refuses to make the religious arrangement when it is his duty to do so,[16] or postpones the religious ceremony indefinitely.[17] Such behaviour has been held to amount to wilful refusal to consummate the marriage, because, in all three instances, the defaulting party knows that, by failing to fulfil the requisite religious requirements, that in effect he is refusing to have sexual intercourse.

---

13 In the Green Paper on divorce *Looking to the Future: Mediation and the Ground for Divorce* (HMSO, 1993) one of the questions asked in the consultation exercise was whether wilful refusal to consummate should cease to be a ground for nullity.

14 Prior to the 1971 Act, the common law operated a bar whereby a petitioner could not plead his own impotence when he knew of it, and concealed it from the respondent; see *Morgan v Morgan* [1959] 1 All ER 539. It is suggested that this rule disappeared when the old common law bars were swept away with the introduction of the Act, and that a petitioner can plead incapacity despite having deceived the respondent as to his sexual capacities.

15 *Jodla v Jodla* [1960] 1 WLR 236.

16 *Kaur v Singh* [1972] 1 WLR 105.

17 *A v J (Nullity Proceedings)* [1989] 1 FLR 110.

Young people of a different ethnic origin, who have been brought up in England, and been subject to English schooling, culture and traditions, may find it difficult to conform to an expectation on the part of their parents that they will be parties to an arranged marriage. Cases have arisen in which such a young person has gone through a ceremony of marriage, but has subsequently failed to consummate the marriage. The question has then arisen whether such failure arose from incapacity to consummate, or whether it arose from wilful refusal. It is only in the former case that the petitioner can rely on his or her own failure to consummate. The test for incapacity was established by the Court of Appeal in *Singh v Singh*.[18] It is a rigorous test, requiring the petitioner to establish an invincible repugnance to the respondent due to a psychiatric or sexual aversion. The difficulty faced by a petitioner in satisfying such a test was illustrated by the facts of *Singh v Singh* itself. The wife had never seen the husband until the day of the civil ceremony. Although she went through with it, she then went back to her parents' house, and thereafter refused to take part in a Sikh religious ceremony. She did not see the husband again, or go near him. She petitioned for a decree of nullity on two grounds, one of which was her incapacity to consummate due to her invincible repugnance for the husband. Her petition was dismissed. The court found that it was understandable that the wife did not want to have sexual intercourse with her husband, as she did not wish to marry him. However, the court held that this was a very long way away from having an invincible repugnance to sexual intercourse.

In *D v D*,[19] by contrast, the evidence was much stronger. The wife had had a very restricted upbringing, and was only allowed to leave home unaccompanied when going to school. She had been subjected to violence from her father and was very frightened of him. When she was shown a photograph of her husband-to-be she protested, but was prevented from leaving her room until she agreed to marry him. All the rest of the family supported the marriage. She went through both a civil ceremony and a Hindu religious ceremony. She stayed living with her parents, the husband moving in to join them, but the marriage was never consummated. After two months she ran away to a refuge and only returned on being told her husband had gone. On finding that he was still there she subsequently escaped again. She was granted a decree of nullity on grounds of incapacity to consummate due to her invincible repugnance.

Should failure to consummate, regardless of the reason, permit the grant of a nullity decree?

It has been seen that the mere fact that the marriage has not been consummated, does not mean that a petitioner will be granted a decree,

---

18 [1971] 2 All ER 828.
19 (1982) 12 Fam Law 150.

despite the fact that the relationship is so bad that he or she feels compelled to petition for nullity.[20] A more liberal approach would permit the grant of a decree simply on the basis that the marriage has not been consummated. Unfairness between the parties can arise where non-consummation connotes fault on the part of one of them, or can lead to a humiliating examination of intimate details such as occurred in *Potter v Potter*.[1] In *Singh v Singh*,[2] what purpose was served by the finding that the wife did not have an invincible repugnance to consummate the marriage? Applying a subjective test she undoubtedly did. A simple, non-judgmental, finding that the marriage has not been consummated would avoid the distasteful and fault-orientated approach to nullity which persists under the present law. The arguments against such a proposal are that it has the potential to place more marriages at risk, it could be unjust to the respondent, and that it strikes at the root of those marriages entered into for companionship only. Nonetheless there is considerable merit in such a suggestion, for it should surely be up to the spouses to decide whether their non-consummated marriage should continue. If one of them decides it should not, this is no different from the situation in divorce. As the law presently operates, refusing the petitioner a decree is not aimed at mending the marriage, and will not do so except, perhaps, in the most extraordinary of cases. It is true that one of the parties may suffer emotional consequences as a result of a nullity decree being granted, but it is hard to disentangle these consequences from those arising from the failure in the parties' relationship. Either party can be protected from the financial consequences of a decree through the provision of financial relief in ancillary proceedings. Where appropriate, a decree could always be denied under the bar in section 13(1) if injustice would otherwise be caused.[3]

Lack of consent

Where a person marries under duress, or by mistake, or is of such unsoundness of mind that he or she does not understand the nature of marriage, in each case there is no consent to the marriage. Lack of consent goes to the root of a marriage, and at common law made the marriage void. Conceptually this was correct. However, the Law Commission recommended that such a marriage should become voidable only. They reached this conclusion because of the need for certainty. Such a marriage cannot, in practice, be treated as void without the court first investigating the circumstances, and being satisfied that there was indeed no consent. The law was therefore changed in 1971 to make such a marriage voidable only.

---

20 See *Singh v Singh* [1971] 2 All ER 828; *Potter v Potter* (1975) 5 Fam Law 161; *S v S (Otherwise W) (No 2)* [1962] 3 All ER 55.
1 (1975) 5 Fam Law 161.
2 [1971] 2 All ER 828.
3 See below.

People sometimes marry out of fear, or because they are subjected to enormous pressure from others. The issue then arises as to what degree of duress is sufficient to vitiate consent. In *Szechter v Szechter*[4] in deciding whether a decree should be granted, Simon P applied the following test:

'In order for the impediment of duress to vitiate an otherwise valid marriage, it must, in my judgment, be proved that the will of one of the parties thereto has been overborne by a genuine and reasonably held fear caused by threat of immediate danger (for which the party is not himself responsible), to life, limb or liberty, so that the constraint destroys the reality of consent to ordinary wedlock.'[5]

Simon P thus laid down three requirements for a petition to be successful: reasonable fear, innocence of the petitioner, and danger to life, limb or liberty. However, there is some confusion over exactly how far proof of each of these requirements is necessary to establish duress. In *Buckland v Buckland*[6] Scarman J had similarly found that the fear of the petitioner must be reasonably entertained. This requirement was contrary to the very old decision of *Scott v Sebright*,[7] where a young woman of some means was induced to marry through fear of bankruptcy, brought about by her villainous suitor. In setting aside the marriage, Butt J commented: 'whenever from natural weakness of intellect or from fear – whether reasonably entertained or not – either party is actually in a state of mental incompetence to resist pressure improperly brought to bear, there is no more consent than in the case of a person of stronger intellect and more robust courage yielding to a more serious danger'.[8] When considering duress, the Law Commission was clear that the test of whether the will was overborne is a subjective one, and does not depend on whether the fear was reasonably entertained.[9] It is suggested that this is the preferable view. Provided that the party does indeed marry out of fear, its reasonableness or otherwise should not be an issue. The petitioner has clearly demonstrated that he or she does not truly consent to the marriage, and his or her will has been overborne.

The 'innocence' of the petitioner raises more difficult questions. This issue arose in *Buckland v Buckland*.[10] The petitioner was falsely accused of seducing a young girl in Malta. He was strongly advised by his solicitor to marry the girl or face two years' imprisonment. In granting a decree on the ground of duress, Scarman J stated: '[fear] will not vitiate consent

---

4   [1970] 3 All ER 905.
5   Ibid, at p 915.
6   [1967] 2 All ER 300.
7   (1886) 12 PD 21.
8   Ibid, at p 24.
9   Law Com No 33, para 62(b).
10 [1967] 2 All ER 300.

unless it arises from some external circumstance for which the petitioner is not himself responsible'.[11] In its report, the Law Commission recognised the basic principle that marriage should be absolutely voluntary.[12] However, and perhaps unfortunately, it failed to go on to state unequivocally that threats to expose a party's misdeeds should inevitably lead to a successful petition, as it felt that the decisions that had so far been reached on duress 'seem to be about right.' It confirmed 'illegitimate' threats as including those whereby a false charge is made against the person threatened. Some 'legitimate' threats it felt would not vitiate consent, such as mere exposure to, or legal proceedings against, a man who has made a girl pregnant. However, it felt that some threats of exposure could vitiate consent. It gave as an example: 'we doubt ... whether any court would hold that it is a legitimate threat not capable of vitiating consent for an employer to tell the office-boy who has robbed the till that unless he marries the employer's ex-mistress he will be prosecuted'. The Law Commission concluded that 'any attempt to define duress with the precision appropriate to a statute would, in our view, be likely to do more harm than good. We think that the courts can safely be left to deal with each case on its merits.'[13]

A number of authorities have established that the fear to which the petitioner is exposed must be real and grave, and that there must be an immediate threat to life, limb or liberty.[14] This approach has also been applied in cases involving arranged marriages. So in *Singh v Singh*[15] where the wife was put under pressure to enter into an arranged marriage, this was held to be insufficient to amount to duress. In *Singh v Kaur,*[16] where a young man petitioned on the ground that the pressure put upon him by his parents was so great that his consent had no validity, the Court of Appeal made it clear that, even if it was not bound by precedent, it would not wish to see the test watered down. Thus, despite expressing considerable sympathy for the petitioner, Ormrod LJ commented that there were many arranged marriages in this country, and this meant that a rigorous standard must be applied. However, in *Hirani v Hirani,*[17] the most recent decision of the Court of Appeal, a different test was applied. The wife, an Indian Hindu, formed an association with an Indian Muslim. Her parents were horrified and arranged for her to marry a man whom none of them had met. The wife subsequently petitioned for nullity on the ground of duress. She claimed she was wholly dependent on her parents, and that they had threatened to throw her out of the house if she did not go through with the marriage. The Court of Appeal held that a threat to

11 [1967] 2 All ER 300, at p 302.
12 Para 64.
13 Para 65.
14 See, for example, *Szechter v Szechter* [1971] P 286; *Singh v Kaur* (1981) 11 Fam Law 152; *Singh v Singh* [1971] 2 All ER 828; *Buckland v Buckland* [1967] 2 All ER 300.
15 Above.
16 (1981) 11 Fam Law 152.
17 (1982) 4 FLR 232.

life, limb or liberty was not necessary. The crucial question was 'whether the threats, pressure or whatever it is, is such as to destroy the reality of consent and overbear the will of the individual'.[18] As it thought the parents had clearly overborne the girl's will, her consent was held invalid.

There is now no clear decision one way or the other as to the correct test, as both *Singh v Kaur* and *Hirani v Hirani* are decisions of the Court of Appeal. However, there has been some recent litigation in Scotland. In *Mahmud v Mahmud*[19] the petitioner claimed that pressure from his family over a period of years, including holding him responsible for the stroke which killed his father, had finally forced him to go through with the marriage. In the Court of Session, Lord Prosser said it was clear that the greatest pressure upon him related to the shame and degradation which would afflict his mother and family if he persisted in his refusal. The court accepted that arranged marriages did not necessarily involve an overbearing of the will, and that if a child did change his mind and consent, albeit resentfully, the marriage was valid. But, if there was no genuine change of mind, then it held the marriage would be invalid. It is suggested that *Hirani v Hirani* and *Mahmud v Mahmud* are the better decisions, and the ones to be preferred. The threat of matters such as social degradation, financial ruin, total rejection by the family, or ostracism by the community are all immensely powerful pressures, well capable of completely overbearing a person's will.[20]

Some marriages are entered into expressly for an ulterior motive, for example to evade immigration laws, or to be allowed to leave another country. Generally speaking the motive of the petitioner is irrelevant; provided that there is a real intention to marry the marriage is valid. However, such a marriage may also take place because of duress. *Szechter v Szechter*[1] provides a compelling illustration. The respondent divorced his wife and married the petitioner in order to effect her release from prison where she would almost certainly have died. All three parties then managed to escape from Poland and come to England. The nullity petition was presented so that the respondent could remarry his first wife. In *Szechter v Szechter* there was a real intention on the part of the petitioner to marry, so that she could benefit from the consequences of the marriage. It was by this means that she could escape a worse fate. However, it was held that the reality was that the marriage was not entered into freely at all, and that there was no true consent. However, where there is a free consent then, according to the House of Lords in *Vervaeke v Smith*,[2] such

---

18 Ibid, per Ormrod LJ at p 234.
19 1994 SLT 599. See also *Mahmood v Mahmood* 1993 SLT 589.
20 In *Mahmud v Mahmud* above, the court was clear that there is no basis for the general view that arranged marriages involve an inherently forceful imposition of the will of the parents. Also, that both the age and the sex of the person consenting is important, but does not justify any generalisation. It is interesting to note that in a number of cases the petitioner has been a young man.
1   [1970] 3 All ER 905. See also *H (Otherwise D) v H* [1953] 2 All ER 1229.
2   [1982] 2 All ER 144.

a marriage is perfectly valid. The petitioner in that case married in order to escape being deported from England. The parties had no intention of ever living together; the reason for the marriage was simply to enable the petitioner to apply for British citizenship.

Where such a 'sham' marriage is held to be valid it gives rise to the particular problem that two different areas of English law operate in conflicting ways. Immigration laws will dictate that where a marriage is a sham a party to such a marriage may be deported. Yet so far as family law is concerned, the parties are validly married. This mismatch of domestic law could well lead to difficult problems in the conflict of laws, as well as to acute personal difficulties. Also, the dividing line between where there is a real intention to marry, and where there is not, may be perilously difficult to draw. For example, where an asylum seeker marries in an attempt to avoid deportation to a country where he reasonably fears that he will be imprisoned, probably tortured, and even killed, is this a sham marriage, or a marriage entered into as a result of duress?

Mistake can take one of two forms: it can relate to the identity of the other person, or to the nature of the ceremony. It is important to distinguish between making a mistake as to the identity of a person, and as to the attributes of that person. Only a mistake as to the former will invalidate the marriage. However, it is not always easy to distinguish between a person's identity and his attributes. In the New Zealand decision of *C v C*,[3] the respondent pretended that he was a well-known boxer, and the petitioner married him under this erroneous belief. It was held that she was simply mistaken as to his attributes, and that she intended to marry the man who stood in front of her. Yet in the recent English decision of *Militante v Ogunwomoju*[4] the petitioner married believing the respondent to be Richard Ogunwomoju, whereas in fact he was Anthony Osimen, an illegal immigrant. Her marriage was declared a nullity.[5] It is difficult to discern any real difference between the two cases, and it is arguable that either case could have been decided the other way. Where the petitioner does not realise that the ceremony is a marriage ceremony, as in *Mehta v Mehta*,[6] where the wife thought the marriage ceremony was one of conversion to the Hindu religion, the marriage could be annulled on the ground of mistake.[7]

A person who is of unsound mind, such that he or she is unable to understand the nature of the contract of marriage, and the duties and

---

3   [1942] NZLR 356.
4   [1993] 2 FCR 355.
5   The judge himself made a fundamental mistake, as he declared that where a person marries another under a mistake 'then that marriage is void'. He should, of course, have stated that such a marriage is voidable.
6   [1945] 2 All ER 690.
7   See also *Hall v Hall* (1908) 24 TLR 756, where the petitioner who married in a registry office thought that she was putting her name down to be married in church in the future; and *Valier v Valier* (1925) 133 LT 830, where an Italian gentleman, of limited intelligence, had no idea that he was getting married.

responsibilities it creates, cannot consent to the marriage.[8] This is a protective measure. For example, in the case of the elderly it means that those who have lost their mental capacity, and who have married 'fortune hunters' not realising what they were doing, may have their marriage annulled.[9] Because such a marriage is voidable rather than void, it means that third parties, such as relatives, cannot take steps to have it annulled. However, with the leave of the court, it is possible for a third party to institute nullity proceedings as the insane person's next friend, and it is also possible for the Court of Protection to direct that matrimonial proceedings be brought on behalf of a patient.

Mental disorder rendering a person unfitted for marriage

A marriage can be annulled where, at the time of the marriage, either party is so mentally ill as to be 'unfitted' for marriage. This was defined in *Bennett v Bennett*[10] as arising where the illness renders a person 'incapable of carrying out the ordinary duties and obligations of marriage'. It is distinguishable from unsoundness of mind in that the party is capable of giving a valid consent, but the state of his or her mental health is such that it would be right to annul the marriage. The illness must be present at the date of the marriage. If it arises subsequently, divorce is the remedy. A petitioner may rely on his or her own mental disorder when applying for a nullity decree. It is suggested that this ground is outmoded and offensive, and stems from the days when mental illness was misunderstood and those suffering from such illness were regarded with fear and suspicion.[11]

Venereal disease

A marriage is voidable where the respondent was suffering from venereal disease in a communicable form at the time of the marriage. The basis of this ground clearly ties in with the non-consummation grounds, as it is looked upon as an impediment to sexual intercourse. It is difficult to know what to make of this ground in the new millennium. When it was first introduced in 1937, antibiotics were not available. At that time venereal

---

8   *Re Park's Estate* [1954] P 112.
9   See (1987) 137 NLJ 538 where a news item reported that on 13 May 1987, the marriage of 83-year-old Mr Frank Yarwood to his housekeeper Mary was annulled on the ground that he did not validly consent to it. He was senile and remembered nothing of the ceremony, at which there had been no flowers or family witnesses, and which had not been followed by any celebration drink.
10 [1969] 1 All ER 539.
11 Why single out mental illness? Is not an adult who is prone to violence, or paedophilia, equally unfitted for marriage?

disease could be an extremely serious complaint. The two most important diseases were gonorrhoea and syphilis. Gonorrhoea was undoubtedly unpleasant, and could have serious consequences, such as resulting in a woman becoming infertile. It was not, however, a fatal disease. Syphilis was more serious as it could lead to debilitating illness, or even death.[12] After the Second World War, penicillin, and other antibiotics, became widely available, and thereafter venereal disease became treatable, if not curable. In 1970 the Law Commission wisely recommended the abolition of epilepsy as a ground for nullity. (Previously epilepsy had existed as one of the grounds of mental disorder.) It said: 'whatever the medical position in 1937, today epilepsy responds to treatment and can be kept under control'.[13] The same could be said of venereal disease. Presumably, therefore, it was the fundamental basis of the ground which was the reason for its retention,[14] namely that it was still looked upon as an impediment to sexual intercourse.[15]

Since 1970 there have been many medical advances and changes. One of these is that medical practitioners no longer even talk about 'venereal diseases'. No longer are there venereology clinics. The modern equivalent are clinics dealing with sexually transmissible diseases. That immediately raises a problem of classification. What nowadays is meant by the phrase 'venereal disease'? Does it mean the same thing as a sexually transmissible disease? If it does, should that still represent a ground for nullity? The range of sexually transmissible diseases varies enormously. Pubic lice are transferred sexually. Such a condition can be fully treated, with no adverse consequences whatsoever. Should it therefore be possible to petition for nullity if the spouse is found to be suffering from pubic lice? At the other end of the scale what about a disease such as AIDS? One of the ways that AIDS can be transmitted is through sexual intercourse. This raises an acute moral and ethical issue which needs to be addressed. If a person gets married knowing that he or she is infected with AIDS, and that this is transmissible by sexual intercourse, but conceals this information from his or her partner, should the marriage be voidable at the instance of the 'innocent' party? It would certainly appear to conform with the fundamental ethos underlying the law of nullity that it should,

12 However, it was clearly not the consequences of venereal diseases that led to the ground being introduced since, if that was the rationale, other equally serious diseases would have allowed the marriage to be avoided. For example, tuberculosis was widespread in the 1930s, and it was undoubtedly fatal in some instances.

13 Law Com No 30, para 73.

14 There is no discussion of this ground in the Law Commission report. It is simply stated that venereal disease will continue to be a ground.

15 The infertility consequence of gonorrhoea could still arise in the 1970s, as indeed it can today, as a woman might be irreparably damaged before she was treated for the disease. However, the chances of the other highly unpleasant, or debilitating, consequences of venereal disease had by then been radically reduced.

as it is undoubtedly an impediment to sexual intercourse.[16] It may be controversial, but it seems logical to suggest that AIDS, or any other disease which is sexually transmissible, should in principle be a ground for nullity.[17]

Pregnancy by another man

Where, at the time of their marriage, the wife conceals from her husband the fact that she is pregnant by another man, he can subsequently seek an annulment. However, the petition must be presented within three years of the date of the marriage.[18] If the wife keeps the child's true paternity secret for more than three years, the marriage cannot be annulled on this ground. The Law Commission's explanation for this ground was that a husband who marries in these circumstances has given conditional consent only to the marriage. The ground therefore appears to rest on one of two bases. Either the husband has married a woman knowing her to be pregnant and believing that he is the father of the child, in which case he might then argue that, but for the pregnancy, he would not have married her. Alternatively, he might argue that he was marrying a woman who was chaste, but the lack of chastity has self-evidently been demonstrated. Whichever of these two bases applies, it is suggested that such thinking has no place in the law today. In 1937, when the ground was first introduced, men might well be forced to marry if they were believed to be responsible for the pregnancy of a woman.[19] This would not normally be the case nowadays; but if it was, the ground of duress might apply. The chastity basis is not relevant or sensible in today's society. There are other forms of behaviour by a spouse which could just as easily be said to strike at the fundamental root of a marriage, in the sense that a spouse is giving conditional consent to the marriage. For example, the woman who marries a man not knowing that he is a convicted rapist, or paedophile, could claim her consent to the marriage should be characterised as conditional. However, her escape route is to use the law of divorce. It is suggested that, similarly, divorce is a more appropriate response in the case of pregnancy by another man.

---

16 Another particular disease, unfortunately prevalent in the 1990s, which would also spring to mind as being in the category of an impediment to sexual intercourse is hepatitis B.

17 A further demonstration of how medically absurd the position has become is if the issue of a person being HIV positive is considered. Such a person is in the incubation period of the disease AIDS, but does not as yet have the disease. Is such a person suffering from venereal disease?

18 S 13(2); see further below.

19 In the American 'shot-gun' wedding case *Lee v Lee* 3 SW 2d 672 (1928) it was stated that 'if there had not been a wedding there would have been a funeral'.

Nevertheless, bringing an alien child into the marriage undoubtedly strikes at the heart of the marriage. A man is unquestionably entitled to say that he certainly would not have married his wife had he known she was carrying another man's child. But is not a woman equally entitled to state that she would not have married her husband if, at the time of the marriage, she had known that another woman was pregnant by him? It is suggested that the law should treat spouses in an equal manner in this regard.[20]

Bars to relief where the marriage is voidable

At common law a petitioner could be denied a decree if she had either approbated, that is accepted, the marriage, or colluded in the presentation of grounds for the decree.[1] Additionally, public policy could operate as a bar even though the parties themselves would suffer no injustice if a decree were to be granted. However, this was altered when the law was reformed in 1971, when statutory bars to relief were introduced. These are now in section 13 of the Matrimonial Causes Act 1973. Section 13(2) states that a petition for nullity must be instituted within three years of the date of the marriage unless the petitioner is relying on incapacity, or wilful refusal, to consummate the marriage.[2] In addition, where the grounds relied upon are venereal disease, or pregnancy by another man, the petitioner must be ignorant of the true facts at the date of the marriage.[3]

A general bar applies to all nullity petitions. Section 13(1) provides that:

'The court shall not ... grant a decree of nullity on the ground that a marriage is voidable if the respondent satisfies the court—
(a) that the petitioner, with knowledge that it was open to him to have the marriage avoided, so conducted himself in relation to the respondent as to lead the respondent reasonably to believe that he would not seek to do so; and
(b) that it would be unjust to the respondent to grant the decree.'

The use of the word 'shall' means that the court has no discretion if facts giving rise to the bar are established and must refuse the decree. However,

---

20 The Law Commission pointed out that this was the position under the Law of New Zealand, but commented that it had been criticised.
1   The principle behind refusing a decree in such a case was expressed in *G v M* (1885) 10 App Cas 171, per Lord Watson at pp 197-198: 'In a suit for nullity of marriage there may be facts and circumstances proved which so plainly imply, on the part of the complaining spouse, a recognition of the existence and validity of the marriage, as to render it most inequitable and contrary to public policy that he or she should be permitted to go on to challenge it with effect.'
2   This is subject to the proviso that the period may be extended where the petitioner has suffered from a mental disorder during the three years, and it is just to do so (s 13(4)).
3   S 13(3).

the burden is on the respondent to raise the question whether the bar applies, and if the respondent does not raise the matter, the court must grant the decree even if it thinks that the bar would apply.[4] Moreover, the conduct of the petitioner can only give rise to the bar provided that he or she knows that the marriage is potentially voidable and yet behaves in a way to affirm the marriage.[5] It has been stated that public policy can no longer raise the bar.[6]

Behaviour which could give rise to the bar is illustrated in *D v D (Nullity)*[7] where the marriage had never been consummated owing to the incapacity or wilful refusal of the wife to consummate it. Nine years after the marriage took place the parties adopted two children, but a year later the husband left in order to live with another woman, and subsequently petitioned for a nullity decree. Dunn J held that the husband knew that it was open to him to have the marriage annulled, and that by agreeing to the adoption he had so conducted himself as to lead the wife to believe he would not seek to do so. However, he nonetheless granted the decree as he found that it would not be unjust to the wife to do so. It is this requirement of injustice to the respondent which makes it most unlikely that any respondent will be able to establish the requirements of the general bar. All the court's powers are available to the parties in ancillary proceedings on the granting of a decree of nullity, and even if unable to obtain a decree of nullity, the petitioner will eventually be able to obtain a decree of divorce.[8] There would, therefore, seem to be little point in failing to grant the nullity petition. Indeed, there has been no case reported since the inception of the Act where the bar has been successfully pleaded.

Should the concept of the voidable marriage be abolished?

Very few marriages come to an end on the ground that the marriage is voidable, partly because the facts upon which a petition to avoid the

---

4   In *D v D (Nullity)* [1979] 3 All ER 337, Dunn J failed to take this into account, although he did grant a decree of nullity on the basis that it would not be unjust to the respondent wife. The wife had originally raised the bar, but subsequently withdrew it and the case came on for hearing undefended.

5   For example, if a man is not initially aware that the child his wife has given birth to is not his, and it is only on discovering the truth that he petitions for nullity, his wife cannot rely on his treatment of the child prior to that discovery as giving rise to the bar.

6   See Dunn J in *D v D (Nullity)* [1979] 3 All ER 337, at p 343, where he said: 'the common law rules are abrogated and replaced by the statutory bar, and therefore I would be prepared to hold on the ordinary natural meaning of the words of the statute, that public policy has no place in the statutory bar'.

7   [1979] 3 All ER 337, which appears to be the only reported case on this area of law.

8   Except in those extremely rare cases where grave (or substantial) financial or other hardship is established, Matrimonial Causes Act 1973, s 5; Family Law Act 1996, s 10. See below.

marriage can be based do not often arise, and partly because of the ease with which it is now possible to obtain a divorce. In many cases the spouses have already separated when the nullity proceedings are heard. They are eligible to set divorce proceedings in motion once a year has elapsed from the celebration of their marriage.[9] Many spouses find it preferable to seek a divorce rather than to rely on the grounds of incapacity, or wilful refusal, to consummate the marriage, which are the facts relied on for the majority of nullity petitions. Is it therefore sensible to retain a separate law of nullity in respect of voidable marriages?[10]

Arguing for retention of the voidable marriage, the Law Commission put forward a number of propositions in its Report in 1970.[11] It took the view that nullity and divorce were conceptually quite different. A decree of nullity recognised an impediment to the marriage, which prevented it from being an effective marriage. Divorce recognised that a valid marriage had come into being, and that a cause to terminate it had arisen since the celebration of the marriage.[12] It commented that the Christian Church drew a distinction between divorce and nullity, and would not welcome any attempt to abolish nullity. For some people, not necessarily members of the Church, there is a stigma associated with divorce, whereas for some of the nullity grounds, such as mental illness, and some cases of incapacity to consummate, no stigma can be attached. And, finally, there was no advantage to anyone in abolishing the voidable marriage, whereas there would undoubtedly be disadvantages.

In favour of abolishing the voidable marriage it can be counter-argued that the view that there is a fundamental conceptual difference between a marriage which has failed to come into existence for the reasons in section 12, and a marriage which has irretrievably broken down, cannot be sustained. It has already been explained why reliance on venereal disease has no place in a modern law of nullity. Similarly, the suggestion that a person who is ill within the meaning of the Mental Health Act is 'unfitted for marriage' is offensive and distasteful. Pregnancy by another man is a gender-biased ground both because the converse does not apply to a man who has made another woman pregnant, and because it concentrates on a particular facet of human relationships between men and women. As a nullity decree has prospective, but not retrospective, effect,[13] it appears odd to claim that the remaining grounds in section 12 prevent

---

9 To obtain a consensual divorce, the parties need to have lived apart for a period of two years and the respondent must consent to the decree; Matrimonial Causes Act 1973, s 1(2)(d). When the Family Law Act 1996 comes into force, parties will be able to obtain a divorce after attending an information meeting and complying with the relevant period of reflection and consideration, which in the case of a childless marriage is a total period of just over a year; see the extensive coverage of divorce below.

10 Voidable marriages have been abolished in Australia: Family Law Act 1975, s 51.

11 Law Com No 33, para 24.

12 This causative view has since become outmoded. The basis for divorce since 1969 has been the irretrievable breakdown of the marriage.

13 S 16.

the marriage coming into existence. This is indeed true of marriages voidable through lack of consent, but it is suggested that such marriages should be restored to the void category, where they properly belong despite the difficulties relating to lack of certainty. Wilful refusal to consummate the marriage must arise after the marriage has taken place, it cannot be a pre-existing impediment. The bar in section 13 enables spouses to attempt a reconciliation without necessarily losing their right to a decree, yet the concept of reconciliation is not consistent with the concept that the marriage is fatally flawed by a fundamental defect. Moreover, it is arguably anomalous that the actions of the parties can somehow overcome a defect going to the root of the marriage in respect of a voidable marriage, and raise a bar to the marriage being annulled, when they clearly cannot do so in the case of a void marriage.[14]

In relation to the issue of stigma, whilst some of the grounds for nullity may not have stigma attached to them, that certainly cannot be said for all of them. There is stigma attached to a finding that a person has wilfully refused to consummate the marriage, or deceived a man into marrying by concealing the true paternity of a baby. Conversely, whilst some facts relied on for divorce under the Matrimonial Causes Act 1973 do have adverse connotations, some do not. There is no stigma attached to a finding that parties have lived apart for two or five years. In any event, that law has been replaced by the Family Law Act 1996 which has swept away notions of fault. As regards the position of the Church, it can be said that this is in an increasingly secular society, and the religion of many members of society is not Christian. Why, therefore, should the Church have any say in the law relating to marriage, when only a minority of the population attend organised Christian worship?

The last argument presented by the Law Commission in favour of retaining the concept of the voidable marriage, namely that there is no advantage to be achieved in abolishing the concept, but to do so would undoubtedly have disadvantages for some persons is persuasive. Where a mechanism exists which can terminate a marriage which has fundamentally failed why do away with that mechanism? This was a formidable argument, and may have outweighed the counter-arguments outlined above until the law of divorce was reformed by the Family Law Act 1996. However, the new divorce law, which requires spouses to reflect and consider, and to sort out the arrangements for their children and financial affairs before ending their marriage, makes retention of the voidable marriage appear even more anomalous than hitherto. Failure or refusal to consummate a marriage does not necessarily mean that there are no children of the family, they may have been adopted, or conceived through treatment for infertility.[15] Where the wife was pregnant by another man

---

14 If, for example, one party to a marriage discovers that the other was a bigamist or under age at the time of its celebration, that party can lead the other reasonably to believe that the marriage will not be annulled as much as he or she wishes, but that will not override the fundamental defect in the marriage.

15 See *D v D (Nullity)* [1979] 3 All ER 337.

at the time of its celebration, the counselling process envisaged by the reformed divorce law is entirely appropriate to assist the parties *and the child* to adjust to this discovery; and access to counselling might be welcomed by, and overcome the difficulties experienced by, parties to a non-consummated marriage. It is suggested that, in truth, voidable marriages are not flawed by an impediment at their inception, but that they are marriages which have failed for reasons, just as marriages which end in divorce fail for reasons. Surely a process of reflection and consideration is appropriate to ending all such marriages whatever the reason for their failure?

The law of divorce

A brief history

Divorce has only been generally available as a means of ending a marriage since the middle of the nineteenth century. Prior to that the Ecclesiastical Courts could grant a decree *a mensa et thoro*, but although this relieved the parties of the duty to live together, it did not permit them to remarry. For a very few it was possible to end a marriage and thereby obtain the right to remarry, but this could only be achieved by private Act of Parliament. It was not until the Matrimonial Causes Act 1857 that a law of divorce applicable to the public at large was passed.[16] This Act, and the subsequent legislation up until 1969, was strictly fault based.[17] Divorce law was built around the notion that one spouse was guilty of a matrimonial offence.[18] Parties were referred to as 'guilty' and 'innocent' and divorce was a remedy for a legal wrong. This conceptual base led to the inclusion in legislation, and the development by case law, of an infrastructure of 'black letter law' rules and principles which often bore little relationship to the physical, mental and emotional circumstances of marriage breakdown. The three matrimonial offences were difficult to prove whether or not the petition was defended.[19] Divorce was barred where the respondent had connived at the commission of the offence relied upon. Attempts at reconciliation raised the bar of condonation. Any evidence that the parties were in agreement that

16 The law discriminated against wives. Husbands could divorce their wives for adultery; wives were required to prove adultery with aggravating features, such as incest, rape, sodomy or bestiality. Divorce in practice was only available to the financially well off as the process was very costly. For a fascinating and detailed account of the history of the law of divorce, see L Stone *Road to Divorce* (OUP, 1991).

17 Matrimonial Causes Act 1923; Matrimonial Causes Act 1937.

18 Between 1937 and 1969 the grounds for divorce were adultery, cruelty, desertion for a continuous period of three years or more, and incurable insanity on the part of the respondent. This last ground was the only concession to the notion that a marriage could be terminated despite there being no 'fault' by either party.

19 See, for example, *Bastable v Bastable* [1968] 1 WLR 1684.

divorce was the solution to their matrimonial difficulties resulted in the decree being denied on the ground of collusion. This structure was damaging because it polarised the position of the parties. It led to spurious cases where the husband provided false evidence of adultery (often allegedly committed in an hotel), and to snooping and gross invasions of privacy in order to obtain evidence of adultery where this was denied. It prevented divorce where marriages had clearly broken down, and it prevented spouses from making realistic attempts at reconciliation.[20] In short, the law was disinterested and out of touch with natural human responses to marital difficulties. It positively encouraged acrimony. It allowed the notion that one spouse was guilty and the other innocent to influence arrangements about the children, and it penalised sensible agreements arrived at by consent. Moreover, it made no provision for those men and women who had left their spouses and formed a new family unit. It was impossible for such men and women to marry for a second time where their first spouse refused to divorce them. By the middle of the twentieth century change was clearly long over due.

In 1956 a Royal Commission, the Morton Commission,[1] published a report advocating reform of the law and included in its recommendations the introduction of the concept of a no-fault divorce. Ten years later a group appointed by the Archbishop of Canterbury published their report, *Putting Asunder*, which advocated that divorce should be based on a single concept, namely the breakdown of the marriage. *Putting Asunder* recommended that, in every case, there should be a judicial enquiry to ensure that a breakdown had really occurred, and that no abuse of the system had taken place. This was followed by a discussion paper issued by the Law Commission,[2] which similarly advocated breakdown as a basis for dissolving a marriage, but recommended that this should be inferred from one or more of five specified facts. Discussions took place between the two groups, and as a result of their deliberations the law was amended in 1969 by the Divorce Reform Act 1969, which represented a compromise between the positions taken in the two reports.

The underlying purpose of the reformed divorce law was:

'(i) to buttress, rather than to undermine, the stability of marriage; and
(ii) when, regrettably, a marriage has irretrievably broken down, to enable the empty legal shell to be destroyed with the maximum fairness, and the minimum bitterness, distress and humiliation.'[3]

---

20 Sexual intercourse between the spouses after the respondent had become aware of the matrimonial offence automatically raised the bar of condonation.
1 *Royal Commission on Marriage and Divorce* Cmd 9678.
2 *Reform of the Grounds of Divorce: the Field of Choice* Cmd 3123.
3 Ibid, para 15.

Provisions were therefore introduced which were designed to assist parties to remain together and to resolve their differences. Parties were no longer to be barred from petitioning if they should live together after adulterous or other behaviour which would otherwise enable them to obtain a decree.[4] Some encouragement was given to parties to consider reconciliation rather than proceeding to a divorce. A solicitor acting for the petitioner would be obliged to file a certificate stating whether or not he had discussed reconciliation with his client, or given the client names and addresses of people qualified to help.[5] A court could adjourn the proceedings at any time if it appeared that there was a reasonable prospect of successful reconciliation.[6]

Parliament properly took the view that it would be wrong to liberalise divorce law without at the same time ensuring that dependent spouses could be protected from suffering some of the more serious economic consequences of divorce.[7] Therefore, legislation was introduced, the Matrimonial Proceedings and Property Act 1970, which gave the courts wide powers to make financial provision and property adjustment orders on the grant of a decree.[8] Implementation of the Divorce Reform Act 1969 was delayed and the two Acts came into force together. They were subsequently consolidated in the Matrimonial Causes Act 1973. Further pressures for reform led to the passing of the Family Law Act 1996 which entirely altered the basis for divorce. Implementation of the Family Law Act 1996 has been delayed, however, pending evaluation of research into some of its more radical provisions. This research is being piloted in different parts of England and Wales, and doubts have since been expressed as to whether some of the Act's provisions will be brought into force in their original form because of difficulties exposed by the researchers' findings. In the meanwhile, therefore, the law of divorce continues to be found in the Matrimonial Causes Act 1973.

Divorce under the Matrimonial Causes Act 1973

When Parliament accepted the notion that irretrievable breakdown of marriage provided the proper basis for divorce, it was forced to acknowledge that consensual divorce, and divorce after lapse of time were

4   Matrimonial Causes Act 1973, s 2; though in relation to adultery see s 2(1), which raises a bar where the parties live together for longer than six months after the discovery of the adultery.

5   Matrimonial Causes Act 1973, s 6(1).

6   S 6(2). It was subsequently established that these provisions had limited value, see the Booth Report, paras 4.42-4.43; Law Com No 170, para 3.9; G Davis and M Murch *Grounds for Divorce* (Clarendon Press, 1988), ch 4.

7   There was particular concern about the so-called 'Casanova's charter' provision, which enables an 'innocent' spouse to be divorced against her will after the parties have lived apart for at least five years.

8   See ch 8.

both acceptable methods of establishing such breakdown. Parliament nonetheless retained the principle that the remedy of divorce should be available where there had been matrimonial misbehaviour, on the ground that such behaviour was also evidence that a marriage had broken down irretrievably. Irretrievable breakdown of marriage is the sole ground for divorce under the Matrimonial Causes Act 1973. However, the Law Commission recognised, and Parliament accepted, that it would be impossible for courts to adjudicate on the individual circumstances of every marriage which had allegedly broken down. Therefore Parliament enacted that proof of breakdown must be shown by proof of one or more of five facts.

Section 1(2) of the Matrimonial Causes Act 1973 provides:

'The court hearing a petition for divorce shall not hold the marriage to have broken down irretrievably unless the petitioner satisfies the court of one or more of the following facts, that is to say—

(a) that the respondent has committed adultery and the petitioner finds it intolerable to live with the respondent;

(b) that the respondent has behaved in such a way that the petitioner cannot reasonably be expected to live with the respondent;

(c) that the respondent has deserted the petitioner for a continuous period of at least two years immediately preceding the presentation of the petition;

(d) that the parties to the marriage have lived apart for a continuous period of at least two years immediately preceding the presentation of the petition … and the respondent consents to a decree being granted;

(e) that the parties to the marriage have lived apart for a continuous period of at least five years immediately preceding the presentation of the petition.'

It must also be appreciated at the outset that a petition for divorce cannot be presented within the first year of marriage,[9] despite the fact that the marriage has irretrievably broken down, and even though the petitioner can establish adultery or behaviour within section 1(2)(b). The one year bar is an absolute bar. It matters not how extreme a petitioner's case may be. However, the petitioner may rely on adultery or behaviour which occurred during the first year of marriage when she presents her petition once that time has elapsed.

When the reformed divorce law was first introduced, courts continued to treat divorce as a process requiring careful judicial scrutiny. As a result, where a petitioner could not bring her case within one of the five facts she could not obtain a divorce, even though there could be no doubt

9   S 3(1).

that the marriage had irretrievably broken down. This was illustrated by *Stringfellow v Stringfellow*.[10] The husband and wife had been married for six years and had two children. The husband suddenly announced he no longer loved his wife, and ceased showing any interest whatsoever in her or the family. Shortly afterwards he left home, and three months later the wife petitioned on the basis that her husband had behaved in such a way that she could not reasonably be expected to live with him.[11] Mr Stringfellow did not defend the petition. Mrs Stringfellow was nonetheless refused a divorce because the court found that the facts relied on showed nothing more than the breakdown of a marriage, and desertion by the husband, and the wife could only petition for desertion after two years had elapsed. The behaviour provision had not been established.[12]

Stringfellow v Stringfellow remains good law: simple desertion on its own does not amount to behaviour within section 1(2)(b). However, the case provides a useful illustration of the difference between the 'law in the books' as laid down when a petitioner for divorce was required to give evidence, and the contents of the petition was subjected to close judicial scrutiny, and the law in practice as it now is. A wife in the position of a Mrs Stringfellow today would probably succeed in obtaining a divorce in reliance on the behaviour fact, provided that she took steps to draft her petition with care. She could include additional facts to support the allegation that her husband had behaved in such a way that she could not reasonably be expected to live with him, whether true or exaggerated, secure in the knowledge that it would usually be impracticable for her husband to challenge such allegations of fact.[13] The wife, and those advising her, would also be aware that she would not have to appear in court and be questioned about what she had alleged. This difference between the law in the books and the law in practice was brought about because the law of divorce was trans-formed in 1973 by the introduction of the special procedure.

The special procedure

Since the mid-1970s[14] divorce has been obtainable under a 'special procedure', the objectives of which are 'simplicity, speed and economy'.[15]

---

10 [1976] 2 All ER 539.
11 S 1(2)(b).
12 See also *Birch v Birch* [1992] 1 FLR 564; *Buffery v Buffery* [1988] 2 FLR 365; *Richards v Richards* [1972] 3 All ER 695. The converse is also true. Provided the petitioner can prove one of the five facts she need not prove it was that fact which caused the marriage to break down irretrievably, and see *Stevens v Stevens* [1979] 1 WLR 885.
13 G Davis and M Murch, *Grounds for Divorce* (Clarendon Press, 1988).
14 In 1973 for all cases based on the fact of two years' separation; in 1977 for all other undefended petitions based on the remaining four facts.
15 *R v Nottingham County Court, ex p Byers* [1985] 1 All ER 735, per Latey J at p 737.

Wherever a case is undefended the requirement to give evidence in court is dispensed with. A district judge, sitting in private, scrutinises the divorce application, and where satisfied that the ground is made out, issues a certificate to that effect.[16] The divorce is then formally granted in open court by a judge. Neither the parties nor their representatives need appear in front of either the district judge in private, or the judge in open court. The advent of the 'special procedure', which is now far from being special but is in fact the norm,[17] has had a profound impact on the extent to which the court can make an effective enquiry into an undefended suit.[18] In addition, in the vast majority of cases the cost of litigation makes it impossible for a privately paying respondent to defend a petition for divorce, and legal aid to defend will not normally be granted where it is clear that the marriage has irretrievably broken down.[19] As a consequence, litigation relating to the proper interpretation of the law almost never occurs and in recent years there have been very few reported divorce cases.[20] It is nonetheless necessary to understand the substantive law, mainly because the petitioner must, of course, make out a case on paper which falls within one of the five facts when presenting her petition under the special procedure, and partly because an accurate understanding of the law is essential in those few defended cases which do arise.

Adultery by the respondent

A petition based on adultery must establish the fact that the respondent has committed adultery, and that the petitioner finds it intolerable to live with the respondent. It is not enough for the petitioner simply to allege the respondent's adultery. However, under the special procedure there is no requirement placed on the petitioner to state why she finds the adultery intolerable.[1] Consequently, although, theoretically, her mere assertion should not suffice,[2] in practice it almost invariably will. What is meant by adultery? It is the voluntary act of sexual intercourse[3] between a married spouse and another person not being married to him or her, who is of the

16 Family Proceedings Rules 1991, r 2.36.
17 *Report of the Matrimonial Causes Procedure Committee*, para 2.8. Under the chairmanship of The Hon Mrs Justice Booth, (HMSO, 1985).
18 See the extraordinary case of *Moynihan v Moynihan (Nos 1 and 2)* [1997] 1 FLR 59.
19 See the Booth Report, para 2.16. Legal aid is not available for undefended divorces.
20 But see *Butterworth v Butterworth* [1997] 2 FLR 336 where the Court of Appeal stated that a respondent to a defended divorce petition has the right to have his case properly tried, preferably by a judge, and that any allegations made against him must be properly proved to the requisite standard.
1   A petitioner is simply required to answer the question: 'Do you find it intolerable to live with the respondent?' Family Proceedings Rules 1991, Appendix 1.
2   *Cleary v Cleary* [1974] 1 WLR 73; *Roper v Roper* [1972] 3 All ER 668.
3   Which must involve some penetration of the female by the male: *Dennis v Dennis* [1955] 2 All ER 51. Artificial insemination would not therefore amount to adultery.

opposite sex, and who may or may not be married. Homosexual intercourse between the respondent and a person of the same sex does not, therefore, come within the definition.[4] The requirement that the act of intercourse be voluntary obviously excludes a rape victim.[5] Difficult questions could, however, arise if a woman was so drunk or drugged at the time of the act of sexual intercourse that she was either incapable of giving her consent, or only consented due to the influence of the intoxicant. Where the intoxicant was consumed voluntarily with knowledge of its 'liberating' effects, it seems that a spouse will be guilty of adultery.[6]

Proof of adultery

Adultery may be established to the satisfaction of the court in a number of ways. The acknowledgment of service form used in relation to petitions based on adultery asks the question: 'Do you admit the adultery alleged in the petition?'[7] If the respondent answers 'Yes', and signs the form, that is sufficient proof. Where the respondent does not admit the adultery, and fails to file an answer, the petitioner will have to prove the adultery in other ways. This could be established by evidence such as that the respondent is living with another person as husband and wife. Other evidence could be that the respondent and the alleged co-respondent had both the inclination and the opportunity to commit adultery, such as where they spent the night in the same room.[8] An admission by the wife that a child is not her husband's child, despite the husband being named as father on the birth certificate, clearly amounts to an admission of adultery.[9] A conviction of the husband for rape means that adultery has taken place, even though his victim's part in the act of sexual intercourse was non-consensual. A finding by a court that the husband is the father of a non-marital child conceived after the marriage establishes his adultery.

The standard of proof of adultery has never been formally established,[10] and in view of the special procedure is never likely to be. As proceedings for divorce are civil proceedings it could be expected that the standard of proof for adultery would be the normal civil standard of the balance of probabilities. However, in *Serio v Serio*[11] the Court of Appeal declared

4   Although a spouse who wished to divorce her partner because of his homosexual activities would normally be able to petition under s 1(2)(b) instead.
5   Sadly, in some communities, the victim of a rape may nonetheless be ostracised by other members of the community, and looked upon as being a guilty party.
6   See dicta in *Goshawk v Goshawk* (1965) 109 Sol Jo 290.
7   Family Proceedings Rules 1991, Appendix 1.
8   By virtue of the Family Proceedings Rules 1991, r 2.7(1), it is no longer necessary to cite the name of the person with whom the respondent is alleged to have committed adultery. Where a person is named they will be made a co-respondent to the petition.
9   *R v King's Lynn Magistrates' Court, ex p M* [1988] 2 FLR 79.
10 In *Blyth v Blyth* [1966] 1 All ER 524 the House of Lords was divided in its obiter views as to the correct standard.
11 (1983) 4 FLR 756.

that a mere preponderance of probabilities was not sufficient and that the standard of proof was commensurate with the seriousness of the issue involved. This judgment reflected a tendency in the past to treat adultery as akin to a criminal offence, and therefore to require a higher standard of proof closer to the criminal standard.[12] *Serio v Serio* does not sit easily with the law relating to legitimacy. The Family Law Reform Act 1969, section 26, provides:

> 'Any presumption of law as to the legitimacy or illegitimacy of any person may ... be rebutted by evidence which shows that it is more probable than not that that person is illegitimate or legitimate.'

Theoretically, in view of *Serio v Serio*, a woman might be held not to have committed adultery because the high standard of proof could not be overcome yet her child might be held to be illegitimate on the basis of the lower standard found in section 26. However, this is patently absurd, and it is suggested that there is no reason why the standard of proof for adultery should be anything other than the normal civil standard. Indeed, should the issue ever arise in practice, it seems probable that the court would so hold.

The petitioner finds it intolerable to live with the respondent

The test applied to whether the petitioner finds it intolerable to live with the respondent is subjective rather than objective.[13] Accordingly, once it is found that the petitioner is telling the truth about his or her feelings that is sufficient, regardless of whether a reasonable person would find it intolerable to live with the respondent.[14] Initially there was some doubt as to whether the adultery and the intolerability of living with the respondent needed to be causally linked. This was resolved in *Cleary v Cleary*[15] where it was held that the adultery and the intolerability needed to have nothing whatsoever to do with each other.[16] On its face this was a curious decision,

---

12 Beyond all reasonable doubt.

13 *Goodrich v Goodrich* [1971] 2 All ER 1340.

14 Thus, theoretically, if the wife alleges that her husband blows his nose too often and she finds this intolerable, providing that the court accepts that this is truly the case it is bound to find this part of her petition made out. See the comments of Faulks J in *Roper v Roper* [1972] 3 All ER 668 at p 670.

15 [1974] 1 All ER 498. In *Cleary* the wife had committed adultery. The husband forgave her, and she went back to live with him. However, subsequently she continued to correspond with the man, she kept going out at night, and she finally left and went back to live with her mother. The husband petitioned for divorce as 'there was no future in the marriage at all.' It was clear that it was the behaviour post the adultery that he found intolerable. The husband was held entitled to a decree, the Court of Appeal holding the Act must be interpreted literally, the two factors not being linked.

16 And see *Carr v Carr* [1974] 1 All ER 1193 where a differently constituted Court of Appeal reluctantly followed the decision of the Court in *Cleary*. They suggested that the matter ought to go to the House of Lords to be resolved.

which could, in theory at least, lead to some odd results. A petitioner who finds her spouse intolerable to live with may be entirely indifferent to his adultery. However, despite her indifference, she is able to base her petition on his adulterous behaviour.[17] It is also difficult to square *Cleary v Cleary* with section 2(2) which provides that where the parties continue cohabiting for a period of up to six months after the discovery of the adultery, this should be disregarded in determining whether or not the petitioner finds it intolerable to live with the respondent. The rationale of the provisions in section 2 is to encourage attempts at reconciliation by the parties, by allowing a period of time in which they can try and resolve their problems without this affecting the divorce process. However, section 2(1) provides that where parties live together for a period in excess of six months after the discovery of adultery this operates as a complete bar to the presentation of a petition in reliance on that adultery. This provision is clearly premised on the notion that it is the adultery which has led to the petitioner finding living with the respondent intolerable, rather than any other behaviour.[18]

It is suggested that the Court of Appeal was correct in concluding that the two clauses are not linked despite these difficulties with a non-causative construction. The two parts of section 1(2)(a) are not linked on a natural reading of the wording. Parliament did not intend there to be any linkage. In Parliamentary debates surrounding the section, an attempt to link the two clauses with the addition of the words 'by reason of which' was rejected.[19] On its face, reliance by a petitioner upon adultery which is not intolerable may appear very unjust to a respondent, particularly where it was an isolated act which occurred in response to the distress to the respondent that the far more serious misbehaviour of the petitioner was causing. However, divorce law is not concerned with justice between the parties, but with recognising the irretrievable breakdown of a marriage. If the petitioner does indeed find it intolerable to live with the respondent then she satisfies the requirements of the section and the marriage has clearly broken down. Such a petitioner should not be denied a decree because an objective outsider might consider she was in fact far more to 'blame' for the breakdown of the marriage than the respondent. Moreover, one aim of the Act was to try and remove the bitterness, distress and humiliation from divorce. If the two factors are linked, enquiry must then be made as to whether it is actually the adultery which has made the

---

17 Though indifference is arguably a stronger sign of breakdown than jealous anger.
18 Of course, in the vast majority of divorces based on adultery it is indeed the adultery which makes living with the respondent intolerable. This also is another example of how 'law in the books' differs from 'law in practice'. *Cleary v Cleary* arose at an early stage in the newly reformed divorce law, when parties to divorce petitions expressed their feelings in court with painful honesty, and where judges were still grappling with how to interpret adultery as evidence of irretrievable breakdown of marriage rather than treating it as a matrimonial offence. A wise petitioner today would simply assert in writing that she finds it intolerable to live with the respondent because of his adultery.
19 See Hansard (HL), Vol 303, cols 1222-1249.

marriage intolerable. Dissection of the marriage must therefore take place to find out the answer. This is not in keeping with the fundamental objectives of the law.

Behaviour by the respondent

More petitioners rely on the fact that 'the respondent has behaved in such a way that the petitioner cannot reasonably be expected to live with the respondent' than any of the other four facts.[20] This is highly regrettable. The policy of terminating the marriage with the minimum bitterness, distress and humiliation is undermined where either party sets out to prove the behaviour fact. Petitions frequently contain a catalogue of incidents in support of the allegation in order that, cumulatively, they should add up to sufficient behaviour to satisfy the court that the fact is established. One incident, without more, will not usually be sufficiently serious to establish the requisite behaviour. Because of its pejorative connotations, a petition based on behaviour may be hotly contested.[1] As the Booth Committee commented:

> 'We are satisfied that the bitterness and unhappiness of divorcing couples is frequently exacerbated and prolonged by the fault element in divorce and that this is particularly so where the fact relied upon is behaviour, whether or not the suit is defended. Great hostility and resentment may be generated by the recital in the petition of allegations of behaviour, often exaggerated and some-times stretching back over many years, to the extent that no discussion can take place between the parties or any agreement be reached on any matter relating to their marriage or their children.'[2]

Section 1(2)(b) is often shortened, colloquially, to 'unreasonable behaviour'. This shorthand is inapt, as it suggests that the subsection is only about blameworthy behaviour. This is incorrect. In the majority of cases the behaviour is indeed 'unreasonable', but on a proper construction of the paragraph, the behaviour need be neither unreasonable nor blameworthy. What section 1(2)(b) requires is that, as regards this particular petitioner, it is not reasonable to expect her to continue living with this particular respondent. This is a far more flexible test than the incorrect shorthand. Unfortunately, courts have on occasion fallen into the trap of applying

---

20　In 1994 54% of all divorces granted to wives were granted on the basis of behaviour. 71% of all divorces awarded to a single party were granted to wives. See J Haskey *Divorce Statistics* [1996] Fam Law 301.

1　It is normal human behaviour to deny prime responsibility for the breakdown of a marriage.

2　Booth Report, para 2.10.

the shorthand test, rather than the correct wording of the statute, and by so doing have affected the way that petitions are presented. In the early decision of *Archard v Archard*,[3] both parties were originally of the Roman Catholic faith. The wife was medically advised not to become pregnant for two years and, having lost her faith, she insisted that the husband use contraceptives. Due to his religious convictions he refused, and was advised by his priest that the way to resolve the dilemma was to stop sleeping with his wife. The wife's petition for divorce was refused on the basis that the husband was not behaving unreasonably. It was undoubtedly the case that the husband, because of his religious beliefs, was acting perfectly reasonably. However, it is suggested that had the correct test been applied, namely whether the wife could reasonably have been expected to continue to live with the husband, then it is clear that she could not.[4]

Other early cases under the Act adopted a similar approach and appeared to require 'bad' behaviour on the part of the respondent.[5] In *Pheasant v Pheasant*[6] the only allegation by the husband was that the wife was unable to give him the spontaneous, demonstrative affection which he said his nature demanded and for which he craved. It was held that he had failed to prove behaviour, as the wife had not been guilty of any breach of the obligations of marriage. This ruling supplied a clear invitation to petitioners to prove fault. By considering whether or not the wife had been in 'breach' of her 'obligations' of marriage, rather than concentrating on whether the husband could be expected to live with her, the emphasis of the court's judgment became concentrated on the nature of the wife's behaviour. It is suggested that this and other early cases thereby encouraged petitioners to drag up as many incidents as possible to ensure that the behaviour fact was established, and affected subsequent behaviour petitions to the detriment of the underlying purpose of the Act.[7]

---

3   (1972) Times, 20 April.
4   Equally, the husband could not reasonably be expected to live with the wife. They were both reasonable in their views, but, it is suggested, neither could reasonably be expected to live with the other.
5   See *Stringfellow v Stringfellow* [1976] 2 All ER 539; *Dowden v Dowden* (1978) 8 Fam Law 106. However, in *Bannister v Bannister* (1980) 10 Fam Law 240, the trial judge was criticised on appeal for falling into the 'linguistic trap' of speaking of unreasonable behaviour and dismissing the wife's petition. Accordingly where the wife alleged that the husband had not taken her out for two years, did not speak to her except when it was unavoidable, stayed away for nights giving her no idea where he was going, and had been living an entirely independent life ignoring her completely, it was found to be behaviour that she could not reasonably be expected to live with.
6   [1972] 1 All ER 587.
7   The reality, in many instances, will be that both parties have contributed significantly to the breakdown of the marriage. The Law Commission, in its examination of the law in 1990, recognised that in the vast majority of cases the court does not conduct an enquiry into the truth of the facts alleged, and that the fault-based facts can therefore be intrinsically unjust: Law Com No 192, paras 2.8-2.14. See too, G Davis and M Murch *Grounds for Divorce* (Clarendon Press, 1988) ch 5, for a compelling account of the difficulties encountered and exacerbated by the presentation of a behaviour petition.

In some cases a single incident of behaviour, for example, a serious assault leading to medical treatment, may be sufficient to establish the petitioner's case. Furthermore, in some circumstances conduct which is not actually directed at the marriage itself, but has a serious effect on the petitioner, could also give rise to a decree being granted. Thus conviction for a very serious criminal offence, such as murder or rape, would undoubtedly give a petitioner the facts on which to base a petition. More minor violence, such as shoves, pushes and slaps will require more than one incident in order to satisfy the subsection. Behaviour such as drunkenness, alcoholism and drug addiction is frequently relied upon by a petitioner. Other types of behaviour have included boorishness and constant criticism adhered to over a long period of time; and deliberate persecution of the wife.[8] In *O'Neill v O'Neill*,[9] the husband's 'DIY' behaviour caused so much stress to the petitioning wife that her health suffered. The final straw for her had been when the husband embarked on prolonged renovation work on their bungalow which involved mixing cement on the living-room floor, and having no door on the toilet for eight months![10] In *Carter-Fea v Carter-Fea*[11] the wife complained that her husband was incapable of managing his own affairs, and she was faced with mounting debt due to his failure to take any action in response to his financial difficulties. She was held entitled to a decree because of the evidence she brought as to the effect that the stress was having on her health. However, somewhat unsympathetically, Lawton LJ commented that it would be a sad day when wives thought they could come to court just because their husbands conducted their financial affairs in way which upset them. It is suggested that this comment displayed a remarkable lack of sensitivity to the very considerable strain that financial profligacy, or incompetence, imposes on a family. For many living under the shadow of debt, the stress of living in highly straitened circumstances due to a person's behaviour is every bit as worthy of the court's sympathy as other forms of behaviour.

Where the respondent refuses to live with the petitioner, logically it could be argued that this is behaviour such that the petitioner cannot reasonably be expected to live with the respondent. However, in *Stringfellow v Stringfellow*[12] it was held that such an allegation amounts to an allegation of simple desertion by the husband, and nothing more, and that the petitioner must therefore wait the requisite two years to petition under the

---

8   *Livingstone-Stallard v Livingstone-Stallard* [1974] 2 All ER 766. The husband was apparently 'rude, boorish and critical' of the wife even during their honeymoon. See also, *Stevens v Stevens* [1979] 1 WLR 885.
9   [1975] 3 All ER 289.
10 The husband had also written to the wife's solicitors casting doubt on the paternity of the couple's two children, which incident the Court of Appeal thought in itself was enough to ground the fact.
11 [1987] Fam Law 131.
12 [1976] 2 All ER 539.

desertion fact. The court held that to find differently would render the desertion fact otiose, because all cases would be subsumed under the behaviour head.

Sometimes a petition brought under section 1(2)(b) is based on the sexual incompatibility of the parties. In such cases the petition may allege forms of conduct which are deemed to amount to sexual perversions, or that one party is making excessive sexual demands on the other. This aspect of a couple's intimate private life is obviously an extremely hurtful and damaging matter to expose to judicial scrutiny, usually for both parties. It is also a very difficult matter on which to require a court to pass judgment, because whether or not the behaviour was reasonable will depend on so many different factors. In *Mason v Mason*[13] the husband alleged that the wife refused to have sexual intercourse more than once per week over a particular period of time. His petition was refused. Considerable evidence was presented in court as to the reasons for the wife's reluctance to engage in sexual intercourse, and as to the various contraceptive issues which were relevant to the parties. That the court should get involved in such intimate details of other people's sexual lives seems nothing other than distasteful and damaging. However, in *Mason v Mason* Ormrod LJ expressed the opinion that: 'where refusal of sexual intercourse is the main ground alleged in support of a petition under section 1(2)(b), in my judgment it requires very careful investigation by the court into the allegations on both sides and into the reasons on both sides'.[14] It is suggested that this statement was perhaps reflective of the times, and that should such a petition be defended today the court should endeavour to concentrate its efforts on discovering whether or not the marriage had indeed irretrievably broken down because of sexual problems, rather than trawling through the parties' sexual history.

The test for behaviour is both subjective and objective

A mixture of both an objective and a subjective test is applied when a court is deciding whether the behaviour fact has been established. The test is clearly objective in that the court must decide whether the petitioner can *reasonably* be expected to live with the respondent. However, the essence of the subsection is subjective. The question that must be asked is: 'Can this particular petitioner be expected to live with this particular respondent?'[15] The respondent's knowledge of the damaging effect of his behaviour on the petitioner will therefore be a relevant factor to take into account. When considering the subsection in *Ash v Ash*,[16] Bagnall J stated that the question the court must ask is:

13 (1981) 11 Fam Law 143.
14 Ibid, at p 144.
15 *Birch v Birch* [1992] 1 FLR 564.
16 [1972] 1 All ER 582.

'Can this petitioner, with his or her character and personality, with his or her faults and other attributes, good and bad, and having regard to his or her behaviour during the marriage reasonably be expected to live with the respondent?'

In elaborating on this he expressed the view that:

'... a violent petitioner may reasonably be expected to live with a violent respondent; a petitioner who is addicted to drink can reasonably be expected to live with a respondent similarly addicted; a taciturn and morose spouse can reasonably be expected to live with a taciturn and morose partner; a flirtatious husband can reasonably be expected to live with a wife who is equally susceptible to the attractions of the other sex; and if each is equally bad, at any rate in similar respects, each can reasonably be expected to live with the other.'[17]

In *Livingstone-Stallard v Livingstone-Stallard*[18] Dunn J formulated the test rather differently. He said:

'I ask myself the question: would any right-thinking person come to the conclusion that this husband has behaved in such a way that this wife cannot reasonably be expected to live with him, taking into account the whole of the circumstances and the characters and personalities of the parties?'[19]

It is suggested that the elaboration in *Ash v Ash* was unfortunate and the better formulation is that of Dunn J in *Livingstone-Stallard v Livingstone-Stallard*. In *Birch v Birch*,[20] the Court of Appeal quoted with approval the following passage from a leading practitioners' text:

'Allowance will be made for the sensitive as well as for the thick-skinned; ... conduct must be judged *up to a point*[1] by the capacity of the complaining partner to endure his or her spouse's conduct ... the court would consider to what extent the respondent knew or ought reasonably to have known of that capacity.'[2]

A similar approach was adopted in *Stevens v Stevens*,[3] where the behaviour of the wife had led to the irretrievable breakdown of the marriage, and

---

17   Ibid, at pp 585-586.
18   [1974] 2 All ER 766.
19   Ibid, at p 771.
20   [1992] 1 FLR 564.
1   Emphasis added.
2   *Rayden on Divorce* (15th edn), Vol 1, p 255.
3   [1979] 1 WLR 885.

the husband had subsequently set out to be deliberately unpleasant to the wife. Although the wife could not complain simply because he reacted to her behaviour, when his behaviour went beyond that, she was entitled to a decree. It is suggested that where, for example, one spouse attacks the other with a kitchen knife, whether the other's response is to flee in terror, or to pick up the nearest handy implement to attack back, should not be regarded as the relevant issue, despite what was said in *Ash v Ash*. The 'right-thinking' person would surely conclude that the victim of such an attack should not be expected to live with the attacking spouse. In such a case the parties are a danger to each other, and neither can reasonably be expected to live with the other.

Behaviour arising through illness

Cases involving illness, particularly mental illness, have posed problems for the courts, who have grappled with the difficulty of when to grant a decree against a spouse who is not morally responsible for his behaviour. Whilst it is generally accepted that marriage entails the taking on of certain obligations, including the burdens of illness, it is nonetheless recognised that the toll that mental illness can exact from a spouse can be very severe. The courts have made it clear that the granting of a decree does not necessarily involve blameworthiness. In *Thurlow v Thurlow*,[4] Rees J held that the court must take into account:

> '... all the circumstances including the disabilities and temperaments
> of both parties, the causes of the behaviour and whether the causes
> were or were not known to the petitioner, the presence or absence of
> intention, the impact of it on the petitioner and the family unit, its
> duration, and the prospects of cure or improvement in the future.'

Clearly in some cases the behaviour is so damaging the petitioner must be granted a decree, such as where one spouse attacks the other. Thus in *Katz v Katz*[5] a decree was granted because, even after making allowances for the husband's mental illness (he suffered from manic-depression) his behaviour, and its impact on the wife, was sufficiently serious to warrant granting her a decree. The wife was so distressed by the situation she found herself in that she had made a very serious suicide attempt. However, the courts have adopted a fairly strict interpretation of the law where illness is involved. Thus in *Richards v Richards*[6] where the husband was very moody, sat staring into space, and had assaulted the wife on two occasions (one incident was very trivial) the court found that, after taking

---

4   [1975] 2 All ER 979, at p 988.
5   [1972] 3 All ER 219. See also *White v White* [1983] 2 All ER 51.
6   [1972] 3 All ER 695.

into account the fact of the husband's mental illness, the wife had not established sufficient cause for granting her a decree.

A more difficult problem of statutory interpretation arises where the respondent's behaviour is passive. Establishing the ground may be hard in view of the wording of the section which requires 'behaviour' on the part of the respondent. It was established in *Katz v Katz*[7] that conduct may take the form of either an act or an omission, but that some type of behaviour must take place. Baker P commented: 'behaviour is something more than a mere state of affairs or a state of mind ... in this context [it] is action or conduct by one which affects the other.' In *Thurlow v Thurlow*[8] the issue of negative and positive behaviour brought about by the illness of one of the spouses was considered in considerable detail. Rees J commented that spouses may often, but not always, be expected to tolerate more in the way of inactivity than activity. However, he went on to say that the contrast between positive and negative conduct was not a helpful distinction, and that an omission to act, in most cases, was at the same time a commission.[9] He said that the petitioner's health may be gravely affected by certain kinds of negative behaviour, which may be due to the respondent's mental or physical illness, or an injury, and which may be involuntary. He concluded that 'negative' as well as 'positive' behaviour was capable of forming the basis of a decree and he expressly disapproved *Smith v Smith*,[10] where a decree was refused to the husband as the wife's 'cabbage-like' existence was due solely to pre-senile dementia. Rees J also raised, but did not answer, the hypothetical question of whether it is possible to divorce a spouse who becomes a 'human vegetable'. His view was that a petitioner might face very considerable difficulties in establishing that there was any, or any sufficient, behaviour, or alternatively that to draw the conclusion that the petitioner could not reasonably be expected to live with the respondent would be hard to justify.

Living together after the behaviour

Where a petitioner continues to live with her spouse for a period of up to six months after the date of the last incident relied on in her petition

---

7 [1972] 3 All ER 219, at p 223.
8 [1975] 2 All ER 979. In *Thurlow v Thurlow* the husband complained of both negative and positive behaviour on the part of the wife. The negative behaviour was that the wife had gradually become a bedridden invalid. She was unable to perform the role of a wife in any way, and had become unfit to reside at home. The positive behaviour alleged was that she became very bad tempered, threw things, burnt various objects, and wandered around the streets causing her carers alarm and stress.
9 In so doing, Rees J quoted with approval the decision of the Court of Appeal in *Gollins v Gollins* [1963] 2 All ER 966, a case decided under the old law requiring proof of cruelty.
10 (1973) 118 Sol Jo 184.

brought under section 1(2)(b), this period must be disregarded by the court when determining whether she can reasonably be expected to live with him.[11] The idea of this provision is to facilitate reconciliation between the parties. No party should be put under pressure to reject reconciliation overtures for fear that by so doing she will lose her right to petition. Where the period exceeds six months the court must take it into account, but this does not provide an automatic bar to the granting of a decree; the court must look at each case individually. In *Bradley v Bradley*[12] the trial judge had refused the wife a decree where she had continued living in a four-bedroomed council house with her husband and seven children pending the hearing. Allowing the wife's appeal, the Court of Appeal held that she should be entitled to prove that it was unreasonable for her to continue living with her husband. This ruling was a vital recognition of the grave difficulties that many poor women with children find themselves in. Housing issues may well force a couple to stay together unwillingly. Unless the petitioner applies for an occupation order, both parties are entitled to continue residing in the matrimonial home. It may well be that neither party has anywhere else to go and, in any event, both spouses may wish to stay in the home in order to share in the care of their children. It is therefore commonplace for a petitioner to claim that she had no choice in the matter but to continue living together under the same roof.[13]

Desertion by the respondent

In order to establish desertion, the petitioner must show that the respondent has deserted her for a period of at least two years immediately preceding the presentation of the petition. This fact is rarely relied on, as normally parties who have separated for more than two years will use the fact of two years' separation with consent.[14] Therefore a petitioner will only need to use this fact where the deserting spouse refuses to consent to a divorce and has not behaved in such a way as to enable the petitioner to avail herself of the provisions of section 1(2)(a) or (b). Desertion occurs where one spouse abandons the other, leaving the home with the intention of not returning. Where there is no agreement to part this gives rise to desertion even though the one deserted is thoroughly glad to see the other go. It is also possible for one party to desert the other whilst still living under the same roof.[15] In *Pulford v Pulford*[16] desertion was described as 'not the withdrawal from a place, but from a state of things'. Thus desertion

---

11 S 2(3).
12 [1973] 3 All ER 750.
13 See ch 6 on orders regulating the occupation of the matrimonial home.
14 Less than 1% of all divorces granted in 1994 were based on this ground. See J Haskey *Divorce Statistics* [1996] Fam Law 301.
15 *Naylor v Naylor* [1961] 2 All ER 129; *Hopes v Hopes* [1948] 2 All ER 920.
16 [1923] P 18, per Lord Merrivale at p 21.

can be established where there is a total cessation of cohabitation between the parties, even though they remain living under the same roof.[17] Where the parties are forcibly absent from one another, for example because the respondent is in prison, or on a posting abroad, or where the parties agree to separate, that will not normally amount to desertion, unless evidence can be brought to show that the respondent intended to have nothing more to do with the petitioner. In *Nutley v Nutley*[18] the wife originally left the home to look after her aged and ailing parents with the consent of the husband. Some time after that, while her parents were still alive, she formed the intention never to return, but did not inform the husband. After the deaths of her parents she still did not return home, and the husband petitioned on the ground of her desertion. The issue arose as to the date from which her desertion commenced. It was held by the Court of Appeal that communicating the intention never to return was not essential. However, because the husband had continued to consent to the wife's absence, no desertion could have taken place. The court recognised that had the wife communicated her intention then perhaps things would have been different, and the husband would not have continued to consent to her withdrawal. However, until he no longer consented, desertion had not occurred.

The intention to desert

Proof of an intention to desert is necessary in order to establish desertion. This may be difficult to establish where the respondent suffers from mental illness or incapacity. For example, the amnesiac who disappears for two years cannot be held to have formed the intention to desert if he has no memory that he has a wife to return to. The onus of proof is on the petitioner to establish that she has been deserted. However, by virtue of section 2(4):

> '... the court may treat a period of desertion as having continued at a time when the deserting party was incapable of continuing the necessary intention if the evidence before the court is such that, had the party not been so incapable, the court would have inferred that his desertion continued at that time.'

Where the respondent is suffering from mental delusions he must be treated as if the delusions are true in assessing whether he is in desertion. So in *Perry v Perry,*[19] where the wife believed that the husband was trying to murder her, she was held not to be in desertion. Clearly if the delusions were true she would have been entitled to leave.

---

17 See below on the meaning of the phrase 'living apart'.
18 [1970] 1 All ER 410.
19 [1964] 1 WLR 91.

Sometimes behaviour by a spouse is such that the other is entitled to leave. In that event the departing spouse is not in desertion. The test for deciding whether a departure is justified was originally described by Lord Penzance in *Yeatman v Yeatman*[20] as being where the behaviour of one party is so 'grave and weighty' as to entitle the other to leave. In *Hall v Hall*[1] a more modern wording of the test was expressed as 'whether the conduct of this husband was sufficient to justify his wife in leaving him and saying that she finds it impossible to live with him'. An interesting example arose in *Quoraishi v Quoraishi*.[2] The parties had validly entered a potentially polygamous marriage in Pakistan. They had lived in England for a number of years, and were educated people, both being doctors. The husband wished to marry a second wife, but the wife steadfastly protested against him so doing. When he did marry another woman, the wife left. The Court of Appeal held that the onus was on the petitioner to establish desertion without just cause. An English court must apply English law, and therefore even if a Muslim woman had no ground for complaint under Islamic law it did not follow that she may not have just cause for leaving. In each case what must be considered was the particular husband and wife, the law of their marriage and personal lives, and most importantly their personal circumstances. Here the wife had consistently protested against her husband taking a second wife. This justified her in leaving and she was not in desertion.

Where a spouse leaves with the intention never to return because she has been driven out by the other she is not in desertion, and she can herself petition on the basis of constructive desertion. Constructive desertion has been recognised since 1864.[3] It occurs either when a spouse has been physically forced out, or where she has felt compelled to leave because of the respondent's actions. In order to establish constructive desertion, the petitioner must show that the respondent's behaviour has been sufficiently grave to drive her out.[4] A petition based on constructive desertion can also, therefore, give rise to a petition under section 1(2)(b).[5] Had it been the wife who wanted a divorce in *Quoraishi v Quoraishi*, she could have petitioned on the ground either of her husband's behaviour or his constructive desertion.[6] Should a petition based on behaviour fail, the

---

20 (1868) LR 1 P & D 489.
1 [1962] 3 All ER 518, per Ormrod LJ at p 523.
2 [1985] FLR 780.
3 See *Graves v Graves* (1864) 3 Sw & Tr 350.
4 *Hall v Hall* [1962] 3 All ER 518. See for example *Lang v Lang* [1955] AC 402, where the husband had assaulted and abused the wife, and where (as a court would recognise today) he had raped her.
5 The wording of the test in *Hall v Hall*, above, bears a strong resemblance to the requirements of the fact of s 1(2)(b).
6 *Quoraishi v Quoraishi* demonstrated that where a member of an immigrant community objected to behaviour, which other members of the community found an ordinary incident of their lives, there was no reason in principle to treat that person any differently from any other divorce petitioner or respondent.

petitioner is not able to plead constructive desertion in the alternative, because the conduct will not have been sufficiently grave for her to have left. In *Morgan v Morgan*[7] the only allegation against the husband was that he had ordered the wife to leave. It was held that 'simple desertion or an order to go' should be considered under fact (c) only and could not amount to constructive desertion. This is a similar approach to that adopted in *Stringfellow v Stringfellow*.[8]

Termination of desertion

Termination of desertion can arise in different ways. Most obviously it occurs where the parties resume cohabitation with each other. However, provision is made in section 2(5) that a period of up to six months' cohabitation for reconciliation purposes shall not terminate the desertion, but the period of failed reconciliation must be added on to the two years required to establish desertion for divorce purposes. Desertion also comes to an end where both parties agree to separate. If the deserting spouse makes a genuine offer to resume cohabitation, desertion on his part ceases. Furthermore, if the deserted spouse refuses to accept the deserter's offer then, unless she has good grounds for refusing the offer, for example, because the deserter has committed adultery in his absence, she will herself be in desertion.[9]

Two years' separation with consent, and five years' separation

Where the parties have lived apart for at least two years (section 1(2)(d)), or at least five years (section 1(2)(e)), a decree of divorce will be granted despite the fact that neither party is alleged to have been at fault. Where the petitioner relies on two years of living apart, he or she must first obtain the respondent's consent before a decree will be pronounced; where reliance is placed on five years of living apart no such consent is required. Prior to 1969 divorce by consent was completely forbidden.[10] Thus the recognition in section 1(2)(d) that parties should be entitled, indeed should be encouraged, to end their marriage by agreement brought about a real change in the law. When the measure was introduced it was the hope of law reformers that this simple, non-judgmental state of affairs, with no

---

7   (1973) 117 Sol Jo 223.
8   [1976] 2 All ER 539.
9   *Everitt v Everitt* [1949] 1 All ER 908.
10 If the parties colluded in a divorce it was an absolute bar to proceedings. Thus, pre-
    1969, the more both parties wanted a divorce the less chance they had of obtaining
    one, a state of affairs which was clearly mad, and to giving an account of which only
    Lewis Carroll could probably have done justice!

allegations of any kind against the respondent being required, would become the main fact relied on for divorce purposes. Unfortunately this has not been the case. Paragraph (d) has never accounted for more than 27% of all divorces.[11]

Positive consent is required, mere passive non-objection is not sufficient.[12] Consent must be freely given with understanding of what it entails,[13] and it can be withdrawn at any time before a decree nisi is pronounced.[14] A respondent can refuse to consent unless the petitioner agrees that he or she does not have to pay costs.[15] This can clearly give one party a better bargaining position if the other is desperate for a divorce. Costs of the actual divorce are not high, because of the special procedure, but where the spouses' resources are limited, costs can still operate as a significant factor. The respondent cannot, however, refuse to pay the costs of ancillary proceedings.

Section 1(2)(e) was the other radical departure from the previous entirely fault-based divorce system. Where the parties have lived apart for a period of at least five years proof of this fact alone allows a decree to be granted. The introduction of non-consensual divorce in reliance on living apart for five years was highly controversial because it permitted divorce against the respondent's will even though the respondent had done nothing 'wrong', a consideration of particular significance to those who were opposed to divorce on religious grounds. Such persons were, and still are, helpless to prevent a divorce.[16] The five-year fact supplies the ultimate escape from an unwanted marriage for those petitioners who cannot establish any of the other facts. For example, where the respondent spouse has become seriously mentally ill it is likely that a court would take the view that he or she does not have sufficient comprehension to consent to being divorced; and where the respondent's mental illness manifests itself in passive behaviour it may be that the petitioner would have difficulty in establishing 'behaviour' for the purposes of paragraph (b).[17] Consequently, reliance on five years of living apart may be the only way of ending the marriage.

---

11 The Law Commission in *Facing the Future* Law Com No 170 published the figures for the years 1971-1986 in Appendix B. The peak year was 1979, when 26.7% of all divorces were granted under fact (d).

12 In *McG (formerly R) v R* [1972] 1 All ER 362 the contention that a letter from the husband's solicitors amounted to consent failed. Part of the letter read: '[the husband] is not in the least concerned with the procedural problems that have arisen. [The husband] simply wants this affair to be brought to finality as soon as possible.' The court held that although this might be an indication that the husband did not object, there was nothing in the letter which amounted to consent by the husband.

13 See s 2(7) and the Family Proceedings Rules 1991, r 2.10(1).

14 Family Proceedings Rules 1991, r 2.10(2).

15 *Beales v Beales* [1972] 2 All ER 667.

16 Unless able to raise a defence to the petition under s 5, which requires the respondent to establish grave financial or other hardship. Such a defence is highly unlikely to succeed; see below.

17 Such as where a spouse is reduced to the state of a 'human vegetable', the example and description given in *Thurlow v Thurlow* [1975] 2 All ER 979; see above under para (b).

Living apart

What is meant by 'living apart' for the purposes of section 1(2)(d) and (e)? Section 2(6) states that a husband and wife:

'... shall be treated as living apart unless they are living with each other in the same household.'

Living with each other in the same household is not the same as living with each other in the same house. Where parties remain together under the same roof they may nonetheless be living apart for divorce purposes. The question for the court is 'has all form of common life between the parties ceased?'[18] Unless it has, the parties remain living together. This strict interpretation of living apart was applied in *Mouncer v Mouncer.*[19] The husband and wife were on very bad terms and from November 1969 they slept in separate bedrooms. They continued to eat meals cooked by the wife, often together and in the company of one or both of their children. They shared the cleaning, but the wife no longer did any washing for the husband. The only reason that the husband stayed was because he wished to live with and help care for the children. He eventually left in May 1971, and petitioned for a divorce in November 1971. The petition was dismissed on the basis that the parties were not living apart until May 1971. In *Hollens v Hollens,*[20] by contrast, the husband and wife continued living in their two-bedroomed council house, but had not spoken or eaten together since a violent quarrel more than two years previously. Neither party had done anything for each other since the quarrel. This degree of separation was sufficient to satisfy the court that all common life between them had ceased and that they were living apart.[1]

It is depressing and somewhat ironic that the more civilised the parties, and the more willing they are to behave well, co-operate with each other, and share the care of their children, the less chance there is of them obtaining a divorce under paragraph (d). Many couples, through financial constraints, cannot afford for one of them to move out of the home until arrangements are made for a financial and property settlement after the divorce. The ruling in *Mouncer v Mouncer* has the effect of driving parties who remain under the same roof to behave in an unnatural and selfish manner, which each is likely to experience as stressful and distressing,

---

18 The same test as in desertion.
19 [1972] 1 All ER 289.
20 (1971) 115 Sol Jo 327.
1   Difficulties might arise where a spouse wishes to end the marriage but continues to look after the other party because he or she is incapacitated in some way. It is suggested that the wisest course in such a situation would be for the caring spouse to lodge a formal declaration of the intention to live apart with a solicitor. The fact that the parties then continued to live under the same roof, with one supplying a variety of services to the other, should not prejudice the obtaining of a divorce, as the parties would not be living with each other as husband and wife. See *Fuller v Fuller* [1973] 2 All ER 650.

and which may cause untold damage to any children of the family.[2] The courts should acknowledge that if there is blame to be allocated for the failure of parties to rely on paragraph (d) and choose instead to rely on paragraphs (a) or (b), that they have played a part in this by interpreting the law on living apart in such a rigid and unimaginative manner.[3]

In order to facilitate attempts at reconciliation section 2(5) permits the spouses to resume living together for one or more periods totalling up to six months without this being taken into account in assessing whether the parties have lived apart for the requisite period. This period of cohabitation does not count as part of the two years but must be added on to it. This means, for example, that where parties have made one or more attempts at reconciliation which have lasted in total for five months they can seek a divorce after two years and five months have elapsed. If they stay together for longer than six months the time must start to run from the beginning again if they subsequently separate and decide to divorce.

The mental element in living apart

Parliament did not intend there to be any mental element to living apart for the purposes of the two and five year separation facts; an amendment to this effect was defeated in the House of Lords.[4] However, there was an early landmark decision, *Santos v Santos*,[5] where the Court of Appeal held that to establish living apart not only must there be a physical separation, but there must also be a mental element of wishing to live apart on the part of at least one of the spouses. Where spouses agree to separate, or where one deserts the other, the mental element is obviously present. But where spouses are physically apart due to reasons such as illness, imprisonment, or an overseas posting, importing a mental element means that the spouses are not 'living apart' until the decision to live apart is taken, and it is only then that time begins to run. It was held in *Santos v Santos* that the decision to live apart need not be mutual; it can be unilateral. Furthermore, the party taking the decision need not communicate it either by word or deed to the other party. However, failure to communicate could clearly lead to evidential difficulties. Sometimes it is possible to determine the mental element by external factors such as a cessation of visits to an ill or imprisoned spouse, or cohabitation with a

---

2   The type of behaviour held sufficient to found a decree in *Hollens v Hollens* (1971) 115 Sol Jo 327 would surely be extremely emotionally damaging to any children of the family.

3   See Law Com No 192, para 2.12, where the Commission comment: 'It is unjust and discriminatory of the law to provide for a civilised "no-fault" ground for divorce which, in practice, is denied to a large section of the population. A young mother with children living in a council house is obliged to rely upon fault whether or not she wants to do so and irrespective of the damage it may do.'

4   Hansard (HL), Vol 304, col 1082-1130.

5   [1972] 2 All ER 246.

third party, but if there is no such evidence it would appear that some sort of corroboration of the petitioner's assertion is required.[6]

In view of the express wish of Parliament not to include a mental element in the definition of 'living apart' the reasons given in *Santos v Santos* for holding that such an element should be included need to be examined. Sachs LJ gave five reasons. First, he said that a survey of Commonwealth statutes, and decisions on similar provisions to the ones contained in the Divorce Reform Act 1969, revealed that the stream of authority ran uniformly and clearly in favour of mere physical separation not constituting 'living apart'. Secondly, he stated that English decisions on other statutes concerning the meaning of the phrase had also uniformly reached the same decision.[7] This prima facie led to the conclusion that the phrase meant something more than mere physical separation, and that there must be good reasons for holding differently. Thirdly, he said absurdities could arise if a mental element was not an integral element of living apart. He gave as an example the case of a man who came home on leave for less than 20 per cent of the two to two and a half years immediately preceding the filing of the petition, who would be able to satisfy the fact even though the parties had been on excellent terms until they had a row on the last day of his leave. As petitions under fact (d) are normally undefended there would be no evidence to rebut the presumption of irretrievable breakdown. Of this Sachs LJ said: 'Unless – contrary to our view – the Act intended to permit divorce by consent simpliciter such a result would be absurd. On the contrary the tenor of [section 1(2)][8] is to ensure that under heads (c), (d) and (e) breakdown is not to be held irretrievable unless and until a sufficiently long passage of time has shown this to be the case.'[9] Fourthly, he held that section 2(6) did not drive the court to conclude that only physical separation counted. The subsection merely made it clear that where parties were living in the same house they could nonetheless be living apart if not living in the same household.[10] Finally, Sachs LJ asserted that petitions founded on heads (d) and (e) needed careful judicial scrutiny. It was not correct to say that the object of the Act was to make divorce easy. It was designed to assist maintenance of marriages other than those reduced to a mere shell.

It was the view of most commentators that the Court of Appeal reached an unfortunate decision in *Santos v Santos*, and that the better inter-pretation of the law is that no mental element is required in order to live apart for divorce purposes. It was disingenuous to argue that a mental

---

6   However, this requirement is perhaps more theoretical than real with the advent of the special procedure. Where a petitioner states that she has formed the intention for the requisite period it is difficult to imagine how that statement will be subjected to close scrutiny.

7   He mentioned the Larceny Act 1916, and also said that two revenue statutes had been cited to him.

8   At the time s 2(1) of the Divorce Reform Act 1969.

9   [1972] 2 All ER 246, at p 255.

10 *Hopes v Hopes* [1948] 2 All ER 920.

element should have been included because of the decisions of Common-wealth countries and pre-1969 English cases. Those drafting the legislation would have been well aware of those decisions, and yet chose not to include any wording importing a mental element. Although absurdities, as the Court of Appeal saw them, can arise if there is no mental element,[11] they can equally arise if there is a mental element. Sachs LJ himself pointed out some of the difficulties: 'How, for instance, does a judge in practice discharge the unenviable task of determining at what time the wife of a man immured long-term in hospital or one serving a 15-year sentence changes from a wife who is standing by her husband ... to one who realises the end has come but visits him merely from a sense of duty arising from the past?'[12] Extending this example, suppose that the wife of a prisoner decides to stand by her husband but almost immediately on his release realises that there is no possibility of resuming their marital relationship. She has become independent, and he has been damaged by his prison experience. Because a mental element is required the wife will have to wait a further five years before she can obtain a divorce. Many would regard this outcome, which inevitably arises when a mental element is required, as equally absurd.

The advent of the special procedure radically affected Sachs LJ's last reason because there is no longer the judicial scrutiny of divorce petitions which he envisaged. However, even at the time of the ruling in *Santos v Santos*, when the special procedure did not exist, it was possible to criticise a construction of section 1(2)(d) and (e) which required the close examination of both parties' thought processes. To encourage the dissection of a marriage on a petition based on separation was counter to the ethos underlying the Act, namely the avoidance of bitterness, distress and humiliation.

Special protection for certain respondents

Where the only fact relied on for divorce is under section 1(2)(e), namely that the parties have lived apart for a continuous period of at least five years, the petitioner can be refused a decree under section 5 on the ground that the dissolution of the marriage will result in grave financial or other hardship to the respondent, and that it would be wrong in all the circumstances to dissolve the marriage. This safeguard has been included

---

11 Although the example they gave is arguably not as absurd as they suggest. The fact that one of the parties has actually gone ahead and petitioned for a divorce suggests that there must have been something radically wrong with the marriage in any event. It is difficult to imagine that any spouse would petition for divorce on the basis of one quarrel, when it is going to involve him or her in all the complications that a divorce inevitably entails. It is also to be hoped that any solicitor faced with such a spouse would at the very least discuss the possibility of reconciliation, and supply a list of people able to help, in accordance with the provisions of s 6.

12 [1972] 2 All ER 246, at p 254. Other difficulties occur in cases involving mental illness.

in slightly altered form in section 10 of the Family Law Act 1996, and it is discussed in that context.[13] Suffice to say that for the purposes of the Matrimonial Causes Act 1973, the bar to divorce in section 5 has hardly ever been applied in practice, but its availability has been useful to exert pressure on the petitioner to offer the respondent a reasonable financial settlement.[14]

The disadvantage of defending a divorce under section 5 is that the only relief available is the refusal of a decree. But the respondent, as well as the petitioner, may not wish to remain bound up in a marriage which has irretrievably broken down. A respondent wife's fear of divorce may relate to its financial consequences rather than to her change in status. In this situation section 10 of the 1973 Act may come to her aid. Section 10 gives special protection to the respondent in divorce cases where a decree nisi has been obtained in reliance on either the two or five year separation fact only. It is *not* given to spouses who divorce in reliance on one of the other three facts. Moreover, protection is only given to the *respondent* to the application, although in practice the choice of who is the petitioner and who is respondent in a divorce action based on the two-year separation fact may be entirely fortuitous. It may, therefore, be important to have all this in mind at the outset of divorce proceedings when determining which fact should be relied on to establish the irretrievable breakdown of the marriage, and who should be the petitioner.

Section 10(1) empowers the court to rescind the decree nisi in a case where the petitioner has misled the respondent (whether intentionally or unintentionally) about any matter which the respondent took into account in deciding to give consent to the decree being granted. Whilst the risk of this happening appears to be remote, in some circumstances a petitioner could be well advised to take advantage of section 7 in order to ensure that section 10 cannot be raised. Section 7 enables either party to a divorce to bring before the court any agreement or proposed agreement, and the court can express its opinion on its reasonableness. Such a step might also prevent the petitioner falling foul of section 10(2) and (3).

Under section 10(2) a respondent may apply to a court for consideration of her financial position after divorce, in which case, by virtue of the provisions contained in section 10(3), the court hearing the application:

'... shall consider all the circumstances including the age, health, conduct, earning capacity, financial resources and financial obligations of each of the parties, and the financial position of the respondent as, having regard to the divorce, it is likely to be after the death of the petitioner should the petitioner die first; and, subject to subsection (4) ... the court shall not make the decree absolute unless it is satisfied:

---

13 See below.
14 A useful illustration is found in *Le Marchant v Le Marchant* [1977] 3 All ER 610.

    (a) that the petitioner should not be required to make any financial provision for the respondent, or

    (b) that the financial provision made by the petitioner for the respondent is reasonable and fair or the best that can be made in the circumstances.'

These safeguards afford the respondent valuable protection where the petitioner is being unreasonable, or obdurate, over financial arrangements, or where he is in arrears with payments due under an existing order. In *Griffiths v Dawson & Co,*[15] Ewbank J said that the first step any competent solicitor should take when consulted by a wife in her late middle age who has been married for many years to a man in pensionable employment, and who is being divorced against her will, is to make an application under section 10 to protect the wife's position. He said that the purpose of making such an application was not to obtain a hearing in court; it was to hold up the decree absolute, whilst financial matters were being looked into. This step prevents a wife from ceasing to be a wife, and thereby losing her right to a widow's pension, until an investigation and compensatory provision has been made. In *Garcia v Garcia,*[16] the wife was able to use section 10(3) to delay the grant of decree nisi because her Spanish husband owed her £4,000 in unpaid maintenance for their child. In *Wilson v Wilson*[17] the Court of Appeal ruled that a petitioner cannot circumvent the protection afforded by subsection (3) by making mere proposals. The court pointed out that the subsection requires the provision to have been made, and that to allow it to be satisfied by proposals only might enable the husband subsequently to resile from them, leaving the wife without protection.

    However, the court has some discretion over whether or not to make the decree absolute once the inquiry under subsection (3) has been conducted. Subsection (4) states that:

'The court may if it thinks fit make the decree absolute notwithstanding the requirements in subsection (3) if—

    (a) it appears that there are circumstances making it desirable that the decree should be made absolute without delay, and

    (b) the court has obtained a satisfactory undertaking from the petitioner that he will make such financial provision for the respondent as the court may approve.'

The courts have been careful to ensure that subsection (4) does not undermine the overall protective purpose of section 10. In *Grigson v Grigson*[18] the husband had failed, even in outline, to give an indication of

---

15 [1993] 2 FLR 315.
16 [1992] 1 FLR 256.
17 [1973] 2 All ER 17.
18 [1974] 1 All ER 478.

the kind or amount of financial provision he would make. He merely said he would do so. It was held that on a true construction of the subsection the court must approve proposals submitted by the petitioner at least in outline, and then obtain an undertaking from him that they will be given effect before proceeding to decree absolute. It was not sufficient for the petitioner merely to give an undertaking that he would 'make such financial provision as the court may approve' at some specified date in the future. Essentially, the provisions in section 10 provide the respondent to a divorce based on the two or five year separation facts with a 'bargaining chip', and where the petitioner is being unreasonable when negotiating financial and property arrangements, it is a bargaining chip which may sometimes usefully be exploited.

The decrees nisi and absolute

Being married gives a person status which is not just of relevance to the particular individual, but is also of importance to other individuals and to the state. The status of being married gives rise to both rights and obligations. A married person may, for example, have the right to a pension as a surviving spouse, or to inherit when his or her spouse dies intestate. He or she may have the obligation to provide financial support for a spouse. The point at which the marriage is finally terminated can therefore be of crucial importance. The decree nisi does *not* terminate the marriage; it is of a purely provisional nature. It is not until decree absolute has been granted that the marriage finally comes to an end. This can be granted six weeks after decree nisi on the application of the party in whose favour the decree nisi was pronounced. If the petitioner fails to apply, the respondent may apply for the decree to be made absolute three months later.[19] If no application has been made after twelve months, the court may require the applicant to provide evidence accounting for the delay. The court then has a discretion whether to make the decree absolute or to rescind it altogether.[20] The period between decrees nisi and absolute is normally used to sort out outstanding issues relating to the children and financial and property matters. However, there is no requirement that these should be resolved before the divorce is finalised.[1]

The importance of the two-stage process was graphically illustrated in *Re Collins*.[2] In 1978 Mrs Collins married a man with an exceptionally violent nature. She was granted a decree nisi, but died before the decree was made absolute. Her daughter and son were taken into care and her

---

19 S.9(2). However, the court may refuse to grant the application if the petitioner would be financially prejudiced by so doing. See *Wickler v Wickler* [1998] 2 FLR 326.
20 See *Court v Court* [1982] Fam 105.
1   In complete contrast to the position under the Family Law Act 1996, see below.
2   [1990] 2 All ER 47. It also reveals how the change of status brought about by adoption may have financial implications.

son was subsequently adopted. Mrs Collins died intestate, leaving an estate worth a net total of about £27,000. Under normal intestacy rules, Mr Collins was entitled to the whole of her estate as a surviving spouse. Had the decree been made absolute the daughter would have inherited her mother's entire estate, which is surely what Mrs Collins would have preferred.[3] This case illustrates the importance of each spouse making a will, or revising an existing will, when their marriage has broken down, so that the inheritance rights of family members are not governed by the vagaries of the intestacy laws as affected by divorce law rather than by their own wishes.[4]

Judicial separation

Some spouses who have conscientious objections to divorce, but whose marriage has effectively come to an end, may wish to separate from each other, to sort out their financial and property affairs and to make arrangements about their children. A decree of judicial separation provides such spouses with the judicial assistance they may need. The decree can be obtained in reliance on exactly the same facts as those for divorce.[5] However, unlike for divorce, these facts supply the *grounds* for a decree of judicial separation and there is no requirement that the marriage should have irretrievably broken down.[6] The decree does not terminate the marriage and can indeed be rescinded. The special procedure applies in the same way as it does for divorce and the vast majority of petitions are handled in this way. If one of the grounds is made out the court must grant the decree, which comes into effect immediately.[7] There is no two-stage process as in divorce, it is not possible to raise the defence of grave financial or other hardship,[8] nor does section 10 apply[9] because the parties' status as a married couple does not alter. Importantly also, the bar which prevents a party presenting a petition for divorce within the first year of marriage does not apply,[10] so the petition can be presented at any time

---

3   The daughter was awarded a lump sum payment of £5,000 under the Inheritance (Provision for Families and Dependants) Act 1975.

4   And, in this case, adoption law, for Mrs Collins would probably have wished her son to inherit too.

5   S 17. Prior to the Divorce Reform Act 1969 the grounds for judicial separation were similar, but not identical, to those for divorce.

6   See s 17(2). The reconciliation provisions of s 6 may therefore be more apposite to petitions for judicial separation.

7   S 41.

8   S 5.

9   Which makes provision for the rescission or withholding of a decree of divorce where the petitioner has misled the respondent to a petition based on the two or five year facts.

10 S 3(1).

which could be invaluable where a decree is needed as a matter of urgency almost immediately after the marriage took place.[11]

Consequences of a decree of judicial separation

A decree of judicial separation relieves spouses from the duty of cohabitation with each other. The legal significance of this old-fashioned concept of marital duty is that once the decree has been obtained, neither party is in desertion for refusing to live with the other party. Consequently, desertion cannot be relied upon should a divorce petition subsequently be presented. A spouse normally seeks a decree of judicial separation in order to take advantage of the court's ancillary powers to make financial provision and property adjustment orders[12] and, where appropriate, orders in relation to the upbringing of the children.[13] Pending the grant of the decree the petitioner may also be well-advised to apply for an occupation order under Part IV of the Family Law Act 1996.[14] For succession purposes, the parties are treated as if they have pre-deceased one another. Consequently, they are not entitled to succeed to one another's property on intestacy.[15] However, where one party is a beneficiary under the other party's will the position is different to that on divorce. On divorce any gift made to a spouse in a will automatically lapses,[16] but this rule does not extend to where the parties are judicially separated.

A petitioner who successfully petitions for a decree of judicial separation is entitled to petition for divorce in reliance on the same facts.[17] Where the respondent to the decree of judicial separation is the petitioner for divorce, he or she must, of course, establish one of the five facts which evidence the irretrievable breakdown of the marriage.

Criticisms of divorce under the Matrimonial Causes Act 1973 and proposals for reform

It has been seen that the underlying purpose of divorce reform in 1969 was to buttress rather than to undermine the stability of marriage, and

11 For example, where there is extreme domestic violence and where a swift property transfer order is appropriate.
12 See ch 8.
13 Pursuant to s 41.
14 See ch 6.
15 Matrimonial Causes Act 1973, s 18(2). However, they are still entitled to make an application for reasonable financial provision under the Inheritance (Provision for Family and Dependants) Act 1975.
16 Wills Act 1837, s 18A.
17 Matrimonial Causes Act 1973, s 4(1).

to enable marriages which had broken down irretrievably to be ended with the minimum of bitterness, distress and humiliation.[18] In the years following the implementation of the new law there was growing disquiet in some quarters that this aim was not being achieved. This disquiet, coupled with a large increase in the divorce rate, provided fertile ground for a fresh examination of the legal framework. In 1982 a committee chaired by Booth J was established to examine the procedures associated with matrimonial causes. The committee was displeased with what it discovered, particularly with regard to divorces based on the behaviour fact, and in its Report published in 1985[19] the committee recommended that changes be made which would lead to the reduction in acrimony between the parties. The Law Commission, taking the lead from the Booth report, carried out an examination of the law in operation since 1973 against the background of its professed objectives, and found it wanting.[20] It published a discussion paper, *Facing the Future: A Discussion Paper on the Ground for Divorce*, in 1988 and invited views on different suggestions for how the law might be altered.[1] In the light of the responses it received, the Law Commission made proposals for reform in *Family Law: The Ground for Divorce*.[2]

The aims of the law of divorce as expressed in both Law Commission papers were encapsulated in four major propositions. First, to support those marriages capable of being saved; secondly, to enable those not so capable to be dissolved with the minimum of avoidable distress, bitterness and hostility; thirdly, so far as possible to encourage the amicable resolution of practical issues relating to the couple's home, finances and children, and the proper discharge of their responsibilities to one another and their children; and fourthly, to minimise the harm the children of the family might suffer, both at the time of the divorce and in the future, and to promote, so far as possible, the continued sharing of parental responsibility for them. The Law Commission discussion paper contained three possible models for reform: a mixed system with both fault and no fault as under the Matri-monial Causes Act 1973, but with some modifications; divorce after a fixed minimum period of separation; and divorce after a fixed minimum period for reflection and consideration, known as 'process over time'. The last model was the one it preferred and which it recommended in its final report.

The Lord Chancellor's Department took up many of the Law Commission's suggestions and published its own Green Paper *Looking to*

---

18 *Reform of the Grounds of Divorce: The Field of Choice* Cmd 3123, para 15.
19 Report of the Matrimonial Causes Procedures Committee (1985).
20 Indeed, the criticisms were devastating: the law was found to be confusing and misleading; to be discriminatory and unjust; to exacerbate hostility; to distort the parties' bargaining positions; to do nothing to save marriages; and to make matters worse for the children, this last criticism probably being the most important in the eyes of the Lord Chancellor's Department.
1 Law Com No 170.
2 Law Com No 192.

the Future: Mediation and the Ground for Divorce, in 1993.[3] In its introduction to the Green Paper the Government's objectives in relation to the law and procedure surrounding the dissolution of marriages were expressed rather differently from those put forward by the Law Commission. These objectives were: (i) to support the institution of marriage; (ii) to include practicable steps to prevent the irretrievable breakdown of marriages; (iii) to ensure that the parties understand the practical consequences of divorce before taking any irreversible decision; (iv) where divorce is unavoidable, to minimise the bitterness and hostility between the parties and to reduce the trauma for the children; and (v) to keep to the minimum the cost to the parties and the taxpayer.

Objections to the law found in the Matrimonial Causes Act 1973, and the reasons for wishing for change, were spelt out in some detail.[4] The Green Paper claimed that the law found in the Matrimonial Causes Act 1973, and particularly the manner of its application in practice, allowed divorce to be obtained quickly and easily without the parties being required to have regard to the consequences. It stated that the system did nothing to save the marriage; it could make things worse for the children; it was unjust and exacerbated bitterness and hostility; it was confusing, misleading and open to abuse; it was discriminatory; and it distorted the parties' bargaining positions. The Consultation Paper listed nine possible options for reforming the law, the preferred option being the Law Commission model, that the sole ground for divorce should be the irretrievable breakdown of the marriage to be established by the passage of time. During this time, the parties would be expected to use the allotted period as an opportunity for consideration and reflection.

A considerable number of comments were received in response to the Consultation Paper, and in the spring of 1995 the Government published a White Paper setting out fresh proposals for change. In his foreword to the Paper, the then Lord Chancellor, Lord Mackay of Clashfern, stated that 'there have been worries that these proposals are to make divorce easier', and he made it plain that he shared these concerns.[5] Not surprisingly, therefore, the key aspects of the Government's proposals concentrated as much on 'marriage saving' as 'marriage ending'. It was stated that their proposals would:

3   HMSO, 1993.
4   *Looking to the Future* (1993) ch 5. A more comprehensive analysis of the defects in the current system was provided in both Law Commission papers. See also, A Bainham *Divorce and the Lord Chancellor: Looking to the future or getting back to basics* (1994) 53 CLJ 253.
5   Lord Mackay made an unusually private statement of his personal beliefs in the foreward. It included the sentences: 'Personally I strongly adhere to the view that marriage should be for life. I believe that a husband and wife with such an ideal should provide the most stable and secure background for the birth and development of children ... I think the reference I gave in my foreword to the Consultation Paper to the teaching of Jesus ... supports this responsibility for the legislator ... I consider we have a heavy responsibility to ensure that our law recognises the importance of the institution of marriage and also to ensure that it does not impose unnecessary damage on the personal relationships with which it deals, particularly those of parents with their children.'

- review present arrangements for marriage preparation;
- examine how couples with marital problems can be encouraged to seek help as early as possible;
- ensure greater integration of Government policies supporting marriage with those on divorce;
- require couples to attend a compulsory information-giving session before starting the divorce process;
- remove the incentive for couples to divorce quickly by making allegations of fault;
- require a twelve-month period for reflection on whether the marriage can be saved – better protection for domestic violence victims would be available during this period;
- require couples to think through and face the consequences of divorce before it happens;
- ensure that arrangements for children and other matters are settled before divorce is granted;
- allow divorce to be barred where the dissolution of the marriage would cause grave financial or other grave hardship; and
- introduce comprehensive family mediation as part of the divorce process.

It was claimed in the White Paper that the Government's proposals would have many beneficial outcomes, including ensuring that couples with marriage difficulties would be informed about the options available to them. Saveable marriages would be identified; referrals for marriage guidance, and opportunities to explore reconciliation would be facilitated; adequate time would be given to test whether the marriage had genuinely broken down; acrimony, hostility and conflict would be removed or minimised, thereby reducing the worst effects of divorce on children;[6] parents would be encouraged to focus on their joint responsibility to support and care for their children; couples would be encouraged to meet these responsibilities before the marriage was dissolved; and couples would be assisted in this process through family mediation.[7]

The resultant Family Law Bill had a difficult progress through Parliament.[8] A large number of amendments were made in response to

6   See M Richards, *But what about the children? Some reflections on the divorce White Paper* (1995) 7 CFLQ 223, for a consideration of the White Paper proposals relating to children.
7   Preface to the White Paper. Whether these are realistic aspirations for the divorce process is open to question. As one commentator has noted, 'there is a need to recognise that the feelings associated with divorce cannot be swept away simply because the law has decided that they are undesirable. Feelings will continue to demand expression and we should not be afraid of them.' See S Day Sclater *Narratives of divorce* (1997) 19 JSWFL 423.
8   Made more difficult because what is now Part IV of the Act was originally contained in a separate Bill (Family Homes and Domestic Violence Bill 1995) which was knocked back at a very late stage by a small, but vociferous, number of Conservative MPs. As a consequence, reform of divorce law and reform of the law relating to non-molestation and occupation orders were both considered together.

pressure from both Houses. However, the Lord Chancellor was determined that the Bill should become law and it received the Royal Assent in July 1996.

Divorce under the Family Law Act 1996

The Family Law Act 1996 is a radical piece of legislation. It sweeps away the divorce provisions in the Matrimonial Causes Act 1973. Divorce is no longer a remedy for marital misbehaviour, or because parties agree and have demonstrated breakdown by living apart for two years, or for five years where there is no agreement. The 1996 Act reaffirms that a divorce order may only be obtained where a marriage has broken down irretrievably,[9] but instead of requiring factual evidence to substantiate this assertion, the Act substitutes a process with which the parties *must* comply before a divorce order will be made.[10]

General principles underlying the divorce legislation

Because divorce under the Act is purely procedural an attempt has been made to promote good practice in the carrying out of these procedures by incorporating general principles in section 1 of the Act 'to which the court and any person, in exercising functions under or in consequence of Parts II and III *shall* have regard'.[11] These are:

'(a) that the institution of marriage is to be supported;
(b) that the parties to a marriage which may have broken down are to be encouraged to take all practicable steps, whether by marriage counselling or otherwise, to save the marriage;
(c) that a marriage which has irretrievably broken down and is being brought to an end should be brought to an end-
  (i) with minimum distress to the parties and to the children affected;
  (ii) with questions dealt with in a manner designed to promote as good a continuing relationship between the parties and any children affected as is possible in the circumstances; and
  (iii) without costs being unreasonably incurred in connection with the procedures to be followed in bringing the marriage to an end; and

---

9   S 39(1)(a).
10 For a fascinating overview, see S M Cretney, *Family Law – a bit of a racket?* (The Joseph Jackson Memorial Lecture, 1996, (1996) 146 NLJ 91.
11 Emphasis added. Part II concerns divorce and separation; Part III concerns legal aid for mediation.

(d) that any risk to one of the parties to a marriage, and to any children, of violence from the other party should, so far as reasonably practicable, be removed or diminished.'

Attendance at information meetings

A spouse contemplating divorce cannot set the process in motion until he or she has first attended an information meeting.[12] The content of the meeting has yet to be prescribed by regulations, but section 8 makes it plain that spouses can expect to be given information about matters which may arise under the Act's provisions which relate to all aspects of the divorce process.[13] The giving of some information will be mandatory. Section 8(9) states that regulations made in relation to the information meeting *must* make provision for the giving of information about marriage counselling and other marriage support services; the importance to be attached to the welfare, wishes and feelings of children; how the parties may acquire a better understanding of the ways in which children can be helped to cope with the breakdown of a marriage; the nature of the financial questions which may arise on divorce or separation, and services which are available to help the parties; protection against violence and how to obtain support and assistance; mediation; the availability to each of the parties of independent legal advice and representation; the principles of legal aid and where parties can get advice about legal aid; and the divorce and separation process. In addition, the meeting must ensure that the spouse or spouses are given the opportunity to have a meeting with a marriage counsellor and are encouraged to attend that meeting.[14]

There is reason to believe that the requirements made of the information meeting will prove to be impractical. The resources in terms of personnel and finance to meet the demands made are considerable, particularly in view of the requirement that different information meetings must be arranged with respect to different marriages.[15] Many of the matters specified are complex, and the notion that they can be absorbed and understood in the space of a single meeting is unrealistic. As one commentator has said: 'But how long is the information meeting to last? How detailed is the written information to be? Will *Rayden* be handed out? Will the poor be given the *National Welfare Benefits Handbook*? Will the dispensers of information have the legal expertise? What are spouses to

---

12 S 8. Where the spouses are contemplating making a statement of marital breakdown jointly, they may attend separate meetings or the same meeting (s 8(4)).

13 S 8(6)(a).

14 S 8(6)(b). The form and structure of information meetings is the subject of pilot studies. For a critique of the information giving and mediation provisions of the new procedure see S M Cretney, *Lawyers under the Family Law Act* [1997] Fam Law 407.

15 S 8(3).

be told about mediation?"[16] In some instances, the requirement to attend an initial meeting will be experienced as oppressive, distressing or both; in others, attendance at the meeting will be a futile exercise which needlessly consumes time and money. It is known that when in distress people can find it enormously difficult to comprehend even the most basic information, and often need to be given the facts and their implications on several occasions before they can fully grasp what is being said. On a more positive note, many will find it helpful to receive information at the outset of the divorce process which guides them through its practical reality, tells them what to expect, explains whom they would be well-advised to see, and assists them to respond with sensitivity to the reactions of their children to the marriage breakdown. It is, however, suggested that useful knowledge about children coupled with understanding cannot be gleaned from an information meeting. The person imparting the information will not know the children concerned and thus can only speak in generalities. People who lack skills in handling inter-personal relationships will not suddenly acquire such skills by being given information about them. At best, all such information can do is raise a parent's level of awareness of the needs of his or her children. There is a risk, however, that forcing some parents to focus on their children's suffering will increase their sense of failure, add to pre-existing feelings of guilt and cause them to spiral downwards into a level of depression which makes it even harder for them to function effectively as parents than hitherto.

Where only one of the parties makes a statement of marital breakdown, the other must attend an information meeting before making any application to a court with respect to a child of the family or of a 'prescribed description' relating to property or financial matters, or contesting any such application.[17] Thus only the spouse determined on setting the divorce process in motion must attend the requisite meeting; the other can simply bury his or her head in the sand unless, or until, he or she wishes to obtain a court order. Some spouses, probably those who are housebound, disabled, in custody, or who risk violence by going to a particular place, will be excused from attending an information meeting.[18] It seems inevitable, therefore, that some spouses will be divorced without taking any active part in the process.[19]

16 M D A Freeman, commentary on the Act in Current Law Statutes.
17 S 8(5).
18 S 8(2); the exempted parties have yet to be prescribed, but see *Hansard* (HL) Vol 568, cols 983-984.
19 Is there a real risk, therefore, that some non-applicant spouses who have no beneficial interest in the matrimonial home, or other property rights, will not apply for a financial provision and property adjustment order and as a consequence lose entitlement to a share in the family assets which they could normally expect in the exercise of the court's discretionary powers under the Matrimonial Causes Act 1973, ss 22A-25D? Will the provisions of s 9 be sufficient to prevent this outcome occurring? (See below for an explanation of s 9.)

Statement of marital breakdown

A statement of marital breakdown sets the divorce process in motion. A party (or both parties where the statement is jointly made) cannot make the statement until at least three months have elapsed since attendance at the information meeting.[20] The statement must declare that the party or parties making it are aware of the purpose of the period of reflection and consideration[1] and wish to make arrangements for the future.[2] Rules made under section 12 will prescribe the matters with which the statement must comply. These matters include: the information which must accompany the statement; whether the person making the statement has made any attempt at reconciliation since attending the information meeting; requirements relating to service on the other party; information about the arrangements which need to be made in consequence of the breakdown; requirements relating to the preparation and production of documents, and attendance in person; and the information and assistance which is going to be given to the parties and the way in which it will be given.

The court's jurisdiction to entertain marital and related proceedings is exercisable only if:

(a) at least one of the parties was domiciled in England and Wales on the statement date;
(b) at least one of the parties was habitually resident in England and Wales throughout the period of one year ending with the statement date; or
(c) nullity proceedings are pending in relation to the marriage when the marital proceedings commence.[3]

In addition a court continues to have jurisdiction where a separation order is in force or an order preventing divorce has been cancelled.[4]

Statement of breakdown cannot be made in the first year of marriage

The bar on divorce within the first year of marriage is perpetuated by the Family Law Act 1996. Indeed, the period before which a divorce can be obtained has been extended. This is because of the manner in which the bar has been retained. Section 7(6) provides that a statement of breakdown which is made before the first anniversary of the marriage is ineffective for the purposes of any application for a divorce order. As a

---

20 S 8(2).
1   As described in s 7.
2   S 6(2), (3).
3   S 19(2).
4   S 19(3), (4). Orders preventing divorce, and the conversion of separation orders into divorce orders, are explained below.

result, where a marriage quickly fails, the parties will nonetheless have to wait for at least one year before either party can make a statement of breakdown, and it will be seen below that the mandatory period for reflection and consideration does not start to run until the statement is made.[5] However, there appears to be nothing to prevent a spouse attending at an information meeting during the first year of marriage. The Law Commission made no serious attempt to justify the retention of the one-year bar.[6] Is it wise to encourage spouses to work at a marriage which has gone so badly wrong in the first twelve months that at least one party wants a divorce? Is it likely that such a marriage will survive the normal stresses and strains of married life? It is surely better for parties who have made a mistake in their chosen partner to recognise this swiftly before too much emotional, and sometimes physical, harm is done. Those who do not wish to encourage precipitate divorce, but would prefer newly married but estranged spouses to receive counselling with a view to attempting a reconciliation, should bear in mind that one possible outcome of a failed attempt at reconciliation is a baby.

Period(s) for reflection and consideration

Once a statement of breakdown has been made the period for reflection and consideration starts to run. The purpose of this period is to give time for the parties 'to reflect on whether the marriage can be saved and to have an opportunity to effect a reconciliation, and to consider what arrangements should be made for the future'.[7] In this way, divorce is treated as a process over a significant period of time in which parties will face up to the emotional and practical consequences of staying together or deciding to part.[8] There will undoubtedly be a large number of sad cases where one party seeks information and assistance in effecting a reconciliation, and postponing the divorce for as long as possible, while the other seeks information and assistance in ending the marriage and sorting out arrangements for the future as swiftly as possible. The decision to divorce is rarely mutual, at least at the outset.

The minimum period for reflection and consideration is nine months beginning with the fourteenth day after the day on which the statement of breakdown is received by the court.[9] This period applies in all cases.[10] It will be extended for a further six months where one party applies for a

---

5 Consequently, the minimum time in which a divorce can be obtained after marriage is one year, nine months and two weeks.
6 Law Com No 192, para 5.82.
7 S 7(1).
8 The information meeting will have explained to the parties where they can obtain information and assistance during this period.
9 S 7(3).
10 S 7(10).

divorce order and the other party applies to the court within a prescribed period for time for further reflection.[11] The prescribed period will inevitably be brief because the opportunity unilaterally to request an extension of time only arises once all the requisite conditions for applying for a divorce order have been satisfied; and the extension will not be granted unless arrangements for the future as required by section 9 have been made.[12] The applicant is not required to give a reason for his or her request, except to say that time for further reflection is wanted. The period of reflection and consideration is *automatically* extended by six months if there is a child of the family who is under the age of sixteen when an application for a divorce order is made.[13] However, the six-month extension will not occur in either case if:

'(a) at the time when the application for a divorce order is made, there is an occupation order or a non-molestation order in force in favour of the applicant, or a child of the family, made against the other party; or

(b) the court is satisfied that delaying the making of a divorce order would be significantly detrimental to the welfare of any child of the family.'[14]

The period of reflection and consideration stops running if at any time during that period the parties *jointly* give notice to the court that they are attempting a reconciliation but require additional time. It resumes running on the day on which either of the parties gives notice to the court that the attempted reconciliation has been unsuccessful.[15] However, where the period stops running for a continuous period of more than 18 months any application for a divorce order must be made 'by reference to a new statement received by the court at any time after the end of the 18 months'.[16] It is therefore essential that one of the spouses informs the court that the attempt at reconciliation has failed where a request was made for additional time. Unless the court is notified, the parties may find when they come to seek a divorce that they are out of time, and must

---

11 S 7(10), (13). The prescribed period is not yet known.

12 S 7(10)(b).

13 S 7(11), (13). A divorce order is made at the end of the process. The extended period comes to an end on there ceasing to be any children of the family under 16, s 7(14). The Law Commission did not support the proposal that the period of reflection and consideration should automatically be longer where there were dependent children. They took the view that considerable harm and additional bitterness may be caused by prolonged uncertainty and delay because there are children, Law Com No 192, para 5.28.

14 S 7(12). This is one of the few ways in which the impact of domestic violence on the applicant is recognised. It seems likely that there will be an increase in applications under Part IV partly in order to facilitate swifter divorce.

15 S 7(8).

16 S 7(9).

start the process all over again.[17] Moreover, parties risk being out of time where they informally extend the period of reflection and consideration. Section 5(3)(b) provides that an application may not be made for a divorce order where a period of one year has passed since the end of the period for reflection and consideration. At that point the statement lapses and should the parties still wish to divorce one or both must make a fresh statement of breakdown.

Thus to summarise: the minimum period for reflection and consideration is nine months. Where there is a child of the family under the age of 16 the minimum period increases to 15 months. Where there is no such child, but at the 'eleventh hour' the non-applicant spouse applies for more time, the minimum period increases to 15 months. The only way in which an applicant for divorce can avoid the period for reflection and consideration lasting for 15 months rather than the minimum 9 months is either through obtaining an order under Part IV of the Act, or by satisfying the court that delay would be significantly detrimental to the welfare of any child of the family.[18] Where both parties want further time to reflect and consider whether to divorce they can do so for 18 months without jeopardising their right to obtain a divorce order, but once the period of reflection and consideration is interrupted for more than 18 months, they are back to square one. Where no formal application for additional time has been made an application for a divorce order must be made within 12 months of the expiration of the period of reflection and consideration.

What happens during the period of reflection and consideration?

The answer to the question 'what happens during the period of reflection and consideration?' depends on how each party views that period,[19] and whether they choose to make use of the facilities on offer to which their attention will have been drawn at the information meeting.[20] It is clear that they *must* use this period to make financial arrangements for the future because unless they have made such arrangements to the satisfaction of the court by the end of the period a divorce order will not be made.[1] It is also clear that the intention of the Act is that the majority of

---

17 They will not have to attend another information meeting, but will have to make a new statement of breakdown.

18 S 7(12).

19 See the marvellously measured irony of the comments by S M Cretney in Divorce Reform in England: Humbug and Hypocrisy or a Smooth Transition, in M D A Freeman (ed) *Divorce: Where Next?* (Dartmouth, 1996).

20 Such information may, of course, only come to the attention of one spouse as the non-applicant is not required to attend a meeting. He is, however, likely to do so at some stage during the process, for unless he does he cannot make any application, or contest any application, to the court about a child or property and financial matters.

1 S 3(1)(c).

couples will resolve disputes between them through the process of mediation. Section 13 provides that after a statement of breakdown has been received by the court, it may direct each party to attend a meeting at which an explanation of the facilities available for mediation will be given, and at which they will be provided with an opportunity to agree to take advantage of these facilities.[2]

Marriage counselling may be provided free of charge during the period of reflection and consideration, but only to those who would not be required to make any contribution towards the cost of mediation. Moreover, it will only be provided free where it appears to the marriage counsellor to be suitable in all the circumstances.[3]

Settling arrangements is a pre-condition for divorce

Marriages under the 1996 Act cannot be terminated as quickly as under the Matrimonial Causes Act 1973. The Government took the view that making the parties settle their arrangements for the future a pre-condition for divorce would emphasise the responsibilities of marriage and parenthood.[4] Part of the Government's thinking behind this pre-condition was that:

> '... when faced with the problems of dealing with the practical consequences of divorce, some couples may come to realise that they need to reconsider their position and, perhaps with the help of counselling, find some way of re-negotiating their relationship so that they and their children can have a future together.'[5]

The Government recognised that there were genuine concerns that pre-conditions could be abused, and could give an advantage to an unreasonable or malevolent spouse, or provide a formidable bargaining chip for the more powerful or determined party, and it stressed in the White Paper that it would take steps to ensure that weaker or vulnerable parties and their children were sufficiently protected. [6]

---

2   S 13(1). Parties will be required to attend the same meeting unless one or both asks for separate meetings or the court considers separate meetings are more appropriate, s 13(3). A spouse who is a victim of domestic violence is likely to wish to attend at a separate meeting. However, there appears to be no method open to the court to identify such a spouse, and she may be too frightened or disempowered to identify herself.
3   S 23(1)-(5).
4   The Law Commission, by contrast, recommended that making arrangements should not be a pre-condition of divorce, as this might rush the parties into making unsuitable arrangements and play into the hands of one of the parties.
5   *Facing the Future*, para 4.33.
6   Ibid, paras 4.29 and 4.30. For this reason there are exemptions built into the statute; see below.

Arrangements about the children

For many spouses, the most painful aspect of their failed marriage is coming to terms with the realisation that they will not be able to parent their children in the same manner as hitherto. Normally this change affects both parties, and each must be willing to negotiate over their new relationship with their children. Unless any disagreement is resolved during the period of reflection and consideration, the parties risk the divorce order being delayed.[7] The court will scrutinise the arrangements for the children which have been, or are proposed to be, made for their upbringing and welfare in order to determine whether it should exercise any of its powers under the Children Act 1989.[8] Where the court is not in the position to exercise its powers without giving further consideration to the case, and where there are exceptional circumstances which make it desirable in the interests of the child, the court may direct that the divorce order is not made until the court orders otherwise.[9]

The court must treat the welfare of the child as paramount when arriving at these decisions.[10] When determining whether to exercise any of its powers under the Children Act 1989, section 11(4) provides that it must also have particular regard, on the evidence before it, to:

'(a) the wishes and feelings of the child in the light of his age and understanding and the circumstances in which those feelings were expressed;

(b) the conduct of the parties in relation to the upbringing of the child;

(c) the general principle that, in the absence of evidence to the contrary, the welfare of the child will best be served by-

  (i) his having regular contact with those who have parental responsibility for him and with other members of his family; and

  (ii) the maintenance of as good a continuing relationship with his parents as possible; and

(d) any risk to the child attributable to-

  (i) where the person with whom the child is living or proposes to live;

---

7 S 3(1)(c) states that the court may only make a divorce order where the requirements of s 9, concerning financial arrangements, are satisfied, and s 9(5) states that the requirements of s 11 must have been satisfied. See also, s 11(2)(c).

8 S 11(1)(b). The private law orders available under the Children Act 1989 are explained in ch 2. Under that Act the court should not make an order relating to the upbringing of a child unless it considers that doing so would be better for the child than making no order at all (s 1(5)). When making an order the court is guided by the checklist in s 1(3).

9 S 11(2).

10 S 11(3).

      (ii) any person with whom that person is living or with whom
          he proposes to live; or
      (iii) any other arrangement for his care and upbringing.'

How far the provisions in section 11(2)-(4) will encourage courts to become
more interventionist where children are affected by divorce remains to be
seen. It is clearly stated in section 11(2)(c) that a divorce order should
only be delayed where the circumstances are 'exceptional', so courts will
normally be able to terminate the marriage despite there being outstanding disagreement over the children's upbringing. Moreover, any delay
must be in the interests of the child; it appears, therefore, that holding up
a divorce order should not be used to force the parties to make use of the
mediation or other facilities provided under the Act.

    Settlement of arrangements about the children may be made easier with
the introduction in section 11(4)(c) of what amounts to a statutory presumption in favour of contact between a child and his parents, and the
extension of this presumption to other members of the child's family.[11] A
provision of this kind was long overdue,[12] and it should help to put the final
nail in the coffin of one parent treating the children as part of the property
allocated on divorce over whom she or he now has absolute rights. An
opportunity was, however, missed to state clearly that the presumption of
contact is displaced where either the child, or the parent looking after the
child, was treated with violence by the non-residential parent.[13] Including
the wider family within the presumption also comes to the aid of grandparents and other relatives who often suffer deeply from loss of regular, or
sometimes any, contact with grandchildren, nephews, nieces and cousins
on the breakdown of a marriage. Where a divorcing spouse refuses to permit
a child to have a relationship with a relative, that relative can point to the
principle enshrined in section 11(4)(c)(i) when seeking the court's leave to
apply for a contact order under section 8 of the Children Act 1989, and can
argue that the provision implies that a contact order to a family member
should normally be made at the substantive hearing of the application.

    Courts are already required to consider any harm which a child has
suffered or is at risk of suffering when making orders under the Children
Act 1989.[14] Section 11(4)(d) supplements this requirement by directing a

---

11 S 11(4)(c)(i) is drafted in terms of 'those who have parental responsibility for him' which,
    on rare occasions, will widen the range of persons affected. Where the couple who are
    divorcing are not the child's parents but have treated him as a child of the family, their
    divorce could have the effect of precipitating an order for contact between the child and
    his actual parents.
12 It is extraordinary that children in care must be allowed to have contact with a parent
    who has caused them to suffer, or to be likely to suffer, significant harm, unless a court
    authorises otherwise, Children Act 1989, s 34 (see ch 3), yet one parent is able to prevent
    the other having contact for months, and sometimes years without giving any cogent
    reason for the refusal, a situation which can continue unless and until a court makes a
    contact order under the Children Act 1989, s 8.
13 See the discussion of the impact of violence on contact orders in ch 4.

divorce court to focus on any risk to the child which is attributable the place where, or persons with whom, the child is living or proposes to live. This could turn out to be an important protective provision for children. New partners of divorcing spouses have not hitherto been directly involved in the statement of arrangements about the children, yet such partners do not always take kindly to the children, and some are resentful of their presence and treat the children with varying degrees of hostility and unkindness. This may come to light under the new divorce process. Much depends on what is made of the phrase the court shall have particular regard, *on the evidence before it*, of the matters listed. It is to be hoped that any statement of arrangements for the children placed before the court will be expected to take account of all of the provisions of section 11. Provided that it does, the statement should draw the court's attention to others living in the household with the residential parent, should tell of the parties' conduct in relation to the upbringing of the children, and should give an account of the children's wishes and feelings.[15] Even where this evidence is provided, there is no provision for an independent person to scrutinise the veracity of what is said, or to report on the children's views, and without such a safeguard the protective provisions in section 11(4) may serve little practical purpose.[16] However, children may sometimes be involved in mediation, and mediators are required to make arrangements to encourage the parties to consider the welfare, wishes and feelings of each child, and whether each child should be given an opportunity to express his feelings at the mediation.[17] Where during the course of mediation a child expresses fears about his own safety, the code of practice with which the mediator must comply will surely make provision for this eventuality, and allow the mediator to draw the matter to the attention of the relevant authorities.[18]

Financial arrangements

A court will not make a divorce order unless the requirements in section 9 of the 1996 Act about the parties' financial arrangements for the future

---

14 Children Act 1989, s 1(3)(e).

15 S 11(4).

16 Where the court does have concerns about risk to a child it can direct a report from a court welfare officer, Children Act 1989, s 7, and where significant harm is suspected, it can ask the local authority to investigate with a view to pursuing care proceedings (s 37).

17 S 27, which inserts s 13B into the Legal Aid Act 1988. S 13B(8) is silent on how the mediator should respond if no account is taken by the parties of the child's views. C Piper in *Divorce reform and the image of the child* (1996) 23 JLS 364, criticises the rather simplistic approach, as she sees it, to the welfare of the child contained within the Act, the preceding White Paper and the Law Commission Report. As she points out: 'The welfare of children has been identified so closely with the reduction of conflict that mediation is equated with welfare'.

18 See Law Commission Report No 192, para 5.48.

are satisfied.[19] Section 9(2) states that one of the following must be produced to the court:

'(a) a court order (made by consent or otherwise) dealing with their financial arrangements;[20]
(b) a negotiated agreement[1] as to their financial arrangements;
(c) a declaration[2] by both parties that they have made their financial arrangements;
(d) a declaration by one of the parties (to which no objection has been notified to the court by the other party) that -
(i) he has no significant assets and does not intend to make an application for financial provision;
(ii) he believes that the other party has no significant assets and does not intend to make an application for financial provision; and
(iii) there are therefore no financial arrangements to be made.'

These provisions are amplified in a limited manner in Schedule 1 of the Act. However, the details of what information the parties will be expected or required to provide have yet to be clarified in regulations.[3] Moreover, it is not clear what status these arrangements will have should one party subsequently wish to resile from them. If compliance with paragraphs (b) and (c) is treated as analogous to having obtained an order within paragraph (a) then parties must take great care before they submit such arrangements for court approval. Once a consent order has been approved it is extremely difficult to persuade a court to overturn it and to substitute fresh terms, and the same principles may be applied to negotiated agreements and declarations.[4] Unless courts keep tight control over whether, and when, financial and property arrangements can be re-opened after divorce, there is a strong possibility that there will be a significant increase in post divorce applications for court orders.[5]

---

19 'Financial arrangements' has the same meaning as in s 34(2) of the Matrimonial Causes Act 1973.
20 A pending appeal against the order is to be disregarded (Sch 1, para 5(2)).
1   That is, a written agreement which has been reached as a result of mediation or any other form of negotiation involving a third party (Sch 1, para 7).
2   The declaration must be in a prescribed form, and in prescribed cases be accompanied by prescribed documents and satisfy other requirements (Sch 1, para 8). Where the parties' arrangements include a division of pension assets or rights any declaration must be a statutory declaration (s 9(8)).
3   For a comment on one of the pilot schemes, operating in Bristol, see District Judge John Frenkel *Ancillary relief pilot scheme in operation* [1997] Fam Law 726.
4   See the discussion of consent orders in ch 8.
5   See ch 8 for an account of when financial provision and property adjustment orders must be applied for under the Family Law Act 1996. It is clear that just because mediation clients reach a written agreement it should not therefore be taken that they are necessarily satisfied with the decision that has been reached. See C Richards *Managing conflict and resolving disputes* [1998] Fam Law 169.

Persons exempted from making financial arrangements

A party may be excused from complying with section 9(2), and a divorce order may be made, if the circumstances fall within one of four exemptions specified in Schedule 1. The first is where the other party has delayed in complying with requirements of the court or has otherwise been obstructive, or where, for reasons beyond the applicant's control, or that of the other party, the court has been prevented from obtaining the information which it requires to determine the financial position of the parties. The second is where because of the ill health or disability (whether physical or mental) of the applicant, the other party or a child of the family, or an injury suffered by any of them, the applicant has not been able to reach agreement with the other party about their financial arrangements and is unlikely to be able to do so in the foreseeable future. In addition, the court must be satisfied that a delay in making a divorce order would be significantly detrimental to any child of the family, or would be seriously prejudicial to the applicant. The third is where the applicant has found it impossible to contact the other party, and as a result it has been impossible for the applicant to reach agreement with the other party about their financial arrangements. The fourth is where an occupation order or a non-molestation order is in force in favour of the applicant or a child of the family, made against the other party, and the applicant has, during the period of reflection and consideration, taken such steps as are reasonably practicable to try to reach agreement about the parties' financial arrangements, but has been unable to do so and is unlikely to be able to do so in the foreseeable future. As with the second exemption, the applicant must also show that a delay in making the divorce order applied for would be significantly detrimental to the welfare of any child of the family, or would be seriously detrimental to the applicant.[6]

The potential for litigation over these provisions, particularly those in the first exemption, are immediately apparent. The other party may object to being accused of delaying the proceedings, or may be angered by being labelled obstructive, and wish to defend his name.[7] It seems that powerful and convincing evidence will be needed to satisfy the tests of 'significant detriment' to the welfare of a child, or 'serious prejudice' to the applicant. The exemptions were included in response to criticisms that the Government's determination that financial matters should be settled before any divorce order was made would 'play into the hands of an unreasonable, spiteful or malicious spouse or provide a formidable bargaining chip for the more powerful or determined party'.[8] It is not stated whether an applicant will be entitled to legal aid to assist her in obtaining an exemption.[9]

6 The requirements of s 11 must be satisfied in all four cases.
7 Will he be given legal aid to do so?
8 White Paper, para 4.29.
9 Will the exemption provisions be brought to the parties' attention at the information meeting?

Mediation

Mediation, according to the Government's White Paper, can encourage couples to seek marital counselling, accept responsibility for the ending of the marriage, acknowledge that there may be conflict and hostility and a strong desire to allege fault and attribute blame, deal with feelings of hurt and anger, address issues which may impede the spouse's ability to negotiate settlements amicably, particularly the conduct of one spouse, and focus on the needs of their children rather than on their own personal needs.[10] Moreover, there is evidence that mediation is effective at reducing bitterness and tension, improving communication between couples, and helping couples reach agreement on a wide range of issues.[11] It therefore came as no surprise that the Government formed the view that mediation should be a central part of the new divorce process.

Mediation is not defined in the Act, nor is its purpose other than in outline,[12] but there is no doubt that it is aimed at securing a more constructive approach to marital breakdown and divorce.[13] In the White Paper the Government saw mediation as 'a process in which an impartial third person, the mediator, assists couples considering separation or divorce to meet together to deal with the arrangements which need to be made for the future'.[14] The mediator is a facilitator as distinct from an adviser, and the process of mediation is intended to empower the parties to reach their own decisions, rather than to have decisions imposed upon them. As one commentator has said: 'the subjective standards of the parties are as important, if not more important, than external standards of fairness, such as the law; the quality of the process and satisfaction of the parties is more important than reaching an agreement for the sake of settlement.'[15]

Will mediation bring about improvement in the divorce process?

It is easy to to credit mediation with more positive outcomes than it merits, and to gloss over the very real concerns which have been expressed about

---

10 *Looking to the Future, Mediation and the Ground for Divorce*, Cm 2799 (HMSO, 1995), para 5.4. It does, however, appear as though the Government failed to understand the distinct and separate concepts of reconciliation and mediation. Reconciliation is about helping spouses to resolve their differences with the aim of cementing the marriage; mediation is about assisting spouses to negotiate an agreed settlement.

11 Ibid, para 5.15.

12 Legal Aid Act 1988, s 13B(7) which briefly states the main principles of the code of practice with which mediators must comply.

13 For an account of the range of family mediation services, and the ways in which they are regulated, in England and Wales, France, Ireland, Scotland and the USA, see L Webley, *A Review of the Literature on Family Mediation* (Institute of Advanced Legal Studies, 1998). The review was prepared for the Lord Chancellor's Advisory Committee on Legal Education and Conduct.

14 *Looking to the Future*, para 5.4.

15 C Richards, *The expertise of mediating* [1997] Fam Law 52.

the process.[16] Reservations about the fairness and impartiality of mediation have arisen even where mediation was carried out by trained personnel with self-selected and willing participants. There is cause for real concern that standards of professionalism will fall when the Family Law Act 1996 comes into force and the process is widely recommended; demand for the service is almost certain to out-strip the supply of appropriately trained people. Certainly it is worrying that there has been no large empirical study which demonstrates that mediation will be able to operate successfully in the ways envisaged.[17]

The mediator is required to comply with a code of practice,[18] which requires the mediator to have in place arrangements designed to ensure:

'(a) that parties participate in mediation only if willing and not influenced by fear of violence or other harm;
(b) that cases where either party may be influenced by fear of violence or other harm are identified as soon as possible;
(c) that the possibility of reconciliation is kept under review throughout mediation; and
(d) that each party is informed about the availability of independent legal advice.'

Paragraphs (a) and (b) only partly address the most serious reservations which have been expressed about mediation, namely whether it is an acceptable process in cases where there has been domestic violence.[19] Mediation is not a partisan exercise; the mediator is neutral and he or she may not appreciate that the mediation sessions are being dominated by one party of whom the other is in fear.[20] The requirement in section 13B(7)(a) of the Legal Aid Act 1988 that the mediator's code of practice must ensure that 'parties participate in mediation only if willing' creates

16 There is extensive literature, see the bibliography to L Webley, *A Review of the Literature on Family Mediation* (Institute of Advanced Legal Studies, 1998). For useful background research, see G Davis, *Partisans and Mediators: The Resolution of Divorce Disputes* (OUP, 1988). See also, University of Newcastle Conciliation Project Unit *Report to the Lord Chancellor on the Costs and Effectiveness of Conciliation in England and Wales* (1989); J M Eekelaar and R Dingwall (eds) *The Development of Conciliation in England*, in *Divorce Mediation and the Legal Process* (Clarendon Press, 1988).
17 A false dichotomy was presented in the White Paper between a non-adversarial system of mediation, as opposed to an adversarial system involving lawyers. Most family law solicitors are members of the Solicitors Family Law Association and adhere to its code of practice. Consequently, many assert that they go to great lengths to ensure that their clients do not enter into bitter adversarial disputes, and that they make every effort to persuade clients to negotiate sensibly.
18 Legal Aid Act 1988, s 13B(6). The code has not yet been drawn up.
19 See also, Legal Aid Act 1988, s 15(3F), below.
20 This difficulty also raises the issue of who should assess a party's capacity to mediate. Where the mediator takes on this function does this come into conflict with the neutral and facilitative nature of the mediator's role?

the danger that a false sense of confidence will be induced that victims of domestic violence will screen themselves out. This is unlikely. Research suggests that many victims of violence are not identified, and there is a real risk, therefore, that abused and fearful spouses will arrive at arrangements with which they are in disagreement because of the gross power imbalance between the parties.[1] Indeed, any power imbalance gives rise to this risk and few unhappy marriages are evenly matched. Moreover, it is notorious that divorcing spouses are frequently temporarily psychologically impaired,[2] and a party who is suffering from guilt or low self-esteem, or who simply cannot cope with any more conflict, may concede on key issues because this offers the easiest way out of a painful process.[3]

The original scheme proposed under the Family Law Bill required all those spouses who qualified for legal aid to mediate rather than to have legal representation unless they could show 'acceptable reasons' for not participating in the process. However, there was considerable opposition to this proposal and it was not carried forward into legislation. Instead, a new provision (section 15(3F)) was inserted into the Legal Aid Act 1988 which states:

'A person shall not be granted representation for the purposes of proceedings relating to family matters, unless he has attended a meeting with a mediator-
(a) to determine-
    (i) whether mediation appears suitable to the dispute and the parties and all the circumstances, and
    (ii) in particular, whether mediation could take place without either party being influenced by fear of violence or other harm; and

---

1   Indeed, victims of domestic violence may be incapable of engaging properly in mediation, see the analysis in L Webley, *A Review of the Literature on Family Mediation* (Institute of Advanced Legal Studies, 1998), pp 92-94; F Kaganis and C Piper *Domestic violence and divorce mediation* [1994] JSWFL 265; C Piper and F Kaganis *The Family Law Act 1996, section 1(d) – how will 'they' know there is a risk of violence?* (1997) 9 CFLQ 269; M Roberts, *Family mediation and the interests of women – facts and fears* [1996] Fam Law 239; contrast M Black and D Price, *Mediation and the shadow of the past* [1996] Fam Law 693.

2   See further S Day Sclater *Divorce – coping strategies, conflict and dispute resolution* [1998] Fam Law 150. In a small-scale study of 11 people going through a divorce, completed over a period of 8 months, researchers administered a general health questionnaire at 2-monthly intervals. The average scores of the respondents throughout the study period were more than double the score which is accepted in general practice as indicative of possible psychiatric morbidity.

3   There is also a cultural dimension. How, for example, can a mediator with a Christian faith and background realistically engage with parties from a totally different background and faith, let alone have the awareness of what amounts to an acceptable, as distinct from improper, power imbalance?

(b) if mediation does appear suitable, to help the person applying for representation to decide whether instead to apply for mediation.'[4]

Thus choice whether to use mediation rather than to seek assistance from a lawyer will continue to be available to all divorcing couples, including those eligible for legal aid.[5] However, it is probable that the professed advantages of mediation will be strongly stressed at the initial information meeting, and that those couples who are required to attend a meeting under section 15(3F) of the Legal Aid Act 1988 will normally be advised to engage in the process.

Mediation is carried out by either a single mediator or by two mediators working together. In the latter case, one is likely to have professional experience of counselling, conciliation or work with children and the other to have knowledge and experience of family law. Both should be trained as mediators, and the College of Family Mediators has been established which accredits mediation courses.[6] Family mediation is a growth industry, and its proper regulation is essential if clients are to receive the kind of service the White Paper claimed that mediation can offer.[7]

Mediation in family matters originated in the setting up of voluntary and often charitable services to provide marriage counselling,[8] and to assist parties to reach amicable agreement about the care and upbringing of their children through conciliation.[9] The extension of mediation to cover financial and property arrangements after divorce has thrown into relief how far it is necessary for mediators to have knowledge of this complex area of family law.[10] Mediators are told in their training that they should

---

4   An assisted party has to make a contribution to the costs of mediation just as he does for legal representation, and a statutory charge will attach to property 'recovered or preserved' (s 13C).

5   See A King, *No legal aid without mediation* [1998] Fam Law 331 in which some of the many implications of the implementation of the new system, arising out of a pilot scheme in the Bristol area, are discussed.

6   The Lord Chancellor's Advisory Committee on Legal Education and Conduct overviews education, training and regulatory standards for family mediation.

7   See further C Richards, *Why do mediators need further supervision?* [1998] Fam Law 105, who sets out very pithily some of the pitfalls mediators may fall into during the mediation process.

8   Such as the Marriage Guidance Council, later renamed Relate. The various different churches offer their own marriage counselling facilities.

9   The first independent family conciliation service was piloted in Bristol in the late 1970s. Subsequently, both in court and out of court conciliation schemes were developed, and most major towns acquired voluntary conciliation agencies, later known as mediation agencies. However, the dependency of these agencies on discretionary local authority funding, and personal donations from members of the public, has made them vulnerable to closure through lack of adequate resources. New provisions in the Legal Aid Act 1988 (s 13B inserted by s 27 of the Family Law Act 1996) empower the Legal Aid Board to make contracts to secure the provision of mediation.

10 See ch 8.

not advise the parties; their role is to facilitate, to see 'fair play' and to diffuse anger and other obstructive emotions. Mediation is based on the notion that an acceptable outcome is achieved where parties arrive at their own agreement about arrangements for the future, whether or not those arrangements would have been arrived at had they been negotiated by solicitors, or imposed by a court. This notion is very disturbing to lawyers. They find it flawed because the process may lead to parties giving up important legal rights for the simple reason that they did not appreciate that they had these rights.

Lawyers bargain for their clients within the shadow of the real law. Spouses, by contrast, may mediate with one another within the shadow of a law which is nothing more than folk lore. Their articulated or unarticulated understanding of their respective rights may therefore distort their vision of whether the agreement reached is fair and just. A lawyer acting for one party has the means to force the other party to disclose his property and financial holdings. It is unclear whether, and how, full disclosure of assets will be accomplished in mediation. How can a mediated agreement be fair where one party does not know the nature and extent of the resources under discussion? Even where full disclosure is achieved, unless parties are advised about the significance of the various assets and the options open to them, how can they be expected to make an informed decision on how money and property should be distributed and divided between them? The likelihood is that parties will reach agreements which fail to take adequate account of the law relating to such matters as mortgages, debts, tax, social security, housing, pensions, child support and spousal maintenance. Consider the following simple examples. How can a spouse who agrees psychologically that a clean break is the appropriate outcome appreciate the importance of having at least a nominal sum in periodical payments?[11] How can parties be expected to negotiate the intricacies of pension splitting? Where it is clear that the wife needs the family home in the foreseeable future because the parties have agreed that the children will live with her, is not the husband (particularly if he feels guilt about the breakdown of the marriage) likely to concede that the property is transferred into her sole name? How can a lay client be expected to understand the availability of such alternatives as *Mesher* and *Martin* orders?[12] Is there not a real risk that parties who reach their own solution will in practice restrict the options open to them through lack of knowledge about available alternatives? Parties will not be content with an agreed outcome if they subsequently discover that a far preferable and fairer arrangement could have been arrived at if only it had been drawn to their attention.

Existing mediation schemes have acknowledged some of these anxieties, and as a consequence before, or during, the mediation process it may be suggested to both parties that it would be advisable for each to obtain

11 See ch 8.
12 Ibid.

independent legal advice. In addition, each spouse is usually invited to ask his or her own lawyer to check the terms of an arrangement agreed at the conclusion of the mediation sessions. This response, of course, pre-supposes that parties who have chosen to engage in mediation rather than litigation will have their own lawyers.[13] Moreover, it places a heavy burden on lawyers who are unlikely to have full knowledge of the facts upon which the agreement was based, or what alternatives have been considered and rejected, and why. There will also be psychological pressure on lawyers not to unpack, or look too closely, at agreements freely reached in mediation. It will take a strong-minded solicitor to undermine an agreement arrived at after a number of mediation sessions.[14]

Breakdown counselling and child-focused mediation have undoubtedly assisted children and families to cope with the distress caused by divorce, and professionals skilled in the art of engaging parents in how they can best minimise their children's suffering have performed, and will continue to perform, an invaluable function.[15] It will therefore be disastrous if the entire mediation process falls into disrepute because of loss of public confidence in its ability to handle property and financial arrangements. Yet there is a real risk that this may happen as a result of some mediators being asked to engage in activities which are beyond their competence. Would not public money better be spent on raising the standards of family law solicitors?[16]

Circumstances in which divorce orders are made

Section 3 of the Act provides that if an application to the court for a divorce order is made by one or both of the parties to a marriage, the court shall make the order if (but only if):

'(a) the marriage has broken down irretrievably;
(b) the requirements of section 8 about information meetings are satisfied;
(c) the requirements of section 9 about the parties' arrangements for the future are satisfied; and
(d) the application has not been withdrawn.'

Evidence of irretrievable breakdown is provided by compliance with the process in Part II of the Act, and the application must be accompanied by

---

13 Where one has and one has not, this is almost bound to exacerbate any power imbalance.
14 Where the parties have been legally aided for mediation, it is not clear how far a solicitor giving independent legal advice will also be eligible to receive payment. Presumably he or she will have to be included in a scheme for which the Legal Aid Board has entered into a franchising arrangement.
15 See ch 4 for further discussion of the role of mediation in children cases.
16 Which are already high with regard to minimising conflict because of the sterling efforts of the Solicitors Family Law Association.

a declaration by the party making the application that having reflected on the breakdown, and having considered the requirements relating to the parties' arrangements for the future, the applicant believes that the marriage cannot be saved.[17] It is clear that either party may apply for the divorce order, not simply the spouse who set the process in motion by filing a statement of breakdown.[18] A joint application has the advantage that it allows for joint acknowledgement that the marriage should be brought to an end. The order, which dissolves the marriage, comes into force on being made.[19] However, a divorce order may not be made if an order preventing divorce is in force under section 10.[20]

Orders preventing divorce

Section 10(1) provides that if an application for a divorce order has been made by one of the parties, a court may, on the application of the other party, order that the marriage is not to be dissolved. This order, which is called 'an order preventing divorce', may be made only if the court is satisfied:

'(a) that dissolution of the marriage would result in substantial financial or other hardship to the other party or to a child of the family; and

(b) that it would be wrong in all the circumstances (including the conduct of the parties and the interests of any child of the family), for the marriage to be dissolved.'[1]

Background to orders preventing divorce

When, in 1969, the law was extended to include non-consensual divorce where the parties had lived apart for at least five years there was considerable concern that the financial consequences of divorce could cause grave financial or other hardship to some women being divorced in middle age. Consequently a court was required to refuse a decree based on the fact of five years of living apart where such hardship was established, and where it would in all the circumstances be wrong to dissolve the marriage.[2] It was essential to establish the causative link between the hardship alleged and the divorce. Often much hardship would already

---

17 S 5(1)(d).
18 S 5(2).
19 S 2.
20 S 3(2).
1   S 10(2).
2   Matrimonial Causes Act 1973, s 5. In determining the issue, the court had first to consider all the circumstances, including the conduct of the parties to the marriage and the interests of those parties and of any children or other persons concerned; s 5(2)(b). At the time of

have been caused by the breakdown of the marriage, but the concern of section 5 was with whether the *divorce* would be causative of grave financial or other hardship.[3] There was no indication in the Act of the type of hardship contemplated, but section 5(3) provided that hardship included the loss of the chance of acquiring any benefit which the respondent might acquire if the marriage were not dissolved. Case law on section 5 focused on a wife's loss of pension rights. Some of that case law has since been overtaken by new powers to divide pension assets and rights, which mean that a spouse's loss of the benefit of a pension is no longer automatically occasioned by divorce.[4]

The Law Commission took the view that as the original rationale of the hardship bar was to safeguard the position of the innocent spouse who did not want to be divorced, there was clearly a case for extending the protection of the bar to all who wished to invoke it.[5] As the Commission pointed out, the fact that the bar had rarely been invoked did not mean that it had been ineffective. However, the manner in which the Commission recommended retention of the bar was somewhat lukewarm: 'It provides an important protection for a small group of people who may still face serious hardship which the law is unable at present to redress in other ways. If it retains substantially the same form as the present bar, it is unlikely to be invoked, and even less likely to succeed, in any but a tiny minority of cases.'[6] The Government accepted the Law Commission's recommendation, expressing the view that the extent and usefulness of the bar may not necessarily be clear from previously decided cases, and that it may well be useful as a 'bargaining chip' for the weaker partner.[7] However, the Government also stated that it did not intend to change the present statutory wording or the way in which the law in this area has been applied.[8] What then should be made of the revised drafting of section 10?

Will orders preventing divorce be available in more than a minority of cases?

There are two substantive differences in the wording of section 10. The hardship must be 'substantial' not 'grave', and it includes hardship to a

---

writing, the law of divorce is still to be found in the Matrimonial Causes Act 1973, and s 5 still applies. Reference to s 5 is nonetheless written in the past tense in order to distinguish the law developed under s 5 from the new provisions under s 10 of the Family Law Act 1996.

3 As a result the bar was rarely invoked and rarely successful. No divorce was refused on the 'other hardship' ground. See *Banik v Banik* [1973] 1 WLR 860; *Rukat v Rukat* [1975] 1 All ER 343.

4 Matrimonial Causes Act 1973, s 25B-D.

5 Law Com 192, para 5.73. However, part of their reasoning was founded on there being no method of dividing occupational pensions, which has since been overcome.

6 Ibid, para 5.75.

7 White Paper, para 4.47.

8 Ibid.

child of the family. These changes undoubtedly have the potential to widen the scope of the defence; substantial is a lesser standard than grave, and children as well as adults are included. Nonetheless, many of the principles derived from the law relating to section 5 of the 1973 Act appear pertinent to the proper interpretation of section 10. Thus the notion that there is little to be gained in keeping alive a marriage which has become an empty shell will probably continue strongly to influence the judges.[9] The substantial financial hardship claimed will almost always relate to loss of income from a pension or otherwise, and it will usually be possible to compensate a spouse for this type of financial hardship by making more generous lump sum and property adjustment orders; or provision which falls outside the court's powers to order, such as paying the premiums on insurance policies, can be secured through undertakings (which have binding force).[10] Sometimes state benefits will make up the shortfall, and a spouse cannot complain about loss of pension rights where she obtains the same income from a different source. As Finer J emphasised in *Reiterbund v Reiterbund*,[11] there is no shame to be attached to the receipt of state benefits, and the law has a duty to foster this attitude.

The chances of a young wife being able to persuade a court to refuse to make a divorce order on the ground of substantial financial hardship appears remote.[12] Its main purpose is to protect wives who have reached middle age from losing financial security. In *Julian v Julian*[13] the loss of pension could not be compensated from the husband's other resources, and there was a substantial monetary gap between the financial provision the husband could provide and the financial benefits the wife would receive if she remained married. As this loss would cause the wife grave financial hardship a divorce was refused. But as has been explained, pension earmarking and pension splitting are now possible. Moreover, a spouse cannot expect to be compensated pound for pound for what she will lose by divorce; it is the *substantial* nature of the hardship which she must establish, not that divorce will cause her financial loss.[14]

Other substantial hardship to a party or a child of the family flowing from divorce also gives the courts discretion to make an order preventing divorce. Several unsuccessful attempts were made to invoke this safeguard under section 5 of the Matrimonial Causes Act 1973, and it never

---

9 *K v K (Financial Relief: Widow's Pension)* [1997] 1 FLR 35.
10 On the use of undertakings, see ch 8. In *Parker v Parker* [1972] 1 All ER 410 the wife's loss of pension rights amounted to grave financial hardship, but the court found that this could be alleviated by the husband purchasing a deferred annuity for her and securing his obligation to pay the annual insurance premium by taking out a second mortgage on his house.
11 [1974] 2 All ER 455.
12 *Mathias v Mathias* [1972] 3 All ER 1.
13 (1972) 116 Sol Jo 763; see too *Johnson v Johnson* (1982) 12 Fam Law 116 where a divorce was also refused. These appear to be the only successful cases.
14 *Le Marchant v Le Marchant* [1977] 3 All ER 610. Though it must be conceded that courts are likely to be more ready to find 'substantial' hardship than 'grave' hardship.

succeeded.[15] The cases reflected the multi-cultural nature of English society, and courts clearly found it difficult to know how properly to respond to assertions that a woman would become an outcast in her own community, in her country of origin, or even within her close family should she be divorced. They stated that the matter should be determined by adopting an objective standard, and that it was one of 'fact and degree'.[16] However, these early decisions put an end to applications made in reliance on the defence of grave other hardship. The reduction of the level of hardship from grave to substantial may give rise to fresh attempts to protect members of ethnic communities who allege that divorce will lead them to be shunned or otherwise discriminated against. Such applicants will, of course, have to show that the hardship stems from the divorce and not the breakdown of the marriage or the separation of the parties.

The applicant, whether alleging substantial financial hardship or substantial other hardship, must overcome the additional hurdle of persuading the court that it would be 'wrong, in all the circumstances (including the conduct of the parties and the interests of any child of the family), for the marriage to be dissolved'.[17] In *Reiterbund v Reiterbund*[18] the court ruled that wrong must be construed as meaning unjust, and that the court must exclude from its consideration the fact that the divorce application had been brought by a 'guilty' husband against a non-consenting wife.[19] However, where the the other party had behaved in a wrongful manner towards the applicant this could lead to the grant of a decree despite a finding that the applicant would suffer grave financial hardship.[20] It is difficult to know whether this approach will be carried forward into the new law or to speculate on how courts might select the circumstances which demonstrate that dissolving the marriage would be wrong. By making conduct a relevant consideration, the bitterness and hostility which the new legislation was intended to avoid could be reintroduced with a vengeance.

An order preventing divorce has no time limit. However, an application to cancel the order can be made by one or both parties and the court must cancel the order unless still satisfied that the conditions for making the order still exist.[1] An order preventing divorce may include conditions which must be satisfied before an application for cancellation can be made. This provision could prove useful. The conditions will give guidance to the

---

15 *Banik v Banik* [1973] 3 All ER 45; *Banik v Banik (No 2)* (1973) 3 Fam Law 174; *Parghi v Parghi* (1973) 117 Sol Jo 582; *Rukat v Rukat* [1975] 1 All ER 343; *Balraj v Balraj* (1981) 11 Fam Law 110.
16 *Banik v Banik*, above.
17 S 10(2)(b).
18 [1974] 2 All ER 455.
19 Any other approach would have been tantamount to striking out the five-year living apart fact as a basis for divorce under the Matrimonial Causes Act 1973.
20 *Brickell v Brickell* [1973] 3 All ER 508; disapproving dictum to the contrary in *Dorrell v Dorrell* [1972] 3 All ER 343.
1 S 10(3).

spouse seeking a divorce on how he or she is expected to mitigate the substantial financial or other hardship to the other spouse, or child, which will flow from the divorce, and will indicate what other factors, if any, make it wrong in the court's view for the marriage to be dissolved. Moreover, the provision prevents repeated applications for cancellation of the order, as the application will not be entertained unless the conditions have been complied with.

The real value of section 10 will be its use to prevent divorce unless and until adequate financial arrangements are made in compliance with section 9. It has the unusually attractive feature of placing a bargaining chip in the hands of the financially weak spouse,[2] and this arguably compensates for the provision's disadvantages. It undoubtedly has the potential to give rise to unpleasantly contentious hearings, and it is anticipated that there will be a significant number of applications made in reliance on section 10 until case law establishes the type of threshold which must be overcome before 'substantial financial or other hardship' and 'wrongfulness' will be found. However, it seems unlikely that the court's powers to prevent a divorce will be brought to the attention of many spouses who settle their financial arrangements through mediation. Thus the people whom section 10 was designed to protect may be the very same people who do not know of the provision's existence or do not appreciate its significance.[3]

Separation orders

The Family Law Act 1996 continues to make provision for those who wish formally to separate but not to divorce for reasons of conscience or other motives. What might these other motives be? It will often be financially unwise for spouses to divorce. Their property and other financial resources will rarely allow both to retain the same standard of living as hitherto; indeed, divorce often impoverishes at least one of the parties.[4] However, where spouses are young or in middle age, the perceived advantages of divorce in putting an end to a failed marriage and of giving each the

---

2   *Le Marchant v Le Marchant* [1977] 3 All ER 610 provides a useful example of the Court of Appeal compelling a husband to 'volunteer' a solution, by withholding the divorce decree until he made an acceptable proposal to alleviate the wife's hardship. See also *K v K (Financial Relief: Widow's Pension)* [1997] 1 FLR 35.

3   It seems probable that poorer people will be referred to mediators, and that the better off will choose to spend their money on a 'partisan' lawyer rather than a 'neutral' mediator. Yet paradoxically, loss of pension rights may hit poor spouses more than rich spouses, for in the case of the latter, the loss can often be mitigated by other orders and arrangements.

4   Where an ex-husband has more children by a new partner he will often be unable to provide adequate support for his ex-wife and children. He will, however, be obliged to provide some child support, and this deduction from his income is likely to result in his second family having little money to spare either; see ch 9.

emotional and legal freedom to form fresh relationships and to remarry are likely to outweigh the economic disadvantages of divorce, at least in the mind of one of the parties. Where spouses are in late middle age or elderly, it may be particularly unwise for them to divorce because of the financial consequences. Either or both may have been contributing to a pension fund for many years which makes provision for a surviving spouse. This widow's or widower's benefit will be lost by divorce, and compensatory provision may have to be made for the benefit of the losing spouse out of existing resources, an outcome which reduces the total assets available to be distributed between both parties, and thus both lose as a result. A separation order does not affect rights under a will, and anticipated inheritance rights may also depend on a potential beneficiary retaining the status of the other party's spouse. However, the Act retains the rule that where a separation order is in force, and while the parties to the marriage remain separated, where one of them dies intestate his or her property devolves as if the surviving party had died before the intestacy occurred.[5]

A separation order may give spouses the assistance they need by giving them access to the court's ancillary jurisdiction without formally ending the rights to which they are entitled as spouses.[6] The procedure for obtaining the order mirrors that for obtaining a divorce order, with the following differences. A statement of marital breakdown may be made during the first year of marriage, and the period for reflection and consideration lasts for nine months in all cases. It is not extended where there are children of the family and cannot be extended on application by one of the parties. Nor can an order preventing a separation order be made. Thus a separation order allows for earlier and speedier relief and will be made where the marriage has broken down irretrievably, where the requirements of section 8 about information meetings are satisfied, and where the requirements of section 9 about the parties' arrangements for the future are satisfied.[7] Where the court is considering an application for a divorce order and an application for a separation order in respect of the same marriage it must proceed as if it were considering only the application for the divorce order unless there is an order preventing divorce in force, or the court makes such an order,[8] or the statement of marital breakdown was made before the first anniversary of the marriage,[9] or the extended period of reflection and consideration for divorce purposes has not expired.[10]

---

5 S 21. The drafting of s 21 does, however, appear to allow for succession on intestacy where the parties have resumed cohabitation. This must surely be desirable, since it is unlikely that parties would formally apply for the cancellation of a separation order.
6 For further comment, see the discussion of the decree of judicial separation under the Matrimonial Causes Act 1973, above.
7 S 3(1).
8 S 3(3).
9 S 7(6). Such a statement is ineffective for the purposes of an application for a divorce order.
10 S 7(13).

Conversion of a separation order into a divorce order

A separation order may subsequently be converted into a divorce order on application, provided that the second anniversary of the marriage has elapsed and there is no order preventing divorce in force.[11] However, where there is a child of the family under the age of 16, or where the divorce application has been made and the other party applies within a prescribed period for time for further reflection, the separation order may not be converted into a divorce order unless there is an occupation order or non-molestation order in force, or the court is satisfied that delaying making the divorce order would be significantly detrimental to the welfare of any child of the family.[12] The restraints on conversion of the order cease to apply 'at the end of the period of six months beginning with the end of the period for reflection and consideration by reference to which the separation order was made; or earlier, on there ceasing to be any children of the family'.[13] It can be seen that these restraints mirror the requirements which must be complied with before a divorce order can be made, and appear to be designed solely to secure that the divorce order requirements are not evaded. No additional period for reflection and consideration is imposed where a formally separated spouse wishes to divorce.

11 S 4(1), (2).
12 S 4(4), (5).
13 S 4(4)(c).

Chapter 8

Money and property on marriage breakdown

Provision for a spouse in the immediacy of marriage breakdown
 Financial provision orders
Protecting the right of occupation in the matrimonial home
 'Matrimonial home rights'
 A spouse with an equitable interest
 Registration of matrimonial home rights
Financial provision and property adjustment orders – the statutory framework
 The role of discretion in orders for financial and property provision
Financial provision and property adjustment orders – their link with the
  court's powers to make divorce orders
 Timing of applications for orders
Periodical payments for an ex-spouse
 Why should one ex-spouse continue to provide income for the other?
 Clean-break and periodical payments
 Circumstances where periodical payments are likely to be ordered
 Circumstances where periodical payments are not likely to be ordered
 Duration of an order for periodical payments
 Rehabilitative periodical payments
 Limiting the duration of orders – variation traps
Quantification of orders for periodical payments
 A nominal sum order
 'One-third rule'
 'Net effect' approach
 'Subsistence level' approach
Secured periodical payments
Lump sum orders
 Lump sums and clean break
 Lump sum or periodical payments?
Property adjustment orders
 Property transfer orders
 Sale orders
 Settlement orders
The statutory guidelines in section 25(1) and (2)

Chapter 8

Money and property on marriage breakdown

Provision for a spouse in the immediacy of marriage breakdown

During marriage spouses normally live together in the same home and, as time goes by, they are likely to accumulate possessions for their joint and separate use. The income of the household, which may be derived from earnings, investments or both, will be provided by one or both of the spouses. When neither is employed, the means for their support usually comes from state benefits. Where there are children of the family the home, possessions and income are used for the children's benefit as well. When families are functioning harmoniously such an informal arrangement works well. The fact that the spouses' rights, interests, responsibilities and claims have become tangled together, without resort to any of the formalities which usually accompany transactions between strangers involving property and money, is not a problem. However, when a marriage breaks down informal arrangements no longer work; the tangle must be untangled. Suddenly it becomes essential to identify the nature of the financial obligations, if any, which each spouse owes to the other, and to the children of their family. Suddenly it becomes important to know what rights each spouse has in relation to the matrimonial home and its contents; whether one or other can continue to live there, or whether it must be sold; and whether a dependent spouse can continue to receive the benefit of the other's income and future earnings.

Financial provision orders

On marriage breakdown a spouse may be in need of immediate financial assistance in the form of periodical payments.[1] She may also need a lump

---

1 Where her only source of income is state benefits she may also be under pressure from the Department of Social Security to institute proceedings for a periodical payments order, because such an order will lead to the reduction, or elimination, of the burden of her support from state funds.

sum to enable her to pay existing debts and to reimburse her for other expenditure. A spouse seeking periodical payments during the subsistence of the marriage has a choice of proceedings open to her. She can apply to the family proceedings court under the Domestic Proceedings and Magistrates' Courts Act 1978, section 1, for an order to be made for periodical payments and/or a lump sum not exceeding £1,000.[2] Alternatively, she can apply to a county court, or to the High Court, under the Matrimonial Causes Act 1973, section 27, for an order for secured or unsecured periodical payments, and a lump sum, unlimited in amount. In either case she must establish that the respondent has failed to provide her with reasonable maintenance. The family proceedings court may be the most appropriate forum in a case when the applicant believes that the breakdown of the marriage may prove to be only temporary, and where she is reluctant to institute divorce proceedings at this stage. Research reveals that, with rare exceptions, parties to proceedings brought under the Domestic Proceedings and Magistrates' Courts Act 1978 have low incomes. Research also tells us that, in the past, the majority of orders made in family proceedings courts were for small sums and mainly for the benefit of any children of the family.[3] The advent of the Child Support Act 1991 has resulted in the role of the family proceedings court being substantially reduced. The Child Support Act 1991 prevents a court making an order for periodical payments for a child of the family except in very limited circumstances, so reducing the role of the courts. The impact of the Act means that the majority of spouses will approach the Child Support Agency where an agreement over how much the absent parent should pay to the parent with care of the children cannot be negotiated. However, a spouse can apply in his or her own right to the family proceedings court for financial support for himself or herself, whether or not there are children requiring maintenance.[4]

Section 1 of the Domestic Proceedings and Magistrates' Courts Act 1978 provides:

> 'Either party to a marriage may apply to a magistrates' court for an order under section 2 of this Act on the ground that the other party to the marriage—
> (a) has failed to provide reasonable maintenance for the applicant; or
> (b) has failed to provide, or to make a proper contribution towards, reasonable maintenance for any child of the family.'

---

2 The order would be made under s 2. However, where the parties agree that a financial provision order should be made, the application should be brought under s 6.

3 See O R McGregor, L Blom-Cooper and C Gibson *Separated Spouses* (Duckworth, 1970); S Garlick *Judicial separation: a research study* (1983) 46 MLR 719; C Smart *The Ties that Bind* (Routledge and Kegan Paul, 1984). Although this research is dated, there is no reason to believe that magistrates' courts attract a different group of separated spouses nowadays than they did hitherto.

4 For ease of writing, henceforth it will be assumed that the applicant is the wife unless otherwise stated.

In practice it is unlikely that the respondent will litigate over whether he has wilfully neglected to maintain the applicant. Instead he is likely to concede the ground, and any contest will be over whether an order should be made in the light of the parties' respective financial circumstances and, if so, how it should be quantified. In relation to failure to provide reasonable maintenance for the applicant, this is relatively easy to establish in a case where the wife has no income, or only a limited income, of her own. There is an obligation on spouses to maintain one another during marriage, and even where a respondent has no source of income from which he can pay his wife maintenance, such as where he is unemployed and living on state benefits, the ground of failure to provide reasonable maintenance can nonetheless be established. The family proceedings courts have a long-standing tradition of making nominal orders, for example for 10 pence per annum, in favour of wives in cases where their husbands lack the means to make reasonable financial provision for them.[5] The advantage to the wife of a nominal order is that it recognises that the husband has an obligation to maintain her, and it is an order which can be varied upwards should his circumstances subsequently improve. Paragraph (b) has been rendered virtually obsolete because the Child Support Act 1991 prevents a court making an order in favour of a child.[6]

Where the grounds for making an order are established or conceded the court, in deciding whether to exercise its powers and, if so, in what manner, must have regard to all the circumstances of the case, give first consideration to the welfare while a minor of any child of the family, and have regard to the several matters which are listed in section 3. These are virtually the same matters as those to which a court must have regard in the exercise of financial provision and property adjustment powers on the grant of a decree of divorce, nullity or judicial separation.[7] The differences are that, because the parties are still married, the clean break principle does not apply, and the spouses' mutual obligation to maintain one another continues. Also, of course, there is no need to consider benefits which might be lost by reason of the marriage being terminated. The powers of the family proceedings court are also much more circumscribed than those of the divorce court. The family proceedings court may only order unsecured periodical payments and/or a lump sum.

Proceedings may also be brought in the county court for periodical payments and/or a lump sum on the grounds of failure to provide reasonable maintenance for a spouse, or a child of the family, under section 27 of the Matrimonial Causes Act 1973.[8]

---

5   See, for example, *Chase v Chase* (1983) 13 Fam Law 21.
6   Child Support Act 1991, s 8. On the Act, and financial and property provision for children generally, see ch 9.
7   Matrimonial Causes Act 1973, s 25: see below.
8   In relation to children, the court's powers are similarly negated by s 8 of the Child Support Act 1991.

Where the breakdown of the marriage appears to be more permanent, and where the process of divorce and separation has been formalised by a statement of marital breakdown which has been received by the court, the court may make an order for financial provision in favour of either spouse.[9] A financial provision order is for periodical payments and a lump sum only. Periodical payments and lump sum orders may provide essential support for the applicant in the immediacy of marriage breakdown where she has no income, or only a small income, of her own. Such payments may be of particular value where one party has left the matrimonial home and there is a risk that he will default on paying the mortgage or the rent. The other party can pay the rent, mortgage or other outgoings out of the periodical payments and such payments are as good as if made by the spouse who is liable to pay; the mortgagee, landlord or other creditor cannot refuse to accept such payments.[10]

Protecting the right of occupation in the matrimonial home

In the immediacy of marriage breakdown swift attention should be given to the nature of each spouse's rights in relation to the matrimonial home. Where the matrimonial home is vested in the name of one spouse alone, there is a danger that the owning spouse may enter into some kind of transaction with a third party in relation to the property without either the knowledge or consent of the non-owning spouse. Such a transaction may give rights in the matrimonial home to the third party which are binding on the non-owning spouse. A non-owning spouse has 'matrimonial home rights' in the matrimonial home, and may have other rights too. Where she fails to protect her rights by registration she may be at risk of losing them, or of finding that they are subordinated to those of the third party; in some cases this is likely to mean that she will lose the roof over her head.

At common law each spouse had a personal right to live in the matrimonial home because he or she was married. This right was a right flowing from status and personal to the spouses only. It was not a property right and therefore it could not bind third parties. This meant that a purchaser who had notice that a spouse with merely a personal right of occupation was living in the matrimonial home could nonetheless enforce any claims he might have against the property. This doctrine left spouses, usually wives, and any dependent children living with them, vulnerable to third party claims. An extreme example arose in *National Provincial Bank Ltd v Ainsworth*,[11] when a deserting husband, and father of four children, mortgaged the family home to a bank and then defaulted on the payments due. The bank brought proceedings for possession and was successful,

---

9   Matrimonial Causes Act 1973, s 22A. For statements of marital breakdown, see ch 7.
10 Family Law Act 1996, s 30(3).
11 [1965] AC 1175.

even though it had notice of the wife's occupation of the house. As a consequence the Matrimonial Homes Act 1967 was enacted to remedy this situation.[12] It conferred a right of occupation which was binding not only on the other spouse but which, by registration, would bind third parties.

Matrimonial home rights

The current law is contained in sections 30-33 of the Family Law Act 1996.

Section 30 provides:

'(1) This section applies if -
(a) one spouse is entitled to occupy a dwelling house by virtue of
    (i) a beneficial estate or interest or contract; or
    (ii) any enactment giving that spouse the right to remain in occupation; and
(b) the other spouse is not so entitled.
(2) Subject to the provisions of this Part, the spouse not so entitled has the following rights ("matrimonial home rights")—
(a) if in occupation, a right not to be evicted or excluded from the dwelling house or any part thereof by the other spouse except with the leave of the court given by an order under section 33;
(b) if not in occupation, a right with the leave of the court so given to enter into and occupy the dwelling house.'

Thus it can be seen that a spouse who has no property right which entitles her to occupy the matrimonial home nonetheless has a personal right to live there. This is an important safeguard when a marriage breaks down because it prevents the owner spouse from asserting a claim to have exclusive possession of the property as sole owner. A spouse who has left the matrimonial home continues to have a right of occupation despite the fact that he or she has not obtained the leave of the court to enter into and occupy the dwelling house. But the right of entry is conditional on leave being obtained.[13] Any other construction of the words of the statute would render the protection it affords relatively useless since, in the main, it is when relationships break down, and one spouse leaves, that recognition of the right of occupation becomes imperative.

Section 30 subsections (3)-(5) give important protection to the spouse with matrimonial home rights. Subsection (3) states that any payments or tender made in respect of rent, mortgage payments or other outgoings by that spouse must be treated as if made by the other spouse. Subsection (4) states that occupation by a spouse with matrimonial home rights is

---

12 Replaced by the Matrimonial Homes Act 1983, a consolidating Act.
13 *Watts v Waller* [1972] 3 All ER 257.

treated as occupation by the other spouse for the purposes of certain Rent Act and Housing Act provisions which give security of tenure. Subsection (5) states that any payment of mortgage instalments by the spouse with matrimonial home rights may be treated by the mortgagee as having been made by the other spouse. However, this does not affect any claim of the paying spouse to an interest in the house by virtue of the payment.

A spouse with an equitable interest

The Family Law Act 1996 extends to those cases where a spouse has matrimonial home rights by reason of the other spouse being a beneficiary under a trust. In that event, the trustees are bound by all the provisions in subsections (3)-(5). Where the legal estate is vested in one spouse alone, but where both have a beneficial interest in the property, section 30(9) provides that:

> '... a spouse -
> (a) who has an equitable interest in a dwelling-house or in its proceeds of sale, but
> (b) is not a spouse in whom there is vested (whether solely or as joint tenant) a legal estate in fee simple or a legal term of years absolute in the dwelling house,
> is to be treated, only for the purpose of determining whether he has matrimonial home rights, as not being entitled to occupy the dwelling-house by virtue of that interest.'

This, on its face, seems strange because a spouse with a beneficial interest in the property already has a right of occupation by virtue of that interest. Why therefore should such a spouse be given a separate right of occupation under the Family Law Act 1996? The reason is that, because of the law relating to the registration of equitable interests, a spouse with an equitable interest could otherwise be in a more vulnerable position than a spouse with a mere right of occupation.

A distinction must here be drawn between unregistered and registered land. In the case of unregistered land, a spouse with an equitable interest could be particularly vulnerable. This is because an equitable interest is not registrable as a land charge under the Land Charges Act 1972 and therefore, if the interest is to be protected against a purchaser for value, notice of that interest must be given to such a third party by some other means. However, unless the spouse with the equitable interest is aware that a transaction involving the land is about to take place, she does not know whom to notify, or how to set about drawing her equitable interest to the purchaser's attention. She is afforded some assistance by the doctrine of 'constructive notice'. The courts have stated that, in some situations, a purchaser ought to have known about the existence of an equitable interest in the land even if in fact he did not know of it.[14] In particular, provided that a spouse remains living on the premises, it is likely that a purchaser for value will be deemed to have constructive notice of a spouse's equitable interest in the property even where the other spouse is also in occupation.[15] But of course when marriages break down one spouse usually leaves the home. When it is the spouse with an equitable interest only who leaves, then her equitable interest, and with it her right of occupation flowing from that interest, will probably be defeated by a purchaser for value without notice of it.[16] Section 30(9) of the Family Law Act 1996 recognises that it is important, therefore, that a spouse with an equitable interest should be given an independent statutory right of occupation, matrimonial home rights, which she can register, and thereby protect, against third parties.

In the case of registered land (which now covers most of the land in the country) a spouse with an equitable interest is in a better position because she can protect that interest through registration. Indeed, equitable interests are minor interests requiring protection on the register, and the general principle applying to registration is that a purchaser takes free of any interest which is not protected on the register. But where a spouse with an equitable interest is in actual occupation of the land, then even if she has not registered that interest it may still be protected on the basis that it is an overriding interest, which therefore binds a purchaser.[17] It is nonetheless suggested that, despite these safeguards, a spouse with an equitable interest should register her matrimonial home rights flowing from her status as a spouse. There is always the risk in a case where a spouse claims that she has an equitable interest in the property that a court might rule that she has acquired no such interest.[18] By contrast, a spouse's right of occupation in the matrimonial home through having matrimonial home rights is conferred by statute. It cannot therefore be questioned, and affords her exactly the type of protection she needs in the immediacy of breakdown, namely it maintains the roof over her head.

---

14 And see the Law of Property Act 1925, s 199(1).
15 See *Hodgson v Marks* [1971] Ch 892, at pp 934-935; *Williams & Glyn's Bank Ltd v Boland* [1981] AC 487, at pp 505-506, 511; *Kingsnorth Finance Ltd v Tizard* [1986] 2 All ER 54; cf *Caunce v Caunce* [1969] 1 All ER 722. Minor children of the legal owner with a beneficial interest are not in actual occupation, 'they are only there as shadows of occupation of their parents', *Hypo-Mortgage Services Ltd v Robinson* [1997] 2 FLR 71, per Nourse LJ at p 72; he also stated, obiter, that *Caunce v Caunce* had been disapproved so far as spouses were concerned.
16 Cf *Kingsnorth Finance Ltd v Tizard*, above, where the spouse with the equitable interest returned regularly at weekends to the former matrimonial home.
17 Land Registration Act 1925, s 70(1)(g); *Williams & Glyn's Bank Ltd v Boland* [1981] AC 487.
18 Cf *Gissing v Gissing* [1971] AC 886; and see further ch 9 where the establishment of an equitable interest by an unmarried partner is discussed.

Registration of matrimonial home rights

Section 31 provides that if at any time during a marriage one spouse is entitled to occupy a dwelling house by virtue of a beneficial estate or interest, then the other spouse's matrimonial home rights are a charge on that estate or interest.[19] A spouse can protect her matrimonial home rights by registering them in the appropriate manner. In the case of unregistered land the right is registrable as a class F land charge under the Land Charges Act 1972.[20] In the case of registered land a notice must be lodged under the Land Registration Act 1925.[1]

The only way of protecting matrimonial home rights against third parties who acquire an interest in the land for value is by registration, and registration only. Failure to register these rights could prove disastrous for a spouse whose only entitlement to live in the matrimonial home depends on having such rights. In the case of unregistered land the doctrine of notice does *not* apply, so that a third party who is aware that a spouse with matrimonial home rights is living on the premises does not take his interest in the land subject to her right of occupation *unless it has been registered*.[2] Similarly, in the case of registered land, matrimonial home rights are *not* an overriding interest under the Land Registration Act 1925 notwithstanding that a spouse is in actual occupation of the dwelling house.[3] So, for example, if the owner spouse were to execute a legal charge over the home in favour of a bank, that mortgage would take priority in any subsequent legal proceedings *unless* the non-owner spouse had first registered his or her matrimonial home rights. Consequently it is imperative to register these rights as soon as the marriage starts to run into serious difficulties. Conversely, once registered, the statutory matrimonial home rights provided by section 30(2) take priority and are effective against all third parties who subsequently acquire an interest in the property.[4] This gives very real protection to the non-owner spouse because no purchaser is likely to be interested in buying, or leasing, a property which is subject to matrimonial home rights; and no mortgagee

---

19 Section 30 does not apply to a dwelling-house which has at no time been, and which was at no time intended by the spouses to be, a matrimonial home of theirs, s 30(7).

20 S 2(7).

1 Family Law Act 1996, s 31(10).

2 Land Charges Act 1972, s 2(8); *Midland Bank Trust Co Ltd v Green* [1981] AC 513.

3 Family Law Act 1996, s 31(10)(b).

4 Exceptionally, in the case of unregistered land, a purchaser who correctly searches the register, and who receives an official search certificate which does not disclose the registered class F charge, will take free: see the Land Charges Act 1972, s 10(4). The defeated spouse will be left with an action in negligence against the Chief Land Registrar or other employee of the Registry: see *Ministry of Housing and Local Government v Sharp* [1970] 2 QB 223.

is likely to lend money when property subject to an occupation right is offered as security for the loan.[5]

Financial provision and property adjustment orders – the statutory framework

The Matrimonial Causes Act 1973 establishes a specific regime for dealing with financial and property provision for spouses and children where a marriage is ended by a divorce order, or where a separation order or a decree of nullity are granted. A court has extensive powers: it can alter existing property rights, give or remove occupation rights, and generally rearrange the spouses' financial affairs in the light of their past, present and anticipated future circumstances.

It is helpful at the outset to have an overview of the main features of the statutory framework. Part II of the Matrimonial Causes Act 1973 provides a comprehensive code for the provision of financial relief for the parties to a marriage and any children of the family.[6] Sections 21-25D specify the nature of the courts' powers. Orders can be made for secured and unsecured periodical payments, for a lump sum or sums, for the sale of property, for the creation and variation of settlements, and for rights in property to be transferred from one spouse to the other. Section 25 sets out what are sometimes referred to as the 'statutory guidelines'. These identify an extensive list of matters to which a court must have regard in deciding how to exercise its powers. Section 25A contains what are commonly known as the 'clean break' provisions. These direct a court, in all cases of divorce and nullity, to consider whether and, if so, how and when it would be just and reasonable to terminate the financial obligations of each party towards the other. Section 25B-D is concerned with pension provision and division. Section 28 is concerned with the duration of continuing financial provision orders in relation to the parties to the marriage, and the effect of remarriage. Section 29 deals with the duration of orders for children.[7] Section 31 empowers courts to vary or discharge certain orders. Sections 33A, 34, 35 and 36 govern a court's powers in relation to consent orders, and the validity and alteration of maintenance agreements. Section 37 enables the court to restrain, or set aside, dispositions of property made with the intention of defeating a claim for financial relief.[8]

---

5   The protection is not absolute; a spouse may lose a registered right of occupation because the court decides to terminate it under the Family Law Act 1996, s 33(3)(e). Indeed, a court may decide to terminate the right of occupation where a purchaser has purchased property with notice of it, because it may, inter alia, take the purchaser's circumstances into account: see *Kaur v Gill* [1988] 2 All ER 288.

6   Although in relation to the children, the courts' powers have been curtailed by the Child Support Act 1991: see above, and also ch 9.

7   See ch 9.

8   References to statutory provisions in this chapter will henceforth be to the Matrimonial Causes Act 1973, unless otherwise stated.

From this brief overview it can be seen that all aspects of the spouses' financial and property affairs need to be considered within the totality of the court's powers. In practice other considerations are also likely to be influential such as how the costs of the proceedings are to be paid, whether any lump sum payment will be used to reimburse the legal aid fund, and whether such a payment will be treated as a resource for social security purposes.

The role of discretion in orders for financial and property provision

It is important to realise that the law relating to financial provision and property adjustment is not a rule-based area of law which has as its chief aim the goals of certainty and parity between one case and another. Rather agreements and orders are made within the framework of a statutory code which allows courts to exercise broad discretionary powers.[9] It will be seen in the analysis which follows that there are no definite and settled answers to some fundamental questions of principle and policy about the nature of the spouses' rights once their marriage comes to an end. Nor can the continuing nature of their obligations to one another be stated with confidence. Thus there is no easy and straightforward answer to the question 'how will property jointly acquired and paid for during a marriage be divided and distributed between the spouses when their marriage is terminated by decree?' A reply certainly cannot be given in the absence of a substantial amount of information about each of the spouses' current and future financial and personal circumstances. Even where all relevant information has been obtained,[10] there is a wide range of possible solutions which could either be negotiated between the spouses, or ordered by a court. Similarly, it is extraordinarily hard to respond to the question 'is there a support obligation owed by one spouse to the other after their marriage has come to an end and, if so, how will it be quantified?' The answer to this question turns on a variety of considerations, and there can often be no certainty in the response. This means that the law in this area is more than usually unpredictable. It also explains why it may take some considerable length of time to reach a negotiated settlement. Moreover, judges tend to limit their judgments to the facts before them and appear reluctant to articulate universal principles to be applied in all cases. Even where a court articulates the principles to be applied, the judgment usually does not contain directions about how these principles should be translated into practical solutions. Furthermore, the courts have not always been consistent in the application of principles when faced

9 See *Dart v Dart* [1996] 2 FLR 286 at p 294 where Thorpe LJ commented: 'Parliament might have opted for a community of property system or some fraction approach. It opted instead for a wide judicial discretion that would produce a bespoke solution to fit the infinite variety of individual cases'. See also *Thomas v Thomas* [1995] 2 FLR 668.
10 The difficulties faced by practitioners in obtaining full disclosure of the opposing party's assets and income is clearly illustrated in *Baker v Baker* [1995] 2 FLR 829.

with similar facts;[11] and it is sometimes difficult to identify which rulings point to general principles, and which are confined to the facts of the case before the court.

This is not to assert that discretionary decision-making is the same as unprincipled decision-making.[12] However, for principles to emerge and to be followed, there needs to be some kind of shared understanding and consensus amongst the judiciary about how particular questions of law and policy might best be resolved, and sometimes this appears to be lacking. It is suggested that the judges themselves do not always feel confident about how best to determine some of the fundamental questions of principle and policy which may arise in a particular case. This may be because the guidance given in the statutory framework contains principles, and policy directives, which may pull in opposing directions when applied to a particular set of facts.[13] Rather, the judges have tended to emphasise that each case must be determined on its own merits and that cases have limited precedent value. The cautious approach of the judiciary to precedent in this context was clearly expressed by Ormrod LJ in *Martin v Martin*[14] when he said:

> 'I appreciate the point [counsel] has made, namely, that it is difficult for practitioners to advise clients in these cases because the rules are not very firm. That is inevitable when the courts are working out the exercise of the wide powers given by a statute like the Matrimonial Causes Act 1973. It is the essence of such a discretionary situation that the court should preserve, so far as it can, the utmost elasticity to deal with each case on its own facts. Therefore it is a matter of trial and error and imagination on the part of those advising clients. It equally means that the decisions of this court can never be better than guidelines. They are not precedents in the strict sense of the word.'

Financial provision and property adjustment orders – their link with the court's powers to make divorce orders

As the Family Law Act 1996 was passing through Parliament, the Lord Chancellor made it clear that he was determined that all matters relating

---

11 For example, contrast the approach taken to the obligation to provide periodical payments for children in *Tovey v Tovey* (1978) 8 Fam Law 80 with that in *Delaney v Delaney* [1990] 2 FLR 457.

12 For further discussion, see G Davis, S M Cretney and J Collins, *Simple Quarrels* (Oxford: Clarendon Press, 1994); E Jackson, F Wasoff, M Maclean and R Emerson Dobash, *Financial support on divorce: the right mixture of rules and discretion* (1993) 7 IJLF 230.

13 For example, the clean break provisions in s 25A lean towards a spouse not receiving periodical payments, but the direction to give first consideration to the welfare of the children in s 25(1) leans towards the residential parent obtaining substantial support in her own right, since any diminution in her income will normally inevitably rebound on the children.

14 [1978] Fam 12, at p 20.

to the parties financial arrangements should be resolved before a divorce order could be made.[15] In this he was successful, and the outcome is reflected in section 3 of the Family Law Act 1996. This provides, inter alia, that a court may only make a divorce order where the requirements of section 9 about the parties' arrangements for the future are satisfied. Section 9(2) states that one of the following must be produced to the court:

'(a) a court order (made by consent or otherwise) dealing with their financial arrangements;

(b) a negotiated agreement as to their financial arrangements;

(c) a declaration by both parties that they have made their financial arrangements;

(d) a declaration by one of the parties (to which no objection has been notified to the court by the other party) that:

(i) he has no significant assets and does not intend to make an application for financial provision;

(ii) he believes that the other party has no significant assets and does not intend to make an application for financial provision; and

(iii) therefore there are no financial arrangements to be made.'

The rule that the parties must have first settled their financial arrangements before they can obtain a divorce can be avoided in limited circumstances only.[16]

What is meant by 'financial arrangements'? The term is all-embracing and must not be confused with the more limited meaning given to 'financial provision'.[17] Section 34(2) of the Matrimonial Causes Act 1973 provides that:

'"Financial arrangements" means provisions governing the rights and liabilities towards one another when living separately of the parties to a marriage (including a marriage which has been dissolved or annulled) in respect of the making or securing of payments or the disposition or use of any property, including such rights and liabilities with respect to the maintenance or education of any child, whether or not a child of the family.'[18]

Thus financial arrangements include both 'financial provision' and 'property adjustment' orders.

What is meant by a 'financial provision order'? Section 21(1) of the Matrimonial Causes Act 1973 provides that financial provision orders

---

15 Hansard, 30 November 1995, Vol 567, col 703.

16 Where the court is satisfied that one or more of the exemptions in Sch 1, paras 1-4 apply. These exemptions are discussed in ch 7.

17 See below.

18 Family Law Act 1996, Sch 1, para 6 provides that for the purposes of the schedule and s 9 of the Act 'financial arrangements' has the same meaning as in s 34(2) of the 1973 Act.

are orders made under sections 23 and 27 of the Act in favour of a party to a marriage or in favour of a child of the family. These are:

'(a) a periodical payments order;
(b) a secured periodical payments order;
(c) an order for the payment of a lump sum.'

What is meant by a property adjustment order? Section 21(2) provides that 'property adjustment orders'[19] are orders made under section 24 of the Matrimonial Causes Act 1973. These are:

'(a) an order for the transfer of property to the other party or a child;
(b) an order for settlement of property in favour of a spouse or child;
(c) an order varying any marriage settlement;
(d) an order extinguishing or reducing either parties' interest in a marriage settlement.'[20]

Timing of applications for orders

The timing of applications for financial provision and property adjustment orders, and the circumstances in which orders can be made, are closely monitored by the legislation. In relation to financial provision orders, section 22A(3) provides:

'The court may make -
(a) a combined order against the parties on one occasion,
(b) separate orders on different occasions,
(c) different orders in favour of different children,
(d) different orders from time to time in favour of the same child,[1]
but may not make, in favour of the same party, more than one periodical payments order, or more than one order for the payment of a lump sum, in relation to any marital proceedings, whether in the course of the proceedings or by reference to a divorce order or separation order made in the proceedings.'

What is the effect of this provision? First, it means that only one periodical payments order and one lump sum order can be made, but the orders do not have to be obtained on the same occasion. Secondly, it means that once an order for periodical payments has been made it cannot be altered except on an application to vary the order. Thirdly, it reaffirms that a lump sum order is a final order. There is no power under the Matrimonial Causes Act 1973 for a court to vary a lump sum order.

---

19 'Property' means property to which a party is entitled either in possession or reversion: s 21(4).
20 A marriage settlement means an ante-nuptial or post-nuptial settlement.

Similar provision is made in respect of property adjustment orders. Section 23A(1) provides that a court may make one or more property adjustment orders. Section 23A(2) provides:

'If the court makes, in favour of the same party to the marriage, more than one property adjustment order in relation to any marital proceedings, whether in the course of the proceedings or by reference to a divorce order or separation order made in the proceedings, each order must fall within a different paragraph of section 21(2).'

Section 23A(3) encourages the court to make all such orders on the same occasion.

What is the effect of these provisions? They make it clear that more than one type of property adjustment order can be made, and that they can be made at different times.[2] But because a court can make one type of property adjustment order on one occasion only it is reaffirmed that property adjustment orders are final orders. However, the full effect of these provisions is unclear. Does the requirement that only one property adjustment order of a particular type can be made once only mean, for example, that if an order is made under section 21(1)(a) transferring the matrimonial home from the husband to the wife, that the wife cannot apply at a later date[3] under section 21(1)(a) for an order that the family car is transferred to her as well? It appears that it does. Conversely, where, for example, the court has ordered that the matrimonial home be transferred into the sole name of the wife because she is looking after the children, and after the divorce the children all move to live with their father, can the father apply under section 21(2)(b) for the matrimonial home to be settled on him until the children's dependency comes to an end? Prima facie, this appears to amount to an application to vary a property adjustment order, which the Act does not permit. Moreover, no property adjustment order may be made under section 23A after a divorce order has been made except in response to an application made before the divorce order was made, or on a subsequent application made with the leave of the court. However, there appears to be scope for argument that where the circumstances are compelling, the requisite leave should be given, since the court has the power to make a settlement order under section 21(2)(b) provided that no settlement order has already been made.

Applications for orders must be made at an 'appropriate time'.[4] These times are:

---

1 Although in relation to orders for children, see the restrictions imposed by the Child Support Act 1991, s 8, see further ch 9.
2 Although so far as is practicable the court should exercise all of its powers on one occasion only.
3 But at an 'appropriate time', s 22A(2).
4 Matrimonial Causes Act 1973, ss 22A (2) and 23A(1).

'(i) after a statement of marital breakdown has been received by the court and before any application for a divorce order or separation order is made;

(ii) when an application for a divorce order or separation order has been made and has not been withdrawn;

(iii) when an application has been made to convert a separation order into a divorce order and has not been withdrawn;

(iv) after a divorce order has been made; and

(v) when a separation order is in force.'

These provisions reflect the Lord Chancellor's determination that the parties' future financial arrangements should be resolved during the period of reflection and consideration and before a divorce order is made. However, although orders can be made during the subsistence of the marriage, they cannot normally take effect until after divorce. Section 22B(1) provides that no financial provision order, other than an interim order, may be made so as to take effect before the making of a divorce order or separation order, unless the court is satisfied:

'(a) the circumstances of the case are exceptional; and

(b) that it would be just and reasonable for the order so to be made.'

Section 23B(1) imposes an identical restriction on when a property adjustment order can take effect. However, there is no power to make an interim property adjustment order.

It has been seen that financial provision orders include orders for the payment of a lump sum.[5] The court's unrestricted power to make a lump sum order when making an interim financial provision order is new. Hitherto, as now, spouses were able to obtain an interim periodical payments order whilst awaiting a divorce. However, a spouse could only obtain a lump sum order to meet liabilities or expenses reasonably incurred. The new power permits a court to make any type of interim financial provision order. An interim lump sum payment could be invaluable to a spouse who has no financial or property resources of her own. In an appropriate case, and guided by the considerations in section 25,[6] it appears that a court could order payment of a lump sum order of sufficient size to enable one party to put down a deposit on a new house (or even purchase a property outright) before any divorce order is made. However, it appears likely that courts will respond cautiously when exercising this power. Courts are required to have in mind the impact of an interim order on 'the ability of the court to have regard to any matter and to make appropriate adjustments when subsequently making a financial provision order which is not interim'.[7]

---

5   S 21(1)(c), above.
6   Which contains the matters to which the court must have regard when exercising its powers to make financial provision and property adjustment orders.
7   Matrimonial Causes Act 1973, s 25(5).

In other words, the court must consider the effect of an interim order on its power to make an appropriate final order, and this will undoubtedly operate as a restraining factor when interim orders are made.

The timing of orders is subject to further constraints. Neither financial provision nor property adjustment orders can be made where the period of reflection and consideration has been interrupted,[8] or where the application process has lapsed.[9] And it has been seen already that an application for an order can only be made after divorce with the leave of the court.[10]

The changes made to the Matrimonial Causes Act 1973 by the Family Law Act 1996 are relatively complicated and they require the parties and their lawyers to be carefully observant of the rules relating to when orders must be applied for and what orders can be obtained. Practitioners should be particularly alert to the fact that the normal rule is that some kind of financial arrangement *must* be made to the court's satisfaction before a divorce order can be made.[11] Indeed, where parties delay in making financial arrangements sufficient to satisfy the court for the purposes of section 9(2) of the Family Law Act 1996, they could find that the time limit for obtaining a divorce order has expired.[12]

Periodical payments for a spouse

Section 22A(1) empowers a court to make orders for secured and unsecured periodical payments. An unsecured periodical payment order is:

> '... an order that a party must make in favour of another person such periodical payments, for such term, as may be specified (a 'periodical payments order').'[13]

A secured periodical payments order is:

> '... an order that a party must, to the satisfaction of the court, secure in favour of another person such periodical payments, for such period, as may be specified (a 'secured periodical payments order').'[14]

---

8   Ss 22B(2)and 23B(2).
9   Ss 22B(3)and 23B(3).
10 Ss 22B(4)(b) and 23B(4)(b).
11 Unless the applicant falls within some exception to the rule, Family Law Act 1996, s 9(2)(7) and Sch 1, paras 1-4.
12 Particular regard must be had to s 5 of the Family Law Act 1996 which defines when a marriage has broken down irretrievably for divorce order purposes under s 3. An application for a divorce order may not be made if a period of one year has passed since the end of the period for reflection and consideration, s 5(3)(b). Should the parties still be intent upon divorcing, they must start the procedure all over again, see ch 7.
13 S 21(1)(a).
14 S 21(1)(b).

In either case the order directs the payer to pay the payee a sum on a periodic basis, normally weekly or monthly.

Why should one spouse continue to provide income for the other?

There is widespread agreement that a parent should continue to have financial responsibility for his or her children where a marriage ends in divorce. The reason for this is almost self-explanatory: a child is not self-supporting, someone must be responsible for providing the income to cater for a child's daily needs, and the state takes the view that this duty should be borne by the parents.[15] By contrast, there is no widespread agreement that it is the duty of one spouse to provide periodical payments for the other spouse where a marriage ends in divorce. The essence of divorce is to bring all aspects of the legal relationship of husband and wife to an end. But, while one spouse continues to be financially dependent on the other, there cannot be a clean break with the past. What then are the reasons which can justify requiring one ex-spouse to make provision for the other ex-spouse's daily needs in the form of periodical payments? Why should the law make provision for this obligation to be imposed merely because, at one time, the parties were married to each other?

Before attempting to answer this question it is necessary to consider how marriage may have the effect of financially disadvantaging one of the spouses, and lead to the dependence of that spouse on the other. It is true to say that, before marriage, unmarried men and women are equal in the sense that each has an earning capacity unaffected by traditional approaches to the division of family responsibilities between men and women. After marriage this equality of opportunity is liable to alter. It is often the case that one spouse pursues his or her career while the other acts as home-maker, career-supporter and child-rearer. Usually it is the man who goes to work and climbs up the promotion ladder. Where the wife is employed, she will have time off for the birth of any children, and may spend several years out of the labour market bringing up the children and running the household. If either spouse has elderly parents, or other close relatives, who require care and frequent visiting, it is likely to be the wife who takes over the substantial burden of providing such attention. Where the wife remains in, or returns to, full-time employment after the birth of children, she is likely to remain at a lower level on the promotion rung than a man or a woman without a young family, and to be less well paid than her husband. Where she works part-time, she is less likely to enjoy the range of benefits associated with full-time work, such as a company car, a pension scheme, private health insurance and holiday pay.

---

15 The Child Support Act 1991 is built around this simple philosophy, which breaks down in practice where children live in re-constituted families, and where parents cannot afford to support both their step-children and the children to whom they are related by blood, see ch 9.

In a situation of this kind, it may be very difficult for the wife to be financially self-sufficient where the marriage ends in divorce, and she has the day-to-day care of the children. Where the children are young, she will need to pay for child care while she is at work, and this may absorb all, or the majority, of her earnings. Where they are older, she may find it difficult to obtain well-paid employment. Where she is seeking to return to work, she is often competing with people who are already in employment, and whose skills have not become rusty through lack of use.[16] Consequently such a wife may be able to demonstrate a need for periodical payments for herself, the alternative being that her standard of living will otherwise be drastically diminished. It can be seen that there is a tension here between the idea that courts should give recognition to the fact that marriage often leads to one spouse being economically disadvantaged in the labour market, and the idea that a spouse should be able to make a fresh start after divorce, and be able to cast aside the duties and obligations owed to a spouse once the relationship is legally over.

It could be maintained that the reasons why a divorced woman often finds it relatively hard to obtain adequately paid employment are structural within society, and that the law should not impose responsibility for this on her husband. Also, that for so long as women are expected to turn to men to make provision for their daily needs, these structures will not be broken down. However, the countervailing argument is that unless, and until, society makes provision for carers of dependent children to be paid, provides care facilities for pre-school and school-age children, expects men and women to share child care, and the care of the elderly, on an equal basis, and does not expect women to give primacy to the career ambitions of their husbands (who may, for example, have to move from one part of the country to another in order to be promoted), then husbands should continue to shoulder part of the financial cost of marriage, namely the ongoing dependency of the wife. The alternative is to let the loss lie where it falls, that is solely on her shoulders.[17]

Clean break and periodical payments

The first question to be resolved in respect of periodical payments for a spouse is whether an order ought to be made, or whether any financial

---

16 *G v G (Periodical Payments: Jurisdiction)* [1997] 1 FLR 368, at p 371 provides a particularly graphic illustration of the difficulties faced by a wife at the end of a twenty year marriage. It is a good illustration because of the very normality of the position in which the wife found herself. The case also shows the impact on a wife where she receives legal advice of a poor standard.

17 See further, R Deech *The principles of maintenance* (1977) 7 Fam Law 229; R Deech *Financial relief: the retreat from precedent and principle* (1982) 98 LQR 621; K O'Donovan *The principles of maintenance: an alternative view* (1978) 8 Fam Law 180; P Symes *Indissolubility and the clean break* (1984) 48 MLR 44; J M Eekelaar and M Maclean *Maintenance After Divorce* (Clarendon Press, 1986).

dependency of one spouse on the other should immediately be brought to an end. If it is thought appropriate to make an order, the two matters then to be resolved are for how long should the order last, and how should it be quantified. It has already been indicated that periodical payments are one part of a package, one piece in the large jigsaw of principles, powers and policy considerations applying to financial provision and property adjustment orders. Particular account must be taken of the clean break provisions in section 25A, and the reference to a spouse's potential to increase her earning capacity in section 25(2)(a), when assessing whether it is appropriate for one spouse to make periodical payments to the other. The clean break provisions and the direction to consider potential earning capacity were introduced into the Matrimonial Causes Act 1973 in 1984,[18] and they have been highly influential on the development of the law during the last decade. Indeed, case law on periodical payments which precedes the clean break approach should be read with some caution, because it may reflect outdated ideas.[19]

In the past a 'blameless' wife was entitled to life-long periodical payments from her husband, and this entitlement survived divorce. The clean break provisions mark a shift in thinking away from the desirability of requiring a husband to provide continuing maintenance for his wife for the rest of her life, which had hitherto been a commonplace feature of court orders, towards an approach which, in appropriate cases, leads to each spouse becoming financially independent of the other. This shift had already started to permeate the reasoning of the courts before it received legislative approval. The motive for the change was to enable the spouses truly to terminate their marriage ties by settling their financial affairs in a manner which left each one free to start afresh without any continuing obligations to a former spouse.[20]

Section 25A provides:

'(1) If the court decides to exercise any of its powers under any of sections 22A to 24A above in favour of a party to a marriage ... it shall be the duty of the court to consider whether it would be appropriate so to exercise those powers that the financial obligations of each party towards the other will be terminated as soon after the grant of a divorce order or decree of nullity as the court considers just and reasonable.

---

18 By the Matrimonial and Family Proceedings Act 1984.
19 It is suggested that Lord Denning's ruling in *Wachtel v Wachtel* [1973] 1 All ER 829, which led to the revival of the 'one-third rule' for the assessment of spousal maintenance, and which for a time was highly influential, has been overtaken by fresh thinking, and an approach to periodical payments which sees them as primarily rehabilitative in the case of a relatively young spouse, or a spouse with an earning capacity.
20 This motive was succinctly expressed by Lord Scarman in *Minton v Minton* [1979] 1 All ER 79, at p 87 when he said: 'The law now encourages spouses to avoid bitterness after family breakdown and to settle their money and property problems. An object of the modern law is to encourage the parties to put the past behind them and to begin a new life which is not over-shadowed by the relationship which has broken down.'

(2) Where the court decides in such a case to make a periodical payments or secured periodical payments order in favour of a party to the marriage, the court shall in particular consider whether it would be appropriate to require those payments to be made or secured only for such term as would in the opinion of the court be sufficient to enable the party in whose favour the order is made to adjust without undue hardship to the termination of his or her financial dependence on the other party.

(3) If the court-

(a) would have power under section 22A or 23 to make a financial provision order in favour of a party to a marriage ('the first party'), but

(b) considers that no continuing obligation should be imposed on the other party to the marriage ('the second party') to make or secure periodical payments in favour of the first party,

it may direct that the first party may not at any time after the direction takes effect, apply to the court for the making against the second party of any periodical payments order or secured periodical payments order and, if the first party has already applied to the court for the making of such an order it may dismiss the application.'[1]

The following salient features should be noted about the clean break provisions: subsection (1) of section 25(A) imposes a duty on a court to consider whether the parties' obligations towards each other should be terminated as soon after decree as the court considers just and reasonable in all cases.[2] This is a strong directive, but it is ameliorated by the language in which the court's discretion is couched. The court must ask itself whether it is *appropriate* so to exercise its powers; and whether the outcome will be *just and reasonable*. It can be seen that neither spouse is given preferential treatment. Rather the requirement is couched in terms which allows the court to consider the circumstances of both parties. The court's duty under subsection (2) is slightly different. It arises in a case when the court has found it appropriate to make an order for periodical payments. The court is then required to consider whether it would be appropriate to limit the term of these payments only to such term as would be sufficient to enable the recipient to adjust *without undue hardship* to the termination of his or her financial dependence on the other. Thus although the court will be considering the financial position of both parties when deciding whether it is appropriate to make an order of limited duration, the court's attention must focus on the payee when applying the undue hardship test.

---

1   Sub-s 3A further provides that 'If the court – (a) exercises, or has exercised, its power under s 22A at any time before making a divorce order, and (b) gives a direction under sub-s (3) above in respect of a periodical payments order or a secured periodical payments order , it shall provide for the direction not to take effect until a divorce order is made'.

2   See *Suter v Suter and Jones* [1987] 2 All ER 336.

An order must of course come to an end when it expires. However, the initial decision to set a time-limit on the periodical payments is not necessarily final, for there is a possibility of the order being varied in the future under section 31, and this could include the extension of the term during which payments are to be made.[3] Clearly, the knowledge that such an application might be made could undermine the purpose of a clean break order which is intended to bring finality to the financial dependence of the payee, albeit postponed for the duration of the order. Section 25A(2) should therefore be considered alongside section 28(1A). This provides:

'At any time when-
  (a) the court exercises, or has exercised, its power under section 22A or 23 ... to make a financial provision order in favour of a party to a marriage,
  (b) but for having exercised that power, the court would have power under one of those sections to make such an order, and
  (c) an application for a divorce order or a petition for a decree of nullity of marriage is outstanding or has been granted in relation to the marriage
the court may direct that that party shall not be entitled to apply under section 31 for the extension of the term specified in the order.'

Section 28(1A) is an important provision. Where such a direction is made it prevents the party in receipt of periodical payments from applying in variation proceedings for an extension of the order. In this way a postponed clean break can truly be achieved. Conversely, where a direction under section 28(1A) is not made, a spouse can apply for an extension of the order even if it was the parties' intention that no such application could be made.[4]

Subsection (3) of section 25A contains the most Draconian provision from the point of view of an applicant for a periodical payments order. It entitles a court to dismiss an application for periodical payments, and to direct that the applicant shall not be entitled to make any further application for an order for either secured or unsecured periodical payments. There are no words of guidance in subsection (3) on how a court should determine whether or not a continuing obligation should be imposed on one party to make, or secure, periodical payments in favour of the other, which seems to be a weakness in the drafting of this provision. The court will, of course, follow the statutory guidelines provided in section 25 in the exercise of its powers in general, but they are not specifically focused on periodical payments orders. It seems paradoxical that a court

---

3   *T v T (Financial Provision)* [1988] 1 FLR 480; *Richardson v Richardson* [1993] 4 All ER 673. See also *B v B (Consent Order: Variation)* [1995] 1 FLR 9 where Thorpe J held that a limited order should not have been agreed in a consent order, as the wife could not possibly adjust to termination without suffering undue hardship.
4   *B v B (Consent Order: Variation)* [1995] 1 FLR 9.

must consider the issue of the payee's adjustment without undue hardship to an order being terminated when limiting the duration of a periodical payments order, but not when refusing to make one altogether.

Circumstances where periodical payments are likely to be ordered

Whilst in theory husband and wife are afforded equal treatment under the law, in practice it is almost always the wife who is the applicant for an order for periodical payments.[5] When are periodical payments orders in favour of a wife likely to be made? Case law suggests that she can expect to be maintained by her husband for the rest of her life where the marriage has been long-lasting, where the husband has taken on the traditional role of breadwinner, and where the wife has been a housewife.[6] This is particularly true where the husband is wealthy.[7] A wife can also expect to be maintained where she has undertaken paid employment, but where her earnings are small, and her future employment opportunities are either limited, or non-existent.[8] Periodical payments may also be made in cases where the marriage has been of short duration, but where to deprive the wife of the income on which she has become reliant, at least in the short term, would be suddenly, and drastically, to reduce the standard of living to which she has become accustomed.[9] Whether this maintenance is provided in the form of periodical payments will probably depend on whether or not there are sufficient resources to capitalise them into a lump sum which, when invested, will produce an adequate income for the wife.[10] Where this is the case, a clean break arrangement of this nature is likely to be made.[11] However, only those with relatively substantial incomes and assets are able to offer sufficient funds to finance a clean break order of this nature; the majority of husbands do not have these resources and they will therefore be required to continue to support their wives on a periodical basis out of income.

---

5 For an example when the husband was the applicant, but where his application failed because his inability to work had largely been self-induced: see *K v K (Conduct)* [1990] 2 FLR 225.

6 *M v M (Financial Provision)* [1987] 2 FLR 1; *Boylan v Boylan* [1988] 1 FLR 282; *B v B (Consent Order: Variation)* [1995] 1 FLR 9.

7 *Dart v Dart* [1996] 2 FLR 286; *A v A (Financial Provision)* [1998] 2 FLR 180.

8 *Leadbeater v Leadbeater* [1985] FLR 789; *M v M (Financial Provision)* [1987] 2 FLR 1; *Flavell v Flavell* [1997] 1 FLR 353.

9 *Khan v Khan* [1980] 1 All ER 497; *C v C (Financial Relief: Short Marriage)* [1997] 2 FLR 26, but one matter influencing the court was that the child of the family had serious health problems.

10 See *Attar v Attar* [1985] FLR 649, in which the court ordered capitalised periodical payments of £30,000 to enable the wife to adjust to the ending of her six-month marriage to a millionaire. See also, *Fournier v Fournier* [1998] 2 FLR 990, where a lump sum order in the form of capitalised periodical payments was substituted for a periodical payments order because the husband had wilfully tried to defeat the wife's claims.

11 *C v C (Financial Provision)* [1989] 1 FLR 11.

When the wife is looking after a dependent child of the family it is usual for an order to be made for periodical payments for her as well as the child. The reason for this is that it is impossible to anticipate how the wife's obligations to the child will affect her future earning capacity.[12] However, the Court of Appeal in *N v N (Consent Order: Variation)*[13] stated that this approach was not intended to discourage wives with children from going out to work and bringing to an end their financial dependency on their former husbands as soon as possible. A wife may also be well advised to seek periodical payments for herself in a case where the husband refuses to make a maintenance agreement for the children, and where there is likely to be a delay before her application for a maintenance assessment is processed by the Child Support Agency.

Circumstances where periodical payments are not likely to be ordered

The clean break approach has encouraged courts to make orders which bring to an end the dependence of one spouse on the other as a source of income. They have felt able to do this, even in cases when the wife is not in the position to achieve financial self-sufficiency, and even where she has children to look after, for a variety of reasons. One reason is because they have extensive powers to redistribute the spouses' property holdings, irrespective of who owns what as a strict matter of law. These powers enable courts to make sure that a wife obtains a fair share of the family assets, which in itself may enable her to be financially independent.[14] Often too, a wife may be awarded more in the way of capital provision than her husband because she has more pressing needs. For example, when there are several children of the family whom the wife is looking after, and where sale of the former matrimonial home is ordered, it is likely that the wife will receive substantially more than a half share in the proceeds of sale to enable her to rehouse the family nucleus.[15] In a case where resources are limited, which often makes sale of the matrimonial home inappropriate, she is likely to be permitted to occupy the house at least during the period of the children's minority. Sometimes a court may give the wife a life interest in the former matrimonial home; or even transfer the husband's entire interest in the property to her. As a consequence of making one of these orders, a court may then seek to balance its comparative generosity towards the wife in capital terms, by relieving

---

12 *Waterman v Waterman* [1989] 1 FLR 380.
13 [1993] 2 FLR 868. See also *Mawson v Mawson* [1994] 2 FLR 985 where the child was aged five. Having heard evidence as to the wife's earnings over the past twelve months, Thorpe J thought the right balance had been struck by limiting a periodical payments order for a finite term, but not including a s 28(1A) direction prohibiting an application for an extension.
14 *C v C (Financial Provision)* [1989] 1 FLR 11; and see below.
15 Cf *Chaudhuri v Chaudhuri* [1992] 2 FLR 73.

the husband of his obligation to make continuing provision for her out of income.[16]

Another reason why courts have not made orders for periodical payments for a spouse is because they have been prepared to take account of the availability of state benefits. A wife who is unemployed, and who has insufficient resources to meet her needs under criteria applied under social security legislation, will normally be entitled to claim income support. Courts have recognised that the availability of state benefits can enable them to release a husband from his obligation to support his wife.[17] A court is most likely to adopt this reasoning where the husband has acquired new dependants. The court may take the view that to require the husband to continue to pay towards the support of his wife will be to place him under too onerous a financial burden. This view was adopted in *Ashley v Blackman*[18] in proceedings to vary an existing order, but the approach has equal force to an application for an original order. The wife in *Ashley v Blackman* was in receipt of both periodical payments and state benefits.[19] The husband had remarried and had two young children. He and his second wife had a very modest income, and his obligation to make periodical payments to his first wife was putting him under considerable financial pressure. If the husband's order were to be reduced, or extinguished, the loss to the wife would be made up by an increase in her benefit payments. Therefore she would suffer no hardship from the termination of the order. The issue for the court was whether the wife should become entirely dependent on public funds, or whether the husband should be required to continue to pay for her support. This case is illustrative of the tension which frequently arises between the court's duty to preserve the public purse from unnecessary expenditure, and its duty to consider the private interests of the parties, and to authorise a clean break arrangement in appropriate cases. Waite J held that the two duties do not necessarily conflict, and that a court can strike the balance which the particular circumstances of a case appear to dictate. He said that flexible orders, including phased termination, can give proper weight to both heads of policy. On the particular facts of the case before him, he found that it was a classic instance when the clean break approach should be applied, and for no order at all to be made against the husband.

The Child Support Act 1991 has resulted in fewer orders for periodical payments being made in favour of a spouse who is caring for the children of the family. Prior to the Act, a wife could expect to receive periodical payments for herself as well as periodical payments for the children. Since

---

16 *Scallon v Scallon* [1990] 1 FLR 194; *Martin v Martin* [1977] 3 All ER 762; *Hanlon v Hanlon* [1978] 2 All ER 889.

17 *Allen v Allen* [1986] 2 FLR 265; *Delaney v Delaney* [1990] 2 FLR 457. More controversially, in *Delaney* the court also said the availability of benefits could release a husband from his child support obligations. This approach has been overtaken by the Child Support Act 1991.

18 [1988] 2 FLR 278.

19 She was disabled and incapable of earning her own living.

1991, the first call on the absent parent's resources has been to meet his financial obligations to his children. Consequently, it may be that the wife does not obtain an order for herself because the husband's spare income is entirely absorbed by child maintenance, which includes an amount for the parent with care.[20] Even where the wife was married to a man of reasonable means, it seems unlikely that she will obtain more than a nominal, or very small, order for herself in a case where there are several children to be maintained, because the quantification of the child support obligation increases for parents on higher incomes.[1]

Another reason why orders for periodical payments are not made is because a wife is sometimes reluctant to pursue her claim in a case where the husband is unwilling voluntarily to make payments. Although she would be likely to obtain an order, she may value her new-found independence from her husband, and wish to bring to an end any reliance upon him. In a case where the husband has a high income, a wife may find it demeaning to pursue an application based on her continuing needs, and prefer instead to receive a lump sum settlement. She may wish for a clean break because any other arrangement is likely to be emotionally draining. A reluctant payer is likely to be an unreliable payer, and the wife may not be prepared to become embroiled in litigation which will probably be long-lasting and acrimonious, which has the potential to lead to never-ending variation and enforcement proceedings, and where there is no certainty about its outcome.

Duration of an order for periodical payments

An order for periodical payments can last for whatever period the court thinks fit, subject to two qualifications: the term cannot begin earlier than the date of making an application for an order, and it cannot extend beyond the death of either of the parties to the marriage. Furthermore, remarriage of the payee brings the order to an end.[2] The power to back-date orders is one to which the court's attention can usefully be drawn when the paying spouse has been obdurate during the negotiations leading to court proceedings, and has refused to make periodical payments on a voluntary basis in the meanwhile. A back-dated order enables the loss suffered by the applicant eventually to be reimbursed. However, it is important to make an application for back-dating at an early stage if a back-dated order is to be of any real benefit to the applicant. Otherwise the applicant may find that the court is reluctant to back-date the order, especially when the respondent is a person of limited means, because the effect of so doing is immediately to put the respondent into arrears with respect to the payments. Therefore, it may be sensible where the respondent refuses

---

20 See *Mawson v Mawson* [1994] 2 FLR 985.
1   See ch 9.
2   Matrimonial Causes Act 1973, s 28(1).

to pay voluntarily, to bring it to his attention that an application will be made for a back-dated order, and to record this in any documentation which will eventually be placed before the court.

Section 25A(2) requires a court to consider whether it would be appropriate to require periodical payments to be made for such term as would, in the opinion of the court, be sufficient to enable the party in whose favour the order was made to adjust without undue hardship to the termination of his or her financial dependence on the other. In *Barrett v Barrett*[3] the trial judge read section 25A(2) as requiring the wife's dependency to be terminated 'unless there was a reason why it should not be'. It was held that he had misdirected himself, and that by doing so had placed too great an emphasis on termination. As Butler-Sloss LJ pointed out: 'if there is to be determination unless there is good reason not to be, then in my judgment it should have been set out in the Act. But it is not.'[4] This was a significant statement from the Court of Appeal about where the balance should lie between finding it appropriate to terminate obligations owed to a spouse, and finding it appropriate to require them to continue. In *Barrett* the difficulties experienced by women in middle age of obtaining employment was the main foundation of the court's determination that the clean break provisions should not be imposed too readily. This was reiterated by the Court of Appeal in *Flavell v Flavell*.[5] Approving the statement that it is not usually appropriate to provide for the termination of periodical payments in the case of a woman in her mid-fifties, Ward LJ added:

> 'The words of the section do not impose more than an aspiration that the parties should achieve self-sufficiency ... There is, in my judgment, often a tendency for these orders to be made more in hope than in serious expectation. Especially in judging in the case of ladies in their middle years, the judicial looking into a crystal ball very rarely finds enough of substance to justify a finding that adjustment can be made without undue hardship. All too often these orders are made without evidence to support them.'

The key phrase in section 25A(2) is 'undue hardship'. Moreover, in *C v C (Financial Relief: Short Marriage)*[6] Ward LJ emphasised that the question is 'can she adjust, not should she adjust'. Section 25A(2) ties in with section 25(2)(a) which requires a court to consider each of the parties' earning

---

3   [1988] 2 FLR 516.
4   Ibid, at p 519.
5   [1997] 1 FLR 353, at p 358. Following divorce, the husband was ordered to make periodical payments to his wife for a period of two years. In variation proceedings, the Court of Appeal approved the decision of the trial judge to vary the order so that there was no longer a termination date.
6   [1997] 2 FLR 26.

capacity, including any increase in that capacity which it would be reasonable to expect each spouse to acquire. These provisions provoke three questions: first, to what extent can periodical payments be used to compensate one of the spouses for having an earning capacity which has been diminished by marriage; secondly, will she be required to increase her earning capacity; and thirdly, for how long a period will she be allowed to adjust to making provision for herself before the periodical payments come to an end?

Rehabilitative periodical payments

One compromise solution to the tension between giving recognition to the continuance of financial obligations between spouses after divorce, and the clean break principle, is for a court to order what can loosely be called 'rehabilitative periodical payments'. Here the term of the order is limited in duration, its purpose being to provide temporary support for the recipient until she can adjust to the change in circumstances brought about by the divorce. Is a limited term order of this nature likely to cause hardship? It was recognised in *M v M (Financial Provision)*,[7] *Barrett v Barrett*[8] and *Flavell v Flavell*[9] that in the case of some women who have never had paid employment, or who permanently give up work once the children are born, any order which is limited in duration is likely to cause them hardship. Such women are unlikely to obtain employment in middle age, and even less likely to do so when approaching retirement age. Also, women who have never had paid employment tend to have been married to relatively affluent men, and to move in professional circles. It may arguably be a hardship in itself to expect the ex-wife of a professional man to obtain unskilled work in her middle years, for example in a shop, or factory, or in a domestic capacity.

The relativism of hardship to the standard of living previously enjoyed by the spouses has been recognised by the courts. In *Boylan v Boylan*[10] the wife had been married to a man of substantial wealth and had enjoyed a high standard of living. After the parties had been divorced for several years the wife sought an increase in her existing order for periodical payments. The husband, who had assets in excess of £1.2 million and an income of £100,000, offered a lump sum of £40,000 in return for an order terminating the wife's periodical payments forthwith. Booth J found this offer to be quite inadequate and ordered him to pay the wife £16,000 per annum. Booth J held that it was by the wife's previous high standard of living that her reasonable requirements should be judged, and an assessment made of whether she could adjust without undue hardship to the

---

7   [1987] 2 FLR 1.
8   [1988] 2 FLR 516.
9   [1997] 1 FLR 353, at p 358.
10 [1988] 1 FLR 282.

termination of periodical payments. The court also considered whether it should limit the duration of the wife's order. It recognised that a wife's employment opportunities are bleak when she has no formal qualifications, and has never been required to apply her mind to the question of earning her living. The court therefore ruled that the only circumstances in which the wife's periodical payments could be terminated in such a way as not to cause her undue hardship would be upon payment of a lump sum sufficient to provide her with an income comparable to that which she would receive by way of periodical payments.

Rehabilitative periodical payments orders may be particularly appropriate in relation to short-term marriages where no children have been born. It has long been the case that a young and childless wife either cannot expect to receive periodical payments at all,[11] or that any order will be of short duration.[12] However, where the parties have married in later life, or where the husband is especially wealthy, it may be thought necessary, and appropriate, to give the wife time in which to adjust to her suddenly reduced standard of living.[13] One way in which this can be achieved is by making a periodical payments order for a limited period, coupled with a direction under section 28(1A) prohibiting the wife from applying for an extension. Unless such a direction is made, the wife can make an application under section 31 to vary the order during its currency by extending its term, and the variation court has a free discretion as to whether or not to do so, although it is likely to be influenced by the fact that the original court thought a limited term order was appropriate.[14]

It can be more difficult to assess the appropriate duration of a periodical payments order where the marriage has been short-lived, but where a child or children have been born. On the one hand a wife who is a party to a short-term marriage cannot reasonably expect to be supported by her husband indefinitely, or even for very long. On the other hand, the wife's earning capacity is likely to be impaired for a significant length of time by her child care commitments. In *Waterman v Waterman*[15] the parties were divorced after their marriage had lasted a mere 17 months. Their child, who was aged five, was living with the wife. The wife had been trained as a secretary, and had been previously employed until just before she began to live with the husband. Since the divorce she had been on training courses

11 *Graves v Graves* (1973) 117 Sol Jo 679; *Brady v Brady* (1973) 3 Fam Law 78.
12 See *Khan v Khan* [1980] 1 All ER 497 where periodical payments of £18 per week were ordered for a young wife for one year, thereafter reducing to £5 a week. The purpose of the initial year was to give her time to train and to find employment.
13 *Hedges v Hedges* [1991] 1 FLR 196, where 18 months was held to be the appropriate adjustment period because the marriage had been of short duration.
14 *Richardson v Richardson (No 2)* [1996] 2 FLR 617.
15 [1989] 1 FLR 380. See also, *C v C (Financial Relief: Short Marriage)* [1997] 2 FLR 26 where substantial provision was made for the wife of a wealthy business man where the marriage had lasted for a mere nine months but where the child of the marriage had health problems.

in order to enhance her earning capacity. The trial judge made various orders, including an order for periodical payments for the wife, which he limited in duration to five years. He also gave a direction under section 28(1A) that the wife was not entitled to apply for an extension of the term of the order. Allowing the wife's appeal in part, Sir Stephen Brown P stated that the question whether the order should be limited in duration had been one for the judge to decide in the exercise of his discretion. He expressed the view that the Court of Appeal might have come to a different conclusion, namely that it was inappropriate to set any term to the periodical payments order had it been considering the matter at first instance. But he reaffirmed the principle that before an appellate court can interfere with a trial judge's discretionary decision it must come to the conclusion that he was plainly wrong. He continued 'so far as the period of five years is concerned, I am bound to confess to some hesitation in accepting that assessment of the appropriate period on the facts of this case, but I am unable to say that the judge was plainly wrong in coming to that conclusion'.[16] However, the Court of Appeal did find that the judge was plainly wrong when he added the direction that the wife should not be entitled to apply for an extension of the term of the order. It described an order under section 28(1A) as a Draconian prohibition, and held that the judge had been wrong to add a prohibition preventing the wife from applying for an extension under any circumstances having regard to the fact that she was caring for a child of tender years, and the uncertainty of what her position might be in five years' time.

It is important not to approach the ratio decidendi of *Waterman v Waterman* too narrowly. It is suggested that there are two strands to the decision. The first is concerned with whether it is normally appropriate for a court to make a limited term order for a parent who is looking after a young child. It is clear that the Court of Appeal did *not* positively endorse such an approach even though the wife's appeal on that point was rejected. Rather it held that the judge had carefully reviewed the financial position and circumstances of the parties, and for this reason his decision could not be faulted. But the tenor of Sir Stephen Brown P's judgment was that he himself would not have made such an order. The second strand was whether the court should truly make a clean break order by upholding the direction under section 28(1A), or whether it should leave the door open for the wife to apply for the order to be extended should she find herself unable to support herself at the end of the five-year period. By allowing the wife's appeal against the section 28(1A) direction, the court gave significant recognition to the important truth that lack of earning capacity brought about by child care responsibilities may be a continuing problem for the wife.[17]

---

16 Ibid, at p 386.
17 See also *Mawson v Mawson* [1994] 2 FLR 985. See further J Harcus *Periodical payments – end of term?* [1997] Fam Law 340.

Limiting the duration of orders – variation traps

The court's variation powers under section 31 are unfettered. The applicant is not required to establish exceptional circumstances or a material change in circumstances before an order can be made, but the exercise of the discretion may, of course, be affected by that consideration.[18] In *B v B (Consent Order: Variation),*[19] Thorpe J rejected the submission that different principles applied where the application for variation was in breach of an express of implied provision in a consent order, and held that the court had the same powers whether the original order was made by consent or in contested proceedings. However, in *Richardson v Richardson (No 2)*[20] the Court of Appeal, following *Edgar v Edgar,*[1] held that where the original consent order imposed a finite term, and where the agreement between the parties was properly and fairly arrived at with competent legal advice, the terms of the order should not be displaced unless there were good and substantial reasons for concluding that an injustice would be done by holding the parties to their terms.[2]

It is essential to ensure that an application to vary a limited term order is made before the order expires, for otherwise there will be no order in existence which is capable of being varied. In *T v T (Financial Provision)*[3] a periodical payments order had been made in favour of a wife which was expressed to take effect 'until such date as the wife shall remarry or until the husband retires or further order'. After the husband retired the wife applied to vary the order. It was conceded that the court would have had jurisdiction to extend the order to beyond the husband's retirement date had the wife made her application before the husband retired.[4] However, the court ruled that its jurisdiction had come to an end once the retirement took place. The addition of the words 'or further order' did not come to the wife's assistance because the Court of Appeal held that these words meant 'a further order in the meantime'. It is all too easy for a spouse to delay for too long before seeking a variation of the original order, with the consequence that her variation application will fail because it falls into a time-limit trap. This was illustrated by *G v G (Periodical Payments: Jurisdiction).*[5] A consent order was made which contained the following terms: 'The respondent to pay or cause to be paid to the petitioner ...

18 *Flavell v Flavell* [1997] 1 FLR 353.
19 [1995] 1 FLR 9.
20 [1996] 2 FLR 617.
1 [1980] 3 All ER 887.
2 The court held that it had been correct in variation proceedings to extend the term of a periodical payments order for a further five years, but to make an order under s 28(1A) preventing any application for a further extension.
3 [1988] 1 FLR 480.
4 This concession was confirmed in *Richardson v Richardson* [1993] 4 All ER 673.
5 [1997] 1 All ER 272. At p 284 Ward LJ added the further rider: 'Although no argument has been addressed to us, I incline to the view that it is essential not only that application be made but that an order be made before the expiration of the term.'

periodical payments at the rate of £14,000 per annum ... until the petitioner shall remarry, cohabit with another man for a period of 6 months ... or until the child of the family, C, shall attain the age of 18 years whichever shall be sooner or until further order.' There was no direction given under section 28(1A) that the wife could not apply for an extension of the term specified in the order, so provided she made her application in time she could have obtained a variation of the order under section 31. However, the wife made her application to vary the original order one month after C reached her eighteenth birthday. Accordingly, and with considerable regret, the Court of Appeal ruled that the court had no jurisdiction to vary the original order because it had already expired.

In the light of the rulings in *T v T (Financial Provision)* and *G v G (Periodical Payments: Jurisdiction)*, it can be seen that very great care must be taken to ensure that a term is not included in an order for periodical payments which brings it to a premature end without due regard for whether the payee's need for periodical payments is a continuing one. An order comes to an end not only when it expressly stands dismissed, but also when it ceases, or is discharged, or where the payer has complied with all his obligations under the order. Consequently in *G v G (Periodical Payments: Jurisdiction)*[6] Ward LJ advised practitioners specifically to provide that nominal periodical payments should continue to be made after the expiration of any term included in a substantive periodical payments order so as to give a peg on which to hang any late variation application.

A contingency which is sometimes included in consent orders for periodical payments is that the order will cease if the wife should cohabit with another man for longer than a specified period.[7] The risk to the wife of an order containing such a clause is that her new partner may not be in the position to maintain her himself. This is particularly likely to be the position when he has children whom he is maintaining under the Child Support Act 1991. The calculations made under the formula make no allowance for the cost of maintaining an adult partner.[8] Although courts have clearly stated that cohabitation should not be equated with re-marriage when a periodical payments order is made,[9] or when an application has been made in variation proceedings to discharge the order,[10] there seems to be nothing to prevent the inclusion of a clause of this type in a periodical payments order. The wife can apply for a variation of this (or any other) term before the cut-off date has been reached, provided that no direction to the contrary has been made under section 28(1A). But once the specified period of cohabitation has been fulfilled it seems that the order for periodical payments terminates automatically. Moreover,

---

6   Ibid, at p 284.
7   See, for example, *G v G (Periodical Payments: Jurisdiction)* above.
8   See ch 9.
9   *Atkinson v Atkinson (No 2)* [1996] 1 FLR 51.
10 *Atkinson v Atkinson* [1987] 3 All ER 849.

the order cannot be revived even if the cohabitation subsequently ceases, and there is a general rule against repeat applications being made for orders.[11]

It is suggested that orders containing a clause that periodical payments should cease automatically if a former wife should cohabit with another man should be avoided. Such provisions are the modern equivalent of the old *dum casta* orders, which at one time used to stipulate that the wife must remain 'chaste' if she wished her periodical payments to continue.[12] They are objectionable in that they may lead to snooping, and may restrain the wife from forming an intimate relationship out of fear that she will lose her source of income from her ex-husband. Whereas cohabitation may provide good cause to apply for variation or termination of an order for periodical payments, for an order to terminate automatically in the event of the wife cohabiting, irrespective of her partner's income, could cause such a wife a great deal of financial hardship.[13]

Quantification of orders for periodical payments

The quantification of periodical payments orders tends to alter in the light of social change, and to changing views on what can reasonably be expected of spouses. In all cases the assessment of how much should be paid, and for how long, will be influenced by the weight given to the various paragraphs in the statutory guidelines in section 25, by the nature of other orders or agreements which are being made, and by the clean break approach. While in any particular case one or more of the statutory guidelines may be highly pertinent, in a large number of cases the reality is how properly to allocate limited resources between spouses who each have needs, obligations, and responsibilities, when these resources are insufficient to meet each spouse's requirements.

As noted above, the availability of state benefits is often an important factor in the court's calculation. Where the court knows that the first family will be equally well provided for from state funds, whether or not the husband makes periodical payments, it will often be prepared to take this into account. In this way a court is able to 'widen the purse' when considering the spouses' resources, and to refrain from making orders against the husband which will be financially onerous.[14] An extreme case was *Delaney v Delaney*[15] where Ward J, after commenting that there should be 'life after divorce' for the husband who wished to set up home

---

11 S 22A(3).
12 Cf *Squire v Squire* [1905] P 4.
13 See further on this issue, M Hayes *Cohabitation clauses in financial provision and property adjustment orders: law, policy and justice* (1994) 110 LQR 124.
14 See *Whiting v Whiting* [1988] 2 All ER 275 where the former wife would be eligible for state benefits and therefore her claim to continuing support was displaced by the needs of the man's second family.
15 [1990] 2 FLR 457.

with his new partner, made nominal orders only for his wife and children. Ward J felt able to make this decision because any order against the husband would merely reduce the wife's benefits pound for pound. However, the advent of the Child Support Act 1991 no longer allows for such an approach. Child support cannot be avoided when the state has an interest in payments being made. Where the parent with care is drawing state benefits she must authorise the child support agency to take action to recover child maintenance from the other parent.[16]

A nominal sum order

In cases where resources are limited, the requirement that a parent must first honour his obligations to his children makes it less likely that there will be money available for the support of his wife. The question then arises whether any order at all should be made in favour of the wife where there seems to be no likelihood that the husband will be able to pay a realistic amount towards her support in the foreseeable future. This is an important question to which consideration should always be given. Any order for periodical payments, however small,[17] is capable of being varied upwards should either of the spouses' circumstances alter in the future. Thus an order for a nominal sum is a form of insurance against falling on hard times. Whether a court would be prepared to increase a nominal sum order in variation proceedings will turn on a variety of circumstances.[18] But the fact that an order for a nominal sum has been made indicates a willingness by the original court to allow the variation court to give the matter proper consideration. For example, in *Whiting v Whiting*[19] the Court of Appeal held that the trial judge had been entitled to take the view that periodical payments should be kept alive by a nominal sum order, in case unforeseen contingencies, such as illness or redundancy, should prevent the wife from making adequate provision for her own needs, and make it necessary for her to look again to her ex-husband for support. Hence the making of a nominal sum order may have profound implications for both parties.

Where there are insufficient resources to make an order in favour of the wife, because the absent parent's obligations to make payments to his children under the Child Support Act 1991 leave nothing to spare, it may nonetheless be vital to obtain a nominal sum order in the wife's favour. Children eventually grow up and stop being a call on the absent parent's income. The wife, as the caring parent, may then find that her own income is drastically reduced by the discontinuance of child support payments.[20] However, if the wife obtains

---

16 Child Support Act 1991, s 6(1); and see ch 9.

17 Even 1p a year.

18 S 31(7).

19 [1988] 2 All ER 275; see too *Scallon v Scallon* [1990] 1 FLR 194; *Hepburn v Hepburn* [1989] 1 FLR 373.

20 The formula for the quantification of child support contains an element of support for the caring parent too: see ch 9.

a nominal sum order in her favour at the time of the original divorce settlement, she is entitled to apply at a later stage for her order to be increased.

'One-third rule'

Over the years, various rules of thumb have been applied to the quantification of periodical payments orders. These have varied according to the social circumstances of the time, and it can be misleading to seek to extrapolate principles from what was, in truth, an attempt by a higher court to provide pragmatic guidance for the lower courts on how to quantify their orders. Such rules of thumb include the so-called 'one-third rule'.[1] At one stage this rule was used quite widely by courts as a starting point for assessing how much a wife should receive in the way of capital and income. When the one-third rule is applied to periodical payments, the amount for the wife is calculated as follows: the income of the husband and wife is added together, and the wife is awarded an amount which will bring her income up to one-third of the total sum. For example, if the husband earns £14,000 a year, and the wife earns £4,000 a year, one-third of the total of their combined incomes is £6,000. Consequently, applying the one-third rule, the wife will receive £2,000 a year in periodical payments from the husband.

According to Lord Denning MR in *Wachtel v Wachtel*[2] the rationale behind awarding the wife one-third, rather than a different fraction, is because there are other demands on the husband's income, including the obligation to make periodical payments to the children, and because the wife will also obtain a share of the capital assets. However, although the rule gives a starting point for making calculations it has restricted value. As Sir John Arnold P subsequently stated, the one-third rule has little use either where the spouses' resources are very limited, or where there is great wealth.[3] This is because the calculation simply does not work in practice in these situations. Also, the rule has largely been overtaken by the clean break approach to periodical payments for a wife, and by the impact of the Child Support Act 1991 on maintenance calculations for children. However, the rule may still have value in a particular case, the most likely being when there are no children of the family to be maintained.

'Net effect' approach

Another calculation method is the 'net effect' approach, which in essence involves working out the husband's available resources after making various deductions, and working out the wife's resources, including the amount of a hypothetical order. The two figures can then be compared

---

1 Given a new lease of life in *Wachtel v Wachtel* [1973] 1 All ER 829.
2 Above.
3 *Slater v Slater* (1982) 3 FLR 364; see too *Furniss v Furniss* (1981) 3 FLR 46.

and related to their respective needs, and the hypothetical order adjusted accordingly.[4] However, as Thorpe LJ said when stating that cases needed to be evaluated taking a broad perspective: 'It has never been the custom in ancillary relief litigation to look with scrupulous care at the budget items of the prospective payer'.[5] While the 'net effect' approach is an acceptable method of calculating quantum, it begs the fundamental question of how to calculate the spouses' respective needs. Unless the chosen system acknowledges the importance of a base line against which to measure such needs, it is inevitable that there will be discrepancies between courts in the amount of resources which a husband is allowed to keep for his own use before making payments to the wife.

'Subsistence level' approach

The 'subsistence level' approach does provide a base line against which to measure needs. It advises courts to ensure that the impact of any order for periodical payments should not be such as to push the remaining income of the payer below the level of income he would receive if drawing social security benefits on the income support scale rates; and not to make an order, other than a nominal order, against someone who is unemployed and living on state benefits.[6] However, the courts have not always adhered to this approach, and they have refused to elevate it to a statement of principle.[7] Rather, the judges have chosen to assess for themselves how much of his income a husband needs to retain in order to support himself and any new dependants. One reason for this has been a determination by some Court of Appeal judges to impress on fathers that they have a moral obligation to support their own children, even when they clearly do not have the means to do so.[8] That moral imperative is no longer a driving force behind orders for periodical payments, because child maintenance has been transferred from the courts to the Child Support Agency. Consequently some of the pressure on courts to make orders against unemployed and poor men has been lifted. Nonetheless, applications for spousal maintenance, for variation of existing orders, and for maintenance for any children of the family to whom the Child Support Act 1991 does not apply, must still come before the courts. Therefore whether or not the

---

4 See *Stockford v Stockford* (1981) 3 FLR 58 in which a more detailed explanation of this calculation is given; see too *Slater v Slater* above.
5 *Campbell v Campbell* [1998] 1 FLR 828.
6 *Ashley v Ashley* [1968] P 582; *Chase v Chase* (1983) 13 Fam Law 21.
7 See *Stockford v Stockford* (1981) 3 FLR 58, in which the Court of Appeal said that the registrar and judge had both misdirected themselves when they had expressed the view that the wife's application must fail if its effect would be to reduce the husband's income below income support scale rates; see too *Freeman v Swatridge* [1984] FLR 762 where more than a nominal order was made against an unemployed man by the Court of Appeal.
8 See, for example, Ormrod LJ in *Tovey v Tovey* (1978) 8 Fam Law 80; *Freeman v Swatridge* [1984] FLR 762.

subsistence level approach is adopted as a minimum base line may still be a matter of critical importance.[9]

It is suggested that in refusing to rule that an order should not depress the payer's income below the income support scale rate, the courts have been both seriously misguided and extraordinarily harsh. The income support scale rate is designed to meet the shortfall which exists between a man's resources and his requirements. It leaves nothing to spare over and above normal family expenditure, and indeed few would argue that income support levels provide other than a sum just adequate to cover basic needs. An order which depresses the payer's income to below this amount displays a breathtaking lack of awareness of the financial difficulties of poor people. As Finer J pointed out two decades ago: 'it is a hardship to live at [income support][10] level. It allows no extras. It is not possible to save. As time goes by, clothes, furniture, linoleum, wear out and having to replace them increases the hardship.'[11] Indeed, when a working man's income is depressed to income support level, let alone below, he will actually be in a worse financial position than a man who is entitled to draw benefits. This is because benefit claimants are automatically entitled to receive free dental treatment, free spectacles and free prescriptions. Any children are entitled to free school meals. Claimants may also be entitled to other payments, and to earn a small amount without this leading to a reduction in their benefit payments. By contrast, the working man who is required to pay maintenance enjoys no such allowances, and when he has a new family, his expenditure on his former family is not normally a deductible expense for the purpose of claiming any means-tested benefits to which he might be entitled, such as family credit.

What are the possible consequences for a man and any new family he may have if the family's income is depressed for any length of time below subsistence level because of a court order? It is likely that some of their basic living requirements may not be met. For example, an adult may go short of food, a child of clothing and shoes, and the whole family of adequate heating. It is also likely that his new relationship will be put at serious risk. Statistics reveal that one in two second marriages break down, and it is well known that financial stress is very destructive of family life. Because there is not enough money to meet all the demands on the husband's income, the order will probably fall into arrears, and enforcement proceedings may then be taken. In these proceedings the husband may then be required to pay an additional sum each week to

---

9　In *E v C (Child Maintenance)* [1996] 1 FLR 472, a case involving former cohabitees, Douglas Brown J held that magistrates might usefully have asked themselves what the Child Support Agency assessment would be in the circumstances. If a nil assessment would be made, this factor, although not binding on the court, would be strongly persuasive when the court was determining whether any order should be made,

10　Previously supplementary benefit.

11　*Williams v Williams* [1974] 3 All ER 377, at p 383.

discharge the arrears, as well as the amount originally ordered. As a result, his income decreases, his maintenance debt increases, and his ability to make proper provision for himself and any current dependants is put in even greater jeopardy. Ultimately he risks imprisonment for non-payment.[12]

Secured periodical payments

A secured periodical payments order is one in which payments are secured against specific property belonging to the payer. Sometimes the chosen property is income producing, and sometimes it is property against which the charge can be enforced with the sum due should the payer default on the payments. Usually the payer is required to transfer the property to trustees and to execute a deed of security. Normally the trusts of the deed provide that, so long as the payer makes the payments ordered to the payee, the income from the property on which the payments are secured should be paid to the payer. In this way the payer is allowed to retain some choice and control over how he fulfils the requirements of the order. The security will, of course, revert to the payer on the payee's death or remarriage; or to his estate when these events occur after the payer's death.

The main advantage of a secured order over an unsecured order is that it can last for the payee's lifetime,[13] which means that when the payer dies the payee can still look to the security as a source of income. It is suggested that full advantage should be taken of the opportunity to apply for a secured periodical payments order which lasts for the lifetime of the payee. It should be borne in mind that usually it is the wife who is the recipient of a periodical payments order; that a woman usually marries a man who is older than herself; and that the husband is statistically likely to predecease the wife. An order which survives the husband's death may make provision for a divorced woman for many years after that death occurs. Furthermore, a divorced woman is not her ex-husband's widow, which means she will lose all entitlement to a widow's pension from his pension fund. This is a major loss of income for divorced women, particularly those divorced at an age when it is too late to establish an entitlement to an adequate pension in reliance on their own pension contributions. A secured order may be one method of compensating a wife for this loss of pension income.[14]

The other main advantage of a secured order is to be found in the improved opportunities for enforcement. The payee is not burdened by

12 See, for example, *R v Slough Magistrates' Court, ex p Lindsay* [1997] 1 FLR 695.
13 Matrimonial Causes Act 1973, s 28(1)(b); this is by contrast with an unsecured order, which can last only for the spouses' joint lives.
14 Pensions are discussed in greater detail below when paragraph (h) of s 25(2) is considered.

the enforcement problems which are often associated with unsecured orders.[15] When an unsecured order is in existence, and the payer is determined to be obdurate in refusing to pay, one response, therefore, might be to make a fresh application for a secured periodical payments order, rather than to attempt to enforce the original order. In the case of a secured order, normally the payer is able to pay the sums due under the order from whatever source of income he chooses. But should he default on the payments, the trustees of the security must make payments directly to the payee from the income produced by the security. Should that income prove to be insufficient, the trustees have power to resort to the capital. In cases where the order is secured on property which does not produce income, the amount of the arrears will be charged on the property, and the payee can realise her charge by forcing a sale. Either process could be invaluable to the payee when the payer is refusing to pay, has disappeared, has emigrated, or has defaulted for some other reason. Sometimes it might be appropriate for the order to be secured on the payer's interest in the former matrimonial home. It is relatively commonplace for sale of the former matrimonial home to be postponed to some future date when the proceeds will then be divided between the spouses in predetermined amounts, and for one spouse to be given a right to live in it in the meanwhile. In a case of this kind, the periodical payments order could be secured on the payer's postponed share and, in the event of his default, his eventual share in the proceeds of sale would be reduced by the arrears outstanding. While this arrangement would not directly assist the payee to obtain a regular income, it would ensure that the payer ultimately pays for his default, and would give the payee a growing share in the proceeds of sale of the matrimonial home, which she might need where her income has been reduced.

Lump sum orders

An order for the payment of a lump sum is 'an order that a party must make a payment in favour of another person of such lump sum or sums as may be specified'.[16] Although section 21(1)(c) refers to sums in the plural, only one lump sum order can be made.[17] The plural allows for it to be paid in instalments, in which case the payments can be secured,[18] and interest can be ordered on the amount deferred.[19] An application can be made for a lump sum on the grant of a decree or at any time thereafter, but it must

---

15 See, for example, *C v C* [1997] 2 FLR 26, at p 46, per Ward LJ: 'Given the husband's lies and deception, given the difficulties there were in obtaining information as to his means and given some move of residence and relocation from this country to Athens, it is not, in my judgment, wrong to secure the periodical payments as [the judge] did.'
16 S 21(1)(c).
17 *Coleman v Coleman* [1972] 3 All ER 886.
18 S 22A(5)(b).
19 S 22A(8).

be remembered that the right to apply for lump sum and property adjustment orders is lost in the event of the applicant's remarriage.[20] However, provided that the application has been made before the re-marriage, the court has jurisdiction even though the application is not heard until after the remarriage.

One consequence of the rule that an application for financial provision and property adjustment orders cannot be made after remarriage is that it is normal practice to make an application for all types of relief at the time of the divorce. Generally speaking, this practice is sensible and desirable, and it deals with the danger of a swift remarriage depriving a spouse of his or her claim to a share in the property. However, it is clearly inadvisable to apply for an order when it is obvious that the respondent is in no position to make a lump sum payment. This is because it must also be remembered that when an application for a lump sum payment is dismissed, no further application can subsequently be made. The applicant may, therefore, have everything to lose and nothing to gain from making a comprehensive application at the time of the divorce. In a case where the respondent has no capital resources, but is likely to acquire them at a later date, for example when he will probably inherit under his parent's will or intestacy, it may be wiser not to make an application at the time of the divorce, but to take the chance that leave will be granted by the court at some time in the future. Alternatively, a court may be prepared to adjourn the application for a lump sum where there is a real possibility that the respondent will shortly obtain capital out of which it can be paid.

Lump sums and clean break

A lump sum order has the advantage that it may achieve a clean break between the parties. A lump sum can be invested to produce a regular income for the applicant; consequently it may obviate the need to order periodical payments in addition. Clean break arrangements have psycho-logical benefits for both spouses because each knows exactly what his or her financial position is, both now and in the future, and each can plan accordingly. Whilst financial dependence of one spouse on the other continues, the spouses do not usually experience their marriage as truly having been dissolved, despite the formal existence of a divorce decree. The ending of financial dependence is what truly liberates the parties from one another. It may also bring a source of acrimony to an end.[1] From the point of view of the payee, a lump sum order has the additional advantage over an order for periodical payments that it is not affected by remarriage. This principle applies whether or not the lump sum is paid all at once, or by instalments. Once made, a lump sum order cannot be

20 S 28(3).
1   *C v C (Financial Provision)* [1989] 1 FLR 11.

varied.[2] Where the court orders that a lump sum be paid by a specific date, and payment is tendered late, the question arises whether the extension of time amounts to a variation of the original order. In *Masefield v Alexander (Lump Sum: Extension of Time)*[3] the Court of Appeal held that there was jurisdiction to extend the time allowed for payment of a lump sum where the payee was not prejudiced by the delay, where it was not the payer's fault, and provided that time was not of the essence and thus going to the substance of the order.

Lump sum orders are particularly appropriate when the marriage has been short-lived, but where the applicant needs temporary support to enable her to find employment, and otherwise adjust to the termination of the marriage. The amount of money ordered will reflect the short-term nature of the marriage. In *Leadbeater v Leadbeater*[4] the wife, who was aged 47, had been married to a very wealthy man for four years, and she had enjoyed a much enhanced lifestyle during this period. There were adequate funds to make a clean break order, but the amount the wife received when measured against her needs was reduced by 25% because of the short duration of the marriage. In *Attar v Attar*[5] the wife's marriage to her millionaire husband lasted a mere six months. Prior to the marriage she had been an air hostess earning £15,000 per annum. The court ordered that she receive a lump sum of £30,000 to enable her to adjust to the ending of the marriage. In the case of less wealthy spouses, a relatively small lump sum order (which can be paid in instalments) may be an appropriate way of assisting a financially dependent party to adjust without undue hardship to the termination of that dependence. For example, it could be used to pay for her education and training to enable her to re-enter the labour market.

Lump sum or periodical payments?

Before the advent of the Child Support Act 1991, courts would sometimes make lump sum orders against husbands which were financially onerous, but in return would relieve the husband of all, or most, of his obligation to make periodical payments for the benefit of his wife and children. Nowadays it would be most unwise for a husband to offer a large lump sum in return for an agreement by his wife not to pursue him for periodical payments, either for herself, or for the children, or to reduce the amount which would otherwise be payable. Such a husband is exposing himself to the risk that the wife may resile on the arrangement. Any term in an

2 By contrast, an order for periodical payments ends automatically if the wife remarries. Where she lives with a new partner, such cohabitation may lead to the order being reduced, or extinguished, in variation proceedings.
3 [1995] 1 FLR 100.
4 [1985] FLR 789.
5 [1985] FLR 649.

order, or agreement, which purports to restrict the right of a parent with care to apply to the Child Support Agency for a maintenance assessment is void.[6] Should the agency become involved at a later date, and the wife would have no choice about this if she was in receipt of state benefits,[7] the absent parent's obligation to his children would be quantified in accordance with the agency's strict arithmetical formula. This formula includes an amount which covers some of the adult carer's needs. The fact that, at an earlier agreed settlement, the caring parent has traded a lower income for higher capital provision is of no interest or concern to the agency; the absent parent will still be liable for the full amount. [8]

It is normally in the interests of a husband not to be liable to make continuing financial provision for his former wife, for he will usually wish to sever their financial as well as their legal links. But there may be occasions when he would prefer an order for periodical payments rather than to make generous capital provision for her. Lump sum and property adjustment orders once made cannot be varied.[9] In a case where the wife has, or is likely to develop, a close personal relationship with another man leading perhaps to cohabitation or remarriage, the husband may take the view that to pay his wife a substantial lump sum is like giving her a 'dowry' to spend on the other man. This was the belief of the husband in *Duxbury v Duxbury*.[10] He did not wish his wife to have a lump sum order because she was living with another man and was likely to spend the money on him. Also, the man was likely to inherit the residue of the money should the wife predecease him. The wife wanted to be free to live her own life in whatever manner she chose, and to spend her money on whomsoever she wished. It is when this type of conflict occurs that a question of principle arises. Does a wife have a right to a lump sum, or is it merely a claim, with the court having a free discretion to choose between a lump sum order and one for periodical payments? In *Duxbury v Duxbury* the Court of Appeal took the view that the trial court had assessed the reasonable needs of the wife, which they found in the circumstances could be provided for by a lump sum order, and that 'how she spent the money was her affair'. It therefore concluded that the husband's objection to a lump sum order, and his wish instead to make periodical payments, was

6   Child Support Act 1991, s 9(4).
7   Child Support Act 1991, s 6(1).
8   See *Crozier v Crozier* [1994] 1 FLR 126 in which a husband had transferred his half share in the matrimonial home in exchange for a nominal order for child maintenance. This arrangement had been embodied in a consent order. Subsequently the Child Support Agency found that he was liable to pay the sum of £29 per week in child support. The husband was refused leave to appeal out of time against the consent order. The Child Support Act 1995 recognised that injustice may have been caused to spouses like the husband in *Crozier* who had reached an agreement prior to the implementation of the Child Support Act 1991. Such a spouse is entitled to apply for a departure direction provided that any agreement was made before 5 April 1993. See further ch 9.
9   S 31.
10   [1990] 2 All ER 77.

ill-founded.[11] In *B v B (Financial Provision: Leave to Appeal)*[12] the husband was attempting to appeal out of time against a lump sum order because the wife had remarried a wealthy man. Of the lump sum Ward J said, 'she has her lump sum, which is the result of her contribution during the marriage, and her remarriage does not affect that in any way at all, see, for example, Mrs Duxbury'.[13]

Property adjustment orders

In many families their most valuable asset is the family home, followed by such items as a car, furnishings and investments. Their assets may also include items jointly owned with a third party,[14] and property acquired since the termination of the marriage.[15] Section 23A enables a court to adjust the spouses' interests in the ownership of such property, so that it can make provision for the current circumstances of all the family members. This can be done either by ordering the out-and-out transfer of property, or that property is sold and the proceeds of sale divided between the parties, or that property is settled on one of the parties. These property adjustment orders can also be made for the benefit of any children of the family.[16] It cannot be emphasised too strongly that there is no power to vary a property adjustment order. Consequently, very close attention must be paid to ensuring that any such order makes fair and just provision for each party, both immediately and in the future.[17]

Property transfer orders

Section 21(2)(a) provides that the court may order 'that a party must transfer such of his or her property as may be specified in favour of the other party or a child of the family', such property being property to which that party is entitled, either in possession or reversion.[18] Property transfer orders, like lump sum orders, may be used to bring about a clean break between the parties. When consideration is being given to making a property

---

11 See too *O'Donnell v O'Donnell* [1975] 2 All ER 993, in which the husband suggested a smaller lump sum and higher periodical payments. This was rejected by the court for various reasons, including that large periodical payments are a strong disincentive 'if not a prohibition' to remarriage.
12 [1994] 1 FLR 219.
13 Ibid, at p 222.
14 See *Harwood v Harwood* [1991] 2 FLR 274 in which the husband was ordered to assign to the wife the whole of his share of the assets of a dissolved partnership.
15 See *Schuller v Schuller* [1990] 2 FLR 193.
16 See ch 9. But such an order is highly unusual, see *Lord Lilford v Glyn* [1979] 1 All ER 441.
17 The only possibility open to an aggrieved party is to seek leave to appeal out of time, see below.
18 S 21(4).

adjustment order it is usually important to establish how each party's capital assets were acquired. In *H v H (Financial Provision: Capital Assets)*[19] Thorpe J held that the fact that the wife's capital holdings had been provided by her husband's parents was a relevant consideration, influencing him not to make any further capital provision for her. However, the size of the parties' respective contributions to the acquisition of property is by no means determinative of how that property will be divided between them. Therefore, the estimation of the nature and extent of the spouses' interests in the family assets does not normally need to be given the same close attention as it would if the court was assessing their respective beneficial entitlements under a resulting or constructive trust.[20] Indeed, the courts have warned practitioners against making prolonged investigations into the exact nature of each spouses' property holdings, because this often gives rise to very considerable and unnecessary expense.[1] Rather, a court will be influenced in a loose sense by whether one spouse contributed to the acquisition of capital by the other, for example by assisting with the building up of a business belonging in law to one of them only.[2] Where this has been the case, the court will approach the distribution of the property between the parties in a manner which is more favourable to the applicant than it would be in a case where her contribution has been confined to domestic matters only. A too loose approach does, however, create the danger that a judge will fail to give proper weight to each spouse's respective rights in their joint property holdings,[3] and recently there has been a shift towards a more careful evaluation of each parties' rights in any property holdings. Thus in *M v B (Ancillary Proceedings: Lump Sum)*[4] Thorpe LJ stated that 'any decision as to how the proceeds of sale are to be divided to give effect to the section 25 criteria must start from an accurate assessment of what the parties' respective proprietary interests are'.

Sale orders

Section 24A provides that:

> 'Where the court makes ... a secured periodical payments order, an order for the payment of a lump sum or a property adjustment

19 [1993] 2 FLR 335.
20 See ch 9.
1   *P v P (Financial Provision)* [1989] 2 FLR 241; *B v B (Financial Provision)* [1989] 1 FLR 119.
2   For an extreme example of going from 'rags to riches' see *Gojkovic v Gojkovic* [1990] 2 All ER 84; see too *Preston v Preston* [1982] Fam 17; *Kokosinski v Kokosinski* [1980] 1 All ER 1106; *Conran v Conran* [1997] 2 FLR 615; *W v W (Judicial Separation)* [1995] 2 FLR 259.
3   See *White v White* [1998] 2 FLR 310, where the trial judge failed to acknowledge the wife's property rights were involved when he transferred a substantial proportion of the assets to the husband.
4   [1998] 1 FLR 53, at p 58. The Court of Appeal held that the trial judge's finding that the wife had been the major financial contributor was simply unsustainable.

order, then, on making that order or at any time thereafter, the court may make a further order for the sale of such property as may be specified in the order, being property in which or in the proceeds of sale of which either or both of the parties to the marriage has or have a beneficial interest, either in possession or reversion.'

This provision is an essential adjunct to those other orders, and used imaginatively it can extend and complement the court's other powers. At its simplest level it may, for example, only be possible to order a lump sum payment if property is sold to raise the necessary cash. Sometimes one spouse is obdurate about complying with an existing lump sum order. In these circumstances, provisions in section 24A may come to the assistance of the other spouse. Thus the court can order sale, but direct that the sale shall not take effect until a specified event occurs, or until after a specified period of time has expired.[5] This power could be used to coerce the obdurate spouse into compliance. For example, a court could order that his own home be sold if the lump sum has not been paid within a specified time. Various factors are influential in determining whether a sale order is appropriate, and sometimes such orders are clearly inappropriate. Thus if ordering the sale of the former matrimonial home will result in both spouses and their children being homeless, such an order would almost certainly be unwise. Similarly, it may be counterproductive to liquidate assets which are income-producing when this will destroy the owning spouse's means of earning his livelihood.[6]

Where a sale order is made, it can contain a provision requiring the proceeds to be invested in a fund designed to secure an order for periodical payments for one of the parties, but such an order will cease to have effect on the death or remarriage of that party.[7] The court can require specified property to be offered for sale to a specified person.[8] In effect, this means that the court can give one spouse the first option to buy out the other spouse's share in the matrimonial home (or other specified property). This is a valuable provision where one spouse is hostile to the other acquiring a particular family asset, and where he or she plans to dispose of it to someone else. Where someone other than the spouses has a beneficial interest in the property in question, this does not prevent an order for sale being made. But that person's position must be respected by the court, which must take account of his or her representations alongside the other matters it is required to consider under section 25.[9]

5   S 24A(4).
6   *Martin v Martin* [1976] 3 All ER 625; *P v P (Financial Provision: Lump Sum)* [1978] 3 All ER 70; *P v P (Financial Provision)* [1989] 2 FLR 241.
7   S 24A(5).
8   S 24A(2)(b).
9   S 24A(6).

Settlement orders

Section 21(2)(b), (c) and (d) provide that the court may make:

> '(b) an order that the settlement of such property of a party as may be specified must be made, to the satisfaction of the court, for the benefit of the other party and of the children of the family, or either or any of them;
>
> (c) an order varying, for the benefit of the parties and of the children of the family, or either or any of them, any marriage settlement;
>
> (d) an order extinguishing or reducing the interest of either of the parties under any marriage settlement.'

A settlement arises where any property has been purchased in the spouses' joint names, or where they each have a beneficial interest in it. It includes any disposition made in favour of the spouses as spouses which makes continuing provision for them.[10] A settlement creates successive interests in land, and can be invaluable where the spouses' resources are insufficient to make adequate provision for them both, and where one spouse needs the immediate use of property more urgently than the other. It may, for example, be appropriate to direct that the matrimonial home be jointly owned, that one spouse should have exclusive use of the property for a period of time, and that the other should become entitled to his or her share in the proceeds of sale of the property when the settlement period comes to an end. In this way a settlement enables a court to make provision for one of the party's needs without entirely taking away the other party's rights in the property concerned.

Where a court wishes to extinguish the interests of one spouse under a settlement, for example where they are joint owners of the matrimonial home, it will normally do this by making a property transfer order under section 21(2)(a). However it should be noted that an order under paragraph (a) directs one of the parties to transfer property to the other, consequently it requires the transferor's co-operation. This can create difficulties where that co-operation is not readily forthcoming, or where the transferor has disappeared. By contrast, under paragraphs (c) and (d) it is the court's order which varies, or extinguishes, a spouse's interest under an existing settlement. It may, therefore, be to the applicant's advantage to apply under either of these paragraphs rather than for a property transfer order. For example, a court could order that the settled property be held on trust for the wife absolutely. As a result, the husband's interest is extinguished immediately by operation of the court's order. The court could couple its order with a direction that the matter be referred to one of the

---

10 *Young v Young* [1962] P 27. However, an outright transfer is not a settlement, see *Prescott v Fellowes* [1958] P 260.

conveyancing counsel of the court for him to execute a proper instrument to be executed by all necessary parties.[11]

The statutory guidelines in section 25(1) and (2)

Section 25(1) and (2) give guidance to the courts on the matters to which a court must have regard when deciding whether and how to exercise its broad and discretionary financial provision and property adjustment powers. The judge is not told what objective the guidelines are designed to achieve,[12] although the courts have adopted the general target of making orders which are fair, just and reasonable.[13] However, what amounts to fairness varies in the light of all the circumstances of the case, and should not be confused with achieving broad equality between the parties.[14] Section 25(1) does have a weight attached to it, but no particular weight attaches to any of the eight specific factors listed in section 25(2)(a)-(h); consequently some factors will assume great importance in some cases, and lesser or no importance in others.

Section 25(1) provides that:

'It shall be the duty of the court in deciding whether to exercise its powers under any of sections 22A to 24A and, if so, in what manner, to have regard to all the circumstances of the case, first consideration being given to the welfare while a minor of any child of the family who has not attained the age of eighteen.'

Section 25(2) provides that:

'As regards the exercise of the powers of the court under section 22A or 23 ... to make a financial provision order in favour of a party to a marriage or the exercise of its powers under section 23A, 24 or 24A ... in relation to a party to the marriage, the court shall in particular have regard to the following matters—

(a) the income, earning capacity, property and other financial resources which each of the parties to the marriage has or is likely to have in the foreseeable future, including in the case of earning capacity any increase in that capacity which it would in the opinion of the court be reasonable to expect a party to the marriage to take steps to acquire;

(b) the financial needs, obligations and responsibilities which each of the parties to the marriage has or is likely to have in the foreseeable future;

---

11 S 30.
12 Contrast with the position under the original statute, the Matrimonial Proceedings and Property Act 1970, where the judicial target was (broadly) to place the parties in the financial position they would have been if the marriage had not broken down.
13 *Page v Page* (1981) 2 FLR 198.
14 *Burgess v Burgess* [1996] 2 FLR 34.

(c) the standard of living enjoyed by the family before the break-down of the marriage;

(d) the age of each party to the marriage and the duration of the marriage;

(e) any physical or mental disability of either of the parties to the marriage;

(f) the contributions which each of the parties has made or is likely in the foreseeable future to make to the welfare of the family, including any contribution by looking after the home or caring for the family;

(g) the conduct of each of the parties, whatever the nature of the conduct and whether it occurred during the marriage or after the separation of the parties or (as the case may be) dissolution or annulment of the marriage, if that conduct is such that it would in the opinion of the court be inequitable to disregard it;

(h) the value to each of the parties of any benefit which by reason of the dissolution or annulment of the marriage, that party will lose the chance of acquiring.'

The welfare of the children must be the court's first consideration

Sometimes legislation requires the welfare of any child affected by it to be given 'paramount' consideration by the court,[15] and sometimes that it should be the court's 'first' consideration.[16] Where the child's welfare is paramount, it overrides all other considerations and determines the course to be followed. Where the child's welfare comes first, it means that the court must give it greater weight than other considerations, but it will not necessarily prevail over the other matters which the court must bear in mind. In the case of financial provision and property adjustment orders, section 25(1) provides that 'first' consideration must be given to the welfare of any child of the family who has not attained the age of 18. In *Suter v Suter and Jones*[17] the Court of Appeal noted the distinction between 'first' and 'first and paramount', and ruled that any order must be just between the parents as well as making provision for their children. However, in many cases the resources available for distribution between the parties are such that they can only cover the needs of the children, and in cases of this kind other considerations in the statutory guidelines are likely to be superfluous.

Providing for the welfare of the children means ensuring that they have adequate financial support and adequate housing. When, in the past, courts had jurisdiction to make periodical payments orders for children,

---

15 See Children Act 1989, s 1(1).
16 See Adoption Act 1976, s 6.
17 [1987] 2 All ER 336.

judges were often determined to ensure that fathers made some contribution to the upbringing of their own children, even when they could ill afford, or arguably not afford, to pay anything at all.[18] This determination has now been taken over by the Child Support Agency, and it is undoubtedly the case that priority will continue to be given to the provision of periodical payments for children during their dependency, whether this is obtained through an application to the Agency, or through a maintenance agreement which is embodied in a consent order. The provision of periodical payments for children normally cannot be disentangled from the provision of periodical payments for the parent who is looking after the children. If the parent with care has an insufficient income in her own right, this will rebound on the children, and be prejudicial to their welfare. Orders for a spouse have therefore tended to be based on a mother's need for continuing financial support, and the impact of this need on the needs of the children.[19] However, as a result there may be a conflict between the focus on the welfare of the children in section 25(1) and the clean break provisions in section 25A, because an order which limits, or terminates, periodical payments for a spouse will reduce the family's income as a whole. It is suggested that the interrelationship between the welfare of the children, and the claim of the caring parent to continue to receive periodical payments, can easily be overlooked. The modern trend is towards the promotion of self-sufficiency for the adults, and there is no established theory that a parent with care should be entitled to receive financial support in that capacity. Indeed, the trend may be the other way, as can be seen in the comments about encouraging mothers to work which were made by the Court of Appeal in *N v N (Consent Order: Variation)*,[20] where a mother was refused a variation of a consent order which deprived her, and indirectly her children, of much needed financial support.

In relation to housing, it is often the case that the spouse who is looking after the children is allowed to retain the use of the matrimonial home. This may be harsh on the other spouse who is forced to live in far inferior accommodation, and who cannot obtain his share in the property at least until the children grow up, and often beyond that date. But, as was said in *Browne v Pritchard*,[1] the courts must direct their attention in the first instance to the provision of homes for all concerned. Ormrod LJ pointed out that it is a complete misapprehension

---

18 In *Freeman v Swatridge* [1984] FLR 762 and *Tovey v Tovey* (1978) 8 Fam Law 80 the husband's income in each case was reduced by the Court of Appeal to below subsistence level; but cf *Delaney v Delaney* [1990] 2 FLR 457 in which a far more generous, indeed arguably a far too generous, approach was taken to the husband's new liabilities when assessing what he should pay to his first family.

19 *Waterman v Waterman* [1989] 1 FLR 380.

20 [1993] 2 FLR 868, at p 875. Compare this approach with the Child Support Act 1991 formula which includes an amount for the caring parent in the calculation of child support.

1 [1975] 3 All ER 721.

to think in terms of one spouse being kept out of his or her share in the fund tied up in the property, because 'investment in the home is the least liquid investment one can possibly make. It cannot be converted into cash while the children are at home and often not until one spouse dies unless it is possible to move into a much smaller and cheaper accommodation'.[2]

When making orders about the home the courts have tended to adopt one of two approaches to giving extra weight to the welfare of the children, although the thinking in each is liable to merge. Sometimes they have taken an essentially legalistic approach, looking at the words of the statute, pointing out that the obligation to give first consideration to the children ends at 18, and then giving greater weight to the rights in waiting of the spouse with an interest tied up in the property. Thus they have ordered that the property should be retained as a home for the children until they are approaching adulthood, and that the proceeds should then be shared between the spouses. The courts have done this even though they have recognised that, from the point of view of the children, the ages of 16, 17 and 18[3] are too early for the house to be sold.[4] At other times the courts have taken a broader view of family life, and have acknowledged that children do not stop needing a home merely because they reach adulthood. In some cases they have extended the period until all the children have ceased to receive full-time education.[5] In others, they have recognised that the spouse who has cared for the children during their minority will continue to wish to provide a home for the children until the children themselves marry, and to which the children can return with their own spouses, and eventually the grandchildren. When influenced by the latter approach, the courts have been inclined to transfer the entire interest in the property to the parent with care of the children as in *Hanlon v Hanlon*.[6]

Once children have reached 18 their welfare is no longer the court's first consideration. But of course children do not stop needing a home or financial provision at that age; indeed they may be entering upon a particularly expensive stage of their lives. The courts have formally recognised that children continue to need support when they have embarked on further and higher education. A parent can therefore be required both to continue to contribute towards the children's financial needs, and in addition to make a contribution towards his ex-wife's reasonable expenditure on keeping a home going for the children during their period of study.[7]

---

2   Ibid, at p 725.
3   All of these ages have been chosen in reported cases.
4   See, for example, *Browne v Pritchard* [1975] 3 All ER 721.
5   See, for example, *Chamberlain v Chamberlain* [1974] 1 All ER 33.
6   [1978] 2 All ER 889. This issue is discussed below under the heading 'The matrimonial home – what order is the most appropriate?'.
7   *G v G (Periodical Payments: Jurisdiction)* [1997] 1 All ER 272.

The financial resources of each spouse

Paragraph (a) of the guidelines concentrates attention on the spouses' resources, that is on their real and personal property and on their income and earning capacity. It provides that the court must have regard to:

'... the income, earning capacity, property and other financial resources which each of the parties to the marriage has or is likely to have in the foreseeable future, including in the case of earning capacity any increase in that capacity which it would in the opinion of the court be reasonable to expect a party to the marriage to take steps to acquire.'

Because the court's decision will influence the parties' financial affairs for many years, it is not just the present levels of income and property that must be considered; the court must also think about what these are likely to be in the foreseeable future,[8] and include any benefits under a pension scheme which a party to a marriage has or is likely to have.[9] The courts have determined that all resources are relevant. Not surprisingly, therefore, it will be seen that this maximisation of resources approach has brought into question some fundamental issues of principle.

The initial burden is on the applicant for an order to prove that there are resources available to meet his or her claim. However, unless a court is provided with correct, complete and up to date information about each spouse's income and assets the judge cannot properly exercise his discretionary powers under the Matrimonial Causes Act 1973. Consequently, each party is under a duty to make full and frank disclosure of all material facts to the other party and to the court. What can a judge do where he forms the opinion that one party has deliberately failed or refused to make full and frank disclosure and has concealed his true financial position from the other party? Courts have been encouraged by the Court of Appeal to adopt a robust response to deliberate non-disclosure, to draw adverse inferences against the recalcitrant party and to make findings about his actual financial circumstances applying a simple balance of probabilities test. Where this results in the non-disclosing party being assumed to have more assets than is the true position he has only himself to blame.[10] The courts are conscious that

8   Cases in the law reports, in the main, are concerned with disputed orders involving the distribution of fairly substantial assets. However, the reality for many spouses is that their resources are small, especially when there are dependent children. Indeed, many have debts rather than assets: see J M Eekelaar and M Maclean *Maintenance after Divorce* (Clarendon Press, 1986).

9   S 25B(1).

10   *Baker v Baker* [1995] 2 FLR 829; *Payne v Payne* [1968] 1 WLR 390; *J-PC v J-AF* [1955] P 215; *Fournier v Fournier* [1998] 2 FLR 990, where the husband's deliberate concealment of his assets and his failure to pay an order for periodical payments led to the capitalisation of the wife's periodical payments.

the integrity of the legal process would be severely undermined if a party were able deliberately to evade the duty to disclose.

A related difficulty occurs where a spouse enjoys access to wealth but is not entitled to it, or where he has substantial means but has an immediate liquidity problem. In *Thomas v Thomas*[11] the husband was a prosperous businessman and the court would normally have made a substantial financial order for the benefit of the wife and children. However, he had a large loan secured on the family home and he claimed that he was unable to offer any alternative security which would be acceptable to the bank. He also stated that his immediate income was modest. However, this was because it was derived from a family business of which he was joint managing director, and the company had a policy of ploughing back profits and paying relatively modest salaries to the directors, while at the same time making very generous provision for them by way of pension provision. Once again the Court of Appeal adopted a robust approach. Waite LJ made it plain that 'the court is not obliged to limit its orders exclusively to resources of capital or income which are shown actually to exist. The availability of unidentified resources may, for example, be inferred from a spouse's expenditure or style of living, or from his inability or unwillingness to allow complexity of his affairs to be penetrated with the precision necessary to ascertain his actual wealth or the degree of liquidity of his assets.' Moreover 'there will be occasions when it becomes permissible for a judge deliberately to frame his orders in a form which affords judicious encouragement to third parties to provide the maintaining spouse with the means to comply with the court's view of the justice of the case.'[12]

Where the respondent to an application is extremely rich he can plead what is known as the 'millionaires' defence'. The respondent concedes that his wealth is more than adequate to meet any order the court might make for the wife's reasonable requirements, and this shields him from having to make full and frank disclosure of all his assets.[13] This has the advantage to the respondent that he can keep the details of his financial affairs confidential, and it spares him the costs that are involved when assets have to be explored in minute, and often contested, detail. However, raising the millionaires' defence does not necessarily allow the respondent to give no details at all. In *Van G v Van G (Financial Provision: Millionaires' Defence)*[14] it was held not to be sufficient for the husband merely to state 'my assets amount to no less than £10m and therefore I can meet any order that can be made', as this did not give

---

11 [1995] 2 FLR 668.
12 Ibid, at p 670. The husband was appealing against a lump sum order of £150,000 plus £8,000 for a car and periodical payments of £1,500 month on the ground that he had neither the capital nor income to pay because his resources were all absorbed by the family business. His appeal was dismissed.
13 *Thyssen-Bornemisza v Thyssen-Bornemisza (No 2)* [1986] Fam 1; applied in *Dart v Dart* [1996] 2 FLR 286.
14 [1995] 1 FLR 328.

the court enough information on which to carry out the balancing operation inherent in section 25(2).

When considering the spouses' earnings, the court is not only concerned with what each spouse is actually earning, it is also engaged in estimating what each spouse could reasonably be expected to earn. If a spouse deliberately reduces his working hours, gives up a job, or is paid less than the normal rate for the work he is doing, the court can base its order on what he could earn.[15] A court may deem a man to be deliberately unemployed and make an order on the assumption that he could obtain work if he tried.[16] However, there is a risk that a court will make the assumption that a spouse could obtain work if he or she makes the effort, without there being any real evidence to substantiate this approach. The danger to the spouse who is wrongly labelled as 'work shy' by a court, and being ordered to make periodical payments on the basis of what the court believes him to be capable of earning, was graphically spelt out by Finer J in *Williams v Williams,*[17] when he reminded courts that the ultimate sanction for non-payment of periodical payments is imprisonment. He also stated that it is wrong for courts to make decisions on the footing of impressions about demeanour or generalised local knowledge, important as these factors may be, unchecked by all the hard information that may be available about a man's earning capacity and his chances of employment.

These were salutary words, which should be borne in mind particularly at times of high unemployment. There is a real risk that orders may be based on hunch and prejudice, especially if the political climate is one in which those persons who cannot obtain work are labelled as lacking the requisite initiative and drive to seek the employment which is allegedly available. Particular care also needs to be taken when an assessment is made of a non-working wife's earning capacity, and any increase in that capacity which it would be reasonable to expect her to take steps to acquire. This provision in section 25(2)(a) reinforces the clean break provisions in section 25A, and the thinking that, where appropriate, the aim should be to enable the spouses to become financially independent of one another. A spouse who is not hampered by child care responsibilities is not entitled simply to lapse into apathy with regard to obtaining employment, she is expected to make real efforts to obtain work.[18] However, the Court of Appeal, in a number of judgments,[19] has recognised the difficulties experienced by middle-aged women in obtaining employment. However, courts have also been prepared to find that a non-working wife has an earning capacity, and to quantify it on what is, in reality, a speculative

---

15 *Hardy v Hardy* (1981) 2 FLR 321.
16 *McEwan v McEwan* [1972] 2 All ER 708.
17 [1974] 3 All ER 377.
18 See the comments of Singer J in *T v T (Financial Provision: Pensions)* [1998] 1 FLR 1072, at p 1080.
19 *M v M (Financial Provision)* [1987] 2 FLR 1; *Leadbeater v Leadbeater* [1985] FLR 789; *Barrett v Barrett* [1988] 2 FLR 516.

basis.[20] The danger of an approach which is not backed by hard evidence is that the resulting financial provision and property arrangements may prove to be insufficient to cater for the wife's needs, because account is taken of her potential earnings which never in fact materialise. It should also be borne in mind that it is much easier for a parent with young children to work when living in a two-parent household than when living as a single parent. Such matters as school holidays, and a child being ill, or off school, can more easily be coped with when parenting is shared with another.

The courts were initially hesitant about whether damages awarded for pain, suffering and loss of amenity could be treated as a resource, but eventually they ruled that personal injuries damages awarded under all heads of damage, including for pain and suffering and loss of amenity, could be taken into account.[1] The manner of the distribution of such damages is, of course, still a matter within the court's discretion, and likely to be influenced by paragraph (e), which looks to any mental or physical disability of either party. Moreover, where the injured party has very considerable needs there may be no readily available capital which is transferable to the other party.[2] Courts have taken account of inherited wealth acquired after the parties separated, and which in no way formed part of the original matrimonial assets.[3] Expectations of inheritance give rise to difficulty because there is no knowing when the testator will die and whether his or her will may be altered. These expectations have therefore sometimes been deemed too uncertain to be included.[4] However, the courts have been prepared, in principle, to take account of all present and future resources and they have been prepared to widen the purse to the maximum extent.

Capital resources

The first question to be asked when considering the parties' capital resources is whether there is any reason to make an order involving capital adjustment. In *H v H (Financial Provision: Capital Allowance)*[5] Thorpe J expressed the view that 'the discretionary powers of the court to adjust capital shares between the spouses should not be exercised unless there is a manifest need for intervention upon the application of the section 25 criteria'. Similar thinking was approved by Waite LJ in *Burgess v Burgess*[6] when he said: 'when the court is dealing with the joint assets of working

20 *M v M (Financial Provision)* above, at p 4.
1   *Daubney v Daubney* [1976] 2 All ER 453; *Wagstaff v Wagstaff* [1992] 1 All ER 275.
2   *C v C (Financial Provision: Personal Damages)* [1995] 2 FLR 171.
3   *Schuller v Schuller* [1990] 2 FLR 193.
4   *Michael v Michael* [1986] 2 FLR 389; *K v K (Conduct)* [1990] 2 FLR 225.
5   [1993] 2 FLR 335, at p 348.
6   [1996] 2 FLR 34, at p 39.

spouses, common sense and equity require that equality of interest should be adopted as a starting point'.

The unfairness of departing from an approach which recognises the actual entitlement of each spouse to his or her share in the capital in a case where each spouse is financially independent is well-illustrated by *White v White*.[7] The parties came before the court as equal partners in a farming business and between them they had substantial assets which meant they could be financially independent of one another. Both parties wished to continue to farm. Instead of determining what belonged to the wife in law and in equity, the trial judge decided that the wife's desire to continue farming was impracticable, but that this ambition was reasonable in the case of the husband. The judge therefore considerably reduced the wife's share in their joint capital assets so that the husband could continue farming in a worthwhile way. The judge's approach was castigated on appeal. As Thorpe LJ said: 'the justification for ordering the wife to transfer substantial assets for no consideration is hardly reasoned'.[8] Any transfer of property order in favour of the husband had to be justified on the basis of fairness and 'it offends [a] sense of fairness that a wife who has worked for over 30 years equally and not nominally in partnership should exit with anything less than her legal entitlement in the absence of extraordinary features'.[9]

Determining what amounts to a proper redistribution of capital resources where the capital has mainly accumulated as a result of the exertions of an extremely wealthy husband has exercised the courts in several cases. A crucial issue is how far the husband's success has been brought about with the assistance of his wife because where it has, the wife's share in the capital has been calculated in terms of 'what is her entitlement' rather than 'what are her reasonable needs'.[10] Expressed succinctly, a partnership case, where the wife is found to be an equal partner, or to have contributed substantially to the accumulation of assets, is wholly different from a 'big money' case where the origin of the wealth is clearly on one side only. In the former case the courts look to entitlement, whereas in the latter type of case the emphasis has been placed on the wife's contribution to the marriage, and what she should reasonably obtain on its breakdown applying all the criteria in section 25.[11]

Resources provided by a new spouse or partner

One of the most difficult issues of principle and policy which a court may have to grapple with is to what extent, if at all, it should take account of

---

7   [1998] 2 FLR 310; see also, *M v B (Ancillary Proceedings: Lump Sum)* [1998] 1 FLR 53.
8   Ibid, at p 319. Thorpe LJ said the the judge's assessment of the husband's reasonable requirements 'might be said to be discriminatory', which indeed it was.
9   Ibid, at p 320.
10 *Gojkovic v Gojkovic* [1990] 1 FLR 140; *Conran v Conran* [1997] 2 FLR 615. See also *Page v Page* (1981) 2 FLR 198.
11 *Dart v Dart* [1996] 2 FLR 286; *A v A (Financial Provision)* [1998] 2 FLR 180.

the income, earning capacity and property of a new partner when considering the spouses' resources. This difficulty is exacerbated when the new relationship is an unmarried relationship. The simple answer to the question whether property belonging to a new spouse or partner can be treated as a resource is 'yes'. There is a body of case law in which this has happened. But the extent to which a new spouse or partner's resources will influence the way the parties' own assets are distributed is not easy to assess, and the policy reasons why resources provided by such persons are taken into account are not always easy to discern, the reason being that 'the Court of Appeal has said again and again that these matters are, as Parliament intended them to be, questions for the discretion of the judge. They are not to be circumscribed by declarations of principle which run the risk of fettering the future exercise of what was meant to be a very flexible discretion indeed'.[12]

Accommodation provided by a new spouse, or intended spouse, for one of the parties has been taken into account either as a resource under paragraph (a) or as affecting that party's financial needs under paragraph (b). When balancing the claims of each spouse to the former matrimonial home, the fact that one spouse has accommodation provided by a new spouse may lead to the postponement of the realisation of his or her interest in the property, and to the quantification of his or her share in the value of the property being reduced. For example, in *H v H (Financial Provision: Remarriage)*[13] the wife was claiming a half share in the matrimonial home on the basis of her contribution to the welfare of the family under paragraph (f). She had remarried, her second husband was wealthy, and their new home had been conveyed into their joint names. She was also being supported by her second husband's income. The court for this reason (and other reasons) rejected her claim to a half share in the property, and instead awarded her one-twelfth of its value, not to be payable until the youngest child was 18. In *Martin v Martin*[14] the husband was living with a woman, whom he intended to marry, in her council house. He gave evidence that the tenancy could be transferred into their joint names. The court took account of the husband's occupation of the council house and treated it as part of his resources affecting his needs. Consequently, it gave the wife a life interest in the former matrimonial home, followed by an equal division of the proceeds of sale.[15] Provision made for the husband by a second partner was taken into account in *Mesher v Mesher and Hall*.[16] Here the woman whom the husband intended to marry had provided a deposit for their new home. Her injection of these resources

---

12 *Atkinson v Atkinson (No 2)* [1996] 1 FLR 51, at p 54.
13 [1975] 1 All ER 367.
14 [1977] 3 All ER 762.
15 This case was heavily influenced by the policy target under s 25 as originally drafted. However, the principle is clear, namely that housing provided by a new partner is a relevant consideration.
16 [1980] 1 All ER 126n.

meant that the husband's housing needs were being met, whereas the wife needed to live in the former matrimonial home. The wife's greater needs led to the husband's entitlement to receive his share in the proceeds of sale of the former matrimonial home being postponed until the spouses' youngest child reached 17.

It is suggested that when a court is assessing the resources of the parties and how much the applicant wife should receive, or the respondent husband retain, what in reality it is usually doing is conducting a balancing exercise between recognising their rights under paragraph (f) and making provision for their needs under paragraph (b). Strictly speaking re-marriage, or cohabitation, or their prospect, is irrelevant if the courts are solely concerned with the parties' accumulated rights at the time of marriage breakdown. Thus in *Wachtel v Wachtel*[17] there was dicta to the effect that where a wife can expect to receive a one-third share in the proceeds of sale of the former matrimonial home, then whether or not she may remarry is immaterial.[18] Similarly, in *Duxbury v Duxbury*[19] the court held that the wife was entitled to a lump sum order despite the fact that she was living with another man, and was likely to spend the money on him. So, adopting a 'rights' approach to financial provision and property adjustment orders, a court might take the view that, in order to give fair recognition to a wife's claim for a share under paragraph (f),[20] she should be entitled to any amount up to a half share in the former matrimonial home, and that any resources provided by a new spouse or partner should be discounted.

Paragraph (a), however, requires the court to take into account resources which the divorcing couple are likely to have in the foreseeable future, and it does not specify from where these should come; and paragraph (b) requires the court to consider the parties' respective needs. Consequently, if sale of the home, and an equal distribution of the assets, is insufficient to provide for two households, a 'needs' approach is likely to predominate. Accordingly, the position appears to be that where the resources available for distribution are being stretched, then the actual, or anticipated, contribution by a new spouse or partner will be taken fully into account by the court when it decides what orders to make. But where there is substantial wealth to be shared between the parties, and where the applicant spouse has built up an entitlement to a share in that wealth because the marriage has been long-lasting, then resources provided by a new spouse or partner are likely to be ignored in making any strictly arithmetical calculation of the parties' respective shares, but is simply a factor to be taken into account.[1] Indeed, it will normally not be possible for a court accurately to quantify the extent of a new spouse's, or partner's,

---

17 [1973] 1 All ER 829.
18 See too *Trippas v Trippas* [1973] 2 All ER 1.
19 [1987] 1 FLR 7.
20 Because of her contribution to the welfare of the family.
1 *S v S* [1987] 1 FLR 71.

assets, because he or she cannot usually be compelled to give precise evidence of means to the court.[2] However, as the court pointed out in *Frary v Frary*,[3] where the husband cannot persuade his partner to give such evidence, he takes the risk that the court will base its order on general assertions and assumptions about the extent of the new partner's means.[4]

Periodical payments where a spouse is living with a new partner

An order for periodical payments automatically comes to an end when a spouse remarries.[5] But what is the position where the wife is living with another man? Where there is little money to provide for both households, money provided by a new partner may enable the court better to make provision for each spouse. For example, in *Suter v Suter and Jones*[6] Mr Jones spent every night at the wife's home (but had breakfast at his mother's house). The Court of Appeal said that he should therefore make a contribution towards the household expenses. This anticipitated contribution, which of course the court could not order Mr Jones to make, enabled the court to relieve the husband of his maintenance obligation towards the wife, and it therefore only made a nominal periodical payments order in her favour.[7]

In *Atkinson v Atkinson*[8] the argument was put that a wife who cohabits permanently with another man should not be in a better position than a wife who remarries. It was pressed on the court that this argument becomes even stronger if the motive for cohabitation rather than remarriage is financial. In *Atkinson* the wife was receiving £6,000 per annum in periodical payments which she would automatically lose if she remarried. The man with whom she was living had only a very modest income, and she was therefore heavily reliant on the money she was receiving from her ex-husband. The Court of Appeal held that the fact of cohabitation is a matter to be taken into account by the court, and is conduct which it would be inequitable to disregard under paragraph (g). It referred to *Suter v Suter and Jones* and said that the financial consequences of cohabitation may be

2   *Wynne v Wynne and Jeffers* [1980] 3 All ER 659; *Frary v Frary* [1993] 2 FLR 696.
3   Above.
4   See too *W v W (Disclosure by Third Party)* (1981) 2 FLR 291.
5   S 28(1)(a).
6   [1987] 2 All ER 336.
7   It would be interesting to know what happened next. Did the court's order bring the relationship between the wife and Mr Jones to a premature end? Mr Jones was very much younger than the wife, and may not have wished to pay 'rent' for spending the night with her. If the relationship did end the wife could have applied for an increase in her periodical payments, as the court had refused to make a clean break order. Thus the burden of supporting the wife may not have entirely been lifted from the husband. Interestingly in *Atkinson v Atkinson* [1995] 2 FLR 356 Thorpe LJ commented that it would be 'unworldly' to ignore the 21-year age gap between the wife and the younger man she was now living with in assessing the future of the relationship.
8   [1987] 3 All ER 849.

such that it would be inappropriate for maintenance to continue because the cohabitant can be expected to contribute to the running costs of the household. However, the court stated that in general there is no statutory requirement to give decisive weight to the fact of cohabitation and that it should *not* be equated with remarriage without legislative sanction.[9]

A fresh attempt to persuade the Court of Appeal that it was manifestly unjust for a cohabiting wife of a wealthy ex-husband to receive anything other than nominal periodical payments was made in *Atkinson v Atkinson (No 2)*.[10] The court rejected this submission, stating that it was 'too crude a view', and held that Thorpe J had been entitled to take into account 'the length of the marriage, the contribution made during the marriage by the wife to the care of the home, the upbringing of the children ... and the opportunity she provided to the husband to pursue his very successful business activities'.[11] On the broader policy issue of what are the proper principles to be adopted in cases where a spouse is living in a new and permanent relationship, the Court of Appeal responded that Parliament had intended that this should be a matter for the discretion of the judge, and that the discretion should not be circumscribed by declarations of principle which ran the risk of fettering the exercise of what was meant to be a very flexible discretion indeed.[12]

A different question arises when the respondent to an application for periodical payments, usually the husband, has remarried, or is living with another woman who has an income of her own. To what extent can the new partner's income be taken into account when assessing how much the husband ought to pay for the support of his first family? It has been held that a court cannot require a second wife directly to contribute to the periodical payments paid by a husband for the support of his former wife and children. Consequently, if the husband has no income at all of his own, and his second wife is the breadwinner in the family, no order for periodical payments can be made against the husband.[13] In *Macey v Macey*[14] it was held that a magistrates' court had erred in law when taking into account the second woman's income as part of the available funds from which an order for periodical payments could be paid. However, the position is a subtle one. In *Macey v Macey* the court held that where the husband derives benefits from his new partner's income, which means that a greater part of his own income is available to pay maintenance to his first wife and children, an order can be made on the basis that the husband does not need his money to support his new family.[15] This has

9   The wife's payments were reduced to £4,500.
10   [1996] 1 FLR 51.
11   Ibid, at p 54.
12   See too *S v S* [1987] 1 FLR 71 where Waite J held that the weight given to a new partner's income will turn on such factors as the permanency of the relationship, the amount of support the wife is obtaining, and how much she needs.
13   *Brown v Brown* (1981) 3 FLR 161; *Berry v Berry* [1986] 1 FLR 618.
14   (1981) 3 FLR 7.
15   See too *Wilkinson v Wilkinson* (1980) 10 Fam Law 48.

the practical consequence that a husband can be ordered to pay more by way of periodical payments to his first family when his new partner has her own income, than he would be required to do where she has not.

Policy and a second partner's income

Whether the income of a second wife, or partner, should be taken into account when assessing a husband's ability to pay for the support of his first wife and children is a contentious issue, which tends to give rise to considerable animosity and strongly held views. On the one hand, the husband and his new partner may enjoy quite a good income when their resources are pooled, but on the other hand, if a court orders the husband to pay a large amount by way of periodical payments to his ex-wife, as well as to his children, the second wife or partner is likely to be extremely resentful that her earnings are treated as a relevant consideration. The Law Commission, when conducting a review of the working of the Matrimonial Causes Act 1973 at the beginning of 1980, wrote in their discussion paper that they had been told of cases in which second wives alleged that they had postponed having children, and in which husbands claimed to have been sterilised, because they could not afford to start a new family.[16] In their final report, the Commission observed that responses to the discussion paper revealed that such feeling was indeed widespread.[17]

Many first wives complained equally strongly to the Law Commission that they, and their children, were living in poverty, because the amount they were receiving in periodical payments was totally inadequate to provide for their needs, whereas, by contrast, the husband and his new partner were enjoying a far higher standard of living.[18] Many first wives deeply resented being forced to rely on inadequate state benefits, and the severe drop in their living standards, caused by the breakdown of the marriage. They felt this particularly strongly where the husband had remarried, and was able to enjoy a comparatively high standard of living with his new partner.[19] Many first wives were angered by the fact that their children had a very low standard of living compared to other children. They found that, as divorced mothers, they did not have the earning capacity to lift their children out of poverty. Consequently they saw no reason why the children's father should not take proper financial responsibility for his children, and for his ex-wife as the parent with care.

Although some of the concerns of husbands and second partners were addressed when the clean break provisions were introduced,[20] in essence

---

16 Law Com No 103, para 26.
17 Law Com No 112, para 41.
18 Law Com No 103, paras 27 and 28.
19 Note the wide discrepancy in the spouses' incomes in *Macey v Macey* (1981) 3 FLR 7.
20 By the Matrimonial and Family Proceedings Act 1984.

the conflict between these two opposing points of view remains. Is the law unfair, as many second wives or partners, and many first wives, would continue to claim? It could be argued that a second wife must take her husband 'subject to all existing encumbrances'.[1] Only a lawyer would choose to express personal relationships in these terms, but the terminology is apt. It is suggested that a second marriage cannot be a fresh start because prior obligations have been incurred which are continuing. It is wrong that a husband should be allowed to escape his liability to his first wife and children by pleading he needs his income to support himself and his second family, when his second wife has her own means of support. But equally it is wrong for a first wife to continue with her dependency unnecessarily. Surely the questions for the court should be: what are the husband's needs in the light of the resources provided by his new partner; how do the second family's resources compare with those of the first family; and how can the claims of each family fairly be balanced one against the other?

It is suggested that the basis of the conflict between the two households arises from the fact that, generally speaking, motherhood forces women into financial dependency. During marriage a wife is therefore forced to look to her husband both for the support of their children, and for her own support, and this situation does not alter simply because the couple divorce. Where a man remarries, or lives, with another woman, and children are born, an almost identical relationship of dependency often comes into being. Hence each woman may properly complain that the husband has insufficient resources to provide herself, and her children, with adequate support. The first wife will complain that the husband's income is being absorbed by his new responsibilities. The second wife will complain that her earnings are being used to keep the husband's first family in addition to her own. It is suggested that both points of view are equally valid. They reveal the sad, but inescapable, fact that the vast majority of men and women neither earn enough, nor own enough, to be able to afford to move from one relationship to another, and to have more children by second partners, without the income of both households being drastically reduced.

Financial needs, obligations and responsibilities

Paragraph (b) of the guidelines requires the court to take account of:

> '... the financial needs, obligations and responsibilities which each of the parties to the marriage has or is likely to have in the foreseeable future.'

---

1   *Roberts v Roberts* [1968] 3 All ER 479, per Rees J.

It is a paragraph to which the courts tend to give great weight. Thus in *S v S*[2] Ormrod LJ said that if the court's attention is concentrated primarily on needs, the calculation of financial provision and property adjustment orders then becomes easier, more logical and more constructive. Certainly where resources are limited, paragraph (b) tends to take priority.[3] And giving primacy to needs is particularly pertinent when there are dependent children, as their welfare must be the court's first consideration.[4] The concentration on needs almost always persuades the courts to make an order under which each spouse is housed. Thorpe LJ neatly expressed the importance given to housing when he said: 'In all these cases it is one of the paramount considerations, in applying the section 25 criteria, to endeavour to stretch what is available to cover the need of each for a home, particularly where there are young children involved.' Significantly, he added: 'Obviously the primary carer needs whatever is available to make the main home for the children, but it is of importance, albeit of lesser importance, that the other parent should have a home of his own where the children can enjoy their contact with him ... in any case where there is, by stretch and a degree of risk-taking, the possibility of a division to enable both to rehouse themselves, that is an exceptionally important consideration and one which will almost invariably have a decisive impact on the outcome.'[5]

The concept of needs becomes complicated in those cases where the resources are ample. 'Reasonable requirements' has been introduced as an appropriately broader concept in 'big money' cases.[6] Because what a wife of a very wealthy spouse requires is likely to be greater than what a wife needs the court will pay particular attention to the word 'reasonable', in order objectively to appraise what the wife subjectively requires.[7]

The words 'obligations and responsibilities' embrace obligations not only to the ex-spouse and children, but also other family obligations, such as to elderly parents or other relatives. And of course it is these words which allow the claims of any new dependants to be brought into the weighing-up process. Thus if by the time the court makes its order one of the parties has remarried and undertaken financial responsibility for a

---

2   [1977] 1 All ER 56.
3   See, for example, *Smith v Smith* [1975] 2 All ER 19n; *Suter v Suter and Jones* [1987] 2 All ER 336; *Wells v Wells* [1992] 2 FLR 66.
4   S 25(1).
5   *M v B (Ancillary Proceedings: Lump Sum)* [1998] 2 FLR 53 at p 60.
6   *O'D v O'D* [1976] Fam 83; *Preston v Preston* [1982] Fam 17.
7   *Dart v Dart* [1996] 2 FLR 286; *A v A (Financial Provision)* [1998] 2 FLR 180; cf *Conran v Conran* [1997] 2 FLR 615, where the wife had made an 'exceptional' contribution to the marriage. See also, *R v R (Financial Provision: Reasonable Needs)* [1994] 2 FLR 1044 where Sir Stephen Brown P held that it was reasonable for the wife of a very wealthy man to stay in a 'superb Queen Anne-style house' worth £1.3m, but he may have been influenced by the fact that the husband had himself bought a house costing £2.7m where he lived with his mistress; and cf *W v W (Judicial Separation)* [1995] 2 FLR 259.

new spouse and her children, or if he is cohabiting and has taken on similar obligations, this must be taken into account.

The court is looking not only at the parties' current needs when their children are dependent, but also at their likely future needs when the children have grown up. The relevance of future needs to financial provision and property adjustment arrangements is one reason why an agreed solution may be difficult to reach. How far, for example, should the parties try to anticipate future events such as ill-health, remarriage, cohabitation and employment prospects? Here there is uncertainty. The Act is undoubtedly concerned with likelihoods rather than mere possibilities. However, the pressure to look to the future is only acute in respect of lump sum and property adjustment orders because these cannot be varied at a later date should the parties' circumstances alter significantly.[8] By contrast, periodical payments orders can be varied if either of the spouses' circumstances change. Consequently, courts are inclined to look to the immediacy of the parties' needs when quantifying the amount of a periodical payments order, and tend to leave the door open to make provision for change should their needs alter.[9]

The prospect of a wife's remarriage or cohabitation causes particular difficulties.[10] Arguably it is irrelevant. If the wife can properly expect to receive a share in the proceeds of sale of the former matrimonial home then whether or not she may remarry is immaterial, and it has been held to be so.[11] However, property adjustment orders are often made not only in recognition of a wife's legitimate expectation to receive a fair share of the family assets, but also in response to her needs, and the needs of the parties' children. Where the wife remarries, the main reason for making a substantial order in her favour may be brought to an end, because her new husband has his own resources. It may then seem manifestly unfair that a lump sum order, or a property adjustment order, which was made to reflect the spouses' respective needs at the time of breakdown, has the effect not only of depriving the husband for all time of his share in the spouses' capital assets, but also, in some cases, of endowing the wife's second husband, or partner, with a house paid for by the first husband.[12]

This point is well illustrated by *Chaudhuri v Chaudhuri*[13] which provides a salutary example. Here the home had been transferred to the wife subject to a charge for one-quarter of the proceeds of sale in favour of the husband. The wife, who was caring for the children, had remarried a

8　S 31(2). Furthermore, a lump sum or property adjustment order cannot be made on an application to vary a periodical payments order: s 31(5).

9　See above.

10　The House of Lords has made it plain that a spouse must state whether or not she intends to remarry, see *Livesey v Jenkins* [1985] 1 All ER 106.

11　See the dicta in *Wachtel v Wachtel* [1973] 1 All ER 829; *Trippas v Trippas* [1973] 2 All ER 1.

12　Cf *Wells v Wells* [1992] 2 FLR 66 (but decided in June 1980) where the husband was fortunate in being granted leave to appeal out of time against such an order.

13　[1992] 2 FLR 73.

year after this order had been made, and the elder child had gone to live with the husband. Leave to appeal out of time was refused, because the original order had contemplated the possibility of the wife remarrying, and because too much time had elapsed since the original order was made. In *Clutton v Clutton*[14] the Court of Appeal referred to the resentment a husband may feel when his house is occupied by the wife and her new husband or partner. The court approved the custom of making provision for this contingency occurring by making property adjustment orders under which the husband's interest in the house is postponed and becomes realisable in the event of the wife's remarriage or cohabitation.[15]

The standard of living before the breakdown of the marriage

Paragraph (c) of section 25(2) requires the court to take account of:

> '... the standard of living enjoyed by the family before the breakdown of the marriage.'

In the case of families of limited, or average, means it is inevitable that the standard of living of each spouse will fall because resources, which are adequate to keep one family at a standard of living which allows for small luxuries, when divided between two households will often barely keep each household in necessities. However, the issue to be resolved in the case of a divorced wife of a rich man is whether she can expect to maintain the standard of living which she enjoyed when married to him. Cases which occurred before 1984 must be treated with caution, because the policy of the legislation was to sustain the wife's standard of living so far as this was possible in the circumstances. However, a wife in circumstances like the wife in *Preston v Preston*[16] would still receive a similar settlement.[17] In that case Ormrod LJ said 'the wife of a millionaire and 23 years married is entitled to expect a very high standard of living which would include a home in a house or flat at the top end of the market, and probably a second home in the country or abroad, together with a very high spending power'.[18] In *Boylan v Boylan*[19] the wife's standard of living was considered in the context of the clean break provisions. Here it was held that it would be wrong to construe the words 'undue hardship' as

---

14 [1991] 1 All ER 340.
15 See below.
16 [1982] 1 All ER 41.
17 See, for example, *Dart v Dart* [1996] 2 FLR 286; *A v A (Financial Provision)* [1998] 2 FLR 180; *R v R (Financial Provision: Reasonable Needs)* [1994] 2 FLR 1044. Particular 'rules' appear to have developed in relation to 'big money' cases, see P George *In all the circumstances – section 25* [1997] Fam Law 729; C Willbourne *Reasonable requirements and the millionaires' defence* [1997] Fam Law 337.
18 [1982] 1 All ER 41, at p 48.
19 [1988] 1 FLR 282.

referring solely to the needs of a former wife when assessing her ability to adjust to the termination of periodical payments. Rather her reasonable requirements should be judged by the standard that she was the former wife of a man of substantial wealth.[20]

The age of each party and the duration of the marriage

Paragraph (d) directs the court's attention to:

'... the age of each party to the marriage and the duration of the marriage.'

In the light of this provision, a court is likely to want to be given information about the following matters: the impact of an unemployed wife's age on whether she can be expected to obtain work; how old she will be when the children cease to be dependent; where the husband is unemployed, whether, at his age, he can expect to gain further employment; where both parties are in middle age, what their financial positions will be on retirement. A wife in middle age with no, or only a limited, earning capacity, is likely to be awarded a more substantial share in the capital assets than a younger wife, as in *Martin v Martin*,[1] where the wife was given a life interest in the former matrimonial home. In *Jones v Jones*[2] the entire interest in the matrimonial home was transferred to the wife because she might be rendered homeless in middle age if the husband retained an interest in the property.[3] A property transfer order was made in *Hanlon v Hanlon*[4] mainly because a middle-aged wife needed the home for the four children of the marriage.

The age of the husband was an important consideration in *Greenham v Greenham*.[5] The trial judge had ordered that the former matrimonial home, in which the husband was living, should be sold when the husband attained the age of 70. He was held to have been wrong to include this provision. Even though the husband would probably be in a secure financial position at that age, and would be able to afford to pay the wife her share in the property, it was unreasonable to force him to move house at the age of 70.

---

20 It was therefore held that the only way in which the wife's right to periodical payments could be terminated, in such a way as not to cause her undue hardship, would be by the payment to her of a lump sum sufficient to provide her with an income comparable to the amount she was receiving in periodical payments; see too *B v B (Financial Provision)* [1990] 1 FLR 20; *R v R (Financial Provision: Reasonable Needs)* [1994] 2 FLR 1044.
1 [1977] 3 All ER 762.
2 [1975] 2 All ER 12.
3 Although this decision was also strongly influenced by the fact that the husband's violence had deprived the wife of her earning capacity.
4 [1978] 2 All ER 889.
5 [1989] 1 FLR 105. Cf *W v W (Judicial Separation: Ancillary Relief)* [1995] 2 FLR 259.

In *S v S*[6] the parties had married when both were aged over 50, and because of her age and circumstances the wife had pressing housing needs. However the marriage had lasted a mere two years, which made it unreasonable to expect the husband to make very substantial financial provision for her. The court arrived at an imaginative solution. It ordered the husband to settle on the wife a sufficient sum to buy a house, the object being that the capital invested in the house would revert to the husband, or to his estate, on the wife's death. This would mean that, in the long run, the husband's family would not be deprived of the capital represented by the house, whereas the wife would have a reasonable home to live in during her lifetime.

The weight given to the duration of the marriage is liable to vary in accordance with whether the fact of marriage has brought about adverse financial circumstances for one of the spouses. If the wife is young and the marriage has been short-lived she cannot expect much, if anything at all, in the way of periodical payments or property adjustment provision.[7] As Balcombe LJ said in *H v H (Financial Provision: Short Marriage)*[8]

'[With] short marriage[s] between two young persons, neither of whom has been adversely affected financially by the consequences of the marriage and [where] each ... is fully capable of earning his or her own living, the approach which the court would normally adopt is to allow for a short period of periodical payments to allow the party ... in the weaker position ... to adjust herself to the situation, and thereafter to achieve the wholly desirable result of a clean break.'

However, if the wife has given birth to a child, then she will need periodical payments for herself as well as the child, and she will have a greater need than the husband to occupy the former matrimonial home.[9] In *C v C (Financial Relief: Short Marriage)*[10] the wife's marriage to a very wealthy man had only lasted for a little over nine months, but the parties had a child who was beset by health problems. The wife, too, had a 'fragile personality', and 'at the age of 40 [was] in that uncertain period in which it may be said she is not young and so her position in the labour market is obviously less favourable than when she was 30'.[11] The Court of Appeal, while acknowledging that the judge's award was at the very top end of the bracket, refused to interfere with the trial judge's decision to award her a lump sum of £195,000, and secured periodical payments of £19,500 per annum for herself, without limit of time, and £8,000 per annum for

6 [1977] 1 All ER 56.
7 *Graves v Graves* (1973) 117 Sol Jo 679; *Brady v Brady* (1973) 3 Fam Law 78.
8 (1981) 2 FLR 392, at p 399.
9 *Cumbers v Cumbers* [1975] 1 All ER 1.
10 [1997] 2 FLR 26.
11 Ibid, at p 32.

the child.[12] Normally, however, in a case where a wife has been married for a short period to a wealthy husband, the court is likely to apply the clean break provisions. Thus in *Attar v Attar*[13] and *Hedges v Hedges*[14] the court made orders designed to give the wives time in which to adjust to their suddenly reduced standard of living, and then terminated the husbands' obligations entirely. In *Leadbeater v Leadbeater*[15] the court ordered the payment of a lump sum, which was less than the wife could have expected if the marriage had lasted for longer.

Giving weight to the duration of the marriage enables courts to do justice between the spouses in relation to their respective property holdings. Under the general law, where property is conveyed into the parties' joint names both legally and beneficially, and where there is an express declaration of trust as to the distribution of the proceeds of the trust for sale, this is conclusive in respect of their entitlement.[16] But this may be quite unjust having regard to their financial contribution to its acquisition, and when the purpose for its joint acquisition has failed to materialise, namely a happy marriage. Thus if, for example, the husband buys a house using all his resources, and perhaps inherited wealth, which is conveyed to him and his wife jointly, then the starting position is that they are joint owners of the property. But if their marriage is short and childless, why should the wife receive a half share in the proceeds of sale? In *Taylor v Taylor*[17] the husband alone had paid for the spouses' jointly-owned property. The marriage lasted for four months and the parties actually lived together for a mere 20 days. Reeve J ordered the whole of the wife's interest to be transferred to the husband.[18]

It is becoming increasingly commonplace for couples to live together as husband and wife before they marry. Consequently the issue has arisen in various cases whether pre-marital cohabitation can be taken into account. This is a particularly important issue in a case where the wife has given birth to the husband's children during the period of cohabitation, so that she has pressing needs for financial assistance. In *Kokosinski v Kokosinski*[19] the parties lived together for 25 years and had a son. Then

---

12 The husband was determined to pay his wife very little. He had met her when she was working as a 'high-class call-girl'. The husband deliberately concealed the extent of his assets and income. This led the judge to assume that he had capital assets of £1m and an income of £100,000. Ward LJ commented more than once that he would not necessarily have made the same high level of provision as the judge. He emphasised the point which applies to all appeals, namely that it does not matter what the appeal court would have done, the question is whether the trial judge was plainly wrong.

13 [1985] FLR 649.

14 [1991] 1 FLR 196.

15 [1985] FLR 789.

16 See for example *Goodman v Gallant* [1986] Fam 106; and see ch 9.

17 (1974) 119 Sol Jo 30.

18 It is interesting to note that, in the case of cohabitants, the courts have no power to redress this type of injustice.

19 [1980] 1 All ER 1106.

they were married, but after marrying they only lived together for about four months. The court held that the period between the ceremony and the breakdown was likely to be the most material consideration. It also held that the 'welfare of the family' in paragraph (f) referred only to events which had occurred after the marriage took place. However, the judge pointed out that the court also must have regard to conduct,[20] and to all the circumstances of the case, and under both of these it could take account of behaviour which had occurred outside the span of marriage, at least in a case where the conduct had affected the finances of the other spouse.[1] In *Foley v Foley*[2] the parties had lived together for seven years and had three children, and then were married for eight years. The court treated the period when they were living together as 'one of the circumstances' to which the court was required to have regard, the weight to be attached to it being a matter for the court's discretion. It held it was entitled to give less weight to the period of cohabitation than to events occurring during the marriage, although the court also said that, where the parties cannot marry, the court could regard their cohabitation as a very weighty factor.[3] In *W v W (Judicial Separation: Ancillary Relief)*,[4] Ewbank J neatly took the issue of pre-marital cohabitation into account by simply stating 'the marriage itself lasted from 1971 but they were living together from 1932 and they themselves have regarded themselves as being married since 1932'.

Cases of post-marital cohabitation can also give rise to the question whether such cohabitation should be taken into account. Such cases are less likely to arise under property adjustment powers, as normally there will have been a comprehensive settlement at the time of the divorce. In that situation the applicant will have to rely on the normal rules governing cohabitation.[5] However, where there has been no final settlement the applicant can ask for leave to apply for a property adjustment order. In *Hill v Hill*[6] the parties had cohabited for 25 years after they divorced. Commenting on the relevance of this, Ward LJ said

---

20 Now under para (g), then under the final target in s 25(1).
1   But it should be noted that the wife did not obtain the type of order she would have obtained had the marriage lasted for 25 years. She obtained a lump sum which was less than the amount she was seeking, and might have expected to obtain, and no periodical payments. Amendments made by the Family Law Act 1996 have since made it explicit that conduct during and after the marriage can be taken into account, but make no mention of conduct before the marriage.
2   [1981] 2 All ER 857.
3   In *Foley v Foley* the wife was awarded a lump sum payment of £10,000, rather than £14,000 which she claimed to be her one-third share of the spouses' combined assets.
4   [1995] 2 FLR 259.
5   See ch 9.
6   [1998] 1 FLR 198, at p 211; see also *S v S (Financial Provision) (Post-Divorce Cohabitation)* [1994] 2 FLR 228 where Douglas Brown J, setting aside an earlier order, held that the parties' subsequent cohabitation undermined the fundamental basis upon which the order had been made.

'I do not see how a distinction can be drawn in principle between pre-marital cohabitation and post-divorce cohabitation. Neither period can count as part of the duration of the marriage but if the court is bound to take the pre-marital cohabitation into account and have regard to it in arriving at a solution which is reasonable and which does justice between the parties, then I do not see how the court can deny that cohabitation after the divorce is not a similar circumstance to take into account.' Thus the court concluded that the wife should be granted leave to apply for a property adjustment order, where the husband and wife had divorced in 1969, prior to the availability of the remedy of property adjustment.[7]

Any physical or mental disability of either of the parties to the marriage

Paragraph (e) requires the court to take account of:

'... any physical or mental disability of either of the parties to the marriage.'

There does not appear to be any case in which this factor has been directly referred to.[8] It sometimes happens that a disabled spouse has resources in the form of damages for personal injuries. In principle damages are treated as any other property available for reallocation after divorce, although the courts are likely to take account of their compensatory nature when determining the order to be made.[9] The courts have yet to determine to what extent the needs of a disabled party should impose an obligation on the other spouse to provide financial support which exceeds the norm.[10] For example, should there be a life-long obligation to provide periodical payments for a disabled spouse where the marriage has been relatively short-lived, and where an immediate or deferred clean break order would normally be considered appropriate? This raises the broader question of when the private obligations of ex-spouses to one another should end, and when those of the welfare state should take over. This is an issue of principle which has not been directly addressed by either the Law Commission or the courts.

7   Which was introduced on 1 January 1971 by the Matrimonial Proceedings and Property Act 1970, the Act having retrospective effect.
8   The needs of the *child* of the marriage who had a serious kidney complaint were an important consideration in *Smith v Smith* [1975] 2 All ER 19n.
9   *Daubney v Daubney* [1976] 2 All ER 453; *Wagstaff v Wagstaff* [1992] 1 All ER 275; *C v C (Financial Provision: Personal Damages)* [1995] 2 FLR 171.
10 In *Chadwick v Chadwick* [1985] FLR 606 the Court of Appeal declined to take account of the wife's disability when determining what order to make in respect of the matrimonial home: see below.

Contributions made to the welfare of the family

Paragraph (f) focuses attention on:

'... the contributions which each of the parties has made or is likely in the foreseeable future to make to the welfare of the family, including any contribution by looking after the home or caring for the family.'

It is designed to correct the imbalance that often exists in the parties' strict property rights under the general law. In many marriages the spouses arrange their finances on the basis that the husband is the sole or main breadwinner, and the wife makes no direct contribution to the purchase of the matrimonial home and other substantial items such as the furniture and the car. Where property is owned solely by the husband, the fact that the wife has contributed towards the general well-being of the family by looking after the children, running the household, and paying for various small items does not give her any beneficial entitlement to a share in the property under the general law.[11] This was expressed with compelling imagery by Lord Simon of Glaisdale when he wrote: 'The cock bird can feather his nest precisely because he is not required to spend most of his time sitting on it.'[12]

The principle that each spouse should normally be entitled to receive a share in the family assets on marriage breakdown is sharply illustrated by the facts of *Smith v Smith*.[13] A lump sum order of £54,000 had been made in favour of the wife under which she received a little less than half of the combined value of the matrimonial home (which was in the husband's sole name), and investments made up partly from savings and partly from the husband's pension lump sum. The purpose of the order had been to give the wife sufficient resources from which to buy a house in order to meet her needs. She had no capital assets of her own. Six months after the order was made the wife committed suicide, leaving her estate to her daughter. The husband appealed against the order and the judge set it aside on the ground that the wife no longer had any needs. On a further appeal by the daughter, the Court of Appeal ruled that the basis of the wife's award had not only been to make provision for her needs, it had also been to reflect her significant contribution to the spouses' long marriage, and that a wife who had few, or no, needs had a right to have

---

11 *Gissing v Gissing* [1970] 2 All ER 780; *Lloyds Bank plc v Rosset* [1990] 1 All ER 1111; and see ch 9.

12 *With All My Worldly Goods* (1964, Holdsworth Club). See too *Conran v Conran* [1997] 2 FLR 615 at p 625 where Wilson J commented that 'in its analysis the court will no doubt strive to perceive, among other features, the nexus between the wife's contribution and the creation of the resources'.

13 [1991] 2 All ER 306.

that contribution recognised in money terms. However, since a significant proportion of the lump sum had been to make provision for the wife, and since the husband was the only one now with future needs, it would be just to the husband to make a substantial downward adjustment of the wife's award. It was reduced to £25,000.

However, it can be misleading to describe the non-owner spouse's claim to a share in the matrimonial assets as a 'right' or an 'entitlement'.[14] Rather, what she has is a claim which will almost certainly be recognised in some manner if presented to a court. But until she presents her claim she has no rights in relation to property owned solely by her husband. Thus if the wife remarries before making an application for a property adjustment order, any 'rights' she has will be lost, because the court no longer has jurisdiction to make an order. If she dies before her application is heard her 'rights' die with her; her claim for a property adjustment order does not accrue for the benefit of her estate.[15] Because the claiming spouse is dependent on a court exercising its discretion to award her a share in the family assets, she is also vulnerable to her claim being denied for moralistic reasons. In *H v H (Financial Provision: Remarriage)*[16] the court applied the concept of earning to the wife's claim to receive a share in the proceeds of sale of the matrimonial home. The wife had deserted the husband and gone to live with another man. Sir George Baker P awarded her merely one-twelfth of the value of the matrimonial home because 'if the job is left unfinished you do not earn as much'. It is suggested that it is very unlikely that the court could properly have used that reason for reducing the wife's interest in the property from one-half to one-twelfth had the spouses been beneficial joint owners of the matrimonial home.[17]

Where one of the parties is wealthy, the spouse who has contributed to the welfare of the family in other than financial terms cannot expect to receive the kind of sum which a spouse who has contributed financially would receive.[18] A critical factor affecting quantification is whether the husband has built up his business with the significant support of his wife, or whether the business has prospered mainly because of the husband's own acumen and effort.[19]

---

14 See Bagnall J in *Harnett v Harnett* [1973] 2 All ER 593, at p 601.
15 On this, see the note by R Spon Smith *Property adjustment and lump sum applications – a catch* [1992] Fam Law 421.
16 [1975] 1 All ER 367; the court's decision was also strongly influenced by the fact that the wife had remarried by the time of the hearing and her new husband was making provision for her needs.
17 See too *Schuller v Schuller* [1990] 2 FLR 193 where the wife, who had been married for 21 years, was awarded only 6% of the value of the house, because she had inherited property after the parties parted.
18 *F v F (Duxbury Calculation)* [1996] 1 FLR 833.
19 Contrast *Conran v Conran* [1997] 2 FLR 615 with *Dart v Dart* [1996] 2 FLR 286. See also *W v W (Judicial Separation: Ancillary Relief)* [1995] 2 FLR 259, where the court held that a half and half share would not be an appropriate starting point where the parties had lived together since 1932, married in 1971, and separated when the wife was 78 and the husband 87. The wife had never directly contributed to the acquisition of the capital assets.

Conduct

The extent to which the conduct of the parties should be taken into account when making financial provision and property adjustment orders is a controversial issue. When, in 1980, the Law Commission issued a discussion paper which included the question of what policy ought to be adopted on the impact of conduct,[20] it received a large amount of conflicting comment in reply. Many individuals felt a considerable sense of injustice because the court had not been prepared to take account of the other spouse's behaviour.[1] Despite this the Law Commission expressed the view that courts cannot reasonably be expected to apportion responsibility for breakdown in any save exceptional circumstances. It relied in particular on the words of Ormrod J in *Wachtel v Wachtel*[2] when he said:

> 'The forensic process is reasonably well adapted to determining in broad terms the share of responsibility of each party for an accident on the road or at work because the issues are relatively confined in scope, but it is much too clumsy a tool for dissecting the complex inter-actions which go on all the time in a family. Shares in responsibility for breakdown cannot be properly assessed without a meticulous examination and understanding of the characters and personalities of the spouses concerned, and the more thorough the investigation the more the shares will, in most cases, approach equality.'

The Law Commission also gave more pragmatic reasons for rejecting an inquiry into the parties' mutual recriminations in other than exceptional cases. These included that it would be expensive of court time and legal aid; that resurrecting past matters, sometimes stretching back over many years, for forensic investigation would not assist the parties to come to terms with their deep feelings about the breakdown of their marriage; and that such feelings are better dealt with during conciliation.[3] However, during the Parliamentary debates on the Family Law Act 1996, some MPs were concerned by the perceived lack of attention being paid to matters of conduct. As a consequence paragraph (g) was amended in a way which suggests that in future more attention may be paid to conduct than has been the case in recent years. The paragraph now requires courts to take account of:

> '... the conduct of each of the parties, *whatever the nature of the conduct and whether it occurred during the marriage or after the separation of the parties or (as the case may be) dissolution or*

---

20 Law Com No 103.
1   Law Com No 112, para 36.
2   [1973] 1 All ER 113, at p 119.
3   Law Com No 112, para 37.

annulment of the marriage,[4] if that conduct is such that it would in the opinion of the court be inequitable to disregard it.'

One view is that all that the new wording does is to clarify the already existing law, as conduct has always been construed broadly, and conduct after separation has been taken into account where it has been deemed appropriate. An alternative view is that by altering the wording Parliament must have intended the law to change in some way and this will encourage parties to litigate issues of conduct.[5] Whichever view proves to be correct, the wording still leaves wide open the question of when it is inequitable for a court to ignore conduct. The courts have generally been reluctant to give weight to immoral conduct except when it has been 'obvious and gross';[6] or where it has been 'of the kind that would cause the ordinary mortal to throw up his hands and say, "surely that woman is not going to be given any money" or "is not going to get a full award"'.[7] Consequently, judges have refused to penalise a spouse who has committed adultery, or otherwise behaved in a manner which has caused offence or distress to the other party, taking the view that the conduct is not of sufficient seriousness and that this would be to 'impose a fine for supposed misbehaviour in the course of an unhappy married life'.[8] However, reasonable people apply different moral standards to certain forms of behaviour, and some may be more prepared than others to find that the conduct is susceptible of forgiveness.[9] The assessment of when conduct will be regarded as relevant is made more difficult by the fact that the courts have held that conduct does not necessarily carry any imputation of moral blame, rather it means behaviour of the greatest importance in the marriage.[10] Thus determining when a court is likely to take the view that it would be inequitable to disregard conduct is not easy.[11]

---

4   New words in italics.
5   See generally D Burles *Conduct and ancillary relief* [1997] Fam Law 804.
6   Per Lord Denning in *Wachtel v Wachtel* [1973] 1 All ER 829.
7   *W v W (Financial Provision: Lump Sum)* [1976] Fam 107, per Sir George Baker P at p 114.
8   *Wachtel v Wachtel* [1973] 1 All ER 829; *A v A (Financial Provision)* [1998] 2 FLR 180.
9   Compare the approach of Bagnall J in *Harnett v Harnett* [1973] 2 All ER 593 with that of Lawton LJ in *Blezard v Blezard* (1979) 9 Fam Law 249.
10 *West v West* [1977] 2 All ER 705.
11 See *R v R (Disclosure to Revenue)* [1998] 1 FLR 922, where it is suggested that a somewhat curious approach to morality was adopted. At an earlier hearing Wilson J had made findings that the husband had not disclosed all his income to the Inland Revenue over a number of years. When reallocating resources between the parties Wilson J did so on the basis that 'the undeclared area of the husband's income was likely to remain as well hidden from the inspector as it had hitherto been'. Subsequently, the wife allegedly disclosed a transcript of the court's judgment to the Inland Revenue without first obtaining the court's leave. Censuring this behaviour in variation proceedings, Wilson J held that this was conduct on the part of the wife which it would be inequitable to disregard. Yet the husband's criminal behaviour in concealing his income from the Inland Revenue appeared to be accepted without censure.

As an illustration of how difficult it is to predict when a court will give weight to one spouse's apparent misconduct it is instructive to look at *Kyte v Kyte*[12] as it passed through the hierarchy of the court system. The registrar found that it would be inequitable to disregard the wife's conduct, yet the judge held that conduct was not relevant and did not apply. Finally, the Court of Appeal held that there had been such an imbalance of conduct as between the husband and wife that it would be inequitable to ignore it. This divergence of opinion reflects research findings made in the 1970s which revealed that registrars tended to differ considerably in the account they took of conduct when choosing the level of their orders.[13] In *Kyte v Kyte* Purchas LJ said that the wording of paragraph (g) may give courts a broader discretion than they had hitherto enjoyed when applying the test of 'gross and obvious conduct'.[14] This may be even more marked with the additional changes brought about under the Family Law Act 1996.[15]

The moral imperative to have regard to conduct probably commands very wide acceptance when the facts of a case are very heavily weighted in favour of one spouse and against the other. An example is *Evans v Evans,*[16] in which the facts were particularly sympathetic towards the husband. He had conscientiously paid maintenance for his ex-wife for many years, and it was only when she was convicted of inciting others to kill him that he applied to have the order terminated. Not surprisingly the court granted his application. Similarly, it was clearly inequitable to disregard conduct where the husband had maliciously attacked his wife with a knife.[17] In *A v A (Financial Provision)*[18] the husband's violent conduct was partly attributable to his uncontrollable psychological state. Allowing the husband's appeal against an order which reduced his share in the parties' jointly owned property to 10%, and increasing it to one-third, Thorpe J held that although an incident of serious violence could not be disregarded, particularly where it had long-standing effects on the

---

12 [1987] 3 All ER 1041.
13 W Barrington Baker, J Eekelaar, C Gibson and S Raikes *The Matrimonial Jurisdiction of Registrars* (1977) Wolfson College, Oxford, Centre for Socio-Legal Studies, SSRC, pp 20-27.
14 He said it was not necessary to decide whether this was the case because the behaviour of the wife satisfied the test under either approach.
15 In two recent cases the Court of Appeal denied the 'wrongful spouse' any remedy at all. However, both were special in that they involved void marriages. In *J v S-T* [1997] 1 FLR 402 the applicant, a transsexual, had deceived his 'wife' as to his true female status for the 17 years of their marriage. The Court of Appeal took the view that the gravity of the deceit was so serious that he should not be entitled to any order for financial or property provision. However Potter LJ and Sir Brian Neill drew back from endorsing the rigorous approach taken by Ward LJ in *Whiston v Whiston* [1995] 2 FLR 268 where it was held that a bigamous spouse should never be able to profit from her crime. They limited the absolute nature of the rule in *Whiston* to cases of bigamy, where the marriage itself constituted the criminal act.
16 [1989] 1 FLR 351.
17 *Jones v Jones* [1975] 2 All ER 12.
18 [1995] 1 FLR 345.

psychological well-being of the injured spouse, conduct was only one of the factors to be considered, and it should not drive the court to conclude that a violent husband should be deprived of his entire capital.

More controversial is the situation when one of the parties has allegedly behaved badly and the other has been blameless, but when that behaviour cannot be characterised as totally immoral. An example arose in *Robinson v Robinson*[19] when the wife had deserted her husband because she was unhappy with army life overseas. The Court of Appeal upheld a ruling by magistrates that the amount of maintenance awarded to the wife should be reduced and limited in time to reflect the blamelessness of the husband, and the blameworthy behaviour of the wife. This ruling appeared to cut across the thinking in *Wachtel v Wachtel,* namely that the legal process is not suited to the allocation of blame for marriage breakdown because of the complexity of the married relationship. *Robinson v Robinson* was arguably nothing more than a case of simple desertion, and it is suggested that to characterise the wife as 'blameworthy' and husband as 'blameless' may have been to fall into the trap which the Court of Appeal had hitherto been anxious to avoid.[1] The relationship between husband and wife is usually too subtle to be analysed in the black and white terms of being 'at fault' and 'faultless'. As Singer J said in *A v A (Financial Provision)*[2] 'I am far from persuaded that the wife's adultery was the cause of the breakdown of this marriage. I regard it rather as symptomatic of the developing incompatibility inherent in the parties' relationship from the outset'.

Probably the least questionable circumstance in which this provision has been satisfied is when the conduct of one spouse has had a direct bearing on the spouses' financial and property position. In *Jones v Jones*[3] the husband had attacked his wife, injuring her so severely that he impaired her earning capacity. The Court of Appeal found that it would be repugnant to justice not to take the husband's conduct into account when securing the position of the wife in the future. In *H v H (Financial Provision: Conduct)*[4] the husband violently assaulted his wife as a result of which he was sent to prison for wounding and attempted rape. This meant that the husband was no longer able to support his wife and children to the standard which had preceded the attack. She had been left in a psychologically vulnerable position. The husband's conduct was one of the factors which influenced Thorpe J to transfer the husband's half share

19 [1983] 1 All ER 391.
1   The ruling also indirectly penalised the child of the family. The mother's maintenance was reduced and limited in time, and she therefore was left with insufficient resources to provide for them both.
2   [1998] 2 FLR 180, at p 185.
3   [1975] 2 All ER 12.
4   [1994] 2 FLR 801.

in the matrimonial home to the wife.[5] In *Martin v Martin*[6] the husband had not behaved in an immoral manner, but he had lost money in successive unsuccessful business ventures. The court held that he could not claim the same share in the family assets as he would have been entitled to had he behaved reasonably.[7] In each of these cases there was a causative link between the conduct of one of the spouses and the parties' current financial circumstances which it was inequitable for a court to disregard.[8]

In *H v H (Financial Relief: Conduct)*[9] it was the conduct of the applicant, the husband, that was in issue. His wife's father, who was very wealthy, had made substantial provision for his daughter and she owned the matrimonial home worth £1.75m. The husband in the last three years of an eighteen year marriage had deceitfully used capital provided by his father-in-law for his own purposes, including placing some of it in a Swiss bank account and financing an adulterous association. However, the court found that his breach of trust was out of character, and that the children had a good relationship with him. Singer J held that it was in the children's interests that their father should be securely and adequately housed even if this meant selling the former matrimonial home in which the children lived with their mother. Accordingly he ordered that £375,000 should be settled on the husband for the purchase of a house to be held on trust. However, because it was inequitable to disregard the husband's conduct Singer J ordered that the property should revert to the children on the husband's death, and not pass to his estate.[10]

Paragraph (g) is but one of the several matters to be taken into account, and the courts have, in the main, made efforts to minimise litigation which focuses on conduct. But, while it is a factor, it provides spouses with a financial motive to litigate. The disadvantage of treating conduct as a

---

5   In *A v A (Financial Provision: Conduct)* [1995] 1 FLR 345, where the husband had attacked the wife, his share in the capital was reduced to one-third and settled on the children as some sort of alleviation for the husband's inevitable feeling that he had lost everything. The husband successfully appealed against the settlement order, which was manifestly contrary to the principles contained in s 25.

6   [1976] Fam 335. See too *Beach v Beach* [1995] 2 FLR 160.

7   See too *Bryant v Bryant* (1976) 120 Sol Jo 165; *Weisz v Weisz* (1975) Times, 16 December; *Hillard v Hillard* (1982) 12 Fam Law 176.

8   In *Tavoulareas v Tavoulareas* [1998] 2 FLR 418 it was stated by the Court of Appeal, per incuriam, that paragraph (g) is aimed at marital conduct, and if misconduct is limited to misconduct within the ancillary relief proceedings, whilst this might affect the award of costs, it was doubtful whether it should diminish the quantum of the financial award. This approach was followed in *Young v Young* [1998] 2 FLR 1131 where the Court of Appeal ruled that the husband's financial misconduct had already been taken into account in a reduced lump sum order, and that it should not have been brought into account a second time to increase his liability for costs.

9   [1998] 1 FLR 971.

10 The husband also received a lump sum of £100,000, principally to cover his debts. The exceptional nature of the capital order for the benefit of the children was emphasised. Cf *Lord Lilford v Glyn* [1979] 1 All ER 441.

discrete consideration is that to do so may foster further animosity between the parties. It has been recognised that it was unhelpful for divorce petitions to contain allegations and counter-allegations about behaviour, and reform of the divorce law by the Family Law Act 1996 has eliminated this process.[11] However, lawyers and mediators are likely to be pressed into hearing details about the parties' conduct while ever it is a relevant matter. The law is also in danger of being perceived as unfair because it is unclear which kind of conduct should be ignored, and which it is inequitable to disregard.

This raises the question whether, as a matter of policy, it would be more beneficial for issues of conduct to be subsumed within the other paragraphs in section 25(2). It is suggested that this might help to avoid allegations being made which can be both inflammatory and distressing to the spouses personally, and may be damaging to their children. For example where, as in *Robinson v Robinson*[12] and *West v West*,[13] one spouse deserted the other at an early stage in the marriage, these allegations could have been considered under paragraphs (d) or (f), which focus on the duration of the marriage, and each spouse's contributions to the welfare of the family. Even extreme cases like *Jones v Jones*,[14] in which the husband attacked the wife with a knife, or *H v H (Financial Provision: Conduct)*,[15] where the husband's attack on his wife had led to his imprisonment, and to her being psychologically harmed, could probably have adequately been considered under paragraphs (a),(b) and (e). These focus on each spouse's earning capacity, resources, needs and any physical or mental disabilities. The fact that the husband's conduct had caused the wife's loss of earning capacity, and increased her needs, would clearly have been relevant, yet the resultant order, if perceived as a matter of causation rather than reflecting guilt and innocence, could not have been characterised as punishing him twice, which was arguably unfair.[16] Where a spouse has squandered resources, as in *Martin v Martin*,[17] this could be considered as a matter relating to the spouses' resources. While some situations would not easily fall within the other paragraphs in the section,[18] abolishing conduct as a separate category would be more in keeping with the moral neutrality of the Family Law Act 1996 which adopts a purely procedural process in relation to divorce.[19] The counter-argument to this is that it is highly offensive if persons who have behaved in a

11 See ch 7.
12 [1983] 1 All ER 391.
13 [1977] 2 All ER 705.
14 [1975] 2 All ER 12.
15 [1994] 2 FLR 801.
16 See the note on *Jones v Jones* by E Ellis 'The discretion to adjust property rights after divorce' (1976) 39 MLR 97.
17 [1976] Fam 335.
18 It is hard to see where *Evans v Evans* [1989] 1 FLR 351 would fall, but it might have been considered under the clean break provisions in s 25A.
19 See ch 7, but see also s 10(2) of the Family Law Act 1996 under which conduct is a relevant consideration where the court is considering whether to make an order preventing divorce on the ground of hardship.

violent manner, such as the husbands in *Jones v Jones*[20] and *H v H (Financial Provision: Conduct)*,[1] do not have their conduct positively condemned in proceedings ancillary to the divorce itself.

Loss of pension

Paragraph (h) directs the court to have regard to:

'... the value to each of the parties of any benefit which, by reason of the dissolution or annulment of the marriage, that party will lose the chance of acquiring.'

For many people who are divorcing the two most valuable assets they possess are the matrimonial home and any expectation they may have under a pension scheme.[2] The loss of an occupational pension scheme entitlement therefore usually represents a real deprivation to a spouse, particularly one divorced in middle age. This is because a divorced wife is no longer her husband's widow for the purposes of his pension scheme and therefore, if he should predecease her, she will not obtain a widow's pension. Similarly, if the wife has a pension scheme which pays benefits to a widower, the husband will not be able to benefit from it if the parties divorce. Where spouses divorce fairly late in life their opportunity to make adequate substitute pension arrangements is likely to be limited. Indeed, it may often be sensible to discuss the alternative of obtaining a separation order with a middle aged or elderly person whose marriage has broken down and who wishes to rearrange his or her financial and property affairs. Orders for financial provision and property adjustment are available in the same way as they are to divorcing spouses, but a separation order does not lead to the automatic loss of pension entitlements.

There are many types of benefits which can accrue under pension schemes. These include lump sum benefits, a regular income entitlement, a widow/widower's pension, death in service benefits and life cover. The valuation of a person's interest in his pension scheme is by no means problem free even though the process of gathering information is assisted by regulations.[3] For example, future interest, inflation and taxation rates can only be predicted. This can therefore give rise to differing valuations, depending on the expectations and assumptions of the actuary doing the

20 [1975] 2 All ER 12.
1   [1994] 2 FLR 801.
2   See the comments of Lord Nicholls in *Brooks v Brooks* [1995] 2 FLR 13 at p 15. A full account of pensions law and how it applies to divorcing couples is beyond the scope of this book. For more detailed consideration, see S Gailey *Pensions in Marriage Breakdown* (CLT Publishing, 1996); R Ellison and M Rae *Family Breakdown and Pensions* (Butterworths, 1997).
3   Occupational Pension Schemes (Disclosure of Information) Regulations 1996; the Divorce etc (Pensions) Regulations 1996.

calculation.[4] This necessarily makes it difficult for any adviser to reach a conclusion as to the worth of a pension.

When courts are making orders, their powers are limited to those contained within sections 22A-24A and these may be inadequate properly to deal with the parties' circumstances.[5] Recompensing a spouse for an indeterminate loss arising some years in the future under a pension scheme may therefore be more effectively handled by the pensioner spouse giving undertakings to the court. Undertakings are enforceable in the same way as court orders, but they allow for more imaginative responses.[6] For example, a pensioner husband could undertake to purchase an annuity for his wife, or he could undertake to take out a policy of insurance on his own life for his wife's benefit, or under an existing pension scheme he might be able to allocate a sum towards a pension after his death for his wife where she would not otherwise be entitled.[7]

Pensions – the statutory framework

The law relating to pensions after divorce was amended by section 166 of the Pensions Act 1995 which inserted sections 25B-25D into the Matrimonial Causes Act 1973, and by section 16 of the Family Law Act 1996 which amended sections 25B and 25D, and established pension splitting. Pension rights have always been a relevant consideration when making financial provision and property arrangements, but a court is now specifically required to have regard to 'any benefits under a pension scheme which a party to the marriage has or is likely to have' when considering the spouses' resources under paragraph (a) of section 25(2);[8] and when considering paragraph (h) the court must have regard to 'any benefits under a pension scheme which, by reason of the dissolution or annulment of the marriage, a party to the marriage will lose the chance of acquiring'.[9]

The simplest means by which a court can take account of the potential loss of pension rights is for the court to seek to compensate the loser when adjusting the division of the parties' present financial and property assets. For example, where the husband can anticipate a lump sum payment and a regular income under his pension scheme, this might persuade a court to transfer the entire beneficial interest in the former matrimonial

---

4   For a helpful analysis of how to assess the value of a pension, see *T v T (Financial Relief: Pensions)* [1998] 1 FLR 1072.
5   See, for example, *K v K (Financial Provision)* [1997] 1 FLR 35, where the court's hands were tied because it had no power to order the husband to take out an insurance policy or to allocate part of his pension to the wife.
6   Undertakings are further discussed below.
7   See the use of undertakings in *W v W (Periodical Payments: Pensions)* [1996] 2 FLR 480.
8   S 25B(1)(a).
9   S 25B(1)(b).

home to the wife, and/or to order that her periodical payments should last for the parties joint lives, and/or to make a lump sum order. In appropriate cases, it could defer payment of the lump sum until the pension lump sum becomes payable.

In many cases, however, it is not possible to make present provision for lost pension rights which adequately take account of the pensioner's future entitlement. The court's new powers enable it to earmark part of the pensioner's entitlement for the benefit of the other spouse. A court 'may require the trustees or managers of the pension scheme in question, if at any time any payment in respect of any benefits under the scheme becomes due to the party with pension rights, to make a payment for the benefit of the other party'.[10] Thus once the pensioner begins to draw benefits, a proportion of the pension can immediately become payable to his ex-spouse.[11] Similarly, the court may require the trustees or managers to pay the whole or part of a lump sum, when it becomes due, to the other party.[12] A disadvantage of earmarking arrangements is that it ties the parties together financially although their marriage has ended, and the receiving spouse is vulnerable should the pensioner spouse die prematurely as this brings any earmarking arrangements to an end. She may also be vulnerable where the pensioner delays taking his pension entitlement.

The aim of Parliament, therefore, when legislating for change was to provide for full pension splitting at the time of the divorce proceedings.[13] Pension splitting allows each party thenceforth to make their own pension arrangements, and ties in with the principle that it is normally desirable to achieve a clean break between them at the time of the divorce. Section 25B(2)(c) states that where the court decides to make a financial provision order, it must consider in particular 'whether the order should provide for the accrued rights of the party with pension rights ("the pension rights") to be divided between that party and the other party in such a way as to reduce the pension rights to the party with those rights and to create pension rights for the other party'. Although this section, which was introduced by the Family Law Act 1996 alongside the major changes to divorce law, provided in principle for pension splitting, there was no provision introduced into the Matrimonial Causes Act 1973 which gave a court the power to make an *order* which splits pension rights between the

---

10 S 25B(4).
11 Pension payments are periodical payments and therefore they do not survive either the death or remarriage of the payee: s 28. Applications to vary the order can be made under s 31. See also, *T v T (Financial Relief: Pensions)* [1998] 1 FLR 1072, at p 1085.
12 S 25C(2). In common with ordinary lump sums, lump sum payments from a pension are treated as capital payments and are therefore unaffected by the remarriage of the receiving spouse.
13 S 25D(2)(aa) therefore provides that the Lord Chancellor has power to supplement the courts' existing powers in relation to pensions by regulations, and this regulatory power includes the right to 'make such consequential modifications of any enactment or subordinate legislation to give effect to the provisions in section 25B'.

parties. The implementation of pension splitting was deferred for further consultation and consideration.[14] This led to the Welfare Reform and Pensions Bill.[15] Under the Bill, the discretionary criteria in section 25 will not be altered, but the court will be able to make a new order, a 'pension sharing order', which will empower it to direct the trustees or managers of a pension scheme to allocate part or all of the pension rights to be awarded to the other spouse at divorce.

In *T v T (Financial Relief: Pensions)*[16] it was argued on behalf of a wife that the earmarking provisions of section 25 B-D did not merely enable the court to compensate her for loss of pension benefits, they *required* the court to compensate her. Singer J rejected this argument. He stated that giving consideration to pension provision was simply included as part of the conventional discretionary balancing exercise the court was required to perform.[17] The wife had applied for an order directing the trustees of the husband's pension fund to pay her a proportion of his pension. Singer J declined to earmark part of the husband's pension in this fashion as he foresaw that such a direction could give rise to a number of potential 'pitfalls, disadvantages, complications and distractions'. These included the fact that it was impossible to predict the appropriate quantum of periodical payments so far ahead; the husband might delay the date when he took his pension rights; an application to vary the order could be made even before it came into effect; the court would be in a far better position to determine the amount of an order at the time when the husband took his pension rights; and there was no reason for supposing that the husband would not meet an appropriate periodical payments order from his pension receipts after retirement. For similar reasons, the court declined to require the husband to commute part of his pension benefits[18] so that a deferred lump sum could be paid to the wife. However, the pension trustees were ordered to pay a lump sum equal to ten times her annual maintenance payable from any death in service benefits, as these benefits might not fall into the husband's estate and would therefore not be available to the wife as a dependant in an application made under the Inheritance (Provision for Family and Dependants) Act 1975.[19]

---

14 A Green Paper, *The Treatment of Pension Rights on Divorce* (Cm 3345), was published in July 1996, followed by a White Paper, *Pension Rights on Divorce* (Cm 3564), in February 1997 which together set out the complexities of pension splitting.

15 At the time of writing the Bill was not due to come into force until late in the year 2001.

16 [1998] 1 FLR 1072.

17 See also *Burrow v Burrow* [1999] 1 FLR 508.

18 S 25B(7).

19 See also, *W v W (Periodical Payments: Pensions)* [1996] 2 FLR 480 where periodical payments to the wife were ordered secured against the husband's pension scheme, the security to consist of an undertaking given by the husband and an attachment of earnings order addressed to the pension provider.

The matrimonial home – what order is the most appropriate?

Often the parties' only major asset is the matrimonial home and it may require some ingenuity to make adequate provision for each spouse from one main resource, particularly where they have dependant children. The dilemma faced by those assisting the parties to reach an agreement, and the court when determining what order to make, is how can arrangements be made which give proper recognition to the rights of both spouses in the property, protect a financially dependant spouse and any children of the family, create a clean break where appropriate, bring finality, and allow for an adjustment of the position if the circumstances of the parties should significantly alter? Clearly these very different objectives nearly always conflict. Moreover, there is a real risk that any property they own will be worth much less than it was originally by the time the parties have finished negotiating over what should happen to it, because of escalating legal costs. Indeed, how the costs will be paid is often a factor which influences the final order.[20] Where a spouse is legally aided, if any property is recovered or preserved for the assisted person, the costs payable are a first charge on the property, with interest accumulating the longer the charge remains unredeemed.[21]

The main methods of disposition of the matrimonial home are described below, and the analysis which follows is aimed at assisting the processes of negotiation, 'Family Dispute Resolution'[1] and mediation. Reported financial provision and property adjustment cases usually involve parties who have significant assets. The reality for many divorcing couples, however, is that their resources are very limited. The discussion which follows therefore focuses on the factors which should be borne in mind when determining what arrangements about the disposition of the home might reasonably be agreed between spouses, as well as giving an account of orders which the courts have made. A realistic approach to orders should mean that unnecessary costs are avoided by parties who can ill-afford to pay them. When considering the appropriateness of particular orders, and choosing between them, the advantages and disadvantages inherent in the different types of order need to be identified and weighed in the light of the range of the court's other powers, the parties' particular circumstances, and the application to them of the statutory guidelines.[2]

---

20 See, for example, *H v H (Financial Relief: Costs)* [1997] 2 FLR 57.
21 Cf *Mortimer v Mortimer-Griffin* [1986] 2 FLR 315. The husband's lump sum was limited to £2,500 as any larger sum would have been recouped by the Legal Aid Fund. By taking account of the impact of Legal Aid in this manner, and not reimbursing the Board's expenditure, the courts have widened the purse of the resources available to the parties.
1 See below for a description of the FDR pilot scheme.
2 See too, M Hayes and G Battersby *Property adjustment: order or disorder in the former matrimonial home* (1985) 15 Fam Law 213; M Hayes and G Battersby *Property adjustment: further thoughts on charge orders* (1986) 16 Fam Law 142.

The property to be sold and the proceeds of sale divided

The attractive feature of an agreement, or order, under which the matrimonial home is sold and the proceeds of sale divided between the parties is that each spouse is able to realise his or her investment in the property. It is particularly appropriate where there are no children, and where each spouse can be adequately housed in alternative accommodation from his or her share of the proceeds. It is also appropriate where the spouses are young. They can go their separate ways, using their shares in the money realised as a down payment on fresh property should they so wish. Sale promotes a clean break and finality. It also allows for flexibility because the division of the proceeds of sale can reflect the criteria in the statutory guidelines. In *M v B (Ancillary Proceedings: Lump Sum)*[3] Thorpe LJ stated that in any case where by stretching the parties' resources and a degree of risk-taking there was a possibility of both parties being rehoused that such an outcome would almost invariably have a decisive impact on the order selected.

In *Scallon v Scallon*[4] the spouses were beneficial co-owners. The Court of Appeal took the view that it was fairer to divide the proceeds of sale of the matrimonial home between the spouses than to transfer the property to the wife only and make no order for periodical payments. It approved an order that the house be sold, and that the net proceeds be divided three-fifths to the wife and two-fifths to the husband. The court found that this division would enable both spouses to be housed in alternative accommodation, which, the court said, was the correct objective. In addition, it ruled that the wife should have the additional protection of a nominal periodical payments order in case she should need maintenance in the future.[5]

With a sale order, the spouse with care of the children (the residential parent) can receive a larger percentage of the proceeds than the other spouse (the non-residential parent), reflecting the requirement that the

3   [1998] 1 FLR 53.
4   [1990] 1 FLR 194.
5   *Scallon v Scallon* was also concerned with the vexed issue of legal aid, and whether the loan from the Legal Aid Fund must be repaid when the property is sold. If any property is 'recovered or preserved' for a person who has been assisted by legal aid, the Legal Aid Fund has first charge on any such property in order to recoup its expenditure on legal fees. Only the first £2,500 of a lump sum, or the value of any property, is exempt. However, since 1989 the Legal Aid Board has had the power to postpone the enforcement of its charge where the money, or property, is to be used for the purchase of a home for the assisted person. In *Scallon v Scallon* the wife asserted that the court had failed to take account of the impact of the charge on her means, and that once she had paid her legal aid contribution she would have insufficient money with which to buy a new home. However, the Court of Appeal, while recognising that postponement of the realisation of the charge is a discretionary power, said that it was right to assume that the Board would not seek to frustrate the order of the court by refusing to exercise its discretion, and by realising its charge immediately.

children's interests must be put first.[6] In some cases, the size of the non-residential parent's share of the sale proceeds may be sufficient for him to set himself up in a home which is of adequate size to provide a setting where his children can enjoy staying contact with him. The objective of securing homes where the children can stay with either parent may override other considerations in the statutory guidelines, as in *H v H (Financial Relief: Conduct)*[7] where the matrimonial home was sold in order to release a sufficient sum with which the husband could purchase a property. The husband's deceitful behaviour would normally have amounted to misconduct which debarred him from a generous settlement.[8] However, his children had a good relationship with him, and the court found that it was in their interests that their father was securely housed.

The disadvantage of immediate sale is that the proceeds may be insufficient for the purchase of two new properties, particularly at times of rapidly inflating house prices. Sale, where there are children, also means that the children lose their home at a time when they are likely to be suffering distress at the termination of their parents' marriage, and experiencing the loss of the day-to-day presence of one parent. When moving to a new house will involve losing the companionship and support of friends in the neighbourhood, or going to a new school, this may be to deprive the children of much needed emotional security. It may also make more difficult the position of the caring parent who is in, or who is seeking, employment because she may have built up a network of persons on whom she can rely to assist her with care of the children while she is at work.[9]

Adults who do not have dependant children may also have sound reasons for resisting sale of the family home. In *R v R (Financial Provision: Reasonable Needs)*[10] Sir Stephen Brown P held that it was wholly unreasonable to order the sale of the former matrimonial home in which the wife had lived for 17 years simply because it provided her with accommodation in excess of her needs. The husband, who was extremely wealthy, had rehoused himself in luxurious accommodation. Sir Stephen Brown P ruled that as it was not necessary for the wife to leave the home because of a lack of resources, it would therefore be unreasonable to require her to do so.[11]

---

6   S 25(1).
7   [1998] 1 FLR 971.
8   S 25(2)(g).
9   Cf *Chaudhuri v Chaudhuri* [1992] 2 FLR 73, in which it had been a central part of the wife's case that she needed to stay in the matrimonial home in order to provide a secure home for the children in a neighbourhood where she would have the support of friends.
10 [1994] 2 FLR 1044.
11 Cf *W v W (Judicial Separation: Ancillary Relief)* [1995] 2 FLR 259.

The property to be transferred into the sole name of one of the spouses

Transferring the matrimonial home into the sole name of one spouse, like sale, has the advantage that it helps to achieve a clean break. It also has the beneficial outcome that the owning spouse is not in the position of being fearful that she will have to sell the property at some date in the future in order that the other spouse can have his share.[12] Courts have been willing to order that the matrimonial home should belong solely to one of the parties where it formed only one part of the spouses' total financial resources. Thus where one spouse enjoyed secure accommodation as part of his employment, as in *Hanlon v Hanlon*,[13] or had acquired an interest in property through marriage to another, as in *H v H (Financial Provision: Remarriage)*,[14] or had additional wealth as a result of inheritance, as in *Schuller v Schuller*,[15] the property was vested in the name of the other spouse alone. Essentially, what the court was doing in those cases was taking account of all available resources under section 25(2)(a), and using the matrimonial home to house one of the parties secure in the knowledge that the other was provided for. Although one spouse was obtaining a disproportionate share in the matrimonial home, this could be justified by reference to each spouses' needs under section 25(2)(b) and, where there were children, by the requirement under section 25(1) to give first consideration to their interests.

Where the other spouse can be compensated for his or her loss by a lump sum payment, raised perhaps through the property being mortgaged, or remortgaged, that solution may be accepted as fair by both parties, and can bring about a parity between them. An order requiring the spouse to whom the property is transferred to pay the other spouse a lump sum is similar in effect to one in which sale of the home is ordered, because in each case both acquire a share in the value of the property.[16] However, a transfer of property has the advantage that the original property is retained thus preserving familiarity of surroundings and continuity for any children of the family.

Another way of compensating a spouse for giving up his or her claim to a share in the matrimonial property is to make no order for periodical payments. In *Hanlon v Hanlon*[17] the husband, who was living rent free in a police flat, was ordered to transfer his entire interest in the matrimonial home to his wife who was looking after their four children, and in return he was no longer required to make periodical payments for the two children

---

12 See *Hanlon v Hanlon* [1978] 2 All ER 889; *Mortimer v Mortimer-Griffin* [1986] 2 FLR 315.
13 [1978] 2 All ER 889. The husband lived rent-free in a police flat.
14 [1975] 1 All ER 367.
15 [1990] 2 FLR 193.
16 In many instances, however, the owner spouse will not have sufficient resources to make any, or any substantial, payment.
17 [1978] 2 All ER 889.

who were still dependant.[18] However, *Hanlon v Hanlon* preceded the Child Support Act 1991. Nowadays a husband could sensibly agree that in return for him transferring his share in the home to his wife, she will not seek an order for periodical payments for herself either now or in the future.[19] But a husband would be extremely unwise to accept such an arrangement in relation to his financial responsibility for his children. He would be vulnerable to an application for child support being made at any time to the Child Support Agency by his former wife.[20] The fact that a transfer of property had taken place on the basis that child support would not be claimed would be of no relevance to how the Agency would assess his maintenance obligation. The Agency would apply the maintenance formula as though no such agreement had ever been made.[1]

The conduct of one of the parties may lead the court to make an order which secures the matrimonial home solely for the other with no compensatory arrangement. In *Jones v Jones*[2] the husband had attacked the wife with a knife severing the tendons of a hand. The trial judge had ordered that the house be transferred to the wife, but that she should pay the husband a sum equal to one-fifth of the equity when the youngest of their five children ceased to be a dependant. The wife appealed on the ground that at that time she would be aged 50, and incapable of earning a living by reason of the injuries inflicted on her by her husband. Clearly the husband had behaved in a manner which it would be repugnant to justice to disregard,[3] and the Court of Appeal found that it would be unjust to the wife that she should be required to sell the house and to find somewhere else to live in order to pay the husband his share. Accordingly, the court ordered that the whole beneficial interest be vested in her. In *Jones v Jones* the conduct of the husband had a direct bearing on the wife's financial circumstances. Similarly, where the husband had dissipated the family assets or failed to make periodical payments in the past, courts have chosen to make an order transferring the home to the wife.[4] Here the courts were influenced by conduct not so much because it was immoral, but because it had the effect of reducing the spouses' assets on divorce, and therefore the range of orders available.

In *A v A (Financial Provision)*[5] the matrimonial home, which the parties jointly owned, had a net value of £50,000 and as the wife had overall

---

18 In *Smith v Smith* [1975] 2 All ER 19n the husband was ordered to transfer his half interest in the matrimonial home to his wife despite the fact that he had no other secure accommodation. His wife had a pressing need for the home because their child had a serious kidney complaint. In return, no periodical payments were ordered for the wife, and only a modest sum for the child.
19 The transferor should ensure that an order is made under s 25A(3) directing that the transferee shall not be entitled to make any further application for periodical payments.
20 The position would, of course, be identical if the parties' roles were reversed.
1 For the position where such an arrangement was made before 5 April 1993, see ch 9.
2 [1975] 2 All ER 12.
3 Under what would now be s 25(2)(g).
4 *Bryant v Bryant* (1976) 120 Sol Jo 165.
5 [1995] 1 FLR 345.

responsibility for the care and upbringing of the parties' three children, she needed all the capital until they achieved independence. Consequently, the husband's realisation of his share had to be postponed until the children reached adulthood. The most difficult decision for the court was how to balance the wife's need for the immediate use of all the capital against the husband's claim to receive his adjusted portion at the end of that term.[6] Normally, the court would have made an order for a deferred charge. However, there was a history of violence by the husband, and he continued to have obsessional feelings about his wife. Thorpe J therefore took the view that it would be unwise to perpetuate a financial relationship between the parties for many years to come, and instead he ordered the wife to make a lump sum payment of £15,000 to the husband. There were various methods by which the wife might raise the lump sum, but because of her responsibilities and the uncertainties of her resources he held that it would be wrong at this stage to specify a date for payment.[7]

The disadvantage of an order which transfers the parties' only substantial asset into the name of only one spouse is that, unless it is made with compensating provisions, it may give unfair weight to one spouse's needs at the expense of the other spouse's rights. This position is exacerbated when the order has been based on the parties' respective needs, and if the needy spouse's circumstances change for the better after the order in her favour has been finalised, for example if she remarries,[8] comes into an inheritance, or obtains gainful employment. At this stage there is no way of re-opening the matter and correcting the imbalance of the original distribution of the property.[9]

Retaining an interest for each spouse in the matrimonial home

Satisfying the immediate needs of one spouse at the time of divorce should not necessarily outweigh the legitimate expectation of the other spouse to have some share in the property, the purchase of which he has paid towards. If both spouses have contributed towards the purchase of the house, either financially or in kind by looking after the home and caring for the family, then, applying paragraphs (c) and (f) (looking to the parties' standard of living and contribution to the welfare of the family) it may seem inequitable to deprive one spouse of any share in the parties' only substantial asset.[10] Indeed, it will often be the fairest solution that each

---

6   The husband's share was reduced from a half to a third.
7   Each party was given liberty to apply as to the date of payment, but Thorpe J expressed the hope that the lump sum would be paid without either party having to exercise their liberty to apply.
8   Cf *Wells v Wells* [1992] 2 FLR 66.
9   *Chaudhuri v Chaudhuri* [1992] 2 FLR 73; *Omielan v Omielan* [1996] 2 FLR 306.
10 It is suggested that in *Schuller v Schuller* [1990] 2 FLR 193 the refusal of the Court of Appeal to give a wife married for 21 years, who had worked except when the children were young and pooled her resources with the husband, more than a 6% share in the matrimonial home was unfair. She had come into a windfall inheritance after the couple

spouse should retain, or be awarded, a proprietary interest in the former matrimonial home. There are two main ways of achieving this outcome. Where the parties are joint owners of the property at the time of the divorce a court can order that their co-ownership should continue, but that the right of occupation should be given solely to the spouse who remains in occupation. Alternatively, one sole or co-owner can be ordered to transfer his or her interest in the property to the other. In return, the (now) sole owner spouse can be required to execute a charge over the property in favour of the other spouse. In either case a court can order that realisation of the non-occupying or non-owning spouse's interest in the property should be postponed until the earliest date at which one or more of various contingencies should occur.

One of the most difficult questions to be determined in cases where the property is held in co-ownership, or where a former spouse has the benefit of a charge over the property, is 'when should the spouse kept out of his share in the former matrimonial home be entitled to realise his share?' When that share is substantial, its realisation will often mean that the house must be sold, so the chosen time has very serious implications for the spouse who has remained living in the property. Equally, the party kept out of his share in the property has a very real interest in the choice of eventualities which will lead to him being able to realise that share.

Various eventualities present themselves as an appropriate date. These include:

1. the youngest child of the family reaching a specified age, or completing full-time education;
2. the death of the wife;
3. the remarriage of the wife;
4. the wife's cohabitation with another man;
5. the sale of the property.

Postponing realisation of one party's share until the children reach adulthood (a *Mesher* order)

An order that the property remain in co-ownership, with the sale postponed, or the charge not to be redeemable, until the youngest child reaches a specified age, is often referred to as a *Mesher* order.[11] The original *Mesher* order involved a settlement of the property on the spouses on trust for

parted. There were other options which would have given greater recognition to the wife's claim to an entitlement to share in the family assets under s 25(2)(d) and (f). For example, an order in which the husband would be allowed to live in the property for the remainder of his life, with the wife receiving a far greater proportion than 6% of the proceeds of sale on his death, could have ensured that his needs were met during his lifetime, and at the same time could have given proper recognition to the wife's right to a fair share in the family assets accumulated during the marriage.

11 *Mesher v Mesher and Hall* [1980] 1 All ER 126n.

sale in equal shares, sale postponed until the youngest child reached 17.[12] But the term a *'Mesher* order' has been used by lawyers and judges to describe any order under which one of the spouses is kept out of his or her share in the former matrimonial home until a specified event relating to the children occurs.[13] When *Mesher* orders were first introduced the chosen age was typically 18, coinciding with the child reaching majority, and the statutory obligation to give first consideration to the welfare of minor children coming to an end.[14] Sometimes it has been fixed less generously at 17 or even 16.[15] However, in recent years there has been a tendency to select the date when the youngest child reaches 18 or completes full-time education, including further and higher education which ever is the later.[16]

Mesher orders are not popular with the judiciary. They have dropped out of favour because they are said to store up problems for the future.[17] Obiter dicta in *Clutton v Clutton*[18] suggest that a *Mesher* order may be appropriate where the spouses' assets are amply sufficient to house both parties if the home is sold immediately, but where it is in the interests of the children that they remain in the same home for the time being. In such a case, said Lloyd LJ, it may be sensible and just to postpone sale until the children have left home, since the wife's share in the proceeds of sale when that time arrives will be sufficient to enable her to rehouse herself. However, he continued, 'where there is doubt as to the wife's ability to rehouse herself, on the charge taking effect, then a *Mesher* order should not be made'.[19] This statement highlights the reservations which the courts have expressed about *Mesher* orders in recent years. When the children reach the specified age the parent who has been looking after them in the former matrimonial home, usually the wife, may not have enough remaining money after sale of the property, or redemption of the charge, to buy a new property.[20] Hence the anxiety that *Mesher* orders store up trouble for the future.

Another disadvantage of a *Mesher* order is that children do not stop needing a family home merely because they leave school, complete further education or start work. It is noticeable that in those cases where the children were not expected to go into higher, or further, education the courts have sometimes chosen 17 as the date for sale.[1] Yet orders which

---

12 The concept of a trust for sale has since been overtaken by the concept of a trust in land, see the Trusts of Land and Appointment of Trustees Act 1996. However, the principles applying to postponement of sale of jointly owned property after divorce remain the same.
13 See, for example, *Carson v Carson* [1983] 1 All ER 478, in which the property was ordered to be held on trust for sale for the spouses jointly until the youngest child attained 18, or completed full-time education.
14 S 25(1).
15 *Hector v Hector* [1973] 3 All ER 1070, which seems an incredibly young age to choose.
16 *Richardson v Richardson (No 2)* [1994] 2 FLR 1051; *B v B* [1995] 1 FLR 9.
17 *Carson v Carson* [1983] 1 All ER 478.
18 [1991] 1 All ER 340.
19 Ibid, at p 343.
20 *Hanlon v Hanlon* [1978] 2 All ER 889.
1   As in *Mesher v Mesher and Hall* [1980] 1 All ER 126n itself.

lead to the family home being sold when children are on the threshold of adulthood, or have attained their majority, are based on inappropriate expectations of independence at such a young age, and they fail to recognise that the crucial date may arise at a time when a child is taking important examinations.[2] It is suggested that 21 is a more suitable age,[3] or the completion of the youngest child's education, which ever is the later.[4]

The age of 21 is, of course, a higher age than the ages of 17 or 18 which bring to an end the obligation of parents to make periodical payments for their children (unless the child is receiving further education or training).[5] Also, once the children of the family reach majority, they are no longer the court's first consideration under section 25(1). However 'adult children' can still be characterised as an obligation and responsibility under section 25(2)(b). Moreover, it is suggested that the higher age is justifiable because there is a difference between an obligation to maintain a child through the provision of income, and an obligation to continue to provide him with a home. Whilst it may be realistic to expect a child to be able to earn a living once he attains his majority, it is usually not realistic to expect him to earn sufficient income to rent, or buy, adequate accommodation. There are sound social policy reasons for enabling young adults to remain in the family home for some period of time after reaching 18. These include that they will continue to benefit from the influence and guidance of their parents. They are less likely to become involved in crime or drug abuse when living in a steady environment. They are more likely to delay marrying, or cohabiting, and having children of their own before they have sufficient resources to make proper provision for their own family. And, in the case of students in higher education, they need a home to return to in vacations.[6]

A significant disadvantage of a *Mesher* order is that it makes the assumption that the children will continue to make their permanent home with the parent who is living in the property throughout their minority. But this may sometimes come into conflict with reality, and with the philosophy of the Children Act 1989. The Act is founded on the premise that after divorce both parents continue to have parental responsibility for their children. It also builds on the notion that parents should be encouraged to make their own arrangements about their children, and that court orders should not be made which settle the arrangements as to the person with whom the children are to live unless making such an

---

2   Relying, probably, on the fact that a parent will normally not try to force a sale at an inappropriate stage in his child's life. But should the date of sale, which relates so directly to the welfare of the child, be left to the goodwill of the non-residential parent?

3   As in *Alonso v Alonso* (1974) 4 Fam Law 164.

4   It would usually be appropriate to state that education includes undergraduate, but not post-graduate, education.

5   S 29(1)–(3).

6   Contrast the approaches to the continuing need of the children for the family home taken in *Hanlon v Hanlon* [1978] 2 All ER 889 and *Chamberlain v Chamberlain* [1974] 1 All ER 33.

order is better for the children.[7] In the case of an order where the non-owning spouse's interest in the former matrimonial home is preserved by a charge over the property, there is no power to re-transfer the home should either the children wish, or a court order, that they move from one parent to the other.[8] A co-ownership order which simply contains a provision that one spouse is entitled to remain in the matrimonial home until the children reach a specified age similarly does not provide for this eventuality. Rather, in either case, the spouses are locked into a fixed property arrangement which cannot be departed from unless both agree.

Another of the reasons why *Mesher* orders have fallen into so much disfavour is because the original orders were settlement orders. The courts seemed to proceed on the assumption that in cases of co-ownership, where the original conveyance directed an equal division of the proceeds of sale,[9] that this division should be preserved, so that the only effect of the *Mesher* order was to postpone the sale. Clearly, if the proceeds of sale must be evenly divided between the parties when the property is sold then such an order can quite properly be described as one in which the 'chickens come home to roost',[10] because it does not make adequate provision for the occupying spouse to purchase an alternative home. But the court, when making a *Mesher* order, has the power to redistribute the proceeds of sale in whatever proportions it thinks fit, so as to make adequate provision for the occupying spouse when the time for sale arrives. Where there is an outright transfer to one spouse, with the interest of the other spouse preserved by means of a charge over the property, the charge can be for any amount. It is normal for the charge to be for a proportion of the proceeds of sale of the property, rather than for a fixed sum, because this arrangement has the advantage that it anticipates the effects of both inflation, and reduction, in house values.

Where the non-residential spouse's share is for a relatively small proportion of the total value of the property, its realisation when the children grow up may not cause the owning or occupying spouse too much hardship. Even where a wife does not have the means to buy out the husband's share so that she is forced to sell the property in order to pay the husband the money due to him, she may be able to buy adequate alternative accommodation for herself, and any remaining children living with her, with her own share of the sale proceeds. At this stage she will probably no longer need a property with so many rooms because one or more of the children will usually have left home. A *Mesher* order may be a fairer order than an out and out transfer order into the sole name of one spouse, in view of the impact of the Child Support Act 1991 on the courts' property adjustment powers. It has been seen that property transfer orders

---

7 Children Act 1989, s 1(5). See further ch 2.
8 See, for example, *Omielan v Omielan* [1996] 2 FLR 306; *Chaudhuri v Chaudhuri* [1992] 2 FLR 73.
9 Whether as joint tenants or tenants in common.
10 See *Carson v Carson* [1983] 1 All ER 478 at p 482.

cannot be 'traded' for no, or low, periodical payments orders for children. It is suggested that it is the quantification of each spouse's share which should be approached with extreme caution, rather than the order itself. There may be sound reasons as to why the independence of the children should be the factor which precipitates sale.

Remarriage or cohabitation precipitating sale or realisation of the charge (a *Martin* order)

One spouse, usually the wife, may have a particularly pressing need to be accommodated in the former matrimonial home. Sometimes this need is likely to continue for the rest of her life. Because one of the main concerns of the court is to make sure that, wherever possible, each spouse is securely housed, it has sometimes been thought appropriate to order that the wife should be allowed to live in the property for the rest of her life. This means that the husband will never himself obtain his share in the property if he predeceases her. He must draw what comfort he can from the knowledge that his share will at some time enure to the benefit of his estate. However, usually such an order contains the contingencies that the property should be sold, or the charge be realisable, 'if the wife should remarry or cohabit with another man'. This is often described as a *Martin*[11] order.

In *Clutton v Clutton*[12] the Court of Appeal ruled that the trial judge had been wrong to order the transfer of the matrimonial home to the wife free of any charge in favour of the husband. It emphasised that the clean break approach did not mean that the court should disregard other considerations, and deprive one spouse for all time of any share in the matrimonial home. In *Clutton v Clutton* both spouses were aged 48 and were divorcing after a 20-year marriage. Their only asset of substance was the matrimonial home, the equity in which was worth about £50,000. The husband was earning about £20,000 per annum but had substantial debts. The wife had an income of £66 per week working part-time as a typist. She was having a stable sexual relationship with a man, but she said that she did not intend either to marry him, or to cohabit with him. The Court of Appeal considered whether remarriage, or cohabitation, should affect the wife's future position, and found that it should. The essence of the court's judgment was that it would be unfair to the husband if he lost his entire interest in the property through the wife obtaining an outright transfer order, if she was later joined in the house by a new husband, the latter having contributed nothing towards its acquisition. In relation to cohabitation, Lloyd LJ said that, if the reason underlying the clean break principle is the avoidance of bitterness, 'then the bitterness felt by the husband when he sees the former matrimonial home occupied by the wife's cohabitee must surely be greater than the bitterness felt by

---

11 After *Martin v Martin* [1977] 3 All ER 762.
12 [1991] 1 All ER 340.

the wife being subject, as she fears, to perpetual supervision'.[13] The court therefore ordered that the sale of the house should be postponed until the wife died, remarried or cohabited with another man, and that the proceeds should then be divided on the basis of two-thirds to the wife and one-third to the husband.

Consider the effect of such an order, namely that the charge should be enforceable by the husband, or that the property should be sold, in the event of the wife's remarriage, and measure it against the principle that it is normally fair that each spouse is entitled to a share in the value of the former matrimonial home. Look at it first from the point of view of the husband. His position was succinctly expressed by Ormrod LJ in *Leate v Leate*[14] when he recognised that it is 'very galling' for a husband if the family assets are handed over to the wife who then remarries. It could strongly be asserted on behalf of the husband that remarriage is a new relationship which should not be subsidised in any way by an ex-husband. He could argue that a wife who has remarried has all the protection of the legal code which surrounds that new marriage, and that her ex-husband's obligation to provide her with housing should now be brought to an end. Indeed, on behalf of the husband it could be asserted that, if remarriage is not a contingency which should precipitate him acquiring his share in the property, it is hard to think of what other change of circumstance should bring this about.

But now consider such a clause from the point of view of the wife. It could be asserted that it may act as a serious restraint on her remarrying, or on her being able to do so only at the cost of losing her home and, where there are children, the children's home too.[15] Such a clause is based on the assumption that her new husband will either be able to provide her with accommodation, or that he will be able to buy out the husband's share in the former matrimonial home. But this may prove to be incorrect. It could also be pointed out that, where the wife is in receipt of periodical payments, her entitlement to these comes to an end on remarriage.[16] Thus remarriage, for her, will mean that not only will she lose her source of income, she may also lose the roof over her head and, when there are children, over their heads too. Yet, the wife is not at risk of losing her home (and may continue to receive periodical payments) provided that she does not remarry. It could be maintained on behalf of the wife that the insertion of the contingency of remarriage is liable to perpetuate the wife's tie to her ex-husband, it is liable to dissuade her from making a fresh start, and that it is a restraint on marriage which is arguably contrary to public policy.[17]

13 Ibid, at p 345.
14 (1982) 12 Fam Law 121.
15 See *Omielan v Omielan* [1996] 2 FLR 306.
16 S 28(1)(a).
17 Is there even a faint chance that it could be found to be contrary to Art 8 of the European Convention on Human Rights, namely that 'everyone has a right to respect for his private and family life'?

In *Clutton v Clutton* the Court of Appeal not only made remarriage a reason for the property being sold, it also said that the wife's 'cohabitation with another man' should have the same effect. In *Chadwick v Chadwick*[18] the Court of Appeal specifically endorsed the inclusion of such a cohabitation clause.[19] Here, after divorce, the trial court had ordered that the former matrimonial home be held in joint names with the parties as trustees, with the wife to have sole occupation of the property unless she decided to move, or to remarry, or to cohabit with another man. On the occurrence of any of these events the house was to be sold and the proceeds divided equally between her and her former husband. The wife, who was severely disabled, appealed on two grounds: (i) that she might wish to move in order to live nearer the hospital where she had regular medical appointments; and (ii) that any new spouse or partner might not have enough resources to be able to assist her with the purchase of the specially adapted accommodation which she needed. She argued that, in either situation, her share in the proceeds of sale might not be sufficient to enable her to buy a new home, and therefore that the order put her at risk of being rendered homeless. The husband's position was that he had no other major resources, and he was purchasing a new property with the assistance of a 100% mortgage.

Approving and upholding the trial judge's order, Cumming Bruce LJ stated that in order to do justice to the husband it was necessary to impose some 'real inconvenience' on the former wife, which here meant that if she remarried or cohabited the house must be sold. He continued:

> 'That imposes on her the necessity, if she decides either to marry another gentleman or to cohabit with another gentleman, to select as her consort a gentleman who is in a position to provide her with accommodation suitable to her needs. [If] she does decide to marry or to cohabit with a gentleman who cannot provide her with such accommodation, that must be regarded as a grave misfortune which she will bring upon herself. Although material considerations are sometimes not the main considerations that lead spouses to the altar, they are not irrelevant.'[20]

The practice of equating cohabitation with remarriage may give rise to problems of definition. First, it will not always be clear whether or not the wife is cohabiting. For example, is a woman cohabiting when a long-distance lorry driver spends part of the week at his parents' home and the other part at the wife's home? Was Mr Jones, the third person involved in *Suter v Suter and Jones*,[1] who slept each night with the wife but had his

---

18 [1985] FLR 606; see too *Simpson v Simpson* [1984] CA Transcript 119; *Hendrix v Hendrix* [1984] CA Transcript 57.
19 See also, *Omielan v Omielan* [1996] 2 FLR 306.
20 Ibid, at p 608.
1 [1987] 2 All ER 336.

breakfast at his mother's house, cohabiting with the wife? It may also not be clear for how long the cohabiting relationship must last before it can precipitate sale of the property. Sometimes a time provision is included in the order such as 'the property to be sold if the wife should cohabit with another man for a period exceeding six months'. But even this may be uncertain in its application. For example, what would be the position if the cohabitation continued for more than six months, but then came to an end. Would the husband nonetheless be entitled to demand that the property now be sold in accordance with the court's order? It appears after *Omielan v Omielan*[2] that the answer to this question is 'yes'. An order to that effect had been made and the wife had cohabited for more than six months in *Omielan*. The Court of Appeal ruled that she was bound by the terms of the order. This places the wife, and any children living with her, in a very vulnerable position, for now she can turn to neither man for a roof over her head or other forms of financial assistance.

It appears both anomalous, and contradictory, that the courts have equated cohabitation with remarriage for the purposes of precipitating sale of the matrimonial home, but not for the purposes of terminating periodical payments in an application brought in variation proceedings. In *Atkinson v Atkinson*[3] the Court of Appeal was emphatic that it is for Parliament, not the courts, to determine whether the fact of cohabitation should automatically bring to an end the right of a wife to receive periodical payments, and it refused either to extinguish, or even substantially to reduce, the cohabiting wife's order, despite evidence that the wife had deliberately refrained from marrying because remarriage would lead to the termination of her periodical payments. This view has since been reiterated on several occasions.[4] Courts also appear to have lost sight of the principle expounded in *Duxbury v Duxbury*[5] that, after divorce, a wife should be free to live as she chooses and to spend money on, or provide a home for, whomsoever she wishes. In *Clutton v Clutton*[6] the wife argued that a cohabitation clause would encourage constant surveillance of her private life by her husband. This fear was dismissed by the court, but it seems likely that steps to obtain evidence to confirm his suspicions will sometimes be taken by a husband who suspects that his wife is cohabiting when this is denied. This type of 'snooping' is at best distasteful and, at worst, may amount to an invasion of her privacy.

It is suggested that it is most unfortunate that courts have advocated the making of orders in which cohabitation is a factor which automatically precipitates sale of the home, or the right to realise the charge. Cohabitation does not give a wife the same security as remarriage. She has no right to live in any new property purchased solely by her cohabitant. If her cohabiting

---

2   [1996] 2 FLR 306.
3   [1987] 3 All ER 849.
4   See, for example, *S v S* [1987] 1 FLR 71; *Atkinson v Atkinson (No 2)* [1996] 1 FLR 51.
5   [1987] 1 FLR 7.
6   [1991] 1 All ER 340.

relationship comes to an end, she has no claims against her new partner for financial provision and property adjustment orders. Should her co-habitant die, she has no automatic succession rights and no pension rights. Thus there are no safeguards, let alone guarantees, that a cohabiting relationship will make provision for a wife's future needs, which was the fear of the wife in *Chadwick v Chadwick*.[7] It would be more acceptable, and less gender-biased,[8] if orders were made in such a manner as to allow the courts to respond in the most appropriate manner to the eventualities of the wife's remarriage, or cohabitation, if and when they occur. This could be achieved by giving the husband 'liberty to apply' to the court for an order that jointly-owned property should now be sold, or that he should be entitled to realise his charge, if the wife should remarry, or cohabit with another man. This allows the court to deal with the issue, on its merits, at the time when it happens. In some cases it will be appropriate to order immediate sale. In others the needs of the wife compared to those of the husband may be such as to persuade the court that to order sale, or the realisation of the charge, would cause her too much hardship. It should be recalled that unless the wife remarries, or cohabits, the husband will, in any event, be deprived of his share of the property. Making these eventualities automatic factors precipitating sale is arguably to put a strong and unacceptable restraint on an ex-wife forming an intimate relationship with a new partner.[9]

Mesher and *Martin* orders are final orders

Property adjustment orders are final, and cannot be varied. Questions have arisen, however, over whether the specified date for sale of the former matrimonial home, or the realisation of a charge over it, can be altered. In *Thompson v Thompson*[10] spouses remained co-owners of the matrimonial home, and sale of the property was postponed until the children reached 17 or further order. The wife wanted to move and therefore wished to sell the property while the children were still young. The husband refused to agree to sale because he feared losing contact with his children. The wife therefore applied to the court for a further order compelling the husband to consent to the sale of the property. It was held by the Court of Appeal that provided the order included a 'liberty to apply' provision, the court had jurisdiction to order a sale

7   [1985] FLR 606. See further M Hayes *Cohabitation clauses in financial provision and property adjustment orders: law, policy and justice* (1994) 110 LQR 124.
8   It is suggested that it is most unlikely that a court would order that a husband who remains in occupation of the matrimonial home under a *Martin* or *Mesher* order should be forced to sell the home if he should remarry, or cohabit, with another woman. The assumption is more likely to be made that such a union will add to the husband's responsibilities, rather than provide him with additional resources.
9   Indeed, it could be asked whether such orders are a modern version of the much discredited *dum sola et casta* (while unmarried and chaste) clauses.
10 [1985] 2 All ER 243.

under section 24A.[11] But it also held that a sale order must be seen as a *working out* of the original order and not a *variation* of it. It held that an early sale at the instance of the party (here the wife) for whose protection the order had been made would give effect to the original order rather than vary it.

Thompson v Thompson should, however, be contrasted with *Taylor v Taylor*,[12] in which the Court of Appeal held that there was jurisdiction to hear an application for an earlier sale under section 24A, whether or not the original order gave liberty to apply for an earlier sale. However, it was held that the trial judge had been wrong to order an earlier sale under section 24A without hearing evidence, or exercising his discretion, on the merits of the case. More significantly, it was held that the discretion to order an earlier sale would not be exercised if the consequence would be to displace rights which had already vested under the earlier order.

This line of reasoning was followed by the Court of Appeal in *Omielan v Omielan*.[13] The court made it plain that section 24A is purely procedural and that it was inserted into the Act to clarify or expand the court's powers of implementation and enforcement. It further made it plain that it is not possible to amend a property adjustment order by making an order under section 24A. In *Omielan* the parties made a consent order whereby the wife was entitled to occupy the former matrimonial home with their four children, but the property was to be sold on the occurrence of one of four events. These included the wife's cohabitation with another man for a period of not less than six months.[14] Subsequently, two of the children went to live with the husband, and the wife gave birth to a child by a man with whom she had been cohabiting for more than six months. The husband applied for an order that the matrimonial home be sold, which the wife resisted. She applied for an order varying the original order and postponing sale until the youngest child reached 18. Ordering that the property be sold and dismissing the wife's application, the Court of Appeal held that there was no jurisdiction to vary the original order. The effect of the wife's cohabitation for more than six months was to bring to an end her beneficial interest in possession and to bring into possession the vested beneficial interests in reversion.

---

11 S 24A: 'Where the court makes ... a secured periodical payments order, an order for the payment of a lump sum or a property adjustment order, then, on making that order or at any time thereafter, the court may make a further order for the sale of such property as may be specified in the order, being property in which or in the proceeds of sale of which either or both of the parties to the marriage has or have a beneficial interest, either in possession or reversion.'

12 [1987] 1 FLR 142.

13 [1996] 2 FLR 306.

14 The other three were the wife's remarriage, her death, or her ceasing to reside at the property on a full-time basis. Unusually, the husband divested himself of any beneficial interest, and the wife's was reduced to 25%. The children had a vested 75% beneficial interest in reversion, subject to the wife's prior right of occupation. The husband and wife were joint owners of the legal estate and trustees of the proceeds of sale.

Overcoming the 'moving house' problem

In cases of co-ownership, the courts seem invariably to have ordered that the parties' respective interests in the fund tied up in the matrimonial home must be shared between them on sale of the property. When making charge orders, almost invariably the courts have provided that the charge will be realisable when the property is sold. However, the contingency that sale of the property leads to distribution of the proceeds of sale may cause particular hardship to the owning or occupying spouse who wishes to move house. Whether there has been a limited term order, as in the case of a *Mesher* order, or a *Martin* order giving the wife a right to live in the house for life, the security afforded by that order disappears if the property is sold at an earlier date, and the proceeds of sale are divided. The wife may wish to move for various reasons such as to take up an offer of employment, to be closer to the children's schools, to care for elderly parents, or to be near to a hospital.[15] Yet the effect of the order may prevent her from moving.

How might the moving-house problem be overcome? In co-ownership cases the property is already vested in trustees (usually the husband and wife). It is suggested that any order or agreement should impose a specific duty on the husband and wife to reinvest the proceeds of sale in a new property, where the wife makes such a request.[16] But in order to be fair to the husband, the order or agreement could include a provision allowing him liberty to apply for the proceeds to be divided when the sale occurs. This would enable the court to consider the respective merits of the spouses' positions at that time. In cases where there is a charge, provision could be made that the charge should not be realisable on sale of the property, provided that the proceeds of sale are reinvested in new property which is similarly intended to provide a home for the wife, and any dependent children who are living with her, the charge to be attached to the new property. Again, in order to be fair to the husband, liberty to apply for realisation of the charge when the property is sold could be given.

Does it seem likely that courts would be willing to accept such a flexible approach? There is no reason in principle why they should not. The answer probably would depend on how they perceive the way in which it would affect the balance of interests between the husband and wife.[17] On the one

15 Cf *Chadwick v Chadwick* [1985] FLR 606.
16 See, for example, *Omielan v Omielan* [1996] 2 FLR 306. The order, which included the provision that the property be sold if the 'wife ceased to reside in the property on a full-time basis,' contained a paragraph which enabled the wife to substitute for the former matrimonial home an alternative property.
17 For an unusual example see *Greenham v Greenham* [1989] 1 FLR 105, in which the Court of Appeal deleted a provision requiring a husband who was occupying the former matrimonial home to pay his wife 20% of its value when he reached his 70th birthday. The court said that although he would have sufficient capital and income to do so, it would still involve him in having to move house at an age when he might not wish to do so.

hand, if the main focus of the original order was to make provision for the wife's needs, then an order which would ensure that those needs will continue to be provided for, should she wish to move house, might well be considered desirable. It could usefully be pointed out that one reason for the wife's desire to move might be because she has employment opportunities elsewhere and that, were she to obtain employment, this could bring about a clean break from any periodical payments requirements imposed on the husband. Thus both parties would gain from such an arrangement. On the other hand, if the court's focus has been on the preservation of the absent spouse's share in that particular piece of property, then it would be likely to be reluctant to allow for such a scheme. In *Chadwick v Chadwick*,[18] which appears to be the only reported case which directly deals with this matter, the Court of Appeal was entirely unsympathetic to the wife's position.

More open-ended *Mesher* and *Martin* orders

It has been seen that the insertion in orders of specific contingencies which give rise to the enforcement of sale of the propery, or the entitlement to demand that the charge over the property should now be realisable, have the potential to cause hardship for the occupying or owning spouse. This potential may dissuade a court from making an order containing a specific contingency, as in the case of *Mesher* orders, which have fallen out of favour for this reason. Yet a refusal to contemplate a *Mesher* order may cause equal hardship for the non-occupying spouse if the other option is a *Martin* order. Such an order often means that the husband never realises his share in the property during his lifetime. An alternative approach is for courts to make more open-ended orders. Sometimes they have done this by inserting a contingency in an order, but also including a clause which gives either spouse 'liberty to apply to the court for an earlier sale of the property, or earlier realisation of the charge'. An even more open-ended order is one in which sale is postponed until 'the parties consent to the sale or until further order of the court, with liberty to apply'.[19]

The disadvantage of a more open-ended type of order is that it is vague and leaves the parties in a state of uncertainty. It is difficult for either of them to make plans if they do not know what events might precipitate sale. Also, when they cannot agree that the appropriate time for sale has now been reached, they may then become embroiled in further litigation, which is costly. However, an open-ended order has the advantage that the merits of ordering a sale can be reviewed at the time of the application. Thus where, for example, the youngest child has not yet reached 18, but where the husband has a particularly pressing need to realise his share in the property, this would allow the husband to take the matter back to

---

18 [1985] FLR 606.
19 See *Re Evers Trust, Papps v Evers* [1980] 3 All ER 399, in the context of postponing the enforcement of a trust for sale (now a trust in land): see ch 9.

court. Where the wife is in fact in the position to be able to accommodate herself from her share in the property, or able to buy the husband out, the court could take account of this when reaching its decision. Equally, if the youngest child has reached 18, but where both the wife and the 'child' have pressing needs to remain in the property, and where the husband is adequately accommodated elsewhere, this too could be borne in mind by the court when determining whether sale should be ordered. It has been argued that an order which states that the property must be sold where the wife cohabits with another man may be unduly restrictive. But a more open-ended order, which would give the husband liberty to apply in the event of his wife's cohabitation would be fair to him, but would also allow the wife to form a relationship with a man of limited means, without the fear of automatically losing the roof over her head.

Normally, the proportion each spouse will receive in the proceeds of sale of the property is fixed at the time when the order is made. However this is not imperative, and in *Sakkas v Sakkas*[1] Wood J ordered that the property be held on trust for sale, sale to be postponed until the younger child attained the age of 20. He further ordered that before the house was sold the matter should be brought back before the court for directions to be given as to the proportions in which the proceeds were to be divided. Again there is uncertainty, and the potential for further litigation is actually built into the court's order; however such an order has the advantage of flexibility and gives the opportunity to achieve fairness when the date for sale arrives.

Choosing between co-ownership or a charge over the property

It has been seen that there is a choice to be made where each spouse retains an interest in the former matrimonial home. Should they be co-owners, or should the property be transferred into the sole name of one party and the interest of the other be protected by giving him a charge over the property?

Co-ownership

There are various considerations which might usefully be borne in mind when making this choice. In many cases co-ownership will be the starting position because it has become increasingly common for the matrimonial home to be conveyed into the spouses' joint names, usually as beneficial joint tenants. When determining what should happen to the matrimonial home it may be the easiest solution simply to maintain the joint tenancy.

---

1 [1987] Fam Law 414.

This has two significant consequences: first, on the death of one joint tenant the whole beneficial interest enures to the benefit of the survivor; and secondly, each spouse's share in the proceeds of sale is fixed at 50%. Therefore, when a marriage breaks down and the parties are joint tenants of the matrimonial home, one of the first matters to consider is whether the joint tenancy should be severed. Succession rights through operation of the doctrine of survivorship may represent what the parties wish, especially where the home is being used for the children, or where each spouse agrees that, in the event of death, the surviving parent should own the house. However, where there is no such joint intention, a spouse who fails to sever the joint tenancy and then dies is likely to have his or her testamentary wishes defeated by operation of the right of survivorship.[2]

It is suggested that a conscious decision should always be made about whether to sever the joint tenancy at an early stage in divorce proceedings. If the divorce proceedings are concluded before the death, presumably questions of severance will be dealt with by the court under section 24. The danger lies if either party dies before the conclusion of the divorce proceedings. Here, in the absence of severance, the survivor takes all. For example, in *McDowell v Hirschfield Lipson & Rumney and Smith*[3] the husband and wife were joint tenants of the matrimonial home. The husband had petitioned for divorce after living apart from his wife for more than five years. He had been living with another woman, the plaintiff, and she had borne him two children. The husband had died while the divorce proceedings were pending, and there had been no express severance of the joint tenancy. The court held that, for severance to be implied, there must be shown a course of dealing in which both parties clearly evince an intention that the property should henceforth be held in common and not jointly, and this the plaintiff had failed to establish. The husband's interest therefore passed to the wife. The other danger in simply allowing a joint tenancy to continue is that such an arrangement is dependent on trust and co-operation between ex-spouses in circumstances which cannot be foreseen. There is always the risk that one of the spouses might sever the joint tenancy at some future date, and devise his or her share to a third party, without the other spouse being aware of the implications of severance for succession purposes.

Another problem associated with preserving the joint tenancy is that if the property is sold during the lifetime of the spouses the proceeds of sale must be equally distributed between them. This may mean that one of the parties has insufficient resources with which to purchase a new property. It may therefore be more appropriate to retain co-ownership, but for the parties, or the court, to convert the joint tenancy into a tenancy in common and to alter the proportionate share of each

---

2   Failure by a lawyer to ensure the severance of a joint tenancy could lead to an action in negligence, see *Carr Glyn v Frearsons (A Firm)* [1999] 1 FLR 8. See *Kinch v Bullard* [1999] 1 FLR 66 for discussion of when notice to sever a joint tenancy becomes effective.
3   [1992] 2 FLR 126; see too *Harris v Goddard* [1983] 3 All ER 242.

spouse's beneficial interest in the property, after taking account of the different factors in section 25.

Where it is agreed that the spouses are already co-owners in equity, but where the legal title is in the name of one spouse alone, say the husband, it is important to ensure that the name of the wife is added to the legal title so that she is equally in control of the property for the future. Otherwise the wife's position as against a purchaser could be put at risk. There is some danger that her beneficial interest could be defeated by sale of the property without her knowledge, or she might find that the property has been used as security for a loan without her consent.[4] Of course, where each spouse's name is on the legal title, then each must be involved in any future transactions concerning the property. The advantages and disadvantages of such an arrangement need to be considered when deciding whether co-ownership or a charge is the better way of maintaining an interest in the property for both spouses. Where the spouses are hostile to one another, or where there is likely to be disagreement over sale or other transactions concerning the property, then any arrangement which depends on the parties' future co-operation is to be avoided. However, such lack of co-operation may be able to be overcome where the obduracy of one co-owner threatens to defeat the court's original order. In *Harvey v Harvey*[5] the husband flatly refused to join with the wife in applying for a second mortgage and improvement grant to effect repairs to the property. The court ordered the appointment of a receiver of the husband's interest in the property, who would be invited to act on the husband's behalf on the applications which the wife wished to make.

The advantage of co-ownership over a charge order is that it allows for more flexibility, because it is possible to create the settlement in such a way that it can be responsive to changes in circumstances. This could be particularly valuable where there are dependant children of the family, and when any order must reflect the needs of the parent caring for the children to provide them with a home. The Children Act 1989 places considerable emphasis on the continuing parental responsibility of each parent after divorce, and where both parents maintain involvement with their children there may be a real possibility that the children may wish to move from one parent to the other during the course of their upbringing. It would be unfortunate, and not in the interests of the children which section 25(1) requires should be given first consideration, if such a move was impossible because of inflexible arrangements about the use of the matrimonial home during their minority. Where it seems likely that the parties will agree, or a court may wish to order, a change of residence for a child, then continuing co-ownership of the property may best provide for this eventuality. It would be possible (although apparently unprecedented) to

4   The wife's position would turn on the application of the doctrine of notice.
5   [1987] 1 FLR 67.

settle the property so that the right of occupation is vested in whichever parent is providing a home for the children, with liberty to apply for the transfer of the right of occupation right if that situation should alter. This would allow for the situation where the children move from one parent to the other after the financial and property arrangements have been completed.

A charge over the property

In most cases the preferred method of preserving the absent spouse's interest in the former matrimonial home is by means of a charge. The legal estate and entire beneficial interest in the property is vested in the sole name of one spouse, but she is required to execute a charge over it in favour of the other spouse to secure to him the payment of a sum of money. It is particularly popular where the property is mortgaged. Many mortgagees, that is the banks and building societies, will release a husband from his personal covenants under the mortgage on the wife giving an undertaking to take full responsibility for these, provided that she is in the financial position to do so. If the husband should then wish to obtain a fresh mortgage to purchase a new home, he will be in a better position to do so because he has no liabilities. Indeed, he may even be able to claim that he is particularly creditworthy because he has a charge on property which he will be able to enforce at some time in the future. Thus a charge order is usually advantageous for the husband.

The advantage of a charge order from the wife's point of view is that she now has full control over the property, and can deal with it without consulting the husband. This is in contrast to her position where there is co-ownership. She is also entitled to redeem the charge at any time, thereby ending the husband's claim over the property.[6] However, the wife could well find herself in the position of owning property subject to two, and possibly three, charges, namely the original mortgage, the husband's charge and, in cases when she has been legally aided, the charge in favour of the Legal Aid Fund. Consequently she would be unlikely to be able to raise any further loan for such things as improvements and repairs using the home as security.

Transfer of tenancies

A court has power under section 53 of the Family Law Act 1996 to make an order transferring a relevant tenancy from one spouse to the other at any time where it has the power to make a property adjustment order. Consequently, the order may not take effect before a divorce or separation order is made, or a decree of nullity is made absolute, unless the circum-

6   *Popat v Popat* [1991] 2 FLR 163.

stances are exceptional.[7] A relevant tenancy means a protected or statutory tenancy within the meaning of the Rent Act 1977, a statutory tenancy within the meaning of the Rent (Agriculture) Act 1976, a secure tenancy within the meaning of section 79 of the Housing Act 1985, or an assured tenancy or assured agricultural occupancy within the meaning of Part I of the Housing Act 1988.[8] The provisions in schedule 7 of the Family Law Act 1996 only apply if one spouse is entitled, either in his own right or jointly with the other spouse, to occupy a dwelling house by virtue of a relevant tenancy. As with any other property adjustment order, an application for a tenancy transfer cannot be made if the applicant has remarried.[9] The court is given guidelines on the matters to which it must have regard when determining whether to make a tenancy transfer order. These are not the same as those detailed in the Matrimonial Causes Act 1973. Rather, the court's attention is directed towards the circumstances in which the tenancy was granted, the criteria for making occupation orders specified in section 33(6)(a), (b) and (c)[10] and the suitability of the parties as tenants[11] but, interestingly, conduct is not a relevant consideration.

Financial and property agreements

Spouses are encouraged to settle their financial and property affairs without recourse to litigation, and most financial and property arrangements are arrived at through negotiation, mediation and agreement, such bargaining taking place in the shadow of what a court would be likely to do.[12] Where the parties draw up an agreement which states their future rights and liabilities and otherwise settles their financial affairs, this is known as a 'maintenance agreement' and is governed by sections 34-36 of the Matrimonial Causes Act 1973. Where there is a dispute over whether the parties agreed terms, the court has a discretion to determine whether accord was reached. Ordinarily, heads of agreement signed by the parties or a clear exchange of solicitors' letters will establish the consensus.[13] However, spouses do not have power to oust the jurisdiction of the courts[14] and any

---

7   Matrimonial Causes Act 1973, s 23B(1).
8   Family Law Act 1996, Sch 7, para 1.
9   Family Law Act 1996, para 13.
10 See ch 6.
11 The Family Law Act 1996 extends the court's property adjustment jurisdiction to cohabitants where they are tenants of property, and the details of the provisions in Sch 7 are more fully discussed in ch 9.
12 See the research on the pressure on parties to reach agreements in G Davis, S M Cretney, and J Collins, *Simple Quarrels* (Oxford: Clarendon Press, 1994).
13 *Xydhias v Xydhias* [1999] 1 FLR 683.
14 *Hyman v Hyman* [1929] AC 601. The state has an interest in ensuring that divorce settlements are just and reasonable, and that arrangements are not made which improperly impose the burden of providing housing and income for a spouse and children onto income support or other state funds.

provision within a such an agreement which purports to do so is void.[15] Consequently, even an express agreement by one spouse not to apply for financial and property provision after divorce does not preclude that spouse from seeking such relief in the courts. This is not, however, to say that the court will ignore the terms of the parties' agreement. On the contrary, the agreement reached is highly relevant to the court's deliberations, and a party to an agreement who wishes to resile from it must satisfy the court that the terms were unfair and that injustice would arise unless the court were to depart from them. Thus the parties are in the paradoxical position that the court may refuse to give effect to an agreement which has not yet been incorporated in a consent order, but the parties themselves are not able to resile from the agreement except where normal contractual principles would allow this, such as fraud, misrepresentation or undue influence.[16]

Edgar v Edgar[17] is the leading case on whether and when a court will allow a party to obtain a court order which departs from an agreed arrangement. The husband and wife executed a deed of separation under which the wife agreed not to apply for a lump sum or property transfer order on divorce. The husband was very wealthy, and the wife's solicitors advised her that she could obtain a far better settlement in divorce proceedings. The wife, however, was eager to separate from the husband and therefore was insistent upon concluding matters between the parties. Nearly three years later the parties divorced and the wife sought a lump sum payment. The trial judge declined to give effect to the agreement and ordered the husband to pay the wife £670,000. Allowing the husband's appeal, the Court of Appeal held that in deciding what weight to give to the parties' prior agreement, the court must take account of the circumstances surrounding the making of the agreement. Had there been undue pressure by one party on the other? Had one party exploited a dominant position? Did one party have inadequate knowledge? Were there any unforeseen or overlooked changes in circumstances existing at the date of the agreement?[18] The crucial question when dealing with parties who had unequal bargaining power was whether the wealthy husband had exploited this power unfairly to the disadvantage of the wife. Since there was no evidence of pressure by the husband to force the wife to accept the

---

15 Matrimonial Causes Act 1973, s 34(1). Such arrangements are normally embodied in a deed, which resolves any difficulties over whether there was a final binding agreement, cf *Standley v Stewkesbury* [1998] 2 FLR 610, or whether the agreement was supported by consideration.

16 The unsatisfactory nature of the law in this area is neatly analysed by Hoffmann LJ in *Pounds v Pounds* [1994] 1 FLR 775, at p 791.

17 [1980] 3 All ER 887.

18 See *B v B (Consent Order: Variation)* [1995] 1 FLR 9, where a consent order was set aside because the wife was in a depressed and confused state when agreeing to it. She was also given bad legal advice, but cf *Harris v Manahan* [1997] 1 FLR 205. The difficulty with allowing a spouse to repudiate an agreement where she has received bad legal advice is that the other spouse has not been responsible for the wrongful advice being given, yet it is he who will affected by the agreement being overturned.

terms of the deed, and since the wife had received advice from her lawyers which she had refused to take, it had not been shown that justice required the court to relieve her of her agreement.

The principles applied in *Edgar v Edgar* continue to govern how courts approach applications to set aside agreements which have been reached.[19] Where such agreement has been arrived at with the benefit of legal advice and with none of the vitiating factors outlined by the Court of Appeal, a court will normally make a financial provision and property adjustment order in identical terms. However, where a party to an agreement is not wilfully or capriciously seeking to depart from a formal agreement freely negotiated, and where the circumstances are totally different from the circumstances contemplated by the contracting parties, the court will not adhere rigidly to the agreement as this would be to depart from the criteria in section 25.[20]

Consent orders

A consent order has the same binding force as a court order made after litigation.[1] A consent order cannot increase the range of possible disposals of the parties' assets.[2] The House of Lords has made it clear that the order may only contain terms which fall within the court's powers to make financial provision and property adjustment orders under the Matrimonial Causes Act 1973.[3] Where parties agree to the provisions of a consent order, and the court subsequently gives effect to their agreement by approving the provisions and embodying them in an order of the court, it is important to appreciate that the legal effect of those provisions is derived from the court order itself. It does not depend any longer on the agreement between the parties.[4] Consequently, consent orders do not have a contractual basis, they are court orders just like any other court orders.[5] Therefore they must be treated in the same way as non-consensual orders.[6]

---

19 See also, *Camm v Camm* (1983) 4 FLR 577.
20 *Beach v Beach* [1995] 2 FLR 160.
1   In practice lawyers tend to consult practitioners' texts and manuals. These contain examples and precedents around which to model a consent order. See too, Law Com Nos 103 and 112.
2   *Livesey v Jenkins* [1985] 1 All ER 106.
3   Matrimonial Causes Act 1973, ss 21-25D.
4   *de Lasala v de Lasala* [1979] 2 All ER 1146.
5   *Thwaite v Thwaite* [1982] Fam 1. Although, as the court has not adjudicated on the evidence, a consent order cannot be challenged on the ground that the court has reached a wrong conclusion on the evidence before it.
6   So, for example, in *Masefield v Alexander* [1995] 1 FLR 100 an application to extend the agreed period under which a lump sum payment should be made was granted by the court. As Butler-Sloss LJ explained, if the order had been imposed by a court and not made by consent there would have been no doubt that the time could be extended. See also, *B v B (Consent Order: Variation)* [1995] 1 FLR 9 where a periodical payments order was extended contrary to the terms of the original agreement.

Parties are wrong, however, to rely on judges being assiduous in examining the terms of a consent order. Section 33A provides:

'(1) ... [O]n an application for a consent order for financial relief[7] the court may, unless it has reason to think that there are other circumstances into which it ought to inquire, make an order in the terms agreed on the basis only of the prescribed information[8] furnished with the application.'

Thus, although a judge is no 'mere rubber stamp', he is under no obligation to make enquiries or require evidence. The effect of section 33A is to confine the function of the court to a broad appraisal of the parties' financial circumstances, and only to probe more deeply where that survey puts the court on inquiry.[9] 'The fact that [the judge] was not told facts which, had he known them, might have affected his decision to make a consent order, cannot of itself be a ground for impeaching the order.'[10] The judge's position was pithily expressed by Ward LJ in *Harris v Manahan*:[11] 'Whilst the court is no rubber stamp, nor is it some kind of forensic ferret.'[12]

With the growing pressure on parties to reach a consensual settlement of their property and financial affairs, it is all the more important that the strictures of the House of Lords in *Livesey v Jenkins*[13] concerning full and frank disclosure are properly observed. Parties are under a duty in both contested proceedings and where a consent order is being negotiated to make proper disclosure of all the material facts. Material facts include those matters in section 25 to which the court must have regard when exercising its discretion, for unless the court has such information it is not in the position properly to exercise that discretion. In *Livesey v Jenkins*, the parties reached a final agreement about the form and the terms of a consent order under which the husband agreed to the transfer to the wife of his half share of the matrimonial home for the express purpose of providing her and their two children with a home. A week later the wife became engaged to be married, but she failed to disclose this fact either to her solicitor, or the husband or his solicitor. Shortly afterwards the

---

7   This means any financial provision order, any property adjustment order, any order for sale of property or any interim order for maintenance: s 33A(3).

8   That is prescribed by rules of court. The information which must be given includes the duration of the marriage; the parties' ages and the ages of their dependent children; an estimate of the value of their property and their respective net incomes; their intended accommodation arrangements; and whether either party has remarried or intends to remarry.

9   *Pounds v Pounds* [1994] 1 FLR 775.

10 *Tommey v Tommey* [1983] Fam 15, at 21. This statement was approved by the House of Lords in *Livesey v Jenkins* [1985] 1 All ER 106 (although the implication that there was no duty to make full and frank disclosure was disapproved).

11 [1997] 1 FLR 205, at p 213.

12 As Ward LJ explained, 'officious inquiry may uncover an injustice but it is more likely to disturb a delicate negotiation and produce the very costly litigation and the recrimination which conciliation is designed to avoid'. Ibid.

13 [1985] 1 All ER 106.

agreement was embodied in a consent order, the wife remarried and within two months she advertised the matrimonial home for sale. Setting aside the consent order, the House of Lords held that the wife's engagement was a material circumstance which was directly relevant to the parties' agreement. She had therefore been under a duty to disclose her engagement and her failure to do so invalidated the consent order which would accordingly be set aside.[14] However, Lord Brandon concluded his speech with 'an emphatic word of warning':

> 'It is not every failure of frank and full disclosure which would justify a court setting aside an order of the kind concerned in this appeal. On the contrary, it will only be in cases when the absence of full and frank disclosure has led to the court making, either in contested proceedings or by consent, an order which is substantially different from the order which it would have made if such disclosure had taken place that a case for setting aside can possibly be made good.'[15]

It is clear that a consent order will be set aside where there has been fraud[16] or mistake, as well as where there has been non-disclosure, as in *Livesey v Jenkins*. In *Middleton v Middleton*[17] the entire basis upon which the order had been made, namely that the family home was also a business asset with considerable goodwill, had been undermined by the husband secretly separating the business from the house, resulting in the house plummeting in value. The Court of Appeal set the order aside and made fresh provision for the wife. Outside these rather extreme circumstances, however, there is a deep reluctance to interfere with such orders. Consequently in *Harris v Manahan*,[18] despite having real sympathy for the wronged wife, the Court of Appeal reiterated that only in the most 'exceptional case of the cruellest injustice' would the public interest in the finality of litigation be overriden, and that the bad legal advice which the wife had clearly been given was no reason for setting the consent order aside.[19]

---

14 See also, *Robinson v Robinson* [1982] 2 All ER 699n.

15 [1985] 1 All ER 106, at p 119.

16 See, for example, *T v T (Consent Order: Procedure to Set Aside)* [1996] 2 FLR 640, where the husband, by his deliberate concealment that he was engaged in active negotiations to acquire shares in a private company at the time when the consent order was being negotiated, was held to have acted fraudulently. Where there is fraudulent non-disclosure, the court is deprived of the opportunity properly to exercise its powers under s 25. Thus the situation is different from where there is a supervening event after the original order was made, as in *Barder v Caluori* [1987] 2 All ER 440, see above.

17 [1998] 2 FLR 821.

18 [1997] 1 FLR 205.

19 See also, *Tibbs v Dick* [1998] 2 FLR 1118, where the Court of Appeal held that bad or negligent legal advice per se could never be a ground for setting aside a consent order. However, a party may have a remedy in negligence, *Frazer Harris v Scholfield Roberts & Hill (A Firm)* [1998] 2 FLR 679; but cf *Kelley v Corston* [1998] 1 FLR 986 which gives immunity from suit in respect of settlements reached 'at the door of the court'.

It must, however, be appreciated that where a provision in a consent order includes an order for periodical payments of limited duration that such a limitation does not prevent the payee seeking an extension of the term of the order under section 31. Unless a direction is included in the consent order under section 28(1A) such an application is not debarred, despite it being contrary to the terms of the original agreement.[20]

Undertakings

Undertakings given to the court enable spouses to promise the court to do certain things which the court cannot order them to do because they fall outside the scope of the statutory framework.[1] For example, it is commonplace for a husband to undertake to make the mortgage repayments on the former matrimonial home, to use his best endeavours to secure the release of the wife from her own obligations to the mortgagee, and to indemnify her should she be pursued for payments owing. Or he might undertake to take out insurance on his life in order to compensate his wife for her loss of expectation of a widow's pension;[2] or to pay the children's school fees,[3] or to be solely responsible for specified debts. The advantage of arrangements agreed in this manner is that they can be more flexible, and more imaginative, than the range of orders available to courts. Importantly, such undertakings are enforceable just as effectively as direct orders,[4] but of course a court cannot require a party who is not willing to do so to give undertakings. Undertakings, particularly when combined with consent orders, allow for consideration of a wide range of proposals about how best to untangle spouses' financial affairs, and how best to make financial and property provision for their future.

Appeals and rehearings

A rigorous approach is taken to appeals or applications for a rehearing. An appeal must be lodged within days of the order being made, and not the date from when the order is to be implemented, as must an application for a rehearing.[5] Appeals or a rehearing are occasionally allowed out of time,

---

20 *B v B (Consent Order: Variation)* [1995] 1 FLR 9. For discussion of clean break orders, section 28(1A) and time limit traps, see above.
1   For a general review on undertakings, see D Burrows *Undertakings and consent orders* [1998] Fam Law 158.
2   *Le Marchant v Le Marchant* [1977] 3 All ER 610.
3   *Gandolfo v Gandolfo* [1980] 1 All ER 833. See too *Omielan v Omielan* [1996] 2 FLR 306 where the husband gave up his share altogether in the house, and the wife's share was reduced from 50% to 25%, the children to gain the remaining 75%. Such an arrangement was one which could not properly have been ordered by the court.
4   *Livesey v Jenkins* [1985] 1 All ER 106.
5   *B v B (Financial Provision: Leave to Apply)* [1994] 1 FLR 219.

but only if the stringent conditions laid down by the House of Lords in *Barder v Caluori*[6] are satisfied. These are that new events must have occurred since the order was made; that these events invalidate the basis on which the order was made so that an appeal would be certain, or very likely, to succeed; that the new events have occurred within a relatively short time of the order being made; that the application for leave to appeal out of time has been made reasonably promptly; and that the granting of leave does not prejudice third parties who have acquired interests in good faith and for value in the property which is the subject of the order.[7] Lord Brandon explained why the question whether leave to appeal out of time should be given on the ground that assumptions or estimates made at the time of the hearing had been invalidated or falsified by subsequent events was a difficult one. It involved a conflict between two important principles: the principle that it is in the public interest that there should be finality to litigation, and the principle that justice required cases to be decided on the true facts, and not on assumptions or estimates which were conclusively shown by later events to have been erroneous.[8]

Subsequently, appeals have occurred where orders have been made on the basis that property or business assets have a particular value, and where the actual value has proved to be considerably higher, as in *Thompson v Thompson*;[9] or considerably lower, as in *Heard v Heard*.[10] In *Thompson v Thompson*, Mustill LJ, when applying the *Barder v Caluori* principles, emphasised the severity of the requirements laid down by Lord Brandon. He said that the reviewing court should look in broad terms at the balance of the financial relationship created by the order under review, and ask itself how this balance had been affected by the new state of affairs. Broadly speaking, it should make no difference whether something had happened to alter the original evaluation of the parties assets or liabilities, or whether an entirely new factor had come into play, such as

---

6   [1987] 2 All ER 440. In *Power v Power* [1996] 3 FCR 338 the Court of Appeal stated that the same test should be adopted where there is an application for a rehearing; see too *B v B (Financial Provision: Leave to Apply)* [1994] 1 FLR 219. For a clear example of the application of the test see *Heard v Heard* [1995] 1 FLR 970.

7   The circumstances of *Barder v Caluori* were particularly distressing. A consent order was made, under which the husband was ordered to transfer the matrimonial home and its contents to the wife. The order had been agreed on the tacit assumption that the wife and the two children would require a home for many years. Tragically, before the order had been executed the wife killed the two children of the family and committed suicide. The wife had devised her estate to her mother. Clearly, the assumption on which the order had been made had been totally invalidated. The husband's appeal against the order was therefore allowed despite the fact that it was out of time.

8   [1987] 2 All ER 440, at p 451.

9   [1991] 2 FLR 530. Note should be taken however, that by the very nature of things a valuation can only be an approximate estimate of the value of the property.

10 [1995] 1 FLR 970. The main family asset, the matrimonial home, could only be sold at about half its estimated value, and since the intention had been that the husband would be able to rehouse himself out of the proceeds of sale this amounted to a new event invalidating the basis of the original order. The husband's delay in appealing could be explained and his appeal was therefore allowed and the case remitted.

the receipt of an unexpected legacy. The cause of the change should not have been foreseen and taken into account when the order was made. However, Mustill LJ also expressed the view that the change should not have been brought about by the *conscious* fault of the person who sought to take advantage of it. He explained that 'merely to say that the applicant must not have brought the change on himself is not enough, for this would disqualify an applicant who had been ruined by an honest error of business judgment'.[11] Despite this concession, the whole tone of the judgment laid emphasis on the exceptional nature of the circumstances which had to be established before leave out of time would be granted, 'otherwise the whole basis of this essentially practical jurisdiction will be put out of joint'.[12]

In *Benson v Benson*[13] six months after a consent order was made the wife died from cancer. A compromise agreement was reached between the husband and those acting on behalf of the wife's estate concerning the enforcement of parts of the order. Meanwhile, the husband was also having business difficulties. The husband delayed seeking leave to appeal out of time until a year after his wife's death. Bracewell J was satisfied that the first three requirements in *Barder v Caluori* were satisfied with respect to the wife's premature death. However, she rejected the husband's contention that his deteriorating financial circumstances amounted to a new event, as the potential seeds for disaster had been sown and were plain to the husband prior to him entering into the consent order. She further found that the delay in mounting the appeal had been lengthy and lacked the promptness which cases of this kind requires, and that the reason was that the compromise arrangement was originally acceptable to the husband, and that it only became unpalatable at a later date. Bracewell J dismissed the husband's application on two grounds. Applying the principle in *Edgar v Edgar*[14] that an agreement which had been freely entered into should not be displaced unless there are compelling grounds, she held that the husband had reached an agreement after receiving both legal and financial advice, and therefore the principle applied. Moreover, by delaying so long, he failed to satisfy the fourth test in *Barder v Calouri* that an application for leave to appeal should be made reasonably promptly.[15]

---

11 [1991] 2 FLR 530, at p 538.
12 The other key factor influencing the court was that the trial judge had found that the wife's appeal would be certain to succeed. Cf *Ritchie v Ritchie* [1996] 1 FLR 898 where the Court of Appeal held that the new events which had occurred, namely for the husband to accept redundancy and fail to pay the mortgage, could not invalidate the fundamental assumption upon which the order had been made and therefore the proposed appeal was neither certain nor very likely to succeed.
13 [1996] 1 FLR 692.
14 [1980] 3 All ER 887, discussed above.
15 Cf *Wells v Wells* [1992] 2 FLR 66 where six months after the husband was ordered to transfer his entire interest in the matrimonial home to his wife, the wife remarried and went to live with the children in the second husband's house. The husband was granted leave to appeal out of time on the ground that the wife's situation had fundamentally changed, and the whole basis of the order had been vitiated. The husband in *Chaudhuri v Chaudhuri* [1992] 2 FLR 73 failed when relying on similar facts because, crucially, the order appealed against contemplated the possibility of the wife remarrying.

Costs and the Ancillary Relief Pilot Scheme

The fact that parties are divorcing does not mean that they must adopt a confrontational stance. It is often the case that one, or both, parties wants to secure an arrangement which is fair to each of them, but they need guidance on how this can best be achieved. Prolonged negotiation, and extensive litigation, over financial provision and property adjustment arrangements after divorce is very expensive for the parties.[16] Cases abound in which the spouses' resources have been relatively limited, and in which the costs of the proceedings have absorbed a sizeable percentage of their assets. For example, in *P v P (Financial Provision)*[17] Anthony Lincoln J said: 'Once again I am confronted with the fact that the total realisable funds of the family have been severely reduced by the incurring of vast costs by both sides in order to resolve an issue as to the value of their respective shareholding.' In *C v C (Financial Provision)*[18] Ewbank J commented, almost in passing, that the costs of the financial part of the case amounted to £160,000, with more costs owing for the divorce. In *H v H (Financial Relief: Costs)*[19] the parties were described as having the lifestyle of a comfortable middle-class family, yet between them they had incurred costs of about £175,000. Clearly, neither party gains if money and resources which could be used to benefit the spouses and their children are unnecessarily spent on paying lawyers' fees.

At various times the judges have issued guidance to lawyers on how they should seek to minimise the costs of matrimonial proceedings, about which the judges have frequently expressed concern.[20] The magnitude of the problem was demonstrated by the need to issue a Practice Direction that the court will require an estimate of the approximate amount of costs on each side before it can make a lump sum award.[1] Very specific guidance was provided for practitioners by Booth J, in concurrence with the President of the Family Division, in *Evans v Evans*.[2] This was designed to promote the efficient handling of cases, to identify and define the issues to be resolved, and to encourage the reaching of a settlement. Lawyers were instructed to keep their clients informed of the costs at all stages of the proceedings. One process which can assist is to issue what is known as a *'Calderbank* letter'[3] in which the right is reserved to draw the court's attention to an offer to settle the arrangements on

---

16   See, for example, *B v B (Financial Provision)* [1989] 1 FLR 119, in which some £50,000 was spent by the spouses in support of their conflicting views of the extent and value of the husband's assets.
17   [1989] 2 FLR 241, at p 242.
18   [1989] 1 FLR 11.
19   [1997] 2 FLR 57.
20   See particularly *P v P (Financial Provision)* [1989] 2 FLR 241.
1   *Practice Direction* [1982] 2 All ER 800.
2   [1990] 2 All ER 147.
3   Stemming from *Calderbank v Calderbank* [1975] 3 All ER 333. See too *A v A (Costs Appeal)* [1996] 1 FLR 14.

specified terms, after the court has made its judgment. If the amount ordered by the court is equal to, or less than, the amount offered, the court can order the successful party to pay the other side's costs as from the date of the letter. However, the difficulties of *Calderbank* exchanges were highlighted in *H v H (Financial Relief: Costs),*[4] in which the costs had become a very large sum in proportion to the available assets, and the *Calderbank* procedure is gradually being replaced.

An ancillary relief pilot scheme which is applicable only in certain designated courts across England and Wales has introduced procedures designed to reduce delay, force parties into more openness at an early stage, facilitate settlements, limit costs, and give the court more control over the conduct of proceedings. It has been formally incorporated into the Family Proceedings Rules.[5] The new rule provides for an early first directions appointment at which directions are given with the object of defining issues and saving costs. Written estimates of costs must be provided at each hearing so that the parties are fully aware of the costs which are being incurred. The purpose of piloting the scheme is to enable the procedure to be monitored and an evaluation made of the operation of the rule. A practice direction explains that a key element in the procedure is the 'Family Dispute Resolution' (FDR) appointment, which is treated as a meeting for the purposes of conciliation. Because the meeting is treated as part of the conciliation process anything said, or any admission made, in the course of an FDR appointment is not admissible in evidence, and the judge before whom the meeting is held can have no further involvement with the application other than to conduct a further FDR appointment. Parties must attend all appointments and must provide the court with relevant information about their financial resources. They must respond promptly to any questionnaire from the other party designed to elicit further information. At the FDR meeting, the court expects parties to make offers and proposals and recipients of the offers and proposals to give them proper consideration.[6] This process will often lead to a consent order being made. Where agreement cannot be reached, each party must file with the court, and serve on the other party, a concise statement setting out the nature and amount of orders which he or she proposes to invite the court to make. At this stage, no privilege attaches to the parties' statements. This new procedure is part of the movement away from the normal forensic process towards mediated settlements in divorce cases.

---

4 [1997] 2 FLR 57; and see further District Judge Stephen Gerlis *Don't bank on Calderbank* [1997] Fam Law 624.
5 SI 1997/1056. See also, *Practice Direction (Ancillary Relief Procedure: Pilot Scheme)* [1996] 2 FLR 368.
6 See Judge John Frenkel *Ancillary relief pilot scheme in operation* [1997] Fam Law 726 for a critical comment on the efficacy of the scheme; see also L Singer, *FDR and the Holy Grail* [1996] Fam Law 751.

Negotiating and mediating a fair settlement

Negotiation over financial and property provision should concentrate on what would be the most fair and reasonable arrangement for both parties, bearing in mind that the Act provides that the welfare of the children must come first, and that the appropriateness of a clean break arrangement should always be considered. It does neither of the parties a service to raise false expectations about how much property and income he or she can expect to retain or receive. Where unrealistic expectations have been raised, these can prove to be a real impediment to obtaining a reasonable negotiated settlement. Yet if the parties are forced to litigate, the legal costs will often outweigh any advantage accruing to a spouse who obtains a more beneficial order than the one which could be agreed upon. It can be seen from the above analysis of the courts' powers, and the various ways in which the courts have chosen to exercise them, that there are no easy and obvious answers as to how agreements and orders for financial provision and property adjustment should be determined. Conscious of the difficulties, the courts have increasingly striven to attempt to ensure that the parties do not waste funds by arguing 'irresponsibly'.[7] In *N v N (Valuation: Charge-Back Order)*[8] a valuation of the matrimonial home by an independent third party was imposed on the husband and wife and both were required to accept it. Singer J commented: 'We are moving very strongly towards greater court intervention in ancillary relief proceedings, and not leaving the parties to get on with it and muddle along as they like but positively to direct and control their expenditure and resources not only on things like valuations but on the extent to which documentary detail should be sought and accepted in relation to long past financial dealings'.[9] In recent years, the process whereby a mediator, who may be a lawyer, helps to mediate a settlement between the parties has become increasingly used, and mediation is a central feature of the changes brought about by the Family Law Act 1996. Mediation will not work for all people, but the process can work well when spouses are willing to try to sort out their affairs in a non-adversarial manner. Mediation also has the advantage which attaches to any genuinely agreed settlement, namely that each of the parties takes responsibility for the decision which is finally reached, and resentment and bitterness may consequently be minimised.

---

7   Hence, for example, the limitations on appeals and rehearings imposed by *Barder v Caluori* [1987] 2 All ER 440.
8   [1996] 3 FCR 459.
9   Ibid, at p 467.

Chapter 9

Money and property for unmarried partners and all children

Chapter 9

Money and property for unmarried partners and all children

Beneficial entitlement to the family home when unmarried partners separate

Where an unmarried partnership comes to an end the man and woman face identical problems to those which usually confront a married couple whose marriage breaks down, namely, how is one home to be shared between two persons who each have rights and needs, and how is provision to be made for housing the children? However, at this point the similarity between married and unmarried couples ends. Although their problems are the same, the solutions are different. Spouses have the benefit of a statutory regime which takes regard of their married status and which allows courts to respond flexibly to their specific circumstances. A spouse who has no right to occupy the matrimonial home flowing from a proprietary interest (and not merely an equitable interest) has a statutory right of occupation of the matrimonial home while ever married;[1] and where the marriage is ended by divorce, a separation order or a nullity decree, the court has power to alter the parties' existing property rights.[2] It is therefore comparatively unusual nowadays for disputes between spouses relating to their rights in the home to be determined by the application of principles which are not specific to their marital status.[3]

There is no such statutory right of occupation or property adjustment regime available to unmarried couples. Courts have no power to make an order about the house, or any other property, on the basis that an adjustment of the parties' respective rights would be fair and reasonable between them and would make proper provision for their children. Instead

---

1 Family Law Act 1996, s 30. Such rights are known as 'matrimonial home rights' (s 30(2)); see ch 8.
2 Under the Matrimonial Causes Act 1973: see ch 8.
3 Where a third party has a claim on the property then the spouses' respective rights in the property take on a different significance, as in *Lloyds Bank plc v Rosset* [1990] 1 All ER 1111, which is discussed below. A detailed account of third party claims on the property of spouses and cohabitants is beyond the scope of this book.

the entitlement of unmarried partners to ownership and occupation of the family home is governed by principles of law and equity.[4] These are principles of general application irrespective of the status of the parties involved, and the fact that the parties to a dispute are spouses or cohabitants is merely fortuitous.[5] However, because disputes over rights in property normally arise between parties who share that property it is not surprising that much of the case law has concerned husbands and wives or unmarried cohabitants.[6]

A declaration of trust respecting land must be in writing

The starting point for determining the parties' respective rights in the land is to look at the conveyance or other document of title; this establishes who has legal title to the property. It may be alleged that the person with the legal title (assumed here to be the man) has made a gift of the land to the woman. However, a basic rule of property law is that:

'... all conveyances of land or of any interest therein are void for the purpose of conveying or creating a legal estate unless made by deed.'[7]

Thus with regard to the legal estate there is certainty, and any informal written transaction designed to dispose of the legal estate is void.[8]

It is where one of the parties (assumed here to be the woman) alleges that the man holds the property on trust for her beneficially that the law

---

4   *Burns v Burns* [1984] 1 All ER 244.
5   In the case of spouses, the outcome may, however, be influenced by the presumption that the husband intended to make a gift to his wife, the 'presumption of advancement', and therefore the husband cannot claim under a resulting trust. The strength of this presumption has considerably diminished as the economic dependence of wives on husbands has undergone radical social change, and is readily rebutted by comparatively slight evidence, see *Pettitt v Pettitt* [1969] 2 All ER 385. In *McGrath v Wallis* [1995] 2 FLR 114, the Court of Appeal held that slight evidence can rebut the presumption of advancement between parent and child. In *Tribe v Tribe* [1995] 2 FLR 966 the Court of Appeal allowed a father to rebut the presumption of advancement to his son. The father had made the transfer in order to defeat his creditors, but his illegal purpose had not been carried out. Commenting on the complexity of the proper application of the rule in *Tinsley v Milligan* [1994] 1 AC 340, namely that a man who has made a gratuitous transfer of property to another for an illegal purpose is not allowed to rely on his purpose in making the transfer in order to rebut the presumption of advancement, Millett LJ said: 'genuine repentance is not required. Justice is not a reward for merit; restitution should not be confined to the penitent ... voluntary withdrawal from an illegal transaction is sufficient' ([1995] 2 FLR 966, at p 990).
6   See further P Rippon *Mistresses I have known – unmarried cohabitants and land ownership* [1998] Fam Law 682.
7   Law of Property Act 1925, s 52(1).
8   See *Crago v Julian* [1992] 1 WLR 372 in which it was held that a deed is necessary even to assign an informal weekly tenancy.

becomes more complex. Section 53(1)(b) of the Law of Property Act 1925 states that:

> '... a declaration of trust respecting land or any interest therein must be manifested and proved by some writing signed by some person who is able to declare such a trust or by his will.'

Section 53(1)(c) states that:

> '... a disposition of an equitable interest or trust subsisting at the time of the disposition, must be in writing signed by the person disposing of the same or by his agent thereunto lawfully authorised in writing or by will.'

Without such writing, any purported declaration of a trust of land is unenforceable.[9] This was well illustrated in *Lloyds Bank plc v Rosset*.[10] The wife claimed a beneficial entitlement to a share in the matrimonial home which had been conveyed into the sole name of her husband on the basis that this had been agreed between the parties. Responding to her claim, Lord Bridge said:

> 'Even if there had been the clearest oral agreement between Mr and Mrs Rosset that Mr Rosset was to hold the property in trust for them both as tenants in common, this would of course have been ineffective since a valid declaration of trust by way of gift of a beneficial interest in land is required by section 53(1) of the Law of Property Act 1925 to be in writing.'[11]

Sometimes there is an express declaration of beneficial entitlement in the conveyance; where there is, that concludes the question of title as between the parties for all time, and in the absence of fraud or mistake at the time of the transaction the parties cannot go behind it at any time thereafter.[12] For example, in *Leake v Bruzzi*[13] the wife successfully appealed against an order that she was entitled to a one-third share, and her husband to a two-thirds share, in the beneficial interest in the matrimonial home. The house had been conveyed into the sole name of the husband, but on the same day a trust deed had been executed by the parties which declared that the husband held the property on trust for both parties as joint tenants beneficially. The trial judge had made his order for unequal

---

9   The requirement of writing may not be enforced in a case of fraud, *Rochefaucauld v Boustead* [1897] 1 Ch 196.
10 [1990] 1 All ER 1111.
11 At p 1116.
12 Per Lord Upjohn in *Pettitt v Pettitt* [1969] 2 All ER 385, at p 407; *Re John's Assignment Trusts* [1970] 2 All ER 210n.
13 [1974] 2 All ER 1196.

apportionment on the basis of the parties' respective contributions to the purchase of the property. Allowing the wife's appeal, the Court of Appeal held that the court was not entitled to go behind the terms of the trust deed, that it was conclusive of the parties' respective beneficial interests in the home and that therefore the wife was entitled to a half share. Thus in an extreme case, where the man alone has paid for the property but where it was conveyed into the parties' joint names with an express declaration that it is held by them as beneficial joint tenants, each is entitled to a half share in the proceeds of sale of the property despite the fact that the woman has made no financial contribution towards its acquisition.

Resulting, implied or constructive trusts

The more difficult cases are those where one party is claiming that it would be unconscionable to allow the other to retain the entire beneficial interest in the property, but where there is no written declaration of trust falling within section 53(1)(b). Section 53(2) makes provision for this. It states that:

> 'This section does not affect the creation or operation of resulting, implied or constructive trusts.'

The concepts of resulting, implied or constructive trusts enable equity to require the legal owner of land to hold the property on trust for another where it would be inequitable to allow him to deny the other a beneficial interest in the land. The broad determining principle is that equity will step in and impose a trust where not to do so would allow the legal owner unjustly to enrich himself at the expense of the other. However, the subsection is silent on how courts should decide whether one of these trusts has arisen. It is the courts themselves which have created the principles, and it will be seen that they have adopted an approach which makes little allowance for the vague and haphazard way in which couples often deal with their financial and property affairs when they are living together in harmony.[14] In *Pettitt v Pettitt*[15] the House of Lords made it clear that beneficial ownership of land is determined by principles which have universal application and that where spouses are involved they are not entitled to receive special treatment. The courts have ruled on several occasions that the fact that the parties are married, or that they have lived together as husband and wife, or that the woman has brought up

---

14 Yet surely such a trusting approach is to be encouraged; there is something rather clinical and pessimistic about the modern trend to draw up contracts at the start of a relationship to determine how the parties' assets will be distributed if the relationship breaks down.

15 [1969] 2 All ER 385.

the parties' children and generally run the household, is of no relevance when applying general principles of law and equity to determine their respective rights in the family home.[16]

Direct financial contribution to the purchase price

Consider first the situation where the legal title is in the joint names of an unmarried couple, but where there is no express declaration of the parties' beneficial entitlement. In *Bernard v Josephs*[17] the Court of Appeal held that there is no presumption that they are beneficial joint tenants or that they are beneficial tenants in common. Rather, the court will consider all the circumstances to ascertain their intentions including their respective contributions to the purchase price and other subsequent contributions. It may conclude that a different apportionment than half and half reflects the parties' intentions. But where the house has been purchased in joint names in order to provide the parties with a home, where each has contributed to the purchase price and where they have subsequently pooled their resources, the proper inference to draw is that they intended to have equal shares in the house.

Consider now the situation where the property is conveyed into the sole name of one party, and where there is no declaration of beneficial entitlement. Here equity presumes that the owner of the legal estate has the sole beneficial entitlement. In order to rebut this presumption and to be beneficially entitled, the party without the legal estate must establish that the legal owner holds the property as trustee for both parties in equal or unequal shares. How can this be done? The most straightforward case is where the property is purchased outright and where the person whose name is not on the legal title makes a direct financial contribution to the purchase price. This could be intended to be a gift, or a loan, or as consideration for a share in the beneficial interest in the land. If the evidence is neutral equity will assume the latter and find that there is a resulting trust. As Lord Diplock said in *Gissing v Gissing,* 'the prima facie inference is that their common intention was that the contributing spouse should acquire a share in the beneficial interest in the land in the same proportion as the sum contributed bears to the total purchase price'.[18]

Where, as is more common, the financing of the transaction is out of moneys advanced on mortgage repayable by instalments, if the person whose name is not on the legal title contributes to the mortgage instalments, even

---

16 The leading cases are *Pettitt v Pettitt* [1969] 2 All ER 385; *Gissing v Gissing* [1970] 2 All ER 780; *Burns v Burns* [1984] 1 All ER 244; and *Lloyds Bank plc v Rosset* [1990] 1 All ER 1111.

17 [1982] 3 All ER 162.

18 [1970] 2 All ER 780, at p 791. For an example of where various properties had been conveyed into the sole name of the husband, but where the wife had provided all the money, see *Heseltine v Heseltine* [1971] 1 All ER 952. It was held that the husband held the entire beneficial interest in the properties on resulting trust in favour of the wife.

if she did not contribute to the original deposit, it may be reasonable to infer a common intention from the outset that she should share in the beneficial interest, or to infer a fresh agreement reached after the original conveyance that she should acquire a share.[19] Furthermore, the contribution need not be directly to the mortgage instalments; where a person contributes to the initial deposit and then uses her money to meet joint household expenses so as to enable her partner to pay the mortgage, this would be consistent with a common intention that the parties will share the beneficial interest in the property.[20] It is, however, essential that such a contribution releases the partner's income to pay the mortgage instalments, and that without it he would not be able to afford to keep up payments and fulfil his other financial commitments.[1]

Common intention and detrimental reliance

More difficult is the situation where one of the parties makes an indirect contribution to the acquisition of the property and claims that this gives rise to a constructive trust. In three leading cases,[2] the House of Lords has emphasised that the key issue to be resolved is whether the parties had a common intention at the time that the property was acquired that its ownership should be shared between them, and whether the non-owner acted to her detriment, or significantly altered her position, in reliance on that common intention. It is only where both common intention and detrimental reliance are established that a constructive trust arises.

The courts are not permitted to ascribe a common intention to the parties which they never had, but which the court is satisfied they would have had if they had thought about the matter.[3] Thus the issue to be resolved is 'what did the parties actually intend?' not 'what can it be assumed that they intended?' But how can a person prove that the parties intended that the property should be jointly owned where there is no written evidence to this effect and where she has made no direct financial contribution to its acquisition? Lord Hodson acknowledged in *Pettitt v Pettitt*,[4] that 'the

---

19 *Gissing v Gissing*, above, per Lord Diplock at p 792. See too *Burns v Burns* [1984] 1 All ER 244, per Fox LJ at p 251: '[There is] a possibility that while, initially, there was no intention that the claimant should have any interest in the property, circumstances may subsequently arise from which the intention to confer an equitable interest on the claimant may arise (eg the discharge of a mortgage or the effecting of capital improvements to the house at his or her expense). Further subsequent events may throw light on the initial intention.'

20 See too *Grant v Edwards* [1986] 2 All ER 426.

1 *Gissing v Gissing* [1970] 2 All ER 780; *Burns v Burns* [1984] 1 All ER 244.

2 *Pettitt v Pettitt* [1969] 2 All ER 385; *Gissing v Gissing* [1970] 2 All ER 780; and *Lloyds Bank plc v Rosset* [1990] 1 All ER 1111.

3 *Pettitt v Pettitt* above. But see *Midland Bank plc v Cooke* [1995] 2 FLR 915, discussed below.

4 [1969] 2 All ER 385, at p 403.

conception of a normal married couple spending the long winter evenings hammering out agreements about their possessions appears grotesque...'. Even if unmarried partners are more cautious than spouses, and more aware that they need to have some kind of understanding about their respective ownership of property, normally they will not formalise any arrangement, and they too will tend to act on tacit understandings. As Waite LJ has pointed out: 'despite the efforts that have been made by many responsible bodies to counsel prospective cohabitants as to the risks of taking shared interests in property without legal advice, it is unrealistic to expect that advice to be followed on a universal scale. For a couple embarking on a serious relationship, discussion of the terms to apply at parting is almost a contradiction of the shared hopes that have brought them together.'[5] This failure to communicate gives rise to difficulties both in determining whether a trust arises, and in quantifying the extent of the claiming party's beneficial interest.

When an unmarried couple part, particularly where their parting is accompanied by feelings of hostility, their respective memories are likely to become selective and self-serving about what they agreed about the family home. In *Bernard v Josephs*[6] it was said that the nature of the relationship was an important factor when considering the inference to be drawn from the way in which the parties had conducted their affairs. Moreover, the court held that it was essential for the court to be satisfied that the relationship between the parties was intended to involve the same degree of commitment as a marriage before applying the principles applicable to a married couple. The fact that the relationship is one of cohabitation, rather than marriage, may therefore have an important bearing on the ascertainment of the couple's common intention, and on the determination of the appropriate apportionment of their respective rights in the property. As Griffiths LJ said, 'each case will depend on its own facts, and I only warn against a blithe assumption that all couples living together are to be regarded as no different from a married couple'.[7]

It is clear from Lord Bridge's speech in *Lloyds Bank plc v Rosset*[8] that the evidence to establish a constructive trust can relate either to oral statements or to conduct. He said that the first question to be resolved is whether:

'... there has at any time prior to acquisition, or exceptionally at some later date, been any agreement, arrangement or under-standing reached between [the parties] that the property is to be shared beneficially. The finding of an agreement or arrangement

---

5   *Midland Bank plc v Cooke* [1995] 2 FLR 915, at p 927.
6   [1982] 3 All ER 162.
7   Ibid, at p 170. In *Midland Bank plc v Cooke* [1995] 2 FLR 915, the fact that Mrs Cooke was married was an important fact influencing the Court of Appeal's conclusion that husband and wife could be presumed to have intended to share the beneficial interest in the property in equal shares; see p 929.
8   [1990] 1 All ER 1111, at p 1118.

to share in this sense can only, I think, be based on evidence of express discussions between the partners, however imperfectly remembered and however imprecise their terms may have been.'

This emphasis on express discussions between the parties means that:

'The tenderest exchanges of a common law courtship may assume unforeseen significance many years later when they are brought under equity's microscope and subjected to an analysis under which many thousands of pounds of value may be liable to turn on fine questions as to whether the relevant words were spoken in earnest or in dalliance and with or without representational intent.'[9]

An example of such an informal oral arrangement arose in *Eves v Eves*.[10] An unmarried couple, who had a child, decided to buy a house. The man provided the deposit and paid the mortgage. At the time of the purchase the man told the woman that 'it was to be their house and a home for themselves and their children'. He said that as she was under 21 it could not be in joint names but had to be in his name alone. He said that, but for her age, it would have been purchased in joint names. In fact he was being dishonest, and all along he intended that the property should be his alone. However, the woman accepted his explanation. The house itself was in a very dirty and dilapidated condition, and the woman did a great deal of work in both the house and garden to make it habitable.[11] Subsequently the man left her and married someone else.[12] The Court of Appeal held that the man clearly led the woman to believe that she would have some undefined interest in the property. This in itself was not enough to create a beneficial interest in her favour. But where it was part of the express or implied agreement between the parties that the woman would contribute some of her labour towards the renovation of the house in which she was to have some beneficial interest, then the law would impose a trust.[13]

In *Grant v Edwards*[14] the house was conveyed into the sole name of the man because the woman was married. Here, too, the man falsely led the woman to believe that her name was being excluded from the title deeds for good reason; he told the woman that were she to be a joint legal owner this might prejudice her position in the matrimonial proceedings which were pending between her and her husband. Subsequently the woman made substantial indirect contributions towards the mortgage repayments

---

9   *Hammond v Mitchell* [1992] 2 All ER 109, at p 121, per Waite J.
10 [1975] 3 All ER 768.
11 She did a considerable amount of painting and decorating, broke up concrete in the garden, demolished and rebuilt a shed and prepared the garden for turfing.
12 The woman by then had given birth to their second child.
13 Quantified here as one-quarter of the equity.
14 [1986] 2 All ER 426.

by applying her earnings towards the joint household expenses, without which the mortgage instalments could not have been paid by the man. The Court of Appeal held that the man's statement that the woman's name would be on the title deeds but for the matrimonial proceedings was sufficient to show the necessary common intention that the ownership should be shared.[15]

It is clear that all that is required for the creation of a constructive trust is that there should be a common intention that the party who is not the legal owner should have a beneficial interest, and that that party should act to his or her detriment in reliance thereon. It should, however, be noted that in *Lloyds Bank plc v Rosset,*[16] Lord Bridge concluded that a constructive trust arose in both *Grant v Edwards* and *Eves v Eves* because of an express common intention. He was of the opinion that such a common intention could not be inferred from the conduct of the parties.

Quantification of shares under a trust

When quantifying the claimant's interest under a constructive trust, the court takes account of both direct and indirect contributions by the claimant, including contributions by way of labour or to joint household expenses.[17] In *Drake v Whipp*[18] the issue for the court was the quantifi-cation of the woman's share in a barn which had been conveyed into her male partner's sole name. She had made a substantial contribution to the purchase price and had also contributed in money and labour towards its subsequent conversion into a home for both parties. The Court of Appeal stated that the distinction between a constructive trust and a resulting trust was crucial. In the case of a constructive trust the court could adopt a broad brush approach in determining the parties' respective shares. In the case of a resulting trust, the woman would only be entitled to a share in the beneficial interest which was equivalent to the money she had invested in the property. It held that the woman's interest arose under a constructive trust, because there was evidence of a common intention that she would share ownership of the property followed by detrimental reliance on her part. Accordingly, the court awarded the woman a one-third share, rather than the 19.4% share which was the proportion of her financial contribution.

In *Midland Bank plc v Cooke,*[19] by contrast, the Court of Appeal concluded that the wife had a beneficial interest in the matrimonial home

---

15 At one stage the man paid insurance moneys relating to the house into a savings account in the parties' joint names, which reinforced the evidence of how the parties intended the property to be shared, namely that each should be entitled to a half share.

16 [1990] 1 All ER 1111. See further D Hayton 'Equitable rights of cohabitees' [1990] Conv 370.

17 *Grant v Edwards* [1986] 2 All ER 426.

18 [1996] 1 FLR 826. For further comment, see A Dunn *Whipping up resulting and constructive trusts* [1997] Conv 467.

19 [1995] 2 FLR 915.

by way of a resulting trust. The property had been conveyed into the sole name of her husband, but the wife contributed her share in a joint wedding gift from her husband's parents. This represented only a small percentage of the total purchase price.[20] The question for the court was 'should the proportion of the wife's beneficial interest be fixed solely by reference to the percentage of the purchase price which she contributed directly so as to make all other conduct irrelevant?' The Court of Appeal answered this question with an unequivocal 'no'. Giving the judgment of the Court, Waite LJ held that where the party without legal title had successfully asserted an equitable interest through direct contribution, the court was not bound to deal with the matter on the strict basis of the trust resulting from the cash contribution. In such a case, where there was no express evidence of the parties' intentions, it was, he said, the duty of the judge to undertake a survey of the whole course of dealing between the parties. That scrutiny should relate to matters relevant to the parties' ownership and occupation of the property and their sharing of its burdens and advantages, and should not confine itself to the limited range of acts of direct contribution of the sort that were needed to found a beneficial interest in the first place. Instead, the court should take into consideration all conduct which threw light on what shares were intended. Moreover, in a case where the parties 'had been honest enough to admit that they never gave ownership a thought or reached any agreement about it' such absence of an express agreement did not preclude the court from inferring an agreement. Here there was evidence that the wife, in addition to bringing up the parties' three children, had worked and paid household bills, had undertaken joint and several liability to repay a second mortgage, and had undertaken liability under a second charge on the property for the benefit of the husband's business. This led Waite LJ to conclude that 'one could hardly have a clearer example of a couple who had agreed to share everything equally: the profits of his business while it prospered, and the risks of indebtedness suffered through its failure; the upbringing of their children; the rewards of her own career as a teacher; and, most relevantly, a home into which he had put his savings and to which she was to give over the years the benefit of the maintenance and improvement contribution'.[1] He added that when in addition the parties had taken on the commitment of marriage, the conclusion was inescapable that their presumed intention was to share the beneficial interest in the property in equal shares.

There is much to be welcomed in Waite LJ's reasoning in *Midland Bank v Cooke*. He rejected the submission that where there was no express agreement between the parties 'there is no scope for equity to make one for them'. He said that such a submission 'runs counter to the very system of law – equity – on which it seeks to rely', and supported this view by

---

20 6.47%.
1   [1995] 2 FLR 915, at p 928. The wife's contribution to the 'maintenance and improvement of the property' was through redecoration, alterations and improvements and repairs carried out with or without the assistance of contractors, whose bills she paid.

declaring that 'equity has traditionally been a system which matches established principle to the demands of social change'.[2] A particularly desirable feature of the ruling was Waite LJ's recognition of the manner in which people share their lives in joint homes, and his appreciation that the lack of any discussion and agreement about each person's respective share in the family home was typical of the behaviour of many young couples. He refused to countenance that such a large number of home-buyers should be 'beyond the pale of equity's assistance in formulating a fair presumed basis for the sharing of beneficial title'.[3] At the conclusion of his judgment Waite LJ stated that the fact that Mr and Mrs Cooke were married was important in his determination that Mrs Cooke should have a beneficial one-half interest in the property. Thus although Waite LJ acknowledged, and was empathetic to, the striking change in social attitudes to home sharing by unmarried couples, it is questionable whether, had the case concerned an unmarried couple, he would have quantified a cohabitant's share so generously.[4]

It is, however, hard to reconcile *Midland Bank plc v Cooke* with the earlier Court of Appeal ruling on quantum in *Springette v Defoe*.[5] An unmarried couple 'of mature years' lived together first in a council house of which Miss Springette was the sole tenant, and subsequently in a council house which they held on a joint tenancy. They bought the house as joint tenants at law, but the transfer was silent as to their beneficial interests in the property, and Miss Springette and Mr Defoe (like Mr and Mrs Cooke) never had any discussion about what their respective beneficial interests were to be. Miss Springette provided 75% of the purchase money, and Mr Defoe 25%. The trial judge found that after the purchase the mortgage was paid in equal shares and from this he drew the inference that there was a common intention between the parties that the property should be owned in equal shares. This view was firmly rejected by Dillon LJ: 'the fact that after the purchase the mortgage was paid in equal shares is not evidence that they had a common intention that the property itself should belong to them in equal shares beneficially. It is merely evidence that ...

---

2   [1995] 2 FLR 915, at p 927.
3   Ibid.
4   The difficulty with Waite LJ's judgment is that it appeared to run counter to Lord Bridge's speech in *Lloyds Bank plc v Rosset* [1990] 1 All ER 1111 in which he stated that a beneficial interest in property must be founded on a direct contribution to its purchase or a specific agreement. Moreover, Lord Bridge said that a court was not entitled to presume an intention where none existed. For critical commentary on the manner in which precedents were handled in *Midland Bank plc v Cooke*, see G Battersby, *How not to judge the quantum (and priority) of a share in the family home* (1996) 8 CFLQ 261. See also, P O'Hagan *Quantifying interests under resulting trusts* (1997) 60 MLR 420; M Dixon *A case too far?* [1997] Conv 66; P Wylie *Computing shares in the family home* [1995] Fam Law 633; M Pawlowski *Midland Bank v Cooke – a new heresy?* [1996] Fam Law 484; D Wragg *Constructive trusts and the unmarried couple* [1996] Fam Law 298.
5   [1992] 2 FLR 388.

they had agreed that they would each pay half of the mortgage payments; it goes no further than that.'[6]

The Court of Appeal had no hesitation in holding that the parties held the property on a resulting trust for themselves in the proportions in which they had contributed directly or indirectly to the purchase price. There was no evidence that the parties had a common intention that they should be entitled in equal shares notwithstanding their unequal contributions, so the presumption of a resulting trust was not displaced.[7]

Conduct which is insufficient to give rise to a trust

It has been seen that failure to establish an agreement or arrangement is not necessarily fatal to the claimant's case. Evidence relating to the parties' conduct may be sufficient to establish a constructive trust where the conduct is such that the court can infer that the parties commonly intended that the beneficial ownership of the property should be shared. However, in *Lloyds Bank plc v Rosset*[8] Lord Bridge stated that:

> 'In this situation direct contributions to the purchase price by the partner who is not the legal owner, whether initially or by payment of mortgage instalments, will readily justify the inference necessary to the creation of a constructive trust. But, as I read the authorities, it is at least extremely doubtful whether anything less will do.'

In *Lloyds Bank plc v Rosset* the issue to be resolved was whether Mrs Rosset had acquired a beneficial interest in the matrimonial home, a derelict farmhouse, which had been purchased in her husband's sole name, and which she had helped to renovate. Mr Rosset had used the property as security for a bank loan without Mrs Rosset's knowledge and when he was unable to repay the loan the bank started proceedings for possession and sale of the property. Mrs Rosset resisted the bank's claim. She alleged that she had made a significant contribution to the acquisition of the property by the work she had personally undertaken in the course of its renovation. This included doing some painting and decorating (for which

---

6   Ibid, at p 392.
7   Commenting in *Midland Bank plc v Cooke* [1995] 2 FLR 915, at p 924 on *Springette v Defoe* [1992] 2 FLR 388, and on *McHardy and Sons (A Firm) v Warren* [1994] 2 FLR 338, in which the judge held the parties were beneficially entitled in equal shares despite the fact that the wife's contribution to the purchase price amounted to 8.97%, Waite LJ said 'I confess that I find the differences of approach to these two cases mystifying. In the one a strict resulting trust geared to mathematical calculation of the proportion of the purchase price provided by cash contribution is treated as virtually immutable in the absence of express agreement; in the other displacement of the cash-related trust by inferred agreement is not only permitted but treated as obligatory'.
8   [1990] 1 All ER 1111, at p 1119.

she had a particular expertise), designing two rooms, co-ordinating work with the builders and engaging in various other tasks connected with the house. She claimed that the parties had a common intention that she should share in the ownership of the property and that therefore she had a beneficial interest under a constructive trust.[9] The trial judge and the Court of Appeal were each satisfied that Mr and Mrs Rosset had had the necessary common intention that she should have an interest in the property, that she had acted on the basis of that common intention to her detriment, and that therefore she had acquired an equitable interest under a constructive trust. However, Lord Bridge, stating the unanimous opinion of the Law Lords, ruled that the two inferior courts had been wrong. Why?

Mrs Rosset failed in her claim because she could not establish that the spouses had a common intention that ownership of the property be shared either by proving that the parties had informally agreed to this, or by establishing conduct on her own part such that the court should infer an agreement. Lord Bridge reasoned in the following manner: he stressed that there must be a common intention between the parties to share the ownership of the property where it is alleged that there is a common intention that the property should be shared beneficially. He said that 'the expectation of parties to every happy marriage is that they will share the practical benefits of *occupying*[10] the matrimonial home whoever owns it. But this is something quite distinct from sharing the *beneficial interest*[11] in the property asset which the matrimonial home represents.'[12] He emphasised this further when he said 'neither a common intention by spouses that a house is to be renovated as a "joint venture" nor a common intention that the house is to be shared by the parents and children as the family home throws any light on their intentions with respect to the beneficial ownership of the property'.[13]

In relation to Mrs Rosset's efforts in respect of the renovation of the property, from which the trial judge had drawn the inference of a common intention that she should have a beneficial interest, Lord Bridge said:

> 'By itself this activity, it seems to me, could not possibly justify such an inference. It was common ground that Mrs Rosset was extremely anxious that the new matrimonial home should be ready for occupation before Christmas if possible. In these circumstances it would seem the most natural thing in the world for any wife, in the absence of her husband abroad, to spend all the time she could

9   She therefore claimed that she had an overriding interest under s 70(1)(g) of the Land Registration Act 1925 which would prevail against the bank because she had been in actual occupation of the land on the date when the bank's charge was created. The third party aspects of this and other cases are beyond the scope of this book.

10 Emphasis added.

11 Emphasis added.

12 Ibid, at p 1115.

13 Ibid, at p 1117.

spare and to employ any skills she might have, such as the ability to decorate a room, in doing all she could to accelerate progress of the work quite irrespective of any expectation she might have of enjoying a beneficial interest in the property. ... On any view the monetary value of Mrs Rosset's work expressed as a contribution to a property acquired at a cost exceeding £70,000 must have been so trifling as to be almost de minimis.'[14]

Thus Lord Bridge not only took the view that this conduct could not justify the inference that there had been a common intention that Mrs Rosset should have a beneficial interest in the matrimonial home, he also characterised her contribution as so trifling that it was doubtful whether it amounted to sufficient detriment.

The courts have not been prepared to recognise that when a woman runs the household and looks after the children, this releases the man to be able to devote his energies to earning.[15] It is suggested that they have reached decisions within a framework which fails to recognise the realities of domestic life where there are children living in the household. It is extremely difficult to combine full-time employment with child care responsibilities, and many men would not be able to remain in employment and pay the mortgage if they had to combine their employment responsibilities with looking after the children and doing domestic tasks.

The clearest example of courts giving no monetary value to the contribution which women make to the successful running of a household arose in *Burns v Burns*.[16] The couple were unmarried but had lived together as husband and wife for 19 years. They were known as Mr and Mrs Burns and Mrs Burns had had two children. There was no express declaration that Mrs Burns should have a share in the beneficial ownership of the matrimonial home, nor had she made any direct financial contribution to its acquisition such as to give rise to a resulting trust. At no time did Mr Burns ask her to contribute to the household expenses in order to relieve the financial burden on him, and her purchases did not release his earnings to enable him to pay the mortgage. Mrs Burns nonetheless sought to establish a common intention that she should have a beneficial interest on the grounds that she had brought up the children, done domestic tasks, had redecorated the interior of the house, had used her earnings to contribute towards the housekeeping expenses and had bought fixtures and fittings and various consumer durables. The Court of Appeal held that none of this expenditure was referable to the acquisition of the house. It held that paying for chattels[17] and decorating the property

---

14 Ibid, at p 1117–1118.
15 The House of Lords made this plain in *Gissing v Gissing* [1970] 2 All ER 780. During the 1970s Lord Denning made efforts in this direction, but these have been overtaken by the return to narrow orthodoxy.
16 [1984] 1 All ER 244.
17 See too Viscount Dilhorne in *Gissing v Gissing* [1970] 2 All ER 780, at p 786.

did not amount to evidence of a common intention that she should have an interest in the house.[18] It had no hesitation in dismissing her claim based on her domestic contributions and role as mother of the children.

Thus Mrs Burns, who properly fulfilled her parental responsibilities to her children by spending their formative years in caring for them, was nonetheless denied any share in the property which had been the family home for 19 years. Mr Burns, on the other hand, was entitled to retain the entire beneficial interest in a property which Mrs Burns had cleaned, decorated and otherwise looked after and in which she had laboured for his benefit as well as for the benefit of herself and their children. The Court of Appeal felt some limited sympathy for Mrs Burns' position, but held that it was not for the courts to attempt to remedy any inequity; this was a matter for Parliament. It could be maintained, however, that it was the courts which created the inequity in the first place by adopting a narrow and money-based approach to contributions towards the acquisition of the matrimonial home. Parliament imposed no restrictions on their powers when it enacted section 53(2) of the Law of Property Act 1925. If courts take the view that they are reaching inequitable decisions surely it is up to them to think again about when a resulting, implied or constructive trust should be imposed? If the Court of Appeal was unhappy with the decision it reached in *Burns v Burns*, bound as it was by *Gissing v Gissing*,[19] it could at least have granted leave to appeal to the House of Lords, with the suggestion that fresh consideration should be given to the imposition of a trust on facts of this kind. It was the House of Lords which created the unfairness to women like Mrs Burns by requiring that evidence to establish a trust must be directly referable to the purchase of the property, and that detrimental reliance must consist of making substantial contributions to the purchase or improvement of the property.[1] As a consequence they have denied many non-earning women who live with men to whom they are not married any security in the form of continuing shelter for themselves and their children if the relationship breaks down.[2]

In *Springette v Defoe*[3] in response to the suggestion that the parties must have communicated an intention that they should have equal shares at a subconscious level, Steyn LJ (understandably) commented 'our trust law does not allow property rights to be affected by telepathy'. However, courts, by adopting a cool and rational attitude towards human behaviour, and demanding specific evidence of the parties' common intention, have developed the law of trusts in a manner which ignores reality. Couples, in

---

18 See too *Pettitt v Pettitt* [1969] 2 All ER 385, at p 416, where Lord Diplock was dismissive of the notion that handiwork around the house by a husband should give rise to him acquiring a beneficial interest in the property owned by the wife.

19 [1970] 2 All ER 780.

1 *Gissing v Gissing* above; *Pettitt v Pettitt* [1969] 2 All ER 385.

2 Although a married woman would be treated in an identical manner, cf *Gissing v Gissing* above, under the Matrimonial Causes Act 1973 she is entitled to apply for a lump sum, settlement and property transfer orders where her marriage breaks down; see ch 8.

3 [1992] 2 FLR 388, at p 394.

practice, often do not communicate their private thoughts about financial and property matters. Indeed, they may not even think about the nature of their respective beneficial shares until a crisis occurs in their relationship. The Court of Appeal's ruling in *Midland Bank plc v Cooke*[4] took a more realistic approach to how couples with children order their lives, and the failure of the parties to communicate was not fatal to proof that they shared a common intention. Moreover, when determining the parties' respective beneficial interests in the matrimonial home, Waite LJ placed considerable emphasis on the fact that the couple had shared the financial ups and downs of married life, and he singled out their shared responsibility for the upbringing of their children as a relevant factor.

Midland Bank v Cooke gives some small degree of hope that courts will gradually be persuaded to adopt a less gender-biased approach to the acquisition of a beneficial share in the family home.[5] It is suggested that any civilised modern legal system would award a Mrs Gissing, or a Mrs Burns, a beneficial share in the property in which they had lived for many years, whether or not their direct and indirect contributions to the family budget and the general welfare of the family were directly referable to the purchase of the property.[6] It is hard to understand why courts are so anxious to ensure that they do not 'sit as under a palm tree, to exercise a general discretion to do what the man in the street, on a general overview of the case, might regard as fair'.[7] If the general public would regard it as fair to give a spouse or cohabitant a beneficial share in the family home, it is unfortunate that courts tend to dismiss in pejorative terms the proposal that courts should set out to achieve this outcome.[8] Parliament has given courts the discretion to develop the law of implied, resulting and constructive trusts,[9] and there could be benefits in the law in this

---

4 [1995] 2 FLR 915.

5 The accusation of gender bias is made on the grounds that only material contributions to the acquisition and maintenance of property are valued. Courts ignore how women contribute to a man's use and enjoyment of his land when carrying out the role of home-maker, child rearer, cook, cleaner and companion. Moreover, courts ignore the fact that women tend to spend their earnings on the children, food and clothing for all members of the household, bills for utilities, and such enjoyable pursuits as holidays, presents and entertainment, all of which enhance the man's quality of life. Such expenditure, although it may not release the husband's income to pay for the purchase of property, which is the crucial test after *Gissing v Gissing* [1970] 2 All ER 780, nonetheless enables him to spend his earnings on items of personal interest and enjoyable pursuits.

6 The contribution of married women to the welfare of the family through the performance of such tasks has long been recognised by the courts when altering the spouses' property rights on divorce, Matrimonial Causes Act 1973, s 25(2)(f); see ch 8.

7 *Springette v Defoe* [1992] 2 FLR 388, per Dillon LJ at p 393.

8 Lord Denning had no hesitation in attempting to use the law of trusts to make fair and just provision for wives in the days before they could claim a share in the matrimonial home on marriage breakdown. He was strongly criticised for doing so, but his determination led to improvements in the position of wives after divorce. For further comment, see U Riniker *The fiction of common intention and detriment* [1998] Conv 202.

9 Law of Property Act 1925, s 53(2)(b).

area advancing on a case by case basis and gradually developing in response to social change. The issues to be resolved do not readily lend themselves to a legislative response except through the introduction of a property adjustment regime, and it is clear that the Law Commission is not finding it easy to recommend a solution.[10]

Orders under the Trusts of Land and Appointment of Trustees Act 1996

Where beneficial entitlement to land is shared the Trusts of Land and Appointment of Trustees Act 1996 provides that any trust of property, whether express or implied, or arising under a resulting or a constructive trust, must take effect behind a trust of land.[11] The trust of land has replaced the trust for sale, and section 4 provides that in the case of every trust for sale of land, the trustees have power to postpone sale of the land for an indefinite period whether the trust was created before or after the commencement of the Act. Section 6 confers on the trustees all the powers of an absolute owner. Section 12 states that a person with a beneficial interest in possession in land subject to a trust of land is entitled to occupy the land, thus ending any uncertainty over whether a cohabitant with a beneficial interest in land under a trust for sale has such a right.[12] Section 13 provides that where two or more beneficiaries are entitled under section 12 to occupy land, the trustees of land may exclude or restrict the entitlement of any one or more (but not all) of them. Where this power is exercised, the occupying beneficiary may be required to make payments by way of compensation to the beneficiary whose entitlement has been excluded or restricted.[13] However, the power to exclude may only be exercised with the consent of the excluded beneficiary or where the court has given its approval.[14] In determining whether to give its approval, the court must have regard to the intentions of the person(s) who created the trust, the purposes for which the land is held, and the circumstances and wishes of each of the beneficiaries who is entitled to occupy the land under section 12.[15] Section 14(1) states that any person who is a trustee of land or has an interest in a property subject to a trust of land may make an application to the court for an order. The order will either relate to the exercise by the trustees of any

---

10 The Law Commission has embarked on a study of the property rights of 'home sharers', see Law Com No 232, para 2.78 (1994). At the time of writing its promised working paper was well overdue. For commentary on the position in New Zealand, see B Atkin, *De factos down-under and their property* (1999) 11 CFLQ 43.

11 S 1(2).

12 Beneficiaries of an implied, resulting or constructive trust, whenever created, will almost always have an interest in possession.

13 S 13(6).

14 S 13(7).

15 S 13(4).

of their functions, or it will declare the nature or extent of a person's interest in the property subject to the trust, and in either case the court may make any such order as the court thinks fit.

Criteria for determining applications made under the Trusts of Land and Appointment of Trustees Act 1996

It must be emphasised at the outset that the 1996 Act is not a property adjustment regime. Although under section 14 the court is empowered to make 'such order as it thinks fit', it cannot alter the parties' respective beneficial interests. Section 15 details the matters to which the court must have regard when determining an application. They include:

'(a) the intentions of the person or persons (if any) who created the trust,
(b) the purposes for which the property subject to the trust is held,
(c) the welfare of any minor who occupies or might reasonably be expected to occupy any land subject to the trust as his home, and
(d) the interests of any secured creditor of any beneficiary.'

Section 15(2) further provides that where the application concerns the power of the trustees to exclude or restrict the right of a beneficiary to occupy the land,[16] the court must also have regard to the circumstances and wishes of each of the beneficiaries who is entitled to occupy the land.

How do the provisions in the Act affect the special difficulties faced by cohabitants when their relationship breaks down? Can the Act assist them where they are unhappy living together under the same roof? What are the implications for cohabitants who enjoy a shared beneficial entitlement as equitable joint tenants or tenants in common where one wishes to realise his beneficial share in the property and the other wishes to remain in occupation?

Consider first a dispute between beneficially entitled cohabitants over occupation of the land. There is overlap here with the powers of the courts to make occupation orders under the Family Law Act 1996, section 33.[17] It is suggested that a cohabitant would be ill-advised to apply for an order under section 14 of the Trusts of Land and Appointment of Trustees Act 1996 because the courts' powers under the Family Law Act 1996 are far more extensive. Furthermore, under the Family Law Act 1996 the criteria guiding the court's decision-making focus on such matters as the parties' respective resources, the likely effect of any order on the health, safety or well-being of the parties and any relevant child and, where significant

16 S 13.
17 Occupation orders are explained in ch 6.

harm is alleged, a balance of hardship test is applied.[18] These welfare-orientated criteria are more appropriate to disputes over occupation of the family home than those contained in section 15 of the Trusts of Land and Appointment of Trustees Act 1996. A cohabitant may well face difficulty in persuading a court to exclude or restrict her partner's right to occupy the family home under the Family Law Act 1996, because courts regard ouster and restriction orders as Draconian. However, she has more chance of success under that Act than under the Trusts of Land and Appointment of Trustees Act 1996. The court's powers under section 14(1) only relate to the exercise by the trustees of any of their functions, and trustees may not unreasonably exclude or restrict entitlement to occupy the land.[19]

Disagreement over sale of the family home

It is where cohabitants cannot agree over whether the land should be retained or sold that the provisions of the Trusts of Land and Appointment of Trustees Act 1996 may come to their assistance. The Act repeals section 30 of the Law of Property Act 1925 (which governed the execution of the trust for sale), and the criteria in section 15 are aimed at consolidating and rationalising the approach hitherto adopted by courts when applying section 30.[20] The framers of the Act did not intend to change the law on how courts had exercised their powers under section 30; rather it was their intention to mirror the position which had been reached through the development of case law.[1] Nevertheless, an important difference between the old law and the new Act is that cases prior to the Act which involved a trust for sale were decided against a background of a duty to sell. That duty no longer exists, meaning that courts should now enjoy greater flexibility when determining whether to postpone sale. Another difference is the introduction of statutory criteria to guide the courts in the exercise of their discretion.[2] There is no requirement that any child affected by an application should be a beneficiary under the trust, which

---

18 Family Law Act 1996, s 33(6), (7).

19 Trusts of Land and Appointment of Trustees Act 1996, s 13(2). The trustees must take account of the intentions of the person(s) who created the trust, the purposes for which the land is held and the circumstances and wishes of each of the beneficiaries (s 13(4)).

20 Following proposals for reform made in *Transfer of Land, Trusts of Land*, Law Com No 181 (1989). Section 30 provided: 'If the trustees for sale refuse to sell or to exercise any of [their] powers ..., or any requisite consent cannot be obtained, any person may apply to the court for a vesting or other order for giving effect to the proposed transaction or for an order directing the trustees for sale to give effect thereto, and the court may make such order as it thinks fit.'

1 The long title makes the limited intentions of the Act plain. These are to make new provisions about trusts of land, to phase out the Settled Land Act 1925, to abolish the doctrine of conversion, to otherwise amend the law about trusts for sale of land, and to amend the law about the appointment and retirement of trustees.

2 S 15. These criteria are given equal weight.

was a critical factor in applications made under section 30 of the 1925 Act.[3] The 1996 Act makes it clear that the welfare of a child who occupies, or might reasonably be expected to occupy, any land subject to the trust as his home is a matter for independent consideration.

When exercising their discretionary powers to postpone sale under section 30, courts focused their attention on the underlying purpose of the trust. Where the parties' relationship had broken down, so that the purpose of providing a family home had come to an end, sale would be ordered.[4] As Salmon LJ said in response to a claim by a husband that sale of the home in which he was living should be postponed, 'the test is not what is reasonable, but whether it is inequitable for the wife, now that the marriage is dead, to want to realise her investment'.[5] However, where that purpose was to provide a home for the family, the Court of Appeal was divided over whether immediate sale would be ordered while that purpose still existed. In *Rawlings v Rawlings*[6] Salmon LJ was clear that a sale would not generally be ordered where one of the purposes of the trust was to provide a home for the children, whilst that purpose still existed. However, in *Burke v Burke*,[7] in a particularly harsh ruling, the Court of Appeal rejected this view and held that the interests of the children would only be taken into account 'so far as they affect the equities in the matter as between the two persons entitled to the beneficial interests in the property'. In *Williams v Williams*,[8] Lord Denning MR and Roskill LJ distinguished the approaches taken in *Jones v Challenger* and *Burke v Burke* which they described as 'outdated, narrow and old-fashioned'. In *Re Holliday (A Bankrupt)*[9] the Court of Appeal said it preferred the approach taken in *Burke v Burke*.[10]

In *Re Evers' Trust, Papps v Evers*,[11] the Court of Appeal rejected once more the uncompromising line taken in *Burke v Burke*. It adopted the

3   Thus the harshness of the ruling in *Burke v Burke* [1974] 2 All ER 944 that an order for sale must be made where the children are not beneficiaries under the trust appears to have been ameliorated; see also *Re Holliday (A Bankrupt)* [1980] 3 All ER 385.

4   *Jones v Challenger* [1960] 1 All ER 785.

5   [1964] 3 WLR 294, per Salmon LJ at p 310. He emphasised that it was not the function of the court to punish the wife for the 'matriminial wrong' of desertion by keeping her out of her share in the property. However, where one party was carrying on a business from home so that immediate sale would cause particular hardship, sale was refused, although an occupation rent became payable, *Bedson v Bedson* [1965] 3 All ER 307.

6   [1964] 3 WLR 294. His view was dictum only because the only child of the marriage was of full age.

7   [1974] 2 All ER 944.

8   [1977] 1 All ER 28.

9   [1980] 3 All ER 385.

10   Goff LJ said 'in my view the preservation of the house as a home for the children can no more be an object [of the trust] than its preservation as a home for the spouse'. In relation to Lord Denning and Lord Justice Roskill's opinions, he said 'this seems to me not so much to be distinguishing cases as saying that having regard to modern thinking and circumstances the court should have regard to differerent considerations in exercising its discretion,' ibid, at p 393.

11   [1980] 3 All ER 399.

dictum of Lord Denning MR that 'the court, in executing the trust, should regard the primary object as being to provide a home and not a sale',[12] and held that this approach to the exercise of discretion had considerable advantages in 'family' cases. In *Re Evers' Trust, Papps v Evers*, the family home was conveyed to an umarried couple on trust for sale as joint tenants. The parties separated, and the mother remained in the home with the three children. The father applied for the property to be sold.[13] The Court of Appeal held that in exercising its discretion, the court had to consider both the primary purpose of the trust, that of sale,[14] and its underlying purpose, that of providing a home not only for the parents but also for the children. Crucially, in the context of the position of unmarried cohabitants, Ormrod LJ observed that such an approach brought the exercise of the discretion into line, so far as it was possible, with the exercise of discretion by the divorce courts, and that it went some way to eliminating the differences between marital and non-marital children.[15] The Court of Appeal confirmed the judge's order that sale of the property should be postponed. Moreover, it did not fix the date at which the parties' child reached 16 as the date for sale because such a date was purely arbitrary. It simply dismissed the application, leaving it open to the father to apply again if the circumstances should alter.[16]

In situations where third parties have a financial interest in the proceedings, or where one of the parties is bankrupt, the courts had, and still have, wider concerns. Section 15(1)(d) of the 1996 Act directs the courts to consider 'the interests of any secured creditor of any beneficiary' when exercising their discretion. A trustee in bankruptcy has the duty to realise the debtor's assets for the benefit of his creditors, and this may involve seeking a sale of the matrimonial home. *Re Holliday (A Bankrupt)*[17] appeared to give a spouse some protection where her and her children's interests conflicted with those of the husband's creditors. Divorce proceedings had been issued, and the husband had filed a bankruptcy petition. The trustee in bankruptcy applied for an order directing sale of the matrimonial home which had been conveyed to the spouses on trust for sale as beneficial joint tenants. The wife resisted sale on the ground that she had no resources and needed to continue to live in the home with the three children of the family. The Court of Appeal held that the need to preserve the home for the children where they were not beneficiaries under the trust for sale was not a purpose of the trust. It therefore held that the

12 *Williams v Williams* [1977] 1 All ER 28, at p 30.
13 Law of Property Act 1925, s 30.
14 Which, of course, no longer applies now that all trusts are included under the broad framework of a trust of land under the Trusts of Land and Appointment of Trustees Act 1996, s 1.
15 See also, *Chhokar v Chhokar* [1984] FLR 313.
16 The mother was required to give an undertaking that she would discharge liability under the mortgage, pay outgoings and maintain the property and indemnify the father so long as she was occupying the property.
17 [1980] 3 All ER 385.

claim of the trustee in bankruptcy must prevail over that of the wife. However, the effect of the court's order that the property must be sold was not as harsh as it first appeared. After balancing the interests of the wife against those of creditors, the court ruled that the house should not be sold immediately. Instead, it allowed the wife and children to occupy the property for a period of five years, so that by the time the property was sold, two of the children would have passed their seventeenth birthday.

Unfortunately, the postponement of sale in *Re Holliday (A Bankrupt)* must be treated as exceptional and, in this regard, a precedent which is most unlikely to be followed. It was distinguished in *Re Citro (A Bankrupt)*,[18] where the Court of Appeal held that the rights of creditors would usually prevail over the rights of a spouse, regardless of whether the property was still being used as a matrimonial home.[19] An order for sale of the home would be made unless there were exceptional circumstances, and the fact that a wife and children faced eviction which would cause them hardship did not amount to an exceptional circumstance which would either prevent sale or justify its postponement. In addition, section 335A(3) of the Insolvency Act 1986 provides that once a year has elapsed since the first vesting of the bankrupt's estate in a trustee, the court must assume, unless the circumstances of the case are exceptional, that the interests of the bankrupt's creditors outweigh all other considerations. Thus Parliament, as well as the courts, has made it clear that the rights of creditors will normally defeat the interest of the spouse or partner of the bankrupt and her children in postponing sale of the family home.[20]

It is in cases where bankruptcy or other claims by third parties are *not* involved, and where children *are* involved, that the sympathetic approach taken in *Re Evers' Trust, Papps v Evers* to postponement of sale until the children no longer have need of the family home appears likely to be followed.[1] There is no excuse for courts failing to recognise that it is for the welfare of *all* children that they should enjoy the benefit of a secure roof over their heads, not just children of divorcing parents. Children of unmarried parents cannot benefit from the property adjustment regime open to spouses. When their parents' relationship breaks down, arguably

---

18 [1990] 3 All ER 952; see also *Re Lowrie (A Bankrupt)* [1981] 3 All ER 353.
19 In *Chhokar v Chhokar* [1984] FLR 313 the primacy of the creditor was displaced. He was a 'scoundrel' who had attempted fraud and other devices to frustrate and destroy the wife's equitable interest.
20 Wider consideration of how bankruptcy affects the rights of beneficial owners of property is beyond the scope of this book. The law is governed by the Insolvency Act 1986. See further, N V Lowe and G Douglas, *Bromley's Family Law* (Butterworths, 9th edn, 1998) pp 168-171; J G Miller, *Family Property and Financial Provision* (Tolley, 3rd edn, 1993) ch 8.
1 This was epitomised in the reasoning of Ormrod LJ in *Browne v Pritchard* [1975] 3 All ER 721, at p 725. Rejecting an application by a husband in divorce proceedings for an order that the matrimonial home should be sold so that he could realise his investment tied up in the property, Ormrod LJ responded: 'investment in the home is the least liquid investment one can possibly make. It cannot be converted into cash while the children are at home.'

bringing the purpose of a trust of land to an end, the only manner in which they can be assisted under the limited discretion available to courts under sections 14 and 15 of the Trusts of Land and Appointment of Trustees Act 1996 is for courts to give considerable weight to their needs. Children of unmarried parents will continue to be discriminated against unless judges willingly acknowledge their continuing need for a family home, as Ormrod LJ recognised as long ago as 1980.[2] Now that all beneficial co-ownership is held under a trust of land, without any duty to sell, it will be easier for courts to give greater importance to the wish of the residential parent to remain living in the property than to the wish of the non-residential parent to realise his share in the capital tied up in the property. It is hoped that courts will sieze this opportunity.[3]

Proprietary estoppel

The law relating to proprietary estoppel is complex and 'the doctrine has rarely been defined in one clear analytical formula, but has instead been expounded at different times by different judges in slightly divergent terms'.[4] Proprietary estoppel prevents the owner of land from insisting on his strict legal rights. It arises where a person is deliberately misled into believing, or mistakenly believes, that she has a present interest in property owned by another, or that she will be given such an interest in the future. The owner of the property must have assured, encouraged or acquiesced in her wrongful or mistaken belief. The non-owner must further establish that she relied on this belief and that, as a consequence, she has suffered detriment or otherwise been prejudiced. Hence the notions of justice and fairness which have informed decisions on proprietary estoppel are similar to those which have persuaded courts to find an implied, resulting or constructive trust, namely that it would be unconscionable if equity did not intervene.[5]

Reliance will usually, but not necessarily, involve the expenditure of money. Thus in *Greasley v Cooke*,[6] Doris Cooke had lived all her adult life with the same family, living as man and wife with one brother, working in the house without payment, looking after a mentally ill member of the household, and remaining there after several members of the family had left or died. She had been encouraged by the family to believe that she could regard the property as her home for the rest of her life and she

---

2   *Re Evers' Trust, Papps v Evers* [1980] 3 All ER 399, at p 403.
3   See also, L M Clements *The changing face of trusts: the Trusts of Land and Appointment of Trustees Act 1996* [1998] 61 MLR 56.
4   K Gray *Elements of Land Law* (Butterworths, 2nd edn) pp 313-314. Ch 11 provides a detailed exposition.
5   *Re Basham (Deceased)* [1987] 1 All ER 405. See also, A Lawson *The things we do for love: detrimental reliance in the family home* (1996) 16 Leg St 218.
6   [1980] 3 All ER 710.

therefore did not ask for payment for what she did. At the age of 62 she was told to leave the house by the one surviving brother. The trial judge held that her belief that she could remain in the house for as long as she lived had been induced by assurances given to her by family members, but that she had failed to prove that she had acted to her detriment in reliance on these assurances. The Court of Appeal held that it was to be presumed that she had acted on the faith of these assurances, and that it was up to those who wished to evict her to prove that she had not acted to her detriment or otherwise been prejudiced by remaining in the house, and they had failed to do so. It therefore granted her a declaration that she was entitled to remain rent free in the house for the rest of her life.[7]

In *Wayling v Jones*[8] promises were made followed by conduct by the plaintiff from which inducement could be inferred. The trial judge nonetheless held that the plaintiff had failed to prove that the detriment he had suffered (not receiving adequate wages and continuing to serve the deceased until his death) had been in reliance on his belief that he would inherit the deceased's property, a hotel. Allowing the plaintiff's appeal and giving the judgment of the court, Balcombe LJ held that the following principles applied: first, there must be a sufficient link between the promises relied upon and the conduct which constituted the detriment;[9] secondly, the promises relied upon did not have to be the sole inducement for the conduct, it was sufficient if they were an inducement; and thirdly, once it had been established that promises had been made, and that there had been conduct by the plaintiff of such a nature that an inducement could be inferred, then the burden of proof shifted to the defendant to establish that the plaintiff did not rely on the promises.[10]

Where a woman has been assured that she will be able to remain in property owned by her partner, and where she spends money on the property in reliance on that assurance, equity may grant her a remedy. In *Pascoe v Turner*,[11] after the breakdown of their relationship, Mr Pascoe told Mrs Turner, with whom he had been living for ten years, that the house and its contents were hers. However, no conveyance of the property was ever drawn

---

7   See also, *Re Basham (Deceased)* [1987] 1 All ER 405, where the plaintiff also worked without receiving payment.

8   [1995] 2 FLR 1029. For comment on *Wayling v Jones* see C J Davis *Estoppel – reliance and remedy* [1995] Conv 409.

9   Balcombe LJ made particular reference to the passages in *Grant v Edwards* [1986] 2 All ER 426 where Browne-Wilkinson V-C equated the principles applying in cases of constructive trusts to those applying in cases of proprietary estoppel.

10 The plaintiff was awarded the net proceeds of sale of the hotel. See also *Greasley v Cooke* [1980] 3 All ER 710; *Grant v Edwards* [1986] 2 All ER 426. Cf *Gillett v Holt* [1998] 2 FLR 470, where the important proviso was emphasised by Carnwath J that in the application of the principles of proprietary estoppel to statements about the contents of a will, the facts must be looked at against the ordinary presumption that such intentions were subject to change. The plaintiff's claim failed on the basis that the testator had not made an irrevocable promise. See also *Taylor v Dickens* [1998] 1 FLR 806.

11 [1979] 2 All ER 945.

up. Therefore, although there was evidence of intention by Mr Pascoe to make a gift of the house to Mrs Turner, it was an imperfect gift.[12] However, Mrs Turner, having been told that the house was hers, set about improving it and spent a substantial sum on the property. Mr Pascoe allowed this to happen and at no time suggested that she was putting her money and her labour into his house. Subsequently he brought proceedings for possession. The court found that Mrs Turner had not acquired a beneficial interest under a constructive trust because there had been no common intention that the ownership be shared at the time when the property was acquired. However, it ruled that Mr Pascoe had encouraged or acquiesced in the manner in which Mrs Turner had changed her position for the worse and therefore that equity should grant her a remedy. The nature of the remedy was at large. It was clear that the beneficial ownership of the property still remained with Mr Pascoe. The Court of Appeal therefore took the view that the choice lay between two alternatives: either the equity could be satisfied by granting a licence to Mrs Turner to occupy the house for her lifetime, or there should be a transfer to her of the fee simple. The court chose the latter and required Mr Pascoe to perfect his gift by conveying the fee simple.[13]

It is suggested that the outcome in *Pascoe v Turner* was generous and clearly influenced by the fact that the court regarded Mr Pascoe as a man who would pursue his purpose of evicting Mrs Turner from the house by any legal means at his disposal, and that therefore Mrs Turner needed a remedy which would be effective to protect her against future manifestations of Mr Pascoe's ruthlessness. It rejected the remedy of granting her a licence to live in the house for the rest of her life because she could not protect this right against a purchaser for value without notice.[14] Also, a licensee cannot charge property as security for a loan, which the court thought she might need in order to effect repairs. A licence has the further disadvantage that the legal owner is entitled to enter the property in order to carry out necessary maintenance and repairs, and this right could have been used by Mr Pascoe as an excuse to act in ways which would have derogated from Mrs Turner's enjoyment of the use of the property.

Satisfying the equity in a case of proprietary estoppel

It is clear, once the equity has been established, that it is for the court to decide how it should be satisfied in the light of the assurances and the

---

12 Law of Property Act 1925, s 52(1): see above.
13 It is surprising that the court took the view that there were only two options available. There were, of course, others. For example, Mrs Turner could have been given a life interest in the property, or a lease for a limited duration, as in *Griffiths v Williams* (1977) 248 Estates Gazette 947.
14 At the time the court's concern was with her inability to register the licence, but since then it has been made clear that a licence is not anyway a proprietary interest; see below.

nature of the detrimental reliance.[15] Despite the Court of Appeal's strictures in *Pascoe v Turner,* an irrevocable licence may appear, on its face, to be the most appropriate remedy in a case of proprietary estoppel arising between unmarried partners. In many cases it may be thought most closely to mirror the assurance given to the aggrieved party that she will always have a home in the property.[16] It also seems likely that a claim that the owner intended to make an out-and-out gift of the property will normally be difficult to substantiate. Moreover, a court will probably be reluctant to make an order which requires the legal owner to transfer the legal estate and entire beneficial interest to the other, for such an order is Draconian, and one which courts are hesitant to make even in cases where they have property adjustment powers, unless the circumstances are compelling.[17] However, where the claim was made against the defendant's estate, the Court of Appeal was willing to enforce the defendant's promise to provide for the plaintiff in his will, even though this resulted in the beneficiaries under the will being deprived of almost the entire estate.[18]

However, the remedy of a licence should be avoided at all costs. As the Court of Appeal recognised in *Pascoe v Turner*, a licence does not afford the licensee adequate protection against a determined owner who is prepared to act with 'ruthless disregard of the obligations binding on conscience'.[19] It has subsequently been made clear in *Ashburn Anstalt v Arnold*[20] that a licence does not bind third parties at all. Irrespective of notice, a purchaser is not bound by a licence because the Court of Appeal held that a licence does not create a proprietary interest in land. Although the ruling concerned contractual licences, it appears inconceivable that a court would take a different approach and give proprietary status to a licence granted by a court in a case of proprietary estoppel.

It is suggested instead that the non-owner should seek an order which grants her one of the traditional estates in land, because such an estate would protect her against the claims of third parties. It would also provide her with better protection against harassment by the other party than would a licence. The court has a range of options at its disposal when determining the nature of the equity to which the estoppel gives rise, and it is suggested that it should look to the ways in which the courts have

---

15 Thus in *Re Basham (Deceased)* [1987] 1 All ER 405 the plaintiff had been encouraged to believe that she would inherit a cottage in return for caring for the deceased. Since the plaintiff had subordinated her own interests and wish to move away in reliance on this belief it was held that she was entitled to inherit the cottage.

16 Cf *Greasley v Cooke* [1980] 3 All ER 710; see too *Inwards v Baker* [1965] 1 All ER 446. In *Matharu v Matharu* [1994] 2 FLR 597, in an action brought by a daughter-in-law against her father-in-law, the Court of Appeal held that a licence for life, rather than an unquantifiable beneficial interest, was the most appropriate remedy.

17 See ch 8.

18 *Wayling v Jones* [1995] 2 FLR 1029.

19 [1979] 2 All ER 945 per Cumming-Bruce LJ, at p 951.

20 [1989] Ch 1.

handled orders relating to the former matrimonial home under the Matrimonial Causes Act 1973 when considering models for orders.[1] For example, where there is evidence of substantial detrimental reliance, the court could have recourse to its powers under section 14 of the Trusts of Land and Appointment of Trustees Act 1996 and order that the property be transferred to trustees, the woman to be allowed to live there for life (or until some fixed date), and no sale to take place without her consent during her lifetime (or until the fixed date).[2] Or it could order the owner to transfer the property to the woman, but preserve an interest in it for him by requiring the woman to execute a charge over the property in his favour, not to be realisable until some future date. Perhaps the nearest equivalent to the grant of a licence would be to order the owner to grant the non-owner party a lease at a nominal rent.[3] Where the owner has succeeded in driving the woman from the home the court could require him to pay compensation.[4]

Conduct found insufficient to give rise to proprietary estoppel

Although the plaintiffs were successful in the cases outlined above, in each instance the facts in favour of the plaintiff were particularly strong. It is important to appreciate that courts have not easily been satisfied that the case is one in which the courts should prevent the owner from exercising his strict legal rights. As with the constructive trust, the courts have maintained a tight control over when equity will intervene to assist an unmarried partner who is relying on proprietary estoppel to remain in occupation of the former family home. Thus in *Coombes v Smith*,[5] Mrs Coombes, a married woman, formed a relationship with Mr Smith, a married man, and had his child. Mr Smith bought a house intended for them both, but although Mrs Coombes moved in, he never did. He refused her requests to put the property in joint names, but reassured her that he would always look after her. He paid the bills and the mortgage and frequently visited her and their child. Mrs Coombes decorated the house on a number of occasions and tidied the garden. When their relationship eventually broke down Mrs Coombes sought an order that Mr Smith transfer the property and its contents to her absolutely, or alternatively a declaration that he was bound to allow her to occupy the property and to use its contents for the rest of her life.

Mr Smith conceded that Mrs Coombes had an equity to remain in the property until their daughter reached 17. (No explanation is given as to why this concession was made, but it seems likely that it was made because

1   See ch 8.
2   Cf *Allen v Allen* [1974] 3 All ER 385.
3   *Griffiths v Williams* (1977) 248 Estates Gazette 947.
4   Cf *Tanner v Tanner* [1975] 3 All ER 776.
5   [1986] 1 WLR 808.

Mrs Coombes was relying on *Tanner v Tanner*,[6] where the Court of Appeal had found that a woman with twins had a contractual licence to remain in the property so long as the children were of school age.) However, Mr Smith asserted that Mrs Coombes had no entitlement to remain in the property after that time. The court upheld his claim. It held that Mrs Coombes' belief that Mr Smith would always provide her with a roof over her head was quite different from a belief that she had the legal right to remain there against his wishes, and therefore she was unable to establish that she had acted under a mistaken belief that she had security of tenure. It distinguished *Pascoe v Turner*[7] on the grounds that there were no words of gift, and there were no improvements made to the property made in the mistaken belief that the property was hers.

The most significant feature of the judgment from the point of view of a woman who claims that she has a licence to remain in her ex-partner's house, was the manner in which the court approached the assurance given by Mr Smith to Mrs Coombes that 'he would never see her without a roof over her head'. It held that all that amounted to was an assurance that Mrs Coombes was a licensee at the will of Mr Smith. It did not provide evidence of what would happen in the event of the relationship breaking down. The court further held that, even if Mrs Coombes had been led to believe that she had a right to remain in the property for the rest of her life, she had not behaved in a way which was detrimental to her, or changed her position in reliance on Mr Smith's representation. It held that it would be wholly unreal to find that she had allowed herself to become pregnant in reliance on some mistaken belief as to her legal rights, and in any event allowing oneself to become pregnant could not amount to detriment in the context of proprietary estoppel. There was no evidence that Mrs Coombes left her husband and moved into the property in reliance on Mr Smith's assurance that he would continue to provide for her if and when their relationship came to an end. Nor did any prejudice arise from her having decorated the property, as this was done in the context of her continuing relationship with Mr Smith. Thus even if the court assumed the existence of the requisite mistaken belief about her legal rights, Mrs Coombes failed in her claim because she was unable to establish that she had acted in such a way as to give rise to an equity in her favour.

There was certainly a realism in the court's view that assurances made by the owning party about property rights when an unmarried cohabiting relationship was happy was almost certainly not intended to have binding force when the relationship broke down. Proprietary estoppel, like the constructive trust, cannot handle the disadvantageous situation in which an unmarried partner, usually the woman, finds herself when her relationship with her partner comes to an end, and where she has not paid for, or contributed towards, the cost of the roof over her head. The law relating to the acquisition of a beneficial interest in the family home, and the law of

6 [1975] 3 All ER 776.
7 [1979] 2 All ER 945.

proprietary estoppel, are not truly a part of family law; they are about property law and its amelioration by equity. It is persons who have been living in a family relationship who usually need to rely on equity at its most generous, but it has been seen that this generosity is limited by doctrines which have universal application. Equity has a part to play in assisting the unmarried where there is unfairness, but this part is limited. Only the introduction of a property adjustment scheme, similar to that available to spouses, would be able to rearrange the rights of unmarried partners.[8]

Transfer of tenancies between cohabitants

Section 53 and schedule 7 of the Family Law Act 1996 introduce for the first time a form of property transfer order between unmarried cohabitants. The existing power to transfer specified tenancies on making divorce or separation orders, or a nullity decree, is re-enacted and extended to cohabitants where they separate. Where a cohabitant is entitled either in his own right or jointly with the other cohabitant to occupy a dwelling-house by virtue of a relevant tenancy, and where the cohabitants cease to live together as husband and wife, the court may make an order transferring the tenancy from one to the other, provided that the dwelling-house was a home in which they lived together as husband and wife.[9]

A relevant tenancy means:

(a) a protected tenancy or statutory tenancy within the meaning of the Rent Act 1977;
(b) a statutory tenancy within the meaning of the Rent (Agriculture) Act 1976;
(c) a secure tenancy within the meaning of section 79 of the Housing Act 1985; or
(d) an assured tenancy or assured agricultural occupancy within the meaning of Part I of the Housing Act 1988.

In determining whether to exercise its power to transfer the tenancy, the court must have regard to all the circumstances of the case including when

---

8   Whether such a scheme would be more just than the present law is a matter of debate, see R Deech 'The case against the legal recognition of cohabitation', and E Clive 'Marriage: an unnecessary legal concept' in J M Eekelaar and S M Katz (eds) *Marriage and Cohabitation in Contemporary Societies* (1980, Butterworths, Toronto). See also, S Gardner *Rethinking family property* (1993) 109 LQR 263; R Bailey-Harris *Financial rights in relationships outside marriage: a decade of reform in Australia* (1995) 9 Int J of Law and Family 233. And see more generally, R Bailey-Harris *Law and the unmarried couple – oppression or liberation?* (1996) 8 CFLQ 137; and R Probert, *Widening the home-sharing debate* [1999] Fam Law 153 in which the author considers the position of adult relatives. At the time of writing, the rights of home sharers are under consideration by the Law Commission. For a comment on a Chancery Bar organised workshop on home sharing see M P Thompson *Home sharing – reforming the law* [1996] Conv 134.
9   Sch 7, paras 3 and 4.

and how the tenancy was granted or otherwise acquired, the housing needs and housing resources of the parties and any relevant child, their financial resources, and the likely effect of an order, or the decision not to make an order, on the health, safety or well-being of the parties or any relevant child. Where only one cohabitant is entitled to occupy the dwelling-house by virtue of the tenancy the court, in addition, must take account of the conduct of the parties in relation to each other and otherwise, the nature of their relationship, the length of time during which they have lived together as husband and wife, whether there are or have been children who are children of both parties or for whom both parties have or have had parental responsibility, and the length of time that has elapsed since the parties ceased to live together.[10] The court must also consider the suitability of the parties as tenants,[11] and the landlord must be given an opportunity to be heard.[12]

The transferor can be compensated for his loss. The transferee may be directed by the court to make payments to the transferor.[13] The court when deciding whether to make such an order must have regard to the financial loss which would otherwise be suffered by the transferor, the parties' needs, their financial resources and their financial obligations.[14] Such payments may be deferred, or made in instalments, but only where immediate payment of the sum by the transferee would cause the transferee greater financial hardship than any financial hardship to the transferor caused by postponement.[15] In addition, the court may direct that both cohabitants are to be jointly and severally liable to discharge or perform the liabilities and obligations in respect of the dwelling house.[16] It may further direct that one cohabitant is to indemnify the other against payments made, or expenses incurred, in discharging or performing such liabilities and obligations.[17]

These provisions significantly extend a court's powers to come to the assistance of a cohabitant where the parties' relationship has broken down and the applicant has greater need to remain in the property than his or her former partner. Not only do they allow a tenancy in joint names to be transferred into the applicant's sole name, they also confer power on the court to transfer a tenancy to her where the other cohabitant is the sole tenant. The criteria which guide the court, although different from the criteria which guide courts when making property adjustment orders between spouses on divorce,[18] nonetheless direct the court to engage in a

---

10 Sch 7, para 5. These criteria are the same as those which the court must take into account when determining whether to make an occupation order under ss 33 and 36 of the Family Law Act 1996; see ch 6.
11 Ibid, para 5(c).
12 Ibid, para 14(1).
13 Ibid, para 10(1).
14 Ibid, para 10(4).
15 Ibid, para 10(2), (5).
16 Ibid, para 11(1).
17 Ibid, para 11(2).
18 Matrimonial Causes Act 1973, s 25; see ch 8.

similar exercise, namely to discover the nature and extent of their resources and to balance their respective needs. Moreover, a cohabitant has two advantages over a spouse when making an application under Schedule 7. First, an order in favour of a cohabitant has immediate effect, whereas in the case of spouses the order takes effect as if the court was making a property adjustment order on divorce;[19] and secondly, remarriage prevents a spouse applying for a transfer of the tenancy, but the marriage of the cohabitant does not affect her right to apply.[20]

The commonest form of security of tenure is in public sector housing, and one aim of these provisions was to enable courts to direct the transfer of local authority tenancies so as to ensure the efficient and beneficial use of council housing. It is only in the context of tenancies that cohabitants are being treated in the same manner as spouses in relation to re-distribution of their property rights.[21] Cohabitant men and women can be required to transfer rights in their rented homes, but no equivalent property transfer orders can be made against owner occupier cohabitants. For this reason, although the purpose behind the provisions is desirable, they give rise to a sense of unease. Most people who live in council houses are relatively poor. The question must be asked, why are public sector and other secure tenancies being treated as a different species of property right from other home ownership rights? A council tenancy is a very valuable asset, particularly when account is taken of the 'right to buy' provisions in the Housing Act 1985.[22] There seems to be an element of class bias here.

Child support

When a marriage breaks down, and where there are dependent children of the family, the parent who is looking after the children will normally expect his or her ex-spouse to contribute towards the children's maintenance until they complete their education. Similarly, when an unmarried couple with children separate the children need to be maintained, and the parent with care is likely to wish to look to his or her ex-partner for child maintenance. Sometimes a child is the product of a more casual intimate relationship between his or her mother and father; indeed, in some cases the mother may be uncertain who the father is, the father may be married to someone

---

19 Sch 7, para 12.
20 Ibid, para 13. Although this is consistent with the provisions in the Matrimonial Causes Act 1973, s 28(3), which prevent an application for a property adjustment order being made where the applicant has remarried, it is hard to see why a former spouse, particularly where she has care of the children, is prevented from applying for the transfer of the tenancy. Her remarriage may in no way have diminished her greater need for the property. It is unfortunate that the opportunity to lift this bar was not taken with regard to the transfer of tenancies between spouses.
21 This is not an entirely accurate statement; the factors in s 36(6) influencing the exercise of judicial discretion are slightly different with regard to cohabitants.
22 The right to buy provisions were first introduced by the Housing Act 1980.

else, or the father may not know that he is a father. But of course a child of a casual union has just as much need of financial support as does a child born into a more conventional family unit containing two parents. All such children are treated in an equal manner under the Child Support Act 1991. Provided that appropriate steps are taken by a parent, or other person with care of the child, to obtain child support maintenance, the law will oblige the child's 'absent parent'[23] to make regular payments for the benefit of his or her own child. These payments will be quantified applying the same principles and the same criteria irrespective of the circumstances surrounding the child's birth.

The Child Support Agency

Although, on their face, various statutes appear to give powers to courts to order parents to make periodical payments for the benefit of their children, these statutes are misleading.[24] They must be read in conjunction with the Child Support Act 1991, which has drastically curtailed the scope of the courts' powers. Since 1993 new claims for child maintenance have been handled outside the court system by an administrative agency called the Child Support Agency, which was established by the Child Support Act 1991. The Child Support Agency is a part of the Department of Social Security. Its role is to make a maintenance assessment and to collect and enforce maintenance payments for children. It is staffed by child support officers who must apply rules rather than exercise discretion when making decisions, and a formula is used to calculate how much child maintenance is payable. Court orders for periodical payments for children can no longer be made except in a residue of cases.[25]

Terms used in the Child Support Act 1991

A child for whom child maintenance is payable under the Child Support Act 1991 is called a 'qualifying child'. A qualifying child is a child who is the natural child of both parents, or who has been adopted by both parents.[1] A child is defined as being under 16, or under 19 but in receipt of full-time education.[2] The jurisdiction of a child support officer extends to those

---

23 See below for discussion of the meaning of this term.
24 Matrimonial Causes Act 1973, s 23; Domestic Proceedings and Magistrates' Courts Act 1978, s 2; Children Act 1989, s 15 and Sch 1.
25 S 8(3) of the Child Support Act 1991 provides that a court shall not exercise any power which it would otherwise have to make, vary or revive orders for child maintenance in any case where a child support officer would have jurisdiction to make a maintenance assessment.
1   S 3.
2   S 55.

cases where the child, the absent parent and the parent with care are all habitually resident in the United Kingdom.[3] The Child Support Act 1991 uses specific language to describe the relationship between a 'qualifying child' and his parents, or between the child and the person who is looking after him.

Section 3 provides:

'(1) A child is a "qualifying child" if—
    (a) one of his parents is, in relation to him, an absent parent; or
    (b) both of his parents are, in relation to him, absent parents.
(2) The parent of any child is an "absent parent", in relation to him, if—
    (a) that parent is not living in the same household with the child; and
    (b) the child has his home with a person who is, in relation to him, a person with care.
(3) A person is a "person with care", in relation to any child, if he is a person—
    (a) with whom the child has his home;
    (b) who usually provides day to day care for the child (whether exclusively or in conjunction with any other person); and
    (c) who does not fall within a prescribed category of person.'

Language used in legislation designed to deal with family situations may have symbolic and emotional significance for the persons concerned and therefore the selection of words in such legislation is important. It is suggested that the choice of language in the Child Support Act 1991 is unfortunate because it is insensitive to the feelings of so-called 'absent parents'. Many parents who are so described find the term offensive. They claim that the term could be understood to carry with it the connotation that the 'absent parent' has in some sense abandoned his child, is feckless in his dealings with the child, or is otherwise failing to show the child any love, care, affection or interest. It is suggested that it would have been preferable if the Child Support Act 1991 had been drafted in a manner which emphasised the continuing responsibility of both parents for the financial support of their child without using language which is arguably pejorative of one of them.[4]

---

3   S 44.
4   For further comment see J Wallbank *The compaign for change of the Child Support Act 1991: reconstructing the "absent father"* (1997) 6 Soc and Leg Studies 191. The House of Commons Social Security Committee has recognised the offensive nature of this terminology: *The Performance and Operation of the Child Support Agency* 2nd report of the House of Commons Social Security Committee, Session 1995-96, para 54.

Assessment of maintenance by the Child Support Agency

Applications for child maintenance are made on a maintenance application form by the parent or other person with care. The applicant must provide a substantial amount of information including detailed information about her personal circumstances and those of her partner; the circumstances of any children under 19 who are living with her; the circumstances of the absent parent; her income from all sources; and her housing arrangements. Once a properly completed maintenance application form has been received by the Child Support Agency the absent parent will be sent a maintenance enquiry form. The absent parent too must provide the Agency with a substantial amount of information, including detailed information about his personal circumstances and whether he accepts that he is the parent of the child or children named;[5] the circumstances of any children under 19 who are living with him; his own income and that of his partner from all sources; and his housing arrangements. He must complete and return the maintenance enquiry form to the Child Support Agency within 14 days. Should he fail to do so the Agency is entitled to make an interim maintenance assessment. Since such an assessment is usually higher than the amount of child maintenance the absent parent would be required to pay if it was calculated under the formula, he has a strong incentive to reply swiftly. All of this data is used to calculate, with the use of the formula, how much child support maintenance should be paid.

Calculations made under the formula progress through five stages:

1. the maintenance requirement;
2. the exempt income calculation;
3. the assessable income calculation;
4. the maintenance assessment calculation; and
5. the protected income calculation.

There are various rules which relate to the calculation of the formula at each of these five stages, and identifying the relevant information which is needed at any stage can be extremely complicated. Detailed provisions, which influence the calculation of the formula, are contained in several sets of regulations. Only a rough calculation can be made of how much each parent will be required to contribute to the support of his or her child unless full account is taken of these provisions, which are very complex. Basic guidance only is given below on how each stage of the formula is calculated.[6]

---

5 A parent cannot delay the payment of child maintenance by falsely denying parentage. His liability to pay will be back-dated to the effective date of the maintenance assessment, and arrears will simply accrue.

6 For a detailed consideration of the operation of the Act, and worked examples, see R Bird, *Child Maintenance, The New Law* (Family Law, 1996); E Jacobs and G Douglas, *Child Support: The Legislation* (Sweet and Maxwell, 1997); E Knights and S Cox *Child Support Handbook* (CPAG 5th edn, 1997). It should be noted, however, that there have

The maintenance requirement

The maintenance requirement is the minimum amount considered necessary for the maintenance of a child or, where there is more than one qualifying child, all of them. The calculation is based on income support rates. Once that basic requirement has been met a parent will be required to pay an additional amount towards the support of his child where he has sufficient income to do so.

Exempt income

A parent is entitled to keep a limited amount of income, known as 'exempt income' before being required to pay child maintenance. The Child Support Act 1991 recognises that the first call on a parent's income is to make provision for his own needs and for the needs of any of his own children who are living with him, and allowance is made for this. However, although an absent parent's exempt income includes an allowance for any child of his own whom he is supporting, this provision may not be as beneficial as it first appears. Where the absent parent has a child by a new partner, that person's liability to support their child is taken into account when the absent parent's exempt income is calculated. Where the new partner can be expected to contribute to the support of their child the allowances made in relation to the child are divided between them, and the absent parent's exempt income is reduced proportionately. The formula is strictly rule-based and makes no allowance for individual financial pressures on an absent parent unless these financial pressures fall within the scope of the data used to calculate the application of the formula. The system gives no scope for the exercise of discretion except in a few clearly defined circumstances.[7]

Assessable income

A parent's assessable income is the income available for child maintenance. It is calculated by taking the parent's net income and subtracting his exempt income; the remainder is his assessable income. A parent's net income is almost invariably less than his gross income because certain

been amendments to the formula and to the level of allowances under the formula since these books were published. A computer program has the advantage that it can be updated when benefit rates alter, or if other changes to the formula are made. E Knights prepares regular updates for Family Law of the decisions of the Child Support Commissioners. At the time of writing, a Green Paper, *Children First, A New Approach to Child Support* Cm 3992 (1998) has proposed changes which will greatly simplify the formula.

7   In a narrow range of circumstances an application may be made for a departure direction; see below.

sums can first be deducted.[8] Each parent is liable to maintain his or her children who are living with the parent with care and therefore the assessable income of each parent must be calculated; but of course only the absent parent actually makes a payment of child maintenance.

The maintenance assessment

The maintenance assessment is calculated by adding together the assessable income of each parent and dividing the total by two; the final figure is the sum available for the support of the child. (Where the parent with care has no assessable income, such as when she is living on income support, only the assessable income of the absent parent is divided by two.) The maintenance assessment is then compared with the maintenance requirement. Where it is less than, or equal to, the maintenance requirement, the absent parent is required to pay 50% of his assessable income.[9] Where the maintenance assessment is more than the maintenance requirement, the formula allows for an additional amount of maintenance to be payable. The parent then has two assessable incomes, in effect, out of which he must make a contribution. Basic assessable income, which will be paid on a 50% basis and which will be put towards the maintenance requirement, and additional assessable income. The additional assessable income is the balance left over after the parent has met his share of the maintenance requirement. He is then required to contribute on a 25% basis out of this extra income until a maximum figure is reached; this ceiling is calculated with reference to income support rates. Thus where one or both parents have high incomes the child benefits accordingly, because his maintenance is assessed with regard to that income.

Protected income

No allowance is made for the cost of maintaining a new spouse or partner and any step-children living in the absent parent's household when the absent parent's assessable income is calculated. In some cases this could mean that a 50% deduction from the absent parent's assessable income could push his remaining income for the support of his present household to below subsistence level. Therefore, before finalising how much an absent parent must pay, it is necessary to establish his protected income level. The protected income calculation is made with reference to income support rates. The amount the couple would receive if they were deriving their income from income support are added together plus a fixed margin above these rates and a further margin of a percentage of the family's income

---

8   The calculation of a parent's net income is governed by regulations which specify which income must be included and which can be excluded.

9   Subject to his protected income.

above the income support level. The absent parent's protected income is then calculated by adding together all income coming into his current family, including the income of a partner and any children living in the household. If the maintenance contribution which the absent parent is required to make reduces his remaining disposable income to below the level of his protected income, his contribution will be reduced by the difference between the two amounts.

Who must use the Child Support Agency?

When marriages and unmarried relationships break down and the parent with care of the children has no source of income, or where her income is insufficient for the family's requirements, she will usually turn to the state for assistance, and she will normally be eligible for some form of welfare benefits. Clearly the cost of maintaining single parents and their children imposes a heavy burden on state funds, and one of the main factors which motivated the establishment of the Child Support Agency was to save public expenditure on welfare benefits. It was asserted by the government that if parents have the means to maintain their own children, the cost of such maintenance should not fall on the taxpayer.[10] When the parent with care and her children are supported by benefits the state gains financially from the pursuit of an absent parent for maintenance because the money recovered is used to reimburse the state for its expenditure. However, the children only gain financially where either the amount which the absent parent is required to pay in child support maintenance exceeds the amount in benefits which is being paid to the parent with care, and they receive the surplus amount, or where the policy is adopted that part of the child support payment should always allocated for the support of the children irrespective of whether the remaining sum is sufficient to reimburse the state.

Because of the strong state interest in the recovery of child maintenance, the Act imposes a degree of compulsion on the parent with care to co-operate with the Agency. Section 6(1) states that a parent with care of a child who is in receipt of income support, family credit or disability working allowance *shall* authorise the Child Support Agency to take action to recover child support from the absent parent if required to do so by the Agency. Where she refuses to do so, and where she refuses to provide information required by the Agency under section 6(9) to enable the absent parent to be traced and a maintenance assessment to be made, she is at risk of a direction being made under section 46 that her benefits be reduced.

These are Draconian provisions. They present the parent with care with a stark choice: either co-operate with the Agency or suffer a reduction in benefits as a penalty for non-compliance. As any reduction in an already

---

10 See the White Paper which preceded the Act, *Children Come First* Cm 1264, Vol 1, para 2.1.

very low income is likely to cause the parent with care and her children very real financial hardship, the threat of such a reduction is likely to persuade her to comply with the Agency's demands. However, the Act recognises that there are some situations in which the parent with care will have good cause to refuse to authorise the Agency to take action to recover child support maintenance from the absent parent, and good cause to refuse to identify the father. Section 6(2) provides that the parent with care who is supported by state benefits shall not be required to authorise the Agency to recover child support maintenance where she can persuade a child support officer that there are reasonable grounds for believing that:

'(a) if the parent were to be required to give that authorisation; or
(b) if she were to give it,
there would be a risk of her, or of any child living with her, suffering harm or undue distress as a result.'

Similarly, where a child support officer is considering whether to impose a benefit reduction for failure to comply with section 6(1) or (9), section 46(3) provides that these same matters must be considered.

No guidance is given in the Act on the meaning of 'harm or undue distress' and sections 6(2) and 43(6) are rare examples of provisions in the Act which allow scope for the exercise of discretion. However, statements of policy have been issued to child support officers on how that discretion should be exercised. It has been stated that a child support officer would be justified in deciding not to proceed in the following cases: the parent has been the victim of rape; the absent parent has sexually assaulted a child living in the household of the parent with care; the child was conceived as a result of incest; the absent parent is a 'celebrity' and unwelcome publicity might result which would be adverse to the welfare of parent and child. Domestic violence, as such, is not singled out. However, during the passage of the Bill through the House of Lords, Lord Henley expressed the view that '... if on the evidence before us we are satisfied that there has been a history of violence in a case or a parent has a well-founded fear that seeking maintenance will put her or the child at risk of violence that will amount to good cause'.[11] While there is evidence to suggest that such an approach has been adopted, it appears that it is only a risk of real physical harm which can exempt a parent with care from her obligation to authorise the Agency to take action.[12] However, there is also evidence to suggest that there is a lack of consistency in how cases of this kind are approached, with some child support officers requiring very strong reasons, accompanied by proof, before they are satisfied that harm

11 *Official Report*, 14 March 1991, col 386.
12 A Garnham and E Knights, *Putting the Treasury First* (Child Poverty Action Group, 1994) pp 84-92.

or distress is likely to be suffered, and others being willing simply to accept the word of the parent with care.[13]

Guidance on when a child support officer should proceed despite the reluctance of the parent with care has also been given. Matters which are not considered distressing enough to count as a reason for non co-operation include: that the absent parent may seek contact; the parent with care wants to sever all links with the absent parent; the absent parent is, or was at the time of the conception, under 16; the absent parent is married to someone else; a voluntary agreement exists.[14] The following, therefore, are examples of situations which would almost certainly not amount to sufficient cause for the purposes of establishing harm or undue distress: a fear that if the absent parent were to be required to support the child he might also demand to have contact with the child although he has not had contact for many years; a fear that a positive relationship between the child and the absent parent would be jeopardised if the Agency were to require the absent parent to maintain the child, or to increase the amount that he has been paying voluntarily; a wish not to reveal the name of the father because he is a married man and such a revelation would be likely to cause the breakdown of his marriage; a fear that the parent with care's current family relationships would be disrupted. These are very real fears and concerns, and a substantial body of evidence is emerging that parents with care are being pressurised into making a maintenance application for their children against their own wishes and better judgment. Many parents have alleged that rather than improving the lot of their child, the Agency's involvement in their lives has led to their children suffering harm and distress.[15] It is suggested that insufficient thought was given to the impact of the Child Support Act 1991 on the stability of family life, and that one of the sad outcomes of the Act is likely to be the breakdown of those family units which are particularly vulnerable to strain brought about by the inflexibility of the Act's requirements.

Departure directions

One of the many criticisms of the Child Support Act in its original form was that the formula failed to take account of the plight of a parent, almost always a father, who on the breakdown of a marriage had transferred the

13 Ibid.
14 See R Bird, *Child Maintenance* (Family Law, 3rd edn, 1996).
15 Ibid. See also reports of early research on the effect of the Child Support Act, G Gillespie *Child Support – the hand that rocks the cradle* [1996] Fam Law 162; D Abbott *The Child Support Act 1991: the lives of parents with care living in Liverpool* (1996) 18 JSWFL 21; C Glendinning, K Clarke and G Craig *Implementing the Child Support Act* (1996) 18 JSWFL 273.

former matrimonial home, or other capital, to the mother. Other criticisms related to the total inflexibility of the formula and the inability of child support officers to have regard to the unavoidable costs faced by some absent parents. These criticisms, and the much publicised failure by the Child Support Agency to come anywhere near its target of securing adequate child support for all children, resulted in a review of the working of the Act. Subsequently a White Paper *Improving Child Support*[16] was published which was followed by the Child Support Act 1995 which amended the 1991 Act.[17]

The White Paper recognised that there were a few exceptional cases where departure should be permitted from the application of the usual formula. Under sections 28A-I of the amended Act, where a maintenance assessment is in force, the person with care or the absent parent may apply for a 'departure direction' which has the effect of departing from the arithmetical formula to determine child support liability. Such a direction is only allowed under tightly defined circumstances which fall into three categories: special expenses, which were not, and could not have been, taken into account in determining the current assessment;[18] property or capital transfers made prior to 5 April 1993;[19] and a final group of cases which are gathered together under the broad heading of 'additional cases'.[20]

The special expenses which permit departure from the standard formula are costs incurred in travelling to work; an absent parent's costs in maintaining contact with the child; costs attributable to illness or disability; debts incurred while the couple were still living together; pre-1993 financial commitments from which it is impossible or unreasonable to expect the parent concerned to withdraw; and the costs of supporting step-children, provided that they were first incurred *before* the Child Support Act 1991 came into force. Regulations clarify the factors which can be taken into account in assessing what costs and other commitments fall within the scope of the departure provisions. Regulations also make provision for the group of 'additional cases' and allow a departure direction to be given with respect to cases where assets which do not produce income

---

16 HMSO, 1995.
17 Before the new provisions came into force they were preceded by a pilot project.
18 Child Support Act 1991, Sch 4B, para 2.
19 Sch 4B, paras 3 and 4. Thus undoing the unfairness to the father who had transferred the entire beneficial interest in the matrimonial home to the mother in exchange for a much reduced child maintenance liability, as in *Crozier v Crozier* [1994] 2 All ER 362. But see *AMS v Child Support Officer* [1998] 1 FLR 955, where the Court of Appeal held that a payment of £35,000 by a father did not constitute a secured maintenance order or agreement under s 8(11) or s 9(1) of the Act but was a lump sum payment. Accordingly, the father had not discharged his liability for the purposes of s 4(10) which prevents applications being made to the Agency where a maintenance order or agreement is in force, and therefore the lump sum payment would not be recognised in the formulaic assessment. See further, J Priest *Capital settlements and the Child Support Act* [1998] Fam Law 115 and 170.
20 Sch 4B, para 5.

are capable of producing income;[1] a person's life-style is inconsistent with his level of income; or where housing or travel costs are unreasonably high or should be disregarded.

The formula and the very poor

The Act is based on the principle that all absent parents are expected to make some contribution towards the maintenance of their own children. Even when an absent parent's only source of income is income support he will be required by the Agency to pay a minimum amount in child support from the income support personal allowance for an adult. Only the very poorest absent parents are exempt.[2] Thus even when under the normal rules of the formula an absent parent's contribution would be nil, or less than the minimum amount, he is nonetheless required to make this minimum payment. Where such an absent parent is in receipt of income support, which will normally be the case, the minimum payment will be deducted directly from the amount which he receives. Moreover, the deduction can be made from a partner's income support where the partner is claiming income support for them jointly as a couple.

The minimum payment provision resiles from the principle that an absent parent should pay child support only in those cases where he can afford to pay. Pushing an absent parent's income to below the minimum amount deemed sufficient for income support purposes is to push him below the poverty line, and the effects of this will be cumulative. Losing a small percentage of the income support personal allowance for one week may not create undue difficulty for an absent parent; but losing that income for an indefinite period is likely to cause him extreme financial hardship. It is suggested that it is of no benefit to a child to impoverish his absent parent through the token gesture of requiring the absent parent to pay child support. Indeed, a parent who has no spare money at all, and who lives some distance away from his child, is unlikely to be able to afford to maintain contact with his child. From the child's point of view, it is far more important that his absent parent fulfils his duty to show the child affection, care and interest by visiting the child and otherwise being involved in the child's upbringing than that he pays small sums of money

---

1   *Phillips v Peace* [1996] 2 FLR 230 was an extreme, indeed an extraordinary, example. As Johnson J commented: 'most people would think that a mother should have no difficulty in obtaining financial support for her child from a father who lives in a house worth £2.6m and whose standard of living is illustrated by his three cars worth respectively £36,000, £54,000 and £100,000'. However, the child support officer calculated the weekly amount payable as nought pounds. Such a decision should no longer be reached. For a useful analysis of the departure provisions in relation to the non-standard earner, see J Priest *Child support and the non-standard earner – pass the Heineken please! Phillips v Peace* (1997) 9 CFLQ 63.

2   Namely those who are in receipt of certain sickness and disability benefits; supporting other children; prisoners; under 18 and in receipt of income support; and defined by the Act as children.

towards the child's maintenance. It is suggested that the minimum payment requirement is unacceptable and that the law here is engaging in the symbolic assertion of parental responsibility at the expense of those who can least afford it, and at the expense of the emotional well-being of the children concerned.

The formula and step-children

Normally the provisions of the formula disregard any financial obligations which an absent parent has taken on in relation to step-children when calculating how much he must pay towards the support of his own children. The formula takes account of the fact that the absent parent is supporting step-children, or that his new partner is supporting her own children from a previous relationship, only when the protected income level is assessed[3] or, for the purposes of a departure direction, where costs of supporting the step-child were first incurred prior to 5 April 1993. All other aspects of the formula are premised on the assumption that step-children are being supported by their own absent parent, whether or not they are in fact being so supported. This is the case even where the step-child's absent parent is dead.

It is suggested that the approach of the Child Support Act 1991 to the financial support of step-children is unrealistic in financial terms and damaging in family policy terms. Bringing up a child is expensive, and providing a child with opportunities to develop his full potential by extending his knowledge, experience and skills usually costs a considerable amount of money. Where a step-child forms part of a household in which there are other children it is particularly important in the interests of the welfare of such a child that he is treated in the same manner as a child who is the child of both parents. Yet no allowance is made in the formula for the costs incurred by a step-parent in making provision for a step-child; even in those cases where the child's own absent parent is not maintaining him, or where the amount of support which the absent parent is providing is below the child's maintenance requirement, no corresponding adjustment is made. It is therefore suggested that the Child Support Act 1991 does not treat all children equally, but that, on the contrary, it discriminates financially against step-children.

Furthermore, although the Child Support Act 1991 is consistent in its approach to the step-parent relationship, the reality of the effect of the formula on different family units containing step-children may be significantly different. As has been seen, the fact that an absent parent is providing support for step-children is disregarded when his exempt income is calculated. Thus an absent parent may be supporting several children out of his income, but the law will treat him as if the only financial liability

---

3   See above.

he has is towards his own children.[4] By contrast, the parent with care may have no income of her own but she may be receiving support for her child from a new partner (who may be very wealthy). However, the new partner's contribution to the support of the child is treated as irrelevant when the formula is calculated. The law treats the parent with care and the absent parent as the only persons who are maintaining their child. For the formula totally to disregard the benefits of income provided by a step-parent for the support of a step-child is just as unwise as it is to disregard a step-parent's obligations to step-children living in his household. Where disregarding a new partner's income leads to considerable disparity between the total income of the family unit in which the parent with care is living, and the total income of the family unit in which the absent parent is a member, this is likely to be perceived as unfair, and therefore as unjust.

In family policy terms, one of the more depressing features of the Child Support Act 1991 is that it has entirely discarded the concept of a 'child of the family'. This concept has been a feature of child maintenance legislation for decades. It is particularly apposite to families in which there are step-children. It is based on the notion that a spouse who has treated a child who is not his own child as a child of the family has responsibilities to that child. In the past, when courts made maintenance orders for children, it meant that courts could make orders against a spouse for the maintenance of a child who was not his own child, and indeed this power survives the Child Support Act 1991.[5] But it also meant that financial obligations and responsibilities taken on in relation to step-children could be taken into account when a court was assessing how much a parent should pay for the support of his own children by a prior marriage or relationship. The competing claims of the children in both families could be balanced one against the other, and the law turned its face away from making fine distinctions between 'legal' and 'moral' responsibilities.[6]

It is suggested that the Child Support Act 1991 is refusing to recognise the reality of family life in modern Britain, in which large numbers of first family units break down and in which large numbers of persons form second family relationships. As a result, there is a real danger that the Act will cause the breakdown of some of these second family units. Lack of money is often a cause of family strife, and the simplistic reasoning in the Act that step-children should be provided for by their own absent parent ignores the reality that sometimes they are and sometimes they are not. It is suggested that it is likely that there will be a strong link

---

4   Unless his income is very low so that such obligations are taken into account when calculating his exempt income. In such a case the income of any partner is taken into account which correspondingly reduces the amount of the absent parent's exempt income.

5   See below.

6   See particularly *Roberts v Roberts* [1968] 3 All ER 479 for an historical analysis of the law on this issue.

between the source of financial support for children and the quality of the inter-personal relationships within families, particularly where natural children and step-children are members of the same household. If this conjecture is correct, it is highly desirable for law to encourage step-parents to take on some financial responsibility for step-children. Such a policy assists in promoting commitment to a step-child by a step-parent and the cohesion of second family units.

Proposed reform of the child support system

The task of calculating child support maintenance applying the formula is a nightmare, even with the assistance of software. The formula is difficult to understand and apply and a large percentage of the calculations made by child support officers have been wrong.[7] This has led to a lack of confidence in the system and strong pressure for reform. The changes made in 1995 converted what was originally a relatively straightforward, but rigid, formula scheme into a formula which is almost incapable of sensible management, and which has been described by one commentator as a 'Byzantine labyryinth'.[8] A Government Green Paper, *Children First, a New Approach to Child Support*[9] has therefore suggested further change. It proposes what the same commentator has called 'a formula of almost infantile simplicity', namely that the non-residential parent should pay 15% of his net income where there is one child; 20% where there are two children; and 25% where there are three or more. However, it has been asserted that the proposed scheme has features which make it fundamentally unfair.[10] Thus should the suggested changes be made they are likely to please some parents but to dismay others.

Options available to parents with care who are not living on benefits

A parent with care of a child who is not in receipt of benefits cannot be compelled to authorise the Child Support Agency to pursue the absent

---

7 See the *Report of the Chief Child Support Officer 1996/97* where it was stated that 22% of calculations monitored were incorrect and that it was impossible to determine the accuracy of a further 15%.

8 N Mostyn, *The Green Paper on child support* [1999] Fam Law 95.

9 Cm 3992 (1998).

10 N Mostyn, in his analysis of the new scheme in *The Green Paper on child support* [1999] Fam Law 95, claims it is unfair because it will result in substantial and arbitrary reductions in the amount of child support that will be payable; it completely fails to take account of the income of the parent with care; and there is no maximum income on which child support can be assessed. See also, C Barton *Third time lucky for child support? – The 1998 Green Paper* [1998] Fam Law 668.

parent for maintenance. If the parent with care chooses to support her child entirely from her own resources she is entitled to do so, even though the child would receive considerably more in child support if his absent parent were required by the Agency to make provision for him. In some cases pursuing child support maintenance carries with it the attendant risk that the absent parent may, as a consequence, wish to have other types of involvement in his child's upbringing, and the parent with care may not wish to take this risk. An example might be where the child was born at a time when the mother was unmarried, where she has subsequently married another man, and where the child's natural father does not know of the child's existence. Where the mother does not want the child's natural father to play any part in the life of the child for fear that this will disrupt the new family unit she has a choice: she can decide whether she is willing to take on the entire financial burden of raising the child, perhaps with the assistance of her husband or partner, or whether to involve the natural father by authorising the Agency to make a maintenance assessment against him. However, it has been seen that this choice is taken from the parent with care if, for any reason, she, or any new partner with whom she is living, should be forced to claim state benefits at some time in the future.

Child maintenance agreements

In most cases the parent with care is likely to wish to obtain financial provision for the child from the other parent. However, where parents are able to agree over child maintenance they may not wish to involve the Agency in the regulation of their financial affairs. Some parents may find submitting their personal lives and financial circumstances to the scrutiny of government officials distasteful and intrusive. The Agency has extensive powers to obtain information from a variety of sources, including employers, local authorities and the Inland Revenue, and a parent may prefer not to risk such enquiries being made.[11] Instead parents may prefer to make their own agreement about financial provision for their children. The private ordering of the parents' financial arrangements for their children may be in the interests of both parents. Fees are payable where the services of the Agency are used, and each parent can therefore save money by not using the Agency.[12]

However, there are pitfalls in making a maintenance agreement. Whilst section 9(2) of the Child Support Act 1991 provides that nothing in the Act shall be taken to prevent any person from entering into a maintenance agreement, subsections of section 9 provide that:

---

11 Child Support Act 1991, s 14 and Sch 2.
12 Only the poorest parents are exempt from paying fees, which are based on the full economic cost of running the Agency.

'(3) The existence of a maintenance agreement shall not prevent any party to the agreement, or any other person, from applying for a maintenance assessment with respect to any child to or for whose benefit periodical payments are to be made or secured under the agreement.

(4) Where any agreement contains a provision which purports to restrict the right of any person to apply for a maintenance assessment, that provision shall be void.

(5) ... no court shall exercise any power that it has to vary any agreement so as—

(a) to insert a provision requiring the absent parent to make or secure the making of periodical payments by way of maintenance ... to or for the benefit of that child; or

(b) to increase the amount payable under such a provision.'

Thus the Act makes it clear that the jurisdiction of the Child Support Agency cannot be ousted by a maintenance agreement.

The effect of section 9 is to put the parent with care in a powerful position in a case where the absent parent fails to pay the amount agreed under the terms of the agreement. Where that amount exceeds the amount which the parent with care would receive were she to apply to the Agency, she can rely on the contractual force of the agreement and take steps to enforce it just like any other contract. Where the amount she receives is less than that which she would receive under a maintenance assessment, the combined effect of section 9(3) and (4) is to enable her to go behind the terms of the agreement and to apply to the Agency for child support maintenance at any time. Indeed, in a case where the parent with care later applies for state benefits she will have no choice but to resile on the agreement and to authorise the Agency to pursue her claim.[13] It is suggested that it is therefore essential that the amount of child support maintenance which the parent with care would receive under a maintenance assessment is calculated before a child maintenance agreement is finalised. Otherwise any maintenance agreement in favour of a child has the potential to be unfair to one of the parties, particularly the absent parent.

Child maintenance orders

Since the coming into force of the Child Support Act 1991, courts have been prevented from making orders for periodical payments for children who fall within the ambit of that Act.[14] However, this prohibition does not apply in four specified circumstances.

13 S 6(1), see above.
14 Child Support Act 1991, s 8(1)-(3).

The four exceptions under the Child Support Act 1991

Where there is a maintenance agreement

Where a written maintenance agreement has been made to secure the making of periodical payments for the child, a court may make an order which is in the same terms as the agreement in all material respects.[15]

Top up orders

Where the absent parent is wealthy, and where a court is therefore satisfied that the amount of child support maintenance payable makes it appropriate for the absent parent to make periodical payments under a maintenance order *in addition* to child support maintenance, it may so order.[16]

Children undergoing education and training including children over the age of eighteen

An order may be made where a child 'is, will be, or (if the order were to be made) would be receiving instruction at an educational establishment or undergoing training for a trade, profession or vocation (whether or not while in gainful employment)'.[17] The order made must be for the purpose of securing the making of periodical payments to meet some or all of the expenses incurred in connection with the provision of the instruction or training. This exception is designed to enable a court to order the payment of school and other education and training fees. An order under this exception also has the advantage that it can last for longer than child support under the Child Support Act 1991. A child continues to be a 'child' under the 1991 Act until he reaches the age of 19 provided that he is receiving full-time education, but not advanced education.[18] Court orders for children, by contrast, can extend beyond the age of 18 years where the child is undergoing education or training, or where there are other 'special circumstances'.[19]

A 'child' over the age of 18 who is receiving education or training can apply in her own right for an order either under the Children Act 1989,

---

15 S 8(5).
16 S 8(6). Often referred to as 'top up' orders. The child support assessment must have been made under the alternative formula mentioned in Sch 1, para 4(3).
17 S 8(7).
18 S 55.
19 Matrimonial Causes Act 1973, s 29(3); Children Act 1989, Sch 1, para 2. Moreover, there is no requirement for the court to take account of any student award the child may be receiving, see *B v B (Adult Student: Liability to Support)* [1998] 1 FLR 373. See further, T Costley-White *Maintenance liability for students* [1999] Fam Law 45.

schedule 1, or by intervening in her parents' matrimonial proceedings.[20] But a child over 18 may not apply for an order to be made against a step-parent.[1] An order may not be made at a time when the child's parents are living with each other in the same household.[2] Nor may the child apply for an order where immediately before he reached the age of 16 a periodical payments order was in force with respect to him.[3] Instead, where the order is in force the child must apply for it to be varied, and where it has expired he must apply for it to be revived.[4] The court's powers in relation to children over 18 are limited to making orders for periodical payments and lump sums, reflecting the view that a parent does not have the responsibility to make ongoing capital provision for his child.[5]

Disabled children

The fourth exception gives a court the power to make a maintenance order where a child is disabled and a disability living allowance is being paid to or in respect of the child, or if no such allowance is being paid. The purpose of the periodical payments order must be to meet some or all of the expenses connected with the child's disability.[6] An order can be made under the Children Act 1989[7] before or after the child attains the age of 18. In *C v F (Disabled Child: Maintenance Orders)*[8] the Court of Appeal was clear that the duration of any orders made by a court under the four exemption provisions were not limited to the child's nineteenth birthday at the latest, which is the latest date for payments made under the Child Support Act.[9] Such a restriction would undermine the purpose of some of the exemption provisions. In particular, they enable the terms of maintenance agreements to be embodied in court orders, and there is no reason why some such agreements should not provide for child maintenance beyond the age of 16 even though the child is not receiving full-time education. Moreover, they specifically empower courts to make orders in respect of children in tertiary education and children, including adult children, under a disability, and it would be absurd if an order had to come to an end when, for example, a child had just completed his first year at university. However, the Court of Appeal held with regret that the court's powers under these exemptions were limited by the conditions imposed within each exemption,

---

20 *Downing v Downing* [1976] 3 All ER 474.
1   Sch 1, para 16(2).
2   Ibid, para 2(4).
3   Ibid, para 2(3).
4   Ibid, para 6(4)-(7).
5   Ibid, paras 2 and 4(4)(b), and see below.
6   S 8(8). Disabled is defined in s 8(9).
7   Sch 1, para 2(1)(b).
8   [1998] 2 FLR 1.
9   S 55.

and in the case of a child under a disability, or in further or higher education, the order must be designed simply to meet expenses attributable to these circumstances. However, Thorpe LJ expressed the view, obiter,[10] that the limits imposed by the Child Support Act 1991 would continue to apply until the child reached an age when that Act no longer applied, and thereafter the broader provisions of schedule 1 of the Children Act 1989 would prevail.

Maintenance orders for children of the family

Because a qualifying child must be biologically related to both parents for the purposes of the Child Support Act 1991, children who have been treated as children of the family are excluded from its scope. A 'child of the family' is a concept which applies only to parties to a marriage; it does not apply to unmarried unions.[11] It means in relation to the parties to a marriage:

'(a) a child of both of those parties; and
(b) any other child, not being a child who is placed with those parties as foster parents by a local authority or voluntary organisation, who has been treated by both of those parties as a child of their family.'[12]

A step-child is the most obvious child to fall within this definition. Indeed, there appear to be no reported cases where an application has been made on behalf of any child other than a step-child.[13]

Orders for financial provision for children of the family may be made in divorce proceedings, in proceedings between spouses brought before magistrates, and under the Children Act 1989, schedule 1. The court, in deciding whether to exercise its powers and to make an order,[14] and if so in what manner, must have regard to the financial and other circumstances of all parties including the child.[15] Paragraph 4(2) of Schedule 1 is of particular relevance to orders for children of the family. It provides:

---

10 With which Butler-Sloss and Hutchinson LJJ were inclined to agree but expressed no firm conclusion.
11 *J v J (A Minor: Property Transfer)* [1993] 2 FLR 56.
12 Children Act 1989, s 105(1); the same definition appears in the Matrimonial Causes Act 1973, s 52(1) and the Domestic Proceedings and Magistrates' Courts Act 1978, s 88(1).
13 However, there is no reason why other children should not be able to look to the parties to a marriage for periodical payments if the marriage breaks down. Examples might be an orphaned relative who has lived with the parties and has been treated as a child of their family; or a foster child who was placed privately, who has been treated as a child of the family for some considerable time, and whose parents cannot support him financially.
14 The orders can include lump sum, settlement and property transfer orders, see below.
15 Sch 1, para 4(1), set out in detail below where a court's discretion to make capital orders is considered.

'In deciding whether to exercise its powers under paragraph 1
against a person who is not the mother or father of the child, and
if so in what manner, the court shall in addition have regard to—
  (a) whether that person assumed responsibility for the child and,
       if so, the extent to which and the basis on which he assumed
       that responsibility and the length of the period during which
       he met that responsibility;
  (b) whether he did so knowing that the child was not his child;
  (c) the liability of any other person to maintain the child.'[16]

In this respect the legislation acknowledges that the obligation owed to a
child of the family may be different from that which is owed by a parent
to his or her own child. Nonetheless, the concept of the child of the family
recognises that a person who chooses to marry someone who already has
children takes on responsibility for the children as well as for his spouse.
If the marriage ends, this responsibility may involve making financial
and property provision for these children, which is tempered only by the
liability of anyone else to maintain the child.

Before any obligation can be imposed, it must first be established that
the non-parent has treated the child as a child of the family. This is a
question of fact turning on evidence of how he behaved towards the child.[17]
Where a child lives in the same household with a step-parent for some
considerable period of time it is almost inevitable that he or she will be
treated as a child of the family.[18] On the other hand, if the child has his
home with other family members, but visits his parent and step-parent,
this does not make him a child of the family and the step-parent is not
financially responsible for him if the marriage breaks down.[19] A child can
be treated as a child of the family where a husband has treated him as
such in the mistaken belief that the child is his own child. In *W(RJ) v
W(SJ)*[20] a husband was deceived by his wife about the paternity of their
two children, and after the marriage broke down blood tests revealed that
he was not the father. Prior to that the husband had treated the children
as his own children. The question for the court was could the children be
treated as children of the family despite the husband's lack of knowledge
about their true paternity? Park J held that both children had been treated
as children of the family and that the husband's lack of knowledge of the
facts relating to the children's paternity was immaterial to their status.

However, lack of knowledge on the part of a deceived husband is highly
material to whether he should be ordered to make provision for a child
who is a child of the family but not his own. The court is required to
consider the basis on which such a husband had assumed and discharged

16 This provision is replicated in the Matrimonial Causes Act 1973, s 25(4).
17 *Teeling v Teeling* [1984] FLR 808.
18 *Carron v Carron* [1984] FLR 805.
19 *D v D* (1981) 2 FLR 93.
20 [1971] 3 All ER 303.

his financial responsibility for the child and whether he did so knowing that the child was not his own. It was implicit in the judgment in *W(RJ) v W(SJ)* that no order for financial provision would be made against the husband. Where a husband is deceived before the child's birth into believing that he is the father of his wife's expected child, but where when the child is born it is clear to him that the child is not his child, and where he has nothing further to do with the child, then the child is not a child of the family. As the court held in *A v A (Family: Unborn Child)*,[1] it is only possible to behave towards a child, and therefore to treat it as a child of the family, after it is born.

In relation to a step-child who has been treated as a child of the family, the obligation of the step-parent to make provision for the child is tempered by the liability of any other person to maintain the child. Whilst this liability has always been of relevance, it has taken on greater significance in the light of the changes brought about by the Child Support Act 1991.[2] It has been seen that this Act emphasises that primary responsibility for child support remains with the natural parent regardless of events, and regardless of the length of time for which a step-parent has been providing for the child. A step-parent who is pursued for child maintenance in the courts will therefore normally be well advised to insist that the applicant first seeks to obtain support for the child from his natural parent through the intervention of the Child Support Agency.

There is a real risk that the concept of the child of the family, and with it the concomitant financial responsibility for such a child, will wither and die in response to the radical change of approach to child maintenance brought about by the Child Support Act 1991. Now that a structure has been established under which all natural parents are obliged to make provision for their own children according to a universal formula, it may be perceived as unfair to burden step-parents and deceived husbands with financial responsibility for children who are not their own through the mechanism of court orders. The notion that this is unfair and unduly burdensome is particularly likely to be expressed in those cases where such men are already supporting their natural children in accordance with the provisions of the formula, and where no allowance has been made in the formula for the costs of maintaining a step-child. However, if this approach were to take root, many step-children could find that they are deprived of adequate financial support when the marriage between their parent and step-parent breaks down. Such children are often financially dependent on their step-parents, and unless step-parents are required to provide step-children with support, the household in which the children live after the breakdown may be reduced to relying on income support payments as their only source of income. Where this would lead to a drastic reduction in the step-child's standard of living the welfare of such a child would be liable to suffer disproportionately to other children. While the majority of children

---

1   [1974] 1 All ER 755.
2   As explained above.

experience some material deprivation after divorce, it is suggested that step-children may be particularly vulnerable to this unless full use is made of the courts' powers under the child of the family provisions.

Maintenance orders in favour of a person with a residence order

An application for child maintenance under the Children Act 1989 may be made by any person in whose favour a residence order is in force.[3] This is an important provision which comes to the assistance of relatives or friends of the child who have undertaken the burden of responsibility for caring for the child but do not have the means to support the child.[4] It seems likely that the power of the courts to make orders in favour of a person with a residence order is not generally known. This is unfortunate because it might persuade relatives and others interested in the child to look after the child where the parents are unable or unwilling to do so. Moreover, those who are already looking after a child on an informal basis in a case where parents are refusing, or failing, to contribute towards the costs of their child's upbringing would sometimes be well-advised to apply for a residence order so that they can obtain income, and possibly a capital, contribution towards the child's upkeep.[5]

Capital orders in favour of *all* children

Parents may be required to make substantial capital provision for the benefit of their children. All children need homes in addition to financial support, and courts have powers to make orders which require a parent to settle property for the benefit of a child, to make a lump sum payment for the benefit of a child, and to transfer property for the benefit of a child. Orders can also be made that property is transferred, or a lump sum payment is made, directly to the child.[6] These powers, which are derived from section 15(1) and Schedule 1 of the Children Act 1989, exist in relation to *all* children irrespective of whether their parents are or were married, are or were unmarried cohabitants, or the child was

---

3 Sch 1, para 1(1). A residence order confers parental responsibility for the child on the person in whose favour the order is made; Children Act 1989, s 12(2).

4 Persons with a residence order can apply for capital orders as well as orders for periodical payments; see below.

5 The court would, of course, have to be satisfied that a residence order was in the best interests of the child (Children Act 1989, s 1(1)), and that the order would be better for the child than making no order (s 1(5)).

6 A court has power to make an order under Sch 1 notwithstanding the bankruptcy of the respondent, *Re G (Children Act 1989, Schedule 1)* [1996] 2 FLR 171. As Singer J said, at p 177: 'It would be quite wrong ... for the mother and, of course in particular the child, to be left with no order simply because a third party had got round to the exercise of their rights to obtain a bankruptcy order against the father.'

conceived as a result of a fleeting relationship.[7] Moreover, a '.. the purposes of the Children Act 1989 includes any party to a marriage (whether or not subsisting) in relation to whom the child concerned is a child of the family.[8] Thus an order may be made against a step-parent; and a step-parent who has care of the child is entitled to apply for an order against the natural parent(s). Any person in whose favour a residence order is in force with respect to a child may also apply for a capital order.[9] The Court's powers under the Act may be exercised at any time.[10]

Children of divorcing parents and capital orders

Children of parents whose marriage is brought to an end by divorce, and children of a marriage which ends in divorce who have been treated as children of the family, have an advantage over other children. In addition to benefiting from the exercise of the court's powers under the Children Act 1989, they are likely to gain from orders made within the divorce proceedings between the spouses. Also, orders in divorce proceedings can be made directly to benefit the child (although this is unusual). When spouses divorce, under provisions of the Matrimonial Causes Act 1973 capital orders in the form of orders for the payment of a lump sum, the creation or variation of settlements and the transfer of property can be made in favour of a party to the marriage.[11] When determining whether to make an order, or orders, the court must give first consideration to the welfare of any children of the family under the age of 18.[12] In practice, capital orders on divorce are almost invariably made in favour of the spouses, but the nature of the order is strongly influenced by the needs of the children. In particular, a court will be anxious to ensure that the parent who is looking after the children of the family has adequate housing during the children's minority, and often beyond that date where the children are at university or other places of higher education.[13] Where resources are

---

7   The law refuses to distinguish between 'wanted' and 'unwanted' childre; see *J v C (Financial Provision)* [1999] 1 FLR 152 where a father who had won the Lottery was ordered to settle property on his 'unwanted' child during his dependency. For an example of where a man had to bear part of the costs entailed in bringing up a child conceived by artificial insemination, see *Re B (Parentage)* [1996] 2 FLR 15. Despite the fact that the relationship with the mother had ended, the respondent (who was married with a son) engaged in a joint enterprise with the mother to secure her insemination with his sperm. She gave birth to twins. The court ruled that the respondent was the father of the twins, and found that it was a case where a judge might well find it appropriate to make an order for a capital sum.

8   Children Act 1989, Sch 1, para 16(2). Once the child attains the age of 18 the obligation of anyone other than a parent ceases.

9   Sch 1, para 1(1).

10 Sch 1, para 1(3).

11 For a full account of these orders, and when they may be made, see ch 8.

12 Matrimonial Causes Act 1973, s 25(1).

13 See, for example, *Richardson v Richardson (No 2)* [1994] 2 FLR 1051; *B v B* [1995] 1 FLR 9.

limited the court will normally postpone the claim of the non-residential parent to realise his or her share in the capital invested in the matrimonial home until the children reach adulthood. In this way, although lump sum, settlement and property transfer orders are not made directly in favour of the children of the family, they are nonetheless designed to benefit the children.

The Matrimonial Causes Act 1973 makes it clear that a parent's duty to make provision for his or her children normally comes to an end once the child attains adulthood. No financial provision order may be made in favour of a child who has attained the age of 18, save where the child is continuing to receive education or training, or unless there are special circumstances.[14] Nor may a property transfer order under section 21(2)(a) be made in favour of a child over the age of 18.[15] This has led courts to turn away from making capital orders for children which will benefit them beyond the stage where they complete their full-time education. In *Lord Lilford v Glynn*[16] the Court of Appeal stated that the wealth of a parent did not amount to special circumstances, and held that it had been wrong to order a millionaire father to settle a lump sum on trust for each of his children to make provision for the payment of an income to them for their lifetime. As Orr LJ said, 'even the richest father ought not to be regarded as under "financial obligations and responsibilities" to provide funds for the purposes of such settlement as are envisaged in this case on children who are under no disability and whose maintenance and education are secure'.[17] In *Kiely v Kiely*[18] a father living in more modest circumstances had been ordered to pay a lump sum to each of his children when the younger child reached 18. Allowing the father's appeal, the Court of Appeal reaffirmed the principle that a parent's obligations end when his child reaches 18. It held that there was nothing special about the circumstances which entitled these children to different treatment.[19] Courts have also refused to allow a capital order to be made in favour of the children of the parties rather than to one of the parties themselves where the purpose of this arrangement was to defeat the statutory charge imposed by the Legal Aid Board.[20]

In the light of these rulings it is difficult to know what weight to give to the statement by Thorpe LJ in *Tavoulareas v Tavoulareas*[1] that 'in an infinite number of cases since [*Lilford (Lord) v Glynn*]*[2] settlements have been ordered during the dependency of a child or children and *the court*

---

14   S 29(1), (3).
15   There is, however, no prohibition on a settlement order being made under s 21(2)(b).
16   [1979] 1 All ER 441.
17   Ibid, at p 447. See too Scarman LJ in *Chamberlain v Chamberlain* [1974] 1 All ER 33, at p 38.
18   [1988] 1 FLR 248.
19   The father had originally been ordered to make periodical payments for his wife and children. Shortly afterwards he ceased to make such payments, and they were subsequently reduced to a nominal sum.
20   *Draskovic v Draskovic* (1981) 11 Fam Law 87.
1   [1998] 2 FLR 418, at p 429.
2   [1979] 1 All ER 441.

invariably chooses, at the conclusion of the dependency, whether the reversion should be for the settlor, for the parties in some shares, or to the child.[3] In *Tavoulareas v Tavoulareas* the trial judge ordered the husband to settle on the wife a lump sum of £250,000 to provide for housing for both the wife and their child, which sum would revert to the husband at the end of the child's dependency. The Court of Appeal substituted an order that the sum of £250,000 should be paid to trustees to hold the same for the benefit of the wife during the child's dependency for the purpose of providing them both with accommodation, but that at the conclusion of the child's dependency the reversion would be to the child. Thorpe LJ stated that this was an exceptional case where the reversion to the child was fully justified. The parties' capital had been derived from their respective families, and neither had made any contribution to the sum which would go into the settlement, and neither had a foreseeable need for that sum when the settlement came to an end.

Had it not been for Thorpe LJ's statement that courts exercise wide choice as to who will benefit from the reversion when a settlement is made, *Tavoulareas v Tavoulareas* could be confined to its own rather unusual facts. Indeed, Thorpe LJ himself stated that the order in favour of the child could be justified on the basis that the case was 'exceptional'. Nevertheless, he appeared confident that courts have a choice as to who will obtain the reversion when a settlement ends. *Tavoulareas v Tavoulareas* does appear to run counter to authority, however, and to be out of line with the decision of the Court of Appeal in *C v C (Financial Relief: Short Marriage)*.[4] The facts were equally unusual, if not more so. The parties had met when the wife was working as a high class prostitute. They married, had a child and separated. The husband, who was very wealthy, wanted any lump sum that he was required to pay to be settled on the wife for the purpose of providing her and the child with a home, and for that sum to revert to the child when the settlement came to an end. The trial judge refused to accede to this request for the reason that the wife should have more than a limited interest in the property. The Court of Appeal dismissed the husband's appeal on two grounds. It found that the trial judge had not been plainly wrong with regard to the needs of the wife; and it held that there was a long line of authorities from *Chamberlain v Chamberlain*[5] to *Lord Lilford v Glynn*[6] that the powers to make lump sum and settlement orders were not normally exercised to provide funds directly for the children.

Capital orders for children of unmarried parents

Whilst children of the family of divorcing parents can be provided with a roof over their heads by orders made between the spouses, children of

---

3   Emphasis added.
4   [1997] 2 FLR 26.
5   [1974] 1 All ER 33.
6   [1979] 1 All ER 441.

unmarried parents enjoy no such advantage. However, since the implementation of the Family Law Reform Act 1987, courts have had wide powers to make capital orders in favour of all children on an application made on their behalf by adults.[7]

These powers were extended by the Children Act 1989, Schedule 1 which added to the persons who are entitled to apply for an order on behalf of a child. It is now the case that any parent (including a step-parent), guardian or person in whose favour a residence order is in force can apply to the court to make one or more orders for the benefit of the child, or to the child himself.[8] These orders are:

'(c) an order requiring either or both parents of a child—
    (i) to pay to the applicant for the benefit of the child; or
    (ii) to pay to the child himself,
such lump sum as may be so specified;[9]
(d) an order requiring a settlement to be made for the benefit of the child, and to the satisfaction of the court, of property—
    (i) to which either parent is entitled (either in possession or in reversion); and
    (ii) which is specified in the order;
(e) an order requiring either or both parents of a child—
    (i) to transfer to the applicant for the benefit of the child; or
    (ii) to transfer to the child himself,
such property to which the parent is, or the parents are, entitled (either in possession or in reversion) as may be specified in the order.'[10]

The exercise of the court's discretion

The principle of the paramountcy of the child's welfare does not apply to orders for financial and property provision made under Schedule 1. This is made plain in section 105 which states that a child's 'upbringing' does not include a child's maintenance.[11] A court when making orders for financial and property provision for children must have regard to all the circumstances of the case, including:

---

7   The Family Law Reform Act 1987 inserted ss 11B and C into the Guardianship of Minors Act 1971.

8   S 15(1) and Sch 1, para 1(1). Children over 18 may only obtain an order for periodical payments and/or a lump sum.

9   The court's powers are wider than under the Matrimonial Causes Act 1973. It can order more than one lump sum, vary its amount, order it to be paid by instalments and vary those instalments (Sch 1, paras 1(5) and 5).

10   Sch 1, para 1(2)(c),(d) and (e).

11   Indeed, as Ward J said in *A v A (A Minor) (Financial Provision)* [1994] 1 FLR 657, at p 667: 'Somewhat to my surprise and for reasons I cannot understand, welfare plays no express part in the considerations to which I have to have regard.'

'(a) the income, earning capacity, property and other financial resources which each person mentioned in sub-paragraph (4) has or is likely to have in the foreseeable future;

(b) the financial needs, obligations and responsibilities which each person mentioned in sub-paragraph (4) has or is likely to have in the foreseeable future;

(c) the financial needs of the child;

(d) the income, earning capacity (if any), property and other financial resources of the child;

(e) any physical or mental disability of the child;

(f) the manner in which the child was being, or was expected to be, educated or trained.'[12]

The persons mentioned in sub-paragraph (4) are any parent, the applicant and any other person in whose favour the court proposes to make the order. Where the court is deciding whether to make an order against a person who is not the child's parent additional considerations apply.[13]

In *K v K (Minors: Property Transfer)*[14] the trial judge ordered a father of four children to transfer his interest in a joint tenancy of the council house in which the family were living to the children's mother for the benefit of the children of the family.[15] When arriving at his decision, the judge omitted to refer to the criteria governing orders for children. In particular he did not take account of the father's nine years of accrued rights under the right to buy provisions of the Housing Act 1980, his ability to find and pay for other accommodation, and his very low income. Ordering a retrial, the Court of Appeal emphasised that the balancing exercise contemplated by paragraph 4 must always be carried out, and that the needs of the parents should not simply be subordinated to those of the children. It held that the judge had erred in principle in failing to conduct this balancing exercise, and therefore that his decision was one with which the Court of Appeal could and must interfere. No guidance was given to the court conducting the retrial on how much weight a court should give to the needs of the children when balancing these against the needs and accrued rights of the father.[16]

K v K (Minors: Property Transfer) was an important ruling in an area of law which, until then, had generated surprisingly little case law. Although the Court of Appeal ordered a retrial, it nonetheless accepted that such an order was for the benefit of the children and that it therefore fell within the court's powers under schedule 1. Where a tenancy is

---

12 Sch 1, para 4(1).
13 Sch 1, para 4(2), see above under maintenance for a child of the family.
14 [1992] 2 All ER 727.
15 Under s 11B(2)(d) of the Guardianship of Minors Act 1971.
16 See also, *Pearson v Franklin* [1994] 2 All ER 137, where the Court of Appeal advised a mother, who had failed to obtain an injunction to oust the children's father from the home, to apply for the transfer of the tenancy under s 15 and Sch 1.

transferred from one parent to the other it will, of course, benefit the transferee long after the children have ceased to be dependent on her. Thus tenancy transfer orders made for the benefit of the children not only provide secure housing for the children and the parent looking after them, but also extend that protection to beyond the stage where the children reach adulthood and the parenting role comes to an end. However, the willingness of the Court of Appeal in *K v K (Minors: Property Transfer)* to contemplate making a property transfer order for the benefit of children, as distinct from a settlement order with reversion to the settlor, seems to have been unique, and is probably limited to cases involving the transfer of a council or other tenancy.[17]

In *Phillips v Peace*[18] the manner in which Johnson J exercised his discretion under Schedule 1 was strongly influenced by provisions in the Child Support Act 1991. The case arose because of the extraordinary (but technically accurate) finding by an officer of the Child Support Agency that a father who had assets running into millions of pounds had no income and therefore could not pay child support. The mother, who had discovered she was pregnant after the parties' six-month relationship ended, therefore applied under Schedule 1 for a lump sum order for the benefit of their child. Johnson J found that this was a case where the Child Support Act 1991 applied so that the court was barred from making an order for periodical payments to provide the child with regular support. He held that when exercising his remaining jurisdiction under Schedule 1 of the Children Act 1989, he should do so only in order to meet the needs of the child in respect of a particular item of capital expenditure. Here the child needed a home. Therefore, Johnson J ordered the father to settle £90,000 on the child, the property purchased to be held by trustees until the child grew up and completed her education.[19] He built into the order provisions making the mother responsible for the repair, upkeep and outgoings on the property; provisions which would enable her to move to another property; and provisions enabling the matter to be reconsidered by the court if the mother was to marry or cohabit with someone. It was agreed that at the end of the child's right of occupation, the mother would have the right to buy the property from the father at its then open market price.

The decision in *Phillips v Peace* is an illustration of the courts' determination that orders for the benefit of children should make provision for them during their minority, but should not be designed to extend beyond

17 The power to order one unmarried cohabitant to transfer the tenancy in the family home to the other has since been introduced under Sch 7 of the Family Law Act 1996; see above.
18 [1996] 2 FLR 230.
19 He also made lump sum provision of £15,000 for furnishings for the house, the medical and nursing costs associated with the birth and a sum of £9,000 for clothing and baby equipment (despite finding that this sum was extravagant, which it undoubtedly was!).

that stage in their lives.[20] This principle has been applied despite the fact that the parent against whom the order is made is extremely wealthy and can well afford to make life-long provision for the child, as was demonstrated in *A v A (A Minor: Financial Provision)*.[1] The father of one child of a family of three children was a multi-millionaire. The mother applied, inter alia, for an outright transfer of property either to herself for the benefit of the child, or to the child herself. Ward J rejected her application, and ordered that the house owned by the father, in which the mother and the three children were living, should be settled on the child during her minority or until she completed full-time education. In relation to the child's mother, he said:

> 'The mother's obligation is to look after [the child], and [the child's] financial need is to provide a roof over the head of her caretaker. It is, indeed, a father's obligation to provide the accommodation for the living-in help which [the child] needs. Consequently, it must be a term of the settlement that while [the child] is under the control of her mother and thereafter for so long as [the child] does not object, the mother shall have the right to occupy the property to the exclusion of the father and without paying rent therefor for the purpose of providing a home and care and support for [the child].'[2]

It is suggested that this was an extraordinarily legalistic and insensitive approach to a mother's role in caring for her child. The reasoning that led the judge to state that a child should be entitled to object to her mother continuing to occupy the family home once the child reached the age when she was no longer under the control of her mother is truly horrifying. It cannot be in the interests of a child that she should have this kind of power over her mother, and the order made had the potential to be extraordinarily damaging to the relationship between the child, her mother and her siblings.

Sadly, however, giving children on whom property is settled the authority to treat their mothers in an immoral fashion once the mother's caring role comes to an end mirrors the power of unmarried fathers who are sole owners of the family home to treat the mothers of their children in an identical manner. A father has no obligation to make either financial or capital provision for the mother of his children in her own right, and he

---

20 See *Chamberlain v Chamberlain* [1974] 1 All ER 33; *Lord Lilford v Glynn* [1979] 1 All ER 441; *Kiely v Kiely* [1988] 1 FLR 248; *H v P (Illegitimate Child: Capital Provision)* [1993] Fam Law 515. But cf *Tavoulareas v Tavoulareas* [1998] 2 FLR 418 where, in divorce proceedings, property settled on the mother and child would eventually revert to the child.

1   [1994] 1 FLR 657.

2   Ibid, at p 663.

can literally cast her into the street once his children have reached their majority and any settlement comes to an end. This was illustrated by *T v S (Financial Provision for Children)*.[3] A district judge ordered the father of five children to buy a small property for the mother and the children, the property to be held by trustees with a power of sale postponed until the youngest surviving of the children reached 21, or ceased full-time education, whichever was the sooner. In that event, the property was to pass to the five children, or to such of them as survived, in equal shares. The father took the view that the property was his property and that it should eventually be restored to him. He also asserted that the judge's order would almost certainly result in the children together allowing their mother to continue to live in the house. Allowing the father's appeal, Johnson J held that the children had no continuing claim on their father after they had ceased full-time education. He therefore extended the duration of the settlement by postponing the father's interest until the youngest child had completed full-time education, including tertiary education, but ordered that upon the trust for sale[4] coming into effect, the property should revert to the father and should not be the property of the children equally. He rejected the option that the father should pay a lump sum to the mother for the benefit of the children because, he said, it would provide 'a windfall' to the mother. In relation to the settlement, he recognised that it was extremely unlikely that the children would insist on their share of the settlement being released if this had the consequence that their mother would be put out of their home, but he took it out of the power of the children to make continuing provision for her. As he said: 'The sadness here is that, after a long and seemingly happy relationship, this mother of five children, never having been married to their father, has no rights against him of her own. She has no right to be supported by him in the short, still less the long term; no right in herself to have even a roof over her head.'[5]

Thus an unmarried parent who brings up the children has no continuing claim for support and shelter in her declining years and can literally be turned out into the street once her mothering role has ended. This is indefensible. Radical proposals for legislative change are urgently needed. Pending such legislation the judiciary should find ways of protecting mothers in the position of the mother in *T v S (Financial Provision for Children)*. One solution would be to adopt the response of the trial judge and where there is a settlement to order that the reversion should be divided between the children.[6] This would give the children the opportunity to make provision for the parent who has looked after them. Another option

---

3   [1994] 2 FLR 883.
4   As it then was.
5   Ibid, at p 889-890. For further comment on *T v S* and *A v A*, see E Cooke, *Children and real property – trusts, interests and considerations* [1998] Fam Law 349.
6   See *Tavoulereas v Tavoulereas* [1998] 2 FLR 418, where the reversion in property settled during the child's minority went to the child.

would be to make a property transfer order for the benefit of the child at the outset rather than a settlement. Parliament has given courts the discretion to make property transfer orders in favour of children, and it is the courts which have fettered this discretion. They have applied the values relating to property ownership rather than values relating to parental responsibility, and the responsibility to make provision for a parent who has undertaken the caring role. This type of reasoning is not conducive to the development of an acceptable system of family law. It is hoped that reform of the law relating to unmarried parents and their children will have occurred well before this book appears in its third edition.[7]

---

7   The first edition of this book was completed in December 1994. At that time the Law Commission was examining the rights of home sharers. Its working paper is still awaited in the summer of 1999.

Index